1250
4-3

PL. I

BASKET SHIELD FROM A CLIFF DWELLING

STEWART CULIN

GAMES OF THE NORTH AMERICAN INDIANS

Dover Publications Inc., New York

Published in Canada by General Publishing Company, Ltd., 30 Lesmill Road, Don Mills, Toronto, Ontario.

Published in the United Kingdom by Constable and Company, Ltd., 10 Orange Street, London WC 2.

This Dover edition, first published in 1975, is an unabridged republication of the Accompanying Paper, "Games of the North American Indians," of the *Twenty-Fourth Annual Report of the Bureau of American Ethnology to the Smithsonian Institution, 1902-1903, by W. H. Holmes, Chief,* originally published by the Government Printing Office in 1907. Plates I and IV were in color in the original edition and are here reproduced in black and white.

International Standard Book Number: 0-486-23125-9
Library of Congress Catalog Card Number: 74-12653

Manufactured in the United States of America
Dover Publications, Inc.
180 Varick Street
New York, N. Y. 10014

CONTENTS

ILLUSTRATIONS

6

GAMES OF THE NORTH AMERICAN INDIANS

By STEWART CULIN

PREFACE

In the spring of 1891 the writer was invited by Prof. F. W. Putnam to prepare and take charge of an exhibit illustrative of the games of the world, at the Columbian Exposition at Chicago. During the course of the exposition his attention was directed by Mr Frank Hamilton Cushing to the remarkable analogies existing between the oriental and modern European games in the collection and those of the American Indians. A joint work in which Mr Cushing should discuss the American games and the writer those of the Old World was then projected. Mr Cushing's ill health delayed and finally prevented his proposed collaboration. Deeply impressed with the importance of the subject, the present author took up the systematic study of American games, constantly aided by Mr Cushing's advice and suggestions. In 1895, at the request of Dr G. Brown Goode, Assistant Secretary of the Smithsonian Institution, in charge of the United States National Museum, he prepared a collection of games for the exhibit of the National Museum at the International and Cotton States Exposition at Atlanta, Ga. A catalogue of this collection, including a comparative study of the Indian stick-dice games, which is incorporated in the present volume, was published in the report of the United States National Museum for 1896. Stimulated by this work, increased attention was paid to Indian games by collectors and students in the field. Dr George A. Dorsey, curator of anthropology in the Field Columbian Museum, undertook the systematic collection of specimens of gaming implements of all the existing tribes. To his efforts and those of his assistants, Rev. H. R. Voth, Dr J. W. Hudson, Dr C. F. Newcombe, Mr S. C. Simms, and Mr Charles L. Owen, is chiefly due the great wealth of material on which the writer has been enabled to draw in the preparation of his work. Doctor Dorsey not only encouraged the widest use of the collections in the Field Columbian Museum, but made many special

29

inquiries of the Indians, and freely placed the field notes and manuscripts which he himself had intended for publication, in the hands of the writer. A trip through the Indian reservations made with Doctor Dorsey in the summer of 1900 resulted in the collection of much new material, and subsequent trips made by the writer alone in 1901, 1902, 1903, 1904, and 1905 yielded satisfactory results.

In 1898, on the invitation of Dr W J McGee, of the Bureau of American Ethnology, the writer arranged with the Bureau for the publication of the present volume. It contains a classified and illustrated list of practically all the American Indian gaming implements in American and European museums, together with a more or less exhaustive summary of the entire literature of the subject. The collection has been confined to games in which implements are employed, and the argument rests directly on the testimony afforded by them. Indian children have many amusements which they play without implements, such as tag, etc., corresponding to those of civilization, but these belong to a different category from those herein described, and their exclusion does not affect the questions under discussion. Since the relation and, in no small degree, the significance of the games become through comparison self-evident, the writer has retained the catalogue form for his work, prefacing the whole with a general dissertation and each of the several divisions into which the games naturally fall, with a short introduction.

In conclusion, the writer desires to express his obligations to American and foreign students and collectors, who have generously placed at his disposal material which they have zealously collected. His thanks are due also to the Chief of the Bureau of American Ethnology and the curators of the United States National Museum, who have in every way aided and facilitated his work.

INTRODUCTION

The games of the American Indians may be divided into two general classes: I, games of chance; II, games of dexterity. Games of pure skill and calculation, such as chess, are entirely absent. The Indian games of chance fall into two categories: 1, games in which implements of the nature of dice are thrown at random to determine a number or numbers, and the sum of the counts is kept by means of sticks, pebbles, etc., or upon an abacus, or counting board, or circuit; 2, games in which one or more of the players guess in which of two or more places an odd or particularly marked lot is concealed, success or failure resulting in the gain or loss of counters. The games of dexterity may be enumerated as: 1, archery in various modifications; 2, a game of sliding javelins or darts upon the hard ground or ice; 3, a game of shooting at a moving target consisting of a netted wheel or a ring; 4, the game of ball in several highly specialized forms; 5, the racing games, more or less related to and complicated with the ball games. In addition, there is a subclass related to the games of shooting at a moving target, of which it is a miniature and solitaire form, corresponding to the European game of cup and ball.

Games of all the classes designated are found among all the Indian tribes of North America and constitute the games par excellence of the Indians. Children have a variety of other amusements, such as top spinning, mimic fights, and similar imitative sports, but the games first described are played only by men and women, or youths and maidens, not by children, and usually at fixed seasons as the accompaniment of certain festivals or religious rites.

There is a well-marked affinity and relationship existing between the manifestations of the same game, even among the most widely separated tribes. The variations are more in the materials employed, due to environment, than in the object or method of play. Precisely the same games are played by tribes belonging to unrelated linguistic stocks, and in general the variations do not follow differences in language. At the same time, there appears to be a progressive change from what seems to be the oldest forms of existing games from a center in the southwestern United States, along lines north, northeast, and east. Similar changes probably occurred along lines radiating from the same center southward into Mexico, but in the absence of sufficient data this conclusion can not be verified.

There is no evidence that any of the games described were imported into America at any time either before or after the Conquest. On the other hand, they appear to be the direct and natural outgrowth of aboriginal institutions in America. They show no modifications due to white influence other than the decay which characterizes all Indian institutions under existing conditions. It is probable, however, that the wide dissemination of certain games—for example, the hand game—is of comparatively recent date, due to wider and less restricted intercourse through the abolition of tribal wars. Playing cards and, probably, the simple board game called by the English nine men's morris are among the few games borrowed by the Indians from the whites. On the other hand, we have taken their lacrosse in the north and racket in the south, and the Mexicans on the Rio Grande play all the old Indian games under Spanish names.

My first conclusions as to the interrelation and common origin of Indian games were based upon a comparative study of the stick-dice game, published in the report of the United States National Museum for 1896. [a] I was then, in default of other data, inclined to view the question from its objective side and to explain the manifold inter-relationships of the dice games as due chiefly to the progressive modifications of the implements employed. This explanation, however, failed to account for the manifest relations which I afterward discovered between the dice game and most of the other games, as well as those which exist between the gaming implements and many ceremonial appliances, and I was led to the conclusion that behind both ceremonies and games there existed some widespread myth from which both derived their impulse.

References to games are of common occurrence in the origin myths of various tribes. They usually consist of a description of a series of contests in which the demiurge, the first man, the culture hero, overcomes some opponent, a foe of the human race, by exercise of superior cunning, skill, or magic. Comparison of these myths not only reveal their practical unity, but disclose the primal gamblers as those curious children, the divine Twins, the miraculous offspring of the Sun, who are the principal personages in many Indian mythologies. They live in the east and in the west; they rule night and day, winter and summer. They are the morning and evening stars. Their virgin mother, who appears also as their sister and their wife, is constantly spoken of as their grandmother, and is the Moon or the Earth, the Spider Woman, the embodiment of the feminine principle in nature. Always contending, they are the original patrons of play, and their games are the games now played by men. I shall reserve for another work the task of attempting to untwine the

---

[a] Chess and Playing Cards.

tangled web in which the myth of the Twins is interwoven. These tales are involved with those of two other similar cosmical personages, who occupy places midway between them. We find the following description of the Twins in their relation to games in Mr Cushing's account of the Zuñi War Gods:[a]

Lo! and of Chance and Fate were they the masters of foredeeming, for they carried the word-painted arrows of destiny (shóliweátsinapa), like the regions of men, four in number. And they carried the shuttlecocks of divination (hápochiwe), like the regions of men, four in number. And they carried the tubes of hidden things (íyankolotómawe), like the regions of men, four in number, and the revealing balls thereof (íyankolote tsemak'ya móliwe), like the regions of men, four in number. Yea, and they bore, with these, other things—the feather bow and plume arrow of far-finding, tipped with the shell of heart-searching; and the race sticks of swift journeys and way-winning (móti-kwawe), two of them, the right and the left, the pursuer and the pursued of men in contention. All these things wherewith to divine men's chance, and play games of hazard, wagering the fate of whole nations in mere pastime, had they with them.

The significant emblems of the Twins are their weapons. These consist of a throwing-club made of heavy wood, their bows and cane arrows, the bows interchangeable with a lance, and a netted shield. These objects are distinguished one from the other by their markings, which again are commonly fourfold, one pair referring to one of the Twins, and one to the other. In this fourfold division we find included those other interrelated twins of whom mention has been made. Gaming implements are almost exclusively derived from these symbolic weapons. For example, the stick dice are either arrow shafts or miniature bows, and a similar origin may be asserted for the implements used in the hand game and in the four-stick game. Counting sticks in general and sticks for the stick game are arrows. The engraved and painted tubes used in the guessing game are arrow shaftments. In the games of dexterity we find again bows and arrows and the netted shield with bows. Snow-snakes are either the club, the bows, or arrows. Ball seems to be less sure, but the racket may be referred to the net shield. The painted sticks of the kicked-billet race are miniature bows. The opposing players are frequently the representatives of the two War Gods. We find gaming implements, as things pleasing to the gods, among the objects sacrificed upon the altar of the Twins in Zuñi.

This is well illustrated in the model of the shrine of the War God arranged for exhibition by Mrs Matilda Coxe Stevenson in the United States National Museum (plate II).[b]

---

[a] Outlines of Zuñi Creation Myths. Thirteenth Annual Report of the Bureau of Ethnology, p. 423, 1896.

[b] The following is a descriptive label of the altar of the War God in the Museum, furnished by Mrs Stevenson: Idol and paraphernalia of the Zuñi war god Ahaiyuta, employed in the worship of the deity and forming a petition for rain. The plumes surround-

The games on the altar are as follows: Set of four cane dice (figure 284) ; set of four long cane dice (figure 2) ; set of four wooden cylinders for hidden-ball game (figure 493) ; two corncob feather darts with ball made of yucca leaves (figure 549) ; sticks for kicked-billet game (figure 913).

From the account of the altars of the twin War Gods among the Hopi given by Doctor Fewkes,[a] it would appear that the games are absent, but we find them upon the altars in the Flute ceremony. For example, on the altar of the Drab Flute (Macileñya) from Oraibi, as reconstructed in the Field Columbian Museum at Chicago, four little flowerlike cups, yellow, green, red, and white, rest upon the floor at the base of the effigy. Between them are two wooden cylinders, painted black, corresponding to the kicked sticks of the Zuñi race game. A corn-husk ring, tied to a long stick, precisely like one used in certain forms of the ring-and-dart game, stands on each side of the principal figure.[b]

In addition, stuck on sand mounds at the right and left, are artificial trees or plants covered with flowers. These flowers are wooden gaming cups, 16 in number—4 white, 4 green, 4 red, and 4 yellow. The four cups are seen again, surmounted with birds, resting upon cloud symbols on the Hopi Oáqöl altar (figure 1).

In general, games appear to be played ceremonially, as pleasing to the gods, with the object of securing fertility, causing rain, giving and prolonging life, expelling demons, or curing sickness. My former conclusion as to the divinatory origin of games, so far as America is concerned, was based upon Mr Cushing's suggestion that

---

ing the image and the objects before it are offerings from the Bow, or War, society and certain members of the Deer clan. They are displayed as they appear in the house of the director of the Bow society, where they are set up previous to being deposited at the shrine of Ahaiyuta on Uhana Yäällänĕ, Wool mountain, southwest of the pueblo of Zuñi.

1. Carved figure of Ahaiyuta, a very old original, collected by Col. James Stevenson, redecorated.

2. Shield of Ahaiyuta ; hoop and network of cotton.

2. Symbolic feather bow and arrow.

3, 3. Ceremonial staffs.

4. Symbolic war club.

5. Ceremonial tablet, with symbol of crescent moon, sun, morning star, lightning, and house of Ahaiyuta.

6, 7, 8, 9, 10. Games supposed to have originated with the gods of war, and made by the Deer clan.

11. Plumes of offerings made by two members of the Bow society.

12. Four plume offerings of a member of the Deer clan.

13. Sacred meal bowl containing prayer meal.

14. Red bread, food offering to the god of war.

15. Turquoise and shell-bead offerings in corn husks.

16. Feathered staff, offering to the god of war by the Bow society. Included in this case, but presented at a different ceremonial.

17. Oraibi basket for holding the prayer plumes afterward deposited in connection with the ceremony.

18. Old handled vase and medicine plume box, personal property of the director of the Bow society.

[a] Minor Hopi Festivals. American Anthropologist, n. s., v. 4, p. 487, 1902.

[b] It is carried by two girls in the public ceremony on the ninth day, the ring being tossed with the stick.

the gaming implements which are sacrificed upon the Zuñi altar were symbols of the divination with which the ceremonies were originally connected. From that point of view the divination might be regarded as an experiment in which the dramatization of war, the chase, agriculture, the magical rites that secured success over the enemy, the reproduction of animals and the fertilization of corn, is performed in

FIG. 1. Oáqöl altar, Hopi Indians, Oraibi, Arizona; from model in the Field Columbian Museum.

order to discover the probable outcome of human effort, representing a desire to secure the guidance of the natural powers by which humanity was assumed to be dominated. As opposed to this view, it should be said that I have no direct evidence of the employment of games in divination by the Indians apart from that afforded by Mr Cushing's assertion in regard to the Zuñi sholiwe. This game is ceremonially played to-day to secure rain.

Column groups — **Games of chance:** Dice games; *Guessing games* (Stick games, Hand game, Four-stick game, Hidden ball game or Moccasin). **Games of dexterity:** Archery, Snow-snake, Hoop and pole, Ring and pin; *Ball* (Racket, Shinny, Double ball, Ball race, Football, Hand-and-foot ball, Tossed ball, Foot-cast ball, Ball juggling, Hot ball).

Tabular Index to Tribes and Games	Dice games	Stick games	Hand game	Four-stick game	Hidden ball game, or Moccasin	Archery	Snow-snake	Hoop and pole	Ring and pin	Racket	Shinny	Double ball	Ball race	Football	Hand-and-foot ball	Tossed ball	Foot-cast ball	Ball juggling	Hot ball
Algonquian stock:																			
Abnaki																708			
Algonkin	49	229																	
Amalecite	49																		
Arapaho	50		268			384	400	441, 445	529		617					705			
Blackfeet	56		269					443											
Cheyenne	58		269			384	400	445	530	563	619	649				705			
Chippewa	61	229			340		401	446	533	564	620	650							
Cree	68	230	270		342		403		535			652							
Delawares	69				342			446	537	567									
Grosventres	70		270			384	404	447	537		621					706			
Illinois	72	230																	
Kickapoo	72																		
Massachuset	73	230													698				
Menominee	73				343		404			567	622	653							
Miami		231			344					569						708			
Micmac	74														698				
Missisauga	80				344		405		538	569		653				708			
Montagnais						384			538							708			
Narraganset	80	231													699				
Nascapee									539									712	
Nipissing	81				344				540	570									
Norridgewock	81	231					406												
Ottawa	82				344														
Passamaquoddy	82						406		540	570									
Penobscot	84						406		541	571									
Piegan	84	231	271					447											
Potawatomi	85					385													
Powhatan		232									622				699				
Sauk and Foxes	85	232			345		407	448	542	572	622	654							
Shawnee										573									
Athapascan stock:																			
Apache (Chiricahua)						385		449											
Apache (Jicarilla)					345			449											
Apache (Mescalero)								449											
Apache (San Carlos)	86							450											
Apache (White Mountain)	87							450											
Ataakut		233																	
Chipewyan			272			385													
Colville								457											
Etchareottine			272																
Han Kutchin			272																
Hupa	91	233							542			656							
Kawchodinne	92		272						543										
Kutchin			272																
Mikonotunne		236									623								
Mishikhwutmetunne		236									623								
Navaho	92				346	385		457			623		668						
Sarsi			272					460											
Sekani	97	236																	
Takulli	97	236	272				409	460											
Thlingchadinne									543										
Tielding		238																	
Tsetsaut											624								
Tututni		239																	
Umpqua			274																
Whilkut		239																	
Beothukan stock:																			
Beothuk	97																		
Caddoan stock:																			
Arikara	97							461			624	657							
Caddo	98							462											
Pawnee	99		274			386	409	463			625	657							
Wichita	102		276			386		470			625	658							
Chimmesyan stock:																			
Niska		240	281					471			628							709	
Tsimshian		240																	

							Minor amusements								Games derived from Europeans	Running races
Shuttlecock	Tipcat	Quoits	Stone-throwing	Shuffleboard	Jackstraws	Swing	Stilts	Tops	Bull-roarer	Buzz	Popgun	Bean shooter	Cat's cradle	Unclassified games		
						730		733		751						
								734								
								734			758					
								734							791	
								734							791	
								734		751						
														781		
		722													792	
																803
								735								
															792	
								735			758		762			
																803
													762			
													763			
		722											763	781		804
														781		
													767			
											758					
						730										
						730	731									804
								736								
								736								

Column groups: **Games of chance** — Dice games; *Guessing games* (Stick games, Hand game, Four-stick game, Hidden ball game, or Moccasin). **Games of dexterity** — Archery, Snow-snake, Hoop and pole, Ring and pin; *Ball* (Racket, Shinny, Double ball, Ball race, Football, Hand-and-foot ball, Tossed ball, Foot-cast ball, Ball juggling, Hot ball).

TABULAR INDEX TO TRIBES AND GAMES	Dice games	Stick games	Hand game	Four-stick game	Hidden ball game, or Moccasin	Archery	Snow-snake	Hoop and pole	Ring and pin	Racket	Shinny	Double ball	Ball race	Football	Hand-and-foot ball	Tossed ball	Foot-cast ball	Ball juggling	Hot ball
Chinookan stock:																			
Chinook		240	281							573									
Clackama				328															
Clatsop			282																
Wasco			282					472											
Chumashan stock:																			
Santa Barbara								472			628								
Copehan stock:																			
Winnimen		241																	
Wintun			283									658							
Costanoan stock:																			
Rumsen			283					472											
Eskimauan stock:																			
Eskimo (Central)	102							472	544						701	709	712		
Eskimo (Central: Aivilirmiut and Kinipetu)	102							473	547										
Eskimo (Ita)									549						701		712		
Eskimo (Koksoagmiut)															700				
Eskimo (Labrador)			283						548						699				
Eskimo (Western)	104					386		474			629				701	706			
Iroquoian stock:																			
Caughnawaga	105							474		573									
Cherokee	105							475		574									
Conestoga	105																		
Huron	106	241					409		549	588									
Mohawk	110									590									
Onondaga	111				349					592									
St Regis										592									
Seneca	113				350		410	476		592									
Tuscarora	118						413	477			629								
Wyandot	118				351									702					
Kalapooian stock:																			
Calapooya			283																
Keresan stock:																			
Keres	119				351	388		478			629		668						
Kiowan stock:																			
Kiowa	124		284			388	413	478			629								
Kitunahan stock:																			
Kutenai			285																
Koluschan stock:																			
Chilkat		243	287																
Stikine		244																	
Taku		244																	
Tlingit	130	245	288													709			
Yakutat																			
Kulanapan stock:																			
Gualala			289							594									
Pomo	131	247	289				413	478	550	594									
Lutuamian stock:																			
Klamath	136	247	291	328				479	550			659							
Modoc			293	332															
Mariposan stock:																			
Chukchansi	138							482			630			702			711		714
Koyeti								482			630								
Mixed tribes											630								
Pitkachi								482											
Tejon	138																		
Wiktchamne	129																		
Yaudanchi								501											
Yokuts	140		293				414	483		595	630								
Mayan stock:																			
Kekchi	141																		
Maya	143																		
Moquelumnan stock:																			
Aplache																	712		
Awani	143										630						712		
Chowchilla			294					484			631								
Costanoan		248																	
Cosumne													669						

	Minor amusements														Unclassified games	Games derived from Europeans	Running races
Shuttlecock	Tipcat	Quoits	Stone-throwing	Shuffleboard	Jackstraws	Swing	Stilts	Tops	Bull-roarer	Buzz	Popgun	Bean shooter	Cat's cradle				
															782		
								736		751					767	782	
								737		752					769	783	
										752							
								737									
		723			729			737		753							805
	721																
																	805
		724						740							770	792	
								740									
								740								793	
															771		
								740									
								741			759					793	
								741							772	783	

TABULAR INDEX TO TRIBES AND GAMES	Games of chance					Games of dexterity													
			Guessing games							Ball									
	Dice games	Stick games	Hand game	Four-stick game	Hidden ball game, or Moccasin	Archery	Snow-snake	Hoop and pole	Ring and pin	Racket	Shinny	Double ball	Ball race	Football	Hand-and-foot ball	Tossed ball	Foot-cast ball	Ball juggling	Hot ball
Moquelumnan stock—Continued.																			
Miwok	143									596									
Olamentke	144	248																	
Topinagugim			294			388	414	484		597				702					
Tulares	145																		
Wasama								485			631	659	670						
Muskhogean stock:																			
Bayogoula								485											
Chickasaw										597									
Choctaw	146							485		598						709			
Huma								486											
Mugulasha								485											
Muskogee								486		605									
Seminole										608									
Natchesan stock:																			
Natchez	146							488								710			
Piman stock:																			
Opata	146										631		670						
Papago	146		295		353							659	670						
Pima	148		295		355	389		489	551			660	671						
Tarahumare	152					389					631		672						
Tepehuan	153											660							
Zuaque	154				356						631		678						
Pujunan stock:																			
Kaoni												660							
Konkau			296																
Maidu			297																
Nishinam	154		298					489		608		661		703		710			
Ololopa		248	299																
Salishan stock:																			
Bellacoola	155	249	299					489											
Chilliwhack		249																	
Clallam	155	249	299								632								
Clemclemalats		249																	
Nisqualli	156	250	299																
Okinagan			300																
Pend d'Oreilles		250						490			632								
Penelakut			301																
Puyallup		250	302																
Quinaielt	156																		
Salish								491											
Shuswap	156	252	302				390	491			632								
Skokomish		253								609				703					
Snohomish	156	253																	
Songish	157	254	302					491			632								
Thompson Indians	157	254	302				390	491	552	609						710			
Twana	158	256	303																
Shahaptian stock:																			
Klikitat	158	257																	
Nez Percés			304					493			632								
Umatilla			305					493	553		633								
Yakima	158		307																
Shastan stock:																			
Achomawi		257	307	332				494			633	661		703				712	
Shasta		258							553			662							
Shoshonean stock:																			
Bannock	159		307					495					678					713	
Comanche	159		309																
Hopi	160				357	390		495			633		678						
Kawia	165		310																
Mono	166		310					498			635		679		704				714
Paiute	166		311	333				498	553			662			704				
Saboba	171		313																
Shoshoni	168		309, 313					499	554		635	662						713	
Tobikhar	172		314					500					680						
Uinta Ute	172		315					500			636	663						713	
Uncompahgre Ute								501											
Ute								501	554										
Yampa Ute			315																

					Minor amusements									Unclassified games	Games derived from Europeans	Running races
Shuttlecock	Tipcat	Quoits	Stone-throwing	Shuffleboard	Jackstraws	Swing	Stilts	Tops	Bull-roarer	Buzz	Popgun	Bean shooter	Cat's cradle			
																805
															794	806
717		724														
		724														
717																
717								741					772			
													773			
717													773			
													773			
								742					773			806
			728					742								
							731	743		755		760	774		794	807
										756		760			796	
								744								
							732	744								

Tabular Index to Tribes and Games	Games of chance					Games of dexterity													
	Dice games	Guessing games				Archery	Snow-snake	Hoop and pole	Ring and pin	Ball									
		Stick games	Hand game	Four-stick game	Hidden ball game, or Moccasin					Racket	Shinny	Double ball	Ball race	Football	Hand-and-foot ball	Tossed ball	Foot-cast ball	Ball juggling	Hot ball
Siouan stock:																			
Assiniboin	173	258	316			391	415	502	555	610	636				707	710			
Catawba		258								611					704				
Congaree		258																	
Crows	177		317			391	415	502			637				707				
Dakota																			
Dakota (Brulé)	179								556										
Dakota (Oglala)	179				364	391	415	503	556		637								
Dakota (Santee)	180				365					611		663							
Dakota (Sisseton)	183																		
Dakota (Teton)	181	258				392	416	508	557		638								
Dakota (Wahpeton)	183																		
Dakota (Yankton)	184		317				418	508			639								
Dakota (Yanktonai)	185									614									
Eno								510											
Hidatsa	186		318		365			511			641					710			
Iowa	186				365					615									
Mandan	187					393	419	511							707				
Omaha	187	259			366	393	419	514			641	663							
Osage	188							516			642								
Oto										615									
Ponca	188							517											
Winnebago	189				366				557	615						708			
Skittagetan stock:																			
Haida	189	259	318			395		517	557		642								
Tanoan stock:																			
Tewa	190 192				367	395			558		643		680						
Tigua	190 195				369			518			642								
Wakashan stock:																			
Bellabella		263																	
Clayoquot	196		319						558										
Hesquiaht																			
Kwakiutl	196	263	319		370			519	559										
Makah	197	263	321			395		522	559		643								
Nimkish																			
Nootka	198		322					523											
Opitchesaht																			
Washoan stock:																			
Pao				335															
Washo	199	265	322	335		396		523				664			704				
Weitspekan stock:																			
Yurok	199	265										664							
Wishoskan stock:																			
Batawat	199	266										665							
Yukian stock:																			
Huchnom			323																
Yuman stock:																			
Cocopa	199												681						
Diegueño			323																
Havasupai	200																		
Maricopa	201				370	396						665	681						
Mission Indians	204		325								644								
Mohave	205		326					523	560		644		682						
Walapai	207				371			525			645								
Yuma	208		327					526			646		682						
Zuñian stock:																			
Zuñi	210	266			372	396		526	560		646		682			710			714

Minor amusements															Games derived from Europeans	Running races
Shuttlecock	Tipcat	Quoits	Stone-throwing	Shuffleboard	Jackstraws	Swing	Stilts	Tops	Bull-roarer	Buzz	Popgun	Bean shooter	Cat's cradle	Unclassified games	Games derived from Europeans	Running races
				728												
								745		756						807
								745	750	756	759					
	721			728		731		746	750	757	759					
				728				746								
				729				747								
								747	750		759				797	808
																809
		725			730			747						784		
			728					747					774		797	
								748					775		798	
718								748								
718		725						748				760		784		
718								748				761	776			
719								749								
719												761				
										757			776			809
		726														
719	721	726					732	749		757		761	777	787	799	

GAMES OF CHANCE

The ultimate object of all Indian games of chance is to determine a number or series of numbers, gain or loss depending upon the priority in which the players arrive at a definitive goal. The Indian chance games, as before mentioned, may be divided into dice games and guessing games—that is, into those in which the hazard depends upon the random fall of certain implements employed like dice, and those in which it depends upon the guess or choice of the player; one is objective, the other subjective. In general, the dice games are played in silence, while the guessing games are accompanied by singing and drumming, once doubtless incantations to secure the aid and favor of the divinity who presides over the game.

The guessing games consist of four kinds:

I. Those in which a bundle of sticks, originally shaftments of arrows, are divided in the hands, the object being for the opponent to guess in which hand the odd stick or a particularly marked stick is held; these for convenience I have designated stick games.

II. Those in which two or four sticks, one or two marked, are held in the hands, the object being to guess which hand holds the unmarked stick; for these the common name of hand game has been retained.

III. Those in which four sticks, marked in pairs, are hidden together, the object being to guess their relative position; these I have designated four-stick games.

IV. Those in which some small object—a stone, stick, or bullet—is hidden in one of four wooden tubes, in one of four moccasins, or in the earth, the object being to guess where it is hidden; for these I have accepted Mr Cushing's designation of the hidden-ball game, and for a particular form of the game, the common descriptive name of the moccasin game.

DICE GAMES

Under this caption are included all games in which number is determined by throwing, at random, objects which, for convenience, may be termed dice. A game or games of this type are here described

44

as existing among 130 tribes belonging to 30 linguistic stocks, and from no one tribe does it appear to have been absent.

The essential implements consist, first, of the dice, and, second, of the instruments for keeping count. The dice, with minor exceptions, have two faces, distinguished by colors or markings, and are of a great variety of materials—split canes, wooden staves or blocks, bone staves, beaver and woodchuck teeth, walnut shells, peach and plum stones, grains of corn, and bone, shell, brass, and pottery disks. They are either thrown by hand or tossed in a bowl or basket, this difference giving rise to the two principal types of the game. Both are frequently found among the same tribe, and the evidence goes to show that the basket-dice game, which is most commonly played by women, is a derivative from the game in which the dice are thrown by hand. In the latter the dice are cast in a variety of ways—tossed in the air against a hide or blanket, struck ends down upon a stone or a hide disk, struck ends down upon a stone held in the hand, or allowed to fall freely upon the earth or upon a hide or blanket.

There are many variations in the method of counting, but they can all be divided into two general classes—those in which the score is kept with sticks or counters, which pass from hand to hand, and those in which it is kept upon a counting board or abacus. In the first the counters are usually in multiples of ten, infrequently of twelve, and vary from ten up to one hundred and twenty. They commonly consist of sticks or twigs, and, from the fact that arrows are employed by some tribes and that many others use sticks bearing marks that may be referred to those on arrow shaftments, they may be regarded as having been derived from arrows, for which the game may have originally been played. The game terminates when one of the opposing sides wins all the counters. The counting board or abacus consists either of stones placed in a square or circle upon the ground, of a row of small sticks or pegs, or of an inscribed cloth, hide, stone, or board. It is almost invariably arranged in four divisions, consisting of ten places each, the number of counts in the circuit varying from forty to one hundred and sixty. In connection with the counting board, men, or pieces, frequently known as "horses," are used to indicate the positions of the several players. It is an invariable rule that when a man, or piece, falls upon a place occupied by a man of an opponent, the latter piece is said to be killed, and is sent back to its starting place. The number of players varies from two, one on each side, up to an indefinite number, depending upon those who desire to take part. Two or four are most common, the spectators betting upon the result. Both men and women participate in the dice games, but usually apart. In their ceremonial forms these are distinctively men's games. As mentioned in the introduction, the dice game was one of the games sacred to the War God in Zuñi, and the cane dice were sacrificed upon his shrine. Figure 2 represents a set of such sacrificial dice, collected by the writer from the shrine of the War God on Corn mountain, Zuñi, in 1902.

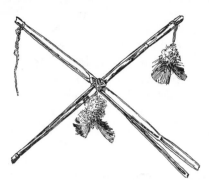

FIG. 2. Sacrificial gaming canes from shrine of War God, Zuñi Indians, Zuñi, New Mexico; length, 15 inches; cat. no. 22681, Free Museum of Science and Art, University of Pennsylvania.

They consist of four split canes 15 inches in length, painted black on the outside, and bound in pairs, one fitting into the other, to form a cross. The middle and two ends are tied with cotton cord, to which down feathers are attached. These canes appear to have been used in a different form of the dice game from that described in the present volume as played in Zuñi.

Dr J. Walter Fewkes [a] mentions a bundle of gaming reeds being placed with other objects upon the Tewa kiva altar (plate III) erected at the winter solstice at Hano, and in a letter [b] to the writer says that the markings on these canes resemble very closely those on the set (figure 200) which he found in the old altar at Chevlon.

A comparison of the dice games of the Indians throughout the United States led the writer at first to refer them all to canes, such as are employed in the Zuñi game of sholiwe. These canes in their original form consist of split arrow shaftments, and are marked both inside and out with bands or ribbonings corresponding with the markings on the arrows of the four world quarters. Many of the wooden dice, which the Zuñi call "wood canes," bear an incised mark on the inner side, corresponding to the inner concave side of the canes. The chevron pattern on the outer face of many of the staves

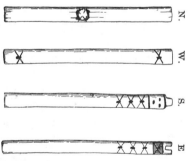

FIG. 3. Cane dice (reproductions); length, 5¼ inches; Zuñi Indians, Zuñi, New Mexico; cat. no. 16543, Free Museum of Science and Art, University of Pennsylvania.

agrees with, and appears to be derived from, the crosshatching on the sholiwe. When the staves are differentiated by marks, these, too, agree more or less closely with those on the canes. It will be observed that in many of the sets one of the dice is distinguished from the others by marks on the face, or convex side, as well as on the reverse.

[a] American Anthropologist, n. s., v. 1, p. 272, 1899.   [b] January 27, 1899.

ALTAR OF WAR GOD; ZUÑI INDIANS, ZUÑI, N. MEX.; FROM PHOTOGRAPH
OF REPRODUCTION IN THE UNITED STATES NATIONAL MUSEUM

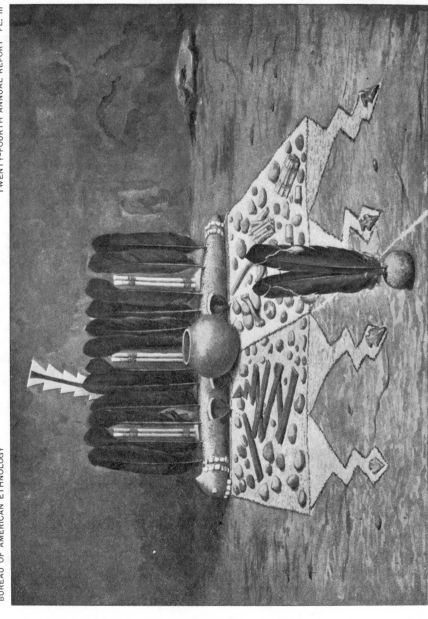

TEWA KIVA ALTAR AT HANO, SHOWING GAMING REEDS; TEWA INDIANS, ARIZONA; FROM FEWKES

When this piece falls with this side uppermost it augments the count in the play.

Figure 3 represents the obverse of a set of Zuñi canes for sholiwe, reproduced from memory by Mr Cushing for the writer in the summer of 1893. The athlua, or "sender," the uppermost cane in this set, corresponding with the north, is marked on the convex side with a cross, agreeing in this respect with one of the sticks of the Tewa game, figure 255.

This peculiarity, in one form or another, is repeated throughout the implements hereafter described, the obverse of one of

Fig. 4. Handle of atlatl, showing crossed wrapping for the attachment of finger loops; cliff-dwelling, Mancos canyon, Colorado; Free Museum of Science and Art, University of Pennsylvania.

the sticks in many of the sets being carved or burned, while in others the stave is tied about the middle. This specially marked die is the one that augments the throw. In attempting to account for it, it occurred to the writer to compare the Zuñi cane bearing the cross marks with the atlatl, or throwing stick, from a cliff-dwelling in Mancos canyon,

Fig. 5. Atlatl (restored); length, 15 inches; cliff-dwelling, Mancos canyon, Colorado; Free Museum of Science and Art, University of Pennsylvania.

Colorado, in the University of Pennsylvania museum (figures 4 and 5). Mr Cushing had suggested that the athlua, placed beneath the other canes in tossing them, corresponded to the atlatl. The comparison seemed to confirm his suggestion. The cross mark is possibly the cross wrapping of the atlatl for the attachment of finger

Fig. 6. Stick die; length, 7 inches; cliff-dwelling, Mancos canyon, Colorado; Free Museum of Science and Art, University of Pennsylvania.

loops. According to this view, the Zuñi canes may be regarded as symbolic of the atlatl and three arrows, such as are carried by the gods in Mexican pictures. From the evidence furnished by the implements employed, I concluded at first that the games with tossed canes, staves, etc., must all be referred to the regions of cane arrows and the atlatl, probably the southwestern United States.

Later observations upon other Indian games, in which it is apparent that the implements represent the bows of the War Gods, caused me to reexamine the stick dice, with the result that I am inclined to believe that many of them are to be indentified with bows rather than with arrows.   At any rate, whether as arrows or bows,

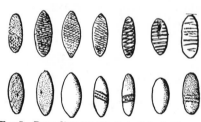

the four dice are to be referred to the War Gods. It will be seen that the counting circuit agrees with the gaming wheel, which in some instances is notched at its four quarters in agreement with the dice marks.

FIG. 7. Bone dice; length, ¹¹⁄₁₆ to ¹⁵⁄₁₆ inch; Tanner springs, Arizona; cat. no. 22770, Free Museum of Science and Art, University of Pennsylvania.

The wide distribution and range of variations in the dice games point to their high antiquity, of which objective evidence is afforded in the prehistoric stick die (figure 6) from the cliff-ruins of Colorado.   Similar evidence exists in the pottery bowls (figures 197–199) decorated with representations of gaming sticks, with their peculiar markings, from prehistoric Hopi graves in Arizona.

Small bone dice are found in the prehistoric graves and ruins of Arizona, New Mexico, and Utah.   Seven such dice in the Free Museum of Science and Art of the University of Pennsylvania (cat. no. 22770), collected by Henry Dodge at Tanner springs, Arizona, are lenticular in form and from eleven-sixteenths to fifteen-sixteenths inch in length.   The flat sides are marked— five with fine diamonds formed of cross lines, and two with straight transverse lines, as shown in figure 7. Four are plain, and three have transverse bands on the rounded side.   Four of them have also traces of blue and three of red paint.   There are several such dice in the American Museum of Natural History. Eight from pueblo Peñasca Blanca, Chaco canyon, New Mexico, are similar to those above described. With them are a similar object of limonite, two small circular bone disks, and three small rectangular pieces of thin bone, which also appear to have been used as dice. From Grand Gulch, Utah, in the same museum, are three similar lenticular bone dice, plain on their flat side, and two somewhat smaller ones with the flat side inscribed with four transverse lines.   With them are four small bone disks, the flat sides of which show grooves, the natural cavities of the bone, and one somewhat smaller that is marked on the flat side with a cross.

From Grand Gulch also, in the same museum, are a number of

FIG. 8 a, b, c. Cane and wood dice and wooden dice cups; Grand Gulch, Utah; American Museum of Natural History.

other dice. Nine consist of small fragments of cane (figure 8*a*), made to include a joint, and slightly flattened and marked with notches at each end, on the flat side. Two of these are somewhat shorter than the rest and have the joint smoothed down. Another set of four wooden dice from the same place is accompanied by a finely wrought wooden cup 2 inches in height and 1⅞ inches in diameter. These dice are three-fourths of an inch in length, slightly flattened on one side, the rounded part being marked with burned devices, as shown in figure 8*b*. Another similar dice cup in the same collection contains three wooden dice (figure 8*c*) and two cane dice like those first described. The wooden dice in these two sets appear to be copies of canes.

ALGONQUIAN STOCK

ALGONKIN.   Three Rivers, Quebec.

Pierre Boucher [a] says:

The game of the dish is played with nine little flat round bones, black on one side, white on the other, which they stir up and cause to jump in a large wooden dish, preventing them from striking the earth by holding it in their hands. Loss or gain depends upon the largest number of one color. The game paquessen is almost the same thing, except that the little bones are thrown into the air with the hand, falling upon a robe spread on the ground like a carpet. The number of one color determines loss or gain.

AMALECITE (MALECITE).   New Brunswick.   (Cat. no. 20125, Free Museum of Science and Art, University of Pennsylvania.)

Set of six disks of caribou bone marked on the flat side (figure 9); a platter of curly maple cut across the grain, 11½ inches in diam-

FIG. 9. Bone dice; diameter, 1 inch; Amalecite (Malecite) Indians, New Brunswick; cat. no. 20125, Free Museum of Science and Art, University of Pennsylvania.

eter; and fifty-two wooden counting sticks about 8 inches in length (figure 10), four being much broader than the others and of different shapes.

These were collected and deposited by Mr George E. Starr, who purchased the game from a woman named Susan Perley, a member

[a] Histoire Véritable et Naturelle des Moeurs et Productions du Pays de la Novelle France, ch. 10, Paris, 1664.

of a tribe calling themselves the Tobique, at an Indian village half
a mile north of Andover, New Brunswick.   Three of the disks and
the counting sticks were made for the collector, while the platter and
three of the disks shown in the upper row (figure 9) are old.   Two
of the latter are made apparently of old bone buttons, there being

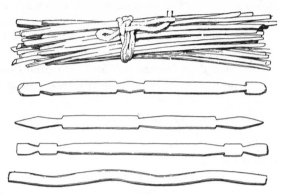

FIG. 10.   Counting sticks for stick dice; length, 8 inches; Amalecite (Malecite) Indians, New
Brunswick; cat. no. 20125, Free Museum of Science and Art, University of Pennsylvania.

a hole in the reverse into which the shank fitted.   The designs on
the faces are not the same.   The woman informed Mr Starr that
the game was called altestagen, and that it was played by two persons,
one of whom places the counting sticks in a pile together.

Then the stones are placed at random in the plate, which is held in both
hands and struck sharply on the ground so as to make the stones fly into the air
and turn before landing in the plate again.   A player continues as long as he
scores, taking counters from the pile of sticks according to his throw.   When
the pile is exhausted, each having obtained part, the game is continued until
one wins them all.   Three plain sticks count one point.   The three carved
sticks count each four points, or twelve plain sticks.   The snake-like stick is
kept to the last.   It is equal to three plain sticks, and a throw that counts three
is necessary to take it.

ARAPAHO.   Wind River reservation, Wyoming.   (Free Museum of
       Science and Art, University of Pennsylvania.)
Cat. no. 36963.   Four willow twigs, marked alike on the flat side,
       painted red; length, 6¾ inches (figure 11).

FIG. 11.   Stick dice; length, 6¼ inches; Arapaho Indians, Wyoming; cat. no. 36963, Free Museum
of Science and Art, University of Pennsylvania.

Cat. no. 36964.   Four others, similar, but marked on the round sides, painted yellow; length, 6½ inches (figure 12).

FIG. 12.   Stick dice; length, 6½ inches; Arapaho Indians, Wyoming; cat. no. 36964, Free Museum of Science and Art, University of Pennsylvania.

Cat. no. 36965.   Five flat shaved twigs, painted orange yellow; one face plain, the other marked with incised lines painted blue; length, 8⅜ inches (figure 13).

FIG. 13.   Stick dice; length, 8⅜ inches; Arapaho Indians, Wyoming; cat. no. 36965, Free Museum of Science and Art, University of Pennsylvania.

Cat. no. 36966.   Four flat willow twigs, one side yellow, with notches painted green and red, all different (figure 14), reverse plain

FIG. 14.   Stick dice; length, 9¼ inches; Arapaho Indians, Wyoming; cat. no. 36966, Free Museum of Science and Art, University of Pennsylvania.

green; accompanied by a thick rawhide disk, 11 inches in diameter, painted green, with the device shown in figure 15a on

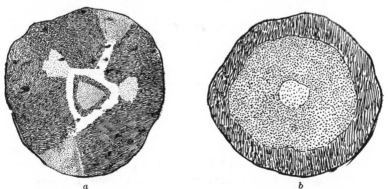

a   b

FIG. 15.   Leather disk used with stick dice; diameter, 11 inches; Arapaho Indians, Wyoming; cat. no. 36966, Free Museum of Science and Art, University of Pennsylvania.

one face; reverse, green with internal ring of red, and blue center (figure 15*b*).   The bets are said to be laid on this.

Cat. no. 36967.   Four flat twigs, having one side painted yellow, with notches painted green and red, all different, as shown in figure

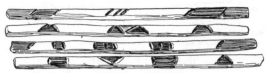

FIG. 16. Stick dice; length, 9 inches; Arapaho Indians, Wyoming; cat. no. 36967, Free Museum of Science and Art, University of Pennsylvania.

16; length, 9 inches; accompanied by a disk of rawhide painted red, yellow, and green, upon which the bets are laid; diameter, 6¼ inches (figure 17).

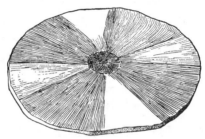

FIG. 17. Leather disk used with stick dice; diameter, 6¼ inches; Arapaho Indians, Wyoming; cat. no. 36967, Free Museum of Science and Art, University of Pennsylvania.

Cat. no. 36968.   Six shaved twigs, ovoid in section, painted red, three marked on the round side with incised line and three with incised lines on both sides, all different; length, 10 inches.

Cat. no. 36969.   Five slender peeled willow twigs, with burnt marks on one side; length, 7 inches (figure 18).

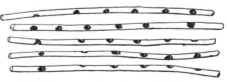

FIG. 18. Stick dice; length, 7 inches; Arapaho Indians, Wyoming; cat. no. 36969, Free Museum of Science and Art, University of Pennsylvania.

Cat. no. 36961.   Eight pieces: Three bone disks with three incised intersecting lines painted red and yellow, diameter about 1 inch; three diamond-shaped bone pieces with incised Greek cross burned and painted green, length, $1\frac{3}{4}$ inches; two rectangular pieces with similar cross burned and painted red, length, $1\frac{1}{2}$ inches. The reverse sides are all plain (figure 19).

FIG. 19. Bone dice; diameter, 1 to $1\frac{1}{4}$ inches; Arapaho Indians, Wyoming; cat. no. 36961, Free Museum of Science and Art, University of Pennsylvania.

Cat. no. 36962. Twenty pieces, contained in a small cotton-cloth bag.

The following are bone, with burnt designs on one face, the reverse being plain: Three diamond-shaped with cross (figure 20a); three diamond-shaped, quartered, the alternate quarters burned (figure 20b); three elliptical, with elongated diamond in field (figure 20c); three elliptical, with cross band and lines at end (figure 20d); one elliptical, with central diamond inclosed by chevrons (figure 20e); two rectangular, with central cross lines and wedge on each end (figure 20f); one rectangular, with lines at the ends (figure 20g); two rectangular, with three dots (figure 20h).

The following are of peach stone: Three with Greek cross (figure 20i); two with dot in circle (figure 20j). All of these specimens were collected by the writer in 1900.

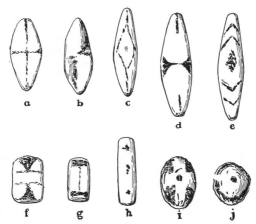

FIG. 20. Bone and peach-stone dice; diameter, $\frac{7}{8}$ inch to $2\frac{1}{4}$ inches; Arapaho Indians, Wyoming; cat. no. 36962, Free Museum of Science and Art, University of Pennsylvania.

ARAPAHO. Cheyenne and Arapaho reservation, Oklahoma. (Cat. no. 152802, 152803, United States National Museum.)

Set of five dice of buffalo bone, marked on one side with burnt designs (figure 21) and basket of woven grass, 9 inches in diameter at top and $2\frac{1}{2}$ inches deep (figure 22). The rim of the basket is bound with cotton cloth, and the inner side of the bottom is covered with the same material. The game is played by women. Collected by Mr James Mooney in 1891.

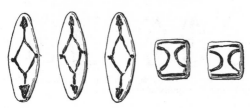

The following account of the game is given by the collector: [a]

FIG. 21. Bone dice; lengths, ⅞ and 1¼ inches; Arapaho Indians, Oklahoma; cat. no. 152802, United States National Museum

The dice game is called ta-u′sĕta′tina (literally, striking or throwing against something) by the Arapaho, and mo′nshimûnh by the Cheyenne, the same name being now given to the modern card games. It was practically universal among all the tribes east and west, and, under the name of hubbub, is described by a New England writer [b] as far back as 1634 almost precisely as it exists to-day among the prairie tribes. The only difference seems to have been that in the east it was played also by the men, and to the accompaniment of a song, such as is used in the hand games of the western tribes. The requisites are a small wicker bowl or basket (hatĕchi′na), five dice made of bone or plum stones, and a pile of tally sticks, such as are used in the awl game. The bowl is 6 or 8 inches in diameter and about 2 inches deep, and is woven in basket fashion of the tough fibers of the yucca. The dice may be round, elliptical, or diamond shaped, and are variously marked on one side with lines or figures, the turtle being a favorite design among the Arapaho. Two of the five must be alike in shape and marking. The other three are marked with another design and may also be of another shape. Any number of women and girls may play, each throwing in turn, and sometimes one set of partners playing against another. The partners toss up the dice from the basket, letting them drop again into it, and score points according to the way the dice turn up in the basket.

FIG. 22. Basket for dice; diameter, 9 inches; Arapaho Indians, Oklahoma; cat. no. 152803, United States National Museum.

The first throw by each player is made from the hand instead of from the basket. One hundred points usually count a game, and stakes are wagered on the result as in almost every other Indian contest of skill or chance. For the purpose of explanation we shall designate two of the five as " rounds " and the other three as " diamonds," it being understood that only the marked side counts in the game, excepting when the throw happens to turn up the three " diamonds " blank while the other two show the marked side, or, as sometimes happens, when all five dice turn up blank. In every case all of one kind at least must turn up to score a point. A successful throw entitles the player to another throw, while a failure obliges her to pass the basket to someone else. The formula is: One only of either kind counts 0; two rounds, 3; three diamonds (both rounds with blank side up),

[a] The Ghost Dance Religion. Fourteenth Annual Report of the Bureau of Ethnology, pt. 2, p. 1004, 1896.

[b] William Wood, New England's Prospect, London, 1634.

3; three diamonds blank (both rounds with marked side up), 3; four marked sides up, 1; five blank sides up, 1; five marked sides up, 8.

A game, similar in principle but played with six dice instead of five, is also played by the Arapaho women, as well as by those of the Comanche and probably of other tribes.

ARAPAHO. Oklahoma. (United States National Museum.)

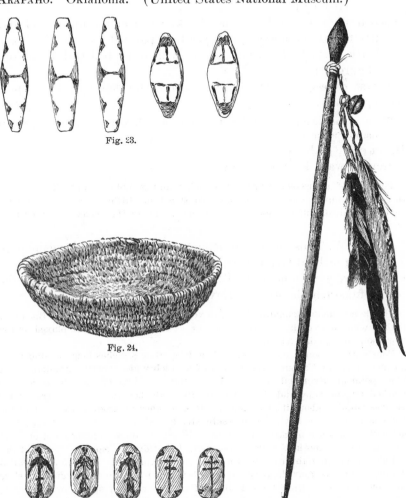

Fig. 23.

Fig. 24.

Fig. 25.   Fig. 26.

FIG. 23. Bone dice; length, 1¾ to 2¼ inches; Arapaho Indians, Oklahoma; cat. no. 165765, United States National Museum.

FIG. 24. Basket for dice; diameter, 10 inches; Arapaho Indians, Oklahoma; cat. no. 165765, United States National Museum.

FIG. 25. Wooden dice; length, 1½ inches; Arapaho Indians, Oklahoma; cat. no. 165765a, United States National Museum.

FIG. 26. Stick representing a man, used by women in dice game; length, 15¼ inches; Arapaho Indians, Oklahoma; cat. no. ₃₇₃⁵⁰, American Museum of Natural History.

Cat. no. 165765. Set of five bone dice, marked on convex side with burned designs (figure 23), and much worn basket of woven grass, 10 inches in diameter at top and 2 inches deep (figure 24).

Cat. no. 165765a. Set of five wooden dice, marked on one side with
    burned designs (figure 25), representing on three a swallow or
    swallow hawk and on two a dragon fly. Both collected by Rev.
    H. R. Voth.

ARAPAHO. Oklahoma. (Cat. no. $\frac{50}{373}$, American Museum of Natural
    History.)

Wooden stick, 15½ inches in length, knobbed at the upper end and
    pointed at the lower, the upper half painted red and the lower
    black, with four feathers and a small brass bell tied at the top
    (figure 26).

It was collected by Dr A. L. Kroeber, who describes it as representing a man:

When women gamble with dice they use this stick as a charm to prevent
cheating in the game.

BLACKFEET. Alberta.

    Rev. Edward F. Wilson [a] says:

Their chief amusements are horse racing and gambling. For the latter of
these they employ dice of their own construction—little cubes of wood with
signs instead of numbers marked upon them. These they shake together in a
wooden dish.

Rev. J. W. Tims [b] gives katsasinni as a general term for gambling.

Dr George Bird Grinnell has furnished me the following account
of the stave game among the Blackfeet, which he describes under the
name of onesteh, the stick, or travois,[c] game:

This is a woman's gambling game, in vogue among the tribes of the Blackfoot
nation, who know nothing of the basket or seed game so generally played by the
more southern plains tribes.

Four straight bones, made from buffalo ribs—6 or 8 inches long, one-fourth of
an inch thick, and about three-fourths of an inch wide, tapering gradually to a
blunt point at either end—are used in playing it. Three of these bones are unmarked on one side, and the fourth on this side has three or five transverse
grooves running about it at its middle, or sometimes no grooves are cut and the
bone is marked by having a buckskin string tied around it. On their other
sides the bones are marked, two of them by zigzag lines running from one end
to the other; another, called the chief, has thirteen equally distant holes
drilled in, but not through, it from one end to the other. The fourth, called
" four," from its four depressions or holes, has four transverse grooves close
to each end, and within these is divided into four equal spaces by three sets
of transverse grooves of three each. In the middle of each of these spaces a
circular depression or hole is cut. All the lines, grooves, and marks are painted
in red, blue, or black [figure 27].

These bones are played with either by two women who gamble against each

    [a] Report on the Blackfoot Tribes. Report of the Fifty-seventh Meeting of British Asso-
ciation for the Advancement of Science, p. 192, London, 1888.

    [b] Grammar and Dictionary of the Blackfoot Language, London, 1889.

    [c] The word travois has been variously explained as coming from travail and from trai-
neau. I believe, however, as stated in The Story of the Indian, p. 156, it is a corruption
from travers or à travers, meaning across, and referring to the crossing of the poles over
the horse's or over the dog's withers (G. B. G.).

other or by a number of women who sit opposite and facing each other in two long lines, each player contesting with her opposite neighbor. Twelve sticks, or counters, are used in the game, and at first these are placed on the ground between the two players.

The player, kneeling or squatting on the ground, grasps the four bones in the right or left hand, holding them vertically with the ends resting on the ground. With a slight sliding motion she scatters the bones on the ground close in front of her, and the sides which fall uppermost express the count or the failure to count. Sometimes, but not always, the players throw the bones to determine which shall have the first throw in the game.

The person making a successful throw takes from the heap of sticks the number called for by the points of the throw—one stick for each point. So long as the throw is one which counts the player continues to throw, but if she fails to count the bones are passed over to the opposite player, and she then throws until she has cast a blank. When the sticks have all been taken from the pile on the ground between them the successful thrower begins to take from her opponent so many of the sticks which she has gained as are called for by her throw. As twelve points must be made by a player before the

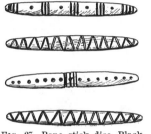   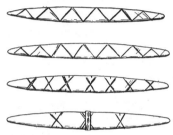

FIG. 27. Bone stick dice, Black-foot Indians, Blackfoot agency, Montana; in the collection of Dr George Bird Grinnell.

FIG. 28. Bone stick dice; length, 5¼ inches; Blackfoot Indians, South Pie-gan reservation, Montana; cat. no. 51693, Field Columbian Museum.

twelve sticks can come into her possession and the game be won, it will be seen that the contest may be long drawn out. A run of luck is needed to finish it.

Some of the counts made by the throws are here given: Three blanks and chief count 6; three blanks and chief reversed, 3; two zigzag, one four, and chief, 4; two blanks, one four, and chief, 2; two blanks, one zigzag, and chief, 0; two blanks, one zigzag, and chief reversed, 0; one zigzag, one blank, one four, and chief, 0.

The women do not sing at this game as the men do at the gambling game of hands.

The game described was obtained by Doctor Grinnell from the Pie-gan of the Blackfoot agency in northwestern Montana, on the eastern flanks of the Rocky mountains. They live on Milk river and Cut Bank, Willow, Two Medicine Lodge, and Badger creeks, being the southernmost tribe of the Blackfeet. It will be observed that the implements for this game are practically identical with those collected by Doctor Matthews from the Grosventres (Hidatsa) in North Dakota (figure 241). Concerning the latter Doctor Grinnell remarks:

The Grosventres of Dakota—by which are meant, of course, the Grosventres of the village, a tribe of Crow stock—are not very distant neighbors of the

Blackfeet, and, in fact, the people of the old Fort Berthold village—the Gros-ventres, Ree, and Mandan—have many customs, and even some traditions, which closely resemble those of the Blackfeet.

BLACKFEET. South Piegan reservation, Montana. (Cat. no. 51693, Field Columbian Museum.)

Set of four bone staves, made of rib bones, 5¼ inches in length and one-half inch wide in the middle, tapering to the ends. The outer rounded sides are cut with lines, which are filled with red paint, as shown in figure 28. Two are alike, and one of the

FIG. 29. Counting sticks for dice; length, 5¼ inches; Blackfoot Indians. South Piegan reservation, Montana; cat. no. 51693, Field Columbian Museum.

others is banded with a narrow thong of buckskin, on which are sewed twelve small blue glass beads. The reverses, which show the texture of the bone, are alike and painted red.

Accompanied by twelve counting sticks (figure 29) made of twigs, 5½ inches in length, smeared with red paint.

———— Blood reserve, Alberta. Cat. no. 51654, Field Columbian Museum.)

Three bone staves, 6⅜ inches in length and five-eighths of an inch in

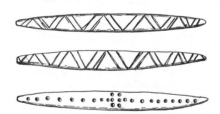

FIG. 30. Bone stick dice; length, 6⅜ inches; Blackfoot Indians, Blood reserve, Alberta; cat. no. 51654, Field Columbian Museum.

width in the middle, tapering to the ends. The outer rounded sides are carved as shown in figure 30, two alike, in which the incised lines are filled with red paint, and one with holes, 10—3 3—9, which are painted blue. The inner sides, which show the texture of the bone, are perfectly plain.

Both of the above sets were collected by Dr George A. Dorsey, who gave me the following particulars regarding the way in which they are used:

I am informed that the Bloods generally use three instead of four bones. They call the game nit sitai epsktpsepinan, we play. The stick marked with holes is called "man" and the other two "snakes." Of the counts I have only this much:

All marked faces up count 4; all unmarked faces up, 4; two unmarked and snake up, 6; one unmarked and two snakes up, 6; one unmarked, snake, and man up, 0.

CHEYENNE. Cheyenne and Arapaho reservation, Oklahoma. (Cat. no. 152803, United States National Museum.)

Set of five bone dice marked on one side with burned designs (figure 31) and basket of woven grass 8½ inches in diameter at top and

2½ inches deep (figure 32).   Both sides of the bottom are covered
with cotton cloth.   Played by women.   Collected by Mr James
Mooney in 1891.

Dr George Bird Grinnell furnished the writer the following account
of the Cheyenne basket game, which he describes under the name of
monshimout:

The Cheyenne seed or basket game is played with a shallow bowl and five
plum stones.   The bowl is from 3 to 4 inches deep, 8 inches across at the top,
flattened or not on the bottom, and woven of grass or strips of willow twigs.
It is nearly one-half inch thick and is strong.   All five seeds are unmarked on
one side, but on the other side [figure 33] three are marked with a figure
representing the paint patterns often used by girls on their faces, the cross being
on the bridge of the nose, the side marks on the cheeks, and the upper and
lower ones on the forehead and chin, respectively.   The other two stones are
marked with a figure representing the foot of a bear.[a]

These plum stones are placed in the basket [figure 34], thrown up and caught
in it, and the combination of the sides which lie uppermost after they have fallen
determines the count of the throw.

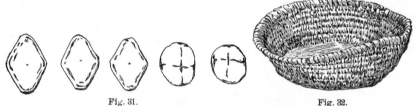

Fig. 31.   Fig. 32.

FIG. 31.   Bone dice; lengths, 1¼ and ⅞ inches; Cheyenne Indians, Oklahoma; cat. no. 152803,
United States National Museum.
FIG. 32.   Basket for dice; diameter at top, 8¼ inches; Cheyenne Indians, Oklahoma; cat. no.
152803, United States National Museum.

The players sit opposite one another, if several are playing, in two rows facing
each other.   Each individual bets with the woman opposite to her.   Each player
is provided with eight sticks, which represent the points which she must gain or
lose to win or lose the game.   When a player has won all the sticks belonging to
her opponent she has won the game and the stake.

There are several combinations of marks and blanks which count nothing for
or against the player making the throw, except that she loses her chance to
make another throw.   Others entitle the thrower to receive one, three, or even
all eight sticks, and each throw that counts anything entitles the player to
another throw.   All the players on the side of the thrower—that is, in the same
row—win or lose from those opposite them as the thrower wins or loses.   If
the person making the first throw casts a blank, she passes the basket to the one
sitting next her; if this one makes a throw that counts, she has another and
another, until she throws a blank, when the basket passes on.   When the basket
reaches the end of the line, it is handed across to the woman at the end of the
opposite row, and in the same way travels down the opposite line.

In making the throw the basket is raised only a little way, and the stones
tossed only a few inches high.   Before they fall the basket is brought smartly
down to the ground, against which it strikes with some little noise.   Some of

---

[a] Mr Cushing identified the mark of the cross with a star and the other with a bear's
track, referring, respectively, to the sky and earth.

the throws are given below, the sides of the seeds being designated by their marks: Two blanks, two bears, and one cross count nothing; four blanks and one bear count nothing; five blanks count 1 point and the thrower takes one stick; three blanks and two bears count 1 point and the player takes 1 stick; one blank, two bears, and two crosses count 1 point and thrower takes one stick; two blanks and three crosses count 3 points and the thrower takes three sticks; two bears and three crosses count 8 points and the thrower takes eight sticks, and wins the game.

The women do not sing at this game, but they chatter and joke continually as the play goes on.

FIG. 33. Plum-stone dice; Cheyenne Indians, Montana; in the collection of Dr George Bird Grinnell.

Doctor Grinnell states that the specimens figured came from the Northern Cheyenne agency, officially known as the Tongue River agency, in Montana, the Indians living on Rosebud and Tongue rivers, which are tributaries of the Yellowstone from the south. At the same time the southern Cheyenne of Oklahoma have the same game.

CHEYENNE. Oklahoma.

Mr Louis L. Meeker, late manual training teacher in the Cheyenne school at Darlington, refers to the Cheyenne dice game in a communi-

FIG. 34. Basket for dice; Cheyenne Indians, Montana; in the collection of Dr George Bird Grinnell.

cation on Cheyenne Indian games made to the Bureau of Ethnology. He says the bone dice, marked differently on one side, are shaken in a basket of Indian manufacture. The game and ordinary playing cards are both called moncimon.

Col. Richard Irving Dodge says:[a]

---

[a] Our Wild Indians, p. 330, Hartford, 1882.

Besides taking part in the round games of the men, the women have games of their own which I have never seen played by men. The most common is called the plum-stone game, and is played by the women and children of nearly all the plains tribes. The stone of the wild plum is polished and the flatter sides are cut or scraped off, making them more flat. Some of these faces are then marked with different hieroglyphics, varying with the tribe, and some are left blank. The game is played with eight such pieces, which are shaken together in a little bowl or a tin cup and then thrown on a blanket. It is really nothing but our game of dice, complicated, however, by a system of counting so curious and arbitrary that it is almost impossible for a white man to learn it. Every possible combination of the hieroglyphics and blanks on the eight stones gives a different count. This varies with the tribe. Among the Cheyenne the highest possible throw is 200, the lowest 0. The game is usually 2,000, though this varies greatly. Each player, having the gambler's superstition as to what is her lucky number, tries to fix the game at that number. If the stakes are valuable, the number fixed for the game is generally a compromise. In some tribes a certain combination of the stones wins and another combination loses the game, even though it be made on the first throw.

CHEYENNE. Cheyenne reservation, Montana. (Cat. no. 69689, Field Columbian Museum.)

FIG. 35. Plum-stone dice; Cheyenne Indians, Montana; cat. no. 69689, Field Columbian Museum.

Implements for women's dice game. Plum-stone dice (figure 35) in sets of three alike, with burnt designs on one side; accompanied by a small basket of twined grass, and counting sticks made of stalks of rushes, about 8 inches in length, dyed yellow, green, red, and blue, each player having six of the same color. Collected by Mr S. C. Simms in 1901.

CHIPPEWA. Bois fort. Near Rainy river, Minnesota. (Cat. no. $\frac{50}{4713}$, American Museum of Natural History.)

Four flat sticks (figure 36), $15\frac{1}{2}$ inches long, burned black on both sides and marked alike in pairs with crosses and cut lines on one face.

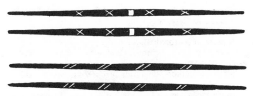

FIG. 36. Stick dice; length, $15\frac{1}{2}$ inches; Chippewa Indians, Bois fort, Minnesota; cat. no. $\frac{50}{4713}$, American Museum of Natural History.

They were collected in 1903 by Dr William Jones, who gives the following counts:

Four points on a flush; 4 points on a cross and striped flush; 2 points on a pair of striped sticks; 20 points on sticks with medial band and ×'s.

CHIPPEWA. Bois fort, Minnesota. (Cat. no. $\frac{50}{4721}$, American Museum of Natural History.)

Wooden bowl (figure 37), 9½ inches in diameter; 80 wooden counters

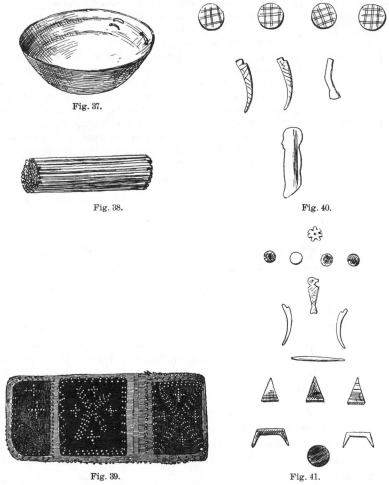

Fig. 37.

Fig. 38.

Fig. 40.

Fig. 39.

Fig. 41.

FIG. 37. Bowl for dice; diameter, 9½ inches; Chippewa Indians, Bois fort, Minnesota; cat. no. $\frac{50}{4721}$, American Museum of Natural History.

FIG. 38. Counting sticks for dice; length, 6 inches; Chippewa Indians, Bois fort, Minnesota; cat. no. $\frac{50}{4721}$, American Museum of Natural History.

FIG. 39. Beaded bag for dice; length, 8 inches; Chippewa Indians, Bois fort, Minnesota; cat. no. $\frac{50}{4721}$, American Museum of Natural History.

FIG. 40. Bone dice; Chippewa Indians, Bois fort, Minnesota; cat. no. $\frac{50}{4721}$, American Museum of Natural History.

FIG. 41. Bone and brass dice; Chippewa Indians, Mille Lacs, Minnesota; cat. no. $\frac{50}{4720}$, American Museum of Natural History.

(figure 38), 6 inches in length; a cloth bag (figure 39), 8 inches in length, ornamented with beads for dice, and the following dice: Four disks, two knives, one gun, and one figure of a man (figure 40).

Another set of dice from Mille Lacs, cat. no. $\frac{50}{4720}$, comprises: One
   star, four disks, one eagle, two knives, one serpent, three arrow
   heads, two yoke-shaped objects, and one brass disk (figure 41).
   With the exception of the last these dice are all of bone and are
   plain on one side and finely crosshatched and painted red on the
   other.

These were collected by Dr William Jones in 1903.

Mr S. C. Simms has kindly furnished the following counts of a
similar game played at Leech lake, Minnesota:

Counts of one: Three white sides up of disks and canoe, rough side of ring,
one rough side of disk and blue side of moose, woman and wigwam; all white
sides up but woman.

Counts of two: Blue sides up of small disks, moose and woman, white sides
of all others and smooth side of brass ring; blue sides of moose and woman,
white sides of all others, and smooth side of ring.

Counts of three: Same as count of two, with exception of moose white instead
of blue side up; four disks white side up, smooth side of ring, white side of
wigwam, blue sides of moose, canoe, and woman.

Count of four: Same as count of three, with exception of rough side of ring up.

Counts of nine: All white sides up and smooth side of ring; all blue sides up
and rough side of ring; white sides of moose, wigwam, canoe, and woman, blue
sides of disks, and rough side of ring.

If canoe stands up on any throw, it counts 2; if on succeeding throw it stands
up, it counts four; if on third throw, it counts 6.

If canoe stands upright on ring, it counts 4, and if remaining dice show blue
sides, an additional count of 9 is made, or 13.

If wigwam stands up on any throw, it counts 3; if on succeeding throw it
stands up, it counts 6; if on third throw, it counts 9.

If moose stands up, it counts 4; if on succeeding throw, it counts 8; if on
third throw, it counts 12, regardless of other dice.

If woman stands up, it counts 5; if on succeeding throw, it counts 10; if on
third throw, it counts 20.

If woman stands up in ring, it counts 10 points, regardless of other dice.

CHIPPEWA. Bear island, Leech lake, Minnesota. (American Museum of Natural History.)

Cat. no. $\frac{50}{4715}$. Four flat sticks (figure 42), $15\frac{1}{2}$ inches long, tapering at the ends, both faces slightly convex and burned black
   on one side and having representations of snakes on the other;
   made in pairs, two alike, distinguished by slight differences in
   the heads.

Cat. no. $\frac{50}{4712}$. Four flat sticks (figure 43), $13\frac{1}{2}$ inches long, tapering
   at the ends, both faces rounded and very slightly convex; made
   in pairs, with faces burned as shown in the figure, and reverses
   burned alike; with four counting sticks (figure 44), 9 inches in
   length.

They were collected in 1903 by Dr William Jones, who gives the
following counts:

The two sticks marked with triangles at the ends may be designated as major, and the other pair as minor. When the pair of major fall face uppermost alike and the minor unlike, the count is 2, but when the minor fall face uppermost alike and the major unlike, the count is 1. When the sticks fall all

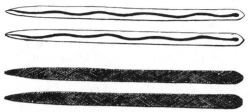

FIG. 42. Stick dice: length, 15¼ inches; Chippewa Indians, Leech lake, Minnesota; cat. no. ₄⁵⁰₇₁₅, American Museum of Natural History.

heads or all tails uppermost, the count is 4. The game is 5, but an extra throw is made when the 5 points are gained. The holder of the 5 points lets the opponent throw first. If the opponent beats him with a pair of majors, then

Fig. 43.   Fig. 44.

FIG. 43. Stick dice; length, 13½ inches; Chippewa Indians, Leech lake. Minnesota; cat. no. ₄⁵⁰₇₁₂, American Museum of Natural History.
FIG. 44. Counting sticks for stick dice; length, 9 inches; Chippewa Indians, Leech lake, Minnesota; cat. no. ₄⁵⁰₇₁₂, American Museum of Natural History.

the 5-point holder throws 2 points back into the pool. If he loses on a flush, he throws 4 points back into the pool. A player wins only on the extra throw.

CHIPPEWA. Mille Lacs, Minnesota. (United States National Museum.)

Cat. no. 204968. Set of four sticks 15 inches in length, flat and plain on one side, and marked as shown in fig. 45 on the other. Two reproductions and two originals, the gift of Mr G. H. Beaulieu, of St Cloud, Minnesota.

The following information about the game was obtained by the writer from a delegation of Chippewa Indians who visited Washington with Mr Beaulieu:

FIG. 45. Stick dice; length, 15 inches; Chippewa Indians, Mille Lacs, Minnesota; cat. no. 204968, United States National Museum.

The game is called shay-mahkewuybinegunug. Men and women play. Each player, of whom the number is not fixed, has five counting sticks. All put up stakes. The counts are as follows: All marked sides count 1; all plain sides, 1; the counts, however, depend upon the previous understanding. If the first throw is two turtles and two tails, it wins the game, but if the other side has won any, then the throw only counts two sticks. A player who does not make a point pays double. The sticks are said to be marked usually with figures of snakes, on account of a dream.

Cat. no. 204967.   Wooden platter (figure 46), 12½ inches long and 7 inches wide, cut from a single piece of wood.

This was described by the collector, Mr G. H. Beaulieu, under the name of bugaysaywin as used in the dice game.

CHIPPEWA.   Minnesota.

J. Long [a] gives the following description of the bowl game:

Athtergain, or miss none but catch all, is also a favorite amusement with

FIG. 46.   Platter for dice; length, 12½ inches; Chippewa Indians, Mille Lacs, Minnesota; cat. no. 204967, United States National Museum.

them, in which the women frequently take part. It is played with a number of hard beans, black and white, one of which has small spots and is called king. They are put into a shallow wooden bowl and shaken alternately by each party, who sit on the ground opposite to one another. Whoever is dexterous enough to make the spotted bean jump out of the bowl receives of the adverse party as many beans as there are spots; the rest of the beans do not count for anything.

——— Wisconsin.

Jonathan Carver [b] describes the game as follows:

The game of the bowl or platter. This game is played between two persons only. Each person has six or eight little bones not unlike a peach stone either in size or shape, except they are quadrangular, two of the sides of which are colored black, and the others white. These they throw up into the air, from whence they fall into a bowl or platter placed underneath, and made to spin round.

According as these bones present the white or black side upward they reckon the game; he that happens to have the greatest number turn up of a similar color, counts 5 points; and 40 is the game.

The winning party keeps his place and the loser yields his to another who is appointed by one of the umpires; for a whole village is sometimes concerned in the party, and at times one band plays against another.

During this play the Indians appear to be greatly agitated, and at every decisive throw set up a hideous shout. They make a thousand contortions, addressing themselves at the same time to the bones, and loading with imprecations the evil spirits that assist their successful antagonists.

At this game some will lose their apparel, all the movables of their cabins, and sometimes even their liberty, notwithstanding there are no people in the universe more jealous of the latter than the Indians are.

——— Apostle islands, Wisconsin.

J. G. Kohl [c] thus describes the game called by the Indians pagessan:

The Canadians call it le jeu au plat (the game of the bowl). It is a game of hazard, but skill plays a considerable part in it. It is played with a wooden bowl and a number of small figures bearing some resemblance to our chessmen. They are usually carved very neatly out of bones, wood, or plum stones, and represent various things—a fish, a hand, a door, a man, a canoe,

[a] Voyages and Travels of an Indian Interpreter, p. 52, London, 1791.
[b] Travels through the Interior Parts of North America, p. 238, Philadelphia, 1796.
[c] Kitchi-Gami, Wanderings round Lake Superior, p. 82, London, 1860.

a half-moon, etc. They call these figures pagessanag (carved plum stones), and the game has received its name from them. Each figure has a foot on which it can stand upright. They are all thrown into a wooden bowl (in Indian onagan), whence the French name is derived. The players make a hole in the ground and thrust the bowl with the figures into it while giving it a slight shake. The more figures stand upright on the smooth bottom of the bowl through this shake, all the better for the player. Each figure has its value, and some of them represent to a certain extent the pieces in the game of chess. There are also other figures, which may similarly be called the pawns. The latter, carved into small round stars, are all alike, have no pedestal, but are red on one side and plain on the other, and are counted as plus or minus according to the side uppermost. With the pawns it is a perfect chance which side is up, but with the pieces much depends on the skill with which the bowl is shaken. The other rules and mode of calculation are said to be very complicated, and the game is played with great attention and passion. My Indians here will lie half the night through round the bowl and watch the variations of the game. It is played with slight divergences by nearly all the Indian tribes, and in many both men and women practise it. How seriously they regard the game and how excited they grow over it I had an opportunity of noticing. Some time ago I seated myself by some Indians who were playing at pagessan. One of them was a very handsome young fellow, wearing broad silver rings on his arms, the carving of which I was anxious to inspect. On turning to him with a question, however, he grew very impatient and angry at this interruption of the game, considered my question extremely impertinent, and commenced such a threatening speech that my interpreter could not be induced to translate it to me. He merely said it was most improper, and then began, for his part, abusing the Indian, so that I had great difficulty in appeasing him. All I understood was that an Indian must not be disturbed when gambling.

Chippewa. Michigan.

Schoolcraft [a] describes the bowl game under the name of pugasaing as follows:

This is the principal game of hazard among the northern tribes. It is played with thirteen pieces, hustled in a vessel called onágun, which is a kind of wooden bowl. They are represented and named as follows:

The pieces marked no. 1 in this cut [figure 47], of which there are two, are called ininewug, or men. They are made tapering or wedge-shaped in thickness, so as to make it possible, in throwing them, that they may stand on their base. Number 2 is called gitshee kenabik, or the great serpent. It consists of two pieces, one of which is fin-tailed, or a water serpent, the other truncated, and is probably designated as terrestrial. They are formed wedge-shaped, so as to be capable of standing on their bases lengthwise. Each has four dots. Number 3 is called pugamágun, or the war club. It has six marks on the handle on the red side, and four radiating from the orifice of the club end, and four marks on the handle of the white side, and six radiating marks from the orifice on the club end, making ten on each side. Number 4 is called keego, which is the generic name for a fish. The four circular pieces of brass,

---

[a] Oneóta, or Characteristics of the Red Race of America, p. 85, New York, 1845. See also, Information respecting the History, Condition, and Prospects of the Indian Tribes of the United States, pt. 2, p. 72, Philadelphia, 1853.

slightly concave, with a flat surface on the apex, are called ozawábĭks. The three bird-shaped pieces, sheshebwug, or ducks.

All but the circular pieces are made out of a fine kind of bone. One side of the piece is white, of the natural color of the bones, and polished, the other red. The brass pieces have the convex side bright, the concave black. They are all shaken together and thrown put of the onágun, as dice. The term pugasaing denotes this act of throwing. It is the participial form of the verb. The following rules govern the game:

1. When the pieces are turned on the red side and one of the ininewugs stands upright on the bright side of one of the brass pieces, it counts 158. 2. When all the pieces turn red side up and the gitshee kenabik with the tail stands on the bright side of the brass piece, it counts 138. 3. When all turn up red, it counts 58, whether the brass pieces be bright or black side up. 4. When the gitshee kenabik and his associate and the two ininewugs turn up white side and the other pieces red, it counts 58, irrespective of the concave or convex position of the brass pieces. 5. When all the pieces turn up white it counts 38, whether the ozawábiks be bright or black. 6. When the gitshee kenabik and his associate turn up red and the other white, it counts 38, the brass pieces immaterial. 7. When one of the ininewugs stands up it counts 50, without regard to the position of all the rest. 8. When either of the gitshee kenabiks stands upright it counts 40, irrespective of the position of the others.

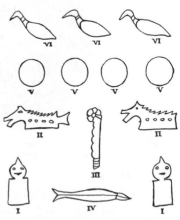

FIG. 47. Bone and brass dice; Chippewa Indians, Michigan; from Schoolcraft.

9. When all the pieces turn up white excepting one, and the ozawábiks dark, it counts 20. 10. When all turn up red except one and the brass pieces bright, it counts 15. 11. When the whole of the pieces turn up white but one, with the ozawábiks bright, it counts 10. 12. When a brass piece turns up dark, the two gitshee kenabiks and the two men red, and the remaining pieces white, it counts 8. 13. When the brass piece turns up bright, the two gitshee kenabiks and one of the men red, and all the rest white, it is 6. 14. When the gitshee kenabik in chief and one of the men turn up red, the ozawábiks bright, and all the others white, it is 4. 15. When both the kenabiks and both men and the three ducks turn up red, the brass piece black, and either the keego or a duck white, it is 5. 16. When all the pieces turn up red but one of the ininewugs and the brass piece black, it counts 2. The limit of the game is stipulated. The parties throw up for the play.

Elsewhere [a] he says:

The game is won by the red pieces; the arithmetical value of each of which is fixed; and the count, as in all games of chance, is advanced or retarded by the luck of the throw. Any number of players may play. Nothing is required but a wooden bowl, which is curiously carved and ornamented (the owner relying somewhat on magic influence), and having a plain, smooth surface.

[a] Information respecting the History, Condition, and Prospects of the Indian Tribes of the United States, pt. 2, p. 72, Philadelphia, 1853.

CHIPPEWA.   Turtle mountain, North Dakota.   (Cat. no. $\frac{5\,0}{4\,7\,2\,2}$, American Museum of Natural History.)

Four flat wooden disks (figure 48), 1 inch in diameter, carved with a cross painted red on one side, and opposite side painted red. Accompanied by a rough willow basket tray, 11 inches in diameter.   Collected by Dr William Jones in 1903.

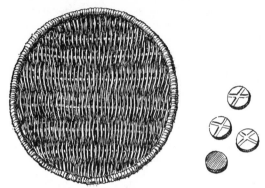

FIG. 48.   Wooden dice and tray; diameter of dice, 1 inch; of tray, 11 inches; Chippewa Indians, Turtle mountain, North Dakota; cat. no. $\frac{5\,0}{4\,7\,2\,2}$, American Museum of Natural History.

CREE.   Muskowpetung reserve, Qu'appelle, Assiniboia.   (Cat. no. 61988, Field Columbian Museum.)

Four wooden staves, 13¾ inches in length, one side plain and the other marked with burned designs, as shown in figure 49.

These were collected by Mr J. A. Mitchell, who describes the game under the name of cheekahkwanuc, dashing down the dice sticks.

Played with four specially marked oblong sticks, each stick having a special counting value according to the marks and according to the number of similar sticks which turn face up at the same time, when thrown down.

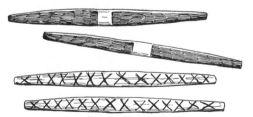

FIG. 49.   Stick dice; length, 13¾ inches; Cree Indians, Qu'appelle, Assiniboia; cat. no. 61988, Field Columbian Museum.

The game is played by any number of men and women, in groups of four each, opposed to similar groups, and is played for stakes, as in our draw poker. The sticks are thrown to the ground, end down, and falling flat are counted by the markings of those which show the marked side uppermost.   The count is as follows: Three plain sides down, one white band up, counts six; two plain sides down, two white bands up, 24; three plain sides down, one X-marked side up,

14; two plain sides down, two X-marked sides up, 56; all marked sides up except the stave with 14 X's, 14; all marked sides up wins game.

CREE. Coxby, Saskatchewan. (Cat. no. 15460, Field Columbian Museum.)

Set of dice consisting of four small bone diamonds and four hook-shaped objects of bone (claws) (figure 50), and a wooden bowl or plate shaped like a tin pan, 8½ inches in diameter (figure 51).

The dice are two-faced, one white and the other black, and are accompanied by a small beaded bag of red flannel. Collected by

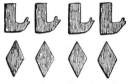

FIG. 50. Bone dice; length, ⅞ inch; Cree Indians, Saskatchewan; cat. no. 15460, Field Columbian Museum.

FIG. 51. Platter and bag for dice; diameter, 8½ inches; Cree Indians, Saskatchewan; cat. no. 15460, Field Columbian Museum.

Mr Philip Towne, who describes the game as follows, under the name of pahkasahkimac, striking ground with wood bowl to shake up the bones:

This game is played by any number of persons, either singly or in partnership. The dice are placed in the bowl, which is then given a sharp downward movement with both hands. The count is determined by combinations of the upper faces of the dice and is as follows: All white sides up counts 100; all dark sides up, 80; 7 white and 1 dark side up, 30; white sides of all hook-shaped dice and of one diamond-shaped die up, 10; dark sides of all hook-shaped dice and of 1 diamond-shaped die up, 8; white sides of 4 diamond-shaped dice and of 1 hook-shaped die up, 6; dark sides of 4 diamond-shaped dice and of 1 hook-shaped die up, 4; each hook-shaped piece on edge, 2. One hundred points constitute the game.

———— Alberta.

In Father Lacombe's Cree Dictionary[a] we find jeu de hasard, pakessewin, and Rev. E. A. Watkins, in his Dictionary of the Cree Language,[b] gives pukasawuk, they gamble with dice.

DELAWARES. Wichita reservation, Okla. (Field Columbian Museum.)

Cat. no. 59376. Four rounded twigs (figure 52), 6¾ inches in length and three-eighths of an inch wide, all grooved on the inner side, three

FIG. 52. Stick dice and counting sticks; lengths, 6¾ inches and 4¼ inches; Delaware Indians, Wichita reservation, Oklahoma; cat. no. 59376, Field Columbian Museum.

a Rev. Albert Lacombe, Dictionnaire de la Langue des Cris, Montreal, 1874.   b London, 1865.

having grooves painted red and one green; outer faces plain; accompanied by seven counting sticks, 4½ inches in length.

Cat. no. 59377. Four rounded strips of cane (figure 53), 6¾ inches long and one-half of an inch wide, with inner sides painted like the preceding. Both of the above sets were collected by Dr George A. Dorsey in 1901.

DELAWARES. Ontario.

Dr Daniel G. Brinton [a] gives the following account derived from conversation with Rev. Albert Seqaqkind Anthony:

FIG. 53. Stick dice; length, 6¾ inches; Delaware Indians, Oklahoma; cat. no. 59377, Field Columbian Museum.

A third game occasionally seen is maumun'di. This is played with twelve flat bones, usually those of a deer, and a bowl of wood constructed for the purpose. One side of each bone is white; the other colored. They are placed in the bowl, thrown into the air, and caught as they descend. Those with the white side uppermost are the winning pieces. Bets usually accompany this game, and it had, in the old days, a place in the native religious rites, probably as a means of telling fortunes.

———— Pennsylvania.

In Zeisberger's Indian Dictionary [b] we find:

Die, to play with, mamandican.

GROSVENTRES. Fort Belknap reservation, Montana. (Field Columbian Museum.)

Cat. no. 60326. Four wooden staves (figure 54) 9¼ inches in length, plain on one side and marked on the other with burnt designs; two alike.

These were collected in 1900 by Dr George A. Dorsey, who gives the following account of the game under the name of tagawatse tothetsan:

The staves are thrown from the hand upon a stone or on the ground, the value of the throw depending on the nature of the combination of uppermost faces. When all faced lots fall uppermost the count is 6. When all unmarked lots fall uppermost the count is 4. When two lots fall face up and two down the count is 2.

This is a woman's game, and formerly heavy stakes were laid on the outcome of the game.

Cat. no. 60295. Four wooden staves (figure 55), 10½ inches in length, two painted green with incised lines painted red, both alike, and two painted red with incised lines painted green; similar but not alike; one of the two red sticks tied with two thongs. The reverses are plain, painted in solid color.

Accompanied with 12 counting sticks, 10 white and 2 with bark on, 9¼ inches in length. They were collected by Dr George A. Dorsey,

[a] Folklore of the Modern Lenape. Essays of an Americanist, p. 186, Philadelphia, 1890.

[b] Cambridge, 1887.

who describes the game under the same name of tagawatse tothetsan:

The staves are thrown from the hand upon the end, on stone or on the ground, the count or value of the throw being as follows: Plain side of banded stave and marked side of other staves, 6; marked side of banded stave and plain side of other staves, 6; all marked or all plain sides uppermost, 4; pair of two marked or plain uppermost, 2. The count is kept with twelve wooden sticks, athsan, the game continuing until one opponent or the other has won all the counters. The stave with the buckskin bands is known as "netha."

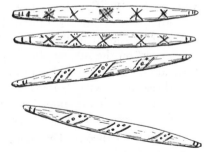

FIG. 54. Stick dice; length, 9¼ inches; Grosventre Indians, Fort Belknap reservation, Montana; cat. no. 60326, Field Columbian Museum.

GROSVENTRES. Fort Belknap reservation. Montana. (American Museum of Natural History.)

Cat. no. $\frac{50}{1869}$. Four wooden staves, 9 inches in length, painted red on one side.

Cat. no. $\frac{50}{1812}$. Four wooden staves, 8 inches in length, painted yellow, with burnt marks on one side; accompanied by 12 counting sticks, 8¼ inches in length, painted yellow.

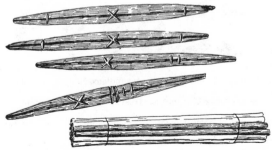

FIG. 55. Stick dice and counting sticks; length of dice, 10½ inches; of counters, 9½ inches; Grosventre Indians, Fort Belknap reservation, Montana; cat. no. 60295, Field Columbian Museum.

Cat. no. $\frac{50}{1768}$. Four wooden staves, 9½ inches in length, painted yellow, and having one side incised with red marks; accompanied by 12 counting sticks, painted yellow, 10 inches in length.

Cat. no. $\frac{50}{1909}$. Four bone staves, 8 inches in length, one side with incised marks; accompanied by 12 counting sticks, cat. no. $\frac{50}{1909}a$, 9½ inches in length, made of willow, pointed at end.

Collected by Dr A. L. Kroeber.

——— Fort Belknap reservation, Montana. (Field Columbian Museum.)

Cat. no. 60332. Set of six triangular bone dice, length 1¾ inches, three alike with spots on one face, and three alike with incised lines as shown in figure 56. One die in each lot has a single spot on the reverse, the other reverses being plain.

Cat. no. 60331. Set of six peach-stone dice, length 1½ inches, three alike with transverse burned bands and three alike with burned marks, shown in figure 57. One die in each lot has two burned marks on the reverse, the other reverses being plain.

Cat. no. 60358. Set of nine plum-stone dice (figure 58), length 1 inch, three alike with transverse bands, three with cross marks, and three with small spots, one die in each lot having a single dot on the reverse, the other reverses being plain.

Collected in 1900 by Dr George A. Dorsey, who gives the following account of the game under the name of besnan-bethetsan.

Six dice are used and tossed in a basket or wooden bowl, the value of the throw being determined when certain combinations fall as follows: All marked faces up or all down count 6; three marked faces up or down, 3; two marked faces up and four down, 2; four marked faces up and two down, 2. In many

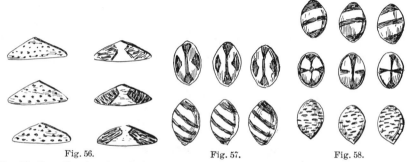

Fig. 56.   Fig. 57.   Fig. 58.

FIG. 56. Bone dice; length, 1½ inches; Grosventre Indians, Montana; cat. no. 60332, Field Columbian Museum.

FIG. 57. Peach-stone dice; length, 1½ inches; Grosventre Indians, Montana; cat. no. 60331, Field Columbian Museum.

FIG. 58. Plum-stone dice; length, 1 inch; Grosventre Indians, Montana; cat. no. 60358, Field Columbian Museum.

sets of this game is found an extra group of three dice; these may be substituted for either of the two other groups of three by any player whenever she desires to change her luck. This is a woman's game, and formerly heavy stakes were wagered on the outcome.

ILLINOIS. It would appear from the manuscript Illinois dictionary of Rev. James Gravier,[a] now in the John Carter Brown library, that this tribe was familiar with the game of plum stones.

KICKAPOO. Kickapoo reservation, Oklahoma. (Cat. no. 70702, Field Columbian Museum.)

Set of eight dice (figure 59), halves of peach stones, one carved to represent a tortoise and one to represent a bird, the carved pieces

---

[a] Andrew McFarland Davis, in Bulletin of Essex Institute, v. 18, p. 187, Salem, 1886.

being painted red on the curved side; accompanied by a wooden bowl, polished by use, 8½ inches in diameter. Collected by Dr George A. Dorsey.

MASSACHUSET. Massachusetts.

William Wood, in his New England's Prospect,[a] relates the following:

> They have two sorts of games, one called puim, the other hubbub, not much unlike cards and dice. . . . Hubbub is five small bones in a small smooth tray, the bones be like a die, but something flatter, black on the one side and white on the other, which they place on the ground, against which violently thumping the platter, the bones mount changing colors with the windy whisking of their hands to and fro; which action in that sport they much use, smiting themselves on the breast, and thighs, crying out, Hub, Hub, Hub; they may be heard play at this game a quarter of a mile off. The bones being all black or white make a double game; if three be of a color and two of another, then they afford but a single game; four of a color and one differing is nothing; so long as the man wins he keeps the tray; but if he lose, the next man takes it.

FIG. 59. Peach-stone dice; Kickapoo Indians, Oklahoma; cat. no. 70702, Field Columbian Museum.

MENOMINEE. . Wisconsin.

Dr Walter J. Hoffman [b] describes the Menominee form of the game under the name akaqsiwok (plate III A):

> It was frequently played in former times, but of late is rarely seen. It is played for purposes of gambling, either by two individuals or by two sets of players. A hemispheric bowl [figure 60] made out of the large round nodules of a maple root is cut and hollowed out. The bowl, wagäq' koman, is symmetric and is very nicely finished. It measures 13 inches in diameter at the rim and is 6 inches in depth. It measures five-eighths of an inch in thickness at the rim, but gradually increases in thickness toward the bottom, which is about an inch thick. There are forty counters, called ma'atik, made of twigs or trimmed sticks of pine or other wood, each about 12 inches long and from one-fourth to one-third of an inch thick. Half of these are colored red, the other half black, or perhaps left their natural whitish color.

FIG. 60. Bowl for dice; Menominee Indians, Wisconsin; from Hoffman.

> The dice, or aka'sianŏk, consist of eight pieces of deer horn, about three-fourths of an inch in diameter and one-third of an inch thick, but thinner toward the edges. Sometimes plum stones or even pieces of wood are taken, one side of them being colored red, the other side remaining white or uncolored. When the players sit down to play, the bowl containing the dice is placed on the ground between the opponents; bets are made; the first player begins a song in

---

[a] London, 1634. Reprint, Boston, p. 90, 1898.
[b] The Menomini Indians. Fourteenth Annual Report of the Bureau of Ethnology, p. 241, 1896.

which the other players as well as the spectators join. At a certain propitious moment the one to play first strikes the bowl a smart tap, which causes the dice to fly upward from the bottom of the bowl, and as they fall and settle the result is watched with very keen interest. The value indicated by the position of the dice represents the number of counters which the player is permitted to take from the ground. The value of the throws is as follows: First throw, 4 red dice and 4 white counts a draw; second throw, 5 red dice and 3 white, 1; third throw, 6 red dice and 2 white, 4; fourth throw, 7 red dice and 1 white, 20; fifth throw, 8 red dice and no white, 40.

The players strike the bowl alternately until one person wins all the counters—both those on the ground and those which the opponent may have won.

MICMAC. Nova Scotia. (Cat. no. 18850, Free Museum of Science and Art, University of Pennsylvania.)

Set of six buttons of vegetable ivory (figure 61) about seven-eighths of an inch in diameter, rounded and unmarked on one side and flat with a dotted cross on the other, being modern substitutes for similar objects of caribou bone. Bowl of wood (figure 62), nearly flat, 11½ inches in diameter. Fifty-one round counting sticks (figure 63), 7¾ inches in length, and 4 counting sticks (figure 64), 7½ inches in length.

They were collected by the donor, Mr Stansbury Hagar. The following account of the game is given by the collector: [a]

A game much in use within the wigwams of the Micmac in former times is

FIG. 61. Bone dice; diameter, seven-eighths inch; Micmac Indians, Nova Scotia; cat. no. 18850, Free Museum of Science and Art, University of Pennsylvania.

that called by some writers altestakun or wŏltĕstakûn. By good native authority it is said that the proper name for it is wŏltĕstŏmkwŏn. It is a kind of dice game of unknown antiquity, undoubtedly of pre-Columbian origin. It is played upon a circular wooden dish—properly rock maple—almost exactly a foot in diameter, hollowed to a depth of about three-fourths of an inch at its center. This dish plays an important rôle in the older legends of the Micmacs. Filled with water and left overnight, its appearance next morning serves to reveal hidden knowledge of past, present, and future. It is also said to have been used as a vessel upon an arkīte trip. The dice of caribou bone are six in number, having flat faces and rounded sides. One face is plain; the other bears a dotted cross. When all the marked or all the unmarked faces are turned up there is a count of 5 points; if five marked faces and one unmarked face or five unmarked faces and one marked face are turned up, 1 point results; if a die falls off the dish there is no count. There are fifty-five counting sticks—fifty-one plain rounded ones about 7½ inches long, a king pin [b] shaped like the

---

[a] Micmac Customs and Traditions. American Anthropologist, v. 8, p. 31, 1895.

[b] Mr. Hagar informs me that the king pin is called kesegoo, the old man, and that the notched sticks are his three wives and the plain sticks his children. The Micmac explains these names by saying that when a stranger calls, the children come out of the wigwam first, then the women, and then the head of the family; and this is the way it happens when one plays at wŏltĕstŏmkwŏn. "The technical name for the king

forward half of an arrow, and three notched sticks, each presenting half of
the rear end of an arrow. These last four are about 8 inches long. Three
of the plain sticks form a count of 1 point; the notched sticks have a value
of 5 points; while the king pin varies in value, being used as a fifty-second
plain stick, except when it stands alone in the general pile; then it has, like
the notched sticks, a
value of 5 points. Thus
the possible points of
the count are 17 (one-
third of fifty-one) on
the plain sticks, and 15
(five times three) on the
three notched sticks, a
total of 32; but by a
complex system the
count may be extended
indefinitely. In playing
the game two players
sit opposite each other,
their legs crossed in
a characteristic manner,
and the dish, or wŏltĕs,
between them usually
placed on a thick piece

FIG. 62. Platter for dice; diameter, 11½ inches; Micmac Indians,
Nova Scotia; cat. no. 18850, Free Museum of Science and Art,
University of Pennsylvania.

of leather or cloth. A squaw keeps the score on the counting sticks [figures 63,
64], which at first lie together. The six dice are placed on a dish with their
marked faces down; one of the players takes the dish in both hands, and raises
it an inch or two from the ground, and brings it down again with considerable
force, thus turning the dice. If all but one of the upturned faces are marked or
unmarked, he repeats the toss and continues to do so as long as one of these com-

FIG. 63. Counting sticks for dice; length, 7¾ inches; Micmac Indians, Nova Scotia; cat. no. 18850,
Free Museum of Science and Art, University of Pennsylvania.

binations results. When he fails to score, the amount of his winnings is withdrawn from the general pile and forms the nucleus of his private pile. His opponent repeats the dice-throwing until he also fails to score. Two successive throws
of either a single point or of 5 points count thrice the amount of one throw—
that is, 3 points or 15 points, respectively. Three successive throws count five

pin is nandaymelgawasch and for the wives tkŏmwoowaal, both of which names mean,
they say, 'it counts five' and 'they count five.' Nan is the Micmac for '5,' but no
numeral of which I know appears in the second name." Mr Hagar regards the polyga-
mous element in the game as a good indication of its antiquity, if, he adds, "such
indeed be necessary." Referring to the passes described by Mrs W. W. Brown, in her
paper on the games of the Wabanaki Indians, he says: "These passes are made by
the Micmac in wŏltĕstŏmkwŏn by passing the right hand rapidly to the left over the
dish, and shutting it exactly as if catching a fly." Wedding ceremonies among the
Micmac were celebrated by the guests for four days thereafter. On the first day they
danced the serpent dance, on the second they played football (tooad ik), on the third
day they played lacrosse (madijik), on the fourth, wŏltĕstŏmkwŏn.

times as much as a single throw, etc. After the pile of counting sticks has been exhausted a new feature is introduced in the count. The player who scores first takes a single plain stick from his pile and places it by itself, with one of its sides facing him to represent 1 point, and perpendicular to this, either horizontally or vertically, to represent 5 points.

He continues to add sticks thus as he continues to score. This use of sticks as counters to indicate unpaid winnings is a device for deferring further set-tlement until the game seems near its end, and also serves to increase the count indefinitely to meet the indefinite duration of the game, as after one player secures a token, his opponent, when he scores, merely reduces the former's token pile by the value of his score. The reduction is effected by returning from the token pile to the private pile the amount of the opponent's score; hence at any time the token pile represents the amount of advantage which its owner has obtained since the last settlement. These settlements are made when-ever either party may desire it. This, however, is supposed to be whenever one player's token pile seems to represent a value approaching the limit of his opponent's ability to pay. If his opponent should permit the settlement to be deferred until he were no longer able to pay his debts, then he would lose the game to the first player; whereas, if one player, after the settlement, retains five plain sticks, but not more, a new feature is introduced, which favors him. If, while retaining his five sticks, he can score 5 points before his opponent scores at all, he wins the game in spite of the much greater amount of his opponent's winnings up to that point. If his opponent scores 1 point only before he obtains his 5 points, he

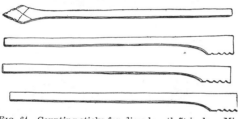

FIG. 64. Counting sticks for dice; length 7¼ inches; Micmac Indians, Nova Scotia; cat. no. 18850, Free Museum of Science and Art, University of Pennsylvania.

still has a chance, though a less promising one. After paying over the three plain sticks that represent a single point, two plain sticks still remain to him, he is then compelled to win 7 points before his opponent wins 1 or he forfeits the game; but if he succeeds in winning his 7 points the game is still his. How-ever, in these last chances he is further handicapped by the rule that he can at no time score more points than are represented in his private pile. Conse-quently, if with only five plain sticks in his possession, he could score only a single point, even if his toss should call for 5; but with six plain sticks he could score 2 points; with nine sticks, 3, etc. The last chances are: With only five plain sticks, 5 points are necessary to win; with four plain sticks, 5 points are necessary to win; with three sticks, 6 points; with two sticks, 7 points; with one stick, 7 points. There are two other minor rules: One, that in counting 5 points on the plain sticks four bundles of four each are given instead of the five bundles of three each, as one should expect; total 16. The other rule is that to count 6 points we use a notched stick plus only two plain sticks, instead of three, as might be expected.

Mr Hagar states that the preceding game was invented and taught by the hero Glooscap. They have also a similar game, called wobuna-runk,[a] which they say was invented and owned by Mikchikch—the turtle—one of Glooscap's companions, to whose shell the dice bear some resemblance.

---

[a] The account of wŏbŭnărunk is from a manuscript by Mr Hagar, which he courteously placed in my hands.

The name wŏbŭnārunk is derived from wŏbŭn, meaning dawn; to which is added a termination signifying anything molded or worked upon by human hands.[a]

The outfit for the game consists simply of six dice, made from moose or caribou bone. One Micmac, at least, is positive that the teeth only of these animals can properly be used. In playing, these dice are thrown from the right hand upon the ground, and the points are counted according to the number of marked or unmarked faces which fall uppermost. It is customary for a player to pass his hand quickly over the dice, if possible, after he has tossed them and before they reach the ground, in order to secure good luck. The shape of the dice is that of a decidedly flattened hemisphere, the curved portion being unmarked. The base or flat surface is about the size of a 25-cent piece and presents three figures (figure 65). Close to its edge there is a circle, touched at four points by a series of looped curves, which form a kind of cross. Within each of the four spaces thus separated is an equal-armed cross composed of nine dots, which, with the dot in the center of the die, make a total of 37 dots upon each piece, or of 222 dots (37 by 6) used in the game.

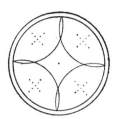

FIG. 65—Bone die; diameter 1¼ inches; Micmac Indians, Nova Scotia; from drawing by Stansbury Hager.

FIG. 66—Engraved shell bead (runtee); Pompey, New York; from Holmes.

The count is as follows: If six marked faces fall face up, it counts 50 points; if five marked faces fall face up, 5; if four marked faces fall face up, 4; if three marked faces fall face up, 3; if two marked faces fall face up, 2; if one marked face falls face up, 1; if six unmarked faces fall face up, 5; total, seven counts and 70 points.

The marks on the Micmac dice are similar to those on some of the inscribed shell beads, known as runtees, found in the state of New York. One of these (figure 66), reproduced from Prof. W. H. Holmes's Art in Shell of the Ancient Americans,[b] is from an ancient village site at Pompey, which Rev. W. M. Beauchamp, of Baldwinsville, New York, attributes to the seventeenth century. Mr Beauchamp writes me that both sides are alike, and that it is pierced with two holes from edge to edge.

MICMAC. Digby, Nova Scotia. (Cat. no. 21642, Free Museum of Science and Art, University of Pennsylvania.)

Set of implements for the game of altestaan, the dice game, consisting of six bone dice, marked on the flat sides as shown in figure 67 and contained in a small velvet bag; a flat wooden dish (figure 68), 10½ inches in diameter, marked with incised lines on

---

[a] From the fact that white shell beads (wampum) are constantly referred to as being used as stakes, not only among the tribes of the Atlantic coast, but in the Southwest (see Cushing's account of the white shell beads used in sholiwe), the writer is inclined to believe that the name of this same wŏbŭnārunk is derived from the use of wampum (wŏbŭn, white, so called from the white beads) as stakes for which it was played. Again, it may refer to the white disks; but, however this may be, a peculiar significance is attached to the use of shell beads as gambling counters or stakes.

[b] Second Annual Report of the Bureau of Ethnology, pl. XXXVI, fig. 4, 1883.

the lower side, as shown in the figure, and fifty-five counting sticks (figure 69) made of bamboo, fifty-one plain and four notched, as described below.

These were collected by Dr A. S. Gatschet, who obtained them from James Meuse, chief of the western counties Indians of Nova Scotia. Meuse claimed that the dish was 300 years old, and, though this is an exaggeration, one can clearly see that it is of old manufacture.

Doctor Gatschet furnished the following account of the game: [a]

The dice, altestá-an—in the plural, altestá-ank—are disk-shaped, flat above and convex below, six in number. They always make them of white bone, and

FIG. 67.—Bone dice; diameter, $\frac{13}{16}$ inch; Micmac Indians, Nova Scotia; cat. no. 21642, Free Museum of Science and Art, University of Pennsylvania.

since the caribou furnishes the hardest bone, they use the bone of this animal only for the purpose. The caribou is still frequent in the woods of Nova Scotia and New Brunswick, and is called χalibû'—in Quoddy, megali'p—from its habit of shoveling the snow with its forelegs, which is done to find the food covered by the snow. χalibû' mulχadéget (Micmac), "the caribou is scratching or shoveling." The bone dice are made smooth by rubbing them on a stone, subigidá-an, whetstone, honing stone; subigidegeí, any object whetted or honed.

The dish, or wáltes, is a heavy platter made of a piece of rock-maple wood, and appears to have no other purpose than to jerk altestá-ank up and receive them when falling down. This is done either by striking the dish upon a table or upon a mat lying on the ground. The rock-maple tree is still found in all the hard-wood ridges of Nova Scotia, and where this useful tree is getting scarce the Nova Scotia white people begin to rear it, as they do also the nimĕnôhen, or yellow birch; the axamúχ, or white ash; the wisxók, or black ash; the midi, or common poplar. When the dish is made of birch bark it is called ulä'n, plural ulânĕl. The Micmac make birch-bark canoes for Annapolis basin, just as in ancient times, and the price they now get for them is $15 to $25.

The wáltes sent to you is made from a piece of rock-maple about one-half inch thick, diameter about 1 foot, and wholly carved with a knife, no machinery having been úsed. The top side is slightly concave and the bottom conspicuously convex. As the biggest rock-maple trees do not exceed 20 inches in thickness, the wáltes was evidently made from one side of the tree and not from across. The wood is cross-grained and extremely smooth, the nerves (opχóχt) of the tree being just perceptible. Round and elliptic figures are carved on the top and bottom side, but have no significance for the game itself. The rubbing smooth or polishing of the wood is called sesubadóχ by the Indians; it has the same effect as sandpaper rubbing with us.

The altestá-ank, or dice, are blank on the convex side and carved with △ figures on the flat side, which converge in the center. The game itself is altestaí; they (two) play the dice game, altestáyek; they (more than two) play the dice game, altestádiyek.

The counters of this game are of two kinds, both being sticks about 7 to 8

---

[a] Bulletin of the Free Museum of Science and Art, University of Pennsylvania, v. 2, p. 191, Philadelphia, 1900.

inches in length: etχamuaweí, flat sticks, with a broadening at one end; (2) kidĕmá-ank, thin, cylindric sticks, about double the thickness of lucifer matches.

The etχamuaweí, plural (ĕ)tχamuawel, slender sticks, are also called "five pointers," because their broadening end shows five notches or points, showing their value as counters, each representing five kidĕmá-ank. The ones sent you are made of bamboo obtained from the West Indies, hence called kesúsk, plural kesuskel. On one of the tχamuawel the end has a double set of notches, the whole resembling a diminutive arrow. It is called the old man; gisigú, plural gisigūk. With this last one tχamuawel are to the number of four. At the final accounting each of the tχamuawel counts 5 points, and it is the privilege of the one who gets the old man to get 5 points more than the others, under the condition that his previous gain exceed 15 points.

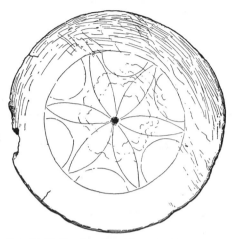

FIG. 68—Platter for dice (obverse); diameter, 10¼ inches; Micmac Indians, Nova Scotia; cat. no. 21642, Free Museum of Science and Art, University of Pennsylvania.

The kidĕmá-ank, or common counters, are fifty-one in number, cylindric, and of the same length as the tχamuawel. Some of those before you are of snaú, or rock-maple, the others of bamboo. Their number is determined by the fact that three times seventeen makes fifty-one, and each three of them represents 1 point in the game.

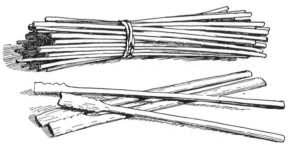

FIG. 69—Counting sticks for dice; length, 9¼ inches, Micmac Indians, Nova Scotia; cat. no. 21642, Free Museum of Science and Art, University of Pennsylvania.

Some of the rules observed in this truly aboriginal game are as follows, according to James Meuse:

Any player in the ring can have three throws of the dice. When, after shaking the wáltes on a table or on the mat, all the dice, or altestá-ank, turn their white or black side up, the player gets 1 etχamuaweí, or 5 points, or 15 kidĕmá-ank. When, after the shake, two altestá-ank turn their marked side up, the player gets no counter, or kidĕmá-an. When one altestá-an turns up with the marked side up, the player gets 1 point, or 3 kidĕmá-ank.

When five dice turn their marked side up and one the blank side, the player makes 1 point, or 3 kidĕmá-ank. When the player finds all six dice with the marked side up he wins 15 counters, or 5 points.

When five marked sides turn up and one blank one he makes 1 point, or 3 counters. But when he makes the same throw again in succession to the above, he wins 3 points, or 9 counters. Whenever a player has all the blanks turned up he has the privilege of throwing again.

MICMAC. New Brunswick. (Peabody Museum of American Archæ-ology and Ethnology.)

Cat. no. 50804. Set of six dice made of antler, three-fourths to seven-eighths of an inch in diameter, marked on flat side with a six-rayed star; bowl of birch wood, 11¼ inches in diameter, and fifty-four counting sticks (figure 70), consisting of fifty plain sticks and four larger sticks. The latter comprise one stick with three serrations on side near one end, two each with four serrations, and one resembling the feathered shaftment of an arrow with three serrations on each side.

FIG. 70. Counting sticks for dice; length, 8 to 8⅞ inches; Micmac Indians, New Brunswick; cat. no. 50804, Peabody Museum of American Archæology and Ethnology.

Cat. no. 50792. Five dice of antler, three-fourths to seven-eighths of an inch in diameter, marked on the flat side with four-rayed star; bowl of birch wood, 9⅛ inches in diameter; 52 counting sticks, consisting of 48 plain sticks and 4 larger sticks.

The latter comprise one stick with five serrations on one side near one end, two with four serrations each, and one resembling a feathered arrow shaftment with serrations on each side. The counting sticks in this and the preceding game are in part of bamboo.

Both were collected by Mr G. M. West.

MISSISAUGA. New Credit, Ontario.

Rev. Peter Jones [a] says:

In their bowl plays they use plum stones. One side is burnt black, and the other is left of its natural color. Seven of these plums are placed in a wooden bowl, and are then tossed up and caught. If they happen to turn up all white or all black they count so many. This is altogether a chance game.

NARRAGANSET. Rhode Island.

Roger Williams, in his Key into the Language of America,[b]

---

[a] History of the Ojebway Indians, p. 135, London, 1861.

[b] London, 1643. (Collections of the Rhode Island Historical Society, v. 1, p. 145, Providence, 1827; also, Collections of the Massachusetts Historical Society, for the year 1794, v. 3, p. 324.) Cited by Andrew McFarland Davis, in Bulletin of the Essex Institute, v. 18, p. 173, Salem, 1886, to whom I am indebted for the reference.

describes the games of the Narraganset as of two sorts—private and public. " They have a kind of dice which are plum stones painted, which they cast in a tray with a mighty noise and sweating." He gives the following words referring to this game: wunnaugonhommin, to play at dice in their tray; asauanash, the painted plum stones which they throw, and puttuckquapuonck, a playing arbor. He describes the latter as made of long poles set in the earth, four square, 16 or 20 feet high, on which they hang great store of their stringed money, having great staking, town against town, and two chosen out of the rest by course to play the game at this kind of dice in the midst of all their abettors, with great shouting and solemnity. He also says:

The chief gamesters among them much desire to make their gods side with them in their games . . . therefore I have seen them keep as a precious stone a piece of thunderbolt, which is like unto a crystal, which they dig out of the ground under some tree, thunder-smitten, and from this stone they have an opinion of success.

NIPISSING. Forty miles above Montreal, Quebec.

Rev. J. A. Cuoq [a] describes the plum-stone game among this tribe under the name of pakesanak, which he says is the usual name given to five plum stones, each marked with several dots on one side only. Four or five women, squatting around on a blanket, make the stones jump about the height of their foreheads, and according to the stones falling on one or the other side the fate of the player is decided. Of late the game has been improved by using a platter instead of a cover (blanket), which caused the name of the game of platter to be given it by the whites.

The name pakesanak is the plural of pakesan, defined as noyau, jeu. Dr A. S. Gatschet has kindly given me the following analysis of this word: Pake, to fall, to let fall; s, diminutive; an, suffix of inanimate nouns.

NORRIDGEWOCK. Norridgewock, Maine.

In the dictionary of Father Sebastian Rasles,[b] a number of words [c] referring to games are defined,[d] from which it appears that the Norridgewock Indians played a game with a bowl and eight disks (ronds), counting with grains. The disks were black on one side

---

[a] Lexique de la Langue Algonquine, Montreal, 1886.

[b] Memoirs American Academy of Arts and Science, n. s., v. 1, Cambridge, 1833.

[c] Je joue avec des ronds blancs d'un côté et noirs de l'autre, nederakké, v. nedanmké, v. neda8é annar. Les ronds, éssé 8anar; les grains, tag8ssak. Les grains du jeu du plat, dicuntur etiam, éssé8anar. Lors qu'ils s'en trouve du nombre de 8, 5 blancs et 3 noirs, v. 5 noirs et 3 blancs, nebarham, keb, etc. (on ne tire rien); idem fit de 4 blancs et 4 noirs. Lors qu'il y en a 6 d'une couleur, et 2 de l'autre, nemes8dam (on tire 4 grains). Lors qu'il y en a 7 d'une même couleur, et qu'un de l'autre, nedéné8i (on en tire 10). Lors qu'ils sont tous 8 de même couleur, n8rihara (on en tire 20). Nesákasi, je plante un bois dans terre p'r marquer les parties. Je lui gagne une partie, je mets un bois p'r, etc., neg8dag8harañ. Nedasahamank8, il me démarque une partie, il ôte un bois, etc. Je joue au plat, n8añradéháma 3. 8an mé. Mets les petits ronds, etc., p8né éssé8anar. Nederakébena, je les mets.

[d] Bulletin of the Essex Institute, v. 18, p. 187, Salem, 1886.

and white on the other. If black and white turned up four and four, or five and three, there was no count; six and two counted 4; seven and one, 10; and all eight of the same color, 20. Davis remarks that, "according to Rasles, the count was sometimes kept by thrusting sticks into the ground. This is shown by Indian words used in the games, which Rasles interprets, respectively: 'I thrust a stick in the ground to mark the games;' 'I win a game from him; I place a stick,' etc.; 'He takes the mark for a game away from me; he removes a stick,' etc.; 'He takes away all my marks; he removes them all.'"

OTTAWA. Manitoba.

Tanner [a] describes the game as follows, under the name of buggasank or beggasah:

The beg-ga-sah-nuk are small pieces of wood, bone, or sometimes of brass made by cutting up an old kettle. One side they stain or color black, the other they aim to have bright. These may vary in number, but can never be fewer than nine. They are put together in a large wooden bowl or tray kept for the purpose. The two parties, sometimes twenty or thirty, sit down opposite to each other or in a circle. The play consists in striking the edge of the bowl in such a manner as to throw all the beg-ga-sah-nuk into the air, and on the manner in which they fall into the tray depends his gain or loss. If his stroke has been to a certain extent fortunate, the player strikes again and again, as in the game of billiards, until he misses, when it passes to the next.

PASSAMAQUODDY. Maine.

The bowl game among these Indians is described by Mrs W. W. Brown,[b] of Calais, Maine, under the name of alltestegenuk:

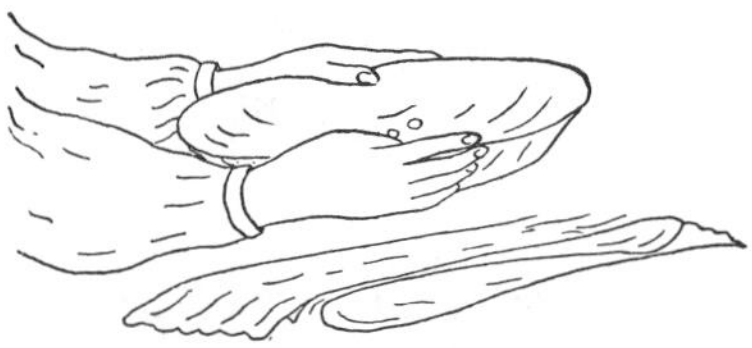

FIG. 71—Manner of holding dish in dice game; Passamaquoddy Indians, Maine; from Mrs W. W. Brown.

Played by two persons kneeling—a folded blanket between them serving as a cushion on which to strike the shallow wooden dish, named wal-tah-hā-mo'g'n. This dish [figure 71] contains six thin bone disks [figure 72] about three-fourths of an inch in diameter, carved and colored on one side and plain on the other. These are tossed or turned over by holding the dish firmly in the hands and striking down hard on the cushion. For counting in this game there are 48 small sticks, about 5 inches in length, named ha-gă-ta-mā-g'n'al; 4 somewhat larger, named t'k'm-way-wāl and 1 notched, called non-ā-da-ma-wuch [figure 73].

All the sticks are placed in a pile. The disks are put in the dish without order; each contestant can play while he wins, but on his missing the other takes the dish. Turning all the disks but one, the player takes 3 small sticks, twice in succession, 9 sticks, three times in succession, 1 big stick or 12 small ones. Turning all alike once, he takes a big stick, twice in succession, 3 big ones, or 2, and lays a small one out to show what is done, three times

[a] A Narrative of the Captivity and Adventures of John Tanner, p. 114, New York, 1830.
[b] Some Indoor and outdoor Games of the Wabanaki Indians. Transactions of the Royal Society of Canada, v. 6, sec. 2, p. 41, Montreal, 1889.

in succession he stands a big stick up—equal to 16 small ones from the opponent—the notched one to be the last taken of the small ones it being equal to 3.

When all the small sticks are drawn and there are large ones left in the pile—instead of taking 3 from the opponent, the players lay one out to show that the other owes 3 sticks, and so on until the large ones are won. Then, unless the game is a draw, the second and more interesting stage begins, and the sticks have different value. Turning all the disks but one, the player lays 1 out—equal to 4 from an opponent. Turning all the disks but one twice in succession, he lays 3 out—equal to 12 from the óther—three times in succession—stands 1 up, equal to 1 large or 16 small ones. Turning all alike, he sets up 1 large one twice in succession; then 3 large ones, or lacking these, 3 small ones for each large one. This would end the game if the opponent had none standing, as there would be no sticks to pay the points. But a run of three times of one kind in succession is unusual. When one has not enough sticks to pay points won by the other comes the real test of skill, although the former has still several superior chances to win the game. If he has 5

Fig. 72—Bone die, Passamaquoddy Indians, Maine; from Mrs W. W. Brown.

sticks, he has 3 chances; if 7 or 9 sticks he has 5 chances; that is, he places the disks in position, all one side up, for each of the tosses; the other contestant takes his turn at playing, but he can not place the disks. Then, giving the dish a peculiar slide, which they call la luk, or running downhill like water, and at the same time striking it down on the cushion, he may, unless the luck is sadly against him, win twice out of three times trying.

To this day it is played with great animation, with incantations for good luck and exorcising of evil spirits, by waving of hands and crying yon-tel-eg-wa-wŭch. At a run of ill luck there are peculiar passes made over the dish and a muttering of Mic-mac-squs ŭk n'me hă-ook (" I know there is a Micmac squaw around ").

One of their legends tells of a game played by Youth against Old Age. The old man had much m'ta-ou-lin (magic power). He had regained his youth several times by inhaling the breath of

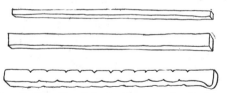

Fig. 73—Counting sticks for dice game; length, 6¼ to 6⅜ inches; Passamaquoddy Indians, Maine; from Mrs W. W. Brown.

youthful opponents. He had again grown old and sought another victim. When he found one whom he thought suited to his purpose he invited him to a game of ăll-tes-teg-enŭk. The young man was also m'ta-ou-lin, and for a pō-he-gan had K'che-bal-lock (spirit of the air), and consequently knew the old man's intention, yet he consented to a game. The old man's wăl-tah-hă-mo'g'n was a skull, and the ăll-tes-teg-enŭk were the eyes of former victims. The game was a long and exciting one, but at each toss off by the young man the disks were carried a little higher by his pō-he-gan until they disappeared altogether. This broke up a game that has never been completed. The legend says that the old man still waits and the young man still outwits him.

Another Passamaquoddy game is described by Mrs Brown under the name of wypenogenuk:

This game, like ăll-tes-teg-enŭk, has long been a gambling game. The disks are very similar, but larger, and eight in number. The players stand opposite each other with a blanket spread on the ground between them. The disks are held in the palm of the hand, and chucked on the blanket. This game is counted with sticks, the contestants determining the number of points necessary to win before commencing to play.

PENOBSCOT. Maine. (Cat. no. 16551, Free Museum of Science and Art, University of Pennsylvania.)

Set of counting sticks of unpainted white wood (figure 74), copied at

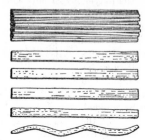

the Chicago Exposition by a Penobscot Indian from those in a set of gaming implements, consisting of dice, counters, and bowl, there exhibited by the late Chief Joseph Nicolar, of Oldtown. The latter kindly furnished the

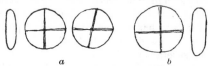

FIG. 74. Counting sticks for dice game; Penobscot Indians, Maine; cat. no. 16551, Free Museum of Science and Art, University of Pennsylvania.

FIG. 75. Limestone disks, possibly used in game; *a* 1 inch in diameter, *b* ⅞ inch in diameter; Nottawasaga, Ontario. Archæological Museum, Toronto.

writer the following account of the game under the name of werlardaharmungun:

The buttons used as dice in this game are made from the shoulder blade of a moose, the counters of cedar wood. The latter are fifty-five in number, fifty-one being rounded splints about 6 inches in length, three flat splints of the same length, and one made in a zigzag shape. A soft bed is made in the ground or on the floor for the dish to strike on. Two persons having been selected to play the game, they seat themselves opposite to each other. The buttons are placed in the dish, and it is tossed up and brought down hard upon its soft bed. If five of the six buttons have the same side up, the player takes three round splints; but if the entire six turn the same side up, it is called a double, and the player takes one of the flat ones. The game is continued until all the counters are drawn.

It might naturally be inferred that remains of the bone disks used

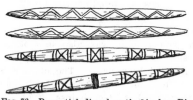

in the bowl game would be found in our archeological museums, but as yet I have not met with any. On the other hand, small disks of pottery and of stone, frequently marked on one face, are not uncommon, and are usually classified as gaming implements. I am in-

FIG. 76. Bone stick dice; length, 8 inches; Piegan Indians, Alberta; cat. no. 69356, Field Columbian Museum.

debted to Mr David Boyle, curator of the Archæological Museum, Toronto, for the sketch (figure 75) representing a small disk of soft white limestone from Nottawasaga, Ontario, in his collection, engraved with a cross on one side and a similar disk with a cross on both sides.

PIEGAN. Alberta. (Cat. no. 69356, Field Columbian Museum.)

Set of four bone staves, 8 inches in length, marked with incised lines, in two pairs, one with chevrons in red and the other with crosses between transverse lines, one of the latter tied with a leather band (figure 76). Collected by Mr R. N. Wilson.

POTAWATOMI. Potawatomi reservation, Oklahoma. (Cat. no. 70701, Field Columbian Museum.)

Set of 8 bone dice (figure 77); six disks, three-fourths of an inch in diameter, one tortoise, and one horse head, with one side rounded and plain and reverse flat and stained red; accompanied by a flat wooden bowl, 11 inches in diameter, and 25 seeds used in counting. Collected by Dr George A. Dorsey.

FIG. 77. Bone dice; diameter, ¾ inch; Potawatomi Indians, Oklahoma; cat. no. 70701, Field Columbian Museum.

SAUK AND FOXES. Tama, Iowa. (Cat. no. 36751, Free Museum of Science and Art, University of Pennsylvania.)

Eight disks of bone (figure 78), gusigonuk, three-fourths of an inch in diameter. Six are marked with two incised circles on one side, and two with a five-pointed star inclosed in a circle, with a brass boss in the center which penetrates to the other side. Except for this the reverses are plain. Accompanied by a wooden bowl, anagai (cat. no. 36752), made of a maple knot, grease-soaked and highly polished; diameter, 11½ inches. Collected by the writer in 1900.

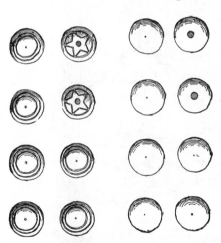

Both men and women play, but this is especially a woman's game. The dice are tossed in the bowl, and the count is kept with ten sticks, 10 being the game. The counts are as follows: Eight marked sides up

FIG. 79. Message sticks for woman's dice game; length, 5¼ inches; Sauk and Fox Indians, Tama, Iowa; cat. no. ₅₀⁵⁰₃₃, American Museum of Natural History.

FIG. 78. Bone dice; diameter, ¾ inch; Sauk and Fox Indians, Tama, Iowa; cat. no. 36751, Free Museum of Science and Art, University of Pennsylvania.

counts 4; eight plain sides up, 4; seven marked sides and one white side up, 2; six marked sides and two white sides up, 1; seven white sides and one marked up, 2; six white sides and two marked up, 1; seven white sides and one star up, 5; seven marked sides and one brass stud up, 5; six white sides and two stars up, 10; six marked sides and two brass studs up, 10. The game is called gusigonogi.

A set of message sticks (figure 79) for the women's dice game, in the American Museum of Natural History (cat. no. $\frac{50}{3533}$), consists of a bundle of eight pieces of reed, 5½ inches in length. Collected by Dr William Jones.

ATHAPASCAN STOCK

SAN CARLOS APACHE. San Carlos, Gila county, Arizona. (Field Columbian Museum.)

Cat. no. 63556. Three wooden staves (figure 80), 9 inches in length,

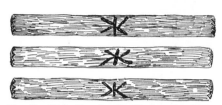 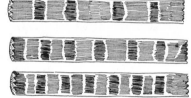

FIG. 80. Stick dice; length, 9 inches; San Carlos Apache Indians, Arizona; cat. no. 63556, Field Columbian Museum.

FIG. 81. Stick dice; length, 8 inches; San Carlos Apache Indians, Arizona; cat. no. 63557, Field Columbian Museum.

flat faces painted red, with incised cross lines painted black in middle and end edges notched, round sides painted yellow.

FIG. 82. San Carlos Apache Indians playing stick dice; Gila county, Arizona; from photograph by Mr S. C. Simms.

Cat. no. 63557. Three wooden staves (figure 81), 8 inches in length, identical with preceding, except that flat faces have alternate painted bands, black and red. They were collected by Mr S. C. Simms, who gives the name of the game as settil.

White Mountain Apache. Arizona. (Field Columbian Museum.)
Cat. no. 61247. Three wooden staves (figure 83), 10¾ inches in
   length, flat on one side, painted yellow, with green band on flat
   face.

These specimens were collected by Rev. Paul S. Mayerhoff, who
gives the following account of the game under the name of tsaydithl,
or throw-sticks:

This is a woman's game and is played with great ardor. The staves are
three in number, from 8 to 10 inches long and flat on one side.

The playground is a circle [figure 84] about 5 feet in diameter. The center
of this circle is formed by a flat rock of any convenient size, generally from
8 to 10 inches in diameter. On the circumference forty stones are arranged
in sets of ten, to be used as counters. Not less than two or more than four
persons can participate in the game at one time.

In playing, the sticks are grasped in the hand and thrown on end upon the
rock in the center with force enough to make them rebound. As they fall,
flat or round face upward, the throw counts from 1 to 10, as follows: Three
round sides up counts 10 points, called yäh; two round sides up, one flat, 1 or
2 points, called tlay; one round side up, two flat, 3 points, called täh geé;

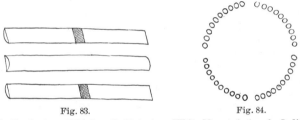

Fig. 83.   Fig. 84.

Fig. 83. Stick dice for tsay-dithl; length, 10¾ inches; White Mountain Apache Indians, Arizona;
   cat. no. 61247, Field Columbian Museum.
Fig. 84. Circuit for stick dice; White Mountain Apache Indians, Arizona.

three flat sides up, 5 points, called dágay. Should one of the players, in making her count, continue from her set of counters to the adjoining set of her
opponent's and strike the place marked by the opponent's tally marker, it
throws the opponent's count out of the game, and she must start anew. Whoever first marks 40 points wins.

Cat. no. 61248. Four sticks (figure 85), 23 inches in length, the
   round sides painted, two alike, with four diagonal black stripes,
   and one with a broad red band in the middle and red ends. The
   first three have flat reverses, painted red, and the fourth, with
   the red band, a black reverse.

Another set, cat. no. 61249, has three with round sides decorated
alike with alternate red and black lines, and one with diagonal black
lines. The first three have red reverses, the fourth a black reverse.

These specimens were collected by Rev. Paul S. Mayerhoff, who
gives the following account of the game under the name of haeegohay,
drop sticks:

This game is played by both sexes together. For it there is no preparation
of a playground. The staves are four sticks 18 to 24 inches in length, round on

the back, flat on the face.   One of the set of four sticks is distinguished from the remaining three and represents a man, the other three being women.   The sticks are dropped and the points counted as follows: Four faces down, sticks lying parallel, counts 10; four faces down, pair of crosses, 10; four faces down,

odd stick crossing the others, 10; four faces up, pair of crosses, 20; four faces up, odd stick crossing others, 20; three faces down, one crossed by the odd stick, face upward, 26; three faces up, one crossed by the odd stick, face down, 26; three faces up, crossed by the odd stick, face down, 39;

FIG. 85. Stick dice for ha-ee-go-hay; length, 23 inches; White Mountain Apache Indians, Arizona; cat. no. 61248, Field Columbian Museum.

three faces up, two crossed by the odd stick, face up or down, 39; four faces up, sticks lying parallel, 40; three faces up, one face down, lying parallel, 52; three faces down, one face up, lying parallel, 52; three faces up, one down, crossing one another six times, 62.

WHITE MOUNTAIN APACHE. White river, Arizona.

Mr Albert B. Reagan furnished the following account of the Apache stick dice game in a communication to the Bureau of American Ethnology in 1901:

This game is usually played by women only, occupying with it their leisure hours.   They bet on it such things as beads, dress materials, and other objects of small value, sometimes even money.   When money is bet it is put under the stone on which the sticks are cast.   In preparing the field a spot of ground is leveled and a small flat stone placed in the center.   Other stones are then piled around this stone to form a circle [figure 86] 3½ feet in diameter, with four openings, 10 stones being placed in each quarter of the circle, the openings corresponding with the northeast, southeast, southwest, and northwest. The stones, which are picked up in the immediate vicinity of the playground,

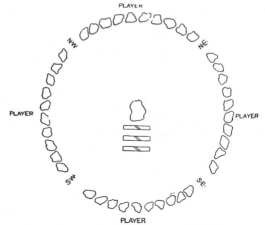

FIG. 86. Circuit for stick dice; White Mountain Apache Indians, Arizona; from drawing by Albert B. Reagan.

are of various shapes and sizes.   The stones being laid, a stick is placed in the opening at the northeast to indicate that this is the starting point.   In counting, a player moves his counting-stick as many stones from the starting point as he has points to count, putting his marker in the space just beyond the last stone counted, unless that count should end in one of the four openings, in which case he puts it in the next preceding space.   The stones in each section are numbered or named.   Those in the two sections on the right of the starting point are numbered from 1 on to the right, and those on the left of the starting point in the same way toward the left.

The playing sticks are about a foot in length, and are the halves of green sticks about 1 inch in diameter, the bark being left on the rounded side and the split surface marked across its face with charcoal bands about 1 inch wide. In throwing, the sticks are carefully held together in the hand, with the marked faces either in or out. They are hurled, ends down, the hand being released just before they strike, so that they are free to fall or bounce in any direction.

The counts are as follows: One marked face up counts 2; two marked faces up, 3; three marked faces up, 5; three marked faces down, 10.

If the player scores 10, she throws again; otherwise she passes the sticks to the next player. When a player makes 10, she always says yak̲! and strikes the center stone with the bunch of three play sticks sidewise before throwing them again. The number of players may be two, three, or four, the last-named num-

FIG. 87. White Mountain Apache women playing stick dice (the sticks in midair); White river, Arizona; from photograph by Mr Albert B. Reagan.

ber being usual. When four play, one sits behind each section of stones, facing the center. When more than two play, the two that face each other play as partners. In moving their counting-sticks, partners always move them in the same direction. The player of the east section and her partner, if she has one, move around the circle toward the south, and the player of the north section moves around toward the west.

If a player's count terminates at, or moves past, a place occupied by an antagonist, she takes her opponent's counting-stick and throws it back, and the latter must start again, losing all her counts.

A game consists of three circuits, or 120 points. Each time a player makes a circuit she scores by placing a charcoal mark on a stone in her section.

Vocabulary: Sĕt dĭlth', the stick game; sĕt dĭlth' bĕd'-dĕn-kák, let us play the stick game; dâk, the sticks used in the stick game; gŭn-ạlsh'nà, the game is finished, won; gŭn-ạlsh-nà She, I have the game.

WHITE MOUNTAIN APACHE. East fork of White river, Arizona. (Field Columbian Museum.)

Cat. no. 68819.   Three wooden staves, 14 inches in length, painted alike, blue on the flat face and rounded backs yellow.

Cat. no. 68822.   Three wooden staves, 11½ inches in length, with incised cross lines, blue and red in the middle of the flat face, the rounded backs plain.

Cat. no. 68821.   Three wooden staves, 12½ inches in length, with diagonal incised black line across the middle of the flat face, the rounded backs plain.

Cat. no. 68824.   Three wooden staves, 9 inches in length, with the middle of the flat sides blackened, and one stave with incised diagonal line in the middle, the rounded backs plain.

These specimens were collected by Mr Charles L. Owen, who describes them as used in the game of tsa-st¢l.

——— Arizona.   (Cat. no. 152696, United States National Museum.)

Set of three sticks of hazel wood, 8 inches in length, three-fourths of an inch wide, and about three-eighths of an inch in thickness, flat on one side, with a diagonal black band across the middle, the other rounded and unpainted.   They show marks of use.

These were collected by Dr Edward Palmer,[a] and were described by

Fig. 88.   Fig. 89.

FIG. 88.   Stick dice; length, 9¼ inches; White Mountain Apache Indians, Fort Apache, Arizona; cat. no. 18619, Free Museum of Science and Art, University of Pennsylvania.

FIG. 89.   Manner of holding stick dice; White Mountain Apache Indians, Arizona; from drawing by the late Capt. C. N. B. Macauley, U. S. Army.

Captain C. N. B. Macauley, U. S. Army, as used in a game played by women in a circle [b] of forty stones divided in four tens with a division to each ten, and having a large flat rock placed in the middle.

Four or six can play.   Two sides are formed of equal numbers, and two sets of sticks are used.   The players kneel behind the rock circle.   The first player takes the sticks in one hand, rounded sides out [figure 89], and slams them end first on the rock.   From this is derived the name of the game, sé-tich-ch, bounce-on-the-rock.[c]

---

[a] A set of sticks (fig. 88) made of a variety of the prickly ash, 9¼ inches in length, but otherwise identical with the above, is contained in the Free Museum of Science and Art of the University of Pennsylvania (cat. no. 18619), and was collected by Capt. C. N. B. Macauley, U. S. Army.

[b] Doctor Palmer says a square ; Captain Macauley, a circle.

[c] Capt. John G. Bourke gave the Apache name of this game to the writer as tze-chis, stone, or zse-tilth, wood, the words referring to the central stone and the staves.   The circle of stones is called, he stated, tze-nasti, stone circle.   Dr Edward Palmer gives the name of the game as satill.

The counts are as follows: Three round sides up counts 10; three flat sides up, 5; two round sides up and one flat, 2; one round side up and two flat, 3.

A throw of 10 gives another throw. Each side has two sticks which are used to mark the count. The two sides count from opposite directions.

WHITE MOUNTAIN APACHE.　Fort Apache, Arizona.　(Cat. no. 84465, Field Columbian Museum.)

Thirteen wooden dice (figure 90), 1⅜ inches in length, flat on one side and rounded on the other, all painted black on the flat side, while three have reddish brown and ten white backs.

Collected in 1903 by Mr Charles L. Owen, who gives the following account of the game, which is played only by warriors:

It is called dă′kă-nādăgíza, or dă′kă gŭstsĕ′gi. Thirteen, or, according to another informant, fourteen dice are used. Two or four players participate. The highest possible throw is 20 points. The dice are shaken in a flat basket, or tsá. The ground, having been hollowed out, is lined with bear grass covered over with a buckskin or blanket. This is to give elasticity and recoil to dice when the basket is struck sharply. The mode of shaking dice is to strike the basket, which is firmly grasped at two opposite sides, down upon the elastic playground, the dice thereby being tossed upward and shaken over well.

FIG. 90. Wooden dice; length, 1⅜ inches; White Mountain Apache Indians, Arizona; cat. no. 84465, Field Columbian Museum.

The counts are as follows: Tā-ilqgái, three white backs, ten black faces, counts 12; itcídĕnkägä, three red backs, ten black faces, —; nĭltŏhä, one red back; twelve black faces, 10; ĕctlái -ilqgái, five white backs, eight black faces, —; gŭstséd-ilqgái or dsĭlqgái, seven white backs, six black faces, —; bā -iscĭnä, three red backs, ten white backs, 20; bēitcihä, — red backs, — white backs, 16; ĕndái, three black faces, ten white backs, —; dōcǎ, three red backs, three white backs, seven black faces, —; năkí-nădá¢lä, two red backs, ten white backs, one black face, 5.

HUPA.　Hupa valley, California. (Free Museum of Science and Art, University of Pennsylvania.)

FIG. 91. Shell dice; diameters, ⅞ to 1⅓ inches; Hupa Indians, California; cat. no. 37199, 37200, Free Museum of Science and Art, University of Pennsylvania.

Cat. no. 37199.　Four disks of mussel shell (figure 91a), two alike, three-fourths of an inch, and two alike, seven-eighths of an inch in diameter. One side is dull and slightly concave, and the other bright and convex.

Cat. no. 37200.　Four disks of abalone shell (figure 91b), similar to the preceding, 1 and 1½ inches in diameter. Collected by the writer in 1900.

They are used by women in a game called by the same name as the dice, yeoul mat.

Two women play. The four dice are shaken together in the hands, the palms clasped together, and the dice let fall upon a blanket. The larger dice are called mi-ni-kiau, and the smaller, mi-ni-skek; the concave sides, tak-ai-tim-it, and the convex, you-tim-it. Two heads and two tails count; four heads count 1; four tails count 1. Other plays do not count. The count is kept with ten sticks, which are put in the center between the two women and drawn out as they win. When the center pile is exhausted they draw from each other until one woman wins the ten sticks. The game is played at any time.[a]

A Crescent City Indian, whom the writer met at Arcata, California, gave the name of the dice described above as tchuthut; large dice, tchaka; small dice, mushnai; concave sides, gaemun; convex sides, youtowitmun; let us play dice, chitat.

KAWCHODINNE. Mackenzie. (Cat. no. 7404, United States National Museum.)

Four wooden blocks (figure 92), 1¼ inches in length, said to be for a

FIG. 92. Wooden dice; length, 1¼ inches; Kawchodinne Indians, Mackenzie; cat. no. 7404, United States National Museum.

game. They have a rounded base, with two transverse cuts, and are perforated, as if for stringing. Collected by Maj. R. Kennicott on the Arctic coast.

NAVAHO. St Michael, Arizona.

Rev. Berard Haile [b] describes the following game:

Ashbí'i, the crossed-stick game. Two sticks are used, about 4 or 5 inches long. One side of the sticks is colored red, the other black. Each stick has on each side four marks, cuts, in the center. A blanket is placed on the ground and another attached above it to the ceiling. The sticks are crossed so that

---

[a] The following vocabulary for the game was collected for the writer by Dr Pliny E. Goddard: Dice, ki wǐl-măt; large dice, mǐ-nǐ kǐ-ā-ō; small dice, mǐ-skǐ-ătz; convex sides, tlā-kŭs; concave sides, mŭk-kŭs.

[b] Under date of June 5, 1902. The information was obtained from a medicine man named Qatqali nadloi, Laughing Doctor.

the marks touch each other, and are held in this position with the index finger and thumb of both hands. The player states how many points he will score and his opponent takes up the challenge by stating his own points. The sticks, held in position with both hands, are thrown up against the blanket above, and according as they fall—that is—as the marks touch each other or are close to one another, a point, great or small, is scored. The highest point is scored if the sticks fall as held when thrown up, otherwise the points count according to the proximity of the mark on the two sticks. The player continues, if he scores a point; contrariwise, his opponent tries.

This was an indoor game and not limited to a particular season. At present it is scarcely known, but our informant remembers it was played quite frequently in his childhood. He remembers, too, that the sticks were not rounded or hollow, but ordinarily round.

In a subsequent letter, from information obtained from Tlissi tso, " Big Goat," whose father was a professional gambler, Father Berard writes:

There are four sticks of different colors, yellow, white, black, and blue. Yellow is called tsī, white whúshi, black ashbíï, and blue nézhi. These names are not those of the colors but of the sticks. White and yellow, black and blue, are partners, respectively. These sticks are placed in a basket and thrown up to the blanket in order to rebound. According as they fall, or not, in proximity to partners selected, points are scored and stakes won.

NAVAHO. Chin Lee, Arizona. (Cat. no. 3621, Brooklyn Institute Museum.)

Three sticks, 3 inches in length, flat on one side and rounded on the other.

One stick (figure 93a), painted half black and half white on the

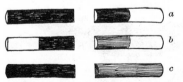

FIG. 93 a, b, c. Stick dice (for ashbíi); length, 3 inches; Navaho Indians, Arizona; cat. no. 3621, Brooklyn Institute Museum.

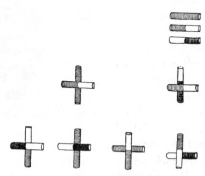

FIG. 94. Order of counts in game of ashbii; Navaho Indians, Arizona.

rounded side, the flat side black, is called tsi'i, head. Another (figure 93b), painted half red and half white, the flat side half black and half white, is called nezhi, and the third (figure 93c), painted entirely red on the rounded side and black on the flat side is called tqelli. Three dice are employed in the game of ashbii. The sticks are held together and tossed, ends upward, against the blanket above the players. A basket is placed below and they do not count unless they fall into it. The counts are agreed upon in advance, and follow the order displayed in figure 94.

NAVAHO. New Mexico. (Cat. no. 9557, United States National Museum.)

Set of three sticks of root of cottonwood, 8 inches in length, about 1¾ inches in breadth, and one-half inch in thickness, one side flat and blackened, the other rounded and unpainted (figure 95); one stick tied near the end to prevent splitting. They show marks

FIG. 95. Stick dice; length, 8 inches; Navaho Indians, New Mexico; cat. no. 9557, United States National Museum.

of continued use. Collected by Dr Edward Palmer.

As observed by the writer at the Columbian Exposition in Chicago, the Navaho play on a circle of forty stones, throwing the staves ends down upon a flat stone placed in the center. Each player has a splint or twig to represent him upon the board, and these are all placed together at one of the four openings in the circle at the commencement of the game. The throws count as follows: Three round side up counts 10; three flat, 5; two rounds and one flat, 0; one round and two flat, 0. The following vocabulary of the game was furnished me by a Navaho at Chicago: The game, set-tilth; the staves, set-tilth; the

FIG. 96. Navaho Indian women playing stick dice, St Michael, Arizona; from photograph by Rev. Berard Haile.

circle of stones, sen-asti; the stone in the center, a-cle-sane.

Dr Washington Matthews[a] describes a game ·played by Navaho women under the name of tsidil or tsindil:

The principal implements are three sticks, which are thrown violently, ends down, on a flat stone around which the gamblers sit. The sticks rebound so

---

[a] Navajo Legends, note 47, p. 219, Boston, 1897.

well that they would fly far away were not a blanket stretched overhead to throw them back to the players. A number of small stones placed in the form of a square are used as counters. These are not moved, but sticks, whose positions are changed according to the fortunes of the game, are placed between them. The rules of the game have not been recorded.

Doctor Matthews tells,[a] among the early events of the fifth or present world, that while they were waiting for the ground to dry the women erected four poles on which they stretched a deerskin, and under the shelter of this they played the game of three sticks, tsindi, one of the four games which they brought from the lower world.[b]

NAVAHO. Arizona. (Cat. no. 62540, Field Columbian Museum.)
Three flat blocks, 6 inches in length, one face painted with equal
    bands of green, blue. and red, and the other face half blue and
    half red.
They were collected by Dr George A. Dorsey, who describes the game under the name of sitih.

The circle is senesti. The game is 40 and the counts are as follows: All with three bands up count 5; all with two bands up, 10; one with three bands and two with two bands, 2; two with three bands and one with two bands, 3; one with two bands and two with three bands, 3.

———— Arizona. (Cat. no. 74735, United States National Museum.)
Set of seven blocks of cedar wood, three-fourths of an inch in length,
    seven-sixteenths of an inch wide, and one-fourth of an inch
    thick (figure 97); section hemispherical. Six have flat sides
    blackened and one painted red; opposite unpainted.
These were collected by Dr Washington Matthews, U. S. Army. The game was " played with counters by women."

Doctor Matthews[c] describes another game similar to the above under the name of taka-thad-sata[d] or the thirteen chips:

It is played with thirteen thin flat pieces of wood which are colored red on

FIG. 97. Wooden dice; length, ¼ inch; Navaho Indians, Arizona; cat. no. 74735, United States National Museum.

one side and left white or uncolored on the other. Success depends on the number of chips which, being thrown upward, fall with their white sides up.

In the gambling contest between Hastsehogan and Nohoilpi the animals came to the relief of the former, and in the game of taka-

[a] Navajo Legends, p. 77, Boston, 1897.

[b] Ibid. The other games were dilkón, played with two sticks, each the length of an arm; atsá, played with forked sticks and a ring; and aspi'n.

[c] Ibid, p. 83.

[d] Taká-thad-sáta was the first of four games played by the young Hastséhogan with the gambling god Nohoílpi. These four games are not the same as the four described as brought from the under world. They comprise, in addition, nánzoz, hoop and pole; tsi'nbetsil, push on the wood, in which the contestants push on a tree until it is torn from its roots and falls, and tsol, ball, the object in which was to hit the ball so that it would fall beyond a certain line.

thad-sata the Bat said: "Leave the game to me. I have made thirteen chips that are white on both sides. I will hide myself in the ceiling and when our champion throws up his chips I will grasp them and throw down my chips instead." The Bat assisted as he had promised the son of Hastsehogan, and the latter soon won the game.

NAVAHO. Keams Canyon, Arizona.

Mr A. M. Stephen describes the following game in his unpublished manuscript:

Ta-ka sost-siti, seven cards, played with seven small chips about 1 inch in diameter, one red, bĭ-tu, on one side and marked with a cross, the other side blackened; six black on one side, hot-djilc, and uncolored on the other side. Thrown up from the hands, when one white side comes up, the one who has been shaking the dice wins, called ün-nai; when only one black disk is exposed, tai-klign; when the red one and all the rest white, hó-ka, a winning card for several amounts, it may be seven times the stakes doubled; when all are black except the red, it is called hot-dje-bi-tci. An even number of players are sought. It is a man's game; but women are also found to play it, though only under protest from the men.

———— Chin Lee, Arizona. (Brooklyn Institute Museum.)

Cat. no. 3622. Seven wooden dice (figure 98a), flat on one side and

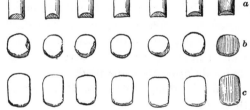

rounded o n t h e other, ends square; length, three-fourths of an inch.

Cat. no. 3623. Seven wooden dice (figure 98b), similar to the above, but circular; diameter, 1 inch.

Cat. no. 3624. Seven

FIG. 98 a, b, c. Three sets of wooden dice; lengths, ¾, 1¼ inches; Navaho Indians, Arizona; cat. no. 3622, 3623, and 3624, Brooklyn Institute Museum.

wooden dice (figure 98c), similar to the above, but oval; diameter, 1¼ inches.

These dice are all painted black on the flat side, with six unpainted and one painted red on the convex side; made by a medicine man named Little Singer, who gave the name as dakha tsostsedi, seven cards.

Rev. Berard Haile describes the preceding game in a personal letter:

Dă'ka tsostse'di, cards seven times or seventh card. There are four sets of chips of seven each. One set is flat on both sides, and square; another has round corners; another is flat below and round above; and the other set tapers to a point on both sides, with rounded back and a ridge in the center. Each of these sets has six chips, colored white or natural on one side, the other side being black. The seventh one is red and white and is called bichi', red, and counts more than all the rest. These chips were made of oak or of a certain species of wood easily polished after removing the bark, perhaps mahogany. The players usually carried four sets with them, together with a basket, in a pouch, from which I conclude it was small, and threw them up. However, they played with only one set at a time, viz., seven chips, either round or flat ones. Accordingly as the color of the chips faced the ground, points were scored. Six white and the seventh red won the game, while all blacks did not score as much.

Frank Walker, one of Father Berard's interpreters, recognized the name taka-thad-sata, or thirteen cards, given by Doctor Matthews as that of a similar game which is so called in legends, but said that daka tsostsedi is more generally known and spoken of.

SEKANI. British Columbia.

Sir Alexander Mackenzie [a] gives the following description of the game of the platter.

The instruments of it consist of a platter or dish made of wood or bark and six round or square but flat pieces of metal, wood, or stone, whose sides or surfaces are of different colors. These are put into the dish, and after being for some time shaken together are thrown into the air and received again in the dish with considerable dexterity, when by the number that are turned up of the same mark or color the game is regulated. If there should be equal numbers the throw is not reckoned; if two or four, the platter changes hands.

TAKULLI. Stuart lake, British Columbia.

The Reverend Father A. G. Morice [b] wrote:

A third chance game was proper to the women and was played with button-like pieces of bone.

It was based on the same principle as dice, and, in common with atlih, it has long fallen into disuse. Its name is atiyéh.

BEOTHUKAN STOCK

BEOTHUK. Newfoundland.

From colored drawings of ancient bone disks attributed to the Beothuk, and presented to the United States National Museum by Lady Edith Blake, of Kingston, Jamaica, it would appear that this tribe may have used gaming disks resembling those of the Micmac.

CADDOAN STOCK

ARIKARA. North Dakota.   (Cat. no. 6342, 6355, United States National Museum.)

Set of eight plum stones, plain on one side, with marks burned on the other, as shown in figure 99. Four have stars on a burnt ground; two, circular marks; two are entirely burned over. Basket of woven grass, 7 inches in diameter at the top and 2 inches deep (catalogued as from the Grosventres). Collected by Dr C. C. Gray and Mr Matthew F. Stevenson.

---

[a] Voyages from Montreal, p. 142, London, 1801.
[b] Notes on Western Dénés. Transactions of the Canadian Institute, v. 4, p. 81, Toronto, 1895.

H. M. Brackenridge,[a] referring to the Arikara, states:

In the evening, about sundown, the women cease from their labors and collect in little knots, and amuse themselves with a game something like jackstones:

five pebbles are tossed up in a small basket, with which they endeavor to catch them again as they fall.

FIG. 99.   Plum-stone dice; diameter, 1⅛ inch; Arikara Indians, North Dakota; cat. no. 6355, United States National Museum.

It seems hardly necessary to point out that he failed to comprehend the object of the game.

CADDO.   Oklahoma.   (Field Columbian Museum.)

Cat. no. 59366.   Four slips of cane (figure 100), 6¼ inches in length, three painted red on the inside and one black.

Cat. no. 59372.   Four slips of cane (figure 101), 11½ inches in length, painted black on the inner side.

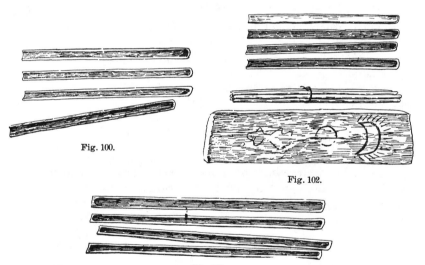

Fig. 100.

Fig. 102.

Fig. 101.

FIG. 100.   Cane dice; length, 6¼ inches; Caddo Indians, Oklahoma; cat. no. 59366, Field Columbian Museum.

FIG. 101.   Cane dice; length, 11¼ inches; Caddo Indians, Oklahoma; cat. no. 59372, Field Columbian Museum.

FIG. 102.   Cane dice board and counting sticks; length of canes, 7¼ inches; length of board, 11 inches; length of counters, 8¼ inches; Caddo Indians, Oklahoma; cat. no. 59370, Field Columbian Museum.

Cat. no. 59370.   Four slips of cane, 7½ inches in length, painted on the inside; one yellow, one red, one blue, one green; with a flat rectangular board, 3½ by 11 inches, with incised and painted

---

[a] Views of Louisiana, together with a Journal of a Voyage up the Missouri River, in 1811, p. 251, Pittsburg, 1814.

designs, on which the canes are thrown, and eight counting sticks, $8\frac{3}{4}$ inches in length (figure 102). Collected by Dr George A. Dorsey.

PAWNEE. Nebraska.

Mr John B. Dunbar says: [a]

The women also were addicted to games of chance, though with them the stakes were usually trifling. The familiar game with plum stones, sŭk'-u, and another, lŭk'-ta-kĭt-au'-ĭ-čŭk-u, played with a bundle of parti-colored rods about a foot in length, were much in vogue among them.

——— Oklahoma.   (Field Columbian Museum.)

Cat. no. 59522.   Set of four stick dice, made of slips of cane, 8 inches in length, entirely plain.

Cat. no. 59413.   Set of four stick dice, made of slips of cane, $12\frac{1}{2}$ inches in length, curved sides plain, concave sides painted, two red and two green.

Cat. no. 59519.   Set of dice, similar to the above, $13\frac{1}{2}$ inches in length, one with concave side painted red and having an incised line painted red on the convex side; one with concave side blue and a line with feather-like marks on the reverse; one with concave side yellow, and an incised line painted yellow on the reverse, and one with the concave side painted white, with a long unpainted line with a cross mark on the reverse.

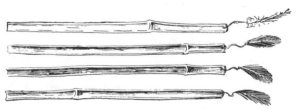

FIG. 103. Cane dice; length, $16\frac{1}{4}$ inches; Pawnee Indians, Oklahoma; cat. no. 59523, Field Columbian Museum.

Cat. no. 59523.   Set of dice, similar to the preceding, $16\frac{1}{4}$ inches in length (figure 103). Insides painted yellow, red, green, and plain, and three crosses incised on reverse. Each has a feather attached by a thong at one end.

Cat. no. 59415.   Four sticks (figure 104), $8\frac{1}{2}$ inches in length, one side rounded and burned with marks, as shown in the figure, the other flat with a groove painted red. Accompanied with a square of buffalo hide, 27 by 32 inches, marked in black with two rows of eight lines, a row on each side, each with seven divisions, on which the bets are laid.

[a] The Pawnee Indians.   Magazine of American History, v. 8, p. 751, New York, 1882.

Cat. no. 59412. Set of four wooden dice (figure 105), 9 inches in
length, one side convex and marked with incised black lines, as
shown in figure. The reverse grooved, three painted red and
plain, and one black and marked with cross lines at the end and
middle. Accompanied by a tablet of sandstone (figure 106), 4
inches square, marked with incised lines, and four counting
sticks, 7 inches in length, painted red, and twelve, 9 inches in
length, painted yellow (figure 107).

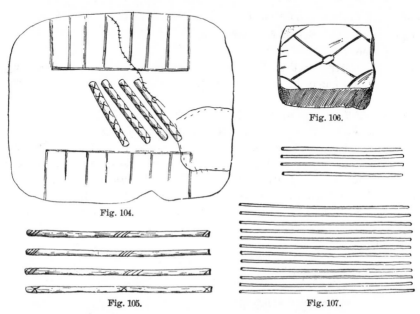

Fig. 104.

Fig. 106.

Fig. 105.

Fig. 107.

FIG. 104. Stick-dice game; length of dice, 8¼ inches; length of hide, 32 inches; Pawnee Indians,
Oklahoma; cat. no. 59415, Field Columbian Museum.

FIG. 105. Stick dice; length, 9 inches; Pawnee Indians, Oklahoma; cat. no. 59412, Field Columbian Museum.

FIG. 106. Stone tablet for stick dice; 4 inches square; Pawnee Indians, Oklahoma; cat. no. 59412,
Field Columbian Museum.

FIG. 107. Counting sticks for stick dice; length, 9 and 7 inches; Pawnee Indians, Oklahoma;
cat. no. 59412, Field Columbian Museum.

Cat. no. 59419. Rattan basket (figure 108), 8½ inches in diameter;
six peach-stone dice, three burned entirely black on one side,
three with crosses on one side, the reverse plain, and four red,
four green, and four yellow counting sticks, all 12 inches in
length.

A number of other peach and plum-stone dice in the same collection are in sets of six, two kinds in each set, all plain on one face
and marked, three alike, on the other, chiefly with stars.

All of the above were collected in 1901 by Dr George A. Dorsey.

PAWNEE. Pawnee reservation, Oklahoma. (Cat. no. 70721, Field
Columbian Museum.)

Set of six plum-stone dice (figure 109), three small, burned black on
    one side, and three large, with a light longitudinal curved band
    with seven dots on one side, reverses plain; accompanied by a
    flat basket of twined rattan, 9 inches in diameter. Collected by
    Dr George A. Dorsey.

In the tale of Scabby Bull, Doctor Dorsey describes the marking of a set of
six magic plum stones for the woman's
game:

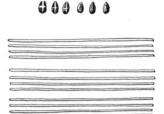

> One of the stones had a new moon pictured
> on it, and a little black star on the decorated
> side. The next stone bore a half moon in black.
> The next stone was decorated with a full
> moon; the next one had upon it one great star,
> which reached from one point of the stone to
> the other. The next stone had two stars
> painted upon it, while the last one had seven
> stars painted upon it. According to the people,
> the man took the stones outside, held them up,
> and through the power of the moon and stars
> the stones were painted black.[a]

FIG. 108. Peach-stone dice, basket, and
counters; diameter of basket, 8¼.
inches; length of counters, 12 inches;
Pawnee Indians, Oklahoma; cat. no.
59419, Field Columbian Museum.

In reply to a letter addressed by the
writer to Dr George Bird Grinnell, of
New York City, he kindly wrote the following account of what the
Pawnee call the seed game:

> I have seen this game played among the Pawnee, Arikara, and Cheyenne, and
> substantially the same way everywhere. The Pawnee do not use a bowl to
> throw the seeds, but hold them in a flat
> wicker basket about the size and shape
> of an ordinary tea plate. The woman
> who makes the throw holds the basket
> in front of her, close to the ground,
> gives the stones a sudden toss into the
> air, and then moves the basket smartly
> down against the ground, and the stones
> fall into it. They are not thrown high,
> but the movement of the basket is
> quick, and it is brought down hard on
> the ground, so that the sound of the

FIG. 109. Plum-stone dice; Pawnee Indians,
Oklahoma; cat. no. 70721, Field Columbian
Museum.

> slapping is easily heard. The plum stones are always five in number, blackened
> and variously marked on one side. The women who are gambling sit in a line
> opposite to one another, and usually each woman bets with the one sitting
> opposite her, and the points are counted by sticks placed on the ground between
> them, the wager always being on the game and not on the different throws.
> It is exclusively, so far as I know, a woman's game.

Z. M. Pike [b] says:

> The third game alluded to, is that of la platte, described by various travelers,

---

[a] Traditions of the Skidi Pawnee, p. 235, New York, 1904.
   [b] An account of an Expedition to the Sources of the Mississippi, Appendix to part 2,
p. 16, Philadelphia, 1810.

and is played by the women, children, and old men, who, like grasshoppers, crawl out to the circus to bask in the sun, probably covered only with an old buffalo robe.

WICHITA. W i c h i t a reservation, Oklahoma. (Cat. no. 59350, Field Columbian Museum.)

Four split canes (figure 110), 6 inches in length, the outer faces plain, the inner sides colored; three red, one green. Collected by Dr George A. Dorsey.

FIG. 110. Stick dice; length, 6 inches; Wichita Indians, Wichita reservation, Oklahoma; cat. no. 59350, Field Columbian Museum.

ESKIMAUAN STOCK

ESKIMO (CENTRAL, AIVILIRMIUT, and KINIPETU). Keewatin.

Dr Franz Boas describes the following game played with bones from seal flippers:[a]

Each bone represents a certain animal or an old or young person. They are divided into two equal parts. One bone is picked up from each pile, held up a few inches, and then let drop. Should one land right side up, it is looked upon as though it had thrown the other down in a fight. The one which fell wrong side up is then set aside, and another from the same pile is tried with the successful one in this way. This is carried on until one side wins. Then the last bone to win is called the bear, being strongest of all. The player who has lost the game so far takes the bone, holds it up to his forehead, and lets it drop. If it should land right side up, it is looked upon as though the bear has thrown him. Otherwise he is stronger than the bear. Children also use these bones for playing house.

ESKIMO (CENTRAL). Frobisher bay, Franklin.

Captain Charles Franklin Hall[b] says:

They have a variety of games of their own. In one of these they use a number of bits of ivory made in the form of ducks, etc.

FIG. 111. Ivory dice in form of women and bird; Central Eskimo, Cumberland sound, Franklin; cat. no. $\frac{60}{3416}$, $\frac{60}{3415}$, American Museum of Natural History; from Boas.

———— Cumberland sound, Franklin. (Cat. no. $\frac{60}{3416}$, $\frac{60}{3415}$, American Museum of Natural History.)

Doctor Boas figures three ivory dice (figure 111) in the form of women, and one representing a bird.[c] Collected by Capt. James Mutch.

Elsewhere[d] Doctor Boas says:

A game similar to dice, called tingmiujang—i. e., images of birds—is

---

[a] Eskimo of Baffin Land and Hudson Bay. Bulletin of American Museum of Natural History, v. 15, p. 112, New York, 1901.

[b] Arctic Researches, p. 570, New York, 1860.

[c] Eskimo of Baffin Land and Hudson Bay. Bulletin of American Museum of Natural History, v. 15, p. 54, New York, 1901.

[d] The Central Eskimo. Sixth Annual Report of the Bureau of Ethnology, p. 567, 1888.

quently played. A set of about fifteen figures, like those represented in figure
522, belong to this game; some representing birds, others men and women. The
players sit around a board or piece of leather and the figures are shaken in the
hand and thrown upward. On falling, some stand upright, others lie flat on
the back or on the side. Those standing upright belong to that player whom

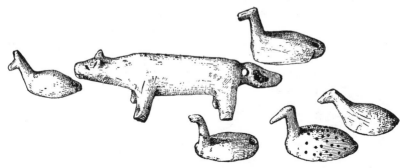

FIG. 112. Game of "fox and geese," Yuit Eskimo, Plover bay, Siberia; from Murdoch.

they face; sometimes they are so thrown that they all belong to the one that
tossed them up. The players throw by turns until the last figure is taken up,
the one getting the greatest number of figures being the winner.

Mr John Murdoch[a] describes similar objects which he purchased
at Plover bay, eastern Siberia, in 1881 (figure 112). They were supposed to be merely works of art. Referring to the account given by
Doctor Boas of their use as a game, he says:

It is therefore quite likely they were used for a similar purpose at Plover
bay. If this be so, it is a remark-
able point of similarity between these
widely separated Eskimos, for I can
learn nothing of a similar custom at
any intermediate point.

In the United States National
Museum (cat. no. 63457) there
is a set of carved water birds
and a seal (figure 113) collected
from the Eskimo at St Law-

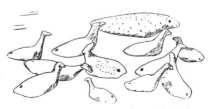

FIG. 113. Ivory water birds and seal; Western
Eskimo, St Lawrence island, Alaska: cat. no.
63457, United States National Museum.

rence island, Alaska, by Mr E. W. Nelson, in 1882. He informs me,
through Prof. Otis T. Mason, that he never saw the flat-bottomed
geese and other creatures used in a game, and all of his specimens
are perforated and used as pendants on the bottom of personal ornaments and parts of clothing.

Prof. Benjamin Sharp, of the Academy of Natural Sciences of
Philadelphia, tells me that he saw the carved water birds used as a
game, being tossed and allowed to fall by Eskimo at St Lawrence
bay, Siberia.

[a] Ethnological Results of the Point Barrow Expedition. Ninth Annual Report of the
Bureau of Ethnology, p. 364, 1892.

In reply to my inquiry in reference to the use of such objects in games by the Arctic Highlanders of Greenland, Mr Henry G. Bryant writes me that small images of birds are rare among them, although representations of men, women, walrus, seal, bears, and dogs are part of the domestic outfit of every well-regulated family.[a]

I understand that the leg bones of the arctic fox are sometimes tied together on a string, and at times these are thrown up and their position noted when striking the ground. Perhaps they attach a significance to the position of the fox bones, which may be analogous to the practice of using wooden or bone dice by other tribes.

Fig. 114. Phalanges of seal used in game; length, 1¼ to 3 inches; Western Eskimo, Point Barrow, Alaska; cat. no. 41841, Free Museum of Science and Art, University of Pennsylvania.

ESKIMO (WESTERN). Point Barrow, Alaska. (Cat. no. 41840, 41841, Free Museum of Science and Art, University of Pennsylvania.)

Two sets, each of twenty-five metatarsal bones (figure 114) of the seal (five sets from as many sets of flippers), employed in a game called inugah. These were collected by Mr E. A. McIlhenny. The following account of the game is given by the collector:

Played by men and women during the winter months. Two persons play, dividing the fifty bones between them, one taking twenty-five from a right flipper and the other twenty-five from a left. The first player lets all his bones fall, and those which fall with the condylar surface upward are withdrawn. The other player then lets his bones fall and withdraws those which fall with the condylar surface upward in the same way. Then the first drops his remainder, and the game proceeds until one or the other has withdrawn all his bones and becomes the winner. Another game is played by two players, each with a single metatarsal bone, the one represented in the foreground of figure 114 being selected preferably. The two players hold the bone aloft at the same time and let it fall on a skin on the floor from a distance of 2 feet. If both bones fall alike, the play is a draw. If one falls with the condylar surface upward, its owner wins and takes the other one. The game is continued in the same way until the bones of one or the other player are exhausted.

Fig. 115. Bone die (stopka); Western Eskimo, Kodiak, Alaska; from Lissiansky.

——— Island of Kodiak, Alaska.

Capt. Uriy Lissiansky [b] says:

There is another favorite game called stopka [figure 115], which is a small figure cut out of bone. It is thrown up into the air, and if it falls on its bottom 2 are counted; if on its back, 3, and if on its belly, 1 only. This game consists in gaining 20, which are also marked with short sticks.

---

[a] Mr Bryant states that these miniature figures, which are made of ivory, are employed to teach children the arts of the chase.

[b] A Voyage Round the World, p. 211, London, 1814.

CAUGHNAWAGA. Quebec.

Col. James Smith [a] describes a game resembling dice or hustle cap:

They put a number of plum stones in a small bowl; one side of each stone is black and the other white; then they shake or hustle the bowl, calling hits, hits, hits, honesy, honesy, rago, rago, which signifies calling for white or black or what they wish to turn up; they then turn the bowl and count the whites and blacks.

CHEROKEE. North Carolina.

I am informed by Mrs Starr Hayes that the Cherokee play a game in a flat square basket of cane, like the lid of a market basket, with colored beans, under the name of black eye and white eye.

The shallow basket used is 1½ feet square. The beans are colored butter beans, a variety of lima, and those selected are dark on one side and white on the other. Twelve beans are kept as counters. Six others are put in the basket, as they come, and the players, who are four in number, and each two partners, play in turn. The basket is held in both hands, slightly shaken, and then with a jerk the beans are tossed in the air. If all turn black, 2 are taken from the counters; if all turn white, 3 are taken. If but one turns up white, 1 is taken from the twelve. When they turn five white, 1 only is taken. The game is played three or six times weekly. Whoever gets twelve beans has the game.

CONESTOGA. Western Pennsylvania and southern New York.

Loskiel [b] gives the following account:

The Indians are naturally given to gambling, and frequently risk their arms, furniture, clothes, and all they possess to gratify this passion. The chief game of the Iroquois and Delawares is dice, which, indeed, originated with them. The dice are made of oval and flattish plum stones, painted black on one and yellow on the other side. Two persons only can play at one time. They put the dice into a dish, which is raised alternately by each gambler and struck on the table or floor with force enough to make the dice rise and change their position, when he who has the greater number of winning color counts 5, and the first who has the good fortune to do this eight times wins the game. The spectators seem in great agitation during the game, and at every chance that appears decisive cry out with great vehemence. The gamblers distort their features, and if unsuccessful mutter their displeasure at the dice and the evil spirits who prevent their good fortune. Sometimes whole townships, and even whole tribes, play against each other. One of the missionaries happened to be present when two Iroquois townships, having got together a number of goods, consisting of blankets, cloth, shirts, linen, etc., gambled for them. The game lasted eight days. They assembled every day, and every inhabitant of each township tossed the dice once. This being done and the chance of each person noted down, they parted for the day; but each township offered a sacrifice in the evening to insure success to their party. This was done by a man going several times around the fire, throwing tobacco into it, and singing a song. Afterward the whole company danced. When the appointed time for the game was at an end they compared notes, and the winner bore away the spoil in triumph.

---

[a] An Account of the Remarkable Occurrences in the Life and Travels of Col. James Smith, p. 46, Cincinnati, 1870.

[b] George Henry Loskiel, History of the Mission of the United Brethren among the Indians in North America, pt. 1, p. 106, London, 1794.

Huron. Detroit, Michigan.

Charlevoix [a] gives the following account:

As I returned through a quarter of the Huron village I saw a company of these savages, who appeared very eager at play. I drew near and saw they were playing at the game of the dish [jeu du plat]. This is the game of which these people are fondest. At this they sometimes lose their rest, and in some measure their reason. At this game they hazard all they possess, and many do not leave off till they are almost stripped quite naked and till they have lost all they have in their cabins. Some have been known to stake their liberty for a time, which fully proves their passion for this game, for there are no men in the world more jealous of their liberty than the savages.

The game of the dish, which they also call the game of the little bones [jeu des osselets], is played by two persons only. Each has six or eight little bones, which at first I took for apricot stones—they are that shape and bigness. But upon viewing them closely I perceived they had six unequal surfaces, the two principal of which are painted, one black and the other white inclined to yellow. They make them jump up by striking the ground or the table with a round and hollow dish, which contains them and which they twirl round first. When they have no dish they throw the bones up in the air with their hands; if in falling they come all of one color, he who plays wins 5. The game is 40 up, and they subtract the numbers gained by the adverse party. Five bones of the same color win only 1 for the first time, but the second time they win the game. A less number wins nothing.

He that wins the game continues playing. The loser gives his place to another, who is named by the markers of his side, for they make the parties at first, and often the whole village is concerned in the game. Oftentimes, also, one village plays against another. Each party chooses a marker, but he withdraws when he pleases, which never happens except when his party loses. At every throw, especially if it happens to be decisive, they set up great shouts. The players appear like people possessed, and the spectators are not more calm. They all make a thousand contortions, talk to the bones, load the spirits of the adverse party with imprecations, and the whole village echoes with howlings. If all this does not recover their luck, the losers may put off the party till the next day. It costs them only a small treat to the company. Then they prepare to return to the engagement. Each invokes his genius and throws some tobacco in the fire in his honor. They ask him above all things for lucky dreams. As soon as day appears they go again to play, but if the losers fancy the goods in their cabins made them unlucky, the first thing they do is to change them all. The great parties commonly last five or six days, and often continue all night. In the meantime, as all the persons present—at least, those who are concerned in the game—are in agitation that deprives them of reason, as they quarrel and fight, which never happens among savages but on these occasions and in drunkenness, one may judge if, when they have done playing, they do not want rest.

It sometimes happens that these parties of play are made by order of the physician or at the request of the sick. There is needed for this purpose nothing more than a dream of one or the other. This dream is always taken for the order of some spirit, and they prepare themselves for the game with a great deal of care. They assemble for several nights to make trial and to see who has the luckiest hand. They consult their genii, they fast, the married persons observe continence, and all to obtain a favorable dream. Every morning they relate what dreams they have had and all the things they have

---

[a] Journal d'un Voyage dans l'Amérique Septentrionnale, v. 3, p. 260, Paris, 1744.

dreamt of which they think lucky, and they make a collection of all and put them into little bags, which they carry about with them, and if anyone has the reputation of being lucky—that is, in the opinion of these people of having a familiar spirit more powerful or more inclined to do good—they never fail to make him keep near the one who holds the dish. They even go a great way sometimes to fetch him, and if through age or any infirmity he can not walk they will carry him on their shoulders.

They have often pressed the missionaries to be present at these games, as they believe their guardian genii are the most powerful.

Nicolas Perrot [a] says:

The savages have also a sort of game of dice, the box of which is a wooden plate, well rounded and well polished on both sides. The dice are made of six small flat pieces of bone, about the size of a plum stone. They are all alike, having one of the faces colored black, red, green, or blue, and the other generally painted white or any different color from the first-mentioned face. They throw these dice in the plate, holding the two edges, and on lifting it they make them jump and turn therein. After having struck the dish on the cloth they strike themselves at the same time heavy blows on the chest and shoulders while the dice turn about, crying " Dice, dice, dice " until the dice have stopped moving. When they find five or six showing the same color they take the gains which have been agreed upon with the opposite party. If the loser and his comrades have nothing more to play with, the winner takes all that is on the game. Entire villages have been seen gambling away their possessions, one against the other, on this game. and ruining themselves thereat. They also challenge to a decision by one throw of the die, and when it happens that a party throws 6 all those of the tribe that bet on him get up and dance in cadence to the noise of gourd rattles. All passes without dispute. The women and girls also play this game, but they often use eight dice and do not use a dice box like the men. They only use a blanket, and throw them on with the hand.

Gabriel Sagard Theodat [b] says:

The men are addicted not only to the game of reeds, which they call aescara, with three or four hundred small white reeds cut equally to the length of a foot, but are also addicted to other kinds of games, as for instance, taking a large wooden platter with five or six plum stones or small balls somewhat flattened, about the size of the end of the little finger, and painted black on one side and white or yellow on the other. They squat all around in a circle and take each his turn in taking hold of the platter with both hands, which they keep at a little distance from the floor, and bring the platter down somewhat roughly. so as to make the balls move about; they take it as in a game of dice, observing on which side the stones lie, whether it goes against them or for them. The one who holds the platter says continually while striking it, " Tet, tet, tet," thinking that this may excite and influence the game in his favor.

For the ordinary game of women and girls, at times joined by men and boys, five or six stones are used; for instance, those of apricots, black on one side and yellow on the other, which they hold in their hands as we do dice, throwing the stones a little upward, and after they have fallen on the skin which serves them as a carpet they see what the result is, and continue to play for the necklaces, ear ornaments, and other small articles of their companions, but never for gold

---

[a] Mémoire sur les Moeurs, Coustumes et Relligion des Sauvages de l'Amérique Septentrionale, p. 50, Leipzig, 1864.

[b] Histoire du Canada, p. 243, Paris, 1866.

or silver coin, because they do not know the use of it, since in trade they barter one thing for another.

I must not forget to mention that in some of their villages they play what we call in France porter les momons, carry the challenge. They send a challenge to other villages to come and play against them, winning their utensils, if they can, and meanwhile the feasting does not stop, because at the least inducement the kettle is on the fire, especially in winter time, at which time they especially feast and amuse themselves in order to pass the hard season agreeably.

Father Louis Hennepin [a] says in describing games of the Indians:

They have games for men, for the women, and for the children. The most common for men are with certain fruits, which have seeds black on one side and red on the other; they put them in a wooden or bark platter on a blanket, a great coat, or a dressed-skin mantle. There are six or eight players. But there are only two who touch the platter alternately with both hands; they raise it, and then strike the bottom of the platter on the ground, by this shaking to mix up the six seeds, then if they come five red or black, turned on the same side, this is only one throw gained, because they usually play several throws to win the game, as they agree among them. All those who are in the game play one after another. There are some so given to this game that they will gamble away even their great coat. Those who conduct the game cry at the top of their voice when they rattle the platter, and they strike their shoulders so hard as to leave them all black with the blows.

The Baron La Hontan [b] says:

Another game which is hazard and chance is perform'd with eight little stones, which are black on one side and white on the other. They're put on a plate which they lay on the ground, throwing the little stones up in the air, and if they fall so as to turn up the black side, 'tis good luck. The odd number wins, and eight whites or blacks wins double, but that happens but seldom.

Marc Lescarbot [c] says:

I will add here, as one of the customs of our savages, games of chance, of which they are so fond that sometimes they bet all they have; and Jaques Quartier writes the same of those of Canada at the time he was there. I have seen one sort of game that they have, but not then thinking to write this I did not pay much attention to it. They place a certain number of beans, colored and painted on one side, in a platter, and having spread a skin on the ground, play upon it, striking the platter on the skin and by this means the before-mentioned beans jump into the air and do not all fall on the colored part, and in this is the hazard, and according to the game they have a certain number of stalks of rushes which they distribute to the winner in order to keep score.

Jean de Brébeuf [d] says:

The game of dish is also in great renown in affairs of medicine, especially if the sick man has dreamed of it. The game is purely one of chance. They play it with six plum stones, white on one side and black on the other, in a dish that they strike very roughly against the ground, so that the plum stones leap up and fall, sometimes on one side and sometimes on the other. The game

---

[a] A Description of Louisiana, p. 300, New York, 1880.
[b] New Voyages to North-America, v. 2, p. 18, London, 1703.
[c] Histoire de la Nouvelle France, p. 788, Paris, 1609.
[d] Relation of 1636. The Jesuit Relations and Allied Documents, v. 10, p. 187, Cleveland, 1897.

consists in throwing all white or all black; they usually play village against village. All the people gather in a cabin, and they dispose themselves on poles, arranged as high as the roof, along both sides. The sick man is brought in a blanket, and that man of the village who is to shake the dish (for there is only one man on each side set apart for the purpose), he, I say, walks behind, his head and face wrapped in his garment. They bet heavily on both sides. When the man of the opposite party takes the dish, they cry at the top of their voice achine, achine, achine, three, three, three, or, perhaps, ioio, ioio, ioio, wishing him to throw only three white or three black. You might have seen this winter a great crowd returning from here to their villages, having lost their moccasins at a time when there was nearly three feet of snow, apparently as cheerful, nevertheless, as if they had won. The most remarkable thing I notice in regard to this matter is the disposition they bring to it. There are some who fast several days before playing. The evening before they all meet together in a cabin, and make a feast to find out what will be the result of the game. The one chosen to hold the dish takes the stones, and puts them promiscuously into a dish, and covers it so as to prevent anyone from putting his hand into it. That done, they sing; the song over, the dish is uncovered, and the plum stones are found all white or all black. At this point I asked a savage if those against whom they were to play did not do the same on their side, and if they might not find the plum stones in the same condition. He said they did. "And yet," said I to him, "all can not win;" to that he knew not how to answer. He informed me besides of two remarkable things: In the first place, that they choose to handle the dish some one who has dreamed that he could win, or who had a charm; moreover, those who have a charm do not conceal it, and carry it everywhere with them; we have, they tell me, one of these in our village, who rubs the plum stones with a certain ointment and hardly ever fails to win; secondly, that in making the attempt, some of the plum stones disappear, and are found some time after in the dish with the others.

Bacqueville de la Potherie [a] says:

The women sometimes play at platter, but their ordinary game is to throw fruit stones with the hands, as one plays with dice. When they have thrown their stones in the air, they move their arms as if making gestures of admiration, or driving away flies. They say nothing, one hears almost nothing, but the men cry like people who fight. They speak only in saying black! black! white! white! and from time to time they make great clamorings. The women have only this kind of game. Children play at cross, never or rarely at platter.

———— Teanaustayae, Ontario.

Father Lalemant [b] says:

One of the latest fooleries that has occurred in this village was in behalf of a sick man of a neighboring village, who, for his health, dreamed, or received the order from the physician of the country, that a game of dish should be played for him. He tells it to the captains, who immediately assemble the council, fix the time, and choose the village that they must invite for this purpose—and that village is ours. An envoy from that place is sent hither to make the proposition; it is accepted, and then preparations are made on both sides.

This game of dish consists in tossing some stones of the wild plum in a wooden dish—each being white on one side and black on the other—whence there ensues loss or gain, according to the laws of the game.

---

[a] Historie de l'Amérique Septentrionale, v. 3, p. 23, Paris, 1722.
[b] Relation of 1639. The Jesuit Relations and Allied Documents, v. 17, p. 201, Cleveland, 1898.

It is beyond my power to picture the diligence and activity of our barbarians in preparing themselves and in seeking all the means and omens for good luck and success in their game. They assemble at night and spend the time partly in shaking the dish and ascertaining who has the best hand, partly in displaying their charms and exhorting them. Toward the end they lie down to sleep in the same cabin, having previously fasted, and for some time abstained from their wives, and all this to have some favorable dream; in the morning, they have to relate what happened during the night.

Finally, they collect all the things which they have dreamed can bring good luck, and fill pouches with them in order to carry them. They search everywhere, besides, for those who have charms suitable to the game, or ascwandics or familiar demons, that these may assist the one who holds the dish, and be nearest to him when he shakes it. If there be some old men whose presence is regarded as efficacious in augmenting the strength and virtue of their charms, they are not satisfied to take the charms to them, but sometimes even to load these men themselves upon the shoulders of the young men, to be carried to the place of assembly, and inasmuch as we pass in the country for master sorcerers, they do not fail to admonish us to begin our prayers and to perform many ceremonies, in order to make them win. They have no sooner arrived at the appointed place than the two parties take their places on opposite sides of the cabin and fill it from top to bottom, above and below the andichons, which are sheets of bark making a sort of canopy for a bed, or shelter, which corresponds to that below, which rests upon the ground, upon which they sleep at night. It is placed upon poles laid and suspended the whole length of the cabin. The two players are in the middle, with their assistants, who hold the charms; each of those in the assembly bets against whatever other person he chooses, and the game begins.

It is then every one begins to pray or mutter, I know not what words, with gestures and eager motions of the hands, eyes, and the whole face, all to attract to himself good luck and to exhort their demons to take courage and not let themselves be tormented.

Some are deputed to utter execrations and to make precisely contrary gestures, with the purpose of driving ill luck back to the other side and of imparting fear to the demon of the opponents.

This game was played several times this winter, all over the country; but I do not know how it has happened that the people of the villages where we have residences have always been unlucky to the last degree, and a certain village lost 30 porcelain collars, each of a thousand beads, which are in this country equal to what you would call in France 50,000 pearls, or pistoles. But this is not all; for, hoping always to regain what they have once lost, they stake tobacco pouches, robes, shoes, and leggins, in a word, all they have. So that if ill luck attack them, as happened to these, they return home naked as the hand, having sometimes lost even their clouts.

They do not go away, however, until the patient has thanked them for the health he has recovered through their help, always professing himself cured at the end of all these fine ceremonies, although frequently he does not do this long afterward in this world.

MOHAWK. New York.

Bruyas [a] in his radical words of the Mohawk language, written in the latter part of the seventeenth century, gives under atnenha,

---

[a] Rev. Jacques Bruyas, Radices Verborum Iroquæorum, p. 37, New York, 1862.

noyau, stone of a fruit, the compounds "t8atnenha8inneton, jouer avec des noyaux comme sont les femmes, en les jettant avec la main, and t8atenna8eron, y jouer au plat."

ONONDAGA. New York.

Rev. W. M. Beauchamp [a] states:

Among the Onondaga now eight bones or stones are used, black on one side and white on the other. They term the game ta-you-nyun-wát-hah, or finger shaker, and from 100 to 300 beans form the pool, as may be agreed. With them it is also a household game. In playing this the pieces are raised in the hand and scattered, the desired result being indifferently white or black. Essentially, the counting does not differ from that given by Morgan. Two white or two black will have six of one color, and these count 2 beans, called o-yú-ah, or the bird. The player proceeds until he loses, when his opponent takes his turn. Seven white or black gain 4 beans, called o-néo-sah, or pumpkin. All white or all black gain 20, called o-hén-tah, or a field. These are all that draw anything, and we may indifferently say with the Onondaga two white or black for the first, or six with the Seneca. The game is played singly or by partners, and there is no limit to the number. Usually there are three or four players.

In counting the gains there is a kind of ascending reduction; for as two birds make one pumpkin, only one bird can appear in the result. First come the twenties, then the fours, then the twos, which can occur but once. Thus we may say for twenty, jo-han-tó-tah, you have one field or more, as the case may be. In the fours we can only say ki-yae-ne-you-sáh-ka, you have four pumpkins, for five would make a field. For two beans there is the simple announcement of o-yú-ah, bird. . . .

The game of peach stones, much more commonly used and important, has a more public character, although I have played it in an Indian parlor. In early days the stones of the wild plum were used, but now six peach stones are ground down to an elliptic flattened form, the opposite sides being black or white. This is the great game known as that of the dish nearly three centuries ago. The wooden bowl which I used was 11 inches across the top and 3 inches deep, handsomely carved out of a hard knot. A beautiful small bowl, which I saw elsewhere, may have been used by children. The six stones are placed in the kah-oón-wah, the bowl, and thence the Onondaga term the game ta-yune-oo-wáh-es, throwing the bowl to each other as they take it in turn. In public playing two players are on their knees at a time, holding the bowl between them. . . . Beans are commonly used for counters. Many rules are settled according to agreement, but the pumpkin is left out, and the stones usually count 5 for a bird and 6 for a field. All white or all black is the highest throw, and 5 or 6 are the only winning points. In early days it would seem that all white or all black alone counted. The bowl is simply struck on the floor. . . . This ancient game is used at the New Year's, or White Dog, feast among the Onandaga yet. Clan plays against clan, the Long House against the Short House, and, to foretell the harvest, the women play against the men. If the men win, the ears of corn will be long, like them; but if the women gain the game, they will be short, basing the results on the common proportion of the sexes. As of old, almost all games are yet played for the sick, but they are regarded now more as a diversion of the patient's mind than a means of healing. The game of the dish was once much used in divination, each piece having its own familiar spirit, but it is more commonly a social game now.

---

[a] Iroquois Games. Journal of American Folk-lore, v. 9, p. 269, Boston, 1896.

ONONDAGA. Grand River reserve, Ontario. (Field Columbian Museum.)

Cat. no. 55785. Set of eight bone disks, burned on one side, 1 inch in diameter.

Cat. no. 55786. Set of eight bone disks, similar to preceding, three-fourths of an inch in diameter.

Cat. no. 55787. Set of eight bone disks, similar to preceding, 1 inch in diameter.

Cat. no. 55788. Wooden bowl, 9¾ inches in diameter.

Cat. no. 55790. Wooden bowl, hemispheric, 12¾ inches in diameter, painted red, with green rim, and yellow dots at the edge.

Cat. no. 55791. Wooden bowl, hemispheric, 10¾ inches in diameter, machine made.

Cat. no. 55789. Set of six worked peach stones, burned on one side, five-eighths of an inch in diameter.

Cat. no. 55807, 55807a. Two sets of peach stones like the preceding, one five-eighths and the other three-fourths of an inch in diameter.

These specimens were collected by Mr S. C. Simms, who informed me that the Onondaga call the bone dice game daundahskaesadaquah, and the Cayuga the peach-stone game daundahqua, and gave the following account of the games:

Game of da-un-dah-ska-e-sa-da-quah (Onondaga), consisting of a set of eight disks, each of a diameter of an inch, made from split beef ribs and blackened by heat upon one side. They are thrown with the hand, the count depending upon the number of faces which turn up of one color. If all are black, for instance, the count is 20; if all turn up but one, 4 is counted; if two, 2. After each successful throw the thrower is given the number of beans called for by his throw, from the bank, which usually begins with 50 beans, and the game continues until one party has won them. This is purely a home game. During the game the buttons are constantly addressed with such remarks as o-han-da, meaning the thrower hopes the buttons will turn up one color; if there should be seven buttons that show the black sides and the remaining one has not yet settled sufficiently to determine the uppermost side, entreaties of hŭn-je, meaning all black, are directed to this one button by the thrower; if, on the other hand, the white sides appear, gan-ja, meaning all white, is sung out, accompanied by derisive shouts of tek-a-ne-ta-wé, meaning two, or scöort, meaning one.

Peach-stone game, da-un-dah-qua (Cayuga). This game is played with a wooden bowl and six peach stones rubbed down and burned slightly on one side to blacken them. In the middle of the one large room of the long house where the game is played a blanket or a quilt is folded double and spread upon the floor. At the south edge of the blanket stands a vessel containing one hundred beans. The bowl is taken by the edge with both hands and is given a sharp rap upon the blanket, causing the peach stones to rebound and fall back within the bowl. There are four winning counts, viz: All white, counting 5; all black, 5; one white, 1, and one black, 1. For each successful throw the representative of the player is handed, from the stock of beans, as many as the throw calls for. A player keeps his place as long as he makes winning throws, but it is taken by another man or woman as soon as he makes an unsuccessful one.

The day before the game is played six men are sent around to collect from the people such things as they care to stake in the peach-stone game. The goods collected—usually wearing apparel—are placed in two piles, the articles being fastened together in pairs with regard to the four brothers' end and the two brothers' end. Two men are selected to call out the male players, and, similarly, two women to call out the female players.

During the game the players are greeted with loud and enthusiastic shouts or with yells of derision, while the opposing player makes comments and grimaces, hoping thus to distract the attention of his or her rival.

Public gambling is permitted by the Iroquois only at the midwinter and fall festivals.

SENECA. New York.

Morgan [a] describes the Iroquois game, under the name of gusga-esatä, or deer buttons:

This was strictly a fireside game, although it was sometimes introduced as an amusement at the season of religious councils, the people dividing into tribes as usual and betting upon the result. Eight buttons, about an inch in diameter, were made of elk horn, and, having been rounded and polished, were slightly

FIG. 116. Bone dice; Seneca Indians, New York; from Morgan.

burned upon one side to blacken them [figure 116]. When it was made a public game it was played by two at a time, with a change of players as elsewhere described in the peach-stone game. At the fireside it was played by two or more, and all the players continued in their seats until it was determined. A certain number of beans, fifty, perhaps, were made the capital, and the game continued until one of the players had won them all. Two persons spread a blanket and seated themselves upon it. One of them shook the deer buttons in his hands and then threw them down. If six turned up of the same color, it counted 2; if seven, it counted 4; and if all, it counted 20, the winner taking as many beans from the general stock as he made points by the throw. He also continued to throw as long as he continued to win. When less than six came up, either black or white, it counted nothing, and the throw was passed to the other player. In this manner the game was continued until the beans were taken up between the two players. After that the one paid to the other out of his own winnings, the game ending as soon as the capital in the hands of either player was exhausted. If four played, each had a partner or played independently, as they were disposed; but when more than two played, each one was to pay the winner the

[a] League of the Iroquois, p. 302, Rochester, 1851.

amount won. Thus, if four were playing independently and, after the beans were distributed among them in the progress of the game, one of them should turn the buttons up all black or all white, the other three would be obliged to pay him 20 each; but if the beans were still in bank, he took up but 20. The deer buttons were of the same size. In the figure [116] they were represented at different angles. . . .

An ancient and favorite game[a] of the Iroquois, gus-kä′-eh, was played with a bowl and peach-stones. It was always a betting game, in which the people,

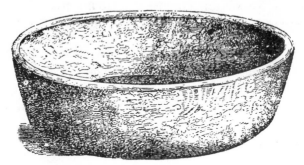

FIG. 117. Bowl for dice; Seneca Indians, New York; from Morgan.

divided by tribes. By established custom, it was introduced as the concluding exercise on the last day of the Green Corn and the Harvest festivals, and also of the New Year's jubilee. Its introduction among them is ascribed to the first To-do dä′ ho, who flourished at the formation of the League. A popular belief prevailed that this game would be enjoyed by them in the future life—in the realm of the Great Spirit—which is perhaps but an extravagant way of expressing their admiration for the game. A dish, about a foot in diameter at the base, was carved out of a knot or made of earthen. Six peach stones were then ground or

FIG. 118. Peach-stone dice; Seneca Indians, New York; from Morgan.

cut down into an oval form, reducing them in the process about half in size, after which the heart of the pit was removed and the stones themselves were burned upon one side to blacken them. The above representation [figures 118, 117] will exhibit both the bowl and the peach stones, the latter being drawn in different positions to show the degree of their convexity.

It was a very simple game, depending, in part, upon the dexterity of the player, but more upon his good fortune. The peach stones were shaken in the bowl by the player, the count depending upon the number which came up of one color after they had ceased rolling in the dish. It was played in the public council house by a succession of players, two at a time, under the supervision of managers appointed to represent the two parties and to conduct the contest. Its length depended somewhat upon the number of beans which made the bank—usually 100—the victory being gained by the side which finally won them all.

A platform was erected a few feet from the floor and spread with blankets.

---

[a] League of the Iroquois, p. 307, Rochester, 1851.

When the betting was ended, and the articles had been delivered into the custody of the managers, they seated themselves upon the platform in the midst of the throng of spectators, and two persons sat down to the game between the two divisions into which they arranged themselves. The beans, in the first instance, were placed together in a bank. Five of them were given each player, with which they commenced. Each player, by the rules of the game, was allowed to keep his seat until he had lost this outfit, after which he surrendered it to another player on his own side selected by the managers of his own party. And this was the case, notwithstanding any number he might have won of his adversary. Those which he won were delivered to his party managers. The six peach stones were placed in the bowl and shaken by the player; if five of them came up of one color, either white or black, it counted 1, and his adversary paid to him the forfeit, which was one bean, the bean simply representing a unit in counting the game. On the next throw, which the player having won, retained, if less than five came up of the same color it counted nothing, and he passed the bowl to his adversary. The second player then 'shook the bowl, upon which, if they all came up of one color, either white or black, it counted five. To pay this forfeit required the whole outfit of the first player, after which, having nothing to pay with, he vacated his seat and was succeeded by another of his own side, who received from the bank the same number of beans which the first had. The other player followed his throw as long as he continued to win, after which he repassed the bowl to his adversary. If a player chanced to win five and his opponent had but one left, this was all he could gain. In this manner the game continued with varying fortune until the beans were divided between the two sides in proportion to their success. After this the game continued in the same manner as before, the outfit of each new player being advanced by the managers of his own party; but as the beans or counters were now out of sight, none but the managers knew the state of the game with accuracy. In playing it there were but two winning throws, one of which counted 1 and the other 5. When one of the parties had lost all their beans, the game was done.

Morgan,[a] referring to games generally, says:

In their national games is to be found another fruitful source of amusement in Indian life. These games were not only played at their religious festivals, at which they often formed a conspicuous part of the entertainment, but special days were set frequently apart for their celebration. They entered into these diversions with the highest zeal and emulation, and took unwearied pains to perfect themselves in the art of playing each successfully. There were but six principal games among the Iroquois, and these were divisible into athletic games and games of chance.

Challenges were often sent from one village to another, and were even exchanged between nations, to a contest of some of these games. In such cases the chosen players of each community or nation were called out to contend for the prize of victory. An intense degree of excitement was aroused when the champions were the most skillful players of rival villages or adjacent nations. The people enlisted upon their respective sides with a degree of enthusiasm which would have done credit both to the spectators and the contestants at the far-famed Elian games. For miles, and even hundreds of miles, they flocked together at the time appointed to witness the contest.

Unlike the prizes of the Olympic games, no chaplets awaited the victors. They were strifes between nation and nation, village and village, or tribe and tribe; in a word, parties against parties, and not champion against champion.

---

[a] League of the Iroquois, p. 291, Rochester, 1851.

The prize contended for was that of victory; and it belonged, not to the triumphant players, but to the party which sent them forth to the contest.

When these games were not played by one community against another, upon a formal challenge, the people arranged themselves upon two sides according to their tribal divisions. By an organic provision of the Iroquois, as elsewhere stated, the Wolf, Bear, Beaver, and Turtle tribes were brothers to each other as tribes, and cousins to the other four. In playing their games they always went together and formed one party or side. In the same manner the Deer, Snipe, Heron, and Hawk tribes were brothers to each other, as tribes, and cousins to the four first named. These formed a second or opposite party. Thus in all Indian games, with the exceptions first mentioned, the people divided themselves into two sections, four of the tribes always contending against the other four. Father and son, husband and wife, were thus arrayed in opposite ranks.

Betting upon the result was common among the Iroquois. As this practice was never reprobated by their religious teachers, but on the contrary, rather encouraged, it frequently led to the most reckless indulgence. It often happened that the Indian gambled away every valuable article which he possessed; his tomahawk, his medal, his ornaments, and even his blanket. The excitement and eagerness with which he watched the shifting tide of the game was more uncontrollable than the delirious agitation of the pale face at the race course, or even at the gaming table. Their excitable temperament and emulous spirits peculiarly adapted them for the enjoyment of their national games.

These bets were made in a systematic manner, and the articles then deposited with the managers of the game. A bet offered by a person upon one side, in the nature of some valuable article, was matched by a similar article or one of equal value by some one upon the other. Personal ornaments made the usual gaming currency. Other bets were offered and taken in the same manner, until hundreds of articles were sometimes collected. These were laid aside by the managers until the game was decided, when each article lost by the event was handed over to the winning individual, together with his own, which he had risked against it.

SENECA. Grand River reserve, Ontario.

Mr David Boyle [a] says:

It is only in connection with the midwinter and fall festivals that the practice of public gambling is permitted. On these occasions there is high revelry.

All the goods collected as stakes by the six men already mentioned are piled in one or two heaps, the articles being tied or pinned in pairs with some regard to their respective values or uses. Thus, there may be two silk neckties, two pairs of moccasins, two shawls, or two strings of onagorha (wampum), which is regarded as taking first place at such times.

The Old Men [b] of the nation appoint two men, one from each side of the long house, to call out the male players, and, similarly, two women for a like purpose.

A sheet is spread on the floor of the long house, and in the middle of this sheet rests the wooden bowl, about 14 or 16 inches wide and 4 to 5 deep, containing six peach stones rubbed down to smooth surfaces and blackened on one side. Near the south edge of the sheet is placed a vessel containing 100

---

[a] Archæological Report, 1898, p. 126, Toronto, 1898.

[b] The pagan Indians when supplying information make frequent mention of the "Old Men," who are not, as would appear, any old men, but certain seniors who, either tacitly or by arrangement, are looked upon as sages. There are six of them; three represent the east end of the long house and three the west. The present Old Men are John Styres, Abraham Buck, and James Vanevery for the east and Johnson Williams, Seneca Williams, and Jacob Hill for the west. Gentes are not taken into account.

beans, from which stock seven are taken by each of the men who act as callers. When everything is ready the arrangement is as shown in the diagram [figure 119], the players invariably sitting east and west.

Before the game is begun all present are exhorted by the speaker to keep their temper, to do everything fairly, and to show no jealousy, " because," says he, " the side that loses this time may be favored by Niyoh the next time, and it will displease him should there be any bad feeling."

The first player takes the bowl by the edge with both hands and after a few preliminary shakes in midair he strikes the bottom sharply on the floor, when the peach stones rebound and fall back within the dish.

Winning throws are of four kinds: All white, all black, one white, or one black. All black or white means that the woman representing the winner receives from him who represents the loser 5 beans, but when only one white or one black bean shows face up, 1 bean is the gain. If, however, any player makes three successive casts, winning 5 each time, he is allowed 15 additional beans, and similarly, after three successive casts winning 1 each, he is allowed 3 more beans.

As long as a player makes winning throws he keeps his place, which when he leaves is immediately taken by another—man or woman. In this way the game is continued until one side wins all the beans, and this may require only an hour or two, or it may take two or three days.

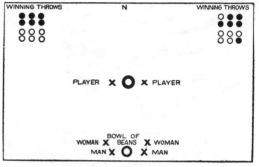

Fig. 119. Position of players in bowl game; Seneca Indians, Ontario; from Boyle.

While the play is going on it is not to be understood that the onlookers exemplify what is known as Indian stoicism. Anything but this. Excitement runs unusually high. Those on the side of the player for the time being encourage him with enthusiastically uproarious shouts of " jagon! jagon! jagon!" "play! play!" or "go on! go on! go on!" while the opponents yell with a sort of tremulous derisiveness " hee-aih! hee-aih!" Nor is this all, for those on the opposing side make faces and grimaces at each other and give utterance to all sorts of ridiculous and absurd things, hoping thus to distract the attention of their rivals, to discourage them, or in some other way to induce loss. . . .

When all the beans have been won, the ceremonial game is at an end and the stakes are divided, each better getting his own article along with the one attached to it.

Similar games may be played afterward " just for fun," as often as the people please.

The peach-stone game is one of the most popular gambling exercises on the Reserve and is often played among friends in each other's houses. The pagans religiously abstain from card playing in accordance, it may be remembered, with the injunctions of Hoh-shah-honh and Sosé-a-wa, the immediate successors of Ska-ne-o-dy'-o, both of whom taught that, as this was a white man's device, it must be shunned.[a]

---

[a] Mr Boyle writes: " The description of the peach-stone game applies to the method of playing by all the pagan nations—Seneca, Cayuga, and Onondaga, although the Seneca are referred to in my report. As the Oneida and Tuscarora are professedly Christian, the game is not indulged in by them."

The implements for a Seneca bowl game collected by Mr John N. B. Hewitt, of the Bureau of American Ethnology (cat. no. 21073, Free Museum of Science and Art, University of Pennsylvania), from the Seneca Indians, Cattaraugus reservation, Cattaraugus county, N. Y., consist of a wooden bowl (figure 120) 9⅜ inches in diameter and six dice made of fruit stones. A set of bone gaming disks from

Fig. 120.    Fig. 121.

FIG. 120. Peach-stone bowl game; diameter of bowl, 9⅜ inches; Seneca Indians, New York; cat. no. 21073, Free Museum of Science and Art, University of Pennsylvania.
FIG. 121. Bone dice; diameter, ⅘ inch; Seneca Indians, New York; cat. no. 21073, Free Museum of Science and Art, University of Pennsylvania.

the same tribe and place are represented in figure 121. As will be seen, they are eight in number and marked on one side, in a way similar to those of the Micmac and Penobscot.

TUSCARORA. North Carolina.

Referring to the North Carolina Indians, John Lawson [a] writes:

They have several other games, as with the kernels or stones of persimmons, which are in effect the same as our dice, because winning or losing depends on which side appears uppermost and how they happen to fall together.

Again, speaking of their gambling, he says: [b]

Their arithmetic was kept with a heap of Indian grain.

He does not specify this game as played by any particular tribe in North Carolina, and it was probably common to all of them.

WYANDOT. Kansas.

Mr William E. Connelley writes me as follows:

There is little I can say about games. The Wyandot are now three-fourths white in blood. There is scarcely a quarter-blood to be found in some neighborhoods. Until they came to Kansas in 1843 they kept up the game between

---

[a] The History of North Carolina, p. 176, London, 1714.   [b] Ibid., p. 27.

the divisions of the tribe at the celebration of the green-corn feast. This game was played with marked plum seeds, and exactly as the Seneca played it and play it yet. The ancient divisions of the tribe are as follows: [a]

First division: 1, Bear; 2, Deer; 3, Snake; 4, Hawk. Second division: 1, Big Turtle; 2, Little Turtle; 3, Mud Turtle; 4, Beaver; 5, Porcupine; 6, Striped Turtle; 7, Highland Turtle, or Prairie Turtle. Mediator, umpire, executive power, the Wolf clan. These are the phratries of the tribe. For the purpose of gambling or playing the final game of the green-corn feast festivities, the tribe separated into its phratries. The Wolf clan was not permitted to take sides. It was always the office of this clan to act as the executive power of the tribe and settle all disputes; but a certain portion of the winnings of the successful party was given to the Wolf clan. The game was played exactly as played by the Seneca. The ending of the game terminated the festivities, as it does to-day in the Seneca. The dances were partly games and partly ceremonies, often engaged in for amusement alone. But I could never get enough information to warrant me in saying where amusement left off and ceremony began. The gambling at the close of the green-corn feast is the only game I could get any definite information about.

KERESAN STOCK

KERES. Acoma, New Mexico. (Brooklyn Institute Museum.)
Cat. no. 4976. Four split canes, 5 inches in length, marked on convex side with cut designs painted black as shown in figure 122.

The reverses are painted with black marks, precisely like those of the Zuñi sholiwe. The cut designs represent a water bug, gamasku, a

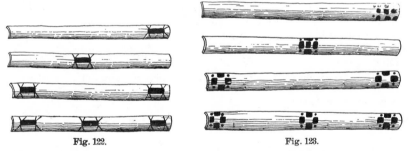

Fig. 122.　　　　　　　　　　Fig. 123.

Fig. 122. Cane dice; length, 5 inches; Keres Indians, Acoma, New Mexico; cat. no. 4976, Brooklyn Institute Museum.
Fig. 123. Cane dice; length, 6¼ inches; Keres Indians, Acoma, New Mexico; cat. no. 4975, Brooklyn Institute Museum.

word which also means spider. The Zuñi call this gannastepi, and use it in precisely the same way as a mark on their sholiwe (see figure 289).

Cat. no. 4975. Four split canes, 6½ inches in length, marked as shown in figure 123.

---

[a] Wyandot Folk-lore, p. 26, Topeka, Kans., 1899.

Both of the above were made for the writer in 1904 by James H. Miller, an Acoma Indian living at Zuñi, who furnished the following particulars:

The game is called bish-i, and the four canes receive the following names:
Stick marked at one end, bish-i, the same as the game, after a great gambler

FIG. 124. Stick dice; length, 5¼ inches; Keres Indians, Acoma, New Mexico; cat. no. 4972, Brooklyn Institute Museum.

of the olden time; stick marked in the middle, tsoi-yo, woman; stick marked at both ends, gosh, the name of a man; stick marked entire length, tel-i, woman.

The first and last two are paired, as if partners. In playing, a basket, o-ta-ni, covered with buckskin, is hung concave side down and the canes tossed against it, so that they fall on a blanket spread beneath it on the ground. In throwing the canes three of them are slid, concave side up, one inside of the other, with the top one projecting and one or the other of the first two crossed beneath them, as in Zuñi.

The counts, which resemble those in Zuñi, although, according to Miller's statement not precisely the same, are extremely complicated. Among them is the following:

Three convex sides up and the stick marked in the middle or at one end concave side up, and crossed beneath others, counts 3.

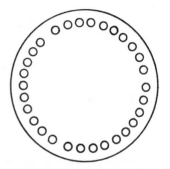

FIG. 125. Circuit for stick dice; Keres Indians, Acoma, New Mexico.

The game is counted with twelve grains of white corn. They blow their breath on the canes before tossing them. The game was invented by Gau-pot. He was the greatest of gamblers, and lost everything. He played against the sun and was beaten, and lost his eyes and became blind. Bish-i is played in winter in the estufas, and there is a society, the Bish-i society, devoted to it. Women don't play and are not even allowed to touch the sticks. Acoma Indians regard it as one of their original games and not as borrowed from Zuñi.

KERES. Acoma, New Mexico. (Cat. no. 4972, Brooklyn Institute Museum.)

Set of three stick dice (figure 124), 5½ inches in length, black on one side and plain white on the other.

They were made for the writer by James H. Miller. He gave the name as owasakut. The counts are as follows:

Three black counts 10; three white, 5; two white, 2; one white, 3. The game is counted around a circle of thirty stones, yow-wu-ni [figure 125], with little sticks called horses. There are three openings in the stone circle, which are called tsi-a-ma, door.

—— Acoma, New Mexico.

The Acoma Indian, James H. Miller, described also the following game to the writer under the name of inaani, to throw up:

A piece of bone, white on one side and black on the other, is tossed with the fingers. Black counts 10 and white 5. Black gives another throw. The count is 30, and is kept by making marks on the ground. Formerly a deer bone was used, but now a sheep bone is substituted. ·

KERES. Cochiti, New Mexico. (Cat. no. 4977, Brooklyn Institute Museum.)

Three sticks, 4 inches in length, flat on one side and convex on the other, one of the flat sticks marked on the round side with fourteen or fifteen notches with two crossed notches, as shown in figure 126.

They were collected by the writer in 1904, and were made by a Cochiti boy at St Michael, Arizona, named Francisco Chaves (Kogit). He gave this account:

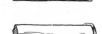

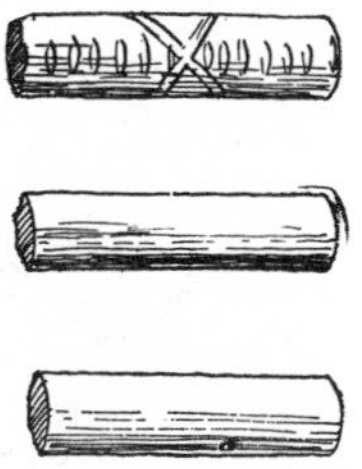

The sticks are thrown, ends down, on a flat stone. The counts are as follows: Three round sides up counts 10; three flat sides up, 5; the marked stick round side up and the other two flat side up, 15; one round side up and two flat, 2; one flat side up and two round, 2. The game is counted around a circle of forty stones with markers called horses.

FIG. 126. Stick dice; length, 4 inches; Keres Indians, Cochiti, New Mexico; cat. no. 4977, Brooklyn Institute Museum.

———— Laguna, New Mexico. (Cat. no. 61819, Field Columbian Museum.)

Three flat wooden blocks, 4¼ by 1⅜ inches, with one side plain and one side painted red. One of the block has fifteen notches, ten of which are on one edge and five on the other, as shown in figure 127. Collected by Dr C. E. Lukens.

The following detailed account of the game, under the name of owasokotz, which was furnished by the collector, appears on the museum label:

FIG. 127. Stick dice; length, 4¼ inches; Keres Indians, Laguna, New Mexico; cat. no. 61819, Field Columbian Museum.

The game is played with three billets of wood, painted black on one side, white on the other, one of the white sides having fifteen notches on it, the other plain. Each player has a small stick to use as a marker, formerly known as o-poia-nia-ma, but of late called a horse, "because it goes so fast;" a flat stone, the size of the hand, used as a center stone, upon which the billets are dropped; and forty small stones, the size of a hen's egg. These forty stones are placed on the ground in the form of a circle, with four openings, or doors, called si-am-ma, always facing the four cardinal points. The play always begins at the east door, but after that they play whichever way they choose. Each player may go a different way if he chooses; as many as wish can play, or they may play partners. At the beginning of the play the horses are placed at the east door. A player takes up the billets and, placing the ends even with one hand, strikes them ends down on the center stone like dice; the count is determined by the manner of the fall, and he then moves his horses up as many stones as he makes; if he gets around to the starting point first, he wins.

There are two ways of playing—one is called pass, the other enter. In pass, if one makes a score which lands him exactly in the starting, or east, door, he must go around again until he lands in the proper place. In enter, if A should

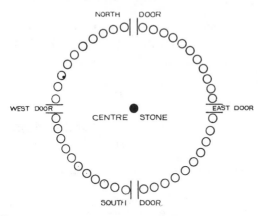

FIG. 128. Circuit for stick dice; Keres Indians, Laguna, New Mexico; from sketch by Dr C. E. Lukens.

land his horse on the top of his opponent's horse, he kills him, and he goes back to the beginning, but if A reaches the starting point first, he falls in and wins, even if the number of stones made should carry him beyond. The count otherwise is just the same in both. The blocks may fall within or without the ring. If one block should fall on edge, not leaning, then the player lays it on the center stone and strikes it with another billet, but if the notched billet is lying face down, it must not be used to strike with; when the notched block stands on edge it must be picked up and thrown on the center stone.

The count is as follows: Two black sides up, with one white notched, 15 stones; three white sides up, 10 (when a player makes 10 or 15 he may strike again, and as many times as he makes these large numbers); two blacks up and one white, not notched, 3; two white and one black up, 2; three blacks up, 5.

KERES. Laguna, New Mexico. (Cat. no. 38500, Free Museum of Science and Art, University of Pennsylvania.)

Three flat blocks (figure 129), 3½ inches in length, painted black on one side the other plain.

One has 15 notches on the edge of the white side. Made for the writer by a Laguna youth, at the Pan-American Exposition, Buffalo, 1903. He describes them as used in the game of patol, or, in their own language, wasokutz.

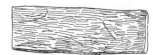

FIG. 129. Stick dice; length, 3¼ inches; Keres Indians, Laguna, New Mexico; cat. no. 38500, Free Museum of Science and Art, University of Pennsylvania.

——— Laguna, New Mexico.

Capt. George H. Pradt, a resident of the pueblo of Laguna for many years, writes as follows:

The game played with a circle of small stones is called, by the Keres Indians, ka-wá-su-kuts.[a] The stones number 40, and are divided into tens by openings called doors or gates called si-am-ma; the doors are placed north, south, east, and west.

In the center of the circle is placed a flat stone, upon which are thrown the three counters. These are flat pieces of wood about 4 inches long, one-half of an inch wide, and one-eighth of an inch thick, painted black on one side, and marked with two, three, and ten marks, respectively. The counters are firmly grasped with the ends down and forcibly thrown, ends down, on the stone in the center in such a manner that they will rebound, and the marks, if any are uppermost, are counted, and the player lays his marker, a small stick like a pencil, between the stones the proper distance from the starting point, to record the number. The starting point is one of the doors, whichever is selected, and the game is played by any number that can assemble around the circle. A player can go around the circle in either direction, but if another player arrives at the 'same point he kills the previous player, and that one is obliged to go back to the starting point; the first one making the circuit successfully wins the game, which is generally played for a small stake. The game is modified sometimes by ruling that if a player falls into one of the doors he must go back, but in this case the player is not obliged to go back if another happens to mark as many points as he.

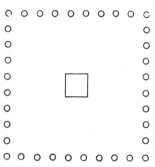

Fig. 130. Circuit for stick-dice game, Keres Indians, Sia, New Mexico; from Mrs Stevenson.

Sometimes a round stone is painted to resemble a face and has a wreath of evergreens placed around it and is used as a mascot; it is placed' to one side of the circle and is appealed to by the players to give them good numbers; this mascot is generally called kûm-mûshk-ko-yo, a traditional fairy, or witch. The name means the old spider woman.

KERES. Sia, New Mexico.

Mrs Matilda Coxe Stevenson [b] gives a description of the game as played by the Sia under the name of wash'kasi, of which the following is an abstract:

Forty pebbles form a square, ten pebbles on a side, with a flat stone in the center of the square [figure 130]. Four flat blocks, painted black on one side and unpainted on the other, are held vertically and dropped upon the stone. The counts are as follows: Four painted sides up, 10; four unpainted sides up, 6; three painted sides up, 3; two painted sides up, 2; one painted side up, —. The players move in opposite directions, both starting at one of the corners. The game is described as the first of four games played by Po'shaiyänne, the Sia culture hero, with the tribal priest. The stake was the latter's house in the north. The second of the four games is of the bowl class, which I have included in this series. The stake in this game was the ti'ämoni, or priest's, house in the west. It was played with six 2-inch cubes, which were highly polished and painted on one side. These were tossed up in a large bowl held with each hand. When three painted sides are up, the game is won; with only two painted sides up, the game is lost. Six painted sides up is equivalent to a march in euchre. The games that followed were, first, a game played with four sticks with hollow ends, under one of which a pebble was hidden. This was played

---

[a] Meaning a punch, or sudden blow, the only name the Lagunas have for it.
[b] The Sia. Eleventh Annual Report of the Bureau of Ethnology, p. 60, 1894.

for the priest's house in the south. Second, a game played with four little mounds of sand, in one of which a small round stone was hidden. This was played for the priest's house in the east. The games were then repeated in the same order, commencing with wash'kasi for the house in the zenith, the game with the six blocks for the house in the nadir, and, finally, the third in order, that with the four sticks with hollow ends, for all the people of the tribe.

Mr Charles F. Lummis informed the writer that he had witnessed the game with the staves or blocks in the following pueblos belonging to this stock: Acoma, Cochiti, Laguna, El Rito (Laguna colony), and San Felipe.

KIOWAN STOCK

KIOWA. Oklahoma. (Cat. no. 16535, 16536, Free Museum of Science and Art, University of Pennsylvania.)

Set of four sticks of willow wood, called ahl (wood), 10 inches in length, five-eighths of an inch in width, and three-eighths of an inch in thickness (figure 131), nearly hemispheric in section, with one side flat.

Three of the sticks have a red groove running down the middle on the flat side, and one has a blue stripe. The last has a burnt design on the reverse, as shown in the figure, while the backs of the others are plain. The flat sides are also burnt, with featherlike markings at the ends.

A cotton cloth, 41 by 48½ inches, marked as shown in figure 133, called the ahl cloth; a flat bowlder, called the ahl stone; two awls, sharpened wires, with wooden handles, 6¾ inches in length; eight sticks, 8¾ inches in length, to be used as counters (figure 132).

These objects were collected by Col. H. L. Scott, U. S. Army, who furnished the following description of the game, under the title of zohn ahl (zohn, creek; ahl, wood), commonly known as the ahl game:

The ahl cloth is divided into points by which the game is counted. The curved lines are called knees, because they are like the knees of the players. The space between the parallel lines 1 and 1 and 20 and 20 is called the creek, and the corresponding spaces between the parallel lines at right angles are called the dry branches. The sticks are held by the players in one hand and struck downward, so that their ends come on the ahl stone with considerable force. If all the sticks fall with the sides without grooves uppermost, the play

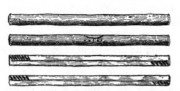

FIG. 131. Stick dice; length, 10 inches; Kiowa Indians, Oklahoma; cat. no. 16536, Free Museum of Science and Art, University of Pennsylvania.

is called white, and counts 10. If all the grooved sides come uppermost, it is called red, and counts 5. Both of these throws entitle the player to another throw. If one grooved side is uppermost, it counts 1; two grooved sides, 2, and three grooved sides, 3. The game is played by any even number of girls or women (never by men or boys), half on one side the line N S and half on the other. The flat ahl stone is placed in the middle of the cloth, and the players kneel on the edge. The two awls are stuck in the creek at 1 1. The player at A makes the first throw, and the throwing goes around the circle

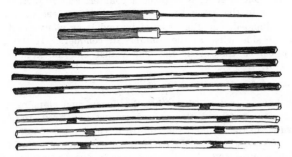

FIG. 132. Counting sticks and awls for ahl (stick-dice) game; lengths, 8¼ and 6¼ inches; Kiowa Indians, Oklahoma; cat. no. 16536, Free Museum of Science and Art, University of Pennsylvania.

in the direction of the hands of a watch, each side counting the results of each throw on the ahl cloth by sticking its awl just beyond the mark called for by the results of the throw. The moves are made in the opposite directions, as indicated by the arrows.

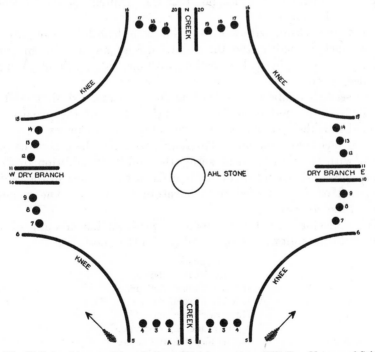

FIG. 133. Cloth for ahl game; Kiowa Indians, Oklahoma; cat. no. 16535, Free Museum of Science and Art, University of Pennsylvania.

If in counting any awl gets into the creek at N, that side must forfeit a counter to the other side and be set back to the creek at S. That side is then said to have fallen into the creek, the object being to jump over. If in their passage around the circle the two awls get into the same division, the last comer is said to whip or kill the former, who forfeits a counter and is set back to the beginning. The counting continues until one gets back to the creek at S. The one first at S receives a counter, and if there is more than enough to take it to the creek the surplus is added to the next round; that is, the creek is jumped, and the awl put beyond it as many points as may be over. When one side wins all the counters, it conquers. If the game should be broken up before this event the side which has the greater number of counters is victor.

Colonel Scott further states:

The Kiowa have a custom of wetting the fingers and slapping them several times on the stone before a throw, and calling out "red, red," or "white, white," according to the number they desire to count; or, if but "one" should be required to throw the opposite party into the "creek," some one puts her finger into her mouth, and, drawing it carefully across the top of the stone, calls out "parko, parko" ("one, one"). Often before the throw the thrower will rub the four sticks in a vertical position backward and forward several times between the palms of the hands, to insure good luck.

The Comanche have a similar game which they play with eight ahl sticks, and the Cheyenne and Arapaho are said to have a game which they play with ahl sticks which are 2 feet or more long.

KIOWA. Oklahoma. (Cat. no. 152908a, United States National Museum.)

Set of four sticks of willow wood, 7 inches in length, three-eighths of an inch in width, and three-sixteenths of an inch in thickness, nearly hemispherical in section, with one side flat, and having a deep groove.

The stick is doubtless a substitute for the cane, like that used by the Zuñi, as suggested by Mr Cushing. Three of the grooves are painted red, these sticks having two oblique marks burnt across the grooved face near each end. The fourth stick has the groove painted black, with three lines burnt across the middle in addition to those at the ends. Its rounded reverse is marked with a star in the center, composed of four crossed lines burnt in the wood. The rounded sides of the others are plain.

The collector, Mr James Mooney,[a] prefaces his account of the game with the following song, employed in the ghost dance:

> Hise' hi, hise' hi,
> Hä' tine' bäku' tha' na,
> Hä' tine' bäku' tha' na,
> Häti' ta-u' seta' na,
> Häti' ta-u' seta' na.
> My comrade, my comrade,
> Let us play the awl game,
> Let us play the awl game,
> Let us play the dice game,
> Let us play the dice game.

---

[a] The Ghost Dance Religion. Fourteenth Annual Report of the Bureau of Ethnology, pt. 2, p. 1002, 1896.

The woman who composed this song tells how, on waking up in the spirit world, she met there a party of her former girl companions and sat down with them to play the two games universally popular with the prairie tribes.

The first is called nĕ'bäku'thana by the Arapaho and tsoñä, or awl game (from tsoñ, an awl) by the Kiowa, on account of an awl, the Indian woman's substitute for a needle, being used to keep record of the score. The game is becoming obsolete in the north, but it is the everyday summer amusement of the women among the Kiowa, Comanche, and Apache in the southern plains. It is very amusing on account of the unforeseen rivers and whips that are constantly turning up to disappoint the expectant winner, and a party of women will frequently sit around the blanket for half a day at a time with a constant ripple of laughter and good-humored jokes as they follow the chances of the play. It would make a very pretty picnic game, or could be readily adapted to the parlor of civilization.

The players sit on the ground around a blanket marked in charcoal with lines and dots and quadrants in the corners, as shown in figure [133]. In the center is a stone upon which the sticks are thrown. Each dot, excepting those between the parallels, counts a point, making 24 points for dots. Each of the parallel lines and each end of the curved lines at the corners also counts a point, making 16 points for the lines, or 40 points in all. The players start at the bottom, opposing players moving in opposite directions, and with each throw of the sticks the thrower moves her awl forward and sticks it into the blanket at the dot or line to which her throw carries her. The parallels on each of the four sides are called rivers, and the dots within these parallels do not count in the game. The rivers at the top and bottom are dangerous and can not be crossed, and when the player is so unlucky as to score a throw which brings her upon the edge of the river (i. e., upon the first line of either of these pairs of parallels) she falls into the river and must lose all she has hitherto gained, and begin again at the start. In the same way, when a player moving around in one direction makes a throw which brings her awl to the place occupied by the awl of her opponent coming around from the other side the said opponent is whipped back to the starting point and must begin all over again. Thus there is a constant succession of unforeseen accidents, which furnish endless amusement to the players.

The game is played with four sticks, each from 6 to 10 inches long, flat on one side and round on the other. One of these is the trump stick and is marked in a distinctive manner in the center on both sides, and is also distinguished by having a green line along the flat side, while the others have each a red line. The Kiowa call the trump stick sahe, green, on account of the green stripe, while the others are called guadal, red. There are also a number of small green sticks, about the size of lead pencils, for keeping tally. Each player in turn takes up the four sticks together in her hand and throws them down on end upon the stone in the center. The number of points depends upon the number of flat or round sides which turn up. A lucky throw with a green or trump stick generally gives the thrower another trial in addition. The formula is: One flat side up counts 1; one flat side up (if sahe), 1 and another throw; two flat sides up (with or without sahe), 2; three flat sides up, 3; three flat sides up (including sahe), 3 and another throw; all four flat sides up, 6 and another throw; all four round sides up, 10 and another throw.

Cat. no. 152908*b*. Set of four sticks (figure 134), of a variety of alder, 5½ inches in length, seven-sixteenths of an inch in width, and one-fourth of an inch in thickness; three with groove painted red on flat side and one with groove painted black.

The former are burned with four diagonal marks, resembling the feathering of an arrow on alternate sides of the groove near each end. The fourth stick has in addition two parallel marks burned directly across the middle. Its rounded reverse is burned with a design in the shape of a diamond. The reverses of the others are plain. Cat. no. 152908*d*. Set of four sticks of willow wood or chestnut sprout, 8¾ inches in length, three-fourths of an inch in breadth, and five-sixteenths of an inch in thickness (figure 135).

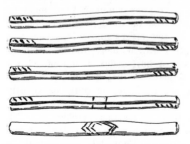

FIG. 134. Stick dice (the lowest stick shows obverse of one next above it); length, 5¼ inches; Kiowa Indians, Oklahoma; cat. no. 152908*b*, United States National Museum.

Three have flat sides with lengthwise groove painted red, with parallel oblique lines like arrow-feathering burned on alternate sides of the groove at the ends, opposite to which are similar marks arranged in triangles. The rounded reverses of these sticks are plain. The fourth stick has an incised device painted black and resembling two feathered arrows, the heads of which meet a transverse band cut across the middle. Its rounded side has three parallel lines burned across the center, on one side of which is an incised design resembling a serpent and on the other an undetermined figure.

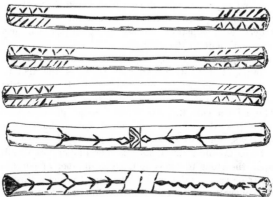

FIG. 135. Stick dice (the lowest stick shows obverse of one next above it); length, 8¼ inches; Kiowa Indians, Oklahoma; cat. no. 152908*d*, United States National Museum.

Cat. no. 152908*c*. Set of four sticks of elm wood, 8⅞ inches in length, nine-sixteenths of an inch in width, and five-sixteenths of an inch in thickness (figure 136); three with groove painted red and one with groove painted black.

The former are burned with two sets of parallel marks about 1⅛ inches apart across the grooved face near each end. The fourth stick has in addition oblique marks burned across the center of the same side, with two pyramidal dotted designs in the center of the opposite side, which on the others is plain.

Cat. no. 152909a. Set of four sticks (figure 137), 5½ inches in length, seven-sixteenths of an inch in breadth, and three-sixteenths of an inch in thickness; section ellipsoidal.

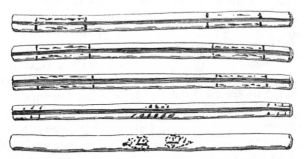

Fig. 136. Stick dice (the lowest stick shows obverse of one next above it); length, 8⅝ inches; Kiowa Indians, Oklahoma; cat. no. 152908c, United States National Museum.

One side, slightly flatter than the other, is grooved and marked with fine cross lines, forming a lozenge pattern. Three are painted red and one dark green. One of the red sticks is burned in the center with two parallel marks obliquely across both the grooved and the opposite side. The green stick has an undetermined figure burned in the center of the rounded side, which on the other two is plain.

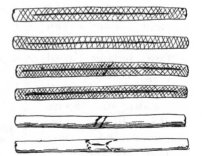

Cat. no. 152909b. Set of four sticks, 3¾ inches in length, five-sixteenths of an inch in breadth, and one-eighth of an inch in thickness; the flat sides grooved and painted, three red and one black.

Fig. 137. Stick dice (the lowest two sticks show obverses of the two next above); length, 5¼ inches; Kiowa Indians, Oklahoma; cat. no. 152909a, United States National Museum.

Cat. no. 152909c. Set of four sticks, 5⅜ inches in length, five-sixteenths of an inch in breadth, and one-eighth of an inch in thickness.

One of the red sticks has an oblique incised line cut across the middle and two parallel lines on the opposite (rounded) side. The black stick has a small triangle cut lengthwise in the center of the rounded side, across which is a transverse incised line.

The flat sides are grooved and have triangular expansions of the groove at each end. Three are painted red and one black; one of the red sticks is marked like the one in the preceding, and the black stick in the same manner.

These Kiowa sticks were all collected by Mr James Mooney. In each set there is an odd stick.

KOLUSCHAN STOCK

TLINGIT. Alaska. (American Museum of Natural History.)

Cat. no. $\frac{19}{650}$. Small ivory die (figure 138d), shaped like a chair;

height 1 inch, twelve-sixteenths of an inch wide at back, and ten-sixteenths of an inch at side, with a vertical hole from top to bottom filled with lead. It is called ketchu and came from Shakan.

FIG. 138. Ivory and wooden dice; Tlingit Indians, Alaska; cat. no. E 894, 19 650, E 1859, 19 650, E 1857, American Museum of Natural History.

Cat. no. $\frac{19}{650}$. Small wooden die (figure 138b), like preceding, the sides engraved with crossed lines. The back of the die has four lead plugs and a hole for a similar plug. The front has an incised rectangular design with three lead plugs.

Cat. no. E 894. Small ivory die (figure 138a), like the preceding; height 1 inch, twelve-sixteenths of an inch wide at back, and eight-sixteenths of an inch at side; front face having small plug of lead.

Cat. no. E 1857. Small wooden die (figure 138e), like the preceding, $1\frac{1}{16}$ inches high, twelve-sixteenths of an inch wide at back and sides; the back and three sides marked with incised lines.

Cat. no. E 1859. Small wooden die (figure 138c), like the pre-ceding, fifteen-sixteenths of an inch high and nine-sixteenths of an inch wide at side; perfectly plain.

FIG. 139. Leather tablet on which dice are thrown; height, 7¼ inches; Tlingit Indians, Alaska; cat. no. E 606, American Museum of Natural History.

All these specimens were collected in Sitka by Lieut. George T. Emmons, U. S. Navy. They are designated as women's gambling dice.

Dr Boas informs me that one die is used.   The counts are:

Either side up, 0; back or front up, 1; bottom up, 2.

The dice are thrown upon a thick tablet of leather about 8 inches square, cut with a totemic device.   One (cat. no. E 606, figure 139) has the device of a bear's head.   Another (cat. no. E 1057) a beaver, and still another (cat. no. E 2404) an unidentified animal.

Similar dice are used by the Haida and possibly by the Kwakiutl.

KULANAPAN STOCK

Pomo.   Tculaki, Mendocino county, California.   (Cat. no. 54473, Field Columbian Museum.)

Six wooden staves (figure 140), 17 inches in length, flat on one side, the other convex, with rounded ends, the convex faces decorated with burned designs, in two slightly different patterns; accompanied with twelve counting sticks, rudely whittled, 11 inches in length.

The collector, Dr George A. Dorsey, who obtained these objects in 1899, describes the game as follows:

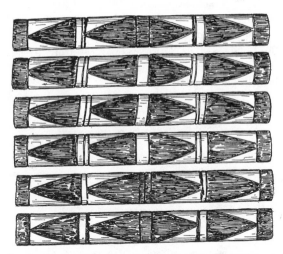

Fig. 140. Stick dice; length, 17 inches; Pomo Indians, Tculaki, California; cat. no. 54473, Field Columbian Museum.

Name, ka-dai.   Twelve is the game.   All white, kule-kule-ka, counts 2; all black, katse-mal da butchin, counts 3; three white, three black, bubu-kule-ka, counts 1.   It is played by women.

——— Ukiah, California.   (Field Columbian Museum.)

Cat. no. 61085.   Six staves (figure 141) of elder wood, 10 inches in length, similar to the preceding, decorated alike on the rounded face with a burned figure, designated as kawinatcedi, turtle-back pattern.

Collected by Dr George A. Dorsey, who gives the counts as follows:

Three plain up counts 3; three plain down, 1; six plain up, 6; six marked up, 2.

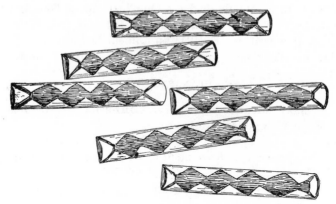

FIG. 141. Stick dice; length, 10 inches; Pomo Indians, Ukiah, California; cat. no. 61085, Field Columbian Museum.

Cat. no. 61086. Six staves (figure 142), similar to preceding, 11 inches in length, four marked alike and two slightly different, with turtle-rib pattern, kawinamisat.

Cat. no. 61087. Six staves (figure 143), similar to the preceding, made of elder, 12 inches in length, marked alike with hododudu-ciba, the milk-snake pattern.

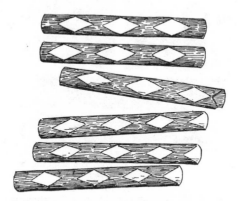

FIG. 142. Stick dice; length, 11 inches; Pomo Indians, Ukiah, California; cat. no. 61086, Field Columbian Museum.

Cat. no. 61146. Six staves (figure 144), similar to the preceding, 10¾ inches in length; four marked alike and two differently, the counts varying much.

Cat. no. 61166. Six staves (figure 145), similar to the preceding, 14¾ inches in length, all marked differently with burnt design.

Cat. no. 61174. Six staves (figure 146), like the preceding, made of elder, 11 inches in length and marked alike. Collected by **Dr** George A. Dorsey.

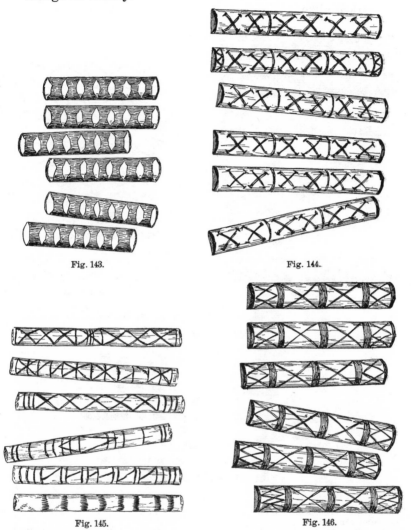

Fig. 143.　　　　　　　　　　　　Fig. 144.

Fig. 145.　　　　　　　　　　　　Fig. 146.

FIG. 143. Stick dice; length, 12 inches; Pomo Indians, Ukiah, California; cat. no. 61087, Field Columbian Museum.

FIG. 144. Stick dice; length, 10¼ inches; Pomo Indians, Ukiah, California; cat. no. 61146, Field Columbian Museum.

FIG. 145. Stick dice; length, 14¼ inches; Pomo Indians, Ukiah, California; cat. no. 61166, Field Columbian Museum.

FIG. 146. Stick dice; length, 11 inches; Pomo Indians, Ukiah, California; cat. no. 61174, Field Columbian Museum.

Cat. no. 61175. Six staves (figure 147), 8 inches in length, of Salix sitchensis, marked alike, designated as kadai kawiatan (toy for child).

Cat. no. 61193. Six staves (figure 148), 12¼ inches in length, all marked alike.

Cat. no. 61194. Six staves (figure 149), 12½ inches in length, all marked alike.

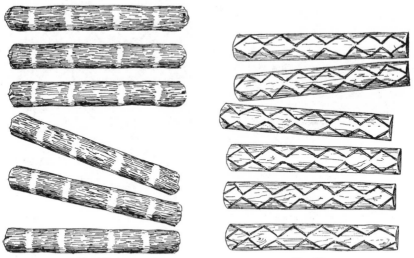

Fig. 147.   Fig. 149.

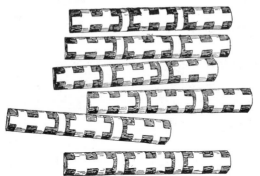

Fig. 148.

FIG. 147. Stick dice; length, 8 inches; Pomo Indians, Ukiah, California; cat. no. 61175, Field Columbian Museum.

FIG. 148. Stick dice; length, 12¼ inches; Pomo Indians, Ukiah, California; cat. no. 61193, Field Columbian Museum.

FIG. 149. Stick dice; length, 12½ inches; Pomo Indians, Ukiah, California; cat. no. 61194, Field Columbian Museum.

Cat. no. 61089. Twelve counting sticks (figure 150), kadai haitai (counters), ash shoots, painted black, 9½ inches in length.

Cat. no. 61090. Twelve counting sticks (figure 151), 10 inches in length, with burnt markings on the end and in middle of the tsupiam, lance pattern.

Cat. no. 61091. Twelve counting sticks (figure 152), 9½ inches in length, with burnt markings of the misakala, black-snake pattern.

Fig. 150.

Fig. 151.

Fig. 152.

Fig. 153.

Fig. 154.

Fig. 155.

FIG. 150. Counting sticks for stick dice; length, 9¼ inches; Pomo Indians, Ukiah, California; cat. no. 61089, Field Columbian Museum.

FIG. 151. Counting sticks for stick dice; length, 10 inches; Pomo Indians, Ukiah, California; cat. no. 61090, Field Columbian Museum.

FIG. 152. Counting sticks for stick dice; length, 9¼ inches; Pomo Indians, Ukiah, California; cat. no. 61091, Field Columbian Museum.

FIG. 153. Counting sticks for stick dice; length, 9⅜ inches; Pomo Indians, Ukiah, California; cat. no 61092, Field Columbian Museum.

FIG. 154. Stick dice; length, 15 inches; Pomo Indians, Lake village, California; cat. no. 54474, Field Columbian Museum.

FIG. 155. Astragalus of deer used as die; Pomo Indians, Ukiah valley, California; cat. no. 70937, Field Columbian Museum.

Cat. no. 61092. Twelve counting sticks (figure 153), 9⅞ inches in length, with burnt markings.

All of the preceding were collected by Dr George A. Dorsey.

Pomo. Lake village, Lake county, California. (Cat. No. 54474, Field Columbian Museum.)

Set of six staves (figure 154) of elder wood, 15 inches in length, similar to the preceding, but each with a different pattern.

They were collected in 1899 by Dr George A. Dorsey, who designates them as kaikadai.

——— Ukiah, Mendocino county, California. (Cat. No. 70937, Field Columbian Museum.)

Astragalus of deer (figure 155), described by the collector, Dr J. W. Hudson, as used as a die.

LUTUAMIAN STOCK

KLAMATH. Upper Klamath lake, Oregon. (Cat. no. 61711, 61722, Field Columbian Museum.)

Four pine staves (figure 156), 7¾ inches long, flat on one side, rather rounded on the other, and tapering to the ends.

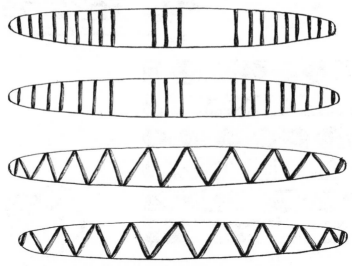

FIG. 156. Stick dice; length, 7¾ inches; Klamath Indians, Oregon; cat. no. 61711, Field Columbian Museum.

Two of the staves are marked by a series of nine parallel lines at each end and three parallel lines in the center, and are known as shnawedsh, women; the remaining two sticks are marked from end to end by zigzag lines crossing back and forth from side to side, and these are called xoxsha or hishuaksk, male person. All these lines have been burnt in by means of a sharp-pointed iron tool.

The counting is as follows: [a]

[a] Certain Gambling Games of the Klamath Indians. American Anthropologist, n. s., v. 3, p. 25, 1901.

All marked sides up or down count 2; both male sticks up with women down, or vice versa, count 1. These are the only counts.

The set no. 61722 differs from the preceding only in the number of parallel lines on the two shnawedsh staves. At the ends of the two staves there are seven parallel lines, while in the center of one are five and of the other six parallel lines. These specimens were collected in 1900 by Dr George A. Dorsey, who furnished the above description of the game under the name of skushash.

KLAMATH. Oregon. (Cat. no. 24126, United States National Museum.) Four woodchuck-teeth dice (figure 157), two, both lefts, stopped at the end with red cloth and marked on the flat side with chevron pattern, and two, somewhat smaller, one right and the other left, apparently from the same animal, marked on the same side with five small holes. Collected by L. S. Dyar, Indian agent.

The game is described by Dr Albert S. Gatschet,[a] under the name of skushash:

> The four teeth of the beaver are marked for this game by the incision of parallel lines or crosses on one side, and a small piece of woolen or other cloth is inserted into the hollow to prevent breaks in falling. The two longer or upper teeth of the beaver are called the male, lakí, the pair of lower and shorter the female teeth, gúlo, kúlu, distributive form: kúkalu. The marked side of the teeth wins, if it is turned up after dropping. The

FIG. 157. Woodchuck-teeth dice; length, 1¼ to 1½ inches; Klamath Indians, Oregon; cat. no 24126, United States National Museum.

> teeth of the woodchuck (mú-i, or mói) serve for the same purpose. . . . In this game of beavers' teeth (pu'man tút) or woodchuck's teeth (múyam tút) they use twelve check sticks to count their gains with. The game is played by two persons, or by two partners on each side.

A further account of the game is found in a text translated by Doctor Gatschet:[b]

> The Klamath lake females play a game with beavers' teeth, letting them drop on a rubbing stone. When all the teeth fall with the right, or marked, side uppermost, they win 2 checks. If both female teeth fall right side up, they win 1 check. If both male teeth fall right side up, they win 1 check. Falling unequally, they win nothing. They quit when one side has won all the stakes. Women only play this game.

The beaver-teeth game may be regarded as a modification of the bone game played by the Blackfeet. The four beaver teeth marked with circles or dots and lines arranged in chevrons clearly replace the four similarly marked staves. Again, the tooth tied with sinew corresponds with the sinew-wrapped stave. The twelve counters agree with those of the Blackfeet.

---

[a] The Klamath Indians. Contributions to North American Ethnology, v. 2, pt. 1, p. 81, Washington, 1890.

[b] Ibid., p. 80.

KLAMATH. Upper Klamath lake, Oregon. (Cat. no. 61536, 61734,
        Field Columbian Museum.)

Set of four woodchuck teeth, the two upper teeth marked on the flat
    side with zigzag lines extending the length of the teeth; these
    are called laki, male.

The lower teeth are marked by four incised dots and are kulu,
female. In another set (61734), figure 158, the markings are as in
the preceding set, except that the lower teeth have five dots instead of

FIG. 158. Woodchuck-teeth dice; Klamath Indians, Oregon; cat. no. 61734, Field Columbian
Museum.

four, and that the incised markings on all four teeth have been filled
with red paint instead of black as in the preceding set. These specimens were collected by Dr George A. Dorsey,[a] who gives the name of
the game as skushash, and says:

In playing the game, which is generally done by women, the teeth are dropped
on a hard level object, such as an under grinding stone. The count is the same
as in the stave game, namely, all marked dice up or down, 2; both males up with
females down, 1.

MARIPOSAN STOCK

CHUKCHANSI. Chowchilly river, Madera county, California. (Cat.
        no. 70890, Field Columbian Museum.)

    Astralagus of deer used as a die. Collected by Dr J. W. Hudson.

These they call ka-nish-nau-she, to flip between thumb and second finger.
The counts are 0, 2, 3, 5.

Doctor Hudson also gave the following description of this game,
obtained from the Tcausilla living on Chowchilly River, about 4
miles west of Ahwahnee post-office.

The bone and the game are called by the same name, kanishnaushe, meaning flipped between thumb and second finger. The bone is thrown like a die.
There are four counts, 1, 2, 4, 12, depending upon the side that turns uppermost.

TEJON. Tule River reservation, California. (Cat. No. 70371, Field
        Columbian Museum.)

Flat basket plaque for dice game, collected by Dr J. W. Hudson, who
        describes it as follows:

This game is played by women with six dice made from halves of walnut
shells. The game, which is played by any number is called ho-watch, the same

a Certain Gambling Games of the Klamath Indians. American Anthropologist, n. s.,
v. 3, p. 26, 1901.

name being applied to the dice. Three up and 3 down count 1; all up or all down, 5. The count is kept with 10 sticks, witchet. The basket plaque is called tai-wan. The designs on this plaque represent the women players, the walnut-shell dice, and the counters.

The game is played also by all other Mariposan tribes in this manner.

WIKTCHAMNE. Keweah river, California. (Collection of Dr C. Hart Merriam.)

Flat basket plaque for dice game (figure 159) 22¼ inches in diameter, with a coil foundation of yellow grass, *Epicampes rigens;* the body material is of the root of the *Cladium mariscus.* It is dec-

FIG. 159. Dice plaque; diameter, 22¼ inches; Wiktchamne Indians, Keweah river, California; in the collection of Dr C. Hart Merriam.

orated with colored designs in red and black; the red twigs with bark on, of redbud (*Cercis occidentalis*), the black, the root of the basket fern (*Pteridium*). Doctor Merriam describes the game as played with eight dice of half walnut shells filled with pitch, inlaid with abalone shell. The flat faces up count when 2, 5, or 8 are up together. Two and five up count 1 each; eight up, 4. The basket is called ti-wan. The man-like figures represent water dogs, the 5-spots, wild-cat tracks, and the double triangles, deer tracks.

The employment of these basket plaques in dice games may in part be explained upon the supposition that the plaques originated in basket shields. The coiled basket trays made by the Hopi Indians at the Second mesa, which suggest shields in their general character, were probably derived from shields. One of the Hopi names for shield is tür′-o-po-o-ta, from tür′-o-ka, enemy, po′-o-ta, the circular tray. An unique example of an ancient basket shield, from a cliff-dwelling in the Canyon de Chelly, Arizona, is represented in plate i.[a]

YOKUTS. Fort Tejon and Tule river, California.

Mr Stephen Powers [b] gives the following account:

The Yokuts have a sort of gambling which pertains exclusively to women. It is a kind of dice throwing, and is called u-chu′-us. For dice they take half of a large acorn or walnut shell, fill it level with pitch and pounded charcoal, and inlay it with bits of bright colored abalone shells. For a dice table they weave a very large fine basket tray, almost flat, and ornamented with devices woven in black or brown, mostly rude imitations of trees and geometrical figures. Four squaws sit around it to play, and a fifth keeps tally with fifteen sticks. There are eight dice, and they scoop them up in their hands and dash them into the basket, counting 1 when two or five flat surfaces turn up. The rapidity with which the game goes forward is wonderful, and the players seem totally oblivious to all things in the world beside. After each throw that a player makes she exclaims, yet′-ni or wí-a-tak or ko-mai-éh, which are simply a kind of sing-song or chanting.

———— Tule River reservation, Tulare county, California. (Cat. no. 70395, 70396, 70397, Field Columbian Museum.)

Eight split reeds (figure 160), 13 inches in length, with backs rudely smeared with seven and eight bands of red paint; four willow

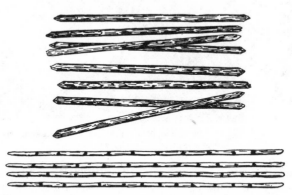

FIG. 160. Cane dice and counting sticks; length of dice, 13 inches; length of counting sticks, 20 inches; Yokuts Indians, Tule River reservation, California; cat. no. 70395. 70396. Field Columbian Museum.

counters, 20 inches long, marked with red stripes; and 25 willow sticks, pointed at one end.

---

[a] This shield, which is 31 inches in diameter, was found by Mr Charles L. Day, of Chin Lee, Arizona, in the cliff-house known as the Mummy cave, in the Canyon del Muerto, July 19, 1904. It is now in the United States National Museum, cat. no. 231778.

[b] Tribes of California. Contributions to North American Ethnology, v. 3, p. 377, Washington, 1877.

These were collected by Dr J. W. Hudson, who describes them as used in the flip-stave game by women.

The game is called tsikehi, to hurdle. Twenty-five sticks are stuck in a row in the ground and receive the same name as the game. The throws are counted around these sticks with four stick counters or horses called witchet. All concave sides up count 16; one concave side up, 1; two concave sides up, 2, and so on; but if an opponent ties your throw you go back as much.

The game appears from Doctor Hudson's description to be played also for counting sticks, when 4 up and 4 down count 1; all up or all down, 4. The sticks are ta-cha. In another dialect they are ka-li-sa.

YOKUTS. Mouth of Mill creek, Fresno county, California. (Cat. no. 70671, 70672, Field Columbian Museum.)

Eight walnut-shell dice (figure 161); basket plaque, 23½ inches in diameter. Collected by Dr J. W. Hudson.

The shells are filled with gum, with pieces of abalone shell inserted as usual, and the basket is old, with colored design.

FIG. 161. Walnut-shell dice; diameter, about 1 inch; Yokuts Indians, Fresno county, California; cat. no. 70671, Field Columbian Museum.

MAYAN STOCK

KEKCHI. Northern Guatemala.

Mr Thomas J. Collins, of Haddonfield, N. J., who spent some time in Guatemala, has communicated to the writer the following account of the corn game of this tribe. He says that it is still in common use among those in the outlying districts. In or near the Spanish-speaking towns, although known, it is rarely, if ever, played.

It is known as bool-ik (from bool, dice, and ik, state of, or meaning of) ; [a] or as batsunk, to play; lain oj ǧuech txe batsunk, I want to play.

---

[a] In reply to my inquiry in reference to the meaning of bool, Mr Collins writes me as follows, under date of December 25, 1899 :

"I have some information as to the Kekchi word bool-ik. I asked for a list of all the words containing the syllable bool from a seminative who has the reputation of knowing the language better than a Guatemalteco. Bool: un pajarito chiquitito, the smallest of birds ; bool : cumbre de las montañas, the summits of mountains ; bool : burbuja, bubble ; bool : granos de maíz marcados, the dice ; bool-ok : jogar ; to play.

"The third (bubble) recalls to me something of interest. A small, turbulent stream near the house at Chama was called the bul-bul-há, and this name was also given to a stream on the opposite mountain when the sound of its roaring reached us during the rains. Superlatives are made by repeating the adjective, and bul-bul-há would signify an extremely bubbling, playful water. The way they throw the dice and the rebounding and rolling of them on the ground are very suggestive of bubbling water and eddies, and if the bird he means be the humming bird, as is likely, its motion would be in line with the same idea. The summits of the mountains are not unlike the irregular up-and-down flight of humming birds. I think that bul (bool) may fairly be taken to mean bubbling, playful, or dancing, in a general sense."

The game is played on the clay floors of houses, usually at night by light of the fire. The ground is swept clean and 15 grains of corn are placed in a straight line, 1½ to 2 inches apart, forming eplix chet, all their places, the 14 spaces between these grains being the board for play.

Four flat-sided grains of corn are selected for dice, and are prepared by digging out with the thumbnail the eye on one side of each grain and either rubbing charcoal in or applying the live end of a glowing stick to the hollow, resulting in each of the four grains, or dice, having a black spot on one side. This operation is called tsep, to mark, ké ru xam, put to the face of the fire, or ké kek sa ix naj ru, put black in the face of his face. The black-spotted side of the dice is called ru bool, face of the dice, and the blank side rit bool, bottom of the dice.

The board and the dice being ready, players select their counters, five for each. Any small articles will do, but preference is shown for five similar twigs, leaf stems, or split sticks, or different lengths and kinds of these. Fragments of leaves of different colors or structure are often used, and where there are many players bits of grass, muslin, or paper; even thread is pressed into service.

Players, any even number, squat around the line of corn, and one of them, taking the four dice in his hand, throws them lightly on the ground, calling the number of black spots, ru bool, showing as they lie. It may be one, two, three, four, or, in case of all blanks, rit bool, five. He plays in a counter to the value of his throw starting from the right end of the line of corn, then throws again and plays farther in; thus, if his first is two and the second five he would leave his counter in the seventh chet, or space, from the right of the board. He is followed by an opponent who plays in from the opposite, or left, end of the board. Then, in turn, a partner (ǧuchben) of the first and a partner of the second player enter, continuing alternately, each throwing twice, entering each at the proper end of the board, until both have played and it is the turn of the first player, who continues the advance of his counter from its position in the seventh space, with the object of ultimately completing his passage of the line. If this is accomplished without taking an adversary or being taken by him he enters again at his own end of the board, exactly as if the board were continuous.

But it is the hope of every player to fall into the space occupied by the counter of an adversary and so take him (xin ket, I struck, or xin chop, I caught). In this case he plays backward toward his entering point and passes out, carrying his captive (ix kam, he is dead).

If he passes out safely without meanwhile being retaken by one of his opponents, the captured counter is retained (ix ǧuak, he is eaten), but his own counter, the captor, is entered again as before. But if he is retaken before passing out, both himself and his captive become the prey of the new captor and are carried by him in the opposite direction. He in his turn may be taken, losing himself and all his prey. Sometimes this taking and retaking continues until the accumulated counters number 6 or 8, the excitement of players increasing until it is a wonderful sight to look upon in the half light of the fire.

All crowded together and moving ceaselessly in a curiously animal way, no muscle or feature at rest. Some are pawing with their hands, some stretching back like cats about to spring, or leaping for an instant upright, but all screaming comments or calling throws in voices entirely unrecognizable. At last the disputed counters are carried out at one end or the other. They are at once separated, those belonging to partners of the winner of them are returned to their owners, who enter them again (tex yolá bi chik, they are living again), while those belonging to the opposing side are put into a hat or some receptacle (lix naj kaminak, there place the dead, or, rotxotx kaminak, house of the dead).

No player loses his throw, for if he has lost his counter, he enters another, but no second can be used until the first is lost. Falling into a space occupied by a partner does not change the play of either, but an adversary would take both should he throw into that space. Players never throw more than twice under any circumstances, but if the first throw takes an opponent's counter, the second throw counts toward carrying him home.

The game lasts from one to three hours and is ended when one side has no more counters to enter (laex chixǧunil xa ǧuak, you have eaten all).

From time to time, toward the close of the game, counters already taken are separated, cham-alni, and counted, ǧuarj lá, the burden of proof lying curiously enough on the victors to show they have caught and eaten all their adversaries.

The whole idea shown by the terms of the game, and still more by the exclamations and remarks of players is that of the pursuit, capture, and safe carrying off of prey. For example: Xin kan, I lay in wait; a án xa ram txé us, you intercepted him well; ta ok laát, enter, thou (ok is used as setting out upon an enterprise); ok ré sikbal kar, to start fishing, or ok ré sikbal tsik, to start the hunt for birds. In the ordinary sense of enter, another word, ojan, is used; a án xin numé sa jumpat, I passed him quickly; ǧwi jun chik xa kam-si ǧwé, if one more, you would have killed me.

Before counters are put in play they are called what they are: Ché, stick; chaj, leaf; ruk-ché, twig; ton chaj, leaf stem. But when put in play they become ǧwe, me, myself; laát, thou; or in the third person are called by name of the player.

MAYA. Chichen Itza, Yucatan.

Dr Alfred Tozzer informs me that he saw grains of corn, blackened on one side, that were used in a game, juego de maiz, presumably similar to that observed among the Kekchi.

The game is called bašal išim (bashal ishim). Four grains of corn, two of them colored black on one side, are thrown. The winning throws are two white and two black or all black.

MOQUELUMNAN STOCK

AWANI. Near Cold Springs, Mariposa county, California.

Dr J. W. Hudson describes the following game under the name of teataȼu:

Six half acorns are cast in a basket plaque. Half face up, half down, count 1; all up or down count 2.

The game was given me by a refugee of the Awani once possessing Yosemite valley, called "Old Short-and-Dirty," a woman about 80 years old, who is one of the five surviving members of that warlike people and lives with her sister and a blind nephew at the above-mentioned place. None of her people have been in Yosemite since about 1870.

MIWOK. California. (Collection of Dr C. Hart Merriam.)

Plaque for dice game (figure 162), 23⅝ inches in diameter, collected by Dr C. Hart Merriam.

The collector states that this plaque was collected from the Miwok, but made by one of the Yuroks tribes. The Miwok call the plaque and game by the same name, chattattoomhe. They use six dice.

OLAMENTKE.   Bay of San Francisco, California.

Louis Choris [a] (1816) says:

Their games consist in throwing small pieces of wood, which fall either in
odd or even numbers, or of others which are rounded on one side, and the game

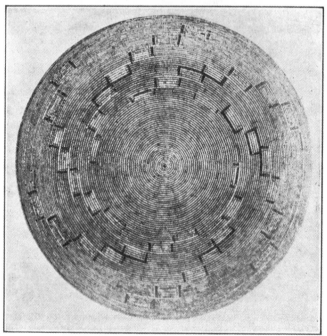

FIG. 162.   Dice plaque; diameter, 23⅜ inches; Miwok Indians, California; in the collection of Dr
C. Hart Merriam.

is lost or won according to whether the pieces of wood fall on the flat or round
side.   [See plate III, *b*.]

MIWOK.   Mariposa   county,   California.   (Cat.   no.   70222,   Field
Columbian Museum.)

Set of six split acorn dice with the shells removed.   Collected by Dr
J. W. Hudson.

——— Tuolumne county, California.   (Cat. no. 70221, Field Columbian Museum.)

Flat basket tray, collected by Dr J. W. Hudson and described by him
as used in a game called chatatha:

Six halves of acorns are used as dice.   Three up or three down, called king-è,
counts 1; all up or down, called a-ti-ka, 2; all other turns, a-wu-ya, nothing.

The flat round basket trays on which the dice are tossed are called hetal, from
a grass used as a warp in this basket.   Eight stick counters, chi-ki-la-hu-hu, oak
sticks, are piled between the opponents.   When one side has won them, they
are all handed to the loser, and must be won again.

[a] Voyage Pittoresque Autour du Monde, p. 5, Paris, 1822.

MENOMINEE INDIANS PLAYING BOWL GAME; WISCONSIN; FROM HOFFMAN

MARY-IRVIN-WRIGHT

OLAMENTKE INDIANS PLAYING STICK GAME; BAY OF SAN FRANCISCO, CALIFORNIA; FROM CHORIS

TULARES. Rancheria near Lemoore, Kings county, California. (Cat.
no. 200069, United States National Museum.)

Flat basket tray (figure 163), 28¾ inches in diameter, worked in
chevron design in colored pattern; accompanied by eight dice

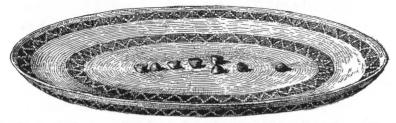

FIG. 163. Basket dice tray and dice; diameter of basket, 28¾ inches; Tulare Indians, California;
cat. no. 200069, United States National Museum.

made of halves of walnut shells, filled with gum and inlaid with
pieces of abalone shell. (From the C. F. Briggs collection. See
Holmes in Report of U. S. National Museum, 1900, plate XLI,
1902.)

MUSKHOGEAN STOCK

CHOCTAW. Mandeville, Louisiana. (Cat. no. 38477, Free Museum of Science and Art, University of Pennsylvania.)

FIG. 164. Corn-grain dice; Choctaw Indians, Louisiana; cat. no. 38477, Free Museum of Science and Art, University of Pennsylvania.

Eight grains of white corn (figure 164), charred on one side. Collected by the writer in 1901.

These are used as dice in the corn game, baskatanje. Two or more men play, throwing the corn with the hand upon the ground. The throws are either white, tobeh, or black, losah, up. The game is twenty-five, and the counts are as follows: All black up, untachaina, counts 8; all white up, 8; seven white up, untokalo, 7; six white up, hanali, 6; five white up, tustslata, 5; four white up, oshta, 4; three white up, tuchaina, 3; two white up, takalok, 2; one white up, chofa, 1.

NATCHESAN STOCK

NATCHEZ. Louisiana.

Le Page du Pratz [a] says, referring to the women's game of the Natchez:

These pieces with which they play are three little bits of cane, from 8 to 9 inches long, split in two equal parts and pointed at the ends. Each piece is distinguished by the designs which are engraved on the convex side. They play three at a time and each woman has her piece. To play this game they hold two of these pieces of cane on the open left hand and the third in the right hand, the round side uppermost, with which they strike upon the others, taking care to touch only the end. The three pieces fall, and when there are two of them which have the convex side uppermost the player marks one point. If there is only one, she marks nothing. After the first the two others play in their turn.

PIMAN STOCK

OPATA. Sonora.

Dr A. F. Bandelier [b] speaks of patol, or quince, as a social game played often on the streets.

PAPAGO. Pima county, Arizona. (Cat. no. 174516, United States National Museum.)

Set of four sticks (figure 165) of saguaro cactus, about $9\frac{1}{4}$ inches in length, three-fourths of an inch in width, and one-fourth of an inch thick.

These are painted solid red on one side, "which is flat and marked with black lines of numerical and sex significance." They were collected by Dr W J McGee and Mr William Dinwiddie. The game is described by the collectors under the name of ghingskoot:

The four marked faces receive the following names: Old man (a), young man (b), old woman (c), young woman (d). In the play the sticks are held verti-

---

[a] Histoire de la Louisiane, v. 3, p. 4, Paris, 1758.
[b] Final Report. Papers of the Archæological Institute of America, Am. series, pt. 1, p. 240, Cambridge, 1890.

cally, bunched in the right hand, and struck from underneath on their lower ends by a stone grasped in the left hand, the blow shooting them vertically into the air [figure 166]. Two backs and two fronts of any sticks up counts 2; three fronts and one back of any sticks up, 3; three backs and the young man up, 4; all fronts up, 5[a]; three backs and the old woman up, 6; all backs, 10; three backs and the young woman up, 14; three backs and the old man up, 15. If the sticks touch or fall on one another, the throw must be repeated. The counts are kept on a rectangle marked on the ground [figure 167], usually approximating 12 by 8 feet, having ten holes, or pockets, counting the corners each time along each side. At two alternate corners are two quadrants called houses (kee) of five holes each not counting the corner holes, called doors (jouta).

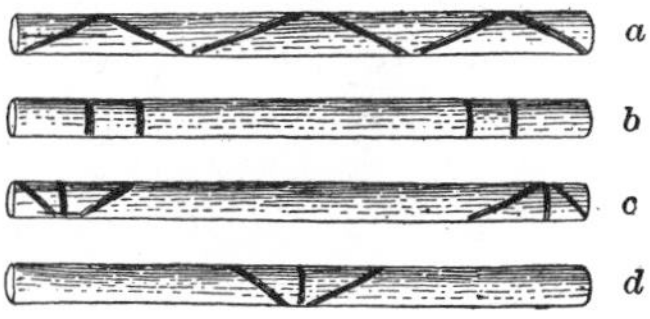

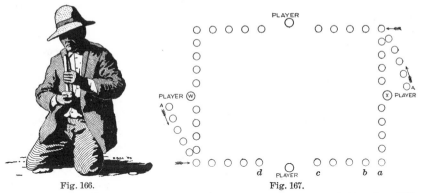

FIG. 165. Stick dice; length, 9¼ inches; Papago Indians, Pima county, Arizona; cat. no. 174516, United States National Museum.

The game is played by two, three, or four players for self or partner, with counters called horses. These usually number two for each player. They are put into play consecutively and by alternate throws of the players. A throw of less than 5, which does not carry the horses out of the door, prevents a player from entering another horse until his aggregate throws are 5+; thus putting his horse into the rectangle proper. After all the horses of a single contestant are in play he may move the same horse continuously. In counting, the pockets from A to either of the nearest corners is 15. It is optional with the player whether he turns to the left or right upon leaving the door, though he

Fig. 166.   Fig. 167.

FIG. 166. Papago Indian striking stick dice in the air; from photograph by William Dinwiddie.
FIG. 167. Circuit for stick dice; Papago Indians, Arizona; from sketch by McGee and Dinwiddie.

must move his horse round the rectangle in the same direction after once starting. If X throws 15, moving to a, and W throws the same number, enabling him to move to the same point, he kills, or throws X's horse out of play, and he must start his piece over again; and again, if he should throw 14, he accomplishes the same result (there is no 1 in the stick count). However, if X should get to c and W throw 10 from house and get to d, he does not kill him. If on the next throw W throws 14 and X has not moved from c, he kills him. A horse must run entirely around the rectangle and back into the house pockets, where he is safe from being killed; but to make him a winning piece, the exact

---

[a] At this play they all laugh, and say the player "has not done skinning himself."

number to count to *a* must be thrown by the sticks. When a horse is on a pocket adjoining *a*, a 2 throw is considered out. The object of the game is to carry all the horses around the pockets and out again at *a*, the first player succeeding in this being declared the winner.

PAPAGO. Cahili, Arizona. (Cat. no. S674, 59, Rijks Ethnographisches Museum, Leiden.)

Set of four sticks (figure 168), 4½ inches in length, rounded on one side, flat, unmarked on the other. Catalogued under the name of quince as a woman's game. Collected by Dr H. F. C. ten Kate, jr, in 1888.

FIG. 168. Stick dice; length, 4½ inches; Papago Indians, Arizona; cat. no. S674, 59, Rijks Ethnographisches Museum, Leiden.

——— Pima county, Arizona. (Cat. no. 174443, United States National Museum.)

Astragalus of bison (figure 169). Collected by Dr W J McGee, who described it as used in a game called tanwan.

The game is played by two persons, who sit facing each other, four or five feet apart.

FIG. 169. Astragalus of bison used as die; Papago Indians, Pima county, Arizona; cat. no. 174443, United States National Museum.

The bone is twirled into the air out of the thumb and forefinger, the back of the hand being held upward. The position in which it falls on the ground controls the count in the game. So long as the player succeeds in throwing the pitted side, or cow hoof, as it is called, upward he retains possession of the bone, and with each throw wins one bean from a prearranged number equally divided between the players. The sides do not count in the play, and the thrower may play again and again without forfeiting the bone until he throws the flat side, opposite the cow hoof, upward, when the bone goes to his opponent to throw, with the same conditions. The winning of the entire number of an opponent's counters constitutes a game won.

PIMA. Arizona. (United States National Museum.)

Cat. no. 27842. Set of four sticks of willow [a] wood, 9 inches in length, three-fourths of an inch in breadth, and one-fourth of an inch in thickness (figure 170); flat on one side, which is incised with transverse and diagonal lines filled in with black paint; the opposite side rounded and painted red.

Cat. no. 27843. Set of four sticks of willow [a] wood, 8⅜ inches in length, three-fourths of an inch in breadth, and one-fourth of an

---

[a] *Salix amygdaloides.*

inch in thickness (figure 171); identical with preceding, except
in the arrangement of the incised lines. Both collected by Mrs
G. Stout.

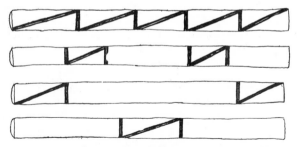

FIG. 170. Stick dice; length, 9 inches; Pima Indians, Arizona; cat. no. 27842, United States
National Museum.

Cat. no. 76017.   Set of four sticks of hazel wood, 7¼ inches in length,
one-half of an inch in breadth, and one-fourth of an inch in

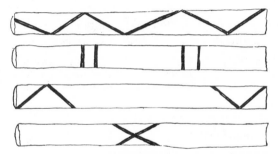

FIG. 171. Stick dice; length, 8⅜ inches; Pima Indians, Arizona; cat. no. 27843, United States
National Museum.

thickness (figure 172); flat on one side, and marked with incised
lines cut at angles across the sticks. These lines are painted red,

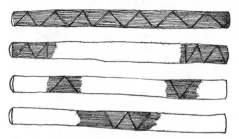

FIG. 172. Stick dice; length, 7¼ inches; Pima Indians, Arizona; cat. no. 76017, United States
National Museum.

and the inscribed part of the faces, black; opposite, rounded
sides, plain. These were collected by Dr Edward Palmer and
described as men's sticks.

Doctor Palmer states:

A space of 10 square feet is inclosed by holes made in the ground [figure 173]. At opposite corners on the outside are two semicircular rows of five holes each. At the beginning a marking-stick is put into the center hole, A, of each semicircle, and the point is to play around the square, and back again to the center hole. Each pair of players moves the pegs in opposite directions, and whenever the count is made that would bring the stick to the hole occupied by that of the antagonist, he is sent back to his original starting place.

The counts are as follows: Four round sides up, counts 10; four flat sides up, 5. When only one flat side is up, it counts whatever is marked on it; any three counts 3, and any two, 2.

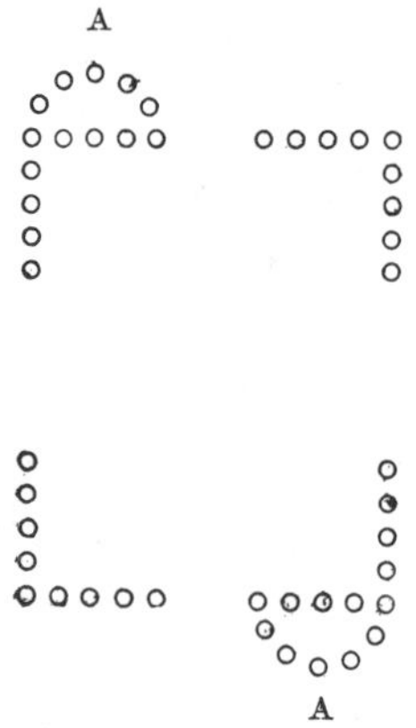

FIG. 173. Circuit for stick-dice game; Pima Indians, Arizona; from sketch by Dr Edward Palmer.

PIMA. Arizona. (Cat. no. 76018, United States National Museum.)

Set of four sticks 7¾ inches long, one-half inch in breadth, and one-fourth of an inch in thickness; flat on one side and painted black; the opposite side rounded and painted red. Collected by Dr Edward Palmer and described by him as women's sticks.

Two play. The sticks are held in the right hand, between the thumb and forefinger, and, with an underthrow, touch the ground slightly, and are let fly.

The counts are as follows: Four blacks, counts 2; four reds, 1; two blacks, out.

Cat. no. 211935.   Squared wooden block, 7⅞ inches long, marked on its four sides, as shown in figure 174.

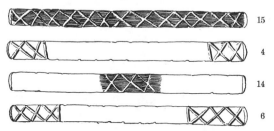

FIG. 174. Four faces of stick die; length, 7⅞ inches;. Pima Indians, Arizona; cat. no. 211935, United States National Museum.

This specimen was collected by Mr Clarence H. Shaw, who describes it as used in the game of kinsgoot:

It is held in the palm of each hand and thrown from the player with a pushing motion. The counts are indicated on figure 174: 15, 4, 14, 6. The game ends at 45.

PIMA. Arizona. (Cat. no. S362, 52, Rijks Ethnographisches Museum, Leiden.)

Three sticks (figure 175), from a set of four, about 5 inches in length, marked on one face with incised lines.

These were collected by Dr H. F. C. ten Kate, jr, and catalogued under the name of kiense (quince), and are similar to the sets from the Pima in the United States National Museum (cat. no. 27842, 27843, 76017).

Dr ten Kate[a] refers to this game as kiensse, and says it resembles the otochei and oetaha of the Yuma and Mohave.

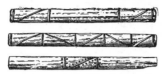

FIG. 175. Stick dice; length, 5 inches; Pima Indians, Arizona; cat. no. S362, 52, Rijks Ethnographisches Museum, Leiden.

PIMA. Arizona. (Cat. no. 218042, United States National Museum.)

Four sticks of mesquite wood, about $8\frac{3}{4}$ inches in length, hemispheric in section and not colored on either side. They were collected by the late Dr Frank Russell, who gives the name of the game as ki^{n}ts and of the sticks as ki^{n}ts kŭt.

The sticks [figure 176] are designated as follows:

No. 1, ki-ik, four. No. 2, tco-otp', six. No. 3, si-ikâ, meaning of word unknown to informants. No. 4, ki^{n}ts, meaning also unknown.

The players sit about 10 feet apart, and put the sticks in play by striking from below with a flat stone held in the left hand. The sticks are held nearly vertical, but are inclined a little forward, so that they will fall in the center of the space between the players, who rake them back with a long stick after each throw.

The count is similar to that described for the Papago game, if we substitute the Pima names for the pieces as follows:

Two backs and 2 faces count 2; 1 back and 3 faces count 3; ki-ik facing up and others down count 4; all faces up count 5; tco-otp' facing up and others down count 6; all faces down count 10; sî-îkâ facing up and others down count 14; ki^{n}ts facing up and others down count 15. The counts are kept upon a rectangle marked upon the ground, usually approximating 12 by 8 feet, having 10 holes or pockets, counting the corners each time along each side. At two alternate corners are two quadrants, called houses (ki), of five holes each, not counting the corner holes, called doors (utpa). The stick used by each player or side to mark its throw is

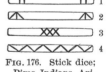

FIG. 176. Stick dice; Pima Indians, Arizona; cat. no. 218042, United States National Museum.

called rsâika, slave or horse. When a player is " coming home " and his count carries his " slave " only to the last hole of his house, it is said to be " in the fire," and remains " burnt " until he throws a less number than 14 or 15.

The corner hole of the rectangle is called tcolût, hip; the second, tcoolrsân, near the corner; the third, rsa-akît, middle; the fourth, kôkĕtam, above the end; the fifth, ko-ok, last; the first hole of the house, tcóoletam, above the hip; the

---

[a] Reisen en Onderzoekingen in Noord Amerika, p. 159, Leiden, 1885.

second, ki-ĭk vakᶜ utra, four hole end; the third, vai-ĭk vakᶜ utra, three hole end; the fourth, sapᶜkᶜ utra, right end or place; the fifth, tai-ĭ utra, fire end or in the fire.

Doctor Russell describes also the following stick dice game, which is played exclusively by women: [a]

Kâ-âmĭsakŭt. This stave game is played with eight sticks, in two sets of four each, which are colored black on the rounded side in one set and black on the flat side in the other, the opposite side being stained red. Two play, each using her own set of sticks, but exchanging them alternately, so that first one set is in use and then the other. They are held loosely in the right hand, and are thrown from the end of the metate or any other convenient stone. If all fall red side up, one point is scored by a mark in the sand. If all are black, two are counted. Four points completes the game.

TARAHUMARE. Pueblo of Carichic, Chihuahua, Mexico. (Cat. no. $\frac{65}{846}$, American Museum of Natural History.)

Set of four split reeds, 6 inches in length and one-half of an inch in width, marked on the inner, flat sides, as shown in figure 177; opposite sides plain.

Collected by Dr Carl Lumholtz, who says: [b]

Their greatest gambling game, at which they may play even when tipsy, is quince, in Tarahumare romavóa. It is played with four sticks of equal length, called romálaka and inscribed with certain marks to indicate their value. They

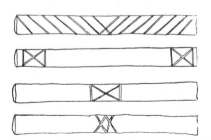

FIG. 177. Stick dice; length, 6 inches; Tarahumare Indians, pueblo of Carichic, Chihuahua, Mexico; cat. no. $\frac{65}{846}$, American Museum of Natural History.

practically serve the same purpose as dice, but they are thrown in a different way. The player grasps them in his left hand, levels their ends carefully, lifts his bundle and strikes the ends against a flat or square little stone in front of him, from which they rebound toward his opponent. The sticks count in accordance with the way they fall. The point of the game is to pass through a figure outlined by small holes in the ground between the two players. The movements, of course, depend upon the points gained in throwing the sticks, and the count is kept by means of a little stone, which is placed in the respective hole after each throw. Many accidents may impede its progress; for instance, it may happen to be in the hole into which the adversary comes from the opposite direction. In this case he is killed, and he has to begin again from the opposite side. The advance is regulated by a number of ingenious by-laws, which make the game highly intellectual and entertaining. If he has the wherewithal to pay his losses, a Tarahumare may go on playing for a fortnight or a month, until he has lost everything he has in this world except his wife and children; he draws the line at that. He scrupulously pays all his gambling debts. (See plate III. c.)

---

[a] From a forthcoming memoir by the collector, to be published by the Bureau of American Ethnology.

[b] Unknown Mexico, v. 1, p. 278, New York, 1902.

TEPEHUAN. Talayote, near Nabogame, Chihuahua, Mexico. (Cat.
no. ₉⁶₁₁⁵, American Museum of Natural History.)

Set of four ash-wood sticks, 18½ inches in length, three-fourths of an
inch broad, and one-eighth of an inch thick, marked on one side
with incised lines smeared with red paint (figure 178a); reverse,
plain.

——— Chihuahua, Mexico. (Cat. no. ₉⁶₁₀⁵, American Museum of
Natural History.)

Set of four ash-wood sticks, identical with the preceding, except that
they are 16¾ inches in length (figure 178b).

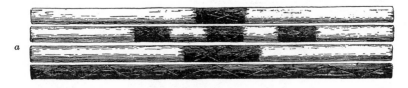

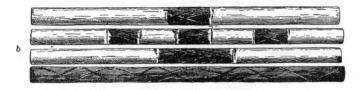

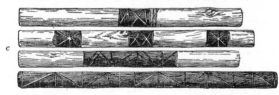

FIG. 178. Stick dice; lengths: a, 18½ inches; b, 16¾ inches; c, 11¼ to 13½ inches; Tepehuan Indians,
Chihuahua, Mexico; cat. no. ₉⁶₁₁⁵, ₉⁶₁₀⁵, ₁₀₃₉⁶⁵, American Museum of Natural History.

Cat. no. ₁₀₃₉⁶⁵. Set of four sticks of canyon walnut, of slightly different lengths, from 11¼ to 13½ inches, eleven-sixteenths of an inch
wide, and one-eighth of an inch thick; one side flat, with incised
designs composed of straight and oblique lines, the incised
places being stained red (figure 178c); opposite sides rounded
and plain.

Cat. no. ₁₀₃₈⁶⁵. Set of four sticks of piñon wood, 6½ inches in length
and three-eighths of an inch square (figure 179).

These last sticks have four instead of two faces. Two opposite sides
are flat and unpainted. One set of the other four sides is unpainted,
with incised lines filled with red paint, as shown in figure 179. The
sides opposite to these are slightly rounded and painted red. The
top stick is marked with a diagonal line across the middle, the next

with two straight transverse lines near each end, the third has a single transverse cut across the middle, and the fourth is plain. The preceding Tepehuan specimens were all collected by Dr Carl Lumholtz. He informs me that the Tepehuan call the game intuvigai zuli gairagai, game straight throwing. It is also generally known by the Spanish name of quince,[a] or fifteen.

He states that it is played by all the tribes in Chihuahua who live in or near the sierra, and by the Mexicans as well, but is not seen

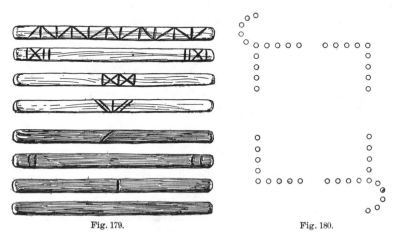

Fig. 179.   Fig. 180.

FIG. 179.   Stick dice; length, 6¼ inches; Tepehuan Indians, Chihuahua, Mexico; cat. no. $\frac{3}{16}\frac{8}{3}\frac{8}{8}$, American Museum of Natural History (lower four show reverses).
FIG. 180.   Circuit for stick dice game; Tarahumare and Tepehuan Indians, Chihuahua, Mexico; from drawing by Dr Carl Lumholtz.

south of the state of Durango. It is not known to the Cora of the state of Jalisco, or to the Tarasco of Michoacan.

ZUAQUE.   Rio Fuerte, Sinaloa, Mexico.

Mr C. V. Hartman, who accompanied Dr Carl Lumholtz, informs me that the Zuaque play the game of quince with four flattened reeds, calling the game kezute.

PUJUNAN STOCK

NISHINAM.   California.

Mr Stephen Powers [b] gives the following account:

The ha is a game of dice, played by men or women, two, three, or four together. The dice, four in number, consist of two acorns split lengthwise into halves, with the outsides scraped and painted red or black. They are shaken in the hands and thrown into a wide, flat basket, woven in ornamental patterns, sometimes worth $25. One paint and three whites, or vice versa, score nothing;

---

[a] Also in French, quinze, " a popular game with cards, in which the object is to make 15 points." The name " quince " does not appear to be confined among the Indians to the game played with staves.

[b] Contributions to North American Ethnology, v. 3, p. 332, Washington, 1877.

two of each score 1; four alike score 4. The thrower keeps on throwing until he makes a blank throw, when another takes the dice. When all the players have stood their turn, the one who has scored most takes the stakes, which in this game are generally small, say a " bit."

NISHINAM. Mokelumne river, 12 miles south of Placerville, California.

Dr J. W. Hudson describes a dice game, played with four half acorns cast into a basket, under the name of ha.

Te'-ŏ, the dice plaque basket is often oval in shape. Two alike up or two alike down count 1; all alike up or down, 2.

SALISHAN STOCK

BELLACOOLA. British Columbia. (Field Columbian Museum.)

Cat. no. 18422. Bone die, copied from a beaver tooth, 1⅝ inches in length, the center tied with a thong and one face decorated with twelve dots in six pairs.

Cat. no. 18434 and 18435. Bone dice, two similar to the above, but with chevron devices; length, 1½ inches.

Cat. no. 18416 to 18419. Wooden dice (figure 181), similar to the preceding, two carved with chevrons and two with dots; length, 2¼ inches.

All these specimens were collected by Mr Carl Hagenbeck.

 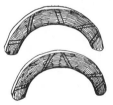

FIG. 181. Wooden dice; length, 2¼ inches; Bellacoola Indians, British Columbia; cat. no. 18416 to 18419, Field Columbian Museum.

CLALLAM. Washington.

A Clallam boy, John Raub, described to the writer the beaver-teeth dice game, as played by this tribe, under the name of smitale. The two teeth marked with dots are called swaika, men, and the two marked with chevrons, slani, women. Playing cards are called smitale.

—— Port Gamble, Washington. (Cat. no. 19653, Field Columbian Museum).

Set of four beaver-teeth dice, two with straight lines and two with circles. Collected by Rev. Myron Eells.

Mr Eells writes:

Precisely the same kind are used by the Twana, Puyallup, Snohomish, Chehalis, and Quenaielt; in fact, by all the tribes on Puget Sound. I have obtained them from the Twana and Quinaielt.

To this list Mr Eells has added the Cowlitz, Lummi, Skagit, and Squaxon, and the Sooke, of British Columbia.

NISQUALLI. Washington.

Mr George Gibbs[a] states:

The women have a game belonging properly to themselves. It is played with four beaver teeth, méh-ta-la, having particular marks on each side. They are thrown as dice, success depending on the arrangement in which they fall.

In his dictionary of the Nisqualli, the name of the game is given as metala, smetali; the highest, or four-point in dice, kes.

QUINAIELT. Washington. (Cat. no. $\frac{16}{4942}$, American Museum of Natural History.)

Four beaver-teeth dice. Collected by Dr Livingston Farrand.

SHUSWAP. Kamloops, British Columbia.

Dr Franz Boas[b] says:

The games of the Shuswap are almost the same as those of the coast tribes. We find the game of dice played with beaver teeth.

SNOHOMISH (?).[c] Tulalip agency, Washington. (Cat. no. 130990, United States National Museum.)

Set of four beaver-teeth dice (figure 182); two, both lefts, stopped at the end and marked on the flat side with rings and dots, and

Fig. 182.   Fig. 183.

FIG. 182. Beaver-teeth dice; length, 1⅟ to 2 inches; Snohomish (?) Indians, Tulalip agency, Washington; cat. no. 130990, United States National Museum.

FIG. 183. Counters for beaver-teeth dice; length, about 3 inches; Snohomish (?) Indians, Tulalip agency, Washington; cat. no. 130990, United States National Museum.

two, rights and lefts, both apparently from the same animal, with both sides plain; 28 radial bones of birds, about 3 inches in length (figure 183), used as counters. Collected by Mr E. C. Cherouse and designated by him as a woman's game.

---

[a] Contributions to North American Ethnology, v. 1, p. 206, Washington, 1877.

[b] Second General Report on the Indians of British Columbia. Report of the Sixtieth Meeting of the British Association for the Advancement of Science, p. 641, London, 1890.

[c] It is not possible to determine the tribe exactly. The tribes at the Tulalip agency are given in Powell's Indian Linguistic Families of America as follows: Snohomish, 443; Madison, 144; Muckleshoot, 103; Swinomish, 227; Lummi, 295.

SONGISH.   Vancouver island, British Columbia.

Dr Franz Boas [a] gives the following account:

Smētalē', a game of dice, is played with four beaver teeth, two being marked on one of their flat sides with two rows of small circles. They are called women, slā'naē smētalē'. The two others are marked on one of the flat sides with cross lines. They are called men, suwē'k·a smētalē'. One of them is tied with a small string in the middle. It is called iнк· ak·· 'ē' sen. The game is played by two persons. According to the value of the stakes, 30 or 40 sticks are placed between the players. One begins to throw. When all the marked faces are either up or down, he wins 2 sticks. If the faces of the two men are up, of the two women down, or vice versa, he wins 1 stick. When the face of the iнк· ak··'ē' sen is up, all others down, or vice versa, he wins 4 sticks. Whoever wins a stick goes on playing. When one of the players has obtained all the sticks he wins the game.

It is considered indecent for women to look on when the men gamble. Only when two tribes play against each other are they allowed to be present. They sing during the game, waving their arms up and down rhythmically. Men and women of the winning party paint their faces red.

THOMPSON.   British Columbia.   (Cat. no. $\frac{16}{993}$, American Museum of Natural History.)

Set of four beaver-teeth dice (figure 184) ; one, partly split, wrapped in sinew; marked on one face with lines and dots, the opposite sides plain.   Collected by Mr James Teit.

The following account is given by the collector: [b]

Women played a game of dice with beaver teeth, which were tossed down on a spread blanket or skin by the player. Each tooth was marked on only one side with carved lines or spots. One, called the man, was marked with eight transverse lines and tied around the middle with a piece of sinew. Its mate was marked with five transverse lines, each having a dot in the middle. The other two were mates, and were each marked alike with a certain number of triangular lines. When the dice were thrown, if all the blank sides or if all the faces came up, it counted 2 points for the thrower ; if a triangular-marked die came face up and all

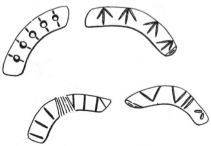

FIG. 184. Beaver-teeth dice; length, 1¼ inches; Thompson Indians, British Columbia; càt. no. $\frac{16}{993}$, American Museum of Natural History.

the others face down, 14 points; if the dotted one fell face up and the other three face down, 8 points; if the man turned face up and the rest face down, 4 points. If the dice fell any other way than as indicated above, it counted nothing, and the opposite party took their turn to throw. If a tooth fell on its edge, it was taken up and let fall to see on which side it would turn. This game is still played by some women, but not nearly as much as it was eight or ten years ago.

[a] Second General Report on the Indians of British Columbia. Report of the Sixtieth Meeting of the British Association for the Advancement of Science, p. 571, London, 1891.

[b] The Thompson Indians of British Columbia. Memoirs of the American Museum of Natural History, v. 2, p. 272, New York, 1900.

TWANA. Washington.

Rev. Myron Eells thus describes the women's game: [a]

The dice are made of beavers' teeth generally, but sometimes from musk-rats' teeth. There are two pairs of them, and generally two persons play, one on each side; but sometimes there are two or three on each side. The teeth are all taken in one hand and thrown after the manner of dice. One has a string around the middle. If this one is down and all the rest up, or up and the rest down, it counts 4; if all are up or down, it counts 2; if one pair is up and the other down, it counts 1; and if one pair is up or down and the other divided, unless it be as above when it counts 4, then it counts nothing; 30 is a game; but they generally play three games, and bet more or less, money, dresses, or other things. They sometimes learn very expertly to throw the one with the string on differently from the others, by arranging them in the hand so that they can hold this one, which they know by feeling, a trifle longer than the others.

SHAHAPTIAN STOCK

KLIKITAT. Washington. (Cat. no. 20955, Free Museum of Science and Art, University of Pennsylvania.)

Three beaver-teeth dice, two marked with five circles with central dot and one with chevrons on flat side. All have ends wrapped with sinew to prevent splitting and one with circles and one with chevrons are wrapped about the middle with sinew. Collected by Mr A. B. Averill.

YAKIMA. Yakima reservation, Washington. (Cat. no. 37512, Free Museum of Science and Art, University of Pennsylvania.)

Four sticks, 5¾ inches in length, triangular in section, one side flat and plain and the other two sides marked with dots and cross

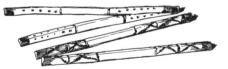

lines as shown in figure 185. Collected by the writer in 1900.

The dice and game are called pomtaliwit. The two sticks marked with cross lines are called walou, man, and the two with dots, woman. It is a woman's game,

FIG. 185. Stick dice; length, 5¾ inches; Yakima In-dians, Washington; cat. no. 37512, Free Museum of Science and Art, University of Pennsylvania.

played by two persons and counted with twenty counting sticks, il quas. The counts are as follows: All heads up counts 2; all tails up, 1; two heads and two tails, 1.

My informant, a Dalles (Wasco) Indian named Jack Long, stated that the game was also played by the Klikitat and Dalles Indians. The former call the game tskaiwit. The game is played on a blanket, and the sticks are tossed up with the hands.

----

[a] Bulletin of the United States Geological Survey, v. III, p. 90, Washington, 1877.

BANNOCK. Fort Hall reservation, Idaho. (Cat. no. 37059, Free
    Museum of Science and Art, University of Pennsylvania.)
Four willow sticks, halves, with pith removed and the groove painted
    red; length, 8½ inches. Three have the flat, grooved side plain,
    and one has burnt cross marks. Two have plain reverses. The
    others, including the one with the flat side, are marked with
    burned designs, as shown in figure 186; with eight willow-twig
    counting sticks 4½ inches in length. These were collected by the
    writer in 1900.

The stick dice and the game are called to-pe-di ; the counters, ti-hope. The two
sticks marked on the rounded convex side with cross lines and triangles are
known, respectively, as pi-au, female, and a-ku-a, male. The counts are as follows : All heads or all tails, 1 ; male and female heads or tails up and the other
two heads or tails down, 2 ; three heads or three tails up, 1.

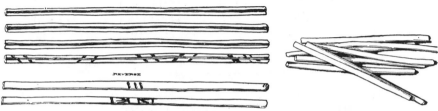

Fig. 186.   Fig. 187.

FIG. 186. Stick dice; length, 8½ inches; Bannock Indians, Idaho; cat. no. 37059, Free Museum of
Science and Art, University of Pennsylvania.
FIG. 187. Counting sticks for stick dice; length, 4½ inches; Bannock Indians, Idaho; cat. no.
37059, Free Museum of Science and Art, University of Pennsylvania.

COMANCHE. Texas.
    J. M. Stanley, in his Catalogue of Portraits of North American
Indians,[a] says in connection with no. 92, a Comanche game, painted
in 1844 :

This game is played exclusively by the women. They hold in their hands
twelve sticks, about 6 inches in length which they drop upon a rock ; the sticks
that fall across each other are counted for the game ; 100 such counts the game.
They become very excited, and frequently bet all the dresses, deerskins, and
buffalo robes they possess.

———— Kiowa reservation, Oklahoma. (United States National Mu-
    seum.)
Cat. no. 152911a. Set of six bone dice, having both faces convex, and
    bearing on one face incised designs (figure 188) filled with red
    paint.

———————————————————————————————————————

[a] Page 55, Washington, 1852. The pictures were destroyed by the fire in the Smithsonian Institution, January 24, 1865.

The reverses are plain, with the exception of the third from the left, which has a cross inscribed upon the back. The device on the face of this die was intended to represent the head of a buffalo, which is more plainly delineated upon one of the Mandan dice (figure 242). The dice are described by the collector as being played by women and shaken up in a basket.

FIG. 188. Bone dice; lengths, 1¼ to 1⅜ inches; Comanche Indians, Oklahoma: cat. no. 152911a, United States National Museum.

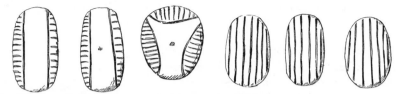

FIG. 189. Bone dice; lengths, 1¼ and 1⅜ inches; Comanche Indians, Oklahoma; cat. no. 152911b, United States National Museum.

Cat. no. 152911b. Set of six bone dice with designs like those on the preceding , but painted green instead of red (figure 189). Both sets were collected by Mr James Mooney.

HOPI. Oraibi, Arizona. (Field Columbian Museum.)

FIG. 190. Cane dice; length, 3¼ inches; Hopi Indians, Oraibi, Arizona; cat. no. 55352, Field Columbian Museum.

Cat. no. 55352. Sandstone slab, inscribed with diagram, 11 inches in length; and four pieces of cane, 3¼ inches in length, with the outer face burned with dots in chevron pattern (figure 190).

These were collected in 1899 by Rev. H. R. Voth, and are described by him as implements for the game of totolospi:[a]

In this game either two or four participate. Each player has one piece, which is placed in the ring seen in the four semicircles. The sticks are then thrown by one party, and as long as either the plain or the figured sides of all the sticks lie upward he moves his piece forward over the cross lines toward the center. As soon as the sticks present different surfaces another player throws.

Cat. no. 55353. Inscribed stone for game of totolospi (figure 191).

[a] Compare with the Aztec totoloque : " Sorte de jeu qui consistait à lancer d'un peu loin de petits jalets coulés en or et très-polis sur des palets également en or ; cinq marques suffisaient pour qu'on perdît ou qu'on gagnât certaine pièce ou joaillerie qui formait l'enjeu (B. Diaz)." R. Simeon, Dictionnaire de la Langue Nahuatl ou Mexicaine (Paris, 1885). The same name, totolospi, is applied by the Tewa at Hano to the foreign Mexican (Spanish) game like Fox and Geese, and the word was probably derived from the Mexican like the analogous patol.

Cat. no. 55354.　Inscribed stone for game of totolospi (figure 192).

Cat. no. 55356.　Two slips of cane, 3¾ inches in length, marked on the round side with burned designs (figure 193), dice used with the above.

These were collected in 1899 by Rev. H. R. Voth, who describes the game as follows:

There are two opposing parties, each of which may consist of one or more persons. The diagram is made smaller or larger, according to the number of players. Each player has one piece, or animal as the Hopi call it, and before starting the pieces are placed on the circles in the space that is depicted running into the center of the diagram. This space is made either in a straight,

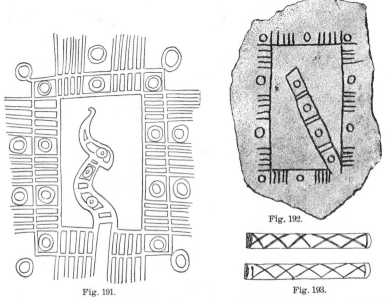

Fig. 192.

Fig. 191.　　　　　　　　　　　Fig. 193.

FIG. 191. Stone board for cane dice; length of diagram, 8 inches; Hopi Indians, Oraibi, Arizona; cat. no. 55353, Field Columbian Museum.

FIG. 192. Stone board for cane dice; length of diagram, 5 inches; Hopi Indians, Oraibi, Arizona; cat. no. 55354, Field Columbian Museum.

FIG. 193. Cane dice; length, 3¾ inches; Hopi Indians, Oraibi, Arizona; cat. no. 55356, Field Columbian Museum.

winding, or coiled form. The number of sticks used varies; generally, however, either two or three are used. These are dropped upon the floor on end. All white or all figured sides up count. The players throw until the sticks do not all present the same side. The pieces are put into the outside circles and move from left to right. Under certain conditions, which have not yet been fully studied, they are put forward over more than one point or are returned to the place of starting.

HOPI. Oraibi, Arizona. (Free Museum of Science and Art, University of Pennsylvania).

Cat. no. 38611.　Sandstone slab, 9 inches long, inscribed with diagram, consisting of an ellipse, with 5 transverse lines on each side and three circles arranged as shown in figure 194.

Cat. no. 38610.   Sandstone slab, 11½ inches long, inscribed with a cross-shaped figure, with five lines on each arm and a circle at each end and in the middle (figure 195).   Collected by the writer in 1901.

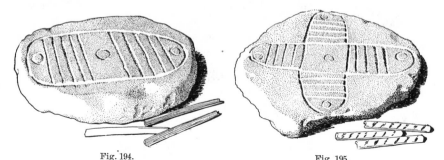

Fig. 194.   Fig. 195.

FIG. 194.   Cane dice and stone board; length of board, 9 inches; Hopi Indians, Oraibi, Arizona; cat. no. 38611, Free Museum of Science and Art, University of Pennsylvania.

FIG. 195.   Cane dice and stone board; length of board, 11¼ inches; Hopi Indians, Oraibi, Arizona; cat. no. 38610, Free Museum of Science and Art, University of Pennsylvania.

Cat. no. 38609.   Stone slab engraved with diagram as shown in figure 196.   Collected by the writer in 1901.

These are counting boards for the game of totolospi.   The first is played by two men and the second by four.   The moves are made according to the throws with cane dice.   The first is accompanied by three slips of cane 4 inches in length, painted red on the inner, hollow

FIG. 196.   Cane dice and stone board; length of board, 12¼ inches; Hopi Indians, Oraibi, Arizona, cat. no. 38609, Free Museum of Science and Art, University of Pennsylvania.

side.   The second also has three dice, with the convex side marked with diagonal burned lines.   The counts are as follows:

Three white up counts 2; three red up, 1.   The players start with their man on the circle nearest to them, advancing line by line across the board.   The one who gets first to the opposite side wins.   The circles are called hwalmai, and the spaces tuwoila.

HOPI.   Walpi, Arizona.

Mr A. M. Stephen in his unpublished manuscript gives tcomakintota as the name of a Hopi man's game, corresponding to the Navaho woman's game of tsĭttĭlc.

HOPI. Mishongnovi, Arizona. (Field Columbian Museum.)

Cat. no. 75568. Pottery bowl (figure 197), 7½ inches in diameter, cream

FIG. 197. Decorated pottery bowl with gambling sticks; Hopi Indians, Mishongnovi, Arizona; cat. no. 75568, Field Columbian Museum.

color, decorated with four marked gambling sticks painted in brown inside of a broken band in the center.

FIG. 198. Decorated pottery bowl with gambling sticks; Hopi Indians, Mishongnovi, Arizona; cat. no. 75892, Field Columbian Museum.

Cat. no. 75892. Pottery bowl (figure 198), 8 inches in diameter, the interior decorated with three marked gambling sticks painted in brown on a plain field inside of a ring with serrated edges having 30 notches; the space outside of the ring spattered. Collected from ancient graves by Mr C. L. Owen in 1900.

HOPI. Shimopavi, Arizona.   (Cat. no. 157735, United States National Museum.)

Pottery bowl (figure 199), containing symbolic pictograph of bird and four marked gaming canes. Excavated from the old cemetery [a] by Dr J. Walter Fewkes.

The symbolic bird, Doctor Fewkes informed me, was identified as Kwataka, Eagle-man, an old crony of gamblers.

FIG. 199.   Decorated pottery bowl with Eagle-man and gaming reed casts; Hopi Indians, Shimopavi, Arizona; cat. no. 157735, United States National Museum.

The bird in this bowl was further identified by Mr Cushing with the Zuñi Misina, referred to in his account of sholiwe (p. 215).

These three bowls serve to establish the existence and antiquity of a cane or reed game, like the Zuñi sholiwe, among the Hopi. Further evidence of the antiquity of this game is furnished by several split gaming reeds excavated by Doctor Fewkes at the Chevlon ruin, near where the Chevlon fork flows into the Little Colorado, about 15 miles east of Winslow, Arizona. The marks on the reeds are shown

---

[a] Doctor Fewkes informs me that old Shimopavi was inhabited up to 1680, but the bowl he regards as older than the middle of the sixteenth century.

in figure 200.　One is apparently without marks on the exterior, and of the four others, two have the same marks, from which it may be inferred that they belonged to two different sets.

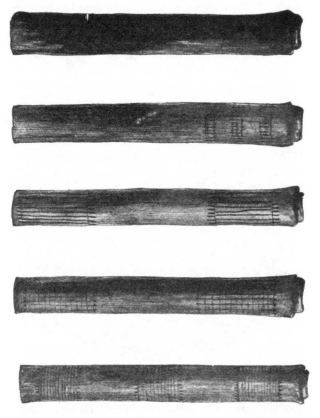

FIG. 200.　Cane dice (restored); Chevlon ruin, Arizona; cat. no. 158030, United States National Museum.

KAWIA.　Indio, Riverside county, California.　(Cat. no. 63589, Field Columbian Museum.)

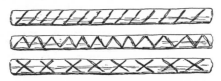

FIG. 201.　Stick dice; length, 16 inches; Kawia Indians, Indio, Riverside county, California; cat. no. 63589, Field Columbian Museum.

Three staves of midrib of palmetto, 16 inches in length, one side rounded, the other flat with burned marks, as shown in figure 201.　Collected by Mr S. C. Simms.

MONO.   Hooker cove, Madera county, California.   (Field Columbian
        Museum.)
Cat. no. 71926, 71927.   Basket plaque, 18½ inches in diameter, and six
    dice, made of acorn calyxes, filled with talc (figure 202).

FIG. 202.   Acorn-cup dice; diameter, seven-eighths of an inch; Mono Indians, Madera county,
California; cat. no. 71927, Field Columbian Museum.

Cat. no. 71178.   Basket dice plaque (figure 203), 25 inches in diam-
    eter, with colored designs.
    Both collected by Dr J. W. Hudson.

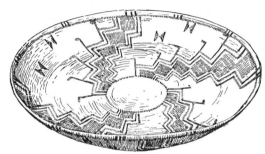

FIG. 203.   Basket tray for dice; diameter, 25 inches; Mono Indians, Madera county, California;
cat. no. 71178, Field Columbian Museum.

PAIUTE.   Southern Utah.   (Cat. no. 14662, United States National
        Museum.)
Slips of cane (figure 204), about 14 inches in length, painted red on
    the inner, concave side.

FIG. 204.   Cane dice; length, about 14 inches; Paiute Indians, southern Utah; cat. no. 14662, United
States National Museum.

Among them are several pairs, made of halves of the same cane,
collected by Maj. J. W. Powell.   A large number of other sets of these
cane dice from the same place are contained in the National Museum.

Paiute. Southern Utah.   (Cat. no. 9411, Peabody Museum of American Archæology and Ethnology.)

Fourteen strips of cane, 5⅝ inches long, with the inner, curved sides painted red (figure 205).   Collected by Dr Edward Palmer and said to be used on the dice principle, the red sides only being counted.

―――― Pyramid lake, Nevada.   (Cat. no. 19045, United States National Museum.)

Eight slips of split cane, painted red on the inside, 11 inches in length.   Collected by Mr Stephen Powers, who describes them as follows:

Tatsungin, gambling pieces.   Ten sticks are stuck into the ground, and two men play by throwing on end eight split pieces of reed, painted red on the

Fig. 205.   Fig. 206.

FIG. 205. Cane dice; length, 5⅝ inches; Paiute Indians, southern Utah; cat. no. 9411, Peabody Museum of American Archæology and Ethnology.

FIG. 206. Stick dice; length, 2¾ inches; Paiute Indians, Pyramid lake, Nevada; cat. no. 37152, Free Museum of Science and Art, University of Pennsylvania.

inside; they count the pieces which fall white side up and there are two pieces serving as counters in addition to the pieces stuck in the ground, the latter representing the ten fingers.

―――― Pyramid lake, Nevada.   (Cat. no. 37150, Free Museum of Science and Art, University of Pennsylvania.)

Eight slips of split reed, painted red on the convex side; length, 13⅜ inches.   Collected by the writer in 1900.

The name of these dice, as reported by Dr George A. Dorsey, is quoquokotateana.

Cat. no. 37152. Eight small willow sticks (figure 206), rounded on one side and flat on the other, the round side plain and the flat side stained red; length, 2¾ inches.   Collected by the writer in 1900 through Miss Marian Taylor.

―――― Pyramid lake, Nevada.   (United States National Museum.)

Cat. no 19054.   Set of twelve sticks of grease wood,[a] one and three-fourths inches in length, five-sixteenths of an inch in breadth, and one-eighth of an inch in thickness (figure 207); both sides rounded, the outer painted red and the inner unpainted.

―――――――――――――――――――

[a] *Larrea mexicana.*

These were collected by Mr Stephen Powers, and are described by the collector under the name of nábago-in, as intended for women to gamble with:

Four players squat in a circle and take turns in tossing these sticks on a basket tray. Five white sides must turn up to count 1. They mark in the sand and five marks count 1 stone; 10 stones end the game.

FIG. 207. Stick dice; length, 2¼ inches; Paiute Indians, Pyramid lake, Nevada; cat. no. 19054, United States National Museum.

Cat. no. 19695. Set of eight dice (figure 208), hoowats, made of canyon walnut shells, split in the middle, and each half filled with pitch and powdered charcoal, inlaid with small red and white glass beads and bits of abalone shell. They are accompanied by a basket tray, chappit (cat. no. 19696).

FIG. 208. Walnut-shell dice; diameter, 1 inch; Paiute Indians, Pyramid lake, Nevada; cat. no. 19695, United States National Museum.

The collector, Mr Stephen Powers, gives the following account of the game:

The women squat on the ground and toss the dice in the tray. When either three or five of them fall flat side up that counts 1. They keep count with sticks for counters. The game is exclusively for women, who bet on it with as much recklessness as men.

SHOSHONI. Wind River reservation, Wyoming. (Free Museum of Science and Art, University of Pennsylvania.)

Cat. no. 36859. Set of stick dice, topedi, slender twigs, two marked alike with grooves the entire length and cross notches in the middle and at the ends on the flat side; the reverse plain; two marked with red grooves and burnt designs on the flat side, and with burnt designs on the reverse, which is otherwise plain; length, 7½ inches.

Cat. no. 36860. Similar to the preceding, except that the designs on the reverses of the two sticks are slightly different; length, 9½ inches.

Cat. no. 36861. Two alike, one side painted red, the reverse plain. One painted red on the flat side, with burnt marks in the center,

and burnt marks and green paint in center on the reverse; one
with the groove painted green and burnt marks on the flat side,
the reverse with burnt marks and green paint; length, 11½ inches;
with eight willow counting sticks, 8 inches in length.

Cat. no. 36862. Two painted yellow on the flat side, the reverse plain;
one painted red on the flat side with burnt marks and blue paint
in the middle, the re-
verse with burnt cross
lines in the middle; one
with groove painted red,
and burnt lines, the re-
verse burnt with cross
marks (figure 209);
length, 11 inches.

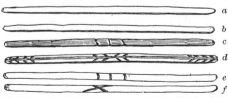

Fig. 209. Stick dice; length, 11 inches; Shoshoni Indians, Wyoming; cat. no. 36862, Free Museum of
Science and Art, University of Pennsylvania. (e, f
are reverses of c, d.)

There are five other sets in
this collection (cat. no.
36863–36867), all varying slightly from the above. Collected by
the writer in 1900. The dice are struck ends down on a flat stone.

SHOSHONI. Fort Hall agency, Idaho. (Cat. no. 22285, United States
National Museum.)

Set of four sticks, 10 inches in length, seven-sixteenths of an inch in
breadth, and three-sixteenths of an inch in thickness; rectangular in section (figure 210), made from grooved box boards, which
Mr Cushing pointed out to the writer were used as a substitute
for split canes; burnt on the inner grooved side with four transverse marks, two near each end. Collected by William H. Danilson.

FIG. 210. Stick dice; length, 10 inches; Shoshoni Indians; Fort Hall agency, Idaho; cat. no.
22285, United States National Museum.

———— Wind River reservation, Wyoming. (Free Museum of Science
and Art, University of Pennsylvania.)

Cat. no. 36836. Dice, bone, marked with incised lines and painted
red and green.

Cat. no. 36837. Dice, bone, three round, three rectangular.

Cat. no. 36838. Dice, blue china, three round, three oval.

Cat. no. 36839. Dice, three blue china, three bone.

Cat. no. 36840. Dice, three bone disks, three plum stones.

Cat. no. 36841.   Dice (figure 211), six bone disks, two sizes.
Cat. no. 36842.   Dice, three bone disks, three bone diamonds.

Fig. 211.   Fig. 212.

FIG. 211. Bone dice; diameter, ⅝ and ⅞ inch; Shoshoni Indians, Wyoming; cat. no. 36841, Free
Museum of Science and Art, University of Pennsylvania.
FIG. 212. Bone dice; diameter, ¾ to ¹⁵⁄₁₆ inch; Shoshoni Indians, Wyoming; cat. no. 36843, Free
Museum of Science and Art, University of Pennsylvania.

Cat. no. 36843.   Dice (figure 212), three bone disks, three bone tri-
    angles.
Cat. no. 36844.   Dice, three china disks, three plum stones.

Fig. 213.   Fig. 214.

FIG. 213. China dice; diameter, ¾ inch; Shoshoni Indians, Wyoming; cat. no. 36847, Free Museum
of Science and Art, University of Pennsylvania.
FIG. 214. China dice; diameter, ½ to ⅞ inch; Shoshoni Indians, Wyoming; cat. no. 36848, Free
Museum of Science and Art, University of Pennsylvania.

Cat. no. 36845.   Dice, three bone disks, three plum stones.
Cat. no. 36846.   Dice, three plum stones, three china triangles.

Fig. 215.   Fig. 216.

FIG. 215. Bag for dice; diameter, 3 inches; Shoshoni Indians, Wyoming; cat. no. 36855, Free
Museum of Science and Art, University of Pennsylvania.
FIG. 216. Basket for dice; diameter, 12½ inches; Shoshoni Indians, Wyoming; cat. no. 36858, Free
Museum of Science and Art, University of Pennsylvania.

Cat. no. 36847.   Dice (figure 213), six china disks, two kinds.
Cat. no. 36848.   Dice (figure 214), seven china dice of three sets.

Cat. no. 36849.   Dice, three bone disks, three bone diamonds.

Cat. no. 36850.   Nine dice of five sets.

All these specimens were collected by the writer in 1900. There are six dice of two different kinds in each set. As will be seen from the above, three may be made of china or bone and three of plum

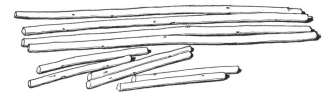

FIG. 217.   Counting sticks for dice; lengths, 5 and 13¾ inches; Shoshoni Indians, Wyoming; cat. no. 36868, Free Museum of Science and Art, University of Pennsylvania.

stones, or three may be round and three diamond-shaped or triangular. The reverses are all plain. Great ingenuity is displayed in the manufacture of these dice, which are made by the women. They are called awunhut. The dice are carried in small buckskin bags ornamented with beadwork, awunhut mogutz. Cat. no. 36852, rectangular, 4 by 3¼ inches; cat. no. 36853, 36854, circular; cat. no. 36855, circular, diameter, 3 inches (figure 215).

The dice are tossed in a flat woven basket, of which there are three specimens in this collection: Cat. no. 36856, diameter, 15 inches; cat. no. 36857, diameter, 11 inches; cat. no. 36858, diameter, 12½ inches (figure 216).

These baskets are called seheouwu. The game is counted with ten counting sticks of peeled willow. Cat. no. 36868 consists of ten such sticks, four of which are 13¾ and six 5 inches in length (figure 217).

SABOBA. California.   (Cat. no. 61940, Field Columbian Museum.)

Set of four wooden staves, 15 inches in length, rounded on one side and flat and marked with incised lines, as shown in figure 218, on the other.

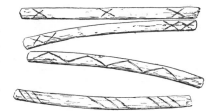

FIG. 218.   Stick dice; length, 15 inches; Saboba Indians, California; cat. no. 61940, Field Columbian Museum.

They were collected by Mr Edwin Minor, who describes the game as follows:

Kun-we'la is played by any number of women seated on the ground in a circle. The players in turn hold the sticks, round side up, with the palms pressing against the ends of the sticks, which are tossed up and allowed to fall on the ground. The count is determined by the number of faces, or flat sides, that turn up. The marks on the sticks are not used in the counting; they merely distinguish them individually.

TOBIKHAR (GABRIELEÑOS). Los Angeles county, California.

Hugo Ried [a] says:

Another game, called charcharake, was played between two, each taking a turn to throw with the points down eight pieces of split reed 8 or 10 inches long and black one side.

UINTA UTE. White Rocks, Utah. (Free Museum of Science and Art, University of Pennsylvania.)

Cat. no. 37109. Four willow sticks, one side flat and painted red, the rounded side burnt with cross marks; length, 10 inches.

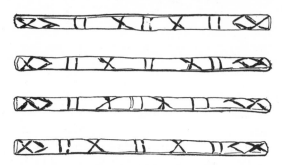

FIG. 219. Stick dice; length, 9¼ inches; Uinta Ute Indians, White Rocks, Utah; cat. no. 37110, Free Museum of Science and Art, University of Pennsylvania.

Cat. no. 37110. Four willow sticks (figure 219), one side nearly flat and painted blue, the opposite sides also nearly flat and marked alike with burnt designs; length, 9½ inches.

Cat. no. 37111. Four willow sticks, one side flat and painted yellow, and the opposite side rounded and painted red; length, 16¼ inches.

FIG. 220. Stick dice for basket dice; length, 2¼ inches; Uinta Ute Indians, White Rocks, Utah; cat. no. 37112, Free Museum of Science and Art, University of Pennsylvania.

These were collected by the writer in 1900. The dice are called toroknop (toropwinuk, Dorsey).

Cat. no. 37112. Twenty oval slips of willow wood (figure 220), flat on one side and rounded on the other, in five sets marked alike on the rounded side; four painted red, four yellow, four green, four

---

[a] Account of the Indians of Los Angeles Co., Cal. Bulletin of the Essex Institute, v. 17, p. 18, Salem, 1885.

black, and four with burnt marks, the reverses plain; length, 2¾ inches. Collected by the writer in 1900.

Doctor Dorsey gives the name as wushanup.

FIG. 221. Uinta Ute women playing basket dice, Ouray, Utah; from photograph by Dr George A. Dorsey.

SIOUAN STOCK

ASSINIBOIN. North Dakota. (Cat. no. 8498, United States National Museum.)

Set of four sticks of polished hickory, 15½ inches in length, about 1 inch in breadth in the center, tapering to three-fourths of an inch at ends, and one-eighth of an inch in thickness. Two are burnt on one side with war calumets, or tomahawks, and with crosses (stars?) at each end, and two each with four bear tracks, with stripes of red paint between (figure 222); opposite sides plain, ends rounded; one notched and tied with sinew, to prevent splitting. Collected by Dr J. P. Kimball.

——— Fort Union, Montana.

In a report to Isaac I. Stevens, governor of Washington territory, on the Indian tribes of the upper Missouri, by Mr Edwin T. Denig, a manuscript in the library of the Bureau of American Ethnology, occurs the following accounts of the bowl and stick-dice game among the Assiniboin:

Most of the leisure time, either by night or by day, among all these nations is devoted to gambling in various ways, and such is their infatuation that it is the cause of much distress and poverty in families. For this reason the name of being a desperate gambler forms a great obstacle in the way of a young man getting a wife. Many quarrels arise among them from this source, and we are well acquainted with an Indian who a few years since killed another because after winning all he had he refused to put up his wife to be played for. Every day and night in the soldier's lodge not occupied by business matters presents

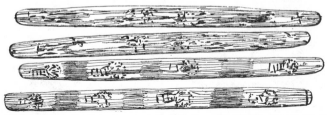

Fig. 222. Stick dice; length, 15¼ inches; Assiniboin Indians, North Dakota; cat. no. 8498, United States National Museum.

gambling in various ways all the time; also in many private lodges the song of hand gambling and the rattle of the bowl dice can be heard.

Women are as much addicted to the practice as men, though their games are different, and not being in possession of much property their losses, although considerable to them, are not so distressing. The principal game played by men is that of the bowl, or cossoó, which is a bowl made of wood with flat bottom 1 foot in diameter or less, the rim turned up about 2 inches, and highly polished inside and out. A drawing and a description of the arithmetical principles of this game is now attached in this place. The manner of counting therein mentioned is the manner in which we learned it from the Indians, but the value of each of the articles composing the dice can be and is changed sometimes in default of some of them being lost, and again by agreement among the players in order to lengthen or shorten the game or facilitate the counting. However, the best and most experienced hands play it as it is represented. It can be played between two or four; that is, either one on each side or two against two. The game has no limit unless it is so agreed in the commencement, but this is seldom done, it being usually understood that the players continue until one party is completely ruined.

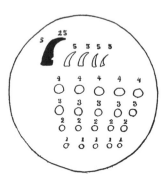

Fig. 223. Bowl game; Assiniboin Indians, Montana; from sketch by Edwin T. Denig.

The dice and their counts [figure 223] are as follows: One large crow's claw, red on one side and black on the other, being the only one that will occasionally stand on end, in which case 25 for it is counted, besides its value of 5 when on its side; four small crow's claws, painted the same as the large one, which count 5 each if the red side turns up; if the black, nothing; five plum stones, black on one side and scraped white on the other, the black sides turned up valued at 4 each, the white sides nothing; five small round pieces of blue china, one-half inch in diameter, which count 3 each for the blue side, for the white side nothing; five vest buttons, the eyes filed off, the eye side turned up counts 2 each, the smooth side nothing; five heads of brass tacks, the concave side turning up counts 1 each, the convex side nothing.

First throw. Big claw on end, 30,. and three red claws, 15, counts 45; two burnt sides up. 0; three blue sides up, 3 each, 9; one eye side up, 0; four concaves up, 1 each. 4: total. 58. [Figure 224a.]

Second throw. Two red. none on end. nothing by claws, counts 0: three burnt sides up, 4 each, 12; five blue sides up, 3 each, 15; three eye sides up, 2 each, 6: two concaves. nothing by tacks, 0: total, 33. [Figure 224b.]

Third throw. Big claw on end, 30, all the rest red, 20, counts 50; five burnt sides up. 4 each, 20; five blue sides up, 3 each, 15; five eye sides up, 2 each, 10; five concave tacks. 1 each, 5; total, 100. This is the best throw that can be made and takes all the stakes when the game does not exceed 100. [Figure 224c.]

The bowl is held by the tips of the four fingers inside the rim and the thumb underneath. The dice being put in, they are thrown up a few inches by striking the bottom of the bowl on the ground, so that each counter makes several revolutions. It is altogether a game of chance, and no advantage can be taken by anyone in making the throws. The counters or dice never leave the bowl, but are counted as the value turns up. One person having shaken it, and the amount of his throw having been ascertained, a requisite number of small sticks are placed before him, each stick counting 1. In this way the game is kept, but each keeps his adversary's game, not his own; that is, he hands him a number of sticks equal to the amount of his throw, which are laid so that all can see them. Each throws in turn unless the big claw stands on end, in which case the person is entitled to a successive throw. By much practice they are able to count the number turned up at a glance, and the principles of the game being stated . . . we will now describe how it is carried on. It has been observed in reference to their gambling that it is much fairer in its nature than the same as carried on by the whites, and this is worthy of attention, inasmuch as it shows how the loser is propitiated, so that the game may not result in quarrel or bloodshed, as is often the case. The game is mostly played by the soldiers and warriors, and each must feel equal to the other in courage and resolution;

Fig. 224. Counts in bowl game; Assiniboin Indians, Montana; from sketch by Edwin T. Denig.

it is often kept up for two or three days and nights without any intermission, except to eat, until one of the parties is ruined. For example, A plays against B; each puts up a knife, and they throw alternately until 100 is counted by the dice: say A wins. B now puts up his shirt against two knives, which is about equal in value; say A wins again, B then stakes his powderhorn and some arrows against the whole of A's winnings; should B now win, the game commences again at the beginning, as A would only have lost a knife; but supposing A wins, B now puts up his bow and quiver of arrows against all A has won. The stakes are never withdrawn, but let lie in front of them. Say A again wins, B then stakes his blanket and leggings, which are about equal in value to all A has won, or, if not, it is equalized by adding or subtracting some article. Supposing A again to be winner, he would then be in possession of two knives. one shirt. one blanket, one powderhorn. one bow and quiver of arrows, and one pair of leggings, the whole of which the Indians value at eight robes. B now stakes his gun against all the above of A's winnings. Now, if A again wins he only retains the gun, and the whole of the rest of the property won by A returns to B, but he is obliged to stake it all against his gun in possession of A, and play again. If A wins the second time he retains the whole, and B now puts up his horse against all of A's winnings, including the gun. If A wins he retains only the horse, and the gun and everything else revert again to B, he being obliged to stake them again against the horse in A's possession. If A wins this time, he keeps the whole, but if B wins he only gets back the horse and gun, and all the rest of the property goes to A. Supposing B again loses and continues losing until all his personal property has passed into the hands of A, then B, as a last resort, stakes his wife and lodge against all his property in the hands of A. If A wins he only keeps the woman; the horse, gun, and all other property returns again to B, with the understanding, however, that he stake it all to get back his wife. Now, if B loses he is ruined, but if A loses he gives up only the woman and the horse, continuing to play with the rest of the articles against the horse until one or the other is broke. At this stage of the game the excitement is very great. The spectators crowd around and intense fierceness prevails. Few words are exchanged and no remarks made by those looking on. If the loser be completely ruined and a desperate man, it is more than likely he will by quarrel endeavor to repossess himself of some of his property, but they are generally well matched in this respect, though bloody struggles are often the consequence.

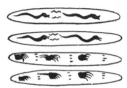

FIG. 225. Stick dice; length 12 inches; Assiniboin Indians, Montana; from sketch by Edwin T. Denig.

We have known Indians to lose everything—horse, dogs, cooking utensils, lodge, wife, even to his wearing apparel, and be obliged to beg an old skin from some one to cover himself and seek a shelter in the lodge of one of his relations. It is, however, considered a mark of manliness to suffer no discomposure to be perceptible on account of the loss, but in most cases we imagine this a restraint forced upon the loser by the character of his adversary. Suicide is never committed on these occasions. His vengeance seeks some other outlet—in war expeditions or some way to acquire property that he may again play and retrieve his losses. There are some who invariably lose and are poor all their lives. A man may with honor stop playing with the loss of his gun. He has also a second opportunity to retire on losing his horse, and when this is so understood at the commencement they do; but when a regular set-to takes place between two soldiers it generally ends as above described.

The usual game which women play alone—that is, without the men—is called chunkandee, and is performed with four sticks marked on one side and blank on the other. The women all sit in a circle around the edge of some skin spread upon the ground, each with her stake before her. One of them gathers up the sticks and throws them down forcibly on the end, which makes them bound and whirl around. When they fall the number of the throw is counted, as herein stated. The implements [figure 225] are four sticks, 12 inches long, flat, and rounded at the ends, about 1 inch broad and one-eighth of an inch thick. Two of them have figures of snakes burned on one side and two the figure of a bear's foot. All the sticks are white on the opposite side. Two painted or marked sides and two white count 2; all the white sides turned up count 10; three burnt sides up and one white count 0; three white sides up and one burnt count 0; four burnt sides up count 10. Each throws in turn against all others, and if the whole of the marked sides or all the fair sides of the sticks are turned up she is entitled to a successive throw. The game is 40, and they count by small sticks as in the preceding. In fine weather many of these gambling circles can be seen outside their lodges, spending the whole day at it, instead of attending to their household affairs. Some men prohibit their wives from gambling, but these take the advantage of their husbands' absence to play. Most of the women will gamble off everything they possess, even to the dresses of their children, and the passion appears to be as deeply rooted in them as in the men. They frequently are thrashed by their husbands for their losses and occasionally have quarrels among themselves as to the results of the game.

Maximilian, Prince of Wied,[a] says:

Another [game] is that in which they play with four small bones and four yellow nails, to which one of each sort is added; they are laid upon a flat wooden plate, which is struck, so that they fly up and fall back into the plate, and you gain or lose according as they lie together on one side, and the stake is often very high.

ASSINIBOIN. Fort Belknap reservation, Montana. (Cat. no. 60161, Field Columbian Museum.)

Set of dice consisting of five claws, one a lion claw larger than the others, five heads of brass tacks, one rectangular piece of copper, and four plum stones having one side burnt and one plain (figure 226).

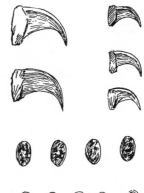

These were collected in 1900 by Dr George A. Dorsey, who describes them as used in the game of kansu and gives the names and value of the objects as follows:

FIG. 226. Claw, plum-stone, and brass dice; Assiniboin Indians, Montana; cat. no. 60161, Field Columbian Museum.

Large crow claw, washage, on end counts 28; red side up, 5; small claws on end, 12; red side up, 4; plum stones, kan-h, black (saap) side up, 4; plain, ska, side up, 0; brass tacks, masiek, concave side up, 4; convex side up, 0; copper plate, hungotunk, big mother, bright side up, 18; other side, 0.

As in other dice games, these objects are tossed in a wooden bowl, the score being kept by counting sticks and 100 constituting game.

CROWS. Wyoming.

Dr F. V. Hayden[b] in his vocabulary gives manopede, a favorite game with women, in which plum pits are used; manuhpe, plum (*Prunus virginiana*) reveals the etymology; badeahpedik, to gamble, evidently referring to the dish, bate; also[c] maneshope, a game with sticks, played by the women.

——— Crow reservation, Montana. (Field Columbian Museum.)

Cat. no. 69691. Four stick dice (figure 227), flat slips of sapling, 11½ inches in length and one-half of an inch wide, with rounded sides plain, and flat sides painted red; two having burnt marks

---

[a] Travels in the Interior of North America, translated by H. Evans Lloyd, p. 196, London, 1843.

[b] Contributions to the Ethnography and Philology of the Indian Tribes of the Missouri Valley, p. 408, Philadelphia, 1862.

[c] Ibid., p. 420.

on both sides; one, two crosses with three dots on the red side opposite, and the other, six diagonal lines with two crosses on the red side opposite.

These were collected by Mr S. C. Simms, who describes them as used in a woman's game. There are 14 other sets of these stick dice in this collection, all of four sticks each, varying in length from 6 to 11½ inches. They are painted red, green, blue, yellow, and black. Two sticks in each set are distinguished by burnt marks on both sides more or less like those figured.

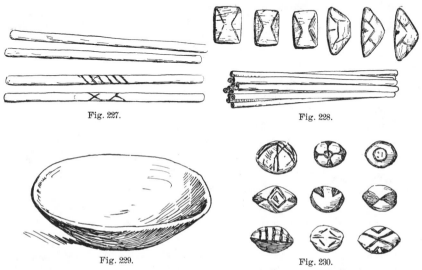

Fig. 227.

Fig. 228.

Fig. 229.

Fig. 230.

FIG. 227. Stick dice; length, 11½ inches; Crow Indians, Montana; cat. no. 69691, Field Columbian Museum.

FIG. 228. Bone dice and counting sticks; length of sticks, 4 inches; Crow Indians, Montana; cat. no. 69711, 69712, Field Columbian Museum.

FIG. 229. Platter for dice; diameter, 9 inches; Crow Indians, Montana; cat. no. 69712, Field Columbian Museum.

FIG. 230. Plum-stone dice; Crow Indians, Montana; cat. no. 69699, 69700, 69701, 69702, 69706, 69707, 69708, 69731, 69732, Field Columbian Museum.

Cat. no. 69711, 69712. Set of implements for woman's dice game, consisting of six bone dice, three triangular and three rectangular, marked on one side with burnt designs; a wooden bowl, 9 inches in diameter, and twelve willow twig counting sticks, 4 inches in length (figures 228, 229). Collected by Mr S. C. Simms in 1901.

There are some fifty sets of these dice in this collection, each consisting of six pieces, of which three and three are alike. They are made of bone, of plum stones (figure 230), and of wood, uniformly marked on one side with burnt designs. A few sets are made of foreign material, such as blue china, brass buttons, etc. They closely resemble the dice used by the Shoshoni in Wyoming.

DAKOTA (BRULÉ). South Dakota. (Cat. no. 10442, 10443, 16552, Free Museum of Science and Art, University of Pennsylvania.)

Eleven plum-stone dice, apparently belonging to two sets; basket in which dice are thrown, made of woven grass, 8 inches in diameter at top and $2\frac{1}{4}$ inches deep, with bottom covered with cotton cloth (figure 231); set of thirty-two sticks used in counting (figure 232), consisting of eleven rounded white sticks, about 13 inches in length, fourteen similar black sticks, made of

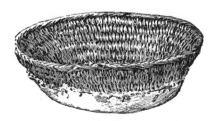

FIG. 231. Basket for plum-stone dice; diameter at top, 8 inches; Brulé Dakota Indians, South Dakota; cat. no. 10443, Free Museum of Science and Art, University of Pennsylvania.

ribs of an old umbrella, about 12 inches in length, and seven iron sticks, about 11 inches in length, consisting of ribs of an umbrella. Collected by Mr Horatio N. Rust in 1873.

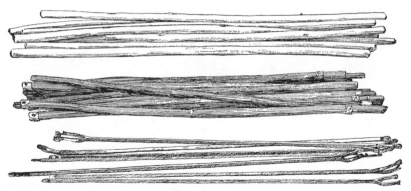

FIG. 232.　Counting sticks for plum-stone dice; lengths, 13, 12, and 11 inches; Brulé Dakota Indians, South Dakota; cat. no. 16552, Free Museum of Science and Art, University of Pennsylvania.

DAKOTA (OGLALA). Pine Ridge reservation, South Dakota. (Free Museum of Science and Art, University of Pennsylvania.) Implements for the game of kansu.

Cat. no. 22119. Set of six dice made of plum stones, polished, with incised and burned marks. Two are marked on one face with a spider and on the reverse with a longitudinal line with three cross marks; two with a lizard, with three transverse marks on the reverse, and two with undetermined marks, as shown in figure 233, the reverses being plain.

Cat. no. 22120. Basket, tampa, $8\frac{1}{2}$ inches in diameter, having the bottom covered with a disk of hide (figure 234).

Cat. no. 22121.   Wooden cup, tampa, 3⅝ inches in diameter and 2 inches deep (figure 235)—a model such as would be used by a child.

These objects were collected by Mr Louis L. Meeker,[a] who says:

The game is played like dice. Each spider [figure 233] counts 4; each lizard, 3, and each turtle, 6.   There is a connection between the native term for spider, inktomi, and the number 4, topa or tom. The turtle presents six visible members when it walks. An old woman here has plum stones marked with the above signs, and also with a face, a thunder hawk, and a bear track. She has

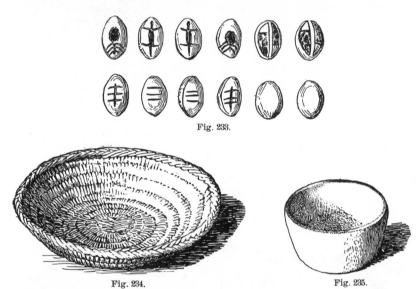

Fig. 233.

Fig. 234.   Fig. 235.

FIG. 233. Plum-stone dice; Oglala Dakota Indians, Pine Ridge reservation, South Dakota; cat. no. 22119, Free Museum of Science and Art, University of Pennsylvania.
FIG. 234. Basket for dice; diameter, 8¼ inches, Oglala Dakota Indians, Pine Ridge reservation, South Dakota; cat. no. 22120, Free Museum of Science and Art, University of Pennsylvania.
FIG. 235. Wooden cup for dice; diameter, 3⅝ inches; Oglala Dakota Indians, Pine Ridge reservation, South Dakota; cat. no. 22121, Free Museum of Science and Art, University of Pennsylvania.

three sets of three pairs each. The third set bears a buffalo face on one and marks that represent the pickets of a buffalo-surround on the others. Those were used only to secure success in the buffalo hunt. The wagers were sacrifices.

DAKOTA (SANTEE).   Minnesota.

Philander Prescott [b] gives the following account in Schoolcraft:

They play with a dish and use plum stones figured and marked. Seven is the game. Sometimes they throw the whole count; at others they throw two or three times, but frequently miss, and the next one takes the dish. The dish which they play in is round and will hold about 2 quarts. Women play this game more than the men and often lose all their trinkets at it.

---

[a] Ogalala Games. Bulletin of the Free Museum of Science and Art, v. 3, p. 31, Philadelphia, 1901.
[b] Information respecting the History, Condition, and Prospects of the Indian Tribes of the United States, pt. 4, p. 64, Philadelphia, 1856.

Schoolcraft [a] describes the game of kuntahso, which he translates as "the game of the plum stones." He figures five sets of stones, each consisting of eight pieces:

In set A [figure 236] numbers 1 and 2 represent sparrow hawks with forked tails, or the forked-tail eagle—*Falco furcatus*. This is the so-called war eagle. Numbers 3 and 4 are the turtle; which typifies, generally, the earth. If 1 and 2 fall upwards, the game is won. If but one of these figures falls upwards, and, at the same time, 3 and 4 are up, the game is also won. The other numbers, 5, 6, 7, and 8, are all blanks. B denotes the reversed sides of A, which are all blanks.

Set C shows different characters with a single chief figure (5) which represents the *Falco furcatus*. This throw indicates half a game, and entitles the thrower to repeat it. If the same figure (5) turns up, the game is won. If no success attends it by turning up the chief figure, the throw passes to other hands. D is the reverse of set C and is a blank throw.

In set E, No. 5 represents a muskrat. The three dots (7) indicate two-thirds of a throw, and the thrower can throw again; but if he gets blanks the second time the dish passes on to the next thrower. Set F is invested with different powers. No. 1 represents a buffalo, and 2 and 3 denote chicken-hawks, fluttering horizontally in the air. The chief pieces, 1, 2, 3, have the same powers and modifications of value as A.

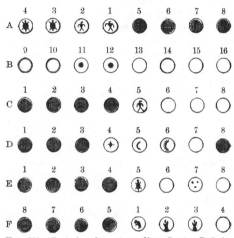

Fig. 236. Casts in plum-stone dice; Santee Dakota Indians, Minnesota; from Schoolcraft.

To play this game, a little orifice is made in the ground and a skin put in it. Often it is also played on a robe. The women and young men play this game. The bowl is lifted with one hand about 3 or 4 inches, and pushed suddenly down to its place. The plum stones fly over several times. The stake is first put up by all who wish to play. A dozen can play at once, if it be desirable.

DAKOTA (TETON). Cheyenne River agency, South Dakota. (Cat. no. 153365, United States National Museum.)

Set of seven plum stones, plain on one side and with marks burnt upon the other.

Collected by Dr Z. T. Daniel,[b] who describes the game as follows under the name of kansu:

᾽ This is a very ancient game of the Sioux Indians, played usually by elderly women, although young women and men of all ages play it. Kansu is an abbreviation of kantasu, which means plum seed. They drop the ta and call the game kansu, because it is played with plum seeds. It is used for gambling and amusement, and is more like our dice than any other of our games. When played, the seeds are thrown up in a basket or bowl, and the markings on the seeds that are up or down decide the throw.

---

[a] Information respecting the History, Condition, and Prospects of the Indian Tribes of the United States, pt. 2, p. 72, Philadelphia, 1853.

[b] Kansu, a Sioux Game. The American Anthropologist, v. 5, p. 215, 1892.

The seeds used are those of the wild plum of the Dakotas, indigenous throughout the northwest region of the United States. They are seven in number. On one side they are all perfectly plain and of the natural color, except some fine marks on four to distinguish them when the burnt sides are down, but on the reverse side of all there are burnt markings. These markings are made by a piece of hot iron, such as a nail, the blade of a knife, or a piece of hoop iron. Before the natives used iron they used a hot stone. Six of the seeds are in pairs of three different kinds, and only one is of a different marking from all the others. One pair is scorched entirely on one side; another pair has an unburnt line about 2 millimeters wide traversing their longitudinal convexity, the remainder of their surfaces on that side being scorched; the remaining pair have one-half of one side burnt longitudinally, the other side of the same unburnt, but traversed by three small burnt lines equidistant, about 1 millimeter wide, running across their short axes. The remaining and only single seed has an hourglass figure burnt on one side, the contraction in the figure corresponding to the long diameter of the seed. They are all of the same size, about 16 millimeters long, 12 wide, and 7 thick, and are oval, having the outlines and convexity on each side of a diminutive turtle shell. When the Sioux first obtained our ordinary playing cards they gave to them, as well as to the game, the name kansu, because they were used by the whites and themselves for the same purpose as their original kansu. The men do not use the seeds or the original kansu now, but they substitute our cards. The women, however, do use the game at the present time. When a ration ticket was issued to them, they gave it the name of kansu, because it was a card; so also to a postal card, business card, or anything of the description of a card or ticket; a railroad, street-car, milk, store, or circus ticket would be called a kansu; so that the evolution of this term as applied to a ticket is a little interesting.

The description of the game kansu, as related by the Sioux, is as follows: Any number of persons may play, and they call the game kansu kute, which literally means to shoot the seeds. When two persons play, or four that are partners, only six of the seeds are used, the hourglass, or king kansu, being eliminated. The king is used when a number over two are playing and each one for himself. The three-line seeds are called sixes, the one-line fours, those that are all black tens. When two play for a wager they each put sixteen small sticks, stones, corn, peas, or whatnot into a common pile between them, making in all 32. The play begins by putting the seeds into a small bowl or basket and giving it a quick upward motion, which changes the positions of the seeds, then letting them fall back into the receptacle, care being taken not to let any one fall out. The markings that are up decide the throw, precisely on the principle of our dice. As they count, they take from the pile of 32 what they make, and when the pile is exhausted, the one having the greatest number wins the game. If all the white sides are up, the throw counts 16. The two tens up and four whites count 16. Two pairs up count 6, and the player takes another throw. Two sixes down count 4. If both tens are down, either side symmetrically, it counts 10. If all burnt sides are up, it is 16. If both fours are down, it is 6. If two pairs are up, it counts 2. One pair up does not count unless all the others are down. When more than two play, and each for himself, the king is introduced. If the king is up and all the others down, the count is 16. If they are all up, the count is the same. If two pairs are up, the count is 6. If the king is down and the remainder up, the count is 16.

DAKOTA (WAHPETON and SISSETON).   South Dakota.

Dr H. C. Yarrow [a] refers to the plum-stone game in his paper on Indian mortuary customs, as described to him by Dr Charles E. McChesney, U. S. Army, as follows:

After the death of a wealthy Indian the near relatives take charge of the effects, and at a stated time—usually at the time of the first feast held over the bundle containing the lock of hair—they are divided into many small piles, so as to give all the Indians invited to play an opportunity to win something. One Indian is selected to represent the ghost, and he plays against all the others, who are not required to stake anything on the result, but simply invited to take part in the ceremony, which is usually held in the lodge of the dead person, in which is contained the bundle inclosing the lock of hair. In cases where the ghost himself is not wealthy, the stakes are furnished by his rich friends, should he have any. The players are called in one at a time, and play singly against the ghost's representative, the gambling being done in recent years by means of cards. If the invited player succeeds in beating the ghost, he takes one of the piles of goods and passes out, when another is invited to play, etc., until all the piles of goods are won. In cases of men, only the men play, and in cases of women, the women only take part in the ceremony. Before the white man came among these Indians and taught them many of his improved vices this game was played by means of figured plum seeds, the men using eight and the women seven seeds, figured as follows and as shown in figure 237. Two seeds are simply blackened on one side [AA], the reverse [aa] containing nothing. Two seeds are black on one side, with a small spot of the color of the seed left in the center [BB], the reverse side [bb] having a black spot in the center, the body being plain. Two seeds have a buffalo's head on one side [C] and the reverse [c] simply two crossed black lines. There is but one seed of this kind in the set used by women. Two seeds have the half of one side blackened and the rest left plain, so as to represent a half-moon [DD]; the reverse [dd]

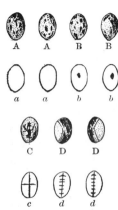

FIG. 237. Plum-stone dice; Wahpeton and Sisseton Dakota Indians, South Dakota; from Yarrow.

has a black longitudinal line crossed at right angles by six small ones. There are six throws whereby the player can win and five that entitle him to another throw. The winning throws are as follows, each winner taking a pile of the ghost's goods:

Two plain ones up, two plain with black spots up, buffalo's head up, and two half-moons up wins a pile. Two plain black ones up, two black with natural spot up, two longitudinally crossed ones up, and the transversely crossed one up wins a pile.

Two plain black ones up, two black with natural spots up, two half-moons up, and the transversely crossed one up wins a pile. Two plain black ones, two black with natural spot up, two half-moons up, and the buffalo's head up wins a pile. Two plain ones up, two with black spots up, two longitudinally crossed ones up, and the transversely crossed one up wins a pile. Two plain ones up, two with black spots up, buffalo's head up, and two long crossed up wins a pile.

The following auxiliary throws entitle to another chance to win: Two plain ones up, two with black spots up, one half-moon up, one longitudinally crossed

---

[a] Mortuary Customs of the North American Indians. First Annual Report of the Bureau of Ethnology, p. 195, 1881.

one up, and buffalo's head up gives another throw, and on this throw, if the two plain ones up and two with black spots with either of the half-moons or buffalo's head up, the player takes a pile. Two plain ones up, two with black spots up, two half-moons up, and the transversely crossed one up entitles to another throw, when, if all the black sides come up excepting one, the throw wins. One of the plain ones up and all the rest with black sides up gives another throw, and the same then turning up wins. One of the plain black ones up with that side up of all the others having the least black on gives another throw, when the same turning up again wins. One half-moon up, with that side up of all the others having the least black on, gives another throw, and if the throw is then duplicated it wins. The eighth seed, used by men, has its place in their game whenever its facings are mentioned above.

The permutations of the winning throws may be indicated as follows: *aa, bb,* c, DD; AA, BB, *c, dd;* AA, BB, *c,* DD; AA, BB, C, DD; *aa, bb, c, dd; aa, bb,* c, *dd.*

DAKOTA (YANKTON). Fort Peck, Montana. (Cat. no. 37604, Free Museum of Science and Art, University of Pennsylvania.)

Set of six plum stones (figure 238), kansu, for playing the game of

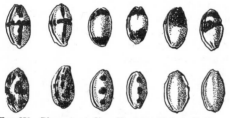

kansukute, plum-stone shooting, marked as follows: One pair marked on one face with a cross, kahdehdega, marked across, reverse black, ata sapa, all black; one pair marked on one face with burnt bands at the end, sanni ska,

FIG. 238. Plum-stone dice; Yankton Dakota Indians, Fort Peck, Montana; cat. no. 37604, Free Museum of Science and Art, University of Pennsylvania.

half white, the reverse, three dots, yamni, threes; one pair marked with two bands near one end, coka, ska, middle white, the reverse plain, ska, white. Collected by the writer in 1900.

The game is played by both men and women. The dice are thrown with the hand. The object is to get a pair uppermost. Bets are made on particular pairs. In old times, when a man died, it was customary to gamble off his property at this game. This was done four or five days after death. The men and women sat in a circle.

———— South Dakota.

George P. Belden [a] says:

They used a kind of dice made of the stones of the wild plum, which grew very plentifully in the deep ravines and canyons a mile or two back from the Missouri river at this point. These stones were first dried hard, then polished by scraping them with a knife. Six were used for the game, four of them being spotted on one side and blank on the opposite, and the other two striped or checked on one side and left blank on the other. These spots and stripes were made on the stones by means of a small iron instrument which they used to paint buffalo robes with. The iron was heated, and the spots and stripes

———————

[a] Belden, the White Chief, edited by Gen. James S. Brisbin, U. S. Army, p. 218, Cincinnati, 1871.

then seared or burnt in the stone. The Indians used a wooden bowl, small and light, for shaking the dice, and never threw them out of the bowl. To play the game they sat on the ground in a circle, and a blanket or robe was doubled up and placed in the middle of the ring—the bowl, containing the six dice, being placed on the folded blanket. The stakes usually were two or four silver earrings, put up by those who engaged in the game, and the sport commenced by some one of the players seizing the edge of the bowl, with his thumb outside and the ends of his forefingers inside the rim, and, raising it an inch or so, bumped it down on the folded blanket three or four times, causing the light plum stones to jump around in the most lively manner. After the player had shaken the bowl thoroughly he sat down and allowed the stones to settle on the bottom, and then they were counted thus: If all the spotted and striped sides were uppermost, the player won, unless some one else tied him; if he threw four spotted ones, it was the same as four aces in cards in the game of bluff; but if he threw three spotted and two striped ones, it was equivalent to a full hand of bluff, and so on, the only difference being that when all the spotted and striped sides were turned up, it showed a higher hand than four aces, and when all the blank sides were turned up it showed a flush that ranked next to the highest hand and above the four aces.

DAKOTA (YANKTONAI). Devils lake, North Dakota. (Cat. no. 23556, 23557, United States National Museum.)

Six plum-stone dice, part of two sets of four each. The designs are burnt, and two—the fourth and fifth—have perforations on both sides (figure 239). Collected by Mr Paul Beckwith in 1876.

The two dice to the left bear a buffalo's head on one side and a pipe or calumet on the reverse. The die on the right has an eagle, or thunderbird, with lightning symbol, on the reverse.

FIG. 239. Plum-stone dice (a, obverse; b, reverse); diameter, about ½ inch: Yanktonai Dakota Indians, North Dakota; cat. no. 23556, 23557, United States National Museum.

————.Devils Lake reservation, North Dakota. (Cat. no. 60369, 60421, Field Columbian Museum.)

Seven plum stones seared on one side (figure 240), and an oblong wooden bowl, with handle, about 14 inches in length.

These were collected by Dr George A. Dorsey, who describes the game as follows:

These are used in the Cut Head [Pabaksa] game of kansu. The dice are plum stones and are seared on one side with various devices, which occur in pairs with an odd stone. The odd stone, with central markings and eight radiating lines, is called echeana, alone; the pair with three parallel lines and seared ends are called okehe, next; the other two pairs are ikcheka, common. To play, the bowl is grasped with two hands and brought down sharply on the ground, so as to cause the dice to jump about. The counts are determined by the character of the upper sides of the dice and are as follows: All marked sides up, sabyaese. black, equal 10; all marked sides down, sakyapese, white. 10; all marked sides down, except alone, 4; all marked sides down, except one, next, 3; all marked sides down, except one, common, 1; all marked sides up, except one, common, 1. This game is played exclusively by women and invariably for stakes.

FIG. 240. Plum-stone dice; Yanktonai Dakota Indians, Devils Lake reservation, North Dakota; cat. no. 60369, Field Columbian Museum.

HIDATSA. North Dakota. (Cat. no. 8425, United States National Museum.)

Set of four bone staves made from cores of elk horn, 8½ inches in length, eleven-sixteenths of an inch in width in middle, and about one-sixteenth of an inch thick; the outer rounded face of the bone marked with lines and dots, filled in with faint red paint, as shown in figure 241, there being two pairs marked alike; the opposite side unmarked and showing texture of bone; ends rounded. Collected by Dr Washington Matthews, U. S. Army, and described as women's gambling instruments.

Doctor Matthews stated in a letter to the writer that these bone staves were not thrown so as to rebound, but gently, ends down, on a blanket.

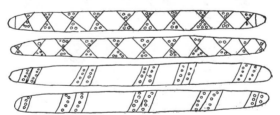

FIG. 241. Bone stick dice; length, 8½ inches; Hidatsa Indians, North Dakota; cat. no. 8425, United States National Museum.

IOWA. Missouri.

Catlin [a] describes a game among the Iowa under the name of konthogra, game of platter.

This is the fascinating game of the women and exclusively their own, played with a number of little blocks of wood the size of a half-crown piece, marked with certain points for counting the game, to be decided by throws, as they are shaken into a bowl and turned out on a sort of pillow. The bets are made after the bowl is turned and decided by the number of points and colors turned.

---

[a] Thomas Donaldson, The George Catlin Indian Gallery. Report of the Smithsonian Institution for 1885, p. 152, 1887.

MANDAN. Fort Berthold, North Dakota. (Cat. no. 8427, United States National Museum.)

Set of five bone dice, with incised designs (figure 242) filled in with red paint, and basket of woven grass (figure 243), 7½ inches in diameter at top and 3 inches deep; with the dice a small clay effigy, 1¼ inches in length, with legs outspread and with arms and head missing (figure 244). Collected by Dr Washington Matthews, U. S. Army.

Catlin[a] mentions the game of the platter among the Mandan.

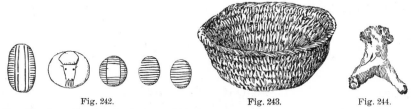

Fig. 242.   Fig. 243.   Fig. 244.

FIG. 242. Bone dice; lengths, 1¼, 1⁵⁄₆, and 1 inch; Mandan Indians, Fort Berthold, North Dakota: cat. no. 8427, United States National Museum.
FIG. 243. Basket for dice; diameter, 7¼ inches; Mandan Indians, Fort Berthold, North Dakota: cat. no. 8427, United States National Museum.
FIG. 244. Clay fetich used with dice; length, 1¼ inches; Mandan Indians, Fort Berthold, North Dakota; cat. no. 8427, United States National Museum.

OMAHA. Nebraska.

Dr J. Owen Dorsey[b] gives the following account under the name of plum-stone shooting, kaⁿ'-si kide:[c]

Five plum stones are provided, three of which are marked on one side only with a greater or smaller number of black dots or lines and two of them are marked on both sides; they are, however, sometimes made of bone of a rounded or flattened form, somewhat like an orbicular button-mold, the dots in this case being impressed. A wide dish and a certain number of small sticks by the way of counters are also provided. Any number of persons may play this game, and agreeably to the number engaged in it, is the quantity of sticks or counters. The plum stones or bones are placed in a dish, and a throw is made by simply jolting the vessel against the ground to make the seeds or bones rebound, and they are counted as they lie when they fall. The party plays around for the first throw. Whoever gains all the sticks in the course of the game wins the stake. The throws succeed each other with so much rapidity that we vainly endeavor to observe their laws of computation, which it was the sole business of an assistant to attend to. The seeds used in this game are called kaⁿ'-si gĕ. Their number varies. Among the Ponkas and Omahas, only five are used, while the Otos play with six. Sometimes four are marked alike, and the fifth is black or white (unmarked). Generally three are black

---

[a] Letters and Notes on the Manners, Customs, and Condition of the North American Indians, p. 147, Philadelphia, 1860.

[b] Omaha Sociology. Third Annual Report of the Bureau of Ethnology, p. 334, 1884.

[c] Miss Alice C. Fletcher gives me the name of the game as gkon'-thi. Gkon is the first syllable of the word gkon'-de, plum; thi means seed. The game is described by Major S. H. Long (Account of an Expedition from Pittsburgh to the Rocky Mountains, v. 1, p. 216, Philadelphia, 1822) under the name of kon-se-ke-da.

on one side, and white or unmarked on the other, while two have each a star on one side and a moon on the other. The players must always be of the same sex and class; that is, men must play with men, youths with youths, and women with women. There must always be an even number of players, not more than two on each side. There are about twenty sticks used as counters. These are made of deska or of some other grass. The seeds are put into a bowl, which is hit against a pillow and not on the bare ground, lest it should break the bowl. When three seeds show black and two have the moon on the upper

FIG. 245. Plum-stone dice (*a*, obverse; *b*, reverse); diameter, ¼ inch; Omaha Indians, Nebraska; cat. no. IV B 2228, Berlin Museum für Völkerkunde.

side it is a winning throw; but when one is white, one black, the third black (or white), the fourth showing a moon, and the fifth a star, it is a losing throw. The game is played for small stakes, such as rings and necklaces.

Figure 245 represents a set of plum stones from the Omaha, collected by Miss Alice C. Fletcher. Two have a star on one side and a crescent moon on the other, the device being in white on a burnt ground, and three are white or plain on one side and black on the other. They are accompanied by a hemispherical bowl made of walnut, 12 inches in diameter, of perfect form and finish, and by about one hundred slips of the stalks of the blue-joint grass, about 12 inches in length, used as counters.

OSAGE. Missouri and Arkansas.

John D. Hunter [a] says:

In common, they merely burn on one side a few grains of corn or pumpkin seeds, which the stakers alternately throw up for a succession of times, or till one arrives at a given number first; that is, counting those only that show of the requisite color when he wins.

A very similar game is played with small flat pieces of wood or bone, on one side of which are notched or burnt a greater or less number of marks, like the individual faces of a die. It is played and counted like the preceding.

FIG. 246. Brass dice; Osage Indians, Oklahoma; cat. no. 59097, Field Columbian Museum.

———— Osage reservation, Oklahoma. (Cat. no. 59097, Field Columbian Museum.)

Six dice, heads of small brass tacks (figure 246), one with a hole punched through the center, all with the inside painted red; diameter, one-fourth of an inch; accompanied by a flat wooden bowl, 9½ inches in diameter. Collected by Dr George A. Dorsey.

PONCA. Nebraska.

According to a Ponca legend published by Dr J. Owen Dorsey,[b] the plum-stone game was invented by Ukiaba, a tribal hero of the

---

[a] Manners and Customs of Several Indian Tribes Located West of the Mississippi, p. 276, Philadelphia, 1823.

[b] The Ƈegiha Language. Contributions to North American Ethnology, v. 6, p. 617, Washington, 1890.

Ponca, who sent five plum stones to a young woman whom he secured by magical arts, afterward telling her: "Keep the plum stones for gambling. You shall always win."

WINNEBAGO. Black River Falls, Wisconsin. (Cat. no. 22157, Free Museum of Science and Art, University of Pennsylvania.)

Wooden bowl, highly polished with use, 9½ inches in diameter, and eight bone disks, five-eighths of an inch in diameter, one side smooth and white, the other stained dark blue (figure 247). Collected by Mr T. R. Roddy.

FIG. 247. Bone dice; diameter, ⅝ inch: Winnebago Indians, Wisconsin; cat. no. 22157, Free Museum of Science and Art, University of Pennsylvania.

—— Prairie du Chien, Wisconsin. Caleb Atwater [a] says:

The women play a game among themselves, using pieces of bone about the size and which have the appearance of a common button mold. They are so cut out that one side is blackish and the other white. A considerable number of these button molds are placed in a small wooden bowl and thrown up in it a certain number of times, when the white sides up are counted.

SKITTAGETAN STOCK

HAIDA. Skidegate, Queen Charlotte islands, British Columbia.

Dr C. F. Newcombe states that this tribe have the chair-shaped dice figured among the Kwakiutl and Tlingit and gives the following account of the game, obtained in 1901, under the name of gadegan:

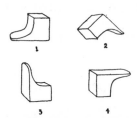

FIG. 248. Positions of die in winning throws; Haida Indians, British Columbia; from sketch by Dr C. F. Newcombe.

Ten counters of slips of wood or of long bones of birds are placed between two players. The first throw in the game is won by the player who scores the highest in the preliminary throwing, which continues until the advantage is gained in the alternate play.

Scoring.—The following are the winning positions [figure 248]: Supine (1), scores 1; prone (2), with the back and under surface uppermost; erect (3), or natural position of a chair, 2; resting on the front edge (4), back uppermost, 4.

Losing positions.—If the die falls and remains on either side. The player continues to throw until the die falls on its side. Until the pot is exhausted winners draw counters from it, and afterward from their opponent's pile. The game goes on until one player has won all the counters. Men and women play indifferently.

---

[a] Remarks Made on a Tour to Prairie du Chien, p. 117, Columbus, 1831.

HAIDA. British Columbia.

Dr J. R. Swanton [a] describes the throwing game:

The Haida name for this game (gu′tgi q!ā′atagañ) means literally "they throw the q!ā′atagaño, 'thing thrown up,' to each other." The "thing thrown up," figure 5 [Swanton], was a piece of wood, bone, or ivory, about 3 inches high, with a base measuring, say, 1½ by 1¼ inches, and most of the upper part cut away, leaving a thin flange extending upward on one side. It was held by the thin flange, with the thicker part up, and flipped over and over. If it fell upon either side, called q!ā′dagaño, marked o in figure 5 [Swanton], the opponent took it; if on the long flat side, or on the concave side, it counted the one who threw it 1; if on the bottom, 2; or if on the smallest side, 4, as indicated in the figure. The game was usually played at camp, in the smokehouse, and the winner had the privilege of smearing the looser's face with soot. It may be played by two or more, each for himself or by sides.

TANOAN STOCK

TEWA. Hano, Arizona. (Cat. no 38618, Free Museum of Science and Art, University of Pennsylvania.)

Three wooden blocks, 4½ inches long and 1½ inches wide, painted black

on one side and plain on the other (figure 249). Collected by the writer in 1901.

They are called chi-ti, and are counted around a circle of forty stones laid on the ground and having an opening after every ten. The counts are as follows: Three white count 10; three black, 5; two black, 3; one black, 2.

FIG. 249. Stick dice; length, 4¼ inches; Tewa Indians, Hano, Arizona; cat. no. 38618, Free Museum of Science and Art, University of Pennsylvania.

Mr A. M. Stephen, in an unpublished manuscript, gives edehti as the Tewa name of a seldom-played man's game corresponding with the Navaho woman's game of tsittilc.

TIGUA. Isleta, New Mexico. (Cat. no. 22726, Free Museum of Science and Art, University of Pennsylvania.)

Two sets of three sticks each (figure 250), halves of twigs, flat on one side, and rounded, with inner bark on the other; length, 4½ inches. Collected by the writer in 1902.

One stick in one of the sets has eleven diagonal notches across the rounded side. In the other set all the sticks are plain. They are used as dice in the game of patol.

An Isleta boy, J. Crecencio Lucero, described to the writer the people of this pueblo as playing the game of patol, which they call in their own language cuwee, with three sticks, puo, counting around a circle of stones, hio.

[a] Contributions to the Ethnology of the Haida. Memoirs of the American Museum of Natural History, whole series, v. 8, pt. 1, p. 59, New York, 1905.

Mr Charles F. Lummis [a] gives the following account of the game in Isleta:

The boys gather forty smooth stones, the size of the fist, and arrange them in a circle about 3 feet in diameter. Between every tenth and eleventh stone is a gate of 4 or 5 inches. These gates are called p'áy-hlah rivers. In the center of the circle, pa-tól náht-heh, pa-tol house, is placed a large cobblestone, smooth and approximately flat on top, called hyee-oh-tee-áy. There is your pa-tol ground.

The pa-tol sticks, which are the most important part of the paraphernalia, are three in number. Sometimes they are made by splitting from dry branches, and sometimes by whittling from a solid block. The chief essential is that the wood be firm and hard. The sticks are 4 to 5 inches long, about an inch wide, and a quarter of an inch thick, and must

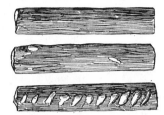

FIG. 250. Stick dice; length, 4½ inches; Tigua Indians, Isleta, New Mexico; cat. no. 22726, Free Museum of Science and Art, University of Pennsylvania.

have their sides flat, so that the three may be clasped together very much as one holds a pen, but more nearly perpendicular, with the thumb and first three fingers of the right hand. Each stick is plain on one side and marked on the other, generally with diagonal notches, as shown in figure [251].

The only other requisite is a kah-níd-deh, horse, for each player, of whom there may be as many as can seat themselves around the pa-tol house. The horse is merely a twig or stick used as a marker. When the players have seated themselves, the first takes the pa-tol sticks tightly in his right hand, lifts them about as high as his chin, and, bringing them down with a smart vertical thrust, as if to harpoon the center stone, lets go of them when they are within some 6 inches of it. The three sticks strike the stone as one, hitting on their ends squarely, and, rebounding several inches, fall back into the circle. The manner in which they fall decides the denomination of the throw, and the different values are shown in figure [251]. Although at first flush this might seem to make it a game of chance, nothing could be farther from the truth. Indeed, no really aboriginal game is a true game of chance; the invention of that dangerous and delusive plaything was reserved for civilized ingenuity.

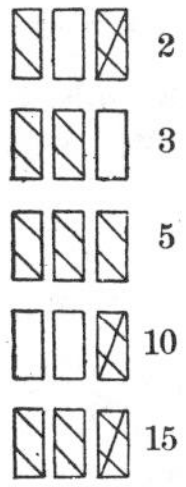

FIG. 251. Counts in stick dice; Tigua Indians, Isleta, New Mexico; from Lummis.

An expert pa-tol player will throw the number he desires with almost unfailing certainty by his arrangement of the sticks in his hand and the manner and force with which he strikes them down. It is a dexterity which anyone may acquire by sufficient practice, and only thus. The five throw is deemed very much the hardest of all, and I have certainly found it so.

According to the number of his throw the player moves his marker an equal number of stones ahead on the circle, using one of the rivers as a starting point. If the throw is five, for instance, he lays his horse between the fourth and fifth stones, and hands the pa-tol sticks to the next man. If his throw be ten, however, as the first man's first throw is very certain to be, it lands his horse in the second river, and he has another throw. The second man may make his starting point the same or another river, and may elect to run his

[a] A New Mexico David, p. 184, New York, 1891.

horse around the circle in the same direction that the first is going or in the opposite. If in the same direction, he will do his best to make a throw which will bring his horse into the same notch as that of the first man, in which case the first man is killed and has to take his horse back to the starting point, to try over again when he gets another turn. In case the second man starts in the opposite direction—which he will not do unless an expert player—he has to calculate with a good deal of skill for the meeting, to kill and to avoid being killed by the first player. When he starts in the same direction, he is behind, and runs no chance of being killed, while he has just as good a chance to kill. But if, even then, a high throw carries him ahead of the first man—for jumping does not count either way, the only killing being when two horses come in the same notch—his rear is in danger, and he will try to run on out of the way of his pursuer as fast as possible. The more players the more complicated the game, for each horse is threatened alike by foes that chase from behind and charge from before, and the most skillful player is liable to be sent back to the starting point several times before the game is finished, which is as soon as one horse has made the complete circuit. Sometimes the players, when very young or unskilled, agree there shall be no killing; but unless there is an explicit arrangement to that effect, killing is understood, and it adds greatly to the interest of the game.

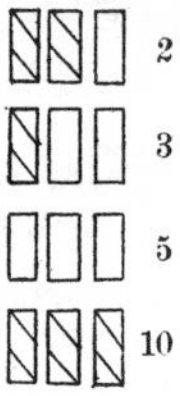

FIG. 252. Counts in stick dice; Tigua Indians, Isleta, New Mexico; from Lummis.

There is also another variation of the game—a rare one, however. In case the players agree to throw fifteens, all the pa-tol sticks are made the same, except that one has an extra notch to distinguish it from the others. Then the throws are as shown in figure [252].

In reply to a letter of inquiry, Mr Lummis wrote me that he distinctly remembers having witnessed this game at Isleta, Santa Clara, San Ildefonso, Tesuque, and Taos (Tanoan); at Acoma, Titsiama, and Cañada Cruz (Acoma colonies), Cochiti, Laguna, El Rito, Sandia, Santo Domingo, and San Felipe (Keresan); and at Zuñi.

I feel quite confident I saw it also in San Juan (Tanoan), though of that I would not be positive. I can not remember seeing the game played in Jemez, Picuris, and Pojoaque (Tanoan); in Sia (Keresan) or any of the Moqui pueblos except Hano (which of course is a village of migration from the Rio Grande). In Nambe (Tanoan) I never saw it, I am sure.

TEWA. Nambe, New Mexico. (Cat. no. 17773, 17774, Field Columbian Museum.)

Set of stick dice, three pieces of split twig, 3⅜ inches in length, one side rounded and the other flat; one of the round sides marked with fifteen notches (figure 253). Collected by Mr L. M. Lampson.

There are two sets, one having the bark left on the back; on the other it is removed. The game is described under the name of tugea, or patol:

This game is played by two or more persons. Forty small stones are laid in a circle with a space or gate between each group of ten. The players throw the billets perpendicularly upon a stone, the surfaces falling uppermost determining the count. One flat and one notched round side up count 1; two flat and one notched round side up, 3; three flat sides up, 5; three round sides up, 10; two flat and notched stick up, 15. When the count is 10 or 15, the player is entitled to another throw. Each player is provided with a small stick for a counter. This is called a horse. All players start from the same place and move their horses forward between the stones according to their score, in the same or opposite directions, as they choose. If one player scores so that his counter comes to a place occupied by the counter of a previous player, the first player must remove his counter or horse and start again, except it be in one of the spaces or gates which may be occupied by two or more horses at the same time. The one who first moves his counter completely round the circle is the winner.

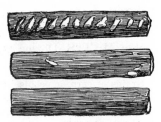

FIG. 253. Stick dice; length, 3⅛ inches; Tewa Indians, Nambe, New Mexico; cat. no. 17774, Field Columbian Museum.

TEWA. Santa Clara, New Mexico. (Cat. no. 60359, Field Columbian Museum.)

Four sticks (figure 254), 4¼ inches in length, one side flat and unmarked and the other round with bark on, two of the rounded sides with incised marks.

They were collected by Mr W. C. B. Biddle, who describes the game as follows:

This game is played with four short two-faced lots, two of which bear special markings on the obverse side. In playing the game forty small pebbles are placed on the ground in the form of a hollow square. Two small sticks or feathers, to be used later on as markers, are placed at the opening in one corner. In the center of the square is a flat stone or inverted cup.

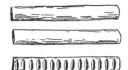

FIG. 254. Stick dice; length, 4¼ inches; Tewa Indians, Santa Clara, New Mexico; cat. no. 60359, Field Columbian Museum.

The game begins by one of the players taking the four staves in hand and casting them on one end on the stone or cup. The count is determined by the character of the uppermost side of the staves, and is as follows: All flat sides down count 10; all round sides down, 5; two flat sides down, 3. In registering the count the counting stick is moved about the stone circuit according to the value of the throw.

The game is ended when one of the counting sticks has made the entire circuit.

———— Santa Clara, New Mexico. (Cat. no. 176707, United States National Museum.)

Set of three blocks of wood, 5¼ inches in length, 1 inch in breadth, and three-eighths of an inch in thickness (figure 255); flat and painted red on one side; the opposite side rounded and painted reddish brown.

One stick has fifteen transverse notches painted green on the rounded side. The notches are divided by an incised cross painted yellow.[a]

The following account of the game, from a manuscript by the collector, Mr T. S. Dozier, was kindly placed in my hands by Mr F. W. Hodge:

Grains of corn or pebbles are laid in the form of a square, in sections of ten each. The two players sit on either side. The sticks, called é-pfe, are thrown in turn on a stone placed in the square. The counts are as follows: Two flat and notched sticks, notches up, count 15; three round sides up, 10; three flat sides up, 5; two flat and one round side, not notched, up, 3; one flat and two round sides, not notched, up, 1.

The players move their markers between the grains or pebbles according to their throw, going in opposite directions. The one first returning to the starting point wins. This is the ordinary way. Sometimes, the markers being con-

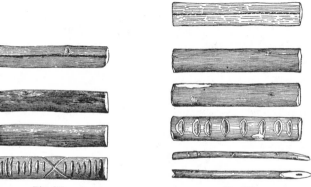

Fig. 255   Fig. 256.

FIG. 255. Stick dice; length, 5¼ inches; Tewa Indians, Santa Clara, New Mexico; cat. no. 176707, United States National Museum.

FIG. 256. Stick dice and marking sticks; lengths, 4¼ and 4⅛ inches; Tigua Indians, Taos, New Mexico; cat. no. 20123, Free Museum of Science and Art, University of Pennsylvania.

sidered as horses, a player will attempt to kill his adversary's horses. In this case he so announces at the commencement of the game, and he then moves his marker in the same direction, and, by duplicating the first throw, or, if at any future stage of the game, always following, he succeeds in placing his marker where his adversary's is, by so doing he kills that horse (marker) and sends him back to the place of beginning. The latter may then elect to move in the same direction as before and kill and send back his adversary, but, if he wishes, he may go in the opposite direction, in which case he does no killing. The game is called tugĭ-é-pfĕ, meaning the thrown stick (tugi, to throw).

Mr Dozier states that the stick with fifteen notches gives rise to the Mexican name of quince (fifteen), which is sometimes given its Tewa equivalent of tadipwa nopfe, and juego de pastor, shepherd's game.

[a] Another set, collected by Mr T. S. Dozier, in the Free Museum of Science and Art of the University of Pennsylvania (cat. no. 20153), has the notches painted green, red, yellow, and blue, and the cross red. These marks appear to imitate wrappings of cord of different colors.

TIGUA. Taos, New Mexico. (Cat. no. 20123, Free Museum of Science and Art, University of Pennsylvania.)

Set of three sticks, 4¼ inches in length, three-fourths of an inch broad, and six-sixteenths of an inch thick (figure 256), one side round, with bark, and the other flat.

One of the sticks has eight transverse cuts on the bark side, as shown in the figure, with the opposite flat side smeared with red paint. They are accompanied by two twigs, 4¾ inches in length, with sharpened ends, one having two nicks cut near one end to distinguish it.

These objects are employed in the game of caseheapana (Spanish, pastor), of which the collector, Dr T. P. Martin, of Taos, has furnished the following account:

A circle, from 2 to 3 feet in diameter [figure 257], is marked on the ground with small stones. One hundred and sixty stones are used, with larger ones at each quarter, dividing the circle into four quarters of forty stones each. A line AB is marked out as a river, and is usually marked from east to west. The line CD is designated as a trail. A large stone is placed in the center.

There are two players, each of whom takes one of the little twigs, which are known as horses. A player takes the three stones, holds them together, and drops them vertically upon the large stone. He counts according to their fall, and moves his horse as many places around the circuit. They throw and move in turn, going in opposite directions, one starting from K and the other from M. If M passes point B before K reaches it, and meets K's horse anywhere around

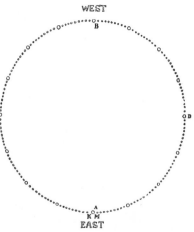

FIG. 257. Circuit for stick dice; Tigua Indians, Taos, New Mexico; from sketch by Dr T. P. Martin.

the circle, K's horse is said to be killed, and has to go back to A and start over again, and vice versa. A chief point in the game is to reach B before the other player, so as to kill him on the second half of the circle.

The counts are as follows: Two flat and notched sticks, notches up, count 15; three round sides up, 10; three flat sides up, 5; two flat and one round side, not notched, up, 1; one flat and two round sides, not notched, up, 1.

This game is usually played all night on the night of November 3 of each year. November 3 is known as "the day of the dead," and this game seems in some way to be connected with it, or rather with its celebration, but I can not find out any tradition connecting the two.

WAKASHAN STOCK

CLAYOQUOT. West coast of Vancouver island, British Columbia. (Cat. no. $\frac{16}{2014}$, American Museum of Natural History.) Set of four beaver-teeth dice, two with dots and two with crossed lines (figure 258). Collected by Mr F. Jacobsen in 1897.

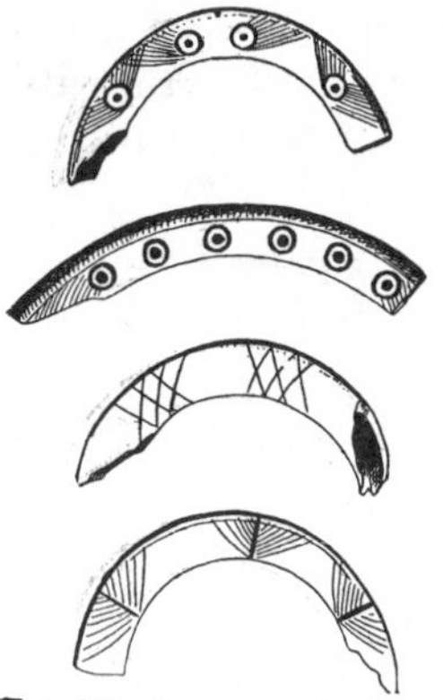

One pair with circular designs are called the women and the other pair with straight lines the men. The one man with the more elaborate designs is trump. Ten counters are placed between the players, one of whom tosses the dice; when two men or two women fall face up he wins one counter; when the trump falls face up and all the others face down, or vice versa, he wins two counters. The game is won by the player who gets all the counters.

Dr C. F. Newcombe writes:

In this game the Clayoquot mark two of the teeth with circular dots, o o o, and two with incised cross lines, x x x or # # #.

FIG. 258. Beaver-teeth dice; length, 2 to 2½ inches; Clayoquot Indians, Vancouver island, British Columbia; cat. no. $\frac{16}{2014}$, American Museum of Natural History.

One of the dotted teeth is also marked by a circular black band, and this is called the man, and the other the woman.

Of the incised teeth, the one with more definite or stronger marks is the man, and the other the woman.

The game is called A. isyEk. No specimens were seen, but the information was obtained from "Annie," the daughter of Atliu, a well-known chief of the tribe.

KWAKIUTL. Dsawadi, Knight's inlet, British Columbia.

Dr C. F. Newcombe describes the beaver-tooth dice game at this place under the name of midale. They say it came from the Stick Indians (Tahlkan). It is now obsolete. It was a woman's gambling game. When all four come up alike they count 2.

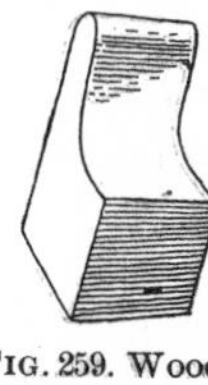

—— Vancouver island, British Columbia.

Dr Franz Boas [a] describes these Indians as using wooden dice (figure 259) in a game called eibayu. "The casts count according to the narrowness of the sides." The dice collected by him were in the World's Columbian Exposition.

FIG. 259. Wooden die; Kwakiutl Indians, British Columbia; from Boas.

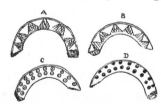

FIG. 260. Beaver-teeth dice; length, 2 to 2½ inches; Makah Indians, Neah bay, Washington; cat. no. 23351, United States National Museum.

[a] Sixth Report on the Indians of British Columbia. Report of the Sixty-sixth Meeting of the British Association for the Advancement of Science, p. 578, London, 1896.

Dr C. F. Newcombe informs me that after very careful inquiry he is unable to find this game among the Kwakiutl. The name eibayu is similar to libaiu, that of the stick game.

MAKAH. Neah bay, Washington. (Cat. no. 23351, United States National Museum.)

Seven beaver teeth, probably part of two or more sets. Two, right and left, apparently from the same animal, are similarly marked on the flat side with chevron pattern (figure 260, *a*, *b*).

Two, also apparently from the same animal, are marked with circles and dots (figure 260 *c*, *d*). Two teeth, right and left, are marked with three chevrons, and one odd tooth has ten circles.

The following account of the game is given by the collector, Mr J. G. Swan:[a]

Four teeth are used; one side of each has marks and the other is plain. If all four marked sides come up or all four plain sides, the throws form a double; if two marked and two plain ones come up, it is a single; uneven numbers lose.

He states also that this game is usually played by the women, and that the beaver teeth are shaken in the hand and thrown down.[b]

——— Neah bay, Washington. (Cat. no. 37378, Free Museum of Science and Art, University of Pennsylvania.)

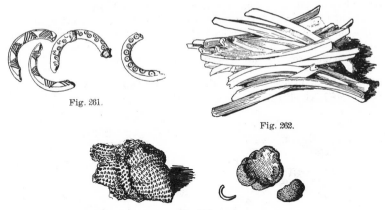

Fig. 261.

Fig. 262.

Fig. 263.

FIG. 261. Beaver-teeth dice; length, 2 inches; Makah Indians, Washington; cat. no. 37378, Free Museum of Science and Art, University of Pennsylvania.

FIG. 262. Counters for beaver-teeth dice; length, 4½ inches; Makah Indians, Washington; cat. no. 37378, Free Museum of Science and Art, University of Pennsylvania.

FIG. 263. Charm used with beaver-teeth dice; Makah Indians, Washington; cat. no. 37378, Free Museum of Science and Art, University of Pennsylvania.

Four beaver-teeth dice (figure 261), two with incised chevrons on one side and two with circles with center dot; reverses plain;

---

[a] The Indians of Cape Flattery. Smithsonian Contributions to Knowledge, n. 220, p. 44, 1870.

[b] The Northwest Coast, or Three Years' Residence in Washington Territory, p. 158, New York, 1857.

length, 2 inches. One tooth, marked with circles, is tied with a string around the middle.

Thirty small bones (figure 262), 4½ inches in length, accompany the dice as counters, katsaiac. Collected by the writer in 1900.

The set is contained in a cotton-cloth bag, in which also was the charm (figure 263), or medicine, koi, used to secure success. This consists of a dried fungus, which is rubbed on the hands, and the tooth of a small rodent.

Dr George A. Dorsey [a] describes the following game:

Ehis This is the well-known game of the beaver-teeth dice, and is played by women throughout the extent of the Northwest Territory. Of this game three sets were collected, one of which is imperfect. There are four teeth in each full set, two of which, usually the lower, are decorated with incised lines, chihlichicotl, which refer merely to the markings. The other pair are variously decorated with a single row of circles or circles arranged in groups. These are known as culkotlith, dotted teeth. In two of the sets, one of the dotted dice is further distinguished by means of a band of black yarn about the center. This is known as quisquis, or snow. The teeth are thrown from the hand upon the ground or upon a blanket. When the marked sides of all four teeth lie uppermost the count is 2 and is known as dhabas or all down. When the four plain sides lie uppermost the count is also 2 and is known as tascoas or without marks. When the two dotted dice fall face down, and the cross-hatch dice fall face uppermost, then the count is 1, chilitchcoas or cross-hatch dice up. The exact reverse of this also counts 1, and is known as kulcocoas or dots down. When one of the teeth is further distinguished by being wrapped with a black band the count is somewhat different: all the marked sides uppermost, counting 4; while the wrapped tooth up with three blank teeth, count 4, also. The remaining counts are as before described.

NOOTKA. Vancouver island, British Columbia. (Cat. no. IV A 1487, Berlin Museum für Völkerkunde.)

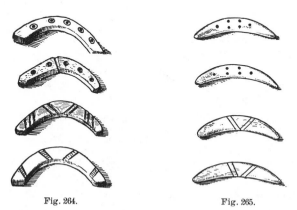

Fig. 264.   Fig. 265.

FIG. 264. Bone dice; length, 2 inches; Nootka Indians, Vancouver island, British Columbia; cat. no. IV A 1487, Berlin Museum für Völkerkunde.
FIG. 265. Bone dice; length, 1⅜ inches; Nootka Indians, Vancouver island, British Columbia; cat. no. IV A 1487, Berlin Museum für Völkerkunde.

---

[a] Games of the Makah Indians of Neah Bay. The American Antiquarian, v. 23, p. 72, 1901.

Set of four flat curved pieces of bone, 2 inches in length, imitations in form of beaver teeth; two marked on one side with spots and two with chevrons (figure 264), the opposite sides plain. Collected by Mr Samuel Jacobsen.

It is described by the collector under the name of todjik as a woman's game. The counts are as follows: Four marked sides up count 2; four blank sides up, 2; two hole sides and 2 blank up, 1; one hole side and three blank up, 0; two line sides and two blank up, 2; two line sides, one blank, and one hole side up, 4. The game is played on blankets, the count being kept with small sticks.

Another set of four flat curved bone dice (figure 265), 1⅛ inches in length, similar to the preceding, but with pointed ends, is included under the same number.

WASHOAN STOCK

WASHO. Carson valley and Lake Tahoe, Nevada.

Dr J. W. Hudson describes the following game played by women:

Twelve small sticks, 4 inches long by three-eighths of an inch wide, of split willow (*Salix agrifolia*), bent, and painted red on the flat side, are cast up and caught in a winnowing basket. The counts are as follows: All red up count 6; two red up, 1; one red up, 2; all plain up, 6.

The sticks are called itpawkaw, the game, pokowa, and the pebble counters, dtek, "stones."

WEITSPEKAN STOCK

YUROK. Hupa Valley reservation, California.

Dr Pliny E. Goddard gave me the Yurok name of the shell dice used by the Hupa Indians as tekgorpos.

WISHOSKAN STOCK

BATAWAT. Blue Lake, California.

An Indian of this tribe who was interrogated by the writer at Blue Lake in 1900 recognized the shell dice (figure 91) which he had collected in Hupa valley and gave the name as goplauwat; large dice, docted; small dice, koshshop; concave sides, tsusarik; convex sides, bokshowarish.

YUMAN STOCK

COCOPA. Sonora, Mexico. (Cat. no. 76165, United States National Museum.)

Set of four sticks of willow [a] wood, 8 inches long, about 1¼ inches broad, and one-half inch thick (figure 266). Flat on one

---

[a] *Salix amygdaloides.*

side, which is uniformly marked lengthwise in the center with a band of red paint about one-half inch in width; opposite side rounded and unpainted. Collected by Dr Edward Palmer.

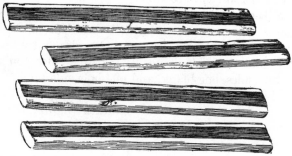

FIG. 266. Stick dice; length, 8 inches; Cocopa Indians, Sonora, Mexico; cat. no. 76165, United States National Museum.

HAVASUPAI. Arizona.

Mr G. Wharton James has furnished the writer an account of the following game (figure 267) :

Squatted around a circle of small stones, the circle having an opening at a certain portion of its circumference called the yam-se-kyalb-ye-ka, and a large flat stone in the center called taä-be-che-ka, the Havasupai play the game called hue-ta-quee-che-ka. Any number of players can engage in the game.

FIG. 267. Havasupai Indian girls playing stick dice; Arizona; from photograph by Mr G. Wharton James.

The players are chosen into sides. The first player begins the game by holding in his hand three pieces of short stick, white on one side and red on the other. These sticks are called toh-be-ya, and take the place of our dice. They are flung rapidly upon the central stone, taä-be-che-ka, and as they fall counts are made as follows: Three whites up count 10; two whites, one red up, 2; two reds, one white up, 3; three reds, 5. Tallies are kept by placing short sticks between the stones, hue, that compose the circle, one side counting in one direction from the opening and the other keeping tally in the opposite direction.

MARICOPA. Arizona. (Cat. no. 2926, Brooklyn Institute Museum.) Four sticks (figure 268), 7 inches in length, one side flat and painted red, and the other rounded. Collected in 1904 by Mr Louis L. Meeker.

The collector describes the game under the name of kainsish:

A joint of cane quartered will serve instead of the sticks. The four flat sides up count 1; the four round sides up count 2; the other throws, nothing, though sometimes they have values agreed upon also. The count is made by marking in the dust. The game is for 6 points, or as many as are agreed upon.

FIG. 268. Stick dice; length, 7 inches; Maricopa Indians, Arizona; cat. no. 2926, Brooklyn Institute Museum.

The following abstract of Maricopa mythology, furnished by Mr Meeker, refers to the game with four sticks:

Table of generations

I. First principles:
  Females: Mat, the Earth
      Hlash, the Moon
  Males: Hyaish, the Sky
      Hlash, the Sun
II. Offspring (originally hermaphrodites):
  (1) Terrestrial (of the Earth by the Sky)
    Kokmat, mud
    Kokmat hairk, his brother
  (2) Celestial (of the Moon by the Sun)
    Hatelowish epash, Coyote man
    Quokosh epash, Fox man

Our man in the moon is Hatelowish, or Quokosh. The Brother seems to have been the first handiwork of Hatelowish epash. He is also identified with the Spider Woman, who spun the web on which the earth was deposited.

Once, when there was yet no earth, a whirlwind came down out of the sky into the turbid water, and they were man and wife.

Twins came. Winds carried them about during their long infancy, childhood, and early manhood.

At length the elder changed the other into a spider and sent him to stretch webs north and south, east and west, and between points. Then a close web was woven outward from the center, where the lines crossed. On this plant the earth was built of sediment deposited by the water. The elder brother then shaped the earth. The sky was so close the sun soon dried and cracked it up into mountain ridges and deep canyons. So he put up his hand and pushed the sky away to its present position. There are five stars where his fingers touched the sky. They are called the hand of God. Then he went about making green things grow, shaping what came forth after subsequent whirlwinds into living things and men and women, teaching these how to build houses, and making the earth fit for them to live upon. So his Pima name is Earth Doctor (Che-o-tma'-ka).[a]

The Brother, ceasing to be a spider, followed and imitated Earth Doctor. Using common clay, he bungled so that misshapen animals were all that he could make.

The man he formed had the palm of his hand extending out to the end of his fingers. Earth Doctor rebuked him, so he threw it down hard against the surface of the water and it swam off in the form of a duck, with a web foot and a very flat breast.

Others were so bad he threw them up against the sky, and they remain there. One of these is Gopher (Pleiades); one is Mountain Sheep (Orion), farther east, and one is the Scorpion of five stars,[b] three in the body and one for each claw, whose place is west of the Gopher. These go in the sun's path. When the Gopher and the Mountain Sheep are east, the Scorpion is west; but when the Gopher and Mountain Sheep are in the west, the Hand is east. Now all the things that were made then were of the first generation. The first flood came because the Brother made so much trouble and claimed to have more power than Earth Doctor, who at length drove him off the earth.

Changing again to a spider, he took refuge in the sky, across which he spun the web of the milky way. Earth Doctor took water into his mouth and spurted it upward at the Spider, but it fell in a spray and remained on the web making a river of the milky way. He took dust in a pouch, and, jerking it, tried to make it go into Spider's eyes. The dust made a road and banks along the river, but some fell in Spider's eyes. Observing that water did not injure him, even when Earth Doctor took handfuls and sprinkled the sky with stars of snow and ice, and also that earth, even in the form of dust, did injure him, Spider tried his own power over the water, calling upon it to rise up and wash away the earth.

The waters rose, washing away all except the mountains and the representative races and animals that took refuge there. A truce was called; it was agreed that Earth Doctor should have power over the earth, the Brother over water. The sun's reflection in water was dipped up with the hand and cast toward the sky, and the flood subsided.[c]

From the mountains that stood, a stronger earth was built. The broken web was mended with strong ropes made of yucca fibers. Eagle feathers were set up around the border. Remnants of the first generation were gathered up, and the second generation began.

In the meantime the Sun, who is a male, had observed what was done by the Sky upon the maiden world of turbid water and visited the Moon in like manner. The Moon's twins were Coyote and his companion the Fox.

When the road and river were complete across the sky along the milky way, Coyote and his companion came down upon the earth. Whatever Earth Doctor did the Coyote imitated, bungling his work as the Brother had done, until at length there was strife again.

---

[a] He is known in Maricopa as Kokmat, which may mean mud or middle earth.

[b] As this constellation rises in the east about August, the three stars of the body are nearly horizontal. The two claws point toward the south, upward and downward.

[c] When a rain doctor wants the rain to cease he still does the same. It is obvious that there must first be a rift in the clouds to get the sun's reflection.

The Brother met Coyote and called him brother, but Coyote would not reply. So a flood was sent to destroy Coyote and the earth and all its inhabitants. Small numbers were saved by clinging to trunks of trees that floated on the water. Coyote insisted the Brother should address him as Elder Brother. This was conceded. Coyote made a ball of mud from the root of the tree on which he floated. He stuck in a bunch of grass from the bill of the duck the Brother had made. This he cast upon the water to be the nucleus of a new world, and the flood subsided.

Then Earth Doctor proceeded to construct the third generation. Coyote helped, or rather hindered. His companion, Fox, made trouble by pranks of his own.

Men increased rapidly. They had no diseases. There were no wars. The few deaths were from snake bites or accidents. The earth was crowded. There was not food for all.

Some killed little children for food. One especially had from girlhood a voracious appetite; as a woman she went from village to village, prowling about houses and carrying off children for food. She had eaten the flesh of all animals and the children of all tribes. A council was held in the skies. The seats of those who were there are in a circle.[a] They agreed to have the great flood, so there would not be too many people.

The cannibal woman was bound and carried away. She was burned alive; all kinds of wood were used for fuel, and the flames were fed seven years. The ashes were then collected, mixed with meal made of all kinds of seeds, and the whole was put into an earthen jar for the seed of the fourth generation.

The flood that followed continued for four years. The Brother, as Spider, sat on the northern end of the milky way[b] opposite Coyote (the Dipper), who tended his fish net, fastened to the immovable star. Coyote's companion, intent upon some prank, ran along the milky way toward the south and fell off, where he may be seen as six stars[c] arranged like the seven stars that represent Coyote. He is generally seen with his head lower than his tail. But when the Moon is full she takes him in her lap, and we can see him there as Rabbit (man in the moon).

Earth Doctor took his seat at the end of the milky way that is south,[d] on the western side, opposite Fox. Only his head may be seen. It is very large and grand. His face is looking toward the west. The lower end of his long braid of hair is in the milky way. When "the moon is dead" and stars are thick two eagle feathers may be seen in his hair, each composed of three very small stars in a row.

The vessel containing the seed of future generations floated upon the water, and, as the waters subsided, touched ground at the highest point; Che-o-tmaka, as the Pima call him, the Maricopa Kokmat, crossed over the sky to get the vessel. But Coyote was just ahead of him, and took refuge in the joint of a great reed that floated upon the water. There were three other joints of reed floating by it, and Coyote having sealed up his reed with resin from the mesquite and chaparral bushes, Kokmat could not tell in which he was concealed.

Now, the earth was barely dry enough to support one who passed over it rapidly, but if he stopped he would sink. As both Coyote and Kokmat wanted the vessel, they ran toward it, Coyote coming forth from his reed when it had floated to a point on the opposite side of the vessel from Kokmat. Coyote challenged Kokmat to exchange places with him and see which could first arrive. The offer was accepted. The two were so nearly equally matched that both arrived at the same time. They tried again, with the same result. When they

---

[a] Corona Borealis.   [c] In Sagittarius (?).
[b] Cassiopeia's Chair.   [d] Scorpio and the others (see Hchuleyuks in constellations).

ran the third time, Coyote being out of breath, sent Fox in his stead, but Kokmat also sent his brother. When the two chief characters ran again, they passed together by the vessel containing the seed, and each tried to kick it on before him, so the race ceased and the contest took on a different form. When they had tried very long and neither had gained any advantage, Fox proposed to cast lots with four sticks, one each for Kokmat, his brother, Coyote, and Fox. He made the sticks half white and half red, and, hiding them, asked Kokmat which color were the sticks for himself and his brother, purporting to turn the sticks in his own favor. But Kokmat made him strike them upward with a stone, to count one if all fell white, two if all fell red, and nothing if they fell mixed.

While they played, Coyote and Fox cheating and quibbling in every conceivable way, the sticks very seldom fell all of a color; Kokmat meantime had the red-headed woodpecker carrying away the seed in his bill to all parts of the world.

From the ashes of the woman and the ashes of all the woods and from all the seeds that were powdered sprang up the present generation.

The mortar, stones, and earthern vessels used were copied by men. Baskets and woven mats were patterned after Spider's webs. The games we play represent the contests between Kokmat and his Brother (Spider) or Kokmat and Coyote.

Each of these four were both male and female, but the female side of Spider became the wife of Kokmat, who alone married.

MISSION INDIANS. Mesa Grande, California. (Field Columbian Museum.)

Cat. no. 62537. Four wooden staves, 12 inches long and 1¼ inches wide, marked on one face with burnt lines as shown in figure 269.

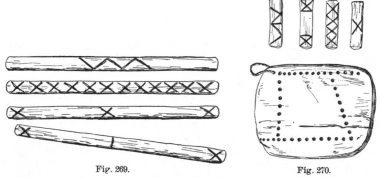

Fig. 269.   Fig. 270.

FIG. 269. Stick dice; length, 12 inches; Mission Indians, Mesa Grande, California; cat. no. 62537, Field Columbian Museum.

FIG. 270. Stick dice and board; length of sticks, 3¼ inches; length of board, 9 inches; Mission Indians, Mesa Grande, California; cat. no. 62536, Field Columbian Museum.

These were collected by Mr C. B. Watkins, who describes them as used in the game of can welso. The sticks are thrown with an overhand movement. The marked sides are counted. The game is played in silence.

Cat. no. 62536. Four wooden sticks, 3¼ inches in length and seven-eighths of an inch wide, round on one side and flat on the other, the latter being marked with burnt cross lines as shown in figure

270; accompanied by a wooden tablet, 7 by 9 inches, marked with holes counting 10 on a side.

These were collected by Mr C. B. Watkins, who describes the game under the name of serup. Each stick has a value known by the marks. The tablet serves to keep the count of the throws.

MOHAVE. Arizona. (Cat. no. 10334, United States National Museum.)

Set of four blocks of cottonwood, 6⅛ inches in length, 2 inches in width, and one-half inch in thickness, section ellipsoidal; one

Fig. 271.   Fig. 272.

FIG. 271. Stick dice; length, 6⅛ inches; Mohave Indians, Arizona; cat. no. 10334, United States National Museum.

FIG. 272. Stick dice; length, 6 inches; Mohave Indians, Lower California (Mexico); cat. no. 24166, United States National Museum.

side painted red, with designs as shown in figure 271, and the opposite side unpainted. Collected by Dr Edward Palmer and described as used by women.

In a letter to the writer Doctor Palmer states:

The game is scored according as the plain or painted sides are up, as each may choose. Three rounds constitute a game. One stick is laid down to indicate which side is to count. The paint on the sticks consists of mesquite gum dissolved in water.

MOHAVE.   Lower California (Mexico).   (Cat. no. 24166, United
    States National Museum.)

Set of four blocks of willow wood,[a] 6 inches in length, 1½ inches in
    width, and five-eighths of an inch in thickness; one side flat and
    painted brown with designs (figure 272) similar to those on the
    preceding, the opposite side rounded and unpainted. Collected
    by Dr Edward Palmer.

Fig. 273.   Fig. 274.

FIG. 273. Stick dice; length, 5⅜ inches; Mohave Indians, Arizona; cat. no. 10090, Peabody Mu-
    seum of American Archæology and Ethnology.
FIG. 274. Stick dice; length, 5¼ inches; Mohave Indians, Arizona; cat. no. 60265, 60266, Field
    Columbian Museum.

———— Arizona.   (Peabody Museum of American Archæology and
    Ethnology.)

Cat. no. 10090.   Set of four gambling sticks, 5⅜ inches in length and
    1¼ inches in width; marked on one face with designs as shown in
    figure 273; the opposite side plain.

Cat. no. 10090, bis.   Set of four gambling sticks, 3½ to 3¾ inches in
    length and eleven-sixteenths of an inch in width; marked on one
    face with red and black designs, the opposite side plain. Both
    collected by Dr Edward Palmer.

———— Fort Mohave, Arizona.   (Cat. no. 60265, 60266, Field Colum-
    bian Museum.)

Four wooden blocks, 5¾ inches in length and 2¼ inches in width,
    round on one side, the other flat and marked with brown paint,
    as shown in figure 274.

---

[a] *Salix amygdaloides.*

Mr John J. McKoin, the collector, describes the game under the name of hotan:

This game is played with four billets, one side of which is flat. The players lay one stick on the ground, flat side down; then they throw the three remaining sticks with the hand and let them fall upon the ground. If all fall with the same side up it counts one. The game is for 4 or 5 points. The sticks are given to different players when two sticks fall the same side up. This is a gambling game, beds, blankets, ponies, and sometimes wives being wagered.

WALAPAI. Walapai reservation, Arizona. (Field Columbian Museum.)

Cat. no. 61099. Three wooden blocks (figure 275), $3\frac{3}{4}$ inches by three-fourths of an inch, one side plain and rounded and the other flat with painted red streak.

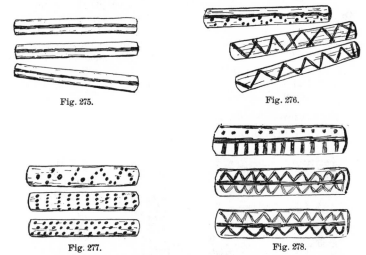

Fig. 275.

Fig. 276.

Fig. 277.

Fig. 278.

FIG. 275. Stick dice; length, $3\frac{3}{4}$ inches; Walapai Indians, Walapai reservation, Arizona; cat. no. 61099, Field Columbian Museum.
FIG. 276. Stick dice; length, 4 inches; Walapai Indians, Walapai reservation, Arizona; cat. no. 61100, Field Columbian Museum.
FIG. 277. Stick dice; length, $4\frac{1}{4}$ inches; Walapai Indians, Walapai reservation, Arizona; cat. no. 63206, Field Columbian Museum.
FIG. 278. Stick dice; length, $4\frac{1}{4}$ inches; Walapai Indians, Walapai reservation, Arizona; cat. no. 63209, Field Columbian Museum.

Cat. no. 61100. Three wooden blocks (figure 276), 4 inches by seven-eighths of an inch, one side plain and rounded, the other flat, with painted designs, two alike and one odd.

Cat. no. 63206. Three wooden blocks (figure 277), $4\frac{1}{4}$ inches by 1 inch, one side plain and rounded, the other flat and painted with brown dots.

Cat. no. 63209. Three wooden blocks (figure 278), $4\frac{1}{4}$ inches by three-fourths of an inch, one side plain and rounded, the other flat with painted designs, two alike and one odd.

These were collected by Mr H. P. Ewing, who gave the following account of the game under the name of tawfa:

The Walapai call this game taw-fa, from the manner of throwing the sticks against a stone. The play is as follows:

Place fifty small stones in a circle about 4 feet in diameter, arranging them

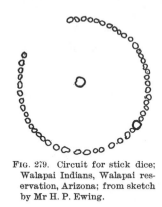

close together except at one point in the circle, which remains open. Opposite this open space a larger stone is placed. These stones are the counters, and the game is counted by moving the stones around the circle. An equal number of stones is placed on each side of the large stone, and whichever contestant gets to the large stone first wins. In playing the game, one person takes the little billets of wood, which are three in number, rounded on one side and flat on the other, and holds them between the thumb and first two fingers so that they are parallel. She throws them so that the three ends will strike on a large stone in the center of the circle. The count is as follows: One flat side up counts 1; two flat sides up, 3; three flat sides up, 5; three flat

FIG. 279. Circuit for stick dice; Walapai Indians, Walapai reservation, Arizona; from sketch by Mr H. P. Ewing.

sides down, 10. This game of taw-fa is little played now among the Walapai, cards having taken its place.

YUMA. Fort Yúma, Arizona. (Cat. no. IV B 1660, Berlin Museum für Völkerkunde.)

FIG. 280. Stick dice; length, 6¼ inches; Yuma Indians, Arizona; cat. no. IV B 1660, Berlin Museum für Völkerkunde.

Set of four blocks of wood, 6½ inches in length, 1¼ inches in width, and five-eighths of an inch in thickness; one side flat and painted with designs, as shown in figure 280, in red; opposite side rounded and painted red.

The collector, Mr Samuel Jacobsen, gives the name as tadak, and states that it is a woman's game.

YUMA. Fort Yuma, San Diego county, Arizona. (Cat. no. 63429, Field Columbian Museum.)

Four wooden blocks, 5⅝ inches in length and 1⅜ inches wide, with flat sides decorated with red paint, as shown in figure 281. The collector, Mr S. C. Simms, describes them as used in the game of otah.

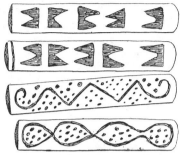

FIG. 281. Stick dice; length, 5⅝ inches; Yuma Indians, Fort Yuma, Arizona; cat. no. 63429, Field Columbian Museum.

——— Colorado river, California.

Lieut. W. H. Emory [a] says:

They play another [game] with sticks, like jackstraws.

——— Colorado river, California. (Cat. no. S362, 76, Rijks Ethnographisches Museum, Leiden.)

FIG. 282. Stick dice; length, 6 inches; Yuma Indians, California; cat. no. S362, 76, Rijks Ethnographisches Museum, Leiden.

Set of four blocks of wood, 6 inches in length and 1 inch in width, one side flat and painted with designs, as shown in figure 282, in dark brown on a whitened surface.

---

[a] Report on the United States and Mexican Boundary Survey, v. 1, p. 111, Washington, 1857.

These were collected by Dr H. F. C. ten Kate, jr, who gives the name as otochei. He refers to this game as played only by women.[a]

In reply to my inquiry in reference to the words tadak and otochei, given by the collector as the names of the preceding Yuman games, Dr A. S. Gatchet writes:

I have not been able to discover any Yuma or Mohave words resembling your otoche-i and tădăk either in the vocabularies in our vaults or in those that I have published myself in the Zeitschrift für Ethnologie. The term "Yuma" refers to a tribe which, during the last forty years, had a reservation at the confluence of the Gila and Colorado rivers, who seem to have resided on New river near the Mohave desert in California. Yuma is also used at present to comprehend all the languages or dialects cognate with the Yuma dialect at the above confluence, under the name of Yuma linguistic family. Your word otoche-i has pretty nearly the ring of an Aztec, or better, Nahuatl word.

ZUÑIAN STOCK

Zuñi. Zuñi, New Mexico.   (Cat. no. 20031, Free Museum of Science and Art, University of Pennsylvania.)

Set of four sticks, 5½ inches in length, in two pairs, each of which consists of a length of reed split in the middle.

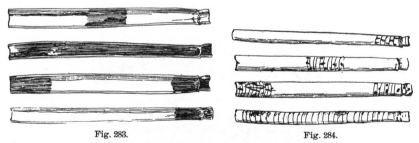

Fig. 283.   Fig. 284.

FIG. 283. Sacrificial cane dice (reverse); Zuñi Indians, Zuñi, New Mexico; cat. no. 20031, Free Museum of Science and Art, University of Pennsylvania.

FIG. 284. Sacrificial cane dice (obverse); length, 5¼ inches; Zuñi Indians, Zuñi, New Mexico; cat. no. 20031, Free Museum of Science and Art, University of Pennsylvania.

The inner sides of the reed are painted as shown in figure 283, and the opposite rounded sides scratched with transverse lines and burnt, as shown in figure 284. These were employed, according to Mr Cushing, in the game of sholiwe, canes, one of the four games[b] which are sacrificed to the twin War Gods, Ahaiyuta and Matsailema. These particular canes were not made to play with, but for the purpose of sacrifice.

---

[a] Reizen en Onderzoekingen in Noord Amerika, p. 114, Leiden, 1885.

[b] In addition to sho'liwe there were lápochiwe, feather dart; i'yankolowe, hidden ball, and mótikawe, kicked stick. Compare with the four Sia games described on p. 123.

ZUÑI. Zuñi, New Mexico. (Cat. no. 69289, United States National
    Museum.)

Two sets, each of four sticks, one 7¾ inches and the other 7 inches
    in length; made in pairs, like the preceding, of split reed.

The inner sides of the reed are painted like the preceding. The
outer sides of the longer set are unmarked, while those of the shorter
set are marked, as shown in figure 285.

FIG. 285. Sacrificial cane dice (obverse); Zuñi Indians, Zuñi, New Mexico; cat. no. 69289, United
States National Museum.

Mr Cushing informed me that these two sets were used together,
also for sacrificial purposes, the longer one being offered to Ahaiyuta
and the shorter to Matsailema.[a]

———— New Mexico. (United States National Museum.)

Cat. no. 69277. Set of four sticks, 6½ inches in length and one-
    half inch in width, made of split cane; the inner sides painted
    like the preceding, and the rounded sides scratched with cross
    marks, as shown in figure 286. Collected by Col. James Ste-
    venson.

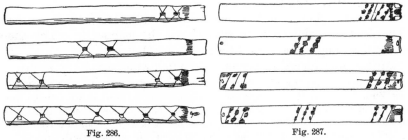

Fig. 286.   Fig. 287.

FIG. 286. Cane dice (obverse); length, 6¼ inches; Zuñi Indians, Zuñi, New Mexico; cat. no.
69277, United States National Museum.
FIG. 287. Cane dice (obverse); length, 6 inches; Zuñi Indians, Zuñi, New Mexico; cat. no. 69278,
United States National Museum.

Cat. no. 69278. Set of four sticks, 6 inches in length and one-half
    inch in width, made of split cane; the inner sides painted like
    the preceding, and the rounded sides marked with cuts, as shown
    in figure 287.

---

[a] Mátsailema is somewhat shorter in stature than his twin brother, and all of his
things are made somewhat shorter. He always wears a shorter war club and a shorter
bow (Cushing).

These sets were intended for actual use and are made of heavy cane, with the inside charred at the edges, unlike the sacrificial sets, which consist of common marsh reed.

FIG. 288.   Cane dice; length, 6⅝ inches; showing method of tying in bundle; Zuñi Indians, Zuñi, New Mexico; cat. no. 22593, Free Museum of Science and Art, University of Pennsylvania.

ZUÑI.   Zuñi, New Mexico.   (Cat. no. 22593, Free Museum of Science and Art, University of Pennsylvania.)

Four split canes, 6¾ inches in length, marked on one side with cross lines and chevrons and on the other with ink, as shown in figure 288.   Collected by the writer in 1902.

These are bound together in a bundle with string, one inside of the other, so that the end of the top cane projects beyond that of the one below it, and so on down.   The sticks are arranged in the following order: Top, black in middle; second, black at one end; third, all black; bottom, black at both ends.

The figure illustrates one of the ways in which the canes are tied up when not in use.   This is one of a number of sets collected in Zuñi by the writer.   The markings vary considerably in detail on the different sets, but are all essentially the same.   In removing the bundle of canes from the cloth in which it was wrapped, the owner took up each cane in turn and breathed on it.

——— New Mexico.   (Cat. no. 4984, Brooklyn Institute Museum.)

Set of four cane dice, 6 inches in length (figure 289).   Collected by the writer in 1904.

The etched figures on the dice represent the water bug, gannastepi. The drawing below (figure 290) shows the manner in which these dice are arranged and bound together when not in use.

Mr Cushing placed in my hands the following account of sholiwe: [a]

The game of sho'-li-we is certainly the most distinctive of any practiced by the Zuñi Indians.   It is not confined to them, but forms of it are found among all the more settled of the present Indians in both our own southwest, and in northern, western, and central Mexico; while variants of it and derived games may be traced over well-nigh the whole western half of our continent.

A study of the distinctive marks of the different sticks or cane slips used in this game by the Zuñi would seem to indicate that this peculiar form of it is the most primitive.   The reason for this will subsequently appear.

---

[a] Mr Owens described sho'-li-we in Some Games of the Zuñi (Popular Science Monthly, v. 39, p. 41, 1891).   The names of the four sticks he gives as follows: The one whose concave side is entirely black, quin, Zuñi for black; the one with one black end, path-tō; with two black ends, kŏ-ha-kwa; and one with a black center, ath-lu-a.   He figures two of the reeds, and the manner of holding the sticks, which he describes as thrown with the right hand against a suspended blanket and allowed to fall on another blanket. Two of the pieces belong to each man and are companions.   There is a pool with twelve markers, and he who wins the markers wins the game.   The winner takes the twelve markers up into his hands and breathes on them.   This is because they have been good to him and allowed him to win.   It is wholly a game of chance, and horses, guns, saddles, and everything are staked upon the throw.

The name sho'-li-we is derived from sho'-o-li, arrow, and we, plural ending, signifying "parts of," sho'-we being the plural of simple arrows. Sho'-o-li, arrow, is derived in turn from sho'-o-le, cane, the termination li in the derived word being a contraction of li-a, and signifying out of, from, or made of. Thus, the name of the game may be translated cane arrows, or cane arrow pieces or parts.

These parts consist of four slips of cane. From the fact that these slips are so split and cut from the canes as to include at their lower ends portions of the joints or septa of the canes, and from the further fact that they are variously banded with black or red paint, or otherwise, it may be seen that they

Fig. 289.   Cane dice; length, 6 inches; Zuñi Indians, Zuñi, New Mexico; cat. no. 4984, Brooklyn Institute Museum.

represent the footings or shaftments of cane arrows in which the septa at the lower ends serve as stops for the footing or nocking-plugs.[a]

A study of the bandings by which these cane slips are distinguished from one another reveals the very significant fact that they are representative of the rib-bandings of cane-arrow shaftments.

I have found that sets of Zuñi, as well as the ancestral cliff-dweller arrows, were thus ribbanded with black or red paint to symbolize, in the arrows so marked, the numerical and successional values of the four quarters, each set, especially of war arrows, consisting of four subsets, the shaftments of each marked differently.   The reasons for this, and for processes of divination by

Fig. 290.   Cane dice, showing method of tying in bundle; Zuñi Indians, Zuñi, New Mexico; cat no. 4984, Brooklyn Institute Museum.

which the members of the different sets among the arrows were determined during their manufacture, I have set forth in a paper on "The Arrow," published in the Proceedings of the American Association for the Advancement of Science, 1895, and also in the American Anthropologist for October of the same year.

---

[a] The canes are split with reference to the notion that one side is masculine or north, and the other feminine or south. This is determined by the direction or character of the natural growth, as well as by the presence or absence of the leaf pocket in the joint on the one side or the other of that particular section which forms the shaftment of the arrow (Cushing). In ancient China, according to the Chow Le (LXII, 37), the arrow maker floated the arrow longitudinally upon water to determine the side which corresponded to the principle of inertia and the side which corresponded to the principle of activity. The former sank, while the latter rose. He cut the notch with reference thereto.

In the second part of that paper, the publication of which was delayed by my Florida explorations, I proceeded to show how these various facts indicated quite clearly that the Zuñi game of sho'-li-we, as its name implied, developed from the use of actual arrows for divination; and I further instanced many ceremonial uses of simple or ceremonial arrows in such divinatory processes as further demonstrating this claim.

It may be well for me to preface a description of the four cane slips constituting the principal apparatus of the game by a statement or two relative to the successional numbers of the four quarters as conceived in Zuñi dramatography.

The chief, or Master, region, as well as the first, is the North, designated the Yellow; believed to be the source of breath, wind, or the element of air, and the place of winter; hence of violence or war, and therefore masculine.

The next, or second region is the West, designated the Blue; believed to be the source of moisture or the element water and the place of spring, or renewal and fertility; hence of birth, and therefore feminine.

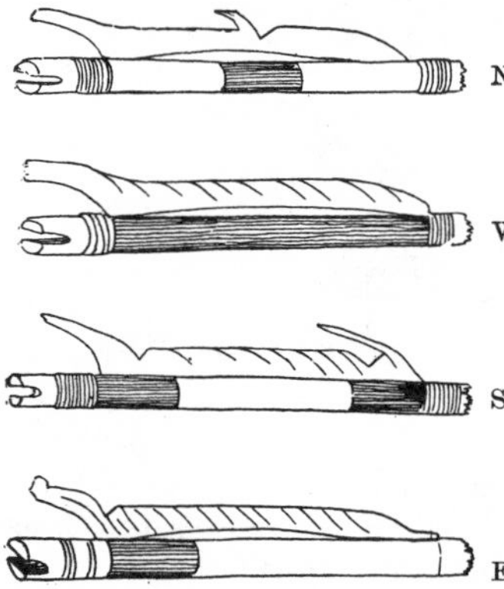

The next, or third, is the South, designated as the Red; believed to be the source of heat or the element fire, and the place of summer, of growth and productivity; hence of fostering, and likewise feminine.

The last, or fourth of the earthly regions represented in the ordinary sheaf of arrows and in the game, is the East, designated the White, and believed to be the source of seeds and the element earth, and the place of autumn, of new years, and hence of creation; therefore masculine again.[a]

These various regions and their numbers and meanings are symbolized on the arrows of the four quarters by differences in their ribbandings [figure 291].

Those of the North were characterized by a single medial ribbanding around the shaftment, sometimes of yellow, but more usually of black, the color of death.

FIG. 291. Arrow shaftments of the four directions, showing ribbanding and cut cock feathers; Zuñi Indians, Zuñi, New Mexico; from sketch by Frank Hamilton Cushing.

Those of the West were also singly ribbanded coextensively with the shaftment, but there was oftentimes a narrow terminal band at either end of this broad band, sometimes of blue or green, but usually of black.

Those of the South were characterized by two bands midway between the two ends and the middle, sometimes of red, but usually of black.

Those of the East were characterized by either two narrow bands at either end, leaving the whole medial space of the shaftment white, or, more often by a single band at the upper end of the shaftment, sometimes composed of two narrow black fillets inclosing white, but usually merely black and not double.

In the highly finished arrows the cock or tail feathers were notched and tufted to correspond numerically and positionally with the bandings, for mythic reasons into which it is not necessary to enter here.

Each of the four cane slips was banded to correspond with the ribbandings of one or another of these sets of the arrows of the four quarters; but the paint bands [figure 283] were almost invariably black and were placed in the concavity of the cane slip, not on the periphery (which was, however, scorched,

[a] See Outlines of Zuñi Creation Myths. Thirteenth Annual Report of the Bureau of Ethnology, p. 369, 1896.

scored, or carved to correspond), evidently to keep the paint from being worn off by handling and casting.

Thus the cane slip of the North was banded only at the middle, and was called a'-thlu-a, or the all speeder, sender (a, all, and thlu-ah, to run, speed, or stand ready).

The cane slip of the West was blackened its full length and was called k'wi'-ni-kwa, or the Black (medicine), from k'wi'-na, black, and ak'-kwa, " medicine " or " sacred."

The cane slip of the South was doubly banded, as was the arrow of the South, and was called pathl-to-a, or divider divided (bordered, enclosed), from pathl-to, border edge, end, and oa, to become, to do, or make to do.

Finally, the cane slip of the East was banded only at one end, and was called ko'ha-kwa ,the white, or the White Medicine (ko'-ha-na, white, and ak'-kwa, " medicine ").

In addition to the banding and scoring of these cane slips, they were, in cases of great importance, as in sets made from the captured arrows of some celebrated foeman, notched at the ends, as I have said the cock feathers were notched; but this old practice has fallen into disuse to such extent that I have seen only one venerated set so notched. In this set, if I observed aright, the notches corresponded in number as well as in place, whether at the sides or in the middle of the ends with the number and positions of the bandings and of the tuftings on the cock feathers of the arrows from which, probably, they were made. The normal numerical value of the cane slips agreed with the successional values of the regions they belonged to—that is, the slip of the North made one; that of the West, two; that of the South, three, and that of the East, four. But as this gave unequal values, other values or counts were added, according as the slips fell concave or convex sides uppermost, and especially according to the thrower.

That this may be understood, the general nature of the game as essentially a sacred tribal process of divination must be considered. Formerly sho'-li-we was exclusively a game of war divination, and was played only by priests of the Bow, members of the esoteric society of war shamans.

These members were, according to their totems and clans, members of the clan groups corresponding to the several quarters or sacred precints of North, West, South, East, Upper, Lower, and Middle regions. But since there were only four regions concerned in the waging of war, clansmen of the upper and nether regions were relegated to the east and west, since the places of the upper and lower regions in the sacred diagram were in the northeast—between the East and North, and in the southwest—between the West and South; while clansmen of the middle might, as determined by the casts of their arrow canes, belong to any one of the other regions, since the midmost was the synthetic region, the all-containing and the all-contained place, either the first, therefore, or the last. This war game of the priests of the Bow was played semiannually at the festivals of the Twin Gods of War, Áhaiyuta and Mátsailema, patrons of the game by virtue of their vanquishment of the creational god of gambling Mi'-si-na, the Eagle star god, whose forfeited head now hangs in the Milky Way, and whose birds are the god servants of war and the plumers of the canes of war.

It is played at such times as a tribal divination; a forecast for war or peace, for prosperity or adversity, and is accompanied by tribal hazards and gambling. But at other times it is played for the determination of peace or war, of the direction or precaution to be taken in defensive or offensive operations or preparations. As thus played, there must be four participants. Each possesses his own canes. In the uppermost room of the pueblo (now fallen), there was formerly a shrine of the game. Here during terrific sand storms or at night the players gathered to divine. To the middle of the ceiling was suspended a jical or large round bowl-basket, over which a deerskin was stretched like a drumhead. Immediately below this, spread over a sacred diagram of prayer meal representing the terrace or cloud bed of the four quarters, on the floor, was a buffalo robe, pelt side up, head to the east, left side to the north, etc. [figure 292]. Upon this pelt a broken circle was traced either in black lines or dots, and with or without grains of corn (forty for each line, the colors corresponding to the quarters as above described), and the openings (canyons or passageways) occurring at the four points opposite the four directions. It

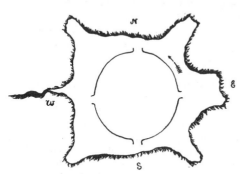

should be observed that a cross (+) was sometimes painted both on the center of the skin on the basket drum and on the hide beneath, the upper symbolic of Áhaiyuta, and the lower of Mátsailema, the Twin War Gods.

FIG. 292. Hide gaming circuit for cane dice; Zuñi Indians, Zuñi, New Mexico; from sketch by Frank Hamilton Cushing.

The four players chose their places according to the clan groups and directions or quarters they represented: the player of the North between the eastern and northern passageway; the player of the West between the northern and western passageway, and so on.

The players of the East and North represented war, and in other modes of the game, masculinity; those of the West and South, peace and femininity.

Before taking their places they muttered prayers, or rather rituals, clasping the playing canes lengthwise between the palms, breathing deeply from, and from the close of the prayers, repeatedly upon them, rubbing and shuffling them vigorously, from which comes the title of a skilled player or a gambler, shos'-li, cane rubber, or cane shuffler. As they took their seats, each placed under the edge of the buffalo hide in front of his place the pool, consisting of sacred white shell beads, or of little tablets representative of various properties and thus forming a kind of currency, since these little symbols were redeemable in the properties they represented or in commodities of equal value by agreement. Each also laid down at his right side on the edge of the robe over the pool two kinds of counters, usually a set of count-

FIG. 293. Manner of holding cane dice in game of sholiwe; Zuñi Indians, Zuñi, New Mexico; from sketch by Frank Hamilton Cushing.

ing straws of broom grass, about six or seven inches long, worn by much use, and varying in number according to the proposed game. From ten to forty or forty-two, or from one hundred to one hundred and two, this latter number divided at random into four bundles, was selected by each player. The additional counters were supplied by beans or corn grains, each set, or the set of each player, being of his appropriate color. Four splints, the moving pieces of the game, were laid in their places by the left sides of the passageways.

Each player then shuffled his cane cards back and forth in his palms, as before described, as though to smooth and heat them, addressed them, especially the stick of his special quarter, as (for the East) "Now then, white one, come thou uppermost!"; then laying the all-sender or his special slip as such across the two middle fingers and the other three slips upon it inside of one another, his thumb pressing over their middle, the ends pointed outward over the index finger, and the bases held down to the base of the palm by the bent-over little finger [figure 293], he quickly breathed or puffed upon them, shouted at them, and cast them skillfully against the stretched skin of the basket, so that they rebounded swiftly and fell almost unerringly within the circle on the pe'-wi-ne or bed of buffalo hide. Now it was noted which slip lay uppermost over the others. If the White man threw, and if the white stick lay uppermost over all the others, he uttered thanks and the cast counted him four and gave him the privilege of another cast. If, moreover, all three slips except his sender lay concave sides upward, they counted him ten and gave him a second additional throw. If all three fell convex sides up, they counted him five; if two concave sides and one convex side up, they counted him three, and if two convex sides and one concave side up, they counted him only one. The player who had the largest number of both kinds of counts after each had tried, led off in the game and was supposed to be favored by the gods at the beginning. With but a slight change in the system of counting, the game was continued; that is, the double counts were kept if the process included gambling, willingness to sacrifice, but only the counts according to the regions, if the game was purely an arrow or war divination. But it is to be noted that in either case an ingenious method was resorted to in order to equalize the counts. Since the North or Yellow man could gain only one and a double throw if his slip came uppermost, he gained the count of his opponent, the South, if his slip fell uppermost on the Red man's slips. The latter thus forfeited alike his double throw and his appropriate number, three. The tally of these purely cosmical counts was kept with the bundle of splints; the tally of the cast-counts or their sums were kept with the grains by counting out, and that of the individual by moving the pointer of the passageway as many dots or grain places to the left as the cast called for. If a player of the East or the North overtook a player of the West or South, if his pointer fell in the same space, he maimed his opponent, sent him back to his passageway, and robbed him of his load; that is, took or made him forfeit his counts.

The completion of the fourth circuit by any one of the players closed the ordinary game, providing the sum of the cosmical counts had been won by him, and the player who, with his partner, had the largest aggregate of both lot and cosmical counts was the winner.

There were many variants of this game as to counts. Some of these were so complicated that it was absolutely impossible for me to gain knowledge of them in the short practice I had in the play. I have given here, not very precisely or fully, the simplest form I know, except that of the lot and diagram, which was quite like that of ta'-sho'-li-we or wood canes, which may be seen by the above description to be an obvious derivative both in mode and name of the older game of canes. It was evidently thus divorced for purposes of exoteric play, as it is practiced not only by men but also by women.

Mrs Matilda Coxe Stevenson [a] gives a number of additional particulars in reference to sholiwe, and her description of the game,

---

[a] Zuñi Games. American Anthropologist n. s., v. 5, p. 480, 1903.

which follows, differs from the preceding in the names of the canes and in the manner in which they are arranged when cast:

Legend says that it was played for rains by the Gods of War and the Ah'-shiwanni[a] soon after coming to this world. The Ah'shiwanni afterward thought the reeds used for the game were too long, so their length was measured from the tip of the thumb to the tip of the middle finger, the fingers extended.

The Ah'shiwanni considered this game so efficacious in bringing rains that they organized a fraternity, which they called Shówekwe, arrow-reed people, while the Ah'shiwi were at Hän'ʻhlipïn'ka, for the express purpose of playing the game for rain. Ten men were designated by the Ah'shiwanni as the original members of the Shówekwe. The prayers of the fraternity were sure to bring rains. . . .

FIG. 294. Split reeds used in shóliwe; Zuñi Indians, Zuñi, New Mexico; from Mrs Stevenson.

Each player takes the side of one of the Gods of War, two pieces of split reed representing the side of the elder God of War and two the younger God of War. The writer for convenience numbers the reeds 1, 2, 3, 4 [figure 294].

No. 1, named knïn'na, black, has the concave side of the reed colored black, indicating morning, noon, and sunset, or the whole day. Three sets of lines on the convex side denote the three periods of the day—morning, noon, and sunset.

No. 2, áthluwa, center, has a daub of black midway of the reed, concave side, denoting midday. The lines on the convex side also denote noon.

No. 3, kóhakwa, white shell, has a baub of black paint at either end of the concave side, indicating morning and evening, or sunrise and sunset. Lines on the convex side denote the same.

No. 4, páhlto, mark on the end, has a daub of black paint on the joint end of the concave side, denoting sunrise, which to the Zuñi is the first light of day, or the white light which comes first; and the lines on the convex side indicate the same. Three dots are sometimes found on the joint of the reed, indicating eyes and mouth of the face, which is not delineated. Other reeds have only two dots for the eyes. Nos. 1 and 3 are said to belong to the elder God of War, and nos. 2 and 4 to the Younger God of War. The player representing the elder god holds no. 3 concave side up, and slides no 2 into the groove of no. 3, the

---

[a] Rain priests.

joint of no. 2 falling below that of no. 3. He then slides no. 4 into that of no. 2, also allowing the joint to extend below. No. 1 is held crosswise, the others at an acute angle (the reeds are sometimes crossed at right angles) with the grooved side against the corresponding sides of the others, the joint to the left, and the opposite end projecting a little more than an inch beyond the group [figure 295]. When the representative of the younger God of War plays, he runs no. 3 into the groove of no. 2 and no. 1 into no. 3, and crosses them with no. 4. The reed which crosses the others is designated as the thrower, but the same reed, as stated, is not used by both players. In this position the reeds are thrown upward against an inverted basket, 10 or 12 inches in diameter, covered with a piece of blanket or cloth and suspended from the ceiling. The reeds strike the cloth over the basket and fall to a blanket spread on the floor to receive them. If played out of doors, which is seldom the case at present, the basket is suspended above the blanket from the apex of three poles, arranged tripod fashion, with sufficient space beneath for the blanket and players.

When the representative of the elder God of War throws and the concave side of no. 1 and the convex sides of the others are up, the trick is won; or if

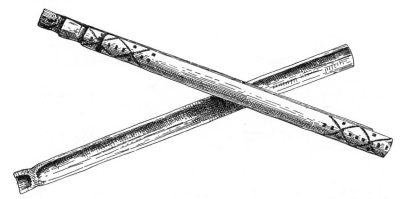

FIG. 295. Method of placing reeds in playing shóliwe; Zuñi Indians, Zuñi, New Mexico; from Mrs Stevenson.

no. 1 be convex side up with the others concave up, the trick is won. If no. 1 crosses no. 3, or vice versa, convex sides up, the trick is won, even should one cross the others by but a hairsbreadth. If nos. 2 and 4 should be crossed as described, the trick goes to the opponent. If all convex sides are up, or vice versa, the trick is lost. If the convex side of no. 3 is up and the others have the concave sides up, the trick belongs to the opponent.

When the representative of the younger God of War plays, the counts are reversed. Silver buttons are the favorite chips for the game. Though shóliwe is the favorite of the lot games of the elder Ah'shiwi, it being the game of the professional gamblers of the pueblo, there is no thought of personal gain when it is played by the Ah'shiwanni for rains. At this time great ceremony is observed and buckskins are used in place of the cloth covering over the basket and the blanket on the floor. The skin on the floor has the head to the east; a broken circle, forming a quadrant, is drawn on the skin. . . .

There is but little ceremony associated with the game when played by the professional or other gamblers. The most abandoned, however, would not dare to play without first offering prayers to the Gods of War, invoking their blessing, and breathing on their reeds.

Zuñi.   Zuñi, New Mexico.   (United States National Museum.)

Cat. no. 69285.   Set of three sticks of larch wood, $3\frac{3}{4}$ inches in length, 1 inch in breadth, and $3\frac{1}{6}$ inches in thickness (figure 296) ; section rectangular ; one side painted red, the opposite unpainted.

Cat. no. 69004.   Set of three sticks of piñon wood (one missing), $3\frac{3}{4}$ inches in length, $1\frac{1}{8}$ inches in breadth, and three-sixteenths of an inch in thickness ; one side flat and blackened, the opposite roughly rounded and unpainted ; ends cut straight across and painted black.

Cat. no. 69355.   Set of three sticks rudely shaped from piñon wood, $5\frac{1}{2}$ inches in length, three-fourths of an inch in breadth, and about one-fourth of an inch in thickness ; section rectangular, with both sides flat ; one painted black, the opposite plain.

Cat. no. 69352.   Set of three sticks of piñon wood, $5\frac{1}{2}$ inches in length, $1\frac{1}{4}$ inches in breadth, and about one-fourth of an inch in thickness ; one side flat and painted black, the opposite rounded and painted red.

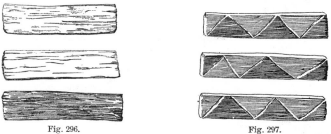

Fig. 296.   Fig. 297.

FIG. 296.   Stick dice; length, $3\frac{1}{4}$ inches; Zuñi Indians, Zuñi, New Mexico; cat. no. 69285, United States National Museum.

FIG. 297.   Stick dice; length, 4 inches; Zuñi Indians, Zuñi, New Mexico; cat. no. 69287, United States National Museum.

Cat. no. 69284.   Set of three sticks of piñon wood, $5\frac{1}{2}$ inches in length, seven-eighths of an inch in breadth, and about three-sixteenths of an inch in thickness ; slightly rounded on both sides, one being painted black and the other red.

Cat. no. 69354.   Set of three sticks of piñon wood, $5\frac{1}{2}$ inches in length, about $1\frac{3}{4}$ inches in breadth, and three-sixteenths of an inch in thickness ; painted black on one side, the opposite side unpainted ; corresponding ends on one side cut straight across and the opposite with one corner rounded.

Cat. no. 69340.   Set of three sticks of pine wood, 6 inches in length, $1\frac{5}{16}$ inches in breadth, and seven-sixteenths of an inch in thickness ; section rectangular ; one side marked with triangles of red and black paint, the opposite side unpainted.

Cat. no. 69287.   Set of three sticks of white pine, 4 inches in length, three-fourths of an inch in breadth, and three-sixteenths of an inch in thickness (figure 297) ; one face flat, with triangles

painted red and black and outlined by incised lines, the opposite
rounded and unpainted.

Cat. no. 69281. Set of three sticks of yellow pine, 5½ inches in length,
   1 inch in breadth, and three-eighths of an inch in thickness (figure 298) ; one face flat and unpainted, the opposite face rounded
   and painted red and black in triangular designs, the triangles on
   one side being red with a black inner triangle, and vice versa,
   the outline of the larger triangles deeply incised.

Cat. no. 69003. Set of three sticks of basswood, 4⅝ inches in length,
   1⅝ inches in breadth, and five-sixteenths of an inch in thickness
   (figure 299) ; flat and painted light red on one side, opposite side
   rounded and painted in triangular designs in red and black, the
   pattern being double that on numbers 69340, 69287, and 69281.

   The preceding Zuñian staves were collected by Colonel James Stevenson. They were all used, as I was informed by Mr Cushing, for
the game of tasholiwe, or wooden canes,
which he described to me as follows:

Ta'-sho'-li-we [a] is played according to the
throws of three wooden blocks, painted red on
one side and black upon the other, around a
circle of stones placed upon the sand. Two or
four players engage, using two or four splints
as markers, and advancing, according to their
throws, around the circle, which is divided into
forty parts by pebbles or fragments of pottery,
and has four openings, called doorways, at its
four quarters. At the commencement of the
game four colored splints are arranged at these
points: At the top (North) a yellow splint, at the
left (West) a blue, at the bottom (South) a red,
and at the right (East) a white splint. The

FIG. 298. Stick dice; length, 5¼
inches; Zuñi Indians, Zuñi, New
Mexico; cat. no. 69281, United
States National Museum.

blocks are tossed, ends down, on a disk of sandstone placed in the middle of the
circle, and the counts are as follows: Three red sides up count 10; three black
sides up, 5; two red and one black, 3; two black and one red, 2.

   A count of 10 gives another throw. When four play, the straws of the North
and West move around from right to left, and those of the South and East from
left to right. When a player's move terminates at a division of the circle
occupied by an adversary's straw he takes it up and sends it back to the beginning. It is customary to make the circuit of the stones four times, beans or
corn of different colors being used to count the number of times a player has
gone around. The colors on the wooden blocks or dice symbolize the two conditions of men: Red, light or wakefulness; black, darkness or sleep.

   The splints have the following symbolism: At top, yellow, north, air, winter;
at left, blue, west, water, spring; at bottom, red, south, fire, summer; at right,
white, east, earth autumn.

---

[a] Ta'-sho'-li-we was described by John G. Owens in the Popular Science Monthly, v. 39,
1891. He gives the name of the central stone as a-rey-ley and the dice ta-mey. For
counting, each player has a horse, or touche. "The horse is supposed to stop and drink
at the intervals between the groups of stones. One game which I witnessed had loaded
rifle cartridges for stakes. Each player places his bet within the circle of stones."

The following is a vocabulary of the game: blocks, ta′-sho′-li-we; literally of wood cones; splints, ti′-we; circle of stones, i′-te-tchi-na-kya-a′-we, literally from one to another succeeding; doorway, a-wena-a-te-kwi-a, literally doorway, all directions of; beans used as counters, a-wi′-yah-na-kya no′we, literally, for keeping count beans.

Mrs Matilda Coxe Stevenson[a] gives the counts in this game as follows:

Three colored sides up count 10; three uncolored sides up, 5; two uncolored and one colored, 3; two colored and one uncolored, 2. The first one around the circle wins the game, provided his count does not carry him beyond the starting point, in which event he must continue going round until his counter reaches the doorway, or spring, as the opening is often called.

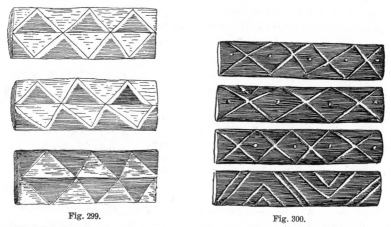

Fig. 299.

Fig. 300.

FIG. 299. Stick dice; length, $4\frac{5}{8}$ inches; Zuñi Indians, Zuñi, New Mexico; cat. no. 69003, United States National Museum.

FIG. 300. Stick dice; length, $5\frac{1}{4}$ inches; Zuñi Indians, Zuñi, New Mexico; cat. no. 22591, Free Museum of Science and Art, University of Pennsylvania.

Mrs Stevenson says that the Zuñi declare that they adopted this game from the Navaho.

ZUÑI. Zuñi, New Mexico. (Cat. no. 22591, Free Museum of Science and Art, University of Pennsylvania.)

Four soft wood blocks (figure 300), $5\frac{1}{4}$ inches long and $1\frac{1}{8}$ inches wide, painted black and marked on the rounded side with diagonal lines and chevrons, two and two alike. Collected by the writer in 1902.

——— New Mexico. (Cat. no. 16531, Free Museum of Science and Art, University of Pennsylvania.)

Reproductions of set of three blocks, originals of piñon wood, 4 inches in length, $1\frac{1}{8}$ inches in breadth, and five-sixteenths of an inch in thickness (figure 301); made by Mr Cushing; rectangu-

[a] Zuñi Games. American Anthropologist, n. s., v. 5, p. 495, 1903.

lar in section; one side painted uniformly white and the opposite side with transverse bands of color separated by black lines of paint, in the following order: yellow, blue, red, variegated, white, speckled, and black.[a]

Mr Cushing informed me that these blocks are used in a divinatory form of tasholiwe, called temthlanahnatasholiwe, of all the region's wood canes.

In this game the counting grains are named for: North, thlup-tsi kwa-kwe, yellow medicine seed people; West, thli'-a kwa-kwe, blue medicine seed people; South, shi-lo-a kwa-kwe, red medicine seed people; East, ko'-ha kwa-kwe, white medicine seed people; Upper region, ku'-tsu-a kwa-kwe, variegated medicine seed people; Lower region, k'wi'-na kwa-kwe, black medicine seed people; Middle or all-containing region, i'-to-pa-nah-na kwa-kwe, of all colors medicine seed people.

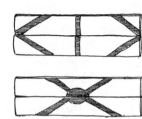

Fig. 301.   Fig. 302.

FIG. 301. Stick dice; length, 4 inches; Zuñi Indians, Zuñi, New Mexico; cat. no. 16531, Free Museum of Science and Art, University of Pennsylvania.
FIG. 302. Stick dice for basket-dice game; length, 4 inches; Zuñi Indians, Zuñi, New Mexico; cat. no. 3035, Brooklyn Institute Museum.

This game is employed in name divination and prognostication of an individual, usually of a youth, the colors being noted for the purpose of determining the rank, and name significant thereof, of the one for whom the divination is made.

Mrs Matilda Coxe Stevenson, commenting upon the above game (figure 301), says that she has not discovered any such form, but that a Zuñi will sometimes, when he wishes to play sholiwe, refer to the canes as temtlanana sholiwe, literally all grandfathers' arrow reeds, i. e., reeds of our forefathers.[b]

ZUÑI. Zuñi, New Mexico.   (Cat. no. 3035, Brooklyn Institute Museum.)

Four very thin flat sticks, 4 inches in length, painted red on one side as shown in figure 302, there being two and two alike, the reverse plain. Collected by the writer in 1903.

The Zuñi described these sticks as used as dice in the game of tsaspatsawe, a woman's game, learned by the Zuñi from the Navaho and regarded as a

[a] The stick with notches (page 194), used in the Tanoan game, suggests the probability that these painted sticks replaced others wrapped with colored thread or fabric.
[b] Zuñi Games. American Anthropologist, n. s., v. 5, p. 496, 1903.

Navaho game. The sticks are tossed up in a small native basket. The counts are as follows: All painted sides up count 4; three painted sides up, 3; two painted sides up, 2; one painted side up, 1.

ZUÑI.   Zuñi, New Mexico.   (Cat. no. 22594, Free Museum of Science and Art, University of Pennsylvania.)

Fig. 303.   Fig. 304.

FIG. 303. Wooden dice for basket-dice game; length, 1¼ inches; Zuñi Indians, Zuñi, New Mexico; cat. no. 22594, Free Museum of Science and Art, University of Pennsylvania.
FIG. 304. Basket for dice; diameter, 10¼ inches; Zuñi Indians, Zuñi, New Mexico; cat. no. 22594, Free Museum of Science and Art, University of Pennsylvania.

Five wooden blocks (figure 303), 1 by 1½ inches and one-fourth of an inch thick, painted black and marked with incised lines on one side, the other side being left plain, accompanied by a Zuñi basket, 10¼ inches in diameter (figure 304). Collected by the writer in 1902.

The name of the game was given as thlaspatsa ananai; that of the basket, tselai.

Men and women play. Two persons engage, and money is bet on the game. The counts are as follows: Five black up counts 10; five white up, 5; four white up, 4; three white up, 3; two white up, 2; one white up, 1. The game is 10.

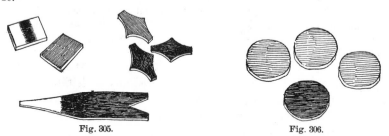

Fig. 305.   Fig. 306.

FIG. 305. Wooden dice and tossing instrument; lengths of dice, 1⅜ and 2¼ inches; Zuñi Indians, Zuñi, New Mexico; cat. no. 3044, 3045, Brooklyn Institute Museum.
FIG. 306. Wooden dice; diameter, 1¼ inches; Zuñi Indians, Zuñi, New Mexico; cat. no. 3046, Brooklyn Institute Museum.

——— New Mexico.   (Brooklyn Institute Museum.)

Cat. no. 3044.   Three diamond-shaped pieces of wood (figure 305), 2⅛ inches long, painted black on one side and red on the other; called moiachua tslemmai, star boards.

Cat. no. 3045.   Two flat wooden blocks (figure 305), 1½ by 1¼ inches, painted red on one side and having a black stripe on the other; called tslemmai kokshi, good boards.

These games are played by two men. The boards are put on the end of a flat forked stick and tossed in the air. They play turn about until one throws all red or all black and wins. The throwing board is called tslem-mai kwil-li ka-so-la, two-forked board.

Cat. no. 3046. Four flat wooden disks (figure 306), $1\frac{1}{2}$ inches in diameter, black on one side and red on the other.

They are called tslai-wai pi-so-li, round boards, and are used like the preceding, except that the boards are thrown by hand.

All of the above-mentioned specimens were collected by the writer in 1903.

TARAHUMARE INDIANS PLAYING STICK-DICE GAME AT THE PUEBLO OF PEÑASCO BLANCO, CHIHUAHUA, MEXICO; FROM PHOTOGRAPH BY LUMHOLTZ

GUESSING GAMES

STICK GAMES

The implements for the stick games are of two principal kinds. The first, directly referable to arrow shaftments, consists (*a*) of small wooden cylinders, painted with bands or ribbons of color, similar to those on arrow shaftments, employed by the Indians of the Athapascan, Chimmesyan, Chinookan, Copehan, Koluschan, Salishan, Skittagetan, and Wakashan stocks of the Pacific coast; (*b*) of fine splints, longer than the preceding, of which one or more in a set are distinguished by marks, employed by the Indians of the Athapascan, Lutuamian, Shastan, Weitspekan, and Wishoskan tribes near the Pacific coast; (*c*) of sticks and rushes, entirely unmarked, employed by the Indians of the Algonquian, Iroquoian, Kulanapan, Siouan, and Washoan tribes. The marks on the implements of the first sort are understood as referring to various totemic animals, etc., which are actually carved or painted on some of the sets.

In the second form of the game the sticks are replaced by flat disks, variously marked on the edges. In this form the game is played by Indians of the Chinookan, Salishan, Shahaptian, and Wakashan stocks, and is confined to the Pacific coast.

The number of sticks or disks varies from ten to more than a hundred, there being no constant number. The first operation in the game, that of dividing the sticks or disks into two bundles, is invariably the same. The object is to guess the location of an odd or a particularly marked stick. On the Pacific coast the sticks or disks are usually hidden in a mass of shredded cedar bark. On the Atlantic coast the sticks are commonly held free in the hands. In one instance it is recorded that the guesser uses a pointer to indicate his choice. The count is commonly kept with the sticks or disks themselves, the players continuing until one or the other has won all.

On the Northwest coast the sets of sticks are almost uniformly contained in a leather pouch, sometimes with the inner side painted, with a broad flap to which a long thong is attached, passing several times around the pouch, and having a pointed strip of bone, horn, or ivory at the end. The latter is slipped under the thong as a fastening. The identification of these sticks with arrow shaftments is aided by comparison with the banded shaftments of actual arrows, as, for example, those of the Hupa (figure 307). Figure 308 represents a cut shaftment of an actual arrow, still bearing bands of red paint, found among the débris of a cliff-dwelling in Mancos canyon, Colorado, which Mr Cushing regarded as having been intended for a game in the manner of the sticks. In this connection the following account of the tiyotipi of the Dakota, by Stephen R. Riggs,[a] will be found of interest:

The exponent of the phratry was the tiyotipi, or soldier's lodge. Its meaning is the lodge of lodges. There were placed the bundles of black and red sticks

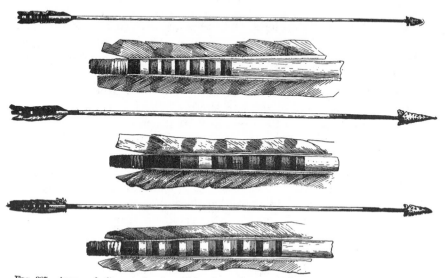

FIG. 307. Arrow shaftment showing ribband ng; Hupa Indians, California; cat. no. 126517, United States National Museum.

of the soldiers. There the soldiers gathered to talk and smoke and feast. There the laws of the encampment were enacted.

Describing the lodge, he says:

A good fire is blazing inside, and we may just lift up the skin door and crawl in. Toward the rear of the tent, but near enough for convenient use, is a large pipe placed by the symbols of power. There are two bundles of shaved sticks about 6 inches long. The sticks in one bundle are painted black and in the other red. The black bundle represents the real men of the camp—those who

FIG. 308. Cut arrow shaftment; length, 6 inches; cliff-dwelling, Mancos canyon, Colorado; Free Museum of Science and Art, University of Pennsylvania

have made their mark on the warpath. The red bundle represents the boys and such men as wear no eagle feathers.

Again, he says:

Then of all the round-shaved sticks, some of which were painted black, and some painted red, four are especially marked. They are the four chiefs of the tiyotipi that were made. And these men are not selected at random for this place, but men who have killed many enemies and are most able are chosen.

---

[a] Dakota Grammar, Texts and Ethnography, edited by James Owen Dorsey. Contributions to North American Ethnology, v. 9, p. 195, 200, Washington, 1893.

In conclusion, Mr Riggs adds:

The special marking of the sticks is done on the line of personal history. Whatever is indicated by the kind of eagle feathers a man is entitled to wear on his head, and by the notches in them, this is all hieroglyphed on his stick in the tiyotipi. Then these bundles of sticks are used for gambling. The question is "Odd or even?" The forfeits are paid in meat for the tiyotipi.

The gambling mat used in the stick game by the Thompson (figure 335) suggests a probable explanation of the origin of the long woven head ornament, consisting of a strip or net made of native hemp (figure 309) worn down the back by the Hupa in one of their dances. From the general resemblance of the two objects and the constant use of other gambling implements as head ornaments, the writer is inclined to connect the Hupa head band with their common game of kin. It may have been used to wrap the sticks or as a mat for the game.

ALGONQUIAN STOCK

ALGONKIN. Three Rivers, Quebec.

Pierre Boucher [a] says:

The game of straw (paille) is played with little straws made for this purpose and which are divided very unequally into three parts, as in hazard. Our Frenchmen have not yet been able to learn this game. It is full of vivacy; and straws are among them what cards are with us.

FIG. 309. Head ornament; length, 38 inches; Hupa Indians, Hupa valley, California; cat. no. 37263, Free Museum of Science and Art, University of Pennsylvania.

CHIPPEWA. Turtle mountain, North Dakota. (Cat. no. $\frac{50}{4717}$, American Museum of Natural History.)

Eleven sticks (figure 310), painted saplings, 18 inches long. These were collected in 1903 by Dr William Jones, who described them as used in a game called agintakunanatiwinani, stick counting.

Two men play. One takes the sticks, five in one hand and six in the other,

FIG. 310. Stick game; length of sticks, 18 inches; Chippewa Indians, Turtle mountain, North Dakota; cat. no. $\frac{50}{4717}$, American Museum of Natural History.

his opponent guessing which hand held the odd stick, touching the hand he selects. The division and guess are effected with great rapidity.

---

[a] Histoire Véritable et Naturelle des Moeurs et Productions du Pays de la Novelle France, ch. 10, Paris, 1664.

CREE. Wind River reservation, Wyoming. (Cat. no. 37027, Free
      Museum of Science and Art, University of Pennsylvania.)

Twenty-nine peeled willow twigs (figure 311), 18 inches in length.

These were collected in 1900 by the writer, for whom they were
made by a Cree of Riel's band, who gave the name as tepashgue ma-
tun and said the game was derived from the Salish.

Played by two persons. One takes the bundle and rolls the sticks in his hands
and divides them into two parts, throwing one bundle to the other player, who
guesses which contains the even number of sticks. If the bundle designated is
odd, the guesser loses. Sometimes the sticks are divided into two bundles and
held crosswise, the other then guessing. They do not sing at this game.

FIG. 311. Stick game; length of sticks, 18 inches; Cree Indians, Wyoming; cat. no. 37027, Free
        Museum of Science and Art, University of Pennsylvania.

————— Muskowpetung reserve, Qu'appelle, Assiniboia. (Cat. no.
       61987, Field Columbian Museum.)

Bundle of twenty-five slender willow splints (figure 312), 19 inches
      in length.

They are used in the game of counting sticks, ahkitaskoomnah-
mahtowinah, and are described as follows by the collector, Mr J. A.
Mitchell:

Played by both men and women or by either separately. Players are divided
into two parties, seated opposite each other. Stakes of money, clothing, etc.,
are then put up in a common lot. The person inviting the players begins the
game by secretly dividing the bundle
of twenty-five sticks into two lots,
holding one bundle in either hand.
If his opponent chooses the bundle
containing the even number of
sticks, he wins; if the odd bundle,
he loses, and the play passes to the

FIG. 312. Stick game; length of sticks, 19 inches;
Cree Indians, Assiniboia; cat. no. 61987, Field
Columbian Museum.

next couple. Play is kept up until either one or the other party desires to
stop, when the wagered articles are taken possession of by the party having
made the most points and are divided among all that party. The game is
sometimes kept up for several days and nights.

ILLINOIS. Illinois.

Mr Andrew McFarland Davis [a] states:

I am indebted to Dr Trumbull for information that a MS. Illinois dictionary
(probably compiled by Gravier, about 1700) gives many of the terms used in
the games of straws and dice.

MASSACHUSET. Massachusetts.

William Wood, in his New England's Prospect,[b] says:

They have two sorts of games, one called puim, the other hubbub, not much
unlike cards and dice, being no other than lottery. Puim is fifty or sixty

[a] Bulletin of the Essex Institute, v. 18, note p. 177, Salem, 1886.
[b] London, 1634; Reprint, p. 90, Boston, 1898.

small bents of a foot long which they divide to the number of their gamesters, shuffling them first between the palms of their hands; he that hath more than his fellow is so much the forwarder in his game: many other strange whimsies be in this game; which would be too long to commit to paper; he that is a noted gambler, hath a great hole in his ear wherein he carries his puims in defiance of his antagonists.

MIAMI. St. Joseph river, Michigan.

P. de Charlevoix [a] says:

That day the Pottawatomi had come to play the game of straws with the Miami. They played in the hut of the chief, and in a place opposite. These straws are small, about as thick as a wheat straw and 2 inches long. Each player takes a bundle of them, usually containing two hundred and one, always an uneven number. After having well shaken them about, making meanwhile a thousand contortions and invoking the spirits, they separate them, with a sort of thorn or pointed bone, into parcels of ten. Each one takes his own, haphazard, and he who has chosen the parcel containing eleven wins a certain number of points, as may have been agreed upon. The game is 60 or 80. There were other ways of playing this game which they were willing to explain to me, but I could understand nothing unless it was that sometimes the number 9 wins the game. They also told me that there is as much skill as chance in this game, and that the savages are extremely clever at it, as at all other games; that they give themselves up to it and spend whole days and nights at it; that sometimes they do not stop playing until they are entirely naked, having nothing more to lose. There is another way of playing, without stakes. This is purely a pastime, but it has almost always bad consequences for morals.

NARRAGANSET. Rhode Island.

Roger Williams, in his Key into the Language of America,[b] says:

Their games (like the English) are of two sorts; private and public; a game like unto the English cards, yet instead of cards, they play with strong rushes.

In his vocabulary he gives the following definitions:

Akésuog: they are at cards, or telling of rushes; pissinnéganash: their playing rushes; ntakésemin: I am telling, or counting; for their play is a kind of arithmetic.

NORRIDGEWOCK. Norridgewock, Maine.

In the dictionary of Father Sebastian Rasles,[c] as pointed out by Mr Davis,[d] one finds corresponding with pissinnéganash, the word pesseníganar, defined as " les pailles avec quoi on joue a un autre jeu."

PIEGAN. Montana.

Mr Louis L. Meeker writes: [e]

A game, described as straws or Indian cards, is played with a number of unmarked sticks. Piegan pupils at Fort Shaw, Montana, used lead pencils for

---

[a] Journal d'un Voyage dans l'Amérique Septentrionnale, v. 3, p. 318, Paris, 1744.

[b] London, 1643. Collections of the Rhode Island Historical Society, v. 1, p. 145, Providence, 1827.

[c] Memoirs American Academy of Arts and Sciences, n. s., v. 1, p. 472, Cambridge, 1833.

[d] Bulletin of the Essex Institute, v. 18, p. 176, Salem, 1886.

[e] In a letter to the author.

the purpose. An odd number was separated into two portions by one player. The other chose one portion. If the number was odd, he won.

POWHATAN. Virginia.

William Strachey [a] says:

Dice play, or cards, or lots they know not, how be it they use a game upon rushes much like primero, wherein they card and discard, and lay a stake too, and so win and lose. They will play at this for their bows and arrows, their copper beads, hatchets, and their leather coats.

In his vocabulary Strachey gives: " To play at any game, mamantū terracan."

Roger Beverley [b] says:

They have also one great diversion, to the practising of which are requisite whole handfuls of little sticks or hard straws, which they know how to count as fast as they can cast their eyes upon them, and can handle with a surprising dexterity.

SAUK AND FOXES. Iowa. (Cat. no. $\frac{50}{3518}$, American Museum of Natural History.)

Bundle of one hundred and two peeled willow sticks (figure 313), 12 inches in length, and a pointed stick (figure 314), with a red-painted tip, 13½ inches in length.

These were collected by Dr William Jones, who describes them as implements for the counting game, agitci kanahamogi. The name

FIG. 313. Stick game; length of sticks, 12 inches; Sauk and Fox Indians, Iowa; cat. no. $\frac{50}{3518}$, American Museum of Natural History.

means to count with an agent; agitasowa, he counts; agitasoweni, counting.

Dr Jones informed me that the game is no longer played, but, from the constant reference to it in stories, the people are all familiar with it and made the above-described implements according to their tradition.

In playing, the entire bundle is held together in the hands and allowed to fall in a pile, which is then divided with the pointed stick, called the dividing stick.

FIG. 314. Dividing stick for stick game; length, 13½ inches; Sauk and Fox Indians, Iowa; cat. no. $\frac{50}{3518}$, American Museum of Natural History.

The object is to separate either 9, shāgäwa; or 11, metāswi neguti, or 13, 15, 17, or 19,[c] but the player must call out which of these numbers he attempts to divide before putting down the dividing stick. If he succeeds he scores 1 point, but if he fails the turn goes to another player.

---

[a] Historie of Travaile into Virginia Britannia, p. 78; printed for the Hakluyt Society, London, 1849.

[b] The History and Present State of Virginia, p. 53, London, 1705; p. 175, Richmond, Va., 1855.

[c] Or 21, 31, 41; 23, 33, 43; 25, 35, 45; 27, 37, 47; 29, 39, 49, etc.

Another set of implements for the same game in this collection (cat. no. $\frac{50}{3517}$) consists of fifty-one sticks (figure 315), 9¼ inches in length, and a finder, a forked twig 18 inches in length. Another name for the game is āteso'kāganăni, from āteso̅ 'kāwa, he tells a story—that is, a myth.

Fɪɢ. 315. Stick game: sticks and finder; length of sticks, 9¼ inches; length of finder, 18 inches; Sauk and Fox Indians, Iowa; cat. no. $\frac{50}{3517}$, American Museum of Natural History.

ATHAPASCAN STOCK

Aᴛᴀᴀᴋᴜᴛ. Hupa Valley reservation, California. (Cat. no. 126905, United States National Museum.)

Set of thirty-one sticks, 8¾ inches in length and tapering to the ends, one having a band of black paint near the middle (figure 316).

These were collected by Lieut. P. H. Ray, U. S. Army, who describes the game under the designation of kinnahelah:

This game is played by any number that wish to engage in betting. Two dealers sit opposite each other on a blanket, each backed by two or more singers and a drummer, and the game commences by one of the dealers taking the sticks in both hands, about equally divided, and holding them behind his back, shuffling them from hand to hand, after which he brings them in front of his body with both hands extended and the sticks grasped so the players can not

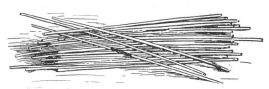

Fɪɢ. 316. Stick game; length of sticks, 8¾ inches; Ataakut Indians, Hupa Valley reservation, California; cat. no. 126905, United States National Museum.

see the centers. The opposite dealer clasps his hands together two or three times and points towards the hand which he thinks holds the stick with the black center. Should he guess correctly, he takes the deal and holds it until his opponent wins it back in like manner. For each failure a forfeit is paid, and one is also demanded when the dealer loses the deal. Friends of each party make outside bets on the dealers, and each dealer's band plays and sings as long as he holds the deal.[a]

Hᴜᴘᴀ. Hupa Valley reservation, California. (Free Museum of Science and Art, University of Pennsylvania.)

---

[a] See Prof. Otis T. Mason, The Ray Collection from Hupa Reservation. Report of the Smithsonian Institution for 1886, pt. 1, p. 234, 1889.

Cat. no. 37201.   Set of one hundred and six fine wooden splints, eight marked in the center with black; length, 8½ inches; tied with a thong.

It was explained by the maker of these sticks that it was customary to put four sticks, aces, marked with black, in a pack, although but one is actually used in guessing. The count is kept with 11 twigs. Two people play. The starter takes 5 and the other player 6, and the game continues until one or the other has the 11 twigs. The name of the game is kiñ, meaning stick. This and the similar sets following are called hō-tchi-kiñ, hō-tchi being explained as meaning correct.

Cat. no. 37202.   Set of sticks for kiñ, hotchikiñ. Fifty-three coarse splints, one marked with black; length, 10 inches.

Fig. 317. Counting sticks for stick game; length, 7 inches; Hupa Indians, California; cat. no. 37206, Free Museum of Science and Art, University of Pennsylvania.

Cat. no. 37203.   Set of one hundred and ninety-three fine splints, four marked with black; length, 8⅝ inches.

Cat. no. 37204.   Set of forty-three fine splints, three marked with black; length, 9 inches.

Cat. no. 37205.   Set of one hundred and thirty-nine fine splints, five marked with black; length, 9¾ inches. Twenty-four splints have spiral ribbons of red the entire length, said to have been added to make the sticks more salable for the white trade.

Cat. no. 37206 (figure 317).   Set of eleven counting sticks for kiñ, called chittistil; half sections, with bark having three spiral lines cut across; length, 7 inches.

A Crescent City Indian whom the writer met at Arcata, California, gave the names of the sticks used in kiñ as tchacti, and the trump as tchacwun.

Fig. 318. Stick game; length of sticks, 4⅛ inches; Hupa Indians, California; cat. no. 37208, Free Museum of Science and Art, University of Pennsylvania.

Cat. no. 37208.   Set of game sticks, missolich (figure 318).   Fifteen small sticks of hard polished wood, 4⅝ inches in length.

Seven of these have three bands around and three rows of dots or points at each end; seven have only three bands and one, two bands. The last is regarded as the ace, or stick which is guessed, hauk.

All collected by the writer in 1900.

HUPA. Hupa Valley reservation, California. (United States National Museum.)

Cat. no. 151673.   Set of ninety-eight slender pointed sticks, 8⅞ inches in length, two marked with a band of black near the middle; collected by Lieut. Robert H. Fletcher, U. S. Army.

Cat. no. 21314.   Set of sixty-two slender pointed sticks, 9¾ inches in length, three marked with black band near the middle.

Cat. no. 21316.   Set of fifty-one slender sticks (figure 319), 9⅜ inches in length, thicker than the preceding and not pointed; three marked with a black band near the middle.

FIG. 319. Stick game; length of sticks, 9⅜ inches; Hupa Indians, California; cat. no. 21316, United States National Museum.

Cat. no. 21315.   Ninety-three slender pointed sticks, 8⅞ inches in length, and two about 8½ inches in length, possibly parts of two or more sets; four marked with band of black near the middle, one carved near the middle, and one carved near the end, as shown in figure 320.

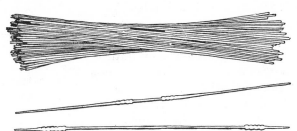

FIG. 320. Stick game; length of sticks, 8⅞ inches; Hupa Indians, California; cat. no. 21315, United States National Museum.

The foregoing specimens from cat. no. 21314 were collected by Mr Stephen Powers, who describes the game as follows:

Kin, one hundred gambling sticks, four of them marked black around the middle. The player holds up two, and his adversary guesses in which hand is the marked one. If he is unsuccessful with this one, he takes another one of the marked ones; if unsuccessful with all of the marked ones in the bunch, he tries another bunch, or scarifies the outside of his legs, cutting them with shallow cross lines. A company, sometimes a hundred people, surround the players, and a drum is beaten with a stick, to which is attached a rattle of deer hoofs, while chanting is kept up.

———— Hupa Valley reservation, California. (Cat. no. 126906, United States National Museum.)

Set of eight cylinders of wood (figure 321), 4⅝ inches in length and five-sixteenths of an inch in diameter, made of twigs. Seven have a band of black paint at both ends and in the middle, while the eighth is painted only in the middle.

These were collected by Lieut. P. H. Ray, U. S. Army, who describes them under the name of kinnahelah:

> The game is essentially the same [as that from the Ataakut] except in the use of a smaller number of sticks and the joker being blackened only in the center, while the balance are blackened at both ends and center. Both games are called kin.

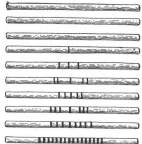

MIKONOTUNNE and MISHIKHWUTMETUNNE. Siletz reservation, Oregon. A. W. Chase [a] says:

> Captain Tichenor played several native games of cards for us, the "pasteboards" being bundles of sticks.

FIG. 321. Stick game; length of sticks, 4⅖ inches; Hupa Indians, Hupa Valley reservation, California; cat. no. 126906, United States National Museum.

SEKANI. Sicanie river, British Columbia. (Cat. no. 688, Peabody Museum of American Archæology and Ethnology.)

Ten sticks of light wood, 4¾ inches in length and one-fourth of an inch in diameter, marked alike with red lines or ribbons (figure 322); collected by J. T. Rothrock, and acquired by the Museum in 1867 with other Athapascan objects.

The use of these sticks is explained clearly by the following reference by Father Morice to the game of atlih. There is another set of gambling sticks in the Peabody Museum, cat. no. 48395, about which nothing is known, but which from their resemblance to the preceding are probably from the same or some adjacent tribe. They number fifty-one, are marked in four different ways with faint black and red lines, and are contained in a flat leather pouch, open at the top, the sticks standing on end.

FIG. 322. Stick game; length of sticks, 4⅖ inches; Sekani Indians, British Columbia; cat. no. 688, Peabody Museum of American Archæology and Ethnology.

TAKULLI. Upper Fraser river, British Columbia. Sir Alexander Mackenzie [b] says:

> We all sat down on a very pleasant green spot, and were no sooner seated than our guide and one of the party prepared to engage in play. They had each a bundle of about fifty small sticks, neatly polished, of the size of a quill, and 5 inches long; a certain number of these sticks had red lines around them, and

---

[a] The Overland Monthly, v. 2, p. 433, San Francisco, 1869.
[b] Voyages from Montreal, p. 311, London, 1801.

as many of these as one of the players might find convenient were curiously rolled up in dry grass, and according to the judgment of his antagonist respecting their number and marks he lost or won. Our friend was apparently the loser, as he parted with his bow and arrows and several articles which I had given him.

TAKULLI. Stuart lake, British Columbia.

The Reverend Father A. G. Morice [a] refers to a game—

atlih, which in times past was passionately played by the Carriers, but is now altogether forgotten except by a few elder men. It necessitated the use of a quantity of finely-polished bonesticks, perhaps 4 or 5 inches long.

Father Morice describes atlih as the original counterpart of the modern netsea, or hand game. In a general sense, the name of the game may be translated gambling. The bones were called alte.

Father Morice [b] gives also the following legend of the game:

A young man was so fond of playing atlih that, after he had lost every part of his wearing apparel, he went so far as to gamble away his very wife and children. Disgusted with his conduct, his fellow-villagers turned away from him and migrated to another spot of the forest, taking along all their belongings, and carefully extinguishing the fire of every lodge so that he might perish.

Now, this happened in winter time. Reduced to this sad fate, and in a state of complete nakedness, the young man searched every fireplace in the hope of finding some bits of burning cinders, but to no purpose. He then took the dry grass on which his fellow villagers had been resting every night and roughly weaved it into some sort of a garment to cover his nakedness.

Yet without fire or food he could not live. So he went off in despair without snowshoes, expecting death in the midst of his wanderings.

After journeying some time, as he was half frozen and dying of hunger, he suddenly caught sight in the top of the tall spruces of a glimmer as of a far-off fire. Groping his way thither, he soon perceived sparks flying out of two columns of smoke, and cautiously approaching he came upon a large lodge covered with branches of conifers. He peeped through a chink and saw nobody but an old man sitting by one of two large fires burning in the lodge.

Immediately the old man cried out, " Come in, my son-in-law ! " The young man was much astonished, inasmuch as he could see nobody outside but himself. " Come in, my son-in-law; what are you doing out in the cold ? " came again from the lodge. Whereupon the gambler ascertained that it was himself who was thus addressed. Therefore he timidly entered, and, following his host's suggestion, he set to warm himself by one of the fires.

The old man was called Ne-yəʀ-hwolluz,[c] because, being no other than Yihta,[d] he nightly carries his house about in the course of his travelings. " You seem very miserable, my son-in-law ; take this up," he said to his guest while putting mantlewise on the young man's shoulders a robe of sewn marmot skins. He next handed him a pair of tanned skin moccasins and ornamental leggings of the same

---

[a] Notes on the Western Dénés. Transactions of the Canadian Institute, v. 4, p. 78, Toronto, 1895.

[b] Ibid., p. 79.

[c] Literally, " He-carries (as with a sleigh)-a-house." The final hwolluz is proper to the dialect of the Lower Carriers, though the tale is narrated by an Upper Carrier, which circumstance would seem to indicate that the legend is not, as so many others, borrowed from Tsimpsian tribe.

[d] Ursa Major.

material. He then called out, " My daughter, roast by the fireside something to eat for your husband; he must be hungry." Hearing which, the gambler, who had thought himself alone with Ne-yəʀ-hwolluz, was much surprised to see a beautiful virgin *a* emerge from one of the corner provision and goods stores and proceed to prepare a repast for him.

Meanwhile the old man was digging a hole in the ashes, whence he brought out a whole black bear cooked under the fire with skin and hair on. Pressing with his fingers the brim of the hole made by the arrow, he took the bear up to his guest's lips, saying, " Suck out the grease, my son-in-law." The latter was so exhausted by fatigue that he could drink but a little of the warm liquid, which caused his host to exclaim, " How small bellied my son-in-law is! " Then the old man went to the second fireplace, likewise dug out therefrom a whole bear, and made his guest drink in the same way with the same result, accompanied by a similar remark.

After they had eaten, Ne-yəʀ-hwolluz showed the gambler to his resting place and cautioned him not to go out during the night. As for himself, he was soon noticed to leave the lodge that and every other night; and as he came back in the morning he invariably seemed to be quite heated and looked as one who had traveled a very great distance.

The gambler lived there happily with his new wife for some months. But his former passion soon revived. As spring came back he would take some alté in an absent-minded way and set out to play therewith all alone. Which seeing his father-in-law said to him, " If you feel lonesome here, my son-in-law, return for a while to your own folks and gamble with them." Then, handing him a set of alté and four tₑtquh,*b* he added: " When you have won all that is worth winning throw your tətquh up over the roof of the house and come back immediately. Also, remember not to speak to your former wife."

The gambler then made his departure, and was soon again among the people who had abandoned him. He was now a handsome and well-dressed young man, and soon finding partners for his game he stripped them of all their belongings, after which he threw his tətquh over the roof of the lodge. He also met his former wife as she was coming from drawing water, and though she entreated him to take her back to wife again he hardened his heart and did not know her.

Yet, instead of returning immediately after he had thrown his tətquh over the roof, as he had been directed to do, his passion for atlih betrayed him into playing again, when he lost all he had won. He was thus reduced to his first state of wretched nakedness. He then thought of Ne-yəʀ-hwolluz, of his new wife, and his new home, and attempted to return to them, but he could never find them.

TLELDING.   South fork, Trinity river, California.

Mr Stephen Powers says: *c*

The Kailtas are inveterate gamblers, either with the game of guessing the sticks or with cords, and they have a curious way of punishing or mortifying themselves for failure therein. When one has been unsuccessful in gaming he frequently scarifies himself with flints or glass on the outside of the leg from the knee down to the ankle, scratching the skin all up crisscross until it bleeds freely. He does this for luck, believing that it will appease some bad spirit who is against him. The Siahs, on Eel river, have the same custom.

---

a Sak-əsta, " She sits apart."
b A long throwing rod which serves to play another game.
c The Overland Monthly, v. 9, p. 163, San Francisco, 1872.

TUTUTNI. Siletz reservation, Oregon. (Cat. no. 63606, Field Columbian Museum.)

A bundle of one hundred and sixty-nine wooden splints (figure 323), pointed at the ends, 12 inches in length, two with black bands in the center, and the remainder plain white; twelve willow counting sticks (figure 324), pointed at the ends, 9¼ inches in length; a tubular wooden pipe (figure 325), 10 inches in length.

These were collected by Mr T. Jay Bufort, who furnished the following description of the game under the name of tussi:

This game is played very much the same as the bone hand game. the only difference being that the reeds are held in the hands behind the back and there

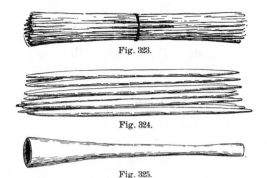

Fig. 323.

Fig. 324.

Fig. 325.

FIG. 323. Stick game; length of splints, 12 inches; Tututni Indians, Siletz reservation, Oregon; cat. no. 63606, Field Columbian Museum.
FIG. 324. Counting sticks for stick game; length, 9¼ inches; Tututni Indians, Siletz reservation, Oregon; cat. no. 63606, Field Columbian Museum.
FIG. 325. Wooden pipe used in stick game; length, 10 inches; Tututni Indians, Siletz reservation, Oregon; cat. no. 63606, Field Columbian Museum.

shuffled and divided, part in each hand. The hands are then held, one beside each leg, and the opposite party guesses by pointing and loses if he indicates the hand holding the marked stick. Tally is kept by means of twelve counters.

WHILKUT. Humboldt county, California. (Free Museum of Science and Art, University of Pennsylvania.)

Cat. no. 37245. Set of forty-five fine splints (figure 326), one marked with black; length, 8 inches.

FIG. 326. Stick game; length of splints, 8 inches; Whilkut Indians, California; cat. no. 37245, Free Museum of Science and Art, University of Pennsylvania.

Cat. no. 37246. Set of sixty-six coarse splints, three marked with black; length, 8⅞ inches.

Cat. no 37247. Set of one hundred and twelve fine splints, three marked with black; length, 8¼ inches.

These were collected by the writer in 1900, and are all designated hotchikiñ.

CHIMMESYAN STOCK

NISKA. Nass river, British Columbia.
Dr Franz Boas [a] describes the game:

Qsan: Guessing game played with a number of maple sticks marked with red or black rings, or totemic designs. Two of these sticks are trumps. It is the object of the game to guess in which of the two bundles of sticks, which are wrapped in cedar-bark, the trump is hidden. Each player uses one trump only.

TSIMSHIAN. British Columbia. (American Museum of Natural History.)

Cat. no. $\frac{16}{785}$. Set of sixty-one wood gambling sticks, $5\frac{3}{16}$ inches in length and six-sixteenths of an inch in diameter, in leather pouch; three plain, others painted with red and black ribbons; four inlaid with small disks and rectangles of abalone shell; ends nipple-shaped and inset with disks of abalone shell. Collected by Dr Franz Boas.

CHINOOKAN STOCK

CHINOOK. Shoalwater bay, Washington.
James G. Swan [b] describes the game of la-hul as follows:

A mat is first placed on the floor, with the center raised up so as to form a small ridge, which is kept in its place by four wooden pins stuck through the mat into the ground. Two persons play at this game, who are seated at each end of the mat. Each player has ten disks of wood, 2 inches in diameter, and a little over an eighth of an inch thick, resembling the men used in playing backgammon, but much larger. The only distinguishing feature about these men, or wheels, is the different manner the edges are colored. There are but two pieces of value; one has the edge blackened entirely around, and the other is perfectly plain, while the others have different quantities of color on them, varying from the black to the white. These disks are then inclosed in a quantity of the inner bark of the cedar, pounded very fine, and called tupsoe. The player, after twisting and shuffling them up in all sorts of forms, separates them into two equal parts, both being enveloped in the tupsoe. These are then rapidly moved about on the mat from side to side, the other player keeping his eyes most intently fixed upon them all the time. He has bet either on the black or the white one, and now, to win, has to point out which of the two parcels contains it. As soon as he makes his selection, which is done by a gesture of his hand, the parcel is opened, and each piece is rolled down the mat to the ridge in the center. He can thus see the edges of all, and knows whether he has lost or won.

Alexander Ross [c] says:

When not employed in war or hunting, the men generally spend their time in gambling. The chief game, chal-e-chal, at which they stake their most valuable property, is played by six persons, with ten circular palettes of polished wood, in size and shape resembling dollars. A mat 3 feet broad and 6 feet long is spread on the ground, and the articles at stake laid at one end, then the parties

---

[a] Fifth Report on the Indians of British Columbia. Report of the Sixty-fifth Meeting of the British Association for the Advancement of Science, p. 582, London, 1895.

[b] The Northwest Coast, p. 157, New York, 1857.

[c] Adventures of the First Settlers on the Oregon or Columbia River, p. 90, London, 1849.

seat themselves, three on each side of the mat, facing one another; this done, one of the players takes up the ten palettes, shuffling and shifting them in his hands, when at a signal given he separates them in his two fists, and throws them out on the mat towards his opponent, and according as the palettes roll, slide, or lie on the mat when thrown, the party wins or loses. This he does three times successively. In this manner each tries his skill in turn, till one of the parties wins. Whole days and nights are spent in this game without ceasing, and the Indians seldom grumble or repine, even should they lose all that they possess. During the game the players keep chanting a loud and sonorous tune, accompanying the different gestures of the body just as the voyageurs keep time to the paddle.

FIG. 327. Stick game; length of sticks, 3¼ inches; Winnimen Indians, California; cat. no. 19338, United States National Museum.

COPEHAN STOCK

WINNIMEN. California. (Cat. no. 19338, United States National Museum.)

Ten willow twigs (figure 327), 3¼ inches in length, nine with bark entire length and one with band of bark removed in the middle.

Collected by Mr Livingston Stone, who describes them as used in a woman's game.

IROQUOIAN STOCK

HURON. Ontario.

Nicolas Perrot [a] says of le jeu des pailles:

The savages lose at the game of straws not only their own property, but also the property of their comrades. To play the game, they procure a certain number of straws or twigs of a certain plant, which are no thicker than the cord of a salmon net. They are made of the same length and thickness, being about 10 inches long. Their number is uneven. After turning and mixing them in their hands, they are placed on a skin or blanket rug, and he who plays first, having an alaine or, more often, a small pointed bone in his hand, contorts his arms and body, saying chok! chok! at frequent intervals. These words mean nothing in their language, but serve to make known their desire to play well and with good luck. Then he pushes the little pointed bone into the pile of straws and takes as many as he wishes. His opponent takes those that remain on the rug and rapidly counts them by tens, making no errors. He who has the odd number of straws wins.

Sometimes they play with seeds which grow in the woods and which are a little like small haricots. They take a certain number of them each, according to the value of the goods wagered, which may be a gun, a blanket, or in fact anything, and he who at the beginning of the game holds nine straws wins everything and takes all that has been wagered. If he finds that he holds an odd number less than nine, he is at liberty to increase his bets to any extent he pleases. This is why in one part of the game he invests, as he pleases, one straw and in another part three, five, or seven, for nine is always supposed; it is the number that wins against all the others, and he who at last finds that he holds nine straws generally takes everything that has been wagered. At the

---

[a] Mémoire sur les Mœurs, Coustumes et Relligion des Sauvages de l'Amérique Septentrionale, p. 46, Leipzig, 1864.

side of the straws on the rug are the seeds with which the players have made their bets. It should be noted that more is bet on the nine than all the others.

When the players have made their bets, he who has been lucky handles the straws often, turning them end for end in his hands, and as he places them on the rug says chank, which means nine, and the other player, who has the alaine or little pointed bone in his hand, plunges it among the straws and, as said before, takes as many as he pleases. The other player takes the rest. If the latter wishes to leave some of them, his opponent must take them, and, both counting by tens, he who has the odd number wins and takes the stakes. But if it happens that the winner is ahead by only one straw he wins only the seeds that belong to that straw; for example, three are more powerful than two, five than three, and seven than five, but nine than all. If several persons play and one of them finds that he holds five, they play four at a time, two against two, or less if there are not four players. Some win the seeds bet on five straws and the others those bet for three and one. When no one holds the odd number of those that remain—that is to say, of one and three—after having carefully counted the straws by tens, when he has not nine, the player must increase his bet, even when he holds five or seven straws, and the deal does not count. He is also obliged to make two other piles; in one he puts five and in the other seven straws, with as many seeds as he pleases. His adversaries draw in their turn when he has done this, and then he takes the rest. Some will be fortunate, but each player takes only the number of seeds belonging to the number of straws, and he who has nine takes only the seeds bet on the nine. When another holds seven he draws what remains, for three and one are the same thing, but not those numbers which are higher. If a player loses everything that he has with him, the game is continued on credit, if the player gives assurance that he has other property elsewhere, but when he continues to lose the winner may refuse him seeds to the extent asked and oblige him to produce his effects, not wishing to continue the game till he has seen that his opponent still has property to risk. To this there is but one reply, and the loser will ask one of his friends to bring to him what remains of his goods. If he continues unlucky, he will continue playing till he loses all that he owns, and one of his comrades will take his place, announcing what he is willing to risk and taking seeds according to its value.

This game sometimes lasts three or four days. When a loser wins back everything and the former winner loses his all, a comrade takes his place and the game goes on till one side or the other has nothing left with which to play, it being the rule of the savages not to leave the game until one side or the other has lost everything. This is why they are compelled to give revenge to all members of a side, one after the other, as I have just stated. They are at liberty to have anyone they wish play for them, and if disputes arise—I mean between winners and losers, each being backed by his side—they may go to such extremes that blood may be shed and the quarrel ended with difficulty. If the winner takes losses calmly, pretending not to notice the sharp practice and cheating which occur frequently in the game, he is praised and esteemed by all; but the cheater is blamed by everyone and can find no one to play with him, at least not until he has returned his ill-gotten gains.

The game is usually played in the large cabins of the chiefs, which might also be called the savages' academy, for here are seen all the young people making up different sides, with older men acting as spectators of the games. If a player thinks he has divided the straws well and that he has drawn an odd number, he holds them in one hand and strikes them with the other, and when he has counted them by tens, without saying anything, he lets the others know that he has gained by taking up the seeds wagered, watching out that his opponent does not do so. If one of them thinks that the straws were not properly counted, they are handed to two of the spectators to count, and the winner, without speaking, strikes his straws and takes the stakes.

All this takes place without dispute and with much good faith. You will notice that this is not at all a woman's game and that it is only the men who play it. [a]

HURON. Ontario.

Bacqueville de la Potherie [b] says:

They have another game which consists of a handful of straws, the number of which is, however, limited. They separate first this handful in two, making certain gestures, which only serve to increase the interest in the game, and in it, as in bowl, they strike themselves heavily upon the naked skin on the shoulders and on the chest. When they have separated the straws, they retain one portion and give the other to their companions. One does not easily understand this game, your lordship, at sight. They seem to play odd and even.

Father Louis Hennepin [c] says:

They also often play with a number of straws half a foot long or thereabouts. There is one who takes them all in his hand; then, without looking, he divides them in two. When he has separated them, he gives one part to his antagonist. Whoever has an even number, according as they have agreed, wins the game.

They have also another game which is very common among little children in Europe. They take kernels of Indian corn or something of the kind; then they put some in one hand and ask how many there are. The one who guesses the number wins.

Baron La Hontan [d] says:

They have three sorts of games. Their game of counters is purely numerical, and he that can add, subtract, multiply, and divide best by these counters is the winner.

KOLUSCHAN STOCK

CHILKAT. Alaska. (United States National Museum.)

Cat. no. 46487. Thirty-four cylindrical wood sticks, part of three sets, ten $4\frac{3}{4}$ inches, fifteen $5\frac{1}{16}$ inches, and nine $5\frac{1}{2}$ inches in length, all marked with black and red ribbons. Collected by Commander L. A. Beardslee, U. S. Navy.

Cat. no. 67909a. Set of fifty-seven cylindrical bone sticks, $4\frac{15}{16}$ inches in length and five-sixteenths of an inch in diameter, with a hole drilled near one end for stringing; all engraved with fine encircling lines. One is set with a rectangular strip of abalone shell and one with a rectangular piece of ivory, having another hole, similarly shaped, from which the ivory has been removed. Six

[a] Rev. J. Tailhan, who edited Perrot's manuscript, after referring to Lafitau's statement that Perrot's description of this game is so obscure that it is nearly unintelligible, says that he has not been more successful than his predecessors, and the game of straws remains to him an unsolved game. (Notes to chap. 10, p. 188.)

[b] Histoire de l'Amérique Septentrionale, v. 3, p. 22, Paris, 1723.

[c] A Description of Louisiana, p. 301, New York, 1880.

[d] New Voyages to North-America, v. 2, p. 18, London, 1703.

others have deep square and triangular holes for the insertion of slips of ivory or shell, and twelve are engraved with conventional animal designs, of which five have holes for the insertion of ivory eyes; ends flat.

Cat. no. 67909b. Set of thirty-nine cylindrical bone sticks, $4\frac{1}{16}$ inches in length and four-sixteenths of an inch in diameter, with a hole drilled near one end for stringing; all engraved with fine encircling lines. One has two deep rectangular holes for the insertion of abalone shell, which has been removed. One has a row of three dots and three dotted circles. Four are engraved with conventional animal designs.

The two sets were collected by Mr John J. McLean.

CHILKAT. Alaska. (Cat. no. $\frac{E}{1019}$, American Museum of Natural History.)

Sixteen maple gambling sticks, $4\frac{3}{16}$ inches in length and five-sixteenths of an inch in diameter, marked with red and black ribbons, and six with burnt totemic designs; ends ovate. With the above are ten odd sticks belonging to six or seven different sets. Collected by Lieut. George T. Emmons, U. S. Navy.

STIKINE. Alaska. (Cat. no. $\frac{19}{1058}$, American Museum of Natural History.)

Set of fifty-three wood gambling sticks, $4\frac{2}{16}$ inches in length and five-sixteenths of an inch in diameter, in leather pouch; all marked with red and black ribbons, and having each end incised with three crescent-shaped marks suggesting a human face; in part inlaid with small pieces of abalone shell and small rings of copper wire; ends flat. Collected by Lieut. George T. Emmons, U. S. Navy.

TAKU. Taku inlet, Alaska. (American Museum of Natural History.)

Cat. no. $\frac{E}{598}$. Set of fifty-seven cylindrical polished maple sticks, $4\frac{15}{16}$ inches in length, in leather pouch; all marked with red and black ribbons.

These were collected by Lieut. George T. Emmons, U. S. Navy, who gave the following designations of the sticks:

Eight are designed as kitē, blackfish; one as tieesh sakh', starfish; four as kah, duck; ten as late-la-ta, sea gull; four as nork, sunfish; four as shuuko, robin; four as heon, fly; three as kar-shish-show, like a dragon fly; three as tseeke, black bear; three as gowh, surf duck; four as larkar; three as yah-ah-un-a, South Southerlee [sic]; three as ihk-ok-kohm, cross pieces of canoe; two as kea-thlu, dragon fly; one as tis, moon.

Cat. no. $\frac{E}{600}$. Set of sixty-six cylindrical polished wood sticks, $4\frac{15}{16}$ inches in length, in leather pouch. Twenty-seven of these sticks are marked with red and black ribbons; thirty-eight are plain, of which some show old bands, obliterated but not removed, while two are inlaid with a small rectangular piece of black horn (plate IV, k), and one with a small ring of copper wire.

These also were collected by Lieutenant Emmons, who gave the following description of the twenty-seven marked sticks:

Three are designated as tuk-kut-ke-yar, humming bird (plate IV, a); three as kark, golden-eye duck (plate IV, b); three as dulth, a bird like a heron without topknot (plate IV, c); three as kau-kon, sun (plate IV, d); four as kite, black-fish (plate IV, e); three as sarish, four-pronged starfish (plate IV, f); three as kok-khatete, loon (plate IV, g); three as ars, stick, tree (plate IV, h); two as ta-thar-ta, sea gull (plate IV, j).

TLINGIT. Alaska. (American Museum of Natural History.)

Cat. no. $\frac{E}{596}$. Set of forty-three gambling sticks, $5\frac{4}{16}$ inches in length and five-sixteenths of an inch in diameter, in leather pouch; one plain, others marked with red and black ribbon; ends nipple-shaped. Fort Wrangell.

Cat. no. $\frac{E}{599}$. Set of forty-six wooden gambling sticks, $5\frac{1}{16}$ inches in length and five-sixteenths of an inch in diameter, in leather pouch; all marked with red and black ribbons. Fort Wrangell.

Cat. no. $\frac{E}{601}$. Set of sixty-two polished maple gambling sticks, $4\frac{4}{16}$ inches in length and one-fourth of an inch in diameter, in leather pouch; painted with red and black ribbons, in part inlaid with abalone shell; one carved with head of a man; ends ovate. Sitka.

Cat. no. $\frac{E}{602}$. Set of sixty-seven maple gambling sticks, $4\frac{4}{16}$ inches in length and five-sixteenths of an inch in diameter, in leather pouch; all marked with red and black ribbons; ends ovate. Sitka.

Cat. no. $\frac{E}{603}$. Set of forty-three wood gambling sticks, $4\frac{12}{16}$ inches in length and four-sixteenths of an inch in diameter, in leather pouch; twenty-two painted with red and black ribbons, others plain, ends having small raised flat disk.

Cat. no. $\frac{E}{2274}$. Set of forty-nine wood gambling sticks, $3\frac{3}{16}$ inches in length and five-sixteenths of an inch in diameter, in leather pouch; all painted with red and black ribbons; ten inlaid with small pieces of abalone shell, copper, and horn; ends flat. Fort Wrangell.

All of the above specimens were collected by Lieut. George T. Emmons, U. S. Navy. The name is given as alhkar.

In a reply to an inquiry addressed by the writer, Lieutenant Emmons wrote as follows:

All of the sets of sticks catalogued in my collection in New York were procured among the Tlingit people, who inhabit the coast of southeastern Alaska from Nass river northward to the delta of Copper river, together with the adjacent islands of the Alexander archipelago, exclusive of Annette and the western portion of Prince of Wales island. The Tlingit are divided into six-teen tribal divisions, but these are purely geographical. They are practically one people, all Tlingit in language, customs, and manners. Gambling sticks are common to all, but are more generally found among the more southern people. The same character of stick is found among the three contiguous peoples, Tlingit, Haida, and Tsimshian, and I should say extended down the west to the extremity of Vancouver island. The Tlingit are the most northen people who use them. I believe the names, which depend upon the sticks, are somewhat arbitrary.

Dr Aurel Krause [a] says:

The Tlingit play with round sticks marked with red stripes, about 4 inches in length. These are mixed by rolling a bundle of from ten to twenty back-ward and forward between the palms of the hands. . . . The sticks are then dealt out, together with a piece of cedar bark, which serves to cover the marks. It is now the point to guess these marks. Two persons or two sides only play.

TLINGIT. Norfolk sound, Alaska.
Capt. George Dixon [b] says:

The only gambling implements I saw were fifty-two small round bits of wood, about the size of your middle finger, and differently marked with red paint. A game is played by two persons with these pieces of wood, and chiefly consists in placing them in a variety of positions, but I am unable to describe it minutely. The man whom I before mentioned our having on board at Port Mulgrave lost a knife, a spear, and several toes [toys] at this game in less than an hour; though this loss was at least equal to an English gamester losing his estate, yet the poor fellow bore his ill fortune with great patience and equanimity of temper.

—————— Port des Français, Alaska.
J. F. G. de la Pérouse [c] says:

They have thirty wooden pieces, each having different marks like our dice; of these they hide seven; each of them plays in his turn, and he whose guess comes nearest to the number marked upon the seven pieces is the winner of the stake agreed upon, which is generally a piece of iron or a hatchet. This gaming renders them serious and melancholy.

—————— Sitka, Alaska.
Otto von Kotzebue [d] says:

Their common game is played with little wooden sticks painted of various colors, and called by several names, such as crab, whale, duck, etc., which are mingled promiscuously together, and placed in heaps covered with moss, the players being then required to tell in which heap the crab, the whale, etc., lies. They lose at this game all their possessions, and even their wives and children, who then become the property of the winner.

---

[a] Die Tlinkit-Indianer, p. 164, Jena, 1885. He gives the name of the game in his vocabulary as alchka, katŏk-kítscha; that of the stick marked with a red ring as nak'-alchká.

[b] A Voyage round the World, p. 245, London, 1789.

[c] A Voyage round the World, in the years 1785, 1786, 1787, and 1788, v. 2, p. 150, London, 1798.

[d] A New Voyage round the World, v. 2, p. 61, London, 1830.

POMO. Ukiah, California. (Cat. no. 3002, Brooklyn Institute Museum.)

Bundle of thirty-five small peeled sticks (figure 328), 4¾ inches in length, and eight counting sticks, split twigs with bark on one side, 7 inches in length. Collected by the writer in 1903.

One player takes the bundle of sticks, forty or fifty, in his hands, and divides them swiftly, and then counts them off in fours, the other player guessing the remainder by calling out yet, pūn, ship, (now obsolete.—J. W. H.), or to, according as he would guess a remainder of one, two, three, or none over. If he guesses correctly, he scores and takes one of the eight counting sticks.

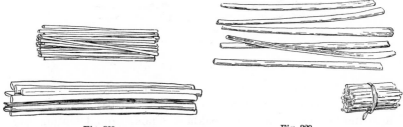

Fig. 328.   Fig. 329.

FIG. 328. Stick game; length of sticks, 4¾ inches; length of counters, 7 inches; Pomo Indians, Ukiah, California; cat. no. 3002, Brooklyn Institute Museum.
FIG. 329. Stick game; length of sticks, 2⅝ inches; length of counters, 7 inches; Pomo Indians, Mendocino county, California; cat. no. 70938, Field Columbian Museum.

———— Seven miles south of Ukiah, Mendocino county, California. (Cat. no. 70938, Field Columbian Museum.)

Bundle of forty-five sticks (figure 329), 2⅞ inches in length, and six counting sticks, 7 inches in length.

These were collected by Dr J. W. Hudson, who describes them as used in a guessing game called wĭtcli.

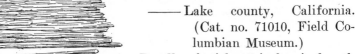

———— Lake county, California. (Cat. no. 71010, Field Columbian Museum.)

Bundle of sticks, 5 inches in length (figure 330), for match game. Collected by Dr J. W. Hudson, who gave the Pomo name for

FIG. 330. Stick game; length of sticks, 5 inches; Pomo Indians, Lake county, California; cat. no. 71010, Field Columbian Museum.

the game as haimasol, sticks mixed up.

KLAMATH. Siletz reservation, Oregon. (Cat. no. 63607, Field Columbian Museum.)

Thirteen fine wooden splints (figure 331), sharp pointed at both ends, 6½ inches in length. Eleven of the sticks have three bands of red alternating with two black (burned) bands in the middle, and on two the band in the middle is white.

These were collected by Mr T. Jay Bufort, who furnished the following account of the game, under the name of tuckinaw.

This game is played on the principle of the bone hand game. The sticks are divided and a wisp of grass is wrapped around each of the bundles, which are laid out in front of the player for the opposite side to guess; in this game the party loses if he guesses the white stick.

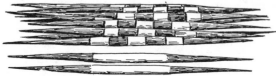

FIG. 331. Stick game; length of sticks, 6½ inches; Klamath Indians, Siletz reservation, Oregon; cat. no. 63607, Field Columbian Museum.

MOQUELUMNAN STOCK

OLAMENTKE and COSTANOAN. San Francisco mission, California.

Otto von Kotzebue,[a] who gives a list of the tribes at this mission, comprising Guimen, Olumpali, Saklan, Sonomi, and Utchium, says:

This being a holiday, the Indians did no work, but, divided into groups, amused themselves with various pastimes, one of which requires particular dexterity. Two sit on the ground opposite each other, holding in their hands a number of thin sticks, and these being thrown up at the same time with great rapidity they immediately guess whether the number is odd or even; at the side of each of the players a person sits, who scores the gain and loss. As they always play for something and yet possess nothing but their clothing, which they are not allowed to stake, they employ much pains and skill on little white shells, which serve instead of money.

Again, he says:[b]

The game is played between two antagonists, at odd or even, with short sticks; an umpire keeps the account with other sticks.

PUJUNAN STOCK

OLOLOPA. California.

A. Delano[c] says:

They are most inveterate gamblers, and frequently play away every article of value they possess, but beads are their staple gambling currency. They have two or three games, one of which is with small sticks, held in the hand, which being suddenly opened, some roll on the fingers, when the opposite player guesses at a glance their number. If he guesses right, he wins; if wrong, pays the forfeit.

---

[a] A Voyage of Discovery (1815–18), v. 1, p. 281, London, 1821.
[b] Ibid, v. 3, p. 44.
[c] Life on the Plains, p. 307, Auburn, 1854.

SALISHAN STOCK

BELLACOOLA. British Columbia. (Field Columbian Museum.)

Cat. no. 18349. Set of fifty-five cylindrical wood sticks, 4¾ inches in length, in leather pouch; variously figured, the ends rounded.

Cat. no. 18348. Set of twenty-four cylindrical wood sticks, 4½ inches in length, in leather pouch; twenty-four painted in various ways, and three carved to represent the human figure.

Cat. no. 18350. Set of forty-two cylindrical wood sticks, 4¾ inches in length, in leather pouch; variously marked with colored ribbons, the ends rounded.

All collected by Dr Franz Boas.

—— British Columbia. (Cat. no. $\frac{16}{6920}$, American Museum of Natural History.)

Set of gambling sticks, collected by Mr George Hunt.

CHILLIWHACK. British Columbia.

Mr Charles Hill-Tout [a] gives the following words in his vocabulary:

Gamble (to), lelähä'l; I gamble, lēlähä'l-tcil; gambling stick, slɛhä'l.

CLALLAM. Washington.

A Clallam boy, John Raub, described this tribe as playing the guessing game with wooden disks, under the name of slahalum. The disk with a white edge is called swaika, man, and that with a dark edge, slani, woman.

—— Fort Vancouver, Washington.

Paul Kane [b] says:

The game is called lehallum, and is played with ten small circular pieces of wood, one of which is marked black; these pieces are shuffled about rapidly between two bundles of frayed cedar bark. His opponent suddenly stops his shuffling and endeavors to guess in which bundle the blackened piece is concealed. They are so passionately fond of this game that they frequently pass two or three consecutive days and nights at it without ceasing.

CLEMCLEMALATS. Kuper island, British Columbia. (Berlin Museum für Völkerkunde.)

Cat. no. IV A 2031. Eleven wooden gaming disks, 2 inches in diameter.

FIG. 332. Wooden gaming disk; diameter, 1¾ inches; Clemclemalats Indians, Kuper island, British Columbia; cat. no. IV A 2381, Berlin Museum für Völkerkunde.

Cat. no. IV A 2381. Ten wooden gaming disks (figure 332), 1¾ inches in diameter.

Both were collected by Mr F. Jacobsen.

[a] Report of the Seventy-second Meeting of the British Association for the Advancement of Science, p. 393, London, 1903.

[b] Wanderings of an Artist among the Indians of North America, p. 220, London, 1859.

NISQUALLY. Washington.

Mr George Gibbs [a] states:

"Another [game], at which they exhibit still more interest, is played with ten disks of hard wood, about the diameter of a Mexican dollar, and somewhat thicker, called, in the jargon, tsil-tsil; in the Niskwalli language la-halp. One of these is marked and called the chief. A smooth mat is spread on the ground, at the ends of which the opposing players are seated, their friends on either side, who are provided with the requisites for a noise, as in the other case. The party holding the disks has a bundle of the fibers of the cedar bark, in which he envelops them, and, after rolling them about, tears the bundle into two parts, his opponent guessing in which bundle the chief lies. These disks are made of the yew, and must be cut into shape with beaver-tooth chisels only. The marking of them is in itself an art, certain persons being able by their spells to imbue them with luck, and their manufactures bring very high prices. The game is counted as in the first mentioned. Farther down the coast, ten highly polished sticks are used, instead of disks."

PEND D'OREILLES. Montana.

The Dictionary of the Kalispel [b] gives the following definition:

Play at sticks, chines zlálkoi.

PUYALLUP. Puyallup reservation, Puget sound, Washington. (Cat. no. 55904, Field Columbian Museum.)

Set of ten wooden disks, 2¼ inches in diameter, with raised edge.

This was collected by Dr George A. Dorsey, who has furnished the following particulars:

Name of game, suwextdz; name of disks, lahalabp; six females, half black and half white; one male, all black; three odd, all white, chatosedn.

I was told by the Indians from whom I got the game that there are generally fifty counters.

——— Tacoma, Washington.

The Tacoma correspondent of the San Francisco Examiner, Mr Thomas Sammons, gives the following account in that paper, February 10, 1895:

The sing gamble is the great contest between two tribes of the Puget Sound Indians for the trophies of the year and for such blankets, wearing apparel, vehicles, and horses as can be spared to be used for stakes, and sometimes more than should be spared. This year the pot at the beginning of the gamble consisted of 12 Winchester rifles of the latest pattern, 11 sound horses, 7 buggies, 100 blankets, 43 shawls, an uncounted pile of mats, clothing for men and women (some badly worn and some in good condition, but mostly worn), and $49 in money.

---

[a] Contributions to North American Ethnology, v. 1, p. 206, Washington, 1877.

[b] A Dictionary of the Kalispel or Flathead Indian Language, compiled by the Missionaries of the Society of Jesus. St. Ignatius Print, Montana, 1877–8–9.

This year the sing gamble was held in the barn of Jake Tai-ugh, commonly known as Charley Jacobs, whose place is 4 miles from Tacoma. At the beginning of the sing gamble, 67 old men and women, many of them wrinkled, many of them gray-headed, gathered at Jake's big barn, which had been cleared of all hay, grain, and other stores.

On the ground, which serves as a floor, were laid two mats woven from straw and weeds and flags. Each of these mats was 3 feet wide and 6 long. Between the mats was a space of about 3 feet. Around these squatted the serious gamblers of the ancient races, many of them wearing brilliantly colored blankets, others arrayed in combination costumes picked up at the reservation or in the town. As a necessary preparation to the game, the drummers, one for each tribe, took positions in front of their drums, made of horsehide drawn over one end of a stout frame 2 feet and 6 inches deep. Beating heavily on these drums with sticks, the sound is similar to that from a bass drum, save that it is more sonorous, and is readily heard at a distance of half a mile. As the drums beat the Indians begin their chants or wails, the men shouting " Hi-ah, hi-ah, hi-ah," and the women moaning an accompaniment between the shouts of their braves, sounding something like this: " Mm-uh, mm-uh, mm-uh."

The players gather around the mats, seven being permitted on each side. One mat is for the Puyallup, the other for the Black Rivers. The dealer for each side sits at the head of his mat, fingering deftly ten wooden chips, about 2 inches in diameter and a quarter of an inch thick. Nine of these are of the same color, but the tenth is different in color, though similar in shape and dimensions. The shuffler handles the chips rapidly, like an experienced faro dealer playing to a big board. He transfers them from one hand to another, hides them under a pile of shavings made from the cedar bark growing close to the sap, resembling much the product called excelsior, He divides the chips into two piles of five each, and conceals each pile under the shavings. Mysteriously he waves his hands forward and backward, crosswise, and over and over, making passes like the manipulations of a three-card monte dealer. The drum keeps up its constant beat; the Indians at the mats and those looking on with interest clap their hands and stamp and chant in time to the drum.

Now is the time for the Indian assigned to guess to point to one of the two piles. The game is entirely one of chance, there being no possible means for the closest observer to detect in which pile the dealer places the odd-colored chip. It is the custom of the game, however, for the guesser to ponder for some time before deciding which pile to select. This adds interest and excitement to the speculation. Finally he decides, and with his finger points to one of the piles. The dealer rolls the chips across the mat to the farther end. If the guess is right the side for which the guesser is acting scores 1 point. If the guess is wrong the tribe to which the dealer belongs scores a point and the other side takes the innings—that is to say, the deal. John Towallis was captain of the Puyallup team, and is now the most popular man in the tribe on account of the remarkable victory of his side after the session of nearly a month, and also on account of the quantity and value of the pot. Captain Jack, the leader of the unsuccessful Black River team, proved a thorough sport; for, in addition to his contribution to the stake of his tribe, he staked and lost his greatest treasure, a big knife; his principal decoration, shiny brass rings, all his money ($60), his watch, his rifle and his harness, his buggy, and his horse. He advised his companions on the team to bet everything they had, except their canoes. He insisted that they should keep those in order that they might have some way to get home. He was not so careful of himself as of them, for he had to walk when the time came. Some of the men and the squaws who paddled home in their canoes felt the sharpness of the weather, for shirts and trousers were exceedingly scarce when the sixtieth stick had gone to the Puyallup end of the board. At the last part of the gamble the Black Rivers plunged wildly. The run of luck of the Puyallup had been constant, and Captain Jack announced to his followers that this could not continue. Luck must turn, and here was a chance for them to get every movable thing, except that which belongs to the Government, transferred from the Puyallup Reservation over to the Black River Reservation. His men were quick to follow his suggestion, and the result is that poverty is intense this year at Black River and the Puyallup are having a boom.

Mr Sammons has kindly furnished the writer with the diagram (figure 333) showing the positions of the players.

Four Indians sit on each side of the two mats, making teams of eight on each side in addition to the Indian who actually does the playing. The position of this Indian is designated A, B. At the time of making the drawing A was shuffling the disk, a piece of wood, glass, or stone, half the size of an ordinary table saucer. The player's two hands rest on the mat, and about them is a bunch of straw, moss, or anything of a like nature that can be had conveniently

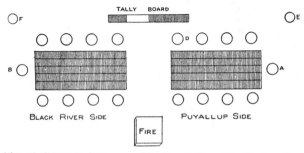

Fig. 333. Position of players in disk game; Puyallup Indians, Washington; from sketch by Mr Thomas Sammons.

and used for the purpose of hiding the player's hands and confusing the opposite team while the disk is being shuffled about. E and F represent tum-tum, or bass-drum, players, who keep up a loud drumming while the shuffling is going on. This is done with the hope of confusing the opposite team, much as coaching is carried in from the coaching line for baseball teams of the present period. A blazing heap of logs at the side warms the warriors and is tended by the women. The women during the game sing monotonously, as do also the four men on each side of the player. The opposing team, who have to do the guessing, remain very quiet and watch very closely every move of the hider's hands. Should the opposing team guess rightly, one stick the size of one's thumb and about 6 inches long is added to the team's credit on the tally board placed between the drummers. Should the opposing team fail to guess, a stick is added to the credit of the team whose captain is doing the shuffling. When either side wins all the sticks the game is over, and the cows, horses, wearing apparel, dogs, harness, cash, watches, and wagons constituting the stakes are delivered to the winners.

SHUSWAP. Kamloops, British Columbia.

Dr Franz Boas [a] says:

Another gambling game is played with a series of sticks of maple wood about

---

[a] Second General Report on the Indians of British Columbia. Report of the Sixtieth Meeting of the British Association for the Advancement of Science, p. 641, London, 1891.

4 inches long and painted with various marks. There are two players to the game, who sit opposite each other. A fisher-skin, which is nicely painted, is placed between them, bent in such a way as to present two faces, slanting down toward the players. Each of these takes a number of sticks, which he covers with hay, shakes, and throws down, one after the other, on his side of the skin. The player who throws down the stick bearing a certain mark has lost.

SKOKOMISH. Washington. (Cat. no. 19648, Field Columbian Museum.)

Set of ten wooden disks, 2 inches in diameter and one-fourth of an inch thick, periphery well rounded and sides concave, colored light red; accompanied by a rough split cedar board, 3 by 10 inches, three-sixteenths of an inch thick, said to go with the game.

Collected by Rev. Myron Eells.

SNOHOMISH (?).[a] Tulalip agency, Washington. (Cat. no. 130981, United States National Museum.)

One hundred and thirty-two wooden disks, part of twenty-three sets. Collected by Mr E. C. Cherouse, United States Indian agent, 1875.

The number of sets may be somewhat less than this, owing to some of the pieces, although bearing different marks, having been combined for use.

The different sets are distinguished by a variety of marks, some of which are so minute as to escape all but careful examination. These marks consist chiefly of minute holes, like pin holes, in ones, twos, and threes, variously arranged on the faces of the disks. Some sets have raised rims, with a line of nicks on each face next to the edge; others are painted with a dark ring near the edge. The edges are either blackened or painted red the entire distance around, or are perfectly plain, or part plain and part blackened, this last kind preponderating. There are but two complete sets of ten disks each in the lot. The disks vary from $1\frac{7}{8}$ to $2\frac{1}{4}$ inches in diameter, those in each set being perfectly uniform and appearing to be cut from the same piece of wood.

The collector gave the following account of the game:

The present casters or trundles are made of a shrub that grows in rich bottom lands and is called by the Indians set-ta-chas. The shrub is the genus *Viburnum*, and I would call it the wild snowball tree. They boil the trundles during three or four hours, and when dried they scrape them with shave grass until they are well shaped, polished, and naturally colored. The common set for a game of two gamblers is twenty apiece. Two of the casters are called chiefs and are edged with black or white, and the others are slaves, or servants. Fine mats are expanded on a level place and fixed to the ground by pins made for that purpose. The two antagonists, surrounded by their respective partners, sit on the ends of the mat, leaving a free space between. Each one keeps his casters hidden under two handfuls of stlowi, or dressed bark, the partners sing-

---

[a] It is not possible to determine the tribe exactly.

ing. The casters are divided, five under the right hand and five under the left. While the counters are running out from the right to the left the opposite antagonist points out to the right or the left before they are out, naming the chief, and if it happens the chief comes out in accord with the guessing the guesser wins the game. If it comes out from a different direction, he loses the game. When Indians gamble they paint their faces with different colors and designs, representing the spirit they invoke for success, and they do their utmost to deceive each other.

SONGISH. Vancouver island, British Columbia.

Dr Franz Boas [a] describes the following game:

SlEhä'lEm, or wuqk·'ats, is played with one white and nine black disks. The former is called "the man." Two players take part in the game. They sit opposite each other, and each has a mat before him, the end nearest the partner being raised a little. The player covers the disks with cedar bark and shakes them in the hollow of his hands, which are laid one on the other. Then he takes five into each hand and keeps them wrapped in cedar bark, moving them backward and forward from right to left. Now the opponent guesses in which hand the white disk is. Each player has five sticks lying in one row by his side. If the guesser guesses right, he rolls a stick over to his opponent, who is the next to guess. If the guesser guesses wrong, he gets a stick from the player who shook the disks and who continues to shake. The game is at an end when one man has got all the sticks. He has lost. Sometimes one tribe will challenge another to a game of slEhä'lEm. In this case it is called lEhälEmē'latl, or wupk·atsē'latl.

Continuing, Doctor Boas says:

In gambling the well-known sticks of the northern tribes are often used, or a piece of bone is hidden in the hands of a member of one party while the other must guess where it is.

It is considered indecent for the women to look on when the men gamble. Only when two tribes play against each other are they allowed to be present. They sing during the game, waving their arms up and down rhythmically. Men and women of the winning party paint their faces red.

THOMPSON INDIANS. British Columbia. (Cat. no. $\frac{16}{4885}$, American Museum of Natural History.)

Set of sixteen willow sticks (figure 334), $5\frac{6}{16}$ inches in length and three-sixteenths of an inch in diameter, all marked with ribbons of red paint, in a small fringed buckskin pouch, stitched with an ornamental figure in red and green silk. Collected by Mr James Teit.

The collector gives the following account: [b]

Another game, engaged in almost altogether by the men, was played with a number of sticks. These were from 4 to 6 inches in length and about a quarter of an inch in diameter, made of mountain-maple wood, rounded and smoothed off. There was no definite number of sticks in a set. Some sets contained only twelve sticks, while others had as many as thirty. Most of the sticks were

---

[a] Second General Report on the Indians of British Columbia. Report of the Sixtieth Meeting of the British Association for the Advancement of Science, p. 571, London, 1891.

[b] The Thompson Indians of British Columbia. Memoirs of the American Museum of Natural History, v. 2, p. 272, New York, 1900.

carved or painted, some of them with pictures of animals or birds of which their posssessors had dreamed. Each man had his own sticks and carried them in a buckskin bag. Two of the sticks were marked with buckskin or sinew thread or with a painted ring around the middle. I do not know exactly the points which each stick won. The players kneeled opposite each other, and each spread out in front of him his gambling mat [figure 335], which was made of deerskin. Each had a bundle of dry grass. The man who played first took one of the sticks with the ring, and another one, generally one representative of his guardian spirit, or some other which he thought lucky, and put them on his mat so that the other player could see them. Then he took them to the near end of

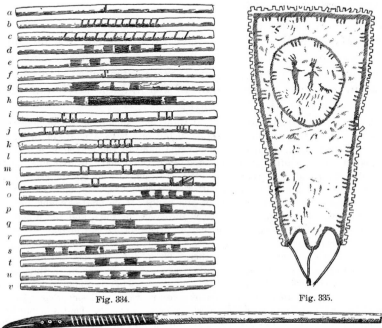

Fig. 334.   Fig. 335.

Fig. 336.

FIG. 334. Stick game; length of sticks, $5\frac{8}{16}$ inches; Thompson Indians, British Columbia; cat no. $\frac{16}{885}$, American Museum of Natural History. *a* and *f*, ska'kalamux, man; *b*, screw of ramrod; *c*, snake; *d*, wolf; *e*, otter; *g*, eagle; *h*, grizzly bear; *i–u*, without names; *v*, one of fifteen sticks, without marks.

FIG. 335. Gambling mat for stick game; length, 31 inches; Thompson Indians, British Columbia; cat no. $\frac{16}{886}$, American Museum of Natural History.

FIG. 336. Pointer for stick game, representing a crane; length, 26 inches; Thompson Indians, British Columbia: cat no. $\frac{16}{887}$, American Museum of Natural History.

the mat, where his knee was, and where the other man could not see them, and rolled each stick up in dry grass until it was completely covered. Then he placed the grass-covered sticks down on the mat again. The other man then took his pointer [figure 336] and, after tapping each of the grass-covered sticks four times with it, moved them around with his pointer four times, following the sun's course. Then he separated one from the other by pushing it with his pointer to the edge of the mat. Then the other man took up this stick and, drawing it back and loosening the grass around it, shoved it back into the center of his set of sticks. Then he took up his sticks and, after shaking them loosely in his hands near his ear, threw them down on the mat, one after another.

After all had been thrown down, and only one trump or ringed stick was found among them, then it was known that the other was the one left in the grass, and therefore that the other player had left the winning stick. But if both trumps came out when the sticks were thrown down then it was known that he had put aside the winning stick and left the other, and thus lost. Afterwards the first player had to guess his opponent's sticks in like manner. The stake was valued, according to agreement, at so many counters, and so many counters a chance. If a man lost four times in succession, he frequently lost the stake. Each player had his own set of sticks, his mat, and his pointer. The names of the designs on the set represented in the figure [334] are given in the legend of the figure. They often accompanied the game with a song. This game has been out of use for many years.

Twana. Washington.

Rev. Myron Eells [a] says they have three methods of gambling— with round blocks or disks, with bones, and the women's game (the beaver-teeth dice game). He gives a more extended account of these games in his paper on the Indians of Washington Territory.[b] Concerning the game with disks he says:

This is the men's game, as a general thing, but sometimes all engage in it. There are ten of these disks in a set. All but one have a white or black and white rim. Five of them are kept under one hand of the player on a mat and five underneath the other hand, covered with cedar bark beaten fine. After being shuffled round and round for a short time, one of the opposite party guesses under which hand the disk with the black rim is. He tells this without a word, but with a peculiar motion of one hand. If he guesses right, he wins and plays next; but if his conjecture is incorrect, he loses and the other side continues to play. The two rows of players are 10 or 12 feet apart. Generally they have six or more sets of these blocks, so that if, as they suppose, luck does not attend one set, they can try another. These different sets are marked on the edges to distinguish them from other sets. Another way of distinguishing them is by having them of slightly different sizes. They are made very smooth of hard wood, sandpapered, and then by use are worn still smoother. In this game they keep tally with a number of sticks used as checks, about 3 inches long. The number of these varies according to the amount bet, twelve of them being used, it is said, when twenty dollars is wagered. I have never seen more than forty used. They begin with an equal number of checks for each party, and then each side tries to win all, one being transferred to the winner each time the game is won. If there is a large number used and fortune favors each party nearly alike, it takes a long time—sometimes three or four days—to finish a game. This game is sometimes played by only two persons, but usually there are many engaged in it. In the latter case, when one player becomes tired or thinks he is in bad luck another takes his place.

Another form of this game is called the tamanous game. A large number of people who have a tamanous, including the women, take part in it, but the men only shuffle the disks. The difference between this form of the disk game and the other form consists in the tamanous. While one man plays the other members of his party beat a drum, clasp their hands, and sing; each one, I believe, singing his or her own tamanous song to invoke the aid of his special guardian spirit. I was lately present at one of these games where forty tally blocks or checks were used, and which lasted for four days, when all agreed to stop,

---

[a] Bulletin of the United States Geological Survey, v. 3, n. 1, p. 88, Washington, 1877.
[b] Annual Report of the Smithsonian Institution for 1887, pt. 1, p. 648, 1889.

neither party having won the game. Very seldom do they play for mere fun. There is generally a small stake, and sometimes from one hundred to two hundred dollars is bet.

The Indians say that they now stake less money and spend less time in gaming than formerly. It is said that in former years as much as a thousand dollars was sometimes staked and that the players became so infatuated as to bet everything they had, even to the clothes on their backs. At present they seldom gamble except on rainy days or when they have little else to do. There is no drinking in connection with it. Outside parties sometimes bet on the game as white people do. There is a tradition that when Dokibatt " came, a long time ago, he told them to give up all their bad habits and things, these among others; that he took the disks and threw them into the water, but that they came back. He then threw them into the fire, but they came out. He threw them away as far as he could, but they returned; and so he threw them away five times, and every time they came back; after which he told the people that they might use them for fun or sport."

SHAHAPTIAN STOCK

KLIKITAT.   Washington.   (Cat. no. 51845, Peabody Museum of
     American Archæology and Ethnology.)
Set of ten wooden disks, 2 inches in diameter, with raised rims and
     incised marks around the inner edge. Two have plain white
     edges, six, edges partly plain and partly burned black, and two
     burned around entire circumference;[a] accompanied by four
     wrought copper pins (figure 337), 11 inches in length, said to
     be used in holding down the mat on which the game is played.
     Presented by Mr A. W. Robinson.

FIG. 337. Copper pins used in holding down gambling mat in disk game; length, 11 inches; Klikitat Indians, Washington; cat. no. 51845, Peabody Museum of American Archæology and Ethnology.

SHASTAN STOCK

ACHOMAWI.   Hat Creek, California.   (Cat. no. $\frac{50}{4113}$, American Mu-
     seum of Natural History.)

FIG. 338. Stick game; length of sticks, 8½ inches; Achomawi Indians, Hat Creek, California; cat. no. $\frac{50}{4113}$, American Museum of Natural History.

Nineteen slender sticks (figure 338), about 8½ inches in length.

Collected in 1903 by Dr Roland B. Dixon, who gave the name as tcupauwiya.

---

[a]As usual, the disks are marked with small punctures. The arrangement is as follows: Two with three marks on each side; three with three marks on one side, two on reverse; two with two marks on each side; three without marks.

SHASTA.   Siletz reservation, Oregon.   (Cat. no. $\frac{50}{3144}$, American Museum of Natural History.

Fourteen sticks (figure 339), 7 inches in length, two plain and twelve

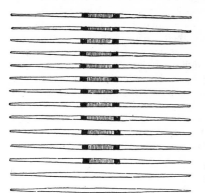

painted in the middle with a broad brown band and black bands outside. Collected in 1903 by Dr Roland B. Dixon.

SIOUAN STOCK

ASSINIBOIN.   Alberta.

Rev. John Maclean[a] says the Stonies have the odd and even game, which is played with small sticks or goose quills.

CONGAREE.   North Carolina.

John Lawson[b] says:

The women were very busily engaged in gaming. The name or grounds of it I

FIG. 339. Stick game; length of sticks, 7 inches; Shasta Indians, Oregon; cat. no. $\frac{50}{3144}$, American Museum of Natural History.

could not learn, though I looked on above two hours. Their arithmetic was kept with a heap of Indian grain.

Elsewhere,[c] presumably referring to the above game, he says:

Their chiefest game is a sort of arithmetic, which is managed by a parcel of small split reeds, the thickness of a small bent; these are made very nicely so that they part, and are tractable in their hands. They are fifty-one in number, their length about 7 inches; when they play they throw part of them to their antagonist; the cut is to discover, upon sight, how many you have, and what you throw to him that plays with you. Some are so expert at their numbers that they will tell ten times together what they throw out of their hands. Although the whole play is carried on with the quickest motion it is possible to use, yet some are so expert at this game as to win great Indian estates by this play. A good set of these reeds, fit to play withal, are valued and sold for a dressed doeskin.

DAKOTA (TETON).   South Dakota.

Rev. J. Owen Dorsey, in Games of Teton Dakota Children,[d] describes a game played by children or adults of either sex:

Chŭn wiyushnan'pi, odd or even. Played at any time by two persons. A like number of green switches must be prepared by each player. Sumac sticks are generally chosen, as they are not easily broken by handling; hence one name for sumac stalks is "Counting-stick stalks." One stick is made the odd one, probably distinguished by some mark. When they begin, one of the players seizes all the sticks and mixes them as well as he can. Closing his eyes, he divides them into two piles, taking about an equal number in each hand. Then crossing his hands, he says to the other player, "Come, take whichever lot you choose."

[a] Canadian Savage Folk, p. 26, Toronto, 1896.
[b] The History of Carolina, p. 27, London, 1714; p. 52, Raleigh, N. C., 1860.
[c] Ibid., p. 176, London ed.; p. 288, Raleigh ed.
[d] The American Anthropologist, v. 4, p. 344, 1891.

Both players are seated. The other makes his choice, and then each one examines what he has. He who has the odd stick wins the game.

OMAHA. Nebraska.

Rev. J. Owen Dorsey [a] gives the following description of the stick-counting game among the Omaha:

Jaⁿ-ḱáwa, stick counting, is played by any number of persons with sticks made of déska or sidúhi. These sticks are all placed in a heap, and then the players in succession take up some of them in their hands. The sticks are not counted till they have been taken up, and then he who has the lowest odd number always wins. Thus if one player had 5, another 3, and a third only 1, the last must be the victor. The highest number that anyone can have is 9. If 10 or more sticks have been taken, those above 9 do not count. With the exception of horses, anything may be staked which is played for in banañge-kide.

SKITTAGETAN STOCK

HAIDA. Skidegate, Queen Charlotte islands, British Columbia. (Cat. no. 37808, Free Museum of Science and Art, University of Pennsylvania.)

Set of forty-eight sticks, $4\frac{3}{4}$ inches in length and three-eighths of an inch in diameter, marked with bands of black and red paint.

Collected in 1900 by Dr C. F. Newcombe, who describes them under the name of sin, or hsin:

The following is a list of the names of the sticks and the number of each: Shadow, hikē haut, 3; red fish, skeitkadagun, 3; black bass, xăsă, 3; mirror (of slate, wetted), xaus gungs, 3; sea anemone, xŭngs kedans, 3; dance headdress, djĭlkiss, 3; puffin, kōxănă, 3; black bear, tăn, 3; devil fish, nŏŭ kwun, 3; guillemot, skădŏa, 3; large housefly, dīdŭn, 3; halibut, xagu, 3; humpback salmon, tsītăn, 3; dog salmon, skă'gī, 3; centipede, gotămegă, 1; chiefs who kiss, i. e., rub noses, skunagĕsilai, 1; supernatural beings of high rank, dsil or djil, 4. The last are trumps.

———— Queen Charlotte islands, British Columbia. (American Museum of Natural History.)

Cat. no. $\frac{16}{682}$. Set of sixty maple gambling sticks, $5\frac{4}{16}$ inches in length and seven-sixteenths of an inch in diameter, in leather pouch; all marked with red and black ribbons.

Cat. no. $\frac{16}{683}$. Set of eighty-eight wood gambling sticks, 5 inches in length and five-sixteenths of an inch in diameter, in leather pouch; all painted with red and black ribbons; two sticks carved at one end with human heads, one having right arm and leg of human figure below and the other their complement; ends flat; a single-pointed paint stick in the pouch.

Both sets were collected by Dr J. W. Powell.

[a] Omaha Sociology. Third Annual Report of the Bureau of Ethnology, p. 338, 1884.

HAIDA.　Queen Charlotte islands, British Columbia.

Francis Poole [a] says:

The game was Odd or Even, which is played thus: The players spread a mat, made of the inner bark of the yellow cypress, upon the ground, each party being provided with from forty to fifty round pins or pieces of wood, 5 inches long by one-eighth of an inch thick, painted in black and blue rings and beautifully polished. One of the players, selecting a number of these pins, covers them up in a heap of bark cut into fine fiberlike tow. Under cover of the bark he then divides the pins into two parcels, and having taken them out, passes them several times from his right hand to his left, or the contrary. While the player shuffles he repeats the words i-e-ly-yah to a low, monotonous chant or moan. The moment he finishes the incantation his opponent, who has been silently watching him, chooses the parcel where he thinks the luck lies for odd or even. After which the second player takes his innings with his own pins and the same ceremonies. This goes on till one or the other loses all his pins. That decides the game.

———— Haida mission, Jackson, Alaska.　(Cat. no. 73522, United States National Museum.)

Set of thirty-two carved polished birch-wood sticks, 4¾ inches in length and eight-sixteenths of an inch in diameter, the ends flat.

Collected in 1884 by Mr J. Loomis Gould. The designs on eight of the sticks are shown on plate v.

———— Queen Charlotte islands, British Columbia.

Prof. George M. Dawson [b] says:

Gambling is as common with the Haida as among most other tribes, which means that it is the most popular and constantly practised of all their amusements. The gambler frequently loses his entire property, continuing the play till he has nothing whatever to stake. The game generally played I have not been able to understand clearly. It is the same with that of most of the coast tribes and not dissimilar from gambling games played by the natives from the Pacific coast to Lake Superior. Sitting on the ground in a circle, in the center of which a clean cedar mat is spread, each man produces his bundle of neatly smoothed sticks, the values of which are known by the markings upon them. They are shuffled together in soft teased cedar bark and drawn out by chance.

James G. Swan [c] says:

The Haida, instead of disks, use sticks or pieces of wood 4 or 5 inches long and a quarter of an inch thick. These sticks are rounded and beautifully polished. They are made of yew, and each stick has some designating mark upon it. There is one stick entirely colored and one entirely plain. Each player will have a bunch of forty or fifty of these sticks, and each will select either of the plain sticks as his favorite, just as in backgammon or checkers the players select the black or white pieces. The Indian about to play takes up a handful of these sticks and, putting them under a quantity of finely separated cedar bark, which is as fine as tow and kept constantly near him, he divides the pins

---

[a] Queen Charlotte Islands, p. 319, London, 1872.

[b] Report on the Queen Charlotte Islands. Geological Survey of Canada, Report of Progress for 1878–79, p. 129B, Montreal, 1880.

[c] Smithsonian Contributions to Knowledge, no. 267, p. 8, 1874.

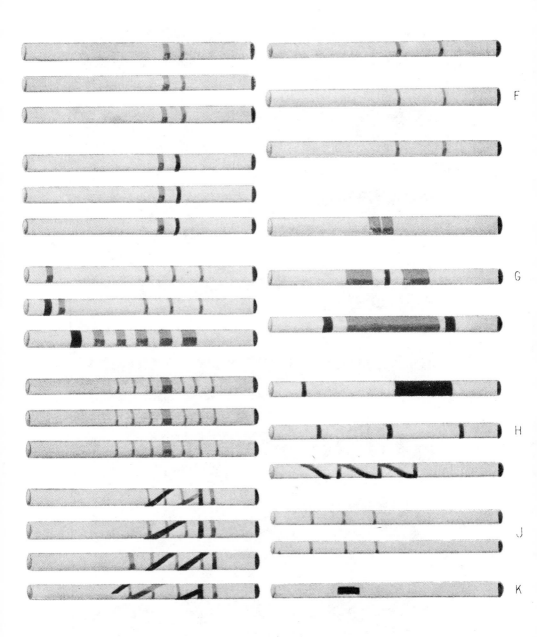

TAKU INDIAN GAMBLING STICKS
ALASKA

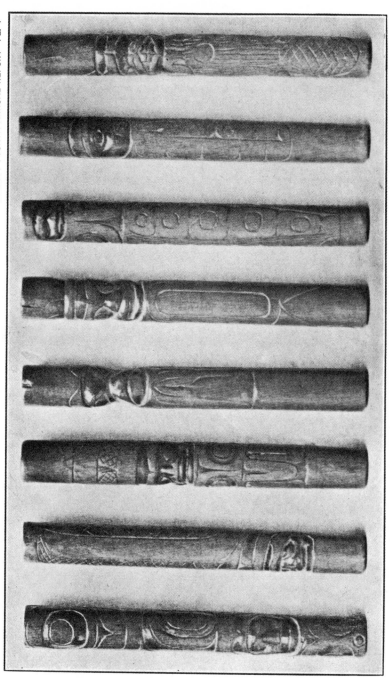

STICK GAME (PART); HAIDA INDIANS, ALASKA; CAT. NO. 73522, UNITED STATES NATIONAL MUSEUM

into two parcels, which he wraps up in the bark, and passes them rapidly from hand to hand under the tow, and finally moves them round on the ground or mat on which the players are always seated, still wrapped in the fine bark, but not covered by the tow. His opponent watches every move that is made from the very first with the eagerness of a cat, and finally, by a motion of his finger, indicates which of the parcels the winning stick is in. The player, upon such indication, shakes the sticks out of the bark, and with much display and skill, throws them one by one into the space between the players till the piece wanted is reached; or else, if it is not there, to show that the game is his. The winner takes one or more sticks from his opponent's pile, and the game is decided when one wins all the sticks of the other. As neither of the players can see the assortment of the sticks, the game is as fair for one as the other, and is as simple in reality as "odd or even" or any child's game. But the ceremony of manipulation and sorting the sticks under the bark tow gives the game an appearance of as much real importance as some of the skilful combinations of white gamblers.

The tribes north of Vancouver Island, so far as my observation has extended, use this style of sticks in gambling, while the Salish or Flatheads use the disks.

Dr J. R. Swanton [a] says under Games:

The great gambling game of the Haida was the same as that used on neighboring parts of the mainland. It was played with a set of cylindrical sticks, four or five inches long. The number of sticks varies in the sets that I have seen, one having as many as seventy. Some of the sets were made of bone, but the most of yew or some similar kind of wood. These were finely polished, and in many cases elaborately carved or painted, but usually were simply divided into sets of from two to four by various lines drawn around them in black and red. One of the sticks was left blank, or nearly so, and was called djîl [bait]. In playing, two men sat opposite each other with their sticks disposed in front of them. Then one rapidly selected one set of sticks and the djîl, shuffled them up concealed in fine cedar bark, divided the sticks into two parcels, and laid them down, one on each side. Sometimes he made three parcels. The opponent had now to guess which of these contained the djîl. If he were successful, the first player did the same thing again with another set. After each guess the sticks were thrown out on a piece of hide in front of both players. When a player guessed right, he in turn laid out his sticks. It is not so true to say that cheating was fair in Haida gambling as to say that it was part of the game. If one could conceal or get rid of the djîl temporarily, so much the better. The people were very much addicted to gambling, and, according to the stories, whole towns were in the habit of giving themselves up to it; but the chances of choosing the djîl were so great that, ordinarily, one could not lose very rapidly. I was told that they sometimes played all day without either side winning. On the other hand, stories tell of how whole families and towns were gambled away.

The entire gambling outfit was quite expensive. There were the gambling sticks themselves; the bag in which they were carried and the bag in which several sets were carried, the skin upon which the sticks were laid out, the mat upon which the actual gambling was done, a thick piece of hide about a foot square upon which the sticks selected by the opponent were thrown so that all could see them; pencils used to mark lines on the sticks. A stone receptacle with two compartments was used for grinding up red and black paint.

[a] Contributions to the Ethnology of the Haida. Memoirs of the American Museum of Natural History, whole series, v. 8, p. 58, New York, 1905.

I obtained the following account of the game from Henry Moody, my interpreter in Skidegate.

The two players sat opposite each other, each generally provided with a number of sets of gambling sticks, so that if one brought him no luck he might use another, just as white men change packs of cards. The person first handling the sticks then laid his set out in front of himself, and rapidly selected one set of sticks, i. e., one set having similar markings on them, along with the djil, or trump. He rolled them up in shredded cedar bark and separated them into two bundles, which he laid down, one on either side of him. The other player then had to guess in which bundle the djil lay; and if successful, it was his turn to play. If he was unsuccessful, his opponent scored one point, and played as before, selecting a second set of sticks. A very skilful manipulator might divide his sticks into four bundles instead of two, in which case the opponent was entitled to select two out of them. One man might lose continually and the other gain up to seven points, and these points (or some of them) received different names entirely distinct from the ordinary numerals, first, second, third, etc. Thus the sixth point was called mā'gʌn; and the seventh, qo'ngu. After one person had reached qo'ngu an eighth count, called sqʌl, had to be scored. The game for this score was played in the following manner: Four bundles were made of one stick each, the djil and three other sticks being used. The guesser was allowed to pick out three of these, and the player won only in case the fourth bundle contained the djil. Otherwise, they began all over again; and on this last count the chances were so greatly in favor of the guesser that they are said often to have played all day without either side winning.

The method of reaching count seven was as follows: After one player had made three points the other was obliged to make ten instead of seven—three to score off his opponent's points, and the usual seven points besides. And so in other cases the player had to catch up with his partner before starting to make his seven.

The gambling sticks had separate names, most of them bearing those of animals. While many sets are marked exclusively with red and black marks, the more elaborate ones are ornamented with representations of the animal figures whose names they bear.

In Marchand's Voyage [a] we find:

Surgeon Roblet remarked that the natives of Cloak Bay have a sort of passion for gaming. They are seen carrying everywhere with them thirty small sticks, three or four inches in length by about four lines in diameter [b] with which they make a party, one against one, in the following manner: Among the sticks there is one distinguished from all the others by a black circle. One of the players takes this single stick, joins to it another taken from among the twenty-nine common ones, mixes the two together without seeing them, and then places them separately under a bit of cloth. That which the adversary chooses, merely by pointing it out, is mixed without looking at it, with all the others, and the adversary wins or loses, if the stick confounded in the mass, in case it happens to be the only stick, is a shorter or longer time in coming out. I admit that I do not see the finesse of this game; perhaps it is ill explained because it has been ill understood. I presume, however, that it may be

---

[a] A Voyage round the World Performed during the Years 1790, 1791, and 1792, by Étienne Marchand, v. I, p. 299, London, 1801.

[b] These little sticks are very nicely wrought, perfectly round and of a beautiful polish; the wood of which they are made appears to be a species of wild plum-tree. It is hard and compact although very light.

susceptible of various combinations, which must have escaped an observer who does not understand the language spoken by the players. I judge so from an assortment of these small sticks which Captain Chanal procured and brought to France. On examining them are seen traced on some, toward the middle of their length, three black parallel circles; on others, the three circles, brought close to each other, occupy one of the extremities. Other sticks bear two, four, five, six, or seven black circles, distributed lengthwise, at unequal distances, and it may be conceived that these varieties, in the number and disposition of the circles which distinguish one stick from the others, may produce several in the combinations. Be this as it may, the time and attention which the natives of Cloak Bay give to this game prove that it has for them a great attraction, and that it warmly excites their interest.

WAKASHAN STOCK

BELLABELLA. British Columbia. (American Museum of Natural History.)

Cat. no. $\frac{16}{744}$. Set of seventy-two wood gambling sticks, $5\frac{4}{16}$ inches in length and six-sixteenths of an inch in diameter, in leather pouch, all marked with red and black ribbons and burnt totemic designs; the ends hollowed; paint stick in pouch.

Cat. no. $\frac{16}{745}$. Set of fifty-four light-colored wood gambling sticks about $4\frac{12}{16}$ inches in length and five-sixteenths of an inch in diameter, lengths slightly irregular, in leather pouch, all marked with red and black ribbons, the ends flat; double-pointed paint sticks, one end red, the other black, in pouch.

Both sets were collected by Dr J. W. Powell.

KWAKIUTL. Nawiti, British Columbia.

Dr C. F. Newcombe describes the stick game (called by the Haida sin) of these Indians under the name of libaiu:

The sticks are mostly made of crab apple, yew, vine, maple, and birch. Some were inlaid with abalone shell. They are in sets of two, three, or four alike, but mostly of two. The same sets of names occur in every village. They were not of families, tribes, or crests, nor of animals or birds. The only name secured was of one having two diagonal bands, which they call k'ĕlpstâle, twisted stalk. There was only one way of playing, and the game was played on small eating mats raised in the middle and sloping toward each of the two players.

—— British Columbia. (Cat. no. 19017, Field Columbian Museum.)

Set of sixty-five polished wood sticks, $4\frac{5}{8}$ inches in length; variously colored, ends rounded. Collected by Mr George Hunt.

MAKAH. Neah bay, Washington. (Free Museum of Science and Art, University of Pennsylvania.)

Cat. no. 37380. Ten plain wooden disks (figure 340a), 2 inches in diameter, one face painted with from eight to ten dots near the edge, the other with a painted ring near the edge. Two have all black edges and one all white.

Cat. no. 37381. Ten plain disks with hole in center (figure 340*b*) ; diameter, 1¾ inches. Three have all black edges and one has all white edges.

Cat. no. 37381. Ten disks with raised rim and nicks around the inner edge (figure 340*c*) ; diameter, 1⅞ inches. Two have all black edges and one all white.

Cat. no. 37382. Ten plain disks (figure 340*d*), 2¼ inches in diameter. One has all black edges and two have all white. Accompanied by a mass of shredded cedar bark in which the disks are manipulated.

Collected by the writer in 1900.

Dr George A. Dorsey [a] thus describes the game:

Sacts-sa-whaik, rolls far. This is the most common and perhaps the best-known game played by the Indians of Washington. It is played with ten disks

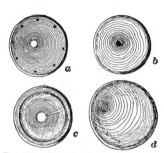

(huliak), while the count is kept with twelve sticks (katsake). Four sets of this game were collected, two of them being made of elder, the other two of maple. None of the sets have any special markings to distinguish them from the ordinary sets of this region, except that in one set one side of the disk has eight small dots near the edge and a black band near the edge on the other side. In all of the sets seven of the disks have perimeters half white and half black. In three sets two of the remaining disks have a perimeter entirely white, while that of the tenth disk is entirely black. In the fourth set the perimeter of two of the disks is entirely black, while that of the third disk is entirely white.

FIG. 340 *a*, *b*, *c*, *d*. Gaming disks; diameters, 2, 1¾, 1⅞, and 2¼ inches; Makah Indians, Neah bay, Washington; cat. nos. 37380 to 37382, Free Museum of Science and Art, University of Pennsylvania.

In the three sets, where there is a single disk with an edge entirely black, it is known as chokope, or man, the disks with white borders being known as hayop, or female. In the fourth set, according to this nomenclature, there would be one female and two men. I was informed by Williams that the object of the game is to guess the location of the female, and, as the nomenclature was given him by me, I am at a loss to reconcile the fact that in the three sets collected there were two females in each set. It is probable that in sets of this sort the black-edged disk may be designated as the female, as without question it is the single disk, distinguished from all others in the set, which is the one sought for in every instance. . . . This game is played only by men.

Charlie Williams informed the writer that the Makah play this game to the accompaniment of singing and drumming.

J. G. Swan,[b] under Gambling Implements, says:

Of these, one form consists of disks made from the wood of a hazel which grows at Cape Flattery and vicinity. The shrub is from 10 to 15 feet high, and with limbs from 2 to 3 inches in diameter. The name in Makah is hul-

---

[a] Games of the Makah Indians of Neah Bay. The American Antiquarian, v. 23, p. 71, 1901.

[b] The Indians of Cape Flattery. Smithsonian Contributions to Knowledge, no. 220, p. 44, 1870.

li-á-ko-bupt, the disks hul-liák, and the game la-hul-lum. The game is common among all the Indians of this territory, and is called in the jargon la-hull. The disks are circular, like checkers, about 2 inches in diameter, and the fourth of an inch thick, and are usually smoothed off and polished with care. They are first cut off transversely from the end of a stick which has been selected and properly prepared, then smoothed and polished, and marked on the outer edge with the color that designates their value. They are used in sets of ten, one of which is entirely black on the outer edge, another entirely white, and the rest of all degrees from black to white. Two persons play at the game, each having a mat before him, with the end next his opponent slightly raised so that the disks can not roll out of reach. Each player has ten disks which he covers with a quantity of the finely beaten bark and then separates the heap into two equal parts, shifting them rapidly on the mat from hand to hand. The opposing player guesses which heap contains the white or black, and on making his selection the disks are rolled down the mat, when each piece is separately seen. If he has guessed right, he wins; if not, he loses.

FIG. 341. Stick game; length of splints, 9½ inches; Yurok Indians, California; cat. no. 37257, Free Museum of Science and Art, University of Pennsylvania.

WASHOAN STOCK

WASHO.   Carson valley and Lake Tahoe, Nevada.

Dr J. W. Hudson describes the following game under the name of dtsudtsu:

A winnowing basket is inverted and held with the left hand while nine small sticks, 2½ inches long, are held in the right and a number of them hidden under it. The opponent guesses whether an odd or even number was hidden. This is a man's game.

WEITSPEKAN STOCK

YUROK.   Klamath river, California.   (Cat. no. 37257, Free Museum of Science and Art, University of Pennsylvania.)

Set of ninety fine splints (figure 341), stained yellow, four marked with black in the center, ten with black spiral in center, and ten with black spiral at the ends; length, 9½ inches. Eleven plain splints in the bundle are 8¾ inches in length.

Collected by the writer in 1900.

The game is called hauk-tsu, the sticks eis-kok, and the marked stick, or ace, pai-kotz.

Another set, cat. no. 37258, consists of forty-seven coarse splints, two marked with black, 9 inches in length.

WISHOSKAN STOCK

BATAWAT.   Humboldt county, California.   (Cat. no. 37269, Free Museum of Science and Art, University of Pennsylvania.)

Bundle of two hundred and fifty fine splints, three with black bands, 8 inches in length, and two hundred and six fine splints, three with black center, two with black center and ends, sixty-six all black, and the remainder plain, 8½ inches in length.

These were collected by the writer in 1900. The sticks are called gutsapi, the trump, schowowick, and the game, bokoworis.

Cat. no. 37287.   Twelve cylinders of hard polished wood (figure 342), 4¾ inches in length, and five-sixteenths of an inch in diameter, painted as follows: Five with broad black band in the middle, five with band at the end, one with bands at ends, and one with two bands nearly midway from the ends.

These specimens were purchased by the writer in 1900 at Arcata, California, and came from an Indian who was probably from Klamath river. A Mad River Indian named Dick, at Blue Lake, California, recognized these sticks and said it was customary to play with six, five alike and one odd one. The sticks were concealed in bundles of grass. He gave the same vocabulary as that recorded above for the fine sticks.

FIG. 342. Stick game; length of sticks, 4¾ inches; Klamath river, California; cat. no. 37287, Free Museum of Science and Art, University of Pennsylvania.

ZUÑIAN STOCK

ZUÑI.   Zuñi, New Mexico.   (Cat. no. 4989, Brooklyn Institute Museum.)

Twenty-one small willow sticks (figure 343), 2⅞ inches in length.

These were collected by the writer in 1904 and are used in a game called sawiposiwai, sticks mixed up.

The sticks are first rolled between the hands and the bundle divided, with the hands behind the back. The hands are then brought forward and the other player, who knows the total number of sticks, tries to guess the number held in the left hand by calling out. A stake is put up, and if the player guesses correctly he becomes the winner. The game is no longer played, and was recalled with difficulty by an old man.

FIG. 343. Stick game; length of sticks, 2⅞ inches; Zuñi Indians, Zuñi, New Mexico; cat. no. 4989, Brooklyn Institute Museum.

HAND GAME

This game, which I have designated by its common English name, is most widely distributed, having been found among 81 tribes belonging to 28 different linguistic stocks. This extensive distribution may be partially accounted for by the fact that, as it was played entirely by gesture, the game could be carried on between individuals who had only the sign language in common.

The name is descriptive, referring to the lots being held in the hand during the play. The game has been designated also the grass game, from the custom in California of wrapping the lots in bundles of grass. The lots are of several kinds. The commonest consist of bone cylinders, some solid, others hollow, between 2 and 3 inches in length. They are made in pairs, one or two sets being used. One piece in each pair is distinguished from the others by having a thong or string tied about the middle. The unmarked bone is sometimes designated as the man and the marked bone as the woman. The object is to guess the unmarked one. Instead of bones, wooden cylinders, one of each pair tied with cord or having a ring of bark left about the center, are used. The Yankton Dakota use two small squared sticks, notched differently. In a degenerate form of the game the players use little strings of beads or a bullet. The Pima employ three twigs with a finger loop at one end, and among some of the tribes of Arizona and southern California, where the game receives the Spanish name of peon, the lots are attached to the wrist with a cord fastened to the middle. This is done to prevent the players from changing them.

The four bones, two male and two female, like the sticks in the four-stick game, probably represent the bows of the twin War Gods.

The game is commonly counted with sharpened sticks, which are stuck in the ground between the players. These are most commonly twelve in number, but, five, ten, fifteen, sixteen, etc., are used. The arrow derivation of these sticks is illustrated in the Wichita game, page 276. The hand game is one for indoors, and is usually played in a lodge or shelter. Both men and women play, but usually quite apart. The number of players varies from two to any number. The opponents seat themselves upon the ground, facing each other, the stakes commonly being placed between the two lines. The side holding the bones sing and sway their hands or bodies. The guesser indicates his choice by swiftly extending his hand or arm. If he guesses correctly, the bones go over to his side.

The bones used in this game are frequently highly valued, being esteemed lucky, their owners thinking that their luck would pass to the person who acquired these bones.

ALGONQUIAN STOCK

ARAPAHO. Wind River reservation, Wyoming. (Cat. no. 61722,
    Field Columbian Museum.)

Four solid bones, 3¾ inches in length, smooth and yellow with age,
    two wrapped with cloth, black with dirt, the edges stitched with
    black thread. Collected by Dr George A. Dorsey in 1900.

ARAPAHO. Oklahoma.

Mr James Mooney in his paper on the Ghost-dance Religion [a] gives
an account of the gaqutit, or hunt-the-button game:

This is a favorite winter game with the prairie tribes, and was probably more
or less general throughout the country. It is played both by men and women, but
never by the two sexes together. It is the regular game in the long winter
nights after the scattered families have abandoned their exposed summer
positions on the open prairie and moved down near one another in the shelter
of the timber along the streams. . . . Frequently there will be a party of
twenty to thirty men gaming in one tipi, and singing so that their voices can be
heard far out from the camp, while from another tipi a few rods away comes a
shrill chorus from a group of women engaged in another game of the same
kind. The players sit in a circle around the tipi fire, those on one side of the
fire playing against those on the other. The only requisites are the button, or
ga'qaä, usually a small bit of wood, around which is tied a piece of string or
otter skin, with a pile of tally sticks, as has been already described. Each
party has a "button," that of one side being painted black, the other being red.
The leader of one party takes the button and endeavors to move it from one
hand to the other, or to pass it on to a partner, while those of the opposing side
keep a sharp lookout, and try to guess in which hand it is. Those having the
button try to deceive their opponents as to its whereabouts by putting one
hand over the other, by folding their arms, and by putting their hands behind
them, so as to pass the ga'qaä to a partner, all the while keeping time to the
rhythm of a gaming chorus sung by the whole party at the top of their voices.
The song is very peculiar and well-nigh indescribable. It is usually, but not
always or entirely, unmeaning, and jumps, halts, and staggers in a most
surprising fashion, but always in perfect time with the movements of the
hands and arms of the singers. The greatest of good-natured excitement
prevails, and every few minutes some more excitable player claps his hands
over his mouth or beats the ground with his flat palms and gives out a regular
war whoop. All this time the opposing players are watching the hands of the
other or looking straight into their faces to observe every tell-tale movement
of their features, and when one thinks he has discovered in which hand the
button is, he throws out his thumb toward that hand with a loud "that!"
Should he guess aright, his side scores a certain number of tallies, and in turn
takes the button and begins another song. Should the guess be wrong, the
losing side must give up an equivalent number of tally sticks. So the play
goes on until the small hours of the night. It is always a gambling game, and
the stakes are sometimes very large.

In the story entitled Split-Feather, Dr George A. Dorsey [b] relates
that one day there was an invitation for the Star society to go to the
head man's tipi to play hand game.

---

[a] Fourteenth Annual Report of the Bureau of Ethnology, p. 1008, 1896.
[b] Traditions of the Arapaho, p. 269, Chicago, 1903.

BLACKFEET. Fort Mackenzie, Montana.
Maximilian, Prince of Wied,[a] says:

They have invented many games for their amusement. At one of them they sit in a circle, and several little heaps of beads, or other things, are piled up, for which they play. One takes some pebbles in his hand, moving it backward and forward in measured time, and singing, while another endeavors to guess the number of pebbles. In this manner considerable sums are lost and won.

—— Montana.
Dr George Bird Grinnell [b] says:

Another popular game was what with more southern tribes is called "hands;" it is like "Button, button, who's got the button?" Two small oblong bones were used, one of which had a black ring around it. Those who participated in this game, numbering from two to a dozen, were divided into two equal parties, ranged on either side of the lodge. Wagers were made, each person betting with the one directly opposite him. Then a man took the bones, and, by skillfully moving his hands and changing the objects from one to the other, sought to make it impossible for the person opposite him to decide which hand held the marked one. Ten points were the game, counted by sticks, and the side which first got the number took the stakes. A song always accompanied this game, a weird, unearthly air—if it can be so called—but, when heard at a little distance, very pleasant and soothing. At first a scarcely audible murmur, like the gentle soughing of an evening breeze, it gradually increased in volume and reached a very high pitch, sank quickly to a low bass sound, rose and fell, and gradually died away, to be again repeated. The person concealing the bones swayed his body, arms, and hands in time to the air, and went through all manner of graceful and intricate movements for the purpose of confusing the guesser. The stakes were sometimes very high, two or three horses or more, and men have been known to lose everything they possessed, even to their clothing.

—— Southern Alberta.
Rev. John Maclean [c] says:

Sometimes the boys and young men of the camp form themselves into a group and play a game of guessing. Two or more persons are opposed, each to each, or one side against the other. A small article is selected, and one of them, passing it from one hand to the other, holds out both hands for his opponent to guess the hand containing the article, which he tries to do by placing in the closed hand, which he supposes is the right one, a small piece of wood. If he has guessed rightly, it becomes his turn to use the article to be sought. The small sticks are kept as a record of the game, until one of the contestants has won them all from his opponent. During the whole time of playing the one who holds the thing to be guessed sways his body, singing and praying for success.

CHEYENNE. Montana.
It appears from Dr Grinnell's [d] account that the game of hand, as played by the Pawnee, is played also by the Cheyenne.

---

[a] Travels in the Interior of North America, translated by H. Evans Lloyd, p. 254, London, 1843.

[b] Blackfoot Lodge Tales, p. 184, New York, 1892.

[c] Canadian Savage Folk, p. 56, Toronto, 1896.

[d] The Story of the Indian, p. 28, New York, 1895.

CREE. Wind River reservation, Wyoming. (Cat. no. 37028, Free Museum of Science and Art, University of Pennsylvania.)

String of eight yellow glass beads in two rows, tied in the middle, and a string of small white and blue glass beads in two rows, one white and one blue, tied in the middle (figure 344); length, 1¼ inches.

These were collected by the writer in 1900 from an Indian of Riel's band, who gave the name as gaiinshwashkwak, and said they were used in the hand game. Four sticks are used as counters. A ring and a cartridge are also employed.

———— Muskowpetung reserve, Qu'appelle, Assiniboia. (Cat. no. 61995, Field Columbian Museum.)

A cartridge shell and a small string of large white and black beads used in the hand game.

These were collected by Mr J. A. Mitchell, who gives the following account of the hand game under the name of meecheecheemetowaywin:

No limit as to numbers or sex of players. The object is so to manipulate one of the two pieces, i. e., the marked cartridge shell, as to puzzle the player's opponent as to the hand in which it is held. Formerly an oblong marked stick was used instead of the cartridge shell; the shell is now used almost exclusively.

FIG. 344. Beads for hand game; length, 1¼ inches; Cree Indians, Wyoming; cat. no. 37028, Free Museum of Science and Art, University of Pennsylvania.

This is one of the most common Indian gambling games, and is valued very highly. The stake usually played for is a pony, or sometimes several of them. The count is kept by means of ordinary pieces of stick, which are thrust into the ground as points are won, and added to or subtracted from by each player, according as he wins or loses, at each guess.

In playing for a horse, the value of the animal is pre-arranged at so many sticks, which are then played for, either one at a time, a few at a time, or all at one stake, as the holder of the sticks may see fit. Four points usually count for one game. Playing is often kept up for days and nights at a time.

Although the cartridge shell and small string of beads seem of but little value, great difficulty is encountered in getting them from the Indians, and then only at an exorbitant price, as they have an impression that when they sell a game they also part with the right to play that game in the future, unless with the consent of the buyer.

———— Manitoba.

Rev. E. A. Watkins, in his Dictionary of the Cree Language,[a] gives the following definitions:

Michĭche ustwatookwuk, they gamble, from michĭche, hand, and ustwatoo-wuk, they bet, referring to the game of hand.

GROSVENTRES. Montana. (American Museum of Natural History.) Cat. no. $\frac{50}{1786}$. String of eleven brass beads and one red glass bead (figure 345a) and another of seven green, one blue, and one red and orange glass beads (figure 345b), about 1½ inches in length,

———
[a] London, 1865.

and 12 counting sticks (figure 346), willow twigs painted red, 18½ inches in length. Collected by Dr A. L. Kroeber in 1901.

Cat. no. $\frac{50}{1931}$. Two bones, cone-shaped (figure 347), 2 and 2¼ inches in length, incised with rings (one with twenty-four), painted red; perforated at the larger end, through which a tied thong is passed. Collected in 1901 by Dr A. L. Kroeber, who describes them as bone hiding buttons.

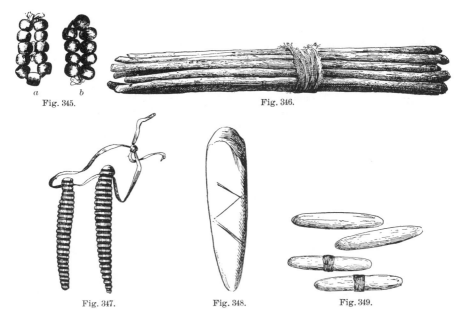

Fig. 345. Fig. 346.

Fig. 347. Fig. 348. Fig. 349.

FIG. 345, a, b. Beads for hand game; length, 1½ inches; Grosventre Indians, Montana; cat. no. $\frac{50}{1786}$, American Museum of Natural History.

FIG. 346. Counting sticks for hand game; length, 18½ inches; Grosventre Indians, Montana; cat. no. $\frac{50}{1786}$, American Museum of Natural History.

FIG. 347. Bones for hand game; lengths, 2 and 2¼ inches; Grosventre Indians, Montana; cat. no. $\frac{50}{1931}$, American Museum of Natural History.

FIG. 348. Bone for hand game; length, 2¼ inches; Grosventre Indians, Montana; cat. no. $\frac{50}{1917}$, American Museum of Natural History.

FIG. 349. Bones for hand game; length, 2¼ inches; Piegan Indians, Alberta; cat. no. 69354, Field Columbian Museum.

Cat. no. $\frac{50}{1917}$. Flat oval bone, highly polished and painted red and incised on one side, as shown in figure 348; length, 2¼ inches. Collected in 1901 by Dr A. L. Kroeber, who describes it as a hiding button.

PIEGAN. Alberta. (Cat. no. 69354, Field Columbian Museum.)

Four bones for hand game (figure 349), solid, with rounded ends, two with black band at the middle, and two plain; length, 2¾ inches. Collected by Mr R. M. Wilson.

CHIPEWYAN. Athabasca.

Father Petitot [a] gives the following definition:

Jeu de mains, udzi.

This name, he states, is general to all the dialects.

ETCHAREOTTINE. Fort Prince of Wales, Keewatín.

Samuel Hearne [b] says:

They have another simple indoor game, which is that of taking a bit of wood, a button, or any other small thing, and, after shifting it from hand to hand several times, asking their antagonist which hand it is in. When playing at this game, which only admits of two persons, each of them have ten, fifteen, or twenty small chips of wood, like matches, and when one of the players guesses right he takes one of his antagonist's sticks and lays it to his own; and he that first gets all the sticks from the other in that manner is said to win the game, which is generally for a single load of powder and shot, an arrow, or some other thing of inconsiderable value.

HAN KUTCHIN. Alaska.

Lieut. Frederick Schwatka, [c] U. S. Army, figures a pair of bones for the hand game as being used by the Aiyan and Chilkat. (See p. 288.)

KAWCHODINNE. Mackenzie.

Father Petitot [a] gives the following definition:

Jeu de mains, udzi.

KUTCHIN. Alaska and Yukon.

Father Petitot [a] gives the following definition:

Jeu de mains, odzi.

SARSI. British Columbia.

Rev. E. F. Wilson [d] describes the following game:

Two men squat side by side on the ground, with a blanket over their knees, and they have some small article, such as two or three brass beads tied together, which they pass from one to another under the blanket; and the other side, which also consists of two persons, has to guess in which hand the article is to be found—very much like our children's " hunt the whistle."

TAKULLI. Stuart lake, British Columbia.

Reverend Father A. G. Morice [e] says:

We find the elegantly carved gambling sticks of the West Coast tribes replaced by simple polished pieces of lynx or other animal's bones without any particular

---

[a] Dictionnaire de la Langue Dènè-Dindjié, Paris, 1876.

[b] A Journey from Prince of Wales's Fort in Hudson's Bay, to the Northern Ocean, p. 335, London, 1795.

[c] Along Alaska's Great River, p. 227, New York, 1885.

[d] Fourth Report on the North-Western Tribes of Canada. Report of the Fifty-Eighth Meeting of the British Association for the Advancement of Science, p. 246, London, 1889.

[e] Notes on the Western Dénés. Transactions of the Canadian Institute, v. 4, p. 77, Toronto, 1895.

design, and with the mere addition to one of the pair of the sinew wrapping necessary to determine the winning stick. The Babine specimens [figure 350] are rather large and must prove awkward in the hand of the gambler. But they have the reputation of being preventive of dishonesty, if distinctions between the honest and the dishonest can be established in connection with such a pastime as gambling. Such of these trinkets as are hollow have generally both ends shut with a piece of wood, and contain minute pebbles and gravel, which produce a gentle rattling sound in the hand of the native, much to his own satisfaction.

FIG. 350. Bones for hand game; length, 3 inches; Babine Indians, British Columbia; from Morice.

Figure 351 represents the Tsiʇꝗoh'tin [Tsilkotin] and figure 352 the Tsé'kéhne [Sekani] equivalent of the Babine gambling sticks. It will be seen from the latter that the Tsé'kéhne, who are the most primitive and uncultured of the three tribes whose technology is under review, are again the only people who in this connection, as with regard to their spoons, have made the merest attempt at bone carving.

The game played with these bone pieces is, I think, too well known to demand a description. The jerking movements and passes of hands of the party operating therewith, as well as the drum beating and the singing of the spectators or partners, are practised among most of the Indian races, especially of the Pacific coast, which have occupied the attention of American ethnologists. The Abbé Petitot says in one of his latest publications that this game is adventitious among the Eastern Dénés, who have borrowed it from the Crees. This

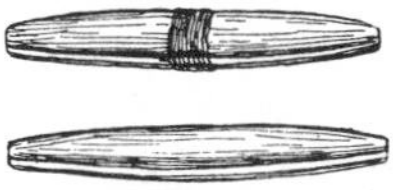

Fig. 351. 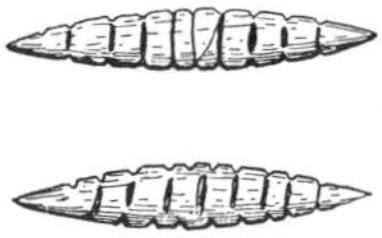   Fig. 352.

FIG. 351. Bones for hand game; length, 3 inches; Tsilkotin Indians, British Columbia; from Morice.
FIG. 352. Bones for hand game; length, 3 inches; Sekani Indians, British Columbia; from Morice.

remark is no less apposite with regard to their kinsmen west of the Rocky mountains. Although no other chance game possesses to-day so many charms for the frivolous Western Dénés, the old men assure me that it was formerly unknown among their fellow-countrymen. That their testimony is based on fact the very name of that game would seem to indicate, since it is a mere verb in the impersonal mood, nət'sə·a, "one keeps in the hand while moving," and is therefore of the fourth category of Déné nouns. The word for "gambling sticks," such as used in connection with nət'sə·a, is nə'ta, which is the same verb under the potential form, and means "that which can be held in the hand." Any of the surrounding races, Tsimpsian, Salishan, or Algonquin, may be held responsible for its introduction among the Western Dénés, for they are all exceedingly fond of it.

The original counterpart of the modern nət'sə·a was the atlih,[a] which in times was passionately played by the Carriers, but is now altogether forgotten except by a few elder men.

---

[a] May be translated by "gambling" in a general sense.

Elsewhere [a] Father Morice contrasts the hand game with the stick

FIG. 353. Bones for hand
game; length, 3¼ inches;
Umpqua Indians, Ore-
gon; cat. no. 3003, Brooklyn Institute Museum.

game as being played silently, while a tambour-
ine or some appropriate substitute, such as a tin
pan, is continually beaten as an accompaniment to the former.

UMPQUA. Oregon. (Cat. no. 3003, Brooklyn
Institute Museum.)

Two hollow bones (figure 353), 3¼ inches in
length and 1¼ inches in diameter, both with
two incised lines near each end and one
with two bands of leather set in grooves around the middle.

CADDOAN STOCK

PAWNEE. Oklahoma. (Field Columbian Museum.)

Cat. no. 59411. Set of eight sticks of smoothed natural brown wood,
21 inches in length.

Cat. no. 59389. Set of ten stick counters, four yellow and four green,
each with feather tied with thong at top, and two plain sticks;
all 16½ inches in length.

Cat. no. 59416. Long bone pipe bead, 2½ inches in length, and eight
counting sticks, 17 inches in length, four painted yellow and
four blue, feathered like arrows, both series differently (figure
354).

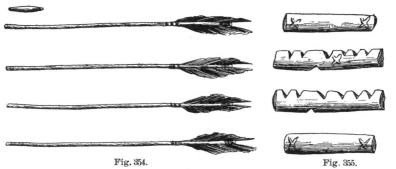

Fig. 354.   Fig. 355.

FIG. 354. Bead and counting sticks for hand game; length of bead, 2½ inches; length of counters,
17 inches; Pawnee Indians, Oklahoma; cat. no. 59416, Field Columbian Museum.
FIG. 355. Sticks for hand game; length, 1¼ inches; Pawnee Indians, Oklahoma; cat. no. 71654,
Field Columbian Museum.

Cat. no. 71588. Set of eight sticks, 22 inches in length, copies of
feathered shafts of arrows, four painted blue and four painted
red, accompanied with a short slender bow.

Cat. no. 71654. Set of four sticks (figure 355), 1¾ inches in length,
marked in pairs alike, one pair with six notches on one side

---

[a] The Western Dénés—Their Manners and Customs. Proceedings of the Canadian Institute, third series, v. 7, p. 154, Toronto, 1889.

and one notch on the other, and the other with incised crosses, one on each side of each end of the stick.

Cat. no. 71650. Two downy crane feathers, one faintly painted red, the other green. Mounted on small twigs; total length about 12 inches.

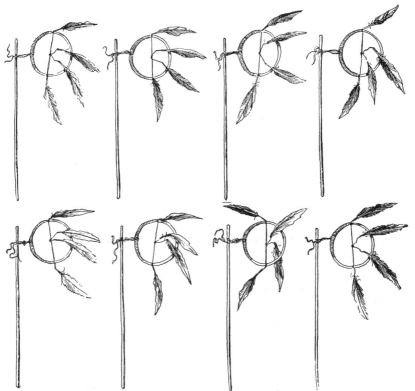

Fig. 356. Counting sticks for hand game; length, 12 inches; Pawnee Indians, Oklahoma; cat. no. 71647, Field Columbian Museum.

Cat. no. 71647. Set of eight sticks (figure 356), 12 inches in length; painted red, with a small cross incised near the top, and each having a hoop, 3¾ inches in diameter, made of a twig, attached by a thong. The inner half of each hoop is wrapped with sinew, and the hoop is bisected with a thong of buckskin having two feathers tied in the middle and one on each side of the rim.

Cat. no. 71649. Two wooden pins, each with four cut feathers tied at top; total length, 12 inches.

Cat. no. 71603. Cane whistle, 16½ inches in length, covered, except near the mouth, with painted buckskin having feathers attached.

Cat. no. 71648. Set of eight counting sticks, peeled twigs; 16 inches in length.

All the foregoing were collected by Dr George A. Dorsey.

PAWNEE. Oklahoma.

Dr George Bird Grinnell [a] says:

Perhaps no gambling game is so widespread and so popular as that known as "hands." It consists in guessing in which of the two hands is held a small marked object, right or wrong guessing being rewarded or penalized by the gain or loss of points. The players sit in lines facing each other, each man betting with the one opposite him. The object held, which is often a small polished bone, is intrusted to the best player on one side, who sits opposite to the best player on the other. The wagers are laid—after more or less discussion and bargaining as to the relative value of things as unlike as an otterskin quiver on one side and two plugs of tobacco, a yard of cloth, and seven cartridges on the other—and the game begins with a low song, which soon increases in volume and intensity. As the singers become more excited, the man who holds the bone moves his hands in time to the song, brings them together, seems to change the bone rapidly from hand to hand, holds their palms together, puts them behind his back or under his robe, swaying his body back and forth, and doing all he can to mystify the player who is about to try to choose the bone. The other for a time keeps his eyes steadily fixed on the hands of his opponent, and, gradually, as the song grows faster, bends forward, raises his right hand with extended forefinger above his head and holds it there, and at last, when he is ready, with a swift motion brings it down to a horizontal, pointing at one of the hands, which is instantly opened. If it contains the bone, the side which was guessing has won, and each man receives a stick from the opposite player. The bone is then passed across to the opposite side, the song is renewed, and the others guess.

In a letter, referring to the hand game, Dr Grinnell writes:

It is popular among all the northern tribes of which I have any knowledge and has a wide vogue in the west. I have seen it among the Arikara, Assiniboin, Grosventres of the Prairie, the three tribes of the Blackfoot Nation, Kootenai, Shoshoni, Ute, Cheyenne, Arapaho, and Pawnee.

WICHITA. Oklahoma. (Field Columbian Museum).

Cat. no. 59316. Set of counting sticks for hand game (figure 357);

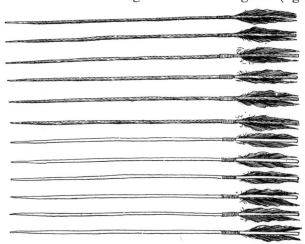

FIG. 357. Counting sticks for hand game; length, 20 inches; Wichita Indians, Oklahoma; cat. no. 59316, Field Columbian Museum.

[a] The Story of the Indian, p. 27, New York, 1898.

twelve unusually well-made arrows about 20 inches in length, with sharp points; the feathering regular and of good workmanship; six painted blue and six yellow.

Cat. no. 59355. Half a set of counting sticks (figure 358); six arrows, uniformly painted and well made, with sharpened points that show evidence of having been repeatedly thrust into the

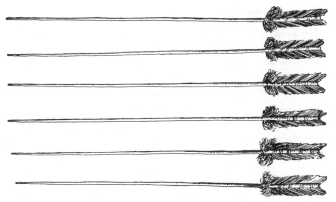

Fig. 358. Counting sticks for hand game; length, 26 inches; Wichita Indians, Oklahoma; cat. no. 59355, Field Columbian Museum.

ground. They are well feathered and painted blue for the greater part of their length. The portion to the extent of about 2 inches nearest to and including the feathering is painted yellow.

Cat. no. 59346. Set of counting sticks (figure 359); eight unpainted arrows, 24¼ inches in length, which terminate abruptly in blunt

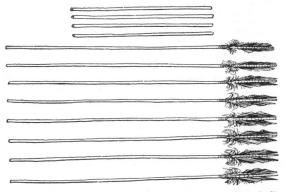

Fig. 359. Counting sticks for hand game; length, 24¼ and 14¼ inches; Wichita Indians, Oklahoma; cat. no. 59346, Field Columbian Museum.

points; the feathering is well done, but unusually short; also four undecorated wooden shafts.

Cat. no. 59227. Set of eight counting sticks, 20 inches long, with blunt points at one end and at the other a bunch of small eagle feathers. One half the shafts in this set are painted blue and the other half red.

Cat. no. 59288. Set of counting sticks (figure 360) ; eight well-made
shafts, 18 inches in length, with no trace of feathering or points,
and four similar shafts, 12 inches in length; all painted dark
blue.

Cat. no. 59266. Set of counting sticks (figure 361) ; eight plain
shafts, 16 inches in length, and four plain shafts, 10 inches in
length; one half the
number of each are
painted blue and the
other half red.

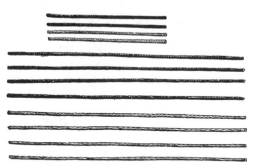

FIG. 360. Counting sticks for hand game; lengths, 18 and
12 inches; Wichita Indians, Oklahoma; cat. no. 59288,
Field Columbian Museum.

The sets were collected
by Dr George A. Dorsey,
who described [a] them as
they are arranged above,
as illustrating the grad-
ual transition of the counting stick used in the hand
game from the actual
practical arrow to the
simple stick. The four shorter undecorated sticks are explained by
the collector as each equivalent to eight of the long ones. Doctor Dorsey stated that the bones used in the game most often consist of two
bone tubes, such as are now purchased from traders for use in the

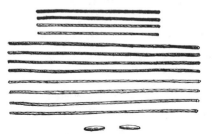

Fig. 361.

Fig. 362.

FIG. 361. Counting sticks and beads for hand game; lengths of sticks, 16 and 10 inches; Wichita
Indians, Oklahoma; cat. no. 59266, Field Columbian Museum.
FIG. 362. Drum used in hand game; diameter, 16 inches; Wichita Indians, Oklahoma; cat. no.
59317, Field Columbian Museum.

manufacture of breast ornaments, and that he was informed that they
use at times even a bullet or some equally unpretentious object.

Cat. no. 59317. Small, double-headed drum (figure 362), 4 inches
deep and 16 inches in diameter, made of two pieces of rawhide,
carefully and evenly stretched over a circular wooden frame and
laced along the median line. One head and half the body are
painted blue, the other half being painted pink with a large
blue circle in the center of the head.

---

[a] Hand or Guessing Game among the Wichitas. The American Antiquarian, v. 23, p.
366, 1901.

This was collected by Dr George A. Dorsey, who states that the peculiar manner of painting was due to its being used in two ceremonies, the blue side being used in the War dance, while the use of the pink side was confined exclusively to the Ghost dance.

Cat. no. 59362.   Large drum (figure 363), constructed similarly to the preceding, 8 inches deep and 30 inches in diameter; accompanied by four forked stakes, upon which the drum is suspended at some distance from the ground, when in use, by four leather thongs, which extend out on the four sides from the center. In addition, the drum bears on the upper surface a braided rawhide handle.

The entire surface of the drum is painted a deep blue, both sides containing similar symbols. The center bears a red circle 6 inches in diameter, upon which is an unusually good drawing of an eagle, the black-tipped white wing and tail feathers being drawn with great fidelity; the body is of course black. Surrounding this red sphere is a narrow blue line from which radiates a white line 5 inches in length, which is crossed at right angles near the outer end by a moon symbol in red. The line terminates in a five-pointed blue star. Between this star and the edge of the drum is drawn in white a pipe with a short stem. Running diagonally across near the outer edge of the

Fig. 363. Drum used in hand game; diameter, 30 inches; Wichita Indians. Oklahoma; cat. no. 59362, Field Columbian Museum.

drum is a yellow star with a pipe in white similar to the one just mentioned. The two diagonally opposite sides are occupied, one by a red and the other by a green star. This specimen was collected by Doctor Dorsey, who states that he was informed that this drum was used not only in the hand game, but in the so-called War dance. It is used also in rain ceremonies, but concerning the latter there was not time to get any detailed information. The pipes have special reference, of course, to the use of the drum during the war ceremony. He gives the following explanation of the symbols:

The red center symbolizes the earth, its light blue boundary being the firmament; the white line leading from the firmament to the blue star representing the way of life which the spirits of the departed travel in their journey to the west, as blue among the Wichitas is symbolic of the west. The color symbolism of the three remaining stars is north for the green, east for the yellow, and south for the red. The deep-blue color of the drum itself represents the heavens.

The following is Doctor Dorsey's account of the game:

The ceremony about to be described took place on the afternoon of Sunday, the 16th of June, 1901, in a very old Wichita grass lodge, about 7 miles north of Anadarko, Okla. This particular house, by the way, I was informed had long been the scene of this and similar ceremonies. Indeed, on the previous day I had here witnessed the ghost dance. Arriving at the lodge about 2 o'clock in the afternoon I found that it was already thronged with people, those of middle or advanced age predominating. The floor had been carefully swept, and both the east and west doors were open. Just outside of the lodge, exposed to the full rays of the sun, was suspended the large drum above described, with its four supports. I was not able to learn on inquiry whether the drum was placed in this position ceremonially or whether it was simply for the purpose of tightening the heads through the action of heat. From the use of the drum, however, later in the ceremony, I am inclined to believe that this first exposure to the sun was ceremonial in character. Within the lodge the occupants assumed positions—some on one side, others on the other—leaving a large open space about the fire hearth in the center. Two old women assumed a position halfway between the hearth and the western side of the lodge, and to one of them was passed the bundle of counting sticks previously described under no. 59288. A number of men then gathered to their left, when the large drum was brought in and placed in their midst, and the smaller drum was placed in the hands of one of their number. The drummers then began a slow and measured beating, all at the same time joining in a sort of chant. This, I was informed, was a supplication to the sun that the game might proceed quietly and orderly, and that whichever side lost should bear no ill will toward the winning side, and that at the conclusion of the ceremony all might be happy. That this, however, does not represent the full meaning of the song is entirely probable. The old women then came forward toward the center of the floor, one of them bearing in her hands two small bone cylinders, around one of which was fastened a black thong. With arms outstretched aloft she turned toward the sun and uttered a prayer which lasted over a minute, all the others in the lodge keeping profound silence. She then passed the cylinders to an old man sitting on the north side of the lodge, who immediately placed one in each hand and began to wave his arms back and forth in front of the body, the members on his side beginning to sing to the accompaniment of the beating of the two drums. After several passes he signified that he was ready, when the other of the two women occupying the center of the lodge guessed at the location of the unmarked cylinder. Her guess proved to be correct, and, as she represented the faction sitting on the south side of the lodge, a red arrow, symbolic of the south, was thrust into the ground in front of and between the two tally keepers. The cylinders were then passed to one of the members of the opposite side, who repeated the performance just described, when the woman who represented the party of the north side hazarded a guess. Before she did this, however, she touched the tips of the fingers of both hands to the side of the hearth, rubbed her hands in front of her face, and then outstretched them in the direction of the sun. Thus the game was continued with varying fortune until about 6 o'clock, at which time the side of the north was in possession of all the counters. I was prepared from what I had observed of this game among other tribes to see some outbreak of joy upon the part of the victors. Instead, however, the game seemed one of intense solemnity. The cylinders were passed back to the woman representing the guesser of the winning side, who held them aloft as before and uttered a prayer. Next she took the bundle of counting sticks and went through the same performance, at the termination of which, without any intimation, both sides joined in a song accompanied by the low beating of the drum. This song was exceedingly beautiful and resembled nothing so much as a subdued but devout hymn of thanksgiving, as indeed I was informed that it was. The song lasted for perhaps ten minutes, when those present began conversing in low tones, which very soon became more animated, and they began to leave the lodge and assemble on the south side of the lodge at a level space cleared of all vegetation, where they gathered in one great circle. The large drum was then brought out by one of the leaders, who held it toward the sun, uttered a prayer, and again all sang a song, which was of the same general character as the one just described. The drum was then returned to its former position just outside the lodge. Five of the older men now began a distribution of food, consisting of meat, bread, and coffee, to all those present, and the ceremony was at an end.

The contrast between this sedate and dignified performance and the loud, boisterous, weird all-night performances, such as are conducted, for example, by the Kootenays, was profound, and no one could have witnessed this game without becoming convinced that a deep religious significance underlies at least one of the games of the American aborigines.

WICHITA. Oklahoma.

In the story of " The Thunderbird and the Water Monster," as related by Dr George A. Dorsey,[a] the hand game is described as the great gambling game of the people of these times. The wagers were generally large, people sometimes betting their lives and weapons, in the former case the winners taking the lives of the losers.

CHIMMESYAN STOCK

NISKA. Nass river, British Columbia.

Dr Franz Boas [b] describes the following game:

Leha'l: the guessing game, in which a bone wrapped in cedar-bark is hidden in one hand. The player must guess in which hand the bone is hidden.

CHINOOKAN STOCK

CHINOOK. Shoalwater bay, Washington.

James G. Swan [c] says:

Another game is played by little sticks or stones, which are rapidly thrown from hand to hand with the skill of experienced jugglers, accompanied all the while by some song adapted to the occasion, the winning or losing the game depending on being able to guess correctly which hand the stick is in. This game can be played by any number of persons and is usually resorted to when the members of two different tribes meet, and is a sort of trial of superiority. Before commencing the game the betting begins, and each article staked is put before the winner, and whoever wins takes the whole pile.

CHINOOK. Near Fort Vancouver, Washington.

Paul Kane [d] says:

The one most generally played consists in holding in each hand a small stick, the thickness of a goose quill and about an inch and a half in length, one plain

[a] The Mythology of the Wichita, p. 102, Washington, 1904.

[b] Fifth Report on the Indians of British Columbia. Report of the Sixty-fifth Meeting of the British Association for the Advancement of Science, p. 582, London, 1895.

[c] The Northwest Coast, p. 158, New York, 1857.

[d] Wanderings of an Artist among the Indians of North America, p. 189, London, 1859; also the Canadian Journal, v. iii, no. 12, p. 276, Toronto, July, 1855.

and the other distinguished by a little thread wound round it, the opposite party being required to guess in which hand the marked stick is to be found. A Chinook will play at this simple game for days and nights together, until he has gambled away everything he possesses, even to his wife.

CHINOOK. Columbia river, Oregon.

John Dunn [a] says:

One of their usual games is this: One man takes a small stone, which he shifts from hand to hand repeatedly, all the while humming a low, monotonous air. The bet being made, according as the adversary succeeds in grasping the hand which contains the stone he wins or loses. The game is generally played with great fairness.

Ross Cox [b] says:

Their common game is a simple kind of hazard. One man takes a small stone, which he changes for some time from hand to hand, all the while humming a slow, monotonous air. The bet is then made, and according as his adversary succeeds in guessing the hand in which the stone is concealed, he wins or loses. They seldom cheat, and submit to their losses with the most philosophical resignation.

CLATSOP. Mouth of the Columbia river, Oregon.

Lewis and Clark [c] give the following account:

The games are of two kinds. In the first, one of the company assumes the office of banker and plays against the rest. He takes a small stone about the size of a bean, which he shifts from one hand to the other with great dexterity, repeating at the same time a song adapted to the game, which serves to divert the attention of the company; till, having agreed on the stake, he holds out his hands, and the antagonist wins or loses as he succeeds or fails at guessing in which hand is the stone. After the banker has lost his money, or whenever he is tired, the stone is transferred to another, who in turn challenges the rest of the company.

FIG. 364. Bones for hand game; length, 3 inches; Wasco Indians, Oregon; cat. no. 60471, Field Columbian Museum.

WASCO. Hood river, Oregon. (Cat. no. 60471, Field Columbian Museum.)

Four bone cylinders (figure 364), from leg bones, yellow and polished from use and age, 3 inches in length; two wrapped in two places by a buckskin thong in a groove which has been cut in for the reception of the band. On each end of the marked bones are five deep, sharp incisions.

These were collected in 1900 by Dr George A. Dorsey, who says:

The game is tlukuma. The unmarked bone is cola, "man," and the marked bone, skaguilak, "woman." The marks on the end of bones are yakimutema. The counters, wowuk, were burned upon the death of the owner's brother.

[a] The Oregon Territory, p. 93, Philadelphia, 1845.
[b] The Columbia River, vol. 1, p. 302, London, 1831.
[c] History of the Expedition under the Command of Lewis and Clark, v. 2, p. 784, New York, 1893.

COPEHAN STOCK

WINTUN.   California.   (Cat. no. $\frac{50}{4187}$, American Museum of Natural
     History.)

Four bones (figure 365), 2¼ inches in length, two tied in the middle
with cord and two plain.   Collected in 1902
by Mr Howard Wilson, who gives the name
as dam.

COSTANOAN STOCK

RUMSEN.   Monterey, California.

    J. F. G. de la Pérouse [a] says:

  The other game,[b] named toussi, is more easy; they
play it with four, two on each side; each in his turn
hides a piece of wood in his hands, whilst his partner
makes a thousand gestures to take off the attention
of the adversaries. It is curious enough to a stander-by
to see them squatted down opposite to each other, keeping the most profound silence, watching the features
and most minute circumstances which may assist them
in discovering the hand which conceals the piece of
wood; they gain or lose a point according to their guess-

FIG. 365. Bones for hand
game; length, 2¼ inches;
Wintun Indians, Cali-
fornia; cat. no. $\frac{50}{4187}$,
American Museum of
Natural History.

ing right or wrong, and those who gain it have a right to hide in their turn;
the game is 5 points, and the common stake is beads, and among the independent
Indians the favors of their women.

ESKIMAUAN STOCK

ESKIMO (Labrador).   Ungava.

    Mr Lucien M. Turner [c] says:

  The young girls often play the game of taking an object and secreting it
within the closed hand.   Another is called upon to guess the contents.   She
makes inquiries as to the size, color, etc., of the object.   From the answers she
gradually guesses what the thing is.

KALAPOOIAN STOCK

CALAPOOYA.   Siletz reservation, Oregon.   (Cat. no. 63605, Field Co-
    lumbian Museum.)

Four bones (figure 366), 3¼ inches in length and 1 inch in diameter
    at ends, two with a leather band around the middle and two
    plain.   Ten counting sticks of willow, 8¾ inches in length,
    pointed at one end, with a black burned band at top.

---

  [a] A Voyage round the World in the years 1785, 1786, 1787, and 1788, v. 2, p. 224,
London, 1798.

  [b] See p. 472.

  [c] Ethnology of the Ungava District.   Eleventh Annual Report of the Bureau of Ethnology, p. 255, 1894.

These were collected by T. Jay Bufort, who gives, under the name of ithlacum, the following account of the game:

Any number of players come together, at which time two captains choose sides. Then the captains divide the bones, each taking one white and one marked bone. The players sit facing each other with the counting sticks lying between them. By lot they decide which side shall play first. The successful man will take a bone in each hand, holding them in front of him, and will exchange them so rapidly that the bystanders are supposed not to know which hand has the marked bone. Then holding both hands still in front of him, exposing the ends, an opposite man makes a guess by pointing at the hand which he thinks contains the white bone. The hands are then opened, exposing the bones to full view. If the guesser has pointed to the marked bone, he loses, and one of the markers is immediately placed to the credit of the player. If he guesses the white bone, he wins, and one of the markers is placed to his credit. Then he proceeds to shuffle the bones for the opposite side to guess.

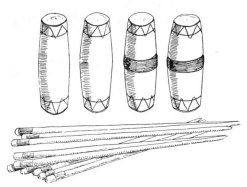

FIG. 366. Bones and counting sticks for hand game; length of bones, 3¼ inches; length of sticks, 8¼ inches; Calapooya Indians, Siletz reservation, Oregon; cat. no. 63605, Field Columbian Museum.

The amount of the stake played for is generally arranged on a series of 12 games, each side putting up the amount collectively, and the winning side dividing at the end of the game. This does not prohibit anyone, however, from betting on a single game or on one hand, which is often done as the game proceeds.

KIOWAN STOCK

KIOWA. Oklahoma.

Mr James Mooney [a] describes the hand game of the Kiowa as follows:

The name dó-á signifies the tipi game; from do, tipi or house, and "a," a game, because, unlike most of their games, it is played inside the tipi, being essentially a game for the long nights when the whole tribe is assembled in the winter camp. A similar game is found among nearly all our wild tribes; it is played by both sexes, but never together. In its general features it resembles our game of "hunt the button," the players forming a circle around the fire of the tipi, one-half of them playing against the others, sitting facing them on the opposite side of the fire. The leader of one party then takes the k'íäbo, or button, a short piece of stick wrapped around the middle with a strip of fur, and small enough to be concealed in the hand. Putting his closed hands together, he raises his arms above his head, clasps them across his chest, or puts them behind his back, endeavoring to pass the k'íäbo from one hand to another, or from his own hand to that of his next partner, without being per-

---

[a] Calendar History of the Kiowa Indians. Seventeenth Annual Report of the Bureau of American Ethnology, p. 348, 1898.

ceived by any of the opposite party, all the while keeping time to the movements of his hands with one of the peculiar dó-á songs, in which the members of his party join.

When the opposing player thinks he has detected in which hand the other has concealed the stick, he indicates it with a peculiar jerk of his thumb and index finger in that direction, with a loud Tsoq! (Comanche for "That!"); if he has guessed correctly, he scores a certain number of points, the account being kept by means of a bundle of green-painted tally sticks. He then takes the k'íäbo and begins a similar set of movements in time to another song, in which his partners join; so the game goes on far into the night, until the contest is decided and the stakes won by one side or the other. It is a most animated and interesting game, of which they are very fond, and frequently at night in the winter camp the song chorus may be heard from several games in progress simultaneously, the high-pitched voices of the women in one tipi making a pleasing contrast to the deeper tones of the men in another.

Mr Mooney gives a picture of the doa game from a Kiowa calendar [figure 367], which he describes as follows:

Winter 1881–82. Ìmdádóá-de Saiá, "Winter when they played the dó-á medicine game." This winter is noted for a great dó-á game played under the auspices of two rival leaders, each of whom claimed to have the most powerful "medicine" for the game. The game was played in the winter camp on the Washita, near the mouth of Hog Creek, the Kiowa leader being Pa-tepte, "Buffalo-bull-coming-out," alias Dátekâñ, now dead, . . . while his opponent was the Apache chief and medicine man Dävéko. The Kiowa leader was recognized distinctively as having "medicine" for this game, and it was said that he could do wonderful things with the "button," making it pass invisibly from one hand to another while he held his hands outstretched and far apart, and even to throw it up into the air and cause it to remain there suspended invisibly until he was ready to put out his hand again and catch it; in other words, he was probably an expert sleight-of-hand performer. His Apache rival, Dävéko, is known as a medicine man as well as a chief, and is held in considerable dread, as it is believed that he can kill by shooting invisible darts from a distance into the body of an enemy. On this occasion he had boasted that his medicine was superior for the dó-á game, which did not

FIG. 367. Hand game; Kiowa Indians, Oklahoma; from a Kiowa calendar: from Mooney.

prove to be the case, however, and as the Kiowa medicine man won the victory for his party, large stakes were wagered on the result and were won by the Kiowa. It is said that this was a part of Pa-tepte's effort to revive the old customs and amusements on a large scale. The game was witnessed by a large concourse, all dressed and painted for the occasion. The picture on the Set-t'an calendar is very suggestive.

KITUNAHAN STOCK

KUTENAI. Bonners Ferry, Idaho. (Cat. no. 51878, Field Columbian Museum.)

Two sets of bones (figure 368), one $2\frac{1}{2}$ inches in length and the other $2\frac{3}{4}$ inches in length; both about three-fourths of an inch in diameter, hollow, and with square ends. In each set one bone is wrapped around the middle with a leather band.

These were collected in 1897 by Dr George A. Dorsey, who bought

them from a Kutenai who belongs to a little renegade band living at Bonners Ferry. Doctor Dorsey writes:

FIG. 368. Bones for hand game; length, 2¼ inches; Kutenai Indians, Idaho; cat. no. 51878, Field Columbian Museum.

This Indian told me that among the Kutenai, or at any rate among his people, whenever they played this game they always had two sets, thus obviating the necessity of passing the set back and forth from side to side, as would be the case if they played with but one set. In connection with these two Kutenai sets I send you some photographs I took of some Kutenai playing this game, taken on the Bitter Root river, near Flathead lake, Mont. [figures 369,

370]. I saw the game played by several different parties among the Flathead Indians, with whom this band of Kutnai is more or less intimately associated.

KUTENAI. British Columbia.

Dr A. F. Chamberlain [a] says:

The Lower Kootenays are very much in love with gambling, which vice, through the efforts of the missionaries, has been entirely suppressed amongst the Upper

FIG. 369. Kutenai Indians playing hand game; Montana; from photograph by Dr George A. Dorsey.

Kootenays. In the gambling dance they chant Hai yā! hai yā! hai yā hē, repeated an infinite number of times, interspersed with yells of hō hō! hā hā!

[a] Report on the Kootenay Indians of South-Eastern British Columbia. Report of the Sixty-second Meeting of the British Association for the Advancement of Science, p. 561, London, 1893.

hē hē hai hai! hē hē hai hai! hū hū! etc. Another gambling refrain is ī ī ī! yā ē e e !

The gambling consists in guessing in which hand one (on which a ring of bark is left) of two sticks of wood is hidden. The players sit in two rows

FIG. 370. Kutenai Indians playing hand game; Montana; from photograph by Dr George A. Dorsey.

facing each other, and a number of them keep beating on a log in front of them with sticks while the sticks are passed from hand to hand. From time to time some of the players sing or contort their limbs in various ways.

KOLUSCHAN STOCK

CHILKAT. Alaska.

Lieut. Frederick Schwatka, U. S. Army,[a] says:

The gambling game which they called la-hell was the favorite during the trip over the Chilkoot trail, although I understand that they have others not so complicated. This game requires an even number of players, generally from four to twelve, divided into two parties which face each other. These "teams" continue sitting about 2 or 3 feet apart, with their legs drawn up under them, à la Turque, the place selected being usually in sandy ground under the shade of a grove of poplar or willow trees. Each man lays a wager with the person directly opposite him, with whom alone he gambles as far as the gain or loss of his stake is concerned, although such loss or gain is determined by the success of the team as a whole. In other words, when a game terminates one team, of course, is the winner, but each player wins only the

_____
[a] Along Alaska's Great River, p. 70, New York, 1885.

stake put up by his vis-à-vis. A handful of willow sticks, 3 or 4 inches long, and from a dozen to a score in number, are thrust in the sand or soft earth between the two rows of squatting gamblers, and by means of these a sort of running record or tally of the game is kept. The implements actually employed in gambling are merely a couple of small bone bobbins, as shown [in figure 371], of about the size of a lady's penknife, one of which has one or more bands of black cut around it near its center and is called the king, the other being pure white. At the commencement of the game one of the players picks up the bone bobbins, changes them rapidly from one hand to the other, sometimes behind his back, then again under an apron or hat resting on his lap, during all of which time the whole assembly are singing in a low measured melody the words, " Oh! oh! oh! Oh, ker-shoo, ker-shoo!'" which is kept up, with their elbows flapping against their sides and their heads swaying to the tune, until some player of the opposite row, thinking he is inspired, and singing with unusual vehemence, suddenly points out the hand of the juggler that, in his belief, contains " the king." If his guess is correct, his team picks up one of

FIG. 371. Bones for hand game; length, 2 inches; Chilkat Indians, Alaska; from Schwatka

the willow sticks and places it on their side, or if the juggler's team has gained, any one of their sticks must be replaced in the reserve at the center. If he is wrong then, the other side tallies one in the same way. The bone " king and queen " are then handed to an Indian in the other row and the same performance repeated, although it may be twice as long, or half as short, as no native attempts to discern the whereabouts of the " king " until he feels he has a revelation to that effect, produced by the incantation. A game will last anywhere from half an hour to three hours. Whenever the game is nearly concluded and one party has gained almost all the willow sticks, or at any other exciting point of the game, they have methods of " doubling up " on the wagers by not exchanging the bobbins, but holding both in one hand or leaving one or both on the ground under a hat or apron, and the guesses are about both and count double, treble, or quadruple, for loss or gain. They wager the caps off their heads, their shirts off their backs, and with many of them, no doubt, their prospective pay for the trip was all gone before it was half earned.

Again, he says:[a]

Another article freely brought to us was the pair of small bone gambling tools so characteristic of the whole northwest country. They have been described when speaking of the Chilkat Indians, and I saw no material difference in their use by this particular tribe.

TLINGIT. Alaska. (Cat. no. $\frac{E}{605}$, American Museum of Natural History.)

Set of four bones (figure 372), solid and very old and stained, $1\frac{7}{8}$ inches in length, not entirely round, but with a raised strip on one side. On two this strip has a fluted edge, ornamented with four circles, with interior dots. One of these is plain and the others are cut to receive a band in the middle. One has a plain strip with two circles with interior dots and is perforated at one end, and the fourth a strip cut away at the sides near the ends,

---

[a] Along Alaska's Great River, p. 227, New York, 1885.

with four dots. The latter has two perforations at right angles and is cut to receive a band. Collected by Lieut. George T. Emmons, U. S. Navy, who describes the specimens as part of the paraphernalia of a shaman.

FIG. 372. Bones for hand game; length, 1⅞ inches; Tlingit Indians, Alaska; cat. no. $\frac{E}{605}$, American Museum of Natural History.

KULANAPAN STOCK

GUALALA. Sonoma county, California.

Mr Stephen Powers [a] says:

While among the Gualala I had an excellent opportunity of witnessing the gambling game of wi and tep, and a description of the same, with slight variations, will answer for nearly all the tribes in central and southern California. . . . They gamble with four cylinders of bone about 2 inches long, two of which are plain and two marked with rings and strings tied around the middle. The game is conducted by four old and experienced men, frequently gray-heads, two for each party, squatting on their knees on opposite sides of the fire. They have before them a quantity of fine dry grass, and, with their hands in rapid and juggling motion before and behind them, they roll up each piece of bone in a little bale, and the opposite party presently guess in which hand is the marked bone. Generally only one guesses at a time, which he does with the word "tep," marked one, "wi," plain one. If he guesses right for both the players, they simply toss the bones over to him and his partner, and nothing is scored on either side. If he guesses right for one and wrong for the other, the one for whom he guessed right is "out," but his partner rolls up the bones for another trial, and the guesser forfeits to them one of the twelve counters. If he guesses wrong for both, they still keep on, and he forfeits two counters. There are only twelve counters, and when they have been all won over to one side or the other the game is ended. Each Indian then takes out of the stake the article which he or she deposited, together with that placed on it, so that every one of the winning party comes out with double the amount he staked.

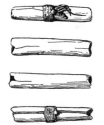

FIG. 373. Bones for hand game; length, 2¼ inches; Pomo Indians, California. cat. no. 200295, United States National Museum.

POMO. Hopland, California. (Cat. no. 200295, United States National Museum.)

Set of four bones (figure 373), 2¾ inches in length and one-half inch in diameter; interior hollow; two tied with thread about the middle and two plain.

---

[a] The Tribes of California. Contributions to North American Ethnology, v. 3, p. 189, Washington, 1877.

Collected by Mr C. F. Briggs, who states that they are used by the Pomo and all other Indians in that part of California.

Pomo. Ukiah, California. (Field Columbian Museum.)

Cat. no. 61144. Four cylindrical bones (figure 374) from legs of mountain lion, 3 inches in length; two bound with native twine,

which passes through the tube and back under wrapping on outside of bone. Smooth and highly polished.

The above specimens were collected in 1900 by Dr George A. Dorsey, who states that the native name is shoduwia.

Sho equals "east;" du-wi equals "night." The game is played by fire light in sweat houses.—(J. W. H.)

Fig. 374. Bones for hand game; length, 3 inches; Pomo Indians, California; cat. no. 61144, Field Columbian Museum.

Cat. no. 61192. Four very old and highly polished bones(figure 375), 2½ inches in length, from the foot of the mountain lion. Two unmarked bones have on the side a row of excavated pits, 9 on one, 6 on the other. The other two bones are bound in the middle with native cordage, which passes also inside and outside the bone. Each of these latter has a circle of black dots near one end, one composed of 7 and the other of 9 dots.

These specimens were collected by Dr J. W. Hudson in 1900, who gives the native name as coka, eastern. Doctor Hudson informed the writer that the pits or dots on the bones represent the king-fisher, bidama chata, the patron of the gamblers.

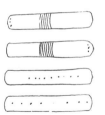

—— Ukiah valley, Mendocino county, California.

Dr J. W. Hudson describes shoka (coka), eastern game, the usual hand or grass game.

Fig. 375. Bones for hand game; length, 2½ inches; Pomo Indians, California; cat. no. 61192, Field Columbian Museum.

The guesser, when calling tĕp, guesses that the plain bone is in the hand in front of the player. If correct he takes the bones. When calling wi, he means the bound bone is in the hand in front. This tribe always keep one of their hands in front and one behind when juggling the bones. A caller can call ko, both, which means that he guesses at both opponents, and the hands are

thus

The call tso'-lo-pa, flicker-head band, means

A "ko," or tso'-lo-pa, if correct, wins both opponents' bones. "Tĕp," or "wi" call refers to the opponent pointed at only, and the other partner must win back the bones lost before the game can proceed in the orthodox way or lose his play. The following archaic calls are very rarely heard in the hand game:

Ŭ'yu equals the high one, the wi bone, or kai-yĕ'; or nau-wa-tca-tcim equals sit-behind-him. Ka-tu'-shĕl equals the short one, the tĕp bone.

POMO. Nabatel village, Mendocino county, California. (Cat. no. 54472, Field Columbian Museum.)

Four highly polished cylindrical bones, 2⅜ inches in length, from the foot of the mountain lion; two bound in the center by ten or more wraps of native cord, which there passes in each direction and enters the hollow of the bone.

This is the most highly polished set ever seen by the collector, Dr George A. Dorsey (1899), who gives the native name as coka, eastern. Another set (cat. no. 54473), similar to the above, is 2½ inches in length.

———— Upper Lake, Lake county, California. (Field Columbian Museum.)

Cat. no. 54468. Two bone cylinders (figure 376), 3 inches in length, one an eagle bone, wrapped with cordage which passes through and back outside the bone. The unmarked bone is one from a mountain lion's foot. Both bones are highly polished and very smooth.

Cat. no. 54470. Two bone cylinders, 2¾ inches in length, similar to above.

Cat. no. 54469. Two eagle-bone cylinders, 3 inches in length, one wrapped with native cordage, nine wraps, which passes through and back to center over ends.

Cat. no. 54471. Four cylindrical bones, 2¾ inches in length, from the legs of wildcats. Two wrapped with twine in center of bone. All highly polished and worn smooth.

FIG. 376. Bones for hand game; length, 3 inches; Pomo Indians, California; cat. no. 54468, Field Columbian Museum.

All of the above-described specimens were collected in 1899 by Dr George A. Dorsey, who gives the native name as duweka at Ukiah.

———— Upper Lake, Lake county, California. (Cat. no. 61215, Field Columbian Museum.)

Two bones, eagle-wing tubes, each about 3 inches in length, one of them wrapped as follows: Eight times around the center with native cord, which also passes out to the end of the tube and back to the other end, then inside the tube and back to the center on the outside.

These were collected in 1900 by Dr J. W. Hudson from Captain Jim Bucknell, a noted Indian character.

LUTUAMIAN STOCK

KLAMATH. Upper Klamath lake, Oregon. (Cat. no. 37496, Free Museum of Science and Art, University of Pennsylvania.)

Four solid bones (figure 377), 3 inches in length, two wrapped about the middle with cord cemented with black gum; six willow counting sticks (figure 378), pointed at one end and painted red; length, 7 inches. Collected in 1900 by Dr George A. Dorsey.

Fig. 377.   Fig. 378.

FIG. 377. Bones for hand game; length, 3 inches; Klamath Indians, Oregon; cat. no. 37496, Free Museum of Science and Art, University of Pennsylvania.

FIG. 378. Counting sticks for hand game; length, 7 inches; Klamath Indians, Oregon; cat. no. 37496, Free Museum of Science and Art, University of Pennsylvania.

KLAMATH. Upper Klamath lake, Oregon. (Cat. no. 61616, Field Columbian Museum.)

Four solid bones (figure 379), 3 inches in length, and tapering to each end. Two of the bones have wound about their centers several wrappings of a buckskin thong; all of them are decorated, the two plain ones having on one side of one end a double cross, while the marked bones have at one end an incision

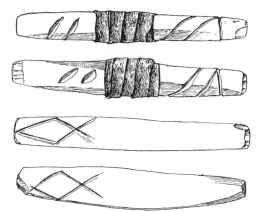

FIG. 379. Bones for hand game; length, 3 inches; Klamath Indians, Oregon; cat. no. 61616, Field Columbian Museum: from Dorsey.

running around the bones, from which spring two parallel incised spirals, terminating under the wrappings. The set of bones is accompanied with twelve neatly made decorated wooden pins, 8¼ inches long.

Collected in 1900 by Dr George A. Dorsey, who describes the game under the name of loipas:[a]

The two marked bones are known as skútash, tied áround, or híshuaksh, male, while the unmarked bones are solsas, female. The twelve sticks serve as counters, kshesh.

---

[a] Certain Gambling Games of the Klamath Indians. American Anthropologist, n. s., v. 3, p. 22, 1901.

Continuing, Doctor Dorsey says:

In connection with the hand game there should be mentioned a lozenge-shaped stone [figure 380], measuring 2¼ inches long by 1½ inches in breadth and an inch in thickness. This stone, with several others similar in shape, was found at Klamath falls, near the foot of Klamath lake, and was obtained by me from a merchant as I was leaving the reservation. The person from whom I procured the specimen said that a number of Klamath Indians had seen the stone and

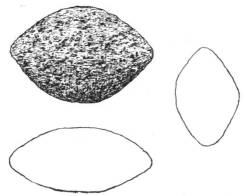

FIG. 380. Stones for hand game; lengths, 1½ to 2¼ inches; Klamath Indians, Oregon; cat. no. 61772, Field Columbian Museum; from Dorsey.

had unanimously declared that it was formerly used in playing the hand game. It was not possible for me to verify this statement, but from the shape of the stone and from my inability to see to what other use it could have been put, I am inclined to the belief that it had been used in the hand game.

MODOC. Yainax subagency, Klamath reservation, Oregon. (Cat. no. 61814, Field Columbian Museum.)

Two slender, tapering wood pins (figure 381), 6¾ inches in length, one marked with two burnt bands and the other plain.

FIG. 381. Sticks for hand game; length, 6¾ inches; Modoc Indians, Oregon; cat. no. 61814, Field Columbian Museum.

They were collected by Mr R. C. Spink, who describes them as used in the hand game under the name of seloogoush and schme.

MARIPOSAN STOCK

YOKUTS. Little Sandy creek, Fresno county, California. (Cat. no. 70866, Field Columbian Museum.)

Four hollow bones, 3 inches long, two wrapped with cord about the middle and two plain.

These were collected by Dr J. W. Hudson, who describes them as used in the grass game.

YOKUTS. Tule River reservation, Tulare county, California. (Cat. no. 70379, Field Columbian Museum.)

Four sticks, 1¾ inches long and one-fourth inch in diameter, two plain and two painted black, with loops for tying to the fingers, and ten unpeeled maple counting sticks, 9 inches in length (figure 382).

These were collected by Dr J. W. Hudson, who describes them as used in the game called tâtât:

Played by two persons, each of whom has a pair of sticks, one white and one black; one player puts his hands behind him and rings two of the four fingers on his right hand with the cords attached to the two sticks. He then brings

FIG. 382. Sticks and counters for hand game; length of sticks, 1¾ inches; length of counters, 9 inches; Yokuts Indians, Tule River reservation, Tulare county, California; cat. no. 70379, Field Columbian Museum.

out his hand, covering the fingers with his left hand. The opposite player endeavors to guess whether the black or white stick is nearest the thumb or whether the two sticks are attached to adjoining or separated fingers.

MOQUELUMNAN STOCK

CHOWCHILLA. Grant Springs, Mariposa county, California.

Dr J. W. Hudson describes these Indians as playing the hand game under the name of hinawu:

The bound bone is called ti-yă-u-ni (female); the plain, nûng-a (man). Ten counting sticks, hû-hû, are used. The call gesture is nĕt, " there ! "

They also play a game called hu'-sa, in which one guesses which hand hides a hidden seed or nut.

TOPINAGUGIM. Big creek, Tuolumne county, California. (Field Columbian Museum.)

Cat. no. 70216. Four bones (figure 383), 3⅞ inches in length, two wrapped with leather thongs and two plain.

Cat. no. 70217. Three bones (figure 384), 3¼ inches in length, two wrapped with thongs and one plain; incomplete set.

Cat. no. 70232. Ten counting sticks of peeled wild cherry, sharpened at one end, 15 inches in length.

All collected by Dr J. W. Hudson, who describes them as used in the grass game. Each side has ten counting sticks.

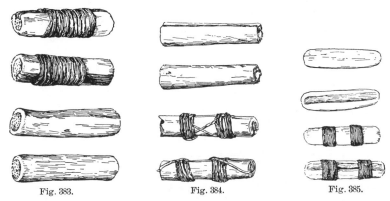

Fig. 383.　　　　　　Fig. 384.　　　　　　Fig. 385.

FIG. 383. Bones for hand game; length, 3⅛ inches; Topinagugim Indians, Tuolumne county, California; cat. no. 70216, Field Columbian Museum.

FIG. 384. Bones for hand game; length, 3¼ inches; Topinagugim Indians, Tuolumne county, California; cat. no. 70217, Field Columbian Museum.

FIG. 385. Bones for hand game; length, 2¼ inches; Topinagugim Indians, Tuolumne county, California; cat. no. 70218, Field Columbian Museum.

TOPINAGUGIM. Big creek, Tuolumne county, California. (Cat. no. 70218, Field Columbian Museum.)

Four bones (figure 385), split panther femur, 2¼ inches in length, two bound with thongs.

These were used by women. They were collected by Dr J. W. Hudson.

PIMAN STOCK

PAPAGO. Mission of San Xavier del Bac, Pima county, Arizona. (Cat. no. 63521, Field Columbian Museum.)

FIG. 386. Sticks for peon; length, 3¼ inches; Papago Indians, Arizona; cat. no. 63521, Field Columbian Museum.

Implements for peon game (figure 386), consisting of three slender sticks, 3¼ inches in length, painted red, black, and yellow, each with a finger loop of colored cloth, the red with a black loop, the black with a white loop, and the yellow with a red loop. Collected by Mr S. C. Simms.

PIMA. Gila River reserve, Sacaton agency, Pinal county, Arizona. (Cat. no. 63300, Field Columbian Museum.)

Implements for a guessing game (figure 387), consisting of three slender round sticks, about 13½ inches in length, each with a loop of cotton cloth tied to one end, and the other end painted black for a distance of 4½ inches; accompanied with twenty counters, fragments of twigs, about 2½ inches in length.

These were collected by Mr S. C. Simms, who gives the name of the game as wahpetah, and states that it is played by six persons, three on each side. The players on one side conceal the sticks under their arms, putting a finger into each loop, the other side guessing whether they have the sticks under the right or the left arm.

FIG. 387. Sticks for wahpetah; length, 13¼ inches; Pima Indians, Arizona; cat. no. 63300, Field Columbian Museum.

PIMA. Arizona.

Dr Frank Russell [a] describes the following game:

Vaputta.—Any number of players may participate, but they are under two leaders who are selected by toss. Each draws up his men in line so that they face their opponents. A goal about 50 yards distant is marked out, and the game begins. A small object, usually a circular piece of pottery such as are so common about the ruins of the Southwest, is carried around behind the line by a leader and placed in the hands of one of his men. The opposite leader guesses which man holds the object. If he guesses wrong, the man at the end of the line in which the object is held, who stands farthest from the goal, runs and jumps over the upheld leg of the man at the opposite end of his line. This moves the winning line the width of one man and the length of a jump toward the goal. If the first guess is correct the object is passed to him and there is no jumping until a guess fails.[b]

PUJUNAN STOCK

KONKAU. California. (Cat. no. $\frac{50}{5185}$, American Museum of Natural History.)

Four bones (figure 388), hollow, two closed with wooden plugs and wound in the middle with cord, the other two plain; length, 2¾ to 3 inches. Collected by Dr Roland B. Dixon.

Mr Stephen Powers [c] relates a myth of the Konkau in which their culture hero, Oankoitupeh (the Invincible), overcame Haikutwotopeh at gambling in a guessing game, and won back his grandfather's

---

[a] In a forthcoming memoir to be published by the Bureau of American Ethnology.

[b] The object is called rsǎiki, slave. It is 40 or 50 mm. in diameter, is pitted in the center " to prevent cheating," and may be of either pottery or stone.

[c] Contributions to North American Ethnology, v. 3, p. 298, Washington, 1877.

tribe, which the latter had lost to Haikutwotopeh through trickery. The original game is described as follows:

They had four short pieces of bone, two plain and two marked. They rolled them up in little balls of dry grass; then one of the players held up one of

FIG. 388. Bones for hand game; length, 2¾ to 3 inches; Konkau Indians, California; cat. no. ₅₁₈₅, American Museum of Natural History.

them in each hand, and the other held up his. If he matched them he counted 2; if he failed to match them the other counted 1. There were sixteen bits of wood as counters, and when one got the sixteen he was the winner.

MAIDU. California. (Cat. no. ₄₀₂₀, American Museum of Natural History.)

Four bones (figure 389), 2½ inches in length, two plain and hollow, and two tied around the middle with thongs and plugged at the ends. Collected by Dr Roland B. Dixon in 1903.

Dr Dixon refers to the game with bones in his Maidu Myths,[a] and describes the adventures of two youths, the sons of a girl and Cloud-Man, created out of two bunches of feathers, and called Always-eating, and Conqueror, or Winner. After a series of exploits, killing

FIG. 389. Bones for hand game; length, 2¼ inches; Maidu Indians, California; cat. no. ₄₀₂₀, American Museum of Natural History.

rattlesnakes, wood bugs, elk, and eagles, Conqueror gambles with an opponent, who has a passage through his body and can pass the gambling bones through this from one hand to the other. Conqueror with the help of the Sun closes this passage, and opens one in his own body, thus winning back his people, who have been lost to his opponent. At the opening of the game the stakes are the players' eyes.

In another story, a variation of the preceding, the person with whom the hero plays is designated as Old-North-Wind. The stakes are eyes and hearts. The hero wins as before.

---

[a] Bulletin of the American Museum of Natural History, v. 17, pt. 2, p. 51, New York, 1902.

MAIDU. Sutters fort, Sacramento valley, California.
    Edwin Bryant [a] says:

The game which they most generally play is as follows: Any number which
may be concerned in it seat themselves crosslegged on the ground in a circle.
They are then divided into two parties, each of which has two champions or
players. A ball, or some small article, is placed in the hands of the players on
one side, which they transfer from hand to hand with such sleight and dexterity that it is nearly impossible to detect the changes. When the players
holding the balls make a particular motion with their hands, the antagonist
players guess in which hand the balls are at the time. If the guess is wrong,
it counts 1 in favor of the playing party. If the guess is right, then it counts
1 in favor of the guessing party, and the balls are transferred to them. The
count of the game is kept with sticks. During the progress of the game all concerned keep up a continual monotonous grunting, with a movement of their
bodies to keep time with their grunts. The articles which are staked on the
game are placed in the center of the ring.

NISHINAM. Mokolumne river, Eldorado county, 12 miles south of
    Placerville, California.
    Dr J. W. Hudson describes the grass game played by this tribe
under the name of helai (hele=maternal cousin), or tep and wo:

The bones are made of the ulna of a panther. Mai'dûk (man), the bound
bone; kü'-le (woman), the plain bone; team'-he-lai (maternal third cousins),
the ten stick counters, each of which represents a value fixed upon them before
playing. Hat! the gesture and call.

In Todd valley Doctor Hudson found the game played under the
same name in the usual manner, but the plain bone was called toloma,
penis, and the bound bone, pekon, vulva.
————— California.
    Mr Stephen Powers [b] says:

The most common mode of gambling (hi'-lai), used by both men and women,
is conducted by means of four longish cylinders of bone or wood, which are
wrapped in pellets of grass and held in the hand, while the opposite party
guesses which hand contains them. These cylinders are carved from several materials, but the Indians call them all bones. Thus they have the phrases
pol'-loam hi'-lai hĭn, toan'-em hi'-lai hĭn, du'-pem hi'-lai hĭn, gai'-a hi'-lai hĭn,
which means, respectively, to gamble with buckeye bones, pine bones, deer bones,
and cougar bones. There is a subtle difference in their minds in the quality of
the game, according to the kind of bones employed, but what it is I can not
discern. This game, with slight variations, prevails pretty much all over California, and as I had opportunity of seeing it on a much larger scale on Gualala
creek, the reader is referred to the chapter on the Gualala [see p. 289].
    The su'-toh is the same game substantially, only the pieces are shaken in the
hand without being wrapped in the grass. . . .
    The ti'-kel ti'-kel is also a gambling game for two men; played with a bit of
wood or a pebble, which is shaken in the hand, and then the hand closed upon it.
The opponent guesses which finger (a thumb is a finger with them) it is under,
and scores 1 if he hits, or the other scores if he misses. They keep tally with
eight counters.

----

[a] What I Saw in California, p. 268, New York, 1848.
[b] Contributions to North American Ethnology, v. 3, p. 332, Washington, 1877.

OLOLOPA. California.

A. Delano [a] says:

Another is with two small pieces of bone, one of which is hollow. These they roll in a handful of grass, and tossing them in the air several times, accompanied with a monotonous chant, they suddenly pull the ball of grass in two with the hands, and the antagonist guesses which hand the hollow bone is in. They have small sticks for counters, and, as they win or lose, a stick is passed from one to the other till the close of the game, when he who has the most sticks is the winner. They will sometimes play all day long, stopping only to eat.

SALISHAN STOCK

BELLACOOLA. British Columbia. (Cat. no. 18396, 18397, Field Columbian Museum.)

Two bones from two sets, $3\frac{3}{16}$ inches in length, and three-fourths of an inch in diameter at the middle; rounded at ends. Neither bone is marked (figure 390). Collected by Capt. Samuel Jacobsen.

FIG. 390. Bones for hand game; length, $3\frac{3}{16}$ inches; Bellacoola Indians, British Columbia; cat. no. 18396, 18397, Field Columbian Museum.

CLALLAM. Washington.

A Clallam boy, John Raub, described this tribe as playing the hand game with four bones, under the name of slahal.

The four bones are used, two plain and two with a black mark around the middle. The former are called swai-ka, "man," and the latter sla-ni, "woman."

NISQUALLI. Washington.

George Gibbs [b] says:

There are several games, the principle of which is the same. In one a small piece of bone is passed rapidly from hand to hand, shifted behind the back, etc., the object of the contending party being to ascertain in which hand it is held. Each side is furnished with five or ten small sticks, which serve to mark the game, one stick being given by the guesser whenever he loses, and received whenever he wins. On guessing correctly, it is his turn to manipulate. When all the sticks are won, the game ceases, and the winner receives the stakes, consisting of clothing or any other articles, as the play may be either high or low, for simple amusement, or in eager rivalry. The backers of the party manipulating keep up a constant drumming with sticks on their paddles, which lie before them, singing an incantation to attract good fortune. This is usually known as the game of hand, or, in jargon, It-lu-kam. . . . Each species of gambling has its appropriate tamahno-ūs, or, as it is called upon the Sound, Skwolalitūd, that is, its patron spirit, whose countenance is invoked by the chant and noise. The tamahno-ūs of the game of hand is called by the Nisqually, Tsaik; of the disks, Knawk'h. It would seem that this favor is not merely solicited during the game, but sometimes in advance of it, and perhaps for general or continued fortune.

---

[a] Life on the Plains, p. 307, Auburn, 1854.

[b] Tribes of Western Washington and Northwestern Oregon. Contributions to North American Ethnology, v. I, p. 206, Washington, 1877.

In his Dictionary of the Nisqualli he gives lahal or slahal as the name of both the game of hand and that played with disks. Again, olahal, or olahalub, means to play.

OKINAGAN. Washington.

Capt. Charles Wilkes [a] says:

The chief amusement of the Okonagan tribes of Indians in the winter and during the heat of the day in summer, when they are prevented from taking salmon, is a game called by the voyageurs "jeu de main," equivalent to our odd-and-even.

Alexander Ross [b] says:

The principal game is called tsill-all-a-come, differing but little from the chall-chall played by the Chinooks or Indians along the seacoast. This game is played with two small oblong polished bones, each 2 inches long, and half an inch in diameter, with twenty small sticks of the same diameter as the bones, but about 9 inches long.

The game does not set any limits to the number of players at a time, provided both sides be equal. Two, four, or six, as may be agreed upon, play this game; but, in all large bets, the last number is generally adopted. When all is ready and the property at stake laid down on the spot, the players place themselves in the following manner: the parties kneel down, three on one side and three on the other, face to face and about 3 feet apart; and in this position they remain during the game. A piece of wood is then placed on the ground between them; this done, each player is furnished with a small drum-stick, about the size of a rule, in his right hand, which stick is used for beating time on the wood, in order to rivet attention on the game. The drumming is always accompanied with a song. The players, one and all, muffle their wrists, fists, and fingers with bits of fur or trapping, in order the better to elude and deceive their opponents. Each party then takes one of the two small polished bones, and ten of the small sticks, the use of which will hereafter be more fully explained. In all cases the arms and body are perfectly naked, the face painted, the hair clubbed up, and the head girt round with a strap of leather. The party is now ready to begin the game, all anxious and on the alert: three of the players on one side strike up a song, to which all keep chorus, and this announces the commencement. The moment the singing and drumming begin on one side the greatest adept on the other side instantly takes the little polished bone, conceals it in one of his fists, then throws it into the other, and back again, and so on from one fist to the other, nimbly crossing and recrossing his arms, and every instant changing the position of his fists. The quickness of the motions and the muffling of the fists make it almost impossible for his opponents to guess which hand holds the bone, and this is the main point. While the player is maneuvering in this manner, his three opponents eagerly watch his motions with an eagle's eye, to try and discover the fist that contains the bone; and the moment one of them thinks he has discovered where the bone is, he points to it with the quickness of lightning: the player at the same time, with equal rapidity, extends his arm and opens his fist in the presence of all; if it be empty, the player draws back his arm and continues, while the guesser throws the player one of the little sticks, which counts 1. But if the guesser hits upon the fist that contains the bone the player throws a stick to him and ceases playing, his

[a] Narrative of the United States Exploring Expedition, v. 4, p. 462, Philadelphia, 1845.
[b] Adventures of the First Settlers on the Oregon or Columbia River, p. 308, London, 1849.

opponent now going through the same operation: every miss counts a stick on either side. It is not the best of three, but three times running: all the sticks must be on one side to finish the game. I have seen them for a whole week at one game and then not conclude, and I have known the game decided in six hours.

It sometimes happens, however, that after some days and nights are spent in the same game, neither party gains: in that case the rules of the game provide that the number of players be increased or diminished; or, if all the players be agreed, the game is relinquished, each party taking up what is put down: but so intent are they on this favorite mode of passing their time, that it seldom happens that they separate before the game is finished; and while it is in progress every other consideration is sacrificed to it: and some there are who devote all their time and means solely to gambling; and when all is lost, which is often the case, the loser seldom gives way to grief.

PENELAKUT (LILMALCHE). Kuper island, southeast of Vancouver island, British Columbia. (Cat no. IV A 2375, Berlin Museum für Völkerkunde.)

Two bone cylinders, 2⅝ inches in length, with incised patterns, as shown in figure 391; both wrapped with fine cord about the middle.

Fig. 391.   Fig. 392.   Fig. 393.

FIG. 391. Bones for hand game; length, 2⅝ inches; Penelakut Indians, Kuper island, British Columbia; cat. no. IV A 2375, Berlin Museum für Völkerkunde.

FIG. 392. Bones for hand game; length, 2¼ inches; Penelakut Indians, Kuper island, British Columbia; cat. no. IV A 2376, Berlin Museum für Völkerkunde.

FIG. 393. Bones for hand game; length, 2¾ inches; Penelakut Indians, Kuper island, British Columbia; cat. no. IV A 2377, Berlin Museum für Völkerkunde.

———— Kuper island, southeast of Vancouver island, British Columbia. (Cat. no. IV A 2376, 2377, Berlin Museum für Völkerkunde.)

Two sets of bone cylinders:

Cat. no. 2376. Two cylinders (figure 392), 2½ inches in length, with incised rings, central dot at the ends, and one incised line around the middle.

Cat. no. 2377. Two cylinders (figure 393), 2¾ inches in length, both with incised rings with central dot at ends, and one with central band of similar rings, with incised lines on both sides.

All these specimens were collected by Capt. Samuel Jacobsen, who gave the name of the game as slahall.

Puyallup. Cedar river, Washington. (Cat. no. 55923, 55924, 55933, 55934, Field Columbian Museum.)

Four sets of gambling bones of two each (figure 394 *a*, *b*, *c*, *d*), 2¾ inches long and an inch in greatest diameter, one in each set having incised lines painted black around the middle, and all marked with incised circles painted red and black. Collected by Dr George A. Dorsey.

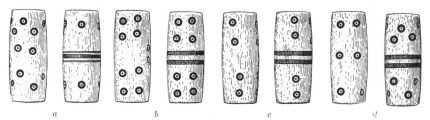

FIG. 394 *a*, *b*, *c*, *d*. Bones for hand game; length, 2¾ inches; Puyallup Indians, Cedar river, Washington; cat. no. 55923, 55924, 55933, 55934, Field Columbian Museum.

Shuswap. Kamloops, British Columbia.

Dr Franz Boas[a] says they play the well-known game of lehal.

Songish. Near Victoria, British Columbia.

Commander R. C. Mayne[b] says:

I have only seen two games played by them, in both of which the object was to guess the spot where a small counter happened to be. In one of these games the counter was held in the player's hands, which he kept swinging backwards and forwards. Every now and then he would stop, and some one would guess in which hand he held the counter, winning, of course, if he guessed right. The calm intensity and apparent freedom from excitement with which they watch the progress of this game is perfect, and you only know the intense anxiety they really feel by watching their faces and the twitching of their limbs.

The other game consisted of two blankets spread out upon the ground, and covered with sawdust about an inch thick. In this was placed the counter, a piece of bone or iron about the size of half-a-crown, and one of the players shuffled it about, the others in turn guessing where it was. These games are usually played by ten or twelve men, who sit in a circle, with the property to be staked, if, as is usual, it consists of blankets or clothes, near them. Chanting is very commonly kept up during the game, probably to allay the excitement. I never saw women gamble.

Thompson Indians. British Columbia.

Mr James Teit[c] says:

Another very common game, played principally by men, was the "guessing game" (known to the whites as "lehal"). Many Spences Bridge women used to play it, and had a different song for it from that of the men. Lower Thompson

---

[a] Sixth Report on the Northwest Tribes of Canada. Report of the Sixtieth Meeting of the British Association for the Advancement of Science, p. 641, London, 1891.

[b] Four Years in British Columbia and Vancouver Island, p. 275, London, 1862.

[c] The Thompson Indians of British Columbia. Memoirs of the American Museum of Natural History, v. 2, p. 275, New York, 1900.

women seldom or never played this game. The players knelt in two rows, facing one another. Each side had two short bones [figure 395], one of which had a sinew thread tied around the middle. The side playing passed these bones through their hands, the opposite side having to guess the hand of the player which held the plain bone. The side playing sang a " lehal " song to the accompaniment of drums. They generally kept time by beating sticks on the floor or on a board. Sometimes neither drums nor sticks were used, but they simply sang. Many of the players wore over their knuckles pieces of weasel or other skin, from which hung many thin strips of buckskin [figure 396]. Some of these skin covers reached up to the wrist, where they were fastened. Other players used strings set with fawn's hoofs around the wrists to make a rattling noise. This game is still often played by the young men.

Fig. 395. Bones for hand game; length, 3 inches; Thompson Indians, British Columbia; cat. no. $\frac{16}{1078}$, American Museum of Natural History.

A note continues:

The stake was generally valued at 12 counters, which were represented by 12 sticks. Each party had 6 of these counters. When one party guessed wrong they forfeited a counter, which was thrown over to the party opposite. When one of the parties guessed right, the gambling bones were thrown over to them, and it was their turn to sing and to hide the bones. When one party won all the counters, the game was at an end. When a large number of gamblers took part in the game, two pairs of gambling bones were used.

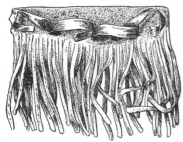

Fig. 396. Knuckle-covering for hand-game players; length, 6 inches; Thompson Indians, British Columbia; cat. no. $\frac{16}{1337}$, American Museum of Natural History.

Mr Charles Hill-Tout [a] says:

Gambling was also a favorite pastime here as elsewhere. The game known as l'tpīq was that commonly practiced. Much betting went on among the players, and all bets were made and " booked " before the game commenced. The method of " booking " was primitive. The objects staked were simply tied or fastened together and set on one side till the game was over, the winner then taking his own and his opponent's property.

TWANA. Washington. (Cat. no. 19748, 19749, Field Columbian Museum.)

Set of two bones (figure 397), $2\frac{7}{8}$ inches in length and $1\frac{1}{4}$ inches in diameter at the middle, the ends flat. The hollow interior of the bones is plugged with wood. One has a line of incised dots encircling it at each end, and the other (the marked one) similar lines of dots at the ends and three lines of dots around the middle. On one side the head of an animal is incised on the opposite sides of the line. Collected by Rev. Myron Eells.

---

[a] Notes on the N'tlaka'pamuq of British Columbia. Report of the Sixty-ninth Meeting of the British Association for the Advancement of Science, p. 507, London, 1900.

Mr Eells [a] describes a game among the Twana played with one or two small bones as follows:

The young men and older boys play this most. The players sit opposite each other about 6 feet apart, from one to six or more on a side, each party in front

of a long pole. Then one person takes one or both of the bones in his hands and rapidly changes them from one hand to the other. One person on the opposite side guesses in which hand one is. If only one bone is used, he guesses which hand it is in, and if both are used, he guesses in which hand a certain one is. If he guesses aright, he wins and plays next; but if not, he loses, and the other continues to play. While each one is playing, the rest of his party beat with a small stick upon the larger one in front of them, and keep up a regular sing-song noise in regular time. Small

Fig. 397. Bones for hand game; length, 2⅞ inches; Twana Indians, Washington; cat. no. 19748, 19749, Field Columbian Museum.

sums are generally bet in this game, from 50 cents to $1.50. Different ones play according as they are more or less successful. Sometimes they grow so expert, even if the guess is right, that the one playing can change the bone to the other hand without its being seen.

Elsewhere [b] Mr Eells says:

The tally is usually kept by two of the players, one for each side, with sticks 8 or 10 inches long, sharpened at one end and stuck in the ground. These sticks are moved according to the success of either party. A modified form of this game is played by using two larger bones or pieces of wood. One of these is marked in some way, either with a string tied around the middle of it, a carved circle, or if it be of wood the bark may be removed except in the middle, where a zone is left. When the small bones are used, it is optional whether one or two be employed, but when they play with the larger ones it is necessary that both be used, for if the player has but one it would plainly be seen in which hand it was.

SHAHAPTIAN STOCK

Nez Perces. Idaho.

It is related by Lewis and Clark: [c]

The Indians divided themselves into two parties and began to play the game of hiding a bone, already described as common to all the natives of this country, which they continued playing for beads and other ornaments.

Capt. B. L. E. Bonneville [d] gives the following account:

The choral chant, in fact, which had thus acted as a charm, was a kind of accompaniment to the favorite Indian game of " Hand." This is played by two parties drawn out in opposite platoons before a blazing fire. It is in some respects like the old game of passing the ring or the button, and detecting the hand which holds it. In the present game the object hidden, or the cache as it

---

[a] Bulletin United States Geological and Geographical Survey, v. 3, p. 89, Washington, 1877.

[b] The Twana, Chemakum, and Klallam Indians of Washington Territory. Annual Report of the Smithsonian Institution for 1887, p. 648, 1889.

[c] History of the Expedition under the Command of Lewis and Clark, v. 3, p. 1008, New York, 1893.

[d] The Adventures of Captain Bonneville, U. S. A., by Washington Irving, p. 376, New York, 1860.

is called by the trappers, is a small splint of wood or other diminutive article, that may be concealed in the closed hand. This is passed backwards and forwards among the party " in hand," while the party " out of hand " guess where it is concealed. To heighten the excitement and confuse the guessers, a number of dry poles are laid before each platoon, upon which the members of the party " in hand " beat furiously with short staves, keeping time to the choral chant already mentioned, which waxes fast and furious as the game proceeds. As large bets are staked upon the game, the excitement is prodigious. Each party in turn burst out in full chorus, beating and yelling and working themselves up into such a heat that the perspiration rolls down their naked shoulders, even in the cold of a winter night. The bets are doubled and trebled as the game advances, and all the worldly effects of the gamblers are often hazarded upon the position of a straw.

NEZ PERCÉS. Lapwai reservation, Idaho. (Cat. no. 60447, Field Columbian Museum.)

Four bones (figure 398), 3 inches in length, highly polished and yellow with age, two with a leather band one-half inch wide. The bones are hollow and resemble a shaft of a human femur.

These were collected by Dr George A. Dorsey, who gives the native name as lokhom.

——— Southern Alberta.

Rev. John Maclean [a] says:

The Nez Percés have a game which I have oftentimes seen played among the Blackfeet, although not in the same fashion, which is guessing with a small piece of wood. Instead of a single pair, as among the Blackfeet, the Nez Percés arrange themselves in two parties, sitting opposite to each other, and a small piece of wood is passed from hand to hand of the other party, the members of which guess, until when rightly guessed, they become the possessors of the article. While the game is in motion, the parties and those not engaged in the game are betting, and some of these bets are quite large. Meanwhile the contestants sing a weird chant, beating on any article with short sticks which will produce a noise. Singing, beating time, guessing, rolling and swaying the body, in a continual state of excitement, the game proceeds until the one party defeats the other members opposed to them. The onlookers, whites and Indians, become deeply interested in the game, and share in the excitement, watching it eagerly, and animated by the furious motions of the parties in the game.

FIG. 398. Bones for hand game; length, 3 inches; Nez Percé Indians, Idaho; cat. no. 60447, Field Columbian Museum.

UMATILLA. Umatilla reservation, Oregon. (Cat. no. 37536, 37537, Free Museum of Science and Art, University of Pennsylvania.)

Four bone cylinders (figure 399), three-fourths of an inch in diameter and 3 inches in length, slightly tapering to ends, two

---

[a] Canadian Savage Folk, p. 42, Toronto, 1896.

wrapped with a thong in the middle.   Twenty willow counting
sticks (figure 400), pointed at one end, 10 inches in length.
These were collected by the writer in 1900.

The bones are called tsko-ma ; the marked one wa-lak-i-ki, and the unmarked
wa-lak-i-kus.

The game was observed by the author at the Fourth of July camp
on the Umatilla reservation in 1900.[a]

In the center of the open space was a large square pavilion built on posts,
covered with green boughs, and sheltered on one side from the sun by young
evergreen trees stuck in the ground.   .   .   .   The women sat in two rows facing
each other, up and down one side of the lodge, the remaining space being occupied
by groups of men playing cards and by spectators.   The stakes, consisting of
blankets, silk handkerchiefs, strings of glass beads, and money in considerable

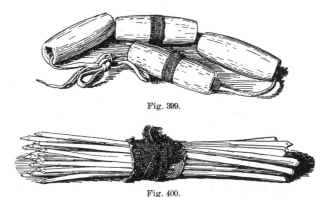

Fig. 399.

Fig. 400.

FIG. 399. Bones for hand game; length, 3 inches; Umatilla Indians, Umatilla reservation,
    Oregon; cat. no. 37536, Free Museum of Science and Art, University of Pennsylvania.
FIG. 400. Counting sticks for hand game; length, 10 inches; Umatilla Indians, Umatilla reser-
    vation, Oregon; cat. no. 37537, Free Museum of Science and Art, University of Pennsylvania.

amounts were deposited in a pile between the rows.   There were 12 women on
each side.   Four bones, about 3 inches long, two having a black band around the
center and two plain, were manipulated by one of the youngest and most vigorous of the women who occupied the center on each side.   The side holding the
bones would sing and sway their arms and hands rhythmically in unison.   The
two sides sang different songs and not always the same one.   The refrain was
very pleasing.   .   .   .   The object seemed to be to guess which player along the
line had the bones, the opposite side leader indicating her choice by a sudden
sideway motion of her hand.   The counts were kept with 20 sticks, each side
having 10, which were stuck in the ground in two rows before the principal
player.   All the participants bet on the result, and at the close of the game, one
or the other side having gained the entire 20 sticks, the winner would divide the
winnings according to the individual bets.   The game seemed interminable, first
one side winning and then the other, and throwing over one or more willow
counting-sticks.   The men card players used small sticks as counters.

[a]A Summer Trip Among the Western Indians.   Bulletin of the Free Museum of Science
and Art, v. 3, p. 160, Philadelphia, 1901.

YAKIMA. Washington.

Jack Long informed the writer that the Yakima call the hand game paliote, and that the Klikitat use the same name, while the Dalles Indians call it pesoguma. The Yakima call the marked bone walakaki and the white one plush, while the Klikitat call them gouikiha and tgope, respectively.

Pandosy [a] gives the following definition:

To play with the hand, pa-li-o-sha.

SHASTAN STOCK

ACHOMAWI. Hat creek, California. (Cat. no. $\frac{50}{4114}$, American Museum of Natural History.)

Four very small sticks (figure 401) about $1\frac{1}{8}$ inches in length, one plain and the other three marked with very fine lines in the middle.

These were collected in 1903 by Dr Roland B. Dixon, who gives the name as yiskukiwa, and says they are used the same as the bones or sticks in the regular grass game. Dr J. W. Hudson gives the name of the hand game played by these Indians as ishkake, and describes the game as played with one plain bone and three marked bones.

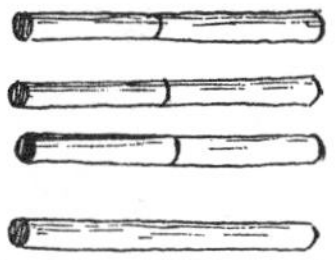

FIG. 401. Sticks for hand game; length, $1\frac{1}{8}$ inches; Achomawi Indians, Hat creek, California; cat. no. $\frac{50}{4114}$, American Museum of Natural History.

———— Fall river, Shasta county, California.

Dr J. W. Hudson describes the following game:

An ovoid stone (bam, stone), 3 inches long, is hidden in the hand behind the back by either of two men, and the location in one of the four hands is guessed at by the opposing side. This stone is used to juggle in the air, and is also considered an amulet of great power. The game is played by men. In every male grave cairn is found one or more sets of these stones. Women are afraid of them.

SHOSHONEAN STOCK

BANNOCK. Rossfork agency, Idaho.

Mr Thomas Blaine Donaldson in a letter [b] to the writer described the Bannock playing the game of hand, as witnessed by him on Thanksgiving Day in 1890.

You may see the willow-stick counters and the betares, or "beaters," with which they marked time on the saplings before them as they chanted a song when the time came for the selected Indian to guess the "right hand" of his opponent.

———— Fort Hall reservation, Idaho. (Cat. no. 37062, Free Museum of Science and Art, University of Pennsylvania.)

[a] Grammar and Dictionary of the Yakama Language, New York, 1862.
[b] February 25, 1901.

Four bones (figure 402), 1 inch in diameter and 3 to 3¼ inches in
    length; two wrapped with a broad leather band.

Cat. no. 37064. Twenty willow sticks (figure 403), pointed at one
    end, 14 inches in length, used as counters.

These were collected by the writer in 1900. The bones are called
tipo.

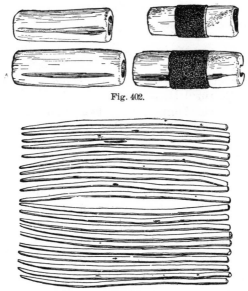

Fig. 402.

Fig. 403.

FIG. 402. Bones for hand game; length, 3 to 3¼ inches; Bannock Indians, Idaho; cat. no. 37062, Free
    Museum of Science and Art, University of Pennsylvania.
FIG. 403. Counting sticks for hand game; length, 14 inches; Bannock Indians, Idaho; cat. no. 37064,
    Free Museum of Science and Art, University of Pennsylvania.

BANNOCK. Fort Hall reservation, Idaho. (Cat. no. 60926, Field
    Columbian Museum.)

Four solid bones, 4⅞ inches in length, beautifully polished from long
    use and yellow with age; two wrapped in the center with a
    piece of calico, black with dirt, and sewed with black thread. All
    the bones, near one end, have a constriction as the result of exca-
    vation when they were fashioned. At each end are two incised
    bands, like the cut of a sharp instrument. Accompanied with
    a long buckskin pouch case, with drawstring and fringe, the
    drawstring long enough to be fastened in belt. Collected by
    Dr George A. Dorsey, who gives the native name as niowin.
    Another set in the same collection (cat. no. 60925) consists of
    four leg bones, 2⅞ inches in length and 1 inch in diameter. The
    bones are cut off square and much worn and polished. Two
    are wrapped in the middle with a piece of buckskin, black from

usage. Accompanied by twenty undecorated counting sticks, made of cottonwood, three-eighths of an inch in diameter and 13 inches long.

BANNOCK and SHOSHONI. Fort Hall agency, Idaho. (Cat. no. 22284, United States National Museum.)

Set of two bones (figure 404), $2\frac{7}{8}$ inches in length, solid and tapering at ends, one wrapped with thread for a length of $1\frac{3}{4}$ inches. Collected by W. H. Danilson, Indian agent.

COMANCHE. Texas.

Robert S. Neighbors[a] says:

Their principal game is the same as all the northern bands, called "bullet," "button," etc., which consists in changing a bullet rapidly from one hand to the other, accompanied by a song to which they keep time with the motion of their arms, and the opposite party guessing which hand it is in. They sometimes stake all they possess on a single game.

FIG. 404. Bones for hand game; length, $2\frac{7}{8}$ inches; Bannock and Shoshoni Indians, Fort Hall agency, Idaho; cat. no. 22284, United States National Museum.

Col. Richard Irving Dodge[b] describes a game somewhat like hide-the-slipper, in which an almost unlimited number may take part:

Two individuals will choose sides, by alternate selection among those who wish to play, men or women. All then seat themselves in the parallel lines about 8 feet apart, facing each other. The articles wagered are piled between the lines. All being ready, the leader of one side rising to his knees holds up the gambling bone, so that all may see it. He then closes it in the two hands, manipulating it so dexterously that it is impossible to see in which hand it is. After a minute or more of rapid motion he suddenly thrusts one or generally both hands, into the outstretched hands of the person on the right and left. This marks the real commencement of the game, no guess of the other watching-side being permitted until after this movement. He may pass the bone to one or the other, or he may retain it himself. In either case, he continues his motions as if he had received it; passing or pretending to pass it on and on to the right and left, until every arm is waving, every hand apparently passing the bone and every player in a whirl of excitement. All this while, the other line is watching with craned necks and strained eyes for the slightest bungle in the manipulation, which will indicate where the bone is. Finally some one believes he sees it and suddenly points to a hand, which must be instantly thrust out and opened palm up. If the bone is in it the watching party wins one point, if not it loses. The other side then takes the bone and goes through the same performance. If during the manipulations the bone should be accidentally dropped, the other side takes a point and the bone. The game is usually 21 points, though the players may determine on any number.

[a] Schoolcraft's Information respecting the History, Condition, and Prospects of the Indian Tribes of the United States, pt. 2, p. 133, Philadelphia, 1852.

[b] Our Wild Indians, p. 329, Hartford, 1882.

KAWIA. Indio, Riverside county, California. (Cat. no. 63591, Field Columbian Museum.)

Four bones (figure 405), 3 inches in length, carved with incised lines, and four pieces of asphaltum of similar size, all having thongs of deerskin with a loop, attached at the end.

Collected by Mr S. C. Simms, who describes them as used in the game of peon.

FIG. 405. Bones and sticks for peon; Kawia Indians, Indio, Riverside county, California; cat. no. 63591, Field Columbian Museum.

MONO. Hooker cove, Madera county, California. (Cat. no. 71443, 71444, Field Columbian Museum.)

Two sets of four bones each, in one set 3 inches and in the other 3⅛ inches long, with two bones in each set plain and two with bands of asphaltum.

Collected by Dr J. W. Hudson, who describes them as used in the grass game, hana.

——— Big Sandy creek, Fresno county, California. (Field Columbian Museum.)

Cat. no. 71227. Four willow wood cylinders (figure 406), 2⅞ inches in length; two with black cloth strip in middle.

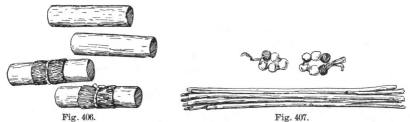

Fig. 406.   Fig. 407.

FIG. 406. Sticks for hand game; length, 2⅞ inches: Mono Indians, Fresno county, California; cat. no. 71227, Field Columbian Museum.

FIG. 407. Beads and counters for hand game; Mono Indians, Fresno county, California; cat. no. 71180, Field Columbian Museum.

Collected by Dr J. W. Hudson, who describes them as used in the grass game, and says that they call the marked bone male, contrary to the usual custom in California.

Cat. no. 71180. Two strings of glass beads, one of five beads, four
white and one blue, and the other of six beads, four white and
two blue, with ten counting sticks (figure 407).

These specimens were collected by Dr J. W. Hudson, who described
them as used only by women in a game called nääkwibi, the object
being to guess which hand contains the beads:

One string is held by each of the two partners. The beads are called o-we'-a,
literally, " excitement." Originally dyed acorns were used.

PAIUTE. Pyramid lake, Nevada. (Cat. no. 37154, Free Museum of
Science and Art, University of Pennsylvania.)

Four bones of mountain sheep (figure 408), 3⅛ inches in length and
three-fourths of an inch in diameter; two wound with black
thread.

Collected by the writer in 1900. The bones are called quoip, meaning " mountain sheep." The game is called tuipo.

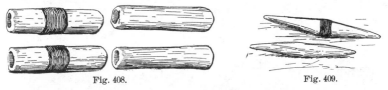

Fig. 408.   Fig. 409.

FIG. 408. Bones for hand game; length, 3⅛ inches; Paiute Indians, Pyramid lake, Nevada; cat.
no. 37154, Free Museum of Science and Art, University of Pennsylvania.
FIG. 409. Bones for hand game; length, 3½ inches; Paiute Indians, southern Utah; cat. no.
10962, United States National Museum.

—— Pyramid lake, Nevada. (Field Columbian Museum.)

Cat. no. 61490. Four billets of elk antler, 3⅞ inches in length, polished and worn smooth; two bound in the center with a band of
black leather one-half of an inch wide.

Cat. no. 61504. Four solid bones, 4 inches in length, beautifully polished with use; two bound with a black leather band.

Cat. no. 61506. Four solid bones, 3¼ inches in length; similar to
next preceding.

Cat. no. 61514. Eight sharpened cottonwood counting sticks, 12
inches long and one-half of an inch in diameter.

All the above specimens were collected in 1900 by Dr George A.
Dorsey, who gives the native name of the game as nayukpui and that
of the counting sticks as semewawak. The players guess for the
white bone (sumuyu).

—— Southern Utah. (Cat. no. 10956, 10959, 10962, 10963, 10968,
10969, 10970, 10975, United States National Museum.)

Sets of bones of two each (figure 409), from 2½ to 4 inches in length,
the ends sharply pointed; one bone in each set wrapped with
sinew or buckskin.

These were collected by Maj. J. W. Powell.

Mr J. K. Hillers, who was a member of Major Powell's expedition, has furnished the writer the following account of the game played with the above-mentioned bones and counters:

It is called ne añg-puki, meaning to kill the bone (pu-ki means to kill; ang or ong being the bone, and ne probably a personal prefix for my, the whole name being equivalent to "my bone to kill"). The "banker" takes two bones, one with a string wound round the middle and the other plain, and places his hands behind his back. His side then chants for a minute or two, during which

FIG. 410. Paiute Indians playing hand game; southern Utah; from photograph by Mr J. K. Hillers.[a]

time he shifts the bones from one hand to the other. On "call," he brings both hands to the front, and crosses them on his breast. The callers now begin their chant. Suddenly one will extend his arm and point to the hand in which he thinks the banker holds the marked bone, at the same time hitting his breast with the other hand. If the guess is correct, the guesser takes the bones after the "rake down," and the game continues until one side or the other has all the counters.

---

[a] Reproduced (fig. 46) without text reference in Maj. J. W. Powell's Exploration of the Colorado River of the West, Washington, 1875.

SABOBA. California. (Cat. no. 61939, Field Columbian Museum.)

Four hollow bones (figure 411), 2¾ inches in length, each having a cord, with a loop at the end, attached to a hole in the middle, and four pieces of charred twig, with similar cords tied around the middle.

Collected by Mr Edwin Minor, who describes them as used in the game of peon:

Peón is a very exciting game, played by four, six, or eight men, seated in two opposing lines. Each line holds a blanket in front, usually in the players' teeth, to hide the hands and the manipulation of the cylinders. Each player has looped to each hand one bone and one wood cylinder. The game is to guess in which hand the bone cylinder is fixed. When a correct guess is made the cylinder must be passed over to the one guessing. When all the bone cylinders are secured by one side the game is won.

All the men who are being guessed at keep up a continual noise and make hideous grimaces to mystify their manipulations. Interested women stand by and sing fantastic and weird songs to encourage their friends. This game is often continued all night before either side wins.

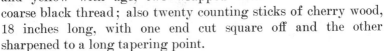

FIG. 411. Bones and sticks for peon; Saboba Indians, California; cat. no. 61939, Field Columbian Museum.

SHOSHONI. Wind River reservation, Wyoming. (Cat. no. 60751, Field Columbian Museum.)

Four solid bones, 5 inches in length, much used and yellow with age, two wrapped with coarse black thread; also twenty counting sticks of cherry wood, 18 inches long, with one end cut square off and the other sharpened to a long tapering point.

These were collected in 1900 by Dr George A. Dorsey, who gives the name of the game as tenzok; of the marked bone as peganata, tie with string; of the unmarked bone, tesaivik, white one; of the counter, tohok.

———— Wind River reservation, Wyoming. (Free Museum of Science and Art, University of Pennsylvania.)

FIG. 412. Bones for hand game; length, 3⅜ inches; Shoshoni Indians, Wyoming; cat. no. 36871, Free Museum of Science and Art, University of Pennsylvania.

Cat. no. 36869. Two polished bones, one covered in the middle for a third of its length with a band of buckskin; length, 3¼ inches.

Cat. no. 36871. Two polished bones (figure 412), one wrapped in the center with a leather thong; length, 3¾ inches.

Cat. no. 36872. Set of twenty counting sticks (figure 413), peeled willow twigs, 18½ inches in length, sharpened to a point, with the bark left at the top for a distance of 4 inches.

All these were collected in 1900 by the writer. The name of the game is tinsok; to play the hand game, nyahwint; the white bone, tonatat; the marked bone, tosabit. The counting sticks are called tohuc.

SHOSHONI. Idaho.

Granville Stuart [a] gives under the term for "gamble or gambling," nyawitch:

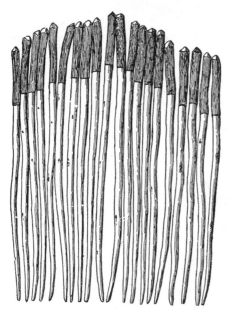

FIG. 413. Counting sticks for hand game; length, 18¼ inches; Shoshoni Indians, Wyoming; cat. no. 36872, Free Museum of Science and Art, University of Pennsylvania.

They take two pieces of bone made for the purpose, about 2½ inches long and a fourth of an inch in thickness, one of which is covered with some dark skin, except about half an inch at each end. Each party then takes a certain number of short pieces of willow sharpened at one end, which they stick in the ground and use to count the game. They take the pieces of bone one in each hand and shift them about rapidly with various contortions and twisting about, accompanied with a kind of monotonous song which they sing in chorus, while some of them generally beat time with a stick on a dry pole. The opposite party (it is played by any number, seated in two rows facing each other) guesses which hand contains the black bone (or the white one as they agree at the commencement of the game). If they guess right, they get the bones, and wrong they give the other side a stick, who keep hiding the bones till it is guessed, when the opposite party takes it, and goes through the same process; whoever wins all the sticks wins the game.

TOBIKHAR (GABRIELEÑOS). Los Angeles county, California.

Hugo Ried [b] says:

Few games, and of a gambling nature. The principal one was called churchúrki (or peón, Spanish). It consists in guessing in which hand a small piece of stick was held concealed, by one of the four persons who composed a side who sat opposite to each other. They had their singers, who were paid by the victorious party at the end of the game. Fifteeen pieces of stick were laid on each side, as counters, and a person named as umpire, who, besides keeping account, settled the debts and prevented cheating, and held the stakes. Each person

[a] Montana as It Is, p. 71, New York, 1865.
[b] Hugo Ried's Account of the Indians of Los Angeles Co., Cal. Bulletin of the Essex Institute, v. 17, p. 17, Salem, 1885.

had two pieces of wood, one black and one white. The white alone counted, the black being to prevent fraud, as they had to change and show one in each hand. The arms were crossed and the hands hidden in the lap; they kept changing the pieces from one hand to the other. Should they fail to guess right, he lost his peón and counters allotted to the others, and so on until the corners were gone or all the peóns killed, when the others had a trial. They bet almost everything they possess. The umpire provided the fine and was paid by the night.

UINTA UTE. White Rocks, Utah. (Cat. no. 37113, Free Museum of Science and Art, University of Pennsylvania.)

Four slender, highly polished bones (figure 414), 3½ inches in length. Two bound with a strip of leather in the middle. Collected by the writer in 1900.

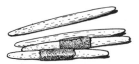

FIG. 414. Bones for hand game; length, 3½ inches: Uinta Ute Indians, White Rocks, Utah; cat. no. 37113, Free Museum of Science and Art, University of Pennsylvania.

YAMPA UTE. Northwest Colorado.

Mr Edwin A. Barber [a] says:

A row of players, consisting of five or six or a dozen men is arranged on either side of the tent, facing each other. Before each man is placed a bundle of small twigs or sticks, each 6 to 8 inches in length and pointed at one end. Every tête-à-tête couple is provided with two cylindrical bone dice, carefully fashioned and highly polished, which measure about 2 inches in length and half an inch in diameter, one being white and the other black, or sometimes ornamented with a black band. At the rear end of the apartment, opposite the entrance, several musicians beat time on rude parchment-covered drums. The whole assembly, sitting "Turk fashion" on the ground, then commence operations. The pledges are heaped up near the players, and each couple soon becomes oblivious of all the rest. One of the gamblers incloses a die in each hand, and, placing one above the other, allows the upper bone to pass into the lower hand with the other die. This process is reversed again and again, while all the time the hands are shaken up and down in order to mystify the partner in the passing of the dice. The other man, during the performance, hugs himself tightly by crossing his arms and placing either hand under the opposite arm, and, with a dancing motion of the body, swaying to and fro, watches the shuffling of the dice with the closest attention. When this has gone on for a few minutes the latter suddenly points with one arm at the opposite arm of his partner and strikes himself under that arm with the other hand. Whichever hand of his rival he chooses is to be opened, and if the dice are in it, the guesser takes them and proceeds in the same manner. If, however, he misses, and the dice are not there, he forfeits one counter, and this is taken from his bundle and stuck into the ground in front of the other. Thus the game continues until one or the other has gained every stick, when he is proclaimed the winner and carries off the stakes. During the entire game the players, as well

[a] Gaming among the Utah Indians. The American Naturalist, v. 11, p. 351, Boston, 1877.

as the musicians, keep time to the accompaniment in their movements, and chant the while a weird, monotonous tune (?), which runs in this wise:

No words are sung, but the syllable "ah" is pronounced in a whining, nasal tone for every note. The entire party keep excellent time, and are always together, rising and falling in the scale with wonderful precision, since the tune itself is so devoid of melody that it is often difficult for a white man to acquire it. This monotonous chant is kept up for hours and even days, and the competitors seem never to grow weary.

SIOUAN STOCK

ASSINIBOIN. North Saskatchewan river, near Carlton, Saskatchewan.

Mr Charles Alston Messiter informs me that the Assiniboin and Cree Indians of the Saskatchewan river, during his residence with them from 1862 to 1864, constantly played the game of hand, using a bit of wood, pebble, or any small object. The man who held the pebble sang, but not those who played against him. Those in the audience, however, sang. There was no drumming. The score was kept by a row of wooden pegs 2 to 2¼ inches in length, which were stuck in the ground in front of each player. Each peg represented a skin. He had seen men lose horses, wife, and children on the game.

———— Fort Union, Montana.

Mr Edwin T. Denig [a] says:

Ordinary gambling for small articles, such as beads, vermilion, rings, knives, arrows, kettles, etc., is carried on by playing the game of hand, which consists in shuffling a pebble from one hand to the other and guessing in which hand the pebble is. They all sit in a ring on the ground, each with whatever stake they choose to put up before them. Both men and women join in the game, and a song is kept up all the time by the whole, with motions of the hands of him who holds the pebble. After singing about five minutes a guess is made by

---

[a] Report to Hon. Isaac I. Stevens on the Indian Tribes of the Upper Missouri. Unpublished manuscript in the library of the Bureau of American Ethnology.

one of the parties as to which hand the pebble is in, and both hands are opened. If the guess has been correct, the one holding the pebble is obliged to pay all the rest an equivalent to the stake before them, but if the hand not containing the pebble be picked upon, all the ring forfeit their stakes to him. Either one man can thus play against the whole, or he has it in his power to pass the pebble to the next, he betting like the others. This is a very common game, and a great deal of property by it daily changes hands, though seldom such large articles as guns, horses, or women.

Maximilian, Prince of Wied,[a] says:

Many games are in use among these Indians; one of these is a round game, in which one holds in his hand some small stones, of which the others must guess the number or pay a forfeit. The game is known also to the Blackfoot.

CROWS. Montana.

Mr Charles Alston Messiter[b] describes their favorite game of hand:

The game consists in holding a shell in one hand, then placing both hands under a buffalo-robe, which is lying in front of all the players, who kneel in a circle, moving the hands about rapidly, changing the shell from one to the other and then holding them both up closed, your adversary having to say in which of them the shell is, losing a peg if he is wrong. A row of pegs stands in front of each man, who either takes one from or gives one to his opponent according to his loss or gain. These pegs represent so much, and everything an Indian possesses is valued at so many pegs—a wife so many, a horse so many, and so on.

DAKOTA (YANKTON). Fort Peck, Montana. (Cat. no. 37605, Free Museum of Science and Art, University of Pennsylvania.)

Implements for hiding game. Two sticks, cut square, $1\frac{7}{8}$ inches in length, one painted red, with two notches, the other black, with four notches (figure 415); accompanied by eight counting sticks (figure 416), peeled twigs, $5\frac{1}{4}$ inches in length, painted black, one with two and one with four notches, the others plain.

These were collected by the writer in 1900.

Fig. 415.   Fig. 416.

FIG. 415. Sticks for hand game; length, $1\frac{7}{8}$ inches; Yankton Dakota Indians, Fort Peck, Montana; cat. no. 37605, Free Museum of Science and Art, University of Pennsylvania.

FIG. 416. Counting sticks for hand game; length, $5\frac{1}{4}$ inches; Yankton Dakota Indians, Fort Peck, Montana; cat. no. 37605, Free Museum of Science and Art, University of Pennsylvania.

The game is called han'-pa-a-pe-e-con-pe, that is, "moccasin game." The stick with two notches is called non-pa-pa, and the one with four notches, to-pa-pa; the counting sticks, can i-ya'-wa. The sticks are concealed in the

---

[a] Travels in the Interior of North America, translated by H. Evans Lloyd, p. 196, London, 1843.

[b] Sport and Adventures among the North-American Indians, p. 316, London, 1890.

hands and the players bet on the red stick with two notches. The game is also played by concealing the sticks under moccasins.

The following particulars about this game were furnished by Dr George A. Dorsey:

Name of game, humpapachapi; stick with two notches, nupahopi; stick with four notches, topapahopi; general name for both as a set, hakenuchkcimi.

HIDATSA. Fort Atkinson, North Dakota.

Henry A. Boller[a] says:

Sometimes they gambled, playing their favorite game of Hand, in which they would get so excited that time passed unheeded.

SKITTAGETAN STOCK

HAIDA. British Columbia. (Cat. no. 53097, Field Columbian Museum.)

Set of two bones (figure 417), 2⅛ inches in length, oval in section (five-sixteenths by nine-sixteenths of an inch), one with a deep, incised cut in the middle wrapped with dark-colored thread, and the other plain.

These were collected by Dr George A. Dorsey from a Haida Indian

FIG. 417. Bones (one false) for hand game; length, 2⅛ inches; Haida Indians, British Columbia; cat. no. 53097, Field Columbian Museum.

at Rivers inlet, British Columbia. Doctor Dorsey writes:

This is the set of which I have already spoken to you as being of the greatest interest, inasmuch as one of the bones is so constructed that it can be made to show up either white or black. I saw the Haida playing this game at Rivers inlet, but I did not see this set in use.

The false bone is made in two pieces, one of which slides on a shoulder over the other. When they are partly slipped apart, this shoulder, wrapped with dark thread is revealed, giving the appearance of the marked bone.

———— Queen Charlotte islands, British Columbia.

Dr J. R. Swanton[b] describes "doing secretly inside of blankets:"

K!itga′ sLlgañ.—The players formed two sides, stationed some distance apart; and the captain of one party, wearing a blanket over his shoulders so as to conceal his movements, passed down his line of players and dropped a wooden or stone ball inside of the blanket of one of them. He did this in such a way as not to excite the suspicions of his opponents. After that he went away to some distance and lay down, so as not to cast suspicious glances at the one who had the ball. Then one of the opposite party who was good at reading character tried to discover from the players' faces who had it. When he had chosen one he said, "You throw that out;" and if he guessed correctly his side got it, and all of them cried "Ā′ ga, ā′ ga!" If he missed, the same thing was done over again.

---

[a] Among the Indians: Eight years in the Far West, 1858–1866, p. 196, Philadelphia, 1868.

[b] Contributions to the Ethnology of the Haida. Memoirs of the American Museum of Natural History, whole series, v. 8, p. 60, New York, 1905.

CLAYOQUOT. Vancouver island, British Columbia. (Berlin Museum für Völkerkunde.)

Cat. no. IV A 1486. Two bones (figure 418), 3 inches in length, one wrapped with thong.

Cat. no. IV A 1492. Two similar bones (figure 419), 3¼ inches in length.

Fig. 418.   Fig. 419.   Fig. 420.

FIG. 418. Bones for hand game; length, 3 inches; Clayoquot Indians, Vancouver island, British Columbia; cat. no. IV A 1486, Berlin Museum für Völkerkunde.

FIG. 419. Bones for hand game; length, 3¼ inches; Clayoquot Indians, Vancouver island, British Columbia; cat. no. IV A 1492, Berlin Museum für Völkerkunde.

FIG. 420. Bones for hand game; length, 3 and 3¼ inches; Clayoquot Indians, Vancouver island, British Columbia; cat. no. IV A 1493, Berlin Museum für Völkerkunde.

Cat. no. IV A 1493. Two bones (figure 420), one flat at ends and the other with rounded ends marked with dice eyes, both unwrapped; length, 3 and 3¼ inches. Collected by Capt. Samuel Jacobson, who gives the name as zoetjeh.

KWAKIUTL. Fort Rupert, Vancouver island, British Columbia. (Cat. no. 21403, 21404, Free Museum of Science and Art, University of Pennsylvania.)

Fig. 421.   Fig. 422.

FIG. 421. Bones for hand game; length, 2¾ inches; Kwakiutl Indians, Fort Rupert, Vancouver island, British Columbia; cat. no. 21403, Free Museum of Science and Art, University of Pennsylvania.

FIG. 422. Bones for hand game; length, 2¾ inches; Kwakiutl Indians, Fort Rupert, Vancouver island, British Columbia; cat. no. 21404, Free Museum of Science and Art, University of Pennsylvania.

Two sets of bone cylinders, composed of two each, one (21403) 2¾ inches long and 1⅝ inches in diameter in the middle, rounded toward the ends. The orifices of the bone are plugged with wood. One is marked with three encircling lines in the middle and the other is plain (figure 421). The other set (figure 422, cat. no.

21404) is of the same length, 1 inch in diameter at the middle, and about the same at the ends, and somewhat flat on four sides. One bone is wrapped with thread at the middle, where an incision is provided to receive it, and has thirty-two large incised rings arranged in pairs on opposite sides of the bands at equal distances around the bone. The other bone has no central band, and corresponding pairs of incised rings are arranged around it near the ends.

These specimens were collected by Mr Harlan I. Smith, who gives the following account of the game:

Two rows of players sit facing each other [figure 423]. Each side has a drum and all sing, to which many keep time by pounding a board with sticks.

Fig. 423. Kwakiutl Indians playing hand game; Fort Rupert, Vancouver island, British Columbia; from photograph by Mr Harlan I. Smith.

The latter is done by the row that hides the bones, while the others rest and watch. One man shuffles the bones, and at last one of the other side guesses in which hand he holds the marked bone. A correct guess is counted with a sharp stick, and the other side takes the bones. When the guessers fail to guess correctly, I believe they go on without a change. They bet on the game a pile of clothes placed in the center.

Dr Franz Boas [a] gives the following:

Ā'laqoa, the well-known game of lehal, or hiding a bone; played with twenty counters.

---

[a] Sixth Report on the Indians of British Columbia. Report of the Sixty-sixth Meeting of the British Association for the Advancement of Science, p. 578, London, 1896.

KWAKIUTL. British Columbia.

Dr C. F. Newcombe gives the name of the hand game as alaxwa,[a] of the bones as alaxwaxin, and of the counters as kwaxklawi. The marked bone is called kilgiuiala and the unmarked or winning bone, kegia.

There are two sides, generally a tribal or family division. Those not manipulating the bones, but belonging to the side which is, sing and drum. The guessing side is quiet until they win all the bones. Each side chooses a man to guess, and he watches the two opponents and endeavors to notify where the two plain bones are concealed. The following gestures are employed in guessing:

Two arms rapidly separated means that the plain bones are held in the outer hands of the pair working them.

The right hand with the forefinger extended, waved to right, means that the plain bones are held in hands toward right of guesser's person, thus—

The right hand with forefinger extended waved to left means that the plain bones are held in hands toward left of guesser's person, thus—

The right hand with forefinger extended, carried with a downward sweep between the two players, means that the plain bones are held in the inner hands, one in the right, and the other in the left hand of the players working them.

Seven or ten counters are used. If the guesser indicates correctly both plain bones, both are thrown to his side, but no markers, and the opposite side now does the guessing. If he guesses one bone correctly it is thrown to him by its player, but the guesser has to pay 1 marker for every guess. If he indicates wrongly both bones, the guesser pays the 2 sticks. The game goes on until all the sticks are won by either one side or the other.

The following note on the Kwakiutl bones was made by Doctor Newcombe at Alert bay:

There is no idea of sex in regard to these bones. That marked with a central zone is called kenoiaule. The plainer one is called lutzuiaule.

MAKAH. Neah bay, Washington. (Cat. no. 37379, Free Museum of Science and Art, University of Pennsylvania.)

Two hollow bones (figure 424), 3 inches in length and 1½ inches in diameter, with decoration consisting of incised rings with central dot painted red, in two rows of 14 each at both ends. One

---

[a] Ale = seek; xwa = gamble (with bone); xak = bone.

bone is wrapped with a broad band of black leather.   Collected
by the writer in 1900.

Dr George A. Dorsey [a] describes the game as follows:

FIG. 424. Bones for hand
game; length, 3 inches;
Makah Indians, Neah
bay, Washington; cat.
no. 37379, Free Museum
of Science and Art,
University of Pennsyl-
vania.

Soktis.—This is the well-known hand or grass game,
of which two sets were collected.   One set consists of
four bone cylinders 2½ inches long and three-quarters of
an inch in diameter.   Two of them have a groove about
the center, one-half inch in width, which has been filled
with many wrappings of black thread.   The other set consists of two bones, the same length as those in the preceding set, but with a diameter not quite as great.   Both
of the bones of this set are plugged at the end with a
piece of wood, while into the other a rifle cartridge has
been thrust.   One of the bones has two grooves one-
quarter of an inch in width and situated from each other
about three-eighths of an inch.   The center of the bone
lying between these grooves is occupied by a band of
nine circles, each one having a hole in the center.   This
set is beautifully polished from long handling and is
yellow with age.   The marked pieces in the Makah game
are known as chokope or men, the unmarked being hayop
or female.   In playing they always guess for the female.   The count is kept
with twenty sticks (katsak).

NOOTKA.   British Columbia.

Dr Franz Boas [b] says:

A guessing game is frequently played between two parties, who sit in two rows
opposite each other.   One party hides a stone, the men passing it from hand to
hand.   The other party has to guess where it is (t'ĕt'ĕt ɛk·tlis).   The following
song, although belonging originally to Cape Flattery, is used all along the west
coast of Vancouver island in playing the game *lehal:*

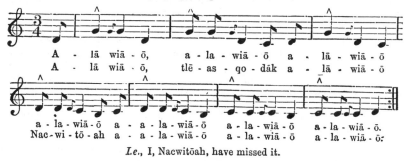

A - lā wiā - ō,   a - la - wiā - ō   a - lā - wiā - ō
A - lā wiā - ō,   tlē - as - qo - dăk   a - lā - wiā - ō

a - la - wiā - ō   a - a - la - wiā - ō   a - la - wiā - ō   a - la - wiā - ō.
Nac - wi - tō - ah   a - a - la - wiā - ō   a - la - wiā - ō   a - la - wiā - ō.

I.e., I, Nacwitōah, have missed it.

WASHOAN STOCK

WASHO.   Carson valley and Lake Tahoe, Nevada.

Dr J. W. Hudson says:

The hand game, hi-nai-yáu-kia, is played by any number, generally six to a
side.   The plain bone is called tĕk-ye'-e'-mĭ, and the bound bone ta-tai'-i-tă.

---

[a] Games of the Makah Indians of Neah Bay.   The American Antiquarian, v. 23, p. 71,
1901.

[b] Second General Report on the Indians of British Columbia.   Report of the Sixtieth
Meeting of the British Association for the Advancement of Science, p. 590, London, 1891.

Each side has five counters, mĕ'-tĕm. The only signal is ha! and is directed to the opponent's hand, which is supposed to hold the tĕk-ye'-e'-mĭ, or plain bone. Ta-tai'-i-tä, the male bone, is merely negative, being fumbled with the plain bone only to confuse the guesser. At the beginning both pairs of bones are held on one side, who begin to sing and slap sticks (their assistants and partners do the latter) on a board before them. Two only of the group manipulate the bones. The guessing opponents are silent, intently regarding the singers. At last one of the opponents stretches forth an arm and often with several frenzied gestures cries ha! at the same time waving his hand to indicate the location of the plain bone. If successful, he takes the bones, and if he guesses both opponents' hands correctly, not only the pair of bones are given him, but counters also. If a guesser happens to guess both plain bones, he receives two counters, and if he guesses right on one only, the one he waves his hand at, he gets but one counter. If he misses both, he and his partner forfeit two counters.

FIG. 425. Bones for hand game; length, 3¾ inches; Huchnom Indians, Eel river, California; cat. no. 21394, United States National Museum.

HUCHNOM. South fork of Eel river, California. (Cat. no. 21394, United States National Museum.)

Four bones (figure 425), 3¾ inches in length, highly polished with use, two wrapped with cord about the middle and two plain.

These were collected by Mr Stephen Powers, who describes them as tep and we; tep, marked ones; we, plain ones.

These are rolled up in pellets of dry grass, and the adversary guesses in which hand is the marked one. They squat on opposite sides of a fire, and keep up a continual chanting, with strange hissing sounds, which confuse the beholder. All the spectators bet on the game if they wish; when one bets he lays down the article, and the one who accepts his bet covers it with articles of equal value, so when the game is done everyone in the victorious party has twice as much as he had at the beginning. The same names exist for these pieces in many tribes [see page 289].

DIEGUEÑO. San Diego, California. (Cat. no. 19757, United States National Museum.)

Four hollow bones, 2⅝ inches long, to which are attached a thick cord about 13 inches in length, terminating in a slip noose, and four wooden twigs, 2½ inches in length, to which is tied a similar noosed cord (figure 426). In the case of the bones the cord passes through a hole in one side and is secured with a knot. Also, fourteen counting sticks (figure 427) of grease wood, about 18 inches in length.

These objects were collected by Dr Edward Palmer, who describes them as used in the game of peon.

The following account of this game, as played by the Luisiño Indians at Agua Caliente, from the Escondito Times, September 26, 1888, was kindly furnished me by Doctor Palmer: [a]

In the evening we again visited the camp. The cooking, eating, and games were in full swing. Candles were lit and stuck around in the most available places. Nearly all the white folks who were tenting or living at the springs were there to see the games, and especially the great game of Peone, which we were told would be played that evening. This game is intensely interesting and a great favorite with this tribe. Each keeper of the game is elected by the tribe, the same as we would a justice of the peace. When a game is to be made up he announces it in a loud voice. It takes eight players, four on a side, and as soon as the bets are made the keeper sits down in front of a small brush fire, takes the money from each side, carefully counting it over. They

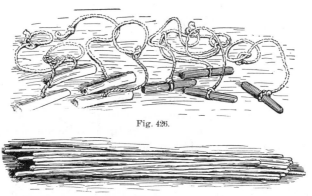

Fig. 426.

Fig. 427.

FIG. 426. Sticks and bones for peon; length of sticks, 2⅛ inches; of bones, 2¼ inches; Diegueño Indians, San Diego, California; cat. no. 19757, United States National Museum.
FIG. 427. Counting sticks for peon; length, 18 inches; Diegueño Indians, San Diego, California; cat. no. 19757, United States National Museum.

usually bet from two to three dollars each, making the full amount from twenty to thirty dollars. When the keeper is satisfied that each side has put in an equal amount, he goes over it carefully, holds it up so all are satisfied, ties it up in a handkerchief, and puts it inside of his shirt. Then he takes up twenty bamboo sticks, a foot long, counts them over carefully; then takes eight pieces of bone, about an inch long, four white and four black; to each is attached a leather thong with a slip noose at the other end large enough

[a] Doctor Palmer writes (in a personal letter, June 2, 1899): "The church fathers in forming the mission of San Luis Rey gathered the Indians from various tribes. In time they became known as the San Luisiño Indians. Afterward in establishing the mission at Agua Caliente, in southern California, the fathers took the Indians from the mission of San Luis Rey (the Luisiños), who, with the Diegueño Indians, living near, were formed into a new mission. As the former predominated, their name was retained. This accounts for both playing the same game." Doctor Palmer continues: "As members of all the tribes of southern California were mixed in forming the mission settlements, their respective games became common, to a greater or less extent, among them all. The fathers kept them, as far as possible, at work, and some curtailed or entirely prohibited the use of their native games, as they were considered as part of their heathen worship, which could not be tolerated. They were thus compelled to discard their tribal games, which are now seldom played."

to go over the wrist. The point in the game is for one side to guess in which hand of each player of the other side the white bone is. The sides arrange themselves opposite each other. They toss to see which has the innings. The umpire gives the bones to the successful side and commences to sing. The squaws of each side arrange themselves behind the players; all are kneeling or sitting on their feet. Each side has a blanket stretched in front of their knees. The side having the bones grasp the side of the blanket in their teeth; it thus forms a curtain, and behind it they slip the leathers over their wrists, without the opposite side seeing which hand the white bone is in. As they take the blanket in their teeth they join in the song with the umpire, swaying their bodies and making all sorts of grimaces with their faces. The squaws sing and keep time with them. The opposite side watches every motion, chatter and talk to each other, and the game becomes exciting as the four drop the blanket from their mouths and join in the song, in a louder key, with the squaws. They have their arms crossed, with their hands under their armpits. The other side at once commences making all sorts of motions at them, pointing to each one, sometimes with one finger, then two, when finally one of them announces which hand the white bone is in of each of the four. If they guess them all, the umpire gives them four of the bamboo sticks as counters; and if they only guess one or two, then the ones they have not guessed go through the same motions until all are caught, when the other side takes the bones, and the performance goes on until one side gets all the counters, and the game is ended with a regular jubilee of the squaws and bucks of the winning side. The umpire, who has watched the game all through and whose decision on any disputed point is law, hands over the money to the winners, who are nearly exhausted, for it takes from three to five hours to play the game. During all that time they are singing and in motion alternately. They divide the money amongst themselves and the squaws of their side. The umpire decides at the top of his not feeble voice that he is ready to start another game.

We should like to be able to picture the intense interest the visitors took in the game, the wild antics of the players, the umpire stolid and watching every motion, the fire burning between the players, lighting up their faces and bringing out in bold relief every expression of disgust or pleasure, making up a picture long to be remembered. To anyone wishing to break himself of the fascinating game of poker, we should recommend Peone.

The game of Peone, described last week, was kept up until about 2 o'clock Sunday morning.

MISSION. Mesa Grande, California. (Cat. no. 62538, Field Columbian Museum.)

FIG. 428. Bones for peon; length, 2½ inches; Mission Indians, Mesa Grande, California; cat. no. 62538, Field Columbian Museum.

Four pieces of bone (figure 428), 2½ inches in length, two tied with cords and two without cords; one perforated and the others notched.

Collected by Mary C. B. Watkins, who describes them as used in the peon game.

MOHAVE. Colorado river, Arizona. (Cat. no. 10333, United States National Museum.)

Five hollow worked bones, 2⅜ inches in length and one-fourth of an inch in diameter (figure 429). The catalogue calls for six specimens.

These specimens were collected by Dr Edward Palmer, who furnished the writer the following account:

FIG. 429. Bone for hand game; length, 2⅜ inches; Mohave Indians, Arizona; cat. no. 10333, United States National Museum.

These bones are made of the leg bones of the white crane. Six pieces constitute the set, there being two sides with three pieces on a side, of different lengths. The game is to guess the length of the pieces held in the hands of the players. A very small end protruded through the fingers. As the opposite sides guess it is an animated game.

Doctor Palmer adds:

These bones are also used by the Yuma (Arizona) and the Cocopa (Sonora, Mexico), and the game is played by them also the same as by the Mohave. One side takes eighteen or twenty sticks as counters. One side has white and the other black bones. The game is to guess in which hand the bones are held.

———— Colorado river, Arizona. (Cat. no. 24179, United States National Museum.)

Fig. 430.

FIG. 430. Sticks for peon; length, 3¼ inches; Mohave Indians, Arizona; cat. no. 24179, United States National Museum.

FIG. 431. Cloth-covered sticks for hand game; length, 3¼ inches; Mohave Indians, Arizona; cat. no. 63337, Field Columbian Museum.

Two worked twigs (figure 430), 3½ inches in length and nine-sixteenths of an inch in diameter, one painted black and the other unpainted, each having a cord attached, ending in a slip noose. This cord passes into a hole in the middle of each stick. A hole runs longitudinally also through the stick.

Collected by Dr Edward Palmer. A similar pair of sticks, also collected by him, is in the Peabody Museum (cat. no. 10093).

Mohave. Parker, Yuma county, Arizona. (Field Columbian Museum.)

Cat. no. 63338. Four bone cylinders, 2¾ inches in length, and four black wooden cylindrical sticks, all with strings with loop at end, attached.

Collected by Mr S. C. Simms, who describes them as used in the game of peon.

Cat. no. 63337. Two cylindrical sticks (figure 431), 3½ inches in length, covered with cotton cloth, one red with black ends, and the other black with red ends.

Collected by Mr S. C. Simms, who gives the name as toothula.

Yuma. Colorado river, California.

Maj. S. P. Heintzelman, U. S. Army, [a] said in 1853:

Another game is with short sticks or pebbles, which one hides in his hands, and another guesses.

———— Fort Yuma, San Diego county, California. (Cat. no. 63331, Field Columbian Museum.)

Four small cylinders (figure 432) made of twigs, 2¼ to 2½ inches in length, uncolored and with ends hollowed out, and four similar cylinders, burned black, with flat ends, all with cords having loop at end, attached.

These were collected by Mr S. C. Simms, who describes them as used in the game of peon, or hohquito.

Fig. 432. Sticks for peon; length, 2¼ to 2¼ inches; Yuma Indians, California; cat. no. 63331, Field Columbian Museum.

Four-stick Game

Unlike almost all of the other Indian games, the four-stick game is confined to a very limited number of tribes: The Klamath and Modoc (Lutuamian), the Achomawi (Shastan), the Paiute (Shoshonean), the Washo (Washoan), and possibly the Chinook. The Klamath and Paiute play in much the same way. As in the hand game, the count is kept with pointed sticks, which are stuck into the ground. Doctor Hudson records the sticks as being regarded as divinities.

[a] House of Representatives, Executive Document 76, Thirty-fourth Congress, third session, p. 49, Washington, 1857.

The four sticks may be referred to the War Gods and their bows. The implements for a prehistoric game from a cliff-dwelling in the Canyon de Chelly, Arizona, which may have been played like the

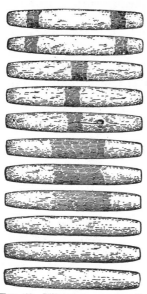

four-stick game are represented in figure 433. These objects consist of eleven wooden billets, 7 inches in length, rounded at the ends, and polished by use. They are painted to correspond with the stick dice and the tubes for the guessing game.

CHINOOKAN STOCK

CLACKAMA. Mouth of the Willamette river, Oregon.

Paul Kane[a] describes the following game:

FIG. 433. Billets for game; length, 7 inches; cliff-dwelling, Canyon de Chelly, Arizona; cat. no. 12061, Brooklyn Institute Museum.

Two were seated together on skins, and immediately opposite to them sat two others, several trinkets and ornaments being placed between them for which they played. The game consists in one of them having his hands covered with a small round mat resting on the ground. He has four small sticks in his hands, which he disposes under the mat in certain positions, requiring the opposite party to guess how he has placed them. If he guesses right, the mat is handed round to the next, and a stick is stuck up as a counter in his favor. If wrong, a stick is stuck up on the opposite side as a mark against him. This, like almost all the Indian games, was accompanied with singing; but in this case the singing was particularly sweet and wild, possessing a harmony I never heard before or since amongst Indians.

LUTUAMIAN STOCK

KLAMATH. Upper Klamath lake, Oregon. (Cat. no. 61537, Field Columbian Museum.)

Four hardwood sticks (plate VI), 12 inches in length. Two of the sticks, skutash, are less than one-half inch in diameter and are closely covered with wrappings extending from end to end of a buckskin thong, which has been painted black; the other two sticks, mu meni, or solses, are one-half inch in diameter at the ends and an inch at the center, and the extremities have been blackened by being charred with a hot iron. Toward the center of these sticks are two bands, 2 inches apart, which have been burnt in. Connecting the two bands are four parallel spirals, also made by burning. There are also six small sticks, 8 inches in length, sharpened at one end and painted red; these are

---

[a] Wanderings of an Artist among the Indians of North America, p. 196, London, 1859. See also the Canadian Journal, p. 276, Toronto, June, 1855.

counters, kshesh, which, at the beginning of the game, are in possession of one or the other side and lie flat on the ground. As points are won by one or the other side, they are taken up and thrust into the ground in front of the winner, according to the number of points gained.

These specimens were collected by Dr George A. Dorsey,[a] who describes the game under the names of shulsheshla, spelshna, or shakla:

In playing this game the four long sticks are arranged in one of a number of possible combinations, the players hiding them under a blanket or large basket tray.

A taking the counters on his side makes the first guess, B manipulating the sticks under a blanket or mat. Should A guess correctly the position of the sticks, he wins and thrusts in the ground one or two counters, according to the value of his guess, and B again arranges the sticks under the blanket. Should A guess wrongly he forfeits one counter and guesses again, but in this case B conceals only two of the sticks, that is, one large and one small wrapped one.

1   2   3   4   5   6

FIG. 434. Possible combinations of large and small sticks in the four-stick game; Klamath Indians, Oregon; from Dr George A. Dorsey.

If A wins, or guesses correctly, the sticks are passed to him, when he manipulates them under the blanket and B guesses. But if A loses, he forfeits a counter and B again manipulates the single pair of sticks. In guessing, when they wish to designate the small wrapped sticks, the index and middle finger are used; for the thick sticks, the index finger alone. In expressing the guess at positions numbered 1 [figure 434] and 2 (vuish), they move the hand sidewise one way or another as they desire to indicate the positions as expressed in numbers 1 or 2. To miss the guess when "vuish is laid," neither side loses nor wins, nor is there any changing to the other opponent of the sticks; but when the position 3 or 4 is laid, with A guessing and winning, the sticks must be passed to him for manipulating and he wins no counters. When the sticks are laid in positions 5 or 6 and A guesses, using two fingers, he obviously loses doubly, and two counters are passed to B.

Another set (cat. no. 61724) is exactly similar to the preceding, except that the buckskin-wrapped sticks are not painted black, while the two large sticks are not painted alike, one having two burnt bands about the center 2 inches apart, from each side of which a row of zigzag lines extends entirely around the stick. On both of the large sticks of this set there are four parallel bands, equidistant from the burnt ends of the stick, the pairs being connected by parallel spirals.

A third set (cat. no. 61723) has two small sticks wrapped with rawhide which has been painted red; the large sticks are charred at

[a] Certain Gambling Games of the Klamath Indians. American Anthropologist, n. s., v. 3, p. 23, 1901.

each end to the extent of about an inch, while in the center are two parallel black bands. The intervening portions of these two sticks are painted red. This set is 11½ inches long and is accompanied with six painted sharpened counting sticks.

KLAMATH. Upper Klamath lake, Oregon. (Cat. no. 37495, Free Museum of Science and Art, University of Pennsylvania.)
Four sticks (figure 435), two of heavy wood tapering from middle to ends and ornamented with burnt designs, 12¼ inches in length,

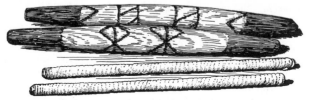

FIG. 435. Four-stick game; lengths of sticks, 12¼ and 11¼ inches; Klamath Indians, Oregon; cat. no. 37495, Free Museum of Science and Art, University of Pennsylvania.

and two smaller sticks, 11¼ inches in length, wound with buckskin. Collected by Dr George A. Dorsey in 1900.

———— Klamath agency, Oregon. (Cat. no. 24132, United States National Museum.)
Two wooden rods (figure 436), 12 inches in length and seven-eighths of an inch in diameter at the middle, tapering to the ends, and

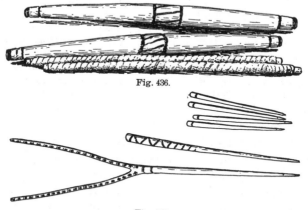

Fig. 436.

Fig. 437.

FIG. 436. Four-stick game; lengths of sticks, 12 and 11¼ inches; Klamath Indians, Klamath agency, Oregon; cat. no. 24132, United States National Museum.
FIG. 437. Counting sticks for four-stick game; lengths, 6¼, 11¼, and 19¼ inches; Klamath Indians, Klamath agency, Oregon; cat. no. 24132, United States National Museum.

marked with burnt designs, as shown in figure 436. These are designated as solchise. Two smaller rods, 11¼ inches in length and five-sixteenths of an inch in diameter, wrapped with a strip of rawhide three-sixteenths of an inch in width except at the extreme ends. These are called skotus. In addition there are six counting sticks, one a forked twig, $19\frac{1}{2}$ inches in length, marked with burnt spots (as shown in figure 437) called teowtis; a pointed stick, $11\frac{1}{4}$ inches in length, also marked with burnt lines, called watch; and four pegs or pins, kice, $6\frac{1}{4}$ inches in length, accompanied by a flat basket (cat. no. 24113, figure 438), 18 inches in diameter, with ornamental patterns in brown and with a bunch of deer thongs tied in the middle on the convex outer side. Collected by L. S. Dyar, Indian agent.

The following description is given by the collector:

Gambling outfit, luck-ulse, thirteen pieces. This game is played by two persons, who sit upon the ground facing each other. The round mat, puh-lah, is used as a cover to hide the four rods, two each of sol-chise and sko-tus. The person performing with these places them side by side on the ground under the mat, and the other guesses their relative positions, whether the large ones are on the outside or in the middle, or if they alternate, etc., and his guess is indicated by certain motions of the hand and fingers. After one guesses a certain number of times he takes the mat and another guesses. The small sharp sticks, kice, are used for the same purpose as points or buttons in billiards, and the other two sticks, te-ow-tis, are stuck in the ground and used to indicate the progress of the game. The package of youcks, medicine, is used as a charm and was formerly considered of much value.

FIG. 438. Basket for four-stick game; diameter, 18 inches; Klamath Indians, Klamath agency, Oregon; cat. no. 24113, United States National Museum.

Commenting on the above description, Doctor Gatschet writes:

The game to which the four sticks belong is the shu'lshesh game, and the two thicker sticks are also called shu'lshesh, while the two slender ones are sko'tas, sku'tash, wrapped up (in buckskin). A blanket is also called sku'tash, sko'-tash, because it wraps up a person. The small kice sticks were called, when I inquired for their name, kshēsh, counting sticks, to count gains and losses, or checks used like our red and white ivory disks used in card games. Watch is wa'kash, a bone awl; wa'tch would be a house. Te-ow-tis is a word I never heard, but it must be te'-utish, stuck in the ground repeatedly, or "stuck in the ground for each one" of the gamesters, for te'wa means to plant, to stick up. The round mat is, in fact, a large tray, called pa'la, or pa"hla, because used for drying seeds by the camp fire or in the sun. Luck-ulse is false for sha'kálóh, (1) gambling outfit for these sticks and also (2) the game itself. "The package of youcks is used as a charm." Yes; that is so, because ya'uks (for ya'-ukish) means (1) remedy, drug used as a medicine, and, in a wider sense, (2) spiritual remedy of the conjurer, consisting in witchcraft, dreams, shamanic songs. The verb of it is ya'-uka, to treat in sickness, and to heal or cure.

Referring to a set of four sticks collected by him at the Klamath agency in 1887, which he says are almost identical with those in the National Museum, Doctor Gatschet writes:

The two shu'lshesh sticks are carefully whittled from the mountain mahogany (*Cerocarpus ledifolius*).

In his work on the Klamath [a] Doctor Gatschet has described this game, as played by the Klamath lake people, under the names of spélshna, shulshéshla, shákla, shákalsha, with four sticks about one foot in length. There are two thick sticks and two slender sticks, the latter wrapped in narrow strips of buckskin leather. They indicate the supposed location of the four game sticks lying under a cover by putting forward fingers. They guess the slender sticks with the index and middle finger; the thick sticks with the index finger alone, and the thicker sticks coupled on one side, and the thinner ones on the other, vû'ish, with a side motion of the hand and thumb. By the last, vû'ish, they win one counting stick; with index and middle finger, two counting sticks.

The name spelshna is derived from speiluish, the index finger. The counting sticks, of which six are commonly used, are called ksē'sh, kshî'sh, from kshéna, to carry off.

MODOC. Fall river, Shasta county, California.

Dr J. W. Hudson describes a game played by women, under the name of ishkake:

Three marked sticks and one plain are used, and their relative position in the hidden hand guessed at.

SHASTAN STOCK

ACHOMAWI. Hat creek, California. (Cat. no. $\frac{50}{4115}$, American Museum of Natural History.)

FIG. 439. Four-stick game; lengths of sticks, 10 and 6¾ inches; Achomawi Indians, Hat creek, California; cat. no. $\frac{50}{4115}$, American Museum of Natural History.

Two sticks, tapering to ends (figure 439), 10 inches in length, and two smaller, thinner sticks, about 6¾ inches in length.

Collected in 1903 by Dr Roland B. Dixon, who gives the name as teisuli. Doctor Dixon writes:

The game is played with the aid of one of the large flat, soft basket plaques, under which the sticks are shifted.

---

[a] The Klamath Indians of Southwestern Oregon. Contributions to North American Ethnology, v. 2, pt. 1, p. 79, Washington, 1890.

ACHOMAWI. Fall river, Shasta county, California.

Dr J. W. Hudson describes the following game [a] under the name of tikali:

Four rods, two bound, 7 inches in length, called tcok'-teă, and two plain, 9 inches in length, called tă-ko'-lĭ, are juggled behind a large, flexible basket plaque, tă-ko'-lĭ tsu-ti'-pa, and the relative position of the rods guessed at. The game is counted with ten counters.

SHOSHONEAN STOCK

PAIUTE. Pyramid lake, Nevada. (Cat. no. 61505, 61519, Field Columbian Museum.)

Four billets of wood, 6 inches in length, two of them 1 inch and two one-half of an inch in diameter, accompanied by ten cottonwood counting sticks, 7 inches in length, sharpened at one end, the upper two-thirds of each stick painted with a spiral band of red.

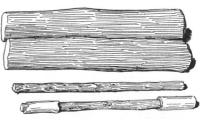

FIG. 440. Four-stick game; length of sticks, 6¼ inches; Paiute Indians, Pyramid lake, Nevada; cat. no. 19044, United States National Museum.

These were collected by Dr George A. Dorsey, who gives the name of the game as witutzi, of the larger billets as biebpe, mother, and of the smaller ones as duaa, young. The counters are called tohu. In playing, the sticks are arranged under a large, flat basket.

———— Pyramid lake, Nevada. (Cat. no. 19044, United States National Museum.)

Two cylindrical billets of wood (figure 440), 6¼ inches in length and 1⅛ inches in diameter, and two smaller ones of the same length and three-eighths of an inch in diameter. The four sticks are

FIG. 441. Counting sticks for four-stick game; length, 8¾ inches; Paiute Indians, Pyramid lake, Nevada; cat. no. 19045, United States National Museum.

uniformly painted red, and one has two tubes of corn stalk slipped over each end. Accompanied with ten willow counting sticks (figure 441), 8¾ inches in length (cat. no. 19045).

[a] The same game, with slight dialectic and local variations, is played by the following tribes, who live on Pit river, Shasta county: Lutwámi, Basi'wi, Amĭts'tci, Pakámali, Hamoáwi, Hádiwiwi, and Săsteitei.—(J. W. H.)

Collected by Mr Stephen Powers, who describes them as follows:

Wuhtatseen, gambling pieces, two large round sticks painted red and two small ones, manipulated by a player who sits on the ground and holds a willow-work tray before him to conceal what he does. The other guesses on which side of the large stick the small ones are. There are ten counters.

FIG. 442. Four-stick game; length of sticks, 6¼ inches; Paiute Indians, southern Utah; cat. no. 14661, United States National Museum.

PAIUTE. Southern Utah. (United States National Museum.) Cat. no. 14661. Two cylindrical billets of willow wood (figure 442), 6¼ inches in length and seven-eighths of an inch in diameter, and two similar sticks, the same length and one-half of an inch in diameter.

The ends of the larger billets are painted blue with a red band in the middle, while the small ones have red ends and a blue band in the middle.

FIG. 443. Paiute playing four-stick game; southern Utah; from photograph by J. K. Hillers.

Another (incomplete) set, catalogued under the same number, consists of three similar billets, unpainted. One of the larger sticks is missing.

Cat. no. 14654. Five twigs of willow, about 12 inches in length, pointed at one end.

Cat. no. 14655. Seven twigs, about 12 inches in length, similar to the above.

Cat. no. 14660. Seven twigs, about 12 inches in length, similar to the above.

These last three numbers are the accompanying counting sticks. All were collected by Maj. J. W. Powell. The above implements are evidently intended for the preceding game. Mr J. K. Hillers writes that they were used in a game (figure 443) played by Indians on the Muddy reservation, a game of odd or even. The sticks are placed under cover in two places. Then a chant begins, as in ne ang-puki. The guessing is done in the same way.

WASHOAN STOCK

PAO. Carson valley, Nevada.

Dr J. W. Hudson describes the following game played by men under the name of tsutsu:

A mu-tal' basket is inverted and held with the left hand touching the ground, while nine small sticks are held in the right hand. The player slips a certain number of these nine sticks under the plaque while juggling and singing. The opponent guesses at the number (even or odd) of sticks under the basket.

WASHO. Carson valley and Lake Tahoe, Nevada.

Dr J. W. Hudson describes the following game under the name of it-dtsu-dtsu: [a]

Four sticks are employed, two large, 10 inches long, bound with buckskin, regarded as female, and called it-tai-ta, and two plain, 7½ inches long, regarded as male, and called it-dtsu-dtsu. The buckskin binding on the longer sticks prevents noise when they are hidden. The four sticks are juggled under a winnowing basket, mu-tal', and then relative positions guessed at by the opponent. The three positions (figure 444) in which the sticks may be placed receive the following names: a, ke-hel-kul; b, ka-hă-tsup; c, kum-de-we, deer, or kum-da-mu. The four sticks are placed in one of these positions under the basket while its holder is singing and invoking Tu-li-shi, the wolf, at the same time violently vibrating the basket against the ground. If guessed right, the sticks are forfeit. An incorrect guess forfeits a counter. Eight counters, me-tĕ-em, are used.

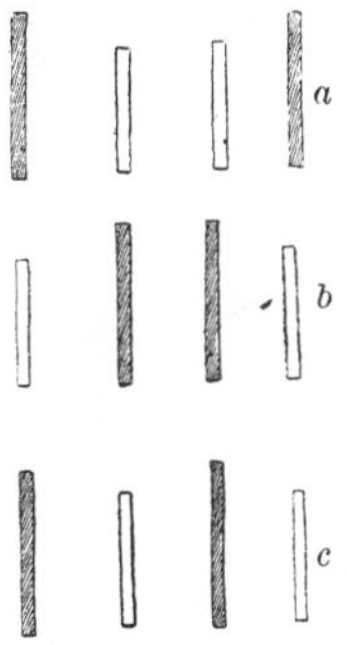

FIG. 444. Position of sticks in four-stick game; Washo Indians, Nevada; from sketch by Dr J. W. Hudson.

HIDDEN-BALL GAME, OR MOCCASIN

A game of hiding something in one of several places, usually four, the opponents guessing where it is concealed. The implements employed are of two kinds: (a) cane tubes or wooden cups derived from the canes, and (b) moccasins. The cane tubes, in their original forms, bear the characteristic marks of the arrows of the four directions, precisely like the canes used in the

---

[a] Compare Kularapan, tsu, arrow; tsu-tsu, arrows.

Zuñi game of sholiwe.   They pass by easy transitions into wooden tubes marked with the same bands, wooden cups similarly marked,

and wooden cups marked or carved with symbols referring to the world quarters.   Finally we have four plain tubes, which at last disappear in a game which consists in hiding a bean or other small object in one of four heaps of sand.   It may be inferred from the sholiwe that the original tubes were butts, or shaftments, of cane arrows.

Fig. 445. Sacrificial tubes for hiding game; height, 2¼ inches; Zuñi Indians, Zuñi, New Mexico; cat. no. 22682, Free Museum of Science and Art, University of Pennsylvania.

The object hidden consists of a small cylindric stick, sometimes painted with bands of color, a bean, or a stone.   Among the Papago

Fig. 446. Drab Flute (Macileña) altar; Hopi Indians, Mishongnovi, Arizona; from Fewkes.

the tubes are filled with sand, which the guesser empties out.   Elsewhere, as in Zuñi, we find the tubes stuck in hillocks of sand.   In Zuñi the guesser used a rod to point to the tubes.   The counters con-

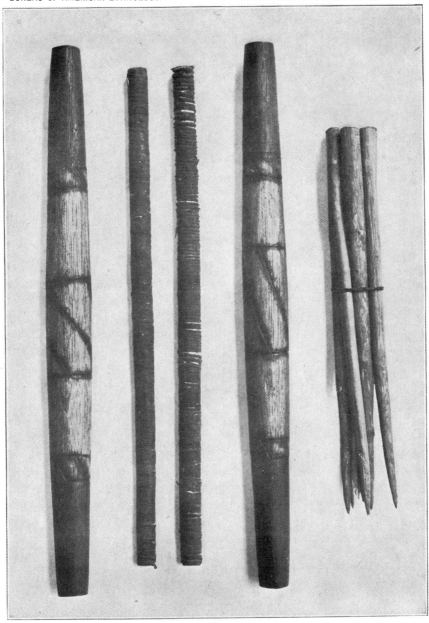

FOUR-STICK GAME; KLAMATH INDIANS, OREGON; CAT. NO. 61537,
FIELD COLUMBIAN MUSEUM; FROM DORSEY

SOYAL ALTAR; HOPI INDIANS, WALPI, ARIZONA; FROM FEWKES

sist of beans or sticks, and number from fifty to one hundred and two, or one hundred and four.

As mentioned in the introduction, the hidden-ball game was one of the five games sacrificed on the altar of the War God in Zuñi. A set of cups (figure 445) for this purpose in the museum of the University of Pennsylvania (cat. no. 22682), collected by the writer in Zuñi in 1902, consists of four wooden tubes, each $1\frac{1}{4}$ inches in diameter and $2\frac{3}{4}$ inches in height. They are painted white, with black tops, and have pink plume feathers stuck in the top of each. As also noted, similar cups, surmounted with effigies of birds, are seen on the Hopi Oáqöl

Fig. 447. Blue Flute (Cakwaleñya) altar; Hopi Indians, Mishongnovi, Arizona; from Fewkes.

altar (figure 1). They occur also on the Soyaluna altar at Walpi, plate VII, as figured by Doctor Fewkes.[a]

Four flowerlike wooden cups—yellow, green, red, and white—appear at the base of the effigy on the altar of the Drab Flute at Oraibi, while sixteen cups of the four colors are stuck like flowers on two

---

[a] The Winter Solstice Ceremony at Walpi. The American Anthropologist, v. 11, p. 79, 1898.

uprights on each side of the figure.   On the Mishongnovi Drab Flute altar (figure 446) there are two upright logs of wood, rounded at the top and pierced with holes, in which are stuck similar flowers. Doctor Fewkes, who has figured this altar, says that these logs correspond with the mounds of sand, covered with meal, of other Flute altars, and were called talactcomos.[a] The sand mounds stuck with flowers occur in the altar of the Blue Flute (figure 447) at Mishongnovi.   These sand mounds [b] should be compared with the sand mountains into which the cane tubes are stuck in the Zuñi game.

The Flute altar at Shumopavi (figure 448) has the flower cups on upright sticks, as at Oraibi, while on that at Shipaulovi (figure 449) they are stuck in sand mounds.   Mention has already been made of

FIG. 448. Flute altar, Hopi Indians, Shumopavi, Arizona; from photograph by Sumner W. Matteson, August 31, 1901.

the gaming-cup flower headdress (figure 569) of the Flute priest at Oraibi.   The Sohu or Star katcina has similar wooden cups in the hair.   Dr J. Walter Fewkes [c] writes:

The Tusayan Tewa of Hanoki, East mesa, call the January moon E'lop'o, wood-cup moon, referring to the e'lo, wooden cups, used by the Tcukuwympkiya or clowns, in their ceremonial games.

---

[a] Journal of American Folk-Lore, v. 9, p. 245, 1896.

[b] These mounds admit of the following explanation.   In many stories of the origin of societies of priests which took place in the under-world, the first members are represented as erecting their altars before the " flower mound " of Müiyinwû.   This was the case of the Flute youth and maid, progenitors of the Flute Society.   These mounds, now erected on earth before the figurine of Müiyinwû in the Flute chambers, symbolize the ancestral mounds of the under-world, the wooden objects inserted in them representing flowers.— Journal of American Folk-Lore, v. 9, p. 245, note, 1896.

[c] In a letter to the author, dated January 27, 1899.

The four cups or tubes, whether wood or cane, may be regarded as representing or referring to the twin War Gods and their female counterparts or associates, who preside over the four world quarters. In the case of the marked and carved tubes, this agreement is suggested at every point: In the banded markings (Hopi, Keres, Papago, Pima, Tarahumare, Tewa, Maricopa), in the burned devices (Hopi), in the cloud terrace and flower symbols carved at the top (Hopi), and in the sex designation (Papago, Pima).

The moccasin game was played by the Algonquian tribes and is found among the Dakota and the Navaho. Two, three, four, six, or eight moccasins are used, but four is the standard number. The

Fig. 449. Flute altar, Hopi Indians, Shipaulovi, Arizona; from photograph by Sumner W. Matteson, September 7, 1901.

objects hidden vary from one to four, and consist either of bullets, stones, or little billets of wood. The players among some tribes indicate their choice by pointing with a rod. The count is kept with sticks or beans, 20, 50, 100, or 102. Mittens are sometimes used instead of moccasins, and the game was borrowed by the whites and played by them under the name of "bullet." Moccasin was a man's game. It was played as a gambling game to the accompaniment of singing and drumming. In the east it retains little of its former ceremonial character. The writer regards it as a direct modification of the hidden-ball game, the Navaho game, with its nodule and striking stick, furnishing a connecting link.

ALGONQUIAN STOCK

CHIPPEWA. Minnesota. (Cat. no. 153033, United States National Museum.)

Set of four buckskin moccasins; four bullets, one plain and three covered with twisted wire (figure 450); and twenty counting sticks, peeled, unpainted twigs , 13⅛ inches in length (figure 451), catalogued as accompanied with a pouch to contain them. Collected by Dr Walter J. Hoffman.

Fig. 450.

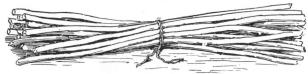

Fig. 451.

FIG. 450. Bullets for moccasin game; diameter, ₁₆⁹ inch; Chippewa Indians, Minnesota; cat. no. 153033, United States National Museum.
FIG. 451. Counting sticks for moccasin game; length, 13⅛ inches; Chippewa Indians, Minnesota; cat. no. 153033, United States National Museum.

———— Bois fort, near Rainy river, Minnesota. (Cat. no. $\frac{50}{4718}$, American Museum of Natural History.)

Four bullets (figure 452), one of white lead, three-eighths of an inch in diameter.

They were collected in 1903 by Dr William Jones, who describes

FIG. 452. Bullets for moccasin game; diameter, three-eighths of an inch; Chippewa Indians, Bois fort, Minnesota; cat. no. $\frac{50}{4718}$, American Museum of Natural History.

them as hidden in the moccasin game. Moccasins are used, and the game has the same name as at Turtle mountain.

———— Mille Lacs, Minnesota.

Mr D. I. Bushnell, jr, describes a moccasin game (figure 453) which he witnessed at Mille Lacs in 1900:

The game lasted thirty-six hours. The stakes were two badly worn neckties. It was played with four metal balls, three of copper and one of lead. The " moccasins " were four pieces of buckskin cut in the shape of moccasin soles. It was played to the beating of a drum, which was passed from side to side.

CHIPPEWA.   Wisconsin.

Prof. I. I. Ducatel [a] says:

Their favorite game is the mukesinnah dahdewog, or moccasin game. It is played with four bullets (one of which is jagged) and four moccasins. The four bullets are to be hid, one under each moccasin, by the first player, whose deal is decided by throwing up a knife and letting it fall on the blanket, the direction of the blade indicating the person who is to hide first. The four bullets are held in the right hand, and the left hand is kept moving from one moccasin to the other; whilst the player, with a peculiar manner calculated to divert the attention of the one with whom he is playing, and with an incessant chant, accompanied by a swinging motion of the head and trunk, passes his

FIG. 453. Moccasin game; Chippewa Indians, Mille Lacs, Minnesota; from photograph by Mr D. I. Bushnell, jr.

bullet hand under the moccasins, depositing a bullet under each. The other is to guess where the jagged bullet is, but not at the first trial; for if he strikes upon it the first time, he loses 4 sticks—there being 20 altogether, that are used as counters; if the second time he makes a similar guess, then he loses 3 sticks; but if he guess the situation of the jagged bullet the third time, then he gains 4 sticks; finally should the bullet remain under the fourth moccasin, the guesser loses 4 sticks. The game continues until the twenty sticks have passed from one hand to the other. At this game, of which they are very fond, they stake everything about them and sometimes come away literally stripped. The groups that are thus collected present the most characteristic of Indian

---

[a] A Fortnight among the Chippewas of Lake Superior. The Indian Miscellany, edited by W. W. Beach, p. 367, Albany, 1877. Reprinted from the United States Catholic Magazine Baltimore, January and February, 1846.

habits. There will be twenty sitting down and as many standing round, intent upon the progress of the game, which is carried on in silence, except on the part of the hider.

Another game of chance, and perhaps the only other after cards, and the one just described, is the pahgehsehwog or pan-play, which consists in guessing at any thing, or number of things, enclosed between two pans.

CHIPPEWA. Turtle mountain, North Dakota. (Cat. no. $\frac{50}{4716}$, American Museum of Natural History.)

Implements for moccasin game (figure 454) : Four black-cloth pads, 8 inches wide, with edges bound with red; eleven counting sticks (saplings), painted red, 18 inches long, and a striking stick (a slender rod), painted red, 36 inches in length.

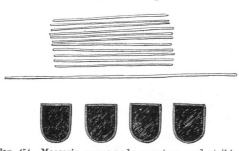

FIG. 454. Moccasin game; pads, counters, and striking stick; width of pads, 8 inches; length of counters, 18 inches; length of striking stick, 36 inches; Chippewa Indians, Turtle mountain, North Dakota; cat. no. $\frac{50}{4716}$, American Museum of Natural History.

These were collected in 1903 by Dr William Jones, who gives the name as makesenatatiweni, or moccasin game.

The game is played with three beads and a bullet, the bullet being trump. Either moccasins or the pads are used.

CREE. Muskowpetung reserve, Qu'appelle, Assiniboia. (Cat. no. 61996, Field Columbian Museum.)

A small tinned iron ring, three-fourths of an inch in diameter, used in the moccasin game, which is described as follows by the collector, Mr J. A. Mitchell, under the name of muskisinastahtowin, concealing an object in a moccasin:

This game is conspicuously a gambling game, and is quite similar to the sleight-of-hand games of the whites. The objects are concealed either together under one of four inverted moccasins or separately under two moccasins, all being placed in a line before the manipulator, who passes his hands under each moccasin in order to confuse the opponents. If the pieces are placed apart from each other under separate moccasins, the player making the guess has the right to another guess should he find one of the pieces at his first guess. Failure at first guess counts him out, and the play goes to the next player.

DELAWARES. Indiana.

I am informed by Mr George S. Cottman, of Irvington, Indiana, that the following is drawn from two articles in a local newspaper,[a] the principal of which was by Robert Duncan, " one of our earliest pioneers, now dead ":

Moccasin was a gambling game much practised among the Delaware Indians, and was borrowed of them by the white settlers. As originally played, a deer

---

[a] Indianapolis News, July 22, 24, 1879.

skin was spread upon the ground and a half dozen upturned moccasins arranged in a semicircle within easy reach of the player. The latter, holding to view a good-sized bullet, then quickly thrust his hand under each moccasin in turn, leaving the bullet under one of them. This was done so skillfully as to leave the onlooker in doubt, and the gambling consisted in betting where the bullet was. This was called moccasin. Subsequently the whites modified the game slightly by placing caps on the table, and the game became changed to bullet. It was played so extensively among the pioneers as to become a recognized evil, and on the early statutes stands a law making gambling at bullet a finable offense.

Mr Cottman writes:

On page 104 of the Laws of Indiana Territory, as revised by John Rice Jones and John Johnson, published in 1807, I find a statute forbidding various gambling games, among them that of bullet, the penalty fixed for practising them being five dollars and costs.

Mr Cottman states also that in the diary of John Tipton, one of the commissioners to locate the Indiana capital, is the following entry:

After dinner we went to the Indian huts, found the men playing a favorite game which they call mockuson, which is played with a bullet and four mockusons.

The locality was near Conner's station, some 16 miles north of the site of Indianapolis, and there can hardly be any doubt that they were Delaware Indians, as this was the Delaware country. The Miami occupied the Wabash region, and the Potawatomi were yet farther north.

MENOMINEE.   Wisconsin.

Dr Walter J. Hoffman [a] describes the moccasin or bullet game, as follows:

Another game that was formerly much played by the Menomini [plate VIII] was the moccasin, or bullet, game, which was probably learned from their Ojibwa neighbors. Five persons participate in this game, four being active players, while the fifth acts as musician, by using the tambourine-drum and singing, the players usually joining in the latter. . . . The articles necessary to play this game consist of four bullets, or balls of any hard substance, one of which is colored, or indented, to readily distinguish it from its fellows; four moccasins also are required, as well as thirty or forty stick counters, similar to those used in the preceding [bowl] game, though uncolored. A blanket also is used, and in addition a stick, about 3 feet long, with which to strike the moccasin under which the bullet is believed to be hidden. When the game is commenced, the players are paired off by two's, who take their places on each of the four sides of the outspread blanket [plate VIII]. The winner of the toss takes the moccasins before him and lays them upside down and about 6 inches apart with the toes pointing forward. The object now is for the player to lift, with his left hand, each moccasin, in succession, and put a bullet under it, making many pretenses of hiding and removing the bullets, in order to confuse the opponents, who are eagerly watching for some slip of the performer whereby they may obtain a clue of the moccasin under which the marked bullet may be placed. While this is going on, the drummer is doing his duty by singing and drumming,

---

[a] The Menomini Indians.   Fourteenth Annual Report of the Bureau of Ethnology, p. 242, 1896.

to which the others are noisily keeping time. When the bullets are all hidden, the player will suddenly call out, " Ho! " in a high note, when the singing drops to a mere murmur, and the striker of the opposing side raises the stick threateningly over the several moccasins, as if to strike them, but each time withdraws as if in doubt. Finally, he will place the end of a long stick under a moccasin, and turn it over. Should the marked bullet be disclosed, he is regarded as successful; if he fails the first time he has another trial, but if the bullet is found only at the second trial, the counters to which he is entitled will be fewer than if he finds the bullet the first time. In event of the opponent making a successful guess of the moccasin under which the marked bullet has been placed, the former player relinquishes the moccasins and bullets and takes his turn at guessing. The game is decided when all the sticks on the blanket are won, those winning the majority taking the bets previously made. The scoring depends on the agreement previously formed.

MIAMI. Indiana.

Mr George S. Cottman obtained for me (July, 1899), from Mr J. H. B. Nowland, the Indianapolis pioneer, the following account of the moccasin game as he saw it played among the Miami, Potawatomi, and Shawnee at an Indian village which stood at the mouth of the Mississineva river, when at the treaty of 1832 he was secretary to Governor Jennings:

The player, seated on the ground with six moccasins arranged in two rows before him and a little painted stick in his hand, would sing an incantation to divert attention from his action, and, thrusting his hand under the various moccasins, secretly and skillfully deposit the stick. The spectators then bet on the moccasin.

MISSISAUGA. Rice lake, Ontario.

G. Copway [a] says:

The Moccasin play is simple, and can be played by two or three. Three moccasins are used for the purpose of hiding the bullets which are employed in the game. So deeply interesting does this play sometimes become, that an Indian will stake first, his gun; next, his steel-traps; then his implements of war; then his clothing; and, lastly, his tobacco and pipe, leaving him, as we say, " Nah-bah-wan-yah-ze-yaid," " a piece of cloth with a string around his waist."

NIPISSING. Forty miles above Montreal, Quebec.

J. A. Cuoq [b] gives the following definition:

Kwate hewin, sorte de jeu de cachette; kazotage, jouer à la cachette.

OTTAWA. Manitoba.

John Tanner [c] thus describes the game:

. . . played by any number of persons, but usually in small parties. Four moccasins are used, and in one of them some small object, such as a little stick or a small piece of cloth, is hid by one of the betting parties. The moccasins are laid down beside each other, and one of the adverse party is then to touch

[a] The Traditional History and Characteristic Sketches of the Ojibway Nation, p. 54, Boston, 1851.

[b] Lexique de la Langue Algonquine, Montreal, 1886.

[c] A Narrative of the Captivity and Adventures of John Tanner, p. 114, New York, 1830.

two of the moccasins with his finger, or a stick. If the one he first touches has
the hidden thing in it, the player loses 8 to the opposite party; if it is not in the
second he touches, but in one of the two passed over, he loses 2. If it is not
in the one he touches first, and is in the last, he wins 8. The Crees play this
game differently, putting the hand successively into all the moccasins, endeavoring to come last to that which contains the article; but if the hand is thrust
first into the one containing it, he loses 8. They fix the value of articles staked
by agreement; for instance, they sometimes call a beaver skin, or a blanket, 10;
sometimes a horse 100. With strangers, they are apt to play high; in such
cases, a horse is sometimes valued at 10.

SAUK AND FOXES. Iowa. (Cat. no. $\frac{50}{3520}$, American Museum of Natural History.)

Twelve peeled willow twigs, 12 inches in length, and a pointed peeled
willow stick, 26 inches in length (figure 455).

These were collected by Dr William Jones, who describes them as
counters and pointing stick for the moccasin game, mama kesä hi
wagi. Four moccasins are used and a bullet is hidden.

FIG. 455. Counting sticks and pointer for moccasin game; length of counters, 12 inches; length
of pointer, 26 inches; Sauk and Fox Indians, Iowa; cat. no. $\frac{50}{3520}$, American Museum of Natural
History.

ATHAPASCAN STOCK

APACHE (JICARILLA). Northern New Mexico.

Mr James Mooney,[a] in his account of the Jicarilla genesis myth,
describes the game as follows:

It was dark in the under-world, and they used eagle plumes for torches. The
people and the animals that go about by day wanted more light, but the night
animals—the Bear, the Panther, and the Owl—wanted darkness. They disputed
long, and at last agreed to play the käyoñ'ti game to decide the matter. It was
agreed that if the day animals won, there should be light, but if the night
animals won, it should be always dark.

The game began, but the Magpie and the Quail, which love the light and have
sharp eyes, watched until they could see the button through the thin wood of
the hollow stick, and they told the people under which one it was. The morning
star came out and the Black-bear ran and hid in the darkness. They played
again, and the people won. It grew bright in the east, and the Brown-bear ran
and hid himself in a dark place. They played a third time, and the people won.
It grew brighter in the east and the Mountain-lion slunk away into the darkness.
They played a fourth time, and again the people won. The Sun came up in the
east, and it was day, and the Owl flew away and hid himself.

In a footnote Mr Mooney describes the game of käyoñti:

A sort of "thimble and button" game, in which one party hides the button
under one of several closed wooden cups or thimbles, and the other tries to guess
under which thimble it is. There is a score of 104 tally sticks.

---

[a] The American Anthropologist, v. 11, p. 198, 1898.

NAVAHO. Keams canyon, Arizona. (Cat. no. 62534, Field Columbian Museum.)

Implements for moccasin game (figure 456), consisting of a ball of

sandstone, 1¼ inches in diameter, marked on one side with a
cross, with one line painted red
and the other black; also one
hundred counting sticks, 8 inches
in length, made of yucca, and a
club of cottonwood, slightly
curved, 13 inches in length.
These specimens were collected
by Mr Thomas V. Keam.

FIG. 456. Moccasin game; diameter of ball, 1¼
inches; length of counters, 8 inches; length of
club, 13 inches; Navaho Indians, Arizona; cat.
no. 62534, Field Columbian Museum.

———— New Mexico. (Cat. no. 74741, United States National Museum.)

Set of 102 splints (figure 457), 8¾ inches in length, made of the root
leaf of the yucca.

Two are notched on the margins to represent a snake, called the
grandmother snake. These were collected by Dr Washington Matthews, U. S. Army, and described as counting sticks for the game of
kescite.

Doctor Matthews [a] describes the game of kesitce [b] as follows:

This is, to some extent, sacred in its nature, for the playing is confined to the
winter, the only time when their myths may be told and their most important
ceremonies conducted. It
is practiced only during
the dark hours. The real
reason for this is probably
that the stone used in the
game can not be hidden
successfully by daylight;
but if you ask an Indian
why the game is played
only at night, he will account for it by referring
you to the myth and saying
that he on whom the sun
shines while he is engaged
in the game will be struck

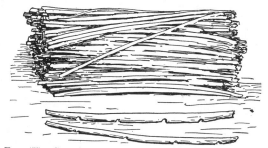

FIG. 457. Counting sticks for moccasin game; length, 8¾
inches; Navaho Indians, New Mexico; cat. no. 74741, United
States National Museum.

blind. I have heard that on some occasions, when the stakes are heavy and
the day begins to dawn on an undecided contest, they close all the apertures
of the lodge with blankets, blacken the skin around their eyes, place a watch
outside to prevent intrusion, and for a short time continue their sport.

The implements of the game are eight moccasins; a roundish stone or pebble
about an inch and a half in diameter; a blanket used as a screen; a stick with

[a] Navaho Gambling Songs. The American Anthropologist, v. 2, p. 2, 1889.
[b] From ke, moccasins, and sitce, side by side, parallel to one another in a row.

which to strike the moccasins; a chip blackened on one side that they toss up to decide which party shall begin the game; and one hundred and two counters, each about 9 inches long, made of a stiff, slender root-leaf of the *Yucca angusti-folia*. Two of these counters are notched on the margins.

The moccasins are buried in the ground so that only about an inch of their tops appear and they are filled to the ground level with powdered earth or sand. They are placed side by side a few inches apart in two rows, one on each side of the fire. The players are divided into two parties, each controlling one row of moccasins. When, by tossing up the chip, they have decided which party shall begin, the lucky ones hold up a screen to conceal their operations and hide the ball in one of the moccasins, covering it well with sand. When all is ready they lower the screen and allow that person to come forward whom their opponents have selected to find the ball. He strikes with a stick the moccasin in which he supposes the ball to lie. If his guess is correct he takes the stone, his comrades become the hiders and his opponents the seekers; but if he fails to indicate the place wherein the pebble is hid the hiders win some of the counters, the number won depending on the position of the moccasin struck and the position of the one containing the stone. Thus each party is always bound to win while it holds the stone and always bound to lose while its opponent holds it.

The system of counting is rather intricate, and though I perfectly comprehend it I do not consider a full description of it in this connection as necessary to the proper understanding of the myth. It will suffice to say that the number of counters lost at any one unsuccessful guess can only be either 4, 6, or 10; these are the only "counts" in the game. When the game begins the counters are held by some uninterested spectator and handed to either side according as it wins. When this original holder has given all the counters out, the winners take from the losers. When one side has won all the counters the game is done. The original holder parts with the two notched counters, called "Grandmothers," last. One of the party receiving them sticks them up in the rafters of the hogan (lodge) and says to them, "Go seek your grandchildren" (i. e., bring the other counters back to our side). The possession of the "grandmothers" is supposed to bring good luck.

A good knowledge of the songs is thought to assist the gamblers in their work, probably under the impression that the spirits of the primeval animal gods are there to help such as sing of them. A song begun during an "inning" (to borrow a term from the field) must be continued while the inning lasts. Should this inning be short it is not considered lucky to sing the same song again during the game.

The following is an epitome of the myth of the kesitce:

In the ancient days there were, as there are now, some animals who saw better, could hunt better, and were altogether happier in the darkness than in the light; and there were others who liked not the darkness and were happy only in the light of day. The animals of the night wished it would remain dark forever and the animals of the day wished that the sun would shine forever. At last they met in council in the twilight to talk the matter over and the council resolved they should play a game by hiding a stone in a moccasin (as in the game now called kesitce) to settle their differences. If the night animals won the sun should never rise again, if the day animals succeeded, nevermore should it set. So when night fell they lit a fire and commenced the game.

In order to determine which side should first hide the stone they took a small weather-stained fragment of wood and rubbed one side with charcoal. They tossed it up; if it fell with the black side up, the nocturnal party were to begin, but it fell with the gray side up and those of the diurnal side took the stone. These raised a blanket to conceal their operations and sang a song, which is sung to this day by the Navajos when they raise a screen in this game . . . and the game went on.

They commenced the game with only one hundred counters but a little whitish, odd-looking snake called lĭc-bitcŏi, i. e., maternal grandmother of the snakes, said they ought to have two more counters. Therefore they made two, notched them so that they would look like snakes, and called them bitcŏi, maternal grandmothers, which name the two notched counters used in the game still bear.

The cunning coyote would not cast his lot permanently with either side. He usually stood between the contending parties, but occasionally went over to one side or the other, as the tide of fortune seemed to run.

Some of the genii of those days joined the animals in this contest. On the side of the night animals was the great destroyer Yeitso, the best guesser of all, who soon took the stone away from the day animals. Whenever the latter found it in the moccasins of their moon-loving enemies they could not hold it long, for the shrewd-guessing Yeitso would recover it. They lost heavily and began to tremble for their chances, when some one proposed to them to call in the aid of the gopher, nasizi. He dug a tunnel under the moccasins leading from one to another and when Yeitso would guess the right moccasin the gopher, unseen by all, would transfer the stone to another place . . . Thus was Yeitso deceived, the day party retrieved their losses and sang a taunting song of him . . .

But when they had won back nearly all the counters, luck appeared to again desert them. The noctivagant beasts came into possession of the pebble, and kept it so long that it seemed as if their opponents could never regain it. Guess as cleverly as they might, the stone was not to be found in the moccasin indicated by those who longed for an eternal day. Then the owl sang a song expressive of his desires . . . and when he had done, one of the wind-gods whispered into the ear of one of the diurnal party that the owl held the stone in his claws all the time, and never allowed it to be buried in the moccasin. So, when next the screen was withdrawn, the enlightened day animal advanced, and, instead of striking a moccasin, struck the owl's claws, and the hidden stone dropped out on the ground.

After this the game proceeded with little advantage to either side, and the animals turned their attention to composing songs about the personal peculiarities, habits, and history of their opponents, just as in social dances to-day the Navajos ridicule one another in song. Thus all the songs relating to animals . . . which form the great majority of the songs of the Kesitce, originated.

Later the players began to grow drowsy and tired and somewhat indifferent to the game, and again the wind-god whispered—this time into the ear of the magpie—and said, "Sing a song of the morning," whereat the magpie sang his song . . . As he uttered the last words, "Qa-yel-ká! Qa-yel-ká!" (It dawns! It dawns!) the players looked forth and beheld the pale streak of dawn along the eastern horizon. Then all hastily picked up their counters and blankets and fled, each to his proper home—one to the forest, another to the desert, this to the gully, that to the rocks.

The bear had lent his moccasins to be used in the game. They were, therefore, partly buried in the ground. In his haste to be off he put them on wrong—the right moccasin on the left foot, and vice versa; and this is why the bear's feet are now misshapen. His coat was then as black as midnight, but he dwelt on top of a high mountain, and was so late in getting back to his lair that the red beams of the rising sun shone upon him, imparting their ruddy hue to the tips of his hairs, and thus it is that the bear's hair is tipped with red to this day.

The home of the wood-rat, létso, was a long way off, and he ran so far and so fast to get there that he raised great blisters on his feet, and this accounts for the callosities we see now on the soles of the rat.

So the day dawned on the undecided game. As the animals never met again to play for the same stakes, the original alternation of day and night has never been changed.

Mr A. M. Stephen, in his unpublished manuscript, gives a lively account of a game of the kesitce which he witnessed on January 23, 1887. The name he gives as keisdje. He describes it as played with one hundred and two yucca-leaf counters, cut off at the taper end, called ketan, a small sandstone nodule, tonalsluci, and a piñon club about 6 inches long, pedilsicli:

The game was played in a hogan erected for a ceremony. Two shallow pits, about 2 feet long, were dug on the north and south sides of the fire. They were just long enough to hold four moccasins each, two pairs, set in alternately. Both pits were covered, only showing the aperture. The moccasins were then filled with sand. These operations were performed very leisurely, with no ceremony apparent. The stakes were then discussed and, after much general talk, produced and laid on both sides of the fire beside the buried shoes. They consisted of saddle, bridle, leggings, buttons, manta, prints, blankets. A young man sat on each of the covered side pits. There was much apparent difficulty in the appraisement of the stakes, but this accomplished they were divided and thrown on each side of the players. After an hour one side held a blanket between them and the fire and sang, then dropped the blanket, and one from the other side struck the shoe and tried to find the nodule. The side failing to find the nodule gives up to the opposing side six or ten counters from the bundle. The sides were about equal in numbers, but this is of little consequence. A piece of corn shuck, black on one side, was tossed up. This was attended with much excitement. In striking, one of the players spat on the stick to hoodoo it for the strikers. There was much droll byplay as the game proceeded. One player, whose side appeared victorious, tried to copulate with the fire. Another, winning, covered his head with his blanket and imitated the cry of the owl(?). One side had a red and the other a black blanket. Much jesting prevailed. One player went around the fire as an old man, followed by another as a Yé, imitating masks, etc., amid great fun and uproar. The players tumbled and rolled in the fire in the roughest kind of horseplay.

To win the maximum number of counters (10, I think) the seeker should strike two shoes and dig them out, i. e., scratch out their contents, and find nothing; then, on striking the third shoe, find it contains the nodule.

IROQUOIAN STOCK

ONONDAGA. New York.

Rev. W. M. Beauchamp [a] says:

A bell is hidden in one of three shoes, by the Onondagas, and the opposing party must guess in which of these it is.

---

[a] Iroquois Games. Journal of American Folk-Lore, v. 9, p. 275, 1896.

SENECA. Ontario.

Mr. David Boyle [a] describes the wake game as follows:

When friends and neighbors are assembled at a wake, it is customary for them to engage in a game to comfort in some measure the bereaved ones, and, to a certain extent, as a mere pastime. It may be premised that in so doing there is no desire that either side engaged should win, and the whole of the proceedings are conducted with seriousness. If, during the progress of the game a young person should forget himself, the Head Man, or master of ceremonies, takes occasion to point out that at such times light behavior is unseemly.

As many players, men and women, may engage as there is room to accommodate when the two sides sit face to face. The game consists in the hiding of a pebble (a marble, or a bullet is now often used) in one of four moccasins or mittens held in the lap of the hider for the time being, the other side trying to guess in which of these the object has been placed.

The Head Man makes a long speech to the players.

A singer having been appointed he sets the pace, accompanied by his drum, by giving one of the three Wake Songs . . . and it is to be noted that these are the only wake songs, and are never used for any other purpose, or at any other time. Indeed, so careful are the people in this respect, that Dah kah-he-dond-yeh, who supplied this account of the game gives this as the reason why children are not allowed to attend wakes—hearing the songs, they might be tempted to sing them thoughtlessly in the course of play.

The singer for the time being may be seated anywhere on his own row, but the hiding must begin at one end, and the guessing at the far away end of the opposite row. To enable the guessers to point out the mocassin supposed to contain the object, a stick or switch, about a yard long is provided and passes from hand to hand. When the hider has done his part the moccasins are placed on the floor, and guessing goes on. As soon as a particular moccasin is pointed out some one who is nearest picks it up and gives it a rap on the floor. Should the sound indicate that the stone or marble, is in the moccasin, one stick is taken from a pile of a hundred splints about the size of lucifer matches, and is placed to the credit of the successful guesser's side. If the guesser desires to make two points in the game, he first lays, one above another, the three moccasins he takes to be empty. Should the remaining one be found to contain the object, his side gains 2. On the other hand, a failure on his part entails the loss of 2. As soon as a correct guess is made the singer ceases his performance and one on the winning side takes it up, and thus the game goes on, each man or woman hiding and guessing in turn.

At midnight the Head Man stops the game until a meal has been served in the usual way, and consisting of the usual kinds of food. On ceasing to play, the two men whose duty it is to keep count, arrange everything to avoid confusion or dispute when the game is resumed. Each puts the little sticks used as counters and won by his side into one of the moccasins; the remaining sticks into a third, and the stone or the marble into a fourth.

Before play begins after the meal the head man repeats his introductory ritual. Should one side win all the counters before daylight, he puts them again into one heap as at the beginning, and play goes on, but as soon as daylight gives the first sign of appearance he makes a change in the manner of conducting the game by appointing two men to act for each row of players, and for the purpose of still further shortening it, he may leave only two moccasins in their hands. Hiding and finding now follow each other quickly, but the sticks

---

[a] Archæological Report, 1899, p. 38, Toronto, 1900.

no longer go to show which side wins, for they are thrown by the head man into the fire, and the hiding and guessing are kept up by the same sides (i. e., without interchange) until all the counters are burnt. The same official then breaks the pointing sticks, which are also put into the fire, and he even treats the drumstick in the same way, having taken it from the hands of the singer. Last of all, he pulls the leather cover off the drum, puts it inside the drum, and replaces the hoop. The instrument should remain in this condition until it is to be again used.

Before the people disperse to their homes in the morning a gun is fired off outside of the door.

WYANDOT. Michigan.

Mr William E. Connelly [a] gives the following description of the moccasin game in an account of a game between a Wyandot and a Chippewa at Detroit in 1773:

Two only can play at this game. They are seated face to face on a buffalo or deer skin. Four new moccasins and a rifle ball make up the implements employed in the game. The moccasins are placed nearly equidistant, like a four-spot on a playing card. The players, seated crosslegged, facing each other, now toss up for the ball, or first "hide." The winner, taking the ball between his thumb and two fingers, proceeds with great dexterity, shuffling his hand under the first, second, third, and fourth moccasins, and humming a ditty, accompanied by some cabalistic words invoking the aid of his patron deity. It now comes to the opposing player to "find" at the first, second, or third "lift." If at the first, it counts a given number in his favor,—say 4; if at second, 2; and the third, 1. The latter player now takes the ball and goes through the same process. Ten usually constitutes the game, but the number is as the players may agree.

KERESAN STOCK

FIG. 458. Tubes for hiding game; height, 6¼ inches; Keres Indians, Acoma, New Mexico; cat. no. 4973, Brooklyn Institute Museum.

KERES. Acoma, New Mexico. (Cat. no. 4973, Brooklyn Institute Museum.)

Four cylinders of cottonwood (figure 458), 6¼ inches in height, painted black on the top and the bottom and having a black band around the middle. They were made for the writer by an Acoma Indian named James H. Miller (Kamitsa), at Zuñi, in 1904. He gave the name of the tubes as aiyawakotai. A small stone ball, yownikototei, is hidden.

———— Laguna, New Mexico. (Cat. no. 61817, Field Columbian Museum.)

Four cane tubes (figure 459), 4¼ inches in height; a small stick, 1¼ inches in length; a bundle of one hundred splint counting sticks, 4⅜ inches in length; and five individual counting sticks, four of them notched at one end, 7¾ inches in length (figure 460).

Cat. no. 61818. Another set of tubes, 3¼ inches in height.

[a] Wyandot Folklore, p. 112, Topeka, 1899. Mr Connelly in a note states that the story of the game was published in the Gazette, of Kansas City, Kansas, by Governor William Walker, some time in the sixties or early in the seventies.

Both sets were collected by Dr C. E. Lukens, who furnished the following account of the game under the name of iyawacutaeyae, to hide away over and over:

The game is played with four small tubes, closed at one end; one little piece of wood or pebble, small enough to hide in one of the tubes, and a bunch of one hundred small sticks and one larger one, which are counters. These counters are at first the common property of both sides, until paid out as forfeits; then each side must play with the sticks they have won. When one side loses all their sticks, they can take the larger one, called the na-catz, scalp, which is common property, and play with it four times. If they yet lose, the other side wins the game.

In beginning play the leaders of the two sides toss up for turns, one side hiding the little object, the other seeking it. B takes the bundle of one hundred counters and goes out. A hides the little object in one of the tubes and arranges them so as to deceive the seeker, placing them on end or side or in fantastic ways. B enters and chooses a tube; if he chooses the full one—that with the object in it—first, he forfeits ten sticks to A, who begins a private

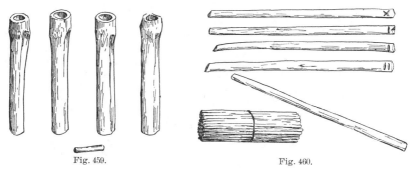

Fig. 459.   Fig. 460.

FIG. 459. Tubes for hiding game; height, 4¼ inches; Keres Indians, Laguna, New Mexico; cat. no. 61817, Field Columbian Museum.
FIG. 460. Counting sticks for hiding game; lengths, 4½ and 7¼ inches; Keres Indians, Laguna, New Mexico; cat. no. 61817, Field Columbian Museum.

bunch with them for his future use. Then A goes out while B hides the object. A enters; if he chooses one empty and next the full one, he pays B 6 sticks forfeit; if he chooses three empty and then the full one, he forfeits 4 sticks, and goes out again. But if A should have chosen two empty and next the full one, then they change sides; B takes what is left of the original one hundred sticks, leaving those he has gained in his bank, and goes out while A hides the object. A hides the object and B seeks, paying forfeits from the bunch as A did, and with these forfeits A begins a private bunch. When B chooses two empty ones and one full one, they change sides as before. When the original bundle is all paid out, they begin on their private store—i. e., the forfeits they have gained.

When one side loses all his sticks he takes up the one large stick, the scalp, and has four chances without paying forfeits. If he is lucky enough to guess so as to change sides, he may win more forfeits, and the game goes on interminably; but if he loses all of the chances he loses the game, and his opponent takes the wager. If one side should lose four, six, or ten, and have only two with which to pay, the two must answer the debt. During the guessing the opposing side sings and dances and prays that the spirits will so deceive the guessers as to make them lose.

KERES. Sia, New Mexico. (Cat. no. 60897, Field Columbian Museum.)
Set of four paper tubes, 2¾ inches in height, open at both ends and
marked with ink, as shown in figure 461. Collected by Annie M.
Sayre.

———— Sia, New Mexico.

Mrs Matilda Coxe Stevenson [a] describes the following game of this
type, as played by Poshaiyänne, the Sia culture hero, in his gambling
contest with the tribal priest:

Four circular sticks, some 8 inches long, with hollow ends, were stood in line
and a blanket thrown over them; the ti'ämoni then put
a round pebble into the end of one, and removing the
blanket asked Po'shaiyänne to choose the stick containing the pebble. "No, my father," said Po'shaiyänne,
"you first. What am I that I should choose before you?"
But the ti'ämoni replied, "I placed the stone; I know
where it is." Then Po'shaiyänne selected a stick and
raising it the pebble was visible. Po'shaiyänne then
threw the blanket over the sticks and placed the stone
in one of them, after which the ti'ämoni selected a stick
and raised it, but no stone was visible. This was repeated four times. Each time the ti'ämoni failed and
Po'shaiyänne succeeded.

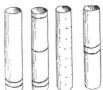

FIG. 461. Paper tubes for
hiding game; height, 2¼
inches; Keres Indians,
Sia, New Mexico; cat.
no. 60897, Field Colum-
bian Museum.

In the third contest the ti'ämoni made four
little mounds of sand, and, throwing a blanket over them, placed in
one a small round stone. The game proceeded in the same manner,
Poshaiyänne placing the stone four times and the ti'ämoni failing
each time. At the seventh and last contest the game of the pebble
and four hollow sticks was repeated with the same result.

PIMAN STOCK

PAPAGO. Mission of San Xavier del Bac, Pima county, Arizona.
(Field Columbian Museum.)

Cat. no. 63539. Four cane tubes, closed at one end with natural joint,
with etched designs filled in with colors, as shown in figure 462;
height, 8¼ inches.

Cat. no. 63511. Four cane tubes, similar to the above, but with incised marks in checker pattern (figure 463); height, 9½ inches.

These specimens were collected by Mr S. C. Simms, who gives the
name of the game as wahpetah, and describes it as follows:

This is a game of four wooden cups, in which something is concealed. One
may use any convenient thing; beans or corn will do. After the object is
concealed, the cups are filled with sand and handed to one's opponent. If he
first hands you back the one containing your bean, you gain 10; if the bean
is in the second, you gain 6; if in the third, 4; but if in the last one you lose
your turn and he conceals the bean. As soon as you give him the cup he

——————————

[a] The Sia. Eleventh Annual Report of the Bureau of Ethnology, p. 61, 1894.

empties it and conceals the bean again. The score is 50, the loser paying from a pile of fifty beans.

PAPAGO. Pima county, Arizona. (Cat. no. 74517, United States National Museum.)

Four single joints of reed (*Phragmitis communis*), each about $7\frac{1}{2}$ inches in length and 1 inch in diameter, having one end open, and the other closed by the natural diaphragm of the joint (figure 464).

They are marked with small squares, cut in simple patterns in the faces of the cylinders. By these designs they are separated into pairs, called the "old people" and the "young people." Scarlet chilacayote beans also belong to the game, each player usually possessing his private bean and one hundred grains of corn, or a greater number, as may be determined by the players prior to the game.

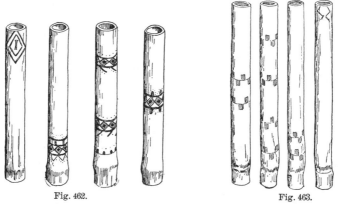

Fig. 462.   Fig. 463.

FIG. 462. Cane tubes for hiding game; height, $8\frac{1}{4}$ inches; Papago Indians, Pima county, Arizona; cat. no. 63539, Field Columbian Museum.
FIG. 463. Cane tubes for hiding game; height, $9\frac{1}{4}$ inches; Papago Indians, Pima county, Arizona; cat. no. 63511, Field Columbian Museum.

The four marked tubes receive the following names: Aks, old woman; kü li, old man; ho tes juk, made black; mä ok ju ool (merely a name).

These specimens were collected by Dr W J McGee and Mr William Dinwiddie in 1894. The following description is given by the collectors under the name of wapetaikhgut:

This is a gambling game much in vogue among the Papago Indians. Two contestants usually engage in the play, though any number may enter the same game. Before the game proper begins there is an initiatory struggle between the two players to gain possession of the reeds. Each of the contestants takes a pair of reeds, and, holding them vertically, with the opening up, in one hand, rapidly passes the other, in which a chilacayote bean is held, over the opening, dropping it into one of them when he considers the adversary sufficiently confused by the motion. Each fills his reeds full of sand from a small heap collected for the purpose, and throws them down before his opponent. Each chooses one of the other's prostrate reeds—the one thought to contain the bean. If both fail, or both succeed, in finding the bean in the same throw, the hiding operation is repeated. If one succeeds and the other fails, the four reeds go to the fortunate finder, and the game begins.

The possessor of all the reeds repeats the shuffling of the bean over their open tops, filling them with sand, and throwing them in front of his antago-nist, who separates them into pairs, usually the "old people" and "young people," though it is not compulsory so to pair them. He next crosses a pair by placing one above the other at right angles, selects one of the un-crossed reeds of the other pair—the one thought to con-tain the bean—and pours the sand from it. If he succeeds in finding the bean in this reed, all the reeds immediately go to him, and he in turn performs the operation just described, his opponent doing the guessing. If he fails to do so, the position of the reed containing the beans counts so many grains of corn to the man who places the bean, the top-crossed reed being worth 10, the under-crossed 6, and the single reed 4.

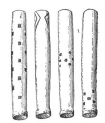

FIG. 464. Cane tubes for hiding game; length, 7½ inches; Papago In-dians, Pima county, Arizona; cat. no. 74517, United States Na-tional Museum.

The counters, or grains of corn, are first placed on one side, all together, and each player draws his winnings from this pile, or bank, until it is exhausted; then the exchange is made directly from the winnings of the players until one or the other has lost all his corn. The possessor of all the grain becomes the winner of the game.

So long as the player attempting to name the reed containing the bean fails to do so, his opponent is winning and holds possession of the reeds, repeating the operation of placing the bean and filling the reeds with sand until the proper reed is guessed.

FIG. 465. Papago Indians playing hiding game; Arizona; from photograph by William Dinwiddie.

PIMA. Gila River reservation, Sacaton agency, Pinal county, Ari-zona. (Cat. no. 63289, Field Columbian Museum.)

Four cane tubes (figure 466), 6¾ inches in length, tops closed with natural joints, faces marked with transverse cuts, painted black, arranged differently to distinguish the tubes.

Collected by Mr S. C. Simms, who gives the name of the game as wakpethgoodt.

PIMA.   Arizona.   (Cat. no. 218043, United States National Museum.)

Four joints of reed (figure 467) engraved with marks, 8½ inches in length.   These were collected by the late Dr Frank Russell, who describes the game played with them as follows:[a]

Vâpûtai, "Lay."   A guessing game in which a number of players act as assistants to two leaders.   A small bean[b] is used by the Papago and a ball of black

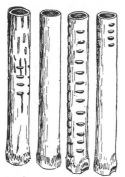

mesquite gum by the Pima.   It is placed in one of four joints of reed.   The reeds are then filled with sand, all being concealed under a blanket, and the opponents guess which reed contains the ball.   The reeds are called vâpûtakŭt, "laying implements."

Reed no. 1, called kuli, "old man," has 17 longitudinal rows of 8 spots each.

Reed no. 2, âks, "old woman," is unmarked.

Reed no. 3, hota stcok, "middle black," has 6 longitudinal rows.

Reed no. 4, ma-atcovolt, has 5 rows around the open end.

FIG. 466. Cane tubes for hiding game; length, 6¼ inches; Pima Indians, Arizona; cat. no. 63289, Field Columbian Museum.

One hundred grains of corn are placed between the players in a hole, from which it is taken as won and placed in a hole in front of each player.   When a player wins all the corn he puts up a stick in the sand.   The number of the sticks may be from 1 to 10, as determined beforehand.   Each player cancels one of his opponent's sticks when he wins one himself.

Two players confine their attention to the guessing; one on each side fills the reeds; one on each side watches the counting.   Four men, one at each corner, hold the blanket under which the filling is done, and sometimes offer suggestions to the leaders.   The "old people," the plain and the marked reeds, are kept together, and the "young people" are used by the opponents.   When the two pairs are filled with sand and a bean or ball is concealed in each pair, the blanket is dropped and the reeds are laid in the center, each filler handing his pair over to the side of his opponent.   If A guesses wrong and B right, they exchange reeds and begin again.   If both guess right, there is no count.   When one guesses right he takes the four reeds and places his ball in one, and the opponent then decides which pair it is in by laying one reed across the other in the pair which he thinks does not contain it.   Then he pours out the sand of first one then the other.   If he has guessed right he does not score, but continues the play by filling and offering to his opponent.   If he guesses wrong, the opponent scores 4 and 6 additional if the ball is in the under reed; 10 if it is in the upper.

FIG. 467. Tubes for hiding game; Pima Indians, Arizona; cat. no. 218043, United States National Museum.

Cheating is done in various ways, but there is reason to believe that this practice has arisen since they have come in contact with the whites.

ZUAQUE.   Rio Fuerte, Sinaloa, Mexico.

Mr C. V. Hartman informs me that a guessing game is played by

---

[a] In a memoir to be published by the Bureau of American Ethnology.

[b] Obtained from Sonora from the tree called paowi by the Pima and chilicoti by the Mexicans.

these Indians on the river banks in conical sand heaps which they form for the purpose.

It is a game with four hollow pieces of reed and a bean [figure 468], el juego de cañulos y chilicote. The four hollow reed pieces are filled with sand, and in one of these the red chilacayote bean is hidden. The four reeds are then placed in the sand heap and guesses are made for the bean. But the reeds are also marked with numbers that are counted and have their value for the players. When a game is finished, the party who have lost have to sing the song of this game, while the winners fill the reeds anew with sand and hide the bean. The song begins : " Wa'-ka-tä'-na-hi'-ǟ, sa-na'-na-na-jä̇ ." The bean is of a small tree, *Erythrina*

FIG. 468. Chilacayote beans for hiding game; Zuaque Indians, Sinaloa, Mexico.

coralloide (D. C.), and has the peculiar property, as a Tarahumare Indian showed me, of becoming burning hot if rubbed only for a second against a somewhat rough stone. The bean is poisonous and is used by the Tarahumare for poisoning dogs, etc.

SHOSHONEAN STOCK

Hopi. Walpi, Arizona. (Cat. no. 166715, United States National Museum.)

Set of four unpainted cottonwood cylinders (figure 469), 6 inches in height and 2¼ inches in diameter, with cylindrical opening at one end, 1¼ inches deep and 1 inch in diameter; marked with burned lines, and having a down feather stuck in the top of each, as shown in figure 469. Collected by Mr James Mooney in 1892.

Fig. 469.

Fig. 470.

FIG. 469. Wooden tubes for hiding game; height, 6 inches; Hopi Indians, Walpi, Arizona; cat. no. 166715, United States National Museum.

FIG. 470. Wooden tubes for hiding game; height, 3½ inches; Hopi Indians, Arizona; cat. no. 21828, Free Museum of Science and Art, University of Pennsylvania.

———— Arizona. (Cat. no. 21828, Free Museum of Science and Art, University of Pennsylvania.)

Four cottonwood cups, 2 inches in diameter and 3½ inches in height, with rounded tops, and marked with burnt lines, having conical holes 1⅛ inches in diameter and 1¼ inches in depth in the bottom, one cup having an additional mark, as shown in figure 470.

Collected by Mr Thomas V. Keam, of Keams canyon, Arizona, who furnished the following account:

Name of tubes, sho-se-vah; name of game, sho-sho-tukia. The game consists of 10 points. It is played during the winter month of January in the kivas (estufas) by two or more individuals. When the tubes are being placed over the object they are hidden from the view of the contesting party by a blanket. A small round sandstone pebble is the object used. It is placed under one of the tubes, and the contesting side calls out the figure marked on the tube under which the pebble is supposed to be, and at the same time lifts the tube. If it exposes the pebble and is done with the right hand, it counts 2 points; if done with the left, it counts 1. Should he turn three and not find the pebble, it counts 1 against him. When the 10 points are won by the outs, they take the stake and assume control of the game, which is sometimes prolonged during the night.

Hopi. Walpi, Arizona. (Cat. no. 41885, United States National Museum.)

Set of four wooden cylinders, 3¼ inches in length and 2 inches in diameter, with hemispherical opening three-fourths of an inch deep and 1 inch in diameter; marked with bands of white paint. Collected by Col. James Stevenson in 1884.

———— Walpi, Arizona. (Cat. no. 55380, Field Columbian Museum.)

Four cone-shaped cottonwood cups, 6¾ inches in height, with rounded tops, marked with burned bands and symbolic designs, as shown in figure 471. They are an ancient set and came from the Powamu altar. Collected by Dr George A. Dorsey.

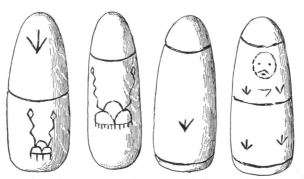

Fig. 471. Wooden tubes for hiding game; height, 6¾ inches; Hopi Indians, Walpi, Arizona; cat. no. 55380, Field Columbian Museum.

———— Oraibi, Arizona. (Cat. no. 22550, United States National Museum.)

Set of four unpainted wooden cylinders (figures 472–475), 6 inches in height and 2¼ inches in diameter, with hemispherical charred opening at one end, seven-eighths of an inch deep and 1¼ inches in diameter. Collected by Maj. J. W. Powell in 1876.

The external surfaces are marked with burned designs of rain cloud and five-pointed star, eagle and butterfly, bear's paw, and eagle and Sho-tuk-nung-wa, the Heart of the Sky god.

HOPI. Oraibi, Arizona. (Cat. no. 67056, Field Columbian Museum.)

Set of four wooden cylinders, 1½ inches in diameter, three of them 3¼ inches in height, with top carved to represent a cloud terrace,

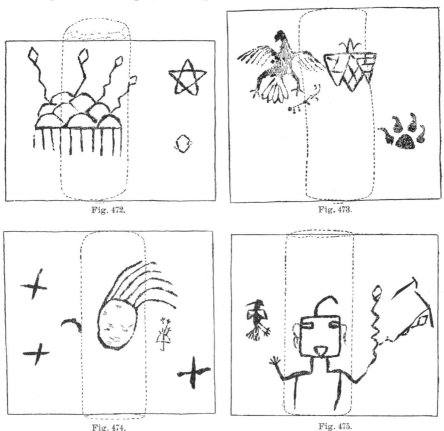

Fig. 472.   Fig. 473.

Fig. 474.   Fig. 475.

FIG. 472-475. Wooden tubes for hiding game; height, 6 inches; Hopi Indians, Oraibi, Arizona; cat. no. 22550, United States National Museum.

and one 3 inches in height, with a deep groove cut near the upper part, within which is tied a string of beads, thirty-four of blue glass and five of coral (figure 476). This last cylinder has a hemispherical opening at both top and bottom, while the others have such an opening only at the bottom. Collected by Rev. H. R. Voth.

———— Oraibi, Arizona. (Cat. no. 67055, Field Columbian Museum.)

Set of four cottonwood cylinders (figure 477), new and unpainted, two of them 3 inches high and 1½ inches in diameter, and two 2¾ inches high and 1¼ inches in diameter.

All have deep conical orifices at the bottom and have tops carved with heads representing masks, the Koyemsi katcina. They were collected by Rev. H. R. Voth, who gave the following description:

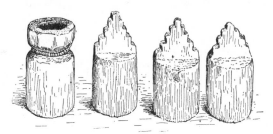

FIG. 476. Wooden tubes for hiding game; heights, 3 and 3¼ inches; Hopi Indians, Oraibi, Arizona; cat. no. 67056, Field Columbian Museum.

Although this is principally a woman's game, men occasionally take part in it. The four wooden objects are hollow at the end which is set in the ground. The form of the upper end differs in different sets; sometimes it represents the Hopi terraced cloud symbol, sometimes that of a particular katcina mask, as in the present example, and sometimes each of the four blocks in a set represents

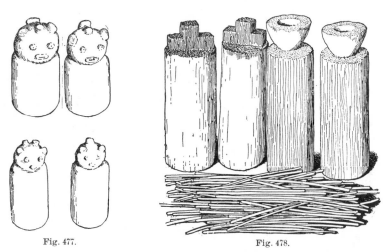

Fig. 477.   Fig. 478.

FIG. 477. Wooden tubes for hiding game; heights, 2½ and 3 inches; Hopi Indians, Oraibi, Arizona; cat. no. 67055, Field Columbian Museum.

FIG. 478. Wooden tubes and counting sticks for hiding game; height, 4½ inches; Hopi Indians, Oraibi, Arizona; cat. no. 38614, Free Museum of Science and Art, University of Pennsylvania.

a different katcina. In playing, two opposing sides are chosen, each of which may consist of several members. The blocks are then placed on the floor and a small ball, a bean, or similar object is hidden in a dexterous manner under one of the blocks. The opposite side is then challenged to guess the block under which the object is hidden. If a correct guess is made, the guessing side plays ; if not, the other side again hides the object, and so on. The object in the game, as well as the details in playing it, have not yet been studied.

HOPI. Oraibi, Arizona. (Cat. no. 38614, Free Museum of Science and Art, University of Pennsylvania.)

Four cottonwood cylinders (figure 478), with carved tops, two alike, with cloud terrace at top painted red, the body of the cylinder being blue; and two with a kind of inverted cone at top painted blue, the body being red; height, 4½ inches; accompanied by fifty counting sticks. Collected by the writer in 1901.

The game, bakshiwu, is played by women. A ball, piliata, nodule, is hidden under one of the four cups, and the object is to guess under which it is concealed. The game is counted with fifty sticks, mori, beans. In guessing the cup is knocked down with the hand, and the game proceeds in rhythm with a song. The cups with the cloud terrace at top are called kopachakitaka, headdress man, and the others with inverted cones like flowers, flute blossom.

—— Walpi, Arizona. (Cat. no. 68874, United States National Museum.)

Set of four cottonwood cylinders (figure 479), two surmounted with cloud terrace symbols, 2¾ and 3¼ inches in height, and two plain, formerly with a projection at the top that has been cut off, 2¾ inches in height. Collected by Col. James Stevenson.

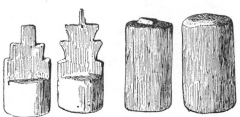

FIG. 479. Wooden tubes for hiding game; heights, 2¾ and 3¼ inches; Hopi Indians, Walpi, Arizona; cat. no. 68874, United States National Museum.

—— Arizona.

Dr J. Walter Fewkes writes as follows in a personal letter :[a]

Although I have not given special attention to the Hopi games, I was able to make a few observations on a cup game which the Tewa of Hano call penici ; the Walpi, cocotukwi. During the month Pamüyawû, or January and part of February, 1900, it was played almost constantly, both in and out of the kivas, in the three towns on the East mesa. The cones used had various markings, and those at Hano had bands called by the following names [figure 480] : a, with three bands on, poyopeni ; b, with two bands, wihipeni ; c, with one band around top, kepeni ; d, with one median band, penopeni. The game was played for several consecutive days in the plaza of Sichomovi by women of different clans, the two sides—one from Hano, the other from Sichomovi—standing opposite each other or seated, as the case may be. Both parties had a wooden drum, and the party having the cones sang vigorously and beat their drums with great

---

[a] July, 1902.

glee. The party not holding cones were silent. The cones were arranged in a row, as shown in the figure [481]. When the stone or marble was placed under one of the cones, all the members of the party owning the cones crowded about them and held up their blankets to prevent the opposite side seeing under which

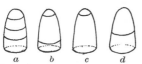

FIG. 480. Tubes for hiding game; Tewa Indians, Hano, Arizona; from sketch by Dr J. Walter Fewkes.

cone the stone was placed. Certain mysterious passes were made when the stone was placed below the cone. The women then seated themselves in a row and invited their opponents to play, or to find the stone concealed under one of the cones. The party then sang loudly, and a man beat the drum as the representative of the opposite party advanced to lift the cone under which he supposed the stone was hidden. There were loud jeers and much bantering back and forth. Bets were made on the game, and it became very exciting, at times lasting the whole afternoon. The details of winning were not noted, but if the one of the opposite party uncovered the stone at the first trial, the cones went to the party to which he belonged. The winners then set up the cones, sang songs, and beat their drum as their opponents before them had done when they held the cones. Figure [481] shows the members of one side with the cones before them and the drummer on one side, made from a group in the plaza, January 12, 1900.

Cocotukwi was played in the Walpi kivas almost continuously from January 12 to February 3; after Powamû began, it was not noted, and it was said to be

FIG. 481. Plaza cocotukwi at Sichomovi, Arizona; from photograph by Dr J. Walter Fewkes.

a game of Pamuyanû—January moon. It always took place at night, never in two kivas on the same night, and followed in rotation from the Moñkiva to the Alkiva. The men gathered first in the kiva and the women came to the hatch and called down to those within that they wanted firewood. The men replied: " Come down and gamble for it at cocotukwi." In the kiva cocotukwi men and women were on opposite sides. If the men lost, they had to " get firewood," but I did not hear what would be the penalty if the women lost. I followed the game one night (January 12) in the Moñkiva. After all were seated, Kakapti, chief of the Sand clan, brought in a bag of sand and emptied it before the fireplace. He took a stick and in a field of this sand which had been carefully spread on the floor made a rectangular figure, across which he drew a pair of lines making a central rectangle, on each side of which he made five parallel grooves [figure 482]. In the smaller central rectangle he made, unknown to me, cabalistic figures, tracing them in the sand, laughingly referring to their names as he did so, the assembled players joking with him or making suggestions. In counting, two short twigs were used, and these were advanced from one to the other of these sand grooves in much the same way that sticks are used in pachtli.[a] Each side had a stick and Kakapti kept account. The mode of counting, as I remember, resembled that of pachtli. The sticks were advanced as one side or the other won. When the party which uncovered the stone did not expose it after two trials it remained with the side which held the cones; to uncover at the first trial counted more than at the second attempt. Different cones seemed to have different values. The cones used were not marked like those at Hano, but were of wood and of about the same shape. There was the same singing, shouting, and laughter as in the plaza game.

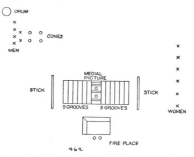

FIG. 482. Plan of kiva hiding game; Hopi Indians, Walpi, Arizona; from sketch by Dr J. Walter Fewkes.

I have found one of these cones made of lava stone in one of the Little Colorado ruins, and Dr Frank Russell has shown me another which he found in the Gila region. I believe that some of the small stone marbles found in the ruins had to do with this game. To relieve the monotony of the long vigils in the kivas between the ceremonies I have sometimes played an informal game of cocotukwi with some youth who was there, picking up the cones from the banquette and trying to see how many times each of us could uncover the stone in the same number of trials. Once or twice I have seen young men play a private game of cocotukwi in this way, but not often.

Mr A. M. Stephen in an unpublished manuscript gives the Hopi name of a game played with a stone nodule concealed under one of four cups as socotüküya and again as socütükiyuñwuh:

The game is played by two parties of grown persons, each usually composed of a large number, seated and facing each other a short distance apart. The implements used are four cylindric wooden cups somewhat resembling large diceboxes, a small stone nodule, and a stout wooden club. After tossing a corn husk or a leaf with a blackened side to decide which shall begin, the party which wins the toss set the four cups in a line in front of their group and conceal them from the opposite side by holding a blanket up as a screen, and then they hide the nodule under one of the cups. The blanket being withdrawn, a person from the challenged side walks across and takes the club in his hand, and after much deliberation turns over one of the cups with the club. If the nodule is not exposed, he turns over another, and the nodule not being found, the crisis of his play is reached, for the object is to uncover the nodule at the third attempt. If then found, his party scores a count, and they take the implements to their side, and conceal the nodule as the first party had done. If, however, the player uncovers the nodule before, or fails to find it

---

[a] Tewa game, corresponding to patolli.

at his third attempt, the challenging party scores a count and again repeats the concealment. The concealing, or challenging, side continue to sing vigorously as long as they continue to gain, ceasing only when they lose, when the other side takes up the songs. These are very numerous and of special interest, as they are wholly of a mythologic character.

SIOUAN STOCK

DAKOTA (OGLALA). Pine Ridge reservation, South Dakota. (Cat. no. 22114 to 22116, Free Museum of Science and Art, University of Pennsylvania.)

A piece of shaved horn (figure 483), nearly round, three-eighths of an inch in diameter and $1\frac{7}{8}$ inches in length; two sharpened sticks of cedar (figure 484), one light and one dark, $8\frac{1}{2}$ inches in length; bundle of twelve counting sticks (figure 485), cuwinyawa, peeled saplings, painted red, 15 inches in length.

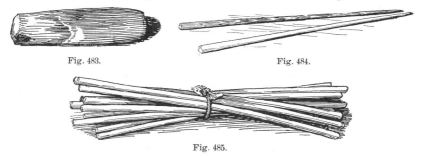

Fig. 483.　　　　　　　　Fig. 484.

Fig. 485.

FIG. 483. Hiding horn for moccasin game; length, $1\frac{7}{8}$ inches; Oglala Dakota Indians, Pine Ridge reservation, South Dakota; cat. no. 22114, Free Museum of Science and Art, University of Pennsylvania.

FIG. 484. Pointing sticks for moccasin game; length, $8\frac{1}{2}$ inches; Oglala Dakota Indians, Pine Ridge reservation, South Dakota; cat. no. 22115, Free Museum of Science and Art, University of Pennsylvania.

FIG. 485. Counting sticks for moccasin game; length, 15 inches; Oglala Dakota Indians, Pine Ridge reservation, South Dakota; cat. no. 22116, Free Museum of Science and Art, University of Pennsylvania.

These objects are described by the collector, Mr Louis L. Meeker,[a] as implements used in the guessing game, hanpapecu, i. e., moccasin game:

A small bit of horn [figure 483] is concealed in one or the other of one player's hands, and the other player guesses which hand; or the same object is concealed in one of two, three, or four moccasins, and the other player guesses which one contains the horn. Should he have doubts, he can draw the game by guessing which does not contain it, and guess on the remaining two for a chance for the next play.

Two sharpened sticks of cedar, cuwinyawa [figure 484], one of the light sapwood, the other of dark heartwood, are held by the guesser, though but one is his. If he uses his own to pull a moccasin toward him, he means that the object concealed is in it. If he uses his partner's stick he pushes the object

[a] Ogalala Games. Bulletin of the Free Museum of Science and Art, v. 3, p. 29, Philadelphia, 1901.

from him, indicating that the object is not concealed in that moccasin. The counters are sticks [figure 485], sometimes used to play odd or even.

Recently this game became so popular upon the Pine Ridge agency that it was necessary to prohibit it entirely.

The moccasin player observes certain physiognomical signs which he regards as indicating which of the moccasins contains the bit of horn or " bullet." The Ogalala dialect contains a long list of words like our smile, sneer, squint, frown, etc., applied to the twitching of the muscles of the limbs as well as to those of the face. It is said that English will not express all or even the greater part of these terms. They seem to have arisen from the necessities of the game.

DAKOTA (SANTEE). Minnesota.

Mr Philander Prescott describes the game in Schoolcraft[a] as follows:

The play of moccasins is practised by the men, and large bets are made. In this game they take sides; one party playing against the other. One side will sing, whilst one man of the other party hides the ball in a moccasin.

There are three moccasins used for the purpose. The man takes the ball or stick between his thumb and forefinger, and slips it from one moccasin to another several times, and leaves it in one of them and then stops, something like thimble-play. The party that have been singing have to guess in which moccasin the ball is; for which purpose one man is chosen. If he guesses where the ball is the first time, he loses. Should the ball not be in the moccasin that he guesses the first time, he can try again. He has now two moccasins for a choice. He has now to guess which one the ball is in. If he is successful, he wins: if not, he loses. So they have only one chance in two of winning. When one side loses, the other side give up the moccasins to the other party to try their luck awhile at hiding the ball. They have no high numbers in the games.

Rev. E. D. Neill [b] says:

One of their games is like " Hunt the Slipper; " a bullet or plum stone is placed by one party in one of four moccasins or mittens and sought for by the opposite.

Riggs [c] gives the following definition:

Haŋ'-pa-a-pe, haŋ'pa-a-pe-ćon-pi—a game in which a bullet is hid in one of four moccasins or mittens, and sought for by the opposite party; han'-pa, moccasins.

IOWA. Missouri.

George Catlin [d] describes the game as follows:
Ing-kee-ko-kee (Game of the Moccasin).

> " Take care of yourself—shoot well, or you lose.
> 　　You warned me, but see! I have defeated you!
> I am one of the Great Spirit's children,
> 　　Wa-konda I am! I am Wa-konda! "

This song is sung in this curious and most exciting, as well as fascinating game, which is played by two, or four, or six—seated on the ground in a circle,

---

[a] Information respecting the History, Condition, and Prospects of the Indian Tribes of the United States, pt. 4, p. 64, Philadelphia, 1854.

[b] Dakota Land and Dakota Life (1853). Minnesota Historical Collections, v. 1, p. 280, St. Paul, 1872.

[c] Dakota-English Dictionary. Contributions to North American Ethnology, v. 7, p. 124, Washington, 1890.

[d] The George Catlin Indian Gallery, p. 151, Washington, 1886.

with three or four moccasins lying on the ground; when one lifts each moccasin in turn, and suddenly darts his right hand under each, dropping a little stone, the size of a hazelnut, under one of the moccasins, leaving his adversary to hit on one or the other, and to take the counter and the chance if he chooses the one under which the stone is dropped. This is, perhaps, one of the silliest-looking games to the spectator, but it all goes to music, and in perfect time, and often for hours together without intermission, and forms one of the principal gambling games of these gambling people.

OMAHA. Nebraska.

Rev. J. Owen Dorsey [a] describes the following game:

In'-utin', Hitting the stone, is a game played at night. Sometimes there are twenty, thirty, or forty players on each side. Four moccasins are placed in a row, and a member of one party covers them, putting in one of them some small object that can be easily concealed. Then he says, "Come! hit the moccasin in which you think it is." Then one of the opposite side is chosen to hit the moccasin. He arises, examines all, and hits one. Should it be empty, they say, "Çiñgĕĕ hă," it is wanting. He throws it far aside and forfeits his stakes. Three moccasins remain for the rest of his friends to try. Should one of them hit the right one (uskan'skan utin' or ukan'ska utin'), he wins the stakes, and his side has the privilege of hiding the object in the moccasin. He who hits the right moccasin can hit again and again until he misses. Sometimes it is determined to change the rule for winning, and then the guesser aims to avoid the right moccasin the first time, but to hit it when he makes the second trial. Should he· hit the right one the first time he loses his stakes. If he hits the right one when he hits the second moccasin, he wins, and his side has the right to hide the object. They play till one side or the other has won all the sticks or stakes. Sometimes there are players who win back what they have lost. He who takes the right moccasin wins four sticks, or any other number which may be fixed upon by previous agreement.

Eight sticks win a blanket; four win leggings; one hundred sticks, a full-grown horse; sixty sticks, a colt; ten sticks, a gun; one, an arrow; four, a knife or a pound of tobacco; two, half a pound of tobacco. Buffalo robes (meha), otter skins, and beaver skins are each equal to eight sticks. Sometimes they stake moccasins.

When one player wins all his party yell. The men of each party sit in a row, facing their opponents, and the moccasins are placed between them.

Mr Francis La Flesche described the same game to the writer under the name of i-u-teh, strike the stone:

Four men play, two against two, sitting on the ground vis-à-vis, and using four moccasins and two balls of buffalo hair about half an inch in diameter. One side hides and the opponents guess, the hiders singing songs, of which there are several. The game is also played with the hands by four players, one of whom tosses the ball from one hand to the other.

WINNEBAGO. Wisconsin.

Mr Reuben G. Thwaites [b] gives the following account, from an interview with Moses Paquette:

The moccasin game is the chief one. It somewhat resembles three-card monte, except that I do not think there is any cheating about it. The players

[a] Omaha Sociology. Third Annual Report of the Bureau of Ethnology, p. 339, 1884.
[b] The Wisconsin Winnebagoes. Collections of the State Historical Society of Wisconsin, v. 12, p. 425, Madison, 1892.

squat on the ground in two groups, facing each other; any number may be on a side—one or a dozen—and the sides need not be equal in numbers. On the ground between the two groups, four moccasins are placed in a row. The leader of the side that has the "deal," so to speak, takes a small bead in his right hand and deftly slides the hand under each moccasin in turn, pretending to leave the bead under each one of them; he finally does leave the bead under one, and the leader of the opposition side, watching him closely, is to guess which moccasin covers the bead. The opposition leader then takes a slender stick and lifts up and throws off the three moccasins under which he thinks nothing has been left, leaving the one under which he guesses the bead has been left. Should the bead be discovered under one of three which he throws off, then he loses 4 points for his side; should he be correct in his guess, and the bead found under the one moccasin left, he gains 4 for his side. Ten small twigs or chips are conveniently at hand, and as each side wins at a play, the leader takes 4 from the pile. When the ten are all taken, by either or both sides, the game is ended, the side having the most sticks being the winner. Usually five such games are played, the side getting the greater number taking the stakes, which are commonly goods—although once in a while they gamble for money.

TANOAN STOCK

TEWA.   Hano, Arizona.

Mr A. M. Stephen in his unpublished manuscript gives the Tewa

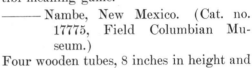

name of the game with a stone nodule concealed under one of four cups as tibi elua, tibi meaning game.

——— Nambe, New Mexico. (Cat. no. 17775, Field Columbian Museum.)

Four wooden tubes, 8 inches in height and 1¼ inches in diameter, marked with lines as shown in figure 486.

These were collected by Mr L. M. Lampson, who describes them as employed in the game of angea, or cañute,[a] played by two parties, each composed of any number of players.

FIG. 486. Wooden tubes for hiding game; height, 8 inches; Tewa Indians, Nambe, New Mexico; cat. no. 17775, Field Columbian Museum.

To begin the game, two of the cups, in one of which a nail is placed, are laid down with the open ends covered. A player from one side chooses a cup, and if the nail is in the first one chosen the cups go to his side. The object of each party of players is to secure and keep the cañates as long as possible.

A bowl containing one hundred and four beans is placed in charge of two men, who act as cashiers for their respective sides. Two heaps of earth are placed in a room at opposite sides and surrounded by the members of the opposing parties. A player from the side which is in possession of the cups, with his arms concealed under a blanket, places the nail in one of them and covers the open ends of all of them with earth.

A player comes over from the other side and endeavors to select at his third choice the cup in which the nail is hidden, with the following result: If found in the first cup taken up, the cashier for his party must pay to the opposing

—————————————————————————————

[a] Spanish cañuto, part of a cane from knot to knot.

party's cashier 10 beans; if in the second, 6 beans; if in the fourth, 4 beans; but if in the third, the player returns to his own side with the cups, which are retained by his party until they are won from them in the manner described.

The cashiers on both sides pay the 10, 6, or 4 beans which may be lost by their players finding the nail in any cup but the third one, from the common pool until the one hundred and four beans have been exhausted, after which they must pay from their winnings until one side or the other obtains the whole number and thereby wins the game, which is usually played for a stake.

The cups are named individually according to the marking on the ends, as follows:

I, one; II, two; + mulato; ∴ cinchado, girded.

These names do not signify different values, but are used in the songs which the party in possession of the cups sing during the game.

TEWA. Santa Clara, New Mexico. (Cat. no. 176706, United States National Museum.)

Four hollow cylinders of wood, closed at one end, $9\frac{1}{2}$ inches long and $1\frac{1}{4}$ inches in diameter, with an internal bore of eleven-sixteenths of an inch. They are marked by burning with the designs shown in figure 487. The closed ends are also differently marked, as in the figure. They are accompanied with a small, round, unpainted stick $2\frac{1}{2}$ inches in length.

Another set in the Free Museum of Science and Art of the University of Pennsylvania (cat. no. 21585) are 11 inches in length and $1\frac{1}{8}$ inches in diameter, and are similarly marked (figure 488). The stick accompanying them, $2\frac{7}{8}$ inches in length, varies in being painted with bands of the colors green, red, black, yellow, green, yellow, black, red, green.

Mr Thomas S. Dozier, of Española, New Mexico, who collected both the above-mentioned sets, writes in reference to the latter that it was made for him by an Indian. He was unable to purchase old sets, because the Mexicans and Indians who own them place an excessive value on them from superstitious motives. Mr Dozier furnished the following account of the game:

Cañute is a winter game and is played usually at night and within doors. The implements are the four hollow tubes of wood, the small stick which passes readily in and out of the hollow tubes, a large cup holding an agreed number of grains of corn, beans, or peas, and two small cups, held by opposing players, which are empty when the game begins.

Two small heaps of loose dry earth, perhaps half a bushel each, are erected at each end of the room, about which the opposing bettors sit or stand. The small stick is inserted secretly in one of the tubes, and then all are buried in that pile of dirt which belongs to the side secreting the stick. A player from the opposing side is then chosen by his side to draw the sticks. The counts are as follows: If the stick is found in the first tube drawn, 10 grains are taken from the large cup and placed in the cup of the side drawing the tubes; if found in the second tube, 6 grains; and if found in the fourth tube, 4 grains are taken; but if the stick be found in the third tube, then the tubes are taken to the opposite pile of dirt, where the opposing side will bury the tubes, and the others must draw. Thus the tubes are moved from one side to the other, as the sides are lucky or unlucky. The players hiding the stick are supposed to have the advantage. There is no count when the tubes are changed. In drawing the tubes, sometimes the drawer announces his choice before he draws. In this case he announces that the stick will be found in such and such a tube,

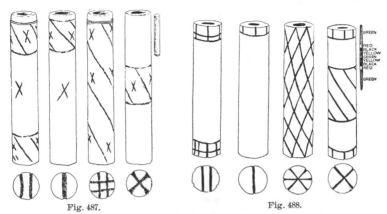

Fig. 487.   Fig. 488.

FIG. 487. Wooden tubes for hiding game; height, 9¼ inches; Tewa Indians, Santa Clara, New Mexico; cat. no. 176706, United States National Museum.

FIG. 488. Wooden tubes for hiding game; height, 11 inches; Tewa Indians, Santa Clara, New Mexico; cat. no. 21585, Free Museum of Science and Art, University of Pennsylvania.

naming the tube. The names of the tubes, which are distinguished by their markings, are pin-do-ĕ (pin-dō-tsĭ-kī), Spanish cinchado, girthed; sĕn-dō', Sp. viejo, old; wĕ-pĭ', Sp. uno, one; wĕ'-gĭ, Sp. dos, two.   This is only an incident in the game, the draws and counts proceeding always in accordance with the rules given. This account might be prolonged greatly by the relation of mere incidents, such as the singing, the hiding of the stick, some peculiar ceremonies antecedent to, and some following after, the game. This is undoubtedly an Indian game, though it can not have originated among the Tewan pueblos. It is known among them as cañute, a name certainly coming from the Spanish caña, a reed. This same name obtains among the Utes and Apaches, tribes closely associated with the Pueblos. The Santa Claras sometimes call the game kä-kū'-wa-ĕ-pfe, meaning the inclosed or shut up (tapado) stick; it does not mean exactly "the hidden stick." Kä-ku-wä means to inclose, shut up, Spanish tapar. This is a mere designation, however appropriate it may sound, there being other designations of a like appropriate nature among other Tewan pueblos and, for that matter, among the Santa Claras themselves.

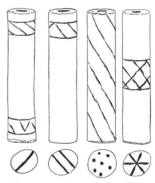

FIG. 489. Wooden tubes for hiding game; height, 6⅜ inches; Tigua Indians, Taos, New Mexico; cat. no. 21593, Free Museum of Science and Art, University of Pennsylvania.

TIGUA. Taos, New Mexico. (Cat. no. 21593, Free Museum of Science and Art, University of Pennsylvania.)

Four hollow cylinders of wood closed at one end, 6⅜ inches in height and 1⅔ inches in diameter, with an internal bore of three-eighths of an inch; marked, by burning, with the designs shown in figure 489.

The closed ends are also differently marked. Except for the slight variations in the markings they are identical with the preceding sets from Santa Clara. They are described by the collector and donor, Dr T. P. Martin, of Taos, as used in the game of cañute.

The sticks, in the same order as the preceding ones, receive the following names: Cinchow (colloquial for cinchado), girthed; mulata (mulato), tawny; una, one; dos, two.

The object concealed is a small stick or sometimes a nail. An Indian takes the four sticks and, placing them under his blanket, conceals the small stick in one of the openings. He then withdraws them and lays them on the ground with the openings either buried in a pile of dirt or pointed toward him. An opposing player, who sits opposite the one who conceals the object, then chooses one. If he selects the tube on his right and it contains the object, he pays the dealer 10 grains of corn, beads, or whatever the game is played for. If he selects the second and it contains the object, he pays 6 to the dealer. If he selects the chinchow and it contains the object, the dealer pays him 4. If he selects the mulata and finds the object, he takes up the sticks and becomes the dealer; the former dealer becomes the player, and the game continues.

WAKASHAN STOCK

Kwakiutl. Vancouver island, British Columbia.

Dr Franz Boas [a] describes a game called mokoa:

This game was introduced from the Nootka. It is played between tribes. An object is given to a member of one tribe, who hides it. Then four members of another tribe must guess where it is. They are allowed to guess four times. If they miss every time, they have lost. This game is played for very high stakes.

YUMAN STOCK

Maricopa. Arizona. (Cat. no. 2923, Brooklyn Institute Museum.) Four cane tubes, 9½ inches in length, with closed joint at one end, cut and painted (figure 490), and small wooden ball painted black.

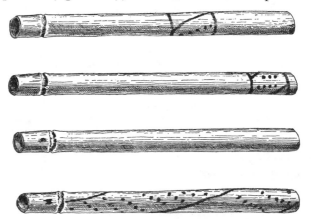

Fig. 490. Cane tubes for hiding game; length, 9½ inches; Maricopa Indians, Arizona; cat. no. 2923, Brooklyn Institute Museum.

[a] Sixth Report on the Indians of British Columbia. Report of the Sixty-sixth Meeting of the British Association for the Advancement of Science, p. 578, London, 1896.

Collected in 1904 by Mr Louis L. Meeker, who describes this game under the name of ta-thulsh:

The speckled reed is called kota-aks, old man, and the blank reed, ako-ash, old woman. The reed marked in the center is called tok-gum-yorsh, and the one marked at the end (mouth marks) hiya quimyorsh. The ball is called ne hatch, pet or live stock.

The ball is concealed in one of the reeds, and the opponent endeavors to guess in which one it is hidden. If he fails, the other player shows which contains the ball, and the original guesser tries once again.

Mr Meeker describes a similar game as follows:

Ch-alh, stick in sand. A stick is concealed in one of four heaps of sand or dust, and the opponent, who has absented himself, returns and guesses which heap contains the stick.

WALAPAI. Walapai reservation, Arizona. (Cat. no. 63210, Field Columbian Museum.)

Implements (figure 491) for the game of nawfa, consisting of a ball and counting sticks.

Collected by Mr Henry P. Ewing, who furnished the following account of the game:

The game of naw-fa is played with sixteen stems of the soap weed, or Spanish bayonet (*Yucca filamentosa*), cut in equal lengths and tied loosely

FIG. 491. Hiding ball and counting sticks; diameter of ball, 2¼ inches; length of sticks, 18¼ inches; Walapai Indians, Arizona; cat. no. 63210, Field Columbian Museum.

together with a wisp of fibers of the same plant, and a small ball cut out of the root of the same plant called me-nat ka-ta-u-ta-ga short yucca, me-nat being the Walapai name for the Spanish bayonet, and the katautaga meaning short, little. The stems serve as counters and are called sa-hu-na-ga.

To play the game, two persons or two sides select a place where the soil is soft and sandy and dig up with a stick or the hands two trenches or holes about 3 or 4 feet long and about 6 or 8 inches deep and a foot wide. The loose soil or sand is left in the trench, and one of the players takes the ball, while the bundle of counters is placed between the two trenches on the ground. The player with the ball takes it in his left hand and buries it, hand and all, in the loose sand at one end; then he draws his hand back, at the same time piling the sand over the buried hand with the other. He gradually withdraws the hand to the far end of the trench, all the time piling up the sand over the trench. When he has withdrawn the hand from the trench the ball is missing, he having hid it somewhere in the loose earth. He divides the earth in the ditch into four piles by piling it up with his hands. One of his opponents now runs his hand into one of the piles. If he finds the ball there, he takes it and hides it in his trench. If he misses, sometimes the hider will say: "Sik a yu cha"—guess again. Of course there are but three chances against him this time, while before there were four, and he nearly always guesses again when allowed to. If he misses his guess, the hider takes one of the counters and puts it in his pile and hides the ball again. After playing a while the counters are usually in possession of the two sets of players, and when there are no more counters in the bundle the man who misses his guess has to give one out of his pile to his opponents. When the counters are all in one pile, the game is won. There is much merriment indulged in while playing the game. A bystander will sometimes rush in, put his hand in the trench and, as the guesser stands undecided which pile to guess, will say: "Here it is in this pile; I am not lying;" but the wary guesser seldom believes him. Sometimes the hider will tell the guesser what pile it is in; he may tell him right or wrong. This game is the jocular game of the tribe and is always a source of great amusement, and when being played always attracts a crowd of onlookers, who laugh, and joke the players continually.

ZUÑIAN STOCK

ZUÑI. Zuñi, New Mexico. (United States National Museum.)
Cat. no. 69468.   Set of four wooden cylinders, 9 inches in height and
    2 inches in diameter, with cylindrical cavity at one end, 1¼ inches
    deep and 1¼ inches in diameter, the upper ends charred for a
    distance of about 1 inch.

These specimens were collected by Col. James Stevenson, and catalogued as articles used in the game of hidden ball, one of the sacred

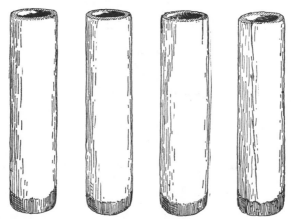

FIG. 492. Wooden tubes for hiding game; height, 12¼ inches; Zuñi Indians, Zu ̄ ̄, New Me ̄ ̄ ̄,
cat. no. 69351, United States National Museum.

games of the Gods of War, played in spring and early summer. One of the cylinders in this set is distinguished from the others by being nicked around the edge at the top.
Cat. no. 69351.   Four wooden cylinders (figure 492), 12¼ inches in
    height and 3 inches in diameter, with a cylindrical cavity in one
    end 2¾ inches deep and 2⅛ inches in diameter, the other end
    charred for a distance of 1⅛ inches, the rest of the external sur-
    face painted white.

Collected by Col. James Stevenson and designated as an especial hereditary set of the tribe.

Cat. no. 69268. Four wooden cylinders (figure 493), 8¾ inches in height and 2¼ inches in diameter, with a cylindrical cavity in one end 2 inches deep and 1¾ inches in diameter, the other end charred for a distance of 1⅞ inches, the other external surface originally painted white; accompanied with a stone ball, a white concretion,[a] 1¼ inches in diameter. Collected by Col. James Stevenson.

Cat. no. 69269. Four wooden cylinders, 6¼ inches in height and 1¾ inches in diameter, with a cylindrical cavity in one end 1¼ inches in diameter, the upper ends blackened to the depth of one-fourth of an inch, the body whitewashed. Collected by Col. James Stevenson.

FIG. 493. Wooden tubes for hiding game; height, 8¾ inches; Zuñi Indians, Zuñi, New Mexico; cat. no. 69268, United States National Museum.

Cat. no. 69270. Four wooden cylinders, 7 inches in height and 1½ inches in diameter, with a cylindrical cavity in one end 1¼ inches deep and 1¼ inches in diameter, the upper ends painted black to a depth of about 1 inch. Collected by Col. James Stevenson.

Cat. no. 69271. Four wooden cylinders, 6½ inches in height and 1⅝ inches in diameter, with a cylindrical cavity in one end 1 inch deep and 1⅛ inches in diameter, the upper ends blackened to a depth of one-half of an inch; accompanied with a bundle of counting straws of broom grass. Collected by Col. James Stevenson.

Cat. no. 69272. Four wooden cylinders, 6 inches in height and 1⅝ inches in diameter, with a conical cavity in one end, the upper ends painted black to the depth of 1⅝ inches. Collected by Col. James Stevenson.

ZUÑI.   Zuñi, New Mexico.   (Cat. no. 32599, Free Museum of Science and Art, University of Pennsylvania.)

Four wooden tubes, 2⅝ inches in diameter and 12¼ inches in height, painted black at the top, the body of the cylinder showing traces of white; accompanied with a stone ball (figure 494) 1½ inches in diameter and a bundle of counting straws (figure 495) 14½ inches in length. Collected by the writer in 1902.

This set is similar to one in the United States National Museum (cat. no. 69351).

---

[a] Quartz grains cemented together by calcium carbonate, like so-called Fontainebleau limestone.

Mr Frank Hamilton Cushing [a] first described the game, as follows:

Eight players went into a ki-wi-tsin to fast, and four days later issued forth, bearing four large wooden tubes, a ball of stone, and a bundle of thirty-six counting straws. With great ceremony, many prayers and incantations, the tubes were deposited on two mock mountains of sand, either side of the "grand plaza." A crowd began to gather. Larger and noisier it grew, until it became a surging clamorous black mass. Gradually two piles of fabrics—vessels, silver ornaments, necklaces, embroideries, and symbols representing horses, cattle, and sheep—grew to large proportions. Women gathered on the roofs around, wildly stretching forth articles for the betting; until one of the presiding priests called out a brief message. The crowd became silent. A booth was raised, under which two of the players retired; and when it was removed, the four tubes were standing on the mound of sand. A song and dance began. One by one three of the four opposing players' were summoned to guess under which tube the ball was hidden. At each guess the cries of the opposing parties became deafening, and their mock struggles approached the violence of mortal combat. The last guesser found the ball; and as he victoriously carried the latter and the tubes across to his own mound, his side scored 10. The process was repeated. The second guesser found the ball; his side scored 15, setting

Fig. 494.   Fig. 495.

FIG. 494. Stone ball for hiding game; diameter, 1¼ inches; Zuñi Indians, Zuñi, New Mexico; cat. no. 32599, Free Museum of Science and Art, University of Pennsylvania.
FIG. 495. Counting straws for hiding game; length, 14½ inches; Zuñi Indians, Zuñi, New Mexico; cat. no. 32599, Free Museum of Science and Art, University of Pennsylvania.

the others back 5. The counts numbered 100; but so complicated were the winnings and losings on both sides, with each guess of either, that hour after hour the game went on and night closed in. Fires were built in the plaza, cigarettes lighted, but still the game continued. Noisier and noisier grew the dancers, more and more insulting and defiant their songs and epithets to the opposing crowd, until they fairly gnashed their teeth at one another, but no blows! Day dawned on the still uncertain contest; nor was it until the sun again touched the western horizon, that the hoarse, still defiant voices died away, and the victorious party bore off their "mountains of gifts from the gods."

Subsequently Mr Cushing, in reply to my inquiries, kindly furnished me the following notes on the game with the four tubes:

I'-yan-ko-lo-we is one of the principal tribal games of the Zuñi. As a public function it is their leading game. It is played by two parties, one representing the East, the other representing the West, or, one representing the North, the other representing the South. Each party is made up, therefore, from members of the clans of its section, region, or direction. But it is to be noted in this connection that the game is played with various motives, all more or less divinatory in object—that is, it is a game of prognostication by victory. As the war dance is a sort of preliminary as well as reminiscent battle, dramatically fought beforehand, to determine victory, so this game is, while celebrating

---

[a] The Century Magazine, v. 26, p. 37, May, 1883.

mythic arbitrations between the gods—the wind gods and the water gods particularly—a means of questioning fate as to which side shall prevail; whether, for example, when the game is played just before the opening of spring [a] the wind gods or the water gods shall control, whether it shall be a wet season or a dry season and, by the relative scorings of the game, how wet and how dry in relation to the growth of the corn that is about to be planted. It will be seen that, since the players on the one side represent North and Winter, the windy and barren season, those on the other side South and Summer, the season of summer showers and fertility, the players on the northern side would represent wind and drought, those on the southern side moisture and growth. Thus, according to the scores of the game, the corn would be planted deep and in well-watered places if the wind men won or throughout various stages of the game "carried the luck."

This will indicate that the game may be played for any variety of purposes, but as a tribal game played annually in the February-March moon [a] it has the above significance. This is because in the myth of the trial of strength between the wind gods and the water gods, when they raced one another, the "racer of the wind gods" was a stick, the arrow billet, that of the water gods a stone, the thunder ball (?). Thus i'-yan-ko-lo-we becomes the water game, just as mo'-ti-kwa-we is the wind game, of the Zuñi, and takes its place as one of the four element games of the tribe, the instrumentalities of which are annually sacrificed or deposited with the effigies of the War Gods A'haiyuta and Ma'tsailema.[b] It follows that there is a tribal set of the tubes, etc. In fact, there are two, for it must be explained in this connection that i'-yan-ko-lo-we is the sho'-li-we (war-arrow game) of the water or peace people, just as for the wind or war people sho'-li-we, or rather ti'-kwa-we, its world or outdoor form, is the i'-yan-ko-lo-we of themselves and their gods, so that in one sense all the four tribal games are one. Thus i'-yan-ko-lo-we may be used for war prognostications, in which case the tribal tubes of oak, or weapon timber, are used. But it is almost always used for peace prognostications, in which the tribal tubes of cottonwood or water timber are used.

The simple name i'-yan-ko-lo-we means hidings and seekings or two and fro hidings, from i'-an, from one another; ya'-na-wa, to divine, guess; ko-lo-a, to hide, cover secretly or by burial; and we, plural sign. I'-yan-ko-lo-we i'-k'osh-na-ne is the game or play of i'yan-ko-lo-we; i is reciprocal or antithetical action; k'o'-sha, to wash, bathe, or to play. Play is so named because it is supposed to refresh or renew as does a bath; but the primitive sense of these expressions must be kept in mind, and the actual fact that none of the games involving tribal participation or contention are played without recourse to baptism or bathing of the face, that the eyes and other senses may be cleared and quickened. It may be noted that this strictly corresponds to the constant "going to water" of ball players among the southern Indians and some tribes of the Mississippi. The idea of renewing or changing personality is also present.

The sacred name is an'-hai-tâ i'-yan-ko-lo-we, by commandment, or appointment i'-yan-ko-lo-we, from an'-to, belonging to or by, and hai-tosh-nan-ne, to point out a ceremonial or the date or mode or regulation thereof. These appointments are made by divine command through the priests by virtue of

---

[a] The regulation game of February-March is always played in spring before the planting, the deer chase, and the tribal billet-race of the priesthood of the Bow. When the game is played with a special motive or reason and for a particular prognostication, it is "called" or "commanded" by the House priesthood; but in such case called only in its appropriate season.

[b] These gods are its chief divinities, but A'haiyuta is holder of the tubes and ball, as Ma'tsailema is holder of the mo'-ti-kwa-we; yet both games belong to both, because one could not play, of course, without the other.

returning dates and are obligatory, as the seasons seem to be, but may be a little earlier or a little later, as the seasons seem to be, exact dates being determined by the priests as keepers and diviners of the calendar of rites. Another sacred name is i'-yan-ko-lo-we te'sh-kwi-ne, from te', space, sh' direction of or throughout, and k'wi'-na, dark, black, made void by darkness— that is, secret, mysterious. The word is applied not only to secret and sacred observances, but also to taboos, forbidden persons or things, places, altars, or precincts.

A semisacred, semimythic name is ku-lu-lu-na-k'ya-al i'-yan-ko-lo-we (thunder stone hide-seek game), from ku-lu-lu, to rumble, thunder, k'ya, that which is for or which does, and a'ale, stone.

There are other names more or less allegorical, chiefly interesting as indicative of the importance of the game and the wealth of lore connected with it.

The name of the tubes is i'-yan-ko-lo-we-kya to'-ma-we, tom'-ma, meaning tube or hollowed wooden billet, and we being the plural ending. Of these tubes there are four, usually plain, though sometimes differentiated by bandings, precisely as are the arrows or cane cards of war, to assign them separately to the four quarters, or "mountains," and sometimes carved to make them rudely and very conventionally representative of the rain or dance gods (A-kâ-kâ) of the four quarters, or rather of their masks or face personalities. The banded tubes are generally made of oak, one of the "weapon woods," and generally pertain to the game as played by the warriors. The carved tubes are, however, made almost invariably of cottonwood, the "wood of water" or of life substance, and pertain to the game as played by the clans at the appointed time in spring or very early summer, just before planting. The war play of this game is not played annually, but only when "called," and it is scarcely ever called at any other season than during the "crescents," or months of the greater and lesser sand storms (April and May). It then immediately follows the great annual war race of the kicked stick or running billet, which is performed in April by the entire priesthood of the Bow, totemically painted; and it thus immediately precedes the annual play of the game by the Seed-and-Water, or Wind-and-Soil, clan leaderships. Usually the mere fact that a tribal set of the tubes is made of "weapon wood" (oak or mountain mahogany) suffices to relegate it without further indication (as, by binding) to war plays, while if made of cottonwood or willow the set is as effectually identified with the peace plays of the game. Both kinds of tubes are said to have been used, one (hard wood) by the war party, the other (soft wood) by the peace party, when questions of war or peace were submitted to divination by means of the game. In all other plays, to be described in due course, only a single set of the tubes was used.

The individual tubes in a set are with one exception, I believe, named precisely as are the canes of sho'-li-we—ko'-ha-kwa, k'wi'-na, pathl-to-a, and not a'-thlu-a, but al'-u-la, the all-container or the container of the stone par excellence. But the tubes also take their names from their "mountains," as designated by color rather than by region or place names; that is, the yellow, the blue, the red, the white. Again, if the game is a strictly sacred or ceremonial peace game, the tubes become the four Kâ-kâ gods of the four regions; or rather, as occasion requires or as the priestly membership of the clans participating in the game determines, four of the many Kâ-kâ gods of the four regions.

The tubes are more often plain than marked, though sometimes they are distinguished by bandings of marks incised and burnt, or simply scorched around them, precisely as are the bands across the four sho'-li-we canes or slips.

Then I have seen one set on which the four principal medicine-animal men or gods were represented, with their appropriate cosmical elements, or rather, the symbols of paraphernalia representing these, attached. But, unfortunately, I noted only that the Bear (He of the West) as God of Thunder and the Eagle-Serpent (He of the Upper Underworld; but here, of Day, therefore of the East) God of Lightning, were represented. I never saw the game played with these tubes, and can not tell from observation what specific form of the game they were designed for. I only know that the tubes were those of one of the particular clan brotherhoods vaguely known as the Badgers (not the totemic Badgers, but the priestly associates of the high-priest of the Badgers, himself, of course, the elder and house priest of the Badger totem). But these particularly and indelibly marked tubes are never used for any other than their one particular form of the game, or by others than their official holders. This explains why the tribal sets are left plain. Like the parts or post slats of the rain altars that correspond to them, they are painted afresh for each occasion on which they are used. Ordinarily all are painted with white kaolin slip and then differentiated by bandings of black, in lieu of the colors they stand for. But when the tubes become gods of the Kâ-kâ, they are distinguished by face delineations, very crude and conventional, in their appropriate colors. In such cases the tubes are merely the timber flesh, ready to be made this set of gods or that other set of gods that is opened to incantation or influence by them through the kind of masks represented on them.

The paint used on the tubes is always sacred. The white is the he-k'o-ha-kya, paint to white make, kaolin slip; the black, the he'-tethl-a-kya, paint to designate (black) make. Both kinds are made from kaolin or coal from particular or sacred places. The paint is, as said above, renewed during preparation for the occasion (the retirement and fasting period of the participants), and at the end of the game is washed off and drunk by the officiators, those who lost spuing it, however (so I was told, but the man who told me was a winner and may have been "crowing"). When only one tube in the set is painted, I suppose it becomes the "all-container" for that special set.

A common name for the hidden ball is i'-yan-ko-lo-kya u'-li-ne, the content, or i'-yan-ko-lo-kya mo'l-u'-li-ne, or ball for placing within, compounded of i'-yan-ko-lo-kya and mo-o-le, ball, rounded object of wood or other substance, u-li, to place within, and n'ne, that which is, or instrument for. Other names are i'-yan-ko-lo-kya a'l'-u-li-ne or i'-yan-ko-lo-kya a'-kya-mo-li-an u'-li-ne, the first from i'-yan-ko-lo-kya, a'l, a stone, pebble, and u'-li-ne, and the second from i'-yan-ko-lo-kya, a'a, a stone (shaped), kya, by water, mo-li-a, rounded by, ne, that which is, and u'-li-ne. The archaic and highly sacred name of the hiding stone, when consisting of a perfectly rounded pebble or concretion found in rain torrent beds or in pot holes, either those of the wind on high mesas or those of the water in mountain torrents, is ku-lu-lu-na-kya-al u'-li-ne or ku-lu-lu-na-kya a'-kya-mo-li-a tsan u'-li-ne, little thunder-stone ball content.

The counters are called ti-we or ti'-po-a-ne. Ti stands for ti'-i-le, a counting straw, from ti-na, to stand or represent, as in or of a procession or group. The second name is composed of ti and po-na-ne, a bundle, bunch, from po-a, to place or lean together. An entire bunch of counters for the game is composed of one hundred and two straws. Of these one hundred are made of clean broom straws; those used in the game of peace being taken preferably from a mealing-trough brush or whisk; those used in the war phases of the game being preferably taken from hair brushes of the enemy made of broom grass. There are also in each complete bunch of counters two counters made of flat splints of yucca blades notched at the ends on opposite sides to represent the feathering of arrows, one retaining the natural spine at the point of the leaf and called father, tim-ta-tchu, or master counter, ti'-mo-so-na, the other plain, made of an inner portion of the leaf, and called a-wa-tsi-ta, their mother, or ho'-ta, maternal grandmother. This is a play on words as well as a symbolic name, ho being the yucca, and Ho'-tethl-okya being the goddess of yucca fiber and of the primeval bowstrings. It may therefore safely be inferred that these two yucca splints represent respectively the arrow and the bow, and that the bunch of straw splints represents the tribal bunch or quiver of arrows.

In addition to the above-mentioned objects there are the staffs of direction, or the feeling staffs or divining wands, one of which is carried by the representative or guesser of either side. The name of one of these staffs is te'-häthl-na-kya thlam-me, from te, region, direction, häthla, to seek understanding, or breast feeling, and thlam-me, slat or wand made for. These wands are now simple slender round rods or sticks, between 2 and 4 feet in length, very slightly flattened, and bent near the tip. Formerly, however, they were more elaborately formed, somewhat longer, more flattened and bent at the tips, and quite elaborately scored, or else wrapped with a continuous platting of fine rawhide, and were intended, it would seem, to represent ceremonially surviving forms of the atlatl. The guesser, when passing to and fro between the two stations, carries one of them in the right hand, held obliquely over the left arm in which the tubes and counters are clasped in the corner of his mantle. When using it, he holds it extended over the tubes, moving its tip rapidly over first one and then another of these tubes, in time to the song of the hiding shamans, until he and it together decide which tube to upset with a sudden sidewise stroke or flip of the wand. There is still another use to which these staffs are put, indicating their supposedly conscious nature. While the guesser for the time being is feeling with his staff, his opponent, who, as aid of the official hider of the content, knows under which of the tubes it is hidden, similarly sways his staff over the tubes, thus seeking to mislead and confuse the movements of the other.

Belonging properly to the movable parts of the game, for it is sometimes carried to and fro between the two stations, is the pa'-u-nu-kya-wem'-ma, covering robe, the mantle of invisibility. It is a buffalo robe or a very large serape, which is held over the hider by four assistants, also official, of his side, when he places the four tubes on their respective mountains of sand and within one of them hides the ball or other content.

In endeavoring to guess, the youth either makes a great variety of passes over the tubes with his slat or staff of direction, poising it over one or another as though to divine with it, or beating the air with it over the tops of the tubes, both in time and out of time, though regularly, to the hiding incantation, until, so suddenly that his motion can scarcely be seen, he switches one of the tubes over. If his guess prove wrong, he continues the motion uninterruptedly until he decides to tip another tube over. Or, again, he may simply hold his staff over his arm; may stand gazing intently and motionless, muffled up to his chin in his serape, now and then making a feint at knocking one of the tubes over with his foot, until he finally spurns the one he has decided on with the toe of his right foot; then, if wrong, he proceeds as before.

If the first tube toppled over contains the ball, a sweeping stake is won, the full count of all the tubes, which is the same as the full count of all the canes in the sho'-li-we game, and the side of the fortunate guesser is allowed to retain the tubes and have another guess.

If he fails at the first and wins the second guess, he wins the count of the particular tube overturned, minus that of the tube he overturned without finding the ball, and so on; so that, unless his second guess happens to catch the ball in a tube of high count, he generally forfeits instead of winning; and his case is of course worse still with the third and fourth guesses, for he is compelled to continue guessing until the ball is found.

The parties which play the game are, of course, two, and they take, year after year, the same stations on the eastern and western sides of the great central plaza of the town, under the walls ; and these stations are called i'-yan-ko-lo-we te'-hua-we, from te', space; aha, to seize, take by choice; ua, or ula, within (some place, the plaza in this case).

Immediately in front of either party are its four mountains, ya'-la-we, of sand, symbolic of the four regions and mountains beyond the plane of this world. They are disposed, contiguously to one another, in a square [figure 497],

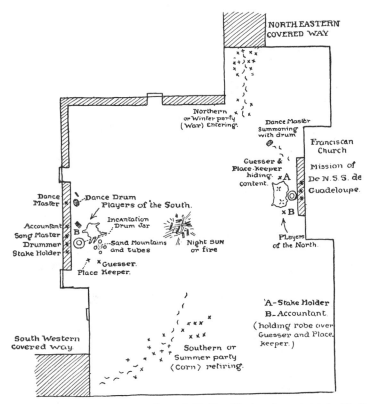

FIG. 496. Plan of hiding game; Zuñi Indians, Zuñi, New Mexico; from sketch by Mr Frank Hamilton Cushing.

each being about a foot in diameter and some 9 inches high. The northernmost mountain is called ya'-la thlup-tsi-na, mountain yellow ; the western, ya'-la thli-a-na, mountain blue ; the southern ya'-la a-ho-na, mountain ruddy ; and the eastern, ya'-la k'o'-ha-na, mountain white.

Sometimes only a single sand mound is raised [figure 498], but in such case it is still the fourfold mountain height, or a-wi-ten te'-yal-la-ne. As indicated in the figures, the tubes are set leaning slightly toward their respective quarters when the guesser and the keeper of the tubes retire together under the mantle or robe before described.

In the two parties to the play there are but two actual players, if the ana-wa-kwe, guessers, may be exclusively so called. They are chosen from their appropriate clans by the clan priests of the game, but are generally experienced old hands or players, and whether middle-aged or young, they are always known as the tsa-wa-ki, youths of the game. They carry the tubes, and counters drawn, to and fro between the stations. When one side loses, the youth of the other side who has come over and made the winning guess, takes the tubes up in the corner of his mantle or in his left arm, grasps the counters won and yielded by the accountant, in his left hand, and, bearing his staff of direction in the right hand, held over all, proceeds very deliberately to his own side, where, with the accountant, or keeper, of his side, who both keeps count and remembers under which tube the ball of his side is hidden, he is concealed under the robe of invisibility or hiding, while together they set the tubes up in the sand mountain or mountains and secrete under one of them the ball. The robe is held over them by the two drum masters, and meanwhile the priest shaman of the game, who is himself an old and celebrated player, makes the invocations and with his assistants sings the incantations of this part of the game. In addition to these functionaries, who are the owners or guardians of the game for their clans (I believe for life), there is a party, usually very large, of singers and dancers for each side. They are composed of all sorts of young or lusty middle-aged members of the clans of their respective sides, and they sing, shout,

Fig. 497.   Fig. 498.

FIG. 497. Sand mounds with hiding tubes; Zuñi Indians, Zuñi, New Mexico; from sketch by Mr Frank Hamilton Cushing.

FIG. 498. Sand mound with hiding tubes; Zuñi Indians, Zuñi, New Mexico; from sketch by Mr Frank Hamilton Cushing.

dance frantically, yell defiance, and taunt and jeer their opponents while the guessing is going on, trying to confuse the guessers or to make the stone stay hidden. When one side is gaining, the dancers of that side generally succeed in driving those of the opposite side out of the plaza; but when the tides of the game vary, both sides are usually drumming, dancing, singing, shouting, and, not infrequently, fighting at once. The game begins at about 2 or 3 o'clock of the appointed day—that is, the fourth day from the final announcement, the fourth day of the retirement of the functionaries of the game and of their fasting and purging. It usually lasts all the afternoon, all night, and not infrequently until late in the forenoon of the day following; but these dance parties, small at first, are continually augmented, and keep up their activity and pandemonium until forced from sheer exhaustion to give up. Some of the strongest endure throughout, but at the end can scarcely speak above dry whisperings and are cadaverous and so exhausted that their feet have to be jerked from the ground in dancing. The songs sung and the taunts yelled are not all traditional, but most of them are, and they are always allusive to the myths of the game and affairs that were connected with it. There are many myths regarding the game. Each tribal division possessing an i'-yan-ko-lo-we has its own account of its own form of the game, while the general myths of its origin are involved in the tradition of all the four tribal games played at creation times by The Two, each as played in some particular manner, as the thunder-ball game of the water gods and water people-animals (i'-yan-ko-lo-we), and the kicked-billet game, or race, of the wind gods and wind people, birds, insects, etc., the mo-ti-kwa-we, stick-ball game.

The game is not played by women or children. It is sometimes mimicked by the latter, although they are not provided with toys for the purpose, nor can they properly play it as a game, for they are not taught the rules or counts, and can therefore only pretend to play the game.

In reply to a direct inquiry of the writer whether he considered that the game was borrowed or regarded it as a fundamental tribal ceremonial, Mr Cushing answered:

It is certainly this latter—more of a function than any other game, for it is accompanied by song and dance and gibes and public betting of the most extravagant nature, is most elaborately and scrupulously prepared for, and seems not to have been played by others than by authorized persons. It is certainly derived by the Zuñi from their ancestors, both those of the Chaco region and those of the farther southwest and was very ancient among them, almost as ancient as sho'-li-we.

Mrs Matilda Coxe Stevenson gives the following account of the game under the name iankolowe: [a]

Implements.—Small stone disk, less than 2 inches in diameter, colored black on one side; four cups, a ball, and straws. "In the old, a grain of corn

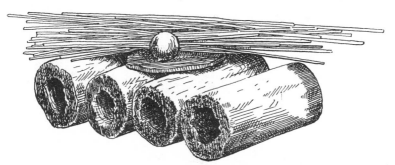

FIG. 499. Arrangement of tubes before playing hiding game; Zuñi Indians, Zuñi, New Mexico; from Mrs Stevenson.

was used instead of the ball;" and the corn is still used when the game is offered to the Gods of War. The four cups are placed on their sides close together in a row, the openings to the east. The disk, ball, and bunch of straws are laid on top of the cups [figure 499]. This arrangement before playing the game is observed by all men of any standing in the tribe, "for it was so with the Gods of War."

Each party chooses a side of the disk before it is thrown. The side up designates the starter of the game, who represents the side of the elder God of War. He sits facing south and forms a square with the four cups before him. The ball is secreted in one of the cups. The elder God of War always placed his cups in the form of a square. The other party, who sits facing north, chooses from the cup nearest to him, taking the one to the west. If the chosen cup contains the ball, he must pay 10 straws to the

[a] Zuñi Games. American Anthropologist, n. s., v. 5, p. 487, 1903.

starter, who again arranges the cups, and the cup to the east and in line nearest the chooser is taken. Should this cup not contain the ball, the chooser lays it with open end to the east and selects another cup. Should this cup contain the ball, he forfeits 6 straws, when the starter again arranges the cups. When a cup containing the ball is chosen, 6 straws must be paid. Should the first, second, and third cups selected be minus the ball, they are laid with the open ends to the east; the fourth cup, containing the ball, is allowed to stand, 4 straws are forfeited, and the cups are rearranged. Should the third cup chosen contain the ball, no payment is made, and the arranging of the game passes to the other party, who represents the side of the younger God of War. He forms three points of a triangle with three cups and places the extra cup to the eastern point, " for so the younger God of War placed his game." When all the straws have passed to one party, the game, upon which heavy wagers are often made, is won.

FIG. 500. Stone disk used to decide which side plays first in hiding game; diameter, 4¼ inches; Zuñi Indians, Zuñi, New Mexico; cat. no. 3028, Brooklyn Institute Museum.

ZUÑI. Zuñi, New Mexico. (Cat. no. 3028, Brooklyn Institute Museum.)

Sandstone disk (figure 500), 4¼ inches in diameter, the edge beveled. One side shows traces of red paint. Collected by the writer in 1903.

It was said to be thrown into the air to decide which side should start the hidden-ball game. The name was given as itapianonnai.

GAMES OF DEXTERITY

The various games of dexterity have been briefly reviewed in the introduction. In one of them—the game of hoop and pole—there are forms in which chance enters, but this is exceptional, and in general the class may be regarded as homogeneous with respect to the skill required in playing the game.

ARCHERY

I have classified under archery games played with arrows, darts, or analogous objects which are shot or tossed at a mark, excepting the hoop-and-pole or ring-and-dart game, to which the majority of other archery games appear to be related. Simple archery, or shooting at a mark, does not hold a very conspicuous place among the Indian games with the bow and arrow, and but three examples (Montagnais, Hopi, Omaha) are found among the following descriptions. The target is usually an important feature and among several tribes is allied to the ring of the ring-and-dart game. This is especially true of the grass targets used by the Grosventres, Crows, and Tetons, and probably also of that used by the Zuñi. The Potawatomi game in which a bark target is buried is similar to the Zuñi game. The yucca ball of the Navaho, the bundle of hay or bark of the Shuswap, and the kelp of the Makah apparently belong to the same category. The Eskimo game in which darts are thrown at a hole in a wooden target is probably a related form. Another common target is an arrow (Tarahumare, Assiniboin, Teton) or a stick set upright (Western Eskimo). In other games a shot arrow is the target (Shuswap, Thompson, Oglala), or arrows are shot out of a ring. The Omaha shoot to dislodge arrows shot into a tree. Cacti, buffalo lights, and moccasins furnish other targets (Omaha). In another type of arrow game, arrows or darts are tossed (Apache, Eskimo, Hopi, Tewa, Zuñi) or shot (Pawnee, Ponca) at an arrow tossed or shot to the ground so that they fall one across the other, usually so that the feathered ends cross. This game may be regarded as the antetype of the Zuñi sholiwe, and possibly of all the Indian dice games.

ALGONQUIAN STOCK

ARAPAHO.   Oklahoma.

In the story entitled " Found-in-Grass," related by Dr George A. Dorsey,[a] the twins, Spring-Boy and By-the-Door, corresponding with the War Gods, are discovered playing a game of arrows. Winning appears to be determined by one arrow touching another.

CHEYENNE.   Cheyenne reservation, Montana.   (Cat. no. 69981, Field Columbian Museum.)

Six arrows, 29 inches in length, with bulging ends weighted by being wound with wire.   Two are blunt and four have wire-nail points.   These arrows are in pairs, distinguished by bands of blue paint, differently arranged on shafts.   Collected by Mr S. C. Simms in 1901.

GROSVENTRES.   Montana.   (Cat. no. $\frac{50}{1859}$, American Museum of Natural History.)

Wisp of grass (figure 501), wound with sinew, 9 inches in length. Collected in 1901 by Dr A. L. Kroeber, who describes it as an arrow target.

FIG. 501.   Arrow target; length, 9 inches; Grosventre Indians, Montana; cat. no. $\frac{50}{1859}$, American Museum of Natural History.

MONTAGNAIS.   Camp Chateau, Labrador.

George Cartwright [b] says:

The Indians were diverting themselves with shooting at a mark with their arrows; but I can not say, that I think them good archers, although their bows are constructed on an excellent principle; for by the assistance of a back-string the bow preserves its elastic power, and by slackening or tightening this string it is rendered weak enough for a child of 5 years old, or strong enough for the most powerful man amongst them.   As there is something particular in their sport of to-day, I shall endeavor to describe it.   They provide two targets of 4 feet square, made of sticks and covered with deerskins.   These they fix on poles about 8 feet high, and at 50 yards distance from each other.   The men dividing themselves into two parties, each party shoots twenty-one arrows at one of the targets, standing by the other.   That party which puts the most arrows into the target, gains the honor, for they have not the least idea of gaming.   The victors immediately set up shouts of mockery and derision at the conquered party; these they continue for some time, when the wives and daughters of the conquerors join in the triumph and walking in procession round the targets, sing

---

[a] Traditions of the Arapaho, p. 364, Chicago, 1903.
[b] A Journal of Transactions and Events during a Residence of Nearly Sixteen Years on the Coast of Labrador, v. 1, p. 238, Newark, 1792.

a song upon the occasion, priding themselves not a little with the defeat of their opponents, who at length join in the laugh against themselves, and all are friends again, without any offense (seemingly) being either given or taken.

POTAWATOMI. Kansas.

Mr Wells M. Sawyer communicated to me the following account secured by him from an Indian interpreter:

Ta-te-wan (gambling). Four players, A, B and C, D, each with a bow and two arrows, play partners. Two strips of bark about 4 inches wide are placed in piles of earth shaped up like a little grave, the mounds being about 200 feet apart. One player of each side takes his place near each mound, A, C and B, D. The arrows of A, C are shot toward the target B, D. If A strikes near the target, but misses with both arrows, and C fails to strike nearer than A, the latter counts 1. If either of C's arrows come nearer than A's, C scores 1. If either hits the target, he scores 5, and if both arrows of A or C hit, the game is won (10 being out). If both A and C hit the target, neither counts. The arrows are returned by B, D.

ATHAPASCAN STOCK

APACHE (CHIRICAHUA). Arizona.

Mr E. W. Davis communicated to the writer the following account of a game played by Geronimo's band at St Augustine, Florida, in 1889:

The game which interested me most, and one which required considerable skill, consisted in tossing arrows, point first, at a mark about 10 feet away. As I recollect, the first man to throw his arrow was required to land on the mark. If he did so, he got his arrow back. His first throw was his misfortune, and the best he could do was to lose. He had no chance to win. Once an arrow in the field, however, the object of the next player was to toss his arrow so that it should cross the first thrown, and so on through the crowd. I have seen as many as six play, and often all would toss around without any one winning. In this case the arrows on the ground remained in the pot, so to speak. The play went on, each player winning as many arrows as he could succeed in crossing with his own, until the whole number were removed.

CHIPEWYAN. Fort Prince of Wales, Keewatin.

Samuel Hearne [a] says:

They have but few diversions; the chief is shooting at a mark with bow and arrows; and another outdoor game called Holl, which in some measure resembles playing with quoits; only it is done with short clubs, sharp at one end.

NAVAHO. St Michael, Arizona.

Rev. Berard Haile describes the following game in a letter of June 27, 1902:

Sä-si" oldó (he shoots the yucca). Bayonet-shaped yucca leaves are placed in hot ashes to make them flexible and moist. Strings of them are then made and wound around bark or something similarly soft. A string of buckskin is

---

[a] A Journey from Prince of Wales's Fort in Hudson's Bay to the Northern Ocean, p. 333, London, 1795.

wound in with the ball when it has nearly the required size. A small piece of an oak twig is fastened to the end of the string, and the "yucca" is finished. The shape, I think, would be shown in the accompanying sketch [figure 502].

The stick and ball are thrown into the air, and the stick, being heavier, has a tendency to steady the ball as it falls to the ground. While it is thus falling, the player shoots at it with bow and arrows, scoring if he is successful.

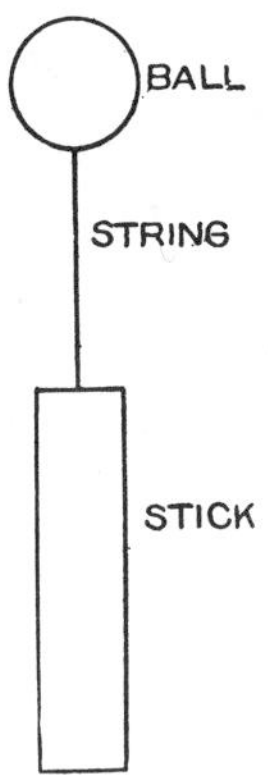

FIG. 502. Arrow target; Navaho Indians, St Michael, Arizona; from sketch by Rev. Berard Haile.

CADDOAN STOCK

PAWNEE. Nebraska.

John B. Dunbar [a] says:

There were also frequent games played with arrows. One person shot an arrow so that it should fall upon the ground at a distance of from 40 to 60 paces. The players then in succession endeavored to shoot so that their arrows should fall immediately across this arrow. Whoever succeeded took all the arrows discharged. If no one lodged an arrow upon it the player whose arrow lay nearest took all. Another game was for several players to take an arrow between the thumb and forefinger of the right hand and throw it so that it should strike in the ground 20 or 30 paces in advance, the feather end of the shaft sloping back toward the thrower. Then stepping forward another was thrown by each, so as to strike 4 or 5 feet beyond the first. Each arrow that failed to strike fast in the ground entailed a forfeit.

WICHITA. Oklahoma.

In the story of "The Deeds of After-birth Boy," as related by Dr George A. Dorsey,[b] reference is made to the two brothers playing an arrow game called "shooting-a-small-plaited-sinew-on-the-fly," lia-kukcs. The game was played for arrows.

ESKIMAUAN STOCK

ESKIMO (WESTERN). Point Barrow, Alaska.

Mr John Murdoch [c] says:

These people have only one game which appears to be of the nature of gambling. It is played with the twisters and marline spikes used for backing the bow, and already described, though Lieut. Ray says he has seen it played with any bits of stick or bone. I never had an opportunity of watching a game of this sort played, as it is not often played at the village. It is a very popular amusement at the deer-hunting camps, where Lieut. Ray often saw it played. According to him the players are divided into sides, who sit on the ground about 3 yards apart, each side sticking up one of the marline spikes for a mark to throw the twisters at. Six of the latter, he believes, make a complete set. One side tosses the whole set one at a time at the opposite stake, and the points which they make are counted up by their opponents from the position of the twisters as they fall. He did not learn how the points were reckoned, except that twisters

---

[a] The Pawnee Indians. Magazine of American History, v. 8, p. 750, New York, Nov., 1882.

[b] The Mythology of the Wichita, p. 92, Washington, 1904.

[c] Ethnological Results of the Point Barrow Expedition. Ninth Annual Report of the Bureau of Ethnology, p. 364, 1892.

with a mark on them counted differently from the plain ones, or how long the
game lasted, each side taking its turn of casting at the opposite stake.
He, however, got the impression that the winning side kept the
twisters belonging to their opponents. Mr. Nelson informs me in a
letter that a similar game is played with the same implements at
Norton sound.

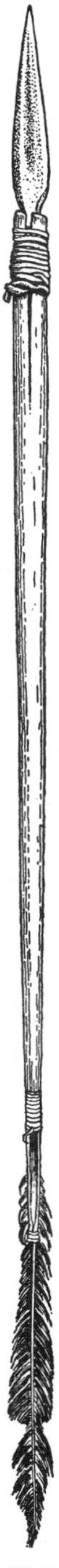

ESKIMO (WESTERN). St Michael, Alaska.

Mr E. W. Nelson [a] describes the following games:

A round block about 6 inches long is cut into the form of a large
spool, but with the flaring rim of one end replaced by a sharpened point.
The top is from 2¼ to 3 inches across and has a deep hole in the center.
This spool-like object is planted in the floor of the kashim with the large
end upward, and an indefinite number of players gather around it
seated crosslegged on the floor. Near the spool is a small pile of
short sticks, of uniform size, used as counters. These, with a small,
pointed wooden dart, in size and shape almost exactly like a sharpened lead pencil, compose the implements of the game. The first
player takes the butt of the dart between the thumb and forefinger,
with its point upward and his hand nearly on a level with the spool.
Then he gives the dart a deft upward toss, trying to cause it to take a
curved course, so that it will fall with the point downward and remain
fast in the hole at the top of the spool. If he succeeds he takes one of
the counting sticks from the pile and tries again; when he misses, the
dart is passed to the next player, and so on, until the counters are all
gone, when the players count up and the one having the most counters is the winner. Ordinarily this game is played by men, women,
or children merely for pastime, but sometimes small articles are
staked upon the outcome. It is a source of much sport to the players,
who banter and laugh like school children at each other's bad play.

Dart-throwing (yokh'-whûk) . . . This is played in the kashim
by two or more persons, usually for a prize or stake. The darts are
small, short, and made of wood, largest at the point and tapering
backward toward the butt, in which is fastened a bird quill for guiding the dart in its flight. In the large end of the dart is fastened a
sharp spike of bone, horn, or sometimes of ivory. The target is a
small, upright stick of some soft wood planted in the floor. This
may be placed in the middle of the room and the players divided into
two parties, seated on opposite sides of the target, or it may be
placed on one side of the room and the players seated together on the
other. In the former case a man is appointed from each side to return
the darts to the throwers and to give each player a counter when a
point is made. Each player has two darts, which he throws one after
the other, and a score is made when a dart remains sticking into the
target. Ten small wooden counting sticks are placed on the floor by the
target, and one of these is given for each score; the side gaining the
most of these counters takes the prize, and the game begins again.

At Cape Nome, south of Bering strait, a similar dart game was seen,
but there the target was a square board-like piece of wood with a dark-
colored bull's-eye painted in the center. This was set up in the kashim
and the men and boys threw their darts at it, scoring when they hit
the bull's-eye. The wooden portion of the darts used in this game,

FIG. 503. Game dart; length, 22¾ inches; Western Eskimo, Cape Nome, Alaska; United States National Museum.

[a] The Eskimo about Bering Strait. Eighteenth Annual Report of the Bureau of American Ethnology, p. 332, 1899.

both at Cape Nome and St Michael, was from 5 to 6 inches in length and from three-fourths of an inch to an inch in diameter at the larger end. Figure [503] represents a dart from Cape Nome, used for throwing at a square board target with a round black bull's-eye painted on its center. The players place the target on one side of the kashim and stand upon the other side to throw, scoring 1 for each dart that sticks in the bull's-eye. These darts are nearly 2 feet in length and have a tapering wooden handle, largest at the front, with an ivory point fastened in the lower end by a tapering, wedge-shape point, which is inserted in the split end and lashed firmly. The upper end of the shaft tapers to a small, round point, on which is fastened the end of a feather from a cormorant's tail, which serves to guide the dart in its flight.

KERESAN STOCK

KERES. Acoma, New Mexico.

An Acoma Indian at Zuñi, named James H. Miller, informed the writer that the Acoma Indians have an arrow game in which they shoot at grass tied up.

KIOWAN STOCK

KIOWA. Oklahoma. (Cat. no. 159913, United States National Museum.)
Six arrows made of a single piece of maple wood, 29¼ inches in length (plate IX).

The heads are carved and painted. According to the collector, Mr James Mooney, the arrows are thrown with the hand, like a javelin, and the player who throws farthest, wins. It is a man's game.

The incised designs, painted red, yellow, green, and blue, are in part easily recognizable as the calumet with primer, bow, and arrow, the lightning, and the symbols of the four directions on the uppermost arrow, which are painted from left to right with the colors red, green, blue, and yellow. Mr Cushing identified others as the war staff, or standard, and shield—day or dawn signs with turkey tracks; day signs with stars; horse tracks and the man sign. Mr Mooney, in reply to my inquiry, informed me that the Kiowa attach no special significance to these carved arrows, and were unable to explain the designs.

MOQUELUMNAN STOCK

TOPINAGUGIM. Big creek, 2 miles north of Groveland, Tuolumne county, California.

Dr Hudson describes these Indians as playing also a game of shooting at an arrow set up, under the name of thuyamship.

The two contestants, armed with bows and blunt arrows, stand beside an arrow stuck in the ground and shoot alternately from a distance of about 170 feet. Two other players stand near the arrow targets and mark the shots. The players shoot back and forth until one of the two arrow targets is struck and broken.

MENOMINEE INDIANS PLAYING MOCCASIN GAME; WISCONSIN; FROM HOFFMAN

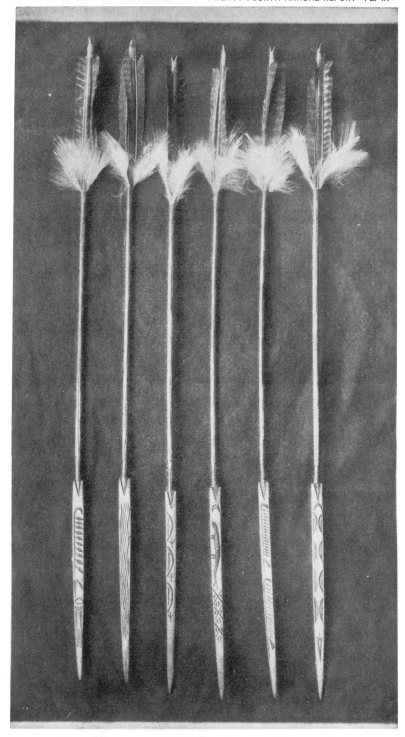

GAMING ARROWS; KIOWA INDIANS, OKLAHOMA; CAT. NO. 159913,
UNITED STATES NATIONAL MUSEUM

PIMAN STOCK

PIMA. Arizona.

The late Dr Frank Russell [a] described the following boys' games:

Vatâmumulītc hukoyoliwia.—The players stand in a circle while a boy runs around the outside, dragging at the end of a string a bundle of rags. When the play begins each boy deposits an arrow in a heap, and the one who trans-fixes the bundle as it flies past is entitled to the pile of arrows. At the end the best marksman may have nearly all the arrows. The same runner con-tinues throughout the game, and receives a few arrows as compensation for his services.

Okmaitcĕkĕ.—A bundle of grass, called woliwikke, is tied with willow bark so that it is about 125 mm. long and 50 mm. in diameter. The player tosses the bundle upward with his left hand while holding the bow in his right, ready to shoot the bundle before it can strike the earth. When the bundle is thrown forward instead of upward, it is called tcomält maitcĕkĕ, "to shoot the bundle low."

Naof towe kukrsa, "prickly-pear standing opposite."—There are usually four players, though sometimes two engage in this shooting game. Prickly-pear leaves are set up opposite each other at a distance of about 30 yards. The game is to pierce the leaf with an arrow, and when four are playing the two partners share equally the winnings or losses. Arrows, bows, and such similar property as these ragged urchins possess are wagered. A bow is considered worth from ten to twenty arrows, according to quality.

Kuorsa.—Either two or four may play. The game consists in shooting an arrow so that it will lie on the ground at a distance of about 100 feet and then shooting two more arrows with the intention of casting them across the first.

TARAHUMARE. Chihuahua, Mexico.

Dr Carl Lumholtz [b] says:

Very common is it to see two young men amusing themselves with shooting-matches, shooting arrows at an arrow which has been shot out into the ground some 50 yards off as a mark. This arrow, as well as the game itself, is called in Mexican Spanish lechuguilla. In Tarahumare the game is called chog'irali, and the target arrow chogira. The arrow coming nearest the chogira counts 1 point; and if it comes within four fingers' width of the aim, it counts 4. The game is for 12 points. The distance is not measured from the points of the arrows, but from the winged parts, one man measuring for all. If a shot strikes so as to form a cross with the chogira, it counts 4. If it only touches the point of the latter in the ground, it counts 2. If two arrows happen to form crosses, neither counts.

Instead of arrows, three sticks may be employed. One is thrown out at a distance and is the chogira, and the other two sticks are thrown toward it and count in a similar way as the arrows. Often while traveling, the Tarahumare play this game, in either form, as they go along the road, perhaps for the entire distance. Two or three pairs may play together.

---

[a] In a memoir to be published by the Bureau of American Ethnology.
[b] Unknown Mexico, v. 1, p. 276, New York, 1902.

SHUSWAP. Kamloops, British Columbia.

Dr Franz Boas [a] says:

Shooting matches are frequently arranged. An arrow is shot, and then the archers try to hit the arrow which has been shot first. Or a bundle of hay or a piece of bark is thrown as far as possible, and the men shoot at it.

THOMPSON INDIANS (NTLAKYAPAMUK). British Columbia.

Mr James Teit [b] says:

A shooting game was played as follows: A steep sandy bank was generally chosen. Each player had two arrows. An extra arrow was fired at the bank by one of the party, to remain there as a target. Each player in turn fired his arrows at this target. The person who struck the notched end of the arrow-shaft or target, thereby splitting it in two, won the greatest number of points. The man who shot his arrow so that it stuck into the bank alongside of the arrow target, touching the latter all along the shaft, won the next highest number. A man was stationed near the target to call out the name of the shooter and the place where the arrows struck. The distance chosen to shoot from was according to the wishes of the archers, generally from 40 to 100 yards. In another game one man shot his arrow as far as he could, the others trying to shoot as near to it as possible, and the game was repeated. The man that could shoot the farthest and truest generally won. A large open space with rather soft ground was best suited for this game.

The Indians used to gather at a bluff close to Nicola river, and about 10 or 12 miles from Spences Bridge. Here they tried to shoot their arrows over the top of the bluff and passers-by did the same. Only the strongest shooters could shoot easily over the bluff.

HOPI. Mishongnovi, Arizona.

Mr Charles L. Owen describes the following game:

The players throw up two sloping embankments at a distance of 200 feet apart. These are 4 feet long and 16 to 18 inches high. In the center of each is placed a conspicuous mark, such as a piece of cotton cloth or a piece of bright tin, at which boys and girls shoot their arrows. The closest shot secures the shooter the first shot at the other target.

Mr A. M. Stephen, in his unpublished manuscript, gives soya nanuveya as the Hopi, and ihŭtiñ as the Tewa name for casting throwing-sticks on the ground in imitation of a game where they cast arrows on the ground, the player trying to cause the fletching of his arrow to lie upon his opponent's in a certain place. The following are terms of the game:

Na-na'-vü-ya, to bet; na-na'-vü-lau-wû, betting, gambling; ho-hüh ak na-na'-vü-ya, to bet arrows; ho'-hü, arrow; pa-vaf-nai-ya, throwing sticks from a short distance to make them lodge in a rock crevice.

---

[a] Second General Report on the Indians of British Columbia. Report of the Sixtieth Meeting of the British Association for the Advancement of Science, p. 641, London, 1891.

[b] The Thompson Indians of British Columbia. Memoirs of the American Museum of Natural History, v. 2, p. 279, New York, 1900.

SIOUAN STOCK

ASSINIBOIN.   Fort Union, Montana.

Edwin T. Denig [a] says:

Another game is played by the boys and young men which consists of plant-ing an arrow in the snow or ground and each throwing other arrows at it until struck, and he who strikes the planted arrow is winner of all the arrows then on the ground.

CROWS.   Crow reservation, Montana.   (Cat. no. 69649, Field Colum-bian Museum.)

FIG. 504.   Arrow target; length, 12 inches; Crow Indians, Montana; cat. no. 69649, Field Colum-bian Museum.

Archery target (figure 504), a wisp of sweet grass bent over in the middle and wound with sinew; length, 12 inches.

This specimen was collected in 1901 by Mr S. C. Simms, who de-scribes the game as follows:

The target is placed 40 feet away from the archer and shot at with an arrow from an ordinary bow. If he hits it, he takes up the target, and placing it be-tween the index and second finger of his left hand, cross-ing and resting on the arrow which is made ready to shoot, but pointed toward the ground. [Figure 505.] Raising the bow and arrow, with the wisp still resting on it, the wisp is released and the arrow discharged at it. If he hits it in the air, he scores an arrow. It is thus used in gambling, and is played in the spring by boys and men. The game is called bah-but-te′-de-o.

FIG. 505. Crow Indian playing grass-target game, Montana; from photograph by Mr S. C. Simms.

DAKOTA (OGLALA). Pine Ridge reservation, South Dakota. (Cat. no. 22130, Free Museum of Science and Art, University of Pennsylvania.)

Toy bow and arrow (figure 506), the bow rudely cut from hardwood, with a single curve and a sinew string, 30 inches in length, and the arrow made of a sapling, with a blunt head, 18 inches in length.

Collected by Mr Louis L. Meeker, who de-

<hr>

[a] Report to Hon. Isaac I. Stevens on the Indian Tribes of the Upper Missouri. Unpub-lished manuscript in the library of the Bureau of American Ethnology.

scribes them under the name of hoksila itazipa. Speaking of the boys,[a] he says:

They play at duels, and the targets for archery are arrows, cactus plants, or the dead body of a small animal.

FIG. 506. Toy bow and arrow; length of bow, 30 inches; length of arrow, 18 inches; Oglala Dakota Indians, Pine Ridge reservation, South Dakota; cat. no. 22130, Free Museum of Science and Art, University of Pennsylvania.

DAKOTA (TETON). Pine Ridge reservation, South Dakota. (Cat. no. $\frac{50}{4236}$, American Museum of Natural History.)

Bow and five arrows with wooden points, collected by Dr J. R. Walker.

One arrow is painted black, and is shot upward so that it falls point down. The player then shoots at it with his other arrows, having four trials.

Doctor Walker [b] describes the game of coat shooting, waskate ogle cekutepi, as played by men in which an arrow painted black or wrapped with a black strip of buckskin, or having a tag attached to it, called ogle, coat, is shot high into the air so that it will fall from 50 to 75 yards away. Then the players stand and shoot at it with bow and arrow.

———— South Dakota.

Rev. J. Owen Dorsey [c] describes the following archery games:

Chun'kshila wanhin'kpe un'pi. Game with bows and small arrows.—These arrows are made of green switches, before the leaves fall in the autumn. The end of each switch-arrow is charred to a point, and when it hits the bare skin it gives pain. The boys used to shoot these arrows at the dogs when they went for water. Played by boys in autumn.

Tachághu yuhá shkátapi, Game with buffalo lights.—The boys used to assemble at the place where they killed the buffalo, and one of them would take a strip of green hide, to which the lights were attached, and drag the latter along the ground to serve as a mark for the rest. As he went along, the others shot at the lights. Sometimes the boy stood still, grasping a long withe fastened to the lights, which he swung round and around his head as he passed around the circle of players, who shot at the lights. Now and then, when a boy sought to recover his arrow, the other boy would strike him on the head with the lights, covering him with blood, after which he would release the player. Sometimes the boy holding the lights would break off all the arrows which were sticking therein, instead of allowing their owners to reclaim them.

Pezhí yuskíl'skíl kutépi, They shoot at grass tied tightly in bunches. Played by the larger boys. Grass is wrapped around a piece of bark till it assumes an oval shape, both ends of the grass being secured together. The grass ball thus

[a] Ogalala Games. Bulletin of the Free Museum of Science and Art, v. 3, pp. 34, 43, Philadelphia, 1901.

[b] Sioux Games. Journal of American Folk-Lore, v. 19, p. 32, 1906.

[c] Games of Teton Dakota Children. The American Anthropologist, v. 4, pp. 337, 339, 340, 341, 1891.

made is thrown into the air, and all shoot at it, trying to hit it before it reaches the ground; when it is hit, the arrow generally penetrates the object very far, leaving only a small part of the feather end visible.   The one who sends his arrow near the heart or mark on the grass ball has the right to toss the ball up into the air; but he who hits the heart on the ball throws the ball on the ground, and then throws it where he pleases, when all shoot at it.   The game is generally played till dark, but there are no stakes put up.

Unkchela kutépi, Shooting at the cactus. This game is always played for amusement, never for gain. On the appointed day the boys assemble on the prairie. One, who must be a swift runner, takes a cactus root into which he thrusts a stick to serve as a handle. Grasping the cactus by this handle, he holds it aloft as he runs, and the others shoot at it. During this game the swift runner himself is regarded as having become the cactus; so when one of the boys hits the cactus they say that it enrages the boy-cactus, who thereupon chases the others. Whenever the boy-cactus overtakes a player he sticks his cactus into him, turns around, and returns to his former place. Again the cactus is held aloft and they shoot at it as before, and again the players are chased. The game is kept up till the players wish to stop it.

Ogléche kutépi, Shooting at an arrow set up. Some boys back their favorites among the players by furnishing them with articles to be put down as stakes. On each side of a hill there is an arrow stuck upright in the ground to serve as a mark. The players on one side shoot at the arrow set up on the other; the players at the front shoot at the arrow in the rear, and then the players in the rear shoot at the arrow set up at the front. The nearer a player sends his arrow to the mark, the more it counts. Sometimes one of the arrows set up is withdrawn temporarily from its place to be used for shooting at the other arrow. Only arrows are staked.

MANDAN. North Dakota.

Catlin [a] describes a favorite amusement which they call the game of the arrow (figure 507):

The young men who are the most distinguished in this exercise, assemble on the prairie at a little distance from the village, and having paid, each one, his entrance fee, such as a shield, a robe, a pipe, or other article, step forward in turn, shooting their arrows into the air, endeavoring to see who can get the greatest number flying in the air at one time, thrown from the same bow. For this, the number of eight or ten arrows are clenched in the left hand with the bow, and the first one which is thrown is elevated to such a degree as will enable it to remain the longest time possible in the air, and while it is flying, the others are discharged as rapidly as possible; and he who succeeds in getting the greatest number up at once, is best, and takes the goods staked.

OMAHA. Nebraska.

Rev. J. Owen Dorsey [b] describes the following games:

Shooting arrows at a mark is called ma[n]kíde. The mark (nacábeg¢e tĕ) may be placed at any distance from the contestants. There must be an even number of persons on each side. Men play with men and boys with boys. Arrows are staked. Sometimes when an arrow hits squarely at the mark it wins eight arrows or perhaps ten, according to previous agreement. When no arrow

---

[a] The Manners, Customs, and Condition of the North American Indians, v. 1, p. 141, London, 1841.

[b] Omaha Sociology. Third Annual Report of the Bureau of Ethnology, p. 339, 1884.

hits the mark squarely and one touches it, that arrow wins. And if there is neither an arrow that hits the mark squarely nor one that barely touches it, then the nearest arrow wins. Should there be no arrow that has gone nearly to the mark, but one that has gone a little beyond it and descended, that one wins. Whichever one is nearest the mark always wins. If there are two arrows equidistant from the mark which belong to opposite sides in the game neither one wins; but if the equidistant arrows are on the same side, both win. Sometimes they say: " Let us finish the game whenever anyone hits the mark squarely." Then he who thus hits the mark wins all the arrows staked.

Shooting at a moccasin.—Hiⁿbe kide is a boy's game. An arrow is stuck in the ground and a moccasin is fastened to it. Each boy rides swiftly by and shoots at the moccasin. The game resembles the preceding one.

Fig. 507. Game of the arrow; Mandan Indians, North Dakota: from Catlin.

Maⁿ-múqpe, The game of dislodging arrows, is common to the Omahas, Poncas, Iowas, Otos, and Missouris. Arrows are shot up into a tree till they lodge among the branches; then the players shoot up and try to dislodge them. Whoever can bring down an arrow wins it. There are no sides or opposing parties. Any number of boys can play. The game has become obsolete among the Omahas, as there are no arrows now in use.

Maⁿ-gádaze is a game unknown among the Omahas, but practised among the Poncas, who have learned it from the Dakotas. It is played by two men. Each one holds a bow upright in his left hand with one end touching the ground, and the bowstring toward a heap of arrows. In the other hand he holds an arrow, which he strikes against the bowstring, which rebounds as he lets the arrow go. The latter flies suddenly toward the heap of arrows and goes among them. The player aims to have the feather on his arrow touch that on some other arrow which is in the heap. In that case he wins as many arrows as the feather or web has touched, but if the sinew on his arrow touches another arrow, it wins not only that one, but all in the heap.

SKITTAGETAN STOCK

HAIDA. British Columbia.

Dr J. R. Swanton [a] describes the following game:

"Arrows stuck up" (Sq!alnā'da). Some one shot an arrow up into the branches of a tree near the town until it stuck there. Then all would try to shoot it down, and generally succeeded in getting more up. He who knocked an arrow down owned it.

TANOAN STOCK

TEWA. Santa Clara, New Mexico.

Mr T. S. Dozier [b] writes as follows:

On the bringing in of the corn and after the dance in honor of that event the first game of the season begins. Then the boys, from the smallest tot able to walk to well grown up ones, and the younger men may be seen at different places about the pueblo with the ah (bow) and tsu (arrow). As you go by you ask: "Hum-bi-o" (what are you doing?) and they reply "I-vi-tsu-ah-wa" (playing the arrow). The game is a very simple one, as played by the Tewa, the bows not being the stronger ones formerly used, nor the very excellent ones now made by the Apache, Navaho, and Ute. A ring, varying in diameter from 5 to 6 inches to 2 or 3 feet, is made on the ground, and the arrows are placed upright in the earth. The players take places around the ring and shoot for position. The ones coming nearest the place, generally marked by a stone or a piece of wood, from which the arrows will be shot at, will shoot first in their order. The shooting then begins, and in order to win, the arrow must be thrown entirely from the ring, and the ones winning the most arrows take positions in the next shooting and go on until the arrows in the ring are exhausted.

WAKASHAN STOCK

MAKAH. Neah bay, Washington.

Dr George A. Dorsey [c] describes the following games:

Tlitsaktsaudl: This game (shoot-arrow) is also played by young men and, generally, in the spring of the year. Two goals are made, situated from 25 to 30 yards apart. As, from the nature of these goals, no specimen could be collected, a description must suffice. Five pieces of kelp are thrust into the earth in a row, the center piece being about 1½ feet high, the outer pieces about 3 inches high, and the two intermediate pieces midway between the center and outer pieces. Over these is placed another piece of kelp, which is bent in a semicircular shape, with its extremities thrust into the earth about 2 feet apart. From two to six play, all standing in front of one goal and shooting at the goal opposite, the object being to hit any one of the upright pieces of kelp. If the representative of one side or the other shoots and strikes the goal, he shoots again. Should he miss, one of the opponents takes the arrow with which he shoots. Should he make a hit, he retains the arrow. The object of this . . . game is to win arrows (quilah).

---

[a] Contributions to the Ethnology of the Haida. Memoirs of the American Museum of Natural History, whole series, v. 8, pt. 1, p. 61, New York, 1905.

[b] Some Tewa Games. Unpublished manuscript in the Bureau of American Ethnology, May 8, 1896.

[c] Games of the Makah Indians of Neah Bay. The American Antiquarian, v. 23, p. 70, 1901.

Tatauas. In this game a goal is also made of kelp, but instead of arrows short spears of red huckleberry, from 3 to 4 inches in length, are used. This game is played by two boys, each one sitting down on the beach facing his opponent, but at one side of him. B takes a piece of kelp stalk (wal'k-a-at) and thrusts it into the ground at his left side, at which A then hurls his spear. Failing to strike the goal, B takes A's spear and passes his piece of kelp to A, who then thrusts it into the ground by his left side, when B hurls the spear. In case he is successful he retains the spear, otherwise the kelp is returned to B and thrown at by A, and the game goes on as before. The object of the game is to win all the spears of the opponent.

WASHOAN STOCK

WASHO. Carson valley, Nevada.

Dr J. W. Hudson describes the following game under the name of tsohotumpesh:

An arrow is stuck in the ground slanting toward the marksman, who, 60 feet away, casts at it a 3-foot blunt arrow. One or more opponents take their turn, standing in the first caster's tracks. The object is to strike the leaning arrow, or knock away an opponent's arrow. Either counts 1. To dislodge the target counts 5, or coup. Several can play, each using any number of darts agreed upon.

YUMAN STOCK

MARICOPA. Arizona.

Mr Louis L. Meeker describes a game of grass shooting in which a wisp of grass is put upon the arrow where it crosses the bow. The bow is drawn and the wisp tossed up and shot in the air or the arrow is forfeited.

ZUÑIAN STOCK

ZUÑI. Zuñi, New Mexico.

Mr John G. Owens [a] describes the following game:

Shō-wē-es-tō-pa. The number of players is unlimited. Each one has several arrows. One throws an arrow on the ground 8 or 10 feet in front of him, the others follow in turn, and, should the arrow thrown by any one cross that of another at the beginning of the feathers, he takes it. The limits of success are very small, and skillful throwing is required to win the arrows of another. This game is but little played at present, and I am doubtful whether the younger men of the tribe know how to play it. . . . The decline of the game is probably due to the decline of the use of the bow and arrow, but I think it has left a descendant in lō-pō-chē-wā. This is played only by the boys. Instead of arrows they use pieces of bone 2 or 3 inches long with feathers tied to them. You may see five or six boys playing this game in all parts of the pueblo at any time during the summer. They generally touch the bone to the tongue before throwing it, to make it stick. The principle of the game is the same as that of the one just described.

Mrs Matilda Coxe Stevenson [b] describes the preceding game as follows:

---

[a] Some Games of the Zuñi. Popular Science Monthly, v. 39, p. 40, New York, 1891.
[b] Zuñi Games. American Anthropologist, n. s., v. 5, p. 490, 1903.

Shówiältowe may be played by any number of persons, each one being provided with several arrows. Holding it between his index and middle finger and

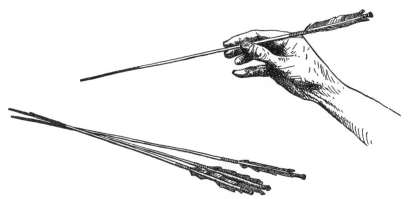

Fig. 508. Method of holding arrows in playing shówiältowe; Zuñi Indians, Zuñi, New Mexico; from Mrs Stevenson.

thumb, the first player throws an arrow a distance of some 10 or 12 feet [figure 508]. Then a second player throws, aiming to have the feathers on his arrow-

Fig. 509. Plumed sticks used in playing lápochiwe; Zuñi Indians, Zuñi, New Mexico; from Mrs Stevenson.

shaft touch those of the one already on the ground. If he is successful he takes both arrows and makes another throw, when the next player aims at the arrow on the ground; if he fails, the arrows remain in place and another player throws; and so on, each man taking the arrows which are touched by his own. Sometimes considerable dispute arises as to whether the feathers are really in contact, the men stooping and examining the arrows with the closest scrutiny.

If the arrows fall apart, each player takes his own from the ground, and a new game is begun. The taker of the full number of arrows wins the game.

Lápochiwe.—Implements [figure 509], three pencil-like sticks; three reeds the length of the sticks, one of them with a sharpened stick projecting, and one longer reed (designated the chief) having a pointed stick attached to the end. Two fluffy feathers are attached to each reed and stick.

Three sometimes play with the number of reeds and sticks mentioned, but when more than two play it is usual to increase the number of sticks, although in the genuine game of the Gods of War the number can not exceed seven.

The one proposing the game divides the six smaller reeds and sticks between his opponent and himself, and throws "the chief." The game is played like shówiältowe, except that the players are seated and throw a comparatively short distance. Lápochiwe is one of the favorite indoor games.

FIG. 510. Lápochiwe; length of darts, about 8¼ inches; Zuñi Indians, Zuñi, New Mexico; cat. no. 3093, Brooklyn Institute Museum

ZUÑI. Zuñi, New Mexico. (Cat. no. 3093, Brooklyn Institute Museum.)

Twelve feathered darts, made of slips of twig (figure 510), about 2½ inches in length, each with three feathers inserted; total length, 8½ inches.

The set was collected by the writer in 1903. The name given was lapochiwe.

———Zuñi, New Mexico. (Cat. no. 3065, Brooklyn Institute Museum.)

Miniature bows, 18½ inches in length, two arrows, and a target made of grass, 5¼ inches in length (figure 511). Collected by the writer in 1903.

The name of the game was given as hapoanpiskwaiwe, from ha-po-an, bunch of grass, and pis-kwai-we, shooting. Two men or two boys play it in summer in the cornfields. The target is covered with sand, which is smoothed over so that the ha-po-an does not show. They shoot in turn, leaving the arrows in the ground. Then they pull out the arrows together, and if neither has pierced the target, it is bad luck; but if one has hit the target and lifts it out on his arrow, he is sure to kill deer. The arrows are old style, not feathered and made of cane with hard-wood foreshafts.

Mrs Matilda Coxe Stevenson [a] describes hapoanne pihlkwanawe:

Implements.—Bow and arrows; an oval roll of green cornhusks.

Any number may play this game. A hä'poänně (roll of husks) is placed upon the ground and arrows are shot at it from a distance of 40 or 50 feet. The first player to strike the roll covers it with a mound of earth, very much larger than the roll itself, while the others turn their backs. The one who places the hä'poänně is almost sure to mark the exact location of it, hence he resorts to various devices to mislead the players. A favorite deception is to leave the

[a] Zuñi Games. American Anthropologist, n. s., v. 5, p. 488, 1903.

mound low where the roll is actually buried, having it more elevated at some other point. The players aim to shoot their arrows into the hä'poänně, and the one who strikes wins the game. The winner draws the husk from beneath the earth with the arrow. When the arrow strikes the mound, but does not touch the hä poänně, it is removed by the one who secretes the object, and a

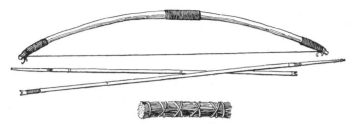

FIG. 511. Target and bow and arrows; length of target, 5¼ inches; length of bow, 18¼ inches; Zuñi Indians, Zuñi, New Mexico; cat. no. 3065, Brooklyn Institute Museum.

second player shoots his arrow. Each player takes his turn until the hä'poänně is struck, the one having the arrangement of it being the last one to shoot, and he is naturally the most frequent winner. This game affords great amusement to the younger men.

SNOW-SNAKE

I have included under the general name of snow-snake all that class of games in which darts or javelins are hurled along snow or ice or free in the air in a competition to see whose dart will go the farthest. They appear to be confined to the northern range of tribes, within the limit of ice and snow.

There are three principal types: First, the snow-snake proper, in which a long polished rod is made to glide on the snow or ice; second, the bone slider, in which a piece of bone or horn, stuck with two feathers, is made to slide along the ice; third, a game in which a javelin, sometimes feathered and commonly tipped with horn, is made to slide along the ground or to dart through the air, after being made to glance by striking the earth or some other obstacle.

The game of snow-snake is played with rods up to 10 feet in length, round or flat, usually highly polished, and not infrequently carved at the end. Shorter sticks, simple javelins or darts with carved heads, are also used. They are made to slide along the frozen crust, or in a rut in the snow. Sides are chosen and stakes bet upon the result, a snake which outdistances all on the opposite side counting a point. Snow-snake is distinctly a man's game, but special forms exist for women.

As suggested by the Omaha game, the first form appears to have been originally a game of sliding bows, and these may be referred to the two bows of the twin War Gods. The hurled snakes may be referred to their war clubs. The bone sliders which have been col-

lected from a number of tribes—Algonquian, Kiowan, and Siouan—
remain unexplained. They are all alike, with two feathers stuck on
pegs, and suggest a bird in their form. The third form of darts is
probably derived from arrows.

ALGONQUIAN STOCK

ARAPAHO. Cheyenne and Arapaho reservation, Oklahoma.

Mr James Mooney [a] says:

The băti'qtûba (abbreviated ti'qtûp) game of the Arapaho and other prairie
tribes somewhat resembles the Iroquois game of the snow-snake, and is played
by children or grown persons of both sexes. It is a very simple game, the contestants merely throwing or sliding the sticks along the ground to see who can
send them farthest. Two persons or two parties play against each other,
boys sometimes playing against girls, or men against women. It is, however,
more especially a girls' game. The game sticks (bătĭqta'wa) are slender willow
rods, about 4 feet long, peeled and painted, and tipped with a point of buffalo
horn to enable them to slide more easily along the ground. In throwing, the
player holds the stick at the upper end with the thumb and fingers, and, swinging it like a pendulum, throws it out with a sweeping motion. Young men throw
arrows about in the same way, and small boys sometimes throw ordinary reeds
or weed stalks.

CHEYENNE. Oklahoma. (Cat. no. 21943, Free Museum of Science
and Art, University of Pennsylvania.)

Feathered bone (figure 512) for throwing on the ice, called hekone-
natsistam, or bone game, consisting of a piece of buffalo or beef
rib, 7 inches in length, with two sticks fitted at one end, each
bearing a hawk feather, dyed red; total length, 25 inches.

It was collected by Mr Louis L. Meeker, who has kindly furnished
the following particulars:

The thumb is placed on one side of the bone, the forefinger between the sticks,
with the end against the end of the
bone, and the other three fingers opposed to the thumb against the other
side of the rib, the convex side of
which is down. It is then thrown
down and forward against a smooth
surface, preferably ice, so that it
glances forward as throwing-sticks
and snow-snakes do.

FIG. 512. Feathered bone slider; length, 7 inches;
Cheyenne Indians, Oklahoma; cat. no. 21943,
Free Museum of Science and Art, University of
Pennsylvania.

The marks etched on the bone represent a horned toad, a tarantula,
the milky way, and the moon. The
four marks invoke the four winds,
while the six legs of the tarantula represent up and down and the cardinal points.

———— Oklahoma. (Cat. no. 67358, Field Columbian Museum.)

Dart points, made of polished horn 3⅝ inches in length, mounted on
sticks 34 and 32 inches in length. The shorter one is notched at
the end like an arrow.

---

[a] The Ghost-dance Religion. Fourteenth Annual Report of the Bureau of Ethnology,
p. 1007, 1896.

Collected by Rev. H. R. Voth in 1890, who gave the following information:

The points are of buffalo horn and are employed as points for sticks from 4 to 6 feet long. The arrows thus formed are used in a game in which a number of girls shoot or hurl the darts along the road or other smooth ground. The object of the contest is to determine who can make the dart go farthest.

CHEYENNE. Cheyenne reservation, Montana. (Field Columbian Museum.)

Cat. no. 69985. Javelin, with conical bone head, 5 inches in length, and wooden shaft painted blue; total length, 66 inches.

This was collected in 1901 by Mr. S. C. Simms, who describes it as used in a woman's game, played on the ice or hard crust of snow and called majestum.

Cat. no. 69984. Arrow tipped with a conical bone point, 4 inches in length, with wooden shaft, painted yellow, and having feathers tied at the end; total length, $27\frac{1}{2}$ inches.

This was collected in 1901 by Mr S. C. Simms, who describes it as used in a man's game.

The stick is seized by one end, whirled rapidly around with a vertical motion, and released when it gains momentum. The object is to make it go as far as possible.

CHIPPEWA. Apostle islands, Wisconsin.

J. G. Kohl [a] says:

The Indians are also said to have many capital games on the ice, and I had the opportunity, at any rate, to inspect the instruments employed in them, which they called shoshiman (slipping sticks). These are elegantly carved and prepared; at the end they are slightly bent, like the iron of a skate, and form a heavy knob, while gradually tapering down in the handle. They cast these sticks with considerable skill over the smooth ice. In order to give them greater impulsion, a small, gently rising incline of frozen snow is formed on the ice, over which the gliding sticks bound. In this way they gain greater impetus, and dart from the edge of the snow mound like arrows.

———— Wisconsin.

Prof. I. I. Ducatel [b] says:

They have their shoshman, or snow stick, about the length of a common walking cane, cut out in the shape of a sledge, which they cause to slide over the snow or ice.

———— Mille Lacs, Minnesota. (Cat. no. 204597, United States National Museum.)

A wooden club, $26\frac{1}{2}$ inches in length, flat on one side and round on the reverse, one end wedge-shaped, with its upper face burned and marked with incised lines painted red and yellow, as shown in figure 513. Collected by Mr G. H. Beaulieu.

---

[a] Kitchi-Gami, Wanderings round Lake Superior, p. 90, London, 1860.
[b] A Fortnight among the Chippewas. The Indian Miscellany, p. 368, Albany, 1877.

This object is stated by the collector to be a rabbit club, which is glanced or thrown along the surface of the snow to kill the animal, "like a snow-snake."

FIG. 513. Snow-snake; length, 26¼ inches; Chippewa Indians, Mille Lacs, Minnesota; cat. no. 204597, United States National Museum.

CHIPPEWA. Bear island, Leech lake, Minnesota. (American Museum of Natural History.)

Cat. no. $\frac{50}{4733}$. Snow-snake (figure 514*a*), a straight stick, pointed at one end, 26 inches in length.

Cat. no. $\frac{50}{4732}$. Snow-snake (figure 514*b*), curved upward and expanding at the farther end, 29½ inches in length.

These specimens were collected in 1903 by Dr William Jones, who describes them as played on the snow and called shoshiman, sliders.

FIG. 514 *a, b*. Snow-snakes; lengths, 26 and 29¼ inches; Chippewa Indians, Bear island, Leech lake, Minnesota; cat. no. $\frac{50}{4733}$, $\frac{50}{4732}$, American Museum of Natural History.

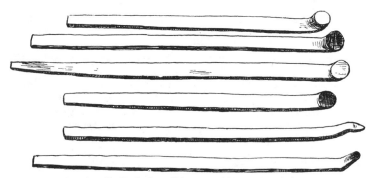

FIG. 515. Snow-snakes; length, 12¼ inches; Chippewa Indians, Bear island, Leech lake, Minnesota; cat. no. $\frac{50}{4719}$, American Museum of Natural History.

Cat. no. $\frac{50}{4719}$. Six snow-snakes (figure 515), 12½ inches in length, with fore ends turned upward and carved differently.

Collected by Dr William Jones, who describes them under the name of shoshiman, sliders:

A small boy's game. Each has an equal number. Played on a ridge of snow, down which a little groove is made. The object is to send the stick the farthest.

CHIPPEWA.   Bois fort, near Rainy river, Minnesota.   (Cat. no. $\frac{50}{4714}$,
    American Museum of Natural History.)

Wooden club (figure 516), made of white cedar, tapering to the point
    and burned black; 22 inches in length.   Collected by Dr Wil-
    liam Jones in 1903.

FIG. 516.   Snow-snake; length, 22 inches; Chippewa Indians, Bois fort, Minnesota; cat. no. $\frac{50}{4714}$,
American Museum of Natural History.

———— Turtle mountain, North Dakota.   (Cat. no. $\frac{50}{4734}$, American
    Museum of Natural History.)

Wooden club (figure 517), 21½ inches long, expanded at the upper end
    and painted red.

Collected in 1903 by Dr William Jones, who describes it as thrown
on the snow with a wrist movement and gives the name as kwashkwa-
shiman, bounding slider.

FIG. 517.   Snow-snake; length, 21½ inches; Chippewa Indians, Turtle mountain, North Dakota;
cat. no. $\frac{50}{4734}$, American Museum of Natural History.

CREE.   Muskowpetung reserve, Qu'appelle, Assiniboia.   (Field Co-
    lumbian Museum.)

Cat. no. 61989.   Wooden dart (figure 518), 7¾ inches in length, the
    shaft decorated with a burnt design; described by the collector,
    under the name of puckitseeman.

Played by any number of persons, of either sex or any age, either singly or by
partners.   A narrow track is made down the side of a hill covered with snow
for a distance of 60 feet or
more.   This track is iced.   The
puck is started at the top of the
track; it is not shoved, but
must start off by its own weight.
The track is barred at four
points, about 10 feet apart, by

FIG. 518.   Snow-dart (puckitseeman); length, 7¾ inches;
Cree Indians, Assiniboia; cat. no. 61989, Field Columbian Museum.

snow barriers.   The object is to pass the puck through as many as possible or
all of the four barriers, and at the same time to have it not leave the track.

To win, the dart must be passed through all four barriers four times by the
same person or partners.   Count is kept, however, according to the number of
barriers passed through.   Considerable skill is acquired in this game in the
handling of the puck.

Cat. no. 61991.   Wooden dart (figure 519), similar to the preceding,
    but longer; length, 18¼ inches.

This is described by the collector, under the name of shooceeman,
throwing to slide:

Played by men only, either singly or in partnership.   Four barriers of loose
snow are constructed at distances of a few feet apart and immediately behind
each other.

The players stand about ten feet distant from the nearest barrier, and the stick is thrown, as in underhand bowling, directly at the nearest barrier, which it approaches with a gliding motion. The object of the game is to pass the stick through the entire set of barriers at one throw, which wins the game; points may be counted, however, according to the number of barriers penetrated by the dart.

In the case of a tie between players, the winner in the play-off must pass his dart through all barriers four times.

FIG. 519. Snow dart (shooceeman); length, 18¼ inches; Cree Indians, Assiniboia; cat. no. 61991, Field Columbian Museum.

Cat. no. 61990. Flat stick (figure 520), one end pointed and curved upward; length, 14¼ inches.

It is described by the collector under the name of esquayopuckitseeman:

Game played by women exclusively. Similar to game cat. no. 61989, except that the ice path is made with numerous turnings and is not impeded by barriers. The ice path is also made much narrower, being but little wider than the dart itself. The passage of the dart around the several turnings is equivalent to the passing of the dart through the snow barriers in the men's games.

FIG. 520. Snow-dart (esquayopuckitseeman): length, 14¼ inches; Cree Indians, Assiniboia; cat. no. 61990, Field Columbian Museum.

All of the preceding specimens were collected by Mr J. A. Mitchell.

GROSVENTRES. Fort Belknap, Montana. (Cat. no. $\frac{50}{1823}$, American Museum of Natural History.)

End of beef rib, having two wooden pegs inserted at one end, upon which feathers are stuck; length, 24 inches. A model collected by Dr A. L. Kroeber.

MENOMINEE. Wisconsin.

Dr Walter J. Hoffman [a] describes the following game:

Another game for both amusement and gambling was termed the snow-snake, and was undoubtedly derived from the Ojibwa. It was played during the winter, either in the snow or on the ice, and the only article necessary consisted of a piece of hard wood, from 5 to 6 feet long and from one-half to three-fourths of an inch thick. The head was bulb-like and shaped like a snake, with eyes and a cross cut to denote the mouth. This rounded end permitted it to pass over slight irregularities in its forward movements. The player would grasp the end, or tail, of the snake by putting the index finger against the end and the thumb on one side, opposite to which would be the remaining three fingers; then stooping toward the ground the snake was held horizontally from

---

[a] The Menomini Indians. Fourteenth Annual Report of the Bureau of Ethnology, p. 244, 1896.

right to left and forced forward in the direction of the head, skimming along rapidly for a considerable distance. [See figure 521.]

The Ojibwa play the game in a similar manner, but they sometimes place a ridge of snow slightly inclined away from the player in order to give the snake an upward curve as it leaves the hands, thus propelling it a considerable distance before touching the snow or ice.

FIG. 521. Menominee Indian holding snow-snake preparatory to throwing; Wisconsin; from Hoffman.

MISSISAUGA. New Credit, Ontario.

Rev. Peter Jones [a] says:

Their principal play during the winter season is the snow-snake, which is made of hard smooth timber, about 6 feet long, having eyes and mouth like a snake. The manner of playing is to take the snake by the tail, and throw it along the snow or ice with all their strength. Whoever sends his snake the farthest a certain number of times gains the prize.

---

[a] History of the Ojebway Indians, p. 134, London, 1861.

NORRIDGEWOCK. Norridgewock, Maine.

Rasles [a] gives, under joüets des enfans:

Sŝhé, c'est un bois plat qu'ils font glisser sur la nége. glace.

PASSAMAQUODDY. Maine.

Mrs W. W. Brown [b] describes the following game (figure 522):

T'so-hâ-ta-ben, or t'so-hē-āc, requires more skill, both in construction and play-ing, than other outdoor games. It is played on the crust or hard-drifted snow of the hillside. If this is the game spoken of by other writers as snow-snakes, there is nothing in the name to so indicate. Each player is supposed to supply himself with the required few t'so-hē-āc, sticks. In that case all the sticks are bunched and thrown up, except five sticks, though it sometimes happens that quite a number will join in the game, each contestant catching what he can as they fall. These sticks have different values, and as distance is what is aimed

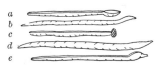

FIG. 522. Snow darts: (a) m-quon, the spoon; (b) at-ho-sis, the snake; (c) ske-gä-weis, the wart; (d) p't'gukwhol-ŭk; (e) be-dupk-t-s, the duck; Passamaquoddy In-dians, Maine; from Mrs W. W. Brown.

at, the one going furthest wins all the others of the same kind. They are set in motion by that peculiar movement which boys use in skipping stones on the water. The shouts of the players, as the stick flies over the snow to the goal of success, or buries itself in the drift of defeat, are deafening. As the sticks are, one by one, set in motion, the player sings " la-hâ-wâ, la-hâ-wâ," calling the stick by name, and this, echoed and reechoed from the valley, is not al-together unmusical. The sticks, or t'so-he-āc, are named m-quon, āt'ho-sis, p-tqŭk whol-êik, ske-ga-weis, and be-dupk-ts. M'quon, the spoon, is about 2 feet long, flat at top and bottom, with one end concave like the bowl of a spoon. A-t'ho-sis, the snake, is long, slender, and round, one end resembling a snake's head, the other pointed. Ske-ga-weis is flat underneath, round on top, about 2 feet in length, one end notched to resemble its name of wart. P't'gŭk-whol-ŭk is the largest of all. From 5 to 7 feet long and nearly round, both ends raised slightly and pointed, going with great force and speed, it drives in and out through the snow, causing much merriment and noisy betting. Be-dupk't's, the duck, is about 3 feet [long], flat on top, round underneath, with an end like the head of a duck. Sometimes these t'so-he-ac are clever imitations, the coloring being also effective. Though this game is not played as much as formerly, even the young boys seem to understand whittling the sticks into a recognizable resemblance to the duck.

PENOBSCOT. Oldtown, Maine. (Cat. no. 48233 to 48235, Peabody Museum of American Archæology and Ethnology.)

Three carved sticks, flat on the under side and curving upward in front, one (48233), snake head, 21 inches in length (figure 523a); another (48234), spoon mouth, 18 inches in length (figure 523b); and the third (48235), 14½ inches in length (figure 523c).

These specimens were made by Big Thunder and collected by Mr C. C. Willoughby, who furnished the following account of the game, which is called suha:

---

[a] Memoirs of the American Academy of Arts and Sciences, n. s., v. 1, p. 472, Cam-bridge, 1833.

[b] Some Indoor and Outdoor Games of the Wabanaki Indians. Proceedings and Transac-tions of the Royal Society of Canada, v. 6, sec. 2, p. 44, Montreal, 1889.

When a man wanted to play this game he took a number of his su-ha sticks and went through the village calling "su ha! su ha!" One or more of the players would take a boy by the feet and drag him down some incline, thus making a track, or path, in the snow. Down this path each player in turn, calling out "su ha!" threw one of his sticks, as a spear is thrown. To mark the distance this stick was stuck up in the snow beside the path, opposite the

Fig. 523 *a,b,c*. Snow-snakes; lengths, 21, 18, and 14½ inches; Penobscot Indians, Oldtown, Maine; cat. no. 48233 to 48235, Peabody Museum of American Archæology and Ethnology.

place where it stopped. When all the sticks had been thrown, they became the property of the man whose stick had covered the greatest distance. He would gather them all up and selecting such as he wanted, calling out at the same time "su ha!" throw the others up in the air, and they became the property of those strong and quick enough to secure them. This game has not been played since 1842.

SAUK AND FOXES. Iowa. (Cat. no. $\frac{50}{2201}$, American Museum of
      Natural History.)

Slender stick of hard wood (figure 524), 25½ inches in length, with
      an egg-shaped end hardened by fire.

Collected by Dr William Jones, who describes it as snow-snake. Prof. Frederick Starr informed the writer that it was swung by the small end to give it impetus.

Fig. 524. Snow-snake; length, 25½ inches; Sauk and Fox Indians, Iowa; cat. no. $\frac{50}{2301}$, American Museum of Natural History.

———— Iowa. (American Museum of Natural History.)

Cat. no. $\frac{50}{3503}$. Three pointed sumac sticks, 46 to 52 inches in length.
      Collected by Dr William Jones, who gives the name as shoskwihani,
sliders.

Fig. 525. Snow-snakes; length, 30 inches; Sauk and Fox Indians, Iowa; cat. no. $\frac{50}{3502}$, American Museum of Natural History.

Cat. no. $\frac{50}{3502}$. Two narrow, flat sticks (figure 525), rounded on the
      upper side, 30 inches in length; one burned black for the entire
      length on the upper side, the other burned only at the head.

Collected by Dr William Jones, who gives the name as manetowagi,
snakes.

They are played on the ice or frozen ground by men, and are thrown with a wrist movement, flat side down, so that they glide along for a great distance.

Cat. no. $\frac{50}{3501}$, $\frac{50}{3500}$. Two sets of sticks, one of each white and the other black, one (figure 526a) having an ovate head, 31 inches in length, and the other (figure 526b) a conical head, 33½ inches in length.

These were collected by Dr William Jones, who gives the name of both as miskwapi and states that they are played on the frozen ground or on the ice.

In throwing they are whirled around the head, and when played on the ground are made to glance from an incline.

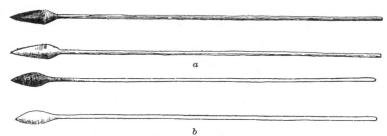

FIG. 526 a,b. Snow-snakes; lengths, 31 and 33½ inches; Sauk and Fox Indians, Iowa; cat. no. $\frac{50}{3501}$, $\frac{50}{3500}$, American Museum of Natural History.

SAUK AND FOXES. Iowa. (Cat. no. $\frac{50}{3507}$, American Museum of Natural History.)

Two darts (figure 527), 26 inches long, with flat wooden heads, one painted blue and the other plain, with a stick 24½ inches long, having a bark cord attached with which the darts are slung. Collected by Dr William Jones.

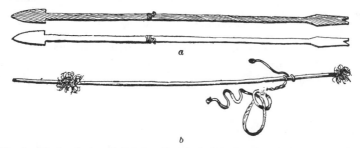

FIG. 527 a,b. Slinging-darts and stick; length of darts, 26 inches; length of stick, 24½ inches; Sauk and Fox Indians, Iowa; cat. no. $\frac{50}{3507}$, American Museum of Natural History.

A summer game. The one whose dart goes farthest wins. The game is called nāneskwapuchuweni, and the darts nāneskwapuchi.

——— Tama, Iowa. (Cat. no. 36756, Free Museum of Science and Art, University of Pennsylvania.)

Two peeled saplings of box elder, 66½ inches in length.

These were collected by the writer in 1900, and described to him as javelins for a game under the name of maskwapihok.

ATHAPASCAN STOCK

Takulli. Stuart lake, British Columbia.

Reverend Father A. G. Morice[a] describes a game called tətquh:

A rod [figure 528] 5 or 6 feet long . . . is thrown through the air so as to fall as far as possible from the initial point of launching, the distance reached determining the measure of success attained. This game . . . is now obsolescent.

A great rival is nəzəz, which is played with sticks of almost the same shape [figure 529], though much stouter near their fore end. As they do duty on the frozen surface of the snow, the finest polish possible is aimed at in their prep-

FIG. 528. Game dart (tətquh); Takulli Indians, Stuart lake, British Columbia; from Morice.

FIG. 529. Snow-snake (nəzəz); Takulli Indians, Stuart lake, British Columbia; from Morice.

aration. These sticks vary in length from 3 to 6 or 7 feet, according to the strength, possessed or assumed, of the player. The Carriers are to-day passionately fond of this game, which is played, as a rule, by adverse bands, the stake going over to the party which first attains the fixed number of points.[b]

CADDOAN STOCK

Pawnee. Oklahoma.

Dr George A. Dorsey [c] says:

In former times, a game was in vogue among the boys somewhat similar to the so-called " snow-snake," common in the central region of the United States. The prize in this game was the javelin itself; and when an individual had won a sufficient number of these long willow javelins they were made up into a mat for him by his grandmother.

IROQUOIAN STOCK

Huron. Ontario.

Bacqueville de la Potherie [d] says:

Girls play with spindles (fuseaux), which they shove beneath a small piece of wood raised above the ground. The game is to push the spindle the farthest. There are games for the winter and games for the summer. Those for all seasons are fruit stones and straws; those for winter are spindles for children. The boys add a tail two feet and a half long to the latter, while the girls use actual spindles. They moisten them with saliva or put them in freezing water, so that they are covered with a slippery coat, and then they push them down the slope of a frozen hill that they may go far. They also use for this purpose long, flat sticks. They paint both the spindles and the sticks.

---

[a] Notes on the Western Dénés. Transactions of the Canadian Institute, v. 4, p. 112, Toronto, 1895.

[b] See also The Western Dénés. Proceedings of the Canadian Institute, 3d ser., v. 7, p. 154, Toronto, 1889.

[c] Traditions of the Skidi Pawnee, p. xvi, New York, 1904.

[d] Histoire de l'Amérique Septentrionale, v. 3, p. 23, Paris, 1753.

SENECA. New York.

Morgan [a] describes the game of gawasa, or snow-snake, as follows:

Among the amusements of the winter season in Indian life was the game with snow-snakes [figure 530]. It was primarily designed as a diversion for the young; but it was occasionally made a public game between the tribes like the other, and aroused a great degree of spirit and the usual amount of betting. The snake was thrown with the hand, by placing the forefinger against its foot and supporting it with the thumb and remaining fingers. It was thus made to run upon the snow crust with the speed of an arrow, and to a much greater distance, sometimes running 60 or 80 rods. The success of the player depended upon his dexterity and muscular strength.

The snakes were made of hickory, and with the most perfect precision and finish. They were from 5 to 7 feet in length, about a fourth of an inch in thickness, and gradually diminishing from about an inch in width at the head to about half an inch at the foot. The head was round, turned up slightly, and pointed with lead to increase the momentum of the snake. This game, like that of ball, was divided into a number of separate contests; and was determined when either party had gained the number of points agreed upon, which was generally from 7 to 10. The players were limited and select, usually not more than six. A station was determined upon, with the line, or general direction in which the snake was to be thrown. After they had all been

FIG. 530. Snow-snake; Seneca Indians, New York; from Morgan.

thrown by the players on both sides, the next question was to determine the count. The snake which ran the greatest distance was a point for the side to which it belonged. Other points might be won on the same side, if a second or third snake was found to be ahead of all the snakes upon the adverse side. One count was made for each snake which outstripped all upon the adverse side. These contests were repeated until one of the parties had made the requisite number of points to determine the game.

With the snow boat [da-ya-no-tä-yen-da-quä] was played one of the winter games of the Iroquois, in which the object was to discover which boat would run the farthest in an iced trench or path. The boat was about 15 inches in length, and made of beech or other hard wood, something in the fashion of a canoe. It was solid, with the exception of an oblong cavity in the center, designed to suspend bells or other rattles upon. In the stern of this little vessel a white feather was inserted for a flag, by which to follow it in its descent. On the bottom the boat was rounded, but with a slight wind lengthwise, as shown in the figure [531], to give it a true direction. A side hill, with an open plain below, was the kind of place selected to try the speed of the boats. Trenches in a straight line down the hill, and about a foot wide, were made by treading down the snow; after

[a] League of the Iroquois, p. 303, Rochester, 1851.

which water was poured into them that it might freeze and line the trenches throughout their whole extent with ice. These trenches to the number of a dozen, side by side, if as many individuals intended to play, were finished with the greatest care and exactness, not only down the hillside, but to a considerable distance across the plain below. At the same time the boats themselves were dipped in water, that they might also be coated with ice.

The people divided by tribes in playing this, as in all other Iroquois games, the Wolf, Bear, Beaver, and Turtle tribes playing against the Deer, Snipe, Heron, and Hawk. At the time appointed the people assembled at the base of the hill and divided off by tribes, and then commenced betting on the result, a custom universally practised on such occasions. The game was played by select players who were stationed at the top of the hill, each with two or

Fig. 531. Snow boat; Seneca Indians, New York; from Morgan.

three boats, and standing at the head of his own trench. When all was in readiness the boats were started off together at the appointed moment, and their rapid descent was watched with eager interest by the people below. . . . If the game was 20 it would be continued until one side had made that number of points. A count of one was made for every boat which led all upon the adverse side, so that if there were six players upon a side it was possible for that number to be made at one trial. On the contrary, if all the boats but one upon one side were in advance of all but one on the adverse side, and the latter was in advance of all, this head boat would win and count one. The principles of the game are precisely the same as in the snow-snake game.

Morgan says also:[a]

There was another game of javelino, gä-ga-dä-yan'-duk, played by shooting them through the air. In this game the javelin used was made of sumac, because of its lightness, and was of the same length and size as in the former [see page 410]. This game was divided into contests, as the ball game, and was won by the party which first made the number agreed upon. The game was usually from 15 to 20, and the number of players on a side ranged from five to ten. When the parties were ready, the one who had the first throw selected the object upon which the javelin was to be thrown, to give it an upward flight, and also its distance from the standing point. If, for example, it was a log, at the distance of a rod, the player placed his forefinger against the foot of the javelin, and, supporting it with his thumb and second finger, he threw it in such a manner, that it would strike the upper part of the log, and thus be thrown up into the air, and forward, until its force was spent. In this manner all the

----

[a] League of the Iroquois, p. 301, Rochester, 1851.

players, in turn, threw their javelins. The one which was thrown the greatest distance won a point. If another upon the same side was in advance of all upon the opposite side, it counted another, and so on for every one which led all those upon the opposite side. In the next contest, the second party chose the object over which to throw the javelin, and the distance. The game was thus continued, until the number of points were gained which were agreed upon for the game.

SENECA. Seneca reservation, Cattaraugus county, New York.

Dr Walter Hough [a] published the following account from information furnished by Andrew John, jr, a member of the tribe:

The game of kow-a-sa, or snow-snake, the national game of the Iroquois it may be called, is still played. A straight well-beaten road is now usually chosen, though sometimes it is played in the open, as formerly. The snakes are brought out, to the great glee of the boys, whose ears are on the alert, when some one says, "dan-di-wa-sa-ye," "let's play snow-snake," because they have the honor to run and bring back for the throwers. The snake is a thin rounded strip of hard wood, from 7 to 10 feet long and 1½ inches wide at most, made very smooth, shod at the forward end with a pewter nose piece, and not curved upward, Mr John says. It is balanced on the left hand and held by the tail in the right hand, the fingers being beneath and the thumb above. Holding it thus, the player runs 3 or 4 rods and, just before he throws he jumps. The stick skips away over the snow like an arrow, or perhaps one could better say like a snake. The skill in the game is in delivering the snake at the best slant, so that none of the original impetus given by the powerful right arm is lost.

The game is usually of four snakes—that is, the best three throws in four.

When skillful players contend, the excitement is very great among the Indians, and there is much betting, sometimes for high stakes; in fact, the game is for betting purposes entirely.

——— New York. (Cat. no. 52241, Peabody Museum of American Archæology and Ethnology.)

Snow-snake, consisting of a highly polished hickory sapling, 7 feet 8 inches in length, the forward end tipped with lead.

This specimen was formerly owned by Chief Two Guns, who won several prizes with this snake, and whose totem, a fish, is cut on one face. Collected by Mr John W. Sanborn.

Another specimen in this collection (cat. no. 52242), made by Indians, has not been used.

——— Grand River reserve, Ontario. (Cat. no. 55798, Field Columbian Museum.)

Snow-snake, made of polished hickory sapling, 7 feet 11 inches in length, shod with lead at forward end for a length of 4½ inches. Collected by Mr S. C. Simms, who gives the following account of the method of play:

The snake, gä-wa-sa, is thrown along a narrow shallow rut in the snow, made by the dragging of a log. The player grasps the end, or tail, of the snake by putting the index finger against the end and the thumb to one side, opposite to

---

[a] Games of Seneca Indians. The American Anthropologist, v. 1, p. 134, 1888.

which would be the remaining three fingers; then, stooping toward the ground, the snake is held horizontally over the rut in the snow, and with a few quick short steps is thrown with considerable force along the rut. Sides are chosen to play the game. The snake which runs farthest wins, and a count is made by each snake which leads all upon the opposite side.

TUSCARORA. New York. (Cat. no. 16340, Free Museum of Science and Art, University of Pennsylvania.)

Four sticks of hard wood, shaved to a point, 41½ inches in length; designated as throwing sticks, ka-te nyä-ta.

KIOWAN STOCK

KIOWA. Oklahoma. (Cat. no. 152906, United States National Museum.)

Bone slider, consisting of a piece of rib bone (figure 532), 4½ inches in length, the upper concave face marked with small holes, having two feathers stuck on wooden pegs in one end; total length, 17 inches. Collected by Mr James Mooney.

FIG. 532. Feathered bone slider; length, 17 inches; Kiowa Indians, Oklahoma; cat. no. 152906, United States National Museum.

KULANAPAN STOCK

POMO. Seven miles south of Ukiah, Mendocino county, California. (Cat. no. 70945, Field Columbian Museum.)

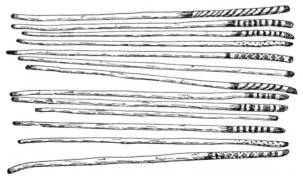

FIG. 533. Ground-coasting arrows; average length, 3 feet; Pomo Indians, Mendocino county, California; cat. no. 70945, Field Columbian Museum.

Thirteen sticks (figure 533), with butt ends marked in pairs with burned devices; average length, 3 feet.

Collected by Dr J. W. Hudson, who describes them as ground-coasting arrows, called mului, a name also applied to a process of etching a rod by holding it in a blaze after it is bound or protected in part by withes of another material, as grapevine, hazel, etc.

The darts are about the size of arrows. Distance only counts. There are five distinct mulu'-i symbols placed on the darts, all named for or as symbols for certain animals.

MARIPOSAN STOCK

YOKUTS. Tule River reservation, Tulare county, California. (Cat. no. 70405, Field Columbian Museum.)

Lance of peeled sapling (figure 534), 66½ inches in length. It is described by the collector, Dr J. W. Hudson, as a snow-snake or ground dart. The butt is weighted by being wound with iron wire.

FIG. 534. Snow-snake; length, 66½ inches; Yokuts Indians, Tule River reservation, Tulare county, California; cat. no. 70405, Field Columbian Museum.

MOQUELUMNAN STOCK

TOPINAGUGIM. Big creek, Tuolumne county, California. (Cat. no. 70230, 70231, Field Columbian Museum.)

Two flat, tapering sticks of wild cherry (figure 535), 38 inches in length, with tips burned with two rings; and whip, with buckskin thong and stock, 31½ inches in length.

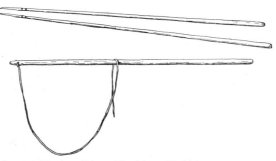

FIG. 535. Throwing- or whipping-sticks, with whip and lash; length of sticks, 38 inches; length of whipstock, 31½ inches; Topinagugim Indians, Tuolumne county, California; cat. no. 70230, 70231, Field Columbian Museum.

Collected by Dr J. W. Hudson, who describes them as throwing- or whipping-sticks used in a game called kuitumsi (kuitu, farthest one).

The lance, la-ma-ku-yi-ta, is one-fourth of an inch in diameter at the butt, expanding to five-eighths of an inch at the tip. The different ones are marked to distinguish them. A buckskin thong, pe-hu-na-ha-a-ta (buckskin to whip), is tied to a wooden handle. The farthest cast wins.

Dr J. W. Hudson describes also these Indians as casting along the ground sticks, 4 feet long, made of willow or calacanthus. Each player has one cast. The one throwing the farthest, wins. The loser is thumped on the head with the knuckles. The game is called pakumship; pakür, lance.

SIOUAN STOCK

ASSINIBOIN. Fort Union, Montana.

Mr Edwin T. Denig [a] says:

The women slide long sticks on the snow.

CROWS. Crow reservation, Montana. (Field Columbian Museum.)
Cat. no. 69657. Feathered dart, a piece of beef rib, painted red and incised with crossed lines, 6½ inches in length, having two long twigs inserted at the squared end, upon which feathers dyed red are stuck; total length, 29 inches.

Collected in 1901 by Mr S. C. Simms, who describes it as played by boys on the ice.

FIG. 536. Game dart; length, 32¼ inches; Crow Indians, Montana; cat. no. 69653, Field Columbian Museum.

Cat. no. 69653. Javelin (figure 536), a thin sapling, painted red and tipped with horn; length, 32¼ inches.

Collected in 1901 by Mr S. C. Simms, who describes it as used in a man's game.

The stick is seized by the end, whirled rapidly with a vertical motion, and released when it gains momentum. The object is to make it go as far as possible.

DAKOTA (OGLALA). Pine Ridge reservation, South Dakota. (Free Museum of Science and Art, University of Pennsylvania.)

FIG. 537. Feathered bone-slider; length, 25 inches; Oglala Dakota Indians, Pine Ridge reservation, South Dakota; cat. no. 22129, Free Museum of Science and Art, University of Pennsylvania.

Cat. no. 22129. A fragment of beef rib (figure 537), 8 inches in length, with feathers stuck on two wooden pegs inserted in one end of the bone; total length, 25 inches.

[a] Unpublished manuscript in the Bureau of American Ethnology.

Collected by Mr Louis L. Meeker,[a] who describes the implement under the name of paslo hanpi, as thrown by boys on the ice.

Cat. no. 22128. A thin straight dart (figure 538), 29¾ inches in length, tipped with a cone of horn and having a bunch of feathers secured with sinew at the shaftment.

FIG. 538. Boys' throwing-arrow; length, 29¾ inches; Oglala Dakota Indians, Pine Ridge reservation, South Dakota; cat. no. 22128, Free Museum of Science and Art, University of Pennsylvania.

Described by the collector, Mr Louis L. Meeker,[b] under the name of pte heste, as thrown underhand by boys against the ground to glance to a great distance. The one whose stick goes farthest takes all the other sticks. This game is described by Dr J. R. Walker [c] among the Tetons under the name of woskate pte heste, game of the young cow.

Any number of persons may play. Each player may have any number of arrows, but all players should have the same number. Two parallel lines are drawn from 20 to 30 feet apart. The players take their position on one side of these lines. A player must throw his horned arrow so that it may strike between the two lines and slide beyond them. The players throw alternately until all the arrows are thrown. At the end the player whose arrow lies farthest from the lines wins the game.

Cat. no. 22132. A slender sapling (figure 539) tipped with a horn point, 63 inches in length.

Described by the collector, Mr Louis L. Meeker,[d] under the name of winyanta paslo hanpi, the girls' throwing-stick.

The sticks, held by the extreme end, with forefinger behind. are cast high in the air. The game is played for small sticks about the size of lead pencils, or larger, the same as are used for counters by the men in the moccasin game.

This game is described by Dr J. R. Walker [e] under the name of woskate hepaslohanpi, game of horned javelins, and the implement he gives as hewahukezala, horned javelin.

The game is played by throwing the javelin so that it will strike and slide on the snow or ice, and the one whose javelin slides the farthest wins.

DAKOTA (TETON). Pine Ridge reservation, South Dakota. (American Museum of Natural History.)

Cat. no. $\frac{50}{4229}$. Two pairs of sticks (figure 540), flat on one side and rounded on the other, slightly expanded, and turned up at the end, one set 48 inches and the other 44 inches in length; one set plain and the other with three dragon flies painted on the upper

---

[a] Ogalala Games. Bulletin of the Free Museum of Science and Art, v. 3, p. 35, Philadelphia, 1901.

[b] Ibid., p. 34.

[c] Sioux Games. Journal of American Folk-Lore, v. 19, p. 32, 1906.

[d] Ogalala Games. Bulletin of the Free Museum of Science and Art, v. 3, p. 36, Philadelphia, 1901.

[e] Sioux Games. Journal of American Folk-Lore, v. 19, p. 36, 1906.

face. Collected by Dr J. R. Walker, who describes them under the name of canpaslohanpi, used in the game of throwing sticks, woskate canpaslohanpi.[a]

FIG. 539. Girls' throwing-stick; length, 63 inches; Oglala Dakota Indians, Pine Ridge reservation, South Dakota; cat. no. 22132, Free Museum of Science and Art, University of Pennsylvania.

Each player has but one throwing stick. Any number of persons may play. The game is played by grasping the stick at the smaller end, between the thumb and second, third, and fourth fingers, with the first finger across the smaller end, the flat side of the stick held uppermost. Then by swinging the hand below the hips the javelin is shot forward so that it will slide on the snow or ice. The game is to see who can slide the stick farthest.

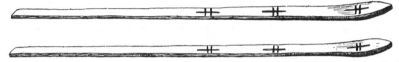

FIG. 540. Snow-snakes; length, 44 inches; Teton Dakota Indians, Pine Ridge reservation, South Dakota; cat. no. $\frac{50}{4239}$, American Museum of Natural History.

DAKOTA (TETON). South Dakota.

Rev. J. Owen Dorsey [b] describes the following games as played by boys in winter:

Ptehéshte un'pi, buffalo horn game: The boys assemble at the corral or some other place where the cattle have been slaughtered, and gather the horns which have been thrown away. They kindle a fire and scorch the horns, noticing how far each horn has been burnt. That part of the horn is cut off, as it is brittle, and they make the rest of the horn very smooth by rubbing. They cut off all the small and pliable branches and twigs of a plum tree and insert the root end into a hole in the horn, tightening it by driving in several small wedges around it. At the small end of the plum stock they fasten a feather by wrapping deer sinew round and round it. The pteheste is then thrown along the surface of the snow, or it often goes under the surface, disappearing and reappearing at short intervals. Sometimes they make it glide over the ice. Stakes are frequently put up by or for the players.

Itázipa kaslóhan iyéya echun'pi, making the bow glide by throwing. They do not use real bows, but some kind of wood made flat by cutting with an ax, with a horizontal curve at the lowest part, and sharpened on the other side. At the head a snake's head is usually made, or else the head of some other object. At the other end the player grasps it and hurls it, making it glide rapidly over the snow or grass. This is a game of chance, but the " bows " are never staked, as they are too expensive. It takes so long to make one that the owner does not sell it, preferring to keep it as long as possible.

The following is played by boys and young men:

In the winter the boys collect the good ribs of animals that are near the village. They make gashes across them, and on one side of each rib they

---

[a] Sioux Games. Journal of American Folk-Lore, v. 19, p. 32, 1906.

[b] Games of Teton Dakota Children. The American Anthropologist, v. 4, p. 338, 1891.

[c] Ibid., p. 343.

make a hole in which they insert two plum sticks. The small end of each plum stick they insert into the hole of a quill feather of some bird. The small end of each plum stick is bent backwards. Just at the fork of the two plum sticks the player grasps the toy, called hutanachute, making it glide over the snow or ice. Stakes are put down when desired, but sometimes they play just for amusement. Occasionally young men join the boys in this game.

The following is an autumnal game of the boys or women:

Paslóhanpi, they shove it along. The boys play this game when the leaves become a rusty yellow. They go to a place where the smallest kind of willow abounds, and there they make a fire. They cut down the straightest of the willows, shaving off the bark with knives. Some color the willow in stripes. Others change the willows into what they call chan kablaskapi, i. e., wood flattened by beating, but what these are Bushotter does not explain. Much of this text is very obscure. Sometimes the young women play the game, at other times the men do; but each sex has its peculiar way of making the paslohanpi glide along. Sometimes they play for stakes.

Dr J. R. Walker [a] gives the following rules for the game with winged bones, woskate hutanacute:

Any number may play. Each player may have from two to four winged bones, but each player should have the same number. A mark is made from which the bones are thrown. The bones are thrown so that they may strike or slide on the ice or snow. The players throw alternately until all the bones are thrown. When all the bones are thrown the player whose bone lies the farthest from the mark wins the game.

Doctor Walker describes woskate paslohanpi as the game of javelins (wahukezala) played by Sioux boys in the springtime, and states that there are two ways of throwing: One to lay the javelin across something, as the arm, or the foot, or another javelin, or a stump of log, or a small mound of earth, or anything that is convenient, and grasping it at the smaller end, shoot it forward; the other way is to grasp the javelin near the middle and throw it from the hand.

DAKOTA (YANKTON). Fort Peck, Montana. (Free Museum of Science and Art, University of Pennsylvania.)

Cat. no. 37610. Three peeled saplings, burnt near the larger end with spiral bands and marks; length, 46½ inches.

Collected by the writer in 1900. The name is pasdohanpi.[b]

FIG. 541. Feathered bone slider; length, 21 inches; Yankton Dakota Indians, Fort Peck, Montana; cat. no. 37612, Free Museum of Science and Art, University of Pennsylvania.

Cat. no. 37612. Two pieces of beef rib, 6½ inches in length, each with two feathers inserted on pegs in one end; total length, 21 inches. One bears incised marks, as shown in figure 541.

---

[a] Sioux Games. Journal of American Folk-Lore, v. 19, p. 31, 1906.
[b] From pa-sdo'-han, to push or shove along.

Collected in 1900 by the writer, to whom they were designated as hutinacute.[a]

MANDAN.　Fort Clark, North Dakota.

Maximilian, Prince of Wied,[b] says:

The children of the Mandans and Manitaries play with a piece of stag's horn [figure 542], in which a couple of feathers are inserted; this is thrown forward, the piece of horn being foremost.

FIG. 542.　Feathered horn dart; Mandan Indians, North Dakota; from Maximilian, Prince of Wied.

OMAHA.　Nebraska.

Mr Dorsey [c] describes the following games:

Man¢in'-bagí, wahí-gasnug'-i¢e (Omaha names), or man-íbagi' (Ponca name) is a game played by an even number of boys. The tall sticks of the red willow are held in the hand, and when thrown towards the ground so as to strike it at an acute angle, they glance off, and are carried by the wind into the air for some distance. Whichever one can throw his stick the furthest wins the game, but nothing is staked. Man dĕ-gasnug'-i¢e is a game similar to man¢in'-bagi, but bows are used instead of the red willow sticks, and arrows are staked, there being an even number of players on each side. Each bow is unstrung, one end being nearly straight, the other end, which is to hit the ground, being slightly curved. When snow is on the ground, the bows glide very far. Sometimes the bow rebounds and goes into the air, then alights and glides still further. The prize for each winning bow is arranged before each game. If the number be two arrows for each and three bows win, six arrows are forfeited by the losing side; if four bows win, eight arrows are lost. If three arrows be the prize for each, when two bows win, six arrows are forfeited; when three win, nine arrows; and so on.

In'-tinbúta, a boy's game among the Omahas, is played in winter. It is played by two, three, or four small boys, each having a stick, not over a yard long, shaped like the figure [543]. The stakes are necklaces and earrings; or, if they have no stakes, they agree to hit once on the head the boy whose stick goes the shortest distance. The sticks are thrown as in man¢in'-bagi.

FIG. 543.　Game dart; Omaha Indians, Nebraska; from Dorsey.

Mr Francis La Flesche described a game to the writer under the name of " wahegusungithae," or bone sliders, in which a bone with a

---

[a] A long stick with a large head which the Dakotas make slide on the snow or ice. (Riggs.) Also, hu-ta'-na-ku-te, v. n., to play with the hutinaćute; to throw a stick so as to make it slide along on the snow, hutanawakute.

[b] Travels in the Interior of North America, translated by H. Evans Lloyd, p. 358, London, 1843.

[c] Omaha Sociology. Third Annual Report of the Bureau of Ethnology, p. 340, 1884.

feather stuck in it is slid along the ice. He said also another game is played in summer, to which the same name is given, with sticks about 3 feet long by one-half of an inch in diameter, which are peeled and burned. They are forcibly thrown down on the ground and fly a great distance. Mr La Flesche described also a game played by Omaha boys under the name of intimbuta, in which a stick of hickory, scraped, polished, and whittled down, is thrown on the frozen ground so that it flies like an arrow.

HOOP AND POLE

The game of hoop and pole, like the dice game, was played throughout the entire continent north of Mexico. It consists essentially in throwing a spear, or shooting or throwing an arrow at a hoop or ring, the counts being determined by the way in which the darts fall with reference to the target.

The game is remarkable for the wide diversity in the form of the implements employed, as well as in the method of play. A number of distinct types may be recognized, of which as many as three are found at the present day among the same tribe. The essential unity of all of these, however, is plainly manifest.

The implements for hoop and pole consist of the hoop or target, the darts or poles, and, in some instances, especially made counting sticks. A common and most widely distributed form of the hoop is twined with a network resembling a spider web, the counts being determined by the particular holes which are penetrated by the darts. In another hoop the net, with the exception of an inner ring, which is attached by cords to the hoop, has disappeared. In still others, among the Takulli, Wasco, Omaha, and Tigua, there remain only four radial spokes or strands. In the Apache game these are reduced to a single median thong or cord, but notches on the hoop suggest the points of contact of the thong lashings. One of the Siouan hoops, known also to the Arapaho, has four sets of equidistant notches on its circumference. These notches agree with the marks of the world quarters on the cane dice and on the tubes of the hidden-ball game.

In another group of the hoop games we find a small ring with beads of different colors set at equidistant points around its inner side. Different values are attributed to these beads, which count accordingly. On other small rings, as among the Pawnee, a single small bead is threaded on the interior of the ring. Marks indicating the quarters are found upon some hoops, while others are entirely plain.

The materials of the rings are equally varied. The netted hoop usually consists of a sapling lashed with rawhide. Other hoops are twined with cord (Mohave) or beads (Ute), and still others have a central core wrapped with rawhide (Navaho, Shoshoni, Tigua) or with bark (Umatilla, Kwakiutl, Makah). The Hopi have rings of corn husks. Again, there are rings of stone (Santa Barbara, Choctaw, Muskogee, Bellacoola, Mandan, Kwakiutl), some of rough lava, as among the tribes of the Pacific, and others of finely finished quartzite, as in the states of the south Atlantic and Gulf coasts. These stone rings are both with and without perforations, and among the Cherokee we read of them being flat on one side and convex on the other. The diameter of the hoop also varies, from 25 inches among the Oglala to 2¾ inches among the Paiute.

The darts employed are of several varieties. Arrows shot from a bow or thrown by hand are common. Simple straight shafts are frequently used, as well as plain long poles made of a single piece. The Hopi and the Thompson have feather darts. For the netted hoop, a sapling with a forked end is commonly employed. The Apache have long jointed poles, the ends marked with rings, which count in accordance with the way they fall upon the hoop. The Navaho use similar jointed poles with a thong attached, the divided ends of which count as they catch in the ring. Among the Tigua (Isleta), the Keres (Laguna), and the Mandan the darts had thongs which caught in the ring. In an Omaha game there is a curved strip of rawhide forming a kind of trident at the end of the pole.

Two short darts attached in the middle by a thong were used with the large hoop of the Dakota, and in a game played by the Caddoan and Siouan stocks the throwing sticks were complicated with arcs and crossbars.

The game was always played by males. There is no record of women participating. The number of players varied from two upward, but two appears to have been the primal number. In the ceremonial forms of the game a complete set of implements consisted of a single ring and two poles. The latter may be explained in many instances as the bows of the twin War Gods. The jointed poles of the Navaho and the Apache may be regarded as the two bows tied together, and the same explanation may be offered for the tied darts used with the large hoop by the Dakota. The implement used by the Caddoan tribes is explained by them as representing a buffalo, the projecting curved head symbolizing the masculine organ. In playing, the long poles were ordinarily thrown after the moving ring by the two contestants; the beaded ring was commonly rolled against some kind of barrier. In the Delaware, Seneca, and Niska games the players stood in two parallel lines, shooting at the hoop as it rolled between them. Among the Makah the lines converge.

For the playing field a level place was selected, and among some tribes especially prepared. Among the Mandan we read of timber floors 150 feet long. The Apache play on a level ground, 100 feet long, with a rock in the center, from which the poles are hurled.

The Creeks had large inclosed courts with sloping sides, on which the spectators were seated. Among the Apache and the Navaho, the direction of the track is from north to south. In reference to the season of the game, we learn that among the Wasco it is played at the time of the first run of salmon, and among the Umatilla in the spring.

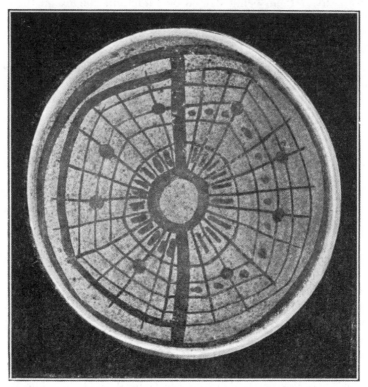

Fig. 544. Pottery bowl with spider-web decoration; diameter, 9¼ inches; Hopi Indians, Mishongnovi, Arizona; cat. no. 75766, Field Columbian Museum.

Morgan describes it as played between different communities among the Iroquois.

Information concerning the counts is meager. The Arapaho used one hundred and the Shoshoni six tally sticks. Among the Apache it is the principal gambling game. It is commonly played for stakes of value, but not infrequently for the arrows and darts used in the play.

The explanation of the origin and significance of the game of hoop and pole rests largely upon the identification of the hoop. The netted gaming hoop is readily seen to be the same as the netted shield, one of the attributes of the twin War Gods, Ahaiyuta and Matsailema,

of Zuñi mythology. Mr Cushing had explained this shield as a
framework, once padded with cotton, and anciently used by the Zuñi
as an actual shield in warfare.[a] Upon the basis of this account the
writer assumed that the game arose from the employment of this

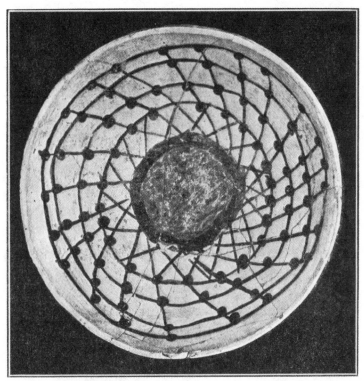

Fig. 545. Pottery bowl with spider-web decoration; diameter, 10 inches; Hopi Indians,
Mishongnovi, Arizona; cat. no. 75675, Field Columbian Museum.

practical shield in connection with the arrow or javelin. A passage
in Cushing's Zuñi Folk Tales,[b] where this netted shield, made only of
nets and knotted cords, is described as the kiaalan, water shield, a

---

[a] The warrior carried also targets or shields of yucca or cotton cord, closely netted
across a strong, round hoop frame and covered with a coarser and larger net, which was
only a modification of the carrying net (like those still in use by the Papago, Pima, and
other Indians of southern Arizona), and which was turned to account as such, indeed, on
hunting and war expeditions. (Outlines of Zuñi Creation Myths. Thirteenth Annual Report of the Bureau of Ethnology, p. 358, 1896.) Elsewhere (A Zuñi Folk Tale of the
Underworld. Journal of American Folk-Lore, v. 5, p. 52) Mr Cushing speaks thus of
their shields :

"Cord shields.—Pī-a-la-we (cord or cotton shields), evidently an ancient style of
shield still surviving in the form of sacrificial net shields of the priesthood of the Bow.
But the shields of these two gods [the twin War Gods] were supposed to have been
spun from the clouds, which, supporting the sky-ocean, that in turn supported the sky-
world as this world is believed to be supported by under waters and clouds, were hence
possessed of the power of floating—upward when turned up, downward when reversed."
This refers to the War Gods covering their heads with their cord shields when descending into the under-world.

[b] P. 337, 376, New York, 1901.

magical implement, led the writer, however, to reconsider the probable identity of this object, with the resulting conclusion that it was never used as a means of physical defense; that it was, in fact, an adaptation

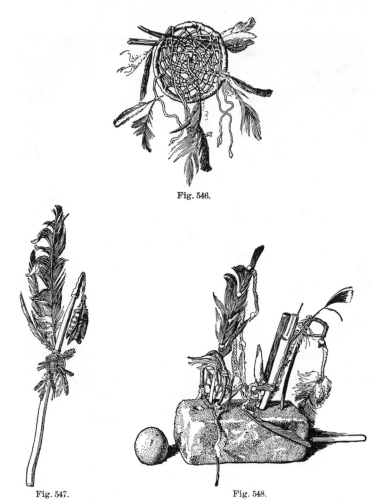

Fig. 546.

Fig. 547.   Fig. 548.

FIG. 546. Netted shield, bow, and arrows attached to plume offering; diameter of shield, 2¼ inches; Zuñi Indians, Zuñi, New Mexico; cat. no. 22678, Free Museum of Science and Art, University of Pennsylvania.

FIG. 547. Plume offering; length, 21 inches; Zuñi Indians, Zuñi, New Mexico; cat. no. 22678, Free Museum of Science and Art, University of Pennsylvania.

FIG. 548. Baho stand with netted shield; length, 5½ inches; Hopi Indians, Oraibi, Arizona; cat. no. 38790, Free Museum of Science and Art, University of Pennsylvania.

of the magical spider web spun by the Spider Woman, the mother of the Twins, the symbol of her protection.   Bowls painted with a web are not uncommon among the ancient fictile ware of the Hopi in Arizona, as shown in figures 544, 545, from Mishongnovi.   The net some-

times appears more or less regularly dotted with spots.[a]   Such figures
I regard as representing the spider web with the dew upon it.   The
" water shield " of Ahaiyuta, from which he shook the torrents, was
suggested, no doubt, by dew on the web.

A miniature netted shield, with or without a tiny bow and arrows,
is of frequent occurrence on objects employed in Zuñi ceremonials.
Such a shield with arrows is represented in figure 546 on a plume
offering secured by the writer in 1902 from the shrine of the War God
on Corn mountain.   As described in the introduction, a similar netted
shield is also seen associated with a male baho attached to each of the
four baho stands (figure 548) placed upon the Hopi Powalawu altar [b]
and the effigy of Pöokong, the lesser War God on the Oraibi snake altar,
has a netted shield on his back.   Feather darts, precisely like those

FIG. 549.   Sacrificial feather darts from altar of War God; length, 18 inches; Zuñi Indians, Zuñi,
New Mexico; cat. no. 22683, Free Museum of Science and Art, University of Pennsylvania.

used in connection with a ring of corn husk among the Hopi (figure
648), are sacrificed upon the altar of the Zuñi War God.   Figure 549
represents a set of four made for the writer in Zuñi in 1902, identical
with those he saw upon the shrine on Corn mountain.   In the Hopi
Oáqöl ceremony at Oraibi, the manas discharge corncob feather darts
at a netted wheel,[c] and in the Oraibi Marau ceremony women shoot
arrows in a similar way into a bundle of vines.[d]   Figure 552 repre-

---

[a] These two bowls were excavated from ancient Hopi graves, at Mishongnovi, by Mr
Charles L. Owen, in 1900.   In one this web is inclosed in a broken circle of brown paint
and divided into two segments by a median line of similar brown paint.   On one side
there are eleven brown strokes in the first set of spaces nearest the center, and on the
other nine red strokes in the corresponding spaces.

[b] Mr Voth states that this particular netted shield is asserted to represent simply a
wheel (ngölla) and the feather with the wheel also serves as a prótection against the
destructive sand storms.   It is called hůkuhtsi, sand storm shutter.   (The Oraibi Powamu Ceremony, p. 77, Chicago, 1901.)

[c] See H. R. Voth, The Oraibi Oáqöl Ceremony, p. 23 and 42, Chicago, 1903.   Mr Voth
relates that on the fifth day of the Oáqöl ceremony, Masátoiniwa, the chief priest, held
a netted wheel, about 12 inches in diameter, of the same pattern as the wheels used on
the last day by the two Oáqöl manas [figure 550], consisting of a wooden ring, about
three-quarters of an inch thick, which was filled with a network of small meshes.   This
is called báchaiyanpi, water sieve, because the cloud deities have such strainers through
which they sift or drop the rain.

[d] Doctor Fewkes, in describing this ceremony at Walpi, says a " small package of
cornhusks."   The two women who shoot the package are called Waühitaka, and their act
of shooting is said to typify lightning striking in the cornfield, an event which is
regarded as the acme of fertilization.   (Hopi Basket Dances.   Journal of American Folk-
Lore, v. 12, p. 91, 1899.)

sents four Marau arrows, Marau hohohu, in the Free Museum of Science and Art of the University of Pennsylvania (cat no. 38810). They are made of reed, 18¼ to 21 inches in length, with wooden points; the feathers are obtained from the wing of the golden eagle. These arrows are described by the collector, Rev. H. R. Voth, as follows:

These arrows are made in the kiva on the 8th day of the Marau ceremony by a man belonging to the Pakat (Reed) clan. In the public ceremony, on the ninth day, they are used by two of the Marau takas, who act as archers in the plaza. The arrows are shot into the bundle, consisting of squash, melon, bean, cotton,

FIG. 550. Netted hoops and feather darts used by the Oáqöl manas; Hopi Indians, Oraibi, Arizona; from H. R. Voth.

and other vines. At the close of the ceremony they are deposited in a shrine north of the village, in which four old stone Pöokong fetiches are sitting on projecting rocks.

Again, in the Lalakonti ceremony, as witnessed by the writer at Walpi in the summer of 1901, the Lakone mana threw feather darts, made of ears of corn, into cloud symbols which the priest, or Lakone taka, traced with meal upon the ground.[a]

_____

[a] See Dr J. Walter Fewkes, Hopi Basket Dances. Journal of American Folk-Lore, v. 12, p. 81, 1899. Doctor Fewkes describes corncobs, instead of ears of corn, stuck with eagle feathers as used in the Lalakonti ceremony at Walpi in 1898. He witnessed also the ceremony at Oraibi, mentioning corncobs as used there, and the one at Shipaulovi, where two halves of corncobs were employed.

Similar ceremonies or games were practised by the cliff-dwellers, as is attested by a number of objects from Mancos canyon, Colorado, in the Free Museum of Science and Art of the University of Pennsylvania. Figure 553 represents a corncob shuttlecock stuck with a grouse feather; figure 554 a feather dart, with a hard-wood point to which a hawk feather is secured by a wrapping of yucca fiber; and figure 555 a ball of coarse yucca stems, the latter identified by Mr Cushing as used in the "arrow-spearing game," all from this locality.

FIG. 551. Oáqöl manas throwing darts into netted hoops; Hopi Indians, Oraibi, Arizona; from H. R. Voth.

The use of the miniature netted shield as a protective amulet is widely distributed. J. G. Kohl [a] describes a wooden ring over which thongs are drawn as a cradle amulet among the Chippewa at Apostle islands, Wisconsin, and an actual cradle charm from the Chippewa, exhibited in the Columbian Exposition at Chicago, was practically identical with the miniature netted shields of the Zuñi and the Hopi. The Hupa employ a similar charm (figure 556) on

---

[a] Kitchi-Gami, Wanderings round Lake Superior, p. 8, London, 1860.

their wicker cradles, a small hexagonal object made by twisting white and black straw around three sticks placed crosswise, with ends equidistant.   Netted shields are also common among the amulets

FIG. 552.   Marau arrows; length, 18¼ to 21 inches; Hopi Indians, Oraibi, Arizona; cat. no. 38810, Free Museum of Science and Art, University of Pennsylvania.

FIG. 553.   Corncob feather dart; length, 7¼ inches; cliff-dwelling, Mancos canyon, Colorado; Free Museum of Science and Art, University of Pennsylvania.

FIG. 554.   Feather dart; length, 10¼ inches; cliff-dwelling, Mancos canyon, Colorado; Free Museum of Science and Art, University of Pennsylvania.

and personal adornments of many of the Plains tribes.   Figure 557 represents a hair ornament collected by Rev. H. R. Voth from the Cheyenne of Oklahoma, in the United States National Museum (cat.

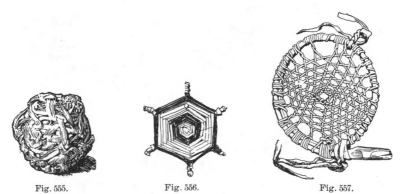

Fig. 555.   Fig. 556.   Fig. 557.

FIG. 555.   Yucca ball; diameter, 2½ inches; cliff-dwelling, Mancos canyon, Colorado; Free Museum of Science and Art, University of Pennsylvania.

FIG. 556.   Cradle charm; diameter, 3 inches; Hupa Indians, Hupa valley, California; cat. no. 37166, Free Museum of Science and Art, University of Pennsylvania.

FIG. 557.   Hair ornament (netted hoop); diameter, 4 inches; Cheyenne Indians, Oklahoma; cat. no. 165859, United States National Museum.

no. 165859), and figure 558 a similar object from the Crows of Montana, in the Free Museum of Science and Art of the University of Pennsylvania (cat. no. 38505).   The latter has a flint arrowhead and a long down feather attached to the face of the net.   Of two similar charms from the Grosventres (Algonquian) of Fort Belknap, Montana, in the Field Columbian Museum (cat. no. 60337, 60334), one is netted (figure 559), while the other is a simple hoop (figure 560) with buckskin thongs crossing at right angles.   These are described by Doctor Dorsey, the collector, as hachieb, formerly much worn on the head and hair as a protection against dangers of various sorts. Analogous hoops are attached to two " medicine cords " (figures 561, 562) from the Chiricahua Apache, figured by Capt. John G. Bourke.[a]

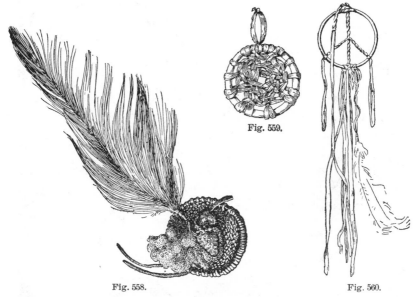

Fig. 559.

Fig. 558.   Fig. 560.

FIG. 558.   Hair ornament (netted hoop); diameter, 2¼ inches; Crow Indians, Montana; cat. no. 38505, Free Museum of Science and Art, University of Pennsylvania.

FIG. 559.   Protective amulet (netted hoop); diameter, 2½ inches; Grosventre Indians, Montana; cat. no. 60337, Field Columbian Museum.

FIG. 560.   Protective amulet (hoop); diameter, 2 inches; Grosventre Indians, Montana; cat. no. 60334, Field Columbian Museum.

Small rings of twisted grass are used as amulets by the Navaho, as illustrated by specimens collected by Dr Edward Palmer (figure 563 a, b), in the United States National Museum (cat. no. 9539).   Similar illustrations of netted hoops and related rings might be multiplied almost indefinitely, and specimens may be found in every considerable collection of modern Indian ceremonial costume.   From a suggestion made by Mr Louis L. Meeker, some, if not all, of these objects may be identified with gaming rings.   He writes that the Cheyenne in Oklahoma use a hair ornament, consisting of a small ring, which

[a] The Medicine Man of the Apache.   Ninth Annual Report of the Bureau of Ethnology, p. 551, 1892.

they wear as a token of prowess in a game called hohtsin, in which a rolling target, consisting of a netted wheel, is used.   Later he transmitted to the writer from the Oglala of Pine Ridge reservation, South Dakota, such a hair ornament, tahosmu, which the Indians of this tribe wear as a token of prowess in the elk game, kaga woskate. It consists of a ring of bent twig (figure 564), 2¼ inches in diameter, wrapped with colored porcupine quills, with an internal cross, and thongs for fastening.[a]

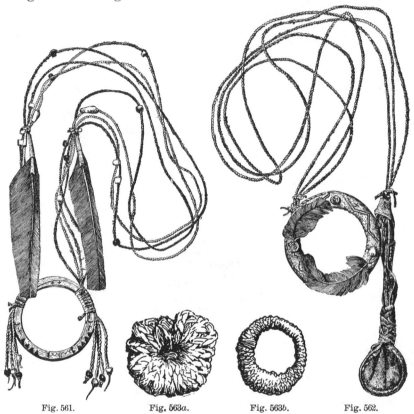

Fig. 561.   Fig. 563a.   Fig. 563b.   Fig. 562.

FIG. 561.   Four-strand medicine cord; Chiricahua Apache Indians, Arizona; from Bourke.
FIG. 562.   Three-strand medicine cord; Chiricahua Apache Indians, Arizona; from Bourke.
FIG. 563a, b.   Amulets of scented grass; diameters, 1¼ and 1⅜ inches; Navaho Indians, New Mexico; cat. no. 9539, United States National Museum.

An examination of two similar hair ornaments collected by the writer in 1900 from the Arapaho of the Wind River reservation, Wyoming, reveals the fact that they are miniature gaming hoops, one (figure 565; cat no. 37003, Free Museum of Science and Art of the

[a] Mr Charles L. Owen informs the writer that the miniature gaming hoops in the Field Columbian Museum, collected by him from the White Mountain Apache in Arizona in 1904, were worn by men who played the pole game, as amulets to secure success in that game.

University of Pennsylvania) a simple hoop with notches, like that used by the Oglala and Yankton Dakota, and the other (figure 566;

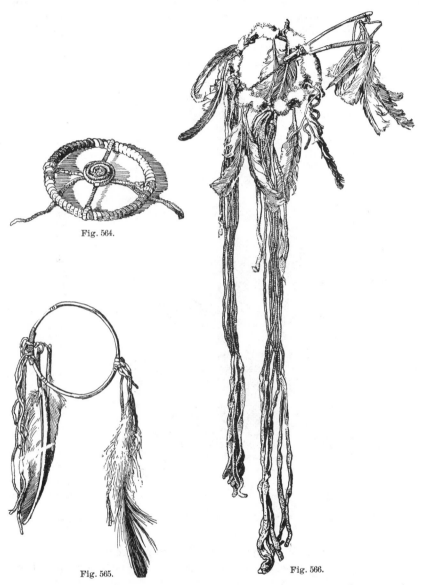

Fig. 564.

Fig. 565.

Fig. 566.

FIG. 564.　Hair ornament; diameter, 2¼ inches; Oglala Dakota Indians, Pine Ridge reservation, South Dakota; cat. no. 21942, Free Museum of Science and Art, University of Pennsylvania.

FIG. 565.　Hair ornament; diameter, 4½ inches; Arapaho Indians, Wind River reservation, Wyoming; cat. no. 37003, Free Museum of Science and Art, University of Pennsylvania.

FIG. 566.　Hair ornament; diameter, 3 inches; Arapaho Indians, Wind River reservation, Wyoming; cat. no. 37004, Free Museum of Science and Art, University of Pennsylvania.

cat. no. 37004) with a median cord, like the gaming hoop of the Apache, and having the two darts secured on the rim.

The ring and feather dart, the netted hoop, and the large buck-skin ring constantly recur in the masks used in the Hopi and Zuñi ceremonials. The nose and mouth of the Hopi Hehea uncle katcina (figure 567) may be regarded as the dart and ring,[a] and the large painted rings which surround the base of so many masks are to be identified with the leather-wrapped gaming hoop.

Fig. 567.   Fig. 568.

FIG. 567. Mask of Hehea tahaamu, or Hehea uncle katcina; Hopi Indians, Arizona; cat. no. 66452, Field Columbian Museum.

FIG. 568. Deerskin plume worn with head ring; length, 18 inches: Hupa Indians, Hupa valley, California; cat. no. 37213, Free Museum of Science and Art, University of Pennsylvania.

We discover a similar object in the heavy ring covered with buck-skin and red woodpecker crests, worn on the head by the Hupa

---

[a] It is not an unreasonable conclusion that the corn-husk rings which supply the place of mouths on other masks, as, for example, the Qötca mana (cat. no. 56288, Field Columbian Museum), are also gaming rings. Again, the ring of network forming part of the Hopi ceremonial head tablet (cat. no. 16993, Field Columbian Museum) may be identified with the netted wheel, and the checkered bands at the base of the Hopi face masks, such as that of the Ana katcina (cat. no. 66286, Field Columbian Museum), with the simple ring which exists entire at the base of the other Zuñi and Hopi masks.

(Athapascan) in northern California. Its derivation from the gaming ring is further borne out by the two long plumes, covered with white deerskin and woodpecker crests, on wooden fore shafts (figure 568) that are stuck on either side in front of the ring.

The Flute priests at Oraibi wear a headdress consisting of a corn-husk ring (figure 569), pierced with two wooden darts, baho, and with four pins, on the ends of which are fastened four gaming cups of four colors.[a]

Fig. 569. Flute priest's headdress; Hopi Indians, Oraibi, Arizona; cat. no. 65789, Field Columbian Museum.

Before returning to the final discussion of the significance of the hoop-and-pole game, let us consider some of the ceremonial uses of rings analogous to the gaming ring. One of the most notable is the conjurer's hoop (figure 570) of the Oglala Dakota. A specimen in the Free Museum of Science and Art of the University of Pennsylvania (cat. no. 22241) consists of a hoop, cangleska, "spotted wood," made of

---

[a] Worn at the fall ceremony of the Flute society. The cup-shaped objects symbolize blossoming, hence the headdress is sometimes called lansi, "flute blossoms." This headdress is worn also by the Flute katcina and by a few others.

a peeled branch about half an inch in diameter, tied with sinew, to form a ring 10 inches in diameter, and painted in four segments—yellow, red, blue, and black. It is accompanied with four sticks, 11½ inches in length, painted like the hoop, one yellow, one red, one blue, and one black. A small calico bag, painted to correspond with the stick and containing tobacco, is tied at the blunt end of each stick. These objects were made for the donor, Mr Louis L. Meeker, by Cangleska Luta, or Red Hoop, an Indian or mixed Cheyenne and Kiuksa Oglala parentage. I append Mr Meeker's [a] account:

According to Indian belief the hoop represents the ecliptic, or zodiac, or, as the Indian would say, the circle of day and night. The yellow segment represents the part between the eastern horizon and the zenith, over which the sun seems to pass between sunrise and noon. The red segment represents the part between the western horizon and the zenith, over which the sun seems to pass from noon to sunset. The blue represents the part from the western horizon to the nadir, the supposed course of the sun from sunset to midnight. The black represents the part from the nadir to the horizon, the supposed path of the sun from midnight to sunrise. The colors ordinarily used are yellow, from the juice of the prickly poppy; red, from blood or red clay; blue, from blue earth; and black, from charcoal. Each color represents a quarter of the globe, or, as an Indian would say, the colors denote the places of the four winds. If the hoop is set up perpendicularly, with the juncture of the red and yellow above, the former to the west and the latter to the east on the plane of the ecliptic, each color will be in its proper position, as above described. If the hoop is laid upon the ground in a horizontal position, with the juncture of the yellow and red to the north, it will give each of the four winds its proper color—from north to east will be yellow; east to south, black; south to west, blue; and west to north, red.

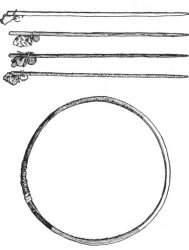

FIG. 570. Conjurer's hoop and sticks; diameter of hoop, 10 inches; Oglala Dakota Indians, South Dakota; cat. no. 22241, Free Museum of Science and Art, University of Pennsylvania.

Each stick belongs to one of the four winds, as indicated by its color. In case of sickness, the hoop, sticks, and tobacco borne by the sticks are offered in the following manner to secure recovery: The hoop is laid in the center of the lodge or on the ground in the position described above. The performer takes each stick and sets it upon its color on the hoop, point down, at the same time chanting the syllables he and e, he e, she, and e e, with or without improvised words of his own, relating to morning or forenoon, hanhanna; dawn, anpao; noon, wicokala; evening, htayetu; midnight, hancokaya; and tate, wind, with or without the name of the color of the stick—zi, yellow; sa, red; to, blue; and sapa, black.

_____

[a] Bulletin of the Free Museum of Science and Art, v. 3, p. 252, Philadelphia, 1902.

Chant

Hi ya ye, hi ye ye, hi ya ye, ya-hi ye ye.
Hi ya ye, hi ye ye, hi ya ye, ya-hi ye ye.

Hi ya ya, hi ye ye, hi ya ye, ya-hi ye ye.
Hi ya ya, hi ye ye, hi ya ye, ya-hi ye ye.

Improvisation

Ta te zi, hi ya ye, ta te sa, ya-hi ye ye.
Ta te to, hi ye ya, ya hi ye, ta-te sa pa.

An pa o, hi ya ya, han han na, wi-co ka la.
Hta ye tu, hi ya ya, ya hi ya, han-co ka ya.

Both chorus and improvisation are repeated and continued at pleasure. The scale is in a minor key and the chant rises and falls, beginning low, becoming higher, and again low. The pupils in the schools say the syllables hi ya ye and hi ye ye are correctly rendered in English by the kindergarten chorus, " Hence this way, hence that way." I believe, however, that " Hence this one, hence that one " is more nearly correct, if, indeed, they have any meaning. Most Indians say they have none.

Two of the sticks laid across the hoop are from north to south; the others from east to west. A light-colored stick is laid from north to south, and a dark-colored one from east to west, either red and black, or yellow and blue. If red and blue are used, and recovery does not take place, red and black will be used when the ceremony is repeated. The other two sticks are held in the hand of the performer, who continues to chant he and e with variations until well-nigh exhausted. The hoop and sticks are then carried away and left on some hill as far away from all forms of animal life as possible.

According to their explanations, the Indians believe the four winds carry incense to the four powers of the universe. The efficacy of the rite is supposed to depend upon the mysterious power of the performer, the weirdness and length of the chant, and the height and solitude of the place where the offering is left. Remains of these hoops may be found on the tops of remote and lonely hills in every Indian community where I have been stationed.

The account here given describes the most common use of the hoop. I have learned that it is used in many ceremonies by the medicine men. In July last I saw one of the hoops and supposed it was used in a game. Evasive answers were given to my inquiries, but there was a young man on his death-bed, and month after month many hoops were required. In order to obtain coloring matter for them it was at last admitted that the hoops were for the benefit of the invalid, and I at last saw the performance, which took place at night. The Indians are unwilling to tell their customs, partly because the medicine men do not approve, and partly because they do not care to have their sacred customs made the object of ridicule.

The Navaho make rings which Col. James Stevenson refers to as gaming rings (figure 571), on the first day of the ceremony commonly called Yebitchai, performed as a healing rite for a member of the tribe. He gives the following account [a] of a performance which he witnessed in October, 1888, at Keams canyon, Arizona:

---

[a] Ceremonial of Hasjelti Dailjis and Mythical Sand Painting of the Navajo Indians. Eighth Annual Report of the Bureau of Ethnology, p. 237, 1891.

During the afternoon of the 12th those who were to take part in the cere-monial received orders and instructions from the song priest. One man went to collect twigs, with which to make twelve rings, each 6 inches in diameter. These rings represented gaming rings, which are not only used by the Navajo, but are thought highly of by the genii of the rocks. [Figure 571.] Another man gathered willows with which to make the emblem of the concentration of the four winds.

The square was made by dressed willows crossed and left projecting at the corners each 1 inch beyond the next. The corners were tied together with white cotton cord, and each corner was ornamented with the under tail feather of the eagle. These articles were laid in a niche behind the theurgist, whose perma-nent seat was on the west side of the lodge facing east. The night ceremony commenced shortly after dark. All those who were to participate were imme-diate friends and relatives of the invalid, excepting the theurgist or song priest, he being the only one who received direct compensation for his professional serv-ices. The cost of such a ceremony is no inconsiderable item. Not only the exorbitant fee of the theurgist must be paid, but the entire assemblage must be fed during the nine days' ceremonial at the ex-pense of the invalid, assisted by his near relatives.

FIG. 571. Gaming ring used in the ceremony called Yebitchai; Navaho Indians, Arizona; from James Stevenson.

A bright fire burned in the lodge, and shortly after dark the invalid appeared, and sat upon a blanket, which was placed in front of the song priest. Previously, however, three men had pre-pared themselves to personate the gods—Hasjelti, Hostjoghon, and Hostjobokon—and one to per-sonate the goddess, Hostjoboard. They left the lodge carrying their masks in their hands, went a short distance away, and put on their masks. Then Hasjelti and Hostjoghon returned to the lodge, and Hasjelti, amid hoots, "hu-hoo-hu-huh !" placed the square which he carried, over the in-valid's head, and Hostjoghon shook two eagle wands, one in each hand, on each side of the in-valid's head and body, then over his head, mean-while hooting in his peculiar way, " hu-u-u-u-uh ! " He then followed Has-jelti out of the lodge. The men representing Hostjobokon and Hostjoboard came in alternately. Hostjobokon took one of the rings, which had been made during the afternoon, and now lay upon the blanket to the right of the invalid, and placed it against the soles of the feet of the invalid, who was sitting with knees drawn up, and then against his knees, palms, breast, each scapula, and top of his head ; then over his mouth. While touching the different parts of the body the ring was held with both hands, but when placed to the mouth of the invalid it was taken in the left hand. The ring was made of a reed, the ends of which were secured by a long string wrapped over the ring like a slip noose. When the ring was placed over the mouth of the invalid the string was pulled, and the ring dropped and rolled out of the lodge, the long tail of white cotton yarn, with eagle plume attached to the end, extending far behind. Hostjoboard repeated this ceremony with a second ring, and so did Hostjobokon and Hostjo-board alternately, until the twelve rings were disposed of. Three of the rings were afterward taken to the east, three to the south, three to the west, and three to the north, and deposited at the base of piñon trees. The rings were placed over the invalid's mouth to give him strength, cause him to talk with one tongue, and to have a good mind and heart. The other portions of the body were touched with them for physical benefit. When the rings had all been rolled out

of the lodge Hasjelti entered, followed by Hostjoghon. He passed the square
(the concentrated winds) four times over the head of the invalid during his
hoots. Hostjoghon then waved his turkey
wands about the head and body of the invalid, and the first day's ceremony was at
an end.

A stone ring from the Cheyenne of
Oklahoma, in the United States National Museum (cat. no. 166029) is
described by the collector, Rev. H. R.
Voth, as a medicine wheel (figure
572). It consists of a flat ring of limestone, 4½ inches in diameter, painted
red, and inscribed with deep grooves,

FIG. 572. Stone medicine ring; diameter, 4½ inches; Cheyenne Indians, Oklahoma; cat. no. 166029, United States
National Museum.

simulating wrappings, extending around it. On the face are engraved
a star and opposite to it a moon. This ring serves to illustrate the transformation of the cloth- or buckskin-wrapped ring into one of stone.

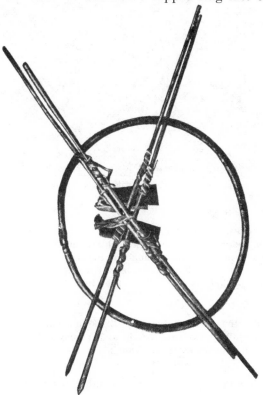

FIG. 573. Gaming wheel and sticks used in Ghost dance; Dakota Indians, South Dakota; from
Mooney.

Actual practical game rings are used ceremonially at the present
day. The writer saw a practical netted hoop worn on the back of

a Yanktonai Dakota at a grass dance at Fort Peck, Montana, in the summer of 1890. Mr James Mooney [a] also relates several instances in his account of the Ghost dance among the Sioux.

At a Ghost dance at No Water's camp, near Pine Ridge . . . four arrows, headed with bone in the olden fashion, were shot up into the air from the center of the circle and afterward gathered up and hung upon the tree, together with the bow, a gaming wheel and sticks [figure 573], and a staff of peculiar shape.

Fig. 574. Arapaho Sun Dance altar with wheel, Oklahoma; from Dorsey.

Elsewhere [b] he says:

In the Ghost dance at Rosebud and Pine Ridge, as usually performed, a young woman stood in the center of the circle, holding out a pipe toward the messiah in the west, and remained thus throughout the dance. Another young woman usually stood beside her holding out a bäqati wheel . . . in the same way. This feature of the dance is said to have been introduced by Short Bull.

Mr Mooney [c] states further:

It is said that the medicine man of Big Foot's band carried such a hoop with him in their flight from the north, and displayed it at every dance held by the band until the fatal day of Wounded Knee. . . . To the Indian it symbolizes the revival of the old-time games.

The ring, or wheel, plays a very considerable part in the ceremony of the Sun dance among the Plains tribes. Dr George A. Dorsey [d]

[a] The Ghost-dance Religion. Fourteenth Annual Report of the Bureau of Ethnology, p. 915, 1896.

[b] Ibid., p. 1064.   [c] Ibid., p. 1075.   [d] The Arapaho Sun Dance, p. 12, Chicago, 1903.

describes it as the object esteemed next after the great tribal medicine, the flat pipe, among the northern Arapaho. The wheel used by them in their Sun dance is described by him as follows:

The object (hehotti) is about 18 inches in diameter [figure 574]. It is made of a rectangular piece of wood, one end of which tapers like the tail of a serpent, the other being rudely fashioned to represent a serpent's head. Near the head of the serpent are several wrappings of blue beads, which have replaced small red berries which formerly occupied this place. At four opposite sides of the wheel are incised designs, two of them being in the form of crosses, the other two resembling the conventionalized Thunderbird. These designs are similar to those found on gaming wheels, used by Arapaho and other Plains tribes. Attached by means of short buckskin thongs are also four complete sets of the tail feathers of an eagle. The spacing of these feathers is not now uniform, but, according to Háwkan, they should have been grouped in equal numbers near the four incised markings on the wheel. As an eagle tail has 12 feathers, there would thus be, in all, 48 feathers on the wheel. At times, however, the wheel does not possess such a large number of eagle tail feathers, but a single tail is divided into four, and there are thus three feathers for each marking. . . . The feathers on the wheel at the present time number 24, there being thus two eagle tails represented, with six feathers to each marking. The inside of the wheel is painted red, while the outer periphery is stained black.

Referring to the symbolism of the wheel, Doctor Dorsey says:

According to Háwkan and one or two other authorities, the disk itself represents the sun, while the actual band of wood represents a tiny water-snake, called henigĕ, and which is said to be found in rivers, in lakes, near ponds, and in buffalo wallows. Later in the ceremony, this lake or pool of sweet water is represented, while near by on a forked stick, is the owner of the pool, a little bird. . . . This serpent is said to be the most harmless of all snakes. The wheel thus, representing this snake, has a derived meaning, and represents the water which surrounds the earth. The additional idea was also put forth that while the wheel represents a harmless snake, all snakes are powerful to charm, and hence the wheel is a sign of gentleness and meekness. The blue beads around the neck of the snake represent the sky or the heavens, which are clean and without blemish; the color blue among the Arapaho is also typical of friendship. The four inside markings (hítanni) on the wheel represent the Four-Old-Men who are frequently addressed during the ceremony, and who stand watching and guarding the inhabitants of this world. The Four-Old-Men may also be called the gods of the four world quarters and to them the Sun Dance priest often makes supplication that they may live to a great age. The Four-Old-Men are also spoken of as the Thunderbird, having power to watch the inhabitants, and in their keeping is the direction of the winds of the earth. They therefore represent the living element of all people. If the wind blows from the north, it is said to come from the Old-Man-of-the-North, who controls the wind of that end or quarter of the world. Another priest states more definitely that the Four-Old-Men are Summer, Winter, Day, and Night, who though they travel in single file, yet are considered as occupying the four cardinal points. Thus, according to direction and the Arapaho color scheme, Day and Summer are the Southeast and Southwest, respectively, and are black in color, while Winter and Night are the Northwest and Northeast, respectively, and are red in color. Inasmuch as Sun is regarded as the grandfather of the Four-Old-Men, it is more than likely that the wheel may be regarded as the emblem of the

Sun. The Four-Old-Men are considered as ever-present, ever-watching sentinels, always alert to guard the people from harm and injury. The same word, hítanni, is also applied to certain markings used in the Old-Woman's lodge, the meaning of which is given variously as the four elements of life, the four courses, the four divides. Thus it is said that when one traveling the trail of life gets over the fourth divide he has reached the winter of old age. The Morning Star is the messenger of the Four-Old-Men, as are also the young men during ceremonies.

The four clusters of feathers also represent the Four-Old-Men. The feathers collectively represent the Thunderbird, which gives rain, and they therefore represent a prayer for rain, consequently for vegetation. . . . The wheel, as a whole, then, may be said to be symbolic of the creation of the world, for it represents the sun, earth, the sky, the water, and the wind. In the great Sun Dance dramatization the wheel itself is represented in the person of the grandfather of the Lodge-Maker, or the "Transferer" as he is called.

In the course of the same paper Doctor Dorsey tells how the wheel is wrapped in calico and buckskin and suspended on a pole or tripod at the back of the lodge of the owner or keeper. It is his duty to preserve the wheel inviolably sacred. The wheel under certain circumstances may be unwrapped by the keeper. This is usually done at the instance of some individual who has made a vow. A new wrapper must be furnished by the person making the vow; hence the term "wrap the wheel" applied to the ceremony. A detailed account is given of this performance. Stories are told of the miraculous movements of the wheel. On one occasion it was seen flying, and changed into an eagle.[a]

The wheel was first kept in the Rabbit tipi.[b] On the second day of the ceremony the wheel was carried into the sweat lodge and placed to the west of the fireplace, the head of the snake facing the east.[c] Later it was carried back to the Rabbit tipi.[d] Here it was placed on its support, a small willow stick, sharpened at one end and split at the other to form a crotch.[e] While it was in the Rabbit tipi a healing ceremony was performed by its aid.[f] On the fifth day it was placed on its support behind the buffalo skull on the sod altar (figure 574).[g] Here, on the seventh day, it was held up to the center pole during the dance, and placed over the head of one of the chief participants.[h] In the origin myth of the wheel [i] the maker of the original is said to have painted it and placed the Four-Old-Men at the cardinal points. Not only were these Old-Men located upon the wheel, but also the morning star (cross); a collection of stars sitting together, perhaps the Pleiades; the evening star (Lone Star); chain of stars (seven buffalo bulls); five stars called a "hand," and a chain of stars which is the lance; a circular group of seven stars overhead, called the "old camp;" the sun, moon, and Milky Way.

[a] The Arapaho Sun Dance, p. 21, Chicago, 1903. [d] Ibid., p. 49. [g] Ibid., p. 122.
[b] Ibid., p. 38. [e] Ibid., p. 68. [h] Ibid., p. 142.
[c] Ibid, p. 47. [f] Ibid., p. 87. [i] Ibid., p. 205.

Taking into consideration all the above facts concerning the hoop or ring, the writer regards the gaming hoop as referable to the netted hoop, which in turn may be regarded as the net shield of the twin War Gods. This object, which the Twins derived from their grandmother, the Spider Woman, is naturally employed, with or without the bows or darts, as a protective amulet. The hoop or ring stands as the feminine symbol, as opposed to the dart or arrows, which are masculine. The implements of the game together represent the shield and the bows or darts of the War Gods.

ALGONQUIAN STOCK

ARAPAHO. Wind River reservation, Wyoming. (Free Museum of Science and Art, University of Pennsylvania.)

Cat. no. 36927. Hoop of sapling (figure 575), 10 inches in diameter,

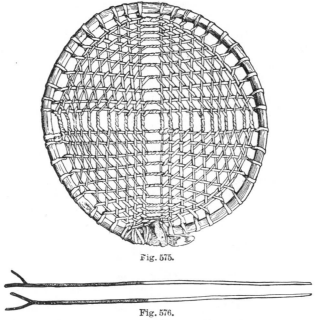

Fig. 575.

Fig. 576.

FIG. 575. Netted hoop; diameter, 10 inches; Arapaho Indians, Wyoming; cat. no. 36927, Free Museum of Science and Art, University of Pennsylvania.

FIG. 576. Darts for netted hoop; length, 42 inches; Arapaho Indians, Wyoming; cat. no. 36973, Free Museum of Science and Art, University of Pennsylvania.

covered with a network of rawhide, which passes over the edge of the hoop forty-five times. The hoop has been painted blue; an old specimen.

Cat. no. 36973. Darts (four), consisting of willow saplings (figure 576) forked at the end; length, about 42 inches.

Collected by the writer in 1900.

ARAPAHO.   Cheyenne and Arapaho reservation, Oklahoma.

Mr James Mooney [a] describes the game of the bäqati, wheel, among the Arapaho, which, he says, " was practically obsolete among the Prairie tribes, but which is being revived since the advent of the Ghost dance.   As it was a favorite game with the men in the olden times, a great many of the songs founded on these trance visions refer to it, and the wheel and sticks are made by the dreamer and carried in the dance as they sing."

The game is played with a wheel (bä'qati, large wheel) and two pairs of throwing-sticks (qa'qa-u'nûtha).   The Cheyenne call the wheel ä'ko'yo or äkwi'u, and the sticks hoo'isi'yonots.   It is a man's game, and there are three players, one rolling the wheel, while the other two, each armed with a pair of throwing sticks, run after it and throw the sticks so as to cross the wheel in a certain position. The two throwers are the contestants, the one who rolls the wheel being merely an assistant.   Like most Indian games, it is a means of gambling, and high stakes are sometimes wagered on the result.   It is common to the Arapaho, Cheyenne, Sioux, and probably to all the northern Prairie tribes, but is not found among the Kiowa or the Comanche in the south.

The wheel is about 18 inches in diameter, and consists of a flexible young tree branch, stripped of its bark and painted, with the two ends fastened together with sinew or buckskin string.   At equal distances around the circumference of the wheel are cut four figures, the two opposite each other constituting a pair, but distinguished by different colors, usually blue or black and red, and by lines or notches on the face.   These figures are designated simply by their colors.   Figures of birds, crescents, etc., are sometimes also cut or painted upon the wheel, but have nothing to do with the game.

The sticks are light rods, about 30 inches long, tied in pairs by a peculiar arrangement of buckskin strings, and distinguished from one another by pieces of cloth of different colors fastened to the strings. There is also a pile of tally sticks, usually a hundred in number, about the size of lead pencils and painted green, for keeping count of the game.   The sticks are held near the center in a peculiar manner between the fingers of the closed hand.   When the wheel is rolled, each player runs from the same side, and endeavors to throw the sticks so as to strike the wheel in such a way that when it falls both sticks of his pair shall be either over or under a certain figure.   It requires dexterity to do this, as the string has a tendency to strike the wheel in such a way as to make one stick fall under and the other over, in which case the throw counts for nothing.   The players assign

---

[a] The Ghost-dance Religion.   Fourteenth Annual Report of the Bureau of Ethnology, p. 994, 1896.

their own value to each figure, the usual value being 5 points for one and 10 for the other figure, with double that number for a throw which crosses the two corresponding figures, and 100 tallies to the game.

The wheel-and-stick game, in some form or another, was almost universal among our Indian tribes. Another game among the Prairie tribes is played with a netted wheel and a single stick or arrow, the effort being to send the arrow through the netting as nearly as possible to the center or bull's-eye. This game is called ana′wati′n-hati, playing wheel, by the Arapaho.

In a myth entitled " Light-Stone," related by Dr George A. Dorsey,[a] the following wheel games are enumerated: Big wheel, running-wheel, and medicine-wheel.

In the story of " The White Crow," related by Dr A. L. Kroeber,[b] there is the following reference to the wheel game:

Close to the camp the people were playing with the sacred arrows and the sacred wheel. Two young men threw the wheel towards an obstacle and then followed it just as if they were running a race.

In Doctor Dorsey's [c] story, entitled " Found-in-Grass," are two twins, Spring-Boy and By-the-Door, who correspond with the twin War Gods. Spring-Boy is blown away by a terrific wind and is found by an old woman, who names him Found-in-Grass. He induces her to make him a bow and arrows and a netted wheel. She went out and cut a green stick and bent it into a ring, and also cut rawhide into small strips. From these articles she made a small netted wheel. One morning he gave his netted wheel to his grandmother and directed her to roll it toward him and say that a fat buffalo cow was running toward him. Sure enough there came running to him a red cow. This cow he shot with his arrows. The operation was repeated, resulting in his shooting a fat buffalo steer and a big fat bull; in this way a supply of meat was procured.

BLACKFEET. Blood reserve, Alberta. (Cat. no. 51641, Field Columbian Museum.)

Ring, 3 inches in diameter, covered with buckskin, painted red, with eight spokes attached inside the rim at equidistant points, four being spirals of brass wire and four alternate ones of beads. Of the latter, one consists of two beads, one red and one blue; another of three, two green and one brass; and the third, of three, one red, one blue, and one red; and the fourth of three red. Collected by Dr George A. Dorsey.

———— Montana. (Cat. no. 22768, Free Museum of Science and Art, University of Pennsylvania.)

Ring (figure 577), 2⅜ inches in diameter, wrapped with buckskin painted red, and having six interior spokes, three consisting

a Traditions of the Arapaho, p. 181, Chicago, 1903.   b Ibid., p. 275.   c Ibid., p. 364.

of two dark-blue glass beads with a bead of spiral brass wire next the center, and three consisting of pyramidal spirals of brass wire, two with red glass beads and one with a yellow glass bead next the center.

This specimen was collected in 1900 by Dr George A. Dorsey, who states that the game is played with two iron-pointed arrows shot from a bow toward the ring, the count being determined by the proximity of the arrow to the ring.

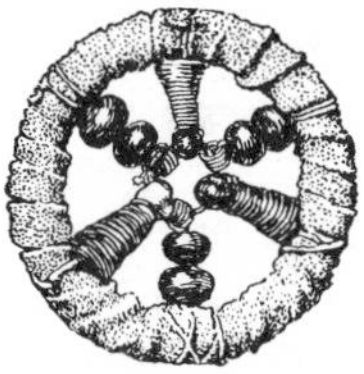

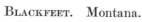

BLACKFEET. Montana.

Dr George Bird Grinnell [a] says:

A favorite pastime in the day was gambling with a small wheel called it-se′-wah. This wheel was about 4 inches in diameter, and had five spokes, on which were strung different-colored beads, made of bone or horn. A level, smooth piece of ground was selected, at each end of which was placed a log. At each end of the course were two men, who gambled against each other. A crowd always surrounded them, betting on the sides. The wheel was rolled along the course, and each man at the end whence it started, darted an arrow at it. The cast was made just before the wheel reached the log at the opposite end of the track, and points were counted according as the arrow passed between the spokes, or when the wheel, stopped by the log, was in contact with the arrow, the position and nearness of the different beads to the arrow representing a certain number of points. The player who first scored 10 points won. It was a very difficult game, and one had to be very skillful to win.

FIG. 577. Gaming ring; diameter, 2⅝ inches; Blackfoot Indians, Montana; cat.no.22768, Free Museum of Science and Art, University of Pennsylvania.

———— Southern Alberta.

Rev. John MacLean [b] describes the hoop-and-arrow game as follows:

A board, 8 or 10 inches in width, is placed on its edge upon the ground, held in place by small stakes driven into the ground; and another, in the same fashion, about 12 feet distant. The contestants play in pairs. Each holds in his right hand an arrow, and one of them a small wheel, having fastened to it a bead, or special mark placed upon it. Standing at one end and inside the board, they run together toward the other board. The contestant having the wheel rolls it on the ground, throwing it with such force that it strikes the board. As the two men run they throw their arrows against the board, and as near the wheel as they can. When the wheel falls, they measure the distance between the point of the arrows and the bead or special mark on the wheel, and the arrow which lies nearest to this point has won the throw. They continue this running and throwing until the one who has reached the number agreed upon as the end of the game has won. The number of points made by the contestants are kept by means of small sticks held in the hands. Several pairs of contestants sometimes play after each other, and for days they will continue the game, surrounded by a large number of men, old and young, who are eagerly betting upon the result.

---

[a] Blackfoot Lodge Tales, p. 183, New York, 1892.
[b] Canadian Savage Folk, p. 55, Toronto, 1896.

CHEYENNE and ARAPAHO. Oklahoma. (Cat. no. 203789, United
    States National Museum.)

Hoop (figure 578), 12 inches in diameter, laced with rawhide, the
    leather passing forty-eight times around the edge. Half the net
    on one side of the principal division is painted blue and the
    other half red; the colors are reversed on the opposite side.
    Collected by E. Granier.

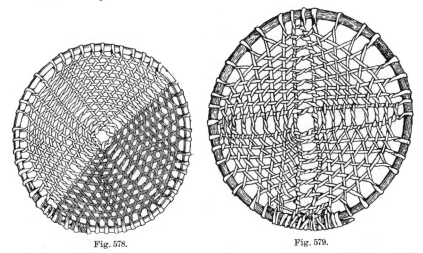

Fig. 578.   Fig. 579.

FIG. 578. Netted hoop; diameter, 12 inches; Cheyenne and Arapaho Indians, Oklahoma; cat. no.
203789, United States National Museum.
FIG. 579. Netted hoop; diameter, 13½ inches; Cheyenne Indians, Oklahoma; cat. no. 165845, United
States National Museum.

CHEYENNE. Oklahoma. (Cat. no. 165845, United States National
    Museum.)

Hoop, a bent sapling laced with a net of rawhide, as shown in figure
    579; diameter, 13½ inches; the thong passes over the edge thirty-
    six times. Collected by Rev. H. R. Voth.

Two other Cheyenne gaming hoops in the United States National
Museum (cat. no. 152814), diameters, 12 and 13 inches, collected by
Mr Mooney, appear to be models. The net is irregular, and does
not seem to be put on with the system and care that characterize the
old hoops.

———— Darlington, Oklahoma. (Cat. no. 18735, Free Museum of
    Science and Art, University of Pennsylvania.)

Hoop, a bent sapling 7 inches in diameter, with a network of raw-
    hide. A red down feather is attached to the hoop by a sinew.
    Apparently a model. The netting, which is coarse, passes over
    the hoop eighteen times. Collected by Mr George E. Starr.

———— Oklahoma.

Mr Louis L. Meeker thus describes the hoop game, ha-ko-yu-tsist:

The player holds a stick, and thrusts it through a wheel with four spokes, made of very light material, and so notched that different counts are made by thrusting in different places.

CHEYENNE. Oklahoma.

Dr A. L. Kroeber[a] in his Cheyenne Tales gives the following account:

There was a large camp near a spring called Old-woman's spring. The people were amusing themselves by games, and were playing the "buffalo game" with rolling hoops. Two young men were standing by, watching. They were painted alike and dressed alike and wore the same headdresses, and both wore buffalo-robes. Finally one of them told the people to call every one and that all should watch him; that he would go into the spring, and bring back food that would be a great help to the people ever after. The other young man also said that he would bring them food. There was an entrance to the spring, formed by a great stone, and by this the two young men descended into the spring, both going at the same time. They found an old gray-headed woman sitting, and she showed them on one side fields of corn, and on the other herds of buffalo. Then one of the young men brought back corn, and the other buffalo meat, and the people feasted on both. And that night the buffalo came out of the spring; and there have been herds of them ever since, and corn has been grown too.

CHIPPEWA. Turtle mountain, North Dakota. (Cat. no. $\frac{50}{4731}$, American Museum of Natural History.)

FIG. 580. Netted hoop and dart; diameter of hoop, 11¼ inches; length of dart, 36 inches; Chippewa Indians, Turtle mountain, North Dakota; cat. no. $\frac{50}{4731}$, American Museum of Natural History.

Hoop (figure 580), 11¾ inches in diameter, netted with buckskin thongs, the thongs painted red, the edge of the hoop wrapped with black cloth, a square orifice in the center of the thongs wrapped with red cloth; accompanied by a straight dart made of a sapling 3 feet long, painted red, with a black band, and a feather tied to the handle end.

This specimen was collected in 1903 by Dr William Jones, who gives the name of the game as tititipanatuwanagi, rollers, and says that it is played by anyone.

DELAWARES. Ontario.

Dr Daniel G. Brinton[b] gives the following account from conversations with Rev. Albert Seqaqkind Anthony:

---

[a] Journal of American Folk-Lore. v. 13, p. 163, Boston, 1900.
[b] Folk-lore of the Modern Lenape. Essays of an Americanist, p. 186, Philadelphia, 1890.

A very popular sport was with a hoop, tautmusq, and spear or arrow, allunth. The players arranged themselves in two parallel lines, some 40 feet apart, each one armed with a reed spear. A hoop was then rolled rapidly at an equal distance between the lines. Each player hurled his spear at it, the object being to stop the hoop by casting the spear within its rim. When stopped, the shaft must lie within the hoop, or the shot did not count.

GROSVENTRES. Fort Belknap reservation, Montana. (Cat. no. 60350, Field Columbian Museum.)

Hoop (figure 581), a bent sapling 10 inches in diameter, netted with hide, which passes over the ring thirty-four times.

Collected in 1900 by Dr George A. Dorsey, who describes it as employed in the game of hatchieb.

In playing, the wheel is rolled forward on the ground, when the players hurl toward it slender spears, or darts, the object being to

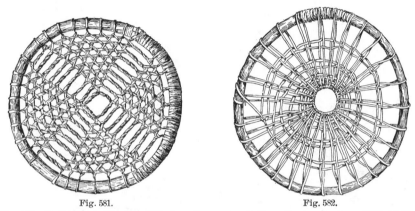

Fig. 581.   Fig. 582.

FIG. 581. Netted hoop; diameter, 10 inches; Grosventre Indians, Montana; cat. no. 60350, Field Columbian Museum.
FIG. 582. Netted hoop; diameter, 16¼ inches; Piegan Indians, Alberta; cat. no. 69353, Field Columbian Museum.

pierce one of the holes formed by the buckskin lacing of the wheel. These holes vary in size, and each has its own proper name and value; the latter, however, could not be learned. The holes are named as follows: Large hole in center, ita, or heart; holes inclosed within the parallel lines crossing at right angles, anatayan, or buffalo bulls; large holes outside the parallel lines, behe, or buffalo cows; small triangles formed at points of cross lacing, wuuha, or buffalo calves; large holes next to the wooden ring, chadjitha, or wolves; small holes formed by the crossing of the thongs next to the wooden ring, caawu, or coyotes.

This game is played by men and formerly stakes of much value were wagered on the result.

PIEGAN. Alberta. (Cat. no. 69353, Field Columbian Museum.)

Hoop of cherry sapling (figure 582), 16¼ inches in diameter, laced with a network of rawhide, which passes around the edge twenty-eight times. Collected by Mr R. N. Wilson. In another similar specimen in the same museum, cat. no. 69352, the thong passes thirty times around the edge.

FIG. 583. Beaded ring; diameter, 3¼ inches; Piegan Indians, Alberta; cat. no. 64350, Field Columbian Museum.

PIEGAN. Alberta. (Cat. no. 64350, Field Columbian Museum.)

Iron ring (figure 583), 3⅛ inches in diameter, wrapped with buckskin and having eight rows of colored glass beads of three each, arranged within, like the spokes of a wheel. The beads are of different colors, as follows: Three white; three red; two black and one dark blue; two green and one black; three yellow; three light blue; two black and one red; two green and one blue. Collected by Mr R. N. Wilson, who describes it as used in a ring-and-arrow game.

SAUK AND FOXES. Iowa. (Cat. no. ₃₅⁵⁰₀₄, American Museum of Natural History.)

Four rings of elm bark (figure 584), 2, 2½, 3, and 3½ inches in diameter, and a little bundle of elm bark (figure 585), 3 inches

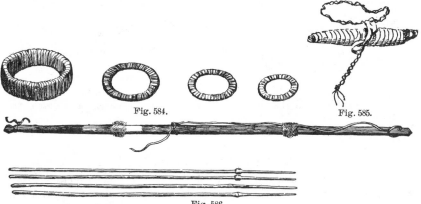

Fig. 584.

Fig. 585.

Fig. 586.

FIG. 584. Game rings; diameters, 3½, 3, 2½, and 2 inches; Sauk and Fox Indians, Iowa; cat. no. ₃₅⁵⁰₀₄, American Museum of Natural History.

FIG. 585. Bundle of elm bark used as target; length, 3 inches; Sauk and Fox Indians, Iowa; cat. no. ₃₅⁵⁰₀₄, American Museum of Natural History

FIG. 586. Bow and arrows used in ring game; length of bow, 38 inches; length of arrows, 25 inches; Sauk and Fox Indians, Iowa; cat. no. ₃₅⁵⁰₀₄, American Museum of Natural History.

long. Bow (figure 586), 3 feet 2 inches in length, with two bands of rabbit fur, designated by its color as the property of the Blacks, one of the two divisions of the people (White and Black); four arrows, 25 inches in length.

The players, men or boys, divide into two sides, each side having four rings and each player four arrows. The rings are rolled, and shot at with the arrows; each arrow must pierce the ring and hang on. The side that hits all the rings first has the right to roll the rings at the arrows. The arrows that have been shot are stuck up in a row, and the winning side rolls the rings at them. Each time that the ring hits an arrow it wins that arrow.

The little bundle of bark is held with the guiding forefinger on the bow, tossed into the air, and shot at in lieu of the ring. In another form of the game the bundle of elm bark or the rings are buried in the sand and shot at with arrows. The game is to hit the concealed bundle or ring so that the arrow shall be held by it. The game is called topagahagi, rings; the little bundle of bark, otawahi; the bow, metaha, and the arrows, owipanoni.

The game is played about the house. People believe there is a spirit of sickness, Apenaweni, always hovering about to get into the lodges, and this game is encouraged in order to keep it away.

ATHAPASCAN STOCK

APACHE (CHIRICAHUA). Arizona.

Mr E. W. Davis gave the writer the following account of a game played by Geronimo's band at St Augustine, Florida, in 1889:

Another game which interested me was played with hoops and poles, and, as I remember, always by two men. The hoops were ordinary pieces of flexible wood, tied into a circle of about 12 inches with leather thongs, and the poles were reeds 10 or 12 feet long. A little heap of hay was placed on the ground and parted in the center. The players stood about 15 feet away, and each in his turn would roll his hoop into the little valley in the hay mound. Waiting until the hoop had nearly reached the hay he would toss the staff through the hay, the object being to pass the hoop so that it might encircle the end of the pole when the hoop reached the hay. This game was very difficult, and misses were more frequent than scores.

APACHE (JICARILLA). Northern New Mexico.

Mr James Mooney,[a] in The Jicarilla Genesis, describes the wheel-and-stick game as having been made by Yolkaiistsun, the White-bead woman, for her two sons, children by her of the Sun and the Moon. She told them not to roll the wheel toward the north. They played for three days, when the Sun's son rolled the wheel toward the east, south, and west. His brother then persuaded him to roll it toward the north. An adventure with an owl follows, and the two boys were set to perform a succession of dangerous feats, which accomplished, they went to live in the western ocean.

APACHE (MESCALERO). Fort Sumner, New Mexico.

Col. John C. Cremony [b] says:

There are some games to which women are never allowed access. Among these is one played with the poles and a hoop. The former are generally about

---

[a] The American Anthropologist, v. 11, p. 201, 1898.
[b] Life Among the Apaches, p. 302, San Francisco, 1868.

10 feet in length, smooth and gradually tapering like a lance. It is [*sic*] marked with divisions throughout its whole length, and these divisions are stained in different colors. The hoop is of wood, about 6 inches in diameter, and divided like the poles, of which each player has one. Only two persons can engage in this game at one time. A level place is selected, from which the grass is removed a foot in width, and for 25 or 30 feet in length, and the earth trodden down firmly and smoothly. One of the players rolls the hoop forward, and after it reaches a certain distance, both dart their poles after it, overtaking and throwing it down. The graduation of values is from the point of the pole toward the butt, which ranks highest, and the object is to make the hoop fall on the pole as near the butt as possible, at the same time noting the value of the part which touches the hoop. The two values are then added and placed to the credit of the player. The game usually runs up to a hundred, but the extent is arbitrary among the players. While it is going on no woman is permitted to approach within a hundred yards, and each person present is compelled to leave all his arms behind. I inquired the reason for these restrictions, and was told that they were required by tradition; but the shrewd old Sons-in-jah gave me another, and, I believe, the true version. When people gamble, said he, they become half crazy, and are very apt to quarrel. This is the most exciting game we have, and those who play it will wager all they possess. The loser is apt to get angry, and fights have ensued which resulted in the loss of many warriors. To prevent this, it was long ago determined that no warrior should be present with arms upon his person or within near reach, and this game is always played at some distance from camp. Three prominent warriors are named as judges, and from their decision there is no appeal. They are not suffered to bet while acting in that capacity. The reason why women are forbidden to be present is because they always foment troubles between the players, and create confusion by taking sides and provoking dissension.

APACHE (SAN CARLOS). San Carlos agency, Gila county, Arizona. (Cat. no. 63535, Field Columbian Museum.)

Hoop of sapling, 9¾ inches in diameter, painted red, divided in half with thong wound with buckskin cord, and having four equidistant notches on both faces on opposite sides of the median thong. Collected by Mr S. C. Simms, who describes it as used in the game of nahlpice (figure 587).

APACHE (WHITE MOUNTAIN). Arizona. (Cat. no. 61246, Field Columbian Museum.)

Two jointed poles in three pieces, 14 feet and 15 feet 4¼ inches in length, and a hoop made of sapling, 9¾ inches in diameter, the latter having a thong wound with cord stretched across the middle. Collected by Rev. Paul S. Mayerhoff, who describes the game under the name of na-a-shosh.

The game is played with two poles, each of which is made up in three sections, and a hoop. The butt end of each pole is marked off into nine divisions or counters. The ring also has marked on its circumference eleven divisions or counters. The spoke bisecting the hoop and wrapped with cord is also used in counting, there being one hundred and four winds of cord, or plus the knot or bead in the center, one hundred and five in all. The total number of points on pole and hoop is one hundred and twenty-five in the average game, but exceeding that in some. The two poles represent the two sexes— yellow representing the male, red the female. They are called mbăshgah. Their three sections are, respectively: Butt, egie-shĕ dĕs-tăh-nēē; middle section, indēē dĕs-tăh-nēē; tip, bĭllăh tăh shĕ dĕs-tăh nēē. The joints are made by wrapping with sinew.

Fɪɢ. 587.　San Carlos Apache Indians playing hoop and pole; San Carlos agency, Arizona; from photograph by Mr S. C. Simms.

The hoop is called băh say; the bead on the center of the bisecting spoke, băh say-bi-yō. The playground (figure 588) is 75 to 100 feet long; the home goal (dō-thēē′-shay-tsay-nee-say-ah) is marked by a flat rock midway between the two ends (dō-thēē′-shay-his-tso).

The ends, toward which the game proceeds alternately, are so built up by means of hay or grass that three parallel ridges, 8 to 10 feet

Fɪɢ. 588.　Plan of pole grounds; White Mountain Apache Indians, Arizona.

in length, are formed. The hoop and poles must be propelled in such a way as to pass into the depressions between the ridges and come to a stop before they have passed to the extreme ends of the ridges. The throw counts only when the hoop falls upon the marked butt of the pole. In playing, one of the two opponents rolls the hoop forward from the home goal toward one of the ends; just as it begins to lose its inertia the opponents throw forward their poles so that they will slide along into the depression in which the hoop has rolled. The same proceeding is repeated in the opposite direction. Then comes the next pair of players, and so on until all have had their turn, when the first set takes its turn once more, the rotation keeping up until the agreed number of points has been made by one opponent or one side.

The method of counting is simple, every mark or counter on pole or hoop counting but one. If the hoop falls against the extreme butt of the pole so that they just touch, it counts 1; if it falls on the

FIG. 589. San Carlos Apache Indians playing hoop and pole, Arizona; from a photograph.

butt, as many points are counted as are inclosed by the hoop; e. g., if it touches the first mark above the butt end, it counts 2; the next higher, 3; the next, 4, etc.

Should marks on the circumference of the hoop touch the pole, points are added to the enclosed points on the butt of the pole, 1 point if one mark, 2 if two marks, etc. Where the spoke of the hoop also crosses the pole, as many points are added to the throw as it takes winds of the cord to cross the thickness of the butt. If the hoop falls upon the pole so that the bar or spoke in it lies exactly above and parallel with the pole, covering all the counters on the pole, such a throw wins the game.

The game has a religious character with the Apache Indians, no festivity being complete without it, and is played with great fervor and persistency. Only those medicine men (called Dēē-yín) deeply versed in their folklore and traditions can give a minute explanation of the original meaning and symbolism of this game, and they are very reluctant to part with their knowledge. Tradition says that one of the Ghons (the minor deities to whom these Indians ascribe their instruction and knowledge in handicrafts and arts, as tilling the soil, raising crops, preparing food, weaving, and manufacturing implements and utensils for camp, chase, or war, the use of medicines, etc.) taught their forefathers the game, with its symbolism.

Fig. 590. White Mountain Apache Indians playing hoop and pole, Arizona; from photograph by George B. Wittick.

There are several short prayers or charms, some sung, some spoken, used by players to neutralize the efforts of their opponents and bring success to themselves. The following may be given as an example:

Hïllchee be-tä hà hïs ēē.
Hïll chēē shä-ō-Ka'-shay näh-ēē-gáy yūl-tläthl.
Dēē-djáy i-dĕs-á-go shï-dáy gush;
Nä-gō-tláy-gō Kä-shay-day-äh.

[Translation.]

The wind will make it miss yours;
The wind will turn it on my pole.
To-day at noon I shall win all;
At night again to me will it fall.

APACHE (WHITE MOUNTAIN). White river, Arizona.

Mr Albert B. Reagan gave the following account of the game in a communication to the Bureau of American Ethnology in 1901:

The pole game is the Apache national game. It is played by the men every day from early morn to late in the afternoon; sometimes to pass the time only,

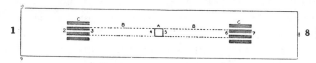

FIG. 591. Plan of pole ground; White Mountain Apache Indians, Arizona; from sketch by Albert B. Reagan. A, base; B B, sliding grounds, length 9 steps; C C, counting fields, length, 3 steps, width 5 feet; spaces between counting fields and end of playground, 1–2, 7–8, length, 6 steps; total length, 1–8, 36 yards; width, 9–10, 6 yards.

sometimes for "medicine," but almost always for gain. They sometimes bet all they have on it, in former times even their women and children.

The pole ground is a level space 36 yards long and 6 wide, laid off in the directions north and south [figure 591]. In its center is the base, usually a rock, from which the poles are hurled. Nine yards from this base, both north and south, are three hay-covered ridges, the center ridge lying on the

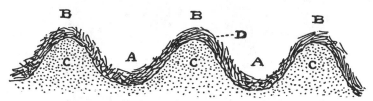

FIG. 592. Cross section of counting field in pole game; White Mountain Apache Indians, Arizona; from sketch by Albert B. Reagan. A A, furrows into which the wheel runs; B B B, ridges on sides of furrows; C C C, earth; D, hay or straw.

center line of the pole ground [figure 592]. These ridges are 3 yards long, with a total width of 5 feet. There are two narrow furrows between the ridges, into which the wheel is rolled.

The two poles are willow, about 15 feet long, made in three sections, which are spliced and tied with sinew. They taper from the butt to a point, being about 1¼ inches in diameter at the butt end. The first 9 inches of the butt,

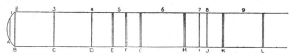

FIG. 593. Counting end of pole for pole game; White Mountain Apache Indians, Arizona; from sketch by Albert B. Reagan.

called the "counting end" [figure 593], is marked with grooves. The counts on this butt are nine in number: The little circular knot, A; the edge, B, of the pole; the lightly cut groove, C; the lightly cut groove, D; the space between the two heavily cut grooves, E F; the space between the two heavily cut grooves, G H; the lightly cut groove, I; the lightly cut groove, J; the space between the two heavily cut grooves, K L. The hoop or wheel [figure 594] is made of willow, about a foot in diameter, the ends being bound with sinew. A buckskin thong, stretched across the ring, is wound its entire length with cord. The center wrap is made larger than the others. These wraps are called beads, because originally beads were used instead of the wrapping cords. These beads are counted to 50 in descending order on each side of the center. Sometimes there are more than fifty turns, but only this number is counted. They are not touched by the hand in counting, but are pointed to with a straw by the player. They are always counted by twos. With the center bead the fifty beads on each side make 101 counts on the diameter of the wheel. The edges on both sides of the circumference of the hoop are notched with nine cuts, which, with the two sinew wrappings, are used in counting. The space, A–B, between the places where the ends are lashed counts 1; and each of the notches, 2, 3, 4, 5, 6, 7, 8, 9, 10, 11, around the ring, 1; making 11 counts, or a

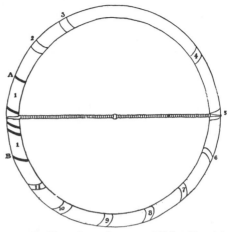

FIG. 594. Hoop for pole game; White Mountain Apache Indians, Arizona; from sketch by Albert B. Reagan.

total of 112 counts on the hoop. With the 9 counts on the butt there is a total of 121 counts in the game; the players learn to count, most of them being able to count to 1,000 in their own language. In rolling the hoop, it is held vertically between the thumb and second finger of the right hand, resting on the

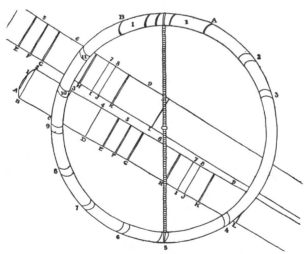

FIG. 595. Counting points in pole game; White Mountain Apache Indians, Arizona; from sketch by Albert B. Reagan.

extended index finger, over which it rolls when it is dispatched. If it is seen to be rolling wide of the furrows, it is sometimes guided to its place by one of the poles. On entering a furrow the loose hay retards its speed and it falls over, only to be slid under the hay by the well-directed poles. If it fails to enter a furrow, which is called a break in the game, it is brought back and rolled again. It is always rolled first to the south and then to the north, and so on for hours until the game is finished.

In throwing the poles, they are propelled by the right hand and guided with the left, the index finger of the right hand being placed against the end of the pole, which is held between the thumb and index finger. The pole, if hurled successfully, slides into the furrow beneath the wheel, and stops with its butt beneath it. If it passes entirely through the furrow or goes to the side this is also called a break in the game, and the poles are taken back to the base and hurled again, the wheel being rolled as before. It takes long practice and much skill to hurl the poles successfully.

In carrying back the poles after they have been hurled they are thrown over the right shoulder. They are then stood on end upon the ground for a moment only, then hurled as before.

In counting, all points on each pole that fall on or within the rim of the hoop are counted, also all the points on the rim of the hoop and all the beads on the cord which fall within the edges of the pole. The points being counted, the game proceeds as before. This is continued for hours, until one side or the other gets the number of points agreed upon as deciding the game. There may be any odd number from 37 to 1,001. The game is sometimes played for the best two out of three or three out of five rounds, etc., two hurls south and one north constituting a play.

Vocabulary: Bâ-na'-e-jōsh', let us play pole; bas'-sā, or pas'-sā, the hoop; bas'-sā-hēū', the counting end of the pole; bas'-sā-hewk', hoop heads, the closely wrapped cord; dá'-des-kīsh', the points on the hoop rim; klō-hō-ká'-nil'-dīsh, the counting field, the three-ridged space; nä'-ē-jōsh', the pole; nä'-ē-jōsh'-ka, the pole ground; sä kō'-shē-

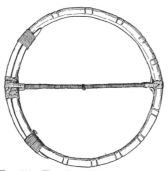

FIG. 596. Hoop for pole game; diameter, 10 inches; White Mountain Apache Indians, Arizona; cat. no. 18618, Free Museum of Science and Art, University of Pennsylvania.

wal'-chēl-kŏt, the base, or center, of the pole ground, from which the hoop is rolled and the poles are hurled; ūk, one of the wraps (beads) on the cord; uk'-chō, the center bead on the cord.

APACHE (WHITE MOUNTAIN). Arizona. (Cat. no. 18618, Free Museum of Science and Art, University of Pennsylvania.)

Hoop of sapling (figure 596), 10 inches in diameter, painted red, the overlapping ends lashed with cords, with a thong lashing between. A thong wound with cord is fastened across the middle of the ring, the outer circumference of which is notched with eleven notches equally disposed in the space between the lashings.

Collected by the late Capt. C. N. B. Macauley, U. S. Army, who described the game to the writer under the name panshka, pole game:

Two men play. The ground is leveled and covered with hay or dried grass. One rolls the wheel and both throw their poles, points first, along the ground beside it, endeavoring to make the wheel fall on the butt of the pole. The counts are most intricate, depending upon the way in which the pole falls in reference to the wheel, the periphery of which is marked with rings of sinew. The details are so complicated that no civilized game nearly compares in complexity with this apparently simple sport.

COLVILLE (CHUALPAY).   Fort Colville, Washington.

Paul Kane [a] says:

The principal game here is called Al-kol-lock, and requires considerable skill. A smooth level piece of ground is chosen, and a slight barrier of a couple of sticks, placed lengthwise, is laid at each end of the chosen spot, being from 40 to 50 feet apart and only a few inches high. The two players, stripped naked, are armed each with a very slight spear about 3 feet long, and finely pointed with bone; one of them takes a ring made of bone, or some heavy wood, and wound round with cord; this ring is about 3 inches in diameter, on the inner circumference of which are fastened six beads of different colors at equal distances, to each of which a separate numerical value is attached. The ring is then rolled along the ground to one of the barriers, and is followed at a distance of 2 or 3 yards by the players, and as the ring strikes the barrier and is falling on its side the spears are thrown, so that the ring may fall on them. If only one of the spears should be covered by the ring, the thrower of it counts according to the colored bead over it. But it generally happens, from the dexterity of the players, that the ring covers both spears, and each counts according to the color of the beads above his spear; they then play towards the other barrier, and so on until one party has attained the number agreed upon for game.

NAVAHO.   Keams canyon, Arizona.   (Cat. no. 62535, Field Columbian Museum.)

Ring (figure 597) wrapped with sheep hide, $6\frac{1}{2}$ inches in diameter, and two poles (figure 598), about 9 feet in length, made in two pieces lashed together with hide, the sticks overlapping about a foot, and the ends of the lashing (figure 599) having crosspieces of hide fastened to them by bands of sheepskin. Collected by Mr Thomas V. Keam.

———— St Michael, Arizona.

The Reverend Father Berard Haile writes in a personal letter:

Ná'azhôzh, stick and hoop. The pole is decorated with buckskin strings, called "turkey feet." The hoop is set in motion and the stick thrown through the rolling hoop. Points score as the stick falls on the turkey feet. Some sticks are decorated with claws of wildcats or of the mountain lion, bear, eagle, etc., which are attached to the strings, and as the claws catch the hoop a point is scored.

Later Father Berard writes:

I find that there were four different forms of ná'azhôzh: First, ná'azhôzh aqá'dest'loni, bound together, in which the stick or pole was cut in two and tied with buckskin, allowing the ends of the string to hang down; second, ná'azhôzh

[a] Wanderings of an Artist among the Indians of North America, p. 310, London, 1859. See also The Canadian Journal, p. 276, Toronto, June, 1855, where Kane describes this game in about the same words under the name of al-kol-loch as one that is universal along the Columbia river. There is a good picture of this game in Kane's collection, no. 65, at Toronto. The original sketches were made at Fort Colville.

dilkô"i, slick or polished, in which the pole was left intact and provided with three strings, one at the point and two at the butt; third, ná'azhôzh dit'lói, strung profusely, in which the pole was profusely decorated with strings, etc.; fourth, ná'azhôzh dilkô', polished, in which the hoop, or wheel, was only about an inch in diameter and thrown toward a mark or point. The players were each provided with a stick, each the length of an arm. In a stooped position they strive to throw the stick through the ring. How many points the winner had to score I could not ascertain, as Mr Big Goat, my informant, claims that in

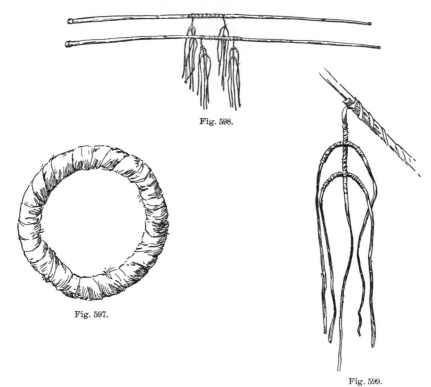

Fig. 598.

Fig. 597.

Fig. 599.

FIG. 597. Ring for pole game; diameter, 6¼ inches; Navaho Indians, Keams canyon, Arizona; cat. no. 62535, Field Columbian Museum.
FIG. 598. Pole for pole game; length, about 9 feet; Navaho Indians, Keams canyon, Arizona; cat. no. 62535, Field Columbian Museum.
FIG. 599. Ends of lashing of pole for pole game; Navaho Indians, Keams canyon, Arizona; cat. no. 62535, Field Columbian Museum.

all these games the points were agreed upon beforehand, and a variation naturally took place according to the value of the article put at stake. To distinguish the first from the fourth game here mentioned, they also called the latter laazē', which means as much as that the pole was varnished (with juice of yucca and paint).

This game is intimated by Dr Washington Matthews in his Navaho Legends [page 219] where he mentions dilkón, played with two sticks, each the length of an arm, as among the four games which the Navaho brought with them from the lower world.

Concerning another game mentioned by Doctor Matthews in this connection, atsa, played with forked sticks and a ring, Father Berard writes:

Atsá also means an eagle, whilst tsā' signifies a needle, awl, or anything similar, ergo, forked sticks? (ts'ā, basket). It was impossible for me to find any clue to this game, unless we assume that it is another form of ná'azhôzh. Many of the games of the legends of the Navaho, they say, are purely mythical or artificial and have not been played by them.

NAVAHO. Arizona, New Mexico.

Dr Washington Matthews [a] refers to the game of nanzoz, as played by the Navaho, as much the same as the game of chungkee played by the Mandan, described and depicted by Catlin (see p. 512).

A hoop is rolled along the ground, and long poles are thrown after it. The Mandan pole was made of a single piece of wood. The pole of the Navaho is made of two pieces, usually alder, each a natural fathom long; the pieces overlap and are bound together by a long branching strap of hide called *th*ági-bĭke, or turkey-claw.

Nanzoz was the second of the four games played by young Hastsé-hogan with the divine gambler or Gambling god named Nohoílpi, or " He Who Wins Men " (at play).

Doctor Matthews [b] says that the game is played with two long sticks or poles of peculiar shape and construction, one marked with red and the other with black, and a single hoop. A long, many-tailed string, called the " turkey claw," is secured to the end of each pole. In this contest the Great Snake came to the assistance of young Hastséhogan. Nanzoz was played out of doors.

The track already prepared lay east and west, but, prompted by the Wind God, the stranger insisted on having a track made from north to south, and again, at the bidding of Wind, he chose the red stick. The son of Hastséhogan threw the wheel; at first it seemed about to fall on the gambler's pole, in the " turkey claw " of which it was entangled; but to the great surprise of the gambler it extricated itself, rolled farther on, and fell on the pole of his opponent. The latter ran to pick up the ring, lest Nohoílpi in doing so might hurt the snake inside; but the gambler was so angry that he threw his stick away and gave up the game, hoping to do better in the next contest, which was that of pushing down trees.

Elsewhere [c] Doctor Matthews describes the personator of Hatdast-sisi as carrying on his back a ring about 12 inches in diameter, made of yucca leaves, and, suspended from this by the roots, a complete plant of the *Yucca baccata*. The ring is like that used in the game of nanzoz and indicates that the god is a great gambler at nanzoz.

---

[a] Navaho Legends, note 76, Boston, 1897.
[b] Ibid., p. 85.
[c] The Night Chant, a Navaho Ceremony. Memoirs of the American Museum of Natural History, whole series, v. 6, p. 15, New York, 1902.

Speaking of the Navaho, Maj. E. Backus, U. S. Army, wrote as follows, in Schoolcraft:[a]

Their favorite game consists in throwing a lance or pole at a rolling hoop, in which they are said to exhibit much skill. I have never seen the game played and can not describe its details.

SARSI. British Columbia.

Rev. E. F. Wilson[b] gives the following account:

The Sarcees, like most other wild Indians, are inveterate gamblers. They will gamble everything away—ponies, teepees, blankets, leggings, moccasins—till they have nothing left but their breech-clout. In my report of the Blackfoot last year I mentioned the use of a little hoop or wheel for gambling purposes. I find that the Sarcees also use this, and two of them showed me how they play the game. A little piece of board, if procurable, or two or three flattened sticks, laid one on the other, are put for a target, at a distance of 18 or 20 feet from the starting-point, and the two players then take their places beside each other; one has the little wheel in his left hand, an arrow in his right; the other one has only an arrow. The play is to roll the wheel and to deliver the two arrows simultaneously, all aiming at the mark which has been set up. If the wheel falls over on one of the arrows, it counts so many points, according to the number of beads on the wire spoke of the wheel that touch the arrow. Nothing is counted unless the little wheel falls on one of the arrows. The articles for which they play are valued at so many points each. A blanket is worth, perhaps, 10 points, a pony, 50, and so on.

FIG. 600. Hoop for game; Takulli Indians, Stuart lake, British Columbia; from Morice.

TAKULLI. Stuart lake, British Columbia.

The Reverend Father A. G. Morice[c] describes the game of keilapəs, encircling willow, or arrow target-shooting, named from the implement required for its performance:

This is a sort of open work disk or wheel [figure 600], principally made of willow-bark strings, though the frame of the hoop is composed of three or four switches very closely fitting each other and kept in position by a strong lacing of strips of bark. Radiating from the axis, or heart, as it is called, are four cords of similar material, stretched so as to form a cross. As this was formerly the great national game of the Carriers, I may be pardoned for giving its rules in full.

A team of five or six men was matched against another of presumed equal force, and after each player had been provided with a given number of pointed arrows, the disk was set wheeling away by one team to the cry of tlép! tlép!

[a] Information respecting the History, Condition, and Prospects of the Indian Tribes of the United States, pt. 4, p. 214, Philadelphia, 1856.

[b] Fourth Report on the North-Western Tribes of Canada. Report of the Fifty-eighth Meeting of the British Association for the Advancement of Science, p. 246, London, 1889.

[c] Notes on the Western Dénés. Transactions of the Canadian Institute, v. 4, p. 113, Toronto, 1895.

This was the signal for the other to shoot at it while it was in motion. Should they fail to hit it, it was returned rolling to the first team, so as to give them an equal chance of making at it with their arrows. As soon as the disk had been shot, the real competitive game commenced. The arrows which had hit it, two, three, or more, became the stake for the rival team to win over. For this purpose the disk was hung upon a short stick planted in the ground near the team who had succeeded in sending home the arrows, and it was aimed at successively by each member of the opposite party. Should anyone be lucky enough to shoot it with his first arrow, the stake played for became his irrevocable property. When the target was hit, but on a subsequent attempt of the marksman, the stake was thereby won over, subject to its being redeemed by any member of the opposing team performing the same feat. In this case the game became a draw; the wheel was set rolling anew, and the nature of the stake was determined as in the first instance.

I have never seen 'keilapəs played by other than children and young men. But in times past it had a sort of national importance, inasmuch as teams from distant villages were wont to assemble in certain localities more favorable to its performance in good style. Indeed, until a few years ago the sporting field of some was literally dotted with small cavities resulting from the fall of the arrows.

CADDOAN STOCK

ARIKARA. South Dakota.

John Bradbury [a] says:

We amused ourselves some time by watching a party who were engaged in play. A place was neatly formed, resembling a skittle alley, about 9 feet in breadth and 90 feet long: a ring of wood, about 5 inches in diameter was trundled along from one end, and when it had run some distance, two Indians, who stood ready, threw after it, in a sliding manner, each a piece of wood, about 3 feet long and 4 inches in breadth, made smooth on one edge, and kept from turning by a crosspiece passing through it, and bended backwards so as to resemble a crossbow. The standers-by kept an account of the game, and he whose piece, in a given number of throws, more frequently came nearest the ring after it had fallen, won the game.

H. M. Brackenridge [b] says:

Their daily sports, in which, when the weather is favorable, they are engaged from morning till night, are principally of two kinds. A level piece of ground appropriated for the purpose, and beaten by frequent use, is the place where they are carried on. The first is played by two persons, each armed with a long pole; one of them rolls a hoop, which, after having reached about two-thirds of the distance, is followed at half speed, and as they perceive it about to fall, they cast their poles under it; the pole on which the hoop falls, so as to be nearest to certain corresponding marks on the hoop and pole, gains for that time. This game excites great interest, and produces a gentle, but animated exercise. The other differs from it in this, that instead of poles, they have short pieces of wood, with barbs at one end, and a cross piece at the other, held in the middle with one hand; but instead of the hoop before mentioned, they throw a small ring, and endeavor to put the point of the barb through it. This is a much more violent exercise than the other.

---

[a] Travels in the Interior of America in the years 1809, 1810, and 1811, p. 126, Liverpool, 1817.

[b] Views of Louisiana, together with a Journal of a Voyage up the Missouri River, in 1811, p. 255, Pittsburg, 1814.

ARIKARA.

Dr George A. Dorsey,[a] in The Origin of the Arikara, describes them as coming in their journeyings to a great lake where they had their village for some time. They made games at this place. Shinny is specified.

At other places they had long javelins to catch a ring with. The side that won began to kill the people who were on the other side, and whose language they could not understand.

Doctor Dorsey,[b] in the story of " The Buffalo Wife and the Javelin Game," relates also the following:

Young man out hunting dreams of two buffalo bulls turning into sticks and of buffalo cow turning into ring. In morning he sees cow and lies with her. Finds ring in grass and wears it on his wrist. He makes sticks and plays game with young men, winning many things. Goes hunting and sees old woman, who induces him to carry her across river on his back. He can not throw her off, and he goes home with her fast to his back. Medicine-men are sent for, but they can do nothing. Poor boy puts on old robe and goes to young man's lodge with bow and four arrows of different colors. He shoots black arrow and splits woman in two. With red arrow he takes her off boy. The other arrows he places on boy's back to remove sore spot. Old woman is then burned. Next day crying and voice are heard near where woman burned. Young man finds ring has gone. White tipi with woman and child inside appears where others were. Young man goes to see it and woman with new buffalo robe passes by him, having child. Young man makes bundle of eagle feathers and follows them. They become buffalo. Calf communicates with father, and woman finally becomes reconciled to him. They come to hill on which Buffalo bull, boy's grandfather, is waiting for them. Man puts two eagle feathers on his horns. He sends them on to next hill and at last they come to hill with four Buffalo bulls, chiefs of Buffalo camp. Man puts feathers on their heads. They are sent into village and Buffalo become mad because man has not feathers enough to go round. Man made to sit on hill until they decide what to do with him. He sticks flint knife into ground and asks gods to form stone around where he sits. Buffalo devise various ways for killing him, but do not succeed in doing so. They decide to send man with Buffalo cow and calf to Indian village with presents. Buffalo bull turns man into Buffalo. Buffalo follow them. Man finds village and tells errand. People bring eagle feathers and native tobacco, which man takes to Buffalo. Buffalo willing to be slaughtered and man tells chiefs. Four times people go and kill Buffalo. Leader of Buffalo gives man sticks to play with. Sticks and ring different kinds of people. Man lives long life. Buffalo calf starts Buffalo ceremony among people.

CADDO. Oklahoma.

In the story of the " Brothers Who Became Lightning and Thunder " Doctor Dorsey[c] tells of two brothers, the elder of whom made two arrows for his young brother; one he painted black and the other he painted blue. They then made a small wheel out of the bark of the elm tree. One of the boys would stand about fifty yards away from the

---

[a] Traditions of the Arikara, p. 15, Washington, 1904.   [b] Ibid., p. 189.
[c] Traditions of the Caddo, p. 35, Washington, 1905.

other and they would roll this little wheel to each other and would shoot the wheel with the arrows. They played with the wheel every day until finally the younger brother failed to hit the wheel, when the wheel kept on rolling and did not stop. They followed its traces and, after a series of adventures, recovered the wheel from an old man, whom they killed. Later they ascended to the sky and became the Lightning and Thunder.

PAWNEE. Nebraska.

Maj. Stephen H. Long [a] wrote as follows:

About the village we saw several parties of young men eagerly engaged at games of hazard. One of these, which we noticed particularly, is played between two persons, and something is staked on the event of each game. The instruments used are a small hoop, about 6 inches in diameter, which is usually wound with thongs of leather, and a pole 5 or 6 feet long, on the larger end of which a limb is left to project about 6 inches. The whole bears some resemblance to a shepherd's crook. The game is played upon a smooth beaten path, at one end of which the gamester commences, and, running at full speed, he first rolls from him the hoop, then discharges after it the pole, which slides along the path pursuing the hoop until both stop together, at the distance of about 30 yards from the place whence they were thrown. After throwing them from him the gamester continues his pace, and the Indian, the hoop, and the pole arrive at the end of the path about the same time. The effort appears to be to place the end of the pole either in the ring, or as near as possible, and we could perceive that those casts were considered best when the ring was caught by the hook at the end of the pole. What constitutes a point, or how many points are reckoned to the game, we could not ascertain. It is, however, sufficiently evident that they are desperate gamesters, often losing their ornaments, articles of dress, etc., at play.

John T. Irving, jr,[b] says:

One of the principal games of the Pawnees, and the one on which the most gambling is carried on, is played by means of a small ring and a long javelin. The ring is about 4 inches in diameter, and the object of the player is to hurl his javelin through the ring, while it is sent rolling over the ground, with great speed, by one of his companions in the game. The javelin is filled with barbs nearly the whole length so that when it has once passed partly through the ring, it can not slide back. This is done to ascertain how far it went before it struck the edges of the ring, and the farther the cast the more it counts in favor of the one who hurled it. It is practiced by the children, young men, and chiefs. The first gamble for single arrows—the second for a bow and quiver— and the last for horses.

John B. Dunbar says: [c]

The most usual game with men was stŭts-au'-ĭ-ka-tus, or simply stŭts-au'-ĭ, played with a small hoop or ring, and stick. The hoop was about 4 inches in diameter, made of several coils of a small strip of rawhide wrapped tightly together with a stout string. At one point on the exterior of the hoop was a bead

---

[a] Account of an Expedition from Pittsburgh to the Rocky Mountains, v. 1, p. 444, Philadelphia, 1823.

[b] Indian Sketches, v. 2, p. 142, Philadelphia, 1835.

[c] The Pawnee Indians. Magazine of American History, v. 8, p. 749, New York, Nov., 1882.

threaded on the wrapping string. The stick was of peculiar structure. Its general shape is shown in the cut . . . [figure 601]. The entire length of the stick was about 5½ feet. It was flattened somewhat in the direction of the crosspieces, and tapered slightly from the heel, *a*, to the point *b*. Directly over the intersection of the crosspieces *c* and *d*, which were upon the upper side, was a small crooked projection (not shown) about the length of a finger, curving over the part of the crosspieces on the same side as the curved heelpiece, *a–e*, i. e., to the right. The entire stick was firmly wrapped with buckskin or rawhide, and the crosspieces and curved attachments held in place by the same means.

At each village there were two or more grounds, about 60 paces long and 15 wide, cleared and smoothed for this game. Two sticks and one hoop were necessary, and the players were arranged by pairs. Two players took the sticks, one of them having also the hoop, and started at full speed from one end of the ground toward the other. When about halfway across, the one carrying the hoop hurled it violently forward, so that it should speed along the ground before them; then instantly changing his stick from his left hand to the right, they simultaneously cast them both at the rolling hoop, in such way that striking flat upon the ground, they should glide along point forward and overtake it. The best throw was to catch the hoop upon one of the small projections over the intersections of the crosspieces. To catch it upon the point of the stick, upon the extremities of the crosspieces or of the curved

Fig. 601.   Fig. 602.

FIG. 601. Dart for ring game; length, about 5½ feet; Pawnee Indians, Nebraska; from Dunbar.
FIG. 602. Dart for boys' ring game; length, about 4 feet; Pawnee Indians, Nebraska; from Dunbar.

heelpiece, was also a good throw. If the hoop was not caught at all, as was usually the case, the value of the throw was determined by its contiguity to certain parts of the stick, and each player was provided with a straw for measuring in such cases. The bead upon the hoop was the point from which every measurement was made. Sometimes spirited debates were had upon the question of the correct measurement, as to whose the throw should properly be. In such case one of the numerous spectators was called in to act as umpire. The value of each throw was reckoned by points, so many points constituting a game. If there were more than two players, the couples alternated in making throws.

By boys this game was played with a smaller and simpler stick [figure 602], about 4 feet long. The aim in their game was to dart the point of the stick directly through the hoop and catch it upon the two prongs at the heel.

The Hon. Charles Augustus Murray [a] describes the hoop-and-dart game as follows:

It is played by two competitors, each armed with a dart, on the smoothest plot of grass they can find. The area is about 50 yards long. They start from one end at full speed; one of the players has a small hoop of 6 inches diameter, which, as soon as they have reached the middle of the course, he rolls on before them, and each then endeavors to dart his weapon through the hoop. He who

_____
[a] Travels in North America, p. 321, London, 1839.

succeeds, counts so many in the game; and if neither pierces it, the nearest javelin to the mark is allowed to count, but, of course, not so many points as if he had ringed it. The game is exceedingly hard exercise; they play with many on a side, and sometimes for five or six hours, in the mid-heat of an August day without intermission. It is made subservient to their taste for gambling, and I have seen them lose guns, blankets, and even one or two horses in a morning.

Zebulon M. Pike [a] says:

They are extremely addicted to gaming, and have for that purpose a smooth piece of ground cleared out on each side of the village for about 150 yards in length, at which they play the following games, viz: one is played by two players at a time, and in the following manner: They have a large hoop of about 4 feet in diameter, in the center of which is a small leather ring attached to leather thongs, which is extended to the hoop, and by that means keeps it in its central position; they also have a pole of about 6 feet in length, which the player holds in one hand, and then rolls the hoop from him, and immediately slides the pole after it, and the nearer the head of the pole lies to the small ring within the hoop (when they both fall) the greater is the cast. But I could not ascertain their mode of counting sufficiently to decide when the game was won.

Another game is played with a small stick, with several hooks, and a hoop about 4 inches in diameter, which is rolled along the ground and the forked stick darted after it, when the value of the cast is estimated by the hook on which the ring is caught. This game is gained at 100.

Dr George Bird Grinnell [b] writes:

Of all the games played by men among the Pawnee Indians, none was so popular as the stick game. This was an athletic contest between pairs of young men, and tested their fleetness, their eyesight, and their skill in throwing the stick. The implements used were a ring, 6 inches in diameter, made of buffalo rawhide, and two elaborate and highly ornamented slender sticks, one for each player. One of the two contestants rolled the ring over a smooth prepared course, and when it had been set in motion the players ran after it side by side, each one trying to throw his stick through the ring. This was not often done, but the players constantly hit the ring with their sticks and knocked it down, so that it ceased to roll. The system of counting was by points, and was somewhat complicated, but in general terms it may be said that the player whose stick lay nearest the ring gained one or more points. In the story which follows, the Buffalo by their mysterious power transformed the girl into a ring, which they used in playing the stick game.

The story related by Dr Grinnell is that of a girl who lived with her four brothers in a lodge by the banks of a river. To the branch of a tree in front of the lodge they had hung a rawhide strap, such as women use for carrying wood, so as to make a swing for the girl. The brothers would swing the girl in the swing to make the buffalo come.

The story relates how, in the brothers' absence, a coyote persuaded the girl to let him swing her, and when the buffalo came they turned her into a ring.

[a] An Account of Expeditions to the Sources of the Mississippi, appendix to pt. 2, p. 15, Philadelphia, 1810.
[b] The Girl Who was the Ring. Harper's Magazine, v. 102, p. 425, February, 1901.

PAWNEE. Oklahoma. (Field Columbian Museum.)

Cat. no. 59400. Hoop of sapling (figure 603), $7\frac{1}{2}$ inches in diameter, with inner concentric ring, $3\frac{1}{4}$ inches in diameter, attached with cord network; all painted green and having an eagle-down feather tied with a thong to the middle.

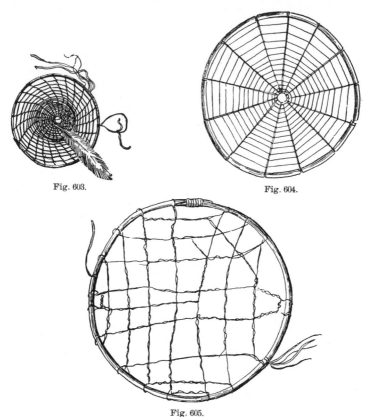

Fig. 603.

Fig. 604.

Fig. 605.

FIG. 603. Netted hoop; diameter, $7\frac{1}{4}$ inches; Pawnee Indians, Oklahoma; cat. no. 59400, Field Columbian Museum.

FIG. 604. Netted hoop; diameter, $5\frac{1}{4}$ inches; Pawnee Indians, Oklahoma; cat. no. 59398, Field Columbian Museum.

FIG. 605. Netted hoop; diameter, 10 inches; Pawnee Indians, Oklahoma; cat. no. 59392, Field Columbian Museum.

Cat. no. 59398. Hoop (figure 604) of sapling, $5\frac{1}{4}$ inches in diameter, netted with fine cord, painted yellow in the center and green outside.

Cat. no. 59392. Hoop (figure 605) of sapling, 10 inches in diameter, netted with twine.

Cat. no. 59394. Hoop (figure 606) of sapling, 13 inches in diameter, bisected by a thong, half the ring on one side of the hoop painted red and the other half black. An eagle tail is tied at each end of the bisecting thong and a piece of otter fur midway between.

Cat. no. 71646. Hoop of sapling, 15 inches in diameter, similar to that last described, but painted in four colors—green, red, blue, and yellow—and having owl and flicker, instead of eagle, feathers.

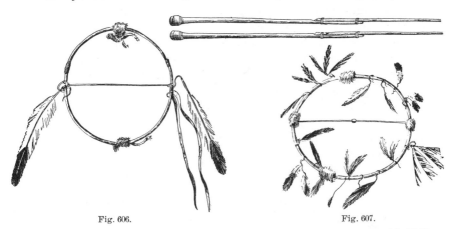

Fig. 606.   Fig. 607.

FIG. 606. Game hoop; diameter, 13 inches; Pawnee Indians, Oklahoma; cat. no. 59394, Field Columbian Museum.

FIG. 607. Hoop and poles; diameter of hoop, 25 inches; length of poles, 50 inches; Pawnee Indians, Oklahoma; cat. no. 59390, Field Columbian Museum.

Cat. no. 59390. Hoop (figure 607) of sapling, 25 inches in diameter, with a buckskin thong bisecting it and a shell bead strung in the center. Twenty-four single feathers and bunches of feathers

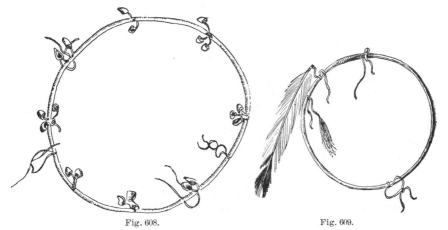

Fig. 608.   Fig. 609.

FIG. 608. Game hoop; diameter, 13 inches; Pawnee Indians, Oklahoma; cat. no. 59393, Field Columbian Museum.

FIG. 609. Game hoop; diameter, 8½ inches; Pawnee Indians, Oklahoma; cat. no. 59395, Field Columbian Museum.

are tied with thongs around the circumference. Accompanied by two poles, 50 inches in length, made in two pieces, joined with thongs and tapering from butt to tip.

Cat. no. 59393.   Hoop (figure 608) of sapling, 13 inches in diameter, entirely covered with hide sewed with the seam on the inner side, one-half of the hoop painted red and the other half black, having eight bunches of deer claws attached by thongs passing through the hide covering.

Cat. no. 59395.   Hoop (figure 609) of sapling, $8\frac{1}{2}$ inches in diameter, tied with cotton cord, having a blue glass bead attached by a thong at the place of juncture and an eagle tail feather and down feather also fastened on by thongs.

Cat. no. 59409.   Ring (figure 610) of hide, wrapped with buckskin, 4 inches in diameter, and two poles, 54 inches in length, each wrapped with buckskin and having two crosspieces lashed across, as shown in figure 611.

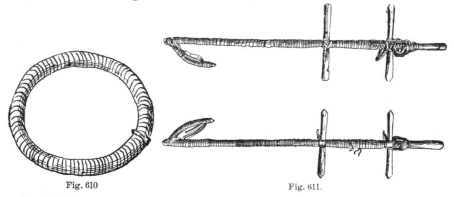

Fig. 610   Fig. 611.

FIG. 610.   Ring for buffalo game; diameter, 4 inches; Pawnee Indians, Oklahoma; cat. no. 59409, Field Columbian Museum.

FIG. 611.   Poles for buffalo game; length, 54 inches; Pawnee Indians, Oklahoma; cat. no. 59409, Field Columbian Museum.

The fore ends of the poles are carved with a kind of knob which is said to represent the penis of the buffalo.   The rear ends have curved pieces attached, which turn forward.   Small wooden forks are lashed to the sides of the crosspieces and a handle-shaped piece in front of the forward fork of each pole.

Another ring in the same collection (cat. no. 71602) has a white shell bead attached to the outer edge.

Cat. no. 71682.   Ring of cloth, wrapped with buckskin, 5 inches in diameter, and a pole, 47 inches long, with two prongs, made of sapling, wrapped with buckskin, each prong with six double strips and one single strip of rawhide wrapped in the buckskin and projecting inward, as shown in figure 612.   These are designated by the collector as implements for the buffalo game.

All of the preceding were collected by Dr George A. Dorsey.

In the story of " Blood-clot Boy " [a] Doctor Dorsey describes the boy

---

[a] Traditions of the Skidi Pawnee, p. 84, New York, 1904.

as making a ring of ash stick, which he wound with a string made of boiled buffalo hide, so that it looked like a spider's web. The grandmother rolled the ring and the boy shot it with arrows and killed buffalo.

Fig. 612.　Ring and pole; diameter of ring, 5 inches; length of pole, 47 inches; Pawnee Indians, Oklahoma; cat. no. 71682, Field Columbian Museum.

Commenting on the above, Doctor Dorsey [a] says:

One of a number of ways for the magic production of a buffalo common to the Plains tribes, the significance of this form resting in the fact that the ring represented the spider-web, thus referring to the belief that the Spider-Woman controlled the buffalo and produced them from her web.

The ring-and-javelin game, according to the Skidi, was originally played for the direct purpose of calling the buffalo, and I have a long account of its origin. According to this account the two sticks represent young buffalo bulls, which turned into the gaming sticks, leaving first full instructions as to how they were to be treated, how the game was to be played, how the songs were to be sung, and how they were to be anointed with the buffalo fat. The ring, according to the story, was originally a buffalo cow, and those in the tribe to-day are said to be made from the skin of the vulva of the buffalo. For the two forms of this so-called buffalo game see figures [610 and 611 in this paper].

In the story "The Coyote Rescues a Maiden" [b] the coyote is described as seeing buffalo playing with sticks and a ring:

A lot of buffalo would line up on the south side of the playing ground. Coyote sat down at the north end of the playing ground. Two buffalo would rise up and take the sticks, one of them taking the ring, and as they ran to the north end, the one with the ring would throw it and both of them would throw their sticks at the ring to see if they could catch it. At the north end they picked up the sticks and the ring, and the one with the ring would throw it again toward the south end of the playing ground, and the two buffalo would throw the sticks at the ring to try to catch it. The two would sit down, and two other buffalo would rise and take up the sticks and ring, and they, too, would run down to the north end of the ground and throw the ring and sticks. They would shout at Coyote to get away, as they might hit him with the sticks. Coyote would rise and limp around, and then would sit down close to the end of the playing ground.

Now, the ring with which they were playing was a girl who had been carried off by the buffalo and transformed by them. During the course of the game the ring rolled toward the Coyote and he took it in his mouth and ran away with it, and finally by the aid of the badger, the fox, the crow, the hawk, and the blackbird the ring was carried back and transformed into a girl again in her brothers' lodge.

---

[a] Traditions of the Skidi Pawnee, p. 343, New York, 1904.　　　[b] Ibid., p. 257.

WICHITA. Oklahoma. (Field Columbian Museum.)

Cat. no. 59365. Wooden hoop (figure 613), 18½ inches in diameter, with an interior network of sinew, which is wrapped around the hoop at thirty points and incloses an inner hoop, 9½ inches in diameter, having also an interior sinew net, accompanied by a dart made of sapling, 35½ inches in length, with a fork at the end. Collected by Dr George A. Dorsey.

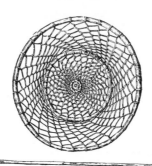

FIG. 613. Netted hoop and dart; diameter of hoop, 18½ inches; length of dart, 35½ inches; Wichita Indians, Oklahoma; cat. no. 59365, Field Columbian Museum.

Cat. no. 59315. Wooden hoop (figure 614), 25¾ inches in diameter, with connecting ends bound with sinew. Collected by Dr George A. Dorsey.

Doctor Dorsey makes several references to the hoop game among the Wichita. In the story of " The Seven Brothers and the Sister," [a]

FIG. 614. Game hoop; diameter, 25¾ inches; Wichita Indians, Oklahoma; cat. no. 59315, Field Columbian Museum.

the chief game of the brothers is described as with the hoop.

In the story of " The Deeds of the After-birth-Boy " [b] the father is described as making a netted ring for his two sons, which he told them not to roll toward the west. They disobeyed him, and were compelled to follow the ring, and ran on until they went into the water of a great lake and found themselves inside of a great monster.

In the story of " Half-a-Boy who Overcame the Gambler," [c] the hero visits a village a two-days' journey north of his own, where there was a cruel gambler who played the wheel game and won the lives of all who visited the village. The village extended east and west and had in the middle an open space, in which he saw many people playing some kind of game. The next morning he commenced to play the game with the gambler. In the game that

[a] The Mythology of the Wichita, p. 69, Washington, 1904.   [b] Ibid., p. 95, 101.   [c] Ibid., p. 194.

they played they used two long sticks and a wheel. First they threw the wheel a long way, then they ran to it and pitched the sticks into the ring. The boy lost from the start and finally staked his life, being told his body was equal to three bets. He lost two of these when it became dark, and the gambler was persuaded by the boy to leave the third part until the next day. From this the man called the boy Half-a-Boy. The boy went to sleep on the ground and was awakened by two women, who revealed themselves as buffalo cows. He ran with them and they traveled part of the night, until they saw a light, which they said was their grandfather and grandmother taking a smoke. When they came up the young women asked the old people to make haste and give the boy powers so that he could get out of his trouble.

Deinde puero præceptum est ut ad tergum tauri iret, et, cum eius membrum semel prehendisset, " palum atrum " posceret; membro iterum prehenso, " palum rubrum " posceret. Hæc igitur fecit. Deinde ei præceptum est ut ad bovem profectus eius volvam prehenderet, anulumque posceret. Hoc facto, puer iam palos duos anulumque habebat.

The black stick remaining in the ring represented the old man and the old woman. He was requested to let the black stick remain in the ring where it belonged and to give the red stick to his opponent. In the game that followed, in which the boy's sticks and ring were employed, the black stick which the boy used never failed to find the wheel, and the boy won back everything in the village and finally the life of the gambler himself. This man was a shadow, and his name was Shadow-of-the-Sun. When the boy won the third and last part of him, he jumped out of the way as he pitched the last stick, and when the stick entered the wheel there arose two great big buffalo, who set after Shadow-of-the-Sun and hooked him until they tore him to pieces. Half-a-Boy burned the gambler's body and ordered all the bones of his victims to be placed in the fire. Then they all came to life in the same manner related in other stories.

CHIMMESYAN STOCK

NISKA. Nass river, British Columbia.

Dr Franz Boas[a] describes the following games:

Sménts, A hoop is placed upright. The players throw at it with sticks or blunt lances, and must hit inside the hoop.

Matldä', A hoop wound with cedar bark and set with fringes, is hurled by one man. The players stand in a row, about 5 feet apart, each carrying a lance or stick. When the ring is flying past the row, they try to hit it.

---

[a] Fifth Report on the Indians of British Columbia. Report of the Sixty-fifth Meeting of the British Association for the Advancement of Science, p. 583, London, 1895.

CHINOOKAN STOCK

WASCO. Washington. (Cat. no. 37501, Free Museum of Science and Art, University of Pennsylvania.)

Ring (seckseck) made of strips of inner bark (figure 615), with an internal cross, 4½ inches in diameter.

Collected by Dr George A. Dorsey, who gives the following account of the game:

Shot at with arrows and played by youths on the appearance of the first run of salmon. When struck on the cross, the play is called tlia-mag-elo, to hit on the tlia-han, the cross; when struck on the periphery, ia-ma-aihth, hits one. The game is played for arrows.

FIG. 615. Game ring; diameter, 4½ inches; Wasco Indians, Washington; cat. no. 37501, Free Museum of Science and Art, University of Pennsylvania.

CHUMASHAN STOCK

SANTA BARBARA. California.

Dr Walter J. Hoffman [a] says that the Indians of Santa Barbara played a game with a barrel-shaped stone ring 3 inches in diameter and 4 in length, at which the players shot arrows, the object being to penetrate the hole while the ring was in motion. The players stood on either side of the course.

COSTANOAN STOCK

RUMSEN. Monterey, California.

J. F. G. de la Pérouse [b] says:

They have two games to which they dedicate their whole leisure. The first, to which they give the name of takersia, consists in throwing and rolling a small hoop, of 3 inches in diameter, in a space of 10 square toises, cleared of grass and surrounded with fascines. Each of the two players holds a stick, of the size of a common cane, and 5 feet long; they endeavor to pass this stick into the hoop whilst it is in motion; if they succeed in this they gain 2 points; and if the hoop, when it stops, simply rests upon their stick, they gain 1 by it; the game is 3 points. This game is a violent exercise, because the hoop or stick is always in action.

ESKIMAUAN STOCK

ESKIMO (CENTRAL). Cumberland sound, Baffin land, Franklin.

Dr Franz Boas says: [c]

A favorite game is the nuglutang [figure 616]. A small, rhomboidal plate of ivory with a hole in the center is hung from the roof and steadied by a heavy stone or a piece of ivory hanging from its lower end. The Eskimo stand

---

[a] Bulletin of the Essex Institute, v. 17, p. 32, note 12, Salem, 1885.

[b] A Voyage around the World in the years 1785, 1786, 1787, and 1788, v. 2, p. 223, London, 1798. La Pérouse refers to two tribes of Monterey, the Achastians (Rumsen) and Ecclemachs (Esselen), the latter belonging to the Esselenian family.

[c] The Central Eskimo. Sixth Annual Report of the Bureau of Ethnology, p. 568, 1888.

around it, and when the winner of the last game gives a signal everyone tries to hit the hole with a stick. The one who succeeds has won. This game is always played amid great excitement.

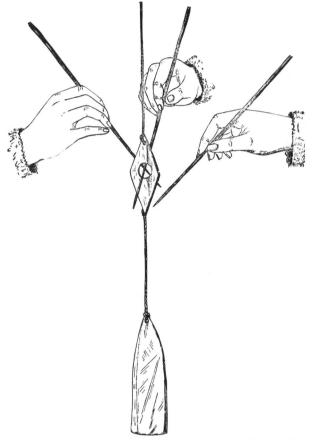

FIG. 616. Game of nuglutang; Central Eskimo, Cumberland sound, Baffin land, Franklin; cat. no. IV A 6821, Berlin Museum für Völkerkunde; from Boas.

CENTRAL ESKIMO (AIVILIRMIUT and KINIPETU). West coast of Hudson bay, Keewatin.

Dr Franz Boas[a] thus describes the game of nugluktuq:

A piece of ivory with a hole in the center is suspended from the top of the snow house. To its lower end a line with a heavy weight is attached, which serves to hold the piece of ivory steady. The men gather around this implement, each holding a small stick with a sharp point. A knife is laid down, which forms the stake of the game; and at the word "a'tē" all the men try to hit the hole in the tooth with their little sticks. Whoever succeeds in hitting the hole wins the knife. Then he places another stake near by, and the play is

---

[a] Eskimo of Baffin Land and Hudson Bay. Bulletin of American Museum of Natural History, v. 15, p. 110, New York, 1901.

resumed, while he himself is barred from taking part in the game. Anyone has the right to take hold of the ivory with his naked hand at the risk of having it gashed with the darts of the spears. If two persons hit the hole at the same time, it does not count.

ESKIMO (WESTERN). St Michael, Alaska. (Cat. no. 33970, United States National Museum.)

Oval hoop (figure 617) of bent twig, 3 inches in diameter, the upper and lower edges wrapped with thongs securing cotton cord network, which covers the interior of the ring, with thong loop for suspension. Two arrows, 22 inches in length, with simple wood shafts and barbed bone points secured with sinew. The arrows are fastened together by a long, twisted sinew cord.

FIG. 617. Netted hoop and darts; diameter of hoop, 3 inches; length of darts, 22 inches; Western Eskimo, St Michael, Alaska; cat. no. 33970, United States National Museum.

These were collected by Mr E. W. Nelson,[a] who describes the game under the name of nugohliganuk:

This is played in the kashim by men only. A small oval wooden frame, about 3 inches long by an inch and a half wide, having the interior finely netted with cord, is hung from the roof and held in place by a cord at each end. It is placed about 4 feet from the floor in front of the summer entrance or under the smoke-hole in the roof. Each player has a long, slender dart, about 3 feet in length and a quarter of an inch in diameter, with a barbed point of bone or deer horn. To the butt end of the dart is fastened a small cord, so that the player can draw it back after throwing. When the point of the dart enters the wooden ring it is held fast by the barbs on the point, and this scores one for the successful player. Under this target each player places some object as a prize. Then all go to one side of the room and throw three darts in succession at the target. Whenever a player pierces the target so that he must remove his dart with his hands, he is entitled to take anything he wishes from the pile of prizes. In this way the game continues until all the articles are disposed of.

IROQUOIAN STOCK

CAUGHNAWAGA. Quebec.

J. Long [b] says:

The boys are very expert at trundling a hoop, particularly the Cahnuaga Indians, whom I have frequently seen excel at this amusement. The game is played by any number of boys who may accidentally assemble together, some driving the hoop, while others with bows and arrows shoot at it. At this exercise

[a] The Eskimo about Bering Strait. Eighteenth Annual Report of the Bureau of American Ethnology, p. 334, 1899.

[b] Voyages and Travels of an Indian Interpreter and Trader, p. 53, London, 1791.

they are surprisingly expert, and will stop the progress of the hoop when going with great velocity, by driving the pointed arrow into its edge; this they will do at a considerable distance, and on horseback as well as on foot.

CHEROKEE. Tennessee.

Lieut. Henry Timberlake (1762)[a] describes the game under the name of nettecawaw:

. . . each player having a pole about 10 feet long, with several marks or divisions, one of them bowls the round stone, with one flat side, and the other convex, on which the players all dart their poles after it, and the nearest counts according to the vicinity of the bowl to the marks on his pole.

——— North Carolina.

Mr James Mooney [b] describes the wheel-and-stick game played with a stone wheel, or circular disk, under the name of gatayusti.

John Ax, the oldest man now living among the East Cherokee, is the only one remaining in the tribe who has ever played the game, having been instructed in it when a small boy by an old man who desired to keep up the memory of the ancient things. The sticks used have long since disappeared, but the stones remain, being frequently picked up in the plowed fields, especially in the neighborhood of the mounds.

This was the game played by the great mythic gambler Uñtsaiyi, Brass.[c]

It was he who invented the gatayûstï game that we play with a stone wheel and a stick.

He lived at Uñtiguhi on the south side of the Tennessee river, and made his living by gambling.

The large flat rock, with the lines and grooves where they used to roll the wheel is still there, with the wheels themselves, and the stick turned to stone.[a]

Mr Mooney relates the story of a boy, the son of Thunder, who played the wheel-and-stick game with Uñtsaiyi, and vanquished him by the aid of his father's magic. The gambler at last staked his life, and was pursued to the edge of the great water, where he was caught by the boy and his brothers, whom he got to help him.

They tied his hands and feet with a grapevine and drove a long stake through his breast, and planted it far out in the deep water. They set two crows on the end of the pole to guard it and called the place Kâgûñ'yï, Crow place. But Brass never died, and can not die until the end of the world, but lies there always with his face up. Sometimes he struggles under water to get free, and sometimes the beavers, who are his friends, come and gnaw at the grapevine to release him. Then the pole shakes and the crows at the top cry Ka! Ka! Ka! and scare the beavers away.[d]

---

[a] Memoirs, p. 77, London, 1765.

[b] Myths of the Cherokee. Nineteenth Annual Report of the Bureau of American Ethnology, p. 434, 1902.

[c] Ibid., p. 311.

[d] Ibid., p. 314.

SENECA. New York.

Lewis H. Morgan [a] describes the game as follows:

The game of javelins, gä-na'-gä-o, was very simple, depending upon the dexterity with which the javelin was thrown at a ring, as it rolled upon the ground. They frequently made it a considerable game, by enlisting skillful players to prepare for the contest and by betting upon the result. The people divided by tribes, the four brothers playing against their four cousin tribes, as in the last case [ball], unless the game was played on a challenge between neighboring communities.

The javelin was 5 or 6 feet in length by three-fourths of an inch in diameter, and was usually made of hickory or maple. It was finished with care, sharpened at one end, and striped as shown in the figure [618]. The ring was about 8 inches in diameter, made either into a hoop or solid like a wheel, by winding with splints. Sometimes the javelin was thrown horizontally, by placing the forefinger against its foot, and supporting it with the thumb and second finger; in other cases it was held in the center, and thrown with the hand raised above the shoulder.

On either side from fifteen to thirty players were arranged, each having from three to six javelins, the number of both depending upon the interest in the game and the time they wished to devote to the contest. The javelins themselves were the forfeit, and the game was gained by the party which won them.

Among the preliminaries to be settled by the managers, was the line on which the ring was to be rolled, the distance of the two bands of players from each other, and the space between each and the line itself. When these points

FIG. 618. Hoop and pole; diameter of hoop, 6 inches; length of pole, 5½ feet; Seneca Indians, New York; from Morgan.

were adjusted and the parties stationed, the ring was rolled by one party on the line, in front of the other. As it passed the javelins were thrown. If the ring was struck by one of them the players of the adverse party were required, each in turn, to stand in the place of the person who struck it, and throw their javelins in succession at the ring, which was set up as a target, on the spot where it was hit. Those of the javelins which hit the target when thus thrown were saved; if any missed, they were passed to the other party, and by them were again thrown at the ring from the same point. Those which hit were won, finally, and laid out of the play, while the residue were restored to their original owners. After this first contest was decided, the ring was rolled back, and the other party, in turn, threw their javelins. If it was struck, the party which rolled it was required, in the same manner, to hazard their javelins, by throwing them at the target. Such as missed were delivered to the other party, and those which hit the target when thrown by them, were won also, and laid

[a] League of the Iroquois, p. 298, Rochester, 1851. See also Report to the Regents of the University upon the Articles furnished to the Indian Collection by Lewis H. Morgan. Third Annual Report of the Regents of the University on the Condition of the State Cabinet of Natural History and the Historical and Antiquarian Collections annexed thereto, p. 79, Albany, 1850.

out of the play. In this manner the game was continued until one of the parties had lost their javelins, which, of itself, determined the contest.

Mr Andrew John, of Iroquois, New York, described the hoop-and-dart game as played at the present day by the Seneca as follows:

The implements for the game consist of a hoop, gah-nuk-gah, made of sapling, without marks; and darts, gah-geh-dok, 4 or 5 feet in length, of which each player has usually two.

The players line up equally on two sides about 10 feet apart. One party throws the hoop and the others launch their darts at it. The object is to stop the hoop as it rolls by impaling it. If a player misses, his dart is forfeited, but if it goes under the hoop, he retains it.

TUSCARORA. New York. (Cat. no. 16338, Free Museum of Science and Art, University of Pennsylvania.)

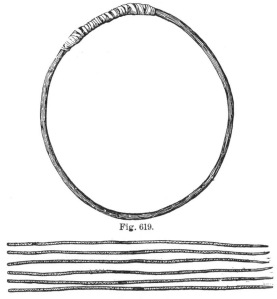

Fig. 619.

Fig. 620.

FIG. 619. Game hoop; diameter, 16 inches; Tuscarora Indians, New York; cat. no. 16338, Free Museum of Science and Art, University of Pennsylvania.

FIG. 620. Poles for hoop game; length, 7 feet; Tuscarora Indians, New York; cat. no. 16338, Free Museum of Science and Art, University of Pennsylvania.

Hoop (figure 619) made of an unpeeled bent sapling, tied with bark, 16 inches in diameter, and six poles (figure 620), 7 feet in length.

Collected in 1893 by the writer, who was informed that they were used in the game of nayearwanaqua.

The ring is called okakna and the poles are called oota. Five or six play. The ring is rolled and all discharge their poles. The one whose pole stops the ring owns it. The others then shoot in turn, and the owner of the ring takes all the poles that miss it and shoots them at the ring, winning those that he puts through it. If two men stop the ring, they divide the poles.

KERES. Laguna, New Mexico. (Cat. no. 3007, Brooklyn Institute Museum.)

Ring (figure 621), covered with buckskin, sewed on inner side with thong and painted white, 8 inches in diameter; and two painted

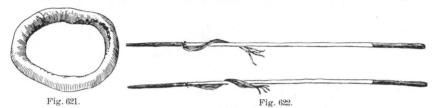

Fig. 621.   Fig. 622.

FIG. 621. Game ring; diameter, 8 inches; Keres Indians, Laguna, New Mexico; cat. no. 3007, Brooklyn Institute Museum.

Fig. 622. Poles for ring game; length, 75 inches; Keres Indians, Laguna, New Mexico; cat. no. 3007, Brooklyn Institute Museum.

poles (figure 622), 75 inches in length, with tips and butts white, middle part red. The tips are pointed, and each has four buckskin thongs, painted red, attached some 15 inches from its end. Collected by the writer in 1903.

Mr John M. Gunn, of Laguna, stated that the game is called

maskurtsh. The ring is rolled and the game is to throw the poles inside of it. The thongs on the poles are used in counting, and when the pole falls with the ring between the two sets of strands the game is won.

KIOWAN STOCK

FIG. 623. Game ring; diameter, 3 inches; Kiowa Indians, Oklahoma; cat. no. 152907, United States National Museum.

KIOWA. Kiowa reservation, Oklahoma. (Cat. no. 152907, United States National Museum.)

Irregular ring (figure 623) of buckskin, 3 inches in diameter, set with four double rows of beads at equal distances on its outer edge, two opposite ones white, and two opposite ones dark blue.

Collected by Mr James Mooney, who furnished the following statement:

Warriors or hunters purchase the privilege of throwing a dart at the ring, and derive auguries from success or failure in sending their darts through the circle.

KULANAPAN STOCK

POMO. Seven miles south of Ukiah, Mendocino county, California. (Cat. no. 70939, 70940, Field Columbian Museum.)

Wooden hoop (figure 624), 20 inches in diameter, with grape binding at joint; and forked-end lance, 8 feet long. Collected by Dr J. W. Hudson.

Doctor Hudson describes the following games:

Da-ko′ kă, da-ko′, the hoop and kă, game. Played with a 16-inch hoop [figure 624] bound with Apocynum cord, by four men usually, each armed with a 9-foot pole. A races the hoop swiftly to B [figure 625], who tries to impale

Fɪɢ. 624. Hoop and dart; diameter of hoop, 20 inches; length of dart, 8 feet; Pomo Indians, Mendocino county, California; cat. no. 70939, 70940, Field Columbian Museum.

it as it passes. (The spear does not leave his hands in the thrust, else he passes out of the game.) If B misses, his place is at once taken by one of the substitutes behind him, who catches the hoop. The player at B rolls to C, who attempts to impale it, thence C to D, and D to A. The player last to miss wins the stakes. When a player misses he forfeits his position and stake money at once, and his chances and stakes are appropriated by his substitute.

In another game a 4-inch hoop is laid upon the ground, and lances 4 feet long are cast upon it from a distance of 50 feet. A transfix counts 5 and a ring strike 2. Twelve counters are used. The game is called da-ko nĭt′-ak or javelin-spearing hoop.

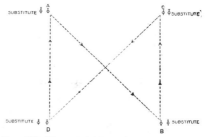

Fɪɢ. 625. Plan of field for hoop game; Pomo Indians, California; from sketch by Dr J. W. Hudson.

A tule butt is erected and a 1-inch ring of twisted fiber hung in its center. Archers stand 60 feet away. A center stroke counts 5, a hoop stroke 2. There are ten counters. This is called da-ko tcox′-tau, ring target.

LUTUAMIAN STOCK

KLÁMATH. Upper Klamath lake, Oregon. (Cat. no. 61682, Field Columbian Museum.)

Ring (figure 626) made of the inner fiber of the tule rush, wrapped with tule bark, 11 inches in diameter.

Collected by Dr George A. Dorsey, who describes it as used in the game of wóshakank.[a] The ring is shot at with arrows, not differing from those used by boys in their hunting. The object of the game is to hit the ring with an arrow.

Another specimen (cat. no. 61681) is 6 inches in diameter. Rings of this size are used chiefly by boys.

[a] Certain Gambling Games of the Klamath Indians. American Anthropologist, n. s., v. 3, p. 17, 1901.

KLAMATH. Oregon. (Cat. no. 37479, Free Museum of Science and
    Art, University of Pennsylvania.)
Ring (figure 627) of bast, 7 inches in diameter.
Collected in 1900 by Dr George A. Dorsey, who describes it as a
ring for woshakank, the kind used by boys.

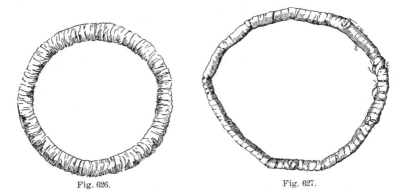

Fig. 626.   Fig. 627.

FIG. 626. Game ring; diameter, 11 inches; Klamath Indians, Oregon; cat. no. 61682, Field Colum-
bian Museum.
FIG. 627. Game ring (boy's); diameter, 7 inches; Klamath Indians, Oregon; cat. no. 37479, Free
Museum of Science and Art, University of Pennsylvania.

———— Upper Klamath lake, Oregon.   (Field Columbian Museum.)
Cat. no. 61641.   Two rings, diameters, 3 and 4 inches, made of flexible
    bast; a small bow, 2 feet in length, and three small reed arrows,
    with long, sharp wooden points, of sage (figure 628).
Collected in 1900 by Dr George A. Dorsey, who describes the
game under the name of shü′kshuks.[a]

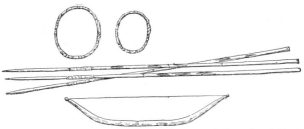

FIG. 628. Rings, bow, and arrows for ring game; diameter of rings, 3 and 4 inches; length of
    bow, 2 feet; Klamath Indians, Oregon; cat. no. 61641, Field Columbian Museum.

It is usually played in a wickiup, by either men or boys, most
commonly in winter, in the following manner: One of two boys sitting from 8 to 10 feet apart rolls a ring toward the other, who shoots
at it with an arrow (ntē′kish).   In case he hits the ring the one who
rolled it endeavors, by shooting, to dislodge the arrow therefrom.

[a] Certain Gambling Games of the Klamath Indians.   American Anthropologist, n. s.,
v. 3, p. 17, 1901.

Should he succeed, there is no count; otherwise the one who first shot gains an arrow, the object of the game being to win arrows.

Cat. no. 61717. Ring, one-half of an inch in diameter, and a small

awl-like object, consisting of a bone point mounted in a sharp wooden handle, 3½ inches in length (figure 629).

This was collected in 1900 by Dr George A. Dorsey, who describes the game under the same name as the preceding—shü′kshuks—which is applied also to the ring. He describes this game as played by persons of both sexes and by

FIG. 629. Game ring and awl; diameter of ring, one-half of an inch; length of awl, 3¼ inches; Klamath Indians, Oregon; cat. no. 61717, Field Columbian Museum; from Dorsey.

all ages, generally in the wickiup. The players sit facing each other, and as one rolls the ring in front of him his opponent endeavors to pierce one or both sides of the ring with the point of his awl. To pierce one side counts 1; both sides, 2.

Cat. no. 61674. Tule fiber ring (figure 630), 11 inches in diameter.

Collected in 1900 by Dr George A. Dorsey, who describes the game as follows:

This is an interesting variation of the ring game, for which I could get no native name to distinguish it from the ones just described. . . . The ring measures 11 inches in diameter and is an inch thick. Across one side of it is fastened a crossbar, measuring 17 inches in length, projecting 3 inches beyond the ring on each side. Both ring and crossbar are made of the inner fiber of the tule rush, closely wrapped with tule bark, the inner surface being placed outside, giving the ring a whitish color. In playing the game two rings of equal size are used; these are placed in an

FIG. 630. Game ring; diameter, 11 inches; Klamath Indians, Oregon; cat. no. 61674, Field Columbian Museum.

upright position, one end of the crossbar resting on a sharp wooden pin firmly fixed in the ground. The interval between the two goals varies according to agreement between the players. There are always two opposing sides, each consisting of one or more individuals. The ring is shot at with arrows from a bow, the object being to pierce both sides of the goal, which is always placed at right angles. Two specimens . . . of this game were collected, the only difference being in the size of the diameter of the ring and the length of the crossbar. This game, I was informed, has not been played for many years, and satisfactory information concerning the method of playing could not be obtained.

Doctor Dorsey describes also a variation called shíkna:

This interesting variation of the ring game is played only by men. It consists of as many spears (shíkna) as there are individual players and two goals (tchedalk), each of which is simply a forked stick thrust in the ground at such interval as may be mutually agreed upon. The spears are of willow, measuring 6 feet in length, and sharpened at one end. They are decorticated, except at the lower extremity. The spears are hurled from the hand, the object being to cause them to fall in such manner that the end of the spear will rest on the fork of the goal. Such a throw counts 5, otherwise the one whose spear falls nearest the goal counts 1; ten usually constitutes the game. The game is still practised to some extent by the Klamath, and in playing they exhibit great skill, one of the players whom I saw not failing to strike the goal oftener than once in six or eight throws. One set of this game (61710) consists of two spears and a pair of forked sticks.

See the Pima game, p. 489.

MARIPOSAN STOCK

CHUKCHANSI. Pickayune, Madera county, California. (Cat. no. 70891, Field Columbian Museum.)

Ring (figure 631), wrapped with buckskin, 3½ inches in diameter, and two maple-wood lances, the longer about 8 feet in length. Collected by Dr J. W. Hudson.

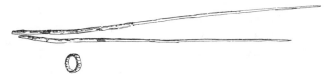

FIG. 631. Ring and poles; diameter of ring, 3½ inches; length of poles, the longer, about 8 feet; Chukchansi Indians, Madera county, California; cat. no. 70891, Field Columbian Museum.

A player rolls the ring along the ground and follows it with the lance, trying to impale it. If he fails, the next tries. One ring is used. Impaling the ring counts 5; if it falls on the pole, the count is 3.

KOYETI.[a] Tule River reservation, California.

Dr J. W. Hudson describes the following game under the name of hoturx:

A lance-and-target game played with a hoop of willow about 3 inches in diameter, laced over with Apocynum with radial cords called ta-koi, and a lance, im-mak, 10 feet long. Two play, using one ring and two poles or lances, one for each. The caster tries to strike the rolling target, and if successful tallies 6. In such case he is allowed to put his hand over the second player's eyes, so that he can not see when he throws. The score is 10, and is kept with sticks.

PITKACHI. Table mountain, Fresno county, California. (Cat. no. 70892, Field Columbian Museum.)

---

[a] Three members only of this tribe are alive.

Ring (figure 632), wrapped with bast cord, 2½ inches in diameter, described by the collector, Dr J. W. Hudson, as used as a moving target for arrows under the name of takumship,[a] " wheel roll."

FIG. 632. Ring and arrow; diameter of ring, 2½ inches; Pitkachi Indians, Fresno county, California; cat. no. 70892, Field Columbian Museum.

Four play. One man rolls the ring by two opponents, one of whom shoots at it with a blunt arrow with a bow, tä-lĭp. If he knocks it over, it counts 1 point ; if he transfixes it, 10. Each part of the arrows used in this game, which are 30 inches long, has a name quite different from those of war, small game, or flight arrows. The foreshaft is literally "come to us." The shaft is literally " tied together" or " links." The feathers are literally " appointed season." I could get no light on the reason for so naming them.

————.[b]   Table mountain, Fresno county, California.

Dr J. W. Hudson describes the following game under the name of xalau :

Two or more men stand before a brush wall or strip of matting, etc., some 10 feet tall, each armed with a 7-foot spear of *Prunus demissa* wood. Each spear is highly decorated with covert feathers from the gray-head eagle and painted. The umpire casts over his spear which sticks in the ground. A player casts after it, trying to make his spear-feathers strike those of the umpire. All follow in order, and the successful caster is assured luck in war or hunting. A wide cast implies catastrophe or death to the caster, who at once makes a new spear and tries " stronger " medicine feathers. This is a ceremonial game of much significance to warriors.

YAUDANCHI.   (See page 501.)

YOKUTS. Tule River reservation, Tulare county, California.   (Cat. no. 70402, 70403, Field Columbian Museum.)

Hoop of fiber, wrapped with buckskin, 4½ inches in diameter; and maple-wood lance (figure 633), about 8 feet long, sharpened at the point and marked with red stripes at the end. Collected by Dr J. W. Hudson, who thus describes the game under the name of hotush :

FIG. 633. Ring and pole; diameter of ring, 4½ inches; length of pole, 8 feet; Yokuts Indians, Tule River reservation, Tulare county, California; cat. no. 70402, 70403, Field Columbian Museum.

Played by four players, two on a side. One player casts the hoop, to-ko-in ho-tush, and his partner casts his lance so that the hoop will fall on it. If he is successful, and the hoop rests entirely on the lance, not touching the ground, he wins the game. If the hoop rests half on the ground, it counts 1. The game is also won at a throw by impaling the ring. Twelve counters are used. The

[a] The etymology of this name is probably not pure Mariposan, part of which seems derived from a northern stock.   (J. W. H.)

[b] Tribe extinct.

lance, hoat, is thrown underhand with both hands. The ring is covered either with buckskin or bark.

Doctor Hudson describes also a ring-and-arrow game under the name of tokoinawas:

This game is played with a hoop or ring, to-ko-in, 6 inches, more or less, in diameter and wrapped with buckskin. One player rolls the ring to another opposite him, while two others on opposite sides, at right angles to the course, shoot at it with arrows. The one who transfixes the ring or strikes it oftenest in ten rolls wins.

YOKUTS. Tule River reservation, Tulare county, California. (Cat. no. 70404, Field Columbian Museum.)

Wooden lance, 8 feet 3 inches long, and a small round wooden block or peg (figure 634).

FIG. 634. Implements for lance-and-peg game; length of lance, 99 inches; Yokuts Indians, Tulare county, California; cat. no. 70404, Field Columbian Museum.

Collected by Dr J. W. Hudson, who thus refers to them as used in a lance-throwing game, aikiwitch:

Each player casts two lances at a peg lying loose on the ground 50 feet away. Six or less play. The lance is call ai-yak-ta-ka and the peg kets-ma-na witch-it. The last man is thumped on the head with the bare knuckles, and the one making the highest score may strike as often as he desires.

MOQUELUMNAN STOCK

CHOWCHILLA. Chowchilly river, Madera county, California.

Dr J. W. Hudson describes the following game under the name of pachitu:

A ring of Asclepias, 2½ inches in diameter, called he-wi′-ta, is rolled, the caster racing, and casting after the ring a 10-foot lance, called hu-wo′-ta. A "lean" counts 3, a "balance" 5, and a "transfix" 12.

TOPINAGUGIM. Big creek, 2 miles north of Groveland, Tuolumne county, California. (Cat. no. 70234, Field Columbian Museum.)

Darts and hoop for a game.

Collected by Dr J. W. Hudson, and described as follows by the collector, under the name of teweknumsia:

The implements consist of a plain lance, ho-cha, 10 feet in length, marked on the butt end with proprietary marks, in paint, and a hoop of oak, 30 inches in diameter, bound with buckskin, te-wek-num-sia. The game is played by four players, who face each other on opposite sides of a square 90 feet across. The casters [figure 635], each of whom have four lances, stand opposite to each other, while two assistants, one for each side, roll the hoop across. As the wheel rolls, both casters throw at it, each trying to transfix it. If one is successful his opponent comes across to his place,

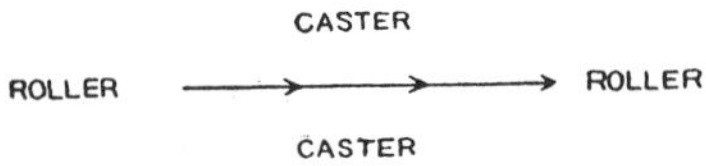

CASTER

ROLLER ———————→———————→ ROLLER

CASTER

FIG. 635. Plan of field for hoop-and-lance game; Topinagugim Indians, Tuolumne county, California; from sketch by Dr J. W. Hudson.

and, standing in the successful caster's tracks, tries to transfix the fallen hoop. After him, the first player tries at the same mark and from the same position. They cast alternately until all have thrown their four lances. The greater number of transfixing spears decides. There are 30 counting-sticks, 15 to a side. The buckskin is to keep the hoop from bounding.

WASAMA. Madera county, California.

Dr J. W. Hudson describes the following game under the name of hewitu numhe:

A hoop, he-wi'-ta, 10 inches in diameter, of Fremontii californica bark bound with buckskin, is rolled toward an opponent, who shoots at it with arrows in passing. A "strike" counts 3 and a "transfix" 10, or coup.

MUSKHOGEAN STOCK

BAYOGOULA and MUGULASHA. Louisiana.

The officer who kept the journal of the frigate [a] when Iberville arrived at the mouth of the Mississippi, 1698–1699, says:

They pass the greater part of their time in playing in this place with great sticks, which they throw after a little stone which is nearly round, like a bullet.

CHOCTAW. Mississippi.

James Adair [b] says:

The warriors have another favorite game called chungke; which, with propriety of language, may be called "running hard labor." They have near their statehouse a square piece of ground well cleaned, and fine sand is carefully strewed over it, when requisite, to promote a swifter motion to what they throw along the surface. Only one or two on a side play at this ancient game. They have a stone about 2 fingers broad at the edge, and 2 spans round: Each party has a pole of about 8 feet long, smooth, and tapering at each end, the points flat. They set off abreast of each other at 6 yards from the end of the playground; then one of them hurls the stone on its edge, in as direct a line as he can, a considerable distance toward the middle of the other end of the square: When they have ran a few yards, each darts his pole anointed with bear's oil, with a proper force, as near as he can guess in proportion to the motion of the stone, that the end may lie close to the stone—when this is the case, the person counts 2 of the game, and, in proportion to the nearness of the poles to the mark, 1 is counted, unless by measuring both are found to be at an equal distance from the stone. In this manner the players will keep running most part of the day, at half speed, under the violent heat of the sun, staking their silver ornaments, their nose, finger, and ear rings; their breast, arm, and wrist plates, and even all their wearing apparel, except that which barely covers their middle. All the American Indians are much addicted to this game, which to us appears to be a task of stupid drudgery. It seems however to be of early origin, when their fore-fathers used diversions as simple as their manners. The hurling stones they use at present were time immemorial rubbed smooth on the rocks, and with prodigious labor; they are kept with the strictest religious care

[a] Journal de la Frégate Le Marin, Margry's Découvertes, v. 4, p. 261, Paris, 1880.
[b] The History of the American Indians, p. 401, London, 1775.

from one generation to another, and are exempted from being buried with the dead. They belong to the town where they are used, and are carefully preserved.

Capt. Bernard Romans [a] says:

Their favorite game of chunké is a plain proof of the evil consequences of a violent passion for gaming upon all kinds, classes, and orders of men; at this they play from morning to night, with an unwearied application, and they bet high; here you may see a savage come and bring all his skins, stake them and lose them; next his pipe, his beads, trinkets and ornaments; at last his blanket, and other garment, and even all their arms, and, after all it is not uncommon for them to go home, borrow a gun and shoot themselves; an instance of this happened in 1771 at East Yasoo a short time before my arrival. Suicide has also been practised here on other occasions, but they regard the act as a crime, and bury the body as unworthy of their ordinary funeral rites.

The manner of playing this game is thus: They make an alley of about 200 feet in length, where a very smooth clay ground is laid, which when dry, is very hard; they play two together, each having a straight pole of about 15 feet long; one holds a stone, which is in the shape of a truck, which he throws before him over his alley, and the instant of its departure, they set off and run; in running they cast their poles after the stone; he that did not throw it endeavors to hit it; the other strives to strike the pole of his antagonist in its flight, so as to prevent its hitting the stone; he counts 1, but should both miss their aim the throw is renewed; and in case a score is won the winner casts the stone and 11 is up; they hurl this stone and pole with wonderful dexterity and violence, and fatigue themselves much at it.

HUMA. Mississippi.

Father James Gravier [b] says:

. . . in the middle of the village a fine level square, where from morning to night there are young men who exercise themselves in running after a flat stone, which they throw in the air from one end of the square to the other, and which they try to have fall on two cylinders that they roll where they think that the stone will fall.

MUSKOGEE. Georgia.

Col. Benjamin Hawkins [c] says:

The Micco, counselors and warriors, meet every day in the public square, sit and drink ä-cee, a strong decoction of the cassine yupon, called by the traders black drink; talk of news, the public, and domestic concerns, smoke their pipes, and play thla-chal-litch-cau, " roll the bullet."

William Bartram, in a manuscript work on the Southern Indians, cited by Squier and Davis,[d] wrote as follows:

Chunk yards.—The ' chunk yards ' of the Muscogulges, or Creeks, are rectangular areas, generally occupying the center of the town. The public square and rotunda, or great winter council house, stand at the two opposite corners of them. They are generally very extensive, especially in the large old towns: some of them are from 600 to 900 feet in length, and of proportionate breadth.

---

[a] A Concise Natural History of East and West Florida, v. 1, p. 79, New York, 1775.

[b] Journal of the Voyage of Father Gravier (1700), in Early Voyages Up and Down the Mississippi, p. 143, John Gilmary Shea, Albany, 1861.

[c] A Sketch of the Creek Country. Collection of the Georgia Historical Society, v. 3, p. 71, Savannah, 1848.

[d] Aboriginal Monuments of the State of New York. Smithsonian Contributions to Knowledge, v. 2, p. 135, 1849.

The area is exactly level, and sunk 2, sometimes 3 feet below the banks or terraces surrounding them, which are occasionally two in number, one behind and above the other, and composed of the earth taken from the area at the time of its formation. These banks or terraces serve the purpose of seats for the spectators. In the center of this yard or area there is a low circular mound or eminence, in the middle of which stands erect the chunk pole, which is a high obelisk or four-square pillar declining upwards to an obtuse point. This is of wood, the heart or inward resinous part of a sound pine tree, and is very durable; it is generally from 30 to 40 feet in height, and to the top is fastened some object which serves as a mark to shoot at, with arrows or the rifle, at certain appointed times. Near each corner of one end of the yard stands erect a less pole or pillar, about 12 feet high, called a "slave post," for the reason that to them are bound the captives condemned to be burnt. These posts are usually decorated with the scalps of slain enemies, suspended by strings from the top. They are often crowned with the white dry skull of an enemy.

It thus appears that this area is designed for a public place of exhibition, for shows, games, etc. Formerly, there is little doubt, most barbarous and tragical scenes were enacted within them, such as the torturing and burning of captives, who were here forced to run the gauntlet, bruised and beaten with sticks and burning chunks of wood. The Indians do not now practise these cruelties; but there are some old traders who have witnessed them in former times. I inquired of these traders for what reason these areas were called "chunk yards;" they were, in general, ignorant, yet, for the most part, concurred in a lame story that it originated in the circumstance of its having been a place of torture, and that the name was but an interpretation of the Indian term designating them.[a]

I observed none of these yards in use in any of the Cherokee towns; and where I have mentioned them, in the Cherokee country, it must be understood that I saw only the remains or vestiges of them among the ruins of the ancient towns. In the existing Cherokee towns which I visited, although there were ancient mounds and signs of the yard adjoining, yet the yard was either built upon or turned into a garden plat, or otherwise appropriated. Indeed, I am convinced that the chunk yards now or lately in use among the Creeks are of very ancient date, and not the work of the present Indians; although they are now kept in repair by them, being swept very clean every day, and the poles kept up and decorated in the manner I have described.

The following plan [figure 636] will illustrate the form and character of these yards: A. The great area, surrounded by terraces or banks. B. A circular eminence at one end of the yard, commonly 9 or 10 feet higher than the ground round about. Upon this mound stands the great rotunda, hothouse, or winter council house of the present Creeks. It was probably designed and used by the ancients, who constructed it for the same purpose. C. A square terrace or eminence, about the same height with the circular one just described, occupying a position at the other end of the yard. Upon this stands the public square. The banks inclosing the yard are indicated by the letters b, b, b, b; c indicates the "chunk pole"; and d, d, the "slave posts."

---

[a] According to Adair, Du Pratz, and other writers, the Cherokees and probably the Creeks were much addicted to a similar game, played with a rod or pole and a circular stone, which was called chungke. Mr Catlin describes this game as still existing under the name of tchung-kee among the Minitarees and other tribes on the Missouri. It also prevailed among some of the Ohio Indians. It has been suggested that the areas called chunk, or chunky yards, by Bartram, derived their names from the circumstance, that they were, among other objects, devoted to games, among which, that of chungke was prominent. This suggestion derives some support from Adair. . . . It is therefore not improbable that these square areas were denominated chungke yards.

Sometimes the square, instead of being open at the ends, as shown in the plan, is closed upon all sides by the banks. In the lately built or new Creek towns, they do not raise a mound for the foundation of their rotundas or public squares. The yard, however, is retained, and the public buildings occupy nearly the same position in respect to it. They also retain the central obelisk and the slave posts.

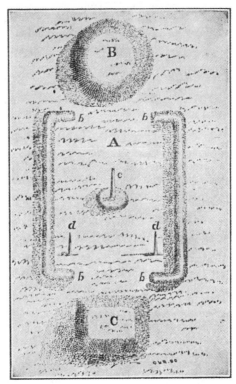

FIG. 636. Chunk yard; Muskogee Indians, Georgia; from William Bartram.

NATCHESAN STOCK

NATCHEZ. Louisiana.

Le Page du Pratz [a] wrote as follows:

The natives of Louisiana have invented but a very few diversions, and these perhaps serve their turn as well as a greater variety would do. The warriors practice a diversion which is called the game of the pole, at which two only play together at a time. Each has a pole, about 8 feet long, resembling a Roman f, and the game consists in rolling a flat round stone, about 3 inches in diameter and an inch thick, with the edge somewhat sloping, and throwing the pole at the same time in such a manner that when the stone rests the pole may touch it or be near it. Both antagonists throw their poles at the same time, and he whose pole is nearest the stone counts 1, and has the right of rolling the stone. The men fatigue themselves much at this game, as they run after their poles at every throw; and some of them are so bewitched by it that they game away one piece of furniture after another. These gamesters, however, are very rare, and are greatly discountenanced by the rest of the people.

---

[a] Historie de la Louisiane, v. 3, p. 4, Paris, 1768.

PIMAN STOCK

PIMA. Arizona. (Cat. no. 76020, United States National Museum.) Stick or arrow with a feather at one end and a corncob at the other, sent by the National Museum, as an exchange, to the Peabody Museum, Salem, Mass.

Collected by Dr Edward Palmer, who thus describes it as used in the game of quins:

Any number can play. A short split stick is first thrown in a slanting direction. Then each one pitches his arrow to see who can come nearest to it. The one who does so holds the stick up while the others pitch. If the arrow touches the split stick and does not catch, the thrower loses nothing. If, however, the arrow remains in the split stick, it becomes the property of the holder. The game ends when one has all the arrows or when the players tire out.

This is the only record of a game analogous to hoop and pole which I find among the tribes of the Piman stock.

PUJUNAN STOCK

NISHINAM. Mokelumne river, 12 miles south of Placerville, California.

Dr J. W. Hudson describes a hoop-and-lance game under the name of nunt:

FIG. 637. Position of players in hoop-and-lance game; Nishinam Indians, California; from a sketch by Dr J. W. Hudson.

The hoop, künûn', consists of an outer hoop of oak wrapped with rawhide, 24 inches in diameter, with a center hoop of rawhide. The former has ten radii of rawhide attached to the inner hoop. The players [figure 637] roll the hoop in turn, and cast a 9-foot lance at it, after springing quickly to right angles of the hoop's course. A bull's-eye counts coup, or 10; between spokes, 5; lean up (by hoop), 2. The dead line and course is laid out previous to play.

SALISHAN STOCK

BELLACOOLA. Dean inlet, British Columbia. (Cat. no. $\frac{16}{1546}$ and $\frac{16}{1551}$, American Museum of Natural History.)

 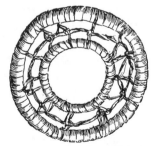

FIG. 638. Cedar-bark game rings; diameter, 7½ inches; Bellacoola Indians, British Columbia; cat. no. $\frac{16}{1546}$, $\frac{16}{1551}$, American Museum of Natural History.

Two rings (figure 638), wrapped with cedar bark, 7½ inches in diameter. Collected by Mr George Hunt and Dr Franz Boas.

BELLACOOLA.   Dean inlet, British Columbia.   (Field Columbian Museum.)

Cat. no. 18490.   Lava ring (figure 639), 3½ inches in diameter, with hole in the center.

Cat. no. 18494.   Lava ring (figure 639), similar to the one last described, but smaller, 2½ inches in diameter.

FIG. 639.   Lava game rings; diameters, 3¼ and 2¼ inches; Bellacoola Indians, British Columbia; cat. no. 18490, 18494, Field Columbian Museum.

PEND D'OREILLES.   Flathead reservation, Montana.   (Cat. no. 51793, Field Columbian Museum.)

Ring, wound with buckskin, 2½ inches in diameter, the interior set with colored beads; and two arrows (figure 640), 23½ inches in length, with iron spike points, the shaft of the arrow being wound with buckskin at ends and middle.   Collected by Dr George A. Dorsey.

FIG. 640.   Beaded game ring and arrows; diameter of ring, 2¼ inches; length of arrows, 23¼ inches; Pend d'Oreille Indians, Montana; cat. no. 51793, Field Columbian Museum.

The Dictionary of the Kalispel [a] gives the following:

Szgolkólégu, the playing at wheels; chgolkoléguten, the play wheels, la roulette; chines golkólégui, I play with small wheels or circles; jouer à la roulette, an Indian play; golkoleguèmen, a gambler at wheels; golko, wheel, wagon.

---

[a] Dictionary of the Kalispel or Flat-head Indian Language, compiled by the Missionaries of the Society of Jesus, St Ignatius Print, Montana, 1877–8–9.

SALISH. Comox, British Columbia.

Dr C. F. Newcombe writes:[a]

I was told of a game called xānăni, played by two sides with a quoitlike disk of twigs, bound with willow or cedar bark, and thrown in the air to be caught on a stick while skimming. At Alert bay (Kwakiutl), the game is called kăni.

SHUSWAP. Kamloops, British Columbia.

Dr Franz Boas [b] says:

A peculiar gambling game is played in the following way: A long pole is laid on the ground, about 15 feet from the players; a ring about 1 inch in diameter, to which four beads are attached at points dividing the circumference into four equal parts, is rolled toward the pole, and sticks are thrown after it before it falls down on touching the pole. The four beads are red, white, blue, and black.

The ring falls down on the stick that has been thrown after it, and, according to the color of the bead that touches the stick, the player wins a number of points.

SONGISH. Vancouver island, British Columbia.

Dr Franz Boas [c] says:

Throwing and catching of hoops is a favorite game.

THOMPSON INDIANS (NTLAKYAPAMUK). British Columbia.

Mr James Teit [d] says:

This game [referring to the stick game] has been out of use for many years, as well as another game, greatly in vogue at one time among the Indians, which was played altogether by men. They found it warm work, and used to strip off all their clothes except the breechcloth when playing. The chief implement in this game was a ring [figure 641] from 2 inches to 4½ inches in diameter, and sewed over with buckskin, the framework often being made of a stick bent round. The buckskin covering was loose, and the space inside not taken up by the stick was filled with sand to make the ring solid and heavy. The player set this ring rolling. Then he followed it, running, and threw a small spear at it. The object of the game was to throw the spear in front of the ring and make the latter fall on it. Generally the playing-ground was marked by two long poles, which prevented the ring from rolling too far. Six different marks, which determined the number of points, were sewed on the buckskin inside of the circle. In later times these were made with different colored beads. The number of beads was six or four. Four were always blue or some other dark color, and two were some light color, generally light blue, but frequently white or red. The light beads counted 10 points each. If both fell on top of the stick, it counted 20. The dark beads counted 5 each. If two fell on top of the stick, it counted 10; if one dark and one light, 15. If the ring did not fall on top of the throwing stick, but stood up against it, it counted 40, which was the highest. The beads were not then counted. Before beads were known, porcupine quills were used as marks on the rings. The two light marks

---

[a] In a letter, March 11, 1901.

[b] Second General Report on the Indians of British Columbia. Report of the Sixtieth Meeting of the British Association for the Advancement of Science, p. 641, London, 1891.

[c] Ibid., p. 571.

[d] The Thompson Indians of British Columbia. Members of the American Museum of Natural History, v. 2, p. 273, New York, 1900.

were in white or yellow, and the four dark marks were black. It seems, therefore, that the colors were not exactly fixed, further than that they had to be light and dark.

Another game was played with the same ring and throwing-stick, and the points were counted as in the game just described. In fact, this game was like that, except that in this the players sat facing each other, and rolled the ring from one to the other. One man started the ring rolling, and then threw his stick in front of it, so as to stop it, if possible, before it reached the other man. Sometimes one man rolled and the other threw, in turn, instead of both men running abreast and throwing their sticks in front of the ring, as in the other game, one after the other. If the player missed, the other man took his turn.

Another game was generally played by boys and girls, but occasionally by adults. It was played out of doors, but also, in cold weather, inside the winter houses. In this a ring from 6 to 10 inches in diameter was used. It was made of pliable sticks, around which bark or dried grass was thickly twisted. Sometimes it was made of reeds (the same as those used in tent-mats) bent in the form of a circle, around which other reeds were twisted. The players sat in two lines, some distance apart, facing one another. At each end of the lines sat a person who set the ring rolling from one to the other between the two lines of players. When the ring was in motion, the players threw darts at it, the object being to make these darts hit the ring. If they passed through the ring without touching, it counted nothing. The darts were about 6 or 7 inches in length, some thick in the middle and small at both ends [figure 642]. One end was feathered, while the other end was brought to a very sharp point. Many darts had the shaft all one thickness to near the point, where it was forked into two sharp points. These darts had property-marks, consisting of notches, dots, circles, or paintings, to indicate the owner. The wood used was that of the wāx·esê'lp-bush.

A peculiar custom in connection with this game was that sometimes the old people would put some of the darts which the boys used for throwing at the ring into the fire of the winter house, the lads not being allowed to get them

FIG. 641. Beaded game ring and spear; diameter of ring, 2 to 4½ inches; length of spear, 29½ inches; Thompson Indians, British Columbia; cat. no. ₁₂⁴⁶₈, ₁₂⁴⁹₈, American Museum of Natural History.

except by catching the ends of them with their teeth. Sometimes all the darts were gathered together and thrown outside. The boys were made to scramble

FIG. 642. Game dart; length, 12 inches; Thompson Indians, British Columbia; cat. no. ₄₁⁶₈₅, American Museum of Natural History.

for them. The one that obtained the most was the victor. A boy who was unlucky in playing, and lost all his darts, could get them back again by putting up his back as a target, every arrow fired at it becoming his property. This game, like the preceding one, has now gone out of use.

In another game a ring the size of a finger ring was placed on the ground about 9 or 10 feet away from the players. Each player had two darts, which he threw so as to hit the center of the ring, if possible. The darts were feathered, had sharp points, and were made rather thin. Boys and girls, in playing these games, won or lost their darts. They did not gamble for anything else. There were no special months for certain games, excepting that some games were better adapted for special seasons than others, and consequently were played only in those seasons.

SHAHAPTIAN STOCK

Nez Percés. Southern Alberta.

Rev. John MacLean[a] mentions "throwing the arrow and wheel" among the games of the tribe.

Umatilla. Oregon. (Free Museum of Science and Art, University of Pennsylvania.)

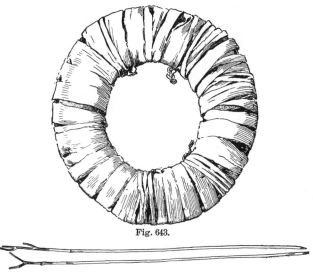

Fig. 643.

Fig. 644.

Fig. 643. Game hoop; diameter, 11¼ inches; Umatilla Indians, Oregon; cat. no. 37538, Free Museum of Science and Art, University of Pennsylvania.

Fig. 644. Poles for hoop game; lengths, 68 and 69 inches; Umatilla Indians, Oregon; cat. no. 37538, Free Museum of Science and Art, University of Pennsylvania.

Cat. no. 37538. Flat hoop (figure 643) made of twigs covered with bark, 11¼ inches in diameter, and two poles (figure 644), 68 and 69 inches in length, forked and painted red at the ends. Collected by the writer in 1900.

The game is played in the spring. The ring is called pasa-pow-i-low-wikes and the poles are designated wai-hutz.

Cat. no. 37539. Ring, wrapped with buckskin, 4 inches in diameter, its interior set with colored beads, as shown in figure 645, and two darts, slender twigs, painted red, 11 inches in length. Collected by the writer in 1900.

---

[a] Canadian Savage Folk, p. 42, Toronto, 1896.

Two men play. The ring is called sow-lai-kai-kas and the darts are known as tuk-tai-pow-ma. The counts depend on the way in which the darts fall in the ring—1, 2, 5, 10, 15, 20, according to the beads to which they are adjacent.

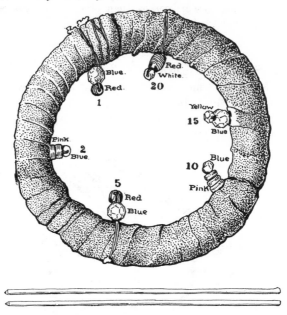

FIG. 645. Beaded game ring and darts; diameter of ring, 4 inches; length of darts, 11 inches; Umatilla Indians. Oregon; cat. no. 37539, Free Museum of Science and Art, University of Pennsylvania.

SHASTAN STOCK

ACHOMAWI. Hat creek, California. (Cat. no. $\frac{50}{4146}$ to $\frac{50}{4148}$, American Museum of Natural History.)

FIG. 646. Bark game disk; diameter, 10 inches; Achomawi Indians, Hat creek, California; cat. no. $\frac{50}{4146}$, American Museum of Natural History.

Bark disk (figure 646), 10 inches in diameter, a bow and ten arrows.

Collected in 1903 by Dr Roland B. Dixon, who describes the disk as used as a rolling target.

SHOSHONEAN STOCK

BANNOCK.　Rossfork, Idaho.

Mr Thomas Blaine Donaldson has given the writer a photograph of the Bannock playing the hoop game, taken by him in 1890.　He says:[a]

The picture [figure 647] shows a boy hurling a spear at a rolling hoop and a smaller youngster watching him.　There were about ten full-grown bucks watching the youngsters playing, and the older men would take the hoop and hurl it along the ground and try to spear it.　They took regular turns, and when they failed to spear the hoop, which was usual, because it took some skill, the other contestants laughed uproariously.

Fig. 647.

Fig. 648.

FIG. 647.　Bannock Indian boy playing hoop and pole, Idaho; from photograph by Mr Thomas Blaine Donaldson.

FIG. 648.　Corn-husk game ring; diameter, 5 inches; Hopi Indians, Arizona; cat. no. 128904, United States National Museum.

HOPI.　Arizona.　(United States National Museum.)

Cat. no. 128904.　Ring of corn husk (figure 648), 5 inches in diameter; accompanied by a number of corncob darts, each with two feathers and sharp points of hard wood.　Collected by Mrs Matilda Coxe Stevenson.

FIG. 649.　Corncob darts; Hopi Indians, Arizona; cat. no. 69024, United States National Museum.

Cat. no. 69024.　Corncob darts (figure 648), similar to the above. Collected by Maj. J. W. Powell.

---

[a] In a letter to the writer, under date of February 25, 1901.

HOPI.   Oraibi, Arizona.   (Field Columbian Museum.)

Cat. no. 66927 to 66932.   Ring of corn husk, 7 inches in diameter,
half overwrapped with white and half with red cord, and four
corncob darts, each with two feathers and wooden points, from
10¼ to 12¼ inches in length (figure 650).

FIG. 650. Corn-husk game ring and corncob darts; diameter of ring, 7 inches; Hopi Indians,
Oraibi, Arizona; cat. no. 66927–66932, Field Columbian Museum.

Collected in 1898 by Rev. H. R. Voth, who furnishes the following
account:

This game is generally designated by the term "throwing the wheel" or
"throwing at the wheel" and is usually played by boys. The wheel is thrown
on the ground, and the spears or arrows, which are held so that the middle
finger runs between the two arrows, are thrown at it. The arrows are often
also thrown into the air; when they descend, the pressure of the air causes them
to rotate rapidly. In the Oáqöl ceremony the women shoot with similar but
somewhat larger arrows at wheels, which are said to represent shields. It was

noticed on several occasions that shortly before and after the Oáqöl ceremony the game was played more than at any other time.

Cat. no. 63176.　Corn-husk ring $2\frac{1}{4}$ inches in diameter; and corncob
　　feather dart, 12 inches in length, with wooden pin (figure 651).
Collected by Dr George A. Dorsey in 1897.　The label reads as follows:

The Hopi variant of a game which has a wide distribution throughout the western part of the United States and Canada.

Fig. 651. Corn-husk ring and corncob dart; diameter of ring, $2\frac{1}{4}$ inches; length of dart, 12
inches; Hopi Indians, Oraibi, Arizona; cat. no. 63176, Field Columbian Museum.

Among the Hopi tribes the game is played almost exclusively by boys. Among other aboriginal tribes of the West men play, often for stakes of considerable magnitude. The wheel used by the Hopi is called wipo-nölla, which simply means corn-husk wheel. The same wheel is also used for many other purposes and in certain ceremonies. At times the arrow is the usual one owned by every Hopi boy, and is shot from a bow. More often a special form of double arrow, passing into a corncob and terminating in a single point, is used. This is thrown at the wheel by hand. The special arrow is called mötöwu. There is no special name for this game, but they say " play with the wheel," or " shoot the wheel," mötöwu.

MONO. Hooker cove, Madera county, California. (Cat. no. 71432, Field Columbian Museum.)

FIG. 652. Lance-and-peg game; length of lances, 6 feet; length of peg, 3 inches; Mono Indians Madera county, California; cat. no. 71432, Field Columbian Museum.

Four lances (figure 652), about 6 feet in length, with butts unpeeled, and a small cylindrical wooden block, 3 inches in length. Collected by Dr J. W. Hudson, who describes them as implements for the lance-and-peg game.

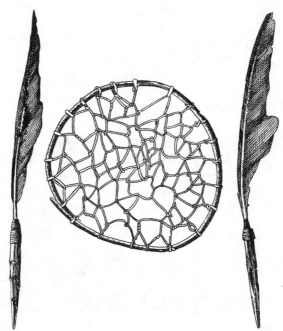

FIG. 653. Netted game hoop and feathered darts; diameter of hoop, 7 inches; length of darts, 12 inches; Paiute Indians, southern Utah; cat. no. 9428, 9429, Peabody Museum of American Archæology and Ethnology.

PAIUTE. Southern Utah. (Cat. no. 9428, 9429, Peabody Museum of American Archæology and Ethnology.)

Small hoop made of a bent twig, about 7 inches in diameter, covered with a net of yucca fiber, as shown in figure 653, and two feather darts, 12 inches in length, consisting of pins of hard wood

about 4 inches in length, to which single feathers, twisted somewhat spirally, are bound with fiber. Collected by Dr Edward
Palmer.

PAIUTE. Pyramid lake, Nevada. (Cat. no. 19059, United States National Museum.)

Small wooden hoop (figure 654), 2¾ inches in diameter, tightly wound
with a strip of buckskin; and a straight, peeled twig, 19 inches in
length.

FIG. 654. Game ring and dart; diameter of ring, 2¾ inches; length of dart, 19 inches; Paiute
Indians, Pyramid lake, Nevada; cat. no. 19059, United States National Museum.

The collector, Mr Stephen Powers, gives the following account of
the game in his catalogue:

Peisheen, ring play. The ring is rolled on the ground, and a rod shot after it
in such a way as to have the ring fall and lie on it.

SHOSHONI. Wyoming. (Cat. no. $\frac{50}{2441-2444}$, American Museum of
Natural History.)

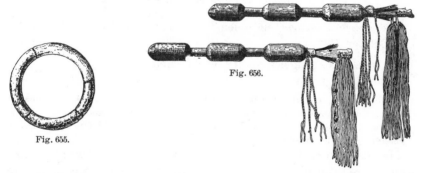

Fig. 656.

Fig. 655.

FIG. 655. Game ring; diameter, 13½ inches; Shoshoni Indians, Wyoming; cat. no. $\frac{50}{2441}$, American
Museum of Natural History.
FIG. 656. Darts for ring game; length, 26 inches; Shoshoni Indians, Wyoming; cat. no. $\frac{50}{2442-2443}$,
American Museum of Natural History.

Hide-covered ring (figure 655), sewed with sinew, the interior filled
with cotton cloth. Diameter of ring, 13½ inches; of section, 2¼
inches. Two wooden clubs (figure 656), 26 inches in length and
about 1½ inches in diameter, with three knobs, 4 inches in length,
one at the extreme end and the others about equidistant along the
body of the club. The first of these knobs is covered with buckskin painted red, the second with buckskin painted yellow, and
the third red. The handle of one is covered with yellow-painted
buckskin and is perforated by a hole through which a thong
is attached, terminating in two long tassels of yellow-painted

cut-buckskin fringe. Black and white horsehair is bound by a strip of buckskin to the handle, four twisted buckskin thongs being attached to this band on the side nearest the knob. The other club is similar, except that the cover of the handle and the cut-leather fringe are stained red. They are accompanied by six willow counting sticks (figure 657), 13¾ inches in length, two painted yellow, two red, and two green.

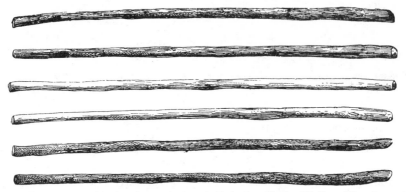

FIG. 657. Counting-sticks for ring game; length, 13¾ inches; Shoshoni Indians, Wyoming; cat. no. ₂₄₄₄⁵⁹, American Museum of Natural History.

The above-described specimens were collected by Mr H. H. St Clair, 2d, in 1901.

TOBIKHAR. Los Angeles county, California.

Hugo Ried [a] says:

Another game, called hararicuar, consisted in throwing rods or canes of the length of a lance, at a ring put in motion, and see who could insert it. The ring was made of buckskin with a twig of willow inside, and 4 inches in diameter. This is not played now.

The same narrative describes divination with rings of willow twigs, which were thrown in turn in the four directions to discover a missing daughter, in a legend of this region.

UINTA UTE. White Rocks, Utah. (Cat. no. 37120, Free Museum of Science and Art, University of Pennsylvania.)

FIG. 658. Game arrow; length, 32½ inches; Uinta Ute Indians, White Rocks, Utah; cat. no. 37120, Free Museum of Science and Art, University of Pennsylvania.

Arrow (figure 658) with wooden shaft and heavy nail point, the shaftment banded with blue and red paint, with three feathers; length, 32½ inches. Collected by the writer in 1900.

[a]Account of the Indians of Los Angeles Co., Cai. Bulletin of the Essex Institute, v. 17, p. 18, Salem, 1885.

The use of this arrow was not ascertained, but from its identity in form with arrows used with the beaded ring, and the fact that it was one of a pair, it was probably used in that game.

UNCOMPAHGRE UTE.   Utah.   (Cat. no. $\frac{50}{1300}$, American Museum of Natural History.)

FIG. 659. Darts for ring game; length, 14¼ inches; Uncompahgre Ute Indians, Utah; cat. no. $\frac{50}{1300}$, American Museum of Natural History.

Two sticks (figure 659), wrapped with buckskin, with buckskin thongs in three sets of three each near one end, length 14¼ inches. Used with a ring 1¼ inches in diameter.

Collected by Dr A. L. Kroeber, who gives the following account:

Two players throw the sticks at the rolling ring, each attempting to make the ring come to rest touching his stick.

UTE.   (Cat. no. 200582, United States National Museum.)

Wooden ring (figure 660), 6 inches in diameter, closely wound with a string of fine colored beads, in four segments, two blue and two white, and having a piece of ermine fur attached. In the E. Granier collection.

FIG. 660. Game ring; diameter, 6 inches; Ute Indians; cat. no. 200582, United States National Museum.

YAUDANCHI.[a] Tule River Indian reservation, California. (Cat. no. 71433, Field Columbian Museum.)

Lances and peg for lance-and-peg game. Collected by Dr J. W. Hudson, who furnishes the following description:

The peg is stuck in the ground, and the lance thrown at it. Played by men and boys. The smaller implements are for boys. The game is called "hot," and is played by young men, not children, and perhaps male adults.

---

[a] This tribe belongs to the Mariposan family, hence the description properly belongs on page 483.

SIOUAN STOCK

ASSINIBOIN. Southern Alberta.

Rev. John Maclean [a] says:

The Stoneys have several games similar to the Blackfeet, including the hoop and arrow game.

CROWS. Wyoming.

Prof. F. V. Hayden [b] mentions the following:

A-ba-tsink′-i-sha, a game somewhat like billiards.

———— Crow reservation, Montana. (Field Columbian Museum.)

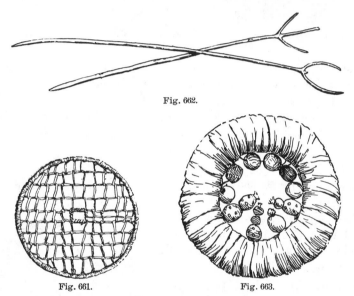

Fig. 662.

Fig. 661.   Fig. 663.

FIG. 661. Netted game hoop; diameter, 11 inches; Crow Indians, Montana; cat. no. 69651, Field Columbian Museum.

FIG. 662. Darts for netted hoop; length, 44½ and 57 inches; Crow Indians, Montana; cat. no. 69651, Field Columbian Museum.

FIG. 663. Beaded ring; diameter, 2½ inches; Crow Indians, Montana; cat. no. 69650, Field Columbian Museum.

Cat. no. 69651. Hoop of sapling (figure 661), covered with a thong network which is attached to the hoop thirty-four times; diameter, 11 inches; accompanied by two darts (figure 662), saplings with trident ends, 44½ and 57 inches in length. Collected by Mr S. C. Simms in 1901.

Cat. no. 69650. Iron ring (figure 663), thickly wound with buckskin, thickly set inside with colored glass beads; diameter, 2½ inches. Collected by Mr S. C. Simms in 1901.

———————————

[a] Canadian Savage Folk, p. 26, Toronto, 1896.

[b] Contributions to the Ethnography and Philology of the Indian Tribes of the Missouri River, p. 408, Philadelphia, 1862.

DAKOTA (OGLALA). Pine Ridge reservation, South Dakota. (Free
Museum of Science and Art, University of Pennsylvania.)
Cat. no. 21945. Hoop of sapling, 25 inches in diameter (figure 664),
with incised marks on both sides, as shown in figure 665.

The first, *a*, nearest the junction, consists of three incised rings
painted red; the next, *b*, is cut on both sides for about 1¼ inches and
marked with black, burnt scratches; the third, *c*, *c*, has a cut on both
sides, marked on one with a cross and on the other with a single notch

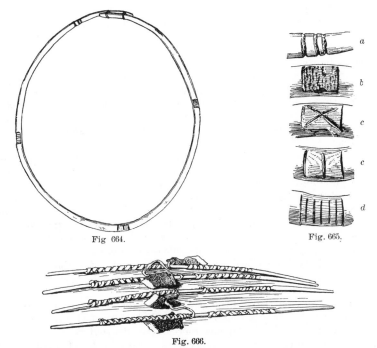

Fig 664.   Fig. 665.

Fig. 666.

FIG. 664. Game hoop; diameter, 25 inches; Oglala Dakota Indians, Pine Ridge reservation, South
Dakota; cat. no. 21945, Free Museum of Science and Art, University of Pennsylvania.

FIG. 665. Marks on game hoop; Oglala Dakota Indians, Pine Ridge reservation, South Dakota;
cat. no. 21945, Free Museum of Science and Art, University of Pennsylvania.

FIG. 666. Darts for hoop game; length, 39¼ inches; Oglala Dakota Indians, Pine Ridge reservation, South Dakota; cat. no. 21945, Free Museum of Science and Art, University of
Pennsylvania.

in the middle, the faces being painted red; the fourth, *d*, is cut with a
similar flat face on both sides, 1¼ inches in length, with five transverse equidistant notches, all painted red.

Four rounded sticks, 39½ inches in length, slightly larger at the butt,
wrapped with thongs, as shown in figure 666, and held in pairs
by thongs 11 inches in length.

One pair has the butts painted red and a small strip of red flannel
tied to the connecting thong, and the other has black butts with a blue

flag. The game is called painyankapi, and is described by the collector, Mr Louis L. Meeker,[a] as follows:

The implements consist of a hoop rather more than 2 feet in diameter, cangleska [figure 664], bent into shape and fastened when green, and two pairs of throwing sticks [figure 666], painyankapi, about 40 inches in length, wrapped with thongs, by which each pair is loosely coupled together, so that in the middle they are about a span apart. Each pair bears a small flag, blue or black on one pair, and red or yellow on the other. The hoop is made of a straight ash stick, 1¼ inches in diameter at the larger end, and is "as long as the tallest man." The hoop bears four flattened spaces on each side at equidistant points. [Figure 665.] Two players, representing two sides, throw two pairs of sticks at the hoop as it rolls past, and the counting is according to the marked or flattened space that lies upon the javelin after the hoop falls. The first mark from the junction, *a*, is called the butt or stump (can huta), and counts 10; the next, *b*, is black (sapa), and counts 20; the next, *cc*, the fork (okaja), counts 10; and the next, *d*, called marks (icazopi), counts 20. When the stick falls across the butt and the fork, it is called sweepstakes. The game is for 40 points. Painyankapi was sometimes called the buffalo game. It is said to have been played to secure success in the buffalo hunt. The hoop figuratively represents the horns of a buffalo and the bone that supports them.

Playing the game is called "shooting the buffalo." Again the hoop represents an encampment of all the Dakota tribes, and the chief's family learn to locate all different tribes upon it. Or it was supposed to represent the rim of the horizon and the four quarters of the earth. The spaces marked are the openings or passes into the circle of the camp. They also represent the four winds and are invoked as such by the thrower before he throws.

In time of much sickness the camp was ranged in two columns, the hoop painted black on one side and red on the other, the sticks painted, two red and two black, and the hoop rolled between the two ranks four times, and then carried away and left in some remote place to bear away the sickness. It was rolled "toward the whites," *i. e.*, south.

The Lakota word for hoop is cangleska. It means spotted wood. No other term for hoop is in use. It follows that the hoop for which all other hoops are named, was spotted. This applies especially to the conjurer's hoop, colored in yellow,[b] red, white, and blue or black as is convenient, to represent the four quarters of the earth. This hoop is laid upon the ground in the medicine lodge, and after necessary ceremonies, the lights are extinguished, when a noise of eating is heard, and a ring cut from a pipe pumpkin, previously placed within the hoop for the purpose, is supposed to be devoured by the Wasicun [c] conjured up by the ceremonies.

Cat. no. 22109. Ring of sinew (figure 667), wrapped with a thong, 3½ inches in diameter, painted red.

Cat. no. 22110. A stick 39½ inches in length, the end lashed with a curved piece of sapling with the points turned toward the

---

[a] Ogalala Games. Bulletin of the Free Museum of Science and Art, v. 3, p. 23, Philadelphia, 1901.

[b] The yellow is always placed north, but the other colors vary.

[c] The term Wasicun, now universally given to white men, means a superior and mysterious being.

handle (figure 668). Two bars of wood, 11½ inches in length, are lashed across the stick, each with a smaller piece of curved wood with points turning toward the handle, as shown in the figure. The curved piece at the end and the body of the stick are wrapped with a thong, and the bars, arcs, and exposed end of stick are painted black. There is a projection above the crossbar, nearest the end to which the curved piece is affixed, against which the forefinger is pressed. A small square of black cloth is tied to the curved end of the stick.

Fig. 667.   Fig. 668.

FIG. 667. Ring for Elk game; diameter, 3¼ inches; Oglala Dakota Indians, Pine Ridge reservation, South Dakota; cat. no. 22109, Free Museum of Science and Art, University of Pennsylvania.
FIG. 668. Darts for elk game; lengths, 39½ and 36 inches; Oglala Dakota Indians, Pine Ridge reservation, South Dakota; cat. no. 22110, 22110a, Free Museum of Science and Art, University of Pennsylvania.

Cat. no. 22110a. A stick similar to the preceding, 36 inches in length, but painted red instead of black, and with a red instead of a black flag. The ends of the arc at the tip are united to the body of the stick by a cord of sinew. The crossbars are 6¼ inches in length.

These are implements for the game of kaga woskate, or haka heciapi, the elk game. Collected by Mr Louis L. Meeker,[a] who states that the ring is tossed into the air, and the player tries to catch it on his stick.

It is held in the hand with the forefinger pressing against a small projection that the best-made sticks bear near the center. Caught upon the point, it counts 10; if on the spur nearest the point, 5; on any other point, 1. The game is for any number of points agreed upon by the players. The Elk Game was played to secure success in the elk hunt.

He continues:

The Lakotas use a special hair ornament as a reward for victory in this game. The Cheyenne award it in the game next described (tahuka cangleska). The ornament [figure 564] is a miniature gaming hoop or wheel, tohogmu, as small as the matter can make it well, with spokes like a wheel, ornamented with porcupine quills and tied to a small lock of hair on one side of the crown by a buckskin string fastened to the center of the ornament.

Col. Garrick Mallery,[b] in his Picture-writing of the American In-

a Ogalala Games. Bulletin of the Free Museum of Science and Art, v. 3, p. 26, Philadelphia, 1901.
b Tenth Annual Report of the Bureau of Ethnology, p. 547, 1893.

dians, gives the accompanying figures referring to the preceding game:

A dead man was used in the ring-and-pole game [figure 669]. American-Horse's Winter Count, 1779–'80. The figure represents the stick and ring used in the game of haka, with a human head in front to suggest that the corpse took the place of the usual stick.

FIG. 669. Haka game; Oglala Dakota pictograph from American-Horse's Winter Count, 1779–80; from Mallery.

It was an intensely cold winter and a Dakota froze to death [figure 670]. American-Horse's Winter Count, 1777–'78.

The sign for snow or winter, i. e., a cloud with snow falling from it, is above the man's head. A haka stick, which is used in playing that game, is represented in front of him. Battiste Good's record further explains the illustration by the account that the Dakota was killed in a fight with the Pawnees, and his companions left his body where they supposed it would not be found, but the Pawnee found it, and, as it was frozen stiff, they dragged it into their camp and played haka with it.

Fig. 670.

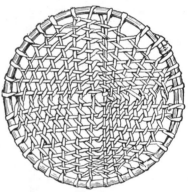

Fig. 671.

FIG. 670. Haka game; Oglala Dakota pictograph from American-Horse's Winter Count, 1779–80; from Mallery.

FIG. 671. Netted hoop; diameter, 11¼ inches; Oglala Dakota Indians, Pine Ridge reservation South Dakota; cat. no. 22112, Free Museum of Science and Art, University of Pennsylvania.

DAKOTA (OGLALA). Pine Ridge reservation, South Dakota. (Cat. no. 22111–22113, Free Museum of Science and Art, University of Pennsylvania.)

FIG. 672. Dart for netted hoop; length, 46 inches; Oglala Dakota Indians, Pine Ridge reservation, South Dakota; cat. no. 22113, Free Museum of Science and Art, University of Pennsylvania.

Hoop (figure 671) of sapling, 11½ inches in diameter, lashed with a rawhide thong, which is passed around the hoop twenty-four times.

Another hoop, also 11¼ inches in diameter, the thong passing around the edge thirty-five times. Both hoops have the edge and the thong net smeared with red paint.

A forked stick (figure 672), consisting of a peeled sapling, 46 inches in length, painted red, with a feather tied at the ends of the forks.

The specimens just described are implements for the game of the buckskin hoop, tahuka cangleska, and were collected by Mr Louis L. Meeker,[a] who describes the game as follows:

Played with several small hoops about a foot in diameter, woven with buckskin thongs with one opening more prominent than the rest, intended to be in the center, called the "heart" [figure 671]. The game is to thrust a small spear [figure 672], with a fork at one end to admit the top of the forefinger, through the "heart" as the hoop is rolled by or flung into the air. When one succeeds, he chases the one who threw the hoop, and endeavors to hit him with it. The one who oftenest pierces the "heart" wins. This is said to be a Cheyenne game played, like the other hoop games, only at the annual summer gatherings, camp against camp, from morning until a crier calls noon, when the victorious camp is feasted by the losers and the individual victor adorned with the hair ornament, good for one year.

The writer has not witnessed the game played in this way, a rain preventing when arrangements were made. The following, however, played by large boys and young men, he has seen as many as fifty times: Two forked sticks, about 4 feet high, to represent men, were set up 30 or 40 paces apart. A prop was placed across, from one foot to the other, both to make them stand erect and to make them easier marks.

Properly, the forks should not be more than an inch or so in diameter at the point and should be split up for a few inches, with a cross stick in the splits, so as to make four points come in contact with the ground and a stick for the hoop to strike, if it rolls under.

Two companies, stationed a very little in front and a little to one side of each "man," take turns rolling the hoops by throwing them against the ground to make them roll towards the "man" on the opposite side, the players of which defend their "man" by thrusting their spears through the rolling hoops.

The side is victorious that oftenest knocks down the "man." The player is victorious who oftenest pierces the heart of the hoop, so the victorious player may not be on the victorious side. My informants do not count this game with their regular hoop games, nor take any pride in the buckskin hoop generally. It was contributed by a full-blood Lakota, but definite knowledge of the manner of playing can not be obtained here.

The name tahuka cangleska means "neck hoop" rather than "deerskin hoop," though it may have the latter meaning, as my informants affirm.

Women say taoga cangleska instead of tahuka cangleska. This would mean "web-hoop" game and make it sacred to Inktomi (the Spider). Women's speech is somewhat different from men's.

The makers of the hoops for the hoop games are not selected at random. White-buffalo-cow River, Pte-sa Wakpa, makes hoops for the "buffalo game." Red Hoop, Cangleska luta, makes the hair-ornament hoop.

The hoops sent herewith were made by these men and by Crazy Horse, Ta-sunk-witko, brother of the desperado Crazy Horse who lost his life while a prisoner some years ago.

---

[a] Ogalala Games. Bulletin of the Free Museum of Science and Art, v. 3, p. 27, Philadelphia, 1901.

DAKOTA (TETON).   South Dakota.

Rev. J. Owen Dorsey,[a] in his account of the games of the Teton Dakota children, describes the game with a rawhide hoop, tahuka changleshka unpi, among those played by boys in the spring:

Occasionally in the early spring the people fear a freshet, so they leave the river bank and camp in the level prairie away from the river. The men hunt the deer, and when they return to camp the boys take part of the hides and cut them into narrow strips, which they soak in water; they make a hoop of ash wood, all over which they put the strips of rawhide, which they interweave in such a way as to leave a hole in the middle, which is called the " heart." The players form sides of equal numbers, and ti-oshpaye or gens usually plays against gens. The hoop is thrown by one of the players toward those on the other side. They are provided with sharp-pointed sticks, each of which is forked at the small end. As the hoop rolls they throw at it, in order to thrust one of the sticks through the heart. When one hits the heart he keeps the hoop for his side, and he and his companions chase their opponents, who flee with their blankets spread out behind them in order to deaden the force of any blow from a pursuer. When the pursuers overtake one of the fugitives they strike him with the hoop as hard as they can; then they abandon the pursuit and return to their former place, while the one hit with the hoop takes it and throws it, making it roll towards the players on the other side. As it rolls he says to them: " Ho! tatanka he gle, Ho! there is a buffalo returning to you." When the stick does not fall out of the heart, they say the hoop belongs to the player who threw the stick. This is not a game of chance, but of skill, which has been played by large boys since the olden times. Bushotter [b] says that it is obsolescent.

DAKOTA (TETON).   Pine Ridge reservation, South Dakota.

Dr J. R. Walker [c] describes the game of " wands and hoops " under the name of woskate pain yankapi.

The name of the wands made of ash or choke-cherrywood, he gives as cansakala, and he says that while anyone may make these wands, it is believed that certain men can make them of superior excellence and give them magic powers, which may be exercised in favor of those who play with them. The rules of the game, with a story of its making and of its use to cause buffalo to come, are given by Dr Clark Wissler.

DAKOTA (YANKTON),   Fort Peck reservation, Montana. (Cat. no. 37606, Free Museum of Science and Art, University of Pennsylvania.)

Hoop of sapling (figure 673), 13 inches in diameter, with four marks at equal distances on both sides of its circumference. These marks are incised, and painted red and blue, as follows: Cross, painted blue, okizati, fork; longitudinal band, painted blue, sapapi, black spot; longitudinal band with transverse cut,

---

[a] The American Anthropologist, v. 4, p. 334, 1891.
[b] George Bushotter, a full-blood Dakota, Mr Dorsey's informant.
[c] Sioux Games. Journal of American Folk-Lore, v. 18, p. 278, Boston, 1905.

painted blue, ska, white; seven transverse notches, the outside and the middle ones blue, the others red, bahopi, notches.

Two pairs of sticks (figure 674), made of saplings, 25 inches in length, wrapped on both sides of the middle with cotton cloth and secured in pairs by a strip of cotton cloth fastened in the middle. One pair is painted red and has a small piece of red flannel fastened to each of the sticks. The other pair is blue, with similar black flags. Collected by the writer in 1900.

These implements were made by Siyo Sapa, Black Chicken, a renegade Hunkpapa and a former member of Sitting Bull's band. He gave the name of the game as pain yanka ichute and that of the darts as ichute.[a]

FIG. 673. Game hoop; diameter, 13 inches; Yankton Dakota Indians, Montana; cat. no. 37606, Free Museum of Science and Art, University of Pennsylvania.

The maker stated also that in the old time buffalo hide and deer skin were never employed in making the implements for this game; always, instead, something of no value, as old rags. He said that many years ago the Indians saw two buffalo bulls rolling this ring.

FIG. 674. Darts for hoop game; length, 25 inches; Yankton Dakota Indians, Montana; cat. no. 37606, Free Museum of Science and Art, University of Pennsylvania.

DAKOTA (YANKTON). Fort Peck, Montana. (Cat. no. 37607, Free Museum of Science and Art, University of Pennsylvania.)

A ring made of cotton cloth, wrapped round and round, and painted red; diameter, 3 inches. Two sticks, 32 inches in length, wrapped with rags, and having a curved piece fastened at one end and a cord stretched across like the string of a bow, connecting it with the stick; also two crosspieces, fastened at about equal distances from the ends, across the stick. These

---

[a] Pa-in'-yan-ka, to shoot or throw a stick through a hoop when rolling; painyanka kiċunpi, the game of shooting through a hoop; i-cu'-te, something to shoot with, as the arrows one uses in a game. (Riggs's Dakota-English Dictionary, Washington, 1890.)

crosspieces are secured by a stout peg placed between them and the stick, and a piece of twig is bent and fastened so that its ends project upward for a distance of about 1½ inches, just above the crossbars. One of the sticks is painted red and has a piece of red flannel attached to the bow, and the other is painted blue, with a black cloth flag.

Collected by the writer in 1900.

The game is called ha-ka'-ku-te, or ha-ka' shooting, receiving its name from the sticks, ha-ká. Each man has a stick; the ring, can-hde'-ska, is rolled and it must go on one of the points to count. The name ha-ka' means branching, having many prongs, like some deer horns.[a] My informant defined it as forked.

Eno.[b] North Carolina.

John Lederer [c] says:

Their town is built round a field, where in their sports they exercise with so much labor and violence, and in so great numbers, that I have seen the ground wet with the sweat that dropped from their bodies; their chief recreation is slinging of stones.

John Lawson [d] says:

These Indians are much addicted to a sport they call chenco, which is carried on with a staff and a bowl made of stone, which they trundle upon a smooth place, like a bowling green, made for that purpose, as I have mentioned before.

———— (?) Camden, South Carolina. (Free Museum of Science and Art, University of Pennsylvania.)

Cat. no. 13602. Biconcave disk of white quartzite (figure 675a), finely polished, 5¼ inches in diameter.

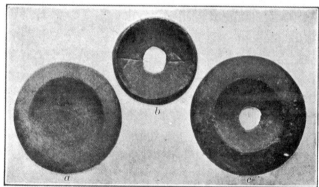

FIG. 675 a, b, c. Chunkee stones; diameters, 5¼, 4, and 4⅜ inches; Eno (?) Indians, Camden, South Carolina; cat. no. 13602, 13556, 13603, Free Museum of Science and Art, University of Pennsylvania.

Cat. no. 13556. Biconcave disk of quartzite, stained yellow and

[a] Riggs's Dakota-English Dictionary, Washington, 1890.
[b] It is doubtful whether the Eno were of Siouan stock; they may have been Iroquoian.
[c] Discoveries of John Lederer, p. 18, London, 1672; Rochester, 1902.
[d] History of Carolina, p. 57, London, 1714.

highly polished by use, 4 inches in diameter and $1\frac{1}{8}$ inches thick at the edge, the edge slightly convex, the interior hollowed in symmetrical cup-shaped cavities, with a hole $1\frac{1}{4}$ inches in diameter in the middle. On one side there are two incised forked marks, as shown in figure 675b.

Cat. no. 13603. Biconcave disk of yellow quartzite (figure 675c), $4\frac{5}{8}$ inches in diameter.

HIDATSA. Fort Clark, North Dakota.

Maximilian, Prince of Wied,[a] describing a visit to a village of this tribe on the 27th of November, 1833, says:

We observed many very handsome young men, in fine new dresses, some of whom were playing the game called billiards [plate x].

——— Fort Atkinson, North Dakota.

Mr Henry A. Boller says:[b]

The favorite game appeared to be one which we called billiards, and a space outside the pickets of the village was beaten as smooth and hard as a floor by those who engaged in it. This game is played by couples; the implements are a round stone and two sticks 7 or 8 feet long, with bunches of feathers tied on at regular intervals. The players start together, each carrying his pole in a horizontal position, and run along until the one who has the stone, throws it, giving it a rolling motion, when each watching his chance, throws the stick. The one who comes nearest (which is determined by the marks on the stick) has the stone for the next throw. Horses, blankets, robes, guns, etc., are staked at this game, and I have frequently seen Indians play until they had lost everything.

Subsequently, in describing a winter camp, he says:[c]

In order to enjoy their amusement of " billiards," some of its devotees cleared off a level piece of ground, between the two lower camps, and planted a line of bushes and underbrush, to form a partial barrier against the wind. Logs were placed on each side of the " alley " to keep the sticks (or cues) from glancing off.

MANDAN. Missouri river, North Dakota.

Lewis and Clark [d] say:

Notwithstanding the extreme cold, we observed the Indians at the village engaged out in the open air at a game which resembled billiards more than anything we had seen, and which we incline to suspect may have been acquired by ancient intercourse with the French of Canada. From the first to the second chief's lodge, a distance of about 50 yards, was covered with timber smoothed and joined so as to be as level as the floor of one of our houses, with a battery at the end to stop the rings; these rings were of clay-stone and flat, like the chequers for drafts, and the sticks were about 4 feet long, with two short pieces at one end in the form of a mace, so fixed that the whole will slide along

[a] Travels in the Interior of North America, translated by H. Evans Lloyd, p. 422, London, 1843.
[b] Among the Indians: Eight Years in the Far West, 1858–1866, p. 159, Philadelphia, 1868.
[c] Ibid., p. 196.
[d] History of an Expedition under the Command of Captains Lewis and Clark to the Sources of the Missouri, v. 1, p. 143, Philadelphia, 1814.

the board. Two men fix themselves at one end, each provided with a stick, and one of them with a ring; then they run along the board, and about halfway slide the sticks after the ring.

Catlin [a] says:

The game of tchung-kee, a beautiful athletic exercise, which they seem to be almost unceasingly practicing whilst the weather is fair and they have nothing else of moment to demand their attention. This game is decidedly their favorite amusement, and is played near to the village on a pavement of clay, which has been used for that purpose until it has become as smooth and hard as a floor. For this game two champions form their respective parties, by choosing alternately the most famous players, until their requisite numbers are made up. Their bettings are then made, and their stakes are held by some of the chiefs or others present. The play commences [figure 676] with two (one from each

Fig. 676. The game of tchung-kee; Mandan Indians, North Dakota; from Catlin.

party), who start off upon a trot, abreast of each other, and one of them rolls in advance of them, on the pavement, a little ring of 2 or 3 inches in diameter. cut out of a stone; and each one follows it up with his "tchung-kee" (a stick of 6 feet in length, with little bits of leather projecting from its sides of an inch or more in length), which he throws before him as he runs, sliding it along upon the ground after the ring, endeavoring to place it in such a position when it stops, that the ring may fall upon it, and receive one of the little projections of leather through it, which counts for game 1, or 2, or 4, according to the position of the leather on which the ring is lodged. The last winner always has the rolling of the ring, and both start and throw the tchung-kee together; if either fails to receive the ring or to lie in a certain position, it is a forfeiture of the amount of the number he was nearest to, and he loses his throw; when another steps into his place. This game is a very difficult one to describe, so as to give an exact

[a] The Manners, Customs, and Condition of the North American Indians, v. 1, p. 132, London, 1841.

idea of it, unless one can see it played—it is a game of great beauty and fine bodily exercise, and these people become excessively fascinated with it, often gambling away everything they possess and even, sometimes, when everything else was gone, have been known to stake their liberty upon the issue of these games, offering themselves slaves to their opponents in case they get beaten.[a]

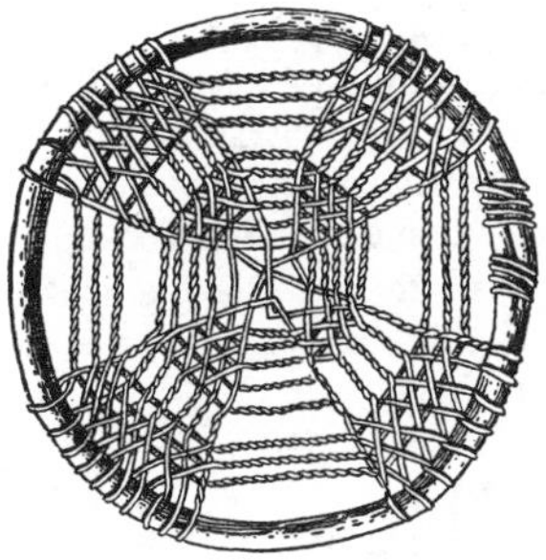

MANDAN. Fort Clark, North Dakota.

Maximilian, Prince of Wied, says: [b]

The game called billiards, by the French Canadians, is played by two young men, with long poles, which are often bound with leather, and have various ornaments attached to them. On a long, straight, level course, or a level path in or near the village, they roll a hoop, 3 or 4 inches in diameter, covered with leather, and throw the

FIG. 677. Netted hoop and pole; Mandan Indians, North Dakota; from Maximilian, Prince of Wied.

pole at it; and the success of the game depends upon the pole passing through it. This game is also practiced among the Manitaries [Hidatsa], and is described in Major Long's Travels to the Rocky Mountains as being played by the Pawnees, who, however, have hooked sticks, which is not the case with the tribes mentioned.

About the middle of March, when the weather is fine, the children and young men play with a hoop, in the interior of which strips of leather are interwoven; its diameter is about a foot [figure 677]. This hoop is either rolled or thrown, and they thrust at it with a pointed stick; he who approaches the center most nearly is the winner. . . .

As soon as the ice in the rivers breaks up, they run to the banks and throw this interlaced hoop into the water.

---

[a] The following account by the Abbé E. H. Domenech, who does not specify the tribe or locality, is probably taken from Catlin. (Seven Years' Residence in the Great Deserts of North America, v. 2, p. 197, London, 1860.)

"Their game of Spear and Ring is extremely curious and difficult. The players are divided into two camps, for Indians are fond of collective parties in which are many conquerors, and consequently many conquered. The stakes and bets are deposited in the care of an old man; then a hard smooth ground, without vegetation of any kind, is chosen, in the middle of which is placed perpendicularly a stone ring of about 3 inches diameter. When all is prepared the players (armed with spears 6 or 7 feet long, furnished with small shields a little apart from each other, sometimes with bits of leather) rush forward, two at a time, one from each camp; they stoop so as to place their spears on a horizontal level with the ring, so that they may pass through it, the great test of skill being to succeed without upsetting it. Each small shield or bit of leather that passes through counts for a point: the victory remains to the player who has most points, or he who upsets the ring at the last hit."

"Some Indians render the game still more difficult by playing it as follows. One of the players takes the ring in his hand and sends it rolling, with all his strength, as far as possible on the prepared ground; his adversary, who is by his side, starts full speed after it to stop it, so as to string it on his spear as far as the last little shield."

[b] Travels in the Interior of North America, translated by H. Evans Lloyd, p. 358, London, 1843.

OMAHA. Nebraska.

Rev. J. Owen Dorsey [a] describes the following game:

Banañ'ge-kíde, Shooting at the banañge, or rolling wheel. This is played by two men. Each one has in his hand two sticks, about as thick as one's little finger, which are connected in the middle by a thong not over 4 inches in length. These sticks measure about 3½ feet in length. Those of one player are red, and those of the other are black. The wheel which is rolled is about 2½ feet in diameter, its rim is half an inch thick, and it extends about an inch from the circumference toward the center. On this side of the rim that measures an inch, are four figures [figure 679]. The first is called máxu, marked with a knife, or mág¢eze, cut in stripes with a knife. The second is sábĕ tĕ, the black one. The third is áki¢ítĕ, crossing each other. The fourth is jiñgá tcĕ, the little one, the little one, or máxu jiñgá tcĕ, the little one marked with a knife. The players agree which one of the figures shall be waqúbe for the game; that is, what card players call trumps. The wheel is pushed and caused to roll along, and when it has almost stopped, each man hits gently at it to make it fall on the sticks. Should the sticks fall on the top of the wheel, it does not count. When a player succeeds in lodging his sticks in such a way that he touches the waqúbe, he wins many sticks or arrows. When figures are touched by one or both of his sticks, he calls out the number. When any two of the figures have been touched, he says: "Naⁿbaⁿ' a-ú hă," "I have wounded it twice." If three figures have been hit, he says, "¢áb ¢iⁿ a-ú hă," "I have wounded three." Twenty arrows or sticks count as a blanket, twenty-five as a gun, and one hundred as a horse.

In the story of "The Man who had a Corn-woman and a Buffalo-woman as wives," translated by Doctor Dorsey,[b] it is related that the "buffalo bulls were playing this game." He defines the name as "to shoot at something caused to roll by pushing."

Doctor Dorsey describes also—

ɟá¢iⁿ-jáhe, or Stick and Ring. ɟá¢iⁿ-jáhe is a game played by two men. At each end of the playground are two búɟa, or rounded heaps of earth.

A ring [figure 678] of rope or hide, the wa¢ígije, is rolled along the ground, and each player tries to dart a stick through it as it goes. He runs very swiftly after the hoop and thrusts the stick with considerable force. If the hoop turns aside as it rolls it is not difficult to thrust a stick in it. The stick [figure 678A] is about 4 feet long. D is the end that is thrust at the hoop. B B are the gaqa or forked ends for catching at the hoop. C C are made of ha násage, wéabasta násage íkaⁿ taⁿ, stiff hide, fastened to the forked ends with stiff wéabasta, or material used for the soles of moccasins. These ha násage

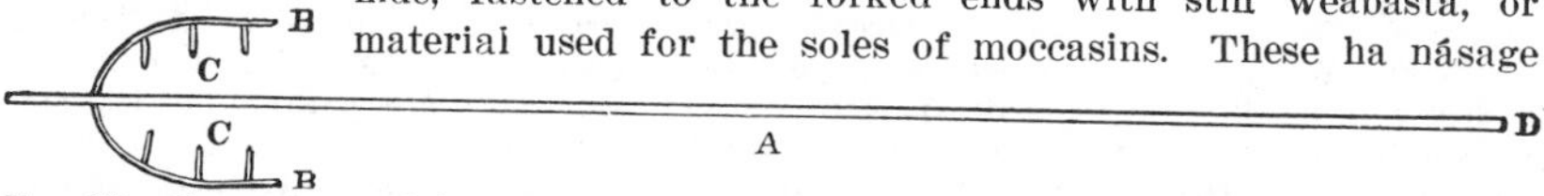

FIG. 678. Game ring and dart; length of dart, about 4 feet; Omaha Indians, Nebraska; from Dorsey.

often serve to prevent the escape of the hoop from the forked ends. Sometimes these ends alone catch or hook the loop. Sometimes the end D is thrust through it. When both sticks catch the hoop neither one wins.

The stakes are eagle feathers, robes, blankets, arrows, earrings, necklaces, etc.[c]

[a] Omaha Sociology. Third Annual Report of the Bureau of Ethnology, p. 335, 1884.

[b] The Çegiha Language. Contributions to North American Ethnology, v. 6, p. 162, Washington, 1890.

[c] Omaha Sociology. Third Annual Report of the Bureau of Ethnology, p. 337, 1884.

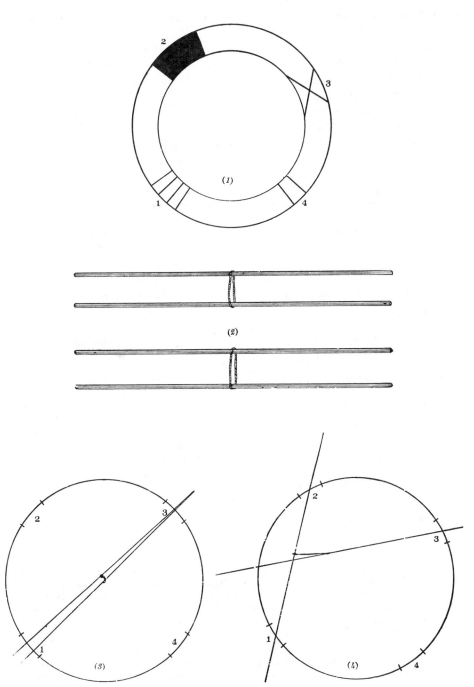

FIG. 679. Ring-and-dart game: Omaha Indians, Nebraska: 1, the wheel, or banañge; 2, the sticks; 3, naⁿ-baⁿ a-ú hă: 4. ¢ábe¢iⁿ a-ú hă; from Dorsey.

OMAHA. Nebraska. (Cat. no. 37776, Peabody Museum of American
    Archæology and Ethnology.)

Implements for the game of bhadhiñ zhahe, consisting of two sticks
    4 feet 2 inches in length, each with an arc attached to one end
    to form a kind of barb, and a flexible ring wrapped with deer-
    skin, about 6 inches in diameter (figure 680).

These were collected by Miss Alice C. Fletcher.

The hoop is called wadhigizi and the sticks are known as wízhahe.

Mr Francis La Flesche described the preceding game to the writer
under the name of pauthin zhahae, or Pawnee zhahae, as played with

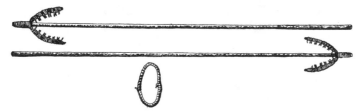

FIG. 680. Game ring and darts; length of darts, 4 feet 2 inches; diameter of ring, about 6 inches;
    Omaha Indians, Nebraska; cat. no. 37776, Peabody Museum of American Archæology and
    Ethnology.

a hoop of buckskin, wathegezhae, about 4 inches in diameter, and a
javelin, waijhahe, about 5 feet long:

The latter has two little branches about 4 inches in length and bent backward
at the point. Four pieces of rawhide are fastened to each of these, turned
inward to form a kind of barbs.

There are two contestants, one of whom throws the hoop, and, as it rolls along
the ground, both endeavor to drive their javelins, which they grasp in the
middle, through it. If the hoop is penetrated it counts 2, but if the hoop catches
on one of the barbs it only counts 1. If the hoop is caught on both of the barbs
it counts nothing. The game is usually 10. The one who scores throws the
hoop. There is a long track, and the players run back and forth. The Omaha
originally had the game under another name.

OSAGE. Missouri and Arkansas.

John D. Hunter says:[a]

Playing the hoop is performed on an oblong piece of ground, prepared
for the purpose. Three parallel lines run the whole length of the plot, at about
15 yards distance from each other. On the exterior ones, the opposing parties,
which generally consist of from twelve to eighteen persons, arrange themselves
about 10 paces apart, each individual fronting intermediate to his two opposite
or nearest opponents. On the central line, extended to a few paces beyond the
wings of the two parties, stand two persons facing each other. It is their part
of the play alternately to roll a hoop of about the diameter of a common
hogshead, with all their strength, from one to the other. The object for triumph between these two is, who shall catch the opponent's hoop the oftenest,

[a] Manners and Customs of Several Indian Tribes located West of the Mississippi,
p. 273, Philadelphia, 1823.

and of the contending parties, which shall throw the greatest number of balls through the hoop as it passes rapidly along the intervening space. Judges are appointed, usually from among the old men, to determine which party is victorious, and to distribute the prizes, which, on some particular occasions consist of beaver and deer skins, moccasins, leggings, etc. but more usually of shells, nuts, and other trifles.

PONCA. Fort Pierre, South Dakota.

Maximilian, Prince of Wied,[a] thus refers to a young Ponca Indian named Ho-Ta-Ma, among the Dakota at Fort Pierre, a handsome, friendly man, who often amused himself with different games:

Frequently he was seen with his comrades playing what was called the hoop game, at which sticks covered with leather are thrown at a hoop in motion.

SKITTAGETAN STOCK

HAIDA. Prince of Wales island, Alaska.

Dr C. F. Newcombe described a game which the Kaigani Haida call k'istaño and the Masset, tulstaonañ. The implements are a flat disk of hemlock twigs bound with cedar bark and a spear of salmon berry.

It is played with a ring. Two sides are chosen and the ring is thrown into the air, the object being to catch it on the point of a stick 9 feet long.

Another game the Kaigani Haida call kokankijao and the Masset, kokijao. A small ring of hemlock twig, with quite a long string tied to the edge, is placed anywhere in a circle of 3 feet drawn on a sandy place. The game is for the opposite player to put a stick, of which ten are given him, inside the ring, which, with the string, is hidden under earth when he is not looking.

Doctor Newcombe describes also the following game:

Ten pieces of kelp, 1 foot long, are placed in the ground at each end of a playing ground 20 feet long. There are two players on each side, each armed with a very sharp spear of salmon berry. The game is to pierce the kelp at the end opposite with the spears. One piece is very small, and if struck, the striker gets all the sticks. The players throw from a crouching position. The game is called hlqamginhlE.

HAIDA. British Columbia.

Dr J. R. Swanton [b] describes the following games:

"A woman's pubic bones" (Gao skū' dji).—This was a boy's game. Late in the spring, when a tall, slim plant called L!al, the pith of which was eaten, was at its best, the boys would collect a great quantity of the stalks. Then two would each drive a couple of sticks into the ground about 5 yards apart. After that, each would take about twenty sticks of the salmon-berry bush, and,

---

[a] Travels in the Interior of North America, translated by H. Evans Lloyd, p. 160, London, 1843.

[b] Contributions to the Ethnography of the Haida. Memoirs of the American Museum of Natural History, whole series, v. 8, p. 60, New York, 1905.

using them as spears, alternately try to drive one of them between the adversary's posts, or stick it into the ground beyond, so that it would rest on their tops. Each boy would then bid a certain number of L!al stalks, and after they had used up all of their spears, he who scored the most hits won all that had been put up by his adversary. If he were one point ahead, he got nothing more; but if he were two points ahead, he won as much again; if he were three points ahead, twice as much, and so on.

"Knocking something over by shooting" (Tc!îtgada'ldaña).—This was played by older people. Toward the end of spring a crowd would go out and set up a piece of board about 3 inches wide and 4 feet high. Then, forming a line some distance away, they would shoot at it with blunt arrows in succession, beginning at one end. He who struck the stake first won all of the arrows shot that time around, except the others that struck. Each person had one shot at every round. Sometimes they played against each other by companies, of which there might be as many as five or six. Indeed, a whole town often seems to have turned out, and the resulting contests to have extended over a long period of time. Toward the end some of the players, their supply of arrows being exhausted, would be compelled to manufacture new ones, often of inferior make. Two of these had to be paid in as an equivalent for one of the better class. For some religious reason they ceased playing with arrows as soon as winter began.

Xatxadī'da (perhaps a name for the pieces of spruce bark used in it).—This game was played in the spring. Two boys provided themselves with ten pieces of spruce bark apiece, each of which was doubled over and fastened along one edge. The opposite edge was the one on which they were to stand. Then they were set up in a row upon the ground, and the players endeavored to drive the same spears as those used in the previous game into each of them. He who first sent a spear into each of his opponent's pieces of bark won, although the opponent was sometimes allowed to have additional pieces.

TANOAN STOCK

Tigua. Isleta, New Mexico. (Cat. no. 22727, Free Museum of Science and Art, University of Pennsylvania.)

Ring of cotton cloth (figure 681), closely wrapped with a buckskin thong, $9\frac{1}{2}$ inches in diameter and $1\frac{1}{4}$ inches thick. The interior is divided into four quarters by two two-ply twisted thongs fastened to the interior and crossing at right angles. Five leather thongs are attached on each side of one of these radial thongs, above and below. The exterior of the ring is painted red, yellow, and blue; red on the sides, then a yellow band, with blue on the edge.

Two poles (figure 681), one 57 and the other 60 inches in length, painted red two-thirds of their length, with blue running zigzag over the red. Eight long buckskin thongs are fastened at a point 14 inches from the end of each pole, and again the same number at another point, 33 inches from the end.

These were collected by the writer in 1902.

The ring is called mar-kur, and the poles shi-a-fit, spears. The ring is rolled, and the poles are hurled at it. The counts are made according to the set of thongs nearest the striking end. If the pole penetrates the ring, and all the thongs pass entirely through it, it counts 10. If one thong remains caught in the ring, it counts 1; if two remain, 2, and so on. The thongs attached to the interior of

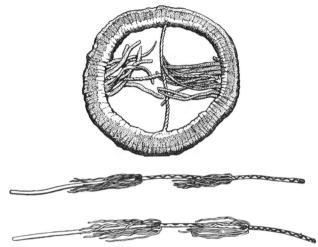

FIG 681. Game ring and darts; diameter of ring, 9¼ inches; length of darts, 57 and 60 inches; Tigua Indians, Isleta, New Mexico; cat. no. 22727, Free Museum of Science and Art, University of Pennsylvania.

the ring do not count, but serve to impede the passage of the pole and entangle its thongs. The game is played by men and boys, but it has not been played in Isleta for the past fifteen years. The writer was told that it is regarded as a Navaho game.

WAKASHAN STOCK

KWAKIUTL. British Columbia. (American Museum of Natural History.)

Cat. no. $\frac{16}{4791}$. Game ring (figure 682), wrapped with cedar bark; diameter, 9½ inches; width, 2 inches; designated as lamagikala gagayaxala, first kane, to be thrown high.

Cat. no. $\frac{16}{4792}$. Game ring like the preceding, 10 inches in diameter; designated as xwaligwagane, second kane, to be thrown high.

Cat. no. $\frac{16}{4793}$. Game ring like the preceding, 8 inches in diameter; designated as tilemyu, third kane, to be thrown very low.

Cat. no. $\frac{16}{4794}$. Game ring (figure 683), like the preceding, 1¾ wide and 8½ inches in diameter; designated as nepayu, the ring, kane, to be thrown at the other player to hurt him.

Cat. no. $\frac{16}{4795}$. Two sticks (figure 684), saplings, 53¼ inches in length; designated as tsatsigalayu, being the sticks for catching the above-mentioned rings.

Collected by Mr George Hunt, who states that the game is played by young men.

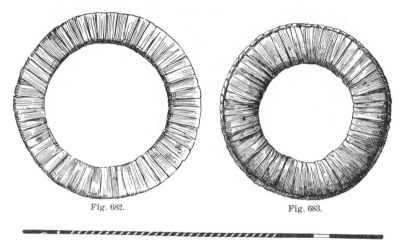

Fig. 682.   Fig. 683.

Fig. 684.

FIG. 682. Game ring; diameter, 9½ inches; Kwakiutl Indians, British Columbia; cat. no. $\frac{16}{4791}$, American Museum of Natural History.

FIG. 683. Game ring; diameter, 8½ inches; Kwakiutl Indians, British Columbia; cat. no. $\frac{16}{4794}$, American Museum of Natural History.

FIG. 684. Dart for ring game; length, 53¼ inches; Kwakiutl Indians, British Columbia; cat. no. $\frac{16}{4795}$, American Museum of Natural History.

KWAKIUTL. Nawiti, British Columbia.

Dr C. F. Newcombe describes the ring-and-dart game under the name of kinxe, the ring being called kani, and the stick, dsadsigala·iu:

Each player has one ring and one stick, 4 to 8 feet long or more, according to taste, and made of willow, partly peeled to show ownership marks. There are two sides of equal numbers, who agree who shall first throw the quoit-like disk. Then each side throw alternately or altogether, as they please. The object is to catch the ring, either in the air or running along the ground, with the stick, and any or all can try at one time, but as all disks can be in the air at once this is not usual. There is no regular scoring. If one disk is caught, it is kept until the whole ten are thrown. If all ten are not caught at one flight or play, they are thrown back to the opposite side. The game is won when one side catches all ten thrown in one play, and the losers are chased by winners, who first say: " Now we have all your kani; " " Now whom will you send out to take the pay? "

If a loser steps out the winners throw their kani at this one as hard as they can from any distance. The victim usually protects himself with a blanket. If he can catch any in his blanket, he can retaliate. If no one comes out to take the penalty the whole side is chased and thrown at.

—— Blunden harbor, British Columbia. (Cat. no. 37907, Free Museum of Science and Art, University of Pennsylvania.)

Perforated lava disk (figure 685), 5 inches in diameter and 1⅜ inches thick.

Collected in March, 1901, by Dr C. F. Newcombe, who describes it, under the name of laua·iu, as used in a game:

The Kwakiutl say that these stone disks are no longer used. According to Mr George Hunt, they were originally rolled in sets of four of different sizes and were shot at with bows and arrows.

Dr Franz Boas, in his Kwakiutl Texts,[a] describes a game played with these stones between the birds of the upper world and the myth people, i. e., "all the animals and all the birds." The four stones were called, respectively, the "mist-covered gambling stone," the "rainbow gambling stone," the "cloud-covered gambling stone," and the "carrier of the world." The woodpecker and the other myth birds played on one side, and the Thunder bird and the birds of the upper world on the other, in two rows, thus · · · · · · ————. The gambling · · · · · · stones were thrown along the middle between the two tribes of birds, and they speared them with their beaks. The Thunder bird and the birds of the upper world were beaten in this contest. This myth is given as an explanation of the reason for playing the game with the gambling stones. They are called laelae.

FIG. 685. Stone game ring; diameter, 5 inches; Kwakiutl (Tenaktak) Indians; cat. no. 37907, Free Museum of Science and Art, University of Pennsylvania.

KWAKIUTL. Nawiti, British Columbia. (Cat. no. 85851, Field Columbian Museum.)

Four wooden darts (figure 686), 38 inches in length, in two pairs, distinguished by burnt designs. One pair has broad flat points and the other tapering blunt points.

Collected in 1904 by Dr C. F. Newcombe, and described by him as used in the spear-and-kelp game, sakaqes.

FIG. 686. Dart for spear-and-kelp game; length, 38 inches; Kwakiutl Indians, British Columbia; cat. no. 85851, Field Columbian Museum.

The game is played by four players armed with spears, sákiåk'ŭs, or darts of yellow cedar like the above, there being two sides with two players to a side. The darts are usually pointed with deer shin bones, 6 inches long, inserted in

[a] Memoirs of the American Museum of Natural History, whole series, v. 5, p. 295, New York, 1902.

the split ends and not barbed. The targets are two piles of kelp, 10 to 15 feet apart. These consist of some twenty pieces, the largest 2¼ inches in diameter, and from that down to less than the diameter of a finger, which lie transversely to the dart thrower. Standing up behind the bunch is a kelp head, which, however, is hidden by the pile from the player. If a thrower impales one or more kelp, both spear and kelp are thrown to him. If he misses, the opposite side throws. The winner is he who first gets all the kelp tubes.

MAKAH. Neah bay, Washington. (Cat. no. 37384, Free Museum of Science and Art, University of Pennsylvania.)

Ring (figure 687) made of a core of grass wrapped with braided cedar bark, 12 inches in diameter. Collected by the writer in 1900.

Dr George A. Dorsey [a] describes a game called dutaxchaias:

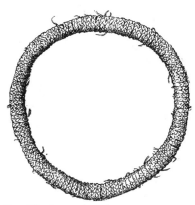

FIG. 687. Game ring; diameter, 12 inches; Makah Indians, Neah bay, Washington; cat. no. 37384, Free Museum of Science and Art, University of Pennsylvania.

This game is played by young men, generally in the spring, or it may be played at any time of the year. The ring (dutapi) is of cedar bark wound tightly and carefully braided. Two specimens were collected, one of which has seen considerable usage. In playing the game, two converging lines of from six to ten men on each side are formed. The man at the apex of the converging lines takes the ring in his hand and rolls it forward between the lines as far as he can; as the ring begins to lose its momentum, and wabbles preparatory to falling, all shoot at it with an arrow (tsik'hati) from an ordinary bow (bistati). When the ring is struck by an arrow of one side or the other (quilah = winner), the losing side pay over an arrow as forfeit. The game ends at any time by mutual consent, or when one side or the other has won all the arrows of the opposing side.

Doctor Dorsey describes also the game of katikas—sharp-stick slanting:

This game is . . . played by boys. On the side of a hill ten or more sharpened sticks are thrust into the ground at intervals of from two to three inches. Each has his individual set of sticks, or goal. One of the players rolls down the slope a large piece of kelp, 6 inches in length. If it so rolls as to impale itself on one of the sticks of one of the other players, he withdraws the stick from the earth and throws the kelp up in the air and attempts to catch it on the point of the stick. If successful, he retains the stick. which constitutes the game.

---

[a] Games of the Makah Indians of Neah Bay. The American Antiquarian, v. 23, p. 69, 1901.

NOOTKA. British Columbia.

Dr Franz Boas [a] says:

The games of the Nootka are identical with those of the neighboring tribes. A favorite game is played with hoops, which are rolled over the ground. Then a spear is thrown at them, which must pass through the hoop (nūtnū'tc).

WASHO. Near Truckee, Nevada.

Dr J. W. Hudson describes the hoop-and-spear game among this tribe, under the name of pululpaiyayapu, the hoop being called by the same name:

The hoop is of willow covered with buckskin, 12 inches in diameter. One player rolls it rapidly past his opponent, who throws at it. Impaling the hoop counts one. Seven is the game, which is counted with sticks. The lance is called mak.

——— Woodfords, Alpine county, California.

Dr J. W. Hudson describes a man's game in which a rolling hoop of willow is shot at with arrows by an opponent, under the name of pululpaiyapa:

Pulul, hoop; baiyap, to shoot at. The game is also played by casting a lance at a target hoop.

In another form of the game called pulultumpes—pulul, hoop; tumpes, to cast, the hoop is held in the hand and the opponent endeavors to catch between his fingers the small dart thrown by his opponent. In this game the outstretched fingers occupy the center of the hoop. In a variation of this an actual arrow is cast, the opponent being often hurt in the hand.

MOHAVE. Fort Mohave, Arizona. (Cat. no. 60264, Field Columbian Museum.)

Ring of bark, 6½ inches in diameter, wrapped with cord (figure 688); and two poles, 12 feet in length, rounded and tapering from butt to tip.

Collected by Mr John J. McKoin, who furnishes the following account of the game:

FIG. 688. Game ring; diameter, 6½ inches; Mohave Indians, Arizona; cat. no. 60264, Field Columbian Museum.

This game is played with two poles and one ring. The poles are called co-tool-wa, and the ring cop-o-cho-ra. These poles are respectively marked with one or two circles carved upon the larger end. Each player chooses an umpire, who rules upon plays. They then agree upon the pole which each is to have and as to who is to make the first trial with the ring. Suppose a player with the pole marked with one circle gets the first trial with the ring. He then throws the pole at the ring while it is rolling or at such point as he believes the ring will fall, the object being to place the pole so that the ring will fall upon it in such a manner that the umpire, standing over the pole at the point where the ring falls and looking perpendicularly downward through the ring, can see the pole. This counts 1 point. If the umpire sees both poles, no points are made, and the player with the ring tries again. He continues to try until he makes the number of points agreed upon with the player of the pole marked with two circles in such a manner that the grave and dignified umpire, making decisions as before explained, decides the point in his favor and awards the ring to him, that player No. 2 may make a trial of his skill. The player who first makes the number of points agreed upon is declared the winner.

MOHAVE. Colorado river, Arizona. (Cat. no. 10116, Peabody Museum of American Archæology and Ethnology.

Implements of ring-and-pole game, consisting of three rings of bark wrapped with twine made of yucca fiber, each about 7 inches in diameter (figure 689). One ring is overwrapped with strips

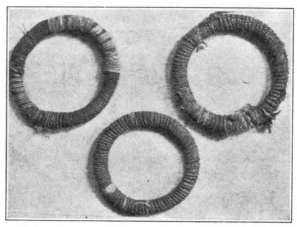

FIG. 689. Rings for ring and pole; diameter, about 7 inches; Mohave Indians, Arizona: cat. no. 10116, Peabody Museum of American Archæology and Ethnology.

of cotton rags of different colors, white, red, and purple, for about two-thirds of its circumference. There are two poles, one perfect, 5 feet 8 inches in length. The other consists of parts of two poles, which have been cut in half for convenience in transportation and do not mate. Collected by Dr Edward Palmer.

Lieut. A. W. Whipple, U. S. Army,[a] describes the following game:

Some of the young men selected a level spot, 40 paces in length, for a playground, and amused themselves in their favorite sport with hoop and poles. The hoop is 6 inches in diameter, and made of an elastic cord. The poles are straight and about 15 feet in length. Rolling the hoop from one end of the course, two

---

[a] Reports of Explorations and Surveys to ascertain the Most Practicable and Economical Route for a Railroad from the Mississippi River to the Pacific Ocean, v. 3, p. 114, Washington, 1856.

persons chase it halfway, and at the same instant throw their poles. He who succeeds in piercing the hoop wins the game.

WALAPAI. Walapai reservation, Arizona. (Cat. no. 15129, Field Columbian Museum.)

Ring (figure 690), interior core wrapped with strips of cotton cloth, with buckskin outside, 6½ inches in diameter; and two cottonwood poles, 12 feet in length. The poles taper to a point and the butts are marked differently.

Two other sets have rings wrapped with cord. One ring (cat. no. 63344, figure 691) is 7 inches in diameter, and another (cat. no. 63345), wrapped with coarse cord, is of the same diameter. Four poles (cat. no. 63344) are 13 feet 8 inches in length.

These were collected by Mr Henry P. Ewing, who gives the following account of the game, which he describes under the name of tutava:

Fig. 690.   Fig. 691.

FIG. 690. Game ring; diameter, 6¼ inches; Walapai Indians, Arizona; cat. no. 15129, Field Columbian Museum.

FIG. 691. Game ring; diameter, 7 inches; Walapai Indians, Arizona; cat. no. 63344, Field Columbian Museum.

The tu-ta-va game is played with two long poles, called tu-a-a, and a hoop, called tav-a-chu-ta. To play, two persons, always men, select a piece of ground about 100 feet long and 20 feet wide, smooth, level, and clear. Standing side by side at one end of this tract, facing the other end, the men hold their poles in both hands and start to run toward the other end of the ground. As they do so the one who holds the hoop throws, or rolls, it along the ground in front of them, and as it rolls each throws his pole, end foremost, giving it a sliding motion, so that it slides along the ground for some distance ahead of the runners. The object is to get the hoop to fall so that one edge of it will rest on the pole, while the other rests on the ground. Should this happen, it counts the contestant using that pole 1. Should the hoop fall so that it rests over the point of the pole, but the pole does not go through it, that counts 4 and wins the game, 4 points constituting the game. If the pole goes through the hoop it does not count anything, and unless the hoop lies fully up on the pole it does not count. It will be seen that this is a game of skill as well as of chance, and is, or was, often played for big stakes—ponies, guns, women, anything, everything.

The game was very popular with the men, and twenty years ago, when the weather was fair, there was not a camp but a game of tu-ta-va could be seen near it all day long. It developed the muscles by running and throwing the pole. The Indians seldom play this game now.

YUMA. Colorado river, California.

Maj. S. P. Heintzleman, U. S. Army, says [a] in 1853:

A favorite amusement is a play called mo-turp, or, in Spanish, redendo [redondo?]. It is played with two poles 15 feet long, an inch and a half in diameter, and a ring wrapped with twine, 4 inches in diameter. One rolls this ring along the ground and both run after it, projecting their poles forward. He on whose pole the ring stops counts 1, and he has the privilege to roll the ring. Four counts game. They do not count when a pole enters the ring. Old and young, chiefs and the common people, all take great delight in this game. They follow it for hours in the hot sun, raising clouds of dust, the perspiration making their dusky skins glossy.

———— Arizona.

Dr H. F. C. ten Kate, jr,[b] says he saw a group of half-naked, painted young men who were intent in the game of otoerboek. This game is played by two men, each armed with a very long wooden pole, who run side by side. One of them rolls a wooden ring, kaptzor, rapidly ahead. At the same time they hastily throw their poles at the ring so that it is stopped. He was not certain whether the sticks had to be thrown through the ring or whether the count depended upon the particular way in which the poles lay beside it.

ZUÑIAN STOCK

ZUÑI. Zuñi, New Mexico. (Cat. no. 3062, Brooklyn Institute Museum.)

Ring of bent twig (figure 692), 5 inches in diameter, wound with blue yarn, and having a piece of blue yarn, 18 inches in length, tied at the point of juncture, and a peeled twig, 30 inches in length, painted red, and tied with blue yarn at four places equidistant along its length. Collected by the writer in 1903.

The game is called tsikonai ikoshnakia, ring play; the ring is called antsikonai, and the stick, tslamtashaikoshai, long stick for play. One man has the ring, which he rolls, and the other the stick, which he throws after it. When the stick penetrates the ring it counts according to the particular string on the stick against which it lies, as shown in figure 692. In going out to play the player carries the ring suspended over his shoulder by the end and the stick held upright in his right hand.

Mrs Matilda Coxe Stevenson [c] describes the game of hotkämonne:

Implements: two slender sticks, each passed through a piece of corncob, the stick sharpened at one end and having two hawk plumes inserted in the other end; ball of yucca ribbons [figure 693].

---

[a] House of Representatives, Executive Document 76, Thirty-fourth Congress, third session, 1857, p. 49. See also Lieut. W. H. Emory in Report of the United States and Mexican Boundary Survey, v. 1, p. 111, Washington, 1857.

[b] Reizen en Onderzoekingen in Noord-Amerika, p. 108, Leiden, 1885.

[c] Zuñi Games. American Anthropologist, n. s., v. 5, p. 491, 1903.

The yucca ball is placed on the ground and the sticks are thrown at it from a short distance. The ball must be penetrated. If the first player strikes the ball, the stick is allowed to remain in place until the other party plays. If both sticks strike the ball, it is a draw. If the second stick fails to strike, it remains where it falls and the first player removes his stick from the ball and throws again. The one who strikes the ball the greater number of times wins the game.

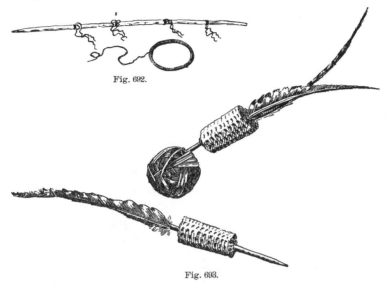

Fig. 692.

Fig. 693.

FIG. 692. Game ring and dart; diameter of ring, 5 inches; length of stick, 30 inches; Zuñi Indians, Zuñi, New Mexico; cat. no. 3062, Brooklyn Institute Museum.
FIG. 693. Yucca ball and corncob darts; Zuñi Indians, Zuñi, New Mexico; from Mrs Stevenson.

Hó'kämonně is one of the most precious games of the Zuñi, it being among those offered to the Gods of War at the winter solstice. The game is frequently played for rains, and when it occurs in this connection sacred meal is sprinkled on the ground before the ball is placed; the one who first penetrates the ball lifts it by the stick, and, drawing a breath from it, offers thanks to the gods that the rains are soon to come.

RING AND PIN

The game which I have designated as ring and pin has a wide distribution, similar to that of the hoop-and-pole-game, of which, as I have stated in the introduction, it may be regarded as a miniature and solitaire form. In the former game the ring or target is attached to a thong or cord by means of which it is swung in the air, the object being to catch it upon a pin or dart fastened to the other end of the thong. It is analogous to the well-known European game of cup and ball (Fr. bilboquet), in which the ball may be caught either in the cup or upon the pointed end of the catching implement. I have employed the name of ring and pin, suggested by Dr George A. Dorsey, as a matter of convenience, for the American game, although rings are among the objects least frequently used. In point of fact, the targets are of the greatest possible variety, both in form and material, ranging from a single hide ring among the Tewa (Hano) to strings of imbricated phalangeal bones (Algonquian, Athapascan, and Siouan tribes), salmon bones (Hupa, Pomo, Umatilla, Shasta), pumpkin rinds (Pima, Mohave), and, finally, to single objects perforated with holes, such as the skulls of small rodents (Eskimo, Paiute), bone copies thereof (Eskimo), seal bones (Eskimo, Clayoquot, Kwakiutl, Makah), or balls of tule (Klamath, Thompson Indians, Paiute) and bundles of pine twigs (Micmac, Passamaquoddy, Penobscot) and moose hair (Penobscot). When we examine the games played with strings of phalangeal bones, from among the northern range of tribes (Algonquian, Athapascan, and Siouan), the most numerously represented in our present collection, we discover that the number of bones is not constant, varying from three to nine, and that not infrequently they are pierced with transverse holes and numbered by means of notches from the bones nearest the pin end. These notches determine the count.

A pretty constant feature of this game is a flap of buckskin or other material attached to the extreme end of the string. This flap is perforated with holes which vary in number, and usually has a large hole in the center. In the Cree game (figure 705) there is the flap alone, a disk of stiff buckskin with twenty-three holes, the direct analogue of the netted hoop. In the Siouan games the flap is replaced with strings of glass beads, which count according to the number caught. The buckskin survives in a vestigial form in the Winnebago game (figure 740), as a piece of ribbon in that of the Sauk and Foxes (figure 713), and again as a tuft of hair in the Umatilla salmon-bone game (figure 731). The buckskin disk survives also as the principal feature of the cedar-bough game of the Passamaquoddy. The Eskimo game, played with a small netted hoop (figure 617), which I have included among the games of hoop and pole, occupies a position midway between the hoop game proper and the ring-and-pin games. The strings of salmon bone are directly analogous to the phalangeal bones, the same being true of the Pima and Mohave disks of pumpkin rind. In general, the material of the target depends upon the culture.

The rabbit and hare skulls occur among both the Paiute and the Eskimo. As is natural, the greatest variation from what may be regarded as the original type is found among the latter people, who copy the hare skull in ivory and make from the same material other implements representing the polar bear and fish. The ball of tule is found among nearly contiguous tribes. The cedar-twig and moose-hair target of the eastern Algonquian tribes is analogous to the archery target of the Crows and the Grosventres (figure 501).

Wire needles are now employed in the Arapaho, Cheyenne, Oglala, and other Algonquian and Siouan tribes, but originally they were all of wood or bone.

The counts are extremely varied. In the phalangeal-bone game the bones count progressively from the one nearest the pin. The loops of beads count 1 or 10; the holes in the leather, 2 or 4; the large central hole, more. The total count of the game also varies from 2, 4, 50, or 100, the commonest number, up to 2,000. The game is played both for stakes and as a child's amusement. The players are usually two in number, women and girls, or a youth and a girl, as suggested by its name of " love game " (Cheyenne) or the " lovers' game " (Penobscot). Mr Cushing informed me that in Zuñi a phallic significance was attached to the ring and pin. This corresponds with the symbolism of the hoop-and-pole game and serves to strengthen and confirm the theory I have advanced as to their interdependence. An object analogous to the ring-and-pin game of the Zuñi is found in a stick with a ring attached by a cord (figure 694), from an ancient shrine of the Little Fire society at Zuñi, in the Brooklyn Institute Museum. The ring represents the net shield of the War Gods, and the object may be considered as the ceremonial antetype of the ring-and-pin game.

ALGONQUIAN STOCK

ARAPAHO. Wind River reservation, Wyoming. (Cat. no. 36981, Free
        Museum of Science and Art, University of Pennsylvania.)
Four phalangeal bones (figure 695), each with ten perforations,

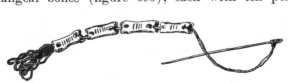

FIG. 695. Chetguetat; length of implement, 16¼ inches; Arapaho Indians, Wind River reservation, Wyoming; cat. no. 36981, Free Museum of Science and Art, University of Pennsylvania.

strung on a thong with a needle attached. The bone nearest the needle has three cuts on one side; the next, four; the next, five, and the last, six. Five beaded loops are at the end opposite the needle.

Another set (cat. no. 36982) in the same collection has three bones, each with eight lateral perforations. One bone has seven notches, another two, while the third is plain. Seven beaded loops and a similar brass ring are attached at the end opposite the needle.

Still another set (cat. no. 36983) has four bones, not perforated laterally, with two, three, four, and five transverse cuts, and three antelope hoofs at the end opposite the needle.

All these are implements for the game of chetguetat. Collected by the writer in 1900.

CHEYENNE. Oklahoma. (Cat. no. 178338, United States National Museum.)

Four phalangeal bones of the deer, perforated, and pierced with lateral perforations and marked with one, two, three, and four scratches; strung on a beaded cord with an iron needle attached, and having eight loops of red glass beads on the end opposite the needle.

These specimens were collected by Mr Louis L. Meeker, when teacher of manual training in the Cheyenne school, Darlington, Oklahoma, who furnished the following particulars concerning it in a communication on Cheyenne Games made to the United States Bureau of American Ethnology:

The ni-to-nis-dot or thrusting game of the Cheyenne is played with the four phalangeal bones from the fore or the hind feet of a deer. Sometimes two of the bones are from a fore foot and two from a hind foot, but this seems to be only when a new set is made of two old ones, part of which are broken.

Each bone is pierced with four rows of holes, four in a row, about equal distances apart, each row being on one of the faces of a bone, for the bones are somewhat quadrangular.

There is a small loop, called an earring, he-wus'-sis, attached on either side of one end of each bone by putting the cord of which it is made through one of the holes or through very small holes nearer the edge and pierced for that purpose.

Thus prepared, the four bones are strung like beads on a buckskin string or on a strand of beads strung on sinews. The larger end of each bone is toward the same end of the string, to which is attached a needle or piece of wire about 6 inches long, one end of which is coiled to make an eye to which the string is fastened. It is generally understood that originally this needle, or bodkin, was of bone and was used for piercing deerskin to sew it with sinews. Large thorns were also used.

The end of the string or strand of beads opposite that to which the needle is attached is composed of a bunch of loops, made, like the earings, of sinews, generally, if not always, strung with beads. The number of loops vary, so that the bunch may be sufficiently large to prevent the bones from slipping off. Perhaps ten loops is the proper number.

In the illustration Hi'-o-ni''-va, "Pipe woman," a camp Indian, is seated on a Government blanket with the game in her hand, ready to throw [figure 696].

The needle is held in the right hand, almost pen-fashion, but against the side of the forefinger at the joint next the nail. The coil that forms the eye of the needle is up, and the other end or point of the needle is where the point of the pen would be, but the needle is held close to the eye that the point may project as far as possible.

The string passes along the under side of the needle; the strand of bones hang down; the tassel of loops is held by the thumb and forefinger of the left hand, which loosen it at the proper moment for a slight movement of the right hand to swing it upward and forward until the chain of bones is in a horizontal position in front of the player. The needle is then thrust forward along the string on which the bones are strung, with the intention of catching one of the bones.

If it passes lengthwise through the first bone, it counts 10; through the second one, 20; the third, 30, and the fourth, 40. Should it enter the end of

FIG. 696. Cheyenne woman playing nitonisdot, Oklahoma; from photograph by Mr Louis L. Meeker.

the bone, but pass out at one of the holes, it counts but 1. If it passes through an earring, it counts but 1. Caught through the tassel of loops at the end it counts 50; or some say it counts 5 or 10 for each loop through which the needle passes. This, and giving a particular value to each hole, is either an innovation or a manner of counting in use only among older players. Children and ordinary players count the same for any hole and 50 for the end loops.

When more than two play, each side takes turns, and each player on a side, but it is not passed from one to another until there is a throw that does not count.

Each side has fifty sticks, which are passed back and forth as the play progresses. When one side has all the sticks, the game is ended. It is said that in olden times the sticks were redistributed and the game continued until exactly noon, when the party having fewest sticks prepared a feast for all.

CHEYENNE. Oklahoma. (Cat. no. 18610, Free Museum of Science and Art, University of Pennsylvania.)

Four phalangeal bones of a deer, perforated, and pierced with lateral perforations, and marked with two, three, four, and five red painted notches, strung on a thong, with an iron needle attached (figure 697). Five loops of blue glass beads are attached to the end opposite the needle.

Collected by Mr George E. Starr.

Another specimen (cat. no. 18682) in the same collection is identical in form with the above, except that the bones have one, two, three, and four notches.

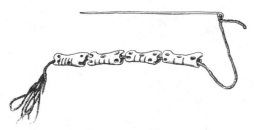

FIG. 697. Nitonisdot; length of implement, 23¼ inches; Cheyenne Indians, Oklahoma; cat. no. 18610, Free Museum of Science and Art, University of Pennsylvania.

Another specimen in the United States National Museum (cat. no. 165800), collected by Rev. H. R. Voth, is practically identical in its details with the preceding.

———— Oklahoma. (Cat. no. 67437, Field Columbian Museum.)

Four phalangeal bones of a deer, perforated and pierced and strung on beaded cord to which an iron needle is attached. At the other end of the cord are loops of strung beads, two pink, three green, and one yellow.

Collected by Rev. H. R. Voth, who describes the game as follows:

These bones are used by the Arapaho as well as the Cheyenne in a game which is sometimes called the love game. The wire bodkin is taken in the right hand and pointed horizontally forward. The four bones are then swung forward, and the bodkin is dexterously thrust through the perforations of one or more of them, each of which represents a certain value. The great aim of the player is to catch all the four bones horizontally on the needle at one time.

Col. Richard Irving Dodge [a] says:

The Cheyenne women have another game of which they are passionately fond. Small white beads are strung on a sinew, 12 or 14 inches long; at one end are fastened in a bunch six loops, about an inch in diameter, of smaller beads similarly strung. Four polished bones of the bear's foot are then strung on this beaded string, the smaller ends toward the loops. Each of these bones is perforated with sixteen holes in rows of four, and at each end are two or three

———————————

[a] Our Wild Indians, p. 331, Hartford, 1882.

very small loops of red beads. The other end of the sinew is now fastened to a sharpened piece of wire, 6 to 7 inches long, and the gambling instrument is complete.

The game is played by any number of players, each in turn. The needle is held horizontally between the thumb and fingers. The bones hanging down are steadied for an instant, then thrown forward and upward, and as they come opposite the point of the needle a rapid thrust is made. If the player be skillful the point of the needle will catch in some of the loops or·perforations of the bones. For each loop at the lower extremity of the instrument caught by the needle the player counts 100. Being put together in a bunch, it is rare that more than two or three are caught, though all six may be. One of the bones caught lengthwise on the needle counts 25; two, 50. Each little loop and perforation penetrated by the needle counts 5. Though the complications are numerous, the count is simple. Thus suppose the needle passed through a little loop on the third bone (5), then through the bone (25), then through a little loop at the other end of the bone (5), then through a loop on fourth bone (5), and finally through three of the terminal loops (300), the count for the throw is the sum of all (340). I have never seen over 500 made at a throw, though it is of course possible to make over 600. If the needle misses or fails to perforate loop or orifice, there is no count. The game is usually 2,000.

CHIPPEWA. Bois fort, near Rainy river, Minnesota. (American Museum of Natural History.)

Cat. no. $\frac{0}{4711}$. Tapering bundle of cedar leaves (figure 698), tied with cotton thread, 7 inches in length, having a wooden pin attached by a cotton cord.

The game is called nāpawăgăn. Catching the bundle counts 1 point.

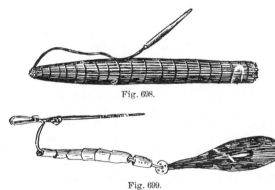

Fig. 698.

Fig. 699.

FIG. 698. Nāpawăgăn; length of bundle, 7 inches; Chippewa Indians, Bois fort, Minnesota; cat. no. $\frac{50}{4711}$, American Museum of Natural History.
FIG. 699. Nāpawăgăn; length of bones, 7½ inches; Chippewa Indians, Bois fort, Minnesota; cat. no. $\frac{50}{4709}$, American Museum of Natural History.

Cat. no. $\frac{50}{4709}$. Seven phalangeal bones (figure 699), strung on a buckskin thong having a wire needle attached at one end, and a metal button with a pear-shaped piece of buckskin, having a vertical slit in the middle and weighted with four small pieces of lead at the edge, at the other; length of bones, 7½ inches.

The game is called năpawăgăn, like the above. Catching any bone but the one nearest the button counts 1; the last bone, 10; the hole in the leather, 1; and a hole in the button, 20.

Both specimens were collected by Dr William Jones in 1903.

CHIPPEWA. Wisconsin.

Prof. I. I. Ducatel [a] says:

. . . Paskahwewog, is a sort of "cup-and-ball," in which a pin is used instead of the ball, and is caught, by a similar arrangement to our game, on its point.

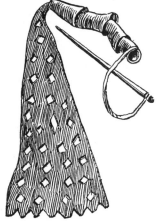

—— Turtle mountain, North Dakota. (Cat. no. $\frac{50}{4710}$, American Museum of Natural History.)

Four bones (figure 700), ends of long bones painted red, strung on a thong with a wooden pin painted red, attached at one end, and a triangular piece of buckskin, cut with diamond-length, 15 inches.

Collected by Dr William Jones, who gives the name of the game as napaaganagi.

FIG. 700. Napaăganăgi; length of implement, 15 inches; Chippewa Indians, Turtle mountain, North Dakota; cat. no. $\frac{50}{4710}$, American Museum of Natural History.

Catching a bone counts 1 point; catching the center hole in the dangle wins the game; the other holes in the dangle do not count.

—— Ontario.

Mr David Boyle [b] describes an old Chippewa game played for gambling purposes:

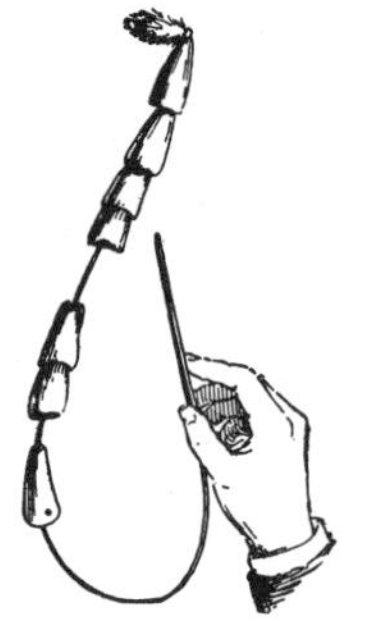

It consists of seven conical bones strung on a leather thong about 8 inches long, which has fastened to it at one end a small piece of fur and at the other a hickory pin 3½ inches long [figure 701]. The game was played by catching the pin near the head, swinging the bones upwards, and trying to insert the point of the pin into one of them before they descended. Each bone is said to have possessed a value of its own; the highest value being placed on the lowest bone, or the one nearest to the hand in playing. This bone has also three holes near the wide end, and to insert the pin into any of these entitled the player to an extra number of points. Above each hole is a series of notches numbering respectively 4, 6, and 9, which were, presumably, the value attached. . . . The one in our possession was presented by Mr J. Wood, an intelligent and influential member of the Missisauga band, near Hagersville.

FIG. 701. Pepenggune-gun; Chippewa Indians, Ontario; from Boyle.

---

[a] A Fortnight among the Chippewas. The Indian Miscellany, p. 368, Albany, 1877.

[b] Fourth Annual Report of the Canadian Institute, p. 55, Toronto, 1891.

Mr Boyle gives the name as pe-peng-gun-e-gun, stabbing a hollow bone.

CREE. Coxby, Saskatchewan. (Cat. no. 15459, Field Columbian Museum.)

Eight phalangeal bones strung on a thong, with a wire needle, 6¼ inches in length, at one end, and an oblong flap of buckskin, 6¼ inches in length, perforated with 14 holes, at the other (figure 702).

These were collected by Mr Phillip Towne, who describes the game under the name of tapa whan, stringing the bone cups:

The object of the game is to catch one or more of the bone cups on the point of the bodkin or to thrust the bodkin into a hole in the buckskin thong. The game is of 50 points, which may be made as follows: One for each bone cup or hole, except the two center holes in the buckskin thong, which count 20. To cause the bodkin to enter one of the four small holes in the last bone cup is equivalent to game.

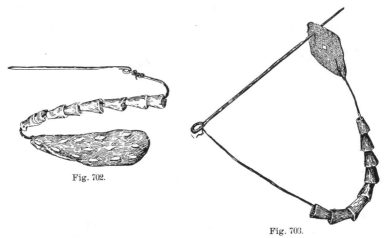

Fig. 702.

Fig. 703.

FIG. 702. Tapa whan; total length of implement, 28 inches; Cree Indians, Saskatchewan; cat. no. 15459, Field Columbian Museum.
FIG. 703. Cup and pin; total length of implement, 40 inches; Cree Indians, Saskatchewan; cat. no. 15130, Field Columbian Museum.

———— Union Lake reserve, Saskatchewan. (Cat. no. 15130, Field Columbian Museum.)

Nine phalangeal bones, painted blue, strung on a thong, with a long wire needle, 12¼ inches in length, at one end, and a diamond-shaped flap of buckskin, 5 inches in length, perforated with fifty-two small holes and a larger hole in the middle, tied at the other end (figure 703). Collected by W. Sibbold.

———— Muskowpetung reserve, Qu'appelle, Assiniboia. (Cat. no. 61993, Field Columbian Museum.)

Eight phalangeal bones strung on a thong, with a wire needle, 5¼ inches long at one end, and a flap of buckskin, perforated with holes, with a large hole in the center, at the other (figure 704). The bone nearest the flap is stained green and has its upper edge serrated. The other bones are plain.

These were collected by Mr J. A. Mitchell, who furnished the following account of the game, under the name of napahwhan:

Played by either men or women, there being no limit to the number of players. The bodkin is held in either hand, the buckskin appendage being held in the opposite hand against the elbow with the needle pointed upward. The whole

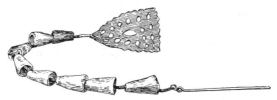

FIG. 704. Napahwhan; total length, 24 inches; Cree Indians, Assiniboia; cat. no. 61993, Field Columbian Museum.

string is then swung outward and upward, the object being to catch one or the whole of the cups as they descend, on the point of the needle, or failing in this, to cause the needle to pass through one or more of the holes in the leather tag.

Of the cups, each counts 2, except the blue-green one, which is called the squay-chagan, last-born child; it scores game and takes all the stakes. The holes in the tag have special values according to position, and combinations of these holes also have certain counting values.

The game is one valued very highly by the Indians and one which they are more loath to part with than with most others.

FIG. 705. Teheapi; length of stick, 9¼ inches; Cree Indians, Wind River reservation, Wyoming; cat. no. 37029, Free Museum of Science and Art, University of Pennsylvania.

CREE. Wind River reservation, Wyoming. (Cat. no. 37029, Free Museum of Science and Art, University of Pennsylvania.)

Disk of rawhide, 3¼ inches in diameter, painted yellow and perforated with holes, attached by a thong to a pointed stick, 9½ inches in length (figure 705).

Collected by the writer in 1900 from an Indian of Riel's band, who gave the name as teheapi:

Played indiscriminately by both sexes as a gambling game. The middle hole counts 10 and the others 2.

DELAWARES. Ontario.

Dr Daniel G. Brinton [a] gives an account of the following game as described to him by Rev. Albert Seqaqkind Anthony:

Qua'quallis. In this a hollow bone is attached by a string to a pointed stick. The stick is held in the hand, and the bone is thrown up by a rapid movement, and the game is to catch the bone, while in motion, on the pointed end of the stick. It was a gambling game, often played by adults.

GROSVENTRES. Fort Belknap reservation, Montana. (Cat. no. 36566, Free Museum of Science and Art, University of Pennsylvania.)

Four phalangeal bones, perforated at top and bottom, strung on a thong with five loops of colored beads at one end and a brass needle at the other (figure 706). The bones are marked on one side with ten, nine, eight, and seven notches; length, 12½ inches.

Collected by Dr George A. Dorsey, who describes the game as follows, under the name of tsaitkusha:

A game and favorite pastime among young men and women, and so often called the matrimonial game. The object of the game is to catch on the point of the long bodkin one or more of the bone cups made from the toe bones of

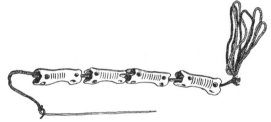

FIG. 706. Tsaitkusha; length of implement, 22 inches; Grosventre Indians, Fort Belknap reservation, Montana; cat. no. 36566, Free Museum of Science and Art, University of Pennsylvania.

deer; or, failing in this, one or more of the loops of beaded thread. Each cup is marked on one side with incised parallel lines; these determine its value and so the count on each cup caught, each loop also counting 1. The number of cups and loops varies in different specimens, four being the most common number.

―――― Fort Belknap reservation, Montana. (Cat. no. 60278, 60286, 60351, Field Columbian Museum.)

Four phalangeal bones, perforated at both ends and having dotted incisions in the middle, strung on a thong with a needle at one end and a loop of colored glass beads at the other.

Three phalangeal bones, similar to the above, but with transverse notches instead of holes.

Four phalangeal bones, similar to the above.

These were collected by Dr George A. Dorsey in 1900.

―――――――――――――――――――――――――――

[a] Folk-lore of the Modern Lenape. Essays of an Americanist, p. 186, Philadelphia, 1896.

MISSISAUGA. New Credit, Ontario. (Cat. no. 178387, United States National Museum.)

Rev. Peter Jones[a] figures a game similar to cup and ball. The actual specimen (figure 707) exists in the United States National Museum, and consists of nine phalangeal bones strung on a thong with a wooden pin.

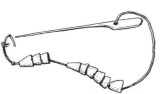

—— Rice lake, Ontario.

G. Copway[b] says:

FIG. 707. Phalangeal-bone game; length, 16½ inches; Missisauga Indians, Ontario; cat. no. 178387, United States National Museum.

The "Tossing Play" is a game seldom seen among the whites. It is played in the wigwam. There is used in it an oblong knot, made of cedar boughs, of length, say about 7 inches. On the top is fastened a string, about 15 inches long, by which the knot is swung. On the other end of this string is another stick, 2¼ inches long, and sharply pointed. This is held in the hand, and if the player can hit the large stick every time it falls on the sharp one he wins. "Bone play" is another indoor amusement, so called because the articles used are made of the hoof-joint bones of the deer. The ends are hollowed out, and from three to ten are strung together. In playing it they use the same kind of sharp stick, the end of which is thrown into the bones.

MONTAGNAIS. Lake St John, Quebec. (Peabody Museum of American Archæology and Ethnology.)

Cat. no. 62326. String of eight large worked phalangeal bones, strung on twine, with a bone pin at one end and a wild-cat tail tied at the other; length, 20½ inches.

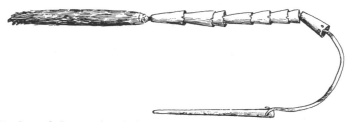

FIG. 708. Cup-and-pin game; length of implement, 26½ inches; Montagnais Indians, Quebec; cat. no. 62327, Peabody Museum of American Archæology and Ethnology.

Cat. no. 62327. String of phalangeal bones (figure 708), similar to the above, but strung on a thong and having a rabbit-skin roll tied at one end; length, 26½ inches. The top bone has four holes near its upper edge. Both collected by Mr Archibald Tisdale about 1892.

---

[a] History of the Ojebway Indians, fig. 7, pl. facing p. 135, London, 1861.
[b] The Traditional History and Characteristic Sketches of the Ojibway Nation, p. 55, Boston, 1851.

MONTAGNAIS. Labrador.

Henry Youle Hind [a] writes as follows:

One evening during our return I observed Michel, who was always doing something when in camp, making some little disks of wood, with a hole in each, and stringing them on a piece of leather; he attached a thin strip of wood to the end of the string, and, with Louis, was soon engaged in a game similar to

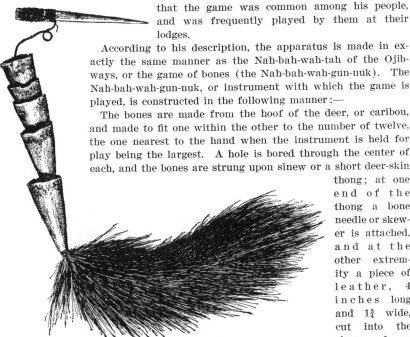

our Cup and Ball. Upon enquiry I found that the game was common among his people, and was frequently played by them at their lodges.

According to his description, the apparatus is made in exactly the same manner as the Nah-bah-wah-tah of the Ojibways, or the game of bones (the Nah-bah-wah-gun-nuk). The Nah-bah-wah-gun-nuk, or instrument with which the game is played, is constructed in the following manner:—

The bones are made from the hoof of the deer, or caribou, and made to fit one within the other to the number of twelve, the one nearest to the hand when the instrument is held for play being the largest. A hole is bored through the center of each, and the bones are strung upon sinew or a short deer-skin thong; at one end of the thong a bone needle or skewer is attached, and at the other extremity a piece of leather, 4 inches long and 1¾ wide, cut into the shape of an oval. Small holes are made

FIG. 709. Cup and pin; length of implement, 14¼ inches; Nascapee Indians, Labrador; cat. no. 3214, United States National Museum; from Turner.

in the piece of leather, which is called the tail, and four holes are drilled into the last 'bone.' The thong is weighted with a piece of lead close to the tail, the last bone slipping over it. The players agree upon the stakes, which are placed before them in the lodge, and one of them takes the bones and begins to play. His object is to catch as many as he can on the needle or skewer in a certain number of trials; the last bone, if caught singly in one of the holes drilled in it, counts the highest; if the tail is caught it also counts next to the last bone.

The other bones count 1 each, and a skillful player will sometimes catch 8 or 10 at one throw.

NASCAPEE. Ungava, Labrador. (Cat. no. 3214, United States National Museum.)

Five cones of polished bone (figure 709), made of phalangeal bones, strung on a thong, with the tail of some small animal fastened

<hr />

[a] Explorations in the Interior of the Labrador Peninsula, v. 1, p. 277, London, 1863.

at one end and a bone pin at the other. Collected by Mr Lucien Turner, who says: [a]

They also have a game corresponding to "cup and ball," but it is played with different implements from what the Eskimo use. . . . The hollow cones are made from the terminal phalanges of the reindeer's foot. The tail tied to the end of the thong is that of a marten or a mink. The player holds the peg in one hand, and tossing up the bones tries to catch the nearest bone on the point of the peg. The object of the game is to catch the bone the greatest possible number of times. It is in no sense a gambling game

NIPISSING. Forty miles above Montreal, Quebec.

J. A. Cuoq [b] gives the following definition:

Pipindjikaneigan, toy, sort of cup and ball, made of several dew-claws of the roebuck strung on a small cord to the end of which is fastened a pointed piece of wood with which they try to catch the dew-claws thrown in the air.

PASSAMAQUODDY. Maine.

Mrs W. W. Brown [c] describes the following game (figure 710):

T'wis. This, which is also an indoor game, is at present oftenest played for amusement. The t'wis is composed of an oblong piece of moose hide, about 4 inches in length, punctured with small holes, the center one being slightly larger than the others. This piece of hide is joined to a bundle of cedar (arbor vitæ)

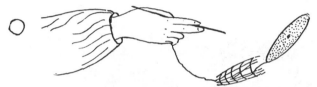

FIG. 710. T'wis; Passamaquoddy Indians, Maine; from Mrs W. W. Brown.

boughs, tightly wound round with cord. To this, by about 6 inches of string, is attached a sharp-pointed stick, tied near the center and held between the thumb and finger like a pen-handle. The game consists in giving the moose-hide a peculiar upward toss and at the same time piercing one of the holes with the point of the stick. The number of points necessary for winning is usually set at 100. Each player can hold the t'wis until he misses a point.

Another kind of t'wis was made of several pieces of bone strung loosely together, each having a certain value, and being counted by catching on the point of the stick, similarly to the holes in the moose hide.

There is a tradition that the first t'wis-ūk were made from that peculiar fungus which grows out from the bark of trees and is known to the Indians as wā-be-la-wen, or squaw-oc-l'moos-wāl-dee—that is, "the swamp woman's dishes." (Squaw-oc-moos is the bête noire of the Indian legends, and even now children will not play with toadstools through the fear of the swamp woman.) "One night," so the story runs, "during a very important game of t'wis, on which everything available had been wagered, both contestants fell asleep. The one having the t'wis was carried by Med-o-lin many miles into a swamp. When he awoke he saw Squaw-oc-moos eating out of the dishes and a t'wis made of boughs in his hands."

---

[a] Ethnology of the Ungava District, Hudson Bay Territory. Eleventh Annual Report of the Bureau of Ethnology, p. 323, 1894.

[b] Lexique de la Langue Algonquine, Montreal, 1886.

[c] Some Indoor and Outdoor Games of the Wabanaki Indians. Transactions of the Royal Society of Canada, v. 6, sec. 2, p. 43, Montreal, 1889.

It seems quite impossible to get a t'wis constructed from these wal-dee. The Indians will describe such a t'wis and promise faithfully to make one, even resenting any insinuations that they are afraid to do so. Their promise, nevertheless, for whatever reason, remains unfulfilled.

PASSAMAQUODDY. Pleasant Point, Maine.

Dr A. S. Gatschet writes from Baddeck, Nova Scotia, August 28, 1899:

The evergreen-bough game is unknown among the Micmac of Cape Breton, where I am now, but I heard of it at Pleasant Point, Me. It is called tu'tuash (plural, tutua'shek). Not only the pine species furnishing the twigs is called so, but also the twigs or needles broken off from it to play the game with, and also the game itself. The twigs, not over 4 or 5 inches long, are made to dance on a table or other level object, and a song, tu'tua, is sung while the dancing lasts.

PENOBSCOT. Kennebunkport, Maine. (Cat. no. 15406, Free Museum of Science and Art, University of Pennsylvania.)

FIG. 711. Artoois; length of cone, 8¼ inches; Penobscot Indians, Kennebunkport, Maine; cat. no. 15406, Free Museum of Science and Art, University of Pennsylvania.

Implement for a game (figure 711), consisting of a pointed stick, 9½ inches in length, attached by a thong to a cone-shaped object 8½ inches in length, made by wrapping leaves of *Arbor vitæ* with thread. The wrapping properly should be of eelskin.

Collected by Mr Henry C. Mercer, who describes it under the name of artoois.

—————— Oldtown, Maine. (Cat. no. 48237, Peabody Museum of American Archæology and Ethnology.)

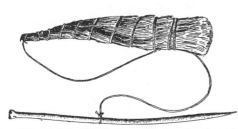

FIG. 712. Ahdu'is; length of cone, 7 inches; Penobscot Indians, Oldtown, Maine; cat. no. 48237, Peabody Museum of American Archæology and Ethnology.

Implement for a game (figure 712), described by the collector under the name of ahduis, and consisting of a pointed bone about 8 inches in length, attached by a thong 14 inches in length to the tip of a cone-shaped object of moose hair, 7 inches in length.

Collected by Mr C. C. Willoughby, who kindly furnished the following description:

Ah-du'-is is the lover's game. This game is played with a very sharp-pointed bone, some 8 inches long, and a roll of moose hair somewhat shorter, of conical form, about 1½ inches broad at base. These are fastened together by a cord about 14 inches long in the same manner as our cup and ball, which this game closely resembles in method of playing. When a man called upon a Penobscot girl to play ah-du'-is, they seated themselves, tailor-fashion, on a robe or skin. The man, taking the sharp-pointed bone, holds it spear fashion, allowing the roll of moose hair to hang down the length of the string. Then, swinging it up, he strikes at it, the object being to impale it on the point of the bone. The game consists of a given number of points. If the first attempt is successful and the bone remains impaled upon the point of the bone, it counts 1, and the player continues until he fails. Then it is passed to the girl. If his company is agreeable to her, she continues the game to the end; but if, on her first successful thrust, instead of continuing, she hands the ah-du'-is to him, it means that his company is not acceptable.

SAUK AND FOXES. Tama, Iowa. (Cat. no. 36755, Free Museum of Science and Art, University of Pennsylvania.)

Six perforated wooden cones (figure 713), strung on a thong with an iron needle made of an arrowhead ground down, attached to a silk ribbon fastened at the opposite end; total length, 11½ inches. Collected by the writer in 1900.

Said to be played by a boy and a girl together, and called ni-bi-quai-ha-ki.

FIG. 713. Nibiquaihaki; length of implement, 11¼ inches; Sauk and Fox Indians, Iowa; cat. no. no. 36755, Free Museum of Science and Art, University of Pennsylvania.

Two specimens of the same implement exist in the American Museum of Natural History (cat. no. $\frac{5\,0}{3\,5\,2\,1}$, $\frac{5\,0}{3\,5\,2\,2}$). Collected by Dr William Jones. He gave the name to the writer as nibiquihok, elm-tree eyes. When the last cone is caught on the pin, it counts 2; any other counts 1. There is a small strip of perforated leather at the extreme end. To catch one of the holes in this counts 5; to catch the thong with the pin between the pin and the first cone counts 10. The first implement has seven and the other six cones.

ATHAPASCAN STOCK

HUPA. Hupa valley, California. (Cat. no. 37209, Free Museum of Science and Art, University of Pennsylvania.)

Implement for game of kiolkis. Four salmon bones (figure 714), vertebræ, perforated and strung on a cord, 17 inches long, fastened at the base or handle of a pointed stick 12 inches long, the object being to throw up and catch the bone on the point. Collected by the writer in 1900.

Men play, one against another, each using an implement. Catching one bone counts 1; two bones, 2; and so on. If a player misses, the other plays. Four points is the game.

A Crescent City Indian, whom the writer met at Arcata, Cal., gave the name of this game as tsluk, while a Mad river (Wishoskan) Indian at Blue lake called it ret-char-i-wa-ten.

FIG. 714. Kiolkis; length of stick, 12 inches; Hupa Indians, Hupa valley, California; cat. no. 37209, Free Museum of Science and Art, University of Pennsylvania.

Dr J. W. Hudson described the preceding game under the name miltokot, " with to stab."

A bone awl held in the right hand jabs at a tightly rolled bunch of grass thrown up on the end of a string. As long as a player succeeds, he continues. There are ten counters. The game is common between youths and maids, and is said to symbolize the desire for a partner. The grass ball is often replaced by fish vertebræ.

KAWCHODINNE. Fort Good Hope, Mackenzie. (Cat. no. 857, United
    States National Museum.)

Eight phalangeal bones (figure 715), worked and polished down to
    conical form, strung on a thong, having a heart-shaped piece of
    buckskin with thirty-two holes cut in it attached at one end and a
    polished bone needle, $7\frac{1}{4}$ inches in length, at the other; total
    length, 26 inches. Collected by Maj. R. Kennicott.

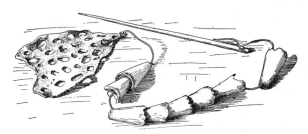

FIG. 715. Phalangeal-bone game; length of implement, 26 inches; Kawchodinne Indians, Fort Good Hope, Mackenzie; cat. no. 857, United States National Museum.

THLINGCHADINNE. Fort Rae, Mackenzie. (Cat. no. 10844, Museum
    of the State University of Iowa.)

The late Dr Frank Russell,[a] the collector, wrote under " ecagoo " in his catalogue of ethnological material secured in the Hudson's Bay Company's territory:

No. 10,844 consists of three small pieces of bone [figure 716] rudely fashioned in hollow cones through which passes a slender thread of twisted sinew. Each cone is 1.5 inches long and 0.8 inch in diameter at the larger end. They are

---

[a] Explorations in the Far North.   State University of Iowa, p. 181, 1898.

hollowed at the base so that they fit into each other. The thread is 6 inches in length and is attached to a strip of caribou skin at one end. This leather

is 4.5 inches long and has nine slits reaching within half an inch of the .ends and in which the point may catch in throwing. The needle is of bone 2 inches long and 0.1 inch in diameter. It is attached to the end of the thread which is towards the base of the cones. In using the ecagoo the thumb and forefinger grasp the end of the needle where it is enlarged by the sinew seizing, and the whole is swung outward and upward. The thread is just long enough to admit the point of the needle into the base of the first cone, where they are crowded into each other. The object to be attained is to pass the needle through the center of the cones or a slit in the leather at the top as the ecagoo falls. In gambling, a score is kept of the points made. Johnnie Cohoyla, from whom I obtained this, in the use of which he was an adept, said that the catching the point in the slits scored 1, on the first cone, 5, in first and second, 10, in all three, 15, and in second and third, 20. I saw it used in his camp as a gambling device, but elsewhere merely as a child's toy.

Doctor Russell precedes this account by saying:

I saw the same apparatus in use among the Stoney Indians of Morley and among the Slaveys at Providence.

ESKIMAUAN STOCK

ESKIMO (CENTRAL). Cumberland sound, Baffin land, Franklin.

Dr Franz Boas [a] writes as follows (references to figures below follow the numbers used in this paper) :

In winter, gambling is one of the favorite amusements of the Eskimo. Figs. 717, 718, 719, 724 represent the ajegaung, used in a game somewhat similar to our cup and ball. The most primitive device is Fig. 724, a hare's skull with a number of holes drilled through it. A specimen was kindly lent to me by

FIG. 716. Ecagoo. Thlingchadinne Indians, Fort Rae, Mackenzie; cat. no. 10844, Museum of the State University of Iowa.

Lucien M. Turner, who brought it from Ungava bay; but in Baffin Land exactly the same device is in use. Fig. 717 represents the head of a fox, in ivory; Fig. 718, a polar bear. The specimen shown in Fig. 719 was brought from Cumberland sound by Kumlien. The neck of the bear is more elaborate than the one shown in figure 718. The attachment of the part representing the hind legs is of some interest. The game is played as follows: First, the skull or the piece of ivory must be thrown up and caught ten times upon the stick in any one of the holes. Then, beginning with the hole in front (the mouth), those of the

[a] The Central Eskimo. Sixth Annual Report of the Bureau of Ethnology, p. 567, 1888.

middle line must be caught. The three holes on the neck of the bear are double, one crossing vertically, the other slanting backward, but both ending in one hole on the neck. After the mouth has been caught upon the stick the vertical hole in the neck is the next, then the oblique one, and so on down the middle line of the animal's body. If, in the first part of the game, the player

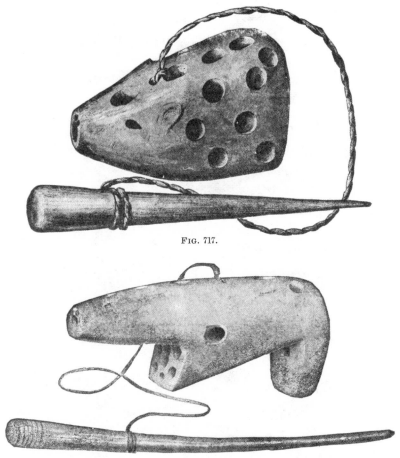

Fig. 717.

Fig. 718.

Fig. 717. Ivory carving representing head of fox, used in the game ajegaung, 1/1; Central Eskimo, Cumberland sound, Baffin land, Franklin; cat. no. IV A 6820, Museum für Völkerkunde, Berlin; from Boas.

Fig. 718. Ivory carving representing polar bear, used in the game of ajegaung, 2/3; Central Eskimo, Cumberland sound, Baffin land, Franklin; cat. no. IV A 6819, Museum für Völkerkunde, Berlin; from Boas.

misses twice, he must give up the pieces to his neighbor, who then takes his turn. In the second part he is allowed to play on as long as he catches in any hole, even if it be not the right one, but as soon as he misses he must give it up. After having caught one hole he proceeds to the next, and the player who first finishes all the holes has won the game.

ESKIMO (CENTRAL).   Kings cape, Repulse bay, Keewatin.   (Cat. no.
10188, United States National Museum.)

Ivory object (figure 720), 4½ inches in length, perforated with holes,
and having an ivory pin, 4 inches in length, attached at top by
a sinew string.

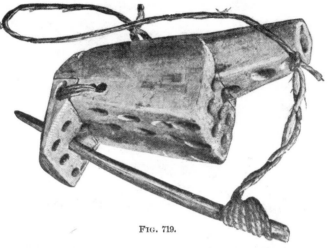

FIG. 719.

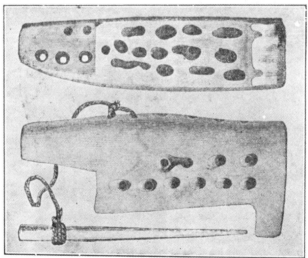

FIG. 720.

FIG. 719. Ivory carving representing polar bear, used in the game ajegaung, 2/3; length of object,
4⅞ inches; length of pin, 5 inches; Central Eskimo, Cumberland sound, Baffin land, Franklin;
cat. no. 34078, United States National Museum; from Kumlien.

FIG. 720. Bone game; length of implement, 4½ inches; Central Eskimo, Repulse bay, Keewatin;
cat. no. 10188, United States National Museum; from Hall.

This specimen was collected by Capt. Charles Francis Hall, U. S.
Navy, who says:[a]

A favorite game was that of cup and ball.

---

[a] Narrative of the Second Arctic Expedition, p. 96, Washington, 1879.

ESKIMO (CENTRAL). West coast of Hudson bay, Keewatin. (Cat. no. 10392, United States National Museum.

Ivory object in the shape of a fish (figure 721), with three holes at the head end and a single hole in the flat tail; length, 4½ inches. An ivory pin, 4½ inches in length, is attached by a cord of plaited sinew to a hole in one side of the fish. The object is to catch the fish at either the head or the tail. Collected by Capt. Charles Francis Hall, U. S. Navy.

FIG. 721. Fish game; length of fish, 4½ inches; Central Eskimo, west coast of Hudson bay, Keewatin; cat. no. 10392, United States National Museum.

ESKIMO (CENTRAL: AIVILIRMIUT AND KINIPETU). West coast of Hudson bay, Keewatin. (Cat. no. $\frac{60}{2547}$, $\frac{60}{2707}a$, American Museum of Natural History.)

Dr Franz Boas [a] describes the above objects as follows:

The game of cup-and-ball is played with an implement quite different from the one used in Cumberland sound. . . . The ball consists of a narrow

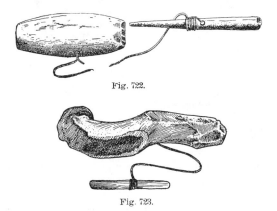

Fig. 722.

Fig. 723.

FIG. 722. Bone game; length of bone, 2¾ inches; Central Eskimo (Aivilirmiut and Kinipetu), west coast of Hudson bay, Keewatin; cat. no. $\frac{60}{2547}$, American Museum of Natural History.

FIG. 723. Seal-bone game; length of bone, 4 inches; Central Eskimo (Aivilirmiut and Kinipetu), west coast of Hudson bay, Keewatin; cat. no. $\frac{60}{2707}a$, American Museum of Natural History.

piece of musk-ox horn with four holes drilled into its short edge. It is caught on a wooden or bone pin [figure 722]. The game is also played with the shoulder bone of a seal [figure 723].

---

[a] Eskimo of Baffin Land and Hudson Bay. Bulletin of the American Museum of Natural History, v. 15, p. 111, New York, 1901.

Eskimo (Labrador). Ungava bay, Labrador. (United States National Museum.)

Cat. no. 90227. Skull of a hare having several holes drilled in the upper part, with a radius of a hare attached by a thong (figure 724). Collected by Mr Lucien M. Turner.

Cat. no. 3478. Similar skull with bone attached. but with no perforations in the cranium.

———— Fort Chimo, Labrador.

Mr Lucien M. Turner [a] says:

A favorite game, something like cup and ball, is played with the following implements: A piece of ivory is shaped into the form of an elongate cone and

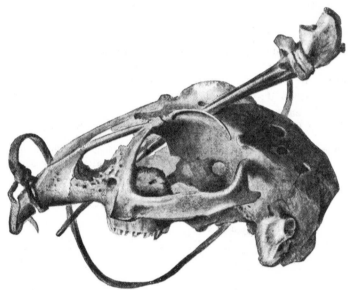

Fig. 724. Skull used in the game of ajegaung, 1/1; length, 3½ inches: Labrador Eskimo, Ungava bay; cat. no. 90227, United States National Museum; from Boas.

has two deep notches or steps cut from one side [figure 725]. In the one next the base are bored a number of small holes and one or two holes in the upper step. The apex has a single hole. On the opposite side of the base two holes are made obliquely, that they will meet, and through them is threaded a short piece of thong. To the other end of the thong is attached a peg of ivory, about 4 inches long. The game is that the person holding the plaything shall, by a dexterous swing of the ball. catch it upon the ivory peg held in the hand. The person engages to catch it a certain number of times in succession, and on failure to do so allows the opponent to try her skill. The skull of a hare is often substituted for the ivory ball, and a few perforations are made in the walls of the skull to receive the peg. It requires a great amount of practice to catch the ball, as the string is 'so short that one must be quick to thrust the peg in before it describes the part of a small circle.

---

[a] Ethnology of the Ungava District, Hudson Bay Territory. Eleventh Annual Report of the Bureau of Ethnology, p. 255, 1894.

Eskimo (Ita). Karma, Inglefield gulf, Greenland. (Cat. no. 18609, Free Museum of Science and Art, University of Pennsylvania.)

Implements consisting of the ulna of a seal (figure 726), 4½ inches in length, perforated at both ends; and a pin, consisting of the radius of a hare, attached by a cord of sinew. Collected by Mr Theodore Le Boutellier.

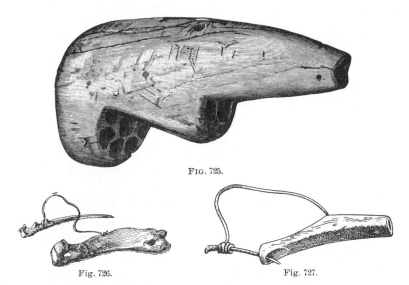

Fig. 725.

Fig. 726.　　　　　　　　　　Fig. 727.

Fig. 725. Bone game; Central Eskimo (Koksoagmiut), Fort Chimo, Labrador; cat. no. 90228, United States National Museum; from Turner.

Fig. 726. Ajagaq; length of seal bone, 4½ inches; Ita Eskimo, Inglefield gulf, Greenland; cat. no. 18609, Free Museum of Science and Art, University of Pennsylvania.

Fig. 727. Ajagaq; length, 6¼ inches; Ita Eskimo, Smith sound, Greenland; cat. no. $\frac{60}{335}$, American Museum of Natural History.

———— Smith sound, Greenland. (Cat. no. $\frac{60}{335}$, American Museum of Natural History.)

A bone 6½ inches in length (figure 727), with a hole bored through each socket and a thin stick tied by a short string to the bone, the latter being thrown up to be caught in either hole with the stick. Figured and described by Dr A. L. Kroeber,[a] who gives the name of the implement as ajagaq and that of the catching stick as ajautang.

IROQUOIAN STOCK

Huron. Ontario.

Father Louis Hennepin,[b] describing the games of children, says:

They also make a ball of flags or corn leaves, which they throw in the air and catch on the end of a pointed stick.

[a] Bulletin of the American Museum of Natural History, v. 12, p. 296, New York, 1900.

[b] A Description of Louisiana, p. 303, New York, 1880.

KULANAPAN STOCK

POMO. Ukiah, California. (Cat. no. 61116, Field Columbian Museum.)

Six pointed oak forks (figure 728) set around a handle, to which they are bound by the bark of the *Cercis occidentales;* total length, 11⅝ inches.

Four vertebral bones of the salmon,[a] 4 inches in length, each composed of from thirteen to fifteen vertebræ, tied with cords of native flax at the base of the points.

Collected by Dr George A. Dorsey, who designates the game as the spearing game, dittcega; from diken, to cast up.[b]

FIG. 728. Dittcega; length, 11⅝ inches; Pomo Indians, Ukiah, California; cat. no. 61116, Field Columbian Museum.

LUTUAMIAN STOCK

KLAMATH. Klamath lake, Oregon. (Cat. no. 61531, Field Columbian Museum.)

A long elliptical ball made of tule pith. The lower end of the ball, which remains loose, consists of a dozen or more strings of tule fiber which project beyond the surface. The upper portion, or body, of the ball is tightly wrapped with the outer bark of the tule rush. Projecting from the upper end of the ball is a small braided loop, one-fourth of an inch in diameter, to which is fastened a 6-inch thread of native grass. At the end of this thread is attached a small bone pin a little more than 1 inch in length.

Collected by Dr George A. Dorsey, who gives the following description of the game under the name of soquoquas:[c]

Taking the pin by the end to which the cord is attached by the thumb and forefinger, and permitting the ball to hang loosely at the end of the string, a sudden downward thrust is given, the object being to strike the braided loop and catch it on the point of the pin. This is known as shapashspatcha ("to split or punch out the moon"). The game is always played in winter and generally only by adults. It is believed that by "punching out the moon" in this fashion the winter months are shortened and the advent of spring is hastened.

Another specimen, cat. no. 61673 (plate XI), is made similarly; the ball is 5 inches in length, while from it project several strands of the inner fiber of tule, also 5 inches in length; the knot, string, and pin are somewhat larger.

---

[a] Doctor Hudson informed the writer that sucker vertebræ are also used.

[b] Doctor Hudson gives the name as di-che-ka, to-stab-at game.

[c] Certain Gambling Games of the Klamath Indians. American Anthropologist, n. s., v. 3, p. 21, 1901.

HIDATSA INDIANS PLAYING HOOP AND POLE; FORT CLARK, NORTH DAKOTA; FROM MAXIMILIAN, PRINCE OF WIED

SOQUOQUAS; KLAMATH INDIANS, OREGON; CAT. NO. 61673, 61712, FIELD
COLUMBIAN MUSEUM; FROM DORSEY

In another specimen, cat. no. 61532, no strands of fiber project from the ball, the two ends being finished alike. Instead of the string being tied in a loop at the upper end, it is simply fastened in one of the wrappings. This ball is not wound from side to side with a circular wrapping of tule bark, but is wrapped about the center from eight to ten times with a tightly woven thread of that material.

The three other specimens, cat. no. 61712 (plate XI), 61713, 61715, are much smaller than the specimens described, the largest being not over 2½ inches in length. They are all made of bark of tule, tightly wrapped from end to end, and are considerably larger about the middle than at either end, thus having a sort of lozenge shape. In each of these three specimens the thread connecting the pin and ball is unusually well made and is very soft and pliable, while the pin consists simply of a porcupine quill. With all of these specimens in which no loop projects from the ball to which the string is attached, the object of the game is to strike the knot where the string is fastened to the ball.

PIMAN STOCK

PIMA. Gila River reserve, Sacaton agency, Pinal county, Arizona. (Cat. no. 63290, Field Columbian Museum.)

Nineteen rings of gourd shell (figure 729), strung on cotton string, with a wooden pin, 9 inches in length, at one end, and a triangular perforated piece of gourd shell, 3½ inches in length, at the other; total length, 23 inches. Collected by Mr S. C. Simms, who gives the name as chelgwegoooot.

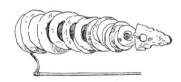

FIG. 729. Chelgwegoooot; length of implement, 23 inches; Pima Indians, Arizona; cat. no. 63290, Field Columbian Museum.

A specimen of the same implement in the United States National Museum (cat. no. 218644), collected by Dr Frank Russell, has thirty-eight rings of dried gourd shell, ranging from 4¼ inches to 1 inch in diameter, with an oval pendant at the end. The catching stick is 8¼ inches in length.

The game is described by the collector [a] under the name of tculi-kiwe′kut:

This is the Gileño of the widespread dart-and-ring game. It is not exclusively a woman's game, but was sometimes played by women. The younger generation knows nothing about it. The apparatus consists of a series of rings cut from cultivated gourds. They vary in diameter from 3 to 12 centimeters, and are strung on a two-ply maguey fiber cord 50 centimeters long. They are kept from slipping off at one end by a rectangular piece of gourd a little larger than the

_____

[a] In a memoir to be published by the Bureau of American Ethnology.

opening in the smallest ring, which is at that end. At the other end of the string is fastened a stick 20 centimeters long, the outer end of which is sharpened. The game is to toss the rings up by a swing and, while holding the butt of the stick, thrust the dart through as many of them as possible. If the thrower fails she hands the apparatus to her opponent, but she continues throwing as long as she scores, and counts the number of rings that are caught on the dart. In the specimen collected there are 14 rings, but only a few may be caught at a single throw. A certain number of marks, 2, 3, or 4, agreed upon in advance, constitute the game. These marks are made upon a diagram laid out in the sand in the form of a whorl. The scoring commences in the center, called the tcunni ki (council house), and runs out to the last hole, called hoholdoga ki (menstrual house), which is on the west side of the diagram; then the score returns to the center before the player is entitled to one point toward game. If the player who is behind throws a number that brings her counter to the same hole as that of her opponent, she "kills" the latter and sends back her counter to the beginning point, but this is not done if she passes her opponent's position.

Two specimens were obtained at Sacaton, which were probably used in games by the Hohokam.

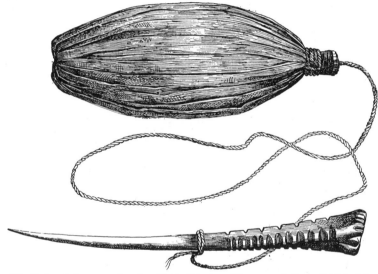

Fig. 730. Ball-and-pin game; length of ball, 4¼ inches; Thompson Indians, British Columbia; cat. no. ₈₁₂₆/₁₆, American Museum of Natural History.

SALISHAN STOCK

Thompson Indians (Ntlakyapamuk). British Columbia. (Cat. no. ₈₁₂₆/₁₆, American Museum of Natural History.)

Egg-shaped ball made of rushes (figure 730), 4½ inches in length, attached at one end by a twisted cord to a notched deer bone.

This specimen was collected by Mr James Teit, who says that the notches on the bone are ornamental, but some boys keep tallies of the greatest number of times they can catch without missing, by notching the pin.

Mr Teit [a] says also:

A boys' game was played as follows: A small, but rather long ball of grass was attached to the hand with a string. In the same hand was held a wooden pin. The ball was thrown away from the .hand, but pulled back again by the string. On the way back, the hand was raised so as to catch the ball on the end of the pin. This was done as often as possible. After the first miss the ball had to be handed to the next boy.

FIG. 731. Pactslewitas; total length of implements, 6¼ inches; Umatilla Indians, Umatilla reservation, Oregon; cat. no. 37540, Free Museum of Science and Art, University of Pennsylvania.

SHAHAPTIAN STOCK

UMATILLA. Umatilla reservation, Oregon. (Cat. no. 37540, Free Museum of Science and Art, University of Pennsylvania.)

Implements for the game of pactslewitas (figure 731), a piece of salmon vertebræ (seven bones) 2½ inches in length, perforated and strung on a cord with one loose bone; wooden pin at one end of the cord and a tuft of fur at the other. Collected by the writer in 1900.

The pin is held in the fingers and the bones are swung in the air. Catching the single bone counts 1; the single bone and the others, 2. The game is 100.

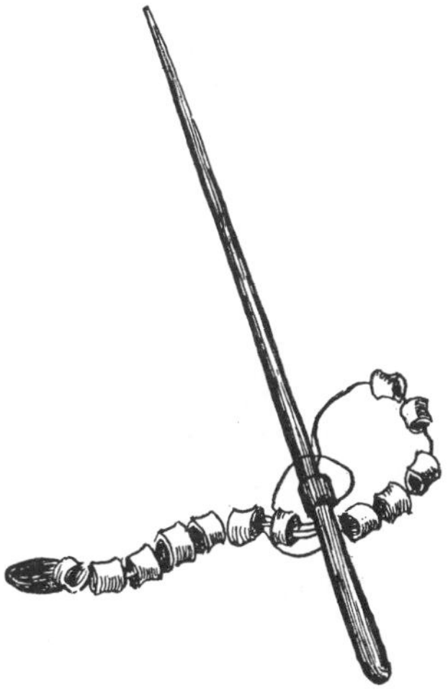

SHASTAN STOCK

SHASTA. Hamburg bar, California. (Cat. no. $\frac{50}{3192}$, American Museum of Natural History.)

Twelve salmon bones (figure 732) strung on a cord which is tied to a pointed stick. A piece of red flannel is attached to the end of the cord. Collected in 1902 by Dr Roland B. Dixon.

SHOSHONEAN STOCK

PAIUTE. Pyramid lake, Nevada. (Cat. no. 19058, United States National Museum.)

A bunch of tule stalks tied at the ends (figure 733), 4¾ inches in length, with a wooden needle attached

FIG. 732. Salmon-bone game; Shasta Indians, California; cat. no. $\frac{50}{3192}$, American Museum of Natural History.

with a cord. Collected by Mr Stephen Powers, who describes it in his catalogue under the name of nadohetin.

Every time the player catches it he has a right to thump his opponent on the forehead.

a The Thompson Indians of British Columbia. Memoirs of the American Museum of Natural History, whole series, v. 2, p. 278, New York, 1900.

PAIUTE. Southern Utah. (Peabody Museum of American Archæology and Ethnology.)

Cat. no. 9434. The skull of the cottontail rabbit attached by a thong to a wooden pin (figure 734a).

The pin is held in the hand and the skull is swung and caught upon its point.

Cat. no. 9433. A small hollow bone (figure 734b), seven-eighths of an inch in length, with a notch cut through one side, strung on a thong, to the other end of which a wooden pin is attached. Evidently intended for a game like the preceding.

Both were collected by Dr Edward Palmer.

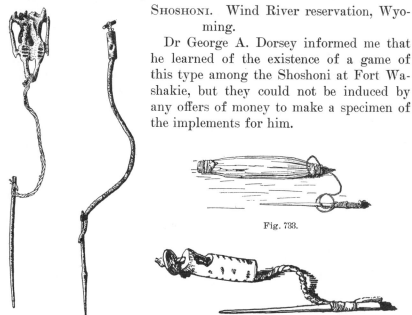

SHOSHONI. Wind River reservation, Wyoming.

Dr George A. Dorsey informed me that he learned of the existence of a game of this type among the Shoshoni at Fort Washakie, but they could not be induced by any offers of money to make a specimen of the implements for him.

Fig. 733.

FIG. 734 a, b.   Fig. 735.

FIG. 733. Nadóhetin; length of reeds, 4⅞ inches; Paiute Indians, Pyramid lake, Nevada; cat. no. 19058, United States National Museum.

FIG. 734 a, b. Skull and pin and bone and pin; Paiute Indians, southern Utah; cat. no. 9434, 9433, Peabody Museum of American Archæology and Ethnology.

FIG. 735. Reed and pin; length of reed, 1¼ inches; Ute Indians, St George, Utah; cat. no. 20934, United States National Museum.

UTE. St George, Utah. (United States National Museum.)

Cat. no. 20934. Small tube of reed (figure 735), 1½ inches in length, with a round hole cut in the side near one end, ornamented with burned marks.

A cord passing through the reed is secured by a knot and a flat glass button at one end. The other end has a wooden pin attached. The object appears to be to catch on the pin either the button, the hole in the side, or the hole in the end of the reed.

Cat. no. 20932. Small bone (probably a bird bone), 1⅝ inches in length, marked with notches, as shown in figure 736, with a cotton cord passing through it having a wooden pin at one end. There are the traces of a tuft of rabbit fur at the end opposite the pin. The object of the game is to catch the bone on the pin at the hollow end nearest the pin, or, possibly, also, in the tuft of fur.

Collected by Dr Edward Palmer.

FIG. 736.   Bone and pin; length of bone, 1⅝ inches: Ute Indians, St George, Utah; cat. no. 20932, United States National Museum.

SIOUAN STOCK

ASSINIBOIN. Fort Belknap reservation, Montana. (Field Columbian Museum.)

Cat. no. 60205. Seven phalangeal bones, perforated and strung on a thong, with a bone needle at one end and a triangular piece of buckskin, perforated with holes, at the other end (figure 737).

Cat. no. 60263. Seven phalangeal bones, like the preceding, but smaller, with wire needle and triangular piece of buckskin.

Collected in 1900 by Dr George A. Dorsey, who describes the game under the name of taseha:

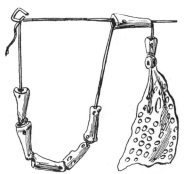

FIG. 737.   Taseha; Assiniboin Indians, Montana; cat. no. 60205, Field Columbian Museum.

A game formerly much played by young men and women, and known as the courting or matrimonial game. The cups (toe bones of the deer, perforated) are swung forward and upward, the buckskin being held by the thumb and forefinger. As the cups descend the attempt is made to catch one or more of them on the end of the bodkin or to thrust the bodkin into one of the perforations in the triangular piece of buckskin attached to the end of the cord beyond the last cup.

The points played are generally 40, the cups having a numerical value, beginning with the first cup, counting 1; the second, 2, etc. According to the owner of the set no. 60263, the last cup counted 40, and so won the game, while the owner of the set no. 60205 [figure 737] claimed that the first cup counted 5. In both games the small holes in the buckskin are worth 4, while the large hole (chaute, heart) has a value of 9.

The game as at present played is almost purely one of pastime. That it formerly had a deep significance there is no doubt.

ASSINIBOIN. Fort Belknap, Montana. (Cat. no. $\frac{50}{2011}$, American Museum of Natural History.)

Seven phalangeal bones strung on a thong, with a triangular piece of buckskin, perforated with holes, attached at one end and a wire needle at the other; total length, 31 inches. Collected by Dr A. L. Kroeber.

DAKOTA (BRULÉ). South Dakota. (Cat. no. 27528, Peabody Museum of American Archæology and Ethnology.)

String of five worked phalangeal bones of deer (figure 738), on a thong, to the end of which a needle is attached.

Collected by Miss Alice C. Fletcher.

They are used only by women. The bones are swung in a circle very rapidly, and caught upon the pin, which in ancient times was made of bone.

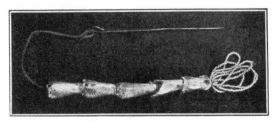

FIG. 738. Cup and pin; Brulé Dakota Indians, South Dakota; cat. no. 27528, Peabody Museum of American Archæology and Ethnology.

DAKOTA (OGLALA). Pine Ridge agency, South Dakota. (Cat. no. 22122, Free Museum of Science and Art, University of Pennsylvania.)

Six phalangeal bones of deer (figure 739), strung on a thong 11 inches in length, with a brass needle, 5 inches in length, attached at one end of the thong, and seven loops of variegated glass beads at the other end.

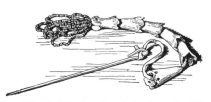

FIG. 739. Tasiha; length of implement, 23½ inches; Oglala Dakota Indians, South Dakota; cat. no. 22122, Free Museum of Science and Art, University of Pennsylvania.

The bones are fluted at the upper edge, except the one nearest the needle, which has small holes around the edge. They were made by Winyanhopa, "Elegant Woman," and collected by Mr Louis L. Meeker, who describes it as an implement from the woman's game of tasiha.

The strand is swung in the air, and the wire thrust into one of the bones, counting from 1 to 4 (or 5) in order, or as many as the number of loops passed through. Some number as many as six bones on one string.

DAKOTA (TETON).   South Dakota.

Rev. J. Owen Dorsey [a] describes the following as a game played by boys, younger married men, or women:

Ta-síha un'pi, Game with the hoofs of a deer.—They string several deer hoofs together and throw them suddenly upward. They jerk them back again by the cord to which they are attached, and as they fall the player who has a sharp-pointed stick tries to thrust it through the holes of the hoofs, and if he succeeds he counts the number of hoofs through which his stick has gone. A number of small beads of various colors are strung together and attached to the smallest hoof at the end of the string. When a player adds a bead to those on the string he has another chance to try his skill in piercing the hoofs. When one misses the mark he hands the hoofs, etc., to the next player. Each one tries to send his stick through more hoofs than did his predecessor. Two sides are chosen by the players. Each player offers articles as stakes for the winner. The season for playing is not specified.

The women, when they play this game, bring their husbands goods without the knowledge of the owners, and sometimes lose all of them. When the men play, they sometimes stake all of their wives' property, and occasionally they lose all. Now and then this game is played just for amusement, without any stakes.

———— South Dakota.

Dr J. R. Walker [b] describes this game under the name of woskate tasi he, game with foot bones, and gives the rules for the play.

FIG. 740. Hokiwaxoxokke; length of implement, 15 inches; Winnebago Indians, Wisconsin; cat. no. 22158, Free Museum of Science and Art, University of Pennsylvania.

WINNEBAGO.   Wisconsin.   (Cat. no. 22158, Free Museum of Science and Art, University of Pennsylvania.)

Seven phalangeal bones strung on a thong (figure 740), with a bone needle attached at one end and two triangular pieces of buckskin at the other; length, 15 inches.

Collected by Mr T. R. Roddy, who says:

The game is called ho-ki-wa-xo-xok-ke.

SKITTAGETAN STOCK

HAIDA.   British Columbia.

Dr J. R. Swanton describes [c] the following game:

Flipping a V-shaped object over and letting it drop (Łgá sLʌ́ñ).—A straight stick was held in one hand, while a V-shaped piece of cedar about 8 inches long was held in the other hand by one of its arms, and so thrown into the air that it would fall astride of the stick. This V-shaped piece is called the łga' sLłgʌ'ño.

[a] Games of Teton Dakota Children. The American Anthropologist, v. 4, p. 344, 1891.
[b] Journal of American Folk-Lore, v. 18, p. 288, 1905.
[c] Contributions to the Ethnology of the Haida. Memoirs of the American Museum of Natural History, whole series, v. 8, pt. 1, p. 60, New York, 1905.

When it fell to the ground, the one who threw it must yield to the next player; but before doing so he was at liberty to pull his opponent's hair violently or punch his knuckles as many times as he had made a catch.

TANOAN STOCK

TEWA. Hano, Arizona. (Cat. no. 38616, Free Museum of Science and Art, University of Pennsylvania.)

Ring of rawhide (figure 741), 5 inches in diameter, attached by a thong to the end of a stick painted red, 13¼ inches in length. Collected by the writer in 1901.

FIG. 741. Ngoila nabapi; diameter of ring, 5 inches; Tewa Indians, Hano, Arizona; cat. no. 38616, Free Museum of Science and Art, University of Pennsylvania.

The ring is swung from the end of the stick and caught on the end. The name of the game was given as ngoi-la na-ba pi.

WAKASHAN STOCK

CLAYOQUOT. West coast of Vancouver island, British Columbia. (Cat. no. ₂₀¹⁶₁₅, American Museum of Natural History.)

Femur of seal (figure 742), 4½ inches in length, with natural perforation; accompanied by a small pointed twig, 6 inches in length. Collected in 1897 by Mr F. Jacobsen, who describes it as a bilboquet.

FIG. 742. Seal-bone game; length of bone, 4½ inches; Clayoquot Indians, Vancouver island, British Columbia; cat. no. ₂₀¹⁶₁₅, American Museum of Natural History.

The following note on a similar game in the Field Columbian Museum (cat. no. 85909) from Clayoquot, was furnished by the collector, Dr C. F. Newcombe:

The game is called shaiyixtsᴇ. It is played with the femur of the common seal and a sharp-pointed twig of a young spruce.

Players arrange themselves in two rows, up to ten a side, opposite one another, and consecutively toss the bone and try to catch it again by a partial rotation. Sometimes the femur is only swung by putting the stick under the projecting edge of the ball of the hip joint and then making the bone to rotate so that the point of the stick will pass into the foramen above the condyle.

The stakes and winning number are arranged according to the number and wishes of the players.

The bone is passed along the whole of one side before being thrown over to the opponents. If the player misses his first attempt he passes it to his next neighbor, but if he succeeds in catching the bone, as required, he goes on trying until he fails.

If a side fails in making 40 wins by the united efforts of all its players, the opponents try. That side which first makes 40 takes all the stake which is equally divided.

Name of femur of seal, hamut; name of stick, quiʟklɛpt.

No string is used, as reported by Dr Dorsey in a similar game amongst the Makahs.

KWAKIUTL. British Columbia. (Cat. no. $\frac{16}{6847}$, American Museum of Natural History.)

Femur of seal (figure 743), 4½ inches in length, with small natural perforations; accompanied by a pointed stick 6¾ inches in length. Collected in 1897 by George Hunt, who describes it as a "seal bone for divining."

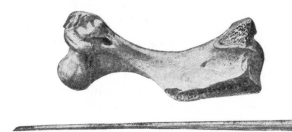

FIG. 743. Seal bone for divining; length, 4¼ inches; Kwakiutl Indians, British Columbia; cat. no. $\frac{16}{6847}$, American Museum of Natural History.

——— Nawiti, British Columbia.

Dr C. F. Newcombe describes a game played by these Indians with a bone perforated with a small hole and a wooden pin:

The bone is not tied to the pin. The point is placed in the hole and the bone tossed up, and the object is to catch it again on the point. There is no score. Both men and women play. The name is dsīchdsk'ia.

MAKAH. Neah bay, Washington.

Dr George A. Dorsey [a] describes a game called kaskas:

This game corresponds to the well-known cup-and-pin game of the Plains Indians, which among the neighbors of the Makahs is modified into a game with a wooden pin and snake or fish vertebræ. With the Makahs a humerus (kashabs) of the hair seal, which is perforated at each end, is attached by means of a

[a] Games of the Makah Indians of Neah Bay. The American Antiquarian, v. 23, p. 72, 1901.

string passing through a hole in the middle of the bone to a wooden pin (ka-a-pick). The bone is tossed upward and as it falls it is caught on the end of the pin. Whatever significance this game may have had in former times has evidently been lost, for, according to Williams, it is played merely for amusement, at any time, and by both sexes.

YUMAN STOCK

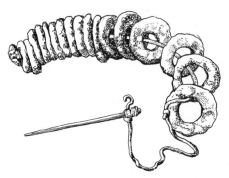

MOHAVE. Colorado river, Arizona. (Cat. no. 10086, Peabody Museum of American Archæology and Ethnology.)

Seventeen rings of pumpkin (figure 744), strung on a deerskin thong, with a wooden pin. Collected by Dr Edward Palmer.

FIG. 744. Pumpkin-rind game; Mohave Indians, Arizona; cat. no. 10086, Peabody Museum of American Archæology and Ethnology.

The wooden pin is held in the hand, and the rings, made from the shell of the pumpkin, are swung and caught upon it. A similar implement from the same tribe is contained in the United States National Museum.

ZUÑIAN STOCK

ZUÑI. Zuñi, New Mexico. (Brooklyn Institute Museum.)

Cat. no. 3061. Ring made of twig wrapped with blue yarn (figure 745), 5 inches in diameter, tied with blue yarn cord to a stick, 21 inches in length. The object is to catch the ring on the end of the stick.

FIG. 745. Ring game; length of stick, 21 inches; Zuñi Indians, Zuñi, New Mexico; cat. no. 3061. Brooklyn Institute Museum.

Cat. no. 3060. Two rings (figure 746), one 2¼ inches and the other 1½ inches in diameter, both wrapped with blue yarn, the larger one suspended over the smaller one and having another yarn-wrapped ring inside of it, and both suspended by a blue yarn cord from the end of a twig 23 inches long; accompanied by a pointed stick, 5¾ inches in length, with a crosspiece tied at one end.

The object is to throw the dart through one or the other of the rings. The smallest ring, tsi-kon tso-na, counts 2, and the large or double ring, tsi-kon kwi-li, 4.

Cat. no. 3059. Ring wrapped with blue yarn (figure 747), $2\frac{1}{2}$ inches in diameter, having three smaller rings, $1\frac{1}{2}$ inches in diameter, suspended from it, and attached to the end of a twig, $17\frac{1}{2}$ inches long, by a blue yarn cord; accompanied by a pointed twig, $21\frac{1}{4}$ inches in length, with a crosspiece tied near one end.

The object is to throw this dart through one of the rings. The large ring, called tsam-mo-so-na, counts 4. One of the small rings, tied with a piece of red yarn and called shi-lo-wa, red, counts 1; another, tied with green, a-shai-na, counts 3, while the third small ring, which is plain black, quin-a, counts 2.

All of these games were collected by the writer in 1903. They all bear the name of tsikonai ikoshnikia, ring play.

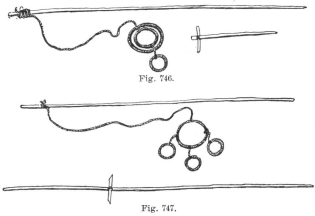

Fig. 746.

Fig. 747.

Fig. 746. Ring game; length of stick, 23 inches; Zuñi Indians, Zuñi, New Mexico; cat. no. 3060, Brooklyn Institute Museum.
Fig. 747. Ring game; length of stick, $17\frac{1}{2}$ inches; Zuñi Indians, Zuñi, New Mexico; cat. no. 3059, Brooklyn Institute Museum.

BALL

Under the general name of ball I have classed all ball games, howsoever played, and all games in which an implement analogous to a ball is employed. In none of them, with trifling exceptions which belong to distinct classes, is the ball ever touched with the hand, to do so being strictly forbidden by the rules of the game.

The Indian ball games may be classified as follows: First, racket, in which the ball is tossed with a racket; second, shinny, in which the ball is struck with a club or bat; third, double ball, a game chiefly confined to women, played with two balls or billets tied together, tossed with a stick; fourth, the ball race, in which a ball or stick is kicked. In addition, subsidiary to the preceding and not general, being confined to a few tribes, we have: Fifth, football; sixth, hand-and-foot ball; seventh, tossed ball; eighth, juggling, and ninth, hot ball.

Games of the first three classes are widespread and almost universal. The ball race appears to be confined to the Southwest. The balls used vary greatly in material. The commonest form is covered with buckskin, but other balls are made of wood, of bladder netted with sinew, and of cordage, bone, or stone.

RACKET

The game of ball with rackets is distinctly a man's game, as opposed to shinny and double ball, which are commonly played by women. It is, however, sometimes played by women, and in one instance by men and women together (Santee).

Racket is less widely distributed than shinny, being confined to the Algonquian and Iroquoian tribes of the Atlantic seaboard and the region of the Great Lakes; and to their neighbors, the Dakota, on the west, and the Muskhogean tribes of the South. It occurs again among the Chinook and the Salish in the Northwest, and in a limited area in California. It is not recorded in the Southwest.

FIG. 748. Miniature racket used by conjurers to look into futurity; length, 8¼ inches; Missisauga Indians, Ontario; cat. no. 178386, United States National Museum.

The game may be divided into two principal classes—first, those in which a single racket or bat is used; second, those in which two rackets are employed. The latter is peculiar to the southern tribes (Cherokee, Choctaw, Muskogee, Seminole), among whom the single racket is not recorded.

The racket may be regarded as a practical contrivance, akin to the throwing stick, but its origin is not clear. Morgan relates that the present netted bat of the Seneca was preceded by a simple stick, with a curved end, and Teit tells how bark strings were used by the Thompson Indians in bending ball sticks to the required crook. The strings, which were sometimes left attached to the bat, furnish an explanation of the present net. On the other hand, it is not unlikely that the racket may be related, with the drum hoop, to the spider-web shield of the twin War Gods, the probable source of the netted wheel.

Rev. Peter Jones[a] figures a miniature racket ball (figure 748), 8¼ inches long, now in his collection in the United States National Museum, as "used by conjurers to look into futurity."

The ball used with the racket was either of wood (Chippewa, Pomo, Santee, Winnebago) or of buckskin stuffed with hair. The

---

[a] History of the Ojebway Indians, London, 1861.

wooden ball appears to be the older and possibly the original form. Morgan states that the Seneca formerly used a solid ball of knot, for which the deerskin ball was substituted. Of the two types of covered ball, the bag-shaped form is more commonly used in racket than that with a median seam. The goals were commonly two sets of posts or poles erected at the extremities of the field, between which the ball had to be driven. Single posts were sometimes used (Miami, Missisauga, Chippewa [Minnesota], Chinook). An early account of the Muskogee describes them as setting up a square mat as a target in their ball play. An analogous object is found in the plat of the racket game at New Orleans. Among the Choctaw the goals were connected by a pole at the top. The length of the field appears to have varied greatly, from 30 rods (Mohawk) to half a league (Miami). In general it was remarkable for its extreme length. Attention appears to have been paid to the direction of the course, which is recorded as laid out from east to west or from north to south (Santee). The season varied in different localities: Summer among the Cherokee, and winter and spring among the Santee Dakota. Racket was commonly a tribal or intertribal contest. Its object, apart from mere diversion, appears to have been the stakes which were invariably wagered. Among the Huron, however, lacrosse is recorded by the Jesuit missionaries as played as a remedy for sickness. The magical rites connected with the game, the dance, scarifications, "going to water," tabus, amulets, and special features of the costume, all appear to refer to success in the contest. Attention may be called to the parallel between the Cherokee myth of ball play of the birds and animals and that of the moccasin game between the day and night animals recorded by Dr Washington Matthews.

There can be no doubt that, though the game of racket may have been modified in historic times, it remains an aboriginal invention. There are those, however, who assert the contrary. Sylva Clapin[a] says that the game of crosse, the national game of Canada since January 1, 1859, is about the same as the soule of the Ardennes mountaineers in France, and in the opinion of many is but a modification of the latter game as brought hither by the first French colonists.

ALGONQUIAN STOCK

CHEYENNE. Colorado.

Prof. F. V. Hayden[b] gives the following description:

O-ho-ni'-wo-ŏḣ, a ball club, with a hoop at the end to hold the ball as it is thrown.

---

[a] Dictionnaire Canadien-Français, Boston, 1894.
[b] Contributions to the Ethnography and Philology of the Indian Tribes of the Missouri Valley, p. 295, Philadelphia, 1862.

CHIPPEWA. Fort Michilimackinac, Michigan.

Alexander Henry [a] says:

Baggatiway, called by the Canadians le jeu de la crosse, is played with a bat and ball. The bat is about 4 feet in length, curved, and terminating in a sort of racket. Two posts are planted in the ground, at a considerable distance from each other, as a mile or more. Each party has its post, and the game consists in throwing the ball up to the post of the adversary. The ball, at the beginning, is placed in the middle of the course, and each party endeavors as well to throw the ball out of the direction of its own post as into that of the adversary's.

Henry describes a game of ball played by the Ojibwa (Chippewa) and Saukies (Sauk), on the King's birthday (June 4), 1763, at Fort Michilimackinac, through which, by strategy, that fort was taken.

———— Michigan.

Baraga [b] gives the following definitions:

Playing-ball or play-ball, pikwakwad, meaning primarily knot on a tree; ball-play, pagaadowewin; pagaádowanak, Indian crozier to play with.

J. Long [c] says:

Playing at ball, which is a favorite game, is very fatiguing. The ball is about the size of a cricket ball, made of deer skn, and stuffed with hair; this is driven forwards and backwards with short sticks, about 2 feet long, and broad at the end like a bat, worked like a racket, but with larger interstices; by this the ball is impelled, and from the elasticity of the racket, which is composed of deer's sinew, is thrown to a great distance: the game is played by two parties, and the contest lies in intercepting each other and striking the ball into a goal, at a distance of about 400 yards, at the extremity of which are placed two high poles, about the width of a wicket from each other: the victory consisting in driving the ball between the poles. The Indians play with great good humour, and even when one of them happens, in the heat of the game, to strike another with his stick, it is not resented. But these accidents are cautiously avoided, as the violence with which they strike has been known to break an arm or a leg.

———— White Earth agency, Minnesota.

Dr Walter J. Hoffman [d] describes the ball play at this place, where, he says, with a population of about 2,000 Indians, it is easy to muster from 80 to 100 ball players, who are divided into sides of equal number.

If the condition of the ground permits, the two posts or goals are planted about one-third of a mile apart. . . . The best players of either side gather at the center of the ground. The poorer players arrange themselves around their respective goals, while the heaviest in weight scatter across the field between the starting point and the goals. The ball is tossed into the air in the center of

---

[a] Travels and Adventures in Canada, p. 78, New York, 1809.

[b] A Dictionary of the Otchipwe Language, Cincinnati, 1853.

[c] Voyages and Travels of an Indian Interpreter, p. 52, London, 1791.

[d] Remarks on Ojibwa Ball Play. The American Anthropologist. v. 3, p. 134, 1890.

the field. As soon as it descends it is caught with the ball stick by one of the players, when he immediately sets out at full speed towards the opposite goal. If too closely pursued, or if intercepted by an opponent, he throws the ball in the direction of one of his own side, who takes up the race.

The usual method of depriving the player of the ball is to strike the handle of the ball stick so as to dislodge the ball; but this is frequently a difficult matter on account of a peculiar horizontal motion of the ball stick maintained by the runner. Frequently the ball carrier is disabled by being struck across the arm or leg, thus compelling his retirement. Severe injuries occur only when playing for high stakes or when ill-feeling exists between some of the players.

Should the ball carrier of one side reach the opposite goal, it is necessary for him to throw the ball so that it touches the post. This is always a difficult matter, because even if the ball be well directed, one of the numerous players surrounding the post as guards may intercept it and throw it back into the field. In this manner a single inning may be continued for an hour or more. The game may come to a close at the end of an inning by mutual agreement of the players, that side winning the greater number of scores being declared victor.

The ball used in this game is made by wrapping thin strands of buckskin and covering the whole with a piece of the same. It is about the size of a baseball, though not so heavy.

The stick is of the same pattern as that used at the beginning of the present century by the Mississaugas, the Ojibwa of the eagle totem of the Province of Ontario.

FIG. 749. Racket; length, 26 inches; Chippewa Indians, Bear island, Leech lake, Minnesota; cat. no. $\frac{50}{4730}$, American Museum of Natural History.

CHIPPEWA. Bear island, Leech lake, Minnesota. (Cat. no. $\frac{50}{4730}$, American Museum of Natural History.)

Racket (figure 749) made of a sapling 26 inches in length, curved at the striking end to form a hoop, netted with buckskin thongs. Collected by Dr William Jones in 1903.

FIG. 750. Racket; length, 34 inches; Chippewa Indians, Wisconsin; cat. no. 22160, Free Museum of Science and Art, University of Pennsylvania.

——— Wisconsin. (Cat. no. 22160, Free Museum of Science and Art, University of Pennsylvania.)

Racket (figure 750), a sapling cut and curved to form an oval hoop at the striking end, lashed at the end, and crossed by two thongs, which are intertwined, but not knotted, in the middle; length, 34 inches. Collected by Mr T. R. Roddy.

CHIPPEWA.   Wisconsin.
Jonathan Carver [a] says:

They amuse themselves at several sorts of games, but the principal and most esteemed among them is that of ball, which is not unlike the European game of tennis. The balls they use are rather larger than those made use of at tennis, and are formed of a piece of deer-skin; which being moistened to render it supple, is stuffed hard with the hair of the same creature, and sewed with its sinews. The ball-sticks are about 3 feet long, at the end of which there is fixed a kind of racket, resembling the palm of the hand, and fashioned of thongs cut from a deer-skin. In these they catch the ball, and throw it a great distance, if they are not prevented by some of the opposite party, who try to intercept it. The game is generally played by large companies, that sometimes consist of more than three hundred; and it is not uncommon for different bands to play against each other.

They begin by fixing two poles in the ground at about 600 yards apart, and one of these goals belongs to each party of the combatants. The ball is thrown up high in the center of the ground, and in a direct line between the goals; towards which each party endeavors to strike it, and whichsoever side first causes it to reach their own goal, reckons toward the game.

They are so exceeding dexterous in this manly exercise, that the ball is usually kept flying in different directions by the force of the rackets, without touching the ground during the whole contention; for they are not allowed to catch it with their hands.

They run with amazing velocity in pursuit of each other, and when one is on the point of hurling it to a great distance, an antagonist overtakes him, and by a sudden stroke dashes down the ball. They play with so much vehemence that they frequently wound each other, and sometimes a bone is broken; but notwithstanding these accidents there never appears to be any spite or wanton exertions of strength to effect them, nor do any disputes ever happen between the parties.

In his Chippewa vocabulary he gives ball as alewin.

―――― Apostle islands, Wisconsin.
J. G. Kohl [b] says:

Of all the Indian social sports the finest and grandest is the ball play. I might call it a noble game, and I am surprised how these savages attained such perfection in it. Nowhere in the world, excepting, perhaps, among the English and some of the Italian races, is the graceful and manly game of ball played so passionately and on so large a scale. They often play village against village, or tribe against tribe. Hundreds of players assemble, and the wares and goods offered as prizes often reach a value of a thousand dollars and more On our island we made a vain attempt to get up a game, for though the chiefs were ready enough, and all were cutting their raquets and balls in the bushes, the chief American authorities forbade this innocent amusement. Hence, on this occasion, I was only enabled to inspect the instruments. They were made with great care and well adapted for the purpose, and it is to be desired that the Indians would display the same attention to more important matters.

The raquets are $2\frac{1}{2}$ feet in length, carved very gracefully out of a white tough wood, and provided with a handle. The upper end is formed into a ring, 4 or 5 inches in diameter, worked very firmly and regularly, and covered by

―――――

[a] Travels through the Interior Parts of North America, p. 237, Philadelphia, 1796.
[b] Kitchi-gami, Wanderings round Lake Superior, p. 88, London, 1860.

a network of leather bands. The balls are made of white willow, and cut perfectly round with the hand: crosses, stars and circles are carved upon them. The care devoted to the balls is sufficient to show how highly they estimate the game. The French call it " jeu de crosse." Great ball players, who can send the ball so high that it is out of sight, attain the same renown among the Indians as celebrated runners, hunters, or warriors.

The name of the ball play is immortalized both in the geography and history of the country. There is a prairie, and now a town, on the Mississippi known as the " Prairie de la Crosse."

CHIPPEWA. Wisconsin.

Prof I. I. Ducatel [a] described boys playing at ball " by throwing it out and catching it with a stick, the end of which is curled up and makes the opening a pocket of network. This is the pahgato-wahnak."

———— Fort William, Ontario. (Cat. no. $\frac{50}{4729}$, American Museum of Natural History.)

A wooden ball (figure 751), painted red, 3 inches in diameter, per-forated with a hole, which emits a whistling noise in the air; and a wooden racket, 36 inches long, curved at the striking end to form a hoop, which is netted with buckskin thongs.

Collected in 1903 by Dr William Jones, who gives the name of the ball as pigwakwatwi and that of the racket and the game as paga-towan.

FIG. 751. Ball and racket; Chippewa Indians, Fort William, Ontario; diameter of ball, 3 inches; length of racket, 36 inches; cat. no. $\frac{50}{4729}$, American Museum of Natural History.

DELAWARES. Pennsylvania.

In Zeisberger's Indian Dictionary [b] we find the definition:

Ball (kugel), gendsítát.

MENOMINEE. Wisconsin.

Dr Walter J. Hoffman [c] describes the following game:

When anyone prepares to have a game of ball, he selects the captains or leaders of the two sides who are to compete. Each leader then appoints his own players, and the ball sticks to be used are deposited at the ball ground on the day before the game is to occur. Then each of the leaders selects a powerful and influential mitä'ⁿ, whose services are solicited for taking charge of the safety of the ball sticks, and to prevent their being charmed or conjured by

<hr />

[a] A Fortnight Among the Chippewas. The Indian Miscellany, p. 368, Albany, 1877.
[b] Cambridge, 1887.
[c] The Menomini Indians. Fourteenth Annual Report of the Bureau of Ethnology, p. 127, 1896.

the opposing mitä'ᵛ. The mitä'ᵛ is not expected to be present at the ground during the night, because he is supposed to have the power to influence the sticks at any distance.

Should one mitä'ᵛ succeed in obtaining such necromantic power over the sticks as to carry them away from the ground—that is, to carry away the power of the sticks—then it is the duty of the opposing mitä'ᵛ to follow him and bring them back. In case the pursuing mitä'ᵛ does not succeed in catching the rival, on account of being outwitted or because of having insufficient power in overcoming him, then the pursuing mitä'ᵛ is killed by his rival's sorcery. It usually happens that the pursuer compels the rival to restore the virtue or power of the sticks before the day approaches.

Four innings are played, and usually the presents, consisting of pieces of cloth, are divided into four parts, one part being given to the victor of each inning. Sometimes, however, the presents are renewed until the end of the game.

The frames from which the presents are suspended are near the middle of the ground, but off toward the eastern side, the tobacco-tray and other accessories being placed on the ground between them and toward the center of the ball ground. The two horizontal parallel poles forming the upper part of the framework are used for the calico and blankets; before them on the ground a cloth is spread, and on this are placed tobacco, pipes, and matches, to which all the participants are at liberty to help themselves.

The accompanying plate [XII] represents the players during a run for the ball. The latter is made of thongs of buckskin tightly wrapped and covered with buckskin or leather, and measures about 2½ inches in diameter. The sticks [figure 752] are made of hickory or ash, and about 3 feet long, the wood being shaved thinner and bent into a hoop or ring at least 4 inches in diameter. Four or five thongs pass through holes in the hoop and cross in the center, forming a netted pocket in which the ball may rest half hidden.

When the ball is caught, the runner carries the stick almost horizontally before him, moving it rapidly from side to side, and at the same time turning the stick so as to keep the ball always in front and retained by the pocket. This constant swinging and twisting movement tends to prevent players of the opposing side from knocking the ball out or dislodging it by hitting the stick.

The manner of preparing for and playing the game is like that of the Ojibwa of northern Minnesota.[a] . . .

FIG. 752. Racket; Menominee Indians, Wisconsin; from Hoffman.

During the intervals of rest the players approach the place of the presents and smoke. The giver of the game also awards to the successful players a part of the presents, the whole quantity being divided into four portions, so that equal portions are distributed at each of the intervals.

The players frequently hang to the belt the tail of a deer, an antelope, or some other fleet animal, or the wings of swift-flying birds, with the idea that through these they are endowed with the swiftness of the animal. There are, however, no special preparations preceding a game, as feasting or fasting, dancing, etc.—additional evidence that the game is not so highly regarded among the Ojibwa tribe.

---

[a] See p. 564.

MIAMI. St Joseph river, Michigan,
Charlevoix [a] says, referring to lacrosse:

It is played with a ball, and with two staffs recurved and terminated by a sort of racket. Two posts are set up, which serve as bounds, and which are distant from each other in proportion to the number of players. For instance, if there are eighty of these, there will be a half league between the posts. The players are divided into two bands, each having its own post; and it is a question of driving the ball as far as the post of the opposing party without falling upon the ground or being touched with the hand. If either of these happens the game is lost, unless he who has committed the mistake repairs it by driving the ball with one stroke to the bound, which is often impossible. These savages are so adroit in catching the ball with their crosses that these games sometimes last several days in succession.

———— Sault de Ste Marie, Michigan.
Mr Alexander McFarland Davis [b] says:

In 1667, Nicolas Perrot, then acting as agent of the French Government, was received near Saut Sainte Marie with stately courtesy and formal ceremony by the Miamis, to whom he was deputed. A few days after his arrival, the chief of that nation gave him, as an entertainment, a game of lacrosse.[c] "More than two thousand persons assembled in a great plain each with his cross. A wooden ball about the size of a tennis ball was tossed in the air. From that moment there was a constant movement of all these crosses which made a noise like that of arms which one hears during a battle. Half of the savages tried to send the ball to the northwest the length of the field, the others wished to make it go to the southeast. The contest which lasted for a half hour, was doubtful."

MISSISAUGA. New Credit, Ontario.
Rev. Peter Jones [d] says:

Ball playing is another favorite amusement.

———— Rice lake, Ontario.
G. Copway [e] says:

One of the most popular games is that of ball-playing, which oftimes engages an entire village. Parties are formed of from ten to several hundred. Before they commence those who are to take part in the play must provide each his share of stakings, or things which are set apart; and one leader for each party. Each leader appoints one of each company to be stake-holder.

Each man and each woman (women sometimes engage in the sport) is armed with a stick, one end of which bends somewhat like a small hoop, about 4 inches in circumference, to which is attached a net work of raw-hide, 2 inches deep, just large enough to admit the ball which is used on the occasion. Two poles are driven in the ground at a distance of four hundred paces from each other, which serves as goals for the two parties. It is the endeavor of each to take the ball to his hole. The party which carries the ball and strikes its pole wins the game.

---

[a] Journal d'un Voyage dans l'Amérique Septentrionnale, v. 3, p. 319, Paris, 1744.

[b] Indian Games. Bulletin of the Essex Institute, v. 17, p. 90, Salem, 1886.

[c] Histoire de l'Amérique Septentrionale par M. de Bacqueville de la Potherie, v. 2, p. 124, Paris, 1722.

[d] History of the Ojebway Indians, p. 134, London, 1861.

[e] The Traditional History and Characteristic Sketches of the Ojibway Nation, p. 49, Boston, 1851.

The warriors, very scantily attired, young and brave, fantastically painted, and women decorated with feathers, assemble around their commanders, who are generally swift on the race. They are to take the ball either by running with it or throwing it in the air. As the ball falls in the crowd the excitement begins. The clubs swing and roll from side to side, the players run and shout, fall upon and tread each other, and in the struggle some get rather rough treatment.

When the ball is thrown some distance on each side, the party standing near instantly pick it up, and run at full speed with three or four after him at full speed. The others send their shouts of encouragement to their own party: "Ha! ha! yah!" "A-ne-gook!"—and these shouts are heard even from the distant lodges, for children and all are deeply interested in the exciting scene. The spoils are not all on which their interest is fixed, but is directed to the falling and rolling of the crowds over and under each other. The loud and merry shouts of the spectators, who crowd the doors of the wigwams, go forth in one continued peal, and testify to their happy state of feeling.

The players are clothed in fur. They receive blows whose marks are plainly visible after the scuffle. The hands and feet are unincumbered and they exercise them to the extent of their powers; and with such dexterity do they strike the ball that it is sent out of sight. Another strikes it on its descent, and for ten minutes at a time the play is so adroitly managed that the ball does not touch the ground. No one is heard to complain, though he be bruised severely or his nose come in close communion with a club. If the last-mentioned catastrophe befel him, he is up in a trice, and sets his laugh forth as loud as the rest, though it be floated at first on a tide of blood.

It is very seldom, if ever, that one is seen to be angry because he has been hurt. If he should get so, they would call him a "coward," which proves a sufficient check to many evils which might result from many seemingly intended injuries.

NIPISSING. Forty miles above Montreal, Quebec.

J. A. Cuoq [a] gives the following definitions:

Pakatowan, jeu de crosse; pakatowanak, bois du jeu de crosse; pikwatwat, balle, pelota pour le jeu de crosse; kawaatikwan, abat-bois, boule à jouer aux quilles.

FIG. 753. Ball; diameter, 3¼ inches; Passamaquoddy Indians, Eastport, Maine; cat. no. 11426, United States National Museum.

PASSAMAQUODDY. Eastport, Maine. (Cat. no. 11426, United States National Museum.)

Hide ball (figure 753), made of a single piece with a thong drawstring at the edge, forming a flattened spheroid; diameter, 3¼ inches. Collected by Dr Edward Palmer.

Mr James Mooney [b] states that the Passamaquoddy use a ball stick (figure 754) with a strong, closely woven netting, which enables the stick to be used for batting. The sticks are ornamented with designs cut or burnt into the wood, and are sometimes further adorned with paint and feathers.

[a] Lexique de la Langue Algonquine, Montreal, 1886.
[b] The Cherokee Ball Play. The American Anthropologist, v. 3, p. 114, 1890.

Mrs W. W. Brown [a] describes the game as follows:

E-bes-qua-mo'gan, or game of ball, seems to have been the most popular and universal of the outdoor games, and played by all North American tribes. Their legends are more or less indebted to it. Tradition gives it a prominent place in their wonderful mythology. The Aurora Borealis is supposed to be Wā-ba-banal playing ball. Among the Wabanaki it was played by women as well as men, but, with few exceptions, never at the same time and place, as hunters and warriors played ball to gain muscular power, to stimulate their prowess, and to augment their fleetness of foot.

The players formed in a circle, proportionate to the number engaged in the game. Each held a stick called e-bes-quā-mo'gan-a-tok. This was made of some flexible wood, about 3 feet in length, crooked to three-fourths of a circle at one end, which was interwoven with stripes of hide after the manner of snowshoes. One man was detached to stand in the centre and on his throwing into the air a chip, upon which he had spat, each one would cry, " I'll take the dry " or " I'll take the wet," thus forming opposite factions. The side of the chip which fell uppermost decided which party should commence play. The ball was never touched with the hand, but thrown and kept in motion by the e-bes-quā-mo'gan-a-tok. The goals were two rings or holes dug in the ground, the distance of the circle of players apart. The game consisted in getting the ball into opponent's goal, and regard for neither life nor limb was allowed to stand in the way of possible success. As they played with little or

FIG. 754. Racket; Passamaquoddy Indians, Maine; from Mooney.

nothing on, few escaped unhurt, but these mishaps were taken as the fortunes of war, and no resentment was felt. The women dress very scantily while playing this game, and the men, having a strict code of honor, never go near their playground. One tradition tells of a man that did so and threw shells and pebbles at the players. They screened themselves as best they could behind bushes and rocks. At the second attack, however, they made a rush in the direction from which the missiles came. The man ran to the water, and, plunging in, was turned into a che-pen-ob-quis (large chubfish), by which transformation they knew he was a Mohawk. They look upon all Mohawks as addicted to sorcery.

PENOBSCOT. Oldtown, Maine. (Cat. no. 48236, Peabody Museum of American Archæology and Ethnology.)

Ball for lacrosse (figure 755), 4 inches in diameter, covered with buckskin and filled with moose hair.

The cover, a nearly circular piece of buckskin about 9 inches in diameter, is drawn up with a buckskin thong, pudding-bag fashion, around the wad of moose hair; over it is placed a second piece of buckskin, 5 inches in diameter, which closes the opening. It was purchased from Big Thunder, one of the very old men of the tribe, when he was on a visit to Cambridge.

---

[a] Some Indoor and Outdoor Games of the Wabanaki Indians. Transactions of the Royal Society of Canada. v. 6, sec. 2, p. 45, Montreal, 1889.

SAUK AND FOXES. Iowa. (American Museum of Natural History.)
Cat. no. $\frac{50}{2206}$. Racket (figure 756) made of hard wood, with the end
shaved thin and turned around to form a circular hoop, which is
laced with cord passing through the edge; length, 29½ inches.
Collected by Dr William Jones in 1901.

Cat. no. $\frac{50}{2203}$. Buckskin-covered ball (figure 757), 2¾ inches in diameter, bag-shaped, with thong attached at the edge of the seam.

Collected in 1901 by Dr William Jones, who describes it as a
lacrosse ball. A bundle of twenty pieces of reed (figure 758), 9½
inches in length, in the same collection, is described as message sticks
for the lacrosse game.

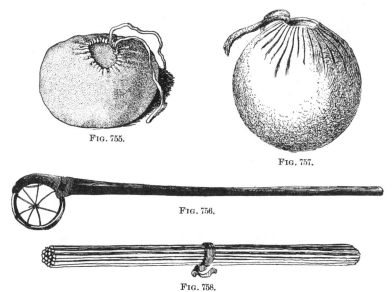

FIG. 755.

FIG. 757.

FIG. 756.

FIG. 758.

FIG. 755. Ball; diameter, 4 inches; Penobscot Indians, Maine; cat. no. 48236, Peabody Museum
of American Archæology and Ethnology.
FIG. 756. Racket; length, 29½ inches; Sauk and Fox Indians, Iowa; cat. no $\frac{50}{2206}$, American
Museum of Natural History.
FIG. 757. Ball; diameter, 2¾ inches; Sauk and Fox Indians, Iowa; cat. no. $\frac{50}{2203}$, American
Museum of Natural History.
FIG. 758. Message sticks for ball game; length, 9½ inches; Sauk and Fox Indians, Iowa; cat.
no. $\frac{50}{3831}$, American Museum of Natural History.

———— Tama, Iowa. (Cat. no. 36753, Free Museum of Science and
Art, University of Pennsylvania.)
Hickory stick (figure 759), with the end turned over to form a small
hoop, which is netted with thong; length, 50½ inches. Collected
by the writer in 1900.

These Indians stated that they no longer make their own balls.
The ball game they call bagahatuwitni, and the stick, otchi.

Dr William Jones informed me that the ball, pekwaki, used in
this game, was bag-shaped and drawn up with a thong.

SAUK AND FOXES. Oklahoma. (Cat. no. $\frac{50}{2253}$, American Museum of Natural History.)

Racket made of hickory, with the end cut thin and turned around to form an oval hoop, as shown in figure 760; length, 42 inches; the circumference is perforated with five holes, through which thongs pass to form a network, as illustrated in the figure. Collected by Dr William Jones.

FIG. 759. Racket; length, 50¼ inches; Sauk and Fox Indians, Tama, Iowa; cat. no. 36753, Free Museum of Science and Art, University of Pennsylvania.

SHAWNEE. Indian Territory.

Dr William Jones informs me that the lacrosse game, while usually played by men alone, is played also by men and women on opposite sides, the men using the sticks and the women their hands. In this latter case the goals, hoop wickets, are nearer together than when men play alone.

CHINOOKAN STOCK

CHINOOK. Fort Vancouver, Washington.

Paul Kane [a] says:

> They also take great delight in a game with a ball, which is played by them in the same manner as the Cree, Chippewa, and Sioux Indians. Two poles are erected about a mile apart, and the company is divided into two bands, armed with sticks, having a small ring or hoop at the end, with which the ball is picked up and thrown to a great distance; each party then strives to get the ball past their own goal. There are sometimes a hundred on a side, and the play is kept up with great noise and excitement. At this game they bet heavily, as it is generally played between tribes and villages.

IROQUOIAN STOCK

CAUGHNAWAGA. Quebec.

Col. James Smith [b] thus describes a game:

> . . . they used a wooden ball about 3 inches in diameter, and the instrument they moved it with was a strong staff about 5 feet long with a hoop net on the end of it, large enough to contain the ball. Before they begin to play, they lay off about half a mile distance in a clear plain, and the opposite parties all attend at the center, where a disinter-

FIG. 760. Racket; length, 42 inches; Sauk and Fox Indians, Oklahoma; cat. no. $\frac{50}{2253}$, American Museum of Natural History.

[a] Wanderings of an Artist among the Indians of North America, p. 190, London, 1859. See also The Canadian Journal, p. 276, Toronto, July, 1855.

[b] An Account of the Remarkable Occurrences in the Life and Travels of Col. James Smith, p. 78, Cincinnati, 1870.

ested person casts up the ball, then the opposite parties all contend for it. If
anyone gets it into his net, he runs with it the way he wishes it to go, and
they all pursue him. If one of the opposite party overtakes the person with
the ball, he gives the stay a stroke which causes the ball to fly out of the net;
then they have another debate for it; and if the one that gets it can outrun
all the opposite party, and can carry it quite out, or over the line at the end, the
game is won; but this seldom happens. When anyone is running away with
the ball and is like to be overtaken, he commonly throws it, and with this
instrument can cast it 50 or 60 yards. Sometimes when the ball is almost at
the one end matters will take a sudden turn, and the opposite party may quickly
carry it out at the other end. Oftentimes they will work a long time back and
forward before they can get the ball over the line, or win the game.

CHEROKEE.   Tennessee river, North Carolina.

John Bartram [a] describes a ball dance in the council house at the Indian town of Cowe:

> This assembly was held principally to rehearse the ball-play dance, this town
> being challenged to play against another the next day.
>
> The people being assembled and seated in order, and the musicians having
> taken their station, the ball opens, first with a long harangue or oration, spoken
> by an aged chief, in commendation of the manly exercise of the ball-play, re-
> counting the many and brilliant victories which the town of Cowe had gained
> over the other towns in the nation, not forgetting or neglecting to recite his
> own exploits, together with those of other aged men now present, coadjutors
> in the performance of these athletic games in their youthful days. This oration
> was delivered with great spirit and eloquence, and was meant to influence the
> passions of the young men present, excite them to emulation, and inspire them
> with ambition.
>
> This prologue being at an end, the musicians began, both vocal and instru-
> mental; when presently a company of girls, hand in hand, dressed in clean white
> robes and ornamented with beads, bracelets, and a profusion of gay ribbands,
> entering the door, immediately began to sing their responses in a gentle, low,
> and sweet voice, and formed themselves in a semicircular file or line, in two
> ranks, back to back, facing the spectators and musicians, moving slowly round
> and round; this continued about a quarter of an hour, when we were sur-
> prised by a sudden very loud and shrill whoop, uttered at once by a company
> of young fellows, who came in briskly after one another, with rackets or hurls
> in one hand. These champions likewise were well dressed, painted, and orna-
> mented with silver bracelets, gorgets and wampum, neatly ornamented with
> moccasins and highwaving plumes in their diadems: they immediately formed
> themselves in a semicircular rank also, in front of the girls, when these changed
> their order, and formed a single rank parallel to the men, raising their voices in
> responses to the tunes of the young champions, the semicircles continually
> moving round. There was something singular and diverting in their step and
> motions, and I imagine not to be learned to exactness but with great attention
> and perseverance; the step, if it can be so termed, was performed after the
> following manner; i. e., first, the motion began at one end of the semicircle,
> gently rising up and down upon their toes and heels alternately, when the first
> was up on tip-toe, the next began to raise the heel, and by the time the first
> rested again on the heel, the second was on tip-toe, thus from one end of the

---

[a] Travels through North and South Carolina, Georgia, East and West Florida, p. 369,
Philadelphia, 1791.

MENOMINEE BALL GAME; WISCONSIN; FROM HOFFMAN

BALL DANCE; EAST CHEROKEE INDIANS, NORTH CAROLINA; FROM PHOTOGRAPH BY MOONEY (1893)

rank to the other, so that some were always up and some down, alternately and regularly, without the least baulk or confusion; and they at the same time, and in the same motion, moved on obliquely or sideways, so that the circle performed a double or complex motion in its progression, and at stated times exhibited a grand or universal movement, instantly and unexpectedly to the spectators, by each rank turning to right and left, taking each others places: the movements were managed with inconceivable alertness and address, and accompanied with an instantaneous and universal elevation of the voice, and shrill, short whoop.

CHEROKEE. North Carolina.

Mr James Mooney described the ball game of the East Cherokee under the name of anetsa: [a]

The ball now used is an ordinary leather-covered ball, but in former days it was made of deer hair and covered with deerskin. In California the ball is of wood. The ball sticks vary considerably among different tribes. As before stated, the Cherokee player uses a pair, catching the ball between them and throwing it in the same way. The stick is somewhat less than 3 feet in length, and its general appearance closely resembles a tennis racket, or a long wooden spoon, the bowl of which is a loose network of thongs of twisted squirrel skin or strings of Indian hemp. The frame is made of a slender hickory stick, bent upon itself, and so trimmed and fashioned that the handle seems to be of one solid round piece, when, in fact, it is double. . . .

The ball season begins about the middle of summer and lasts until the weather is too cold to permit exposure of the naked body, for the players are always stripped for the game. The favorite time is in the fall, after the corn has ripened, for then the Indian has abundant leisure, and at this season a game takes place somewhere on the reservation at least every other week, while several parties are always in training. The training consists chiefly in regular athletic practice, the players of one side coming together with their ball sticks at some convenient spot of level bottom land, where they strip to the waist, divide into parties, and run, tumble, and toss the ball until the sun goes down. . . .

In addition to the athletic training, which begins two or three weeks before the regular game, each player is put under a strict gaktûnta or tabu, during the same period. He must not eat the flesh of a rabbit (of which the Indians generally are very fond) because the rabbit is a timid animal, easily alarmed and liable to lose its wits when pursued by the hunter. Hence the ball player must abstain from it, lest he, too, should become disconcerted and lose courage in the game. He must also avoid the meat of the frog (another item on the Indian bill of fare), because the frog's bones are brittle and easily broken, and a player who should partake of the animal would expect to be crippled in the first inning. For a similar reason he abstains from eating the young of any bird or animal, and from touching an infant. He must not eat the fish called the hog-sucker, because it is sluggish in its movements. He must not eat the herb called atûnka or Lamb's Quarter, (*Chenopodium album*), which the Indians use for greens, because its stalk is easily broken. Hot food and salt are also forbidden, as in the medical gaktûnta. The tabu always lasts for seven days preceding the game, but in most cases is enforced for twenty-eight days—i. e., 4×7—4 and 7 being sacred numbers. Above all, he must not touch a woman, and the player who should violate this regulation would expose himself to the summary vengeance of his fellows. This last tabu continues also for seven days after the game. As before stated, if a woman even so much as touches a

---

[a] The Cherokee Ball Play. The American Anthropologist, v. 3, p. 105, 1890.

ball stick on the eve of a game, it is thereby rendered unfit for use. As the white man's law is now paramount, extreme measures are seldom resorted to, but in former days the punishment for an infraction of this regulation was severe, and in some tribes the penalty was death. Should a player's wife be with child, he is not allowed to take part in the game under any circumstances, as he is then believed to be heavy and sluggish in his movements, having lost just so much of his strength as has gone into the child.

At frequent intervals during the training period the shaman takes the players to water and performs his mystic rites, as will be explained further on. They are also scratched on their naked bodies, as at the final game, but now the scratching is done in a haphazard fashion with a piece of bamboo brier having stout thorns, which leave broad gashes on the backs of the victims.

When a player fears a particular contestant on the other side, as is frequently the case, his own shaman performs a special incantation, intended to compass the defeat and even the disabling or death of his rival. As the contending sides always belong to different settlements, each party makes all these preliminary arrangements without the knowledge of the other, and under the guidance of its own shamans, several of whom are employed on a side in every hotly contested game. . . .

On the night preceding the game each party holds the ball-play dance in its own settlement. On the reservation the dance is always held on Friday night, so that the game may take place on Saturday afternoon, in order to give the players and spectators an opportunity to sleep off the effects on Sunday. . . . The dance must be held close to the river, to enable the players to " go to water " during the night, but the exact spot selected is always a matter of uncertainty up to the last moment, excepting with a chosen few. If this were not the case, a spy from the other settlement might endeavor to insure the defeat of the party by strewing along their trail a soup made of the hamstrings of rabbits, which would have the effect of rendering the players timorous and easily confused.

The dance begins soon after dark on the night preceding the game, and lasts until daybreak, and from the time they eat supper before the dance until after the game, on the following afternoon, no food passes the lips of the players.

Mr Mooney selected for illustration the last game which he witnessed on the reservation, in September, 1889. On the occasion in question the young men of Yellow Hill were to contend against those of Raven Town, about 10 miles farther up the river, and as the latter place was a large settlement noted for its adherence to the old traditions, a spirited game was expected.

Each party holds a dance [plate XIII] in its own settlement, the game taking place about midway between. The Yellow Hill men were to have their dance up the river, about half a mile from my house. . . . The spot selected for the dance was a narrow strip of gravely bottom, where the mountain came close down to the water's edge. . . . Several fires were burning. . . . Around the larger fire were the dancers, the men stripped as for the game, with their ball-sticks in their hands and the firelight playing upon their naked bodies. . . .

The ball-play dance is participated in by both sexes, but differs considerably from any other of the dances of the tribe, being a dual affair throughout. The dancers are the players of the morrow, with seven women, representing the seven Cherokee clans. The men dance in a circle around the fire, chanting responses to the sound of a rattle carried by another performer, who circles around on the outside, while the women stand in line a few feet away and dance to and fro, now advancing a few steps toward the men, then wheeling and dancing away from them, but all the while keeping time to the sound of the drum and chanting the refrain to the ball songs made by the drummer, who is seated on the ground on the side farthest from the fire. The rattle is a gourd fitted with a handle and filled with small pebbles, while the drum resembles a small keg with a head of ground-hog leather. The drum is partly filled with water, the head being also moistened to improve the tone, and is beaten with a single stick. Men and women dance separately throughout, the music, the evolutions, and the songs being entirely distinct, but all combine to produce an harmonious whole. The women are relieved at intervals by others who take their places, but the men dance in the same narrow circle the whole night long, excepting during the frequent halts for the purpose of going to water.

At one side of the fire are set up two forked poles, supporting a third laid horizontally, upon which the ball sticks are crossed in pairs until the dance begins. As already mentioned, small pieces from the wing of the bat are sometimes tied to these poles, and also to the rattle used in the dance, to insure success in the contest. The skins of several bats and swift-darting insectivorous birds were formerly wrapped up in a piece of deerskin, together with the cloth and beads used in the conjuring ceremonies later on, and hung from the frame during the dance. On finally dressing for the game at the ball ground, the players took the feathers from these skins to fasten in their hair or upon the ball sticks, to insure swiftness and accuracy in their movements. Sometimes also hairs from the whiskers of the bat are twisted into the netting of the ball sticks. The players are all stripped and painted, with feathers in their hair, just as they appear in the game. When all is ready an attendant takes down the ball sticks from the frame, throwing them over his arm in the same fashion, and, walking around the circle, gives to each man his own. Then the rattler, taking his instrument in his hand, begins to trot around on the outside of the circle, uttering a sharp "Hĭ!" to which the players respond with a quick "Hi-hĭ′!" while slowly moving around the circle with their ball sticks held tightly in front of their breasts. Then, with a quicker movement, the song changes to "Ehu′!" and the responses to "Hăhĭ′! Ehu′! Hăhĭ′! Ehu′! Hăhĭ′!" Then, with a prolonged shake of the rattle, it changes again to "Ahiye′!" the dancers responding with the same word "Ahiye′!" but in a higher key; the movements become more lively and the chorus louder, till at a given signal with the rattle the players clap their ball sticks together, and, facing around, go through the motions of picking up and tossing an imaginary ball. Finally, with a grand rush, they dance up close to the women, and the first part of the performance ends with a loud prolonged "Hu-ŭ!" from the whole crowd.

In the meantime the women have taken position in a line a few feet away, with their backs turned to the men, while in front of them the drummer is seated on the ground, but with his back turned toward them and the rest of the dancers. After a few preliminary taps on the drum, he begins a slow, measured beat, and strikes up one of the dance refrains, which the women take up in chorus. This is repeated a number of times until all are in harmony with the tune, when he begins to improvise, choosing words which will harmonize with the measure of the chorus, and at the same time be appropriate to the subject of the dance. As this requires a ready wit in addition to ability as a singer, the selection of a drummer is a matter of considerable importance, and that functionary is held in corresponding estimation. He sings of the game on the morrow, of the fine things to be won by the men of his party, of the joy with which they will be received by their friends on their return from the field, and of the disappointment and defeat of their rivals. Throughout it all the women keep up the same minor refrain, like an instrumental accompaniment to vocal music. As Cherokee songs are always in the minor key, they have a plaintive effect, even when the sentiment is cheerful or even boisterous, and are calculated to excite the mirth of one who understands the language. This impression is heightened by the appearance of the dancers themselves, for the women shuffle solemnly back and forth all night long without ever a smile upon their faces, while the occasional laughter of the men seems half subdued. The monotonous repetition, too, is something intolerable to anyone but an Indian, the same words, to the same tune, being sometimes sung over and over again for a half hour or more. Although the singer improvises as he proceeds, many of the expressions have now become stereotyped and are used at almost every ball-play dance. . . .

According to a Cherokee myth, the animals once challenged the birds to a great ball play. The wager was accepted, the preliminaries were arranged, and at last the contestants assembled at the appointed spot—the animals on the ground, while the birds took position in the tree-tops to await the throwing up of the ball. On the side of the animals were the bear, whose ponderous weight bore down all opposition; the deer, who excelled all others in running; and the terrapin, who was invulnerable to the stoutest blows. On the side of the birds were the eagle, the hawk, and the great Tlániwă—all noted for their swiftness and power of flight. While the latter were preening their feathers and watching every motion of their adversaries below, they noticed two small creatures, hardly larger than mice, climbing up the tree on which was perched the leader of the birds. Finally they reached the top and humbly asked the captain to be allowed to join in the game. The captain looked at them a moment, and, seeing that they were four-footed, asked them why they did not go to the animals where they properly belonged. The little things explained that they had done so, but had been laughed at and rejected on account of their diminutive size. On hearing their story the bird captain was disposed to take pity on them, but there was one serious difficulty in the way—how could they join the birds when they had no wings? The eagle, the hawk, and the rest now crowded around, and after some discussion it was decided to try and make wings for the little fellows. But how to do it! All at once, by a happy inspiration, one bethought himself of the drum which was to be used in the dance. The head was made of groundhog leather, and perhaps a corner could be cut off and utilized for wings. No sooner suggested than done. Two pieces of leather taken from the drumhead were cut into shape and attached to the legs of one of the small animals, and thus originated Tlameha, the bat. The ball was now tossed up, and the bat was told to catch it, and his expertness in dodging and circling about, keeping the ball constantly in motion and never allowing it to fall to the ground, soon convinced the birds that they had gained a most valuable ally. They next turned their attention to the other little creature; and now behold a worse difficulty! All their leather had been used in making wings for the bat, and there was no time to send for more. In this dilemma it was suggested that perhaps wings might be made by stretching out the skin of the animal itself. So two large birds seized him from opposite sides with their strong bills, and by tugging and pulling at his fur for several minutes succeeded in stretching the skin between the fore and hind feet until at last the thing was done and there was Tewa, the flying squirrel. Then the bird captain, to try him, threw up the ball, when the flying squirrel, with a graceful bound, sprang off the limb and, catching it in his teeth, carried it through the air to another tree-top a hundred feet away.

When all was ready, the game began, but at the very outset the flying squirrel caught the ball and carried it up a tree, then threw it to the birds, who kept it in the air for some time, when it dropped; but just before it reached the ground the bat seized it, and by his dodging and doubling kept it out of the way of even the swiftest of the animals until he finally threw it in at the goal, and thus won the victory for the birds. Because of their assistance on this occasion, the ball player invokes the aid of the bat and the flying squirrel and ties a small piece of the bat's wing to his ball stick or fastens it to the frame on which the sticks are hung during the dance.[a]   .   .   .

At a certain stage of the dance a man, specially selected for the purpose, leaves the groups of spectators around the fire and retires a short distance into the darkness in the direction of the rival settlement. Then, standing with his face still turned in the same direction, he raises his hand to his mouth and utters four yells, the last prolonged into a peculiar quaver. He is answered by the players with a chorus of yells—or rather yelps, for the Indian yell resembles nothing else so much as the bark of a puppy. Then he comes running back until he passes the circle of dancers, when he halts and shouts out a single word, which may be translated, "They are already beaten!" Another chorus of yells greets this announcement. This man is called the talala, or woodpecker, on account of his peculiar yell, which is considered to resemble the sound made by a woodpecker tapping on a dead tree trunk. According to the orthodox Cherokee belief, this yell is heard by the rival players in the other settlement— who, it will be remembered, are having a ball dance of their own at the same time—and so terrifies them that they lose all heart for the game. The fact that both sides alike have a talala in no way interferes with the theory.

At frequent intervals during the night all the players, accompanied by the shaman and his assistant, leave the dance and go down to a retired spot at the river's bank, where they perform the mystic rite known as "going to water," hereafter to be described. While the players are performing this ceremony, the women, with the drummer, continue the dance and chorus. The dance is kept up without intermission, and almost without change, until daybreak. At the final dance green pine tops are thrown upon the fire, so as to produce a thick smoke, which envelopes the dancers. Some mystic properties are ascribed to this pine smoke, but what they are I have not yet learned, although the ceremony seems to be intended as an exorcism, the same thing being done at other dances when there has recently been a death in the settlement.

At sunrise the players, dressed now in their ordinary clothes, but carrying their ball sticks in their hands, start for the ball ground, accompanied by the shamans and their assistants. The place selected for the game, being always about midway between the two rival settlements, was in this case several miles above the dance ground and on the opposite side of the river. On the march each party makes four several halts, when each player again "goes to water" separately with the shaman. This occupies considerable time, so that it is usually afternoon before the two parties meet on the ball ground. While the shaman is busy with his mysteries in the laurel bushes down by the water's edge, the other players, sitting by the side of the trail, spend the time twisting extra strings for their ball sticks, adjusting their feather ornaments, and discussing the coming game. In former times the player during these halts was not allowed to sit upon a log, a stone, or anything but the ground itself; neither was it permissible to lean against anything excepting the back of another player, on penalty of defeat in the game, with the additional risk of

---

[a] A somewhat different account of this myth is given by Mr Mooney in Myths of the Cherokee. Nineteenth Annual Report of the Bureau of American Ethnology, p. 286, 1900.

being bitten by a rattlesnake. This rule is now disregarded, and it is doubtful if any but the older men are aware that it ever existed.

On coming up from the water after the fourth halt, the principal shaman assembles the players around him and delivers an animated harangue, exhorting them to do their utmost in the coming contest, telling them that they will undoubtedly be victorious, as the omens are all favorable, picturing to their delighted vision the stakes to be won and the ovation awaiting them from their friends after the game, and finally assuring them in the mystic terms of the formulas that their adversaries will be driven through the four gaps into the gloomy shadows of the Darkening Land, where they will perish forever from remembrance. The address, delivered in rapid, jerky tones like the speech of an auctioneer, has a very inspiriting effect upon the hearers and is frequently interrupted by a burst of exultant yells from the players. At the end, with another chorus of yells, they again take up the march.

On arriving in sight of the ball ground, the talala again comes to the front and announces their approach with four loud yells, ending with a long quaver, as on the previous night at the dance. The players respond with another yell, and then turn off to a convenient sheltered place by the river to make the final preparations.

The shaman then marks off a small space upon the ground to represent the ball field, and, taking in his hand a small bundle of sharpened stakes about a foot in length, addresses each man in turn, telling him the position which he is to occupy in the field at the tossing up of the ball after the first inning, and driving down a stake to represent each player until he has a diagram of the whole field spread out upon the ground.

The players then strip for the ordeal of scratching [plate XIV]. This painful operation is performed by an assistant, in this case by an old man named Standing Water. The instrument of torture is called a kanuga and resembles a short comb with seven teeth, seven being also a sacred number with the Cherokees. The teeth are made of sharpened splinters from the leg bone of a turkey and are fixed in a frame made from the shaft of a turkey quill, in such a manner that by a slight pressure of the thumb they can be pushed out to the length of a small tack. Why the bone and feather of the turkey should be selected I have not yet learned, but there is undoubtedly an Indian reason for the choice.

The players having stripped, the operator begins by seizing the arm of a player with one hand while holding the kanuga in the other, and plunges the teeth into the flesh at the shoulder, bringing the instrument down with a steady pressure to the elbow, leaving seven white lines which become red a moment later as the blood starts to the surface. He now plunges the kanuga in again at another place near the shoulder, and again brings it down to the elbow. Again and again the operation is repeated until the victim's arm is scratched in twenty-eight lines above the elbow. It will be noticed that twenty-eight is a combination of four and seven, the two sacred numbers of the Cherokee. The operator then makes the same number of scratches in the same manner on the arm below the elbow. Next the other arm is treated in the same way; then each leg, both above and below the knee, and finally an X is scratched across the breast of the sufferer, the upper ends are joined by another stroke from shoulder to shoulder, and a similar pattern is scratched upon his back. By this time the blood is trickling in little streams from nearly three hundred gashes. None of the scratches are deep, but they are unquestionably very painful, as all agree who have undergone the operation. Nevertheless the young men endure the ordeal willingly and almost cheerfully, regarding it as a necessary part of the ritual to secure success in the game. In order to secure a

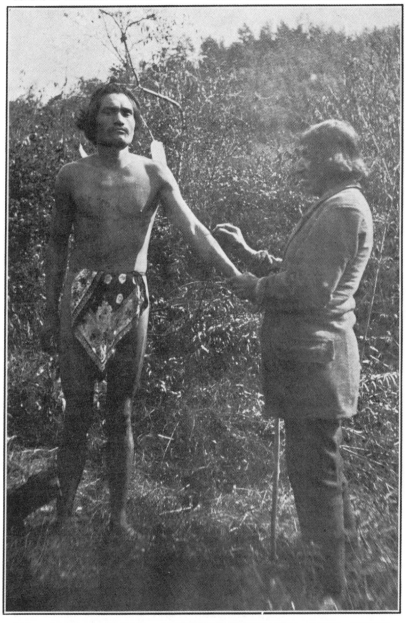

SCRATCHING A PLAYER; CHEROKEE INDIAN BALL GAME, NORTH
CAROLINA; FROM PHOTOGRAPH BY MOONEY (1893)

CHEROKEE INDIAN BALL PLAYER, JOE CROW, READY FOR THE BALL
DANCE; NORTH CAROLINA; FROM PHOTOGRAPH BY MOONEY (1888)

picture of one young fellow under the operation I stood with my camera so near that I could distinctly hear the teeth tear through the flesh at every scratch with a rasping sound that sent a shudder through me, yet he never flinched, although several times he shivered with cold, as the chill autumn wind blew upon his naked body. This scratching is common in Cherokee medical practice, and is variously performed with a brier, a rattlesnake's tooth, a flint, or even a piece of broken glass. It was noted by Adair as early as 1775. To cause the blood to flow more freely, the young men sometimes scrape it off with chips as it oozes out. The shaman then gives to each player a small piece of root, to which he has imparted magic properties by the recital of certain secret formulas. Various roots are used, according to the whim of the shaman, their virtue depending entirely upon the ceremony of consecration. The men chew these roots and spit out the juice over their limbs and bodies, rubbing it well into the scratches; then going down to the water, plunge in and wash off the blood, after which they come out and dress themselves for the game.

The modern Cherokee ball costume consists simply of a pair of short trunks, ornamented with various patterns in red or blue cloth, and a feather charm worn upon the head. Formerly the breechcloth alone was worn, as is still the case in some instances, and the strings with which it was tied were purposely made weak, so that if seized by an opponent in the scuffle the strings would break, leaving the owner to escape with the loss of his sole article of raiment. This calls to mind a similar custom among the ancient Greek athletes, the recollection of which has been preserved in the etymology of the word "gymnast." The ornament worn in the hair is made up of an eagle's feathers, to give keenness of sight; a deer tail, to give swiftness; and a snake's rattle, to render the wearer terrible to his adversaries. If an eagle's feathers can not be procured, those of a hawk or any other swift bird of prey are used. In running, the snake rattle is made to furnish a very good imitation of the sound made by the rattlesnake when about to strike. The player also marks his body in various patterns with paint or charcoal. The charcoal is taken from the dance fire, and whenever possible is procured by burning the wood of a tree which has been struck by lightning, such wood being regarded as peculiarly sacred and endowed with mysterious properties. According to one formula, the player makes a cross over his heart and a spot upon each shoulder, using pulverized charcoal procured from the shaman and made by burning together the wood of a honey-locust tree and of a tree which has been struck by lightning, but not killed. The charcoal is pulverized and put, together with a red and black bead, into an empty cocoon from which one end has been cut off. This paint preparation makes the player swift like the lightning and invulnerable as the tree that defies the thunderbolt, and renders his flesh as hard and firm to the touch as the wood of the honey locust. Among the Choctaws, according to Catlin, a tail of horse hair was also worn, so as to stream out behind as the player ran. Just before dressing, the players rub their bodies with grease or the chewed bark of the slippery elm or the sassafras, until their skin is slippery as that of the proverbial eel.

A number of precautionary measures are also frequently resorted to by the more prudent players while training, in order to make assurance doubly sure. They bathe their limbs with a decoction of the herb *Tephrosia virginiana*, or catgut, in order to render their muscles tough like the roots of that plant. They bathe themselves with a decoction of the small rush (*Juncus tenuis*), which grows by the roadside, because its stalks are always erect and will not lie flat upon the ground, however much they may be stamped and trodden upon. In the same way they bathe with a decoction of the wild crabapple or the ironwood, because the trunks of these trees, even when thrown down, are supported and kept up from the ground by their spreading tops.   To make themselves more supple, they whip themselves with the tough stalks of the wā'takû, or star-grass, or with switches made from the bark of a hickory sapling which has grown up from under a log that has fallen across it, the bark being taken from the bend thus produced in the sapling.   After the first scratching the player renders himself an object of terror to his opponents by eating a portion of a rattlesnake which has been killed and cooked by the shaman.   He rubs himself with an eel skin to make himself slippery like the eel, and rubs each limb down once with the fore and hind leg of a turtle, because the legs of that animal are remarkably stout.   He applies to the shaman to conjure a dangerous opponent, so that he may be unable to see the ball in its flight, or may dislocate a wrist or break a leg.   Sometimes the shaman draws upon the ground an armless figure of his rival, with a hole where his heart should be.   Into this hole he drops two black beads, covers them with earth and stamps upon them, and thus the dreaded rival is doomed, unless (and this is always the saving clause) his own shaman has taken precautions against such a result, or the one in whose behalf the charm is made has rendered the incantation unavailing by a violation of some one of the interminable rules of the gaktûnta.

The players, having dressed, are now ready to go to water for the last time, for which purpose the shaman selects a bend of the river where he can look toward the east while facing upstream.   This ceremony of going to water is the most sacred and impressive in the whole Cherokee ritual, and must always be performed fasting, and in most cases also is preceded by an all-night vigil.   It is used in connection with prayers to obtain a long life, to destroy an enemy, to win the love of a woman, to secure success in the hunt and the ball play, and for recovery from a dangerous illness, but is performed only as a final resort or when, the occasion is one of special importance.   The general ceremonial and the principal formulas are nearly the same in all cases.   I have collected a number of the formulas used on these various occasions, but it is impossible within the limits of this paper to give more than a general idea of their nature.

The men stand side by side looking down upon the water, with their ball sticks clasped upon their breasts, while the shaman stands just behind them, and an assistant kneeling at his side spreads out upon the ground the cloth upon which are placed the sacred beads.   These beads are of two colors, red and black, each kind resting upon a cloth of the same color, and corresponding in number to the number of players.   The red beads represent the players for whom the shaman performs the ceremony, while the black beads stand for their opponents, red being symbolic of power and triumph, while black is emblematic of death and misfortune.   All being ready, the assistant hands to the shaman a red bead, which he takes between the thumb and finger of his right hand; and then a black bead, which he takes in the same manner in his left hand.   Then, holding his hands outstretched, with his eyes intently fixed upon the beads, the shaman prays on behalf of his client to Yûwĭ Gûnahi' ta, the Long Man, the sacred name for the river: " O, Long Man, I come to the edge of your body.   You are mighty and most powerful.   You bear up great logs and toss them about where the foam is white.   Nothing can resist you.   Grant me such strength in the contest that my enemy may be of no weight in my hands— that I may be able to toss him into the air or dash him to the earth."   In a similar strain he prays to the Red Bat in the Sun Land to make him expert in dodging; to the Red Deer to make him fleet of foot; to the great Red Hawk to render him keen of sight; and to the Red Rattlesnake to render him terrible to all who oppose him.

Then, in the same low tone and broken accents in which all the formulas are recited, the shaman declares that his client (mentioning his name and clan) has now ascended to the first heaven. As he continues praying he declares that he has now reached the second heaven (and here he slightly raises his hands); soon he ascends to the third heaven, and the hands of the shaman are raised still higher; then, in the same way, he ascends to the fourth, the fifth, and the sixth heaven, and finally, as he raises his trembling hands aloft, he declares that the spirit of the man has now risen to the seventh heaven, where his feet are resting upon the Red Seats, from which they shall never be displaced.

Turning now to his client, the shaman, in a low voice, asks him the name of his most dreaded rival on the opposite side. The reply is given in a whisper, and the shaman, holding his hands outstretched as before, calls down the most withering curses upon the head of the doomed victim, mentioning him likewise by name and clan. He prays to the Black Fog to cover him so that he may be unable to see his way; to the Black Rattlesnake to envelop him in his slimy folds; and at last to the Black Spider to let down his black thread from above, wrap it about the soul of the victim, and drag it from his body along the black trail to the Darkening Land in the west, there to bury it in the black coffin under the black clay, never to reappear. At the final imprecation he stoops and, making a hole in the soft earth with his finger (symbolic of stabbing the doomed man to the heart), drops the black bead into it and covers it from sight with a vicious stamp of his foot; then with a simultaneous movement each man dips his ball sticks into the water, and bringing them up, touches them to his lips; then, stooping again, he dips up the water in his hand and laves his head and breast.

Below is given a translation of one of these formulas, from the collection of original Cherokee manuscripts obtained by the writer. The formulistic name for the player signifies "admirer or lover of the ball play." The shaman directs his attention alternately to his clients and their opponents, looking by turns at the red or the black bead as he prays. He raises his friends to the seventh heaven and invokes in their behalf the aid of the bat and a number of birds, which, according to the Cherokee belief, are so keen of sight and so swift upon the wing as never to fail to seize their intended prey. The opposing players, on the other hand, are put under the earth and rendered like the terrapin, the turtle, the mole, and the bear—all slow and clumsy of movement. Blue is the color symbolic of defeat, red is typical of success, and white signifis joy and happiness. The exultant whoop or shout of the players is believed to bear them on to victory, as trees are carried along by the resistless force of a torrent:

"THIS IS TO TAKE THEM TO WATER FOR THE BALL PLAY."

"Sgĕ! Now, where the white thread has been let down, quickly we are about to inquire into the fate of the lovers of the ball play.

"They are of such a descent. They are called so and so. (As they march) they are shaking the road which shall never be joyful. The miserable terrapin has fastened himself upon them as they go about. They are doomed to failure. They have become entirely blue.

"But now my lovers of the ball play have their roads lying down in this direction. The Red Bat has come and become one with them. There, in the first heaven, are the pleasing stakes. There, in the second heaven, are the pleasing stakes. The Peewee has come and joined them. Their ball sticks shall be borne along by the immortal whoop, never to fail them in the contest.

"But as for the lovers of the ball play on the other side, the common turtle has fastened himself to them as they go about. There, under the earth, they are doomed to failure.

"There, in the third heaven, are the pleasing stakes. The Red Tla'niwă has come and made himself one of them, never to be defeated. There, in the fourth heaven, are the pleasing stakes. The Crested Flycatcher has come and joined them, that they may never be defeated. There, in the fifth heaven, are the pleasing stakes. The Marten has come and joined them, that they may never be defeated.

"The other lovers of the ball play—the Blue Mole has become one with them, that they may never feel triumphant. They are doomed to failure.

"There, in the sixth heaven, the Chimney Swift has become one with them, that they may never be defeated. There are the pleasing stakes. There, in the seventh heaven, the Dragonfly has become one of them, that they may never be defeated. There are the pleasing stakes.

"As for the other lovers of the ball play, the Bear has come and fastened himself to them, that they may never be triumphant. He has caused the stakes to slip out of their hands, and their share has dwindled to nothing. Their fate is forecast.

"Sgě! Now let me know that the twelve (runs) are mine, O White Dragonfly. Let me know that their share is mine—that the stakes are mine. Now, he [the rival player] is compelled to let go his hold upon the stakes. They [the shaman's clients] are become exultant and gratified. Yû!"

This ceremony ended, the players form in line, headed by the shaman, and march in single file to the ball ground, where they find awaiting them a crowd of spectators—men, women and children—sometimes to the number of several hundred, for the Indians always turn out to the ball play, no matter how great the distance, from old Big Witch, stooping under the weight of nearly a hundred years, down to babies slung at their mothers' backs. The ball ground is a level field by the river side, surrounded by the high timber-covered mountains. At either end are the goals, each consisting of a pair of upright poles, between which the ball must be driven to make a run, the side which first makes 12 home runs being declared the winner of the game and the stakes. The ball is furnished by the challengers, who sometimes try to select one so small that it will fall through the netting of the ball sticks of their adversaries; but as the others are on the lookout for this, the trick usually fails of its purpose. After the ball is once set in motion it must be picked up only with the ball sticks, although after having picked up the ball with the sticks the player frequently takes it in his hand, and, throwing away the sticks, runs with it until intercepted by one of the other party, when he throws it, if he can, to one of his friends further on. Should a player pick up the ball with his hand, as sometimes happens in the scramble, there at once arises all over the field a chorus of "Uwâ'yĭ Gûtĭ! Uwâ'yí Gûtĭ!" "With the hand! with the hand!"—equivalent to our own "Foul! foul!"—and that inning is declared a draw.

While our men are awaiting the arrival of the other party, their friends crowd around them, and the women throw across their outstretched ball sticks the pieces of calico, the small squares of sheeting used as shawls, and the bright red handkerchiefs so dear to the heart of the Cherokee, which they intend to stake upon the game. It may be as well to state that these handkerchiefs take the place of hats, bonnets, and scarfs, the women throwing them over their heads in shawl fashion and the men twisting them like turbans about their hair, while both sexes alike fasten them about their throats or use them as bags for carrying small packages. Knives, trinkets, and sometimes small coins, are also wagered. But these Cherokee to-day are poor indeed. Hardly a man among them owns a horse, and never again will a chief bet a thousand dollars upon his favorites, as was done in Georgia in 1834. To-day, however, as then, they will risk all they have.

Now a series of yells announces the near approach of the men from Raven Town, and in a few minutes they come filing out from the bushes—stripped, scratched, and decorated like the others, carrying their ball sticks in their hands, and headed by a shaman. The two parties come together in the center of the ground, and for a short time the scene resembles an auction, as men and women move about, holding up the articles they propose to wager on the game and bidding for stakes to be matched against them. The betting being ended, the opposing players draw up in two lines facing each other, each man with his ball sticks laid together upon the ground in front of him, with the heads pointing toward the man facing him. This is for the purpose of matching the players so as to get the same number on each side ; and should it be found that a player has no antagonist to face him he must drop out of the game. Such a result frequently happens, as both parties strive to keep their arrangements secret up to the last moment. There is no fixed number on a side, the common quota being from nine to twelve. Catlin, indeed, speaking of the Choctaws, says that " it is no uncommon occurrence for six or eight hundred or a thousand of these young men to engage in a game of ball, with five or six times that number of spectators ;" but this was just after the removal, while the entire nation was yet camped upon the prairie in the Indian Territory. It would have been utterly impossible for the shamans to prepare a thousand players, or even one-fourth of that number, in the regular way, and in Catlin's spirited description of the game the ceremonial part is chiefly conspicuous by its absence. The greatest number that I ever heard of among the old Cherokee was twenty-two on a side. There is another secret formula to be recited by the initiated at this juncture, and addressed to the Red Yahulu, or hickory, for the purpose of destroying the efficiency of his enemy's ball sticks.

During the whole time that the game is in progress the shaman, concealed in the bushes by the water side, is busy with his prayers and incantations for the success of his clients and the defeat of their rivals. Through his assistant, who acts as messenger, he is kept advised of the movements of the players by seven men, known as counselors, appointed to watch the game for that purpose. These seven counselors also have a general oversight of the conjuring and other proceedings at the ball-play dance. Every little incident is regarded as an omen, and the shaman governs himself accordingly.

An old man now advances with the ball, and standing at one end of the lines, delivers a final address to the players, telling them that Uné'lanû'hĭ, the Apportioner—the sun—is looking down upon them, urging them to acquit themselves in the games as their fathers have done before them ; but above all to keep their tempers, so that none may have it to say that they got angry or quarreled, and that after it is over each one may return in peace along the white trail to rest in his white house. White in these formulas is symbolic of peace and happiness and all good things. He concludes with a loud " Ha ! Taldu-gwŭ' ! " " Now for the twelve ! " and throws the ball into the air.

Instantly twenty pairs of ball sticks clatter together in the air, as their owners spring to catch the ball in its descent. In the scramble it usually happens that the ball falls to the ground, when it is picked up by one more active than the rest. Frequently, however, a man will succeed in catching it between his ball sticks as it falls, and, disengaging himself from the rest, starts to run with it to the goal ; but before he has gone a dozen yards they are upon him, and the whole crowd goes down together, rolling and tumbling over each other in the dust, straining and tugging for possession of the ball, until one of the players manages to extricate himself from the struggling heap and starts off with the ball. At once the others spring to their feet and, throwing away their ball sticks, rush to intercept him or prevent his capture, their black hair streaming out behind and their naked bodies glistening in the sun as they run. The scene is constantly changing. Now the players are all together at the lower end of the field, when suddenly, with a powerful throw, a player sends the ball high over the heads of the spectators and into the bushes beyond. Before there is time to realize it, here they come with a grand sweep and a burst of short, sharp Cherokee exclamations, charging right into the crowd, knocking men and women to right and left, and stumbling over dogs and babies in their frantic efforts to get at the ball.

It is a very exciting game, as well as a very rough one, and in its general features is a combination of baseball, football, and the old-fashioned shinny. Almost everything short of murder is allowable in the game, and both parties sometimes go into the contest with the deliberate purpose of crippling or otherwise disabling the best players on the opposing side. Serious accidents are common. In the last game which I witnessed one man was seized around the waist by a powerfully built adversary, raised up in the air, and hurled down upon the ground with such force as to break his collar-bone. His friends pulled him out to one side and the game went on. Sometimes two men lie struggling on the ground, clutching at each others' throats, long after the ball has been carried to the other end of the field, until the drivers, armed with long, stout switches, come running up and belabor both over their bare shoulders until they are forced to break their hold. It is also the duty of these drivers to gather the ball sticks thrown away in the excitement and restore them to their owners at the beginning of the next inning.

When the ball has been carried through the goal, the players come back to the center and take position in accordance with the previous instructions of their shamans. The two captains stand facing each other, and the ball is then thrown up by the captain of the side which won the last inning. Then the struggle begins again; and so the game goes on until one party scores 12 runs and is declared the victor and the winner of the stakes.

As soon as the game is over, usually about sundown, the winning players immediately go to water again with their shamans and perform another ceremony for the purpose of turning aside the revengeful incantations of their defeated rivals. They then dress, and the crowd of hungry players, who have eaten nothing since they started for the dance the night before, make a combined attack on the provisions which the women now produce from their shawls and baskets. It should be mentioned that, to assuage thirst during the game, the players are allowed to drink a sour preparation made from green grapes and wild crabapples.

Although the contestants on both sides are picked men and strive to win [plates xv, xvi], straining every muscle to the utmost, the impression left upon my mind after witnessing a number of games is that the same number of athletic young white men would have infused more robust energy into the play— that is, provided they could stand upon their feet after all the preliminary fasting, bleeding, and loss of sleep. Before separating, the defeated party usually challenges the victors to a second contest, and in a few days preparations are actively under way for another game.

Of the ball game, Mr Mooney relates further:

Some old people say that the moon is a ball which was thrown up against the sky in a game a long time ago. They say that two towns were playing against each other, but one of them had the best runners and had almost won the game when the leader of the other side picked up the ball with his hand— a thing that is not allowed in the game—and tried to throw to the goal, but it struck against the solid sky vault and was fastened there, to remind players never to cheat. When the moon looks small and pale, it is because some one has handled the ball unfairly, and for this reason they formerly played only at the time of a full moon.[a]

In another myth Mr Mooney refers to playing ball as a figurative expression for a contest of any kind, particularly a battle.[b]

CHEROKEE. Walker county, Georgia.

Rev. George White writes: [c]

We have been favored with the following letter from a gentleman, giving an account of an Indian ball-play which took place in this county, and at which he was present:

"We started one fine morning in the month of August, for the hickory grounds, having learned that two towns, Chattooga and Chicamauga, were to have a grand ball play at that place. We found the grounds to be a beautiful hickory level, entirely in a state of nature, upon which had been erected several rude tents, containing numerous articles, mostly of Indian manufacture, which were the stakes to be won or lost in the approaching contest. We had been on the ground only a short time when the two contending parties, composed of fifty men each, mostly in a state of nudity and having their faces painted in a fantastical manner, headed by their chiefs, made their appearance. The war-whoop was then sounded by one of the parties, which was immediately answered by the other, and continued alternately as they advanced slowly and in regular order towards each other to the center of the ground allotted for the contest.

" In order that you may have an idea of the play, imagine two parallel lines of stakes driven into the ground near each other, each extending for about 100 yards and having a space of 100 yards between them. In the center of these lines were the contending towns, headed by their chiefs, each having in their hands two wooden spoons, curiously carved, not unlike our large iron spoons. The object of these spoons is to throw up the ball. The ball is made of deer skin wound around a piece of spunk. To carry the ball through one of the lines mentioned above is the purpose to be accomplished. Every time the ball is carried through these lines counts 1. The game is commenced by one of the chiefs throwing up the ball to a great height, by means of the wooden spoons. As soon as the ball is thrown up, the contending parties mingle together. If the chief of the opposite party catches the ball as it descends, with his spoons, which he exerts his utmost skill to do, it counts 1 for his side. The respective parties stand prepared to catch the ball if there should be a failure on the part of their chiefs to do so. On this occasion the parties were distinguished from each other by the color of their ribbons; the one being red, the other blue.

" The strife begins. The chief has failed to catch the ball. A stout warrior has caught it, and endeavors with all speed to carry it to his lines, when a faster runner knocks his feet from under him, wrests the ball from him, and triumphantly makes his way with the prize to his own line; but when he almost reaches the goal, he is overtaken by one or more of his opponents, who endeavors to take it from him. The struggle becomes general, and it is often the case that serious personal injuries are inflicted. It is very common during the contest to let the ball fall to the ground. The strife now ceases for a time, until the chiefs again array their bands. The ball is again thrown up, and the game is continued as above described. Sometimes half an hour elapses before either side succeeds in making 1 in the game.

[a] Myths of the Cherokee. Nineteenth Annual Report of the Bureau of American Ethnology, pt. 1, p. 257, 1900.

[b] Ibid., p. 245, 433.   [c] Historical Collections of Georgia, p. 670, New York, 1855.

" It is usual at these ball-plays for each party to leave their conjurers at work at the time the game is going on; their stations are near the center of each line. In their hands are shells, bones of snakes, etc. These conjurers are sent for from a great distance. They are estimated according to their age, and it is supposed by their charms they can influence the game. On this occasion two conjurers were present; they appeared to be over 100 years of age. When I spoke to one of them he did not deign even to raise his head; the second time I spoke he gave me a terrible look, and at the same time one of the Indian women came and said, ' Conagatee unaka,' ' Go away, white man.' "

HURON. Ontario.

Nicolas Perrot [a] says, under jeu de crosse:

They have a certain game played with a bat, which greatly resembles our game of tennis. Their custom is to pit one nation against another, and if one is more numerous than the other, a certain number of men are withdrawn to render the sides equal. They are all armed with a bat—that is to say, a stick—the lower end of which is enlarged and laced like a racket. The ball is of wood and shaped very much like a turkey egg.

The goals are laid out in the open country, and face east and west, south and north. One of the parties, in order to win, must make the ball pass beyond the east and west goals, while the other party plays for the north and south goals. If anyone who has won once makes the ball pass beyond the wrong goal, he is obliged to begin again, taking his adversary's goal. If he happens to win again, he gains nothing. Then, the parties being equal and the game even, they begin the deciding game, and the successful side takes the stakes. Men and women, young boys, and girls all play on one side or the other, and make bets according to their means.

These games usually begin after the disappearance of the snow and ice and continue till seed time. The games are played in the afternoon, and the captain of each team harangues his players and announces the hour fixed for beginning the game. At the appointed time they gather in a crowd in the center of the field, and one of the two captains, having the ball in his hand, tosses it up in the air, each player trying to send it in the proper direction. If the ball falls to the ground, they try to pull it toward themselves with their bats, and should it fall outside the crowd of players, the most active of them win distinction by following closely after it. They make a great noise striking one against the other when they try to parry strokes in order to drive the ball in the proper direction. If a player keeps the ball between his feet and is unwilling to let it go, he must guard against the blows his adversaries continually aim at his feet; if he happens to be wounded, it is his own fault. Legs and arms are sometimes broken, and it has even happened that a player has been killed. It is quite common to see some one crippled for the rest of his life who would not have had this misfortune but for his own obstinacy. When these accidents happen the unlucky victim quietly withdraws from the game, if he is in a condition to do so; but if his injury will not permit this, his relatives carry him home, and the game goes on till it is finished, as if nothing had occurred.

As to the runners, when the sides are equal, sometimes neither side will win during the entire afternoon, and, again, one side may gain both of the two games necessary to win. In this racing game it looks as if the two sides were about to engage in battle. This exercise contributes much toward rendering the savages agile and quick to avoid adroitly a blow of a tomahawk in the hands of

---

[a] Mémoire sur les Moeurs, Coustumes et Relligion des Sauvages de l'Amérique Septentrionale, p. 43, Leipzig, 1864.

an enemy when engaged in war, and unless previously informed that they were at play one would truly believe them to be fighting.

Whatever accident the game may cause is attributed to luck, and there is in consequence no hard feeling between the players. The wounded seem as well satisfied as if nothing had happened to them, thus demonstrating that they have plenty of courage and that they are men.

They take what they have wagered and their winnings, and there is no dispute on either side when it comes to a question of payment, no matter what game they play. If, however, anyone who does not belong in the game, or who has bet nothing, hits the ball, thus giving any advantage to either side, one of the players on the other side will upbraid the outsider, asking him if the game is any affair of his and why he meddles with it. They often come to blows, and, if some chief does not pacify them, blood may be spilled or even some one killed. The best way to prevent such disorderly occurrences is to begin the game anew, with the consent of those who are ahead, for if they refuse to do so they have the advantage. When some prominent man takes part in the dispute, it is not difficult to arrange their differences and induce them to follow his advice.

Baron La Hontan says: [a]

They have a third play with a ball not unlike our tennis, but the balls are very large, and the rackets resemble ours, save that the handle is at least 3 feet long. The savages, who commonly play at it in large companies of three or four hundred at a time, fix two sticks at 500 or 600 paces distant from each other. They divide into two equal parties, and toss up the ball about halfway between the two sticks. Each party endeavors to toss the ball to their side; some run to the ball, and the rest keep at a little distance on both sides to assist on all quarters. In fine, this game is so violent that they tear their skins and break their legs very often in striving to raise the ball. All these games are made only for feasts or other trifling entertainments; for 'tis to be observed that as they hate money, so they never put it in the balance, and one may say interest is never the occasion of debates among them.

HURON. Ihonatiria, or St Joseph, near Thunder bay, Ontario.

Jean de Brébeuf says: [b]

Of three kinds of games especially in use among these peoples—namely, the games of crosse, dish, and straw, the first two are, they say, most healing. Is not this worthy of compassion? There is a poor sick man, fevered of body and almost dying, and a miserable sorcerer will order for him, as a cooling remedy, a game of crosse. Or the sick man himself, sometimes, will have dreamed that he must die unless the whole country shall play crosse for his health; and no matter how little may be his credit, you will see then in a beautiful field, village contending against village as to who will play crosse the better, and betting against one another beaver robes and porcelain collars, so as to excite greater interest. Sometimes, also, one of these jugglers will say that the whole country is sick, and he asks a game of crosse to heal it; no more needs to be said, it is published immediately everywhere; and all the captains of each village give orders that all the young men do their duty in this respect, otherwise some great misfortune would befall the whole country.[c]

---

[a] New Voyages to North-America, v. 2, p. 18, London, 1703.

[b] Relation of 1636. The Jesuit Relations and Allied Documents, v. 10, p. 185, Cleveland, 1897.

[c] Brébeuf describes all the affairs of the Huron as included under two heads:

The first are, as it were, affairs of state—whatever may concern either citizens or strangers, the public or the individuals of the village; as, for example, feasts, dances, games, crosse matches, and funeral ceremonies. The second are affairs of war. Now there are as many sorts of Captains as of affairs. (Ibid., p. 229.)

MOHAWK.   Grand river, Ontario.   (Cat. no. 38513, 38514, Free Museum of Science and Art, University of Pennsylvania.)
Racket for lacrosse (figure 761), consisting of a sapling curved at one
end, the bent portion woven with a network of bark cord; length,
48 inches.

FIG. 761.   Racket; length, 48 inches; Mohawk Indians, Grand river, Ontario; cat. no. 38513, Free
Museum of Science and Art, University of Pennsylvania.

Ball covered with buckskin (figure 762), round, 2½ inches in diameter, the cover in one piece cut and sewed like a baseball.   Collected by the writer in 1901.
The name of the racket was given as ki-du-kwa-sta, and that of the
ball as no-hā.   The racket was explained as the old kind, with bast
cords instead of twine, as is now used.

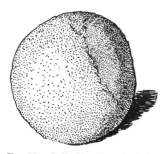

FIG. 762.   Ball; diameter, 2½ inches;
Mohawk Indians, Grand river,
Ontario; cat. no. 38514, Free
Museum of Science and Art, Uni-
versity of Pennsylvania.

Mr J. N. B. Hewitt [a] informed the
writer that the use of bark as a network
was only to replace sinew when that
article was not obtainable.   The bark
of the slippery elm, boiled in water to
make it pliable, was employed.   He says:

The network on the common Iroquois club
was not drawn taut, but it was sufficiently taut
to enable the player to throw the ball to a very
great distance—a successful throw carrying
the ball about 20 rods—and yet the netting
was loose enough to enable a skillful player
oftentimes to carry the ball through a crowd
of opposing players.   On the regulation club
used in the modernized game, which is very
seldom played by the Iroquois, the network is made very taut, so that the network emits a twang when it is picked by the fingers. . . .

The goals or butts for the ball game were marked by poles or stakes, from 10
to 15 feet in length, two in number, driven in the ground from 5 to 15 paces
apart.   The goal therefore was a square or quadrilateral space bounded on two
sides by the two upright poles, on one side by the ground and on the other by a
line connecting either the extreme ends of the poles or two marked points on the
poles at some agreed height from the ground.   The goals were placed from 40 to
80 rods apart, according to the number and skill of the players. . . .

The players to begin the game assemble on the ball-ground at a point midway between the goals, or butts.   The two parties are then divided into couples,
every player being paired with one of the opposite party, those paired being, as
nearly as possible, of equal skill, agility, strength, and fleetness of foot.   One of
the players is placed immediately in front of the goal defended by his side, and
another in front of the opposite goal.   These two are called the door-guards.   It
is their duty to guard the goals against an opposing player who may attempt to

---

[a] See The American Anthropologist, v. 5, p. 189, 1892.

throw the ball through from a distance or to carry the ball into the goal on his club. These two are chosen rather for their skill and vigilance than for fleetness of foot.

It was considered a great feat for a player to take the ball on his bat, elude his pursuers and opponents, outplay the door-guard, and thus carry the ball into the goal, especially if he was able to walk into the goal. The side whose player did this would taunt the other side by saying, " It lay on the club when it entered."

The game was opened by the two captains holding their clubs crossed in the form of a Maltese cross with the ball placed midway between the ends of the network on each club; then by a steady push each captain endeavors to throw the ball in the direction of the goal to which his side must bear it.

Like all other public games of the Iroquois, the ball game was to the spectators a favorite opportunity for betting, and many would wager and lose all their possessions.

The Iroquois prefer the ancient to the modern style of the game, for in the former they had a greater opportunity to exhibit their skill, strength, and fleetness of foot individually, whereas in the modernized form of the game, I believe, there is more team-play.

Previous to a matched game the players would go through a course of stringent fasting, bathing, and emetics. The latter were decoctions of the bark of spotted alder and red willow.

The contending parties of ball players all carried some charm or talisman to insure their victory. Shamans were hired by individual players to exert their supernatural powers in their own behalf and for their side, and when a noted wizard openly espoused the cause of one of the parties the players of the other side felt to a certain extent disheartened.

The game was played during spring, summer, and fall; and formerly the players painted and adorned themselves in their most approved style.

The game generally begins in the afternoon; seldom, if ever, in the forenoon. It is usually followed by a dance at night, accompanied by a feast.

Mohawk. Grand river, Ontario.

Col. William H. Stone,[a] referring to the ball game, which he erroneously declares the Six Nations adopted from the whites, describes a match played at Grand river between the Mohawk and Seneca in 1797:

The combatants numbered about six hundred upon a side. The goals, designated by two pair of byes, were 30 rods apart and the goals of each pair about 30 feet apart. Each passage of the ball between them counted a point, but the tally chiefs were allowed to check or curtail the count in order to protract the game. The ball was put in play by a beautiful girl.

——— Caughnawaga, Quebec.

J. A. Cuoq [b] gives the following definitions:

Atenno, paume, balle, pelote à jouer; atstsikwahe, crosse de jouer, baton recourbè, raquette pour le jeu de crosse; tekatsikwaheks, frapper la balle, jouer à la crosse.

---

a Life of Brant, v. 2, p. 447, Cooperstown, 1844.
b Lexique de la Langue Iroquoise, Montreal, 1882.

The last two are derived from otsikwa, meaning in general anything that has a form almost round and a certain solidity.

ONONDAGA. New York.

The Dictionnaire Français-Onontagué [a] gives this definition:

Bale à jouer, odzikk8a deyeyendakk8a.

In Zeisberger's Indian Dictionary [b] we find:

To play at ball, waszichquaëqua; ball (kugel), ozíchqua.

ST REGIS. St Regis, New York. (Cat. no. 118840, United States
National Museum.)

Leather-covered ball (figure 763), made of a single piece cut and
stitched with thread, containing an interior core of cotton thread;
diameter, 2¼ inches. Collected by R. B. Hough.

FIG. 763. Ball; diameter, 2¼
inches; St Regis Indians, St
Regis, New York; cat. no.
118840, United States National
Museum.

SENECA. New York.

Morgan [c] describes the Iroquois ball
game as follows:

With the Iroquois, the ball game, o-tä-dä-jish'-
quä-äge, was the favorite among their amusements of this description. This game reaches
back to a remote antiquity, was universal among
the red races, and was played with a degree of
zeal and enthusiasm which would scarcely be
credited. It was played with a small deerskin
ball, by a select band, usually from six to eight
on a side, each set representing its own party. The
game was divided into several contests, in which
each set of players strove to carry the ball
through their own gate. They went out into an open plain or field and erected
gates, about 80 rods apart, on its opposite sides. Each gate was simply two
poles, some 10 feet high, set in the ground about 3 rods asunder. One of these
gates belonged to each party; and the contest between the players was, which
set would first carry the ball through its own a given number of times. Either
5 or 7 made the game, as the parties agreed. If 5, for example, was the
number, the party which first carried, or drove the ball through its own
gate this number of times, won the victory. Thus, after eight separate contests, the parties might stand equal, each having won 4; in which case the
party which succeeded on the ninth contest would carry the game. The players
commenced in the center of the field, midway between the gates. If one of them
became fatigued or disabled during the progress of the game, he was allowed to
leave the ranks, and his party could supply his place with a fresh player, but
the original numbers were not at any time allowed to be increased. Regular
managers were appointed on each side to see that the rules of the game were
strictly and fairly observed. One rule forbade the players to touch the ball
with the hand or foot.

---

[a] New York, Cramoisy Press, 1859.
[b] Cambridge, 1887.
[c] League of the Iroquois, p. 294, Rochester, 1851.

In preparing for this game the players denuded themselves entirely, with the exception of the waistcloth.[a] . . . They also underwent, frequently, a course of diet and training, as in a preparation for a foot-race.

When the day designated had arrived the people gathered from the whole surrounding country, to witness the contest. About meridian they assembled at the appointed place, and having separated themselves into two companies, one might be seen upon each side of the line, between the gates, arranged in scattered groups, awaiting the commencement of the game. The players, when ready, stationed themselves in two parallel rows, facing each other, midway on this line, each one holding a ball bat, of the kind represented in the figure, and with which alone the ball was to be driven. As soon as all the preliminaries were adjusted, the ball was dropped between the two files of players, and taken between the bats of the two who stood in the middle of each file, opposite to each other. After a brief struggle between them, in which each player endeavored, with his bat, to get possession of the ball, and give it the first impulse towards his own gate, it was thrown out, and then commenced the pursuit. The flying ball, when overtaken, was immediately surrounded by a group of players, each one striving to extricate it, and, at the same time, direct it towards his party gate. In this way the ball was frequently imprisoned in different parts of the field, and an animated controversy maintained for its possession. When freed, it was knocked upon the ground or through the air; but the moment a chance presented it was taken up upon the deer-skin network of the ball bat by a player in full career, and carried in a race towards the gate. To guard against this contingency, by which one contest of the game might be determined in a moment, some of the players detached themselves from the group contending around the ball, and took a position from which to intercept a runner upon a diagonal line, if it should chance that one of the adverse party got possession of the ball. These races often formed the most exciting part of the game, both from the fleetness of the runners, and the consequences which depended upon the result. When the line of the runner was crossed, by an adversary coming in before him upon a diagonal line, and he found it impossible, by artifice or stratagem, to elude him, he turned about, and threw the ball over the heads of both of them, towards his gate; or, perchance, towards a player of his own party, if there were adverse players between him and the gate. When the flight of the ball was arrested in any part of the field, a spirited and even fierce contest was maintained around it; the players handled their bats with such dexterity, and managed their persons with such art and adroitness, that frequently several minutes elapsed before the ball flew out. Occasionally in the heat of the controversy, but entirely by accident, a player was struck with such violence that the blood trickled down his limbs. In such a case, if disabled, he dropped his bat and left the field, while a fresh player from his own party supplied his place. In this manner was the game contested: oftentimes with so much ardor and skill that the ball was recovered by one party at the very edge of the adverse gate; and finally, after many shifts in the tide of success, carried in triumph through its own. When one contest in the game was thus decided, the prevailing party sent up a united shout of rejoicing.

After a short respite for the refreshment of the players, the second trial was commenced, and continued like the first. Sometimes it was decided in a few moments, but more frequently it lasted an hour, and sometimes much longer, to

---

[a] The gä-kä or waist-cloth, was a strip of deerskin or broadcloth, about a quarter wide and 2 yards long, ornamented at the ends with bead- or quill-work. It was passed between the limbs and secured by a deerskin belt, passing around the waist, the embroidered ends falling over the belt, before and behind, in the fashion of an apron.

such a system had the playing of this game been reduced by skill and practice. If every trial was ardently contested, and the parties continued nearly equal in the number decided, it often lengthened out the game, until the approaching twilight made it necessary to take another day for its conclusion.

On the final decision of the game, the exclamations of triumph, as would be expected, knew no bounds. Caps, tomahawks and blankets were thrown up into the air, and for a few moments the notes of victory resounded from every side. It was doubtless a considerate provision, that the prevailing party were upon a side of the field opposite to, and at a distance from, the vanquished, otherwise such a din of exultation might have proved too exciting for Indian patience.

In ancient times they used a solid ball of knot. The ball bat, also, was made without network, having a solid and curving head. At a subsequent day they substituted the deer-skin ball and the network ball bat [figure 764] in present use. These substitutions were made so many years ago that they have lost the date.

FIG. 764. Racket; length, 5 feet; Seneca Indians, New York; from Morgan.

KULANAPAN STOCK

GUALALA. California.

Mr Stephen Powers [a] mentions tennis among the amusements at the great autumnal games of this tribe.

POMO. California.

Mr Stephen Powers [b] relates the following:

There is a game of tennis played by the Pomo, of which I have heard nothing among the northern tribes. A ball is rounded out of an oak-knot about as large as those generally used by schoolboys, and it is propelled by a racket which is constructed of a long, slender stick, bent double and bound together, leaving a circular hoop at the extremity, across which is woven a coarse mesh-work of strings. Such an implement is not strong enough for batting the ball, neither do they bat it, but simply shove or thrust it along the ground.

The game is played in the following manner: They first separate themselves into two equal parties, and each party contributes an equal amount to a stake to be played for, as they seldom consider it worth while to play without betting. Then they select an open space of ground, and establish two parallel base lines a certain number of paces apart, with a starting-line between, equidistant from both. Two champions, one for each party, stand on opposite sides of the starting-point with their rackets; a squaw tosses the ball in the air, and as it descends the two champions strike at it, and one or the other gets the advantage, hurling it toward his antagonist's base-line. Then there ensues a universal rush, pell-mell, higgledy-piggledy, men and squaws crushing and bumping—for the squaws participate equally with the sterner sex—each party striving to propel

---

[a] Tribes of California. Contributions to North American Ethnology, v. 3, p. 193, Washington, 1877.

[b] Ibid., p. 151; also Overland Monthly, v. 9, p. 501.

the ball across the enemy's base-line. They enjoy this sport immensely, laugh and vociferate until they are " out of all whooping "; some tumble down and get their heads batted, and much diversion is created, for they are very good-natured and free from jangling in their amusements. One party must drive the ball a certain number of times over the other's base line before the game is concluded, and this not unfrequently occupies them a half day or more, during which they expend more strenuous endeavor than they would in a day of honest labor in a squash-field.

Powers describes the Pomo as staking fancy bows and arrows on their ball games. Of these articles they frequently have a number made only for gambling purposes—not for use in hunting.

POMO. Ukiah valley, Mendocino county, California. (Cat. no. 70966, 70977, Field Columbian Museum.)

Racket (figure 765), made of a bent oak stick, 40 inches in length, with twine mesh, and ball, of pepper-wood knot, $2\frac{1}{4}$ inches in diameter. Collected by Dr J. W. Hudson.

FIG. 765. Ball and racket; diameter of ball, $2\frac{1}{4}$ inches; length of racket, 40 inches; Pomo Indians, Mendocino county, California; cat. no. 70966, 70977, Field Columbian Museum.

———— Seven miles south of Ukiah, Mendocino county, California. (Cat. no. 70946, 70947, Field Columbian Museum.)

Racket of dogwood (figure 766), with rawhide lacings, 35 inches long; and ball, a pepperwood knot. Collected by Dr J. W. Hudson, who describes the game as played by tossing the ball in the center of the field and contesting for it with netted sticks, under the name of tsitimpiyem:

FIG. 766. Ball and racket; length of racket, 35 inches; Pomo Indians, Mendocino county, California; cat. no. 70946, 70947, Field Columbian Museum.

The ball sticks, called tsi-tīm', are 3 feet in length. The goals, hui kali dako' (hui!=we win!) are 6 feet high and 25 yards apart. The ball, pikŏ', is usually of laurel (*Umbellaria*), but sometimes a deer knuckle bone.

MARIPOSAN STOCK

YOKUTS. Tule River agency, Tulare county, California. (Cat. no. 70392, Field Columbian Museum.)

Two willow saplings (figure 767), 50 inches in length, with an oak loop lashed on the lower end with sinew; accompanied by two small mistletoe-root balls coated with pitch and painted red.

These are implements for a ball game, collected by Dr J. W. Hudson.

The two balls are laid side by side on the ground at the end of the course, and at a word the captains dip them up with their spoon sticks and cast them forward to their mates, who send them on to the nearest pair of opponents. The course is about 1,200 yards—around a tree and back to the first goal. There are usually eight players, three and a captain on each side.

Fig. 767. Ball and racket; length of racket, 50 inches; Yokuts Indians, Tule River agency, Tulare county, California; cat. no. 70392, Field Columbian Museum.

The game is called wip-i-watch (to lift on the end of a stick); the ball, o-lol; the stick, wi-pat; the starting goal, to-liu, and the turning stake. tsa-lam. It is played only by men.

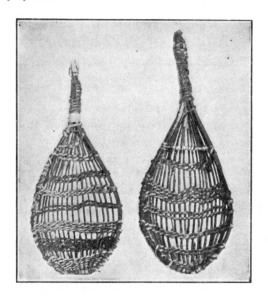

Fig. 768. Ball baskets; lengths, 16 and 18 inches; Miwok Indians, Tuolumne county, California; in the collection of Dr C. Hart Merriam.

MOQUELUMNAN STOCK

Miwok. Bald Rock, Tuolumne county, California. (Collection of Dr C. Hart Merriam.)

Two spoon-shaped willow baskets (figure 768), one 16 and the other 18 inches in length, the longer stiffened by a crosspiece near the handle.

Collected by Doctor Merriam and described by him as used by women in catching the ball, posko, in the game called amtah.

Each woman carries a pair of these baskets, called am-mut'-nah, one in each hand. She catches the ball in the larger one and covers it with the other while she runs off with it toward the goal. The men try to kick the ball, but can not lay hands on it.

TOPINAGUGIM. Big creek, Tuolumne county, California. (Cat. no. 70220, 70226, Field Columbian Museum.)

Two oval wicker baskets (figure 769), 13 inches in length, with handle; and buckskin-covered ball, 3½ inches in diameter.

Collected by Dr J. W. Hudson, who describes them as used in the game of umta, played by both men and women. The baskets resemble the seed-flail baskets used in this region.

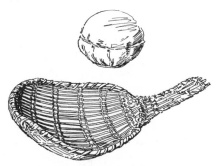

FIG. 769. Ball and ball-casting basket; diameter of ball, 3¼ inches; length of basket, 13 inches; Topinagugim Indians, Tuolumne county, California; cat. no. 70220, 70226, Field Columbian Museum.

———— California.

Mr H. H. Bancroft [a] says:

. . . they have one or two games which require some exertion. One of these, in vogue among the Meewocs, is played with bats and an oak-knot ball. The former are made of a pliant stick, having the end bent round and lashed to the main part, so as to form a loop, which is filled with a network of strings. They do not strike but push the ball along with these bats. The players take sides, and each party endeavors to drive the ball past the boundaries of the other.

———— Big creek, 2 miles north of Groveland, Tuolumne county, California.

Dr J. W. Hudson describes the following game under the name of sakumship:

Two women, standing 50 feet apart, throw a 4-inch ball of buckskin filled with hair, each using two baskets to throw the ball, which they may not touch with their hands. The casting baskets, called shak-num-sia, are made somewhat stronger than the a-ma-ta.

This is a great gambling game between women, and is played for high stakes. It is counted with sticks, and a player forfeits one if she fails to catch or throw the ball so that it goes beyond the other's reach.

MUSKHOGEAN STOCK

CHICKASAW. Mississippi.

Adam Hodgson [b] says:

As we were riding along toward sunset, we saw many parties of Chickasaws repairing to a dance and ball-play. The magnificence of their dresses exceeded anything we had yet seen.

---

[a] The Native Races of the Pacific Coast, v. 1, p. 393, San Francisco, 1874.
[b] Remarks during a Journey through North America, p. 283, New York, 1823.

CHOCTAW. Mississippi.

Capt. Bernard Romans [a] says:

Their play at ball is either with a small ball of deerskin or a large one of woolen rags; the first is thrown with battledores, the second with the hand only; this is a trial of skill between village and village; after having appointed the day and field for meeting, they assemble at the time and place, fix two poles across each other at about an 150 feet apart. Then they attempt to throw the ball through the lower part of them, and the opposite party, trying to prevent it, throw it back themselves, which the first again try to prevent; thus they attempt to beat it about from one to the other with amazing violence, and not seldom broken limbs or dislocated joints are the consequence; their being almost naked, painted, and ornamented with feathers has a good effect on the eye of the bystander during this violent diversion; a number is agreed on for the score, and the party who first gets this number wins.

The women play among themselves (after the men have done) disputing with as much eagerness as the men; the stakes or bets are generally high. There is no difference in the other game with the large ball, only the men and women play promiscuously, and they use no battledores.

James Adair [b] says:

Ball playing is their chief and most favorite game: and it is such severe exercise, as to show it was originally calculated for a hardy and expert race of people like themselves, and the ancient Spartans. The ball is made of a piece of scraped deer-skin, moistened and stuffed hard with deer's hair, and strongly sewed with deer's sinews.—The ball-sticks are about 2 feet long, the lower end somewhat resembling the palm of a hand, and which are worked with deer-skin thongs. Between these, they catch the ball and throw it a great distance, when not prevented by some of the opposite party, who try to intercept them. The goal is about 500 yards in length: at each end of it, they fix two long bending poles into the ground, 3 yards apart below, but slanting a considerable way outward. The party that happens to throw the ball over these counts 1; but if it be thrown underneath, it is cast back, and played for as usual. The gamesters are equal in number on each side; and at the beginning of every course of the ball they throw it up high in the center of the ground, and in a direct line between the two goals. When the crowd of players prevents the one who catched the ball from throwing it off with a long direction, he commonly sends it the right course by an artful sharp twirl. They are so exceedingly expert in this manly exercise, that, between the goals, the ball is mostly flying the different ways, by the force of the playing sticks, without falling to the ground, for they are not allowed to catch it with their hands. It is surprising to see how swiftly they fly, when closely chased by a nimble-footed pursuer; when they are intercepted by one of the opposite party, his fear of being cut by the ball sticks commonly gives them an opportunity of throwing it perhaps a hundred yards; but the antagonist sometimes runs up behind, and by a sudden stroke dashes down the ball. It is a very unusual thing to see them act spitefully in any sort of game, not even in this severe and tempting exercise.

Bossu [c] says:

The Chactaws are very active and merry; they have a play at ball, at which they are very expert; they invite the inhabitants of the neighboring villages to it,

---

[a] A Concise Natural History of East and West Florida, p. 79, New York, 1776

[b] The History of the American Indians, p. 399, London, 1775.

[c] Travels through that Part of North America formerly called Louisiana, by Mr. Bossu, Captain in the French Marines, translated from the French by John Reinhold Forster, v. 1, p. 304, London, 1771.

exciting them by many smart sayings. The men and women assemble in their best ornaments, they pass the whole day in singing and dancing; they even dance all the night to the sound of the drum and chickikois. The inhabitants of each village are distinguished by a separate fire, which they light in the middle of a great meadow. The next day is that appointed for the match; they agree upon a mark or aim about 60 yards off, and distinguished by two great poles, between which the ball is to pass. They generally count 16 till the game is up. There are forty on each side, and everyone has a battledoor in his hand, about $2\frac{1}{2}$ feet long, made very nearly in the form of ours, of walnut or chestnut wood, and covered with roe-skins.

An old man stands in the middle of the place appropriated to the play and throws up into the air a ball of roe-skins rolled about each other. The players then run, and endeavor to strike the ball with their battledoors; it is a pleasure to see them run naked, painted with various colors, having a tiger's tail fastened behind, and feathers on their heads and arms, which move as they run, and have a very odd effect; they push and throw each other down; he that has been expert enough to get the ball, sends it to his party; those of the opposite party run at him who has seized the ball, and send it back to their side; and thus they dispute it to each other reciprocally, with such ardour, that they sometimes dislocate their shoulders by it. The players are never displeased; some old men, who assist at the play, become mediators, and determine, that the play is only intended as a recreation, and not as an opportunity of quarreling. The wagers are considerable; the women bet among themselves.

When the players have given over, the women assemble among themselves to revenge their husbands who have lost the game. The battledoor they make use of differs from that of the men in being bent; they all are very active, and run against each other with extreme swiftness, pushing each other like the men, they having the same dress, except on those parts which modesty teaches them to cover. They only put rouge on their cheeks, and vermilion, instead of powder, in their hair.

Choctaw.   Indian Territory.

Catlin [a] says:

It is no uncommon occurrence for six or eight hundred or a thousand of these young men to engage in a game of ball, with five or six times that number of spectators, of men, women, and children, surrounding the ground and looking on.   .   .   .

While at the Choctaw agency it was announced that there was to be a great ball play on a certain day, within a few miles, on which occasion I attended and made the three sketches which are hereto annexed (see plates XVII, XVIII, XIX); and also the following entry in my notebook, which I literally copy out:

" Monday afternoon at 3 o'clock, I rode out with Lieutenants S. and M., to a very pretty prairie, about 6 miles distant, to the ball-play-ground of the Choctaws, where we found several thousand Indians encamped. There were two points of timber, about half a mile apart, in which the two parties for the play, with their respective families and friends, were encamped; and lying between them, the prairie on which the game was to be played. My companions and myself, although we had been apprised, that to see the whole of a ball-play, we must remain on the ground all the night previous, had brought nothing to sleep upon, resolving to keep our eyes open, and see what transpired through the night. During the afternoon, we loitered about among the different tents and shanties of the two encampments, and afterwards, at sundown, witnessed the ceremony

---

[a] Letters and Notes on the Manners. Customs, and Condition of the North American Indians. v. 2. p. 123, London, 1841.

of measuring out the ground, and erecting the " byes," or goals which were to guide the play. Each party had their goal made with two upright posts, about 25 feet high and 6 feet apart, set firm in the ground, with a pole across at the top. These goals were about 40 or 50 rods apart; and at a point just halfway between, was another small stake, driven down, where the ball was to be thrown up at the firing of a gun, to be struggled for by the players. All this preparation was made by some old men, who were, it seems, selected to be the judges of the play, who drew a line from one bye to the other; to which directly came from the woods, on both sides, a great concourse of women and old men, boys and girls, and dogs and horses, where bets were to be made on the play. The betting was all done across this line, and seemed to be chiefly left to the women, who seemed to have martialled out a little of everything that their houses and their fields possessed. Goods and chattels—knives—dresses—blankets—pots and kettles—dogs and horses, and guns; and all were placed in the possession of stake-

FIG. 770. Choctaw ball player; Indian Territory; from Catlin.

holders, who sat by them, and watched them on the ground all night, preparatory to the play.

The sticks with which this tribe play, are bent into an oblong hoop at the end, with a sort of slight web of small thongs tied across, to prevent the ball from passing through. The players hold one of these in each hand, and by leaping into the air, they catch the ball between the two nettings and throw it, without being allowed to strike it or catch it in their hands.

The mode in which these sticks are constructed and used will be seen in the portrait of Tullock-chish-ko (he who drinks the juice of the stone), the most distinguished ball-player of the Choctaw nation [figure 770], represented in his ball-play dress, with his ball-sticks in his hands. In every ball-play of these people, it is a rule of the play that no man shall wear moccasins on his feet, or any other dress than his breech-cloth around his waist, with a beautiful bead-belt, and a " tail," made of white horsehair or quills, and a " mane " on the neck, of horsehair dyed of various colors.

This game had been arranged and " made up," three or four months before the parties met to play it, and in the following manner:—The two champions who led the two parties, and had the alternate choosing of the players through the whole tribe, sent runners, with the ball-sticks most fantastically ornamented with ribbons and red paint, to be touched by each one of the chosen players; who thereby agreed to be on the spot at the appointed time and ready for the play. The ground having been all prepared and preliminaries of the game all settled, and the bettings all made, and goods all " staked," night came on without the appearance of any players on the ground. But soon after dark, a procession of lighted flambeaux was seen coming from each encampment, to the ground where the players assembled around their respective byes; and at the beat of the drums and chants of the women each party of players commenced the " ball-play dance " [plate XVII]. Each party danced for a quarter of an hour around their respective byes, in their ball-play dress, rattling their ball-sticks together in the most violent manner, and all singing as loud as they could raise their voices; whilst the women of each party, who had their goods at stake, formed into two rows on the line between the two parties of players, and danced also, in an uniform step, and all their voices joined in chants to the Great Spirit; in which they were soliciting his favor in deciding the game to their advantage; and also encouraging the players to exert every power they possessed, in the struggle that was to ensue. In the meantime, four old medicine-men, who were to have the starting of the ball, and who were to be judges of the play, were seated at the point where the ball was to be started; and busily smoking to the Great Spirit for their success in judging rightly, and impartially, between the parties in so important an affair.

This dance was one of the most picturesque scenes imaginable, and was repeated at intervals of every half hour during the night, and exactly in the same manner; so that the players were certainly awake all night, and arranged in their appropriate dress, prepared for the play which was to commence at 9 o'clock the next morning. In the morning, at the hour, the two parties and all their friends were drawn out and over the ground; when at length the game commenced, by the judges throwing up the ball at the firing of a gun; when an instant struggle ensued between the players, who were some six or seven hundred in numbers, and were mutually endeavoring to catch the ball in their sticks, and throw it home and between their respective stakes; which, whenever successfully done, counts 1 for game. In this game every player was dressed alike, that is, divested of all dress, except the girdle and the tail, which I have before described; and in these desperate struggles for the ball, when it is up ([plate xviii], where hundreds are running together and leaping, actually over each other's heads, and darting between their adversaries' legs, tripping and throwing, and foiling each other in every possible manner, every voice raised to the highest key, in shrill yelps and barks)! there are rapid successions of feats, and of incidents, that astonish and amuse far beyond the conception of anyone who has not had the singular good luck to witness them. In these struggles, every mode is used that can be devised, to oppose the progress of the foremost, who is likely to get the ball; and these obstructions often meet desperate individual resistance, which terminates in a violent scuffle, and sometimes in fisticuffs; when their sticks are dropped, and the parties are unmolested, whilst they are settling it between themselves; unless it be by a general *stampedo*, to which they are subject who are down, if the ball happens to pass in their direction. Every weapon, by a rule of all ball-plays, is laid by in their respective encampments, and no man is allowed to go for one; so that the sudden broils that take place on the ground are presumed to be as suddenly settled without any probability of much personal injury; and no one is allowed to interfere in any way with the contentious individuals.

There are times when the ball gets to the ground [plate xix], and such a confused mass rushing together around it, and knocking their sticks together, without the possibility of anyone getting or seeing it, for the dust that they raise, that the spectator loses his strength, and everything else but his senses; when the condensed mass of ball-sticks, and shins, and bloody noses, is carried around the different parts of the ground, for a quarter of an hour at a time, without any one of the mass being able to see the ball; which they are often thus scuffling for, several minutes after it has been thrown off, and played over another part of the ground.

For each time that the ball was passed between the stakes of either party, one was counted for their game, and a halt of about one minute; when it was again started by the judges of the play, and a similar struggle ensued; and so on until the successful party arrived to 100, which was the limit of the game, and accomplished at an hour's sun, when they took the stakes; and then, by a previous agreement, produced a number of jugs of whisky, which gave all a wholesome drink, and sent them all off merry and in good humor, but not drunk.

CHOCTAW. Indian Territory. (Cat. no. 6904, United States National Museum.)

Ball stick, consisting of a stick with a round handle, the end shaved flat and curved to form a kind of spoon-shaped hoop, which is laced with thongs, one running horizontally across, and the other from end to end, the latter serving to lash the turned end of the stick to the handle; length, 30¾ inches. Collected by Dr Edward Palmer in 1868.

—————— Indian Territory. (Cat. no. 21967, Free Museum of Science and Art, University of Pennsylvania.)

Pair of rackets (figure 771), one 30 and the other 28½ inches in length, consisting of a hickory sapling, cut flat at one end, which is curved around to form a spoon-like hoop, the turned-over end, which terminates in a small knob, being lashed to the handle.

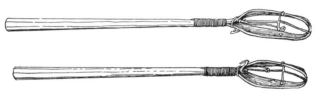

Fig. 771.

FIG. 771. Rackets; lengths, 30 and 28½ inches; Choctaw Indians, Indian Territory; cat. no. 21967, Free Museum of Science and Art, University of Pennsylvania.

FIG. 772. Horse tail worn in ball game; length, 25 inches; Choctaw Indians, Indian Territory; cat. no. 18764, Free Museum of Science and Art, University of Pennsylvania.

Fig. 772.

Also, a tail (figure 772; cat. no. 18764), used in the ball game, consisting of a piece of a horse's tail attached to a strip of wood by a thong and loop at the top; length, 25 inches. This was collected by Mr George E. Starr, who has furnished the following account of the game as witnessed by him at a place about 10 miles southwest of Red Oak, on the line of the Choctaw railroad, in Indian Territory:

The game was between Tobucksey and Sugarloaf counties of the Choctaw Nation. On the night before, the players went into camp near the place agreed upon. The season was the traditional one of the full moon of one of the summer months, and the company slept, without shelter, upon the ground. On their arrival, the new players, who had never been allowed to play before on the county teams, dressed themselves in ball costume, and, while their elders were arranging rules, ran around making themselves conspicuous to their own side in the hope they would be chosen the next day. Before retiring, the managers on each side and the principal players assembled to make regulations to govern the play. They sat in a circle, and, no matter how heated the argument became, a speaker was never interrupted by one of the opposite side. There were about 250 Indians present, about evenly divided on each side, being chiefly men, with a few women and children. Each side brought with them a conjurer, or medicine man. At about 7 o'clock on the following morning the managers assembled for some purpose, after which they collected their sides, and took their places, a little apart, to prepare for the play. They stripped for the game, putting on nothing but a breech clout. Their heads were bare, with the hair cut short, without feathers. Their only ornament was a coon tail stuck up straight along the spine, or a horse tail falling on the breech clout behind. This was attached to the belt, a leather strap or revolver belt. The men carry their weapons to the ball game, but are not allowed to wear them in the field. The majority of the players were of splendid physique, spare and wiry. Several were, in part, of negro blood, and many showed the result of intermixture with the whites. The sides each numbered 30, of ages varying from 18 to 35. Among them were some that were crippled, the result, it may be, of former play.

The goal posts, which the ball must touch, were about 200 to 225 yards apart. They consisted of two trees, lashed together with ropes. They were about 8 inches in diameter, and were cut flat on one side, and were set at an angle so that they presented a face of about 12 inches to the ball. This must hit the post, to which it may be carried between a player's sticks, but it must bounce over a line in front of the posts, otherwise it does not count and is still in play.

The conjurers were conspicuous throughout the game. At the commencement, after the sides were chosen, all went to their goal posts. When within about 10 feet of the posts they broke their formation, and, uttering a cry, ran up to the posts, battering them with their ball sticks. They did this to scare the spirit of bad luck away.

Then they lined up in a kind of alley between the goals. Near the middle of the field, however, there were about eight men of each side ranged opposite to each other in a line running horizontally across the goal line. When all the others were ready, the men who were to take these places crossed the field. A medicine man put the ball in play, tossing it into the air. One of them had his face painted half red and half black, and carried in his hand a small branch of a tree resembling hickory. They both stood near their respective goals and sung and clapped their hands. The game lasted from 10 to 5, with an intermission for luncheon. The score is 12 goals, but if this number is not completed on either side, the one having the highest number is adjudged the winner. Butting with the head is prohibited, under a penalty of 5 goals.

The Indians bet everything they possess upon the game, even to their clothes and boots. The bets are made through stakeholders—four or five Indians—who constantly ride about on horseback. Whatever is bet is put with what is bet against it. If handkerchiefs, they are knotted together and thrown over the stakeholder's shoulder; if money, the sums are put together in his pocketbook. His memory is remarkable, and he never fails to turn over the stakes correctly. Much skill is shown during the game. In a scrimmage the ball is tossed backward through the bent legs of the players, and when the player secures it he utters a signal cry—hogle á! This is repeated by those along the line, and each grabs the opponent nearest to him and holds him. While they are wrestling the player with the ball tries to run with it, so that he can throw it and make a goal.

The ball, it should be observed, is about the size of a golf ball, made of rags and covered with white buckskin. Several are provided, as they are frequently lost in the tall grass. The players on the side with the wind sometimes substitute a ball with a long tail and a loose cover that comes off during the play. The tail then impedes their opponents in throwing it against the wind. The women are extremely active in aiding their side. They are not permitted to touch the ball sticks, but they are constantly running about and giving hot coffee to the men. In one hand they carry a cup of coffee and in the other a quirt with which they whip the players when they think they are not playing hard enough. At times a player will get a woman to give him a pin, with which he will scarify his leg, making from three to five scratches from near the ankle to the middle of the calf, until the blood comes. This, they say, prevents cramps.

When the players return to the game after lunch hour they place their ball sticks in rows opposite each other in the middle of the field, where they are counted by the umpire or the leaders on each side. This is done to see that no more are playing than started in the game. The spectators cry out and encourage the sides. When a goal is made there is a shout. The most exciting point in a close game is when the last goal is neared. Then the play becomes very fast and the rules are not strictly observed. A goal may be made in a few moments or the contest may last for an hour. In wrestling, the players seize each other by the belts, dropping the ball sticks. With the exception of the prohibited butting almost everything is permitted. At the present game five men were crippled, of whom two died. The injuries inflicted upon a man during a game are frequently avenged by his relatives. The result of the game described was a victory for Tobucksey county. The conjurer on the Sugarloaf side was said to have sent his men to the creek to bathe in the morning, which weakened them. They were penalized five goals for butting at the end, and so lost the game. There was no celebration afterwards. All were tired out and went home quietly to their mud-chinked log cabins at the close of the day.

CHOCTAW. Mandeville, Louisiana. (Cat. no. 38476, Free Museum of Science and Art, University of Pennsylvania.)

Racket (figure 773), one of pair, consisting of a sapling, the end cut thin and turned over to form a kind of spoon, which is crossed and tied to the handle with cotton cord; length, 36½ inches.

FIG. 773. Racket; length, 36½ inches; Choctaw Indians, Louisiana; cat. no. 38476, Free Museum of Science and Art, University of Pennsylvania.

Collected by the writer in 1901. The rackets are called kabucha. The ball game is now seldom or never played by these Indians. The game was borrowed from the Indians by the whites in Louisiana, and is still played under the name of raquette.

While in New Orleans in the summer of 1901 I was told that the old game of raquette was still played on Sunday afternoons on a vacant lot east of the town. The players, some hundreds of French-speaking negroes, had assembled in a level, uninclosed field. The majority were armed with rackets (figure 774), each consisting of a piece of hickory bent over at one end to form a spoon, which was netted with a thong, precisely like those used by the Choctaw. A racket was carried in each hand, and the ball was picked up and thrown with them in the same way as in the Indian game. The players appeared to own their own rackets, and I purchased a pair without difficulty. At the same time there was an old man who had a large number of rackets strung on a cord, which he said were reserved for the use of the clubs to which they belonged.

Fig. 774.   Rackets; lengths, 21 and 24 inches; negroes, New Orleans; cat. no. 38480, Free Museum of Science and Art, University of Pennsylvania.

The goals or bases were two tall poles about 600 feet apart, having a strip of tin, about a foot wide and 10 feet long, fastened on the inner side some distance above the ground. These goals, called plats, were painted, one red with a small double ring of white near the top, the other blue with a black ring. Midway in a straight line between was a small peg to mark the center of the field, where the ball was first thrown. The players belonged to two opposing clubs, the Bayous and La Villes. Their colors agreed with those of the goals. Each side was led by a captain, who directed the play. The contest was for a flag, for which three successive games were played. The game appeared to be open, free for all, without reference to number; but in more formal matches the sides are equalized and regulated. The ball was put in play at the center flag, being tossed high in the air, and caught on the uplifted ball sticks. Then there was a wild rush across the field, the object being to secure and carry the ball and toss it against the tin plate, making a plat. The game was played with much vigor and no little violence. A blow across the shins with a racket is permissible, and broken heads are not uncommon. Play usually continues until dark, and, at the close, the winners sing Creole songs, reminding one of the custom at the close of the Choctaw game. Raquette was formerly much played by the Creoles, and the present negro clubs perpetuate the names of the opposing clubs of old Creole days.

MUSKOGEE. Eufaula, Indian Territory.   (Cat. no. 38065, Free Museum of Science and Art, University of Pennsylvania.)
Pair of rackets (figure 775), 37¼ inches in length, each made of a sapling, cut thin at the end, which is curved over to form a

kind of scoop, the cut end being bound to the body of the stick by thongs. The spoon at the end is crossed by two twisted thongs, with a longitudinal thong running through the middle. Made by Matawa Karso and collected by Mr W. H. Ward in 1891.

According to Tuggle,[a] the Creeks and Seminoles have stories of ball games by birds against fourfooted animals. In one story the bat is rejected by both sides, but is finally accepted by the four-footed animals on account of his having teeth, and enables them to win the victory from the birds.

FIG. 775.   Rackets; lengths, 37¼ inches; Muskogee Indians, Indian Territory; cat. no. 38065, Free Museum of Science and Art, University of Pennsylvania.

MUSKOGEE. Georgia.

Réné Laudonnière [b] wrote as follows in 1562:

They play at ball in this manner: they set up a tree in the midst of a place which is 8 or 9 fathoms high, in the top whereof there is set a square mat made of reeds or bulrushes, which whosoever hitteth in playing thereat, winneth the game.

John Bartram [c] says:

The ball play is esteemed the most noble and manly exercise; this game is exhibited in an extensive level plain, usually contiguous to the town; the inhabitants of one town play against another, in consequence of a challenge, when the youth of both sexes are often engaged and sometimes stake their whole substance. Here they perform amazing feats of strength and agility; the game principally consists in taking and carrying off the ball from the opposite party, after being hurled into the air, midway between two high pillars, which are the goals, and the party who bears off the ball to their pillar wins the game; each person having a racquet, or hurl, which is an implement of a very curious construction, somewhat resembling a ladle or little hoop-net, with a handle near 3 feet in length, the hoop and handle of wood, and the netting of thongs of raw-hide, or tendons of an animal.

The foot-ball is likewise a favorite, manly diversion with them. Feasting and dancing in the square at evening ends all their games.

Maj. Caleb Swan [d] says:

Their ball-plays are manly and require astonishing exertion, but white men have been found to excel the best of them at that exercise; they therefore seldom or never admit a white man into the ball-ground. Legs and arms have often

---

[a] Quoted by Mooney in Myths of the Cherokee. Nineteenth Annual Report of the Bureau of American Ethnology, pt. 1, p. 454, 1900.

[b] Hakluyt's Voyages, v. 13, p. 413, Edinburgh, 1889.

[c] Travels through North and South Carolina, Georgia, East and West Florida, p. 508, Philadelphia, 1791.

[d] Schoolcraft, Information respecting the History, Condition, and Prospects of the Indian Tribes of the United States, pt. 5, p. 277, Philadelphia, 1856.

been broken in their ball-plays, but no resentments follow an accident of this kind.

The women and men both attend them in large numbers, as a kind of gala; and bets often run as high as a good horse or an equivalent of skins.

J. M. Stanley,[a] in his Catalogue of Portraits of North American Indians, describes under no. 16, Tah-Coo-Sah Fixico, or Billy Hardjo, chief of one of the Creek towns:

The dress in which he is painted is that of a ball-player as they at first appear upon the grounds. During the play they divest themselves of all their ornaments, which are usually displayed on these occasions, for the purpose of betting on the results of the play; such is their passion for betting that the opposing parties frequently bet from five hundred to a thousand dollars on a single game.

Col. Marinus Willett [b] says:

This day I crossed the Toloposa and went 5 miles to see a most superb ball play. There were about eighty players on a side. The men, women, and children, from the neighboring towns, were assembled upon this occasion. Their appearance was splendid; all the paths leading to the place were filled with people; some on foot, some on horseback. The play was conducted with as much order and decorum as the nature of things would admit of. The play is set on foot by one town sending a challenge to another; if the challenge be accepted, the time and place are fixed on, and the whole night before the play is employed by the parties in dancing, and some other ceremonious preparations. On the morning of the play, the players on both sides paint and decorate themselves, in the same manner as when they are going to war. Thus decorated, and stripped of all such clothing as would encumber them, they set out for the appointed field. The time of their arrival is so contrived, that the parties arrive near the field at the same time; and when they get within about half a mile, in a direction opposite to each other, you hear the sound of the war song and the yell; when, presently, the parties appear in full trot, as if fiercely about to encounter in fight. In this manner they meet and soon become intermingled together, dancing while the noise continues. Silence then succeeds; each player places himself opposite to his antagonist. The rackets which they use are then laid against each other, in the center of the ground appointed for the game. They then proceed to measure a distance of 300 yards, 150 each way, from the center, where they erect two poles, through which the ball must pass, to count 1. The play is commenced by the balls being thrown up in the air, from the center; every player then, with his rackets, of which each has two, endeavors to catch the ball, and throw it between the poles; each side laboring to throw it between the poles towards their own towns; and every time this can be accomplished, it counts 1. The game is usually from 12 to 20. This was lost by the challengers. Large bets are made upon these occasions; and great strength, agility, and dexterity are displayed. The whole of the present exhibition was grand and well conducted. It sometimes happens that the inhabitants of a town game away at these plays all their clothes, ornaments, and horses. Throughout the whole of the game the women are constantly on the alert, with bottles and gourds filled with drink, watching every opportunity to supply the players.

---

[a] Smithsonian Miscellaneous Collections, v. 2, p. 13, 1862.
[b] A Narrative of the Military Actions of Colonel Marinus Willett, p. 108, New York, 1831.

SEMINOLE. Florida. (Cat. no. 18497, 19841, Free Museum of Science and Art, University of Pennsylvania.)

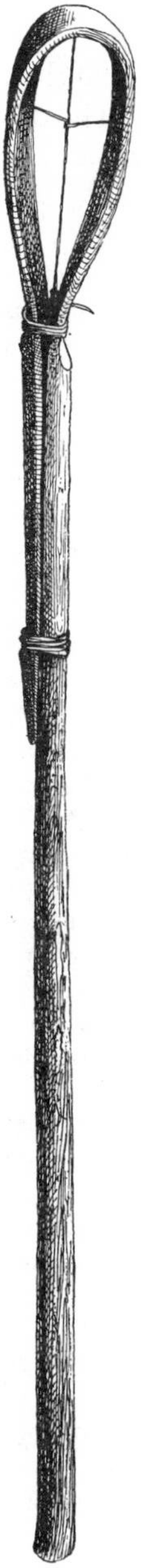

Rackets and ball, the rackets (figure 777) saplings bent to form a scoop-shaped hoop, the ends lashed together for a handle, the hoop crossed by two thongs tied at right angles; the ball (figure 776), of two colors, one hemisphere light, the other dark, made of buckskin, with median seam; diameter, $2\frac{3}{4}$ inches.

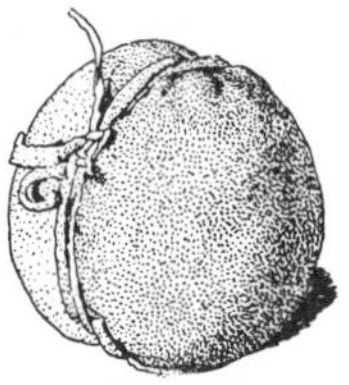

The rackets were collected by Mr Henry G. Bryant and the ball by Lieut. Hugh L. Willoughby in 1896. Mr Bryant gives the name of the rackets as tokonhay.

Fig. 776.

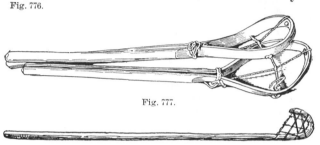

Fig. 777.

Fig. 779.

FIG. 776. Ball; diameter, $2\frac{3}{4}$ inches; Seminole Indians, Florida; cat. no. 19841, Free Museum of Science and Art, University of Pennsylvania.

FIG. 777. Rackets; length, 13 inches; Seminole Indians, Florida; cat. no. 18497, Free Museum of Science and Art, University of Pennsylvania.

FIG. 778. Racket; length, 33 inches; Seminole Indians, Indian Territory; cat. no. $\frac{50}{2288}$, American Museum of Natural History.

FIG. 779. Ball racket; length, 36 inches; Nishinam Indians, California; from sketch by Dr J. W. Hudson.

———— Indian Territory. (Cat. no. $\frac{50}{2288}$, American Museum of Natural History.)

Ball stick (figure 778), made of hickory, one end cut flat and turned over to form a spoon-shaped receptacle, which is crossed by two thongs at right angles; length, 33 inches. Collected by Dr William Jones in 1901.

PUJUNAN STOCK

NISHINAM. Mokelumne river, 12 miles south of Placerville, California.

Dr J. W. Hudson describes the following game under name of patai kato:

Fig. 778.

Pä'-tai is the general name for the flail basket used in harvesting seed; ka-tüm', sling. The implements are a ball of buckskin, 3 inches in diameter, filled with deer hair, called pâs'-ko, and a single club [figure 779], ku-nûn'-teă, 3 feet in length, with its recurved lower end netted. There are four players to a side, each side having its captain. The ball is placed in the center of the field, 20 feet distant from the captains. The umpire calls "Ha!" for the start. The goals, 500 yards apart, consist of wooden arches, 4 feet apart at bottom and 6 feet high.

No interference is permitted, under penalty of individual stakes.

SALISHAN STOCK

SKOKOMISH.   British Columbia.

Mr Charles Hill-Tout [a] mentions two kinds of ball games, kekqua and tcquila.

The former was a kind of lacrosse, and the ball was caught and thrown with an instrument similar to the lacrosse stick.

THOMPSON INDIANS (NTLAKYAPAMUK).   British Columbia.

James Teit [b] says:

The other game was similar to that of "lacrosse." There were two sides and a goal for each, marked by stones or wooden pegs, or by long stakes half the

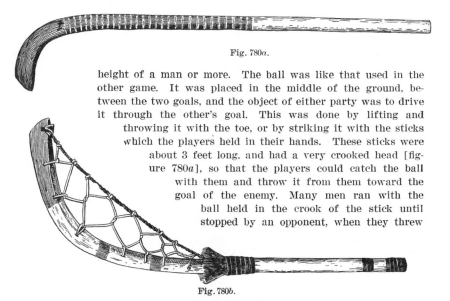

Fig. 780a.

height of a man or more. The ball was like that used in the other game. It was placed in the middle of the ground, between the two goals, and the object of either party was to drive it through the other's goal. This was done by lifting and throwing it with the toe, or by striking it with the sticks which the players held in their hands. These sticks were about 3 feet long, and had a very crooked head [figure 780a], so that the players could catch the ball with them and throw it from them toward the goal of the enemy. Many men ran with the ball held in the crook of the stick until stopped by an opponent, when they threw

Fig. 780b.

FIG. 780 a, b. Ball sticks; lengths, 23½ and 23 inches; Thompson Indians, British Columbia; cat. no. $\frac{16}{4887}$, $\frac{16}{4887}$T, American Museum of Natural History.

the ball toward the intended goal. Others preferred, if they had a chance, to lift the ball with the toe, and before it fell strike or catch it with their stick. One man always tried to take the ball from his opponent with his stick.

---

[a] Notes on the Sk'qō'mic of British Columbia. Report of the Seventieth Meeting of the British Association for the Advancement of Science, p. 488, London, 1900.

[b] The Thompson Indians of British Columbia. Memoirs of the American Museum of Natural History, whole series, v. 2, p. 277, New York, 1900.

When bending the end of the stick to the desired crook, bark string was used, connecting the latter to the straight part of the stick. Some Indians played with the strings still attached, thinking to get a better hold of the ball, but this was considered unfair. In some games all the players used crooks with nets similar to those of lacrosse sticks [figure 780b]. Often a guard stick was used to protect the ball from the players of the opposite party [figure 781]. Any person who touched the ball with his hands while playing went immediately out of the game. Sometimes, to the amusement of the men, the women were persuaded to play the game. Within the last few years this game has fallen altogether into disuse.

The Lower Thompsons had a ball game in which the ball was thrown up by one player. The player who caught it ran with it until overtaken by another player, who in his turn ran with it until a certain goal was reached. . . .

Another boys' game was to take a pebble about 3 inches in diameter and covered with skin, and roll it down a hillside. Other players with scoop-nets, about 1 foot long (including the handle), stood at the bottom, and each tried to catch the bounding ball as it reached him. The nets were made of a pliable stick or wand, bent over the top so as to form a circle, which was filled with a netting of bark twine. A game similar to the last was played with a skin-covered ball, to which a short toggle was attached [figure 782a]. The players held a kind of hoop with handle [figure 782 b, c], by means of which they tried to catch the ball by its toggle.

Fig. 781. Stick for protecting ball; length, 28¼ inches; Thompson Indians (Ntlakyapamuk), British Columbia; cat. no. ₄₈₈₇¹⁶, American Museum of Natural History.

THOMPSON INDIANS (NTLAKYAPAMUK). Thompson and Fraser rivers, British Columbia.

Mr Charles Hill-Tout [a] says:

They were fond of games, like their neighbors, and utilized the level, grassy river benches for various games of ball. One of these games, suk'-kul-lila'-ka, was not unlike our own game of football. The players were divided, as with us, into two groups, and at each end of the field was a goal formed by two poles planted several feet asunder. The play commenced from the middle of the field, and the object was to get the ball through the goal of their adversaries. The ball was made from some kind of tree fungus, cut round, and covered with elkhide. I could not learn anything of the rules of the game; nor was my informant certain whether the feet or hands, or both, were used in propelling the ball.

SIOUAN STOCK

ASSINIBOIN. Fort Union, Montana.

In a report to Isaac I. Stevens, governor of Washington Territory, on the Indian tribes of the upper Missouri, by Edwin T. Denig, a manuscript in the library of the Bureau of American Ethnology, after a description of the game of shinny, occurs this passage:

Another mode of playing the game is by catching the ball in a network attached to the end of the stick, over a small hoop a little larger than the ball.

---

[a] Notes on the N'tlapamuq of British Columbia. Report of the Sixty-ninth Meeting of the British Association for the Advancement of Science, p. 507, London, 1900.

They catch it in this net as it flies through the air and throw it from one to the other towards either goal. The man who catches can run with the ball toward the limit until he is overtaken by one on the other side, when he throws it as far as he can on its way, which is continued by the others.

CATAWBA. South Carolina.

Mrs R. E. Dunbar, of Leslie, York county, South Carolina, informs the writer [a] that the Catawba do not play any of their old games. They used to play a game with two sticks and a ball. The sticks were hollowed out like a large wooden spoon. The ball must not touch the hand or the ground, but must be thrown and kept in the air with the sticks. Any number in excess of two could play. This game was called wahumwah.

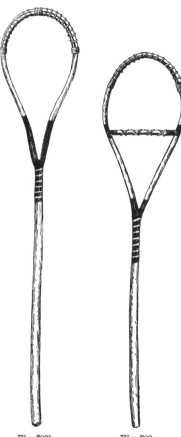

Fig. 782a.   Fig. 782b.   Fig. 782c.

FIG. 782 a, b, c. Balls and catching hoops; lengths of hoops, 22¼ and 20½ inches; Thompson Indians (Ntlakyapamuk), British Columbia; cat. no. $\frac{16}{1870}$, $\frac{16}{1889}$, $\frac{16}{1888}$, American Museum of Natural History.

DAKOTA (SANTEE). Minnesota.

Dr Walter J. Hoffman [b] wrote:

The game played by the Dakota Indians of the upper Missouri was probably learned from the Ojibwa, as these two tribes have been upon amicable terms for many years; the ball sticks are identical in construction, and the game is played in the same manner. Sometimes, however, the goals at either end of the ground consist of two heaps of blankets about 20 feet apart, between which the ball is passed.

---

[a] In a letter, dated September 1, 1901.

[b] Remarks on Ojibwa Ball Play. The American Anthropologist, v. 3, p. 135, 1890.

When the Dakotas play a game, the village is equally divided into sides. A player offers as a wager some article of clothing, a robe, or a blanket, when an opponent lays down an object of equal value. This parcel is laid aside and the next two deposit their stakes, and so on until all have concluded. The game then begins, two of the three innings deciding the issue.

When the women play against the men, five of the women are matched against one of the latter. A mixed game of this kind is very amusing. The fact that among the Dakota women are allowed to participate in the game is considered excellent evidence that the game is a borrowed one. Among most other tribes women are not even allowed to touch a ball stick.

The players frequently hang to the belt the tail of a deer, antelope, or some other fleet animal, or the wings of swift-flying birds, with the idea that through these they are endowed with the swiftness of the animal. There are, however, no special preparations preceding a game as feasting or fasting, dancing, etc.—additional evidence that the game is less regarded among this people.

Mr Philander Prescott [a] gives the following account of the ball game in Schoolcraft:

Ball plays are played by both men and women, and heavy bets depend on the issue. I believe there is but one kind of ball playing. One village plays against another. The boundaries are near a half mile. The ball is started from the middle. Each party strives to get the ball over the respective boundaries; for instance, the boundaries are east and west; one party or village will try to carry the ball west and the other east. If a village or party gets the ball over the eastern boundary, they change sides, and the next time they have to try and get it over the western boundary; so, if the same party propels it over the western boundary, they win one game; and another bet is played for. The ball is carved and thrown in a stick about 2 or 3 feet long, with a little circle at the end to assist in picking it up. This hoop has some buckskin cords across to keep the ball in. I have known an Indian to throw the ball over the boundaries in three throws. When it is seen flying through the air, there is a great shout and hurra by the spectators. They sometimes pick up the ball, and run over the lines without being overtaken by any of the opposite party. Then a great shout is raised again, to urge on the players. Horses, guns, kettles, blankets, wampum, calico, beads, etc., are bet. This game is very laborious and occasionally the players receive some hard blows, either from the club or ball. I once saw a man almost killed with the ball. He stood in front of the player that was going to throw the ball, who threw with great force and aimed too low. The ball struck the other in the side, and knocked him senseless for some time. As to the effects, I do not perceive that any serious evil results, if we except the gambling. Ball is generally played in May and June, and in winter.

Schoolcraft [b] says:

Ball playing.—This game is played by the northwestern Indians in the winter season, after the winter hunts are over, and during summer, when, the game being unfit to kill, they amuse themselves with athletic sports, games of chance, dances, and war. The game is played by two parties, not necessarily equally divided by numbers, but usually one village against another, or one large village may challenge two or three smaller ones to the combat. When a challenge is accepted, a day is appointed to play the game; ball-bats are made, and each party

---

[a] Information respecting the History, Condition, and Prospects of the Indian Tribes of the United States, pt. 4, p. 64, Philadelphia, 1856.

[b] Ibid., pt. 2, p. 78, 1852.

assembles its whole force of old men, young men, and boys. The women never play in the same game with the men. Heavy bets are made by individuals of the opposite sides. Horses, guns, blankets, buffalo-robes, kettles, and trinkets are freely staked on the result of the game. When the parties are assembled on the ground, two stakes are placed about a quarter of a mile apart, and the game commences midway between them ; the object of each party being to get the ball beyond the limits of its opponents. The game commences by one of the old men throwing the ball in the air, when all rush forward to catch it in their ball-bats before or after it falls to the ground. The one who catches it throws it in the direction of the goal of the opposing party, when, if it be caught by one of the same side, it is continued in that direction, and so on until it is thrown beyond the limits ; but if caught by an opponent, it is thrown back in the opposite direction. In this way, the ball is often kept all day between the two boundaries, neither party being able to get it beyond the limit of the other. When

FIG. 783. Santee Dakota Indian ball-play on the ice, Minnesota; from Schoolcraft.

one has caught the ball, he has the right, before throwing it, to run towards the limits until he is overtaken by the other party, when, being compelled to throw it, he endeavors to send it in the direction of some of his own party, to be caught by some one of them, who continues sending it in the same direction.

Figure 783 represents a ball play on the ice. The young man has the ball in his ball-bat, and is running with it toward the limits of the other side, pursued by all the other players.

Fig. 784 represents a ball play on the prairies in summer. The ball is on the ground and all are rushing forward to catch it with their ball-bats, not being allowed to touch it with their hands.

The ball is carved from a knot, or made of baked clay covered with rawhide of the deer. The ball-bat . . . is from 3 to 4 feet long; one end bent up in a circular form of about 4 inches in diameter, in which is a net-work made of rawhide or sinews of the deer or buffalo.

E. D. Neill [a] says:

The favorite and most exciting game of the Dakota is ball playing. It appears to be nothing more than a game which was often played by the writer in school-boy days and which was called shinny. A smooth place is chosen on the prairie or frozen river or lake. Each player has a stick 3 or 4 feet long and crooked at the lower end, with deer strings tied across, forming a sort of pocket. The ball is made with a rounded knot of wood, or clay covered with hide, and is supposed to possess supernatural qualities. Stakes are set at a distance of a quarter or a half a mile, as bounds. Two parties are then formed, and, the ball being thrown up in the center, the contest is for one party to carry the ball from the other beyond one of the bounds. Two or three hundred men are sometimes engaged at once. On a summer's day, to see them rushing to and fro, painted in divers colors, with no article of apparel, with feathers in their heads, bells

FIG. 784. Santee Dakota Indian ball-play on the prairie, Minnesota; from Schoolcraft.

around their wrists, and fox and wolf tails dangling behind, is a wild and noisy spectacle. The eyewitnesses among the Indians become more interested in the success of one or the other of the parties than any crowd at a horse race, and frequently stake their last piece of property on the issue of the game.

DAKOTA (YANKTONAI). Devils lake, North Dakota. (Cat. no. 60362, 60395, Field Columbian Museum.)

Stick of hickory terminating in a ring which supports a buckskin thong net, and a buckskin ball filled with deer hair. These specimens were collected in 1900 by Dr George A. Dorsey, who gives the name of the stick as chianyankapi, and that of the ball as tahpa.

---

[a] Dakota Land and Dakota Life. Collections of the Minnesota Historical Society, v. 1, p. 281, St Paul, 1872.

Iowa. Missouri.

George Catlin [a] says:

Two byes, or goals, are established, at three or four hundred yards from each other, by erecting two poles in the ground for each, 4 or 5 feet apart, between which it is the strife of either party to force the ball (it having been thrown up at a point halfway between) by catching it in a little hoop, or racket, at the end of a stick, 3 feet in length, held in both hands as they run, throwing the ball an immense distance when they get it in the stick. The game is always played over an extensive prairie or meadow.

Catlin says also:

Previous to commencing on the exciting game of ball, as the goods of all playing are more or less at stake, each party must needs invoke the aid of supernatural influence to their respective sides; and for this purpose they give a very pretty dance, in which, as in the Scalp Dance, the women take a part, giving neat and curious effect to the scene. In most of the tribes this dance is given at intervals of every half hour or so, during the night previous to the play, preparing the minds and bodies of the players for this exciting scene, upon which they enter in the morning with empty stomachs and decide before they leave the ground to eat.

Oto. Oklahoma. (Cat. no. 71404, Field Columbian Museum.)

Ball covered with buckskin (figure 785), 2¼ inches in diameter, and racket, a stick 40 inches in length with end bent to form a spoon-shaped hook, which is laced with buckskin. Collected in 1902 by Dr George A. Dorsey.

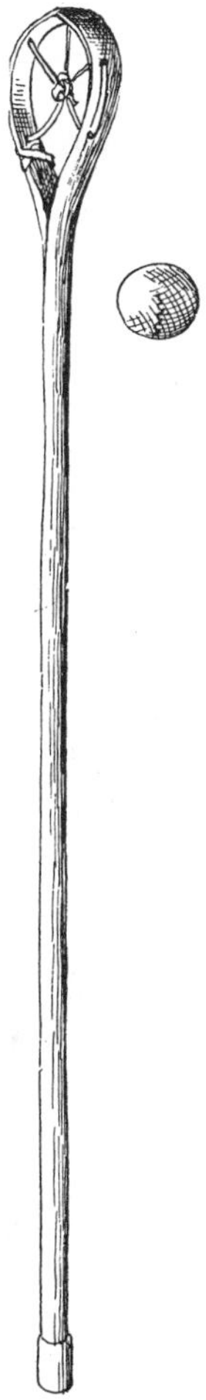

Winnebago. Wisconsin. (Cat. no. 22159, 22160, Free Museum of Science and Art, University of Pennsylvania.)

Wooden ball (figure 786), 3 inches in diameter, perforated with six holes at right angles, and a racket (figure 787), length 26½ inches, consisting of a sapling cut and bent at the striking end to form a hoop, which is laced with a throng and a cord crossing at right angles.

Collected by Mr T. R. Roddy.

The ball stick is called cha-pa-nun-a. The ball, wa-ki-hki, is perforated with holes in order to sound when flying through the air.

Fig. 785. Ball and racket; diameter of ball, 2¼ inches; length of racket, 40 inches; Oto Indians, Oklahoma, cat. no. 71404, Field Columbian Museum.

---

[a] The George Catlin Indian Gallery, p. 151, 1887. Annual Report of the Smithsonian Institution for 1885, 1887.

Caleb Atwater [a] (1829) says:

They also play ball, in which sport great numbers engage, on each side, and the spectators bet largely on each side. The articles played for are placed in view of those who play the game. These consist of beads, paints, jewels, etc. This game is very animated and excites great interest.

In regard to the Winnebago in Wisconsin, Mr Reuben G. Thwaites [b] says:

The vigorous game of lacrosse—nowadays familiar to patrons of state and county fairs of this section, at which professional bands of Chippewas exhibit their skill—was, in earlier days, much played by the Winnebagoes. It was usually played at La Crosse—Prairie la Crosse deriving its name from this fact—during the general rendezvous after the winter's hunt. The Winnebagoes having always clung to the water-courses and heavy timber, during their winter's trapping and hunting, would float down the rivers to La Crosse, and there have their feasts and lacrosse games, meet the traders, and indulge in a big spree. Occasionally they played lacrosse in their villages, but this was not common. It was considered to be more especially a spring festival game. I never hear, nowadays, of the Wisconsin Winnebagoes playing it, and in fact I never saw it in this state, but when I was at the mission on Turkey river I frequently saw the Indians there indulge in it. . . . These games were always for heavy stakes in goods.

Fig. 787.

Fig. 786.

FIG. 786. Ball; diameter, 3 inches; Winnebago Indians, Wisconsin; cat. no. 22159, Free Museum of Science and Art, University of Pennsylvania.
FIG. 787. Racket; length, 26½ inches; Winnebago Indians, Wisconsin; cat. no. 22160, Free Museum of Science and Art, University of Pennsylvania.

SHINNY

Shinny is especially a woman's game, but it is also played by men alone (Assiniboin, Yankton, Mohave, Walapai), by men and women alone (Sauk and Foxes, Tewa, Tigua), by men and women together (Sauk and Foxes, Assiniboin), by men against women (Crows). It may be regarded as practically universal among the tribes throughout the United States. As in racket, the ball may not be touched with the hand, but is both batted and kicked with the foot. A single bat is ordinarily used, but the Makah have two, one for striking and the other for carrying the ball. The rackets are invariably curved, and usually expanded at the striking end. In some instances they are painted or carved.

---

[a] The Indians of the Northwest, p. 118, Columbus, 1850.
[b] The Wisconsin Winnebagoes. Collections of the State Historical Society of Wisconsin, v. 12, p. 426, Madison, 1892.

The ball is either of wood, commonly a knot, or of buckskin. The wooden ball occurs chiefly on the Pacific coast and in the Southwest. The buckskin ball is generally used by the Eastern and Plains tribes, and is commonly flattened, with a median seam, the opposite sides being painted sometimes with different colors. The Navaho use a bag-shaped ball. The goals consist of two posts or stakes at the ends of the field, or two blankets spread side by side on the ground (Crows); again a single post is used (Menominee, Shuswap, Omaha) or lines drawn at the ends of the field over which the ball must be forced (Navaho, Eskimo, Omaha, Makah). The distance of the goals is not recorded, except among the Miwok (200 yards), the Omaha (300 yards), Mono (1,400 yards and return), and the Makah (200 yards).

In a California form of the game the players were lined up along the course and struck their ball along the line, the game corresponding with one in which the ball was kicked, struck, or tossed, played by the same tribe.

The game of shinny is frequently referred to in the myths. It was commonly played without any particular ceremony. Among the Makah it was played at the time of the capture of a whale, the ball being made from a soft bone of that animal. The shinny stick may be regarded as analogous to the club of the War Gods.

ALGONQUIAN STOCK

ARAPAHO. Cheyenne and Arapaho reservation, Oklahoma.

Mr James Mooney [a] describes the woman's game of gugahawat, or shinny, played with curved sticks and a ball like a baseball (figure 788), called gaa-wă'ha, made of buffalo hair and covered with buckskin.

Two stakes are set up as goals at either end of the ground, and the object of each party is to drive the ball through the goals of the other. Each inning is a game.

Mr Mooney gives the Cheyenne name of this game as ohonistuts.

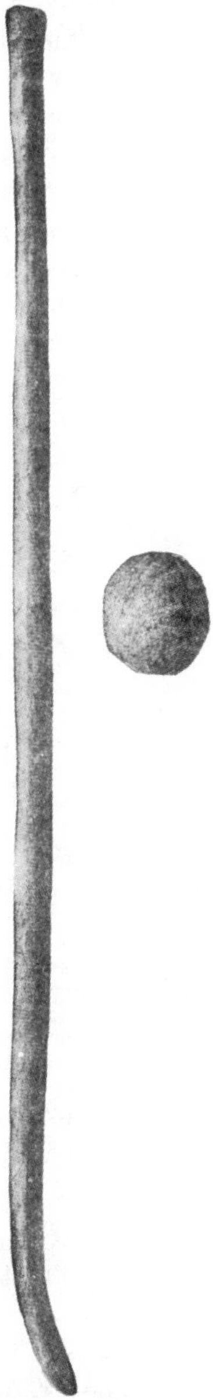

FIG. 788. Shinny ball and stick; Arapaho Indians, Oklahoma; from Mooney.

[a] The Ghost-dance Religion. Fourteenth Annual Report of the Bureau of Ethnology, pt. 2, p. 964, 1896.

ARAPAHO. Wind River reservation, Wyoming. (Cat. no. 36974, Free
    Museum of Science and Art, University of Pennsylvania.)
Ball covered with buckskin (figure 789), flattened, with median seam,
    one face painted with a cross, dividing it into quarters, the
    other with a similar cross, the quarters each containing two dots,
    with a T-shaped mark between; diameter, 4 inches. Three
    metal dangles are attached to the center of one face. There is
    a thong loop for suspension. Collected by the writer in 1900.

——— Wind River reservation, Wyoming. (Free Museum of Science
    and Art, University of Pennsylvania.)
Cat. no. 36976. Shinny stick (figure 791), besh, curved at the end
    and painted red and blue; length, 40 inches. Ball (figure 790)
    covered with buckskin, with median seam, one face painted red
    and one green; diameter, 3½ inches.

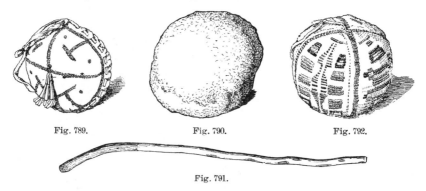

Fig. 789.   Fig. 790.   Fig. 792.

Fig. 791.

FIG. 789. Shinny ball; diameter, 4 inches; Arapaho Indians, Wind River reservation, Wyoming;
    cat. no. 36974, Free Museum of Science and Art, University of Pennsylvania.
FIG. 790. Shinny ball; diameter, 3½ inches; Arapaho Indians, Wind River reservation, Wyoming;
    cat. no. 36976, Free Museum of Science and Art, University of Pennsylvania.
FIG. 791. Shinny stick; length, 40 inches; Arapaho Indians, Wind River reservation, Wyoming;
    cat. no. 36976, Free Museum of Science and Art, University of Pennsylvania.
FIG. 792. Shinny ball; diameter, 3½ inches; Arapaho Indians, Wyoming; cat. no. 200764, United
    States National Museum.

Cat. no. 36975. Shinny stick, besh, curved at the end and painted
    with bands of red and green; length, 34 inches.
    These were collected by the writer in 1900.

——— Wyoming. (United States National Museum.)
Cat. no. 200764. Beaded ball (figure 792), made of buckskin, slightly
    flattened, with buckskin thong for suspension; diameter, 3½
    inches. The ball is completely covered with a ground of white
    glass beads divided by two intersecting lines of red beads into
    four segments, each of which contains a design in colored beads,
    probably representing conventionalized animal figures. The de-
    signs on opposite sides are alike.

Cat. no. 200765.   Beaded ball, similar to the preceding, but only partially covered with beads.   Two intersecting lines of white and red beads divide the ball into four segments, each of which contains a rectangular beaded design, two opposite ones alike of white and red beads with green center, and two of dark blue and white with green center.   It has a loop for suspension.

Cat. no. 200763.   Beaded ball, entirely covered with beadwork.   Two bands of white beads surround the ball at right angles, forming four segments, two on opposite sides composed of beads of different colors—pink, white, blue, yellow, red, and green—and two, also opposite, of blue beads with a white middle line and colored figures on the blue ground.

The three preceding balls belong to the E. Granier collection.

FIG. 793.   Shinny ball; diameter, 4 inches; Cheyenne Indians, Oklahoma; cat. no. 166027, United States National Museum.

ARAPAHO.   Wyoming.

In the tale of " Foot-Stuck-Child " [a] Dr A. L. Kroeber relates how a miraculous girl, who is escaping from her husband, a buffalo, and from a rock who wished to marry her, threw up a ball which she was carrying.   She first threw the ball, and as it came down kicked it upward, and her fathers, in turn, rose up.   Then she threw and kicked it for herself.   She and her fathers reached the sky in one place. They live in a tent covered with stars.

In Doctor Dorsey's [b] version of the same story the girl disobeys her father's injunction not to leave her tipi to take part in a shinny-ball game, and was captured by the buffalo bull.

CHEYENNE.   Oklahoma.   (United States National Museum.)

Cat. no. 166027.   Hide ball (figure 793), disk-shaped, with two hide faces sewed to a strip at the edge, painted brown, with a design of a turkey drawn on one side and on the opposite side a deer, with hills and pine trees; diameter, 4 inches; thickness, 2 inches.

[a] Traditions of the Arapaho, p. 159, Chicago, 1903.   [b] Ibid., p. 172.

Cat. no. 165856.   Another (figure 794), a flattened sphere with median seam, encompassed with thong, with a loop for suspension; diameter, 3 inches.

Both were collected by Rev. H. R. Voth.

Cat. no. 152903.   Shinny stick (figure 795), curved and expanded at

the end, with incised design of an elk and eagle, painted yellow, with half the striking end green; length, 35 inches.   Collected by Mr James Mooney.

CHEYENNE.   Oklahoma.   (Cat. no. 67443, 67445, Field Columbian Museum.)

FIG. 794.   Shinny ball; diameter, 3 inches; Cheyenne Indians, Oklahoma; cat. no. 165856, United States National Museum.

Two shinny sticks; length $33\frac{3}{4}$ and $37\frac{3}{4}$ inches.   Collected by Rev. H. R. Voth in 1890.

The following appears on the label:

Used in an old ball game which was very seldom played, but was revived during the Ghost-dance craze among the Cheyenne and Arapaho, with other games and ceremonies that had been nearly forgotten.   The ball was rolled and struck along the ground, generally within the circle of the dancers.

FIG. 795.   Shinny stick; length, 35 inches; Cheyenne Indians, Oklahoma; cat. no. 152903, United States National Museum.

——— Cheyenne reservation, Montana.   (Cat. no. 69979, Field Columbian Museum.)

Shinny stick and ball (figure 797); the ball of buckskin, flattened, with median seam, $3\frac{3}{4}$ inches in diameter, and painted red; the stick a sapling, curved at right angles at striking end, 31 inches in length.   Collected in 1901 by Mr S. C. Simms, who describes the game as played by young girls.

CHIPPEWA.   Turtle mountain, North Dakota.   (Cat. no. $\frac{50}{4723}$, American Museum of Natural History.)

Buckskin ball, flattened, with median seam, $4\frac{1}{2}$ inches in diameter, painted with a cross in red on both faces and a red circle around the middle.   The ball is very heavy and is probably weighted with clay.

Buckskin ball (figure 798) with median seam, with a Greek cross in yellow beads on one face, a green bead cross on the other, and a band of yellow beads around the seam.

Curved stick (figure 798), painted red, 24 inches in length.

These were collected by Dr William Jones in 1903.

GROSVENTRES.   Fort Belknap reservation, Montana.   (Cat. no. 60356, Field Columbian Museum.)

Buckskin-covered ball with median seam, painted red, 3¼ inches in diameter, and stick made of sapling, curved at one end and painted red, 31 inches in length (figure 799).

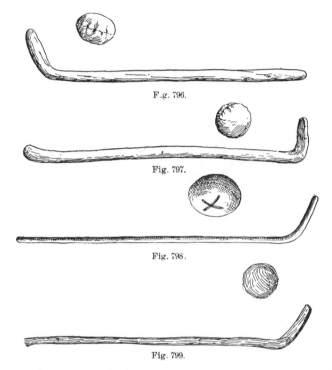

Fig. 796.

Fig. 797.

Fig. 798.

Fig. 799.

FIG. 796. Shinny ball and stick; diameter of ball, 4 inches; length of stick, 38 inches; Cheyenne Indians, Montana; cat. no. 69648, Field Columbian Museum.

FIG. 797. Shinny ball and stick; diameter of ball, 3⅜ inches; length of stick, 31 inches; Cheyenne Indians, Montana; cat. no. 69979, Field Columbian Museum.

FIG. 798. Shinny ball and stick; diameter of ball, 4½ inches; length of stick, 24 inches; Chippewa Indians, Turtle mountain, North Dakota; cat. no. $\frac{50}{4723}$, American Museum of Natural History.

FIG. 799. Shinny ball and stick; diameter of ball, 3¼ inches; length of stick, 31 inches; Grosventre Indians, Montana; cat. no. 60356, Field Columbian Museum.

These were collected in 1900 by Dr George A. Dorsey, who describes them as used in the game of shinny, kakawaasethi, a game of ball played with a curved stick and a buckskin-covered ball, kawa, slightly flattened on two sides.

Formerly this was a popular game among the young men of the tribe, who played among themselves or against a team representing some rival tribe. The object of the game was to advance the ball by batting it with sticks to some goal, against the effort of the opposing team.

GROSVENTRES. Fort Belknap reservation, Montana. (American Museum of Natural History.)

Cat. no. $\frac{50}{1728}$. Buckskin ball with median seam, painted yellow, with a bear's foot in green on one face; diameter, 3 inches.

Cat. no. $\frac{50}{1729}$. Buckskin ball with median seam, one side painted red, with a cross, the other dark; diameter, 4¼ inches.

Cat. no. $\frac{50}{1731}$. Buckskin ball with median seam, a cross in red quill work on one face, a bow and arrow on the other; diameter, 2½ inches.

Cat. no. $\frac{50}{1910}$. Shinny stick, curved at the end; length, 2 feet 3 inches.

These specimens were collected by Dr A. L. Kroeber.

MENOMINEE. Wisconsin.

Dr Walter J. Hoffman [a] wrote:

> The women formerly played a game of ball in which two sides, composed of unlimited numbers, would oppose each other. At each end of the ball ground, which was several hundred yards in length, a pole was erected, to serve as a goal. Many of the players would surround their respective goals, while the strongest and most active women, playing about the middle of the ground, would endeavor to obtain the ball and throw it toward their opponents' goal. The ball was made of deer hair tightly wrapped with thongs of buckskin, and covered with the same material. It measured about 3 inches in diameter. The women used sticks with a slight curve at the striking end, instead of a hoop, as on the sticks used by the men.
>
> The game was more like the well-known game of shinny than anything else, with the addition of having to cause the ball to strike the goal instead of being merely knocked across a certain score line. The guardians of the goals were expected to prevent the ball from touching the post, and a good strike might send it away over the active players' heads, far toward their opponents' goal.

POWHATAN. Virginia.

William Strachey [b] wrote:

> A kind of exercise they have amongst them much like that which boys call bandy in English.

SAUK AND FOXES. Iowa. (Cat. no. $\frac{50}{3505}$, $\frac{50}{3506}$, American Museum of Natural History.)

Leather-covered ball (figure 800) with median seam, flattened, 5 inches in diameter, and stick (figure 800), a sapling, curved at the striking end, 41 inches in length.

Collected by Dr William Jones, who describes them as used in the game of ice hockey. Men and women play apart or together. The goals are lines on opposite sides, across which the balls must be driven from either side to count.

---

[a] The Menomini Indians. Fourteenth Annual Report of the Bureau of Ethnology, pt. 1, p. 244, 1896.

[b] The History of Travaile into Virginia Brittania. Printed for the Hakluyt Society, p. 77, London, 1849.

ATHAPASCAN STOCK

MIKONOTUNNE AND MISHIKHWUTMETUNNE. Siletz reservation, Oregon.

A. W. Chase [a] says:

One of the national games is extremely interesting. It is generally played by rival tribes, and is identical with that in vogue amongst our school-boys called hockey. Sides being chosen, each endeavors to drive a hard ball of pine wood around a stake and in different directions.

NAVAHO. New Mexico. (Cat. no. 9530, United States National Museum.)

Buckskin ball (figure 801), bag shaped, with drawstring; diameter, 1½ inches. Collected by Dr Edward Palmer.

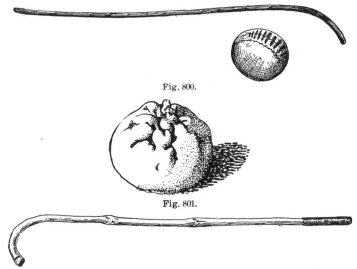

Fig. 800.

Fig. 801.

Fig. 802.

FIG. 800. Ball and stick for ice hockey; diameter of ball, 5 inches; length of stick, 41 inches; Sauk and Fox Indians, Iowa; cat. no. 50/3505, 50/3505, American Museum of Natural History.
FIG. 801. Shinny ball; diameter, 1½ inches; Navaho Indians, New Mexico; cat. no. 9530, United States National Museum.
FIG. 802. Shinny stick; length, 32 inches; Navaho Indians, Arizona; cat. no. 3629, Brooklyn Institute Museum.

——— Chin Lee, Arizona. (Cat. no. 3629, Brooklyn Institute Museum.)

Ball stick (figure 802), a peeled sapling curved at the striking end, with bark at the handle; length, 32 inches. Collected by the writer in 1903.

Dr Washington Matthews describes the game of tsol, or ball, as the last of the games played by the young Hatsehogan with the gambling god Nohoilpi.[b]

[a] Overland Monthly, v. 2, p. 433, San Francisco, 1869.
[b] Navaho Legends, p. 84, Boston, 1897.

The object was to hit the ball so that it would fall beyond a certain line. " I will win this game for you," said the little bird Tsĭlká*l*i, for I will hide within the ball and fly with it wherever I want to go. Do not hit the ball hard; give it only a light tap, and depend on me to carry it." . . . On the line over which the ball was to be knocked all the people were assembled; on one side were those who still remained slaves; on the other side were the freedmen and those who had come to wager themselves, hoping to rescue their kinsmen. No*h*o*f*lpi bet on this game the last of his slaves and his own person. The gambler struck his ball a heavy blow, but it did not reach the line; the stranger gave his but a light tap, and the bird within it flew with it far beyond the line, whereat the released captives jumped over the line and joined their people.

NAVAHO. St Michael, Arizona.

Reverend Father Berard Haile writes as follows in a personal letter: [a]

In shinny, ndashdilkă'*l*, the ball bears the same name, jol, as in the tossed and batted ball game. The stick is the reversed ball stick; however, the filling of the ball is somewhat different, for it is put in a small leather pouch and then sewed at the end and not in the center. This seems immaterial. Shinny is played according to the rules which regulate the game of tossed and batted ball regarding time of year, etc. The Navaho prefer long distances [figure 803] between the opposing lines. The object is to bring the shinny ball over the opponent's line. Whoever is successful first is the winner. The stick is also

Players   one or two miles   Players

FIG. 803. Plan of shinny ball field; Navaho Indians, St Michael, Arizona.

called be-akă'li, and the origin of the game is the same as that of tossed and batted ball.

TSETSAUT. Portland inlet, British Columbia.

Dr Franz Boas [b] mentions these people playing a game with a ball of cedar bark.

CADDOAN STOCK

ARIKARA. Oklahoma.

Dr George A. Dorsey,[c] in the origin of the Arikara, describes them as coming in their journeying to a great lake where they had their village for some time.

They made games at this place. The first game they played was the shinny ball and four sticks. The land was marked out by four sticks, which inclosed an oblong extending from east to west. Each side tried to force the ball through the other's goal. When one side was beaten it immediately began to kill those of the other side.

---

[a] June 27, 1902.

[b] Fifth Report on the Indians of British Columbia. Report of the Sixty-fifth Meeting of the British Association for the Advancement of Science, p. 568, London, 1895.

[c] Traditions of the Arikara, p. 16, Washington, 1904.

Pawnee. Oklahoma. (Cat. no. 59384, Field Columbian Museum.)

Buckskin ball (figure 804), $3\frac{1}{8}$ inches in diameter, flattened, with median seam and painted with concentric rings in color on both faces; on one face an outside ring of green, then red, black, and white, with yellow in the center; on the other, black, yellow, red, black, yellow, and black in the center. It has a thong for suspension and is accompanied with four sticks (figure 805)

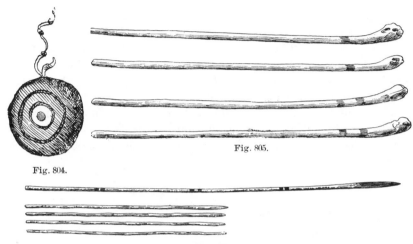

Fig. 804.

Fig. 805.

Fig. 806.

Fig. 804. Shinny ball; diameter, $3\frac{1}{8}$ inches; Pawnee Indians, Oklahoma; cat. no. 59384, Field Columbian Museum.

Fig. 805. Shinny sticks; length, 34 inches; Pawnee Indians, Oklahoma; cat. no. 59384, Field Columbian Museum.

Fig. 806. Goal sticks and pole for shinny; length of sticks, 43 inches; length of pole, 85 inches; Pawnee Indians, Oklahoma; cat. no. 59384, Field Columbian Museum.

made of saplings about 34 inches in length, curved and knobbed at the end, and painted in pairs with bands of color near striking end; two with a green and a red band, and two with one red and two green bands. Also a pole (figure 806) 85 inches in length, with a kind of ferrule at the upper end, and the lower end pointed, and four stakes, 43 inches in length, designated as goal posts. Collected in 1901 by Dr George A. Dorsey.

Wichita. Wichita reservation, Oklahoma. (Cat. no. 59305, Field Columbian Museum.)

Buckskin-covered ball (figure 807), 4 inches in diameter, with median seam and loop for suspension; and ball stick, 34 inches in length, curved, with a knot at the end. Collected by Dr George A. Dorsey.

Dr A. S. Gatschet has kindly furnished the writer with the following list of words relating to ball, from the Wichita language, obtained by him in 1872:

Kasins, ball, plural kasritsa or irha kasintsa; kuyätsits, catching; kakia ti kasints kuyätsik, somebody catches a ball.

In his Wichita Tales [a] Dr George A. Dorsey relates how the first man, Darkness, who began to get power to foretell things after the creation of people, told the woman Watsikatsia, made after his image, that when he was about to go to a certain being, Man-Never-Known-on-Earth, he reached down at his left side with his right hand and brought up a ball. Then he reached down with his left hand at his right side and brought up a belt. Then he reached down in front, touched the ball to the belt, and brought up a shinny stick. He took the ball, tossed it up, and struck it with the stick. As the ball flew, he went with it. Thus guided, he went to the place where he expected to find Man-Never-Known-on-Earth. The object of his visit was that power be given him so that there should be light on the

FIG. 807. Shinny ball and stick; diameter of ball, 4 inches; length of stick, 34 inches; Wichita Indians, Oklahoma; cat. no. 59305, Field Columbian Museum.

face of the earth. He tossed and struck the ball again, but not arriving at the place, he knew he could not depend upon the ball, and so took his bow and arrow and shot an arrow and flew with it. This he did a second, third, and fourth time, but without avail. Then he remembered he could run. He made one long run and stopped to rest. Then he ran again and a third and fourth time. He had made twelve trials and knew he was near the place of his journey.

Later, in the same narrative, it is related how Darkness, arriving at a certain village, instituted the game of shinny:

The crowd came, and he told them they were to have such a game as shinny ball. He reached down with his right hand on his left side and produced a ball, and then reached down on his right side with his left hand and brought up a shinny stick. These he showed the people and told them they were for their use. Then he commanded the people to gather just outside the village at about evening time, and then he set the time for play. They went as he told them. When they were all there he tossed the ball toward the north and traveled with it. It went a long ways. When it lit, he picked it up and struck it with the stick and drove the ball back south, then said that the point

---

[a] Journal of American Folk-Lore, v. 15, p. 215, 1902.

where he stood when he struck the ball would be called "flowing water" (the goal). Then he took the ball, tossed it, went with it, and again struck it southward. Where it hit was the second "flowing water," or goal. Between these two goals or bases was level ground, and in both directions as far as you could see. Then he divided the men into two parties, and placed one at each goal. Between these two parties and in the center of the field he placed two men, one from each of the two parties. He gave one man the ball and told him to toss it up. As the ball was tossed he told the other man to strike it towards the south. He did so and drove the ball towards his opponents on the south. Now they played, and the north side drove the ball to the south goal and won. Then they changed goals, and the other side won. Then Darkness said they had played enough.

Dr George A. Dorsey [a] also relates that in the Wichita creation legend the first man, Having-Power-to-carry-Light, gave the men a ball smaller than the shinny ball.

He told them this ball was to be used to amuse themselves with; that the men were to play together and the boys were to play together. Whenever a child was born, if it was a boy this kind of ball was to be given to it, that he might observe it and learn how to move around. The ball had a string to it. The farther the ball rolled—that is, the older the child should get—the faster it would move around. He went on and taught the men how to play the game, for the people were ignorant and did not know what the things were for. Finally, the men were shown how the ball should be used. He showed them the clubs for the shinny game. He told them they should be divided equally in the game, one party on one side and the other party on the other side. Many were interested, for the game was new to them. Many of the men were fast on their feet. The game was to be won by the side that should get the ball to the goal first. Having-Power-to-carry-Light also told them how to travel with the arrows and ball. This marks the time when they learned to travel fast from one place to another. The men went out hunting animals after they had been taught that animals existed for their use, and they traveled with their arrows and ball. They would shoot an arrow in the direction they wanted to go; then they would go with the arrow as it went up. This is the way they traveled. They would hit the ball, and as it flew the person would be on the ball. When the ball hit the ground they would hit it again, and so they would go from place to place.

In the story of "The Deeds of After-Birth Boy" [b] his father made his boy a shinny ball and stick. This ball was what we call "ball-for-young-boys" (kasintswiks).

Again, in the story of "The Deeds of After-birth-Boy" the father made his two boys a shinny ball and two sticks, with which they played a game against the Headless-Man, the stake to be their own

---

[a] The Mythology of the Wichita, p. 27, Washington, 1904.
[b] Ibid., p. 92.

lives. The ball was finally knocked by After-birth-Boy over a small creek that had been selected as a goal.

The Headless-Man's ball was black and his shinny stick was black. The two boys had a green ball and green sticks, green representing the spring of the year. Since that time the shinny game is played in the spring, under the power of the After-birth-Boy.[a]

There is a similar episode in the story of " The Little Brown Hawks,"[b] in which the four brother Swift-Hawks and their father played successively against Boy-setting-Grass-on-Fire-by-his-Foot-steps, lost their lives and were clubbed with a shinny club. The play-ground extended north and south, and it was a long way from goal to goal. The game consisted in tossing the ball and one hitting it, the first running in the direction they were headed, the other following him. A posthumous brother of the four Swift-Hawks finally over-came Boy-setting-Grass-on-Fire-by-his-Footsteps. When the ball was tossed up, hail began to fall instead of the ball coming down. All of the hail came down on Boy-setting-Grass-on-Fire-by-his-Foot-steps, and on him alone, and killed him. Those whom he had killed were brought to life by burning his body.

CHIMMESYAN STOCK

NISKA. Nass river, British Columbia.

Dr Franz Boas [c] describes the following game:

Gōntl: a ball game. There are two goals, about 100 to 150 yards apart. Each is formed by two sticks, about 10 feet apart. In the middle, between the goals, is a hole in which the ball is placed. The players carry hooked sticks. Two of them stand at the hole, the other players of each party, six or seven in number, a few steps behind them towards each goal. At a given signal, both players try to strike the ball out of the hole. Then each party tries to drive it through the goal of the opposing party.

CHUMASHAN STOCK

SANTA BARBARA. Santa Barbara, California.

Alfred Robinson [d] says:

In front of the house was a large square, where the Indians assembled on Sunday afternoons to indulge their favorite sports and pursue their chief amusement—gambling. Here numbers were gathered together in little knots, who appeared engaged in angry conversation; they were adjusting, as Daniel informed me the boundary lines for the two parties who were to play that afternoon at ball, and were thus occupied till dinner time. When I returned from dinner they had already commenced; and at least two or three hundred

---

[a] The Mythology of the Wichita, p. 99, Washington, 1904.

[b] Ibid., p. 247.

[c] Fifth Report on the Indians of British Columbia. Report of the Sixty-fifth Meeting of the British Association for the Advancement of Science, p. 583, London, 1895.

[d] Life in California, p. 105, San Francisco, 1891.

Indians of both sexes were engaged in the game. It was the " Presidio " against the " Mission." They played with a small ball of hard wood, which, when hit, would bound with tremendous force without striking the ground for two or three hundred yards. Great excitement prevailed, and immense exertion was manifested on both sides, so that it was not till late in the afternoon that the game was decided in favor of the Indians of the Presidio.

ESKIMAUAN STOCK

Eskimo (Western). St Michael, Alaska.

Mr Nelson [a] describes the game which he calls hockey—aiyutalugit or patkutalugit.

This is played with a small ball of ivory, leather, or wood, and a stick, curved at the lower end. The ball and stick are called pat-k'u'-tûk. The ball is placed on the ground or ice and the players divide into two parties. Each player with his stick attempts to drive the ball across the opponents' goal, which is established as in the football game.

IROQUOIAN STOCK

Tuscarora. North Carolina.

John Lawson[b] says:

Another game is managed with a batoon and a ball, and resembles our trapball.

KERESAN STOCK

Keres. Acoma, New Mexico.

A Keres Indian at Zuñi, named James H. Miller, informed the writer in 1904 that the boys played shinny—matashoku—in the fall. The stick they call hopi, and the ball matashoku.

———— Cochiti, New Mexico.

A Keres boy at St Michaels, Arizona, named Francisco Chaves (Kogit), described the Indians at Cochiti to the writer in 1904 as playing shinny under the name of oomatashia. The ball, pelota, they call matashshok, and the stick, oomatash.

KIOWAN STOCK

Kiowa. Oklahoma. (United States National Museum.)

Cat. no. 152903. Buckskin ball (figure 808), a flattened sphere, with median seam; diameter, $3\frac{1}{2}$ inches; wooden stick (figure 809), painted red, curved at the striking end, with a knob at the top; length, 30 inches.

Cat. no. 152904. Hide ball (figure 810), a flattened sphere with median seam, painted red; diameter, $3\frac{1}{4}$ inches.

These specimens were collected by Mr James Mooney.

[a] The Eskimo about Behring Strait. Eighteenth Annual Report of the Bureau of American Ethnology, pt. 1, p. 337, 1899.

[b] The History of Carolina, p. 288, London, 1714 ; reprint, Raleigh, N. C., 1860.

MARIPOSAN STOCK

CHUKCHANSI. Pickayune, Madera county, California. (Cat. no. 70895, Field Columbian Museum.)

Two mountain mahogany balls, 1½ inches in diameter. Collected by Dr J. W. Hudson.

MIXED TRIBES. Tule River reservation, California.

Dr J. W. Hudson describes the following game:

The ball is called o-lol, and the stick, ka-tal. The goals, to-lin, are two pairs of upright sticks, placed at the ends of the course, at a distance of 400 yards.

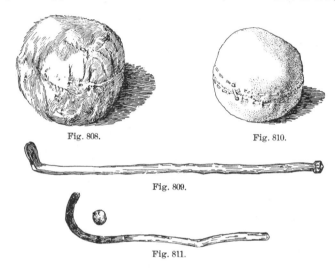

Fig. 808.   Fig. 810.

Fig. 809.

Fig. 811.

FIG. 808. Shinny ball; diameter, 3¼ inches; Kiowa Indians, Oklahoma; cat. no. 152903, United States National Museum.

FIG. 809. Shinny stick; length, 30 inches; Kiowa Indians, Oklahoma; cat. no. 152903, United States National Museum.

FIG. 810. Shinny ball; diameter, 3¼ inches; Kiowa Indians, Oklahoma; cat. no. 152904, United States National Museum.

FIG. 811. Shinny ball and stick; diameter of ball, 2¼ inches; length of stick, 40 inches; Yokuts Indians, Tule River reservation, California; cat. no. 70399, 70400, Field Columbian Museum.

YOKUTS. Tule River reservation, Tulare county, California. (Cat. no. 70399, 70400, Field Columbian Museum.)

Shinny stick, 40 inches in length (figure 811), made of oak, bent and fire seasoned at the lower end, with a red stripe near the crook; and a ball, 2½ inches in diameter, made of an oak knot, rounded and seasoned. Collected by Dr J. W. Hudson.

MOQUELUMNAN STOCK

AWANI. Yosemite valley, Mariposa county, California. (Cat. no. 70229, Field Columbian Museum.)

Four mountain mahogany ball sticks, 4 feet in length, with recurved ends. Collected by Dr J. W. Hudson.

CHOWCHILLA. Chowchilly river, Madera county, California. (Cat.
no. 70233, Field Columbian Museum.)

Two oak-wood balls, 3 inches in diameter. Collected by Dr J. W.
Hudson, who describes the game as follows:

> Played only by men, who are divided in two equal sides,
> say fifteen on a side. The goals, which are each some 200
> yards from the center, are two trees or two posts, a long step,
> or, say, 3 feet, apart. Two men standing side by side cast
> the ball up and strike it to their opponents' goal.

WASAMA. Chowchilly river, Madera county, California.

Dr J. W. Hudson describes the following ball game
under the name of müla:

> Played with a club, mu-lau' of mountain mahogany, and a
> mahogany ball, o-lo'-la.

> Two or more men play in couples or pairs from a start
> line [figure 812]. The captains at station 1 strike their re-
> spective balls toward their respective partners at station 2.
> If the ball falls short of 2, the failing striker must forward
> his ball to station 2 by an additional stroke; when the ball
> passes into the territory of the partner at station 2, he (no.
> 2) must drive it forward from where it stopped. The last
> stationed partner must drive it over the goal line. The small-
> est number of aggregate strokes on a side wins. Station
> keepers must keep within their own territories.

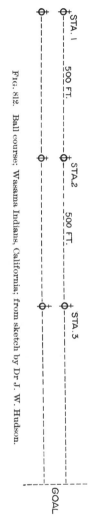

FIG. 812. Ball course; Wasama Indians, California; from sketch by Dr J. W. Hudson.

PIMAN STOCK

OPATA. Sonora, Mexico.

Mr A. F. Bandelier[a] speaks of a game called
uachicori, or shinny.

TARAHUMARE. Chihuahua, Mexico.

Dr Carl Lumholtz[b] states:

> In a game called taquari, a ball is knocked along the ground
> by one party of players toward a goal, while the opposite
> party strives to beat it back to the opposite goal.

ZUAQUE. Sonora, Mexico. (Cat. no. 129853, United
States National Museum.)

Irregular wooden ball (figure 813), somewhat rudely
carved, $1\frac{3}{8}$ inches in diameter; and a roughly
hewn stick, curved and flattened on the inner side at the end, 23
inches in length.

Described by the collector, Dr Edward Palmer, as a boy's shinny
stick and ball.

<hr />

[a] Final Report. Papers of the Archæological Institute of America, pt. 1, p. 240, Cambridge, 1890.

[b] Tarahumari Life and Customs. Scribner's Magazine, v. 16, p. 311, New York, 1894.

SALISHAN STOCK

CLALLAM. Washington.

A Clallam boy described this tribe as playing the game of shinny, skweikuklioise. The ball, smuck, is a cedar knot. The shinny stick is called kuklioisesun. The word for goal is sweikkutum.

PEND D'OREILLES. Flathead reservation, Montana. (Cat. no. 51777, Field Columbian Museum.)

Shinny stick (figure 814), curved and expanding at the striking end into a thin blade, with a knob at the end of the handle; length, 27 inches. Collected by Dr George A. Dorsey.

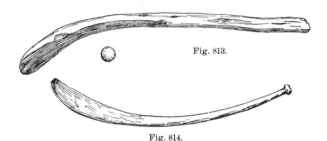

Fig. 813.

Fig. 814.

FIG. 813. Shinny ball and stick; diameter of ball, 1⅝ inches; length of stick, 23 inches; Zuaque Indians, Sonora, Mexico; cat. no. 129853, United States National Museum.

FIG. 814. Shinny stick; length, 27 inches; Pend d'Oreille Indians, Flathead reservation, Montana; cat. no. 51777, Field Columbian Museum.

SHUSWAP. Kamloops, British Columbia.

Dr Franz Boas [a] says:

The following game of ball was described to me: The players stand in two opposite rows. A stake is driven into the ground on the left side of the players of one row, and another on the right side of the players on the other row. Two men stand in the center between the two rows. One of these pitches the ball, and the other tries to drive it to one of the stakes with a bat. Then both parties endeavor to drive the ball to the stake on the opposite side, and the party which succeeds in this has won the game.

SONGISH. Vancouver island, British Columbia.

Dr Franz Boas [b] describes the following game:

K'k·oiä'ls, a game at ball; the ball, which is made of maple knots, is called smuk. It is pitched with crooked sticks and driven from one party to the other.

SHAHAPTIAN STOCK

NEZ PERCÉS. Idaho.

Col. Richard Irving Dodge [c] says:

Among the Nez Percés and other western tribes the women are extremely fond of a game of ball similar to our " shinny," or " hockey," and play with great spirit.

[a] Second General Report on the Indians of British Columbia. Report of the Sixtieth Meeting of the British Association for the Advancement of Science, p. 641, London, 1891.

[b] Ibid., p. 571.

[c] Our Wild Indians, p. 344, Hartford, 1882.

UMATILLA. Oregon. (Cat. no. 37541, 37542, Free Museum of
Science and Art, University of Pennsylvania.)

Ball (figure 815), a flattened spheroid of buckskin, with median
seam, painted yellow, with the sun in red lines on one side and a
similar design, perhaps a star, on the other; diameter, 4 inches.

Stick (figure 816), a club, flattened and curved at one end; length,
29 inches.

These were collected by the writer in 1900. The ball is called
tkaiput, and the bat tkaila.

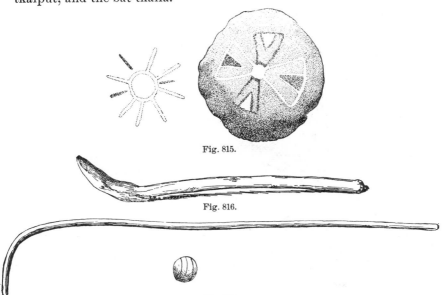

Fig. 815.

Fig. 816.

Fig. 817.

FIG. 815. Shinny ball; diameter, 4 inches; Umatilla Indians, Oregon; cat. no. 37541, Free Museum
of Science and Art, University of Pennsylvania.
FIG. 816. Shinny stick; length, 29 inches; Umatilla Indians, Oregon; cat. no. 37542, Free Museum
of Science and Art, University of Pennsylvania.
FIG. 817. Shinny ball and stick; diameter of ball, 1⅜ inches; length of stick, 42 inches; Achomawi Indians, Hat creek, California; cat. no. $\frac{50}{4117}$, American Museum of Natural History.

SHASTAN STOCK

ACHOMAWI. Hat creek, California. (Cat. no. $\frac{50}{4117}$, American Museum of Natural History.)

Wooden ball, 1⅜ inches in diameter, and curved stick, 42 inches in
length (figure 817). Collected in 1903 by Dr Roland B. Dixon,
who describes them as implements for hockey, popaqwaiwi.

SHOSHONEAN STOCK

HOPI. Arizona. (United States National Museum.)

Cat. no. 23222. Buckskin ball; a flattened spheroid, with median
seam; diameter, 3¼ inches. Collected by Maj. J. W. Powell and
designated as a shinny ball.

Cat. no. 41765.   Buckskin ball, painted red, ovate, with median seam, stuffed with hair; diameter, 3¾ inches.

Cat. no. 68843.   Buckskin ball; a flattened spheroid, with median seam; diameter, 2½ inches.

Cat. no. 68869.   Buckskin ball (figure 818) ; bag-shaped, painted red, with drawstring; diameter, 5 inches.' Designated as a football.

The three foregoing specimens were collected by Col. James Stevenson.

Cat. no. 84286.   Buckskin ball (figure 819) ; a flattened spheroid, with median seam; diameter, 3¾ inches.

Cat. no. 84287.   Buckskin ball, similar to the preceding; diameter, 2½ inches.

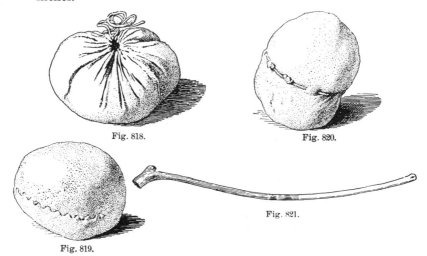

Fig. 818.

Fig. 820.

Fig. 821.

Fig. 819.

FIG. 818. Shinny ball; diameter, 5 inches; Hopi Indians, Arizona; cat. no. 68869, United States National Museum.

FIG. 819. Shinny ball; diameter, 3¾ inches; Hopi Indians, Arizona; cat. no. 84286, United States National Museum.

FIG. 820. Shinny ball; diameter, 3¼ inches; Hopi Indians, Arizona; cat. no. 84289, United States National Museum.

FIG. 821. Shinny stick; length, 28 inches; Hopi Indians, Walpi, Arizona; cat. no. 166718, United States National Museum.

Cat. no. 84288.   Buckskin ball, similar to the preceding; diameter, 3 inches.

Cat. no. 84289.   Buckskin ball (figure 820), spheroidal, with median seam and drawstring around the seam; diameter, 3½ inches.

This and the three specimens preceding were collected by Mr Victor Mindeleff.

HOPI.   Walpi, Arizona.   (Cat. no. 166718, United States National Museum.)

Peeled stick with curved end (figure 821), one-half painted red, with two bands of blue paint near the middle; length, 28 inches.   Collected by Mr James Mooney.

Mr A. M. Stephen, in his unpublished manuscript, gives the following definitions:

Ball, ta-tci; shinny, or hockey, as practiced by white boys, ta-tatc'-la-la-wûh.

Mono. Hooker cove, Madera county, California. (Cat. no. 71435, 71436, Field Columbian Museum).

Mahogany club (figure 822), with flat end slightly curved, 54 inches in length, and small mountain mahogany ball.

Collected by Dr J. W. Hudson, who describes it as of the Yokuts type.

Five other clubs (figure 823) in the same collection (cat. no. 71434) are similar, but the striking part is narrow. Four of these are of oak and one is of mountain mahogany.

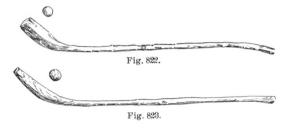

Fig. 822.

Fig. 823.

FIG. 822. Shinny ball and stick; length of stick, 54 inches; Mono Indians, Madera county, California; cat. no. 71435, 71436, Field Columbian Museum.

FIG. 823. Shinny ball and stick; length of stick, 50½ inches; Mono Indians, Madera county, California; cat. no. 71434, Field Columbian Museum.

Doctor Hudson gives the following account of the game under the name of nakwatakoina, to swing strike:

Each opponent starts his mahogany-wood ball, usually 1¾ inches in diameter, forward at a signal. Their partners at the next station forward their respective balls to the next relay station, and so on. Interference with an opponent's ball, even by accident, is protested by loud "Hip! he!!" which is at once apologized for by "He-he-he!!" If a player should forward an opponent's ball, this protesting cry recalls him to seek his own ball, while the distance made by the fouled stroke is kept by the fouled party. Every player has one or more substitute balls in his belt, so that when a ball is lost another is allowed in play. The balls must turn a goal stake, a-na'-na kwi-no hi'-na, "man's circling stake," often a tree, about 400 yards from the starting line, and return to a hole, to'-op, at the starting line. The game may be played also to a goal straight away, several miles. Once a game was played between the Hooker Cove people and Whisky Creeks, in which they started at Hooker Cove, and the goal was in a field beside the road at Whisky Creek, 7½ miles distant.

Shoshoni. Wind River reservation, Wyoming. (Cat. no. 36878, Free Museum of Science and Art, University of Pennsylvania.)

Stick (figure 825), ego, with a broad curved end and a knot at the handle; length, 24½ inches; and a ball (figure 824), covered with buckskin, with median seam, in the form of a flattened sphere, 3½ inches in diameter. Collected by the writer in 1900.

UINTA UTE. White Rocks, Utah. (Free Museum of Science and
Art, University of Pennsylvania.)

Cat. no. 37114. Buckskin ball (figure 826), bag shaped, with drawstring and thong; diameter, 3¼ inches.

Cat. no. 37117. Shinny stick (figure 827), rudely whittled, with
broad curved end; length, 27½ inches.

These specimens were collected by the writer in 1900. The ball is
called pokunump, and the stick, beher. It is a woman's game.

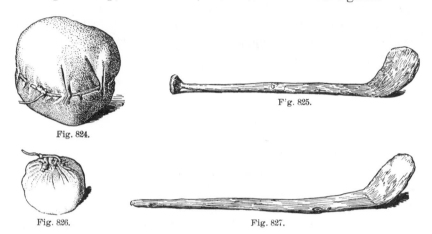

Fig. 824.

F'g. 825.

Fig. 826.   Fig. 827.

FIG. 824. Shinny ball; diameter, 3¼ inches; Shoshoni Indians, Wind River reservation, Wyoming; cat. no. 36878, Free Museum of Science and Art, University of Pennsylvania.

FIG. 825. Shinny stick; length, 24¼ inches; Shoshoni Indians, Wind River reservation, Wyoming; cat. no. 36878, Free Museum of Science and Art, University of Pennsylvania.

FIG. 826. Shinny ball; diameter, 3¼ inches; Uinta Ute Indians, White Rocks, Utah; cat. no.
37114, Free Museum of Science and Art, University of Pennsylvania.

FIG. 827. Shinny stick; length, 27¼ inches; Uinta Ute Indians, White Rocks, Utah; cat. no.
37117, Free Museum of Science and Art, University of Pennsylvania.

SIOUAN STOCK

ASSINIBOIN. Fort Union, Montana.

In a report to Isaac I. Stevens, governor of Washington Territory,
on the Indian tribes of the upper Missouri, by Mr Edwin T. Denig, a
manuscript in the library of the Bureau of American Ethnology,
there occurs the following account:

Most of these tribes, particularly the Sioux, are fond of playing in parties.
The principal game at ball is called tah-cap-see-chah, being the same denominated shinny, or bandy, by the whites. It is generally got up when two different
bands are camped together, and a principal person in each having made a bet
of a blanket or gun, they choose from their bands an equal number of young
men, who are always the most active they can select, the number varying from
fifteen to forty on each side. Sometimes the play is headed by the chief of each
band betting, though they take no part in the game, which is usually played by
men of 20 to 30 years of age. Each of the players stakes something against an

equivalent on the part of one on the opposite side, and every bet, which consists of shirts, arrows, shells, feathers, blankets and almost every article of trade or their own manufacture, is tied together separately, and as fast as the bets are taken and tied together they are laid on a pile about the center of the playground, being given in charge of three or four elderly men, who are chosen as judges of the sport. After this has been concluded two posts are set up about three-quarters of a mile apart and the game consists in knocking the ball with sticks toward these posts, they being the outcome or limit for either party in different directions. They strip naked, except the breechcloth and moccasins, and paint their bodies in every possible variety of manner. Each is furnished with a stick about 3½ feet long, turned up at the lower end, and they range themselves in two lines, commencing at the middle of the ground and extending on either side some distance. The ball is cast into the air in the center of the course, struck as soon as it falls by some one, and the game begins, each party endeavoring to knock the ball to the post designated as their limit. The game is played three times, and whichever party succeeds in winning two courses out of the three is judged conqueror. When the players are well chosen it is often an interesting game, and some splendid specimens of foot racing can be seen; but when one of them, either intentionally or by accident, hurts another by a stroke with the play stick, a general shindy takes place, and the sticks are employed over each others' heads, which is followed by a rush for the stakes and a scramble. We have seen them, when this was the case, arm themselves and exchange some shots, when, a few being wounded, the camps would separate and move away in different directions. Supposing, however, the game proceeds in its proper spirit and humor, each bet being tied separately, the parcels are handed out to the successful party by the judges. This game is not often done by large parties of men, or, if so, it is very warmly contested and very apt to break up in a disturbance. We have seen it also played by both men and women joined, a few men aiding two parties of women; this was amongst the Sioux, but with the other tribes it is generally played by men only.

CROWS. Crow reservation, Montana. (Cat. no. 69648, Field Columbian Museum.)

Shinny stick and ball; the ball a flattened spheroid, with median seam, 4 inches in diameter; the stick an unpainted sapling, curved at the end; length, 38 inches.

Collected by Mr S. C. Simms in 1901, who says:

The game is played only in the spring, when the grass is green, the men on one side and the women on the other. The goals each consist of two blankets, spread side by side on the ground. A man or a woman selects one of the goals. The ball is tossed in the air among the crowd of players, and the object is to drive it to the goal selected.

DAKOTA (OGLALA). Pine Ridge reservation, South Dakota. (Cat. no. 22117, 22118, Free Museum of Science and Art, University of Pennsylvania.)

Stick (figure 828), made of a sapling, 39 inches in length, bent at one end by fire, and a buckskin-covered ball (figure 828), 2½ inches in diameter, the cover made of a single piece and stitched with sinew.

It is described by the collector, Mr Louis L. Meeker,[a] as used in the woman's game of shinny, takapsica:

Many players form two companies and strive to take the ball with their sticks to two different goals in opposite directions. First play is decided by kicking the ball up into the air. The one who can do so oftenest without letting the ball or the foot touch the ground plays first. This is a separate game with the Winnebago.

Shinny is played by women, large girls, and schoolboys. The women of one camp will play against the women of another camp. The boys and girls of one school will play against another school, for, although not quite up to the dignity of men, the game is scarcely limited to women.

FIG. 828. Shinny ball and stick; diameter of ball, 2½ inches; length of stick, 39 inches; Oglala Dakota Indians, Pine Ridge reservation, South Dakota; cat. no. 22117, 22118, Free Museum of Science and Art, University of Pennsylvania.

DAKOTA (OGLALA). Pine Ridge reservation, South Dakota. (Cat. no. 22124, Free Museum of Science and Art, University of Pennsylvania.)

Knobbed stick (figure 829), made of a sapling, 36 inches in length.

Described by the collector, Mr Louis L. Meeker,[b] as used in the boy's game of can takapsica, or wood shinny:

A block of wood, cut from a seasoned stick about 3 inches in diameter, is laid upon the ground. Two players, armed with sticks having a natural enlargement on one end, each paces off 50 steps in opposite directions, and each marks his opponent's goal. Giving the word to each other, they race back to the block of wood, the one who wins placing his foot upon the block to take possession. He then deliberately aims and strikes the block with all his force toward his goal, and both race after it to take possession with the foot and strike it again as before.

FIG. 829. Stick for wood shinny; length, 36 inches; Oglala Dakota Indians, Pine Ridge reservation, South Dakota; cat. no. 22124, Free Museum of Science and Art, University of Pennsylvania.

DAKOTA (TETON). Pine Ridge reservation, South Dakota.

Dr J. R. Walker [c] describes the game of shinny, woskate takapsice, and of woman's shinny, woskate takwinkapisce, and gives the rules for the play.

[a] Ogalala Games. Bulletin of the Free Museum of Science and Art, v. 3, p. 31, Philadelphia, 1901.

[b] Ibid., p. 33.

[c] Sioux Games. Journal of American Folk-Lore, v. 18, p. 283, 1905.

DAKOTA (TETON). Cheyenne River agency, South Dakota. (Cat. no. 168170, United States National Museum.)

Shinny stick (figure 830), a peeled sapling, turned around at one end, 28½ inches in length. The handle is cut away at the end and has four thongs wrapped with colored quill work, and a bunch of strings of glass beads attached. Collected by Mr Z. T. Daniel.

FIG. 830. Shinny stick; length, 28½ inches; Teton Dakota Indians, Cheyenne River agency, South Dakota; cat. no. 168170, United States National Museum.

DAKOTA (YANKTON). South Dakota.

George P. Belden [a] describes the ball game as follows:

A great noise of shouting is heard in the camp, and the young men, with bat, or club, 3 feet long and crooked at the end, go out on the prairie near the camp. Having found a smooth spot they halt, and two of the youths, by common consent, take opposite sides and pick out the players, first one and then the other, until enough are had.

One morning I heard the young men shouting for ball, and I went out with them to the playground. The two chiefs, A-ke-che-ta (Little Dog Soldier) and Ma-to-sac (White Bear), were picking sides, and a number of Indians were already seated facing each other, and bantering on the game. As each man was selected he spread down his buffalo robe and sat upon it, facing his opponent. I was selected by A-ke-che-ta, and silently took my place in the line. Presently all the young men who were to play were selected, and then several old men were appointed to act as umpires of the game. These advanced and seated themselves between the contestants, and then the warriors rose and commenced betting on the game. First one warrior advanced and threw down a robe before the old men; then a warrior from the other side came forward and laid a robe upon it; and so all bet, one against the other. Presently there was a great number of piles of stakes, some having bet moccasins, headdresses, beadwork, earrings, necklaces, bows and arrows, and even ponies. All these were carefully watched over by the old men, who noted each stake and the depositor on a stick. If you did not wish to bet with any particular warrior you laid your wager on the big pile, and instantly it was matched by the judges against some article of corresponding value from the pile of the other side. Thus I bet a hunting knife, half a pound of powder, a pair of moccasins, and a small hand mirror, which articles were appropriately matched with others by the judges. All was now in readiness for the game to begin, and the parties separated. The two lines were formed about 100 yards apart. In front of each side, 20 feet from each other, two stakes, smeared with paint, are driven firmly into the ground, and the object of the game is to drive the ball between the stakes. Whichever side shall first force the ball through the opposite stakes wins the game. The ball, made of rags and covered with buckskin, is carried to the center of the ground between the combatants and there deposited, by one of the old men, who then returns to his post. The judges then give the signal, and

a Belden, the White Chief; edited by Gen. James S. Brisben, U. S. A., p. 37, Cincinnati, 1871.

with loud shouts the players run to the ball, and commence knocking it to and fro with their crooked sticks. The ball is about the size of a large orange, and each party tries to prevent its coming toward their stakes. No warrior must touch the ball with his hands; but if it lies in a hole, he may push it out with his foot and then hit it with his stick.

In the game which I am telling you about, Ma-to-sac's party reached and struck the ball first, lifting it clear over our heads, and sending it far to our rear and close to our stakes. Then we all ran, and Ma-to-sac's and A-ke-che-ta's warriors fell over one another, and rapped each other on the shins with their clubs, and there was great confusion and excitement, but at length one of the party succeeded in hitting the ball, and sent it to Ma-to-sac's stakes. Thither we ran, but no one could find the ball. After much search I discovered it in a tuft of grass, and, bidding one of our men run quickly to the stakes, I hit it and drove the ball to him. Unfortunately it fell in a hole, and before our warrior could get it out and hit it, a dense crowd of Ma-to-sac's men were around the spot and in front of the stakes. The contest was violent, so much so, indeed, that no one could hit the ball, though it was continually tramped over. At length some one called out, "There it goes," and the warriors scattered in all directions, looking to see where it was; but one of Ma-to-sac's men, who had called out, stood fast, and when the crowd had scattered, I saw him attempting to conceal the ball beneath his foot. Running against him from behind with such force as to throw him on his face, before he could recover his feet I hit the ball, and, seeing all Ma-to-sac's men off their guard, with the aid of a young man, easily drove it between their stakes, only a few yards distant.[a]

The judges at once declared the game was ours, and many and loud were the cheers sent up by our party, in token of the victory, while Ma-to-sac's men retired sullen and disappointed. I was declared the winner, and A-ke-che-ta thanked me for my services, while the young warriors gathered around and congratulated me on my success. Then we all smoked, and went over to the stakes to receive our shares. As winner I was entitled to a general share of the spoils; but I declined in favor of the young Indian who had helped me drive the ball, saying that, as he had last hit it, and actually forced it between the stakes, he was, in reality, the most deserving. This argument was loudly applauded by the old men, and the young warrior, who had not been friendly for some time with me, was so touched by my generosity that he came and thanked me, saying, frankly, "You, and not I, won the game." However, I forced the general stakes upon him, at which he was much pleased. I found that the stakes had won a saddle, half a pound of powder, 6 yards of wampum beads, and a handsomely braided knife-scabbard. When the judges had awarded all the winnings, among which were fourteen ponies, each took up his trophies and returned to the village, where for the remainder of the day the game was fought over again and again in the tepees.

DAKOTA (YANKTON). Fort Peck, Montana. (Free Museum of Science and Art, University of Pennsylvania.)

Cat. no. 37609. Ball, tapa, covered with buckskin, slightly flattened, with median seam; diameter, 2½ inches.

---

[a] In this game everyone must keep his temper, and any stratagem is allowed, so the ball is not touched with the hands. It is not suffered, however, for anyone to hit another over the head, or on the body with sticks or the hands, but if you can upset a gamester by running against him it is esteemed fair. When either party cheats, foul is called by the opposite party, when the game ceases until the judges decide the matter. If it is a foul play the play is given to the other side. No one thinks of disputing the judges' decision, and from it there is no appeal.

Cat. no. 37608. Flat, highly finished stick (figure 831), painted red, somewhat wide and slightly spoon-shaped at the striking end; length, 39½ inches.

Collected by the writer in 1900; the stick is one of several that were found in the grass after a woman's ball game.

HIDATSA. Fort Atkinson, North Dakota.

Henry A. Boller [a] says:

The young squaws are playing a game of ball resembling shinny or football, insomuch as curved sticks and feet are called into service.

OMAHA. Nebraska. (Cat. no. IV B 2225, Berlin Museum für Völkerkunde.)

Club (figure 833), curved at end, 39 inches in length, and a buckskin ball (figure 832), with median seam, 4 inches in diameter. Collected by Miss Alice C. Fletcher.

The ball is designated tabe, and the stick tabe gathi.

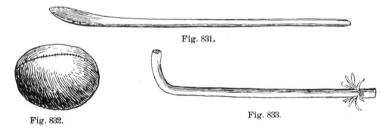

Fig. 831.

Fig. 832.

Fig. 833.

FIG. 831. Shinny stick; length, 39½ inches; Yankton Dakota Indians, Fort Peck, Montana; cat. no. 37608, Free Museum of Science and Art, University of Pennsylvania.
FIG. 832. Shinny ball; diameter, 4 inches; Omaha Indians, Nebraska; cat. no. IV B 2225, Berlin Museum für Völkerkunde.
FIG. 833. Shinny stick; length, 39 inches; Omaha Indians, Nebraska; cat. no. IV B 2225, Berlin Museum für Völkerkunde.

Rev. J. Owen Dorsey [b] describes tabegasi, men's game of ball, as follows:

This is played by the Omahas and Ponkas with a single ball. There are thirty, forty, or fifty men on each side, and each one is armed with a curved stick about 2 feet long. The players strip off all their clothing except their breechcloths. At each end of the playground [figure 834] are two posts from 12 to 15 feet apart. The playground is from 300 to 400 yards in length. When the players on the opposite side see that the ball is liable to reach A they try to knock it aside, either towards B or C, as their opponents would win if the ball passed between the posts at A. On the other hand, if the party represented by A see that the ball is in danger of passing between the posts at D, they try to divert it either towards E or F.

The stakes may be leggings, robes, arrows, necklaces, etc. All are lost by the losing side, and are distributed by the winners in equal shares. One of the elder

[a] Among the Indians: Eight Years in the Far West, 1858–1866, p. 67, Philadelphia, 1868.
[b] Omaha Sociology. Third Annual Report of the Bureau of Ethnology, p. 336, 1884.

men is requested to make the distribution. Two small boys, about 12 years old, stand at the posts A, and two others are at D. One boy at each end tries to send the ball between the posts, but the other one attempts to send it in the opposite direction. These boys are called uhé ginájiⁿ.

The game used to be played in three ways: (1.) Phratry against phratry. Then one of the players was not blindfolded. (2.) Village against village. The Omaha had three villages after 1855. . . . (3.) When the game was played neither by phratries nor by villages, sides were chosen thus: A player was blindfolded, and the sticks were placed before him in one pile, each stick having a special mark by which its owner could be identified. The blindfolded man then took up two sticks at a time, one in each hand, and, after crossing hands, he laid the sticks in separate piles. The owners of the sticks in one pile formed a side for the game. The corresponding women's game is wabaɔnade.

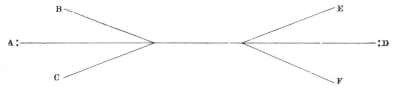

Fig. 834. Plan of shinny ball ground; Omaha Indians, Nebraska; from Dorsey.

OSAGE. Oklahoma. (Cat. no. 59174, Field Columbian Museum.)

Buckskin-covered ball (figure 835) $2\frac{5}{8}$ inches in diameter, cover in one piece, with median seam four-fifths round; and stick, a sapling, bent and squared at the end, $31\frac{1}{2}$ inches in length.

Collected by Dr George A. Dorsey.

FIG. 835. Shinny ball and stick; diameter of ball, $2\frac{5}{8}$ inches; length of stick, $31\frac{1}{4}$ inches; Osage Indians, Oklahoma; cat. no. 59174, Field Columbian Museum.

SKITTAGETAN STOCK

HAIDA. Queen Charlotte islands, British Columbia.

Mr James Deans [a] says:

It has been common from unknown times for all the native tribes on this coast to play the game of shinny, it being played in the same way our fathers used to play it, and as I have often played it myself, with crooked stick and wooden ball.

TANOAN STOCK

TIGUA. Isleta, New Mexico. (Cat. no. 22728, Free Museum of Science and Art, University of Pennsylvania.)

Ball (figure 836), covered with buckskin, flat, with median seam, $2\frac{3}{4}$ inches in diameter; and a stick, a curved sapling, 30 inches in length.

Collected by the writer in 1902.

---

[a] Games of the Haidah Indians.

An Isleta boy, J. Crecencio Lucero, described the people of this pueblo as playing a game of shinny with a soft buckskin ball, poja or pelota, which they hit with a stick, pojatu or chueco. Men and women play.

FIG. 836. Shinny ball and stick; diameter of ball, 2¼ inches; length of stick, 30 inches; Tigua Indians, Isleta, New Mexico; cat. no. 22728, Free Museum of Science and Art, University of Pennsylvania.

TEWA. Santa Clara, New Mexico.

Mr T. S. Dozier [a] writes as follows:

About the middle of January there is played a game that is to the Pueblos what baseball is to the Americans. It is nothing more or less than the old game of shinny, generally played on the ice, as with us. The pu-nam-be, or ball, used is a soft, light affair, made of rags and buckskin or wholly of buckskin. The pu-nam-be pfĕ, stick, is generally of willow, with a curved end, and is about 3 feet long. Men, boys of all sizes, and girls of all ages, and now and then a married woman engage in the pastime. The sexes do not play together, nor the boys with men. Among the men wagers of every description are made. During the past winter, in a game between the men, which lasted nearly a whole day, the side that was beaten had to dance a solemn dance for a whole day. Quite a difficulty arose on account of it.

———— Tesuque, New Mexico. (Cat. no. 23219, 23221, United States National Museum.)

Two shinny sticks (figure 837), made of bent saplings, the bark being left on the handle; lengths, 24 and 26 inches. Collected by Maj. J. W. Powell.

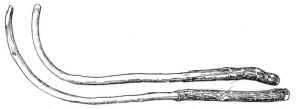

FIG. 837. Shinny sticks; lengths, 24 and 26 inches; Tewa Indians, Tesuque, New Mexico; cat. no. 23219 and 23221, United States National Museum.

WAKASHAN STOCK

MAKAH. Neah bay, Washington. (Cat. no. 37387, 37388, Free Museum of Science and Art, University of Pennsylvania.)

Ball (figure 838), an irregular spheroid, 3 inches in diameter, made of whalebone; and two sticks (figure 839), one a round club,

---

[a] Some Tewa Games. Unpublished manuscript, Bureau of American Ethnology.

curved at the end, 31 inches in length, used for striking the ball, and the other slender, 32 inches in length, hooked at the end, used in running away with the ball.   Collected by the writer in 1900, and described by Dr George A. Dorsey [a] as follows:

Keyuquah.—This is the well-known game of shinny, which is played, as a rule, only by young men.   In former times it was only played at the celebration of the capture of a whale.   Now it is played at any time.   A specimen of bat, lok-whiuk, was collected, which differs from the shinny stick as used by the tribes of the interior, in that it has no broad extended portion.   The bat measures 2 feet 9 inches in length, the lower 6 inches being curved out at an angle of twenty degrees.   One side of this curved extremity is flattened.   The specimen collected of the ball (huoo) is made from the body of some large vertebra. Williams states that in former times the ball was invariably made of whalebone. The goals (loquatsis, for the mark) are two straight lines on the beach, about 200 yards apart, and the starting point of the game is invariably from a point equidistant between the goal lines.

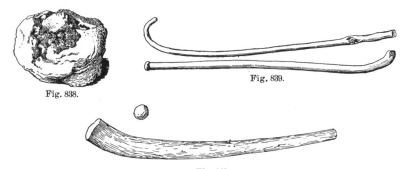

Fig. 839.

Fig. 838.

Fig. 840.

FIG. 838.   Shinny ball; diameter, 3 inches; Makah Indians, Neah bay, Washington; cat. no. 37387, Free Museum of Science and Art, University of Pennsylvania.
FIG. 839.   Shinny sticks; lengths, 31 and 32 inches; Makah Indians, Neah bay, Washington; cat. no. 37388, Free Museum of Science and Art, University of Pennsylvania.
FIG. 840.   Shinny ball and stick; diameter of ball, 1¼ inches; length of stick, 33 inches; Mission Indians, Mesa Grande, California; cat. no. 62539, Field Columbian Museum.

YUMAN STOCK

MISSION INDIANS.   Mesa Grande, California.   (Cat. no. 62539, Field Columbian Museum.)
Ball of wood (figure 840), painted brown, 1¾ inches in diameter, and stick, a rouhd club, 33 inches in length, slightly curved and expanding toward the end.   Collected by Mr C. B. Watkins.

MOHAVE.   Parker, Yuma county, Arizona.   (Field Columbian Museum.)
Cat. no. 63395.   Ball (figure 841), made of cordage, 1⅜ inches in diameter.   Another (cat. no. 63399) is somewhat smaller and unpainted.

[a] Games of the Makah Indians of Neah Bay.   The American Antiquarian, v. 23, p. 70, 1901.

Cat. no. 63357. Ball sticks (figure 841) of cottonwood, 41 inches in length, slender and curved at the end. Half the stick near the striking end is blackened by charring. Another (cat. no. 63359) is also 41 inches in length. The first stick has a notched cross mark on the handle.

Collected by Mr S. C. Simms, who gives the name of the ball as mahlke.

MOHAVE. Fort Mohave, Arizona. (Cat. no. 63194, Field Columbian Museum.)

Slender stick, 42½ inches in length, unpainted and curved at the end.

Collected by Mr S. C. Simms, who gives the name of the stick as unro.

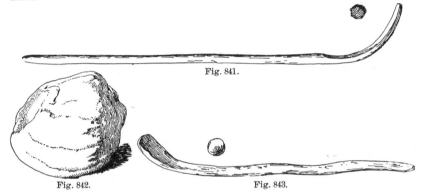

Fig. 841.

Fig. 842.   Fig. 843.

FIG. 841. Shinny ball and stick; diameter of ball, 1⅛ inches; length of stick, 41 inches; Mohave Indians, Arizona; cat. no. 63395, 63357, Field Columbian Museum.
FIG. 842. Shinny ball; diameter, 4¼ inches; Mohave Indians, Arizona; cat. no. 24163, United States National Museum.
FIG. 843. Shinny ball and stick; diameter of ball, 2¼ inches; length of stick, 32 inches; Walapai Indians, Arizona; cat. no. 63140, Field Columbian Museum.

———— Colorado river, Arizona. (Cat. no. 10098, 10117, Peabody Museum of American Archæology and Ethnology.)

Stick, or bat, curved at one end, length, 3 feet 2 inches, and ball consisting of large dried pumpkin stem.

Collected by Dr Edward Palmer, who describes them as a shinny stick and ball for bandy.

———— Colorado river, Arizona. (Cat. no. 24163, United States National Museum.)

Shinny ball (figure 842), a dried pumpkin or squash, an irregular spheroid, about 4½ inches in diameter. Collected by Dr Edward Palmer.

WALAPAI. Walapai reservation, Arizona. (Cat. no. 63140, Field Columbian Museum.)

Buckskin-covered ball (figure 843), 2¼ inches in diameter, the cover a bag brought together by a drawstring; and ten sticks, curved at one end, about 32 inches in length.

They were collected by Mr Henry P. Ewing, who describes the game as follows:

The tas-a-va game is not a Walapai game, particularly, although the young men and boys still play it a good deal. It is essentially the national game of the Mohave. They use a more delicate stick, made of willow, slender and curved perfectly at the end. The men all play it, young and old, and they are very expert, and it has developed them into great runners. They make a ball with a buckskin cover sewed on it exactly like the cover on our baseballs. Their ball is smaller and neater, their sticks trimmer and nicer, and when they play with the Walapai there is always a row about whether the Mohave ball or the Walapai ball shall be used. The Mohave usually give in, because they know that they can win anyway. As many can play as wish, and the distance for the grounds is usually from 300 to 500 yards. In starting the game the ball is buried by a medicine man in sight of all halfway between the home stations, and at a signal the contestants rush in and dig out the ball with their sticks and away they go. It is against the rules to touch it with the hands, or anything but the shinny stick. The sticks are called tas-a-va; the ball tam-a-nat-a, meaning tied in a bundle.

FIG. 844. Shinny ball and stick; diameter of ball, 1¼ inches; length of stick, 38½ inches; Yuma Indians, Fort Yuma, California; cat. no. 63349, Field Columbian Museum.

YUMA. Fort Yuma, San Diego county, California. (Field Columbian Museum.)

Cat. no. 63349. Ball (figure 844), covered with colored yarn, red, white, and black, 1¼ inches in diameter; and slender curved stick, 38½ inches in length, the handle straight, the end crooked, the outside of the curved end painted black, the inner side red, with three sets of bands of colored paint—red, black, and red; black, red, and black; and black, red, and black on the lower half of the stick above the crook.

Cat. no. 63312. Ball and stick similar to the preceding, but uncolored and unpainted.

Collected by Mr S. C. Simms, who gives the name of the ball as etsoat and that of the stick as sahtos.

ZUÑIAN STOCK

ZUÑI. Zuñi, New Mexico. (Cat. no. 3077, 3569, Brooklyn Institute Museum.)

Bag-shaped ball (figure 845), covered with deerskin, 2 inches in diameter; and curved stick, 35 inches in length. Collected by the writer in 1903.

The name of the ball was given as poppun and that of the stick as poppun kapnaki tammai.

Mrs Matilda Coxe Stevenson[a] speaks of the game of popone tkapnane, ball hit, as the same as shinny or bandy, and says that the Zuñi assert that the game came from Mexico long ago.

FIG. 845. Shinny ball and stick; diameter of ball, 2 inches; length of stick, 35 inches; Zuñi Indians, Zuñi, New Mexico; cat. no. 3077, 3569, Brooklyn Institute Museum.

ZuÑI. Zuñi, New Mexico.   (Cat. no. 4999, Brooklyn Institute Museum.)

Buckskin-covered ball (figure 846), ovate, with median seam, 8 inches in greatest diameter. Collected by the writer in 1904.

This is used in the man's game of shinny, po-pone-kap-na-kwai. The goals consist of circles in the sand on the east and west sides of the village. A hole is dug midway between, in which the ball is placed and covered with sand. Each man makes a lightning mark with his stick. The object is to drive the ball into the opponent's circle. They bet on the game. The smaller balls are used by boys.

FIG. 846. Shinny ball; diameter, 8 inches; Zuñi Indians, Zuñi, New Mexico; cat. no. 4999, Brooklyn Institute Museum.

DOUBLE BALL

The game of double ball throughout the eastern United States and among the Plains tribes is played exclusively by women, and is commonly known as the woman's ball game.   In northern California, however, it is played by men.

The implements for the game consist of two balls or similar objects attached to each other by a thong, and a curved stick with which they are thrown.

The balls vary in shape and material. Among the Cheyenne two small slightly flattened buckskin balls are used. The Wichita balls are smaller, with a long cut-leather fringe. Among the Sauk and Foxes and other Algonquian tribes the balls are oblong, weighted with sand, and frequently both, with the connecting thong, are made of one piece of buckskin. These pass by an easy transition into a single long buckskin-covered piece, somewhat narrow in the middle, as among the Paiute.

[a] American Anthropologist, n. s., v. 5, p. 496, 1903.

A distinct variation is found among the Hupa, where, instead of balls, two small bottle-shaped billets tied together at the top are employed. The Klamath use large billets fastened together by a cord passing through a hole in the middle of each stick. The Chippewa, Papago, Tarahumare, Achomawi, and Shasta have short cylindrical billets tied with a thong, and both Papago and Pima, double balls wrought of plaited leather.

The sticks, made of saplings, usually taper to the end and are slightly curved. Ordinarily they are plain, but among the Shoshoni and Paiute they have a small fork or crotch. They vary in length from 23 inches to 6 feet. One stick is almost invariably used, but Catlin describes the Dakota as playing with one in each hand. The bases, two in number, consist of poles (Chippewa) or of two piles of earth (Omaha), and vary in distance from 300 and 400 yards (Omaha) to a mile (Cree) apart. The object of the game is to get the ball over the opponent's base line or to take it to one's home (Missisauga). Bets are made upon the result.

FIG. 847. Yoke-shaped billet; height, 3⅜ inches; cliff-dwelling, Mancos canyon, Colorado; Free Museum of Science and Art, University of Pennsylvania.

Double ball as a woman's game appears at present to have no ceremonial significance. Its implements, however, offer a possible means of identifying the wooden yoke-shaped objects found in the cliff-dwellings, such as are represented in figure 847 from Mancos canyon, Colorado.

This specimen, in the Free Museum of Science and Art of the University of Pennsylvania, was made by bending a straight piece of wood, 8½ inches in length. The ends are cylindrical, each having three knobs, one at the extremity and two equidistant above. The upper part of the yoke, which is 4 inches in height, is squared. A large number of similar yokes, accompanied by many highly finished sticks, which might have been used for throwing them, were found together in a chamber in the Pueblo Bonito, Chaco canyon, New Mexico, by the Hyde exploring expedition. The collection is now in the American Museum of Natural History, New York City. The sticks, numbering several hundred specimens, vary in length from 3 to 4 feet, and are very finely finished. They vary also in form. One series terminates in a kind of hook. Another has a curved end, on some bound with cord or sinew and on others plain. A third series has a flat, shovel-like end. Still others are straight, with a flat, knobbed handle.

A ceremonial analogue of the game may be observed in the tossing of the annulets and cylinder from cloud-terrace symbol to cloud-terrace symbol by the girls and boys in the procession on the ninth day of the Flute ceremony.

Dr J. Walter Fewkes [a] described this performance as witnessed by him at Shipaulovi in the summer of 1891:

These annulets [figure 848] [called yo-yo-ñu-la] were made of wi'-po, a flag leaf, which is twisted into shape around a core of the same material. Into each was bound one or more live insects, bä'-chi-bi, a "skater" which lives on the surface of the water. The annulet was painted black, and to it was attached a handle made of twisted fibers of yucca leaves, forming a hoop across the annulet by which it can be carried. . . .

At the same time that the annulets were manufactured, a small cylinder [figure 849], about the length of the diameter of the annulets, or a little more, was whittled out of wood. This cylinder was painted black. . . . A small handle made of yucca fiber was securely fastened to it.

Fig. 848.

Fig. 849.

In the march to the top of the mesa from the spring two girls each cast an annulet, and the boys the cylinder, into the cloud-terrace symbol [plate xx], which the priest traced with meal on the ground, using for the purpose the long black-snake baho.

A similar cylinder and annulets are described by Doctor Fewkes [b] as employed in the Mishongnovi Flute ceremony in 1896.

A stick with a small ring stands on each side of the altar of the Drab Flute at Oraibi, these being the implements used by the girls in the ceremony described above.

The double or tied billets used in this game may be referred to the two bows of the twin War Gods, and the other forms are probably derived from them. A suggestion as to the origin of the tossing stick may be obtained from the Flute ceremony.

FIG. 848. Annulet baho, used in the Flute ceremony; Hopi Indians, Shipaulovi, Arizona; from Fewkes.
FIG. 849. Cylinder tossed in the Flute ceremony; Hopi Indians, Shipaulovi, Arizona; from Fewkes.

ALGONQUIAN STOCK

CHEYENNE. Oklahoma. (Cat. no. $\frac{50}{24}$, American Museum of Natural History.)

Two buckskin-covered balls (figure 850), 3 inches in diameter, somewhat flattened, with median seam, painted yellow, with red bands on opposite side of the seam and green rings on opposite faces, connected by a thong 5 inches long. Collected by Mr Walter C. Roe and described as thrown with a stick.

[a] Journal of American Ethnology and Archæology, v. 2, p. 131, Boston, 1892.
[b] Nineteenth Annual Report of the Bureau of American Ethnology, pt. 2, p. 999, 1900.

CHIPPEWA.   Wisconsin.

Prof I. I. Ducatel [a] says:

The only play observed among the girls is the pahpahjekahwewog, a sort of substitute for our " graces," which simply consists in catching with two sticks a twine loaded at each end with a ball.

——— Michigan.

Baraga [b] gives the following definitions:

Passikawein, Indian women's play corresponding to the Indian ball play which is played by men only; passikawan, the stick or rod used by the squaws in playing their play.

——— Apostle islands, Wisconsin.

J. G. Kohl [c] says:

Another description of ball play, especially practiced by the women, is what is called the " papassi kawan," which means, literally, " the throwing game." It is played by two large bands, who collect round two opposite poles, and try to throw the object over their opponents' pole. In place of a ball they have two

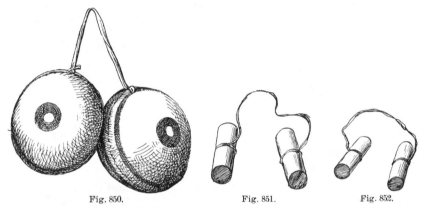

Fig. 850.   Fig. 851.   Fig. 852.

FIG. 850.   Double balls; diameter of balls, 3 inches; Cheyenne Indians, Oklahoma; cat. no. $\frac{8.9}{5}$, American Museum of Natural History.

FIG. 851.   Double billets; length of billets, 3¾ inches; Chippewa Indians, Bear island, Leech lake, Minnesota; cat. no. $\frac{50}{4725}$, American Museum of Natural History.

FIG. 852.   Double billets; length of billets, 4¼ inches; Chippewa Indians, Bear island, Leech lake, Minnesota; cat. no. $\frac{50}{4724}$, American Museum of Natural History.

leathern bags filled with sand, and attached by a thong. They throw them in the air by means of a staff excellently shaped for the purpose, and catch it again very cleverly. The stick is sharp and slightly bent at the end, and adorned like the raquets. I once saw a very neat model of these instruments for the women's throwing game suspended to the cradle of a little girl.

——— Bear island, Leech lake, Minnesota. (American Museum of Natural History.)

Cat. no. $\frac{50}{4725}$. The wooden billets (figure 851), each 3¾ inches in length, tied together with a cord of lin bark. The ends of the billets are painted red.

[a] A Fortnight Among the Chippewas. The Indian Miscellany, p. 368, Albany, 1877.

[b] A Dictionary of the Otchipwe Language, Cincinnati, 1853.

[c] Kitchi-Gami, Wanderings round Lake Superior, p. 90, London, 1860.

Cat. no. $\frac{50}{4734}$. Two wooden billets (figure 852), similar to the preceding, but 4¼ inches in length, diameter 1¼ inches, unpainted, and tied together with a strip of the same bark.

Collected in 1903 by Dr William Jones.

CHIPPEWA. Fort William, Ontario. (Cat. no. $\frac{50}{4727}$, $\frac{50}{4751}$, American Museum of Natural History.)

Double ball (figure 853), two buckskin-covered bags made in one piece, 18½ inches in length; with a stick, a sapling, 44 inches in length, painted red.

Collected in 1903 by Dr William Jones.

———— Turtle mountain, North Dakota. (American Museum of Natural History.)

Cat. no. $\frac{50}{4726}$. Two buckskin-covered bags (figure 854), made in one piece, 20 inches in length, having Greek, crosses made of green beads sewed on the opposite faces. Accompanied by a stick 26½ inches in length, wrapped from the upper end with black

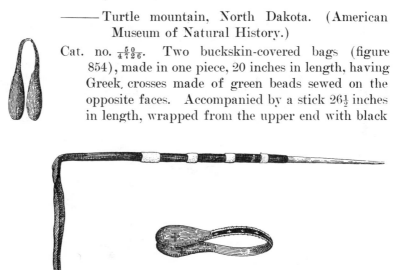

Fig. 853.　　　　　　　　　　　　　Fig. 854.

FIG. 853. Double ball and stick; length of ball, 18½ inches; length of stick, 44 inches; Chippewa Indians, Fort William, Ontario; cat. no. $\frac{50}{4727}$, $\frac{50}{4751}$, American Museum of Natural History.

FIG. 854. Double ball and stick; length of ball, 20 inches; length of stick, 26½ inches; Chippewa Indians, Turtle mountain, North Dakota; cat. no. $\frac{50}{4726}$, American Museum of Natural History.

cloth for the greater part of its length, and ornamented with a band of red and three bands of white beads.

Cat. no. $\frac{50}{4728}$. A double ball, similar to the preceding, but decorated with white, red, and blue beads.

These were collected in 1903 by Dr William Jones, who states that the goal is the bent limb of a tree or a stick that will hold the bag, the goals being from 100 to 200 yards apart. The stick is called wipawaganak; the bag, papasikawanag, meaning thing that is kicked. The game is called by the same name as the bag.

CREE. Muskowpetung reserve, Qu'appelle, Assiniboia. (Cat. no. 61992, Field Columbian Museum.)

Two oblong balls covered with deerskin, connected by a strip of the same material (figure 855); total length, 24 inches.

They were collected by Mr J. A. Mitchell, who describes the game under the name of puseekowwahnuk, kicking game:

The name of kicking game seems to be a misnomer, as the game is in no way played with the feet. The game is played by women only, any number, but not by the old women, as great powers of endurance are required. It is in many respects similar to lacrosse. The players are given various stations in the field and carry sticks. The goals are usually 1 mile or thereabout apart.

Players gather in a circle at the beginning and the double ball is thrown aloft from the stick of one of the leaders, when the scrimmage commences and is kept up until one side passes the ball through its opponent's goal.

The game is a very interesting one and develops much skill. It is, from a hygienic point of view, highly beneficial, as it develops a fine, robust class of women. As with all other Indian games, this game is invariably played for stakes of some kind.

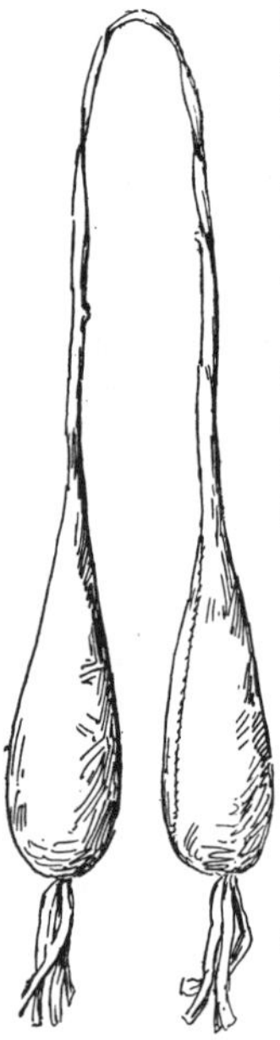

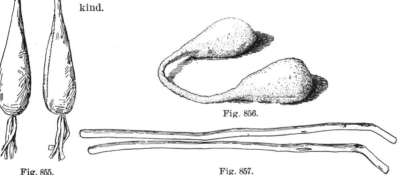

Fig. 856.

Fig. 855.

Fig. 857.

FIG. 855. Double ball; length, 24 inches; Cree Indians, Assiniboia; cat. no. 61992, Field Columbian Museum.

FIG. 856. Double ball; length, 10 inches; Cree Indians, Wind River reservation, Wyoming; cat. no. 37030, Free Museum of Science and Art, University of Pennsylvania.

FIG. 857. Sticks for double ball; length, 31 inches; Cree Indians, Wind River reservation, Wyoming; cat. no. 37030, Free Museum of Science and Art, University of Pennsylvania.

———— Wind River reservation, Wyoming. (Cat. no. 37030, Free Museum of Science and Art, University of Pennsylvania.)

Two oblong bags of buckskin (figure 856), weighted with sand, and attached to each other by a thong made of the same piece; length, 10 inches. Two sticks (figure 857), peeled saplings, slightly curved at one end and painted yellow; length, 31 inches.

These were collected by the writer in 1900 from an Indian of Riel's band, who gave the name of the balls as wepitse and weshikanik, and the name of the sticks as wepitse kana tikwa. The game is said to be played by both men and women. The goal is placed at a distance of 50 yards.

CREE. Edmonton, Alberta. (Cat. no. 15060, Field Columbian Museum.)

A buckskin bag (figure 858), 12 inches in length, the ends filled with sand; and a curved stick, 37 inches in length. Collected by Isaac Cowie and described as used by women in playing handball.

MENOMINEE. Shawano, Wisconsin. (Cat. no. 37958, Free Museum of Science and Art, University of Pennsylvania.)

Double ball (figure 859), consisting of two slender buckskin bags, united in the center by a thong 5½ inches in length; total length, 10½ inches.

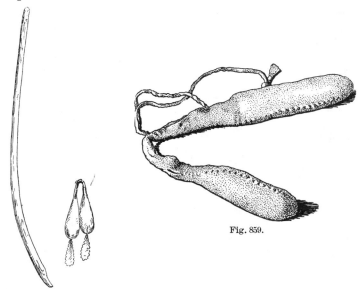

Fig. 859.

Fig. 858.

FIG. 858. Double ball and stick; length of ball, 12 inches; length of stick, 37 inches; Cree Indians, Alberta; cat. no. 15060, Field Columbian Museum.

FIG. 859. Double ball; length, 10¼ inches; Menominee Indians, Shawano, Wisconsin; cat. no. 37958, Free Museum of Science and Art, University of Pennsylvania.

This was collected by F. X. Steinbrecker in 1890 and is described on an appended label as a superstitious toy used by females at joyous feasts.

A Menominee Indian informed the author in Washington that the women of this tribe play the game with the long double ball, which they call cuachiciwuk.

MISSISAUGA. Rice lake, Ontario.

G. Copway [a] says:

Doubtless the most interesting of all games is the Maiden's Ball Play, in the Ojibway language, pah-pah-se-Kah-way. The majority of those who take part in this play are young damsels, although married women are not excluded.

[a] The Traditional History and Characteristic Sketches of the Ojibway Nation, p. 55, Boston, 1851.

The ball is made of deer skin bags, each about 5 inches long and 1 in diameter. These are so fastened together as to be at a distance of 7 inches each from the other. It is thrown with a stick 5 feet long.

This play is practiced in summer beneath the shade of wide-spreading trees, beneath which each strives to find their homes, tahwin, and to run home with it. These having been appointed in the morning, the young women of the village decorate themselves for the day by painting their cheeks with vermilion and disrobe themselves of as much unnecessary clothing as possible, braiding their hair with colored feathers, which hang profusely down to the feet.

At the same time the whole village assemble, and the young men, whose loved ones are seen in the crowd, twist and turn to send shy glances to them, and receive their bright smiles in return.

The same confusion exists as in the game of ball played by the men. Crowds rush to a given point as the ball is sent flying through the air. None stop to narrate the accidents that befall them, though they tumble about to their not little discomfiture; they rise, making a loud noise between a laugh and a cry, some limping behind the others, as the women shout. "Ain goo" is heard, sounding like the notes of a dove, of which it is no bad imitation. Worked garters, moccasins, leggins, and vermilion are generally the articles at stake. Sometimes the chief of the village sends a parcel as they commence, the contents of which are to be distributed among the maidens when the play is over.

I remember that, some winters before the teachers from the pale faces came to the lodge of my father, my mother was very sick. Many thought she could not recover her health. At this critical juncture she told my father that it was her wish to see the Maiden's Ball Play, and gave as her reason for her request that were she to see the girls at play it would so enliven her spirits with the reminiscences of early days as to tend to her recovery.

A description of the game follows in which it is related that the goals were two large spruce trees transplanted from the woods to holes in the ice.

MISSISAUGA. River Credit, Ontario.

Rev. Peter Jones [a] says:

The women have a game called uhpuhsekuhwon, which is played with two leather balls tied with a string about 2 feet long. These are placed on the ground, and each woman, with a stick about 6 feet long, tries to take up uhpuhsekuhwon from her antagonist, throwing it in the air. Whichever party gets it first to their respective goals or stakes counts 1.

FIG. 860. Double ball; length, 18½ inches; Sauk and Fox Indians, Tama, Iowa; cat. no. 36754, Free Museum of Science and Art, University of Pennsylvania.

SAUK AND FOXES. Tama, Iowa. (Cat. no. 36754, Free Museum of Science and Art, University of Pennsylvania.)

Bag of cotton cloth (figure 860), 18½ inches in length, expanded at the two ends and thin in the middle. Collected by the writer in 1900.

Six women play on each side, some 50 yards apart. The side that first gets the ball across wins the game. The ball is called kunanohok.

---

[a] History of the Ojebway Indians, p. 135, London, 1861.

SAUK AND FOXES.   Iowa.   (Cat. no. $\frac{50}{2210}$, American Museum of Natural History.)

Double ball (figure 861), covered with buckskin and filled with sand, the ends ovate; length, 15 inches.

Cat. no. $\frac{50}{2209}$.   Two sticks or clubs (figure 862), slightly knobbed at the end opposite the handle, 36 and 39 inches in length, one blackened and the other white.

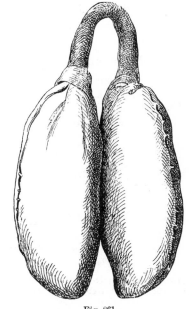

Fig. 861.

Fig. 862.

FIG. 861.   Double ball; length, 15 inches; Sauk and Fox Indians, Iowa; cat. no. $\frac{50}{2210}$. American Museum of Natural History.

FIG. 862.   Sticks for double ball; lengths, 36 and 39 inches; Sauk and Fox Indians, Iowa; cat. no. $\frac{50}{2209}$, American Museum of Natural History.

The foregoing specimens were collected by Dr William Jones, who describes them as used in the woman's ball game:

The game is played only by women. They have two bases, for which almost anything will answer. They like to get two trees some distance apart—say a quarter of a mile—and use outstretched limbs for the goals. The ball must be thrown on the goal. Each goal made counts a point. The color of the sticks corresponds with the division among the people into Whites and Blacks, each side using implements of its appropriate color.

The game is called ko-nen-no-hĭ-wag; the ball, ko-na-no-ha-ki, kidneys; the ball sticks, ot-chi.

ATHAPASCAN STOCK

Hupa. Hupa valley, California. (Cat. no. 37208, Free Museum of
Science and Art, University of Pennsylvania.)

Implements for the game of miskatokitch: Two small bottle-shaped
billets of wood (figure 863), with a knob at each end, attached
to each other by a double thong 3 inches in length; and a slender
stick (figure 864), or bat, of hardwood, 32 inches in length,
slightly curved at the end. Collected by the writer in 1900.

The billets are called yatomil, while the long sticks are called by
the same name as the game.[a]

Dr J. W. Hudson describes another form of this game:

A dumb-bell-shaped piece of buckskin, with big knots at each end, is jerked
with a rod to a tree goal. The buckskin is held in the mouth by one captain,
who finally drops it between the opponents. There are three players to a side.
The game is characterized by fierce interference.

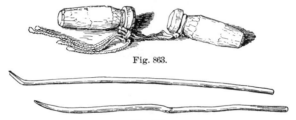

Fig. 863.

Fig. 864.

Fig. 863. Double billets; length of each, 3 inches; Hupa Indians, Hupa valley, California; cat.
no. 37208, Free Museum of Science and Art, University of Pennsylvania.

Fig. 864. Sticks for double-billet game; length, 32 inches; Hupa Indians, California; cat. no.
37208, Free Museum of Science and Art, University of Pennsylvania.

A Crescent City Indian whom the writer met at Arcata, California,
in 1900 gave the name of the tied billets as naustais and that of the
long sticks, or bats, as naustaischin; let us play, natithis.

Dr Pliny Earle Goddard [b] says:

The Hupa have four games. One of these very much resembles shinny.
The contestants are not individuals, but social or ethnic units. Village is pitted
against village or tribe against tribe. The shinny stick, called miʟkitûkûtc, is
about 3 feet long, or, more exactly, the length of the leg of the player. It has
a natural turn at the end. Two round sticks about 5 inches long tied together
with a piece of buckskin are used for a ball. They are called yademil. A
straight course is laid out with a stake at each end. At least six players take
their places in pairs, two at the middle and two at the points halfway between
the middle and the stakes. The pair at the middle have the balls. Those at
the other points stand facing each other with interlocked sticks. They are
said "to tie" each other. One of the two at the middle of the course takes the
two balls in his teeth. Suddenly he drops them and tries to drive them toward

---

[a] Dr Pliny E. Goddard gave the writer the names as follows: Long sticks, mil-tĕ-tŭk-
ketsh; tied sticks, yā-tĕ-mil.

[b] Life and Culture of the Hupa, p. 60, Berkeley, 1903.

his goal by catching the buckskin loop on the end of his stick. If he succeeds, he runs after the balls and tries to strike them again before he is overtaken. If he is overtaken, the next pair of players release one another and start after the balls while the first couple wrestle. The third pair take up the game if the second couple become involved in a wrestling match. The side which succeeds in getting the balls to the stake wins. As the game is described as played in former times, it probably rivaled modern football in roughness.

Dr Goddard [a] relates the story of a miraculous boy, Dug-from-the-ground, whose grandmother made him a shinny stick of blue-stone, with other things of the same material, for his journey to the home of the immortals, at the edge of the world, toward the east. Arriving, he met ten brothers who greeted him as brother-in-law. He played shinny with them, Wildcat, Fox, Earthquake, and Thunder, and won with the aid of the stick and balls his grandmother had made. He returned home to his grandmother and found he had been away as many years as it seemed to him he had spent nights.

F̲ɪɢ. 865. Double ball and stick; length of ball, 25 inches; length of stick, 32¼ inches; Pawnee Indians, Oklahoma; cat. no. 59405, Field Columbian Museum.

CADDOAN STOCK

A̲ʀɪᴋᴀʀᴀ. Fort Berthold, North Dakota.
Susan W. Hall [b] writes:

The women, in their modern Christian sewing meeting, are reviving a pretty and interesting old game of theirs, played with small deerskin-covered balls attached by a couple of inches of deerskin string and tossed by a long stick from one side to another.

P̲ᴀᴡɴᴇᴇ. Oklahoma. (Cat. no. 59405, Field Columbian Museum.)

Two buckskin balls (figure 865), each composed of two small balls conjoined, which have bands of white and blue beads around the middle, with buckskin fringe at the ends, and a string uniting them; total length, 25 inches; accompanied by a stick, painted yellow, 32½ inches in length. Another specimen in the same collection (cat. no. 59408) has single balls, flattened, each about 2 inches in diameter, painted yellow. Collected in 1901 by Dr George A. Dorsey.

[a] Hupa Texts, p. 146, Berkeley, 1904.
[b] A letter to Mr Theodore J. Eastman, dated August 11, 1900. In a subsequent letter to the writer she says that the balls were about the size of a lemon and were thrown with a stick and kept going from opposing sides.

Doctor Dorsey[a] mentions the shinny ball and double ball being used by a boy and a girl to convey them miraculously through space.

WICHITA. Oklahoma.

Implements (figure 866) for a woman's ball game, in the possession of Mr James Mooney, consist of two balls of buckskin, each about 2 inches in the greatest diameter and having white glass beads at the median seam fastened together with a thong, 11 inches in length, with a fringe of cut buckskin attached to each; and a stick, consisting of a bent sapling, 23 inches in length. The balls and stick are painted yellow. These implements are models, made and presented to Mr Mooney by Wichita Indians at the Indian Congress at Omaha in 1898.

FIG. 866. Double ball and stick; length of stick, 23 inches; Wichita Indians, Oklahoma; in the possession of Mr James Mooney.

In the Wichita tales the double ball is frequently referred to as a magical implement used in traveling. Bright-Shining-Woman (the Moon) gave it to women among the things they should use to enjoy themselves. She showed them how to play the game, and told them that the ball was for their use in traveling.[b]

In the story of " The Seven Brothers and the Woman " [c] the woman made her escape, aided by the double ball. When she tossed the double ball she went with it up in the air. Again, in " The Story of Child-of-a-Dog " [d] the woman uses the double ball in escaping from her pursuers. The same incident occurs in the stories of " Young-Boy-Chief and his Sister " [e] and " Trouble Among the Chief's Children." [f] In the story of " Young-Boy-Chief Who Married a Buffalo " [g] two women are described as playing the double-ball game with the other women.

COPEHAN STOCK

WINTUN. California.

Mr Alexander MacFarland Davis[h] says:

I am indebted to Mr Albert S. Gatschet, of Washington, for information concerning a game played among the Wintún Indians, called Ka-rá, which is played by throwing up two disks of wood connected by a string about 3 inches long. They are to be caught when they come down. Mr Gatschet refers to Mr Jeremiah Curtin, Bureau of Ethnology, for authority.

---

[a] Traditions of the Skidi Pawnee, p. 25, New York, 1904.

[b] The Mythology of the Wichita, p. 28, Washington, 1904.

[c] Ibid., p. 65.

[d] Ibid., p. 146.

[e] Ibid., p. 220.

[f] Ibid., p. 237.

[g] Ibid., p. 200.

[h] A Few Additional Notes concerning Indian Games. Bulletin of the Essex Institute, v. 18, p. 184, Salem, 1887.

LUTUAMIAN STOCK

KLAMATH.   Upper Klamath lake, Oregon.   (Cat. no. 61538, Field
    Columbian Museum.)

Willow poles (figure 867), skuekush, 52¼ inches in length, decorated
    and marked throughout the greater part of their length with two
    burnt spiral lines, which run in opposite
    directions; and two wooden billets, 6 inches
    long and 1 inch in diameter, fastened to
    each other by means of a short cord, 10
    inches in length, which passes through the
    center of each billet.

Collected in 1900 by Dr George A. Dorsey,[a]
who describes them as used in the game of
tchimmaash, generally played by women.   Two
goals, anku, are marked, about a hundred yards
apart.   From two to ten generally play.

Dr A. S. Gatschet[b] says:

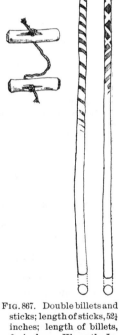

> The tchimmá-ash game is played almost exclusively
> by females.   The tchimmá-ash is a string about 2–3
> feet long, to the ends of which sticks or pieces of cloth
> are tied; it is taken up and thrown forward by two
> flexible willow rods (shuékûsh wá'hlkish) to play-
> mates, who divide themselves into two parties.   Be-
> fore the commencement of the game two limits (yûash)
> are meted out on the ground, which serve as bases.
> Both of them are located between the lines of starting
> (shalχuétgîsh).

MOQUELUMNAN STOCK

WASAMA.   Chowchilly river, Madera county,
    California.

Dr J. W. Hudson describes the following
game under the name of tawilu:

> Two or more women contest with 3-foot sticks for
> a braided buckskin strip 10 inches long.   The goals are
> 150 feet apart.

PIMAN STOCK

PAPAGO.   Mission of San Xavier del Bac, Pima
    county, Arizona.   (Field Columbian
    Museum.)

FIG. 867. Double billets and
sticks; length of sticks, 52¼
inches; length of billets,
6 inches; Klamath In-
dians, Oregon; cat. no.
61538, Field Columbian
Museum.

Cat. no. 63543.   Double ball (figure 868), consisting of two balls
    made of plaited hide, 1½ inches in diameter, united by a plaited

---

[a] Certain Gambling Games of the Klamath Indians.   American Anthropologist, n. s.,
v. 3, p. 19, 1901.

[b] The Klamath Indians of Southwestern Oregon.   Contributions to North American
Ethnology, v. 2, pt. 1, p. 81, Washington, 1890.

thong, total length, 5 inches; and slender stick, made of sapling, tapering to a point, 44 inches in length.

Cat. no. 63506.   Double ball (figure 869), consisting of two oblong wooden balls, 1⅝ inches in longest diameter, tied together by a strip of cotton cloth.

Cat. no. 63507.   Sticks used with the above, tapering to a point, one 6 feet 10½ inches, and the other 4 feet 4 inches in length.

These were collected by Mr S. C. Simms, who describes them as implements used in the woman's game of toakata. The Spanish call it " hobbles."

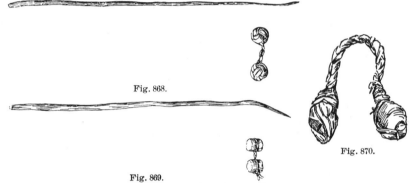

Fig. 868.

Fig. 869.

Fig. 870.

FIG. 868. Double ball and stick; length of balls, 5 inches; length of stick, 44 inches; Papago Indians, Arizona; cat. no. 63543, Field Columbian Museum.

FIG. 869. Double billets and stick; length of billets, 1⅝ inches; length of stick, 52 inches; Papago Indians, Arizona; cat. no. 63506, 63507, Field Columbian Museum.

FIG. 870. Double ball; length, 9¼ inches; Pima Indians, Arizona; cat. no. 63499, Field Columbian Museum.

PIMA.   Salt River reservation, Maricopa county, Arizona.   (Cat. no. 63499, Field Columbian Museum.)

Dumb-bell shaped ball (figure 870) of black painted leather; length (extended), 9½ inches. Collected by Mr S. C. Simms, who describes it as used in a woman's game.

TEPEHUAN. Talayote, near Nabogame, Chihuahua, Mexico. (Cat. no. $\frac{65}{916}$, American Museum of Natural History.)

Two wooden billets (figure 871), 2¼ inches in length, tied together with a cord of twisted white wood.

These were collected by Dr Carl Lumholtz in 1894, who gave the name of the billets as dádayar and that of the sticks as tshibukar. In case the cord of the billets should break it is mended, and the dadayar is buried under some loose earth in order to be thrown again.   Bets are made by the bystanders.

PUJUNAN STOCK

KAONI.   Cosumnes river, 12 miles south of Placerville, California.

Dr J. W. Hudson describes a game played with a buckskin strap, 24 inches long and knotted at the ends, under the name of tikili.

This is contested for by four women armed with clubs 30 inches long. The goals, which are usually trees, are 100 feet apart.

In Todds valley a dumb-bell shaped plaything consisting of pine cones thrust upon each end of a 12-inch stick [figure 872] is called hĕp'-pĕp-do'-kai. It is played by women, three to a side, with goal lines 200 feet apart. Kicking or foot-casting only is allowed.

NISHINAM. California.

Mr Stephen Powers[a] says:

The ti'-kel is almost the only really robust and athletic game they use, and is played by a large company of men and boys. The piece is made of rawhide, or nowadays of strong cloth, and is shaped like a small dumb-bell. It is laid in the center of a wide, level space of ground, in a furrow hollowed out a few inches in depth. Two parallel lines are drawn equidistant from it, a few paces apart, and along these lines the opposing parties, equal in strength, range themselves. Each player is equipped with a slight, strong staff, from 4 to 6 feet long. The two champions of the parties take their stations on opposite sides of the piece, which is then thrown into the air, caught on the staff of one or

FIG. 871. Double billets; length, 2¼ inches; Tepehuan Indians, Chihuahua, Mexico; cat. no. $\frac{65}{916}$, American Museum of Natural History.

the other, and hurled by him in the direction of his antagonist's goal. With this send-off there ensues a wild chase and a hustle, pellmell, higgledy-piggledy, each party striving to bowl the piece over the other's goal. These goals are several hundred yards apart, affording room for a good deal of lively work; and the players often race up and down the champaign, with varying fortunes, until they are dead blown and perspiring like top-sawyers.

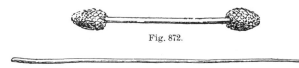

Fig. 872.

Fig. 873.

FIG. 872. Implement for tossing game; Kaoni Indians, California; from sketch by Dr J. W. Hudson.
FIG. 873. Stick for double ball; length, 62 inches; Achomawi Indians, Hat creek, California; cat. no. $\frac{50}{4116}$, American Museum of Natural History.

SHASTAN STOCK

ACHOMAWI. Hat creek, California. (Cat. no. $\frac{50}{4116}$, American Museum of Natural History.)

Stick (figure 873), a peeled sapling, 62 inches in length.

Collected in 1903 by Dr Roland B. Dixon, who describes it as used in a woman's ball game, luswalli. The tied billets, which doubtless accompanied it, are missing.

[a] Tribes of California. Contributions to American Ethnology, v. 3, p. 333, Washington, 1877.

SHASTA. Hamburg bar, California. (Cat. no. $\frac{50}{3194}$, American Museum of Natural History.)

Two wooden billets (figure 874), about 5 inches in length, tied together with a buckskin thong; accompanied with a stick, a peeled sapling, about 40 inches in length. Collected in 1902 by Dr Roland B. Dixon, who describes these specimens as implements for a woman's game.

FIG. 874. Double billets and stick; length of billets, about 5 inches; length of stick, about 40 inches; Shasta Indians, California; cat. no. $\frac{50}{3194}$, American Museum of Natural History.

SHOSHONEAN STOCK

PAIUTE. Pyramid lake, Nevada. (Cat. no. 37157, Free Museum of Science and Art, University of Pennsylvania.)

Ball and stick (figure 875) for woman's game; the ball, of buckskin, nearly cylindrical, and expanding at the ends; length, 11½ inches; the stick a forked, peeled sapling, 40 inches in length. Collected by the writer, through Miss Marian Taylor, in 1900.

FIG. 875. Double ball and stick; length of ball, 11½ inches; length of stick, 40 inches; Paiute Indians, Pyramid lake, Nevada; cat. no. 37157, Free Museum of Science and Art, University of Pennsylvania.

———— Pyramid lake, Nevada. (Cat. no. 19053, United States National Museum.)

Leather ball for woman's game, 12 inches in length, identical with the preceding.

Collected by Mr Stephen Powers, and described by him in his catalogue under the name of tapecool:

It is laid on the ground midway between two base lines, and the contending parties of women, armed with long sticks, seek to propel it beyond each other's base line.

SHOSHONI. Wind River reservation, Wyoming. (Cat. no. 36875, 36876, Free Museum of Science and Art, University of Pennsylvania.)

Ball (figure 876), nazeto, and stick, hope, for a woman's ball game. The ball, a buckskin bag, shaped like a dumb-bell, 10 inches in length; the stick, a peeled willow branch (figure 877), 46½ inches in length, with a projecting twig near the end. Collected by the writer in 1900.

UINTA UTE. White Rocks, Utah. (Cat. no. $\frac{50}{1281}$, American Museum of Natural History.)

Buckskin ball, nearly rectangular, narrowing toward the middle, with padded ends, with design in blue beads on one side, as shown in figure 878; length, 7 inches. Collected by Dr A. L. Kroeber in 1900.

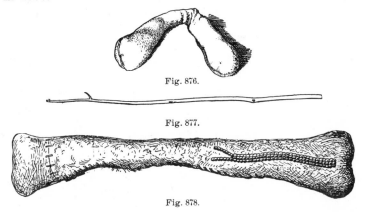

Fig. 876.

Fig. 877.

Fig. 878.

FIG. 876. Double ball; length, 10 inches; Shoshoni Indians, Wyoming; cat. no. 36876, Free Museum of Science and Art, University of Pennsylvania.
FIG. 877. Stick for double ball; length, 46¼ inches; Shoshoni Indians, Wyoming: cat. no. 36875, Free Museum of Science and Art, University of Pennsylvania.
FIG. 878. Double ball; length, 7 inches; Uinta Ute Indians, Utah; cat. no. $\frac{50}{1281}$, American Museum of Natural History.

SIOUAN STOCK

DAKOTA (SANTEE). Prairie du Chien, Wisconsin.

Catlin [a] says:

In the ball-play of the women [figure 879], they have two balls attached to the ends of a string about a foot and a half long; and each woman has a short stick in each hand, on which she catches the string with the two balls, and throws them, endeavoring to force them over the goal of her own party. The men are more than half drunk, when they feel liberal enough to indulge the women in such an amusement, and take infinite pleasure in rolling about on the ground and laughing to excess, while the women are tumbling about in all attitudes, and scuffling for the ball.

OMAHA. Nebraska.

Rev. J. Owen Dorsey [b] describes this game:

Wabáɔnade, the women's game of ball.—Two balls of hide are filled with earth, grass, or fur, and then joined by a cord. At each end of the playground are two gabázu, or hills of earth, blankets, etc., that are from 12 to 15 feet

---

[a] Letters and Notes on the Manners, Customs, and Condition of the North American Indians, v. 2, p. 146, London, 1841.
[b] Omaha Sociology. Third Annual Report of the Bureau of Ethnology, p. 338, 1884.

apart. Each pair of hills may be regarded as the "home," or "base," of one of the contending parties, and it is the aim of the members of each party to throw the balls between their pair of hills, as that would win the game.

Two small girls, about 12 years old, stand at each end of the playground and act as uhe ginajiⁿ for the women, as the boys do for the men in ꞩabe-gasi.

Each player has a webaꞩnade, a very small stick of hard or red willow, about 5 feet long, and with this she tries to pick up the balls by thrusting the end of the stick under the cord. Whoever succeeds in picking them up hurls them into the air, as in playing with grace hoops. The women can throw these balls very far. Whoever catches the cord on her stick in spite of the efforts of her opponents tries to throw it still further and closer to her "home." The stakes are buffalo hides, small dishes or bowls, women's necklaces, awls, etc. The bases are from 300 to 400 yards apart. The corresponding men's game is Labe-gasi.

Fig. 879. Santee Dakota women playing double ball. Prairie du Chien, Wisconsin; from Catlin.

WASHOAN STOCK

Washo.   Carson valley and Lake Tahoe, Nevada.

Dr J. W. Hudson describes the following game played by women under the name of tsikayaka:

A buckskin strap, pĕ-tsil'-tsi, is contested for by the opposing players, each armed with a four-foot rod, tse-kai'-yak. The goals are stakes, two hundred feet apart.

WEITSPEKAN STOCK

Yurok.   Klamath river, California.   (Cat. no. 37259, Free Museum of Science and Art, University of Pennsylvania.)

Two bottle-shaped wooden billets (figure 880), 5½ inches in length, with a knob at the end and two lines of bark left at the center, tied together with a piece of twine, 2½ inches in length; accompanied by two long slender sticks (figure 881) or bats, of hard wood, pointed and slightly curved at the end, 33 and 35 inches in length. Collected by the writer in 1900.

The billets are called wat-tai; the bats, mai-num-in. The latter were obtained from an Indian named Wichapec Billy, 57 years of age, who had used them in matches. He said the game was played by three parties of three each, who stripped and painted. Money was put up, say five dollars on a side. Matches were formerly common between Hupa and Wichapec.

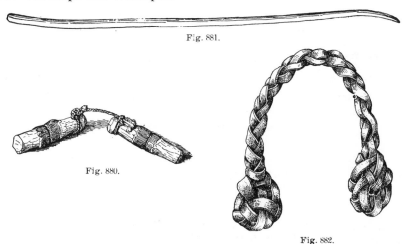

Fig. 881.

Fig. 880.

Fig. 882.

FIG. 880. Double billets; length of each, 5¼ inches; Yurok Indians, California; cat. no. 37259, Free Museum of Science and Art, University of Pennsylvania.
FIG. 881. Stick for double billets; length, 33 inches; Yurok Indians, California; cat. no. 37259; Free Museum of Science and Art, University of Pennsylvania.
FIG. 882. Double ball; length, 8½ inches; Maricopa Indians, Arizona; cat. no. 2924, Brooklyn Institute Museum.

WISHOSKAN STOCK

A Batawat Indian at Blue Lake, California, gave the name of the long sticks as rocosaiyok wataiwat and that of the tied billets as goshwa wik.

YUMAN STOCK

MARICOPA. Arizona. (Cat. no. 2924, Brooklyn Institute Museum.) Double ball (figure 882), made on a plaited leather throng; length, 8½ inches. Collected in 1904 by Mr Louis L. Meeker, who gives the name as tus-ho-al kik, and says that the ball is pitched with sticks.

BALL RACE

The ball race appears to be confined to the Southwestern tribes, extending into Mexico and westward into California, although it was found by the writer among the Shoshonean Bannock in Idaho. It consists of a race in which the contestants kick or toss some small object before them, commonly around a circuit which has been agreed upon, back to the starting place. There are either two individual players or two parties. The object which is kicked or tossed is of three different kinds—first, a ball of stone (Pima, Mono, Tewa, Maricopa) or of wood (Opata, Papago, Pima, Tarahumare, Zuaque, Cocopa, Mohave, Yuma); second, a single billet (Navaho)

or two billets (Keres, Tewa, Zuñi); third, a ring or rings (Tarahumare, Zuñi). In addition, the Bannock are said to kick a beef bladder, and the Hopi use two cubes of hair and piñon gum in a similar race.

The game of kicked stick was one of the games sacred to the War God in Zuñi, and the implements are sacrificed upon his altar. The implements used may be identified readily as conventionalized bows of the War Gods, an explanation which serves likewise for the racing billets used by other tribes. Objects similar to the kicking billets are used by the Hopi in ceremonials, and may be regarded as having a similar origin.

For example, a set of six small wooden cylinders (figure 883), contained in the Field Columbian Museum, is made of cottonwood root, $2\frac{5}{8}$ inches in length and three-fourths of an inch in diameter, painted black, with green ends, and having a feather attached around the middle by cotton cord. They were collected by Rev. H. R. Voth in 1893, and described by him as oönötki. He says:

FIG. 883. Set of sacrificial wooden cylinders; length, $2\frac{5}{8}$ inches; Hopi Indians, Oraibi, Arizona; cat. no. 67049 to 67054, Field Columbian Museum.

Cylinders of this kind are made of different sizes and used in various ceremonies such as the Flute, Marau, and Soyal. They are deposited as offerings in springs and shrines, but generally not before they have been consecrated at the altar during some ceremony. This set of six was made by and obtained from the chief priest of the Marau order. The small feathers attached to them are those of the pin-tail duck.

Another set of two cylinders in the same museum (cat. no. 67086, 67087) are $2\frac{1}{2}$ inches in length, and are mentioned by Mr Voth as having been found by him in a shrine where the Soyaluna fraternity made their offerings to the sun.

The tossing-rings of the Zuñi and Tarahumare game may be explained as representing net shields, and the contest, which in Zuñi is conducted between the clowns with billets and between the women with rings, is analogous to the ceremony in the Flute dance, where the

Flute youth and the Flute maid throw annulets and cylinders, described under " Double ball," to which game the ball race is apparently closely related.

The existence of the ball race at an early period is proved by specimens of the kicking-sticks (figure 884) in the cliff-dwellings. A pair of such billets from Mancos canyon, identified by Mr Cushing, is in the Free Museum of Science and Art of the University of Pennsylvania. They are made of cottonwood, one $4\frac{1}{2}$ inches in length and $1\frac{5}{8}$ inches in diameter, marked around with sharply incised parallel lines about one-fourth of an inch apart; the other 5 inches long and $1\frac{1}{2}$ inches in diameter, with similar incised lines in diamond pattern. Another pair (figure 885) from the same place are simple sections of

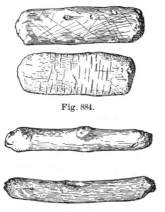

Fig. 884.

Fig. 885.

Fig. 886

FIG. 884. Kicking billets; lengths, $4\frac{1}{2}$ and 5 inches; cliff-dwelling, Mancos canyon, Colorado; Free Museum of Science and Art, University of Pennsylvania.

FIG. 885. Kicking billets; lengths, $4\frac{1}{2}$ and 5 inches; cliff-dwelling, Mancos canyon, Colorado; Free Museum of Science and Art, University of Pennsylvania.

FIG. 886. Clown kicking billet; Mexico, 1583; reverse of Hispano-American playing card, impression, $2\frac{1}{2}$ by 4 inches; from photograph of the original in the Archives of the Indies, Seville, Spain.

twig, $4\frac{3}{4}$ and 5 inches in length and three-fourths of an inch in diameter. Many of the unidentified stone balls found in ruins and graves at various places in the Southwest may have been used in this game.

A picture of a travesty of the kicked-stick game, identified by Mr Cushing, is printed on the reverse of an Hispano-American playing card, engraved in Mexico in 1583 and preserved in the Archives of the Indies at Seville, Spain. This curious and interesting relic represents a clown (figure 886), fantastically dressed in the native ceremonial costume, standing on his head and kicking a huge billet in the air with his feet.

The ball race has been adopted from the Indians by the Mexicans of the Rio Grande. Capt. John G. Bourke, of the United States

Army, informed the writer that they have a game of kicking a cow's horn, which they call juego del cuaco.[a] This game, according to the authority just mentioned, corresponds with the Zuñi, Hopi, Pueblo, and Pima game of the tor stick.

ATHAPASCAN STOCK

Navaho. St Michael, Arizona.

Rev. Berard Haile describes the following game in a letter to the writer:[b]

Iddi is football. This is a gambling game, and there are two parties, five to a side at most. There may be less than five, but not more. The players strip themselves and agree upon a distance, which is regulated by the stake. A stick, about 4 inches long, of green piñon or oak, cut smooth and round, is set into the ground about 2 fingers deep. The best runner works his toes, as hands and fingers are not allowed, under the stick, and kicks it ahead of him. Should he miss, his successor is ready to bring it into his territory again. The required distance being made, the home run begins, and whosoever has the ball at the starting point first wins the game and stake. The game was played only in the spring of the year, because it is not too warm during that season. At present the Navaho do not play it. Some would not allow it, even in the springtime, as they claim it would bring a stormy season and much wind. They say the Great Earth-Winner, Ni'nahuiebi'i, taught them the game.

In a subsequent letter to the author Father Haile gives the name of the game, according to information received from another source, as baaes or iolis, which means " to hop " game, raise and throw with the foot.

The Navaho at Chin Lee, Arizona, informed the writer that this was not originally a Navaho game, but was borrowed by them from the Zuñi.

KERESAN STOCK

Keres. Acoma, New Mexico. (Cat. no. 4974, Brooklyn Institute Museum.)

Fig. 887. Kicking billets; length, 2 inches; Keres Indians, Acoma, New Mexico; cat. no. 4974, Brooklyn Institute Museum.

Two billets (figure 887), 2 inches in length, one painted with black at the ends and the other with a black band in the middle. Collected by the writer in 1904 and made by James H. Miller, an Acoma Indian, at Zuñi.

They are kicked in a racing game called a-cha-wa-ï ta-wa-ka. The one with the black bands at the end is called gosh, man, and the other tsoi-yo, woman. This is a game of the war captains, and is played in the spring in the months from March to May to secure rain. The winning stick is buried in a cornfield. The present sticks are such as are

---

[a] Spanish chueca, pan or hollow of the joints of bones; a small ball with which country people play at crickets.

[b] Under date of June 5, 1902. The information was obtained from a medicine man named Qatali Natloi, Laughing Doctor.

used by boys. The regular kicking sticks are made of oak. Tsa-tio hu-chi made the game first.

KERES. Cochiti, New Mexico. (Cat. no. 4978, Brooklyn Institute Museum.)

Two wooden billets (figure 888), 2 inches in length and about seven-eighths of an inch in diameter, one painted red and the other yellow.

These were made by a Keres boy from Cochiti, named Francisco Chaves (Kogit), at St Michael, Arizona, who describes the billets under the name of tawaka and mentions them as being kicked in the race of the same name.

Boys, girls, and men play. Sides are chosen, and the sticks are kicked with the bare feet.

———— Laguna, New Mexico. (Cat. no. 3006, Brooklyn Institute Museum.)

Two wooden billets (figure 889), 1⅛ inches in length and about 1 inch in diameter. One of these billets has a band of red paint around the middle, and the other is plain, except the ends, which are painted red. These implements were collected by the writer in 1903.

Fig. 888. 　　　　　　　　Fig. 889.

FIG. 888. Kicking billets; length, 2 inches; Keres Indians, Cochiti, New Mexico; cat. no. 4978, Brooklyn Institute Museum.
FIG. 889. Kicking billets; length, 1⅛ inches; Keres Indians, Laguna, New Mexico; cat. no. 3006, Brooklyn Institute Museum.

The sticks are called tow-wa-ka; the one with the red band ku-ka-ni tow-wa-ka, and the other sho-mutz tow-wa-ka. The game is called ka-tcho-wai. The blocks are kicked with the bare feet around a designated course. Sides are chosen and there is one block for each. It may not be thrown with the hands, but they may place it on the toe to give it a good kick.

MOQUELUMNAN STOCK

COSUMNI. California.

Mr James Mooney[a] writes as follows from information obtained from Col. Z. A. Rice, of Atlanta, Ga., who went to California in the

_____

[a] Notes on the Cosumnes Tribes of California. The American Anthropologist, v. 3, p. 261, 1890.

year 1850, where he spent several years in the immediate vicinity of the tribe now under consideration, which formerly lived in the Sacramento basin:

Their football game was more properly a foot race. Two parallel tracks were laid off and each party had its own ball. Two athletic young fellows, representing the two contending parties, took their stand at one end, each with a ball on the ground in front of him, and at the signal each kicks it along his respective track towards the goal. All along the line were stationed relays of players, whose duty it was to assist in getting the ball through. It was a rough-and-tumble game, to see who should kick the ball, for no one was allowed to touch it with his hand. Two posts were put up at each end of the track, and the ball must be driven between these posts. Betting was heavy, the stakes being Indian trinkets of all kinds, and judges and stakeholders presided with a great deal of dignity. The score was kept by means of an even number of short sticks, and as each player drove the ball home, he drew out one of the sticks, and so on until the game was won. It was a very exciting play and aroused as much interest as does a horse race among the whites.

WASAMA. Near Grant Springs, Mariposa county, California.

Dr J. W. Hudson describes these Indians as playing a game with a ball made of deer hair and provided with a buckskin cover, in which two men each contest or race with their ball along a prescribed course to a certain goal.

The name of the game is tĕk′mĕ, to kick; and that of the ball, pu′kŭ, little dog, pup.

PIMAN STOCK

OPATA.   Sonora, Mexico.

Mr A. F. Bandelier[a] says:

The Ua-ki-mari is rather a foot-race than a game of ball, for the runners toss the ball before them with their toes, and the party whose " gomi," or ball of a certain kind of wood, reaches the goal first is declared the victor. . . .

Village plays against village. The Maynates or captains of the runners are important personages on such days, and what is evidently primitive, and shows besides that there is a religious import placed upon the ceremony, is the fact that they formerly used to gather the evening before at a drinking bout, smoking at the same time the fungus of the mesquite, called in Opáta to-ji, in long and big cigar-like rolls.

PAPAGO.   Mission of San Xavier del Bac, Pima county, Arizona. (Cat. no. 63485, Field Columbian Museum.)

Ball of mesquite wood, 3⅛ inches in diameter, designated by the collector, Mr S. C. Simms, as a football, sonecua.

PAPAGO.   Arizona.

Dr H. F. C. ten Kate, jr,[b] says:

One of the few bodily exercises they have is a sort of ball game in which they use a ball made of hard gum, which is kicked without stopping by two men

---

[a] Final Report, pt. 1, p. 240, Cambridge, 1890.
[b] Reizen en Onderzoekingen in Noord-Amerika, p. 29, Leiden, 1885.

who run over a great expanse of country. A large number of spectators follow the two players, either on horseback or on foot, at the same gait.

PIMA. Arizona. (United States National Museum.)

Cat. no. 76014. Two stone balls (figure 894), consisting of tufa, covered with some black vegetable substance, probably mesquite gum; diameters, 2⅛ and 2⅜ inches. Described by the collector, Dr Edward Palmer, as footballs.

Cat. no. 27847. Wooden ball (figure 895), 2½ inches in diameter, covered with mesquite gum. Described by the collector as a football.

FIG. 890. Papago kicking-ball players, Arizona; from photograph by Mr William Dinwiddie.

Dr H. F. C. ten Kate, jr,[a] says the Pima have a football game in which the ball—sonjikjo—is made of the gum of the greasewood and sand.

——— Arizona.

The late Dr Frank Russell [b] described the kicked ball races of this tribe as follows:

These races were frequently intertribal, and in their contests with the Papagos the Pimas nearly always won. The use of these balls in foot races is very widespread in the Southwest, and even yet we hear of races taking place that exceed twenty miles in length.

The kicking ball when of wood resembles a croquet ball in size, but it is usually covered with a creosote gum. They are made of either mesquite or paloverde wood. Stone balls about 6 cm. in diameter are also used, and are covered with the same black gum.

[a] Reizen en Onderzoekingen en Noord-Amerika, p. 159, Leiden, 1885.
[b] In a memoir to be published by the Bureau of American Ethnology.

Each contestant kicks one of these balls before him, doing it so skillfully that his progress is scarcely delayed; indeed, the Pima declare that they can run faster with than without the balls—which, in a sense, is true. Perhaps the occurrence of the stone balls in the ruins gave rise to the idea that they possess magic power to "carry" the runner along, for all things pertaining to the Hohokam have come to have more or less supernatural significance. Two youths will sometimes run long distances together, first one and then the other kicking the ball so that it is almost constantly in the air. The custom of using these balls is rapidly disappearing, as, it is to be regretted, are the other athletic games of the Pima.

The men received thorough training in speed and endurance in running during their raids into the Apache country, but they had few sports that tended toward physical improvement except the foot races. Sometimes a woman ran in a contest against a man, she throwing a double ball by means of a long stick while he kept a kicking ball before him. But the women seldom ran in foot races, though their active outdoor life, engaged in the various tasks that fell to them, kept them in fit condition. However, they had an athletic game which corresponded in a measure to the races of the men and developed skill in running. This game was played as follows:

Âldû.—Two of the swiftest runners among the women acted as leaders and chose alternately from the players until all were selected in two groups. Two goals were fixed about 400 yards apart. One side saying, "To the trail is where we can beat you," while the other party declared, "To that mesquite is where we can beat you." Two lines were formed about 25 yards apart, and the ball was put in play by being tossed up and started toward the opponent's goal. It was thrown with sticks until some one drove it beyond the goal and won the game.[a] To touch the ball with the hands debarred the person from further play. This game was abandoned about 1885.

TARAHUMARE. Chihuahua, Mexico.

Dr Carl Lumholtz describes the foot race of this tribe:[b]

Two districts or pueblos always run against each other. Sometimes there are many runners on each side, and the two parties show in their apparel some distinguishing mark; for instance, one side wears red headbands, while the other wears white ones. I have seen from four to twenty runners taking part on each side. Each party has a small ball, about 2 inches in diameter, carved with a knife from the root of an oak tree, which they have to toss ahead of them as they run. The runner who happens to be ahead is the one whose duty it is to toss the ball with his toes, and at each toss it may be thrown a hundred yards or more in advance. They are not allowed to touch the balls with their hands, but their friends who follow them may point out to the runner where the ball is lying. If the ball lodges in an awkward place, as between two rocks, or in the water, the runners or their friends may pick it up and place it back on the race course. The circuits over which the race is held are circular when the country allows, but generally the course is backward and forward along the top of the ridge, the group of spectators and bettors being at the starting-point, which is always at the middle of the race-track. Each party chooses a manager to represent the runners and to arrange the day and place of the race.

---

[a] The stick in the collection is of willow, 1.230 m. long, with a maximum diameter of 18 mm. The balls are in pairs, 15 cm. apart, connected by a 4-strand, 2-ply leather thong, the balls being mere knotty enlargements of the thong.

[b] Tarahumari Life and Customs. Scribner's Magazine, v. 16, p. 304, New York, 1894.

These managers also decide the number of circuits to be made, and get runners of equal ability, if they can, for each side, the object being to get the best runners possible.

In important races the runners may prepare for a fortnight, but as a rule they do not practice much before the race, for running comes to them as naturally as swimming to ducks. Their training chiefly consists in abstinence from native beer for two or three days before the event. On the day of the race the runners are fed with pinole only; they have tepid water to drink, and their legs are well bathed in warm water and rubbed by the managers. The medicine man also rubs them with a smooth stone to make them strong.

Fig. 891. Papago kicking-ball player, Arizona; from photograph by Mr William Dinwiddie.

A race is never won by natural means. The losers always say that they were influenced by some herb and became sleepy on the race-course, so that they had to lose. The help of the medicine man is needed in preparing the runner for the race. He assists the manager to wash the feet of the runners with warm water and different herbs, and he strengthens their nerves by making passes over them. He also guards them against sorcery. Before they run he performs a ceremony to " cure " them.

The food and the remedies he uses are put under the cross with many kinds of charms, different kinds of woods, and herbs from the barrancas. Some of the herbs are supposed to be very powerful, and they are, therefore, securely tied up in small pieces of buckskin or cotton cloth. If not so tied up, they might break away. The water which the runners drink is also placed near the cross, upon each side of which is put a candle, and the whole outfit is on a blanket. At the ceremony the runners stand, holding the balls in their hand. The doctor, or medicine man, standing near the cross, burns incense (copal) over them. He also sings about the tail of the gray fox, one of their legendary animals, and other songs. After this he makes a speech, warning them against eating pinole or drinking water in other people's houses, for fear of poison; all that they eat and drink must come from their parents or relatives. They are not allowed to eat anything sweet, nor eggs, potatoes, cheese, or fat. Three times they drink from the water near the cross, and three times from the herbs. The eldest and swiftest runner then leads in walking around the cross as many times as there are to be circuits in the race, and the rest follow him. All the things near the cross then remain untouched until morning. The runners sleep near by to keep watch, and they also secure some old men to watch against sorcery, for old men are supposed to discover the approach of sorcerers even when they sleep. After the ceremonies are over the doctor takes each runner aside and subjects him to a rigid examination.

Fig. 892.   Fig. 893.

FIG. 892. Papago kicking-ball race—the start, Arizona; from photograph by Mr William Dinwiddie.

FIG. 893. Papago kicking-ball race, Arizona; from photograph by Mr William Dinwiddie.

More than a hundred kinds of remedies are brought to the contest, some to strengthen the runners and secure success, and others to weaken their rivals. The most efficient thing against the rivals is the blood of the turtle and bat mixed together, dried and ground, and rolled into a big cigar, with a small amount of tobacco added to it. Its smoke makes the rivals stupid. The dried head of a crow or eagle, hikori, a small cactus worshiped by the Tarahumaris, and other herbs and innumerable things are carried around by all who take part in the racing. Some of the women carry small, thin stones to protect them against sorcerers. During the race the runners have their heads ornamented with the feathers of the chaparral-cock, and in some parts with the feathers of the peacock, of which bird the Indians are very fond, because it is supposed to be light footed, and also because it is from another country. Many of them also have their legs ornamented with chalk, and wear belts to which a great number of deer hoofs, beads, or reeds are attached, so as to make a great deal of noise. These belts help them to victory, because they become, as they fancy, as light as the deer itself, and the noise keeps them from falling asleep.

In the afternoon before the race the managers and the runners meet together, the latter bringing the balls with them, to receive an omen as to which party is going to win. Water is put into a big earthen tray, and the two balls are started simultaneously from one end of the tray to the other. The party whose ball reaches the other end first will be the winner, and they repeat this as many times as there are to be circuits. Three or four hours before sunset the chief calls the runners together and makes a speech, warning them against any kind of cheating. Just as in horse racing, rascally tricks are more or less common, especially if the Indians have become half civilized. It may happen that some one will bribe the runners with a cow not to run fast; afterward he may also cheat the runner. It is not uncommon for an important runner to simulate illness. "Our rivals," he may say, "have bewitched us." The whole thing then comes to nothing, and the wagers are divided between the parties, who return to their home to await the next race.

There is no prize given to the runners themselves, and they gain nothing by it unless in helping their friends to win wagers. A good runner is also greatly admired by the women, which may be of some account to him. It is also the custom for a man who has been very lucky with his wagers to give a small part of his winnings to the successful runner, who, however, is allowed to take

Fig. 894.   Fig. 895.

FIG. 894.   Stone kicking balls; diameters, 2¼ and 2⅜ inches; Pima Indians, Arizona; cat. no. 86014, United States National Museum.

FIG. 895.   Wooden kicking ball; diameter, 2½ inches; Pima Indians, Arizona; cat. no. 27847, United States National Museum.

neither beads nor money, but only light-weight things made from wool or cotton; but his father can receive gifts for him and buy something for his son's benefit.

On the day of the race stones are laid on the ground in a row, one stone for each circuit to be run, and as the race progresses count is kept by taking away one stone for each circuit finished by the runners. It is from this practice that the tribe derives its name, Tarahumari—from tara (count), and humari (run), people who run according to count.

Trees are marked with crosses, so as to show the circuit to be run. Three to six watchmen are placed along the circuit to see that no cheating is done during the race. Each party helps the side in which it is interested, so that their runners may win the race.

The women, as the runners pass them, stand ready with dippers of warm water, or pinole, which they offer to them to drink, and for which they stop for a few seconds. The wife of the runner may throw a jar of tepid water over him as he passes, in order to refresh him, and all incite the runners to greater speed by cries and gesticulations. Drunken people must not be present, because they make the runners heavy. For the same reason pregnant women are forbidden to enter the race-course. A runner must not even touch the blanket of such a woman. As the time passes, the excitement becomes more and more intense. Most of the men and women follow the race, shouting to the runners all the time to spur them on, and pointing out to them where the ball is; and if night comes on before the contest has been decided, the men light torches made from the oily pine-wood to show the runners the road, making the scene one of extreme picturesqueness, as like demons these torch-bearers hurry through the forest.

One manager, or chochiame, from each side is appointed stakeholder. They tie the stakes, of whatever nature, together—so much ari [a] against so many arrows, so many blankets against so many balls of yarn, etc., and hold them until the race is over. At big races, where the wagers may amount to small mountains of such articles, and may include cattle and goats, the position of the manager requires a man of decision and memory, as he carries all the bets in his head and makes no written record. The value of such wagers may exceed $1,000.

Describing a race which he witnessed near Guachochic in September, 1892, Doctor Lumholtz says:

The chief race began late, as is generally the case, about 3 o'clock. When all was ready, the two managers threw the balls in the direction in which the men were to go, the runners dropped their blankets and sped away, although not from a line, as with us. They were naked, except for a breech-cloth, and wore sandals on their feet. The race was made in two hours and twenty-one seconds, and the distance covered was 21 miles, according to my calculation. I estimated that the runners covered a distance of 290 feet in nineteen seconds on the first circuit, and in later circuits in about twenty-four seconds. A circuit may measure from 3 to 12 miles in length. They may agree upon from five to twenty circuits. The first three circuits are run at the highest speed, but the speed is never great, although constant. At a race rehearsal I have seen them making 4 miles in half an hour. Filipe, who is now dead, could run from mid-day to sunrise. He was from Marrarachic, and was the greatest runner known in the northeastern part of Tarahumari. Good runners make 40 miles in from 6 to 8 hours.

Women hold their own races, one valley against another, and the same scenes of betting and excitement are to be observed, although on a smaller scale. The women do not toss the balls with their toes, but use a species of long wooden fork, with two or three prongs, with which they propel the ball forward. It must not be touched with the hand. At other times the women use a curved stick, with which they throw before them a ring of twisted fibre, which thus replaces the ball. Neither must this be touched with the hand, although I have seen them cheat when they fancied themselves unobserved, picking it up and running with it in order to save time. This is a very ancient game, as similar rings have been excavated from the cliff-dwellings. The women get even more excited than the men, and it is a strange sight to see these stalwart Amazons racing heavily along, but with astonishing perseverance. They wear nothing but a skirt, which, when creeks or water-holes come in their way, they gather up, à la Diane, and make short work of the crossing.

TARAHUMARE. Chihuahua, Mexico. (Cat. no. 16311, 16312, Free Museum of Science and Art, University of Pennsylvania.)

---

[a] Secretion of a plant-louse, which is eaten by the Indians.

Two wooden balls (figure 896), 2½ and 2⅞ inches in diameter; and
two sticks (figure 897), with curved, fork-like ends, one with
two and the other with three prongs; lengths, 24½ and 26 inches.

Collected by Dr Carl Lumholtz, who gives the name of the sticks
as manijera,[a] and of the game as el patillo. He further says, in a
letter: [b]

The ball game of the Tarahumare women, played by two at a time, is called
by the Tepehuan ke ta-tau-koard. The ball is beaten by a cuchara, or spoon,
called tau-koua-le-ka-re. The game is begun by the ball being thrown up in the
air and then struck to one side.

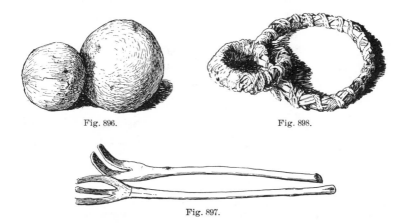

Fig. 896.   Fig. 898.

Fig. 897.

FIG. 896. Tossing balls for women's race; diameters, 2½ and 2⅞ inches; Tarahumare Indians,
Chihuahua, Mexico; cat. no. 16311, Free Museum of Science and Art, University of Pennsylvania.

FIG. 897. Tossing sticks for women's ball race; lengths, 24½ and 26 inches; Tarahumare Indians,
Chihuahua, Mexico; cat. no. 16312, Free Museum of Science and Art, University of Pennsylvania.

FIG. 898. Tossing rings for women's race; diameters, 3½ and 5 inches; Tarahumare Indians,
Chihuahua, Mexico; cat. no. 16314, Free Museum of Science and Art, University of Pennsylvania.

TARAHUMARE. Guachochic, Chihuahua, Mexico. (Cat. no. 16313–
16315, Free Museum of Science and Art, University of Pennsylvania.)

Two rings (figure 898) made of yucca fiber, wrapped with cord
made of native wool, interlinked, one 3½ and the other 5 inches
in diameter, and two similar rings (figure 899), each 5 inches in
diameter; accompanied by two pointed sticks (figure 900),
slightly curved at the end, 28½ and 29½ inches in length.

Collected by Dr Carl Lumholtz, who describes them as used in the
game of la revetta.[c]

---

[a] Probably manejera, from manejar, to handle.
[b] Dated July 23, 1902.
[c] Spanish, revuelta.

ZUAQUE.   Rio Fuerte, Sinaloa, Mexico.

Mr C. V. Hartman writes the author as follows:

These Indians have the same game as the Tarahumare, corrida de la bola, a race in which a wooden ball is tossed with the foot. Its name in their language is ga-hi'-ma-ri.

Their women have a game with similar wooden balls, thrown up in the air with sticks which are spoon-like in the end, not forked, as by the Tarahumare. They call the game a'-tja.

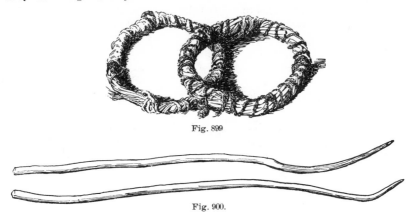

Fig. 899

Fig. 900.

FIG. 899. Tossing rings for women's race; diameter, 5 inches; Tarahumare Indians, Chihuahua, Mexico; cat. no. 16313, Free Museum of Science and Art, University of Pennsylvania.

FIG. 900. Tossing sticks for women's ring race; lengths, 28½ and 29½ inches; Tarahumare Indians, Chihuahua, Mexico; cat. no. 16315, Free Museum of Science and Art, University of Pennsylvania.

SHOSHONEAN STOCK

BANNOCK.   Fort Hall reservation, Idaho.

A kind of foot race, in which a ball made of an inflated beef bladder, watooka, is kicked, was described to the writer in 1900 by the Indians at Rossfork, Idaho.   Two sides choose, sometimes three or four men and sometimes only one on each side.   Each side has its ball.   The runners start at a given point, make a circuit, and return.

HOPI.   Oraibi, Arizona.   (Cat. no. 66084, 66113, Field Columbian Museum.)

Footballs consisting of nearly cubical blocks, 2⅛ inches and 1⅛ inches square, made of pitch and horsehair.

These balls, called qöonah, are described as follows by the collector, Rev. H. R. Voth:

One of the principal sports of the Hopi, in which they indulge every few days in the spring, is a football race, in which the men from different kivas participate and in which balls like these specimens are used. They are made of pitch and horsehair, to which sometimes a little rabbit fur and a few hairs growing over the big toe of men who are known as specially fast runners are added. These toe hairs are chosen because the ball is kicked with the point of the moccasin. The horsehair is taken from fast horses. The racers start on one side of the mesa, each group kicking before them their own ball around the mesa point, ascending on the opposite side. At each succeeding race the circuit is increased, until it reaches a length of from 8 to 10 miles.

Mr Voth informed the writer that the balls are distinguished by having the mark of the kiva to which they belong painted on one side.

FIG. 901. Kicking balls; dimensions, 2 inches square; Hopi Indians, Oraibi, Arizona; cat. no. 38705, Free Museum of Science and Art, University of Pennsylvania.

HOPI. Oraibi, Arizona. (Cat. no. 38705, Free Museum of Science and Art, University of Pennsylvania.) Two black cubes made of hair and piñon gum, with rounded corners, about 2 inches square (figure 901). Collected by the writer in 1901.

They were described as sunkoiungat, footballs, and were used in the spring of the year.

———— Walpi, Arizona. (Cat. no. 38622, Free Museum of Science and Art, University of Pennsylvania.)
Ball of hard white clay stone, 2¼ inches in diameter. Collected by the writer in 1901.

Mr A. M. Stephen in his unpublished manuscript mentions " kicking a nodule ahead during a run; " Hopi, wunpaya nanamüiniwa; Tewa, tibi kwanwino. In his diary he says:

Monday, March 20 [1893] : A cold, blustering day and not many want na-na'-mü-i-nĭ-wa. Still there are a few from each kiva. They ran at usual time and place.

Tuesday, March 21: Last night was rainy and to-day is cloudy, foggy, and showery. The decorations of the different kivas engaged in the na-na'-mü-i-nĭ-wa, I should think, must have been originally of ceremonial significance, but I do not find anyone who can enlighten me on that side. The racers run in

the valley. The women watch the varying positions of the men of the different kivas. When the men are clustered together kicking the nodules, others on the outside of the hurdle watch their legs and distinguish the nodules as kicked.

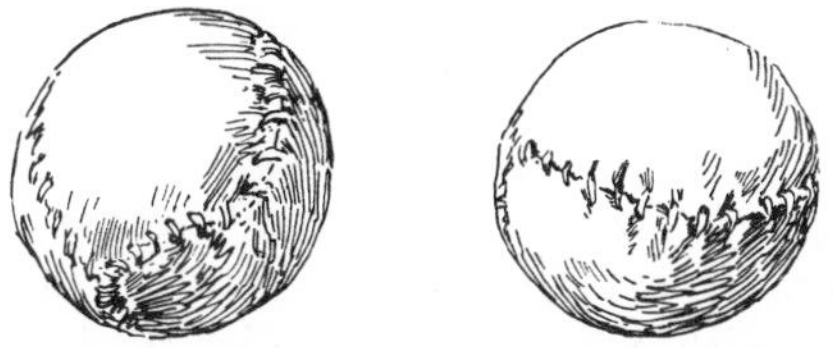

FIG. 902. Footballs; diameter, 4½ inches; Mono Indians, Madera county, California; cat. no. 71440, Field Columbian Museum.

The name of the stone nodule he gives as küüñü; to kick the nodule, wiñpa or wüñpa.

MONO. Hooker cove, Madera county, California. (Cat. no. 71440, Field Columbian Museum.)
Two buckskin-covered balls (figure 902) filled with hair, 4½ inches in diameter. Collected by Dr J. W. Hudson, who describes them as a pair of balls for the ball race.

Two balls are used. They are sometimes kicked as far as 15 miles.

Tobikhar (Gabrieleños). Los Angeles county, California.

Hugo Ried [a] says:

Football was played by children and by those swift of foot. Betting was indulged in by the spectators.

TANOAN STOCK

Tewa. Hano, Arizona. (Free Museum of Science and Art, University of Pennsylvania.)

Cat. no. 38617. Two wooden cylinders (figure 903) about 1 inch in diameter and 3¼ inches long, painted black. One slightly smaller in the diameter than the other. Collected by the writer in 1901.

The Hopi name of these sticks was given to the collector as kohoumpaiah. The large one was designated as yasako kohoumpaiah and the smaller as chihoiya kohoumpaiah. They were described as used in a racing game by two men, who kick them and run down the trail in the woman's dance, majowtikiwe, in July.

Fig. 903.   Fig. 904.

FIG. 903. Kicking billets; length, 3¼ inches; Tewa Indians, Hano, Arizona; cat. no. 38617, Free Museum of Science and Art, University of Pennsylvania.
FIG. 904. Slinging ball; diameter of ball, 3¼ inches; Tewa Indians, Hano, Arizona; cat. no. 38619, Free Museum of Science and Art, University of Pennsylvania.

In the summer of 1905 the writer obtained a single kicking stick from the Tewa at Hano. It was painted red. He was told only one was used. They called it pai-kweh-beh, and gave the Walpi name for the stick as ko-ho-koing-i.

Cat. no. 38620, 38621. Two balls of altered peridotite, apparently approximating closely to serpentine, 2 inches in diameter.

Cat. no. 38623. Balls of iron concretion, slightly shaped, 2⅜ inches in diameter.

Collected by the writer in 1901.

Cat. no. 38619. A ball (figure 904), 3½ inches in diameter, covered with a piece of an old stocking, blackened, and having a braided wool cord, 10 inches in length, with a knot at the end, attached.

This was collected by the writer in 1901, to whom it was described as used in a game in which the contestants lie on their backs and sling the ball backward overhead. In A. M. Stephen's unpublished manuscript, he refers to a game with " a small nodule in a sling fastened to the great toe; player lies on back and kicks or slings it backward overhead;" Hopi, süñü wûñpa; Tewa, konlo kwebe.

---

[a] Account of the Indians of Los Angeles Co., Cal. Bulletin of the Essex Institute, v. 17, p. 18, Salem, 1885.

Dr J. Walter Fewkes,[a] in his account of the Hopi Powamu, describes a curious game of ball called sunwuwinpa played by the kiva chief and the Hehea katcinas. The ball is attached to a looped string. The player lies on his back and, passing the loop over the great toe, projects the ball back over his head. The slinging-ball game would appear to be the clown's travesty of the kicked-stick race.

TEWA. Santa Clara, New Mexico.

Mr T. S. Dozier writes: [b]

The game of the kicked stick, still played at Zuñi, has been discontinued at the Tewa pueblos for some years. This is a game of sacrifice as well as of wager, and would have to be performed at the latter pueblos with too much publicity, owing to the encroachment of the settlers on all sides; the course of the race, taking Santa Clara for an example, could be preserved on the lands of the pueblo, but to the north, in accordance with the old bounds, would have to pass through or beyond thickly settled villages to the north of Española, then it would cross the tracks of the Denver and Rio Grande Railroad, and there would be one continuous obstruction of houses and fenced fields on the homestretch toward the south.

Fig. 905.   Fig. 906.

FIG. 905. Wooden kicking ball; diameter, 3⅜ inches; Cocopa Indians, Sonora, Mexico; cat. no. 152694, United States National Museum.

FIG. 906. Stone kicking ball; diameter, 2⅜ inches; Maricopa Indians, Arizona; cat. no. 2925, Brooklyn Institute Museum.

YUMAN STOCK

COCOPA. Lower Colorado river, Sonora, Mexico. (Cat. no. 152694, United States National Museum.)

Ball of hard wood (figure 905), almost perfectly spherical, and highly polished by use; diameter, 3⅜ inches. Collected by Dr Edward Palmer, who describes it as a football.

MARICOPA. Arizona. (Cat. no. 2925, Brooklyn Institute Museum.) Stone ball (figure 906), 2⅜ inches in diameter.

Collected in 1904 by Mr Louis L. Meeker, who describes the ball under the name of ho nyavik as kicked between goals in a game similar to shinny.

---

[a] Tusayan Katcinas. Fifteenth Annual Report of the Bureau of Ethnology, p. 290, 1897.

[b] Some Tewa Games. Unpublished MS. in the library of the Bureau of American Ethnology.

MOHAVE.   Fort Mohave, Arizona.   (Cat. no. 60267, Field Columbian Museum.)

Ball of mesquite wood, 2½ inches in diameter.

Collected by Mr John J. McKoin, who describes it as used in a game of football, ooy yank:

This game is played with a mesquite ball, about 2 inches in diameter. This ball is called coon ya va. The players wager beads, ponies, wives, blankets, etc. The game is played by two persons, each having a ball. A line is marked out upon the ground and each player puts his ball upon this line, placing them about 5 or 6 feet apart. Then they take positions 8 or 10 feet behind the balls. Each player has a second, who stands behind his principal and follows him throughout the play. These seconds give the player a signal to begin the play. The players then rush forward, each to his own ball, pushes his foot under it and tosses it as far as he can. He continues this performance until he reaches a goal, previously agreed upon and marked, 1 or 2 miles from the starting point. Upon reaching this goal the players turn and play back to the starting point. The one who first puts his ball over the mark is the winner and takes the stakes.

Fig. 907.   Fig. 908.

FIG. 907. Wooden kicking ball; diameter, 2¼ inches; Mohave Indians, Arizona; cat. no. 9980, United States National Museum.
FIG. 908. Wooden kicking ball; diameter, 3¼ inches; Yuma Indians, Fort Yuma, California; cat. no. 63347, Field Columbian Museum.

————— Colorado river, Arizona.   (Cat. no. 9980, United States National Museum.)

Wooden ball (figure 907), rudely carved and slightly flattened; diameter, 2½ inches. Described by the collector, Dr Edward Palmer, as a football.

YUMA.   Fort Yuma, San Diego county, California.   (Cat. no. 63347, Field Columbian Museum.)

Cottonwood ball (figure 908), 3¼ inches in diameter, designated by the collector, Mr S. C. Simms, as a football, esor.

ZUÑIAN STOCK

ZUÑI.   Zuñi, New Mexico.   (United States National Museum.)

Billets of hard wood, in pairs, one of each pair with a band of red paint in the middle and the other with bands at both ends and the middle.

Cat. no. 69273a.   Two billets, 3¾ inches long, 1⅛ inches in diameter.

Cat. no. 69273*b*. Two billets (figure 909), 4½ inches long, seven-eighths of an inch in diameter.

Cat. no. 69274. Two billets, 4 inches long, five-eighths of an inch in diameter.

Cat. no. 69275. Two billets, 6 inches long, one-half inch in diameter.

Cat. no. 69276. Two billets (figure 910), 5 inches long, three-eighths of an inch in diameter.

These are used in the kicked-stick race. They were collected by the late Col. James Stevenson.

Mr F. W. Hodge [a] describes the kicked-stick race as follows:

When the Sun Priest announces the arrival of planting time, and the herald proclaims from the house-tops that the planting has been done, the seasons for foot-racing in Zuñi are at hand.

The first races of the year, while interesting ceremonially, are by no means so exciting as those which follow later in the season when the planting is finished. These preliminary races are over a short course and are participated in by a representative of each of the six estufas. Six prayer-plumes and an

Fig. 909.   Fig. 910.

FIG. 909. Kicking billets; length, 4½ inches; Zuñi Indians, Zuñi, New Mexico; cat. no. 69273*b*, United States National Museum.

FIG. 910. Kicking billets; length, 5 inches; Zuñi Indians, Zuñi, New Mexico; cat. no. 69276, United States National Museum.

equal number of race-sticks are made by the Priests of the Bow, the latter of which are placed in the trail about 2 miles from the starting point. When the time for the race has been decided upon, which may not be until three or four days after the race-sticks have been deposited by the priests, the six representatives of the estufas run to the point where they are, and each man finds and kicks one of the sticks in a small circle homeward. This race is a contest between the six individuals comprising the racing party, and no betting is engaged in.

The great races of Zuñi, and those in which the chief interest is centered, occur after the planting—the time when nearly all the men are at leisure. In selecting the participants in these races, the swiftest-footed of the young men of the northern half of the pueblo are matched against those of the southern, or of the western half against the eastern. The number of racers on a side varies from three to six, and the degree of interest taken in the contest depends upon the reputation of those engaged in it, and particularly upon the extent to which betting has been indulged in.

As soon as the choice of sides has been made, the wagering begins, and increases with good-natured earnestness until the time for the foot-race arrives. Every available hide and pelt is brought to light from beneath the piles of stores secreted in the back rooms and cellars, to be converted into cash or gorgeously colored calico, and the demand upon the trader for goods is unequaled except

[a] A Zuñi Foot-race. The American Anthropologist, v. 3, p. 227, 1890

when a great dance is approaching. Money, silver belts, bracelets and rings, shell necklaces, turquoises, horses, sheep, blankets, in fact anything and everything of value to the Indian, are offered by a resident of one side of the pueblo in support of his favorites against something of equal value held by a champion of the opposing side.

On the evening of the day before a long race takes place, the participants repair to a secluded spot in one of the mesas some miles from the village, where a hole, a foot or two in depth, is excavated, in which is deposited, with due ceremony, a quantity of sacred meal and two cigarettes made of native tobacco (ah-na-té) rolled in the husk of corn. When this portion of the ceremony has been concluded and the hole filled, the Indians move away for a short distance and sit for a while without speaking above a whisper, when they start for the pueblo. On their way should a roosting bird become frightened and take flight, or the hoot of an owl be heard, the sign is a warning to defer the race. But if lightning be seen or a shooting-star observed, the omen is considered a favorable one and the race takes place on the day following.

The racers are greeted on their return by a priest who offers a blessing. A single cigarette is made and passed around among the number, after which one of them recites a prayer. The preparatory ceremonies being now completed, the racers retire into the house of the priest, who extends his hospitality until after the event. The following morning, the day of the race, the runners arise even earlier than usual, take a short run, and return to await the time appointed to start. In the meanwhile they make bets with one another or with anyone who may happen in. About an hour before starting they partake sparingly of paper bread (hé-we) soaked in water, after which they doff their every-day apparel and substitute breech-cloths, the color of which is either entirely white or red, dependent upon the side to which the wearer belongs. To prevent the hair being an impediment to progress, it is carefully and compactly arranged above the forehead in a knot by one of the Priests of the Bow. To this knot or coil an arrow-point is invariably attached as a symbol of flight, or perhaps as a charm to insure to the runner the swiftness of the arrow. The arrow-points having been thus placed, the same priest, holding in each hand a turkey-quill, pronounces a blessing and leads his charges to the starting point.

Without, the excitement is intense. The women discuss with one another the probable outcome, and engage in betting as spiritedly as the men. Here may be seen a fellow who has wagered all he possesses—if he wins, so much the better, and if all is lost he takes the consequences philosophically and trusts success will visit him next time. Another may be seen who has ventured all his own property as well as that of his wife, and if he fails to win a divorce is imminent. The small boys also are jubilant. When the race was first proposed they sought their companions, selected sides, and staked their small possessions on the results of their own races with a zeal that would have become their fathers.

The articles that are to change hands at the close of the race are placed in a heap in the center of the large dance-court near the old Spanish church. Around this pile of valuables a crowd gathers, on horse-back or afoot, to take advantage of the few moments that remain in which to make their final wagers. As the runners emerge from the house under the leadership of the priest, they are followed by the excited crowd to the smooth ground on the opposite side of the river, from whence they usually start.

A Zuñi foot-race is not entirely a contest of swift-footedness, although much, of course, depends upon that accomplishment. In preparing for the start the members of one side arrange themselves several paces apart in an irregular line in the course to be pursued, in such a manner that the movements of their leader at the point of starting can be readily seen, those of the contesting party posting themselves in a similar line a few feet away. The leader of each side places across his foot at the base of the toes a rounded stick measured by the size of the middle finger. Just before the signal is given to proceed a mounted priest goes ahead, sprinkling the trail with sacred meal.

At the signal each of the two leaders kicks his stick as far in advance as possible, when the racer of his side who happens to be nearest its place of falling immediately rushes for and again kicks it, his companions running ahead in order to be in readiness to send the stick on its further flight. This operation is continued throughout the entire course, the racers in the rear each time running in advance as rapidly as possible that they may kick the stick as often as their companions.

Not infrequently the first kicking of the sticks sends them flying over the heads of the second and even the third racers in advance, and they fall near each other. The excitement at this occurrence is very great, for none of the dozen young men spare themselves in scrambling over and pushing one another in order to secure the stick and send it on its course. No difficulty is experienced by a racer in recognizing the stick of his party, that belonging to one side having a band of red paint around the center, the other an additional, though narrower, stripe around both ends.

Considering the extreme lightness of the race-stick, the distance which it is sent by a single kick, or rather toss, with the toes is remarkable. Very often a stick is raised aloft in this manner about 30 feet and falls at least a hundred feet from the point at which it was lifted. Nor is the distance which the stick is sent the only requisite of success. Sometimes a narrow, sandy trail bordered by weeds is to be traversed, and a careless kick will probably send the stick into the brush or into an arroyo, where great difficulty may be experienced in regaining it, since a racer is never allowed to touch a stick with his hands until he reaches the goal. Again, throughout the rough race-trail the character of the land surface varies greatly, and long stretches of deep sand alternate with rocky passes, arroyos, and hills clothed with scrub timber or sagebrush. Indeed, smooth ground is seldom met with over the entire course of 25 miles.

Accompanying the participants may always be seen two or three hundred equestrians—those who, more than any others, are interested in the outcome of the race by reason of the extent of their prospective gains or losses. When one side follows closely in the track of its opponent, the horsemen all ride together; but when, by reason of accident or inferiority in speed, a party falls considerably in the rear, the horsemen separate to accompany their respective favorites. If the season is dry, the dust made by loping horses is blinding; but the racers continue, apparently as unmindful of the mud-coating that accumulates on their almost nude, perspiring bodies as if they were within but a few steps of victory.

On they go from the point of starting over the southern hills, thence eastward to Thunder Mountain, along the western base of which they proceed to the basaltic rocks through which the Zuñi river runs. Keeping close to the mesas that form the northern boundary of the valley, the racers cross the river on their return at a point about 2 miles west of the pueblo, whence they continue to the western end of the southern hills first crossed. These having been skirted, they pass over the low, sandy corn-fields to the goal, followed by the yelling horsemen, who wave yards of brilliant calico as they dash forward with the final spurt of the racers. When the goal is reached, the first racer of the winning side takes the stick into his hands for the first time since starting. With renewed energy the individual members of the successful party put forth every remaining effort to be the first to arrive at the central plaza of the pueblo. He who gains it first is considered the superior racer of all, and his honor is indeed well earned. Running as rapidly as possible once around the heap of stores, at the same time breathing from his hand the " breath of life," the victor, stick in hand, continues at a running pace to his home.

Curiosity prompted me to note the time occupied in performing this feat, which was found to be exactly two hours.

Like almost every undertaking of the Zuñi, the foot-race has more or less of a religious significance, as will be seen from the initiatory ceremonies. The opposing racers who await the signal to give the stick its first toss place turquoises or shell beads beneath the stick that they may be sacrificed at the first lifting of the foot. In the belief of the Zuñi the stick has a tendency to draw the racers on, and as long as it can be kept in advance their success is, of course, assured. The cause thus follows the effect in the same manner as it does when in Zuñiland the summer comes because the butterflies appear, and it departs because the birds take their flight.

Training for a Zuñi foot-race begins at childhood. At almost any time a naked youngster of four or five years may be seen playing at kicking-the-stick outside the door of his home, or, if a year or two older, coming from the cornfield—where he has been dutifully engaged in frightening off the crows—tossing the stick as far as his little feet will allow him.

Mr John G. Owens [a] wrote the following account of the same game:

Ti-kwa-we, or Game of the Kicked Stick.[b]—This is the great national game of Zuñi. Among Zuñi sports it ranks as baseball does among our own. It is indulged in by almost the whole male population, from boys of 5 or 6 to men of 40. Any evening of the summer one can see crowds of twenty or thirty boys skirting the southern hills and kicking the stick. Practiced thus during eight months of the year, they have an especial occasion when they contest for the championship, and this is one of the great jubilees of the tribe. Although the women do not take part, yet they show equal interest with the men and become as much excited.

The time of holding this contest is usually in the spring, between the planting of the wheat and the corn. The Priest of the Bow makes six prayer-plumes and six race-sticks. The prayer-plumes consist of small sticks with the white feathers from the tail of a certain species of hawk tied to one side ; the race-sticks are about the size of the middle finger. The priest then takes these sticks and places them on the trail toward the south, and for four days they remain there untouched. At the end of this time he, and any others who wish to join in the race, will run out to where the sticks have been placed, and as they arrive they breathe on their hands and then kick the sticks home, making a circle of 2 or 3 miles.

Four days later a representative of each clan, each with a picture of his clan painted on his back, will run out in much the same manner. By this time most of the people have returned from their wheat-planting and the ti-kwa-we is in order. At present there are six estufas in Zuñi—Ha-e-que, Ha-cher-per-que,

_____

[a] Some Games of the Zuñi. Popular Science Monthly, v. 39, p. 42, New York, 1891.

[b] This game was described by Mr F. W. Hodge in The Anthropologist for July, 1890. I have thought well to repeat it here in connection with the other games, and also to make some corrections and to add several points not mentioned in that article.

Choo-per-que, Moo-ha-que, O-ha-que, and Uts-ann-que. The contest lies between the members of these different estufas, and not between the members of the different clans or parts of the pueblo, as has been stated by some writers.

Whatever estufas wish to contest select their men. When the men have been selected it is announced in the evening from the house-tops. This generally takes place three or four days prior to the race. This race is generally held at Zuñi, but may be held at one of the farming pueblos, as Pescado, Ojo Caliente, or Nutria; in any case it is estufa against estufa. On the evening of the day before the race each side sends for a Priest of the Bow. Upon arrival he puts into the mouth of each one a piece of glass about 1 inch long; and with some sacred meal, taken from his pouch, he paints a mask on each one's face, then blesses them, and they repair to the hills 3 or 4 miles distant. They depart in absolute silence. Not a word may they speak unless they hear or frighten some wild animal in front of them. If the sound comes from behind, it is considered an ill omen. Having reached the hills, they dig a hole about the length of the arm and deposit in it some sacred meal, native tobacco, hewe, shells, and other things held valuable by the Zuñis, and then retire a short distance and do not speak above a whisper. In a little while one will start for the pueblo, saying nothing, and the rest follow in single file. As they return, any manifestation of power, as thunder or lightning, is considered a good omen, as it will make them strong.

The priest who blessed them before they started awaits their return and accompanies them to the house of one of the racers or that of any member of the same estufa. As they reach the door of the house, those within say, "Have you come?" "We have," they reply. "Come in and sit down." The priest then blesses them, and a single cigarette is made of native tobacco and passed among the number. Then they retire for the night. Next morning everything is alive in Zuñi. Indeed, for several days past the whole population has been somewhat excited over the coming event. Everyone takes sides, from the gray-haired old warrior, who believes the ti-kwa-we to be the greatest game ever held, to the blushing maiden, whose lover is one of the contestants. Excitement runs high, and the gambling disposition of the Indian has its fullest encouragement. The small boy meets his playmate and stakes all his possessions. The veteran gambler once more tries the turn of fortune, and to counteract his heavier betting he makes a long prayer to Ah-ai-u-ta or plants an additional plume. The contestants themselves engage in betting, and every conceivable thing of value to an Indian is either carried to the plaza, south of the old Spanish church, where it is put up against something of equal value held by an opponent, or is hurried off to the trader's store and turned into money. Ponies, sheep, goats, money, beads, bracelets, all are wagered. Sometimes also they sell the race. This is not generally admitted by the Zuñis, but I have it on good authority that it has been done.

The day for the race has arrived; the runners have been up since early morning, and have taken a spin over part of the course. During the morning nearly all the members of the estufa drop in to tell them how much they have wagered on their success and to encourage them. About an hour before the time to start they eat a little hewe, or paper bread, soaked in water. Hewe is one of the chief breadstuffs of the Zuñis, and a good hewe-maker is in reputation throughout the tribe as a good pastry cook is among us. Hewe is made from corn batter spread with the hand on a large flat stone over a slow fire. It takes but a moment to bake it, is almost as thin as paper, very crisp, and will vary in color according to the color of the corn used. This repast of hewe is accompanied by a piece of humming-bird, as the flight of that bird is so very swift.

The runners then bathe in a solution made from a root called que-me-way. The time for the contest is at hand. The every-day attire is exchanged for the simple breech-clout. The hair is done up in a neat knot on the top of the head, and the priest pronounces a blessing as he fastens in it an arrow-point, the emblem of fleetness. He then places a pinch of ashes in front of each racer, and, standing before him, holding an eagle-wing in each hand, he first touches the ashes with the tips of the wings and then brushes the racer from head to foot. Then turning to the north, he touches the wings together and says a prayer, the same to the west, south, east, the earth, and sky. I suppose the idea of the Zuñi in this to be, that as he has sent a prayer to the four points of the compass, the earth, and sky, he has cut off every possible source of misfortune and danger.

Everything being now ready, the priest leads his favorites to the course across the river. Excitement in the pueblo has reached its height; the most venturesome are offering big odds in the plaza, and now all assemble to see the start.

Should a side be at all doubtful of its success in the race, an old woman is procured to sit and pray during the entire race. She sits in the middle of the room. The racers sweep the floor around her and then pile up everything that is used about the fire, such as pokers, ladles, stirring-sticks, and even the stones used to support the pots during cooking: these are to make their opponents warm; also the mullers with which they grind the corn, and the brooms: these will make them tired. A woman is chosen rather than a man, because she is not so fleet of foot. . . .

As each side is brought to the course the priest gives a parting blessing, and the runners take their positions opposite their opponents in single file along the course. The tik-wa, or stick to be kicked, is about the size of the middle finger. That belonging to one side has its ends painted red and that of the other side its center painted red, so that they may be easily distinguished. The rear man of each file places the tik-wa across the base of his toes and sprinkles a little sacred meal upon it. Surrounding the racers will be three or four hundred mounted Indians dressed in the gayest colors. All is now ready; each rider has his eye on his favorite side, an old priest rides in advance and sprinkles sacred meal over the course, the starters kick the sticks, and the wildest excitement prevails. As each racer left his home he put into his mouth two shell beads— the one he drops as a sacrifice as he starts, the other when he has covered about one-half the course. The stick is tossed rather than kicked, and a good racer will toss it from 80 to 100 feet. Over the heads of the runners it goes and falls beyond the first man. He simply points to where it lights, and runs on. The next man tries to kick it, but should he fail to get under it he goes on, and the next man takes it. The race is not to the swift alone, although this has much to do with it. The stick can in no case be touched with anything but the foot, and should it fall into a cactus bush, a prairie-dog hole, or an arroyo much valuable time is lost in getting it out. Not infrequently it happens that one side will be several miles in advance of the other when the stick falls into some unnoticed hole. The wild and frenzied yelling which takes place as those who were behind come up and pass can only be imagined and not described. So skill in tossing it plays a prominent part. On, on they go to the southern hills, east to Ta-ai-yal-lo-ne, north to the mesas, follow these west for miles, then to the southern hills, and back again to the starting-point. The distance traversed is nearly 25 miles, and they pass over it in about two hours. Racing is indulged in by the excited horsemen as they approach the goal, and it is not unusual to see a pony drop over dead from exhaustion as they near the village. The successful runner crosses the river and runs around the heap of wagered goods near the church, then, taking up the tik-wa in his hands for the first time, he inhales, as he thinks, the spirit of the tik-wa, and thanks it for being so good to him. He then runs to his home, and, if he finds a woman awaiting him, hands the stick to her, who breathes on it twice, and he then does the same. Returning it to the woman, she places it in a basket which she has ready for it; and the next day one of the racers wraps it up with some sacred meal in a corn-husk and deposits it about 6 inches below the surface of the ground in an arroyo, where it will be washed away by the rains. Meanwhile the winners have claimed their stakes, and, should another estufa have a set of men to put up, the winners of the first race must compete with them until all have had a chance, and the great Zuñi races are over for that year.

Mrs Matilda Coxe Stevenson [a] says:

There are but two exclusively religious games of tíkwawe played annually. In one, members of the kíwiᵗsiwe (chambers dedicated to anthropomorphic worship) play, and in the other the clans take part. Both of these races are for rains to water the earth that the crops may grow. They take place some days previous to corn planting, which usually occurs from the 10th to the 15th day of May.

Other games of tíkwawe may occur at any time when not forbidden by the retreat of the Ah'shiwanni for rain.

Tíkwanĕ race of the Kíwiᵗsiwe: The Ah'pí'ᵗläshíwanni (Bow priesthood), or warriors, convene at the full moon of April and remain in session throughout the night. On the following morning they prepare télikyináwe (prayer-plumes). These offerings to the Gods of War are deposited at noon the same day at a shrine north of the village. This shrine is on the ground supposed to have been occupied as the home of the Gods of War during their stay at Ítiwanna (the site of the present Zuñi)'. The other prayer-plumes are made into five ᵗkáĕtchiwe (singular, ᵗkáĕtchinĕ) or groups of télikyináwe bound together at the base. The sticks of four groups are colored black, and are offerings to the deceased members of the Ah'pí'ᵗläshíwanni. The ᵗkáĕtchiwe are deposited at midnight on the four sides of the village by such members of the Ah'pí'ᵗläshíwanni as may be designated by the elder brother Bow-priest, or director of the organization, in excavations carefully concealed by stone ledges, set in plaster, which extend along the exterior of houses, furnishing seats for those who like to sit out in the balmy afternoon of a New Mexican winter or to enjoy the cool breezes after sunset in summer time. These ledges are identical with those before many other Zuñi dwellings. The depositors of the plumes know just which slab to remove in order to have access to the depository. The fifth group consists of two télikyináwe, one of which is dotted with the various colors for the zenith, the other is black to represent the nadir. These are offerings to the Sä'lämobia, certain warrior gods of the zenith and the nadir. This group is planted in an excavation, also concealed by a slab seat, on the west side of Síaátéwita, or sacred dance plaza. After the placing of the télikyináwe the Ah'pí'ᵗläshíwanni continue their songs and ceremonies in the ceremonial chamber until sunrise, and soon afterward the elder brother Bow-priest announces from a house-top that the people of the kíwiᵗsiwe will run in four days.

The director of each kíwiᵗsina (plural kíwiᵗsiwe) gives formal notice to his people,[b] and the young men who wish to take part in the race appear at the

---

[a] Zuñi Games. American Anthropologist, n. s., v. 5, p. 469, 1903.

[b] Every male receives involuntary and voluntary initiation into the Kótikili, a fraternity associated with anthropomorphic worship, becoming allied with one of the six kíwiᵗsiwe.

appointed time. Those from the Héiwa (north), Héᵗkapawa (nadir), and Chú-pawa (south) kíwiᵗsiwe represent the side of the elder God of War, while those from the Múhe‘wa (west), Óhe‘wa (east), and Úpᵗsänáwa (zenith) kíwiᵗsiwe represent the side of the younger God of War. After an early breakfast (the runners having exercised before the meal) nothing more is eaten during the day but crushed héwe (wafer-like bread) in water.

In the afternoon the first body of Ah'shiwanni ᵃ (the elder brother Bow-priest being also Rain-priest of the nadir) proceed about a mile south of the village, over the road leading to the present home of the Gods of War, and here the elder brother Bow-priest lays upon the ground a láshowaně (one or more plumes tied together), composed of two upper wing-feathers of a bird called shóᵗkapiso,ᵇ and the younger brother Bow-priest places a similar láshowaně on the ground and west of the other, the distance between the two láshowaně being the length of the extended arms from finger tip to finger tip. The Ah'shiwanni group west and the Ah'piᵗläshíwanni east of the plumes; the elder brother Bow-

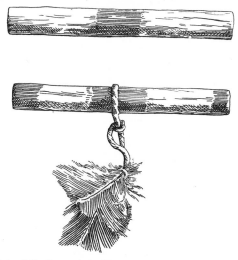

Fɪɢ. 911. Kicking billets of the Bow-priests (the plumes are attached only when the tíkwawe are made as offerings to the Gods of War); Zuñi Indians, Zuñi, New Mexico; from Mrs Stevenson.

priest standing with his fellows of the Ah'piᵗläshíwanni, a line is made south of the plumes by drawing, or rather pushing, the foot over the earth from west to east.

Six members of the Ah'piᵗläshíwanni selected by the elder brother Bow-priest have each a tíkwaně (figure 911), made by himself. Three of the tík-wawe are colored black at either end and midway, indicating the sticks of the elder God of War; and three are painted black midway only for those of the younger God of War.

The six warriors, clad only in breechcloths, stand by the line, the one at the east end having the tíkwaně of the elder God of War, the man at the right having that of the younger God of War, and so they alternate down the line.

ᵃ Mrs Stevenson designates the Ah'shiwanni of the six regions, whose prototypes are the members of the Council of the Gods, as the first body of Ah'shiwanni. There are a number of other Ah'shiwanni in Zuñi.

ᵇ A bird, as the Zuñi say, which flies but never tires. Mrs Stevenson failed to obtain a specimen, but she is almost sure it is a species of hawk.

Each warrior places his right foot on the line and the stick across the foot near the toes; he then sprinkles meal upon the stick and prays for rain and for success in the race. The Ah'shiwanni also sprinkle meal and pray for rain. In the meantime the runners gather at the base, which is south of the pueblo and just across the river which flows by the village.

The racers (the number is not limited) wear only kilts, and the long hair is drawn back and tucked into the handkerchief, or banda, at the back, the hair being brought over the band and tucked in from the top. A member of the Bow-priesthood marks off the line on the earth, similar to the one described, upon which the runners take position, facing south. The warrior who stands some feet beyond the line carries a bow and arrows in his left hand and an arrow in his right. He directs the runners in the course they are to take, and, facing east, prays and sprinkles meal eastward. The meal is thrown four times, the fourth being the signal for the start. No word is spoken. The course is south to the group of Ah'shiwanni and Ah'pi''läshíwanni—a course that must never be deviated from in these races, as this is the road of the Gods of War. On reaching the body awaiting them, each runner passes between the two láshowawe previously described. Bending and extending his hands toward the plumes, he brings his hands to his mouth and draws in a breath from the plumes, that he may run like the shó'kapiso, which flies but never tires. The runners do not halt, but pass right on. Each Pi''läshíwanni in the line calls out the name of the kíwi'sina he represents as he kicks the tíkwanĕ into the air. The runners of each kíwi'sina at once look to their appropriate sticks. They are followed by the first body of Ah'shiwanni and Ah'pi''läshíwanni, except the elder and younger brother Bow-priests. The Ah'shiwanni and Ah'pi''läshíwanni, however, do not attempt to keep pace with the runners, who move in a circuit, but return instead to the láshowawe, which are guarded by the elder and younger brother Bow-priests, passing between the latter and on to the village.

The tíkwawe are kicked into the river, to go to Kó'hluwaláwa (abiding place of the Council of the Gods), and the runners hasten to their homes. The ceremony of washing the hair of the runners occurs before the race and also on the morning after the race.

The younger brother Bow-priest makes an excavation the depth of his arm, and the two láshowawe are deposited therein, with prayers by the elder and younger brother Bow-priests to the úwannami (rain makers) for rains. These two now proceed to the base, where the large crowd gathered to greet the returning runners still remains.

At this point the elder brother Bow-priest cries out that the ä'notiwe (clans) will run in four days.

The race of the ä'notiwe may occur simultaneously at one or more of the farming districts, where most of the Zuñi at this season are gathered. It also takes place in Zuñi, provided a Pí''läshíwanni is present to start the racers. The observances previous to the race of the ä'notiwe are much the same as those for the race of the kíwi'siwe. A member of each clan makes the tíkwanĕ to be used by the racers of his clan, and he is free to select that of either one of the Gods of War. The runners dress as on the previous occasion, and their hair is done up in the same manner. The clan symbol is painted on the breast of each runner, and that of the paternal clan is painted on the back. Those of Píchikwe (*Cornus stolonifera*) clan have a conventional design of the dogwood, including the roots, on the breast, and below a macaw or raven with the head pointing to the left, according to the division of the clan to which the man belongs.

The Pí''läshíwanni makes a line near the river bank, south of the village, by drawing or pushing his foot over the earth, as has been described, and the runners stand upon the line, facing south, each clan being together, the runner at the west end of the line placing the tíkwanĕ across his foot, as before noted. The Pí''läshíwanni stands in advance of the runners, and, facing east, prays and throws the meal four times eastward, the fourth time, as before, being the signal for starting. The same course is followed as that pursued by the people of the kíwi'siwe. Each of these races covers only about 4 miles.

No thought of betting is in the Zuñi mind when these races for rains occur. While deep interest is exhibited by the women, as well as by the men, in these purely religious races, the real enthusiasm occurs at the time of the betting races, when about 25 miles are covered.

The betting race is not confined to the kíwi'siwe, nor to any section of the village, although statements to the contrary have been made. A man approaches another with his plan for a race, and if it be acceptable to the other a race is arranged for. It is heralded from the housetop by a civil officer of the village, who shouts, "To-morrow there will be a race!" Those to be associated with the race gather at the houses of the two managers. The swiftest runners are sure to be present. After some discussion the originator of the race visits the house of the other manager and learns from him how many runners he will have in the contest. He then returns to his house and selects the same number for his side. The number varies from three to six on a side, one side representing the elder, the other the younger, God of War.

Each manager calls at the house of one of the first body of Ah'shiwanni—those of the north and the zenith excepted—and announces, "My boys will run to-morrow. You will come to my house to-night." The friends of each party gather at the two houses, the runners being on one side of the room, the friends on the opposite side. When the Shíwanni (sing. for Ah'shiwanni) bearing a basket tray of broken héwe arrives, he takes his seat on his wadded blanket, the manager sitting opposite to him. The Shíwanni places the basket upon the floor and asks for corn-husks. Preparing as many husks as there are runners for the side, he sprinkles prayer-meal into each husk, and, after adding bits of white shell and turkis beads, folds it and lays it on the héwe in the tray. Raising the tray with both hands to his face, he prays for success, and, drawing four breaths from the contents of the tray, says, "Si" (Ready). The runners approach, the Shíwanni deposits a handful of broken héwe from the tray into the blanket supported by the left arm of each runner, and hands a corn-husk package to each. The body of runners who represent the elder God of War goes to a point north of the village; and the other goes south. An excavation the depth of an arm is made by an ancient corn-planter at each point, when each runner opens his husk package, deposits the contents in the excavation, and drops in the héwe as offerings to the Gods of War and the ancestors. The one who prepares the earth to receive the offerings covers the opening, leaving no trace of the excavation.

All now sit perfectly still and listen for sounds from the departed. When they hear any noise which they suppose comes from the dead, they are gratified, and say, "Éllakwa, nána" "(Thanks, grandfather)."

After walking a short distance they halt and wait again for some manifestation. Should they hear a few notes from the mocking bird, they know the race will be in favor first of one side and then of the other—uncertain until the end. If the bird sings much, they will meet with failure. If they hear an owl hoot, the race will be theirs.

The runners return to the houses which they left and retire for the remainder of the night in a large room, the family having withdrawn to another apartment. Sometimes a runner goes to an arroyo and deposits offerings of precious beads to the Gods of War, or to a locality where some renowned runner of the past was killed by an enemy, and, after offering food to the Gods of War, with a prayer for success in the race, he sits and eagerly listens for some sound from the deceased. After a time he moves a short distance and listens again. He then moves a third time and listens, and if he hears anything from the dead he is quite sure of success. If he hears the whistling of the wind he is also likely to meet with success, and if he hears an owl hoot his success is assured. In this event he imitates the owl during the race, which annoys the opposite side, for they know the reason for the owl-like cries.

At sunrise each runner carries a corn-husk containing bits of precious beads and meal a distance from the village and sprinkles the offering to the úwannam pí‘‘läshíwanni (deceased members of the Bow-priesthood) of the six regions, for success.

It is the custom for the runners to exercise for the race in the early morning, returning to the houses of the managers, where they eat a hearty breakfast; but they must not drink coffee, as this draught distends the stomach. After this early meal nothing is partaken except a small quantity of wafer-bread and water. They remain at the managers' houses until the hour for the race.

By afternoon the betting and excitement have increased until every available object of the bettors is placed in Téwita ‘hlánna (the large plaza). Crowds gather around the managers, who are busy looking after the stakes. Everything is wagered, from a silver button to a fine blanket. Yards of calico are brought out, silver belts and precious beads; in fact, all the possessions of many are staked, especially those of the old gamblers, who, having lost heavily in the gambling den, hope to regain their fortunes.

The objects are stacked in two heaps in Téwita ‘hlánna, the two managers having charge of arranging the articles. A blanket from one heap finds its counterpart in the other, and the two are placed together, forming the base of a third pile. Drawing in this way from the two piles is continued until they are consolidated into one great heap. Much of the forepart of the afternoon is consumed in this work. When the managers return to their houses and announce to the runners that the task of arranging the stakes is completed, the latter remove their clothing and, after donning a kilt of white cotton or some other light material, take medicine of the Shúmakwe fraternity into their mouths, eject it into their hands, and rub their entire bodies, that they may not be made tired from running. A piece of humming-bird medicine, consisting of a root, is passed around; each runner takes a bite, and, after chewing it, ejects it into his hands and rubs his body, that he may be swift like the bird.

The hair is brought forward and a Pí‘‘läshíwanni forms a long knob by folding the hair over and over and wrapping it with yarn. He then places an arrow point in the knot to insure fleetness; and lifting ashes with two eagle wing plumes, he passes them down either side of the body of each racer and sprinkles ashes to the six regions. This is for physical purification.

Medicine is sometimes put into the paint used on the tíkwanĕ, which for the betting races is painted red instead of black; and a bit of this paint is slipped under the nail of the index finger of the right hand. If a runner is observed to keep his thumb pressed to his finger, it is known that he has medicine under the nail, and those making the discovery are apt to bet high on that side, for they believe that the medicine will bring success. Failure in such cases is attributed to the bad heart of the runner.

The wives of the two Ah'shiwanni who were present on the previous night go each to the house visited by the husband and remain while the runners are absent. Several parcels, including two blankets, are removed from the heap in the plaza and carried to each house and deposited beside the woman for good luck to the runner.

The runners are accompanied to their base by their managers and Ah′pi‘‘läsh-
iwanni. Crowds gather. Every man who can obtain a horse is mounted. All
is excitement, the women's enthusiasm being almost equal to that of the men,
for each wife is interested in the side her husband has chosen, and every maiden
is interested in the side of her favorite admirer. While the men gather about
the runners as they prepare for the race, and follow them, the women must
content themselves in the village. The two tíkwawe designating the sides of the
elder and the younger God of War are made by the Pí‘‘läshíwanni of the side
of the second manager, and are carried by a runner of this party to the base,
where he holds the sticks out to the opposite side, one of the party taking the
tíkwaně of his choice. The racers do not form in regular line. Each leader
places the stick across his foot near the toes and sprinkles it with meal; then
they cry out, " Si! " "(Ready!)." The stick must not be touched with the hand
after it is placed on the foot. It is often thrown a long distance, and no matter
where it may rest it must be managed with the foot. There is nothing more
exciting to the Zuñi, except the scalp dance, than this game of tíkwaně. The
equestrians urge their ponies onward to keep pace with the racers, who run
southward over the road of the Gods of War for a distance, then around to the
east, crossing the river. On they go, keeping to the foot-hills.[a] Recrossing the
river several miles west of Zuñi, they bend around to the east, and return by
the southern road to the base, when the members of the successful party vie
with one another in reaching the great plaza, for he who is first to pass around
the heap of wagered articles is the hero of the hour. As they run around this
pool they extend their hands toward it and, bringing them to their mouths, draw
in a breath, and pass on to the house of the manager whence they started, where
the victor deposits the tíkwaně of his side in a basket of prayer-meal, while all
present make offerings of bits of precious beads in a basket.

The wife of the Shíwanni takes the hand of the victor and, standing, brings
her clasped hands four times before his mouth. Each time he draws a breath.
The waving of the hands four times is repeated before each runner, who draws
as many breaths.

After the prayers the victor empties the contents of the basket. which includes
the meal and bead offerings and the tíkwaně, into a corn-husk and carries it to
his home. After each runner returns to his home he drinks a quantity of warm
water as an emetic, and when relieved he retires for the night. It is not uncommon for a runner to be so affected by the race that the manipulations of a
masseuse (the Zuñi are experts in this practice) are necessary to restore him.
The following morning the head of each runner is washed in yucca suds, and
he bathes. After the morning meal the tíkwaně of the Elder God of War is
deposited, with the contents of the corn-husk carried by the runner from his
manager's house, at a shrine on Úhana-yäl′lanně (Wool mountain), while the
tíkwaně of the younger God of War and the other offerings are deposited on
Tówa-yäl′lanně (Corn mountain).

The most prominent religious positions do not debar men from taking part in

---

[a] There are six stone heaps which direct the runners in their course. These monuments, which are some 4 feet high, are supposed to have been made by direction of the
Gods of War, and are distinct from those made by men and women who whirl a stone
or bit of wood around the head in the left hand, from left to right, four times, and
throw it over the shoulder onto the heap, that the fatigue that would otherwise come
to the body may be cast into the stone or chip. The words expressed are " ᵗHlon yúteᵗ-
tchi hánasima tínatu " (" This place tired, unlucky, be settled "). These mounds are
supposed to have been begun by the Gods of War. Vases containing medicine of these
gods are believed to be buried beneath the mounds, though these objects are too sacred
to be commonly referred to.

these betting races. One of the fleetest as well as most enthusiastic runners of the present time is the kómosona (director-general) of the kíwi'siwe.

There are many informal games of tíkwanĕ in which young men hurriedly gather for sport, and sometimes a considerable stake is raised. One race observed by the writer, in which great enthusiasm was exhibited, began at 5 o'clock in the afternoon, the parties returning after 7. There were three racers on a side, the kómosona being one, but he lost on this occasion.

While there is much betting and considerable interest is manifested in these informal races, there is no ceremony associated with them. Each runner bets on his side. Outside parties bet one with another, one holding the stakes; or more frequently, a third party has charge of the stakes, which are heaped in the large plaza. Sometimes the articles are afterward carried to the kíwi'sina to which the successful party belongs, while again they pass to the winner in the plaza, he, in turn, dividing the profits among the runners of his side. While much interest prevails at the informal races, and great enjoyment is derived from them, the excitement is as nothing compared with that of the more formal affairs.

It is interesting to see the very young boys in their foot races and to observe how closely they follow their elders in the rules governing the stakes. Wagers are always made, as the races would be of little interest to the younger boys without the element of chance associated with them.

Beginning at so early an age, there is no wonder that these people develop into the swiftest of runners. The writer has never known the Zuñi to lose a foot-race with other Indians, nor with the champion runners of the troops at Fort Wingate, who sometimes enter into races with them. It is quite common for the Zuñi and Navaho to race. Though these races are always informal, the stakes are often large, and the Navaho leave their precious beads, silver belts, bridles, and valuable blankets behind them when they depart for the pueblo. Their love for gambling prevents them from learning lessons from sad experiences.

ZUÑI. Zuñi, New Mexico. (Cat. no. 4994, Brooklyn Institute Museum.)

Fifteen sticks (figure 912), 4½ inches in length, pieces of sapling with the bark on, this being cut with distinguishing marks. Collected by the writer in 1904.

These are special kicking sticks used in the clan races in the spring. At the sacred foot races at this season the estufas first compete, and four days afterward the clans. Each clan has its own stick, tikwawe, which is cut with a mark to distinguish it. Each clan is represented in this race by as many men as possible.

——— Zuñi, New Mexico. (Brooklyn Institute Museum.)

Cat. no. 3056. Water-worn pebble (figure 913), 3½ inches in length, which has been used as a pestle in a paint mortar.

It was collected in 1903 by the writer, to whom it was described as a kicking stone, atikwannai, originally used in racing, like the kicking stick.

Cat. no. 3064. Ring of twig (figure 914), wrapped with white cotton cord, 3 inches in diameter; and slender wooden rod (figure 915), 27½ inches in length, with a kind of knob at the end.

Collected by the writer in 1903. The following description was given: The game of tsi-koi ti-kwa-wai, or ring ti-kwa-wai, is played by women and Kayemashi at the Rain dance. They start in the

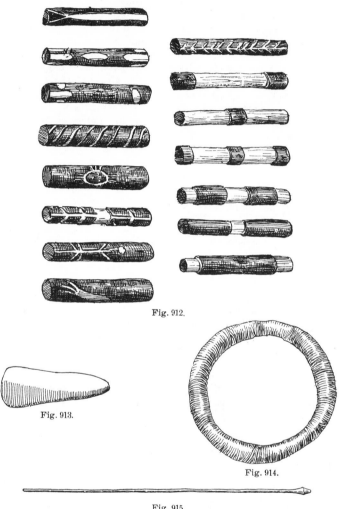

Fig. 912.

Fig. 913.

Fig. 914.

Fig. 915.

FIG. 912. Kicking billets used in clan races; length, 4¼ inches; Zuñi Indians, Zuñi, New Mexico; cat. no. 4994, Brooklyn Institute Museum.

FIG. 913. Kicking stone; length, 3½ inches; Zuñi Indians, Zuñi, New Mexico; cat. no. 3156, Brooklyn Institute Museum.

FIG. 914. Tossing ring for race game; diameter, 3 inches; Zuñi Indians, Zuñi, New Mexico; cat. no. 3064, Brooklyn Institute Museum.

FIG. 915. Tossing rod for race game; length, 27½ inches; Zuñi Indians, Zuñi, New Mexico; cat. no. 3064, Brooklyn Institute Museum.

middle plaza and run some three hundred or four hundred yards in a small circuit down to the Middle of the Earth and back to the plaza. The clowns use a regular kicking stick, only one, and the women use one ring. Each woman has a stick, tslam-mai. They play the game maybe once or twice during a summer. Its object is to cause rain. The game usually follows a dance, but if the cacique orders it, the women play the game without reference to the dance. It is sometimes played by men alone, and sometimes for money. Dick gave the name of this game as ya-mu-nai tsi-ko-nai or ya-mu-nai ti-kwa-wai.

Additional particulars concerning this game are furnished by Mrs Matilda Coxe Stevenson in her paper on Zuñi Games,[a] where she describes it under the name of ᵗsíkon-yä′munĕ tíkwanĕ.

Implements.—Slender sticks [figure 916], the length of an arrow shaft, zigzagged in black, symbolic of lightning; a ring, about 2½ inches in diameter, composed of yucca ribbons, and a tíkwanĕ, or racing stick. . . .

This is a foot race run only by order of the Ah′wan tä′-chu (Great Father) Kóyemshi, and is exclusively for rains. A chosen number of women, each supplied with a stick, stand in line to the left of a number of men. The latter are provided with a tíkwanĕ, which they kick; and the women who play against the men use a yucca ring, tossing it with their sticks. Though the distance covered is short the latter seldom win.

Mr John T. Owens[b] described the following game:

A-we-wō-po-pa-ne.[c]—This is played by only two persons, but each usually has several backers, and considerable betting is done. One place is designated as the stone-home. One hundred stones are placed in a row a certain distance apart. Each stone must be picked up and carried separately and placed, not thrown, in the stone-home. Another point, several miles distant, is taken, and the game is for one to run to the distant spot and return, while the other gathers up the stones. As it is a contest of speed and judgment, not chance, it becomes very exciting.

FIG. 916. Ring, tossing rod, and kicking billet for race game; Zuñi Indians, Zuñi, New Mexico; from Mrs Stevenson.

FOOTBALL

Information concerning the game of football is extremely meager and unsatisfactory. The specimens commonly designated as footballs by collectors are, as a matter of fact, intended mostly for the game of hand-and-football or the ball race.

Football is mentioned as occurring among four Algonquian tribes (Massachuset, Micmac, Narraganset, Powhatan), but particulars are given only for the Micmac. It is spoken of also among the

---

[a] American Anthropologist, n. s., v. 5, p. 493, 1903.

[b] Some Games of the Zuñi. Popular Science Monthly, v. 39, p. 40, New York, 1891.

[c] There is a slight resemblance in this contest to our sport, the potato race.

Wyandot, Catawba (with uncertainty), Eskimo, Chukchansi, Topinagugim, Achomawi, Nishinam, Skokomish, Mono, Paiute, and Washo. The game was played by men (Micmac, Paiute); by men and women opposed (Topinagugim), and by men, women, and children (Eskimo). The balls were of buckskin (Micmac, Eskimo, Topinagugim, Achomawi, Nishinam, Mono, Paiute), or of stone (Chukchansi), and the goals were two sticks, erect (Paiute, Topinagugim, Nishinam, Mono) or placed slantingly (Micmac), or lines drawn at the ends of the course (Eskimo, Chukchansi).

In a California game (Topinagugim, Mono) the ball is kicked by successive players who are lined up along the course, corresponding with a game in which the ball is similarly tossed along the course with curved or spoon-shaped sticks (Mono). In one game (Topinagugim) men and women are opposed, the men kicking the ball and the women tossing it with flail-shaped baskets. The game appears to be most popular among the Eskimo, with whom in one instance it is complicated by the ball being whipped as well as kicked.

ALGONQUIAN STOCK

MASSACHUSET. Massachusetts.

William Wood [a] wrote:

> For their sports of activity they have commonly but three or four, as football, shooting, running, and swimming: when they play county against county there are rich goals, all behung with wompompeage, mowhackies, beaver skins and black otter skins. It would exceed the belief of many to relate the worth of one goal, wherefore it shall be nameless. Their goals be a mile long, placed on the sands, which are even as a board; their ball is no bigger than a handball, which sometimes they mount in the air with their naked feet, sometimes it is swayed by the multitude, sometimes also it is two days before they get a goal; then they mark the ground they win and begin there the next day. Before they come to this sport they paint themselves, even as when they go to war, in policy to prevent mischief, because no man should know him that moved his patience, or accidentally hurt his person, taking away the occasion of studying revenge. Before they begin their arms be disordered and hung upon some neighboring tree, after which they make a long scroll on the sand, over which they shake loving hands and with laughing hearts scuffle for victory. While the men play, the boys pipe, and the women dance and sing trophies of their husbands conquests; all being done, a feast summons their departure. It is most delightful to see them play in smaller companies, when men may view their swift footmanship, their curious tossings of their ball, their flouncing into the water, their lubber-like wrestling, having no cunning at all in that kind, one English being able to beat ten Indians at football.

MICMAC. Nova Scotia.

Mr Stansbury Hagar [b] says:

> The only other Micmac game [than the bowl game] of which I have learned is tooādijik or football. The goals were of two sticks placed slantingly across

---

[a] New England's Prospect, p. 73, London, 1634.
[b] Micmac Customs and Traditions. The American Anthropologist, v. 8, p. 35, 1895.

each other like the poles of the traditional wigwam.   About a score of players, divided into two parties, faced each other at equal distances from the center of the field.   The ball was then rolled in by the umpire, and the object of the game was to kick it between the goal posts.   In more recent times a player may catch his opponent by the neck and thus hold him back until he can obtain the ball himself, but scalping was anciently employed as a means of disposing of an opponent.

NARRAGANSET.   Rhode Island.

Roger Williams[a] gives pasuckquakohowauog, they meet to foot-ball, and says:

They have great meetings of foot-ball playing, only in summer, town against town, upon some broad sandy shore, free from stones, or upon some soft heathie plot, because of their naked feet, at which they have great stakings, but seldom quarrel.

POWHATAN.   Virginia.

William Strachey[b] says:

Likewise they have the exercise of football, in which they only forcibly encounter with the foot to carry the ball the one from the other, and spurned it to the goal with a kind of dexterity and swift footmanship, which is the honour of it; but they never strike up one another's heels, as we do, not accompting that praiseworthy to purchase a goal by such an advantage.

In his vocabulary he gives: "A ball, aitowh."

FIG. 917.   Footballs; diameters, 2¼ and 3¼ inches; Labrador Eskimo, Ungava; cat. no. 90031, 90032, United States National Museum.

ESKIMAUAN STOCK

ESKIMO (LABRADOR).   Ungava.   (Cat. no. 90031, 90032, United States National Museum.)

Buckskin-covered balls, one nearly spherical, 2¼ inches in diameter, and the other rather flattened, 3¼ inches in diameter, both covered with a single piece of buckskin, with a draw string, as shown in figure 917; contained in a net bag, made of knotted thongs, with a thong draw-string at the mouth.

---

[a] Key into the Language of America, London, 1643.
[b] The History of Travaile into Virginia Britannia, p. 77.   Printed for the Hakluyt Society, London, 1849.

Collected by Mr Lucien M. Turner,[a] who describes them as foot-balls.   He says:

Football calls out everybody, from the aged and bent mother of a numerous family to the toddling youngster scarcely able to do more than waddle under the burden of his heavy deerskin clothes.

ESKIMO (KOKSOAGMIUT).   Fort Chimo, Labrador.   (Cat. no. 90285, United States National Museum.)

Buckskin ball, with median seam, 1½ inches in diameter, and whip, consisting of four loops of buckskin, tied in the middle with a single thong, attached to a short wooden handle (figure 918).

Collected by Mr Lucien M. Turner,[b] who says:

FIG. 918.   Football and driver; diameter of ball, 1½ inches; Koksoagmiut Eskimo, Fort Chimo, Labrador; from Turner.

Figure 918 represents the football . . . and the whip for driving it.   The Eskimo are very fond of this game.   All the people of every age, from the tod-dling infant to the aged female with bended back, love to urge the aí uk toúk, as the ball is termed.   The size of the ball varies from 3 to 7 inches in diameter. They have not yet arrived at perfection in making a spherical form for the ball, but it is often an apple shape.   It is made by taking a piece of buckskin or sealskin and cutting it into a circular form, then gathering the edges and stuffing the cavity with dry moss or feathers.   A circular piece of skin is then inserted to fill the space which is left by the incomplete gatherings.   This ball is very light and is driven either by a blow from the foot or else by a whip of peculiar construction.   This whip consists of a handle of wood 8 to 12 inches in length.   To prevent it from slipping out of the hand when the blow is struck, a stout thong of sealskin is made into the form of a long loop which is passed over the hand and tightens around the wrist.   To the farther end of the whip handle are attached a number of stout thongs of heavy sealskin. These thongs have their ends tied around the handle and thus form a number of loops of 12 to 20 inches in length.   These are then tied together at the

[a] Ethnology of the Ungava District, Hudson Bay Territory.   Eleventh Annual Report of the Bureau of Ethnology, p. 255, 1894.
[b] Ibid., p. 256.

bottom in order to give them greater weight when the ball is struck by them. A lusty Eskimo will often send the ball over a hundred yards through the air with such force as to knock a person down.

At Fort Chimo the game is played during the late winter afternoons when the temperature is 30° to 40° below zero. It is exciting and vigorous play where a large crowd joins in the game.

Sometimes the ball is in the form of two irregular hemispheres joined together, making a sphere which can be rolled only in a certain direction. It is very awkward and produces much confusion by its erratic course.

ESKIMO (CENTRAL). Cumberland sound, Baffin land, Franklin.
Dr Franz Boas [a] says:

Another game of ball I have seen played by men only. A leather ball filled with hard clay is propelled with a whip, the lash of which is tied up in a coil. Every man has his whip, and is to hit the ball and so prevent his fellow-players from getting at it.

ESKIMO (ITA). Smith sound, Greenland.
Dr A. L. Kroeber [b] says:

Among amusements is ball-playing. The ball is of sealskin, and is stuffed with scraps of skin, so as to be hard.

ESKIMO (WESTERN). St Michael, Alaska.
Edward William Nelson [c] describes the game:

Football (i-tĭg'-ŭ-mi-u'-hlu-tín).

The ball (ûñ'kak) used in this game is made of leather, stuffed with deer hair or moss, and varies in size, but rarely exceeds 5 or 6 inches in diameter. The game is played by young men and children. The usual season for it is at the end of winter or in spring. I sàw it played in various places from Bering strait to the mouth of the Kuskokwim; at Cape Darby it was played by children on the hard, drifted snow; it is also a popular game on the lower Yukon.

Two of the participants act as leaders, one on each side choosing a player alternately from among those gathered until they are equally divided. At a given distance apart two conspicuous marks are made on the snow or ground which serve as goals; the players stand each by their goal and the ball is tossed upon the ground midway between them; a rush is then made, each side striving to drive the ball across its adversaries' line.

Another football game is begun by the men standing in two close, parallel lines midway between the goals, their legs and bodies forming two walls. The ball is then thrown between them and driven back and forth by kicks and blows until it passes through one of the lines; as soon as this occurs all rush to drive it to one or the other of the goals.

The northern lights (aurora) of winter are said by these people to be boys playing this game; others say it is a game being played by shades using walrus skulls as balls.

[a] The Central Eskimo. Sixth Annual Report of the Bureau of Ethnology, p. 570, 1888.
[b] Bulletin of the American Museum of Natural History, v. 12, p. 300, New York, 1900.
[c] The Eskimo about Bering Strait. Eighteenth Annual Report of the Bureau of American Ethnology, pt. 1, p. 335, 1899.

WYANDOT. Kansas.

Mr William E. Connelley writes the author as follows:

They played a game of ball which they say was much like our modern foot-ball, but I never could get enough information about it to warrant me in describing it as in any way different from the well-known game of Indian ball.

CHUKCHANSI. Table mountain, Fresno county, California.

Dr J. W. Hudson describes the following game under the name of eye: [a]

Two or more men play on a side, using a stone ball, she'-lĕl o'-lol ("stone ball"). At a signal each captain kicks (foot casts) his respective ball forward to his partners, who forward it in the same manner to a goal line, wĕx, 400 yards distant. The one whose ball is first over the line wins.

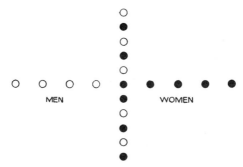

FIG. 919. Plan of ball field; Topinagugim Indians, California; from a sketch by Dr J. W. Hudson.

TOPINAGUGIM. Big creek, 2 miles north of Groveland, California. (Field Columbian Museum.)

Cat. no. 70224. Buckskin-covered ball, filled with deer hair, with median seam, 4½ inches in diameter.

Cat. no. 70225. Buckskin-covered ball, filled with moss, with median seam, 7 inches in diameter.

These were collected by Dr J. W. Hudson, who describes them as footballs.

He also describes the following game under the name of puskaw, football:

The ball is an oblate spheroid, 13 inches long by 8 inches in its shorter diam-eter, and consists of buckskin filled with deer hair. A straight, level course of about 500 yards is laid out, at one end of which the two balls are placed about 12 feet apart. The two opposing starters, pa-chu'-pĕ, stand about 50

---

[a] Ey-ĕ' is name for manzanita tree, and it is probable the ball was once made from this dense, heavy timber.—J. W. H.

feet behind their respective balls, and, at the signal, "Wisaetch!" the two opponents rush forward and kick their balls to their respective partners stationed next to them on the course, also running after the ball to assist, if necessary. No interference or handling of the ball is allowed. The penalty is usually the confiscation of the stakes. The number of players regulates the length of the course. Often fifty play.

Dr J. W. Hudson describes also the following ball game, played between men and women under the name umta:

The ball, pûs'-pûtch-ki, consists of an oblate spheroid 4 by 7 inches in diameter, covered with buckskin and stuffed with deer hair.

The goals are two sets of poles, 3 feet apart and 8 feet high, bent at the top to form an arch, and 600 yards apart. The men are stationed in a line on one side and the women on the other [figure 919]. The starters, five men and five women, arranged alternately, stand in a line in the center of the field, at right angles to the goal course. At a word, a man casts down the ball and each side tries to secure it. The women must advance the ball with their hands, or with a handled basket, a-ma-ta, while the men can kick only, and must not throw or touch the ball with their hands, nor can they interfere with their hands. The women are very expert and throw the ball long distances.

PUJUNAN STOCK

Nishinam. Mokelumne river, 12 miles south of Placerville, California.

Dr J. W. Hudson describes the following game:

Pâs'-ko, football.[a]—The ball, pâs-kö, is oblong, 12 inches in longest diameter, covered with buckskin and stuffed with deer hair. There are eight players to a side. One ball is used. The goals consist of pairs of poles, 3 feet apart, at the ends of a 1,000-foot course. Rough play is the rule, as a player is allowed to run with the ball in his hands, and interference is permissible.

SALISHAN STOCK

Skokomish. British Columbia.

Mr Charles Hill-Tout [b] refers to a kind of football under the name of tcquila.

SHASTAN STOCK

Achomawi. Hat creek, California. (Cat. no. $\frac{50}{4119}$, American Museum of Natural History.)

Ball covered with buckskin (figure 920), 4 inches in diameter. Collected in 1903 by Dr Roland B. Dixon, who describes it as a football, pwatoqwaiwi.

FIG. 920. Football; diameter, 4 inches; Achomawi Indians, Hat creek, California; cat. no. $\frac{50}{4119}$, American Museum of Natural History.

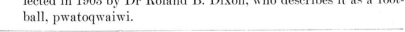

[a] The name of this game, as also probably the game, was of Miwok introduction.—J. W. H.

[b] Notes on the Sk·qo'mic of British Columbia. Report of the Seventieth Meeting of the British Association for the Advancement of Science, p. 488, London, 1900.

SHOSHONEAN STOCK

Mono. Hooker cove, Madera county, California. (Cat. no. 71440, Field Columbian Museum.)

Ball covered with buckskin filled with hair, 4½ inches in diameter.

Collected by Dr J. W. Hudson, who describes it as used in a football game called tanasukwitokoin.

The above ball is not the right shape. It should be oblong, 8 by 6½ inches. It is called o-no-wi, and is filled with deer hair.

Two balls are laid on the starting line, a-na-wi'-a-nu-a-we', 20 feet apart, and at a signal each captain kicks his ball to his partners, who forward it to the goal, a-nă-nă-ko'-i-nă, a hole between a pair of stakes, 350 yards distant. No interference whatever is permitted.

Another football game with the same name, ta-na-sü-kwi-to'-ko-in, is played with one ball, 7 inches in diameter, which is dropped in the center of the field and kicked or carried in almost the same manner as modern football. The goals are pairs of upright poles, 5 feet between and 400 yards apart.

Paiute. Pyramid lake, Nevada. (Cat. no. 37155, Free Museum of Science and Art, University of Pennsylvania.)

Buckskin-covered ball (figure 921), 3 inches in diameter. It was collected by the writer in 1901 through Miss Marian Taylor.

Called wut-si-mo and used in a football game by men, say, four on a side. The object is to kick the ball between two goals, tu-bi, made of willow sticks, and some 8 or 10 feet high. The goals are about 50 yards apart, the players starting in the center. They wear only a loin cloth.

FIG. 921. Football; diameter, 3 inches; Paiute Indians, Nevada; cat. no. 37155, Free Museum of Science and Art, University of Pennsylvania.

SIOUAN STOCK

Catawba. South Carolina.

Mrs R. E. Dunlap,[a] of Leslie, York county, South Carolina, writes the author that the Catawba formerly played a game of football which they called wachippu.

WASHOAN STOCK

Washo. Carson valley and Lake Tahoe, Nevada.

Dr J. W. Hudson describes this tribe using a football, kawmal, 6 inches in diameter, and filled with the inner bark of the sagebrush.

The goals, maw'-tap, consist of two sets of poles, 10 feet high and about 4 feet apart, at either end of the field, which is about 300 feet long. The game is like our football. There are three players to a side, and the ball is cast up in the center of the field by a captain. The game is called pă-lăw'-ya-păw.

HAND-AND-FOOT BALL

I have classified under the name of hand-and-foot ball a woman's game played with a large ball, which is struck down with the hand

---

[a] In a letter, September 1, 1901.

and kicked back with the foot. The ball is covered either with buck-skin (Cheyenne, Eskimo, Mandan) or with bladder netted with sinew (Grosventres, Crows).

It is commonly played by one woman at a time, but among the Eskimo two or four play. The Cheyenne count the game with sticks, and their ball has a thong attached.

The game has been found among two Algonquian tribes (Cheyenne, Grosventres), among the Eskimo, and among four Siouan tribes (Assiniboin, Crows, Mandan, Winnebago). Included in this division is a ball with a thong, from the Arapaho, which is struck only with the hand.

ALGONQUIAN STOCK

ARAPAHO. Wind River reservation, Wyoming. (Cat. no. 36977, Free Museum of Science and Art, University of Pennsylvania.)
Buckskin ball (figure 922), with median seam, 2½ inches in diameter, one face marked with a cross in colored quill work, attached to a thong 19 inches in length.

Fig. 922.   Fig. 923.

FIG. 922. Ball with thong; diameter, 2¼ inches; Arapaho Indians, Wyoming; cat. no. 36977, Free Museum of Science and Art, University of Pennsylvania.
FIG. 923. Hand-and-foot ball; diameter, 9¼ inches; Cheyenne Indians, Montana; cat. no. 69978, Field Columbian Museum.

The end of the thong is held in the hand, and the ball is thrown up and caught.

Collected by the writer in 1900. The name is kowwha; it is used in a girl's game.

CHEYENNE. Cheyenne reservation, Montana. (Field Columbian Museum.)
Cat. no. 69978. Kicking football (figure 923), covered with buck-skin, irregularly elliptical, with two faces, consisting of disks of buckskin sewed to a middle band 2 inches wide and painted red, to which is attached a buckskin thong 24 inches in length; diameter, 9¼ inches.

Collected by Mr S. C. Simms in 1901. The thong is held in the hand and the ball kicked repeatedly. It is used in a woman's game.

Cat. no. 68977. Buckskin ball flattened (figure 924), with median
seam, painted red, 7½ inches in diameter; accompanied by twenty
counting sticks, willow twigs, painted red, 8½ inches in length.

These were collected in 1901 by Mr S. C. Simms, who says the ball is
kicked in the air and caught on the foot, the operation being repeated
until the player misses. A stick is given for each successful stroke.
This is a woman's game.

CHEYENNE. Oklahoma.

Mr Louis L. Meeker writes that girls kick a little ball in the air,
counting the number of times it is done without letting ball or foot
touch the ground.

———— Colorado.

Prof. F. V. Hayden[a] gives under ball: e-hu-a-si-wa-to, to play
ball with the foot.

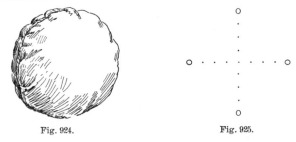

Fig. 924.   Fig. 925.

FIG. 924. Hand-and-foot ball; diameter, 7½ inches; Cheyenne Indians, Montana; cat. no. 68977,
Field Columbian Museum.
FIG. 925. Position of players in women's football game; Western Eskimo, Alaska; from Nelson.

GROSVENTRES. Fort Belknap, Montana. (Cat. no. $\frac{50}{1896}$, American
    Museum of Natural History.)

Ball, covered with a bladder and twined with a network of sinew;
    diameter, 6 inches. Described by the collector, Dr A. L. Kroe-
    ber, as a football.

ESKIMAUAN STOCK

ESKIMO (WESTERN). St Michael, Alaska.

Mr E. W. Nelson[b] describes the following game:

Women's football (ûñ-käl'-û-g'it). . . . This game is played by women
usually during the fall and winter. The ball used is generally considerably
larger than the one used in the men's game. The four players stand opposite
each other [figure 925].

Each pair has a ball, which is thrown or driven back and forth across the
square. The ball is thrown upon the ground midway between the players, so
that it shall bound toward the opposite one. She strikes the ball down and
back toward her partner with the palm of her open hand. Sometimes the ball

———————————

[a] Contributions to the Ethnography and Philology of the Indian Tribes of the Missouri
Valley, p. 295, Philadelphia, 1862.
[b] The Eskimo about Bering Strait. Eighteenth Annual Report of the Bureau of American Ethnology, pt. 1, p. 336, 1899.

is caught on the toe or hand and tossed up and struck or kicked back toward the other side. The person who misses least or has fewer "dead" balls on her side wins. At times this game is played only by two women.

SIOUAN STOCK

ASSINIBOIN. Fort Union, Montana.

Mr Edwin T. Denig [a] says:

The women play hand and foot ball.

CROWS. Crow agency, Montana. (Cat. no. 154335, United States National Museum.)

Football (figure 926), covered with bladder and twined with sinew; diameter, 6 inches. Collected by Dr W. J. Hoffman, who gives the name as buh tse.

Fig. 926.　　　　　　　　　　　　　　Fig. 927.

FIG. 926. Hand-and-foot ball; diameter, 6 inches; Crow Indians, Montana; cat. no. 154335, United States National Museum.

FIG. 927. Hand-and-foot ball; Mandan Indians, North Dakota; from Maximilian, Prince of Wied.

———— Crow reservation, Montana. (Field Columbian Museum.)

Cat. no. 69646. Bladder filled with antelope hair, inclosed in a network of sinew; diameter, $6\frac{3}{4}$ inches.

Cat. no. 69645. Football, similar to the preceding, $8\frac{1}{2}$ inches in diameter.

Cat. no. 69647. Football, similar to the preceding, 7 inches in diameter.

These specimens were collected in 1901 by Mr S. C. Simms, who describes them as juggling footballs, boop tcje, used in a woman's game. The object is to keep the ball in the air the longest time by kicking it or by the greatest number of kicks without a miss.

MANDAN. Fort Clark, North Dakota.

Maximilian, Prince of Wied,[b] says:

The women are expert in playing with a large leathern ball [figure 927], which they let fall alternately on their foot and knee, again throwing it up and

---

[a] Unpublished manuscript in the library of the Bureau of American Ethnology.

[b] Travels in the Interior of North America, translated by H. Evans Lloyd, p. 358, London, 1843.

catching it, and thus keeping it in motion for a length of time without letting it fall to the ground. Prizes are given, and they often play high. The ball is often very neat and curiously covered with dyed porcupine quills.

WINNEBAGO. Wisconsin.

Mr Louis L. Meeker communicates the following description of a game played by the Winnebago girls and some others:

They take a light soft ball, such as a stuffed stocking foot, place it on the toe, and standing on one foot, kick it up a few inches. Then as it falls they kick it back again, so as to send it up as often as possible without letting it fall to the ground, keeping count of the number of times. When it falls to the ground or when the foot is placed on the ground the ball is passed to another player. The first to count 100, or any number agreed upon, wins.

TOSSED BALL

In general, the ball throughout the North American continent was propelled with a bat or racket and not touched with the hands. The following exceptional games have been recorded:

ALGONQUIAN STOCK

ABNAKI. Quebec.

Lafitau [a] says:

Their ball is nothing but an inflated bladder, which must always be kept up in the air and which in reality is upheld a long time by the multitude of hands tossing it back and forth without ceasing; this forms a very pretty sight.

MIAMI. St Joseph river, Michigan.

Charlevoix [b] says, after describing lacrosse:

The second game is very like this one, but not so dangerous. Two boundaries are marked out, as in the first game, and the players take up all the ground which is between them. The one who begins throws a ball up into the air as perpendicularly as possible, so that he may easily catch it again and throw it towards the goal. All the others have their arms raised, and the one who seizes the ball either goes through the same maneuver or throws it to one of his party whom he considers more alert or more skillful than himself, for in order to win the ball must never fall into the hands of the adversaries. Women play this game also, but rarely. They have four or five on a side, and the one who lets the ball fall loses.

MONTAGNAIS. Camp islands, Labrador.

George Cartwright [c] says:

At sunset the Indians amused themselves with playing at ball. This amusement consisted only in tossing the ball at pleasure from one to another, each striving who should get it; but I soon perceived they were very bad catchers.

---

[a] Moeurs des Sauvages Ameriquains, v. 4, p. 76, Paris, 1724.

[b] Journal d'un Voyage dans l'Amérique Septentrionnale, v. 3, p. 319, Paris, 1744.

[c] A Journal of Transactions and Events during a Residence of nearly Sixteen Years on the Coast of Labrador, v. 1, p. 237, Newark, 1792.

CHIMMESYAN STOCK

NISKA.　Nass river, British Columbia.

Dr Franz Boas [a] describes a game:

Tlēt!: a ball game.—Four men stand in a square: each pair, standing in opposite corners, throw the ball one to the other, striking it with their hands. Those who continue longest have won.

ESKIMAUAN STOCK

ESKIMO (CENTRAL).　Cumberland sound, Baffin land, Franklin.

Dr Franz Boas [b] says:

The ball [figure 928] is most frequently used in summer. It is made of sealskin stuffed with moss and neatly trimmed with skin straps. One man throws the ball among the players, whose object it is to keep it always in motion without allowing it to touch the ground.

KOLUSCHAN STOCK

TLINGIT.　Alaska.

Dr Aurel Krause [c] says:

Ball is played by children as well as adults. The young people of the village often passed the time in a game in which two sides placed themselves opposite each other and threw a thick leather ball back and forth, whereby they exerted themselves never to let it come to the earth.

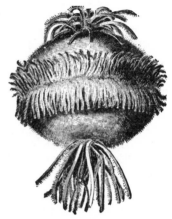

FIG. 928.　Ball; Central Eskimo, Cumberland sound, Baffin land, Franklin; cat. no. IV A 6822, Berlin Museum für Völkerkunde; from Boas.

MUSKHOGEAN STOCK

CHOCTAW.　Mississippi.

Capt. Bernard Romans [d] says:

The women also have a game where they take a small stick, or something else off the ground after having thrown up a small ball which they are to catch again, having picked up the other; they are fond of it, but ashamed to be seen at it. I believe it is this propensity to gaming which has given these savages an idea of a meum and tuum above all other nations of America.

Captain Romans [e] describes also a game played with a large ball of woolen rags, which he says the men and women play promiscuously with the hand only.

[a] Fifth Report on the Indians of British Columbia. Report of the Sixty-fifth Meeting of the British Association for the Advancement of Science, p. 583, London, 1895.

[b] The Central Eskimo. Sixth Annual Report of the Bureau of Ethnology, p. 570, 1888.

[c] Die Tlinkit-Indianer, p. 164, Jena, 1885.

[d] A Concise Natural History of East and West Florida, v. 1, p. 81, New York, 1775.

[e] Ibid., p. 79.

NATCHEZ. Louisiana.

Le Page du Pratz [a] wrote:

The young people, especially the girls, have hardly any kind of diversion but that of the ball: this consists in tossing a ball from one to the other with the palm of the hand, which they perform with tolerable address.

NISHINAM. California.

Mr Stephen Powers [b] describes the following game:

The pos'-kâ huk'-um-toh kom-peh' (tossing the ball) is a boys' game. They employ a round wooden ball, a buckeye, or something, standing at three bases or corners, and toss it around from one to the other. If two of them start to exchange corners, and the third "crosses out" or hits either of them, he scores one, and they count up to a certain number, which completes the game.

THOMPSON INDIANS (NTLAKYAPAMUK). British Columbia.

Mr James Teit [c] says:

The Lower Thompson had a ball game in which the ball was thrown up by one player. The player who caught it ran with it until overtaken by another player, who in his turn ran with it until a certain goal was reached.

ASSINIBOIN. Fort Union, Montana.

Mr Edwin T. Denig [d] says:

The women play hand and foot ball.

HIDATSA. Fort Clark, North Dakota.

Maximilian, Prince of Wied, [e] referring to a visit of this tribe at Fort Clark, on November 27, 1833, speaks of some of the women " playing with a leathern ball, which they flung upon the ice, caught it, and then threw it into the air, catching it as it fell."

ZUÑI. Zuñi, New Mexico. (Cat. no. 5000, Brooklyn Institute Museum.)

Cotton cloth-covered ball (figure 929), ovate, with median seam, 6 inches in diameter.

---

[a] Histoire de la Louisiane, v. 3, p. 5, Paris, 1768.

[b] Tribes of California. Contributions to North American Ethnology, v. 3, p. 331, Washington, 1877.

[c] The Thompson Indians of British Columbia. Memoirs of the American Museum of Natural History, v. 2, p. 278, New York, 1900.

[d] Unpublished manuscript in the library of the Bureau of American Ethnology.

[e] Travels in the Interior of North America, translated by H. Evans Lloyd, p. 422, London, 1843.

This was made for the writer by Nick Graham, as a copy of a ball used by the clowns, or Koyemshi, in a game in the plaza at Zuñi, May 27, 1904, which he described as follows:

The clowns produced a large, soft ball, and one of them made a mark with his foot across the middle of the plaza from north to south. Sides were chosen, half the clowns ranging themselves on one side and half on the other. One side had the ball, and one of the players on that side would run forward with it to the line and try to strike a player on the other. If he hit him, the latter went to the striker's side, but if he missed, the other side threw the ball.

Mrs Matilda Coxe Stevenson[a] says under popone (wool-bag or ball):

This game is also played by the Kóyemshi and the Néwekwe fraternity during the intermission of the dances.

Fig. 929.   Fig. 930.

FIG. 929. Ball; diameter, 6 inches; Zuñi Indians, Zuñi, New Mexico; cat. no. 5000, Brooklyn Institute Museum.
FIG. 930. Stone foot-casting ball; diameter, 4 inches; Chukchansi Indians, Madera county, California; cat. no. 70894, Field Columbian Museum.

Two sides are formed in line, and a man runs out from one side and turns his back to his opponents, one of whom advances and throws a small bag filled with wool. If he succeeds in striking the one who has his back turned, the latter must join the side of the one who strikes; but should the one endeavoring to strike be hit from the other side before he returns to his ranks, he must pass to his opponent's side.

FOOT-CAST BALL

A game of casting a heavy stone ball with the top of the foot, the object being to see who can throw it farthest; observed only in California by Doctor Hudson among the tribes of two stocks (Mariposan and Moquelumnan).

MARIPOSAN STOCK

CHUKCHANSI. Madera county, California.   (Cat. no. 70894, Field Columbian **Museum.**)
Stone ball (figure 930), 4 inches in diameter. Collected by Dr J. W. Hudson, who describes it as used in the foot-putting game.

---

[a] Zuñi Games. American Anthropologist, n. s., v. 5, p. 495, 1903.

MOQUELUMNAN STOCK

APLACHE. Big creek, north of Groveland, Tuolumne county, California.

Doctor Hudson describes the following game under the name of sawa puchuma (sawa, stone; puchuma, to lift or cast with the top of the foot):

A pecked stone ball, about 3 inches in diameter, is cast with the top of the right foot. The left foot must not get out of position. The one who can throw it farthest wins.

BALL JUGGLING

The sport or game of throwing two or more balls into the air at the same time has been observed among the Eskimo and an adjacent Algonquian tribe, among the Bannock, Shoshoni and Ute (Shoshonean), and among the Zuñi. There is no indication that it was borrowed from the whites, and further investigation will doubtless result in its discovery in other parts of the continent.

ALGONQUIAN STOCK

NASCAPEE. Ungava, Labrador.

Mr Lucien M. Turner [a] says:

While walking out the girls generally toss stones or chips in the air and strive to keep at least two of them up at once. The Eskimo often practice this also, and, as it appears to be a general source of amusement among the Innuit, I suspect that the Indian borrowed it from them.

ESKIMAUAN STOCK

ESKIMO (CENTRAL). Cumberland sound, Baffin land, Franklin.

Dr Franz Boas [b] says:

A third game of ball, called igdlukitaqtung, is played with small balls tossed up alternately from the right to the left, one always being in the air.

ESKIMO (ITA). Smith sound, Greenland.

Dr A. L. Kroeber [c] says:

The Adlet among them also juggle, some with as many as five pebbles at once.

SHASTAN STOCK

ACHOMAWI. Pit river, California.

Dr J. W. Hudson describes these Indians as casting up lenticularly-shaped stones over and over, juggling.

[a] Ethnology of the Ungava District, Hudson Bay Territory. Eleventh Annual Report of the Bureau of Ethnology, p. 321, 1894.

[b] The Central Eskimo. Sixth Annual Report of the Bureau of Ethnology, p. 570, 1888.

[c] Bulletin of the American Museum of Natural History, v. 12, p. 300, New York, 1900.

SHOSHONEAN STOCK

BANNOCK. Fort Hall reservation, Idaho. (Cat. no. 37066, Free
    Museum of Science and Art, University of Pennsylvania.)
Two perforated marbles collected by the writer in 1900. They are
called marapai and are said to be used in juggling.

SHOSHONI. Wind River reservation, Wyoming. (Cat. no. 36882,
    Free Museum of Science and Art, University of Pennsyl-
    vania.)
Set of three gypsum balls (figure 931), name tapa, 2 inches in diam-
    eter.
Collected by the writer in 1900. They are used by women in a
juggling game, described by Dr George A. Dorsey [a] as follows:

Occasionally rounded, water-worn stones are used. The Shoshoni name for
the game is nă-wá-tă-pi ta-na-wa-ta-pi, meaning to throw with the hand. The
usual number of balls used is three, although two or four may be used. The object is to keep one or more of the balls, according to the number used, in the air
by passing them upward from one hand to the other, and vice versa, after the
fashion of our well-known jugglers. The balls are about an inch in diameter,

Fig. 931.   Fig. 932.

FIG. 931. Juggling balls; diameter, 2 inches; Shoshoni Indians, Wyoming; cat. no. 36882, Free
Museum of Science and Art, University of Pennsylvania.
FIG. 932. Juggling balls; diameter, 1¼ inches; Uinta Ute Indians, White Rocks, Utah; cat. no.
37121, Free Museum of Science and Art, University of Pennsylvania.

and are painted according to the fancy of the owner, one of the sets collected
having been painted blue, another red, while a third set was white. Contests of
skill with these balls are occasions of considerable betting among the women,
stakes of importance often being wagered. The usual play of the game is when
two or more women agree upon some objective point, such as a tree or tipi, to
which they direct their steps, juggling the balls as they go. The individual who
first arrives at the goal without having dropped one of the balls, or without
having a mishap of any sort, is the winner of the contest. . . . All Shoshoni who were interrogated on this point declared that the art of juggling had
long been known by the women, and that before the advent of the whites into
Wyoming contests for stakes among the women was one of their commonest
forms of gambling. This game was also observed among the Bannocks, the
Utes and the Paiutes. . . .

UINTA UTE. White Rocks, Utah. (Cat. no. 37121, Free Museum of
    Science and Art, University of Pennsylvania.)
Set of three red clay balls (figure 932), 1½ inches in diameter. Used
    by women in a juggling game. Collected by the writer in 1901.

---

[a] Journal of American Folk-Lore, v. 14, p. 24, Boston, 1901.

ZUÑIAN STOCK

ZuÑI.   Zuñi, New Mexico.   (Cat. no. 3085, Brooklyn Institute Museum.)

Four red clay balls (figure 933), 2 inches in diameter.

Collected in 1903 by the writer, to whom they were described as follows:

> Women make balls of red clay as big as hens' eggs for the boys to gamble with. They use two, throwing them up and keeping one in the air. They keep count, and the one who scores highest wins. The game is called ha it-zu-lu-lu-na-wai; the ball, hai-muk-kia-ma-wai.

HOT BALL

Dr J. W. Hudson describes the following game as one for training young men:

> An old man goes out at night and takes a stone ball which he puts in the fire and heats very hot. He then removes the ball from the fire and throws it as far as he can with wisps of straw. A number of youths are lined up, on the

Fig. 933.   Fig. 934.

FIG. 933. Juggling balls; diameter, 2 inches; Zuñi Indians. Zuñi, New Mexico; cat. no. 3085, Brooklyn Institute Museum.
FIG. 934. Hot ball; diameter, 2¼ inches; Mono Indians, Madera county, California; cat. no. 71439, Field Columbian Museum.

alert, heads down, to locate where the ball strikes, and at the moment it falls they run and try to get it. He who finds it first gets the first honor, but he who brings it to the camp gets the stakes.

MARIPOSAN STOCK

CHUKCHANSI.   Fresno county, California.   (Cat. no. 70893, Field Columbian Museum.)

Two stone balls, 2 inches in diameter.

Collected by Dr J. W. Hudson, who describes them as probably used in the game of hot ball.

SHOSHONEAN STOCK

MONO.   Hooker cove, Madera county, California.   (Cat. no. 71439, Field Columbian Museum.)

Four stone balls (figure 934), 2¼ to 2¾ inches in diameter. Collected by Dr J. W. Hudson, who describes them as used in the game of hot ball.

MINOR AMUSEMENTS

From the recorded accounts, meager as they are, it appears that the Indians of North America had the same kinds of minor amusements and children's plays as occur in other parts of the world and survive in our own civilization. Thus, for example, Mr Nelson [a] gives descriptions of twenty-two [b] such amusements in addition to those of which accounts have been extracted for the present work.

Rev. J. Owen Dorsey [c] in the same way describes forty-one such plays, beside those mentioned in this volume, as existing among the Teton Dakota. Of these, thirty-one are readily classified as imitative and dramatic, twelve [d] of these referring to war and combat, six [e] to hunting, four [f] to religion, and nine [g] to social customs and domestic employments; three [h] are ring games, similar to those of civilization, four [i] are simple contests of action, and three [j] may be classified as miscellaneous.

According to Mr Dorsey, each of these games, and of the other children's games which he enumerates, has its own special season or seasons and is played at no other time of the year. Children of one

---

[a] The Eskimo about Bering Strait. Eighteenth Annual Report of the Bureau of American Ethnology, pt. 1, p. 337, 1899.

[b] Rope jumping; blind man's buff; hide and seek; tag; twin tag; ring around; tossing on walrus skin; tug of war; arm pulling; pole pulling; stick raising; finger pulling; foot pulling; neck pulling; head pushing; battering ram; wrestling; knee walking; high jumping; horizontal jumping; hurdle jumping; kaiak racing.

[c] Games of Teton Dakota Children. American Anthropologist, v. 4, p. 329, 1891. For further information about Dakota children's games, see Ogalala Games, by Louis L. Meeker, in Bulletin of Free Museum of Science and Art, v. 3, p. 23, Philadelphia, 1901.

[d] Running toward one another; taking captives from one another; how they are brought up (follow my leader); hide and seek; throwing stones at one another; they hit one another with earth; use mud with one another; throwing fire at one another; throwing chewed leaves into the eyes; they wound one another with a grass which has a long sharp beard, míchapécha; wrestling; they kick at one another.

[e] Hunting for young birds; egg hunting; trampling on the beaver; deer game; grizzly-bear game; goose and her children.

[f] Ghost game; mystery game; pretending to die; playing doctor.

[g] Courting the women; going to make a grass lodge; playing with small things; playing with large objects; they make one another carry packs; sitting on wooden horses; old woman and her dog; causing them to scramble for gifts; flutes.

[h] Howf! howf!: snatching places from one another; they do not touch one another.

[i] Who shall get there first; hopping; jumping from a high object; they play neck out of joint (tumbling, somersaults).

[j] Hoop that is made to roll by the wind; sport with mud horses; ball of mud made to float is thrown at.

715

sex seldom play with those of the other. In accordance with the original plan I shall dismiss with this mere mention the games played without special implements. There is much, however, in them, as well as in the Indian toys and playthings, that would repay comparative study, although our information about them is scanty.

Mr Dorsey says the Teton use sleds of different kinds. Among the Oglala the boys coast down hill on a piece of wood or bark like a barrel stave, with a rein tied to one end, which they hold, standing erect, with one foot advanced and the rein drawn tight for support.[a]

Yankton boys have a kind of sled, huhu kazunta, made of rib bones lashed together with rags (figure 935).

FIG. 935. Bone sled; length, 14 inches; Yankton Dakota Indians, Fort Peck, Montana; cat. no. 37613, Free Museum of Science and Art, University of Pennsylvania.

I have classified the following amusements, all of which may be regarded as games of dexterity, under thirteen different heads, having here restricted myself to those of which more than one mention occurs. It is difficult to decide from present data whether certain of them may not have been borrowed from the whites. Though the Indians generally are a conservative people, they have, at the same time, high powers of mimicry and imitation. Of this gift the anecdotes of the Hopi clowns related by Mr A. M. Stephen in his unpublished manuscript afford many interesting illustrations.

Mr Dorsey describes the skill with which Teton children make playthings of clay, copying animal forms with amazing fidelity. Indian children in general are given to making pictures, often painting or cutting them high up on the rocks. Among other amusements one has been noted where they laid pebbles on the ground to form outline pictures of various objects.

---

[a] Louis L. Meeker, Ogalala Games. Bulletin of the Free Museum of Science and Art, v. 3, p. 35, Philadelphia, 1901.

SHUTTLECOCK

A game of shuttlecock, played with a wooden battledoor, is common among the tribes on the Northwest coast. The Zuñi play with corn-husk shuttlecocks, stuck with feathers, batted with the hand, and a similar object was found in a cliff-dwelling in the Canyon de Chelly. Only the two forms occur, and no other distribution has been observed.

PIMAN STOCK

PIMA. Arizona.

The late Dr Frank Russell [a] described the following game:

Kwaĭtusĭwĭkŭt.—The children sometimes amuse themselves by tossing into the air corncobs in which from one to three feathers have been stuck. They do not shoot arrows at them.

SALISHAN STOCK

BELLACOOLA. Dean inlet, British Columbia. (Cat. no. $\frac{16}{1541}$, $\frac{16}{1542}$, American Museum of Natural History.)

Battledoor, made of thin, unpainted boards, $11\frac{1}{2}$ by $13\frac{1}{2}$ inches, and shuttlecock, consisting of a small piece of twig, stuck with three feathers.

These specimens were collected by Mr George Hunt and Dr Franz Boas, who gave the names as laetsta and koamal.

FIG. 936. Battledoor; length, $12\frac{1}{4}$ inches; Bellacoola Indians, British Columbia; cat. no. IV A 6772, Berlin Museum für Völkerkunde.

———— British Columbia. (Cat. no. IV A 6772, Berlin Museum für Völkerkunde.)

Wooden battledoor (figure 936), made of four wooden slats lashed to a handle; length, $12\frac{1}{2}$ inches. Collected by Capt. Samuel Jacobsen.

CLALLAM. Washington.

A Clallam boy, John Raub, described this tribe as playing the wooden battledoor game like the Makah. The name of the battledoor, he said, was acquiaten; of the shuttlecock, sacquiah.

SKOKOMISH. British Columbia.

Mr Charles Hill-Tout [b] describes a game called tckwie:

This was a kind of shuttlecock and battledore, and a favourite pastime of the girls.

---

[a] In a memoir to be published by the Bureau of American Ethnology.

[b] Notes on the Sk.qŏ'mic of British Columbia. Report of the Seventieth Meeting of the British Association for the Advancement of Science, p. 488, London, 1900.

WAKASHAN STOCK

HESQUIAHT. Vancouver island, British Columbia. (Cat. no. IV
A 1489, Berlin Museum für Völkerkunde.)

Battledoor (figure 937), wooden plaque, with a handle of the same
piece, 14 inches in length; and shuttlecock (figure 938), a twig
tied with three feathers. Collected by Capt. Samuel Jacobsen.

KWAKIUTL. Nawiti, British Columbia.

Dr C. F. Newcombe gives the name of the battledoor of slats as
quemal and of the shuttlecock as quemlaiu. The game is quumla.
Two or more play. If there are many players, they stand in a ring.
They throw always to the right and in front of the body. The one
who lasts longest wins.

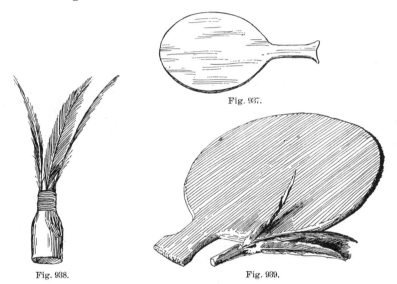

Fig. 937.

Fig. 938.

Fig. 939.

FIG. 937. Battledoor; length, 14 inches; Hesquiaht Indians, Vancouver island, British Columbia;
cat. no. IV A 1489, Berlin Museum für Völkerkunde.
FIG. 938. Shuttlecock; length, 3 inches; Hesquiaht Indians, Vancouver island, British Columbia;
cat. no. IV A 1489, Berlin Museum für Völkerkunde.
FIG. 939. Battledoor and shuttlecock; diameter of battledoor, 9 inches; Makah Indians, Washington; cat. no. 37389, Free Museum of Science and Art, University of Pennsylvania.

MAKAH. Neah bay, Washington. (Cat. no. 37389, Free Museum of
Science and Art, University of Pennsylvania.)

Battledoor (figure 939), consisting of a thin circular board of cedar
wood, 9 inches in diameter, with a wooden handle; and shuttlecock, consisting of a branch of salmon-berry wood having surf-
duck feathers inserted.

These objects were collected by the writer in 1900. The name of
the bat was given as klahaiac; that of the shuttlecock as kokoei;
to play the game, klahatla.

Dr George A. Dorsey [a] describes the game as played equally by boys and girls under the name of thahatla; the bat he gives as tlahayak.

NIMKISH. Nimkish river, British Columbia. (Cat. no. $\frac{16}{81281}$, American Museum of Natural History.)

Battledoor (figure 940), consisting of eight strips of cedar wood lashed with cedar bark to two sticks on either side to form a rectangle 9½ by 10½ inches, with a cedar-wood handle in the center, 17 inches long. Collected by Dr Franz Boas in 1900.

OPITCHESAHT. Vancouver island, British Columbia. (Cat. no. IV A 7119, Berlin Museum für Völkerkunde.)

Wooden battledoor (figure 941), a round plaque of wood with a handle of the same piece, 12 inches in length.

The collector, Capt. Samuel Jacobsen, gives the name as eidzatsek, that of the shuttlecock as tklapaek.

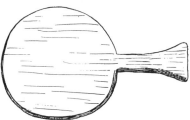

Fig. 940.   Fig. 941.

FIG. 940. Battledoor; length, 17 inches; Nimkish Indians, British Columbia; cat. no. $\frac{16}{81281}$. American Museum of Natural History.

FIG. 941. Battledoor; length, 12 inches; Opitchesaht Indians, Vancouver island, British Columbia; cat. no. IV A 7119, Berlin Museum für Völkerkunde.

ZUÑIAN STOCK

ZUÑI. Zuñi, New Mexico. (Cat. no. 16306, Free Museum of Science and Art, University of Pennsylvania.)

Shuttlecocks (figure 942), square thick bundles of corn husk, tied around at the top, and having four feathers inserted; height, from 5 to 7 inches. Made by Mr Cushing in 1893.

---

[a] Games of the Makah Indians of Neah Bay. The American Antiquarian, v. 23, p. 71, 1901.

Mr John G. Owens [a] describes the game as follows:

Pō-kē-an.—This game is somewhat similar to our popular game called battle-door and shuttlecock. Green corn-husks are wrapped into a flat mass about 2 inches square, and on one side are placed two feathers, upright; then, using this as a shuttlecock and the hand for a battledoor, they try how many times they can knock it into the air. Some become very skillful in this, and as they return the shuttlecock to the air they count aloud in their own language—Tō-pa, quil-ē, hī, ă-wē-ta, ap-ti, etc. The striking resemblance to our European game suggests a common origin, and it may easily have been introduced through contact with the Spaniards. This, however, is doubtful, and I am inclined to think that we must give the Indian the credit of inventing this game rather than borrowing it, as similarity of product by no means proves identity of origin.

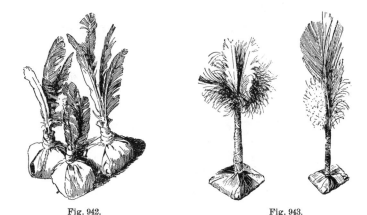

Fig. 942.   Fig. 943.

FIG. 942. Shuttlecocks; height, 5 to 7 inches; Zuñi Indians, Zuñi, New Mexico; cat. no. 16306, Free Museum of Science and Art, University of Pennsylvania.

FIG. 943. Shuttlecocks; height, 8 inches; Zuñi Indians, Zuñi, New Mexico; cat. no. 3087, 3088, Brooklyn Institute Museum.

ZUÑI   Zuñi, New Mexico.   (Cat. no. 3087, 3088, Brooklyn Institute Museum.)

Two delicate packets of woven corn husk (figure 943) stuck with down feathers, 8 inches in height.

Collected by the writer in 1903. The name was given to him as pokianawai.

Mrs Matilda Coxe Stevenson describes this game under the name of po[t]kinanane (plural, po[t]kiannawe), the implements being made of corn husks neatly interlaced, forming a square of about an inch and a half, with two delicate feathers projecting from the center. She says: [b]

So named because the sound produced by the shuttlecock coming in contact with the palm of the hand is similar to the noise of the tread of a jack rabbit upon[l] frozen snow. The game is played as frequently by the younger boys as by their elders, and always for stakes.

---

[a] Some Games of the Zuñi. Popular Science Monthly, v. 39, p. 39, New York, 1901.
[b] Zuñi Games. American Anthropologist, n. s., v. 5, p. 492, 1903.

One bets that he can toss the shuttlecock a given number of times. While ten is the number specially associated with the game, the wagers are often made for twenty, fifty, and sometimes a hundred throws. In case of failure the other player tries his skill, each party alternating in the game until one or the other tosses the shuttlecock (only one hand being used) the given number of times. which entitles him to the game.

The Zuñi claim that this game originated with them.

TIPCAT

The game of tipcat, played with a small billet, usually pointed, which is struck with a club, appears to be known in America, at least to certain tribes. Hennepin's account seems to refer to it, and the cat made by Mr Cushing is similar to those used by boys in our streets. The Zuñi game is peculiar in the ball tied to a stick which is used to hit the billet.

IROQUOIAN STOCK

HURON. Ontario.

Father Louis Hennepin [a] says:

The children play with bows and with two sticks, one large and one small. They hold the little one in the left and the larger one in the right hand; then with the larger they make the smaller one fly up in the air, and another runs after it and throws it at the one who sprung it. This game resembles that of children in Europe.

SIOUAN STOCK

DAKOTA (TETON). South Dakota.

Rev. J. Owen Dorsey [b] describes the game under the name ichapsil echunpi, making the wood jump by hitting it:

When the boys play this game an imaginary stream is marked off on the ground, and the players stand on imaginary ice near the shore. They take turns at knocking at a piece of wood, in order to send it up into the air. He who fails to send up the piece of wood loses his stakes, and he who succeeds wins the stakes.

ZUÑIAN STOCK

ZUÑI. Zuñi, New Mexico. (Cat. no. 16309, Free Museum of Science and Art, University of Pennsylvania.)

Small double-pointed billet (figure 944), 2¾ inches in length, with a bat, consisting of a small bag-shaped buckskin ball (figure 945), attached to the end of a handle made of a small twig, 19 inches in length—a model made by Mr Cushing, who describes it as known in Zuñi as the jumping-toad game.

---

[a] A Description of Louisiana, p. 303, New York, 1880.

[b] Games of Teton Dakota Children. The American Anthropologist, v. 4, p. 341, 1891.

QUOITS

The following games are akin to our game of quoits, but they do not appear to have anything in common with it apart from a general resemblance. At the same time it is not unlikely that the game played with stones by the Tarahumare, Mohave, and Zuñi may have been borrowed from the Spaniards. The last-named play with iron disks, rayuelas. The Zuñi regard their game as Mexican. I have here incorporated a Navaho game like ring-toss, which may have had likewise a foreign origin.

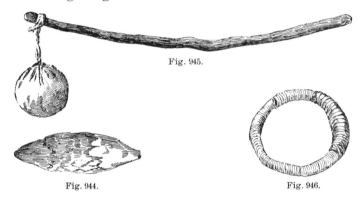

Fig. 945.

Fig. 944.   Fig. 946.

FIG. 944. Tipcat (model); length, 2¾ inches; Zuñi Indians, Zuñi, New Mexico; cat. no. 16309, Free Museum of Science and Art, University of Pennsylvania.
FIG. 945. Bat for tipcat (model); length, 19 inches; Zuñi Indians, Zuñi, New Mexico; cat. no. 16309, Free Museum of Science and Art, University of Pennsylvania.
FIG. 946. Ring for game; diameter, 4½ inches; Navaho Indians, Arizona; cat. no. 3632, Brooklyn Institute Museum.

ALGONQUIAN STOCK

MICMAC. Nova Scotia.
    Dr A. S. Gatschet writes: [a]

They have also the quoit game, and play it as Americans do; subale'wit, he plays the quoit game; nin subale'wi, I play at quoits; subale'-udi, the disk-shaped stone quoit.

ATHAPASCAN STOCK

NAVAHO. Chin Lee, Arizona. (Cat. no. 3632, Brooklyn Institute Museum.)
Yucca-wrapped ring (figure 946), 4½ inches in diameter, half its diameter painted white.
Collected by the writer in 1903. Two common sticks, about a foot high, are set up as pegs about as far apart as one can pitch, and if the ring falls so that its green edge touches the peg it counts twice as much as the white. When it falls on the peg the game is won. The ring is called bas, ring.

---

[a] From Baddeck, Nova Scotia, August 28, 1899.

ESKIMAUAN STOCK

ESKIMO (WESTERN). Liesnoi island, Alaska. (Cat. no. 90436, United
    States National Museum.)

Eleven flat polished ivory disks (figure 947), 1⅜ inches in diameter
    and one-fourth of an inch thick. Five have a single comma-
    shaped hole in the middle, and five three holes in a line across
    the piece. The eleventh piece appears to belong to another set.
    Collected by W. J. Fisher, Coast and Geodetic Survey.

This appears to be the game observed by Mr Ivan Petroff[a] among
the Kaviagmiut:

> The Kaniags were inveterate gamblers. They frequently lost all their pos-
> sessions in a game they called "kaganagah," which was played as follows: Two
> seal-skins were spread out at a distance of 8 or 10 feet from each other, and a
> flat, round piece of bone, about the size of a silver eagle was deposited upon
> each, the edge of the disk being marked with four black dots. The players,
> whose number was never more than four, but generally two, divided into two

FIG. 947. Ivory gaming disks; diameter, 1⅜ inches; Western Eskimo, Alaska; cat. no. 90436,
United States National Museum.

> parties, and each put up some article of value. Each gambler had five wooden
> disks, and these he threw from the edge of one skin to the other, trying to cover
> the bone disk. When all the disks had been thrown, the players examined their
> relative positions. If the bone disk had been covered, the lucky thrower received
> from his opponent three bone sticks, or marks; but if he had covered only one of
> the black dots of the disk he received two marks, and the wooden disk which had
> fallen nearest to the bone procured for the thrower one mark, and the marks
> were subsequently redeemed with valuables.

——— Kodiak island, Alaska.

Capt. Uriy Lissiansky[b] says:

> The Cadiack men are so fond of gaming that they often lose everything they
> possess at play. They have a very favorite game called kroogeki. Four or
> more men play at it; that is, two against two, or three against three. Two
> skins are spread on the ground, at the distance of about 12 feet from each other.
> On each skin is placed a round flat mark made of bone, about 4½ inches in
> circumference, with a black circle and center marked on it. Every player has
> five wooden pieces, like what are called men in the game of draughts or back-
> gammon, and distinguished in the same manner by color. The players kneel,
> and, stretching themselves forward, lean on the left hand, throwing the

---

[a] Tenth Census. Report on the Population, Industries, and Resources of Alaska, p. 143,
Washington, 1884.

[b] A Voyage round the World, p. 210, London, 1814.

draughts with the right, one after another, adversary against adversary, aiming at the round mark. If a man hits the mark, his antagonist endeavors to dislodge the draught by placing his own there. When all the draughts are expended on both sides, it is examined how they lie, and they are counted accordingly: for every draught touching the mark, 1; for that which lodges on it, 2; for that which cuts the black circle, 3, etc. In this manner the game continues till the number 112, which is the point of the game, is gained. The numbers are counted by small sticks made for the purpose.

KERESAN STOCK

KERES. Cochiti, New Mexico.

A Keres boy at St Michael, Arizona, named Francisco Chaves (Kogit), described the following game to the writer in 1904:

Waiso.—A tin can is set up, on which stakes—money, buttons, or matches—are placed. Several boys throw flat stones at the can, and the one who knocks the can down, or comes nearest to it, wins. The stones, waiso, are smooth flat pebbles about 4 inches in diameter, picked up for the occasion.

FIG. 948. Stone quoits; diameters, 3¼ and 3 inches; Tarahumare Indians, Chihuahua, Mexico; cat. no. 16343, Free Museum of Science and Art, University of Pennsylvania.

PIMAN STOCK

PIMA. Arizona.

The late Dr Frank Russell [a] described the following game:

Haeyo.—This game affords considerable amusement for the spectators as well as the participants. Four men provide themselves with moderately large stones, hayakŭt, which they throw between two holes set about 50 feet apart. All stand at one hole and try successively to throw into the other. If but one succeeds in throwing into the hole, he and his partner are carried on the backs of their opponents across to the opposite goal. If both partners throw into the hole they are carried across and then return to the first hole, the "horses" who carry them attempting to imitate the gallop of the horse.

TARAHUMARE. Chihuahua, Mexico. (Cat. no. 16343, Free Museum of Science and Art, University of Pennsylvania.)

Hemispheric disk of quartzite (figure 948), 3½ inches in diameter, and another of lavalike stone, 3 inches in diameter.

Collected by Dr Carl Lumholtz, who describes them [b] as used in a game called cuatro, four, which resembles our game of quoits:

It is called rixiwátali (rixíwala=disk), and two and two play against each other. First one stone is moistened with spittle on one side to make it

---

[a] In a memoir to be published by the Bureau of American Ethnology.
[b] Unknown Mexico, v. 1, p. 277, New York, 1902.

" heads or tails " and tossed up. The player who wins the toss plays first. Each has three stones, which are thrown toward a hole in the ground, perhaps 20 yards off. One of each party throws first, then goes to the hole and looks at it, while the other players make their throws. The stone falling nearest to the hole counts 1 point; if it falls into the hole, it counts 4; if the stone of the second player falls on top of the first stone in the hole, it " kills " the first stone. The game is out at 12. To measure distances, they break off small sticks. Lookers-on may stand around and bet which of the players will win.

SKITTAGETAN STOCK

HAIDA (KAIGANI). Prince of Wales island, Alaska.
Dr C. F. Newcombe describes the following game:

A narrow stone about a foot in length is erected at some 20 feet from a base, and any number of players, from two to six, try to knock it down, each with a round ball-like stone. He who first scores ten knockdowns wins. This game is called q'ūsqEdE'ldŭñ.

FIG. 949. Stones for lükia; lengths, 4¼ and 5 inches; Kwakiutl Indians, Vancouver island, British Columbia; cat. no. 37906, Free Museum of Science and Art, University of Pennsylvania.

WAKASHAN STOCK

KWAKIUTL. Nawiti, Vancouver island, British Columbia. (Cat. no. 37906, Free Museum of Science and Art, University of Pennsylvania.)

Two ovate pieces of worked lava, 4¼ and 5 inches in length (figure 949).

They were collected by Dr C. F. Newcombe, who describes them as used in the game of lükia, played by boys:

Played with oblong stones having one end slightly thin, so as to remain where they fall when thrown, and two mark sticks or goals. The players, from two to twelve, equally divided on two sides, each have one stone, except the last, who has two. Each side begins in turn and plays alternately. The object is to get nearest the mark, and it is allowable to drive an opponent's stone by striking it with one's own. That side wins which first scores 10 nearest.

YUMAN STOCK

Mohave. Colorado river, Arizona.
Capt. John G. Bourke [a] says:

The day was passed in looking in upon the Mojave living close to the fort, and noting what was of most interest. They were nearly all engaged in playing "shinny" or "quoits." The quoits were two round, flat stones, 4 inches diameter; the side which could first throw them both into the hole, 20 paces away, won the game.

ZUÑIAN STOCK

Zuñi. Zuñi, New Mexico.   (Cat. no. 16344, 16345, Free Museum of Science and Art, University of Pennsylvania.)
Thin disks of sandstone, from 2¼ to 5 inches in diameter; a piece of corncob; and two silver buttons (figure 950); implements for a game like quoits, reproduced by Mr Frank Hamilton Cushing in 1893.

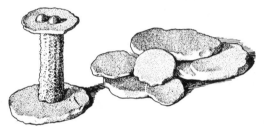

Fig. 950. Standing-cob game; Zuñi Indians, Zuñi, New Mexico; cat. no. 16344, 16345, Free Museum of Science and Art, University of Pennsylvania.

The corncob is set on a sandstone disk with a smaller disk on top of it, the silver buttons, which are used as stakes, being put on the upper disk. The players throw at this target with other disks of sandstone. The game was described by Mr Cushing under the name of the standing-cob game.

Mr John G. Owens [b] describes this game as follows:

Than-kä-lä-wä.—This game is usually played in the spring, and resembles somewhat our game of quoits. In place of the ordinary quoit they use flat stones. Any number may take part. A small stone or even a corn-cob is set up, and on this each places his stake. To determine which shall pitch first they all throw for some distant point. He who comes nearest to the mark chosen pitches first, and each one follows according to his throw; then the game begins. The distance pitched is nearly 100 feet. The object is to knock over the stake or pool. If the pool is knocked over, and the stone pitched goes beyond it, it counts nothing; if just even with it, the one who pitched has another chance; if it remains behind, he takes everything, and all put up again. They count it great sport, and some become very skillful in pitching.

[a] Notes on the Cosmogony and Theogony of the Mojave Indians.   Journal of American Folk-Lore, v. 2, p. 171, 1889.
[b] Some Games of the Zuñi.   Popular Science Monthly, v. 39, p. 40, New York, 1891.

ZUÑI. Zuñi, New Mexico. (Brooklyn Institute Museum.)

Cat. no. 3096. Two stone disks, 4½ and 5 inches in diameter, one a broken upper stone for the metate (figure 951).

Cat. no. 3097. Flat stone disk, 4 inches in diameter; one side flat, the opposite side convex and marked with incised lines, as shown in figure 952.

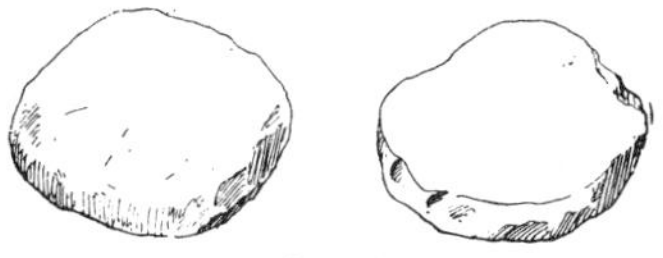

Fig. 951. 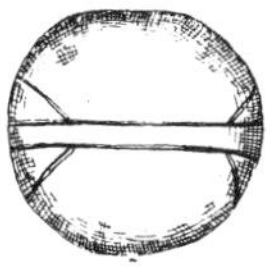   Fig. 952.

FIG. 951. Stone quoits; diameters, 4½ and 5 inches; Zuñi Indians, Zuñi, New Mexico; cat. no. 3096, Brooklyn Institute Museum.

FIG. 952. Stone quoit; diameter, 4 inches; Zuñi Indians, Zuñi, New Mexico; cat. no. 3097, Brooklyn Institute Museum.

The specimens just described were collected by the writer in 1903.

The stones are called tankalanai. It is a winter game for men and boys. Each one has a quoit. They set a corncob up on the ground and put the stakes—turquoises, silver beads or buttons, or money—on top of the cob and throw at it in turn. The first player throws his stone from the cob at some distant mark, about as far as he can. The players then stand at this point and throw at the cob until one of them knocks it down. Then the one whose quoit fell nearest to the stakes (not the cob) wins all. After a player throws he draws a ring around his stone to mark where it fell when he takes it up to throw again. A stone, a chip, or any convenient object is put on the cob to lay the stakes on.

Cat. no. 3098. Sandstone disk (figure 953), 3½ inches in diameter, with a cross incised on one face and on the other the face of the sun.

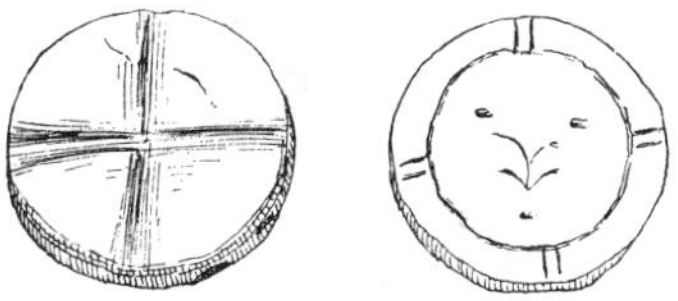

FIG. 953. Sun quoit; diameter, 3½ inches; Zuñi Indians, Zuñi, New Mexico; cat. no. 3098, Brooklyn Institute Museum.

It was presented to the writer by Zuñi Dick in 1903. He gave the name as tankalana yettokia, and said it was anciently used on Corn mountain by the Sun priest.

Mrs Matilda Coxe Stevenson, in her paper on Zuñi Games,[a] states that the Zuñi assert that this game came from Mexico.

---

[a] American Anthropologist, n. s., v. 5, p. 496, 1903.

STONE-THROWING

A game of throwing stones at a mark is reported from two tribes.

SHOSHONEÁN STOCK

BANNOCK. Rossfork, Idaho. (Cat. no. 37065, Free Museum of Science and Art, University of Pennsylvania.)

Stone ball (figure 954) pitted with a hammer stone and perfectly spherical; diameter, $2\frac{7}{8}$ inches.

Collected by the writer in 1900.

The name given was tin-bin ter-ow-a-ko, and it was described as used in a game of throwing at a mark, the players betting which would come nearest.

FIG. 954. Stone ball used to throw at a mark; diameter, $2\frac{7}{8}$ inches; Bannock Indians, Rossfork, Idaho; cat. no. 37065, Free Museum of Science and Art, University of Pennsylvania.

TANOAN STOCK

TEWA. Santa Clara, New Mexico.

Mr T. S. Dozier [a] writes:

The old Tewa game of kou-wa-di has almost passed into disuse. Only two or three times have I seen it played. It consisted in throwing a kou-e (stone) at a target, with about the same rules as are observed in the arrow game. It was played just after that game, the game of marbles and that of tops taking its place now.

SHUFFLEBOARD

A game played on the ice by women, like shuffleboard, has been observed among the Dakota. Four accounts are recorded.

SIOUAN STOCK

ASSINIBOIN. Fort Union, Montana.

Mr Edwin T. Denig [b] says that the women play billiards with flat stones on the ice.

DAKOTA (TETON). Pine Ridge reservation, South Dakota.

Dr J. R. Walker [c] describes the game of woskate icaslohe, played by women on the ice with a stone ball, tapaiyan, and wooden cylinder, cannúbi, calling it the game of bowls.

DAKOTA (YANKTON). Fort Peck, Montana. (Cat. no. 37611, Free Museum of Science and Art, University of Pennsylvania.)

Two small wooden cylinders (figure 955), $1\frac{1}{4}$ inches in diameter and $1\frac{1}{2}$ inches in length; and a flat oval stone about 3 inches in diameter.

[a] Some Tewa Games. Unpublished manuscript in the Bureau of American Ethnology.
[b] Unpublished manuscript in the library of the Bureau of American Ethnology.
[c] Journal of American Folk-Lore, v. 19, p. 29, 1905.

The latter is marked on one side in ink with eyes and mouth simulating a human face. An iron ball, about three-fourths of an inch in diameter, accompanies these specimens.

These objects were collected by the writer in 1900. They were made by Black Chicken. The game, umpapi, is played on the ice exclusively by women. The cylinders are set up and struck with the stone, ihe, or with the bullet, which is shoved with the hand.

FIG. 955. Implements for umpapi; length of cylinders, 1¼ inches; Yankton Dakota Indians, Fort Peck, Montana; cat. no. 37611, Free Museum of Science and Art, University of Pennsylvania.

HIDATSA. Fort Atkinson, North Dakota.

Henry A. Boller [a] says:

The mania for gambling was by no means confined to the men. The women and young girls were equally imbued with it; and, sitting down on a smooth place on the ice, they would roll a pebble from one to the other for hours together. Young infants were often kept on the ice all the while, their mothers, or those who had them in charge, being too much engrossed with their play to pay them any attention.

JACKSTRAWS

The game of jackstraws would seem a natural and logical development from the game of stick-counting. The only intimations the writer has had of it in America are among the Eskimo and the Haida. The first of the two games described by Mr Nelson is somewhat like our game of jackstones; the second is identical with our jackstraws.

ESKIMAUAN STOCK

ESKIMO (WESTERN). St Michael, Alaska. (Cat. no. 178970, United States National Museum.)

FIG. 956. Jackstraws; length, 4½ inches; Western Eskimo, St Michael, Alaska; cat. no. 178970, United States National Museum.

Bundle of 109 small squared pine splints (figure 956), 4½ inches in length.

Collected by Mr E. W. Nelson, who describes the game played with them as follows: [b]

A bundle of from 50 to 75 small, squared, wooden splints, about 4 inches long and a little larger than a match, are placed in a small pile crosswise on the back of the player's outstretched right hand. The player then removes his hand quickly and tries to grasp the falling sticks between his thumb and fingers, still keeping

[a] Among the Indians: Eight years in the Far West, 1858–1866, p. 197, Philadelphia, 1868.
[b] The Eskimo about Bering Strait. Eighteenth Annual Report of the Bureau of American Ethnology, pt. 1, p. 332, 1899.

the palm downward. If one or more of the sticks fall to the ground it is a miss and the next player tries. Every time a player succeeds in catching all of the falling sticks, he lays aside one of them as a counter until all are gone, when each player counts up, and the one holding the greatest number is the winner. These squared splints are similar to those used as markers in the first game described [a game of dart throwing, see page 387]. Small stakes are sometimes played for in this game, as in the first.

The bunch of slender splints already described are also used to play a game exactly like jackstraws. The player grasps the bunch of sticks between the thumb and forefinger of the right hand, resting one end upon the floor; then he suddenly releases them and they fall in a small heap. The players have a small wooden hook, and each in succession removes as many of the sticks as he can without moving any but the one taken. Each player keeps those he succeeds in removing, and the one holding the largest number at the end is the winner. Both men and women play this game, but usually not together.

SKITTAGETAN STOCK

HAIDA. Prince of Wales island, Alaska.

Dr C. F. Newcombe says these Indians have the cheese-straw game (jackstraws) which they call hlketosgan, and play precisely like the European game.

SWING

Only four notices of the swing occur, one of which appears to refer to a late and civilized form.

ALGONQUIAN STOCK

ARAPAHO. Wyoming.

Dr A. L. Kroeber [a] relates a flood myth in which Crow-woman, the wife of a man, urges a girl named River-woman, whom her husband has taken as a new wife, to go with her to a swing which she had hung on a tree that leaned over a pool in the river. After refusing three times, the girl went and swung, when the rope broke and she fell into the pool and was drowned.

CADDOAN STOCK

PAWNEE (SKIDI). Oklahoma.

In the story of "Coyote Rescues a Maiden," Dr George A. Dorsey [b] refers to the girl who had the power of attracting buffalo through being swung by her brothers.[c]

WICHITA. Oklahoma.

Dr Albert S. Gatschet communicated to me the following name for the swing of children: neeniku'yassash.

---

[a] Traditions of the Arapaho, p. 11, Chicago, 1903.
[b] Traditions of the Skidi Pawnee, p. 254, Boston and New York, 1904.
[c] The same story is found among the Caddo. Traditions of the Caddo, p. 51, Washington, 1905.

SIOUAN STOCK

DAKOTA (TETON). South Dakota.

Rev. J. Owen Dorsey [a] describes the following game, as played by girls and boys:

Hóhotéla, Swinging, is an autumnal game. The swing is attached to a leaning tree after the leaves have fallen. When four ropes are used, a blanket is laid on them, and several children sit on the blanket and are pushed forward. Those who push say "Hohote, hohote! Hohotela, hohotela!" as long as they push them. When two ropes are used, only one child at a time sits in the swing.

STILTS

Our information about the use of stilts is extremely meager, the name from the Wichita and two recent specimens, boys' playthings, from Shoshonean tribes, being practically all. They are mentioned as existing among the Maya by Bishop Landa,[b] who refers to a dance on high stilts in honor of the bird deity Yaccocahmut.

This description was suggested to me by Dr Eduard Seler to explain the picture of a figure on what appears to be stilts, that occurs in plate xxi of the Troano Codex (figure 957).

A clue to the origin of these implements may be found in the employment of planting sticks as stilts by boys in Zuñi.

CADDOAN STOCK

WICHITA. Oklahoma.

Dr Albert S. Gatschet communicated to me the following name for stilts among terms for outdoor games from the Wichita language collected in 1892: Hāk i'arits, stilts, walking wood.

FIG. 957. Stilt-walking (?); Maya Indians, Yucatan; from pl. xxi, Codex Troano.

SHOSHONEAN STOCK

HOPI. Oraibi, Arizona. (Cat. no. 38703, Free Museum of Science and Art, University of Pennsylvania.)

Pair of stilts (figure 958), hokia, two cottonwood poles, 54½ inches in length, with a crotch wrapped with colored rags.

Collected by the writer in 1901. They are used by boys.

---

[a] Games of Teton Dakota Children. The American Anthropologist, v. 4, p. 329, 1891.

[b] Relation des Choses de Yucatan, p. 223, Paris, 1864.

SHOSHONI. Wind River reservation, Wyoming. (Cat. no. 36886,
Free Museum of Science and Art, University of Pennsylvania.)

Pair of stilts (figure 959), made of saplings, with a forked crotch,
the lower part of which is bound with willow bark; length, 42½
inches.

Collected by the writer in 1900.

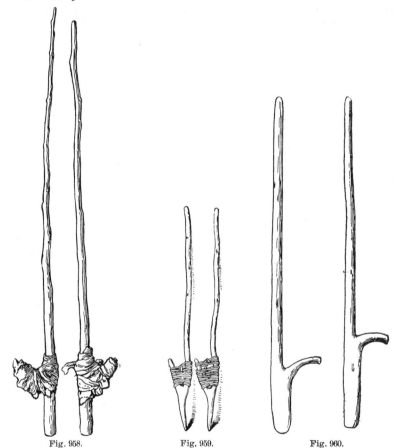

Fig. 958.   Fig. 959.   Fig. 960.

FIG. 958. Stilts; length, 54¼ inches; Hopi Indians, Oraibi, Arizona; cat. no. 38703, Free Museum
of Science and Art, University of Pennsylvania.

FIG. 959. Stilts; length, 42¼ inches; Shoshoni Indians, Wyoming; cat. no. 36886, Free Museum
of Science and Art, University of Pennsylvania.

FIG. 960. Digging sticks (used as stilts); length, 30 inches; Zuñi Indians, Zuñi, New Mexico;
cat. no. 3188, 3189, Brooklyn Institute Museum.

ZUÑIAN STOCK

ZUÑI. Zuñi, New Mexico.

The writer was informed in Zuñi that boys frequently employ a
pair of digging sticks (figure 960); tasakwiwai, to walk on in the
manner of stilts.

TOPS

The top is one of the most widely diffused of Indian children's playthings. The assertion has been made that it is of recent introduction, but its general use, taken in connection with its existence in prehistoric times in Peru, would seem to point to its having been known before the period of contact with the whites.

The most usual form is the whip top, made of wood, horn, stone, or clay, and sometimes painted in colors. Spinning tops is a winter game and is commonly played on the ice. Tops consisting of disks of wood, bone, or ivory, with wooden or bone spindles, also occur. On the Northwest coast a pierced slat is sometimes used to hold the top while the string is being unwound. The strings are of sinew or bark cord.

Top spinning occurs as a game among the Eskimo, the player endeavoring to run round the house while his top is spinning. The Niska try to see who can keep his top spinning longest. Among the Oglala the player tries to whip and hold his top in a square. Some of the wooden peg tops of the Pueblos have a hole in the side to make them hum when they spin. Of all forms, these peg tops seem most likely to be of European introduction. The spindle and cord tops seem to be related in form and mechanism to the spindle employed in weaving, and the whip top appears to be analogous to the whipped ball, but this remains mere conjecture.

FIG. 961. Whip top; height, 3½ inches; Arapaho Indians, Wind River reservation, Wyoming; cat. no. 36980, Free Museum of Science and Art, University of Pennsylvania.

ALGONQUIAN STOCK

ARAPAHO. Wind River reservation, Wyoming. (Cat. no. 36980, Free Museum of Science and Art, University of Pennsylvania.)

Wooden whip top (figure 961); height, 3½ inches. Collected by the writer in 1900.

———— Cheyenne and Arapaho reservation, Oklahoma.

Mr James Mooney [a] says:

Tops are used by all Indian boys, and are made of wood or bone. They are not thrown or spun with a string, but are kept in motion by whipping with a small quirt or whip of buckskin. In winter they are spun upon the ice. The younger children make tops to twirl with the fingers by running a stick through a small seed berry.

---

[a] The Ghost-dance Religion. Fourteenth Annual Report of the Bureau of Ethnology, pt. 2, p. 1006, 1896.

BLACKFEET. Montana. (Cat. no. 16190, Field Columbian Museum.) Two pieces of wood resembling whip tops (figure 962). Collected by J. M. McLean.

CHEYENNE. Oklahoma.

Mr Louis L. Meeker [a] writes:

They have also whip tops (ne'-do-hi-yon''-hsist, or whirling game). They are played in winter. When the ice breaks up in the spring, they are thrown into the water as it rises, with the implements for the other winter games, and carried away. Playing winter games in summer is popularly supposed to make hairs grow on the body where tweezers will be required to remove them—a nursery tale.

FIG. 962. Whip tops; heights 2 and 2¼ inches; Blackfoot Indians, Montana; cat. no. 16190, Field Columbian Museum.

CHIPPEWA. Apostle islands, Wisconsin.

J. G. Kohl [b] says:

The Indian boys manage to make tops out of acorns and nuts as cleverly as our boys do. They also collect the oval stones which are found on the banks of the rivers and lakes and use them on the ice in winter. Barefooted and active, they run over the ice, and drive the stones against each other with whips and sticks. The stone that upsets the other is the victor.

——— Michigan.

Baraga [c] gives the following definitions:

Top (boy's plaything), towéigan; I play with a top, nin towéige.

CREE. Edmonton, Alberta. (Cat. no. 15070, Field Columbian Museum.)

Wooden whip top and whip (figure 963). Collected by Isaac Cowie.

FIG. 963. Whip top and whip; height of top, 2¼ inches; length of whip, 22¼ inches; Cree Indians, Alberta; cat. no. 15070, Field Columbian Museum.

GROSVENTRES. Fort Belknap, Montana. (American Museum of Natural History.)

Cat. no. $\frac{50}{1811}$. Top of solid black horn (figure 964), 2¾ inches in length, accompanied by a whip with four buckskin lashes, and a wooden handle painted red, 13 inches in length.

[a] Notes on Cheyenne Indian Games communicated to the Bureau of American Ethnology.
[b] Kitchi-Gami, Wanderings round Lake Superior, p. 84, London, 1860.
[c] A Dictionary of the Otchipwe Language, Cincinnati, 1853.

Cat. no. $\frac{50}{1878}$.   Top, a disk of wood (figure 965), 4 inches in diameter, painted red, with wooden spindle 7 inches in length.

Both of the above were collected by Dr A. L. Kroeber in 1901.

NORRIDGEWOCK.   Norridgewock, Maine.

Rasles [a] gives the following definitions:

Pébésk8mañgan, toupie sur la glace, &c.; sur la terre, arip8dangan.

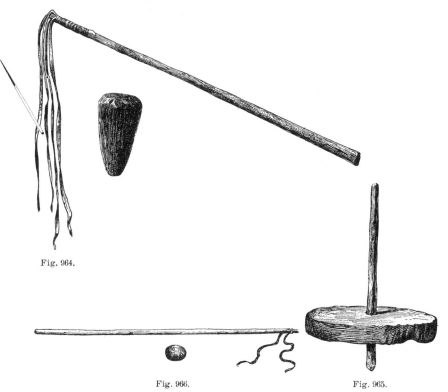

Fig. 964.

Fig. 966.   Fig. 965.

FIG. 964.   Whip top and whip; height of top, 2¼ inches; Grosventre Indians, Montana; cat. no. $\frac{50}{1811}$, American Museum of Natural History.

FIG. 965.   Top; diameter, 4 inches; Grosventre Indians, Montana; cat. no. $\frac{50}{1878}$, American Museum of Natural History.

FIG. 966.   Whip top and whip; diameter of top, 1¼ inches; Sauk and Fox Indians, Iowa; cat. no. $\frac{50}{3519}$, American Museum of Natural History.

SAUK AND FOXES.   Iowa.   (Cat. no. $\frac{50}{3519}$, American Museum of Natural History.)

Ovate ball of stone (figure 966), 1¾ inches in diameter, with a whip made of a peeled stick, 21 inches long, having two leather lashes.

Collected by Dr William Jones, who describes them as whip top and whip, played on the ice. The top is called nimitcihi, dancer.

---

[a] A Dictionary of the Abnaki Language in North America.   Memoirs of the American Academy of Science and Arts, n. s., v. 1, Cambridge, 1833.

CHIMMESYAN STOCK

Niska. Nass river, British Columbia.

Dr Franz Boas [a] describes a top as follows:

Halha'l: spinning top, made of the top of a hemlock tree. A cylinder, $3\frac{1}{2}''$ in diameter and $3''$ high, is cut; a slit is made on one side and it is hollowed out. A pin, $2\frac{1}{2}''$ long and $\frac{1}{4}''$ thick, is inserted in the center of the top. A small board with a wide hole, through which a string of skin or of bear-guts passes, is used for winding up the top. It is spun on the ice of the river. The board is held in the left hand, and stemmed against the foot. Then the string is pulled through the hole with the right. Several men begin spinning at a signal. The one whose top spins the longest wins.

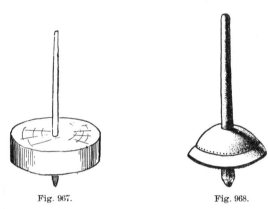

Fig. 967.   Fig. 968.

Fig. 967. Top; diameter, 3 inches; Tsimshian Indians, Hazelton, British Columbia; cat. no. 53115, Field Columbian Museum.
Fig. 968. Top; height, $3\frac{1}{4}$ inches; Central Eskimo, Cumberland sound, Baffin land, Franklin; cat. no. $\frac{60}{3466}$, American Museum of Natural History.

Tsimshian. Hazelton, British Columbia.   (Cat. no. 53115, Field Columbian Museum.)

Top (figure 967), consisting of a disk of wood 3 inches in diameter, with a wooden spindle 6 inches in length. Collected by Dr George A. Dorsey, who describes it as a child's toy.

ESKIMAUAN STOCK

Eskimo (Central). Cumberland sound, Baffin land, Franklin.   (Cat. no. $\frac{60}{3466}$, American Museum of Natural History.)

Wooden top (figure 968), with a wooden whirl and a spindle, $3\frac{1}{4}$ inches in length.

Collected by Capt. James S. Mutch, and figured by Doctor Boas,[b] who says it was probably spun on the ice.

---

[a] Fifth Report on the Indians of British Columbia. Report of the Sixty-fifth Meeting of the British Association for the Advancement of Science, p. 583, London, 1895.
[b] Eskimo of Baffin Land and Hudson Bay. Bulletin of the American Museum of Natural History, v. 15, p. 53, New York, 1901.

Eskimo (Central: Aivilirmiut and Kinipetu). West coast of Hudson bay, Keewatin.

Dr Franz Boas [a] describes the following game:

A large cake of ice is formed in the shape of a top (kipekutuk) with a flat surface and a dull point which fits into a shallow hole. One man sits down on the piece of ice, while two others spin it around by means of sticks. This game is often indulged in at the floe edge, when waiting for the pack-ice to come in with the tide. Generally a man who is the butt of all the others is induced to sit on this top, and is spun around until he is made sick.

Eskimo (Labrador). Ungava bay. (United States National Museum.)

Cat. no. 90281. Wooden top (figure 969), conical, with band of red paint around the top; height, 2 inches.

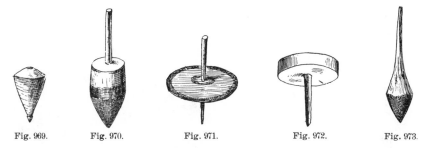

Fig. 969.　　　　Fig. 970.　　　　　　Fig. 971.　　　　　　　Fig. 972.　　　　　　Fig. 973.

Fig. 969. Top; height, 2 inches; Labrador Eskimo, Ungava bay; cat. no. 90281, United States National Museum.

Fig. 970. Top; height, 4¼ inches; Labrador Eskimo, Ungava bay; cat. no. 90282, United States National Museum.

Fig. 971. Top; height, 3¼ inches; Labrador Eskimo, Ungava bay; cat. no. 90283, United States National Museum.

Fig. 972. Top; height, 2¼ inches; Labrador Eskimo, Ungava bay; cat. no. 90284, United States National Museum.

Fig. 973. Wooden top; height, 4¼ inches; Western Eskimo, Bristol bay, Alaska; cat. no. 56045, United States National Museum.

Cat. no. 90282. Wooden top (figure 970), with two bands of red paint, and spindle of the same piece at the top; height, 4½ inches.

Cat. no. 90283. Wooden top (figure 971), a flat disk, 3¼ inches in diameter, with a spindle 3¾ inches in length.

Cat. no. 90284. Wooden top (figure 972), a disk, with a spindle below; the top concave and painted on the upper side with circle of red paint at the edge.

All these specimens were collected by Mr Lucien M. Turner.

Eskimo (Western). Bristol bay, Alaska. (United States National Museum.)

Cat. no. 56045. Wooden top (figure 973), 4¾ inches in height.

---

[a] Eskimo of Baffin Land and Hudson Bay. Bulletin of the American Museum of Natural History, v. 15, p. 110, New York, 1901.

Cat. no. 56045*a*. Wooden top (figure 974), 4½ inches in height, the lower part painted blue with red ring on top and blue above.

Cat. no. 56046. Ivory disk (figure 975), 2¼ inches in diameter, the top decorated with incised lines, and ivory pin, 3⅞ inches in length.

Cat. no. 56047. Wooden top (figure 976), a disk of wood, 4½ inches in diameter, with the top convex and ornamented with incised circles painted red and black, having a wooden spindle, 4½ inches in length.

Cat. no. 56048. Bone disk (figure 977), 1¼ inches in diameter, with the bottom ornamented with nine black spots, and bone pin, 1¾ inches in length.

All the foregoing specimens were collected by Mr Charles L. McKay.

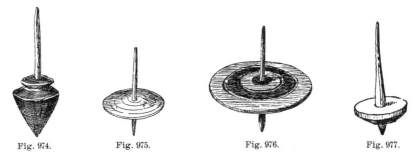

Fig. 974.   Fig. 975.   Fig. 976.   Fig. 977.

FIG. 974. Wooden top; height, 4¼ inches; Western Eskimo, Bristol bay, Alaska; cat. no. 56045*a*, United States National Museum.

FIG. 975. Ivory top; height, 3⅞ inches; Western Eskimo, Bristol bay, Alaska; cat. no. 56046, United States National Museum.,

FIG. 976. Wooden top; diameter, 4½ inches; Western Eskimo, Bristol bay, Alaska; cat. no. 56047, United States National Museum.

FIG. 977. Bone top; height, 1¼ inches; Western Eskimo, Bristol bay, Alaska; cat. no. 56048, United States National Museum.

ESKIMO (WESTERN). Point Barrow, Alaska. (Cat. no. 56491, United States National Museum.)

Top,[a] consisting of a shaft of pine and a disk of spruce (figure 978), 4¼ inches in diameter, ornamented with blacklead marks, forming a border about one-fourth of an inch broad; height, 5¼ inches. It is called kaipsa.

Collected in 1882 by Lieut. P. H. Ray, U. S. Army.

——— Lower Yukon, Alaska.

Mr Edward William Nelson[b] gives, under top spinning (uiwuk), the following description:

In winter, along the lower Yukon and adjacent region to the south, the children of both sexes gather in the kashim, and each child in succession spins

---

[a] The Point Barrow Eskimo. Ninth Annual Report of the Bureau of Ethnology, p. 376, 1892.

[b] The Eskimo about Bering Strait. Eighteenth Annual Report of the Bureau of American Ethnology, pt. 1, p. 333, 1899.

its top. The moment the top is spun the owner runs out through the entrance passage and attempts to make a complete circuit of the house and enter again before the top stops spinning. A score is made every time this is done successfully.

Continuing, Mr Nelson [a] says:

From Kuskokwim river to Cape Prince of Wales, on both the mainland and the islands, children of both sexes were found using tops. These are commonly of disk shape, thin at the edge, and perforated in the center for a peg. One from Cape Prince of Wales [figure 979] is of walrus ivory; it is 2½ inches in diameter and has a hole an inch wide in the middle, which is closed by a neatly-fitted wooden plug of the same thickness as the top, through which passes a spindle-shaped peg 4 inches long. This is the general style of top used in the region mentioned, but another kind is made to be spun with a guiding stick and cord; these are often used by men as well as boys.

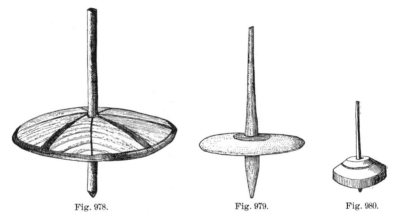

Fig. 978.   Fig. 979.   Fig. 980.

Fig. 978. Top; height, 5¼ inches; Western Eskimo, Point Barrow, Alaska; cat. no. 56491, United States National Museum.

Fig. 979. Top; height, 4 inches; Western Eskimo, Cape Prince of Wales, Alaska; cat. no. 45478, United States National Museum.

Fig. 980. Ivory top; height, 3 inches; Western Eskimo, Kotzebue sound, Alaska; cat. no. 127908, United States National Museum.

Referring to the tops spun by children on the lower Yukon, he says:

These toys are spun between the two hands, the upper part of the spindle being held upright between the palms.

Eskimo (Western). Kotzebue sound, Alaska. (Cat. no. 127908, United States National Museum.)

Disk of ivory (figure 980), 2⅞ inches in diameter, the top convex and marked with an incised line painted red, with a wooden spindle 3 inches in length. Collected by Lieut. George M. Stoney, U. S. Navy.

[a] The Eskimo about Bering Strait. Eighteenth Annual Report of the Bureau of American Ethnology, pt. 1, p. 341, 1899.

KERESAN STOCK

KERES. Sia, New Mexico. (Cat. no. 134362, United States National Museum.)

Wooden top (figure 981) with conical base and flat top, having a hole leading into a small cavity near the top of the base and a nail point; height, 2⅞ inches. Collected by Col. James Stevenson.

KIOWAN STOCK

KIOWA. Oklahoma. (Cat. no. 152905, United States National Museum.)

Wooden top (figure 982), 2⅛ inches in height, with a bone pin. Collected by Mr James Mooney.

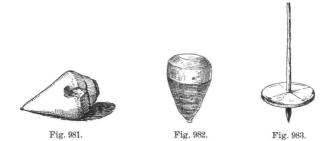

Fig. 981.   Fig. 982.   Fig. 983.

FIG. 981. Top; height, 2⅞ inches; Keres Indians, Sia, New Mexico; cat. no. 134362, United States National Museum.

FIG. 982. Top; height, 2⅛ inches; Kiowa Indians, Oklahoma; cat. no. 152905, United States National Museum.

FIG. 983. Ivory top; height, 3⅛ inches; Yakutat Indians, Port Mulgrave, Alaska; cat. no. 16298, United States National Museum.

KOLUSCHAN STOCK

YAKUTAT. Port Mulgrave, Alaska. (Cat. no. 16298, United States National Museum.)

Ivory disk (figure 983), 3⅛ inches in diameter, with a wooden spindle 3¾ inches in length. Collected by Dr W. H. Dall.

LUTUAMIAN STOCK

KLAMATH. Upper Klamath lake, Oregon. (Cat. no. 61729, Field Columbian Museum.)

Disk of white-pine bark (figure 984), 2½ inches in diameter, through which is thrust a 4-inch stick, sharpened at each end. A second specimen (61728) is similar to the first except that the disk is of cedar bark and instead of being beveled at the edge is cut off square.

These specimens were collected in 1900 by Dr George A. Dorsey and described by him under the name of heshtalxeash.[a]

MARIPOSAN STOCK

YOKUTS. Tule River reservation, Tulare county, California. (Cat. no. 70506, Field Columbian Museum.)

Two wooden hand tops (figure 985); lengths, $4\frac{1}{4}$ and $2\frac{1}{4}$ inches. Collected by Dr J. W. Hudson, who describes them as toys for hand spinning.

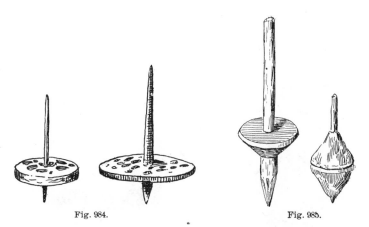

Fig. 984.   Fig. 985.

FIG. 984. Tops; Klamath Indians, Oregon; cat. no. 61728, 61729, Field Columbian Museum.
FIG. 985. Hand tops; lengths, $4\frac{1}{4}$ and $2\frac{1}{4}$ inches; Yokuts Indians, Tule River reservation, Tulare county, California; cat. no. 70506, Field Columbian Museum.

MAYAN STOCK

MAYA. Yucatan.

Dr Alfred Tozzer writes:

A top game is called in Maya polkirich. The tops are made of wood in the common shape and spun in a circle marked on the ground in the center of which is the object to be won or lost. Certain rules govern this.

SALISHAN STOCK

CLALLAM. Washington.

A Clallam boy, John Raub, informed the writer that the boys of this tribe play with tops like those used by the Makah (figures 1002–1004), which they call tsuchichaiootklen.

---

[a] Certain Gambling Games of the Klamath Indians. American Anthropologist, n. s., v. 3, p. 20, 1901.

THOMPSON INDIANS (NTLAKYAPAMUK). British Columbia. (American Museum of Natural History.)

Cat. no. $\frac{16}{8609}$. Fir-wood top (figure 986), with iron pegs at top and bottom and twisted bark cord; height, 3¾ inches.

Collected by Mr James Teit, who says:

Formerly the pins of tops were made of bone instead of iron. Most tops had buckskin thongs instead of bark strings, as they were considered superior for making them spin. Tops were generally spun on smooth ice, and the amusement was indulged in occasionally by adults. Sometimes boys tried to split one another's tops by trying to spin one on top of the other.

Cat. no. $\frac{16}{8644}$. Disk of yellow pine bark (figure 987), 3 inches in diameter and five-eighths of an inch thick, with wooden spindle 5 inches in length.

Collected by Mr James Teit, who gives the name as salelaepten.

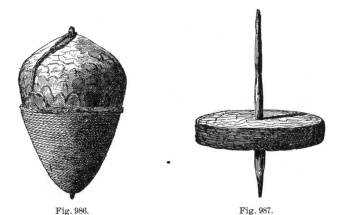

Fig. 986.   Fig. 987.

FIG. 986. Top; height, 3¾ inches; Thompson Indians (Ntlakyapamuk), British Columbia; cat. no. $\frac{16}{8609}$, American Museum of Natural History.

FIG. 987. Top; diameter, 3 inches; Thompson Indians (Ntlakyapamuk), British Columbia; cat. no. $\frac{16}{8644}$, American Museum of Natural History.

Mr Teit [a] further says:

Tops or whirligigs were used. These were generally made of a thin circular piece of wood, or more frequently a piece of yellow-pine bark, through the center of which was inserted a pin a fourth to half an inch in diameter and about 5 or 6 inches long, the circular piece of wood being allowed to remain about the middle of the pin. The one who made his top spin the longest won.

SHOSHONEAN STOCK

BANNOCK. Fort Hall reservation, Idaho. (Cat. no. 37067, Free Museum of Science and Art, University of Pennsylvania.)
Finger top, or teetotum (figure 988), made of the end of a cotton spool, with a peg for twirling; height, 1½ inches.

[a] The Thompson Indians of British Columbia. Memoirs of the American Museum of Natural History, whole series, v. 2, p. 281, New York, 1900.

This was collected by the writer in 1900. The name was given as temeinígakin.

HOPI. Oraibi, Arizona. (Cat. no. 51978, 55308, 67011, 67060, Field Columbian Museum.)

Four tops, made of wood.

These were collected by Rev. H. R. Voth, who furnished the following information:

Top spinning is often indulged in among the Hopi boys. The tops are of different sizes and forms, and are spun with a little whip, which consists of a stick from 10 to 15 inches long, to which any kind of a string is tied. The top is taken between the thumb and forefinger, or sometimes the middle finger, and sent with a twirl spinning over the ground, after which it is kept in motion by quickly striking its lower point with the whip. Sometimes it is started by winding the string of the whip around the point and withdrawing it with a quick motion, being much the same as when a white boy starts his top with a string.

——— Arizona. (United States National Museum.)

Cat. no. 22512. Wooden top (figure 989), made from a billet, the body cylindrical, painted red, the base conical, with traces of green paint, a boss at the top; height, 4¾ inches. Collected by Maj. J. W. Powell.

Cat. no. 68834. Wooden top (figure 990), a flat disk, painted with concentric rings of black, white, blue, and yellow on top, having a wooden spindle 9½ inches in length. Collected by Col. James Stevenson.

Fig. 968.   Fig. 989.   Fig. 990.

FIG. 988. Finger top; height, 1¼ inches; Bannock Indians, Idaho; cat. no. 37067, Free Museum of Science and Art, University of Pennsylvania.
FIG. 989. Whip top; height, 4¾ inches; Hopi Indians, Arizona; cat. no. 22512, United States National Museum.
FIG. 990. Top; height, 9¼ inches; Hopi Indians, Arizona; cat. no. 68834, United States National Museum.

——— Oraibi, Arizona. (Cat. no. 38624, Free Museum of Science and Art, University of Pennsylvania.)

Wooden tops, conical (figure 991), painted blue, white, and red, with black bands between, and the top painted with concentric circles of blue, white, black, and red; height, 4 inches; accompanied by whips consisting of sticks with long single buckskin lashes.

The foregoing were collected by the writer in 1901. The top is called riyanpi; the whips, wowahpi.

PAIUTE. Southern Utah. (Cat. no. 9436, Peabody Museum of American Archæology and Ethnology.)

Two tops (figure 992), with clay whirls $1\frac{1}{2}$ and $1\frac{3}{4}$ inches in diameter, cemented with gum, having wooden pins, 5 inches in length. Collected by Dr Edward Palmer.

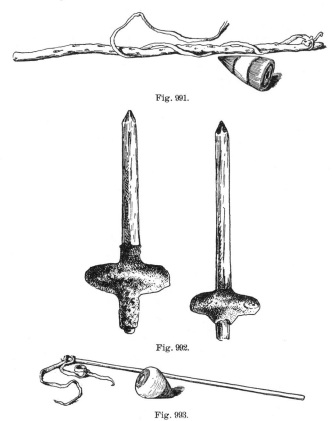

Fig. 991.

Fig. 992.

Fig. 993.

FIG. 991. Whip top and whip; height of top, 4 inches; Hopi Indians, Oraibi, Arizona; cat. no. 38624, Free Museum of Science and Art, University of Pennsylvania.

FIG. 992. Tops; length, 5 inches; Paiute Indians, southern Utah; cat. no. 9436, Peabody Museum of American Archæology and Ethnology.

FIG. 993. Whip top and whip; height of top, $3\frac{1}{4}$ inches; Shoshoni Indians, Wyoming; cat. no. 36885, Free Museum of Science and Art, University of Pennsylvania.

SHOSHONI. Wind River reservation, Wyoming. (Cat. no. 36885, Free Museum of Science and Art, University of Pennsylvania.)

Whip top (figure 993), nara pugi, and whip, temaki. The top made of wood, $3\frac{1}{2}$ inches in length, painted yellow and blue; the whip, a stick, 24 inches in length, with leather thong. Collected by the writer in 1900.

SIOUAN STOCK

CROWS. Crow reservation, Montana. (Field Columbian Museum.)

Cat. no. 69660. Conical wooden top (figure 994*a*), with rounded base and flat top, painted red; height, 3 inches; with whip, a twig with three buckskin lashes.

Cat. no. 69662. Cylindrical wooden top (figure 994*b*), with hemispheric base and flat top, painted black; height, 3 inches; with whip.

Cat. no. 69663. Wooden top, cylindrical billet, pointed alike at both ends; painted red; height, 3 inches.

Cat. no. 69664. Cylindrical wooden top, with conical base, having an iron nail-head in the center; unpainted; height, 4 inches.

Cat. no. 69665. Top, similar to the preceding; height, 2½ inches; with whip.

Cat. no. 69666. Top, similar to no. 69660; unpainted; height, 3¼ inches.

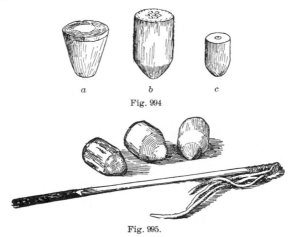

a   *b*   *c*

Fig. 994

Fig. 995.

FIG. 994 *a*, *b*, *c*. Whip tops; heights, 3, 3, and 1⅝ inches; Crow Indians, Montana; cat. no. 69660, 69662, 69667, Field Columbian Museum.

FIG. 995. Whip tops and whip; Oglala Dakota Indians, Pine Ridge reservation, South Dakota; cat. no. 22125 *a*, *b*, *c*, *d*, Free Museum of Science and Art, University of Pennsylvania.

Cat. no. 69677. Catlinite top (figure 994*c*), bullet-shaped, with a wooden plug extending from top to point; height, 1⅜ inches. The plug takes up the shock when the top is thrown.

These specimens were collected in 1901 by Mr S. C. Simms, who gives the name memashscha.

DAKOTA (OGLALA). Pine Ridge reservation, South Dakota. (Cat. no. 22125 *a*, *b*, *c*, *d*, Free Museum of Science and Art, University of Pennsylvania.)

Two wooden tops (figure 995), rudely cut from a sapling, 1¾ inches in diameter at top and 2⅝ and 3 inches in length. One is painted yellow, with red center on top and beveled edge, blue at the top, the lower pointed end painted red and yellow. The other is painted blue on top, with red beveled edge and the pointed end yellow and red. A third top is similar, but unpainted. A whip consists of a stick, 17 inches in length, with a lash made of hide, cut in three thongs, attached with sinew.

These specimens were collected by **Mr Louis L. Meeker,**[a] who gives the name as can wakiyapi, and says:

Players contend for position in a square marked on the ground or on ice. The game is to whip the top into the square and keep it there. On ice a square is marked and each player starts his top outside the square, trying to whip his top inside. When one succeeds, he holds the square while he keeps his top there. Should the top fall or run outside the ring, the others press in. The tops are rudely shaped from hard-wood sticks.

DAKOTA (TETON). South Dakota.

Rev. J. Owen Dorsey [b] gives the following account:

Chan káwachípi, Spinning tops.—Tops are made of ash, cedar, buffalo horn, red catlinite, or of stone. They put a scalp lock on the upper surface, ornamenting the latter with several colors of paint. They make the top spin by twirling it with the fingers, or by whipping. When they make it spin steadily by whipping they redden the scalp lock, and as it revolves very rapidly it seems to be driven into the ground. This game is played on the ice or snow; sometimes on ground which has been made firm and smooth by trampling. For a whip each player takes a tender switch, to the small end of which he fastens a lash of deer hide. He braids one-half of the lash, allowing the rest to hang loosely. They place the tops in a row, after putting up stakes, and say: "Let us see who can make his top spin the longest distance."

Dr J. R. Walker [c] describes the game of tops among the Teton as played by making a square about 5 feet across. The players spin their tops outside of the square, and drive them into the open side of the square with their whips while they are spinning.

DAKOTA (YANKTON). Fort Peck, Montana. (Free Museum of Science and Art, University of Pennsylvania.)

Cat. no. 37614. Two whip tops, rudely carved, peg-shaped, with the top edge beveled; one with the top painted red and beveled edge blue, the other blue, with a red edge; the whip a peeled twig, 15 inches in length, with hide lash.

Cat. no. 37615. Whip top of wood (figure 996), 4 inches in height. It shows much use.

Cat. no. 37616. Whip top of horn (figure 997), a tip of horn, hollowed, 2½ inches in length.

These tops were collected by the writer in 1900. A top is called kawacipi; a wooden top, cankawacipi; the whip, icapsinte.

---

[a] Ogalala Games. Bulletin of the Free Museum of Science and Art, v. 3, p. 33, Philadelphia, 1901.

[b] Games of Teton Dakota Children. The American Anthropologist, v. 4, p. 338, 1891.

[c] Sioux Games. Journal of American Folk-Lore, v. 19, p. 33, 1906.

HIDATSA. Fort Berthold, North Dakota. (Cat. no. 178969, United
States National Museum.)

Wooden top, 2¾ inches in height, with a bone pin (figure 998). Collected by Dr Washington Matthews, U. S. Army, who describes
it as an ice top.

OMAHA. Nebraska.

Mr Francis La Flesche described to the writer a game like whip
top, played with stone balls on the ice. Clay balls and river pebbles
are also used. The name, moodedeska, is an old word and not descriptive. This game is played also by the Dakota and the Ponca.

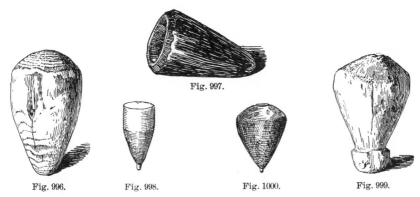

Fig. 997.

Fig. 996.　　　　　　Fig. 998.　　　　　　　　Fig. 1000.　　　　　　　Fig. 999.

FIG. 996. Whip top; height, 4 inches; Yankton Dakota Indians, Fort Peck, Montana; cat. no.
37615, Free Museum of Science and Art, University of Pennsylvania.

FIG. 997. Horn top; height, 2¼ inches; Yankton Dakota Indians, Fort Peck, Montana; cat. no.
37616, Free Museum of Science and Art, University of Pennsylvania.

FIG. 998. Top; height, 2¼ inches; Hidatsa Indians, Fort Berthold, North Dakota; cat. no. 178969,
United States National Museum.

FIG. 999. Top; height, 3¼ inches; Tewa Indians, Santa Clara, New Mexico; cat. no. 46828, United
States National Museum.

FIG. 1000. Top; height, 2¼ inches; Tewa Indians, Santa Clara, New Mexico; cat. no. 151956,
United States National Museum.

SKITTAGETAN STOCK

HAIDA. Queen Charlotte islands, British Columbia.

Dr C. F. Newcombe informed the writer that he had seen this tribe
make little tops, which they spun with the fingers.

TANOAN STOCK

TEWA. Santa Clara, New Mexico. (United States National Museum.)

Cat. no. 46828. Wooden top (figure 999), roughly worked, the base
terminating in a hemispheric knob; height, 3¾ inches. Collected
by Col. James Stevenson.

Cat. no. 151956. Wooden top (figure 1000) with iron point; height,
2¾ inches. Collected by Capt. John G. Bourke, U. S. Army.

Mr T. S. Dozier says:

The Tewa of Santa Clara call a top pfet-e-ne; playing a top, i-vi-pfet-e-ne-o-a-rai-mai. This no doubt is of modern date, but the small boys are the most expert top spinners I ever saw. It is played without gain, but in the old way, where the other fellow may have his top ruined by being knocked out of the ring.

TIGUA. Isleta, New Mexico.

An Isleta boy named J. Crecencio Lucero described the boys of this pueblo as playing with tops, napiri, which they spin with a string.

WAKASHAN STOCK

HESQUIAHT. Vancouver island, British Columbia. (Cat. no. IV A 1490, Berlin Museum für Völkerkunde.)

Wooden top (figure 1001), with handle to hold when spinning; height of top, 2¾ inches; length of handle, 3⅞ inches.

The collector, Capt. Samuel Jacobsen, gives the name as jäh-jäh-jakei.

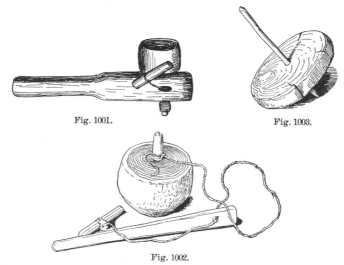

Fig. 1001.   Fig. 1003.

Fig. 1002.

FIG. 1001. Top, with handle; length of handle, 3⅞ inches; Hesquiaht Indians, Vancouver island, British Columbia; cat. no. IV A 1490, Berlin Museum für Völkerkunde.
FIG. 1002. Top; diameter, 2⅝ inches; Makah Indians, Neah bay, Washington; cat. no. 37390, Free Museum of Science and Art, University of Pennsylvania.
FIG. 1003. Top; diameter, 3¼ inches; Makah Indians, Neah bay, Washington; cat. no. 37391, Free Museum of Science and Art, University of Pennsylvania.

MAKAH. Neah bay, Washington. (Free Museum of Science and Art, University of Pennsylvania.)

Cat. no. 37390. Hemispheric wooden top (figure 1002), with spindle at the top in one piece; diameter, 2⅝ inches; accompanied by sinew cord and perforated stick, with which the top is held and through which the cord is drawn.

Cat. no. 37391. Perforated wooden disk (figure 1003), 3¼ inches in diameter, with spindle; accompanied by sinew cord.

Cat. no. 37392.   Peg top of hard wood with wooden peg in one piece
    (figure 1004) ; height, 3¼ inches.

These tops were collected by the writer in 1900 and are called
bo-bus-ca-die.

Charlie Williams described another form of top to the writer, a
kind of teetotum, made of alder bark, perforated, and played with
the fingers.

Dr George A. Dorsey [a] states that the three varieties of tops,
ba-buthl-ka-di, were described to him by Charlie Williams as in use
among the Makah before the advent of the whites, but he thought
that they had been derived from northern Indians.

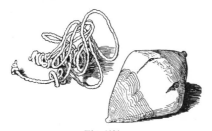  

Fig. 1004.   Fig. 1005.   Fig. 1006.

Fig. 1004. Top; height, 3¼ inches; Makah Indians, Neah bay, Washington; cat. no. 37392, Free
Museum of Science and Art, University of Pennsylvania.

Fig. 1005. Top; height, 2⅛ inches; Nootka Indians, Vancouver island, British Columbia; cat.
no. IV A 1485, Berlin Museum für Völkerkunde.

Fig. 1006. Top; height, 2¼ inches; Nootka Indians, Vancouver island, British Columbia; cat.
no. IV A 1484, Berlin Museum für Völkerkunde.

NOOTKA. Vancouver island, British Columbia. (Berlin Museum
    für Völkerkunde.)

Cat. no. IV A 1485.   Wooden top (figure 1005), 2⅛ inches in
    height.

Cat. no. IV A 1484.   Top with bone whirl and
    wooden pin (figure 1006), 2¼ inches in height.

The collector, Capt. Samuel Jacobsen, gives the
name as jäh-jäh-jakei.

ZUÑIAN STOCK

ZUÑI. Zuñi, New Mexico. (Cat. no. 127698,
    United States National Museum.)

Wooden top (figure 1007) with conical base and
    rounded top, having a hole leading into a small
    cavity at the top of the base, and a nail point;
    height, 4 inches. Collected by Col. James
    Stevenson.

Fig. 1007. Top; height,
    4 inches; Zuñi In-
    dians, Zuñi, New
    Mexico; cat. no.
    127698,   United
    States National
    Museum.

Two others (cat. no. 69146 and 129070) are similar to the preceding, and another (cat. no. 69413) is somewhat smaller, 3 inches

---

[a] Games of the Makah Indians. The American Antiquarian, v. 23, p. 73, 1901.

in length.   Still another similar top, collected by the writer in 1902, is in the Free Museum of Science and Art of the University of Pennsylvania (cat. no. 22603).   The tops are spun with a cord.   The name was given to the writer as moktatonai.

BULL-ROARER

The bull-roarer, or whizzer, used ceremonially by the Hopi, Zuñi, Navaho, Apache, and other tribes, is employed in the same form as a child's toy, the latter being presumably borrowed from the implement used in religious rites.   A few examples will suffice.

SIOUAN STOCK

DAKOTA (OGLALA).   Pine Ridge reservation, South Dakota.   (Cat.
        no. 22127, Free Museum of Science and Art, University of
        Pennsylvania.)
A thin, flat, rectangular piece of wood (figure 1008), $1\frac{1}{4}$ by $5\frac{3}{4}$ inches,
        attached by a thong 36 inches in length, to the end of a stick 31
        inches long.
This is described by the collector, Mr Louis L. Meeker,[a] as a boy's plaything, under the name of tateka yuhmunpi.

FIG. 1008. Bull-roarer; length of stick, 31 inches; Oglala Dakota Indians, Pine Ridge reservation, South Dakota; cat. no. 22127, Free Museum of Science and Art, University of Pennsylvania.

DAKOTA (TETON).   South Dakota.

Dr J. Owen Dorsey [b] describes the instrument as follows:

Chan' kaóbletuntun'pi, Wood having edges, . . . : A straight piece of wood is prepared, with four sides or edges, and is fastened by a strip of hide to another piece of wood which is used as a handle. The boy grasps the handle, whirls it around his head, making the four-cornered piece move rapidly with a whizzing noise.

OMAHA.   Nebraska.

Mr Francis La Flesche described the bull-roarer, as used by Omaha boys as a plaything, under the name of gahoota.   It is made of a stick, 6 inches long, with a notch cut at one end, and fastened to the end of a whip.   Mr La Flesche did not know the meaning of the name.

---

[a] Ogalala Games.   Bulletin of the Free Museum of Science and Art, v. 3, p. 34, Philadelphia, 1901.
[b] Games of the Teton Dakota Children.   The American Anthropologist, v. 4, p. 343, 1901.

BUZZ

A whirling toy made of a flat piece of bone, pottery, or gourd shell, or of a heavy bone, with one or two cords on each side, is a common toy among Indian children. The Plains tribes use a knuckle bone tied with a piece of sinew. A remarkable form, in which a conical piece of wood is made to revolve on a wooden spindle, is found among the Eskimo. Evidence as to the antiquity of the disk-shaped buzz is afforded by a clay-stone disk (figure 1009) with two perforations, from the cliff-ruins in the Canyon de Chelly, in the Museum of the Brooklyn Institute.

Fig. 1009.   Fig. 1010.

FIG. 1009. Stone buzz; diameter, 1½ inches; cliff-ruins in Canyon de Chelly, Arizona; cat. no. 10679, Brooklyn Institute Museum.
FIG. 1010. Bone buzz; Atsina (Grosventre) Indians, Fort Belknap, Montana; cat. no. $\frac{50}{1819}$, American Museum of Natural History.

ALGONQUIAN STOCK

ARAPAHO. Oklahoma. (Cat. no. 165819, United States National Museum.)

Toe bone of cow or ox, painted red and tied with sinew strings, having wooden handles at the ends; length, 20 inches. Collected by Rev. H. R. Voth.

GROSVENTRES. Fort Belknap, Montana. (Cat. no. $\frac{50}{1819}$, American Museum of Natural History.)

Toe bone of cow or ox (figure 1010), tied with sinew, having wooden pegs inserted at the ends of the cord. Collected by Dr A. L. Kroeber.

ESKIMAUAN STOCK

ESKIMO (CENTRAL). Cumberland sound, Baffin land, Franklin. (Cat. no. $\frac{60}{3469}$, American Museum of Natural History.)

Buzz (figure 1011), made of a disk of skin, 2¾ inches in diameter, with serrated edges, having two perforations for the string.

The specimen here described was collected by Capt. James S. Mutch and is figured by Doctor Boas:[a]

_____

[a] Eskimo of Baffin Land and Hudson Bay. Bulletin of the American Museum of Natural History, v. 15, p. 53, New York, 1901.

Eskimo (Central: Aivilirmiut and Kinipetu). West coast of Hudson bay, Keewatin. (Cat. no. $\frac{60}{2531}a$, $\frac{60}{2734}b$, American Museum of Natural History.)

Disk of sandstone (figure 1012), 1½ inches in diameter, and another of bone, each with two perforations, through which pass strings made of sinew. Collected by Capt. George Comer.

Dr Franz Boas [a] figures these objects.

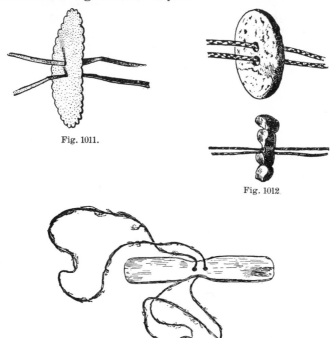

Fig. 1011.

Fig. 1012.

Fig. 1013.

Fig. 1011. Buzz; diameter, 2⅜ inches; Central Eskimo, Cumberland sound, Baffin land, Franklin; cat. no. $\frac{60}{3489}$, American Museum of Natural History.

Fig. 1012. Buzzes; diameter, 1½ inches; Central Eskimo (Aivilirmiut and Kinipetu), west coast of Hudson bay, Keewatin; cat. no. $\frac{60}{2531}a$, $\frac{60}{2734}b$, American Museum of Natural History.

Fig. 1013. Buzz; length, 3⅛ inches; Ita Eskimo, Cape York, Greenland; cat. no. 18391, Free Museum of Science and Art, University of Pennsylvania.

Eskimo (Ita). Cape York, Greenland. (Cat. no. 18391, Free Museum of Science and Art, University of Pennsylvania.)

Hourglass-shaped piece of ivory (figure 1013), 3⅛ inches in length, perforated by two holes, through which an endless sinew string is passed. Collected by Mr Henry G. Bryant.

---

[a] Eskimo of Baffin Land and Hudson Bay. Bulletin of the American Museum of Natural History, v. 15, p. 112, New York, 1901.

ESKIMO (ITA). Smith sound, Greenland. (Cat. no. $\frac{60}{44}$, American Museum of Natural History.)

A flat bone in the shape of an hourglass or figure 8, with a looped string passing through two holes in its middle, described by Dr A. L. Kroeber under the name of hieqtaq, or bull-roarer.

ESKIMO (WESTERN). Wainwright inlet, Utkiavi, Alaska. (Cat. no. 89722, United States National Museum.)

Board of pine wood (figure 1014), $3\frac{1}{2}$ inches long and $2\frac{1}{2}$ inches wide, with two round holes in the middle, through which is passed a piece of stout sinew braid, the ends of which are knotted together.

 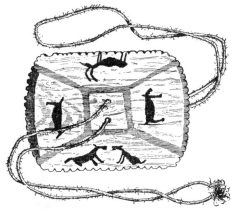

FIG. 1014. Buzz; length, $3\frac{1}{4}$ inches: Western Eskimo, Wainwright inlet, Alaska; cat. no. 89722, United States National Museum.

Collected by Mr John Murdoch,[a] who describes it as follows:

When the board is placed in the middle of the string it can be made to spin around and whiz by alternately pulling and relaxing the ends of the string. The board is rather elaborately painted. One end has a border of black lead on both faces, the other a similar border of red paint, which appears to be red lead. Broad red bands form a square 1 inch across around the holes, with lines radiating from each corner to the corners of the board, on both faces. On the space between these lines are figures rudely drawn with black lead. On one face, in the first space, is a goose; in the second, a man with a staff; in the third, the conventional figure of a whale's tail; and in the fourth, a whale, with line and float attached to him, pursued by a whaling umiak. On the other side, the first space contains a dog or wolf walking; the second, two of these animals, sitting on their haunches, facing each other; the third, another walking; and the fourth, a reindeer in the same attitude.

---

[a] The Point Barrow Eskimo. Ninth Annual Report of the Bureau of Ethnology, p. 378, 1892.

Eskimo (Western). Nuwuk, Alaska. (Cat. no. 89806, United States National Museum.)

Block of spruce (figure 1015a), fitted with a shaft of narwhal ivory.

FIG. 1015 a, b. Whirligigs; lengths, 10¼ and 9 inches; Western Eskimo, Nuwuk, Alaska; cat. no. 89806, 89807, United States National Museum; from Murdoch.

This fits loosely into a tubular handle, which is a section of the branch of an antler with the soft inside tissue cut out. A string of seal thong passes through a hole in the middle of the handle and is fastened to the shaft. This string is about 8 feet long, and about half of it is tied up into the hank to make a handle. The specimen was collected by Mr John Murdoch,[a] who describes it as follows:

It works very much like a civilized child's whirligig. The string is wound around the shaft and a smart pull on the handle unwinds it, making the block spin round rapidly. The reaction, spinning it in the opposite direction, winds up the string again. A couple of loose hawk's feathers are stuck into the tip of the block, which is painted with red ocher for about an inch. Four equidistant stripes of the same color run down the sides to a border of the same width round the base. This was made for sale and appears to be an unusual toy. I do not recollect ever seeing the children play with such a toy. It is called kai'psa (Gr. kâvsâk, " a whirligig or similar toy ").

Another specimen (cat. no. 89807, United States National Museum) is made of a solid tip of a mountain sheep's horn (figure 1015b), and is elaborately ornamented with a conventional pattern of lines and of circles and dots, incised and colored red with ocher. The shaft is of hard bone, and the line has a little wooden handle at the end. . The block is so heavy it will hardly spin. A similar object, collected by Mr E. A. McIlhenny at Point Barrow, Alaska (cat. no. 42369, Free Museum of Science and Art, University of Pennsylvania), is described by him as a whirligig, kaipsak. It differs from the specimens described in being made entirely of wood, and is quite new and unused.

SHOSHONEAN STOCK

HOPI. Oraibi, Arizona. (Cat. no. 128488, United States National Museum.)

Five disks of clay stone (figure 1016), from 1⅜ to 2½ inches in diameter, each perforated with two holes, having a cord of woolen yarn passing through them with its ends tied to form a loop on each side.

FIG. 1016. Buzzes; diameters, 1¼ and 2½ inches; Hopi Indians, Oraibi, Arizona; cat. no. 128488, United States National Museum.

Two of the specimens which are figured are painted in red, white, and black, with star or flower-shaped designs on both sides. The others are plain. These were collected by Col. James Stevenson and were designated as child's toys. Two other specimens in the United

---

[a] Ethnological Results of the Point Barrow Expedition. Ninth Annual Report of the Bureau of Ethnology, p. 376, 1892.

States National Museum (cat. no. 68803 and 128918), both collected by Colonel Stevenson, are similar to those above described.

MONO. Hooker cove, Madera county, California. (Cat. no. 71454, Field Columbian Museum.)

Small bone, pivosy (figure 1017), of a metatarsal bone of a deer, with loops at each end, described by the collector, Dr J. W. Hudson, as a bone whirligig.

FIG. 1017. Bone whirligig; Mono Indians, Madera county, California; cat. no. 71454, Field Columbian Museum.

————Hooker cove, Madera county, California. (Cat. no. 71442, Field Columbian Museum.)

Pottery disk (figure 1018), 2 inches in diameter, decorated with four spots of red paint, with cotton cord. Collected by Dr J. W. Hudson, who describes it as a whirligig.

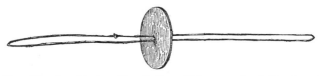

FIG. 1018. Buzz; diameter, 2 inches; Mono Indians, Madera county, California; cat. no. 71442, Field Columbian Museum.

SIOUAN STOCK

CROWS. Crow reservation, Montana. (Cat. no. 69668, Field Columbian Museum.)

Whirling toy, made of a joint bone of an ox, painted red, tied around with a sinew string, extending 8 inches on each side, and having hand grips, made of twigs, at the ends.

Collected by Mr S. C. Simms, who gives the name as ewahpoa-rooahcooah.

FIG. 1019. Bone buzz; length, 11¼ inches; Oglala Dakota Indians, Pine Ridge reservation, South Dakota; cat. no. 22126, Free Museum of Science and Art, University of Pennsylvania.

DAKOTA (OGLALA). Pine Ridge reservation, South Dakota. (Cat. no. 22126, Free Museum of Science and Art, University of Pennsylvania.)

Toe bone of a cow or ox (figure 1019), tied with sinew, with two small sticks inserted at the end of the cord.

This specimen was collected by Mr Louis L. Meeker,[a] who describes it as a boy's toy under the name of hohouh yuhmunpi.

DAKOTA (TETON). South Dakota.

Rev. J. Owen Dorsey [b] thus describes the implement:

Hohú yukhmun'pi, Making the bone hum by twisting the cord.—Bone is not the only material used, for the toy is sometimes made of stone or of a circular piece of wood. The toy is made thus: Some deer or buffalo sinews are twisted together; parts of a deer's foot are cooked till soft, and are strung together on the sinew. To the ends of the sinew are fastened two sticks which serve as handles, one stick at each end, each being at right angles to the sinew. The sinew is twisted, and when pulled taut the toy makes a humming sound.

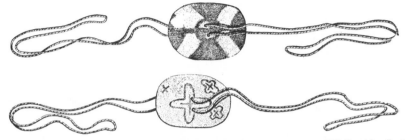

FIG. 1020. Buzz; diameter, 2¼ inches; Maricopa Indians, Arizona; cat. no. 2927, Brooklyn Institute Museum.

YUMAN STOCK

MARICOPA. Arizona. (Cat. no. 2927, Brooklyn Institute Museum.)
Wooden disk (figure 1020), 2¾ inches in diameter, perforated with two holes, through which a cord passes. Collected by Mr Louis L. Meeker in 1904.

FIG. 1021. Buzz; diameter, 3 inches; Zuñi Indians, Zuñi, New Mexico; cat. no. 3069, Brooklyn Institute Museum.

ZUÑIAN STOCK

ZUÑI. Zuñi, New Mexico. (Cat. no. 3069, Brooklyn Institute Museum.)
Disk of dried gourd shell (figure 1021), 3 inches in diameter, pierced with two holes, through which a string passes.

Collected by the writer in 1903. The name was given as huwawananai.

[a] Ogalala Games. Bulletin of the Free Museum of Science and Art, v. 3, p. 34, Philadelphia, 1901.
[b] Games of Teton Dakota Children. The American Anthropologist, v. 4, p. 343, 1891.

POPGUN

The writer has a record of the popgun from seven tribes, of which three are Siouan. The evidence is not sufficient to establish proof of its existence before the time of native contact with the whites. At the same time the two finely finished popguns (figure 1022) excavated by Dr George A. Dorsey at Ancon, Peru, now in the Field Columbian Museum, bring its aboriginal character in North America within the bounds of probability.

ALGONQUIAN STOCK

CHEYENNE. Oklahoma. (Cat. no. 165964, United States National Museum.)

Popgun (figure 1023), consisting of a wooden tube, marked with burned designs, 10 inches in length, and a stick, or plunger, 16¾ inches in length. Collected by Rev. H. R. Voth.

Fig. 1023.

Fig. 1022.   Fig. 1024.

Fig. 1025.

FIG. 1022. Wooden popguns; length, 5 inches; Ancon, Peru; cat. no. 5309, Field Columbian Museum.

FIG. 1023. Popgun; length, 10 inches; Cheyenne Indians, Oklahoma; cat. no. 165964, United States National Museum.

FIG. 1024. Popgun; length, 12¼ inches; Sauk and Fox Indians, Iowa; cat. no. $\frac{50}{3508}$, American Museum of Natural History.

FIG. 1025. Popgun; length, 12⅝ inches; Arikara Indians, Fort Berthold, North Dakota; cat. no. 8424, United States National Museum.

SAUK AND FOXES. Iowa. (Cat. no. $\frac{50}{3508}$, American Museum of Natural History.)

Popgun of elder wood (figure 1024), 12½ inches in length.

This was collected by Dr William Jones, who gives the name as paskesi gani, fighting thing, and says that it was used by boys with a bow and a belt of blue-joint arrows in playing war.

CADDOAN STOCK

ARIKARA. Fort Berthold, North Dakota. (Cat. no. 8424, United States National Museum.)

Wooden popgun (figure 1025), a tube, 12⅝ inches in length, marked with burned designs, and a wooden plunger. Collected by Dr C. C. Gray and Dr Washington Matthews, U. S. Army.

MARIPOSAN STOCK

Yokuts. Tule River reservation, Tulare county, California. (Cat. no. 70505, Field Columbian Museum.)
Popgun of elder (figure 1026), with maple piston, for shooting wads; length, 14½ inches. Collected by Dr J. W. Hudson.

FIG. 1026. Popgun; length, 14½ inches; Yokuts Indians, Tule River reservation, Tulare county, California; cat. no. 70505, Field Columbian Museum.

SIOUAN STOCK

Dakota (Oglala). Pine Ridge reservation, South Dakota. (Cat. no. 22131, Free Museum of Science and Art, University of Pennsylvania.)
Popgun, epahoton (figure 1027), a piece of sapling, three-fourths of an inch in diameter and 6½ inches in length, with a hole burned through the center, the outside being ornamented with burned lines, as shown in the figure.
Collected by Mr Louis L. Meeker, who states that popguns are used by Oglala boys to shoot wads of elm bark.[a]

FIG. 1027. Popgun; length, 6½ inches; Oglala Dakota Indians, Pine Ridge reservation, South Dakota; cat. no. 22131, Free Museum of Science and Art, University of Pennsylvania.

Dakota (Teton). South Dakota.
Rev. J. Owen Dorsey [b] says:

I′pahotun′pi un′pi, Pop-gun game.—In the fall, when the wind blows down the leaves, the boys make pop-guns of ash wood. They load them with bark which they have chewed, or else with wild sage (Artemesia), and they shoot at one another. The one hit suffers much pain.

Dr J. R. Walker [c] describes the popgun under the name of ipahotonpi, and gives the names of the parts as tancan, body; wibopan, ramrod; and iyopuhdi, the wadding. The latter, he says, is made by chewing the inner bark of the elm, and using it while wet.

FIG. 1028. Popgun; Omaha Indians, Nebraska; from drawing by Mr Francis La Flesche.

Omaha. Nebraska.
Mr Francis La Flesche told the writer in 1893 that Omaha boys made popguns (figure 1028), batushi (to push, to crack), of elder, which they stop with two wads of nettle fiber. These Indians were

[a] Bulletin of the Free Museum of Science and Art, v. 3, p. 35, Philadelphia, 1901.
[b] Games of Teton Dakota Children. The American Anthropologist, v. 4, p. 337, 1891.
[c] Journal of American Folk-Lore, v. 19, p. 35, 1905.

probably acquainted with the popgun before white contact. They made them through the winter, and in the summer threw them away. The following, he said, is the order of the boys' games: Shinny (tabegathe, ball to strike) in spring; throwing sticks and target shooting in summer; shinny in the fall; tops, bone sliders, and popguns in winter. The plum-stone dice game is played at all seasons.

BEAN SHOOTER

The implement to which for convenience the name of bean shooter has been given is a mechanical contrivance not unlikely to have been borrowed from the whites, found thus far only in the Southwest and on the Northwest coast.

FIG. 1029. Bean shooter; length, 12¾ inches; Hopi Indians, Oraibi, Arizona; cat. no. 38626, Free Museum of Science and Art, University of Pennsylvania.

SHOSHONEAN STOCK

HOPI. Oraibi, Arizona. (Cat. no. 38626, Free Museum of Science and Art, University of Pennsylvania.)

Bean shooter (figure 1029), made of a piece of cane, 12¾ inches in length, with a spring, consisting of a bent strip of wood, the ends of which are secured in holes cut in the cane. Collected by the writer in 1901.

MONO. Hooker cove, Madera county, California. (Cat. no. 71445, Field Columbian Museum.)

Wooden splint (figure 1030), 10 inches in length, used as a toy for flipping mud balls. Collected by Dr J. W. Hudson.

FIG. 1030. Stone flipper; length, 10 inches; Mono Indians, Madera county, California; cat. no. 71445, Field Columbian Museum.

WAKASHAN STOCK

KWAKIUTL. Alert bay, Vancouver island, British Columbia.

Dr C. F. Newcombe writes as follows, describing what he calls the figure 4 dart shooter:

Among the Kwakiutl, of the Nimpkish tribe, this is called HEndlEm. In use a small stick is placed across the top of the pliant side pieces and is shot to some little distance by pressing on the trigger piece which is horizontal to the figure 4. The figure is held in front of the body with both hands with the short end of the trigger downwards, and the perpendicular stem of the 4 horizontally. It is frequently used when children are sick and small sticks are shot in different directions to chase away the spirit supposed to be causing the sickness. It was used as lately as two years ago at Alert bay. Sets of four of this instrument are employed by grown-up people—relatives of the sick. The sticks are left lying about after the performance, but the guns are burned when done with. This goes on for four nights in succession. The noise of the two flexible sides coming together when the stick is ejected is supposed to aid the good work. At night the four shooters are left loaded near the sick child to scare the ghost or spirit. They are also used as a game by children.

MAKAH. Neah bay, Washington. (Free Museum of Science and Art, University of Pennsylvania.)
Two stone flippers, made of curved pieces of whalebone, one single and the other double, recurved. Collected by the writer in 1900.
OPITCHESAHT. Vancouver island, British Columbia. (Cat. no. IV A 7117, 7118, Berlin Museum für Völkerkunde.)
Curved splint of whalebone (figure 1031), 4 inches in length.
The collector, Capt. Samuel Jacobsen, gives the name as tklamáyek.

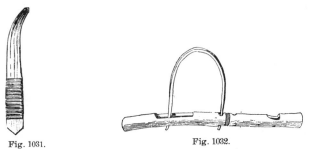

Fig. 1031.   Fig. 1032.

FIG. 1031. Stone flipper; length, 4 inches; Opitchesaht Indians, Vancouver island, British Columbia; cat. no. IV A 7117, 7118, Berlin Museum für Völkerkunde.
FIG. 1032. Bean shooter; length, 10 inches; Zuñi Indians, Zuñi, New Mexico; cat. no. 3066, Brooklyn Institute Museum.

ZUÑIAN STOCK

ZUÑI. Zuñi, New Mexico. (Cat. no. 3066, Brooklyn Institute Museum.)
Bean shooter (figure 1032), consisting of a tube of wood, with a wooden spring; length, 10 inches.
Collected by the writer in 1903. The name was given as keto ananai.

CAT'S CRADLE

Cat's cradle is known to all the tribes of whom direct inquiry has been made. The Zuñi explain it as the netted shield of the War Gods, and as taught to the latter by their grandmother, the Spider. The idea seems to underlie the tradition among the Navaho also that the play was taught them by the Spider people. In addition to cat's cradle the Indians have a variety of tricks and amusements with string.[a] Charlie Williams, at Neah bay, Washington, described the following as a common amusement among the Makah:

A string is tied about the neck with a false knot. It is pulled tight and comes off. This is called tu-a-oss. The string is sometimes tied about the toe.

The writer saw this trick performed with many grimaces by an old Shoshoni woman at Fort Washakie, Wyoming.

Dr Alfred Tozzer described the trick of splicing a cut rope in the mouth, as seen by him among the Maya at Chichen Itza, Yucatan. The rope is arranged as shown in figure 1033, the point *a* being concealed from the audience, who consider the ring an unbroken piece of rope, circled twice. The rope is then cut at *b* and four ends shown, *a* still being concealed from the audience. The two ends below *b* are placed in the mouth, but, the string having been cut at *b*, a small piece only is left around the longer loop at *a*, which the tongue easily frees from the loop of the main string; the string when taken from the mouth thus shows an unbroken surface at *b*, as the small piece cut at *b* and running from *b* to *a* and back to *b* is still concealed in the mouth.

FIG. 1033. Cord arranged for trick of splicing in the mouth; Maya Indians, Chichen Itza, Yucatan; cat. no. 2815, Brooklyn Institute Museum.

Mr Dorsey describes an amusement with string among the Teton Dakota under the name of "String wrapped in and out among the fingers," etc.

ALGONQUIAN STOCK

SAUK AND FOXES. Tama, Iowa.

These Indians described the game of cat's cradle to the writer under the name of sah-sah-nah-ki-á-ti-wi, parcel.

ATHAPASCAN STOCK

APACHE (WHITE MOUNTAIN). Arizona. (Cat. no. 3001, Brooklyn Institute Museum.)

The cat's cradle (figure 1034) figure was collected by the writer from a White Mountain Apache girl at Albuquerque. She called it ikinasthlani.

---

[a] Consult String Figures and Tricks, by Prof. Alfred C. Haddon. American Anthropologist, n. s., v. 5, p. 218, 1903.

HUPA. California.

Mr Pliny Earle Goddard [a] says:

The Hupa make several varieties of cat's cradle.

NAVAHO. St Michael, Arizona. (Free Museum of Science and Art, University of Pennsylvania.)

The following games of cat's cradle were collected by the writer. The figures were made by a single individual, who used his lips and teeth when necessary. The intermediary stages were not considered or exhibited.

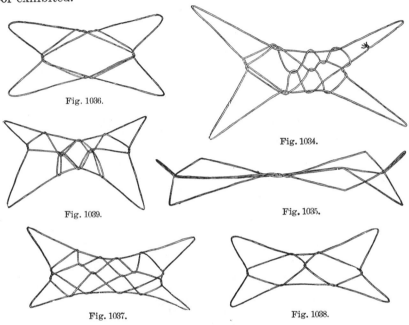

Fig. 1036.

Fig. 1034.

Fig. 1039.

Fig. 1035.

Fig. 1037.

Fig. 1038.

FIG. 1034. Cat's cradle, i-ki-nas-thla'-ni; White Mountain Apache Indians, Arizona; cat. no. 3001, Brooklyn Institute Museum.

FIG. 1035. Cat's cradle, atsinlt'lish, lightning; Navaho Indians, St Michael, Arizona; cat. no. 22712, Free Museum of Science and Art, University of Pennsylvania.

FIG. 1036. Cat's cradle, sûtso, big star; Navaho Indians, St Michael, Arizona; cat. no. 22713, Free Museum of Science and Art, University of Pennsylvania.

FIG. 1037. Cat's cradle, sô' łani, many (group of) stars; Navaho Indians, St Michael, Arizona; cat. no. 22714, Free Museum of Science and Art, University of Pennsylvania.

FIG. 1038. Cat's cradle, sô ahóts'ii, twin stars; Navaho Indians, St Michael, Arizona; cat. no. 22715, Free Museum of Science and Art, University of Pennsylvania.

FIG. 1039. Cat's cradle, sô bide' huloni, horned stars; Navaho Indians, St Michael, Arizona; cat. no. 22716, Free Museum of Science and Art, University of Pennsylvania.

Cat. no. 22712: atsinlt'lish, lightning, figure 1035.

Cat. no. 22713: sûtso, big star, figure 1036.

Cat. no. 22714: sô' łani, many (group of) stars, figure 1037.

Cat. no. 22715: sô ahóts'ii, twin stars, figure 1038.

Cat. no. 22716: sô bide' huloni, horned stars, figure 1039.

[a] Life and Culture of the Hupa, p. 61, Berkeley, 1903.

Cat. no. 22717: dilyehe, Pleiades, figure 1040.

Cat. no. 22718: mâ'i a⅃ts âyilaghu⅃i, coyotes running apart, figure 1041.

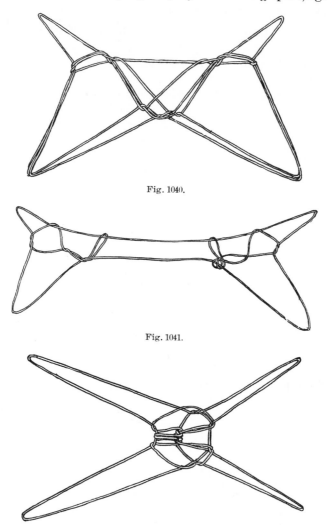

Fig. 1040.

Fig. 1041.

Fig. 1042.

FIG. 1040. Cat's cradle, dilyehe, Pleiades, Navaho Indians, St Michael, Arizona; cat. no. 22717, Free Museum of Science and Art, University of Pennsylvania.

FIG. 1041. Cat's cradle, mâ'i a⅃ts' âyilaghu⅃i, coyotes running apart; Navaho Indians, St Michael, Arizona; cat. no. 22718, Free Museum of Science and Art, University of Pennsylvania.

FIG. 1042. Cat's cradle, nashja, owl; Navaho Indians, St Michael, Arizona; cat. no. 22719, Free Museum of Science and Art, University of Pennsylvania.

Cat. no. 22719: nashja, owl, figure 1042.

Cat. no. 22720: t'lish, snake, figure 1043.

Cat. no. 22721: nashúi dich'izhi, horned toad, figure 1044.

Cat. no. 22722: łesis, poncho, figure 1045.
Cat. no. 22723: hoghan (hogan), figure 1046.
Cat. no. 22724: chizh joyełi, packing (carrying) wood, figure 1047.

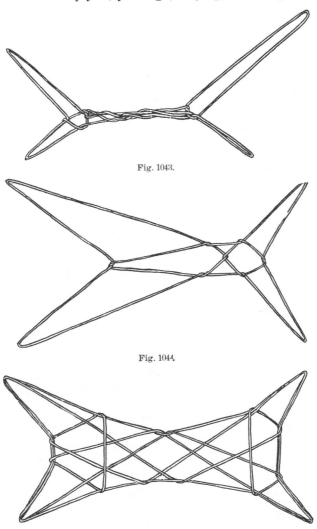

Fig. 1043.

Fig. 1044.

Fig. 1045.

FIG. 1043.   Cat's cradle, t'lish, snake; Navaho Indians, St Michael, Arizona; cat. no. 22720, Free Museum of Science and Art, University of Pennsylvania.

FIG. 1044.   Cat's cradle, nashúi dich' izhi, horned toad; Navaho Indians, St Michael, Arizona; cat. no. 22721, Free Museum of Science and Art, University of Pennsylvania.

FIG. 1045.   Cat's cradle, łesis, poncho; Navaho Indians, St Michael, Arizona; cat. no. 22722, Free Museum of Science and Art, University of Pennsylvania.

Of the specimens just mentioned, cat. no. 22712, lightning, was found by the writer in Isleta (figure 1064) under the same name, and cat. no. 22714, many (group of) stars, at the same place, but the name there was not obtained; cat. no. 22715, twin stars, occurs in Zuñi as lightning (figure 1069), and cat. no. 22724, packing (carrying) wood; also in Zuñi (figure 1068).

The following information about the game was communicated to the writer by Rev. Berard Haile in a personal letter:

Cat's cradle owes its origin to the Spider people. They, the spiders, who in the Navaho's belief were human beings, taught them the game for their

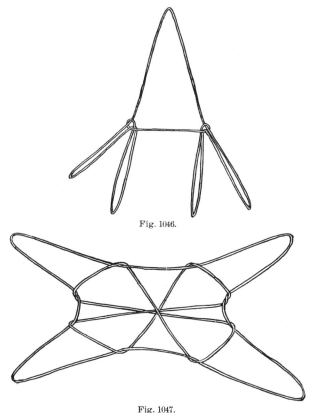

Fig. 1046.

Fig. 1047.

FIG. 1046. Cat's cradle, hoghan (hogan); Navaho Indians, St Michael, Arizona; cat. no. 22723, Free Museum of Science and Art, University of Pennsylvania.
FIG. 1047. Cat's cradle, chizh joyeɬi, packing (carrying) wood; Navaho Indians, St Michael, Arizona; cat. no. 22724, Free Museum of Science and Art, University of Pennsylvania.

amusement. The holy spiders taught the Navaho to play and how to make the various figures of stars, snakes, bears, coyotes, etc., but on one condition—they were to be played only in winter, because at that season spiders, snakes, etc., sleep and do not see them. To play the cat's cradle at any other time of the year would be folly, for certain death by lightning, falling from a horse, or some other mishap were sure to reach the offender. Otherwise no religious meaning is said to attach to the game. Even the above information was only extracted with much patience and scheming. I may add that one Navaho claimed that the cat's cradle is a sort of schooling by which the children are taught the position of the stars, etc. Though this might be a satisfactory explanation, it was not approved by the medicine man from whom I obtained the above. Na' atlo, it is twisted, is the term for cat's cradle.

NAVAHO. Chaco canyon, New Mexico.

Cat's cradle (figure 1048), called carrying wood, chizh joyełi. Figure made for the writer by Dr Alfred Tozzer, who collected the specimen, with others, among the Navaho in 1901.

In addition to the above figure, Dr Tozzer furnished Prof. Alfred C. Haddon [a] with the following list of cat's cradles, which he collected among the Navaho:

Man, děnně; sternum with ribs, ai-yĭt; woman's belt, sĭs; bow, atˡ-ti; arrow, ka; two hogans, naki-hogan or atˡ-sa-hogan; sand-painting figure, ᵏos-shis-chĭ; coyote, ma-ĭ; bird's nest, a-to; horned toad, na-a-sho-ĭ-di-chĭzi; butterfly, ga-hĭ-kĭ; star, so-a-hinatˡsan-ⁿtĭ-ĭ.

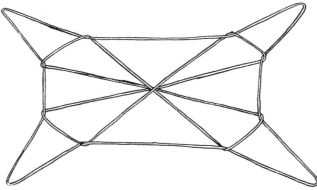

FIG. 1048. Cat's cradle, carrying wood; Navaho Indians, Chaco canyon, New Mexico; cat. no. 22738, Free Museum of Science and Art, University of Pennsylvania.

The general name for these figures is na-ash-klo, according to Mr Tozzer. The term na signifies a "continuous movement;" ash is "I," and klo is the root word of "weaving." Perhaps "continuous weaving" would be a fair translation of the Navaho word.

Professor Haddon gives directions for making the hogan, two hogans, and carrying wood, many (group of) stars, owl, and lightning, and illustrates the perfected figure of each.

TSETSAUT. Portland, British Columbia.

Dr Franz Boas [b] mentions their playing the game of cat's cradle.

ESKIMAUAN STOCK

ESKIMO (CENTRAL). Frobisher bay, Baffin land, Franklin.

Capt. Charles F. Hall [c] says:

The Innuit social life is simple and cheerful. They have a variety of games of their own. In one of these they use a number of bits of ivory, made in the

---

[a] String Figures and Tricks. American Anthropologist, n. s., v. 5, p. 220, 1903.
[b] Report of the Sixty-fifth Meeting of the British Association for the Advancement of Science, p. 568, London, 1895.
[c] Arctic Researches, p. 570, New York, 1860.

form of ducks, etc., such as Sampson's wife gave me, as just mentioned. In another, a simple string is used in a variety of intricate ways, now representing a tuktoo, now a whale, now a walrus, now a seal, being arranged upon the fingers in a way bearing a general resemblance to the game known to us as " cat's cradle." The people were very quick in learning of me to play chess, checkers, and dominoes.

Eskimo (Central).   Cumberland sound, Baffin land, Franklin.

Dr Franz Boas [a] says:

The women are particularly fond of making figures out of a loop, a game similar to our cat's cradle (ajarorpoq). They are, however, much more clever than we in handling the thong, and have a great variety of forms, some of which are

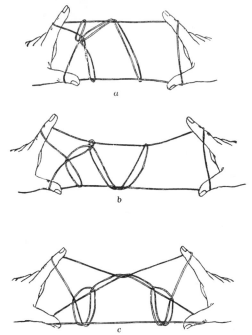

FIG. 1049 *a, b, c*. Cat's cradle; *a*, deer; *b*, hare; *c*, hills and ponds; Central Eskimo, Cumberland sound, Baffin land, Franklin; from Boas.

represented in figure 1049. For example, I shall describe the method of making the device representing a deer [figure 1049*a*]. Wind the loop over both hands, passing it over the backs of the thumbs inside the palms and outside the fourth fingers. Take the string from the palm of the right hand with the first finger of the left, and vice versa. The first finger of the right hand moves over all the parts of the thong lying on the first and fourth fingers of the right hand and passes through the loop formed by thongs on the thumb of the right hand ; then it moves back over the foremost thong and takes it up, while the thumb lets go the loop. The first finger moves downward before the thongs lying on the fourth finger and comes up in front of all the thongs. The thumb is placed into the loops hanging on the first finger and the loop hanging on the first finger of the left hand is drawn through both and hung again over the same finger.

---

[a] The Central Eskimo. Sixth Annual Report of the Bureau of Ethnology, p. 569, 1888.

The thumb and first finger of the right and the thumb of the left hand let go their loops. The whole is then drawn tight.

In addition to the above, Doctor Boas[a] illustrates two other cat's cradles from this locality, one called amaroqdjung, wolf (figure 1050a), and the other ussuqdjung (figure 1050b), and he describes the manner in which all are made.

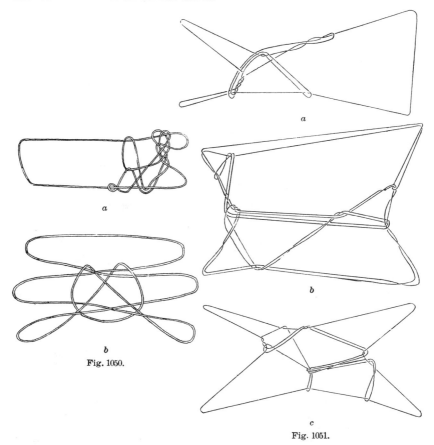

Fig. 1050.

Fig. 1051.

ESKIMO (ITA). Smith sound, Greenland.

Dr A. L. Kroeber[b] figures the following cat's cradles: Fox (figure 1051a), raven (figure 1051b), polar bear (figure 1051c), narwhal (figure 1052a), hare (figure 1052b), and walrus head (figure 1052c).

[a] Internationales Archiv für Ethnographie, v. 1, p. 233, Leiden, 1888.
[b] Bulletin of the American Museum of Natural History, v. 12, p. 298–300, New York, 1800.

KERES. Acoma, New Mexico.

An Acoma Indian at Zuñi named James H. Miller gave the name of cat's cradle as napainet.

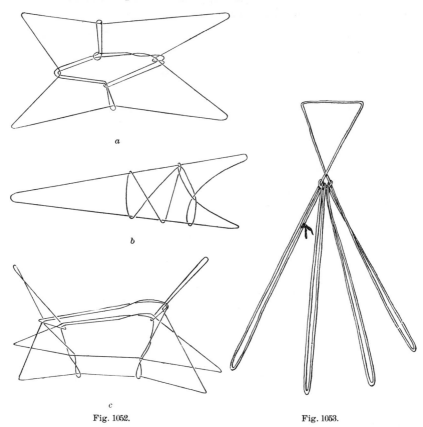

a

b

c

Fig. 1052.   Fig. 1053.

FIG. 1052 a, b, c. Cat's cradle; narwhal, hare, walrus head; Ita Eskimo, Smith sound, Greenland; cat. no. $\frac{60}{913}$, $\frac{60}{911}$, $\frac{60}{914}$, American Museum of Natural History; from Kroeber.

FIG. 1053. Cat's cradle, chicken foot; Keres Indians, Cochiti, New Mexico; cat. no. 4979, Brooklyn Institute Museum.

———— Cochiti, New Mexico. (Brooklyn Institute Museum.)

The following cat's cradles were collected by the writer in 1904 from Francisco Chaves (Kogit), a Keres boy from Cochiti, at St Michael, Arizona:

Cat. no. 4979: spinakaiyaka, chicken foot, figure 1053.

Cat. no. 4980: polaka, butterfly, figure 1054.

Cat. no. 4981: wisdyakka, bow, figure 1055.

Cat. no. 4982: sjonanakka, bat, figure 1056.

He gave the name as kokominnaoowishiyan, string playing; kokomin, string.

KULANAPAN STOCK

POMO.   Ukiah, California.   (Cat. no. 3000, Brooklyn Institute Museum.)

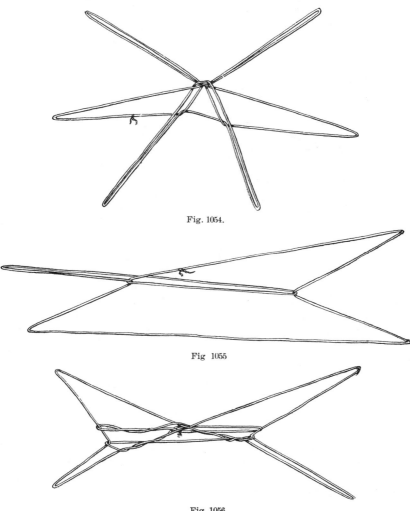

Fig. 1054.

Fig 1055

Fig. 1056.

FIG. 1054.   Cat's cradle, butterfly; Keres Indians, Cochiti, New Mexico; cat. no. 4980, Brooklyn Institute Museum.

FIG. 1055.   Cat's cradle, bow; Keres Indians, Cochiti, New Mexico; cat. no. 4981, Brooklyn Institute Museum.

FIG. 1056.   Cat's cradle, bat; Keres Indians, Cochiti, New Mexico; cat. no. 4982, Brooklyn Institute Museum.

This cat's cradle (figure 1057) was collected by the writer from a Pomo Indian man at Albuquerque. He gave the general name of the amusement as datidatu, tangled up, and of this figure as tsudium, humming bird.

MAYAN STOCK

MAYA. Chichen Itza, Yucatan. (Cat. no. 2813, 2814, Brooklyn Institute Museum.)

Dr Alfred Tozzer has furnished the writer two cat's cradles from this tribe. One (figure 1058) is called a chicken's foot. A is held on the little finger, B on the middle finger, and C on the thumb.

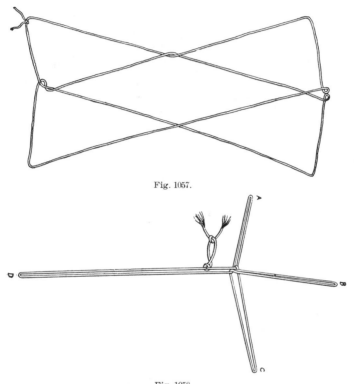

Fig. 1057.

Fig. 1058.

FIG. 1057. Cat's cradle, tsudium, humming bird; Pomo Indians, Ukiah, California; cat. no. 3000, Brooklyn Institute Museum.

FIG. 1058. Cat's cradle, chicken's foot; Maya Indians, Yucatan; cat. no. 2813, Brooklyn Institute Museum.

In another (figure 1059) A is held in the mouth of the operator and D in the hand of an assisting person. B and C, held in each hand by the operator, are pulled outward from the center as D approaches the center. The operation is called sawing wood.

SALISHAN STOCK

CLALLAM. Washington.

A Clallam boy, John Raub, described this tribe as playing cat's cradle, which they call tskusli skutsisen.

Shuswap.   Kamloops, British Columbia.

Dr Franz Boas [a] says:

Children and women play cat's cradle.

Skokomish.   British Columbia.

Mr Charles Hill-Tout [b] says these Indians were acquainted with qauwilts, or the cat's cradle game.

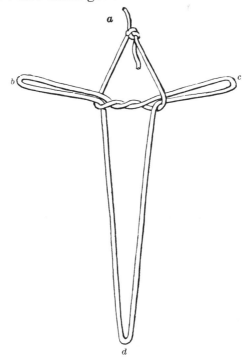

Fig. 1059.   Cat's cradle, sawing wood; Maya Indians, Yucatan; cat. no. 2814, Brooklyn Institute Museum.

Songish.   British Columbia.

Dr Franz Boas [c] says:

Hqwauā'latcis, the game of cat's cradle.—A great variety of figures are made. Only one person is required to make these figures. Sometimes the teeth must help in making them.

Thompson Indians (Ntlakyapamuk).   British Columbia.

Mr James Teit [d] says:

Many children's games were played by the smaller boys and girls. "Cat's cradle" was one of these [figure 1060]. Strings were fixed on the fingers in

[a] Second General Report on the Indians of British Columbia. Report of the Sixtieth Meeting of the British Association for the Advancement of Science, p. 641, London, 1891.

[b] Notes on the Sk·qō'mic of British Columbia. Report of the Seventieth Meeting of the British Association for the Advancement of Science, p. 488, London, 1900.

[c] Second General Report on the Indians of British Columbia. Report of the Sixtieth Meeting of the British Association for the Advancement of Science, p. 571, London, 1891.

[d] The Thompson Indians of British Columbia. Memoirs of the American Museum of Natural History, whole series, v. 2, p. 281, New York, 1900.

different ways, so as to present many forms, such as the " beaver," the " deer," the " buckskin," the " conical lodge," the " women's house," the " man stealing wood," etc.

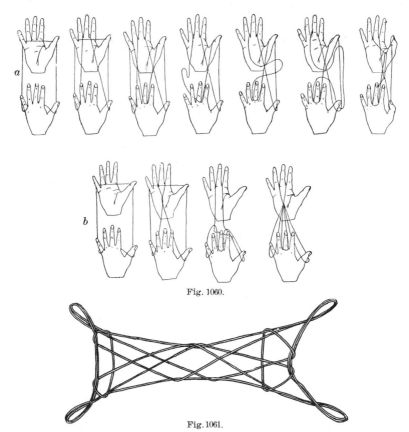

Fig. 1060.

Fig. 1061.

FIG. 1060. Cat's cradle; *a*, dressing a skin; *b*, pitching a tent; Thompson Indians, British Columbia; from sketches by Harlan I. Smith.
FIG. 1061. Cat's cradle; Tigua Indians, Isleta, New Mexico; cat. no. 22729, Free Museum of Science and Art, University of Pennsylvania.

The figure called pitching a tent is found in Zuñi, under the name of brush house (figure 1070).

SHOSHONEAN STOCK

HOPI. Walpi, Arizona.

The Indians at the First Hopi mesa informed the writer, in 1905, that they knew a number of cat's cradles and called them all ma-mal-lac-bi.

TANOAN STOCK

TEWA. Hano, Arizona. (Brooklyn Institute Museum.)

The following cat's cradles were collected by the writer in 1905:
Cat. no. 7129, bo-tāñ-la.
Cat. no. 7130, a-gai-yo-sin-i.

TIGUA.   Isleta, New Mexico.   (Free Museum of Science and Art, University of Pennsylvania.)

The following cat's cradles were collected by the writer at Isleta in 1902:

Cat. no. 22729, figure 1061.

Cat. no. 22730, pakula, star, figure 1062.

Cat. no. 22731, figure 1063.

Cat. no. 22732, vopiridai, lightning, figure 1064.

The only name my informant could give for the amusement was thlu, string.   He did not know names for all the figures he was able to make.

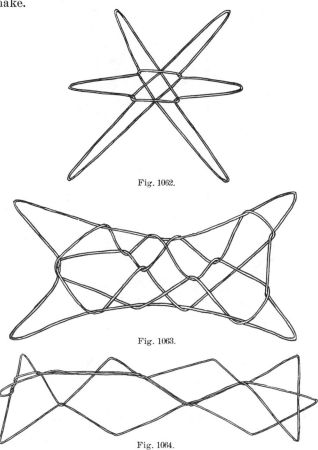

Fig. 1062.

Fig. 1063.

Fig. 1064.

FIG. 1062.   Cat's cradle, pakula, star; Tigua Indians, Isleta, New Mexico; cat. no. 22730, Free Museum of Science and Art, University of Pennsylvania.

FIG. 1063.   Cat's cradle; Tigua Indians, Isleta, New Mexico; cat. no. 22731, Free Museum of Science and Art, University of Pennsylvania.

FIG. 1064.   Cat's cradle, vopiridai, lightning; Tigua Indians, Isleta, New Mexico; cat. no. 22732, Free Museum of Science and Art, University of Pennsylvania.

Cat. no. 22731 occurs among the Navaho as many (group of), stars (figure 1037), and cat. no. 22732 as lightning (figure 1035).

WAKASHAN STOCK

MAKAH. Neah bay, Washington.

Charlie Williams described the Makah as playing cat's cradle under the name of howwutsoksh.

The figures corresponded with those of our common child's play. The first he called bow, bistati; the second, devilfish, tiththupe. Another figure was the frog, wachit. Girls and boys play.

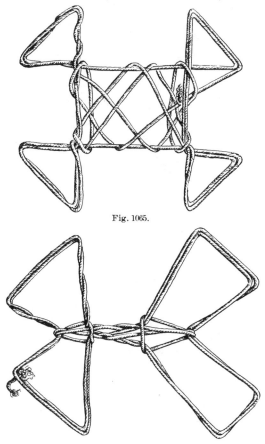

Fig. 1065.

Fig. 1066.

FIG. 1065. Cat's cradle, hpaish, mealing stone; Maricopa Indians, Arizona; cat. no. 2921, Brooklyn Institute Museum.

FIG. 1066. Cat's cradle, kpaitch, turtle; Maricopa Indians, Arizona; cat. no. 2922, Brooklyn Institute Museum.

YUMAN STOCK

MARICOPA. Arizona. (Brooklyn Institute Museum.)

The following cat's cradles were collected for the writer by Mr Louis L. Meeker:

Cat. no. 2921: hpaish, mealing stone (figure 1065).

Cat. no. 2922: kpaitch, turtle (figure 1066).

ZUÑIAN STOCK

ZUÑI.　Zuñi, New Mexico.　(Free Museum of Science and Art, University of Pennsylvania.)

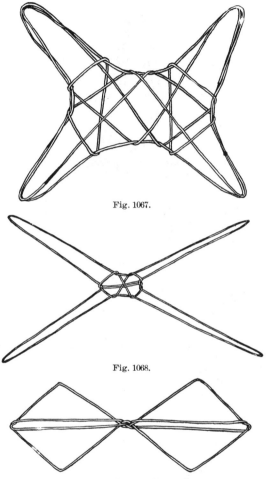

Fig. 1067.

Fig. 1068.

Fig. 1069.

FIG. 1067.　Cat's cradle, pichowainai, netted shield; Zuñi Indians, Zuñi, New Mexico; cat. no. 22604, Free Museum of Science and Art, University of Pennsylvania.

FIG. 1068.　Cat's cradle, pishkappoa pichowainai, netted shield; Zuñi Indians, Zuñi, New Mexico; cat. no. 22605, Free Museum of Science and Art, University of Pennsylvania.

FIG. 1069.　Cat's cradle, pichowai wailolo, lightning; Zuñi Indians, Zuñi, New Mexico; cat. no. 22606, Free Museum of Science and Art, University of Pennsylvania.

The following cat's cradles were collected by the writer in Zuñi in 1902:

Cat. no. 22604: pichowainai, netted shield (figure 1067).

Cat. no. 22605: pishkappoa pichowainai, netted shield (figure 1068).

Cat. no. 22606: pichowai wailolo, lightning (figure 1069).

Cat. no. 22607: pichowai hampunnai, brush house (figure 1070).
Cat. no. 22608: pichowai hampunnai, brush house (figure 1071).
Cat. no. 22609: tslempistonai pichowainai, top crossbeam of ladder
(figure 1072).

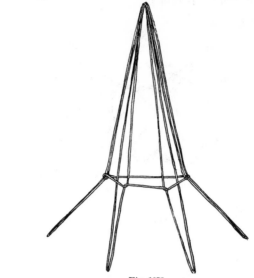

Fig. 1070.

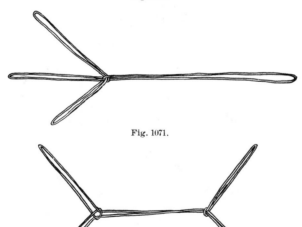

Fig. 1071.

Fig. 1072.

FIG. 1070. Cat's cradle, pichowai hampunnai, brush house; Zuñi Indians, Zuñi, New Mexico;
cat. no. 22607, Free Museum of Science and Art, University of Pennsylvania.
FIG. 1071. Cat's cradle, pichowai hampunnai, brush house; Zuñi Indians, Zuñi, New Mexico;
cat. no. 22608, Free Museum of Science and Art, University of Pennsylvania.
FIG. 1072. Cat's cradle, tslempistonai pichowainai, top crossbeam of ladder; Zuñi Indians, Zuñi,
New Mexico; cat. no. 22609, Free Museum of Science and Art, University of Pennsylvania.

Cat. no. 22610: pichowai atslonononai, sling (figure 1073).
Cat. no. 22605 occurs among the Navaho as packing (carrying) wood
(figure 1047), and cat. no. 22606 as twin stars (figure 1038).

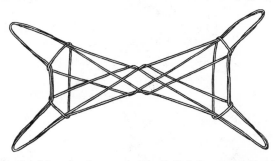

Fig. 1073.   Cat's cradle, pichowai atslonononai, sling; Zuñi Indians, zuñi, New Mexico; cat. no.
22610, Free Museum of Science and Art, University of Pennsylvania.

My informant in Zuñi stated that the cat's cradle was called
pichowainai or pishkappoa, the netted shield, figures 1067 and 1068,
actually representing this shield, which was supposed to have been
carried by the War God.   The idea is borrowed from the spider web,
and cat's cradle was taught to the little boys, the twin War Gods, by
their mother, the Spider Woman, for their amusement.

CHEROKEE INDIAN BALL TEAM; WOLFTOWN, NORTH CAROLINA; FROM PHOTOGRAPH BY MOONEY (1888)

UNCLASSIFIED GAMES

Into this category of unclassified games, arranged by stocks, have been put the miscellaneous games of which but a single record exists, and which, with the information now at hand, can not be assigned to a place in any of the preceding series, nor yet regarded as of foreign origin. It will be seen that these games are few in number and of little apparent significance. One, the Clatsop game described by Lewis and Clark, may be the guessing game played with wooden disks, imperfectly described.

ILLINOIS. Illinois.

Joutel says: [a]

A good number of presents still remaining, they divide themselves into several lots, and play at a game, called of the stick, to give them to the winner. That game is played, taking a stout stick, very smooth and greased, that it may be harder to hold it fast. One of the elders throws the stick as far as he can; the young men run after it, snatch it from each other, and at last he who remains possessed of it has the first lot. The stick is then thrown again; he who keeps it then has the second lot, and so on to the end. The women whose husbands have been slain in war often perform the same ceremony and treat the singers and dancers whom they have before invited.

NAVAHO. St Michael, Arizona.

Rev. Berard Haile describes the following game in a letter:

Tsin beedził, the great game of the Earth-winner. The Earth-winner, Ni'-nahuiłbi'i, plays with the gambler, who lays a wager that he can outdo the Earth-winner in strength. A test is made by placing a pole 6 inches in diameter in the ground about 2 feet deep. The pole is about 8 feet in height, and the gambler pushes it over on a run. The Earth-winner thus loses the game. In consequence of this event, the Navaho, out of respect for their great teacher of games, who, they say, came from Mexico, do not play this game.

TAKULLI. Stuart lake, British Columbia.

The Reverend Father A. G. Morice [b] says:

Tə'ko· is another pastime which is somewhat childish in character. In most cases it is played by the fireside in the camp lodge during the long winter evenings. Its necessary accompaniments [figure 1074] are a blunt-headed stick and two small, thin, and springy boards firmly driven in the ground, one close by each

---

[a] Historical Journal of Monsieur La Salle's Last Voyage to Discover the River Mississippi. French's Historical Collections of Louisiana, v. 1, p. 186, New York, 1846.

[b] Notes on the Western Dénés. Transactions of the Canadian Institute, v. 4, p. 112, Toronto, 1895.

player. The two opposite parties sit facing each other and throw the tə'ko·
against the little board on the other side, upon hitting which it rebounds to the
knees of the successful player, who is then entitled to recommence and continue
as long as luck favors him.   Failing to get at the mark, the tə'ko· is handed to
the other partner. The number of points obtained indicates the winner. The
old men profess to be ignorant of that game, which is probably adventitious
among our Indians.

CHINOOKAN STOCK

CLATSOP.   Mouth of Columbia river, Oregon.

Lewis and Clark [a] describe the following game:

Two pins are placed on the floor, about the distance of a foot from each other,
and a small hole is made between them. The players then go about 10 feet
from the hole, into which they try to roll a small piece resembling the men used
in draughts; if they succeed in putting it into the hole, they win the stake; if
the piece rolls between the pins, but does not go into the hole, nothing is won or
lost; but the wager is wholly lost if the checker rolls outside the pins.

FIG. 1074. Implements for tə'ko·; Takulli Indians, British Columbia; from Morice.

ESKIMAUAN STOCK

ESKIMO (CENTRAL).   Cumberland sound, Baffin land, Franklin.

Dr Franz Boas [b] says:

The sāketān resembles a roulette. A leather cup with a rounded bottom and
a nozzle is placed on a board and turned round. When it stops the nozzle points
to the winner. At present a tin cup fastened with a nail to a board is used for
the same purpose [figure 1075].

Their way of managing the gain and loss is very curious. The first winner
in the game must go to his hut and fetch anything he likes as a stake for the
next winner, who, in turn receives it, but has to bring a new stake, in place of
this, from his hut. Thus the only one who loses anything is the first winner of
the game, while the only one who wins anything is the last winner.

Again, of the Eskimo of the west coast of Hudson bay, Doctor
Boas [c] says:

Women gamble with a musk-ox dipper, which is turned swiftly around. The
person away from whom the handle points wins the stake, and has to place a
stake in her turn.

[a] History of the Expedition under the Command of Lewis and Clark, v. 2, p. 784, New
York, 1893.
[b] The Central Eskimo. Sixth Annual Report of the Bureau of Ethnology, p. 568, 1888.
[c] Eskimo of Baffin Land and Hudson Bay. Bulletin of the American Museum of Natural History, v. 15, p. 110, New York, 1901.

This game corresponds in general principle with roulette, or rather with the spinning arrow.

ESKIMO (CENTRAL: AIVILIRMIUT and KINIPETU). West coast of Hudson bay, Keewatin. (Cat. no. $\frac{9}{2735}b$, American Museum of Natural History.)

Dr Franz Boas [a] says:

Small hoops of whalebone (terkutuk) are joined crosswise [figure 1076]. Then they are placed on the ice or hard snow when the wind is blowing. The young men run to catch them.

A similar game is mentioned by Rev. J. Owen Dorsey among the Teton Dakota (see p. 715).

Fig. 1075.   Fig. 1076.

FIG. 1075. Säketän, or roulette; Central Eskimo, Cumberland sound, Baffin land, Franklin; cat. no. IV A 6854, Berlin Museum für Völkerkunde; from Boas.

FIG. 1076. Whalebone hoops; diameter, 3¼ inches; Central Eskimo (Aivilirmiut and Kinipetu), west coast of Hudson bay, Keewatin; cat. no. $\frac{9}{2735}b$, American Museum of Natural History.

———— West coast of Hudson bay, Keewatin. (Cat. no. $\frac{69}{2731}b$, American Museum of Natural History.)

Dr Franz Boas [a] says:

Boys play hunting seals [figure 1077]. Each of them has a small harpoon and a number of pieces of seal-skin with many holes. Each piece of skin represents a seal. Each of the boys also has a hip-bone of a seal. Then one boy moves a piece of skin which represents a seal under the hole in the hip-bone, which latter represents the blowing-hole in the ice. While moving the piece of skin about under the bone, the boys blow like seals. Whoever catches with the little harpoon the piece of skin in one of the holes retains it, and the boy who catches the last of the pieces of skin goes on in turn with his seals. The little harpoons are made by the fathers of the boys, the pieces of skin are prepared by their mothers.

MAYAN STOCK

MAYA. Yucatan.

Dr Alfred Tozzer [b] describes the following game:

Wäk pel pul, to throw six, is played with six sticks [figure 1078] made of any kind of wood, which has branches directly opposite each other. They each rest

---

[a] Eskimo of Baffin Land and Hudson Bay. Bulletin of the American Museum of Natural History, v. 15, p. 111, New York, 1901.

[b] In a letter to the writer, November 7, 1903.

on the large end, and each has marks on the upper part, running from 1 to 6, which show the count. The one with six notches is placed in the middle, and the others in a circle around it. Rocks, cocoa beans, or money are then thrown in an endeavor to knock down as many as possible.

SKITTAGETAN STOCK

HAIDA (KAIGANI). Prince of Wales island, Alaska.

Dr C. F. Newcombe describes the following game under the name of kwai indao:

A set of 40 or 50 sticks, representing ten different numbers, are placed in a row. The players alternately try to repeat from memory, blindfold, the order in which these ten numbers run.

The same collector describes also the following game:

Twenty or forty small sticks, 6 inches long, are taken in the palm, thrown up in the air, and caught on back of hand. They are then thrown up again, if any are caught, and if possible an odd number caught in the palm. If an odd number—one, three, five, or seven—be so caught, one stick is kept by the player, who

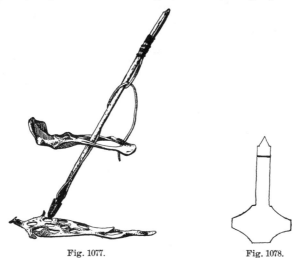

Fig. 1077.   Fig. 1078.

FIG. 1077. Game of sealing; length of harpoon, 12¾ inches; Central Eskimo, west coast of Hudson bay, Keewatin; cat. no. ₂⁹₇₃₁ b, American Museum of Natural History.

FIG. 1078. Stick for wăk pel pul; Maya Indians, Yucatan; from sketch by Dr Alfred Tozzer.

tries again. If none or an even number be caught, the opposite player takes his turn. He who takes the last stick wins all his opponent's sticks and takes them all up and goes on as before. Boys or girls play. The game is called hăl hai' jao, "turn around game."

WAKASHAN STOCK

KWAKIUTL. Nawiti, British Columbia. (Cat. no. 85850, Field Columbian Museum.)

Two flat slats (figure 1079), 1½ inches wide at top, and 15½ and 21 inches long, the lower ends sharpened to a point. Two flat slats, 1½ inches wide at top and 13 inches long, with transverse white lines across the flat sides at top, and lower part cut round to form a handle.

Two wooden darts, with blunt heads, 35 and 38 inches in length, one with a rattle in the handle end.

Collected in 1904 by Dr C. F. Newcombe, who describes the game as follows:

The flat piece is set firmly in the ground at an inclination from the player to form a kind of springboard. The players stand at about 10 feet from the board and throw the darts at it. The game is to catch the dart on the rebound as many times as possible, and he who first catches it ten times, not necessarily without an intervening miss, is the winner. No counters are used. This game is only played in the fall, when drying salmon. The game is k'lemgua, the dart k'lemgwa·iu, and the spring klemgwa·yas.

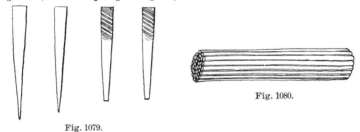

Fig. 1080.

Fig. 1079.

FIG. 1079. Slats for k'lemgua; lengths of slats, 15¼ and 21 inches; Kwakiutl Indians, British Columbia ; cat. no. 85850, Field Columbian Museum.

FIG. 1080. Sticks for mena (stopping-breath game); length, 6¼ inches; Kwakiutl Indians, British Columbia; cat. no. 85857, Field Columbian Museum.

KWAKIUTL. Nawiti, British Columbia. (Cat. no. 85857, Field Columbian Museum.)

Bundle of forty sticks (figure 1080), 6½ inches in length. These were collected in 1904 by Dr C. F. Newcombe, who describes them as used in a game called menă.

The sticks are laid in two parallel rows of twenty each, and one player tries to pick up as many sticks as possible and make two other similar rows while the other player stops his breath by holding his nose and mouth. It is played by men and boys, by two or more players in turns. The counters are called menasu.

———— Nawiti, British Columbia. (Cat. no. 85856, Field Columbian Museum.)

Bundle of forty sticks, 6 inches in length.

These were collected in 1904 by Dr C. F. Newcombe, who describes them as follows:

These sticks—the same as used in menă, are also employed in a counting game. The bundle of forty is arranged in bunches of from one to five, placed in any order in one or two lines. One player tries to commit to memory the number of sticks in each bunch in their order from left to right, and then turns around, and with his back to the sticks calls the number after the watcher says gĭnīts? or "how many?" If correct, each bunch correctly named is put in one place, but if wrong, in another. The sticks are the unit for scoring. He who gets the greatest number of sticks wins. The game is called gĭnīts, and the sticks gĭnītsa·iu.

KWAKIUTL. Nawiti, British Columbia. (Cat. no. 85355, Field
Columbian Museum.)

Ring of whalebone (figure 1081), $2\frac{1}{2}$ inches in diameter, supported
on a stick in a horizontal position, and twenty-four unpainted
sticks, $8\frac{3}{4}$ inches in length.

Collected in 1904 by Dr C. F. Newcombe, who describes them as
used in a game called quaquatsewa·iu.

The players drop the sticks held in one hand through the ring, to see who
can get the highest number through. This is done with the eyes open, blindfolded, and blindfolded after turning round.

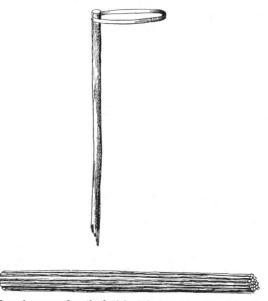

Fig. 1081. Stick-dropping game; length of sticks, $8\frac{3}{4}$ inches; diameter of ring, $2\frac{1}{2}$ inches; Kwakiutl
Indians, British Columbia; cat. no. 85355, Field Columbian Museum.

——— Vancouver island, British Columbia.

Dr Franz Boas[a] describes a game like the first in this series:

Tl'ɛ'mkoāyu.—A stick, about 3 feet long, with a knob at its end, is thrown
against an elastic board which is placed upright at some distance. If the stick
rebounds and is caught, the player gains 4 points. If it rebounds to more than
half the distance from the player to the board, he gains 1 point. If it falls
down nearer the board than one-half the distance, or when the board is missed,
the player does not gain any point. The two players throw alternately. Each
has 10 counters. When one of them gains all the counters, he is the winner of the
stake. When the stick falls down so that the end opposite the knob rests on the
board, the throw counts 10 points.

Another game he mentions as follows:[b]

T'ē'nk·oayu, or carrying a heavy stone on the shoulder to test the strength of
those who participate in the game.

[a] Sixth Report on the Indians of British Columbia. Report of the Sixty-sixth Meeting
of the British Association for the Advancement of Science, p. 578, London, 1896.
[b] Ibid.

ZUÑIAN STOCK

Zuñi. Zuñi, New Mexico. (Cat. no. 3063, Brooklyn Institute Museum.)

Two rings (figure 1082), made of twig, one $3\frac{1}{2}$ inches in diameter, wrapped with green and blue yarn in alternate quarters, and the other, $2\frac{3}{4}$ inches in diameter, wrapped with plain white cord. Collected by the writer in 1903.

Boys play. The large ring is thrown down, and the object of the game is to toss the small ring so that it will fall within the large one. The rings are called tsi-ko-nai.

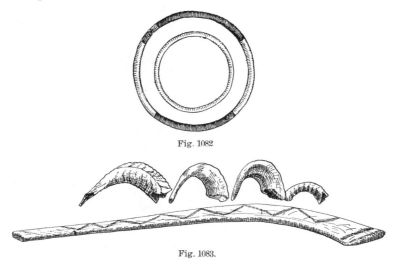

Fig. 1082

Fig. 1083.

FIG. 1082. Ring game; diameter of large ring, $3\frac{1}{2}$ inches; Zuñi Indians, Zuñi, New Mexico; cat. no. 3063, Brooklyn Institute Museum.

FIG. 1083. Implements for "horns kill," or "killing the rabbit;" Zuñi Indians, Zuñi, New Mexico; from Mrs Stevenson.

——— Zuñi, New Mexico.

Mrs Matilda Coxe Stevenson[a] describes a game called saithlä-tawe, horns kill, or killing the rabbit:

Six goat-horns [figure 1083] are placed in line on the ground an equal distance apart, and the players stand some rods away. The game is begun by a player starting to run and throwing a rabbit-stick toward the horns. He is entitled to as many horns as he strikes, and may continue to throw the stick as long as he is successful in striking a horn; but when he fails to strike one, another plays. The one who strikes the largest number of horns wins the game.

[a] Zuñi Games. American Anthropologist, n. s., v. 5, p. 489, 1903.

CHOCTAW INDIAN BALL-PLAY DANCE AROUND THE STAKES; INDIAN TERRITORY; FROM CATLIN

CHOCTAW INDIAN BALL-PLAY—"BALL UP;" INDIAN TERRITORY; FROM CATLIN

CHOCTAW INDIAN BALL-PLAY—"BALL DOWN;" INDIAN TERRITORY; FROM CATLIN

GAMES DERIVED FROM EUROPEANS

It is obvious that there has been steady modification of old Indian customs under the influence of the whites, and that the Indians have absorbed European ideas, many of which have in time become difficult of recognition as foreign in origin. These facts are true to a certain extent of their games. An excellent example of incorporation is found in the Navaho game of baseball. In spite of tribal traditions, it appears that the Navaho learned the game from the whites when they were imprisoned at the Bosque Redondo after 1863. The following account of the game was furnished the writer by Rev. Berard Haile, of St Michael, Arizona:

Aqejólyedi, Run around ball.—This game is not played at present in its original form, but was quite frequently played fifteen or twenty years ago. The ball, joł, was made, before rag time, of the bark of a shrub called azhi' (bark) or awe ts'ál, baby's cradle, which owes its name to the fact that it was used for bedding in cradles. This bark was covered with the hide of deer, goat, horse, or any animal which can be eaten by the Navaho with impunity. Therefore bear, coyote, or dog hides would not be allowed as a covering for the ball. There were two halves to the cover, which were sewed together in the center with the sinews of deer or buckskin strips. The ball is the sign of the evil-spirit wind, and therefore must disappear as soon as vegetation begins and until after the harvest. The stick, or bat, bē-akáli, something to strike with, was an oak stick of this shape: J. Oak is hard and has great resisting power, and is used in nearly all the Navaho religious ceremonies. Though I have no authority for it, I am inclined to believe it is used to signify the power of Godhead. The curvature of one end of the bat is made by placing the stick in hot ashes, and then bending in the forks of another twig. In shinny the reversed stick Γ is used. In this game the batter takes hold of the curved end and strikes the ball with the thin end, which is about of the thickness of the middle finger. In shinny, however, he holds the thin end and strikes the ball with the knotty end of the stick.

The terms of the game and the points to be scored by the winning side having been agreed upon, the players line up in about the position of the subjoined diagram [figure 1084].

I have given the four bases the names of east, south, etc., although they are not thus called by the Navaho. They have a name for east, meaning the first place to run to, and for north, na"ilyed, run is finished.

The pitchers are called ałch'i'náalni', he throws toward him; for the other players there are no names. The pitcher may throw high or low, and the batter may strike at the ball from either direction; there may also be two or three batters at the bat at one time, and a batter may be allowed to retire after two or three strikes and take up the bat at another more opportune time. The fourth strike compels the batter to run for first base, as also when he hits the ball, fair or foul, fly or grounder. Once on the base he is safe until he leaves it, though he may lead off, or until another batsman hits the ball. The runner and his side (one out is sufficient) are retired if the runner is touched or hit with the ball by the enemy, either before reaching first base or while he is making for any of the other points. The chase thus becomes interesting. Anything and everything is allowed to the runner to evade being touched by the ball; he may describe a circle, dodge, jump, or knock the ball out of his enemy's hand to reach his base. Making the circuit scores one point, and whichever side scores most runs, or the number of runs agreed upon, is the winner.

This is another of the Great Earth-winner's games. Being challenged by his Indian followers or companions, they gradually learned the games from him; they staked him for his wife, cheated him, and he lost; whereupon the Indians dispersed and played his games in their newly acquired countries.

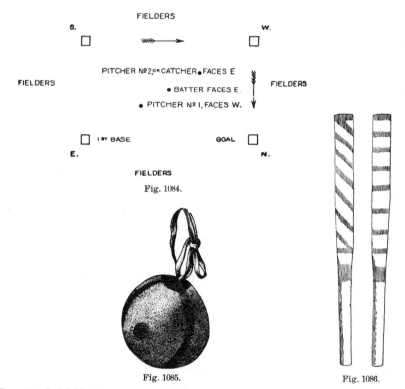

Fig. 1084.

Fig. 1085.

Fig. 1086.

FIG. 1084. Ball field; Navaho Indians, St Michael, Arizona; from sketch by Rev. Berard Haile.
FIG. 1085. Ball; diameter, 2⅜ inches; Thompson Indians, British Columbia; cat. no. ₄₈₆₆, American Museum of Natural History; from Teit.
FIG. 1086. Bat; length, 24¼ inches; Thompson Indians, British Columbia; cat. no. ₄₈₆₆, American Museum of Natural History; from Teit.

In the same category I would place the similar ball game of the Thompson Indians of British Columbia, described by Mr James Teit,[a] who says:

Formerly a favorite pastime was playing ball. The ball used was a kind of knot found on fir-trees. The knot is nicely rounded off, and sometimes covered

---

[a] The Thompson Indians of British Columbia. Memoirs of the American Museum of Natural History, whole series, v. 2, p. 277, New York, 1900.

with buckskin. Other balls were of stone, or of deerskin stuffed with vegetable material [figure 1085]. There were two ways of playing it.

One way was quite similar to that of " rounders." The bat used in this game was a short straight stick, about 4 inches wide at one end [figure 1086]. Each side took turns in batting. Four stones were placed about 20 yards apart, in the form of a square. These were called " houses." The man who held the bat was bowled to by a man of the opposite party, who stood about in the center of the ring. If the batter missed the ball, his place was immediately taken by the next man of his party. If he struck the ball with his bat, he immediately dropped the latter, and ran to the first house, or the second if he could manage it. The object of the opposite party was to catch the ball as quickly as possible, and strike the man with it while he was running from one house to the other, thereby knocking him out of the game. If the man managed to get back to his starting-point, he was allowed another chance to bat. The game is still frequently played by the young men.

I have made no mention of playing cards, which are widely used, games being played either with cards purchased from the traders, or with native copies more or less closely resembling them. The ten flat pieces of cedar bark (plate XXI, cat. no. 11217, United States National Museum) collected by Maj. J. W. Powell from the Uinkaret in northern Arizona, which were figured as dice in the writer's paper on Chess and Playing Cards, proved on comparison to be copies of playing cards. The games played by the Indian with cards are easily recognizable as common Spanish and American games.

The remaining games which I am able to identify as of European origin may be included in a single class—games played on boards or diagrams, like merils. They may be regarded as games of skill and calculation, a kind of game which otherwise appears to be entirely lacking.

ALGONQUIAN STOCK

CREE and CHIPPEWA. Muskowpetung reserve, Qu'appelle, Assiniboia. (Cat. no. 61994, Field Columbian Museum.)

Board and men (figure 1087), the board 9 inches square, with cross diagram with holes in which the men—small green painted pegs, with one larger one—are inserted.

They were collected by Mr J. A. Mitchell, who describes the game under the name of musinaykahwhanmetowaywin:

This game is played by two persons, one playing the king piece or oke-mow, against his opponent's thirteen pawns. Moves can be made in any direction by any of the pieces, provided the lines of the diagram are followed.

The king has the power to take the opposing pieces and can take as many pieces in one move as are left unprotected, but only following the lines of the board. The pawns have no power to take the king, but endeavor so to press it as finally to checkmate. The king is technically known as musinay-kah-whan.

The game is one which has been long known to the Indians and is much admired by them. Many skillful players have been developed, some being more particularly skilled in manipulating the king piece, while others make the pawn their special play. The play is invariably for stakes of some kind.

MICMAC. Nova Scotia.

Dr A. S. Gatschet [a] writes:

The majority of the games they play now are borrowed from the whites. Their checker game is the same as ours and played on a checkerboard. A checker stone is called adena′gan (plural, adena′gank), while the checkerboard is adenagenei′. The checkers are either disk-shaped and smooth (mimusχa-witchink adena′gank) or square (esgigeniχi′tchik adena′gank).

The game is called after the moving of the stones from square to square; nin adnai′, it is my move; kit adnāt, it is your move.

PASSAMAQUODDY. Maine.

Mrs W. W. Brown [b] describes the following game:

Ko-ko-nag′n has a resemblance to the game of checkers, but, although nearly all are more or less proficient at the latter game, there are only a few who understand ko-ko-na-g′n. This, unlike any other game, may be played by male and female opponents. It is the least noisy, the skillful play requiring deliberation and undivided attention. A smooth surface is marked off into different-sized spaces, and pieces of wood, round and square, marked to qualify value, are generally used, though sometimes carved bone is substituted.

Fig. 1087.

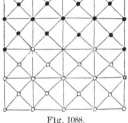

Fig. 1088.

FIG. 1087. Board game and men; dimensions of board, 9 inches square; Cree and Chippewa Indians, Assiniboia; cat. no. 61994, Field Columbian Museum.
FIG. 1088. Board game; Keres Indians, Acoma, New Mexico.

This may be the game referred to by Rasle among the Norridge-wock Indians, where he says:

Un autre jeu où l'on place des grains sur des espèce de lozanges entrelassées, di′r (dicitur), mañmadöañgñ.

KERESAN STOCK

KERES. Acoma, New Mexico.

An Acoma Indian named James H. Miller, employed at Zuñi, described to the writer under the name of aiyawatstani, chuck away grains, the game illustrated in figure 1088. Twenty-two white and twenty-two black pieces are used on each side. He explained that they learned the game in the olden time when they first came out of the ship-pap (si-pa-pu) away in the north. Iyatiko, the mother, made all the games.

---

[a] From Baddeck, Nova Scotia, August 28, 1899.
[b] Some Indoor and Outdoor Games of the Wabanaki Indians. Transactions of the Royal Society of Canada, v. 6, sec. 2, p. 43, Montreal, 1889.

KERES.　Cochiti, New Mexico.

A Keres boy at St Michael, Arizona, named Francisco Chaves (Kogit), described the Indians at Cochiti as playing the game of paitariya on a board represented by the diagram here given:

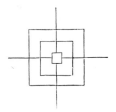

KOLUSCHAN STOCK

YAKUTAT.　Port Mulgrave, Alaska.　(Cat. no. 16300, United States National Museum.)

Twenty-two carved wooden chessmen (figure 1089), from $1\frac{7}{8}$ to $3\frac{3}{8}$ inches in height.　Collected by Dr W. H. Dall.

FIG. 1089.　Chessmen; height, $1\frac{7}{8}$ to $3\frac{3}{8}$ inches; Yakutat Indians, Port Mulgrave, Alaska; cat. no. 16300, United States National Museum.

MARIPOSAN STOCK

YOKUTS.　Tule River reservation, Tulare county, California.　(Cat. no. 70377, Field Columbian Museum.)

Flat stone, 13 by $10\frac{1}{4}$ inches, with top etched as shown in figure 1090, and twenty-four pieces of clay, conoid in shape, twelve black with two small holes in the top, and twelve red.　Collected by Dr J. W. Hudson.

PIMAN STOCK

PAPAGO. Mission of San Xavier del Bac, Pima county, Arizona.

Mr S. C. Simms informs me that he saw the game of coyote and chickens, pon chochotl (figure 1091), played by this tribe on a diagram traced on the smooth ground.

A red bean was used for the coyote and twelve grains of corn for the chickens. Another form of the game was played with twelve chickens on each side. This latter was played for money, the first game being regarded as too easy to bet on. Both Papago and Mexicans play, mostly men.

―――― Pima county, Arizona.

Mr S. C. Simms described the Papago as playing a game (figure 1092) on a star-shaped diagram which they called ohohla (Spanish, jeoda).[a]

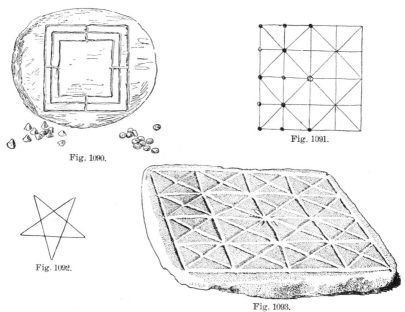

Fig. 1090.

Fig. 1091.

Fig. 1092.

Fig. 1093.

FIG. 1090. Stone game board and men; dimensions, 13 by 10¼ inches; Yokuts Indians, Tule River reservation, Tulare county, California; cat. no. 70377, Field Columbian Museum.
FIG. 1091. Game of coyote and chickens; Papago Indians, Arizona; from sketch by Mr S. C. Simms.
FIG. 1092. Star game; Papago Indians, Arizona; from drawing by Mr S. C. Simms.
FIG. 1093. Stone game board for tuknanavuhpi; length, 9 inches; Hopi Indians, Oraibi, Arizona; cat. no. 38613, Free Museum of Science and Art, University of Pennsylvania.

SHOSHONEAN STOCK

HOPI. Oraibi, Arizona. (Cat. no. 38613, Free Museum of Science and Art, University of Pennsylvania.)
Stone board (figure 1093), 7 by 9½ inches, inscribed with three equidistant cross lines in both directions, dividing the surface into

―――

[a] Probably geoda, geode.

sixteen rectangles, each of which is crossed by diagonal lines. The central point is marked with a star.

Collected by the writer in 1901.

Two men play, using white and black stones, which are arranged as shown in figure 1094. The game, called tuknanavuhpi, is like fox and geese. White leads. The object is to jump over and take an opponent's piece, which is continued until one or the other loses all. A player may jump in any direction. When a line across one end of the board becomes empty, it is not used again, so the players' field becomes more and more contracted.

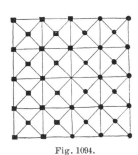

Fig. 1094.

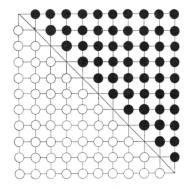

Fig. 1095.

FIG. 1094. Arrangement of men in game of tuknanavuhpi; Hopi Indians, Oraibi, Arizona.
FIG. 1095. The game of totolospi; Hopi Indians, Walpi, Arizona; after drawing by Dr J. Walter Fewkes.

HOPI. Oraibi, Arizona. (Cat. no. 55356, Field Columbian Museum.)

Stone slab inscribed with a diagram similar to the preceding.

This is described by the collector, Rev. H. R. Voth, in 1899, as a gaming board, tûkvnanawöpi.

This game is generally played by either two or four persons, each side having twenty pokmoita, animals, which consist of corn, pieces of corncob, charcoal, etc., and are placed on the board in tiers. First one side moves into the center, this piece being, of course, jumped, and then the moves are made alternately by the two sides. Moves and jumps may be made in any direction, and the latter over as many pieces as may be found with a vacant place right behind them. As soon as a tier of squares is vacant it is abandoned, so that finally the pieces are crowded into three or two squares, and even into one square. The inclosed spaces outside the squares are called houses. In these the killed animals are placed.

——— Walpi, Arizona.

Dr J. Walter Fewkes [a] describes the game of totolospi as follows:

To-to-lós-pi resembles somewhat the game of checkers, and can be played by two persons or by two parties. In playing the game a rectangular figure [figure 1905], divided into large number of squares, is drawn upon the rock, either

[a] Journal of American Ethnology and Archæology, v. 2, p. 159, Boston, 1892.

by scratching or by using a different colored stone as a crayon. A diagonal line, tûh-kí-o-ta, is drawn across the rectangle from northwest to southeast, and the players station themselves at each end of this line. When two parties play, a single person acts as player, and the other members of the party act as advisers. The first play is won by tossing up a leaf or corn husk with one side blackened. The pieces which are used are bean or corn kernels, stones and wood, or small fragments of any substance of marked color. The players are stationed at each end of the diagonal line, tûh-kí-o-ta. They move their pieces upon this line, but never across it. (On this line the game is fought.) The moves which are made are intricate, and the player may move one or more pieces successively. Certain positions entitle him to this privilege. He may capture or, as he terms it, kill one or more of his opponent's pieces at one play. In this respect the game is not unlike checkers, and to capture the pieces of the opponent seems to be the main object of the game. The checkers, however, must be concentrated and always moved towards the southeast corner.[a]

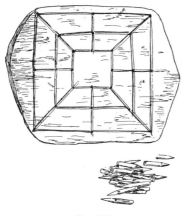

Fig. 1096.

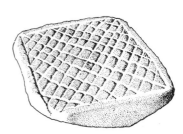

Fig. 1097.

FIG. 1096. Game board and men; length of board, 9 inches; Mono Indians, Madera county, California; cat. no. 71519, Field Columbian Museum.
FIG. 1097. Stone game board for totolospi; length, 4¼ inches; Tewa Indians, Hano, Arizona; cat. no. 38612, Free Museum of Science and Art, University of Pennsylvania.

This game is now rarely played on the East Mesa, but is still used at Oraibi. It is said to have been played in ancient times by the sun and moon, or by other mythical personages. Figures of this game formerly existed on the rocks near the village of Walpi, and may be the same referred to by Bourke.

Mr A. M. Stephen, in his unpublished manuscript, gives this definition: Totolospi, a primitive sort of checkers.

MONO. Hooker cove and vicinity, Madera county, California. (Cat. no. 71519, Field Columbian Museum.)
Board, 9 inches in length, with inscribed design (figure 1096), and holes for pegs at the intersection of lines; accompanied by pegs of two sizes.

Collected by Dr J. W. Hudson, who designates it as yakamaido, square game, or Indian checkers.

---

[a] It would appear from Doctor Fewkes's sketch of the board that only one player moved toward the southeast and that his opponent went in the opposite direction.

OMAHA. Nebraska.

Mr Francis La Flesche told the writer in 1893 that the Omaha learned the game of checkers from the whites about twenty years before and that they called it wakanpamungthae, gambling bowed head, or bowed-head game.

TANOAN STOCK

TEWA. Hano, Arizona. (Cat. no. 38612, Free Museum of Science and Art, University of Pennsylvania.)

Stone board (figure 1097), 4¾ inches square, inscribed with diagonal lines, ten in one direction and fifteen across. Collected in 1901 by the writer, to whom it was described as used in a game like fox and geese, totolospi,[a] and played with little broken sticks, black and white, which are arranged as shown in figure 1098.

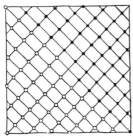

| Fig. 1098. | Fig. 1099. | Fig. 1100. |

FIG. 1098. Arrangement of men in totolospi; Tewa Indians, Hano, Arizona.
FIG. 1099. Game of picaria (pedreria); Tigua Indians, Isleta, New Mexico.
FIG. 1100. Game of picaria (pedreria); Tigua Indians, Isleta, New Mexico.

———— Santa Clara, New Mexico.

Mr T. S. Dozier [b] describes a game of pitarilla (pedreria), said to be of Pueblo origin, but doubtless of Spanish introduction:

In this game the crosses are marked by each player in turn where the men are placed, the object being to get three men in a row, always in a straight line; then one of the opposing player's pieces, the latter being grains of corn or pebbles, may be moved to the center. When all of the men of any player are moved by this process to the center, the other has won them. There are two figures used, the first [figure 1101] being a little more complicated than the other [figure 1102], though the same rule obtains in both.

A boy from Santa Clara at Mother Catherine's school at St Michael, Arizona, described the preceding game (figures 1101, 1102) under the name of bidaria (pedreria), as played at Santa Clara, and, in

_____

[a] See note, p. 160.
[b] Some Tewa Games. Unpublished MS. in Bureau of American Ethnology, May 8, 1896.

addition, the game of kuang, or jack rabbit, played with twelve stones, ku, on a board (figure 1103). Another board game (figure 1104) he described under the name of akuyo, star.

TIGUA. Isleta, New Mexico.

A boy from Isleta, named J. Crecencio Lucero, described the people of this pueblo as playing a board game which they call picaria (Spanish, pedreria), little stone. They use diagrams of two kinds, represented in figures 1099 and 1100.

———— Taos, New Mexico.

Dr T. P. Martin, of Taos, describes the following game, the name of which translated into English is Indian and jack rabbits:

Two play. A diagram of sixteen squares is marked on the sand, as shown in figure [1105]. Twelve small stones are arranged at points where the lines

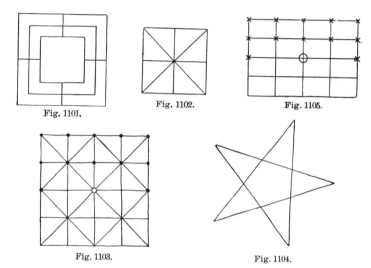

Fig. 1101.

Fig. 1102.

Fig. 1105.

Fig. 1103.

Fig. 1104.

FIG. 1101. Game of pitarilla (pedreria); Tewa Indians, Santa Clara, New Mexico; from sketch by Mr T. S. Dozier.

FIG. 1102. Game of pitarilla (pedreria); Tewa Indians, Santa Clara, New Mexico; from sketch by Mr T. S. Dozier.

FIG. 1103. Game of k'uâng, jack rabbit; Tewa Indians, Santa Clara, New Mexico.

FIG. 1104. Star game (akuyo); Tewa Indians, Santa Clara, New Mexico.

FIG. 1105. Game of Indian and jack rabbits; Tigua Indians, Taos, New Mexico; from drawing by Dr T. P. Martin.

intersect, on one side, as in the figure. The opposing player, occupying the one in the center at the beginning of the game, holds a stick, with which he points at the squares. The small stones are moved one at a time, and the object is to move them square by square without losing any until they occupy corresponding positions on the opposite side of the diagram. The player with the stick, who moves in turn, endeavors to catch the stones by jumping, as in draughts. Vocabulary: Name of the game, ko-app-paw-na, Spanish fuego de la liebre; board, or diagram, whee-e-na, Spanish reyes; pieces, kō-na, Spanish liebre; stick, tu-na-mah; to take a piece, con-con-we-la (the rabbit gets out from the man); some of the old men, however, shout au-gala, eat up.

ZUÑIAN STOCK

Zuñi. Zuñi, New Mexico. (Cat. no. 16550, 17861, Free Museum of
   Science and Art, University of Pennsylvania.)
Cardboard, inscribed with diagram (figure 1106), for the game of
   awithlaknakwe, or stone warriors, and twenty-six pieces, or men
   (figure 1107), consisting of disks made from shards of pottery,
   used in the game.
   The disks are in two sets, twelve plain and twelve perforated,
with a hole in the center, both 1⅛ inches in diameter. In addition,
there are two pieces, one plain and one perforated, somewhat larger
than the others.

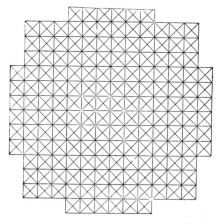

FIG. 1106.   Game of stone warriors; Zuñi Indians, Zuñi, New Mexico; cat. no. 17861, Free
          Museum of Science and Art, University of Pennsylvania.

These implements were made in 1893 by Mr Frank Hamilton
Cushing, who furnished the following account of the game:

Played by two or four persons upon a square board divided into one hundred
and forty-four squares, each intersected by diagonal lines. At the opening of
the game each player places six men in the center of the six squares at his
side of the board. The latter usually consists of a slab of stone pecked with the
diagram [figure 1106]. The men consist of disks of pottery about 1 inch in
diameter [figure 1107], made from broken vessels, those upon one side being
distinguished by being perforated with a small hole, while those on the other
side are plain. The object of the game is to cross over and take the opponent's
place, capturing as many men as possible by the way. The moves are made one
square at a time along the diagonal lines, the pieces being placed at the points
of intersection. When a player gets one of his opponent's pieces between two of
his own, it may be taken, and the first piece thus captured may be replaced by a
seventh man, called the Priest of the Bow, which may move both on the diagonal
lines and on those at right angles. A piece may not be moved backward.
When four persons play, those on the north and west play against those on the
south and east.

Vocabulary: Board, a-te-a-lan-e, stone plain; straight lines, a-kwi-we, canyons or arroyos; diagonal lines, o-na-we, trails; ordinary men, a-wi-thlak-na-kwe; seventh piece, pi-thlan shi-wani (mósona), Priest of the Bow.

The latter piece by power of magic is enabled to cross the canyons. The game is commonly played upon house tops, which are often found marked with the diagram.

The resemblance of the disks employed in this game to the prehistoric pottery disks which are found in the ruins in the southwestern United States and Mexico suggests that the latter may have been employed similarly in games. There is no evidence, however, that the board game existed before the coming of the whites. It was probably introduced by them and does not furnish an explanation of the prehistoric disks.

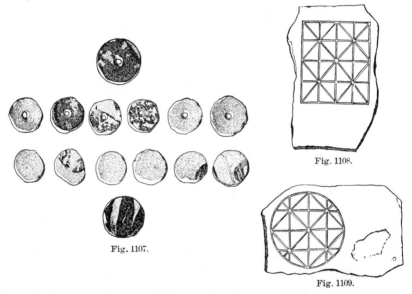

Fig. 1108.

Fig. 1107.

Fig. 1109.

FIG. 1107. Pottery men for game of stone warriors; diameters, 1⅛ and 1⅜ inches; Zuñi Indians, Zuñi, New Mexico; cat. no. 16550, Free Museum of Science and Art, University of Pennsylvania.

FIG. 1108. Stone game board; Zuñi Indians, Zuñi, New Mexico; cat. no. 3099, Brooklyn Institute Museum.

FIG. 1109. Stone game board; Zuñi Indians, Zuñi, New Mexico; cat. no. 3099, Brooklyn Institute Museum.

ZUÑI. Zuñi, New Mexico. (Cat. no. 3099, 3100, Brooklyn Institute Museum.)

Two flat stones inscribed with diagrams, as shown in figures 1108, 1109, and 1110.

Collected by the writer in 1903. The name was given as awithlaknanai. Nick Graham stated that this is a Mexican game. The third form (figure 1110), he said, was introduced into Zuñi the year before by an Indian from Santa Ana, a Keresan pueblo near the Rio Grande.

ZUÑI. Zuñi, New Mexico. (Cat. no. 5049, Brooklyn Institute Museum.)

Long stone slab, inscribed with the diagram shown in figure 1111.

This was found by the writer on a house top in Zuñi, and was explained by the natives as used in a game with white and black pieces, played like the preceding. The positions of the pieces at the beginning of the game are indicated by black and white circles. The name of the game was given as kolowis awithlaknannai, the kolowisi being a mythic serpent. Another form of the same game (figure 1112) was made for the writer by Zuñi Nick (Nick Graham), who described it under the name of awithlaknan mosona, the original awithlaknannai.

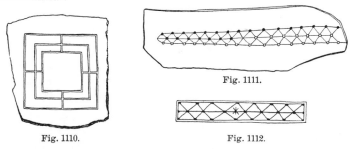

Fig. 1111.

Fig. 1110.   Fig. 1112.

FIG. 1110. Stone game board; Zuñi Indians, Zuñi, New Mexico; cat. no. 3100, Brooklyn Institute Museum.
FIG. 1111. Kolowis awithlaknannai; length of diagram, 33 inches; Zuñi Indians, Zuñi, New Mexico; cat. no. 5049, Brooklyn Institute Muséum.
FIG. 1112. Awithlaknan mosona; Zuñi Indians, Zuñi, New Mexico.

Mrs Matilda Coxe Stevenson [a] describes the game of awe ʻhlacnawe, stones kill, as follows:

Implements.—A number of small stones (a different color for each side), and geometrical markings on a stone slab or on the ground.

There is no specified size for the " board," it being larger or smaller according to the number of angles. The stones are placed on all the intersections of the geometrical drawing except the central one. The first player moves to the center. where his " man " is jumped by his opponent. The stones may be moved in any direction so long as the lines are followed.

In a note Mrs Stevenson says:

Some of the older men of the Zuñi declare that this game, when it came originally to Zuñi from Mexico, was played with one set of stones and a stick for the opposite side, and that the use of the double set of stones is an innovation of their own.

<hr/>

[a] Zuñi Games. American Anthropologist, n. s., v. 5, p. 496, 1903.

M. Wright Gill -

FLUTE CHILDREN THROWING ANNULETS AND CYLINDERS ON RAIN-CLOUD SYMBOLS; HOPI INDIANS, MISHONGNOVI, ARIZONA; FROM FEWKES

APPENDIX

RUNNING RACES

For purposes of comparison with the kicked-stick or ball race, and in order not to lose sight of the fact that the ball race is not the only form of race game practised by the Indian, the writer has inserted the following collection of data in this appendix, confining the body of the text exclusively to games in which implements are employed.

ALGONQUIAN STOCK

MISSISAUGA. New Credit, Ontario.

Rev. Peter Jones [a] says:

Foot races, in which they show much swiftness, are common among them.

——— Rice lake, Ontario.

G. Copway [b] says:

Foot racing is much practised, mostly, however, by the young people. Thus in early life they acquire an elasticity of limb as well as health of body which are of priceless value to them in subsequent years.

ATHAPASCAN STOCK

APACHE (MESCALERO). Fort Sumner, New Mexico.

Maj. John C. Cremony [c] says:

Racing on foot is another diversion frequently resorted to by the active, restless Indians, and the women generally manage to carry off the palm, provided the distance is not too great. The officers at the post offered a number of prizes to be competed for, the fastest runner to take the prize apportioned to the distance for which it was offered. The longest race was half a mile, the next a quarter, the third 300 yards, and the fourth 100. It was open for men under 40 years of age and over 15, and for girls from 15 up to 25. About a hundred Apaches and Navajoes entered for the prizes, and practiced every day for a week. At the appointed time everybody in camp assembled to witness the contest. Among the competitors was the Apache girl, Ish-kay-nay, a clean-limbed, handsome girl of 17, who had always refused marriage, and she was the favorite among the whites. Each runner was tightly girded with a broad belt, and

---

[a] History of the Ojebway Indians, p. 134, London, 1861.

[b] The Traditional History and Characteristic Sketches of the Ojibway Nation, p. 58, Boston, 1851.

[c] Life Among the Apaches, p. 304, San Francisco, 1868.

looked like a race horse. Ten entered for the halfmile stake, which was a gaudy piece of calico for a dress or shirt, as the case might be. At the word they went off like rockets, Nah-kah-yen leading handsomely, and Ish-kay-nay bringing up the rear, but running as clean and easy as a greyhound. Within 400 yards of the goal she closed the gap, went by like a steam engine, and got in an easy winner, 6 yards ahead of all competitors. For the quarter-mile race she again entered, but was ruled out by the other Indians, and their objections were allowed, it being decided that the victor in either race should not enter for another.

NAVAHO. New Mexico.

Dr Washington Matthews [a] describes Hastseltsi, or Hastseiltsi, as a Navaho god of racing. His personator takes no part in the dance or in any act of succor.

His function is to get up foot races; hence a good runner is selected to enact this character. He goes around among the assembled crowd challenging others, who are known to be good racers, to run with him. He does not speak. He approaches the person whom he wishes to challenge, dancing meanwhile, gives his peculiar squeaking call, which may be spelt " ooh ooh ooh'—ooh ooh'," beckons to him, and makes the sign for racing, which is to place the two extended fingers together and project them rapidly forward. If he wins in the race, he whips his competitor across the back with his yucca scourges; if he loses, his competitor may do nothing to him. If the losing competitor asks him to whip gently, he whips violently, and vice versa; but the flagellation is never severe, for the scourges of yucca leaves are light weapons. He races thus some six or seven times or until he is tired; then he disappears. Each race is only about 200 yards. The people fear him, yet a man when challenged may refuse to race with him. He often resorts to jockeying tricks with his opponent, such as making a false start. He may enter a medicine-lodge to get up a race, but for no other purpose. Hastséltsi is a very particular god and likes not to touch anything unclean.

CADDOAN STOCK

WICHITA. Oklahoma.

In The Story of Child-of-a-Dog, as related by Dr George A. Dorsey,[b] the hero is challenged to run a foot race with four brothers, his brothers-in-law. The starting place is a pole stuck in the ground. He wins the race by the aid of magic objects given him by two women, his wives.

Again, in the story of The Swift-Hawks and Shadow-of-the-Sun,[c] there is a description of a foot race between the people of the east and the west sides of a village. The chief of the east side has a dark complexion, is called Shadow-of-the-Sun, and kills those whom he overcomes in the race. He is finally beaten by the last of four brothers.

As in other stories, his body is burned by the victor and his many victims come out alive from the fire.

---

[a] The Night Chant, a Navaho Ceremony. Memoirs of the American Museum of Natural History, whole series, v. 6, p. 25, New York, 1902.

[b] The Mythology of the Wichita, p. 133, Washington, 1904.

[c] Ibid., p. 207.

There is also an account in The Coyote Who Lost his Powers [a] of a foot race between the coyote and a strange man, a Shooting Star, in which the coyote has the choice of running on top of the ground or under the ground. He chooses to run on top of the ground, while his opponent runs under the ground. The coyote wins and kills the other, and then restores the latter's victims to life by gathering their bones and putting them into the fire.

In The Coyote, Prairie Turtle, and the Squirrel [b] the coyote and the prairie turtle run a foot race, which the latter loses.

ESKIMAUAN STOCK

ESKIMO (WESTERN).   St Michael, Alaska.

Mr E. W. Nelson [c] says:

Foot racing, ûk-whaun'. This is a favorite sport among the Eskimo, and is practiced usually in autumn, when the new ice is formed. The race extends from one to several miles, the course usually lying to and around some natural object, such as an island or a point of rocks, then back to the starting point.

IROQUOIAN STOCK

SENECA.   New York.

Morgan [d] states:

Foot races furnished another pastime for the Iroquois. They were often made a part of the entertainment with which civil and mourning councils were concluded. In this athletic game the Indian excelled. The exigencies, both of war and peace, rendered it necessary for the Iroquois to have among them practiced and trained runners. A spirit of emulation often sprang up among them, which resulted in regular contests for the palm of victory. In these races the four tribes put forward their best runners against those of the other four, and left the question of superiority to be determined by the event of the contest. Before the time appointed for the races they prepared themselves for the occasion by a process of training. It is not necessary to describe them. They dressed in the same manner for the race as for the game of ball. Leaping, wrestling, and the other gymnastic exercises appear to have furnished no part of the public amusement of our primitive inhabitants.

MUSKHOGEAN STOCK

MUSKOGEE.   Georgia.

Réné Laudonnière [e] wrote:

They exercise their young men to runne well, and they make a game among themselves, which he winneth that has the longest breath. They also exercise themselves much in shooting.

---

[a] The Mythology of the Wichita, p. 253, Washington, 1904.

[b] Ibid., p. 273.

[c] The Eskimo about Bering Strait. Eighteenth Annual Report of the Bureau of American Ethnology, p. 340, 1899.

[d] League of the Iroquois, p. 307, Rochester, 1851.

[e] Hakluyt's Voyages, v. 13, p. 413, Edinburgh, 1889.

PIMA. Arizona.

The late Dr Frank Russell [a] wrote as follows of relay races:

At various points in Arizona I have found what appear to have been ancient race tracks situated near the ruins of buildings. One of these was seen on the south bank of the Babacomari, 3 miles above the site of old Fort Wallen. It is 5 meters wide and 275 meters long. It is leveled by cutting down in places, and the rather numerous bowlders of the mesa are cleared away. In the Sonoita valley, 2 miles east of Patagonia, there is a small ruin with what may have been a race track. It is 6 meters wide and 180 meters long. At the northern end stands a square stone 37 centimeters above the surface. These will serve as examples of the tracks used by the Sobaipuris, a tribe belonging to the Piman stock. The dimensions are about the same as those of the tracks that I have seen the Jicarilla Apaches using in New Mexico. The tracks prepared by the Pimas opposite Sacaton Flats and at Casa Blanca are much longer.

The relay races of the Pimas did not differ materially from those among the Pueblo tribes of the Rio Grande or the Apaches and others of the Southwest. When a village wished to race with a neighboring one, they sent a messenger to convey the information that in four or five days, according to the decision of their council, they wished to test their fortunes in a relay race, and that in the meantime they were singing the bluebird (or, as the case might be, the hummingbird) songs and dances in preparation. Both had the same time to practice, and the time was short. In this preparation the young men ran in groups of four or five. There were forty or fifty runners in each village, and he who proved to be the swiftest was recognized as the leader who should run first in the final contest. It was not necessary that each village should enter the same number of men in the race; a man might run any number of times that his endurance permitted. When the final race began each village stationed half its runners at each end of the track, then a crier called three times for the leaders, and as the last call (which was long drawn out) closed the starter shouted "Tâ'wai!" and they were off on the first relay. Markers stood at the side of the track and held willow sticks with rags attached as marks of the position of the opposing sides. Sometimes a race was ended by one party admitting that it was tired out, but it usually was decided when the winners were so far ahead that their runner met the other at the center, where the markers also met. The women encouraged their friends with shouts in concert, which were emitted from the throat and ended in a trill from the tongue. At the close of the race the winning village shouted continuously for some time, after which the visitors would go home, as there was no accompanying feast.

THOMPSON INDIANS (Ntlakyapamuk). British Columbia.

Mr James Teit [b] says:

Foot races were frequently run, and bets made on the result. The best runners traveled long distances to meet each other. Sometimes celebrated Okanagan, Shushwap, and Thompson runners competed with one another. The

---

[a] In a memoir to be published by the Bureau of American Ethnology.

[b] The Thompson Indians of British Columbia. Memoirs of the American Museum of Natural History, whole series, v. 2, p. 280, New York, 1900.

largest bets were made on races between champions. It is said that when the Indians were numerous, and almost all the men in constant training, there were some excellent long and short distance runners among them. Two men of the Spences Bridge band were said to be the fastest runners in the surrounding tribes. One of them raced against horses and against canoes paddled downstream.

SHOSHONEAN STOCK.

Hopi. Walpi, Arizona.

Mr A. M. Stephen, in his unpublished manuscript, gives the following vocabulary of racing among the Hopi:

Wa'-zrik-yu'-wü-ta, running; wa-wa'-si-ya, a short-distance race; yüh'-tü, a long-distance race; tcüle'-yüh-tü, race on the eighth morning of the Snake dance; tcu'-tcüb-ti añ'-am-yüh-tü, race on the ninth morning of the Snake dance; le'-len-ti yüh-tü, race on the ninth morning of the Flute ceremony; la-kon'-yüh-tü, race at sunset by women on the eighth day of the Lalakonti; la'-la-kon-ti añ'-am-yüh-tü, race at early sunrise by men on the ninth day of the Lalakonti; ti'-yot-wa'-zri, a race between two youths; ta'-kat-wa'-zri, a race between two men; to'-tim-yüh-tü, a race between many men; ta'-tak-yüh-tü, a race between several men; Ho'-pi ta'-cab-wüt a'-müm wa-zri, a race between a Hopi and a Navaho; Ho'-pi ta'-cab-müi a'-mum-yüh-tü, a race between several of each people (Hopi and Navaho); ka-wai'-yo ak-wa-zri, a race between two horsemen; ka-wai-yo-mü-i ak yüh-tü, a race between several horsemen.

SIOUAN STOCK

Crows. Upper Missouri river, North Dakota.

In a report to Isaac I. Stevens, governor of Washington Territory, on the Indian tribes of the upper Missouri, by Mr Edwin T. Denig, a manuscript in the library of the Bureau of American Ethnology, there occurs the following:

Foot racing is often practiced by the Mandan and Crows. The former nation before they were so much reduced by smallpox had a regular race course 3 miles in length, in which any and all who chose could try their speed, which they did by running three times around this space, betting very high on either side. They still practice the amusement, but not so much as formerly. Foot races among the Crow Indians are usually contested by two persons at a time, a bet being taken by those concerned, and many more by the friends and spectators on either side, consisting of blankets, buffalo robes, or some other article of clothing. They mostly run about 300 yards, and in starting endeavor to take every advantage of each other, a dozen starts being often made before the race begins. These Indians also run horse races, betting one horse against the other. The same trickery and worse is displayed in their horse as in their foot races, and often the loser will not pay.

The Sioux also have foot races, in which anyone may join, provided he bets, which, if they have anything to stake, they are sure to do. The name of being a fast and long runner is highly prized among them all; indeed after that of being a warrior and hunter that of being a good runner is next to be desired, but the principal aim in all these amusements appears to be the winning of each other's property. They, of course, occupy and enable them to pass agreeably some of the long summer days, but we never see these things introduced without the bets or prospects of gain, and from this fact, together with the earnestness exhibited in betting and in the contest, we conclude it to be no more than another mode of gambling, to which they are all so much addicted.

MANDAN. North Dakota.

Prof. F. V. Hayden [a] describes the Mandan foot race as Olympic in character:

A race-course of 3 miles on the level prairie was laid off, cleared of every obstruction, and kept in order for the express purpose. Posts were planted to mark the initial and terminating points, and over the track the young men tested the elasticity of their limbs during the fine summer and autumn months, to prepare themselves for the hardship of their winter hunts. On the occasion when races were determined on by the chiefs, the young men were informed by the public crier, and every one who had confidence in his prowess was admitted to the lists. Each of the runners brought the amount of his wager, consisting of blankets, guns, and other property, and sometimes several judges or elderly men were appointed by the chief of the village, whose duty it was to arrange the bets, regulate the starting, and determine the results of the race. As the wagers are handed in, each is tied to or matched with one of equal value, laid aside, and when all have entered, the judges separate, some remaining with the property staked at the beginning of the race-course, and others taking their station at its terminus. Six pairs of runners whose bets have been matched now start to run the 3-mile course, which is to be repeated three times before it can be decided. The ground is laid out in the form of an arc, describing two-thirds of a circle, the starting point and goal being but a few hundred yards distant from each other, the intermediate space being filled up by the young and old of the whole village. The runners are entirely naked, except their moccasins, and their bodies are painted in various ways from head to foot. The first set having accomplished about half the first course, as many more are started, and this is continued as long as any competitors remain, until the entire track is covered with runners, at distances corresponding with their different times of starting, and the judges award the victory to those who come out, by handing each a feather painted red, the first six winning the prize. These, on presenting the feathers to the judges at the starting-point, are handed the property staked against their own. The first and second heats are seldom strongly contested, but on the third, every nerve is strained, and great is the excitement of the spectators, who with yells and gestures, encourage their several friends and relations. The whole scene is highly interesting, and often continued for two or three days in succession, to give everyone an opportunity to display his abilities. Those who have shown great fleetness and powers of endurance, receive additional reward, in the form of praise by the public crier, who harangues their names through the village for many days afterwards. This is a fine national amusement, and tends much to develop the great muscular strength for which they are remarkable. They also immediately on finishing the race, in a profuse state of perspiration, throw themselves into the Missouri, and no instance is known where this apparent rashness resulted in any illness.

---

[a] Contributions to the Ethnography and Philology of the Indian Tribes of the Missouri Valley, p. 430, Philadelphia, 1862.

WINNEBAGO. Prairie du Chien, Wisconsin.

Caleb Atwater [a] says:

Athletic games are not uncommon among them, and foot races afford great diversion to the spectators. The women and children are present at these races and occupy prominent situations, from which they can behold everything that passes, without rising from the ground where they are seated. Considerable bets are frequently made on the success of those who run.

YUMAN STOCK

MARICOPA. Arizona.

Mr Louis L. Meeker describes the foot race in this tribe as follows:

A whole company run, side against side, from opposite goals, a flagman marking where each two pass. Each side runs in order. The final position of the flag marks victory.

SUMMARY OF CONCLUSIONS

(1) That the games of the North American Indians may be classified in a small number of related groups.

(2) That morphologically they are practically identical and universal among all the tribes.

(3) That as they now exist, they are either instruments of rites or have descended from ceremonial observances of a religious character.

(4) That their identity and unity are shared by the myth or myths with which they are associated.

(5) That while their common and secular object appears to be purely a manifestation of the desire for amusement or gain, they are performed also as religious ceremonies, as rites pleasing to the gods to secure their favor, or as processes of sympathetic magic, to drive away sickness, avert other evil, or produce rain and the fertilization and reproduction of plants and animals, or other beneficial results.

(6) That in part they agree in general and in particular with certain widespread ceremonial observances found on the other continents, which observances, in what appear to be their oldest and most primitive manifestations, are almost exclusively divinatory.

---

[a] Remarks made on a Tour to Prairie du Chien, p. 117, Columbus, 1831

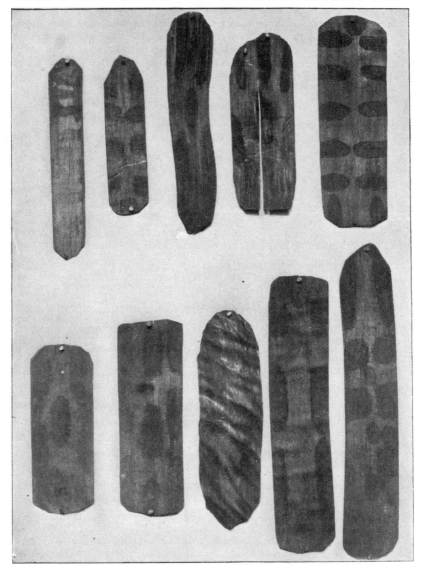

BARK PLAYING CARDS; LENGTHS, 5 TO 10 INCHES; UINKARET INDIANS,
ARIZONA; CAT. NO. 11217, UNITED STATES NATIONAL MUSEUM

INDEX

(Roman numerals in this index refer to the Administrative Report, v-xl, which is not included in this edition.)

(A TABULAR INDEX to TRIBES and GAMES will be found on pages 36–43.)

O